East Africa

Uganda
p381

Kenya
p220

Rwanda
p506

Burundi
p555

Tanzania
p52

Anthony Ham,
Ray Bartlett, Jean-Bernard Carillet, Stuart Butler, Shawn Duthie, David Else,
Mary Fitzpatrick, Anna Kaminski, Tom Masters, Carolyn McCarthy, Helena Smith

PLAN YOUR TRIP

Welcome to East Africa . . . 6

East Africa's Top 16 10

Need to Know 18

If You Like.... 20

Month by Month 23

Itineraries 27

Safaris 32

Gorilla Tracking 41

Travel with Children 47

Countries at a Glance . . 49

TONI TEJON / SHUTTERSTOCK ©

ON THE ROAD

HELL'S GATE NATIONAL PARK, KENYA P245

BEN CRANKE / GETTY IMAGES ©

OL DOINYO LENGAI, TANZANIA P117

ALEKSANDAR TODOROVIC / SHUTTERSTOCK ©

NAIROBI, KENYA P221

TANZANIA 52

Dar es Salaam 53

Jangwani & Kunduchi Beaches 63

Dar es Salaam's Southern Beaches 63

Zanzibar Archipelago . . . 64

Zanzibar Island 65

Pemba 85

Northeastern Tanzania . . . 91

Bagamoyo 93

Saadani National Park 94

Pangani 95

Tanga 97

Usambara Mountains 99

Northern Tanzania 103

Arusha 103

Arusha National Park . . . 109

Tarangire National Park . . . 112

Mto wa Mbu 114

Lake Manyara National Park 115

Lake Natron 117

Karatu 118

Lake Eyasi 119

Ngorongoro Conservation Area 119

Serengeti National Park . . . 123

Moshi 129

Marangu 133

Mt Kilimanjaro National Park 134

Machame 137

West Kilimanjaro 138

Central Tanzania 138

Dodoma 139

Kondoa Rock-Art Sites . . . 141

Babati 142

Lake Victoria 143

Musoma 143

Mwanza 145

Rubondo Island National Park 149

Bukoba 150

Western Tanzania 153

Tabora 154

Kigoma 156

Gombe National Park . . . 159

Mahale Mountains National Park 160

Mpanda 162

Katavi National Park 163

Sumbawanga 165

Southern Highlands . . . 167

Morogoro 168

Mikumi National Park . . . 170

Iringa 171

Ruaha National Park 174

Contents

Makambako 177
Njombe 177
Mbeya 178
Tukuyu 181
Lake Nyasa 182
Songea 184
Tunduru 185
Southeastern Tanzania 185
Mafia 185
Selous Game Reserve . . . 190
Kilwa Masoko 194
Kilwa Kisiwani 196
Mtwara 197
Mikindani 200
Makonde Plateau 201
Understand Tanzania . . . 201
Survival Guide 206

KENYA 220
Nairobi 221
Southern Rift Valley . . . 241
Longonot National Park . . . 242
Lake Naivasha 242
Hell's Gate National Park 245
Nakuru 246
Lake Nakuru National Park 249
Masai Mara & Western Kenya 251
Narok 251
Masai Mara National Reserve 252
Mara North Conservancy 259
Naboisho Conservancy 260
Olare-Orok Conservancy 260
Olderikesi Conservancy 261
Lake Victoria 262
Western Highlands 265
Central Highlands & Laikipia 277
Nyeri 277
Aberdare National Park . . . 279
Laikipia Plateau 281
Mt Kenya Region 289
Southeastern Kenya 300
Amboseli National Park 300
Tsavo West National Park 303
Tsavo East National Park 309
Voi 311
Mombasa & the South Coast 312
Mombasa 312
South of Mombasa 321
Lamu & the North Coast 328
Kilifi 328
Watamu 329
Arabuko Sokoke Forest Reserve 331
Gede Ruins 332
Malindi 332
Lamu 337
Northern Kenya 343
Isiolo to Moyale 344
Maralal to Turkana's Eastern Shore 351
Marich to Turkana's Western Shore 355
Understand Kenya 358
Survival Guide 365

JØRN ERIKSSON/500PX ©

RWENZORI MOUNTAINS NATIONAL PARK, UGANDA P436

Contents

ON THE ROAD

FRILET PATRICK / HEMIS.FR / GETTY IMAGES ©

NUNGWI, ZANZIBAR ISLAND, TANZANIA P78

MARIAN GALOVIC/SHUTTERSTOCK ©

NYIRAGONGO, RWANDA P498

UGANDA.......... 381

Kampala............. 384
Entebbe............... 401
Mabamba Swamp Wetlands............. 406
Mpanga Forest Reserve............... 406
The Equator........... 406
Eastern Uganda 406
Jinja.................. 406
Mbale................. 413
Mt Elgon National Park...415
Sipi Falls.............. 417
Nyero Rock Paintings ... 418
Northeastern Uganda............... 419
Kidepo Valley National Park.......... 419
Kitgum................ 422
Gulu.................. 422
Southwestern Uganda............... 423
Fort Portal............ 424
Crater Lakes........... 428
Kibale Forest National Park.......... 431
Semuliki National Park...433
Semliki Wildlife Reserve............... 434
Kasese................ 435
Rwenzori Mountains National Park.......... 436
Queen Elizabeth National Park.......... 439
Bwindi Impenetrable National Park.......... 445
Kabale................ 451
Lake Bunyonyi......... 453
Kisoro................ 455
Mgahinga Gorilla National Park.......... 457
Lake Mutanda.......... 459
Mbarara............... 460
Lake Mburo National Park.......... 461

Contents

NIGEL PAVITT / GETTY IMAGES ©

KILWA KISIWANI, TANZANIA P196

Masaka.................462
Ssese Islands...........463
Northwestern Uganda...............465
Ziwa Rhino Sanctuary...466
Masindi...............466
Hoima.................468
Murchison Falls National Park..........468
Budongo Forest Reserve...............474
Understand Uganda... 475
Survival Guide........486

DETOUR: DEMOCRATIC REPUBLIC OF THE CONGO...........494
Goma..................495
Parc National Des Virunga............498
Bukavu................501
Understand the Democratic Republic of the Congo.........502
Survival Guide........503

RWANDA.........506
Kigali..................507
Northwestern Rwanda............... 517
Musanze (Ruhengeri)... 517
Volcanoes National Park..........520
Gisenyi (Rubavu).......527
Southwestern Rwanda..............530
Huye (Butare)..........530
Nyanza (Nyabisindu)....533
Nyungwe Forest National Park..........534
Cyangugu (Rusizi).......538
Kibuye (Karongi).......539
Eastern Rwanda......540
Akagera National Park...541
Understand Rwanda...544
Survival Guide........550

BURUNDI.........555
Understand Burundi...556

UNDERSTAND

East Africa Today..............560
History..............562
Life in East Africa..... 568
Environment......... 573
Wildlife & Habitat......581
National Parks & Reserves........... 605
Tribal Cultures........611
The Arts..............619
A Taste of East Africa...623

SURVIVAL GUIDE

Safe Travel.......... 628
Directory A-Z......... 630
Transport........... 640
Health.............. 647
Language............ 652
Index............... 660
Map Legend.......... 670

SPECIAL FEATURES

Safaris.............. 32
Gorilla Tracking........41
Wildlife & Habitat.... 581
National Parks & Reserves.......... 605
A Taste of East Africa...623

Welcome to East Africa

East Africa is the Africa of childhood longings, a wild realm of extraordinary landscapes, peoples and wildlife in one of our planet's most beautiful corners.

Wildlife

Welcome to the true home of the African safari. This is untamed Africa, where wildebeest, shadowed by zebras, stampede in their millions across the earth; where lions, leopards and cheetahs, hyenas and wild dogs roam free in search of their next meal. Such stirring scenes of life and death, such overwhelming scenes of abundance coexist with scenes of surprising fragility, among them chimpanzees and powerful yet gentle silverback male gorillas forced with their families into remote islands of montane forest. To draw near to such wildness is to experience something so profound as to live forever in the memory.

Beautiful Landscapes

This is the land of the Masai Mara and the Serengeti, of an immense red sun setting behind a flat-topped acacia somewhere out beyond eternity. Here on the African savannah, the world remains as it once was, unspoiled by human presence. Nearby are the epic signposts to the Rift Valley, among them Mt Kilimanjaro, the Ngorongoro Crater, the Crater Highlands, Mt Meru, Mt Kenya and the Rwenzoris. By climbing these peaks on foot, by scaling the Rift, you add your own footprints to Africa's marvellous human story and explore in ways unimaginable to those who never leave their vehicles.

Captivating Cultures

Wherever you go, don't miss the chance to get to know East Africa's people. Whether you're exploring Maasailand accompanied by red-shawled Maasai warriors, standing in solidarity with victims of genocide at the sobering Kigali Genocide Memorial, or hunting with the ancient Hadzabe people of Lake Eyasi, there are countless opportunities to immerse yourself in the everyday beauty, realities and vibrancy of East African life. It is, after all, East Africans themselves, with their warmth, hospitality and fascinating history, who will provide you with so many of your journey's most memorable moments.

Beaches & Islands

In few places do fascinating human cultures come together quite so agreeably as they do along East Africa's Indian Ocean coastline. Travel back in time to the days when this part of the world was at the centre of a far-flung trading network whose influences – African, Asian, Middle Eastern – continue to dance their way through modern Swahili culture. From Lamu to Zanzibar and just about everywhere in between, you can also relax on white-sand beaches, dive amid colourful marine life or sail on a dhow (ancient Arabic sailing vessel). Some might call it paradise.

Why I Love East Africa

By Anthony Ham, Writer

East Africa is where my love affair with Africa took hold and promised never to let go. Wildlife (big cats especially) and wilderness rank among the grand passions of my life and it was here that I saw my first lion on the march, my first cheetah on the hunt, my first leopard on a kill, and where I came so close to elephants and black rhinos that I could have reached out to touch them. And this is the home of Maasai friends who give me hope that the old ways can survive.

For more about our writers, see p672

Above: Samburu warrior performing traditional jumping dance, Kenya

East Africa

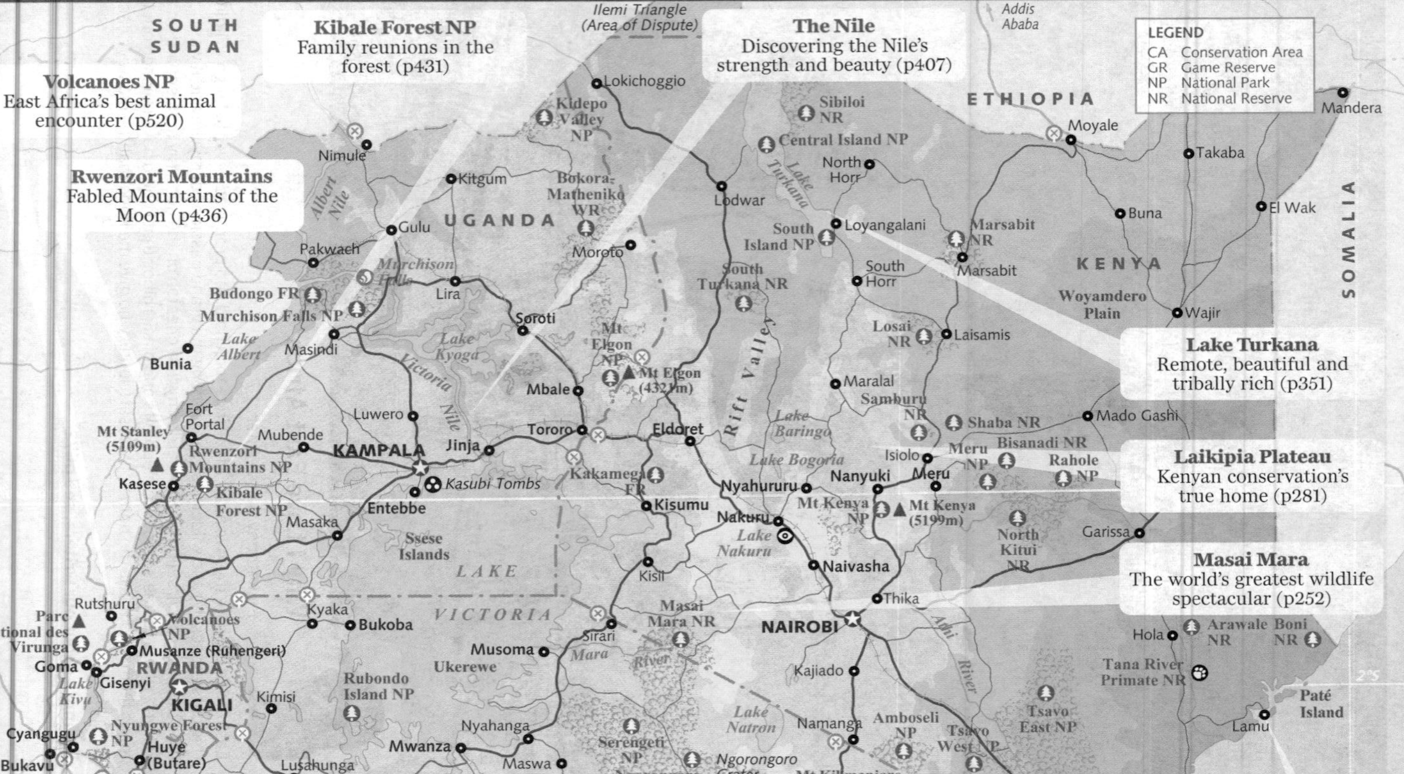

0 150 km
0 90 miles
LEGEND
CA Conservation Area
GR Game Reserve
NP National Park
NR National Reserve
Volcanoes NP
East Africa's best animal encounter (p520)
Kibale Forest NP
Family reunions in the forest (p431)
Rwenzori Mountains
Fabled Mountains of the Moon (p436)
The Nile
Discovering the Nile's strength and beauty (p407)
Lake Turkana
Remote, beautiful and tribally rich (p351)
Laikipia Plateau
Kenyan conservation's true home (p281)
Masai Mara
The world's greatest wildlife spectacular (p252)
SOUTH SUDAN
ETHIOPIA
SOMALIA
UGANDA
KENYA
RWANDA
Ilemi Triangle (Area of Dispute)
Addis Ababa
Lokichoggio
Kidepo Valley NP
Nimule
Kitgum
Bokora-Matheniko WR
Moroto
Gulu
Pakwach
Albert Nile
Murchison Falls
Budongo FR
Murchison Falls NP
Lira
Soroti
Lake Albert
Masindi
Bunia
Lake Kyoga
Victoria Nile
Mt Elgon NP
Mt Elgon (4321m)
Mbale
Luwero
Tororo
Fort Portal
Mt Stanley (5109m)
Mubende
KAMPALA
Jinja
Rwenzori Mountains NP
Kasese
Kibale Forest NP
Kasubi Tombs
Entebbe
Kakamega FR
Kisumu
Masaka
Ssese Islands
LAKE VICTORIA
Kisii
Rutshuru
Parc National des Virunga
Volcanoes NP
Kyaka
Bukoba
Musanze (Ruhengeri)
Goma
Gisenyi
Lake Kivu
KIGALI
Kimisi
Rubondo Island NP
Ukerewe
Musoma
Cyangugu
Nyungwe Forest NP
Huye (Butare)
Bukavu
Lusahunga
Nyahanga
Mwanza
Maswa
Lodwar
Sibiloi NR
Central Island NP
Lake Turkana
North Horr
South Island NP
Loyangalani
South Turkana NR
South Horr
Rift Valley
Eldoret
Lake Baringo
Lake Bogoria
Nyahururu
Maralal
Samburu NR
Losai NR
Laisamis
Marsabit NR
Marsabit
Moyale
Takaba
Buna
El Wak
Mandera
Woyamdero Plain
Wajir
Shaba NR
Isiolo
Meru NP
Bisanadi NR
Rahole NP
Meru
Nanyuki
Mt Kenya NP
Mt Kenya (5199m)
Mado Gashi
Nakuru
Lake Nakuru
Naivasha
North Kitui NR
Garissa
Thika
NAIROBI
Masai Mara NR
Sirari
Mara River
Kajiado
Athi River
Lake Natron
Namanga
Amboseli NP
Tsavo West NP
Tsavo East NP
Tsavo
Serengeti NP
Ngorongoro Crater
Mt Kilimanjaro
Hola
Arawale NR
Boni NR
Tana River Primate NR
Lamu
Paté Island

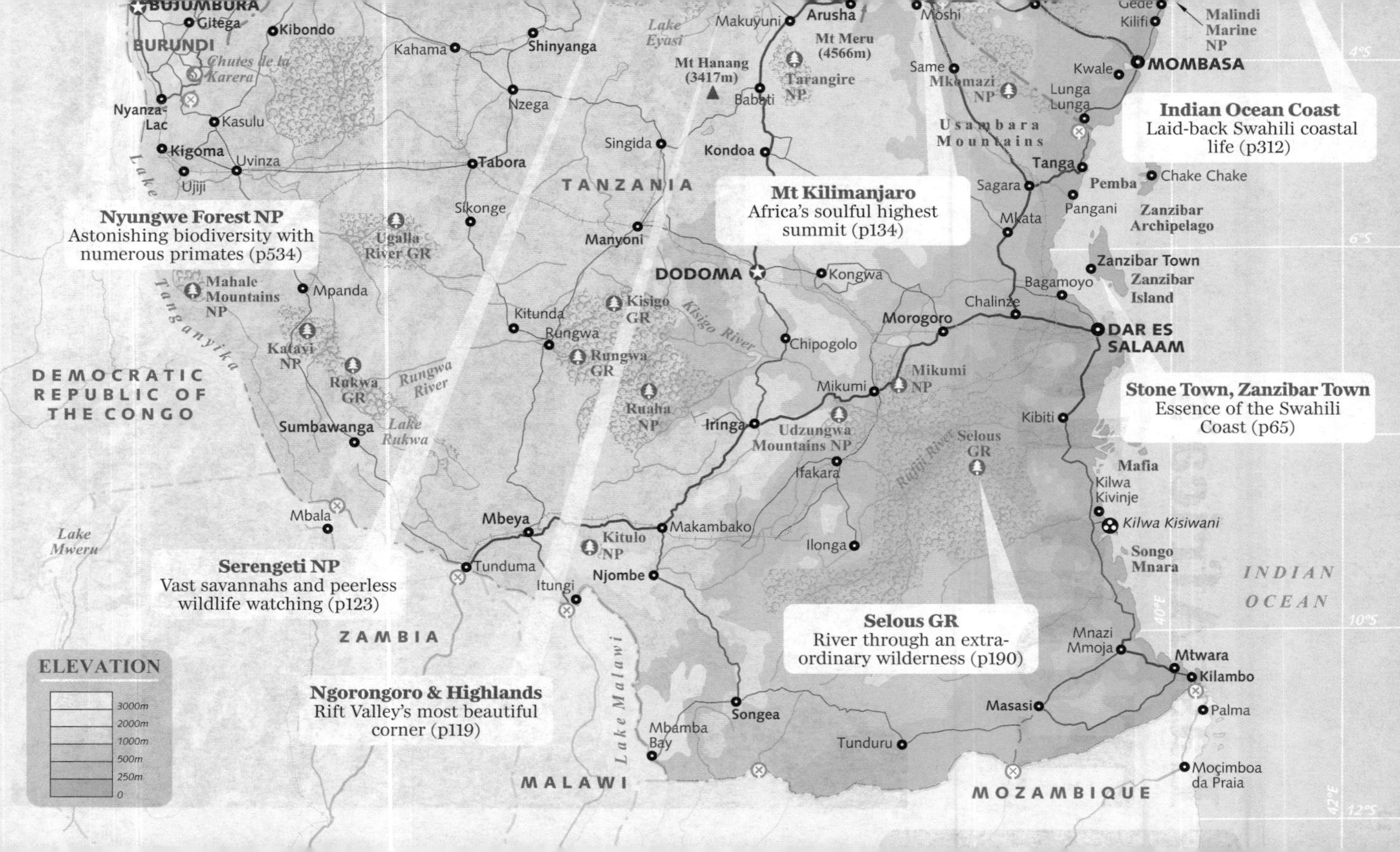
Indian Ocean Coast
Laid-back Swahili coastal life (p312)
Mt Kilimanjaro
Africa's soulful highest summit (p134)
Nyungwe Forest NP
Astonishing biodiversity with numerous primates (p534)
Stone Town, Zanzibar Town
Essence of the Swahili Coast (p65)
Selous GR
River through an extra-ordinary wilderness (p190)
Serengeti NP
Vast savannahs and peerless wildlife watching (p123)
Ngorongoro & Highlands
Rift Valley's most beautiful corner (p119)
ELEVATION
3000m
2000m
1000m
500m
250m
0
BUJUMBURA
Gitega
BURUNDI
Kibondo
Chutes de la Karera
Nyanza-Lac
Kasulu
Kigoma
Uvinza
Ujiji
Lake Tanganyika
Kahama
Shinyanga
Nzega
Tabora
Sikonge
Ugalla River GR
Mpanda
Mahale Mountains NP
Katavi NP
Rukwa GR
Rungwa River
Lake Rukwa
Sumbawanga
DEMOCRATIC REPUBLIC OF THE CONGO
Mbala
Lake Mweru
ZAMBIA
Tunduma
Mbeya
Itungi
Lake Malawi
MALAWI
Kitunda
Rungwa
Rungwa GR
Kisigo GR
Kisigo River
Ruaha NP
Kitulo NP
Njombe
Makambako
Mbamba Bay
Songea
Tunduru
Singida
TANZANIA
Manyoni
Lake Eyasi
Mt Hanang (3417m)
Makuyuni
Arusha
Mt Meru (4566m)
Tarangire NP
Babati
Kondoa
DODOMA
Kongwa
Chipogolo
Iringa
Udzungwa Mountains NP
Ifakara
Ilonga
Mikumi
Mikumi NP
Morogoro
Chalinze
Selous GR
Rufiji River
Moshi
Same
Mkomazi NP
Usambara Mountains
Sagara
Mkata
Tanga
Lunga Lunga
Kwale
MOMBASA
Kilifi
Gede
Malindi Marine NP
Pemba
Chake Chake
Pangani
Zanzibar Archipelago
Zanzibar Town
Zanzibar Island
Bagamoyo
DAR ES SALAAM
Kibiti
Mafia
Kilwa Kivinje
Kilwa Kisiwani
Songo Mnara
INDIAN OCEAN
Mnazi Mmoja
Mtwara
Kilambo
Palma
Masasi
Moçimboa da Praia
MOZAMBIQUE
4°S
6°S
10°S
12°S
40°E
42°E

East Africa's Top 16

Wildebeest Migration (Kenya & Tanzania)

1 Welcome to one of the greatest shows on earth. The pounding hooves draw closer, and then, suddenly, thousands of wildebeest stampede by, sweeping across the plains of the Serengeti National Park in Tanzania (from October to July) and the Masai Mara (pictured, p252) in Kenya (from July to October). Wherever you catch up with them, you'll find up to a million of these ungainly animals along with herds of zebras, elephants and giraffes. With predators never far away, this is natural drama on an epic scale.

Gorilla Tracking, Volcanoes National Park (Rwanda)

2 Nothing can really prepare you for that first moment when you find yourself in the midst of a family of mountain gorillas. It's an utterly humbling experience, sharing the forest with the silverback, whose sheer size and presence will leave you in awe, or with adorable fuzzy babies clowning about and tumbling from trees. The term 'once in a lifetime' is bandied about a lot, but gorilla tracking in Volcanoes National Park (p520) is one experience where it just happens to be true.

GAIL JOHNSON / SHUTTERSTOCK ©

2

DANITA DELIMONT / GETTY IMAGES ©

Mt Kilimanjaro (Tanzania)

3 It's difficult to resist the allure of climbing Africa's highest peak (p134), one of the Holy Grails of East African travel with its snow-capped summit, views over the surrounding plains and otherworldly gravitas. It's at once one of Africa's most rewarding hikes and an iconic African experience. If you can't make the summit, there are other great ways to experience the mountain. Day-hike on the lush lower slopes, spend time learning about local Chagga culture or sip a sundowner from a nearby vantage point with the mountain as a backdrop.

Below: Mt Kilimanjaro as seen from Kenya

Stone Town, Zanzibar (Tanzania)

4 Stone Town, the historic quarter of Zanzibar Town (p65), never loses its beguiling call of the exotic. First you'll see the skyline, with the spires of St Joseph's Cathedral and the Old Fort. Then wander through narrow alleyways that reveal surprises at every turn. Linger at shops scented with cloves, watch men wearing *kanzu* (a white robe-like outer garment) play the game *bao*, and admire intricate henna designs on the hands of women in their black cover-all *bui-bui*. Island rhythms quickly take over as mainland life slips away.

3

4

FREDER / GETTY IMAGES ©

ROBIN NIEUWENKAMP / SHUTTERSTOCK ©

Masai Mara National Reserve (Kenya)

5 Studded with flat-top acacia trees, the rolling savannahs of the Masai Mara National Reserve (p252) support some of the highest concentrations of wildlife on the planet. The great herds of wildebeest may bring sound and movement to the plains, but it's the big cats – the Marsh Pride of lions, lords of their domain, the leopards lurking in riverine thickets and the cheetahs surveying the world from a termite mound before exploding into a chase – who are the Mara's most soulful inhabitants. Above: Cheetah cubs

Serengeti National Park (Tanzania)

6 In this most superlative of East African parks (p123), time often seems to stand still. The Seronera River and its hinterland could just be the easiest place on earth to encounter wildlife at any time of the year. But this is a vast park, one that rewards those who linger with enough time to spare for the southern kopjes standing sentinel out over the eternal plains, the fine rock-and-river prospects of the Grumeti River in the west, and the endless plains and Mara River in the north. Top right: Zebras

Chimp Tracking, Kibale Forest National Park (Uganda)

7 Traversing muddy paths, stumbling over twisted roots and making your way through dense vegetation – chimpanzee tracking can be hard work. But oh my, is it worth it, and the struggle and sweat is all but forgotten as chimpanzees become visible in a clearing ahead and then draw near in curiosity – you could almost reach out and touch them. Of the four places to see habituated chimps in East Africa, Kibale Forest National Park (p431) in Uganda is the best all-round experience.

8

9

Ngorongoro & Crater Highlands (Tanzania)

8 On clear days, the magic of Ngorongoro (p119) begins while you're still up on the rim. Whether concealed from view by morning mists or bathed in the golden light of sunrise, Ngorongoro seems to echo with the beauty of Africa's first morning. Down in the crater itself, amid hues of blue and green, an unparalleled concentration of iconic African wildlife calls to mind the primeval Africa of our imaginations. Nearby, Ol Doinyo Lengai and Lake Natron are the pick of the fabulous Crater Highlands.

Laikipia Plateau (Kenya)

9 In the shadow of Mt Kenya, Laikipia Plateau (p281) hosts a network of conservancies and private wildlife reserves – it's both beautiful and one of the most exciting stories in African conservation. At the forefront of efforts to save endangered species such as lions, African wild dogs (pictured), Grevy's zebras and black rhinos, the plateau's ranches offer an enticing combination of high-end lodge accommodation, big horizons and charismatic megafauna. Best of all, this is a more personal experience than your average national park, with scarcely another vehicle in sight.

Rwenzori Mountains (Uganda)

10 Known in ancient times as the Mountains of the Moon, the Unesco World Heritage–listed Rwenzoris (p436) today retain a powerful sense of being a world apart. Here in tropical Africa, along the continent's highest range of mountains, ice-bound summits swirl into view then disappear, among them Mt Stanley (5109m), Africa's third-highest peak. Rainforest and an extraordinary array of plants, animals and birds – some endemic, a few of them endangered – make for some of East Africa's most challenging yet most rewarding trekking trails. Top: Chameleon

Lake Turkana (Kenya)

11 Amid the deserts and horizonless tracts that characterise so much of Kenya's north, Lake Turkana glitters like a jade and turquoise mirage. Rising from its waters is Teleki, one of the world's most perfectly shaped volcanic cones (pictured), while the shores are dotted with dusty and utterly intriguing villages, such as Loyangalani (p353), that are home to the beguiling mix of traditional peoples – Turkana, Samburu, Gabbra, El Molo – who call this isolated corner of Africa home. And there are crocodiles here. Lots of them.

Amboseli National Park (Kenya)

12 There's possibly no better place in the world to watch elephants (pictured) than Amboseli National Park (p300) in Kenya's south. A big part of the appeal is the setting – Africa's highest mountain, the snow-capped Mt Kilimanjaro, is the backdrop for seemingly every picture you'll take here. Just as significantly, Amboseli was spared the worst of Kenya's poaching crisis and these elephants are remarkably tolerant of humans (allowing you to get really close). And their tusks are among the biggest in Kenya. It's also an excellent place to see lions and cheetahs.

Selous Game Reserve (Tanzania)

13 Vast Selous (p190), with its tropical climate, profusion of greenery and massive Rufiji River, is completely different from Tanzania's northern parks. Take a boat safari, and as you glide past borassus palms, slumbering hippos and cavorting elephants, enjoy the many attractions large and small along the riverbanks. These include birdlife of astonishing richness, vast elephant herds and the largest population of lions on the planet. They're all part of the daily natural symphony in this, one of Africa's largest wildlife reserves. Below: Giraffes

12

13

ARIADNE VAN ZANDBERGEN / GETTY IMAGES ©

AUTHENTIC TRAVEL / SHUTTERSTOCK ©

Nyungwe Forest National Park (Rwanda)

14 With no fewer than 13 species of primates, a rich tapestry of birdlife and a degree of biodiversity seldom found elsewhere, Nyungwe Forest National Park (p534) is one of Africa's most important conservation areas. The vast forest is home to numerous primate species, including habituated chimpanzees and a huge troop of colobus monkeys. Hiking through this equatorial rainforest in search of our evolutionary kin – or just in search of a waterfall – is guaranteed to nurture your inner Tarzan. Above: Black-and-white colobus

White-water Rafting on the Nile (Uganda)

15 With rapids that go by names like A Bad Place or Dead Dutchman, the idea of being flung head-on into surging torrents of water sounds like a nightmare. But for those who've experienced it, it's one of the most exciting things they've done in Africa. Things start off as a leisurely paddle along the source of the Nile River close to Jinja (p409). The next thing you know you're looking up at a towering wave that mercilessly smashes upon you. It's breathtaking stuff and a ridiculous amount of fun.

Indian Ocean Coast (Kenya & Tanzania)

16 East Africa's Indian Ocean coast is one of Africa's prettiest shores. Long stretches of white sand, translucent waters and coves sheltered by palm trees would be sufficient reason for most travellers to visit. But trade winds through the centuries have brought an intriguing mix of African and Arab cultures, resulting in a coastline with attitude: at once laid-back in the finest spirit of *hakuna matata,* yet bristling with ruins and the evocative signposts of Swahili culture. You could pick anywhere, but it's difficult to beat Lamu's Shela Beach (pictured, p337).

Need to Know

For more information, see Survival Guide (p627)

Currency
Kenyan shilling (KSh), Tanzanian shilling (Tsh), Ugandan shilling (USh), Rwandan franc (RFr), Burundi franc (BFr)

Visas
May be available on arrival in Kenya, Tanzania and Rwanda but it's best to arrange in advance; online e-visas available for Kenya and Uganda.

Money
ATMs are widespread and credit cards widely accepted in Kenya, Tanzania and Uganda; less so in Rwanda (Visa only) and Burundi.

Mobile Phones
Local SIM cards are widely available and can be used in most international mobile phones. Mobile coverage is extensive, but patchy in wilderness areas and parks.

Time
Kenya, Tanzania and Uganda are on East Africa Time (GMT/UTC plus three hours); Rwanda and Burundi are one hour behind.

When to Go

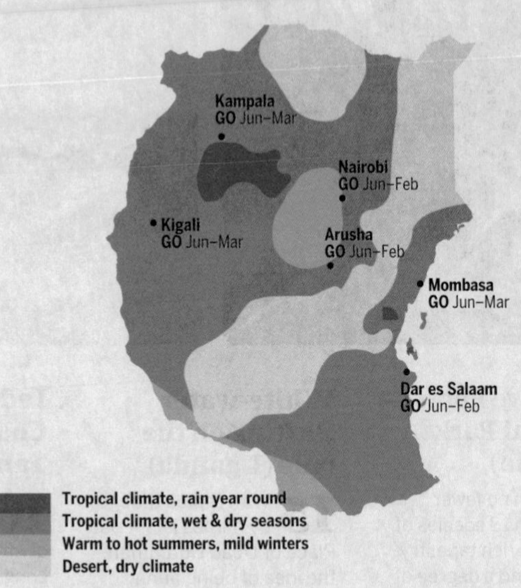

High Season
(Jun–Aug)

- Much of the region is cool and dry.
- Hotels in popular areas are full, many with high-season prices.
- Animal-spotting is easiest, as foliage is sparse and animals congregate around water sources.

Shoulder
(Sep–Feb)

- An ideal travel time, with greener landscapes and fewer crowds.
- Peak-season prices from mid-December to mid-January.
- Short rains in October and November rarely interrupt travel.

Low Season
(Mar–May)

- Heavy rains in much of the region can make secondary roads muddy.
- Some areas are inaccessible but landscapes are wonderfully green.
- Some hotels close; others offer low-season discounts.

Useful Websites

Lonely Planet (www.lonelyplanet.com/east-africa) Destination information, hotel bookings, traveller forum and more.

Kenya Wildlife Service (www.kws.go.ke) Conservation news and information on national parks and reserves.

Tanzania National Parks (www.tanzaniaparks.go.tz) Background info on all of Tanzania's national parks.

Uganda Wildlife Authority (www.ugandawildlife.org) Detailed coverage of Uganda's national parks.

Rwanda Tourism (www.rwandatourism.com) Rwanda's tourist information portal.

Safari Bookings (www.safaribookings.com) Invaluable resource for choosing safari operators and destinations.

Important Numbers

Country	Country Code	Emergency Number
Burundi	☎257	☎117 (police)
DRC	☎243	☎112 (police), ☎118 (fire)
Kenya	☎254	☎999
Rwanda	☎250	☎113
Tanzania	☎255	n/a
Uganda	☎256	☎999 (landline), ☎112 (mobile)

Exchange Rates

For exchange rates, see p53 (Tanzania), p221 (Kenya), p384 (Uganda), p495 (DRC) and p508 (Rwanda).

Daily Costs

Budget: Less than US$50

- Room in basic budget guesthouse: US$10–25
- Local-style meal: US$5
- Nairobi–Arusha bus journey: from US$27

Midrange: US$50–200

- Double room in midrange hotel: US$50–200
- Meal in Western-style restaurant: US$10–20
- Nairobi–Arusha shuttle bus: US$35

Top end: More than US$200

- Upmarket hotel room: from US$200
- All-inclusive safari package per person per day: from US$300
- 4WD rental with driver per day: from US$150

Opening Hours

The following apply, with some variations, in most countries of the region. Many shops and offices close for one to two hours between noon and 2pm, and on Friday afternoons for mosque services (especially coastal areas).

Banks 9am–3pm Monday to Friday, 9am–11am Saturday

Post offices 8.30am–5pm Monday to Friday, 9am–noon Saturday

Restaurants 11am–2pm and 5pm–9pm; some remain open between lunch and dinner

Shops 8.30am or 9am–3pm or 5pm Monday to Friday, 9am–11am Saturday

Supermarkets 8.30am–8.30pm Monday to Saturday, 10am–8pm Sunday

Arriving in East Africa

Jomo Kenyatta International Airport (Nairobi, Kenya) Taxis to the city centre cost KSh1800 to KSh3000 and take 30 minutes to one hour; book at the 'information' desk in the arrivals hall.

Julius Nyerere International Airport (Dar es Salaam, Tanzania) Taxis to the city centre cost Tsh35,000 to Tsh60,000, and will take 40 minutes to 1½ hours, depending on traffic.

Kilimanjaro International Airport (between Arusha and Moshi, Tanzania) Taxis to Arusha or Moshi cost Tsh50,000. Airline minivan shuttles charge Tsh10,000. For both transport types: 45 minutes to Moshi, one hour to Arusha.

Entebbe International Airport (Entebbe, Uganda) Taxis to Kampala cost US$35. Shuttle buses to Kampala's city centre cost USh2500 and take one hour.

Getting Around

East Africa is easy to get around by African standards, with road and air the most comfortable and reliable options.

Air Flying between Kenya, Tanzania, Uganda, Rwanda and Burundi is relatively simple – Kenya Airways has the largest regional network.

Car Driving is on the left in Tanzania, Kenya and Uganda; on the right in Rwanda and Burundi. Four-wheel-drive required in some areas and recommended in some parks. Consider renting a car with a driver.

Bus Buses are the most widespread public transport, but they're sometimes overcrowded and far from luxurious. They're usually (but not always) faster than trains or trucks, and safer and more comfortable than minibuses.

Train The new Nairobi–Mombasa rail link is better than taking the bus.

For much more on **getting around**, see p642

If You Like...

Primates

Tanzania, Uganda and Rwanda have no peers when it comes to watching primates. Encounters with mountain gorillas and chimpanzees are the major draws, but there are also golden monkeys and charismatic colobus.

Bwindi Impenetrable National Park Almost-guaranteed sightings of eastern mountain gorillas. (p445)

Volcanoes National Park Eastern mountain gorillas and golden monkeys. (p520)

Kibale Forest National Park Thirteen species, including red colobus and L'Hoest's monkey. (p431)

Semuliki National Park Nine species, including De Brazza's monkey. (p433)

Queen Elizabeth National Park Chimpanzees in beautiful Kyambura Gorge. (p439)

Nyungwe Forest National Park Chimpanzees and Angolan colobus monkeys. (p534)

Gombe National Park Chimps where Jane Goodall made them famous. (p159)

Mahale Mountains National Park Up-close chimpanzees in a stunning setting. (p160)

Kakamega Forest National Reserve Kenya's best primate reserve. (p268)

Big Cats

Lions sleeping under (or up!) a tree, a lone leopard draped along a branch, a cheetah accelerating across the savannah – these are some of East Africa's most unforgettable experiences.

Masai Mara National Reserve Arguably the best place to spot all three cats, especially from July to October. (p252)

Mara Conservancies All three cats in abundance and without the crowds. (p259)

Serengeti National Park The Seronera River is big-cat central and sightings are likely year-round. (p123)

Ngorongoro Conservation Area What's thought to be the highest lion density in Africa. (p120)

Tsavo East National Park A good spot for relatively easy sightings of all three cats. (p309)

Ol Pejeta Conservancy Go lion-tracking with the experts. (p284)

Queen Elizabeth National Park Leopards and tree-climbing lions in Uganda. (p439)

Murchison Falls National Park Lions and leopards in north-western Uganda. (p468)

Selous Game Reserve Africa's largest lion population, with leopards commonly sighted too. (p190)

Rhinos & Elephants

The African elephant and the rhinoceros are the enduring icons of the continent, whether as a symbol for the gravitas of its wildlife or the natural world's remarkable resilience.

Amboseli National Park As close as you'll get to a big-tusked elephant, with Mt Kilimanjaro in the background. (p300)

Samburu National Reserve Elephants set against one of Kenya's most beautiful regions. (p347)

Ruaha National Park Some of East Africa's largest herds, with 12,000 elephants in total. (p174)

Tsavo East National Park Kenya's largest elephant population with over 11,000. (p309)

Tarangire National Park Large dry-season elephant herds in one of Tanzania's most underrated parks. (p112)

Ol Pejeta Conservancy East Africa's largest population of black rhinos in Kenya's Laikipia. (p284)

Lewa Wildlife Conservancy Both black and white rhinos in central Kenya. (p286)

Nairobi National Park The world's densest concentration of black rhinos. (p221)

Meru National Park Both black and white rhinos without the crowds. (p299)

Top: Dolphin swimming over coral, Zanzibar Archipelago (p64), Tanzania

Bottom: Rhinoceros at Lewa Wildlife Conservancy (p286), Kenya

Ngorongoro Conservation Area Your best chance to see black rhinos in Tanzania. (p120)

Hiking & Trekking

With soaring Rift Valley mountains with accessible summits, snaking forest trails and flatland savannah, East Africa has a range of trekking experiences to suit most time frames and fitness levels.

Mt Kilimanjaro Trek to the roof of Africa. (p134)

Mt Kenya Africa's second-highest mountain with arguably better views. (p289)

Mt Meru Widely considered to be a brilliant alternative to Kili, and it's close to Arusha. (p110)

Rwenzori Mountains National Park Fabulous high-altitude trekking in mist-soaked forests. (p436)

Mt Elgon A vast volcano with quieter hiking trails. (p274)

Usambara Mountains Trails wind through pretty villages and even prettier landscapes. (p99)

Volcanoes National Park Hike through dense forest in search of Rwanda's gorillas. (p520)

Nyungwe Forest National Park Track chimps and other primates along the trails through primeval forest. (p534)

Islands

The islands of East Africa's Indian Ocean coastline capture the essence of the region's appeal. For an utterly different experience, Lake Turkana and Lake Rubondo are remote and rarely visited.

Zanzibar Island A magical name for a magical place, from Stone Town to perfect beaches. (p65)

Pemba Hidden white-sand coves and an intriguing culture. (p85)

Mafia Island Indian Ocean paradise with a marine park and few visitors. (p185)

Lamu Archipelago Manda, Manda Toto and Paté Islands are simply superb. (p337)

Wasini Island One of Kenya's little-known jewels and a real step back in time. (p327)

Central Island National Park An otherworldly volcano rising above the extraordinary Lake Turkana. (p357)

Rubondo Island A beautiful Lake Victoria island with birdwatching, elephants and chimps. (p149)

History & Ruins

East Africa's Swahili coast lies at the confluence of empires and trade routes with some stunning landmarks still in place. The powerful kingdoms of ancient Uganda also left their mark.

Gede Ruins An ancient and exceptional Swahili trading post in Kenya. (p332)

Kilwa Kisiwani Imposing and predominantly 15th-century Arab ruins in Tanzania. (p196)

Mnarani A Medieval Swahili port with fine mosques and massive baobab trees. (p328)

Kasubi Tombs Ancient royal tombs of the Buganda kings with other sites nearby. (p385)

Zanzibar Palaces Crumbling reminders of Zanzibar's past grandeur. (p73)

Kondoa Rock-Art Sites Beguiling ruins of a very different (and more ancient) kind. (p141)

Kigali Genocide Memorial A sobering monument to Rwanda's tragic recent history. (p509)

National Museum, Nairobi A fascinating journey through Kenyan history from an African perspective. (p221)

Beaches

East Africa's coastline is utterly gorgeous and there are some near-perfect beaches, including some with stunning, remote stretches of sand that have yet to be discovered.

Kilifi Fishing village, empty sand and Indian Ocean perfection. (p328)

Zanzibar's East Coast White sand and offshore reefs. (p65)

Watamu Marine National Park Seven kilometres of unspoiled beach with a lovely fishing village nearby. (p330)

Pemba Beautiful white-sand coves with plenty of space to spread your towel. (p85)

Tiwi Beach The alter ego to nearby Diani Beach resorts and its equal in beauty. (p322)

Diving & Snorkelling

Reefs proliferate all along East Africa's coastline and the diving and snorkelling here ranks among the best in Africa, with abundant marine life and an exceptional array of coral.

Pemba Divers in the know swear by Pemba's reefs. (p85)

Zanzibar Archipelago Coral reefs and shipwrecks offshore from Zanzibar Town. (p64)

Kisite Marine National Park Snorkel with dolphins; diving is also possible. (p327)

Watamu Marine National Park Fabulous reefs, fish and sea turtles. (p330)

Diani Beach Professional dive schools and even a purpose-sunk shipwreck. (p323)

Maziwe Marine Reserve Snorkel with dolphins in pristine waters with a sand island nearby. (p206)

Malindi Marine National Park Sharks, turtles and a stunning ocean floor. (p332)

Creature Comforts

East Africa does luxury extremely well. There's nothing quite like returning from a day's safari to luxury accommodation and impeccable standards of personal service out in the African bush.

Ol Donyo An utterly extraordinary place close to Amboseli. (p304)

Segera Retreat An *Out of Africa* experience in Kenya's Laikipia. (p286)

Asilia Naboisho Camp A gorgeous tented camp in Naboisho Conservancy in the Mara. (p260)

Lamai Serengeti A northern Serengeti stunner with vast, beautifully styled rooms. (p127)

Shu'mata Camp Classic safari luxury on a perch near Kilimanjaro. (p138)

Giraffe Manor Top-end luxury with a Rothschild's giraffe looking in your window. (p233)

Cottar's 1920s Camp Safari luxury and nostalgia in overdrive. (p262)

Mara Plains Palatial tents with details no one else thought of. (p260)

Sabyinyo Silverback Lodge An exclusive base for visiting Rwanda's gorillas. (p526)

Month by Month

TOP EVENTS

Sauti za Busara, February

Festival of the Dhow Countries, July

Annual wildebeest migration, July to October

International Camel Derby, August

Mombasa Carnival, November

January

January is a popular month for visiting East Africa, with animals congregating around waterholes and the bird migration under way. Days are usually warm and dry and there's action in the southern Serengeti.

Birds in Abundance

Migratory bird species have by now arrived in their millions, giving Kenya and northern Tanzania close to its full complement of more than 1100 bird species. Rift Valley lakes and other wetlands are, in most years, a birdwatcher's paradise.

Dry-Season Gatherings

It can depend on the October/November rains, but perennial water sources have dried up by January, drawing predators and prey alike to the last remaining waterholes across Kenya and Tanzania. Wildlife watching at this time can be tense, exhilarating and intensely rewarding.

Zanzibar Swahili Festival

This art and cultural festival (www.facebook.com/zanzibarswahilifestival) is held every four months on Zanzibar Island (including in January), each time with a different focus.

February

High season continues; days are hot and dry. The same principles apply as in January, with excellent wildlife watching around waterholes and countless bird species on show.

Orchids in Kitulo National Park

The blooms of orchids (over 40 species have been identified) as well as irises, geraniums and many other wildflowers carpet Kitulo Plateau in Tanzania's Southern Highlands. It's the rainy, muddy season here, but hardy, well-equipped hikers will be rewarded.

Wildebeest Births

The annual wildebeest migration mid-year may grab the headlines, but the species' great calving, a similarly epic yet also heart-warming sight, occurs in February in Tanzania's Serengeti National Park, with approximately 500,000 births occurring in a three-week period.

Sauti za Busara

Zanzibar gets even more rhythm than usual with the three-day Sauti za Busara. Swahili songs from every era fill the night, and dance troupes take over the stages of Stone Town and elsewhere on the island. (p71)

March

March is traditionally when East Africa's big annual rains begin, flooding many areas and making wildlife watching difficult. Prices are low and safaris can be excellent if the rains are late.

Kilimanjaro Marathon

This marathon (www.kilimanjaromarathon.com) is something to do around Kilimanjaro's foothills, in case climbing to the summit isn't enough; it's held in late February or early March in Moshi, with a half-marathon, a 10km wheelchair marathon and a 5km fun run also available.

Late-Rains Safari

The cheapest time to visit the Kenya and northern Tanzania safari circuit – roads can be impassable, mosquitoes are everywhere and wildlife disperses. But if the rains are late, conditions couldn't be better, with wildlife desperate for a drink and most birds still around.

Nyama Choma Festival

Self-described as 'the largest barbecue showcase festival in East Africa' (www.facebook.com/nyamachomafest), this is the place to try one of Tanzania's favourite meals, prepared in seemingly infinite variety by master chefs. Held several times annually in Dar es Salaam and other locations.

April

Unless the rains have failed entirely, this is one month to avoid. The inundation that should have begun in March continues to batter the region into submission. Getting around is difficult, and at times impossible.

Wildebeest Head North

The wildebeest – until now widely scattered over the southern Serengeti and the western reaches of Ngorongoro Conservation Area – begin to form thousands-strong herds that start migrating north and west in search of food.

May

The rains usually continue into May. By late May, they may have subsided; when they stop and you can see the horizon, the country is wonderfully green, although wildlife can still be tough to spot.

June

East Africa emerges from the rains somewhat sodden but ready to make up for lost time. The annual migration of wildebeest and zebra in their millions is usually well under way.

Gorilla Naming Ceremony

Rwanda stages the Kwita Izina (www.rdb.rw/kwitizina), otherwise known as the Gorilla Naming Ceremony, a countrywide event that honours the country's newborn gorillas with local community events and gala balls. Watch out for the odd celebrity conservationist in Kigali. Can spill over into July.

Grumeti Crossing

As the southern Serengeti dries out, vast wildebeest herds continue migrating northwestwards in search of food, crossing the Grumeti River en route. The timing of the crossing (which lasts about a week) varies from year to year, anywhere from May to July.

Lake Turkana Cultural Festival

One of Kenya's biggest cultural events, this fascinating festival focuses on the numerous tribal groups that inhabit northern Kenya, among them the El Molo, Samburu, Pokot and Turkana.

Run with Lions

In late June or early July, Kenya's Lewa Wildlife Conservancy hosts the Lewa Safaricom Marathon, one of the world's more unusual marathons, with a winning combination of wildlife watching and serious fundraising. (p287)

July

The wildebeest migration is in full swing, as is the annual migration of two-legged visitors who converge on Kenya's Masai Mara and Tanzania's Serengeti. Weather is fine and warm, with steaming conditions on the coast.

Festival of the Dhow Countries

Arguably East Africa's premier cultural festival, this Zanzibar extravaganza in early July runs over two weeks with live performances, literary events with an East African focus, and the Zanzibar International Film Festival. (p71)

Kigali Music

In July or August, Rwanda's capital plays host to world music, blues, funk and roots artists from around the globe at its excellent annual music festival. (p512)

Return to Amboseli

When the rains begin in March the herbivores of Amboseli (elephants, antelope, zebras...), followed by the predators, leave for grasslands outside the park. By July they're on their way back to the park confines.

Top: Wildebeest migration, Masai Mara National Reserve (p252), Kenya

Bottom: Swahili Fashion Week (p26), Dar es Salaam, Tanzania

Wildebeest Migration

Wildebeest cross the Mara River en masse, passing from Tanzania's Serengeti National Park to Kenya's Masai Mara National Reserve, with predators following in their wake. It's one cliché that just happens to be true: this is the greatest wildlife show on earth.

August

The mid-year high season continues with the Serengeti and the Mara the focus, although other parks are also rewarding. Europeans on holiday flock to the region, so prices go up and room availability goes down.

Camel Racing

Maralal's International Camel Derby in northern Kenya is at once serious camel racing and a chance to join the fun. It's a huge event. (p351)

Jahazi Literary & Jazz Festival

In late August or early September, Zanzibar presents a long weekend of jazz, blues, poetry and storytelling. Performances take place at the Old Fort and Livingstone Beach Restaurant in Zanzibar Town. (p72)

Kenya Music Festival

The country's longest-running music festival, and one of East Africa's most prestigious, is held over 10 days in Nairobi, drawing some worthy African and other international acts.

Mara River Crossing

By August – often earlier – the wildebeest make their

spectacular crossing of the Mara River into Kenya's Masai Mara, before roaming south again in anticipation of the rains.

September

The weather remains fine and tourist numbers drop off slightly, even though the Serengeti, the Mara and Rwanda's Volcanoes National Park are still filled to bursting with wildlife. Prices remain high.

Royal Ascot Goat Racing

Kampala's expats dress in their finest and funniest for the Royal Ascot Goat Races. It all happens on the shores of Lake Victoria and is the biggest event on the *muzungu* (foreigner) social calendar.

Rwanda Film Festival

One of East Africa's best events for cinephiles, the Rwanda Film Festival takes over cinemas around Kigali in September, showcasing new Rwandan films. (p512)

October

The short rains begin but rarely disrupt travel plans. Wildebeest are still in the Mara until mid-October, it's the best season for diving and snorkelling, and visitor numbers continue to fall.

Here Come the Rains

Unlike the main rainy season from March to May, the short rains that usually begin in October and continue into November cause only minor disruptions to safaris. Rains are generally localised and heavy, but only last for an hour or two each day.

Kampala City Festival

This fun and frenetic Kampala street festival runs through the first week of October with parades and performers celebrating Ugandan culture. Art, fashion and music appear on stages across the city. (p391)

Tusker Safari Sevens

Nairobi hosts the highly regarded international rugby tournament Tusker Safari Sevens. Drawing world-class rugby union players, the tournament spills over into November.

November

The short rains occur almost daily, but disruptions are minimal. Migratory birds arrive in their millions; it's an aerial version of the Serengeti and the Mara wildebeest migration and, for some, every bit as spectacular.

East African Safari Rally

This classic car rally held in late November is more than 50 years old, and there's more than a whiff of colonial atmosphere about it. The rally traverses Kenya, Tanzania and Uganda and is open only to pre-1971 vehicles.

Karibu Music Festival

This lively festival (http://karibumusic.org) has grown fast, and is now one of Tanzania's largest music festivals. It's held in Bagamoyo; dates vary, but it usually happens in November.

Lamu Culture

The Lamu Cultural Festival moves around the calendar a little, but this colourful carnival often falls in November. Expect donkey and dhow races, Swahili poets and island dancing. (p339)

Maulid Festival

This annual celebration (commencing 20 November 2018, 9 November 2019 and 28 October 2020) of the Prophet Mohammed's birthday rouses the Swahili coast from its slumber as Muslims from up and down the coast converge on Lamu, Zanzibar and other Swahili ports. Everyone is welcome.

Migratory Birds

Birdwatchers couldn't hope for a better time to visit, as millions of birds and hundreds of species arrive for their wintering grounds while Europe shivers.

Mombasa Carnival

Mombasa throws its biggest party of the year in November with Mombasa Carnival. Music, dance and other events take over the streets. A similar festival takes place (usually in November, although dates vary) further north in Lamu. (p315)

December

A reasonable month in which to visit, with lower prices and fine weather. There are plenty of migratory birds in residence, and much of the region is swathed in green.

Swahili Fashion Week

The largest showcase for East African design is held in Tanzania during Swahili Fashion Week (www.swahilifashionweek.com).

Itineraries

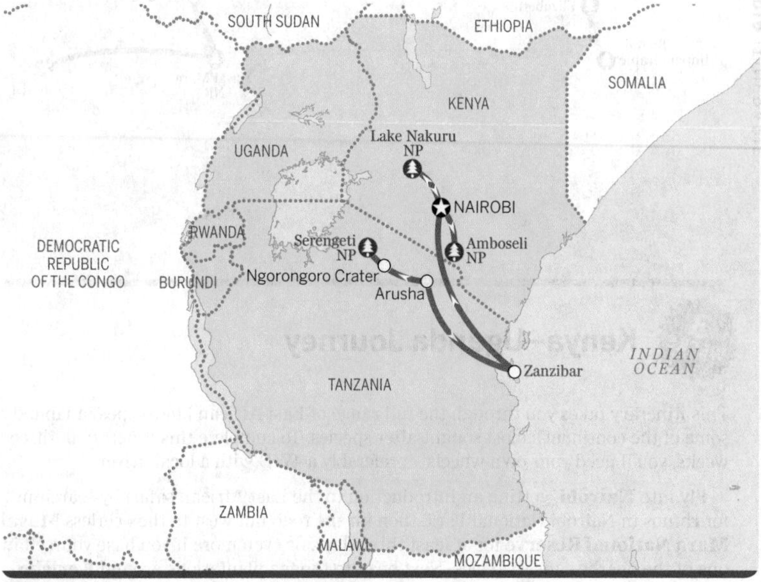

Classic East Africa

Here's what we'd do if we only had two weeks and wanted to see the best East Africa has to offer. This itinerary combines some of Africa's best wildlife watching with beaches and the Swahili coast; to manage it in two weeks, you'll need to travel some legs by air.

After arriving at Tanzania's Kilimanjaro International Airport, visit **Arusha** for a day or two, then head to **Ngorongoro Crater** and **Serengeti National Park** for a combination of fabulous wildlife-watching and iconic East African landscapes; allow at least four days between the two. Catch a flight from the Serengeti to Arusha and then on to the **Zanzibar Archipelago** for diving, snorkelling and relaxing. While you're there, take in the charm and historical attractions of Stone Town in **Zanzibar Town**.

Fly from Zanzibar to **Nairobi**, spend a couple of days enjoying its diverse attractions and restaurants, then head out on safari again, driving north to **Lake Nakuru National Park** for some more wildlife watching. After returning to Nairobi, again by road, take another short flight, this time to **Amboseli National Park** for peerless Mt Kilimanjaro views and some of Africa's best elephant viewing.

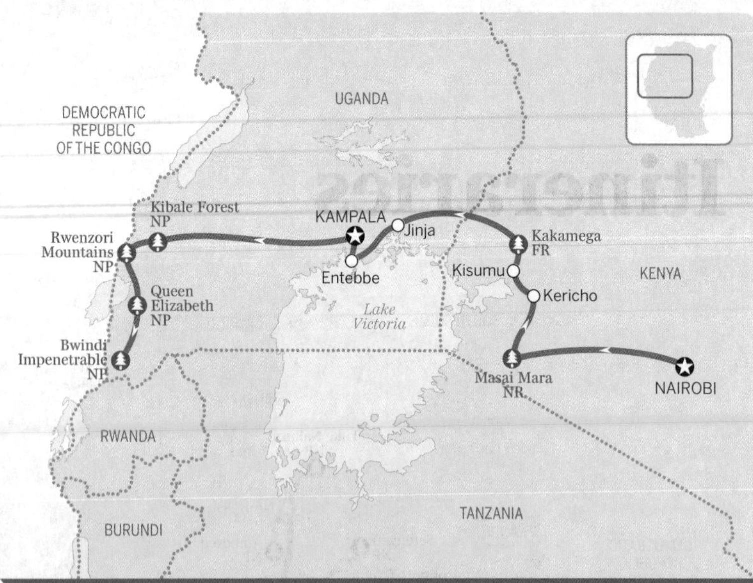

Kenya–Uganda Journey

This itinerary takes you through the full range of East African landscapes inhabited by some of the continent's most sought-after species. To complete this itinerary in three weeks, you'll need your own wheels – preferably a 4WD with a local driver.

Fly into **Nairobi**, getting an introduction to the East African safari by searching for rhinos in Nairobi National Park, then hit the road out west to the peerless **Masai Mara National Reserve** for at least three days, or even more if you base yourself in one of the nearby conservancies. Next head to the tea plantations around **Kericho**, pass through the regional capital of **Kisumu**, then delve into Kenya's last stand of central African rainforest in the **Kakamega Forest Reserve** in search of birdlife and primates.

After crossing into Uganda, set aside a few days to make the most of **Jinja**, East Africa's adrenaline-sports capital and home to the source of the Nile. From here, it's a short hop to **Entebbe**, with its Lake Victoria beaches, and on to **Kampala**, one of Africa's more agreeable capital cities; it's worth spending a couple of days here. Tracking west, explore the rainforests of **Kibale Forest National Park**, with 13 primate species and some of East Africa's best chimpanzee tracking; two days is a minimum here. From here it's a short hop to the mist-shrouded **Rwenzori Mountains National Park**, a soaring range rich in unusual wildlife and equally wonderful for its hiking trails that take you up into the clouds. Three days is a minimum in the Rwenzori.

Away to the south, **Queen Elizabeth National Park** has extraordinarily rich birdlife and tree-climbing lions; take a boat trip on the Kazinga Channel and hike along beautiful Kyambura (Chambura) Gorge in search of chimpanzees and other primates. At journey's end, **Bwindi Impenetrable National Park** is a wonderful place to immerse yourself one last time in the African wilderness. It's also one of the best places in the world to see mountain gorillas, as well as 350 bird species, African golden cats and 10 other species of primate.

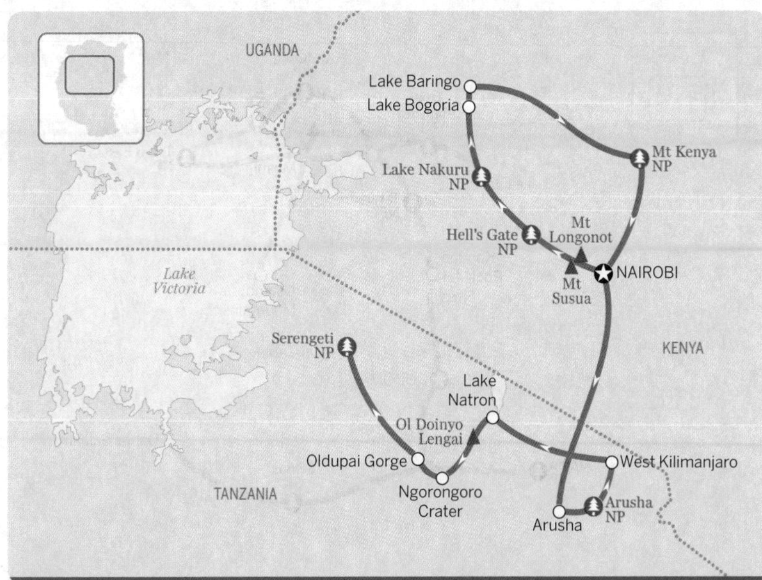

Best of the Rift

The dramatic uplands of the Great Rift Valley have a gravitas all their own – this itinerary is all about some of the region's most spectacular scenery. This trip *could* be accomplished with public transport, supplemented with day or longer tours, and could take a week more or a week less, depending on how many mountains you climb and how far you walk.

Begin in **Nairobi**, and track northwest to **Mt Longonot**, a shapely volcano and one of few Rift Valley crater rims that can be reached and returned from in a day. If you've time and a desire for have-it-all-to-yourself experiences, detour to **Mt Susua**, a Maasai heartland and fabulous Rift Valley formation. **Hell's Gate National Park**, too, is good for day treks, while **Lake Nakuru National Park** is a fine example of a Rift Valley lake that can draw flamingos, not to mention lions, leopards and rhinos. You could detour north from here to **Lake Bogoria** and **Lake Baringo** – the latter is one of Kenya's most prolific birdwatching locations – but your main goal lies east, where **Mt Kenya National Park**, home to Africa's second-highest peak, is a week-long undertaking if you trek to one of its summits.

A day-long road trip south via Nairobi takes you into Tanzania via the border crossing at Namanga and then on to **Arusha**, gateway to **Arusha National Park** and its picturesque Rift Valley volcano of Mt Meru; this is another of East Africa's premier high-altitude trek-climbs. Arusha NP is also the place to begin a trip out into the Crater Highlands, where the Rift's fractures and otherworldly landscapes come alive like nowhere else in Africa. Start by heading across to **West Kilimanjaro** for stunning views of Africa's highest mountain. From there, flamingo-rich and deliciously remote **Lake Natron** is utterly unforgettable, as is **Ol Doinyo Lengai**, surely one of the most perfectly formed mountains on the planet; set aside a day to climb it, and double that to rest in its shadow admiring the view.

Southwest of here is the simply magnificent **Ngorongoro Crater**, the epitome of Rift Valley beauty. Out to the west, **Oldupai Gorge** is one of the cradles of humankind, while the **Serengeti National Park**, the alter ego to all those volcanoes, is an extraordinary place to end your journey.

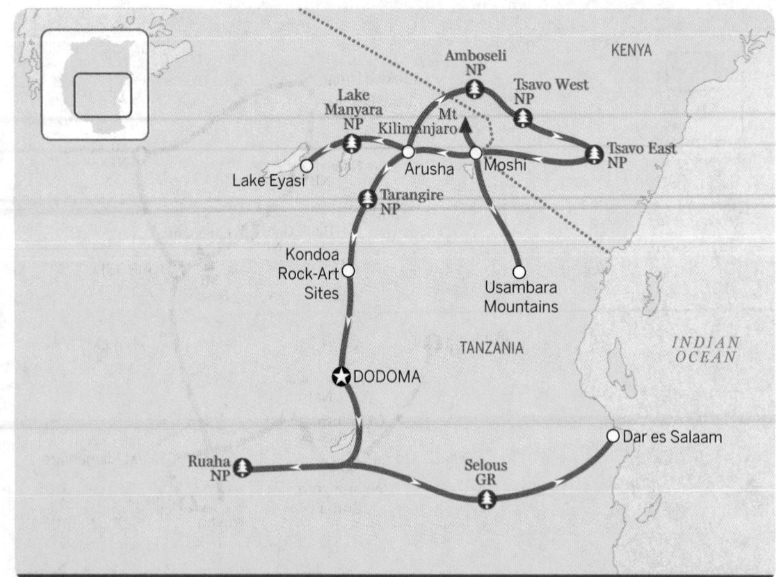

3 WEEKS Tanzanian Trails

This predominantly Tanzanian odyssey could link up with all manner of other itineraries. Three weeks is doable at a leisurely pace in your own vehicle, or in a rush on public transport. Add an extra week if you plan on climbing Mt Kilimanjaro.

Fly into Kilimanjaro International Airport and spend a day or two getting your bearings in **Arusha**. Head north out of town and into Kenya. If you've your own wheels, take the dusty trails that lead into **Amboseli National Park** from Namanga. After a minimum two days with the elephants in Kili's shadow, go east into **Tsavo West National Park** for red soils, man-eating lions, black rhinos and utterly beguiling views. East again, and you're in the sweeping savannahs of **Tsavo East National Park**.

From Voi take the road through the Taita Hills to Tanzania and spend a night or two in **Moshi**. As much as we like this agreeable town, its claim to fame is obvious whenever the clouds part – this is the gateway to **Mt Kilimanjaro**. Plan on at least a week as you climb all the way to Africa's highest point. If you have the mountain-climbing bug, detour southeast for some green-hills trekking in the **Usambara Mountains**.

Back to the north (via Moshi and Arusha), **Lake Manyara National Park** is famous for its tree-climbing lions, while **Lake Eyasi** is a remote side trip that takes you among the Hadzabe, one of East Africa's most ancient of peoples. Back on the main roads, **Tarangire National Park** is a wonderful park, rich in elephants, baobabs and so much more. Continuing south, the Unesco World Heritage–listed **Kondoa Rock-Art Sites** are a fascinating insight into the wisdom of the ancients, while **Dodoma** is a capital in name only but a good place to break the journey.

Ruaha National Park is at once the cultural heartland of the Barabaig and a wildly beautiful park known for its elephants and lions. Away to the east, **Selous Game Reserve** is one of our favourite protected areas in Africa, not to mention one of the largest; it's also home to the biggest lion populations on the planet. From Selous you could either head for the coast or make for **Dar es Salaam** for the journey home or onwards.

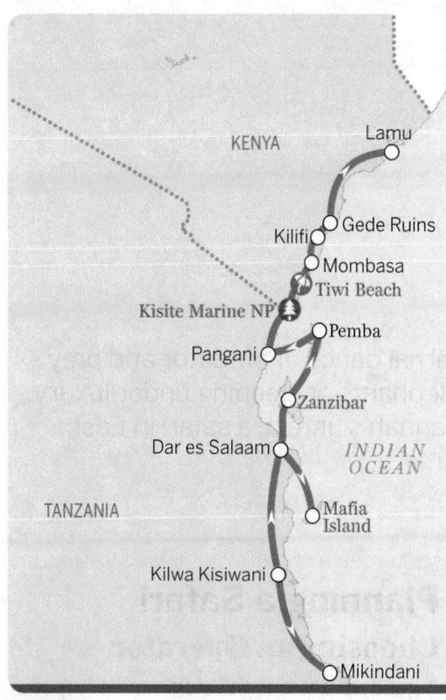

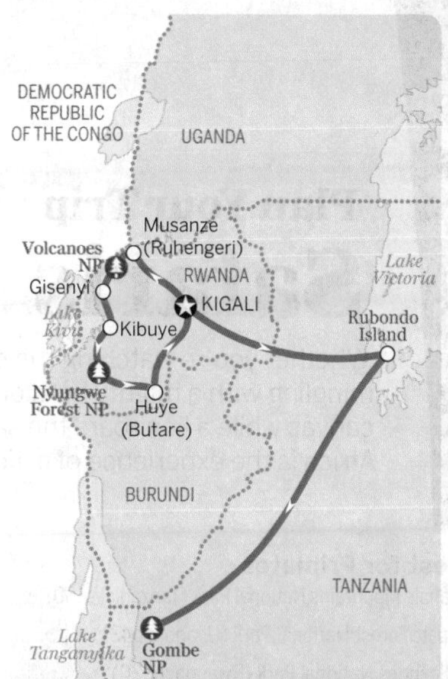

The Swahili Coast

Warning: this itinerary could take far longer if you find your own slice of paradise and never want to leave.

From **Dar es Salaam**, travel south to the ruins at **Kilwa Kisiwani**, and further south still to tiny **Mikindani**, a charming Swahili village. Returning north, **Mafia Island** is like Zanzibar without the crowds. And yet, there's nowhere on earth quite like **Zanzibar**, the essence of East Africa's Indian Ocean coast. **Pemba**, its northern neighbour, is an adventurous detour.

Your last Tanzanian port of call is **Pangani**, while just across the Kenyan border, **Kisite Marine National Park** is home to crocs along the banks of mangrove-lined rivers, dolphins crashing through the surf and humpback whales from August to October. Just before you arrive in the roiling Swahili port city of **Mombasa**, pause in **Tiwi Beach**, a tranquil white-sand paradise away from the resorts. Continuing north, stop in the charming town of **Kilifi** and at the **Gede Ruins**, an ancient Swahili city. But **Lamu Town**, a Swahili heritage gem, is the main event; a dhow (ancient Arabic sailing vessel) trip out into the wonderful Lamu archipelago is a must while here.

Gorillas Out West

Although this itinerary focuses on Rwanda and Tanzania's far west, it can link up seamlessly with the national parks of southwestern Uganda or the other wildlife-rich protected areas of Tanzania's far west.

Rwanda's capital **Kigali** has a lush, mountainous setting and lively nightlife, with the sobering counterpoint of a genocide memorial. From Kigali it's a short hop to **Musanze (Ruhengeri)** and the mountain gorillas of **Volcanoes National Park**. Next, head south along the shores of Lake Kivu and the scenic inland beaches around **Gisenyi** and **Kibuye** to **Nyungwe Forest National Park**, with its chimpanzees and other primates.

Travel east to **Huye (Butare)** before returning to Kigali en route to the shores of lovely Lake Victoria; **Rubondo Island**, with its unlikely populations of chimpanzees and elephants, is a wonderful place to rest from the rigours of the road. But to really understand our primate cousins, make your way to **Gombe National Park**, former home park of legendary conservationist Jane Goodall and one of the best places on earth to view chimpanzees.

Plan Your Trip
Safaris

Whether you're watching the eternal dance of predator and prey, mingling with a mighty herd of elephants or sleeping under luxury canvas while a lion roars the savannah's unrest, a safari in East Africa is the experience of a lifetime.

Best for Primates

Mahale Mountains National Park (Tanzania; p160)

Kibale Forest National Park (Uganda; p431)

Volcanoes National Park (Rwanda; p520)

Bwindi Impenetrable National Park (Uganda; p284)

Best for Elephants

Tarangire National Park (Tanzania; p112)

Amboseli National Park (Kenya; p300)

Samburu National Reserve (Kenya; p347)

Tsavo East National Park (Kenya; p309)

Best for Rhinos

Lake Nakuru National Park (Kenya; p249)

Ol Pejeta Conservancy (Kenya; p284)

Nairobi National Park (Kenya; p221)

Ngorongoro Crater (Tanzania; p122)

Best for Birdwatching

Kakamega Forest Reserve (Kenya; p268)

Rubondo Island National Park (Tanzania; p149)

Selous Game Reserve (Tanzania; p190)

Murchison Falls National Park (Uganda; p468)

Semuliki National Park (Uganda; p433)

Best Times to Go

Dry season (July through September) for spotting the Big Five

Rainy season (March through May) for birdwatching

Dry and shoulder seasons (June to January) for chimpanzee tracking

Planning a Safari

Choosing an Operator

A good operator is the single most important variable for your safari, and it's worth spending time thoroughly researching those you're considering. Competition among safari companies is fierce and standards of professionalism vary greatly. Some companies use glorified matatu or dalla-dalla (minibus or pick-up truck) drivers as guides, offer sub-standard food and poorly maintained vehicles, or underpay and poorly treat their staff, while others are high-quality companies with excellent track records. Following are some things to keep in mind when looking for an operator:

➡ Do some legwork before coming to East Africa. Check out traveller forums and the 'User Reviews' section of the Safari Bookings website (www.safaribookings.com). Get personal recommendations and, once in the region, talk with as many people as you can who have recently returned from a safari or trek with the company you're considering.

➡ Be sceptical of price quotes that sound too good to be true, and don't rush into any deals, no matter how good they sound.

➡ Don't fall for it if a tout tries to convince you that a safari or trek is leaving 'tomorrow' and that you can be the final person in the group. Take the time to shop around at reliable outfits to get a feel for what's on offer. If others have supposedly registered, ask to speak with them.

➡ Don't give money to anyone who doesn't work out of an office, and don't arrange any safari deals at the bus stand or with touts who

KATO, TATO & THE REST

The **Kenyan Association of Tour Operators** (KATO; Map p224; ☎020-713348, 020-271 3386; www.katokenya.org; Longonot Rd, Upper Hill, Nairobi) and the **Tanzanian Association of Tour Operators** (TATO; ☎0754 535637, 027-250 6430, 027-254 5208; www.tatotz.org; Philips St, just off Simeon Rd, Arusha) serve as local regulatory bodies. Reputable safari companies in Kenya and Tanzania will be registered members. While they're not always the most powerful of entities, going on safari with one of their members (both have member lists on their websites) will at least give you some recourse to appeal in case of conflict or problems. They're also good sources of information on whether a company is reputable or not, and it can be worth checking in with them before finalising your plans.

Uganda's equivalent, the **Association of Uganda Tour Operators** (AUTO; ☎Uganda 0414-542599; www.auto.or.ug), has no policing power, but does screen prospective new members to confirm they are at least competent.

Safari Bookings (www.safaribookings.com) is a fabulous online resource for comparing safari operators and destinations.

Other good sources of information on tour operators include the following:

- **Tanzania Tourist Board Tourist Information Centre** (p61)
- **Tourism Uganda** (p399)
- **Kenya Professional Safari Guides Association** (KPSGA; ☎020-2342426; www.safariguides.org)
- **Ecotourism Society of Kenya** (ESOK; Map p224; ☎020-529 2078, 0726366080; www.ecotourismkenya.org; Longonot Rd, Upper Hill, Nairobi)
- **Rwanda Tourism** (p636)

follow you to your hotel room. Also be wary of sham operators trading under the same names as companies listed in guidebooks. Don't let business cards fool you either; they're easy to print up and are no proof of legitimacy.

- Go with a company that has its own vehicles and equipment. If you have any doubts, don't pay a deposit until you've seen the vehicle (and tyres) that you'll be using. Also be aware that it's not unknown for an operator to show you one vehicle, but then on the actual departure day, arrive in an inferior one.
- Especially at the budget level, there's often client swapping between companies whose vehicles are full and those that aren't. You could easily find yourself on safari with a company that isn't the one you booked with; reputable companies will inform you if they're going to do this. Although getting swapped into another company's safari isn't necessarily a bad thing, be sure that the safari you booked and paid for is what you get.
- Unless you speak the local language, be sure your driver and/or guide can speak your language.
- Go through the itinerary in detail, confirming in writing what's expected and planned for each stage of the trip. Be sure that the number of wildlife drives per day and all other specifics appear in the written contract, as well as the starting and ending dates and approximate times.
- Normally, major problems such as complete vehicle breakdown are compensated for by adding additional time onto your safari. If this isn't possible, reliable operators may compensate you for a portion of time lost. However, don't expect a refund for 'minor' problems such as punctured tyres or lesser breakdowns. Park fees are non-refundable.

Safari Style

While price can be a major determining factor in safari planning, there are other considerations that are just as important:

Ambience Will you be staying in or near the park? (If you stay well outside the park, you'll miss the good early morning and evening wildlife-viewing hours.) Are the surroundings atmospheric? Will you be in a large lodge or an intimate private camp?

Equipment Mediocre vehicles and equipment can significantly detract from the overall experience. In remote areas, lack of quality equipment or vehicles and appropriate back-up arrangements can be a safety risk.

Access and activities If you don't relish the idea of spending hours on bumpy roads, consider parks and lodges where you can fly in. To get out

WHAT TO BRING

- Binoculars
- Good-quality sleeping bag (for camping safaris, but check if they're provided)
- Mosquito repellent
- Mosquito net (many lodges and tented camps have nets, but you may need one for budget guesthouses)
- Rain gear and waterproofs for high-altitude trekking and/or wet-season camping safaris
- Sunglasses
- Camera and extra batteries, memory and zoom capacity
- Extra contact lens solution and your prescription glasses (the dust can be irritating)
- Toilet paper, snacks and extra water for budget safaris
- For walking safaris, lightweight, long-sleeved shirts and trousers in subdued colours, a head covering, and sturdy, comfortable shoes

of the vehicle and into the bush, target areas offering walking and boat safaris.

Guides A good driver/guide can make or break your safari. With operators trying to cut corners, chances are that staff are unfairly paid, and are not likely to be knowledgable or motivated.

Community commitment Look for operators that do more than just give lip service to ecotourism principles, and that have a genuine, long-standing commitment to the communities where they work. In addition to being more culturally responsible, they'll also be able to give you a more authentic and enjoyable experience.

Setting the agenda Some drivers feel that they have to whisk you from one good 'sighting' to the next. If you prefer to stay in one strategic place for a while to experience the environment and see what comes by, discuss this with your driver. Going off in wild, hurried pursuit of the 'Big Five' means you'll miss the more subtle aspects of your surroundings.

Extracurriculars In some areas, it's common for drivers to stop at souvenir shops en route; most shops pay drivers commissions to bring clients, which means you may find yourself spending more time souvenir shopping than you'd bargained for. If you're not interested, discuss this with your driver at the outset, ideally while still at the operator's office.

Less is more If you'll be teaming up with others to make a group, find out how many people will be in your vehicle, and try to meet your travelling companions before setting off.

Special interests If birdwatching or other special interests are important, arrange a private safari with a specialised operator.

Booking

Booking (and paying for) a safari before arriving in East Africa is strongly recommended if you'll be travelling in popular areas during peak season or if your schedule is tight or inflexible. Only prebook with operators that you have thoroughly checked out, and take particular care if prebooking at the budget end of the spectrum. Confirm that the operator you're considering is registered with the relevant national regulatory body and get as much feedback as possible from other travellers.

If cutting costs and maintaining flexibility are priorities, then it can work out better to book your safari once you are in East Africa. Allow at least a day to shop around, don't rush into any deals, and steer clear of any attempts at intimidation by touts or dodgy operators to get you to pay immediately or risk losing your place in a departing vehicle.

Costs

- Camping safaris cater to shoestring travellers and those who are prepared to put up with a little discomfort and who don't mind helping to pitch the tents and set up camp. Safaris based in lodges or tented camps cost more, with the price usually directly proportional to the quality of the accommodation and staff.
- Most safari quotes include park entrance fees, accommodation and transport costs to/from the park and within the park, but confirm before paying. Drinks (alcoholic or not) are generally excluded, although many operators provide one bottle of water daily. Budget camping safari prices usually exclude sleeping bag rental (US$5 per day to US$20 per trip). For group safaris, find out how many people will be sharing the vehicle with you, and how many people per tent or room.
- If accommodation-only prices apply, you'll need to pay extra to actually go out looking for wildlife on wildlife drives, boat safaris or walks. There is usually the opportunity for two of these 'activities' per day (each about two to three hours). Costs range from about US$25 per person for a walk up to US$200 or more per day per vehicle for wildlife drives.

ALANF / SHUTTERSTOCK ©

Top: Male lion, Masai Mara National Reserve (p252), Kenya

Bottom: Wildlife at Lake Nakuru National Park (p249), Kenya

➡ There isn't necessarily a relationship between the price paid and the likelihood of the local community benefiting from your visit. Find out as much as you can about an operators' social and cultural commitment before booking.

Budget

At the budget end, reliability is a major factor, as there's often only a fine line between operators running no-frills but good-value safaris, and those that are either dishonest or have cut things so close that problems are bound to arise.

Most budget safaris are camping safaris. To minimise costs, you'll camp or stay in basic guesthouses, travel in relatively large groups and have no-frills meals. In some areas the campgrounds may be outside park boundaries to save on park entry fees and high park camping fees; however, this means you'll lose time during prime morning and evening wildlife viewing hours shuttling to and from the park. Most budget safaris also place daily kilometre limits on the vehicles, meaning your driver may be unwilling or unable to follow certain lengthier routes.

In Tanzania, expect to pay US$150 to US$200 per person per day for a budget safari with a registered operator. The cost in Kenya will be slightly lower. Genuine budget camping safaris are few and far between in Uganda, although a few companies offer reasonably priced three-day trips to Murchison Falls and Queen Elizabeth National Parks for about US$70 to US$100 per person per day, camping or sleeping in dorms.

To save money, bring drinks with you, especially bottled water, as it's expensive to buy in and near the parks. Snacks, extra food and toilet paper are other worthwhile items. During the low season, it's often possible to find lodge safaris for close to the price of a camping safari.

Midrange

Most midrange safaris use lodges, where you can expect to have a comfortable room and to eat in a restaurant. In general, you can expect reliability and reasonably good value in this category. A disadvantage is that the safaris may have a packaged-tour atmosphere, although this can be minimised by carefully selecting a safari company and accommodation, and giving attention to how many other people you'll be travelling with. Expect to pay from about US$200 to US$300 per person per day in Kenya and Tanzania for a midrange lodge safari. During low season, always ask about special deals. In Uganda, plan on anywhere from US$100 to US$150 per person per day.

Top End

Private lodges, luxury tented camps and sometimes private fly camps are used in

FIELD GUIDES

➡ *A Field Guide to the Carnivores of the World* (Luke Hunter; 2011) Wonderfully illustrated and filled with fascinating detail.

➡ *The Kingdon Field Guide to African Mammals* (Jonathan Kingdon; 2nd ed, 2015) The latest edition of the classic field guide covering over 1150 species. There's also the travel-friendly *Kingdon Pocket Guide to African Mammals* (2016).

➡ *The Behavior Guide to African Mammals* (Richard Despard Estes; 1991) A classic study of the behaviour of mammal species. Estes' follow-up *The Safari Companion: A Guide to Watching African Mammals* (1993) is an excellent, slightly more accessible alternative.

➡ *Birds of Kenya and Northern Tanzania* (Dale A Zimmerman, David J Pearson & Donald A Turner; 2005) The birding field guide of choice for Kenya and Tanzania.

➡ *Birds of East Africa: Kenya, Tanzania, Uganda, Rwanda, Burundi* (Terry Stevenson & John Fanshawe; 2004) Broader coverage if a little dated.

➡ *Jonathan Scott's Safari Guide to East African Animals* and *Jonathan Scott's Safari Guide to East African Birds* (Jonathan Scott) Both first published in 1998 but updated since, these are wonderful safari companions with fine photos by Angela Scott.

➡ In the UK, an excellent source for wildlife and nature titles is Subbuteo Natural History Books Ltd (www.wildlifebooks.com), while in Australia, check out Andrew Isles Natural History Books (www.andrewisles.com); both accept international mail orders.

top-end safaris, all with the aim of providing guests with as authentic and personal a bush experience as possible while not forgoing the comforts. For the price you pay (from US$250 or US$300 up to US$800 or more per person per day), expect a full range of amenities, as well as top-quality guiding, a high level of personalised attention and an intimate atmosphere.

In Kenya, private or community-run conservancies are increasingly a part of the mix. Most of these conservancies restrict entry onto the conservancy to those who stay in what is usually a luxury lodge, ensuring a more intimate safari experience. Accommodation prices sometimes (but don't always) include a fee that goes towards the conservancy's conservation and community projects. Most of the conservancies are concentrated in Laikipia, northern Kenya and around the Masai Mara, with just two in Tanzania (close to Lake Manyara and in West Kilimanjaro).

When to Go

Apart from climate considerations, the ideal time to make a safari very much depends on which parks and reserves you want to visit and your particular interests. For example, the wet season is the best time for birdwatching in many areas, although some lowland parks may be completely inaccessible during the rains. Wildlife concentrations also vary markedly, depending on the season.

Climate Considerations

Getting around is easier in the dry season (July to October), and in many parks, reserves and conservancies this is when animals are easier to find around waterholes and rivers. Foliage is also less dense, making wildlife easier to spot. However, as the dry season corresponds in part with the high-travel season, lodges and camps in some areas get crowded and accommodation prices are at a premium.

June is also good (and sometimes considered to be high season), while the short rains in late October and November rarely interrupt travel plans. Unless these rains have been particularly heavy, the recommended safari season extends into February.

As a general rule (unless you're a birdwatcher) avoid March to May, when the region's long rains bucket down, wildlife disperses and many tracks become impassable.

Wildebeest Migration

When it comes to visiting Kenya's Masai Mara or Tanzania's Serengeti to see the wildebeest migration, deciding when to go where always involves some element of risk. What follows is a general overview of what usually happens, but it's a guide only and exceptions are common.

January to March During the rains, the wildebeest are widely scattered over the southern and southwestern section of the Serengeti and the western side of Ngorongoro Conservation Area.

April Most streams dry out quickly when the rains cease, nudging the wildebeest to concentrate on the few remaining green areas, and to form thousands-strong herds that begin to migrate northwest in search of food.

May to early July In early May, the herds cross northwest towards the Western Corridor. The crossing of the crocodile-filled Grumeti River usually takes place between late May and early July, and lasts only about a week.

Mid-July to August By the second half of July, the herds are moving north and northwest into the northern Serengeti and Kenya's Masai Mara. As part of this northwards push, they make an even more incredible river crossing of the Mara River.

September to October In early September, the last stragglers leave the Serengeti and most will remain in the Masai Mara throughout October.

November to December The herds usually begin moving south again in November in anticipation of the rains, crossing down through the heart of the Serengeti and to the south in December.

Safari Itineraries

Wherever you plan to take your safari, don't be tempted to try to fit too much into the itinerary. Distances in East Africa are long, and moving too quickly from park to park is likely to leave you tired and unsatisfied.

Tanzania

Northern Circuit

Half-Week

- Any of the northern parks alone
- Ngorongoro Crater together with Lake Manyara or Tarangire National Parks

One Week to 10 Days

- Lake Manyara or Tarangire National Parks plus Ngorongoro Crater and the Serengeti

- ➡ Serengeti National Park, Ngorongoro Crater and Lake Natron
- ➡ Serengeti and Rubondo Island National Parks
- ➡ One or two of the northern parks plus cultural tourism programs around Arusha or hiking in the Usambara Mountains

Southern Circuit

Half-Week

- ➡ Any one of the following: Mikumi, Saadani or Ruaha National Parks or Selous Game Reserve

One Week

- ➡ Selous Game Reserve and Ruaha National Park
- ➡ Ruaha and Katavi National Parks
- ➡ Selous Game Reserve and the Mafia or Zanzibar islands
- ➡ Mahale Mountains National Park and Lake Tanganyika
- ➡ Katavi National Park and Lake Tanganyika

10 Days

- ➡ Ruaha, Katavi and Mahale Mountains National Parks
- ➡ Kaavi and Mahale Mountains National Parks plus Lake Tanganyika

Western Parks

Half-Week

- ➡ Katavi National Park
- ➡ Gombe National Park
- ➡ Rubondo Island National Park

One Week

- ➡ Mahale Mountains and Katavi National Parks

Kenya

Half-Week

- ➡ Masai Mara National Reserve
- ➡ Lake Nakuru National Park
- ➡ Amboseli National Park
- ➡ Tsavo West or Tsavo East National Parks

One Week

- ➡ Masai Mara National Reserve and Amboseli National Park or Lakes Nakuru and Baringo
- ➡ Laikipia Conservancies and Samburu National Reserve

10 Days

- ➡ Masai Mara National Reserve, Amboseli National Park and Tsavo National Parks
- ➡ Laikipia Conservancies and Masai Mara National Reserve, Amboseli National Park or Tsavo National Parks
- ➡ Rift Valley lakes plus Samburu and Buffalo Springs National Reserves
- ➡ Samburu and Buffalo Springs National Reserves plus Marsabit National Park and Lake Turkana
- ➡ Meru National Park or Shaba National Reserve plus Marsabit National Park and Lake Turkana

Uganda

Most safaris in Uganda last one week to 10 days and focus on the southwest, usually combining a gorilla visit in Uganda or neighbouring Rwanda with wildlife watching in Queen Elizabeth and Murchison Falls National Parks and chimp visits in Kibale Forest National Park.

Rwanda

It's easy to visit the highlight parks – Volcanoes National Park, Nyungwe Forest National Park and Akagera National Park – within one week to 10 days. Most organised safari packages are short (less than a week), and concentrate on trips to Volcanoes National Park.

Types of Safari

Organised Vehicle Safaris

Four to six days on an organised vehicle safari is often ideal. At least one full day will normally be taken up with travel, and after six days you may well feel like a rest. If you pack too much distance or too many parks into a short period, you'll likely feel as if you've spent your whole time in transit. If you can, build in rest days spent at camp or on walking safaris and other non-vehicle-based activities.

Minivans are the most common safari transport throughout Kenya (but they're banned in Tanzanian parks); if you have a choice, go for a good 4WD instead – preferably one with a pop-up style roof (versus a simple hatch that flips open or comes off), as it affords some shade. Minivans accommodate too many people for a good experience, the rooftop opening is usually only large enough for a few passengers to use at once, and at least some passengers will get stuck in middle seats with poor views.

Whatever the vehicle, avoid crowding. Most price quotes are based on groups of three to four passengers, which is about the maximum number of people most vehicles can hold comfortably.

Other Safaris

There are many options for walking, cycling and other energetic pursuits, sometimes on their own, and sometimes in combination with a vehicle safari. At all parks, any out-of-vehicle activities in areas with large wildlife must be accompanied by an armed ranger.

Walking, Hiking & Cycling Safaris

At many national parks (and at almost all of the private and community-run conservancies), you can arrange walks of two to three hours in the early morning or late afternoon, with the focus on watching animals rather than covering distance. Following the walk, you'll return to the main camp or lodge, or to a fly camp.

Multiday or point-to-point walks are available in some areas, as are combination walking-hiking-cycling itineraries with side trips by vehicle into the parks to see wildlife. Popular areas in Kenya include Mt Kenya National Park (p289) and Mt Elgon National Park (p274) for trekking and hiking and Hell's Gate National Park (p245) for cycling. Walking (and sometimes horse-riding) safaris are staples of the Laikipia, northern Kenya and Mara conservancies. Lion tracking is also possible in Ol Pejeta Conservancy (p284).

In Tanzania, places where you can walk in big game areas include Selous Game Reserve (p190) and Ruaha (p174), Mikumi (p170), Katavi (p163), Tarangire (p112),

TRACKING CHIMPANZEES

After hanging out with the mountain gorillas many people carry on up the evolutionary tree to spend a day tracking our even closer relatives, chimpanzees. There are four main national parks in which to see chimps and, as with the gorillas, the experience in each is different.

Mahale Mountains National Park (Tanzania)

With steep forested mountains falling sharply down to beaches of feather-soft white sands and the turquoise waters of Lake Tanganyika, Mahale Mountains (p160) is the park with the most spectacular setting. Lots of chimps here are very used to humans; many will happily walk right up to you. Consequently many rate Mahale as the best park to see chimps. However, getting to Mahale can be time consuming and expensive. You're also limited to one hour a day with the chimps and for the rest of the day there's actually not much else to do. Face masks must be worn when with the chimps.

Gombe National Park (Tanzania)

Located on the shores of Lake Tanganyika, access to Gombe (p159) is relatively easy and the park is good value. The chimps here have been studied for decades (this is where Jane Goodall worked) and couldn't be more used to people. Chimp encounters are limited to an hour a day and there's not much else to do once your time with the chimps is up. Face masks must be worn.

Nyungwe Forest National Park (Rwanda)

One of the most important forest systems in East Africa, Nyungwe (p534) is home to a large number of chimps, but of all the big chimpanzee parks, the apes here are the least habituated and most skittish around people. Access to the park is cheap and easy and there are lots of other things to do when your hour with the chimps is up.

Kibale Forest National Park (Uganda)

Access to this important forest (p431) is cheap and easy and there's an array of brilliant-value accommodation for all budgets. The chimps here are very well habituated and up-close encounters are pretty much guaranteed. The one-hour chimp permit here is more expensive than at any of the other parks, but you can pay a little extra and join a full-day 'chimp experience'. When not with the chimps there are lots of other wildlife and cultural activities available. Face masks not required.

TIPPING

Assuming service has been satisfactory, tipping is an important part of the East African safari experience (especially to the drivers/guides, cooks and others whose livelihoods depend on tips), and it will always be in addition to the overall safari price quoted by the operator. Many operators have tipping guidelines. Depending on where you are, for camping safaris this averages from about US$10 to US$15 per day per group for the driver-guide/cook, and more for upmarket safaris, large groups or an especially good job.

Another way to calculate things is to give an additional day's wage for every five days worked, with a similar proportion for a shorter trip, and a higher than average tip for exceptional service. Wages in East Africa are low, and it's never a mistake to err on the side of generosity when tipping those who have worked to make your safari experience memorable. Whenever possible, give your tips directly to the staff you want to thank, although many safari camps and lodges keep a box for tips that are later shared among all staff.

Lake Manyara (p115), Serengeti (p123) and Arusha (p109) National Parks. There are also several parks – including Kilimanjaro (p134), Mahale Mountains (p160) and Gombe (p159) National Parks – that can only be explored on foot. Short walks are easily arranged in Rubondo Island National Park (p149). Multiday walks are possible in the Crater Highlands, Serengeti National Park and Selous Game Reserve, and cycling is possible in the area around Lake Manyara National Park.

In Uganda, opportunities include everything from tracking gorillas and chimpanzees to birdwatching walks in Bwindi Impenetrable (p445) and Kibale Forest (p431) National Parks, to wildlife walks in Queen Elizabeth (p439), Kidepo Valley (p419) and Lake Mburo (p461) National Parks, and climbing Mt Elgon (p415) or trekking in the Rwenzoris (p436).

Boat & Canoe Safaris

Boat safaris are an excellent way to experience the East African wilderness and offer a welcome break from dusty, bumpy roads. Good destinations include the following:

- Along the Rufiji River in Tanzania's Selous Game Reserve (p190), with two- to three-hour boat safaris
- Uganda's Queen Elizabeth National Park (p439)
- Launch trips up the Victoria Nile to the base of Murchison Falls (p468)

Camel Safaris

Most camel safaris take place in northern Kenya's Samburu and Turkana tribal areas, with Maralal a logical base. Although you may see wildlife along the way, the main attractions are the journey itself, and the chance to immerse yourself in nomadic life and mingle with the indigenous people. You can either ride the camels or walk alongside them. Most travelling is done in the cooler parts of the day. Most operators provide camping equipment or offer it for rental. There are also camel safaris in Maasai areas near Arusha National Park (p109).

Balloon Safaris

The places for balloon safaris are Kenya's Masai Mara National Reserve (p252) and Tanzania's Serengeti National Park (p123). Everything depends on wind and weather conditions; spotting animals can't be guaranteed and flight time is generally limited to a maximum of one hour. But the captains try to stay between 500m and 1000m above ground, which means that if animals are there you'll be able to see them. Most balloon safaris are followed by a champagne breakfast in the bush.

Do-It-Yourself Safaris

It's possible to visit most of East Africa's parks with your own vehicle, without going through a safari operator. Some travellers rave about the experience and the freedom it gives you. For others, unless you're experienced at bush driving, the modest cost savings may be offset by having someone else handle the logistics; if you're renting, hiring a local driver rarely costs a whole lot more.

For most areas, you'll need a 4WD. In addition to park admission fees, there are daily vehicle fees and, in some areas, a mandatory guide fee. You may need to carry extra petrol, as it's not available in all parks, as well as spare tyres. Carrying a tent is also recommended.

Plan Your Trip

Gorilla Tracking

Nothing quite prepares you for the moment when you come upon a gorilla family in the wild. No bars, no windows – you're a humble guest in their domain. Coming face to face with mountain gorillas is one of life's great experiences. And we'll help you make it happen.

Planning Your Trip

There's nothing quite like sharing a few long moments with a mountain gorilla family: the first glimpse of black as a juvenile jumps off a nearby branch, a toddler clings to its mother's back and a giant silverback rises to size you up. To make the most of this life-changing experience, planning ahead is essential.

When to Go

Any time you can. The experience will be incredible no matter when you go, but there are advantages to going at different times of the year.

It's generally easier to track gorillas in the rainy seasons (March to May and September to November) because they hang out at lower altitudes. You may also get better photos in the rainy season, assuming it isn't raining at the time you're with the gorillas, because they love to sunbathe after getting wet. Then again, you'll need to be wearing some serious wet-weather gear.

The busiest times on the mountains are December to February and July to August. Scoring permits takes more effort during these months, but that won't matter if a tour company is handling things for you.

Booking Ahead

Permits are required to visit the gorillas and booking ahead is always a good idea, particularly if you're planning to visit Uganda's Bwindi Impenetrable National

Best for Seeing Gorillas

Bwindi Impenetrable National Park (Uganda; p445)

Volcanoes National Park (Rwanda; p520)

Best for Independent Travellers

Mgahinga Gorilla National Park (Uganda; p457)

Parc National des Virunga (DRC; p498)

Dry Season

When December to February, June to August

Advantages Generally dry weather

Disadvantages Permits more difficult to obtain

Wet Season

When March to May, September to November

Advantages Fewer visitors so permits easier to obtain; permits cheaper at Bwindi Impenetrable National Park; generally easier to track gorillas

Disadvantages Can be extremely wet

Cheapest Permits

Bwindi Impenetrable National Park (Uganda) – US$600 (US$450 April, May, October and November)

Parc National des Virunga (DRC) – US$400

Most Expensive Permits

Volcanoes National Park (Rwanda) – US$1500

RULES FOR GORILLA TRACKING

- Anyone with an illness cannot track the gorillas. In Rwanda you'll get a full refund if you cancel because of illness and produce a doctor's note, while in Uganda you'll get back half.
- Eating and smoking near the gorillas is prohibited.
- If you have to cough or sneeze, cover your mouth and turn your head.
- Flash photography is banned; turn off the autoflash.
- Speak quietly and don't point at the gorillas or make sudden movements; they may see these as threats.
- Leave nothing in the park; you shouldn't even spit.
- Keep a few metres back from the gorillas and promptly follow your guide's directions about where to walk.
- When faced with 200kg of charging silverback, never, ever run away...crouch down until he cools off.
- Children under 15 years of age aren't allowed to visit the gorillas.

Park (p445) and Rwanda's Volcanoes National Park (p520) from December to February or July to August. If you aren't travelling in these months and you only have a very small window of opportunity, you should still make a reservation as far in advance as possible to be safe.

To make a phone booking for Rwanda, you need to pay a deposit by bank transfer, while in Uganda you'll need to provide all the money up front. If you can't get a permit on your own, you'll need to go through a tour operator, which is often a good idea anyway. In the Democratic Republic of the Congo (DRC), you can book online.

Required Fitness Levels

With the combination of mud, steep hills and altitude, gorilla tracking is hard work. Although gorillas sometimes wander near the visitor centres and might be found quickly, you're far more likely to be hiking for two to four hours, and some trackers have wandered across the mountains for an entire day. The authorities sometimes group together visitors of similar age and fitness level, and factor this into which gorilla family they send you out to find, but it can still take hours of hard walking.

What to Bring

For the most part, you don't need anything special beyond the usual outdoor essentials such as sunscreen, insect repellent, and food and water (enough for the whole day, just in case). Good boots are important. Some people like rubber boots because they keep the mud and fire ants at bay, but they have no ankle support. Plan for rain no matter what month you're tracking (you'll be in a rainforest after all). It's also often chilly in the morning, so you might want a warm top.

You may have to trudge through thorns and stinging nettles, so trousers and long-sleeved shirts with some degree of heft may save you some irritation. For the same reason, garden gloves can come in handy.

Finally, bring your passport with you on tracking day; you'll need it during registration.

Costs

For most of the year, demand for gorilla-tracking permits far outstrips supply. Permits cost the following:

- Rwanda US$1500
- Uganda US$450–600
- DRC US$400

The price includes park entry, guides and armed escorts, while porters are available for a little extra. These people are paid very little, and work hard, and so they will expect a small tip.

Understanding Gorillas

Gorillas are the largest of the great apes and share 97% of their biological make-up with humans. Gorillas used to inhabit a

Top: Bwindi Impenetrable National Park (p445), Uganda

Bottom: Volcanoes National Park (p520), Rwanda

MITCHELL KROG / GETTY IMAGES ©

swath of land that cut right across central Africa, but the last remaining eastern mountain gorillas number around 880, divided between two 300-plus populations in the forests of Uganda's Bwindi Impenetrable National Park and on the slopes of the Virunga volcanoes, encompassing Uganda's Mgahinga Gorilla National Park, Rwanda's Volcanoes National Park and the DRC's Parc National des Virunga.

Daily Life

Gorillas spend 30% of their day feeding, 30% moving and foraging, and the remainder resting. They spend most of their time on the ground, moving around on all fours but standing up to reach for food. Gorillas are vegetarians and their diet consists mainly of bamboo shoots, giant thistles and wild celery, all of which contain water and allow the gorillas to survive without drinking for long periods of time. A silverback can eat his way through more than 30kg of bamboo a day.

A group's dominant silverback dictates movements for the day, and at night each gorilla makes its own nest. Gorillas usually travel about 1km a day, unless they have met another group, in which case they may move further.

Families

Gorillas generally live in family groups of varying sizes, usually including one to two older silverback males, younger blackback males, females and infants. Most groups contain between 10 and 15 gorillas, but they can exceed 40. The largest habituated group in Uganda's Bwindi Impenetrable National Park has 26 members, and in Rwanda's Volcanoes National Park the largest group has 28.

There are strong bonds between individuals, and status is usually linked to age. Silverbacks are at the top of the hierarchy, then females with infants or ties to the silverbacks, then blackbacks and other females. Most gorillas leave the group when they reach maturity, which helps prevent inbreeding among such a small population.

Conflict

Gorillas are relatively placid primates and serious confrontations are rare, although violence can flare up if there's a challenge for supremacy between silverbacks. Conflicts are mostly kept to shows of strength and vocal disputes.

Conflict between groups is also uncommon, as gorillas aren't territorial; if two groups meet, there's usually lots of display and bravado on the part of silverbacks, including mock charges. Often the whole group joins in and it's at this point that young adult females may choose to switch allegiance.

If gorillas do fight, injuries can be very serious as these animals have long canine teeth and silverbacks pack a punch estimated to be eight times stronger than that of a heavyweight boxer. If a dominant male is driven from a group by another silverback, it's likely the new leader will kill all the infants to establish his mating rights.

Communication

Gorillas communicate in a variety of ways, including facial expressions, gestures and around two dozen vocalisations. Adult males use barks and roars during confrontations or to coordinate the movement of their groups to a different area. Postures and gestures form an important element of intimidation and it's possible for a clash to be diffused by a display of teeth-baring, stiff-legging and charging.

Friendly communication is an important part of group bonding and includes grunts of pleasure. Upon finding food, gorillas will grunt or bark to alert other members of the group.

Biology

Gorillas are the largest primates in the world and mountain gorillas are the largest of the three gorilla species; adult male mountain gorillas weigh as much as 200kg (440lb). Females are about half this size.

Males reach maturity between eight and 15 years old, their backs turning silver as they enter their teens, while females enter adulthood at the earlier age of eight. Conception is possible for about three days each month, and once a female has conceived for the first time, she spends most of her life pregnant or nursing.

The duration of a gorilla pregnancy is about 8½ months. Newborn infants are highly dependent on adults, and a young infant will rarely leave its mother's arms during its first six months. In its second year, a young gorilla begins to interact with other members of the group and starts to feed itself. Infant gorillas and silverbacks often form a bond, and it's not uncommon for a silverback to adopt an infant if its mother dies. This distinguishes gorillas from other primates, where child-rearing duties are left to females. From about three years, young gorillas become quite independent and build their own nests.

Mountain gorillas are distinguished from their more widespread lowland relatives by longer hair, broader chests and wider jaws. The most obvious thing that sets the gorillas in Bwindi apart from those of the Virungas is that they are less shaggy, most likely due to the lower altitude.

Where to Track Gorillas

Bwindi Impenetrable National Park (Uganda)

Home to around half of the world's eastern mountain gorilla population, Bwindi Impenetrable National Park (p445) remains one of the top spots to track mountain gorillas. The evocatively named park lives up to its name, with stunning scenery comprising dense, steep virgin rainforest. And yes, it means tracking can occasionally be hard work, but with the aid of a good walking stick (or a porter to lend a hand), you'll get there without too much difficulty. And while visibility often isn't as good as it is in the open spaces where the Virunga gorillas hang out, in Bwindi you'll get just as close to them and they're more likely to be seen swinging from the trees.

Arranging Permits

Even though the number of tracking permits has increased to around 96 per day, it can still be difficult to get them. There are 12 mountain gorilla groups spread across four areas of the park.

Permits, which cost US$600, must be booked at the Uganda Wildlife Authority (p485) headquarters in Kampala or through a Ugandan tour operator. It's theoretically possible to arrange permits online via a bank transfer, but UWA is notoriously tricky to get in touch with via email.

Discount permits are available for US$450 for the low season months of April, May, October and November; whether this remains an ongoing approach is yet to be determined.

Mgahinga Gorilla National Park (Uganda)

Mgahinga Gorilla National Park (p457) encompasses Uganda's share of the Virunga volcanoes, which sit squarely on the tri-nation border. This park is popular with independent travellers because reservations aren't possible more than two weeks in advance, due to the only habituated gorilla group's tendency to duck over the border into Rwanda or the DRC. Of course, the downside of this is that it means they can't always be tracked. It often takes longer to find the gorillas here than in Bwindi (p445), but the walking is usually (but not always) much easier.

Arranging Permits

Reservations for the eight places available daily are only taken at the Mgahinga Gorilla National Park Office (p457) in Kisoro. The US$600 fee is paid at the park headquarters on the morning of your tracking.

GORILLA LOCATIONS

COUNTRY	LOCATION	DAILY PERMITS AVAILABLE	COST (US$)	HABITUATED GORILLA GROUPS
Uganda	Bwindi Impenetrable National Park	96	600 (450 Apr, May, Oct & Nov)	12
Uganda	Mgahinga Gorilla National Park	8	600	1
Rwanda	Volcanoes National Park	80	1500	10
the DRC	Parc National des Virunga	26	400	6

Volcanoes National Park (Rwanda)

Rwanda's Volcanoes National Park (p520) ranks up there with Uganda's Bwindi Impenetrable National Park (p445) as one of the best places in East Africa to see gorillas, but a recent price hike has somewhat diminished its appeal. Part of its cachet comes from the fact that this is where Dian Fossey was based and where the film about her work was made. Also, the towering volcanoes form a breathtaking backdrop. Tracking here is usually easier than in Bwindi because the mountains offer a more gradual climb, and the visibility is often better too; remember, however, that the trekking here is still extremely strenuous. One other thing to remember is that visitors here, unlike in Bwindi, are assigned gorilla groups on tracking day, not when reservations are made, so those who aren't in such good shape will get one of the groups requiring the least amount of walking.

Arranging Permits

There are 10 habituated gorilla groups. Eighty tracking permits (US$1500 per person) are available each day.

You can book a permit with the RDB Tourist Office (p636) in Kigali or through a tour operator.

Parc National des Virunga (the DRC)

Established in 1925 by the Belgian colonial government as Albert National Park, Parc National des Virunga (p498) is the continent's oldest and largest protected area. To put things in perspective, Virunga is contiguous with five different national parks in Uganda, and protects an incredible range of endangered animals, from forest elephants to chimpanzees and mountain gorillas.

The park lies at the centre of a war-torn region, and has been threatened by poaching, land invasions, charcoal producers and rebel factions. The park was forced to close in 2012, but parts of it reopened to tourism in 2014. Assuming that the security situation is safe, the DRC receives far fewer visitors than Uganda's Bwindi Impenetrable National Park (p445) or Rwanda's Volcanoes National Park (p520). Given that permits are also easier to come by here (and they are cheaper), this is probably the easiest place for independent travellers to see the gorillas. And the setting is stunning.

Guide, Volcanoes National Park (p520), Rwanda

The habituated mountain gorillas of the Parc National des Virunga can be seen on a gorilla tracking trip (US$400 to US$600). The other drawcard is the chance to climb, and sleep on the rim of (US$300), the Nyiragongo volcano, whose crater contains the world's largest permanent lava lake.

Bookings for all park activities should be made through the impressively organised Virunga **visitor centre** (☎DRC 99 1715401; www.visitvirunga.org; Blvd Kanya Muhanga, Goma, DRC; ⏰8.30am-5pm Mon-Fri, to noon Sat) in Goma or through its website. While tourist visas for the Congo are extremely difficult to obtain, the park can help arrange what is known as a Virunga Visa, which is valid for the park itself, Goma, Bukavu and the Parc National Kahuzi-Biega (www.kahuzibiega.org), home to habituated groups of eastern lowland gorillas (permits US$400). Visas take around a week to issue and cost US$105.

The security situation in this part of the world changes fast and often. Be sure to double-check the latest before venturing here.

Arranging Permits

You can buy permits (US$400) and arrange transport and accommodation directly through the Institut Congolais pour la Conservation de la Nature (p498).

Plan Your Trip

Travel with Children

East Africa is a wonderful destination for families. Yes, there are vaccinations to worry about, distances can be large and there are regions you'll want to avoid. But you might just have the holiday of a lifetime.

East Africa for Kids

Health & Safe Travel

Africa's list of potential health hazards is formidable, although a little preparation can ameliorate most risks – talk with your doctor before departure, take special care with hygiene once you're on the road and make sure your children always sleep under a mosquito net.

Safaris & Cultures

The safari could have been custom-built for older children, but younger kids may not have the patience to sit for long periods in a car. Driving up to within touching distance of elephants and watching lion cubs gambolling across the plains are experiences your kids won't quickly forget. A number of very top-end lodges, particularly in Kenya, operate 'Warrior for a Week' programs, during which, in between safaris, the little darlings get taught how to make fire without matches, track buffalo, shoot their little sister with a bow and arrow and other such things you don't really want a five-year-old boy learning!

If such top-end lodges are beyond your budget, you'll be pleased to hear that throughout the region there are numerous other 'cultural experience' programs that are often easier on the wallet than a safari. More importantly, most of these are likely to leave a stronger imprint in your child's mind than any number of animal encounters.

Best Regions for Kids

Tanzania

Tanzania combines fabulous safari destinations – particularly Ngorongoro Conservation Area (p120), a true place of the imagination, and the Serengeti National Park (p123) – with a lengthy Indian Ocean coastline; safari lodges and beach resorts (especially in Zanzibar) are often family-friendly.

Kenya

Like Tanzania, Kenya combines stirring safaris with fabulous coastline. The Masai Mara National Reserve (p252) during the wildebeest migration (July to October) is an extraordinary spectacle; other national parks such as Nairobi (p221) and Lake Nakuru (p249) are more manageable in size. Anywhere along the coast can be good for families, although Diani Beach and (security depending) Lamu are our pick.

Uganda

With wildlife-rich national parks and a slew of water-based activities at Entebbe and Jinja, Uganda can be a great destination. Queen Elizabeth National Park (p439), with its boat rides and good roads, is ideal for a family safari. Remember minimum age requirements (usually 12 or 15 years old) apply for chimp and gorilla tracking.

Beach Holidays

Beach holidays are a sure-fire way to keep the kids happy, and factoring in some beach time to go with a safari can be a good idea. Kenya's and Tanzania's beaches alone should be sufficient, but some of the water sports on offer, and other pursuits such as snorkelling, may be suitable for children, depending on their age. Packing a picnic lunch and sailing out to sea on a dhow (ancient Arabic sailing vessel) is fun family time.

Children's Highlights

National Parks & Reserves

Masai Mara National Reserve, Kenya Africa's charismatic megafauna in abundance. (p252)

Serengeti National Park, Tanzania Arguably the best national park in East Africa. (p123)

Nairobi National Park, Kenya Good roads, easy access and loads of animals. (p221)

Lake Nakuru National Park, Kenya Flamingos, leopards and monkeys. (p249)

Saadani National Park, Tanzania Perfect combination of beach and bush. (p94)

Beaches

Zanzibar, Tanzania Intriguing island culture and glorious beaches. (p64)

Lamu Archipelago, Kenya Indian Ocean port. (p337)

Pangani & Around, Tanzania Terrific beaches on Tanzania's north coast. (p95)

Entebbe, Uganda White-sand beaches on Lake Victoria's shore. (p401)

Activities

Swimming with dolphins Take the plunge at Kisite Marine National Park, Kenya. (p327)

Snorkelling Snorkel the Indian Ocean at Pemba, Tanzania. (p85)

Sailing Take a dhow trip and sail the trade winds at Zanzibar, Tanzania. (p64)

White-water rafting Enjoy white-water rafting for teens at Jinja, Uganda. (p409)

Planning

Travelling to East Africa with children requires careful planning. It's generally best to avoid the rainy season (March to May) and you'll need to check carefully what vaccinations are required for each country you plan to visit; antimalarial medication is also recommended. Accommodation is generally easy to organise but do your research – some resorts and safari camps are more family-friendly than others and some don't even accept children.

For all-round information and advice, check out Lonely Planet's *Travel with Children*.

What to Bring

Canned baby foods, powdered milk, disposable nappies and the like are available in most large supermarkets, but they are expensive. Bring as much as possible from home, along with child-friendly insect repellent (this can't be bought in East Africa). Child seats for hire cars and safari vehicles are generally not available unless arranged in advance.

For protection against malaria, bring mosquito nets for your children and ensure that they sleep under them.

Accommodation

Although some wildlife lodges have restrictions on children aged under 12 years, most lodges can handle most practicalities with aplomb, whether it's the extra bed or cot, or serving buffet meals for fussy eaters; some lodges even have children's playgrounds and almost all have swimming pools.

Budget hotels are probably best avoided for hygiene reasons. Most midrange accommodation should be acceptable, though it's usually only top-end places that cater specifically for families. Camping can be exciting, but make sure little ones don't wander off unsupervised.

Children under two years usually stay free in most hotels. Children between two and 12 years are usually charged 50% of the adult rate; you'll also get a cot thrown in. Large family rooms are sometimes available, and some places also have adjoining rooms with connecting doors.

Transport

Safari vehicles are usually child-friendly, but travelling between towns on public transport is rarely easy. Functional seatbelts are rare even in taxis and accidents are common. A child seat brought from home is a good idea if you're hiring a car or going on safari.

Countries at a Glance

East Africa is a vast region of astonishing diversity.

Kenya and Tanzania rank among the premier wildlife-watching destinations on the planet. Their savannah parks and conservancies shelter just about every African species of charismatic megafauna, from elephants, rhinos and millions-strong herds of wildebeest to the predators that pursue them. If it's primates you're after, Uganda and Rwanda are the places to go for gorillas, while western Tanzania is one of the best places anywhere for observing chimpanzees in the wild.

Fascinating traditional cultures are another East African speciality (including in Burundi, though it's not currently safe for travellers), while the landscapes – from the continent's highest mountains to volcanic craters, from lush rainforest and palm-fringed coastlines to epic deserts – could just be the most varied of any African region.

Tanzania

Wildlife
Beaches & Islands
Culture

Predators & Prey

Whether you're watching wildebeest on the Serengeti Plains, communing with lions in Ngorongoro Crater or floating past hippos and crocs in Selous Game Reserve, the variety of wildlife in Tanzania is unsurpassed.

Coastal Paradise

Let yourself be seduced by miles of Indian Ocean coastline, magical archipelagos, swaying palms, and fine diving and snorkelling. Once you get hooked, you may never want to leave.

Tribal Insights

Tanzania has a rich array of tribal traditions (including the Maasai, the Barabaig and the Hadzabe) and long Swahili roots. To get to know the cultural melange, travel off the beaten track. Cultural tourism programs offer an accessible introduction.

p52

Kenya

Wildlife
Beaches & Islands
Culture

Animal Abundance

From the predator-filled plains of Masai Mara National Reserve to the elephant-rich landscapes of Amboseli National Park, Kenya offers superb wildlife watching against stunning natural backdrops.

Steamy Swahili Coast

Kenya's coast is enchanting, whether you're relaxing on the beaches around Mombasa or wandering sleepy lanes on Lamu island. Come for a week, but wind up staying much longer.

Tribal Traditions

The beaded Turkana and the red-robed Maasai are just a sampling of Kenya's vibrant tribal mix. Getting to know the different peoples and rich traditions is a highlight, no matter which part of the country you visit.

p220

Uganda

Wildlife
Landscapes
Adventure Sports

Gorillas & Lions

Uganda's Bwindi Impenetrable National Park is home to almost half of the world's surviving mountain gorillas, and a visit here is a highlight. Elsewhere, lions and other predators are plentiful in many parks.

Mountains & Waterfalls

Lovely Murchison Falls National Park, wild Kidepo Valley National Park and the peerless Rwenzoris are just three of the many attractions in this country that's painted in every shade of green.

White-Water Rafting

Uganda's upper Nile stretch, with its Class IV and Class V rapids, is a challenging white-water rafting destination. Or take a family float trip for a gentler introduction.

p381

Detour: DRC

Primates
Nature
Adventure

Gorillas & Chimpanzees

The gorillas of Parc National des Virunga are the main attraction. Get ready for hard, sweaty tracking work, and magical encounters once you find them. Virungas park is also home to chimpanzees, and visits to the park's habituated Tongo population should soon be possible.

Nyiragongo Volcano

Climb to the top of Nyiragongo Volcano for views down into the world's largest lava lake. Plan to overnight on the crater rim, to see the fiery glow of lava light up the night sky.

Off the Tourist Trail

Whether it's meeting gorillas, trekking up Nyiragongo volcano or just getting into the country, everything about the DRC is an adventure.

p494

Rwanda

Wildlife
Landscapes
Culture

Mountain Gorillas

The bamboo- and rainforest-covered slopes of the Virunga volcanoes are home to some of the last remaining sanctuaries of the endangered eastern mountain gorilla. A hike here in search of silverbacks and their families is an unforgettable experience.

Mountains & Lakes

The 'Land of a Thousand Hills' has endless mountains and stunning scenery. Lake Kivu offers lovely inland beaches, while Nyungwe Forest National Park protects extensive tracts of montane rainforest.

Rwanda's People

Rwanda has moved impressively far from its troubled history, and getting to know its vibrant cultural backdrop is a highlight of travelling here.

p506

Burundi

Burundi is unfortunately not a safe destination for travellers right now. Ten years of relative quiet following the end of the civil war in 2005 did enable the adventurous to visit this incredible country, but since 2015, when President Pierre Nkurunziza controversially declared he was to run for an unprecedented third term, the country has been a place of intense political instability and violence.

This environment has further impeded the country's economy, leading to food shortages and some 65% of the population living below the poverty line. If the political woes right themselves and the country becomes a safe place for travellers, tourism will hopefully play a part in contributing to the future prosperity of the country and its people.

p555

On the Road

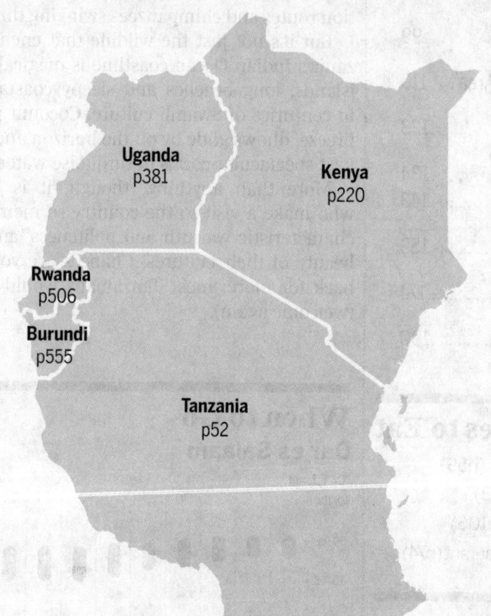
Uganda
p381
Kenya
p220
Rwanda
p506
Burundi
p555
Tanzania
p52

Tanzania

255 / POP 52.5 MILLION

Includes ➡

Dar es Salaam........53
Zanzibar Island.......65
Pemba..............85
Usambara Mountains...........99
Ngorongoro Conservation Area...119
Serengeti National Park.......123
Mt Kilimanjaro National Park.......134
Lake Victoria........143
Gombe National Park.......159
Ruaha National Park.......174
Selous Game Reserve.......190

Best Places to Eat

- Chapan Bhog (p59)
- The Rock (p83)
- Blue Heron (p106)
- Lukmaan Restaurant (p74)

Best Places to Stay

- Lake Shore Lodge & Campsite (p164)
- Old Boma at Mikindani (p200)
- Kisolanza – The Old Farm House (p173)
- Shu'mata Camp (p138)

Why Go?

Tanzania is *the* land of safaris, with wildebeest stampeding across the plains, hippos jostling for space in rivers, massive elephant herds kicking up the dust on their seasonal migration routes and chimpanzees swinging through the treetops.

But it's not just the wildlife that enchants visitors. Tanzania's Indian Ocean coastline is magical, with its tranquil islands, long beaches and sleepy coastal villages steeped in centuries of Swahili culture. Coconut palms sway in the breeze, dhows glide by on the horizon and colourful fish flit past spectacular corals in turquoise waters.

More than anything, though, it is Tanzania's people who make a visit to the country so memorable, with their characteristic warmth and politeness, and the dignity and beauty of their cultures. Chances are you'll want to come back for more: most Tanzanians would say '*karibu tena*' (welcome again).

When to Go

Dar es Salaam

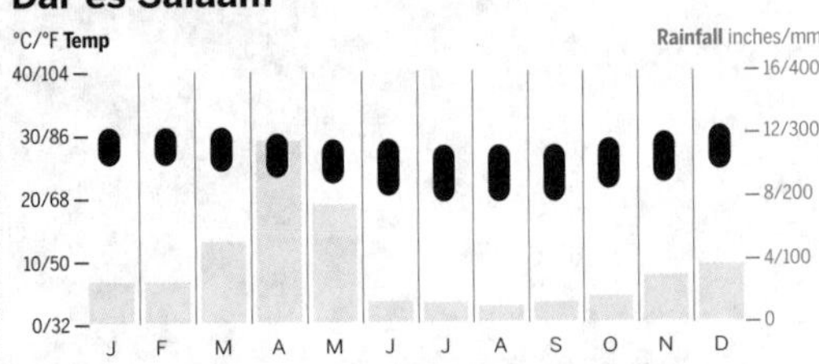

Mar–May Heavy rains bring green landscapes, lower prices, top-notch birdwatching and muddy roads.

Jun–Aug Cool, dry weather, with wildlife watching at its prime.

Sep–Oct Weather remains dry, and wildlife watching is good, without the crowds.

DAR ES SALAAM

☎022 / POP 4.36 MILLION

Over the last century, Dar es Salaam has grown from a sleepy Zaramo fishing village into a thriving tropical metropolis of over four million people. Straddling some of the most important sea routes in the world, it is East Africa's second-busiest port and Tanzania's commercial hub. Despite this, and its notorious traffic jams, the city has managed to maintain a low-key, down-to-earth feel.

Rimming the central area is Kivukoni Front, with a bustling fish market where dhows dock at dawn to offload the night's catch. Excellent craft markets and restaurants abound, and nearby sandy beaches and islands beckon.

Dar es Salaam's architecture is a mixture of African, Arab, Indian and German, although much of this is now dwarfed by towering high-rises. Many travellers bypass 'Dar' completely; those that linger will encounter the city's eclectic cultural mix and languid vibe.

Sights & Activities

Nafasi Art Space GALLERY

(☎0753 334310, 0673 334314; www.nafasiartspace.org; Eyasi Rd, Light Industrial Area, Mikocheni B; ⊙10am-5.30pm Mon-Fri, 10am-2pm Sat) Aiming to be the leading contemporary art centre in Tanzania, Nafasi is a complex of studios housed in an old industrial warehouse in Mikocheni. Many local member artists work there alongside regional and international residencies, all of whom exhibit in the on-site gallery. The centre provides a platform for training and cross-cultural discourse, which it promotes through monthly events such as Chap Chap, which combines an exhibition and open workshops with evening music, theatre and dance.

National Museum & House of Culture MUSEUM

(Map p56; ☎022-211 7508; Shaaban Robert St; adult/student Tsh6500/2600; ⊙9.30am-6pm) The National Museum houses a copy of the famous fossil discoveries of *zinjanthropus* ('nutcracker man') from Olduvai Gorge, plus other archaeological finds. Wander through the History Room and ethnographic collection for insights into Tanzania's past and its mosaic of cultures, including the Shirazi civilisation of Kilwa, the Zanzibar slave trade, and the German and British colonial periods. Despite renovations, however, the museum still has much work to do on appropriate displays and the curation of a coherent narrative.

Village Museum MUSEUM

(Map p58; ☎022-270 0437, 0718 525682; New Bagamoyo Rd; adult/student Tsh6500/2600, dance & drum performance Tsh2000; ⊙9am-6pm) This open-air museum features a collection of authentically constructed dwellings illustrating traditional life in various parts of Tanzania. Each house is furnished with typical items and surrounded by small plots of crops, while 'villagers' demonstrate traditional skills such as weaving, pottery and carving. Traditional tribal dance performances also take place daily, whenever there is sufficient demand.

Sleeping

Friendly Gecko Guesthouse GUESTHOUSE $

(☎0759 941848; www.friendlygecko.com; Africana area; dm US$20, s/d from US$30/50; P❄📶) If you want to stay in Dar a couple of days and

TANZANIA FAST FACTS

Area 943,000 sq km

Capital Dodoma (legislative), Dar es Salaam (economic)

Currency Tanzanian shilling (Tsh)

Population 52.5 million

Languages Swahili, English

Money The easiest way to access money while travelling in Tanzania is at ATMs using a Visa card.

Visas Almost everyone needs a visa, which costs US$50 for most nationalities (US$100 for US citizens) for a single-entry visa valid for a maximum of three months.

Exchange Rates

Australia	A$1	Tsh1753
Canada	C$1	Tsh1725
Europe	€1	Tsh2771
Japan	¥100	Tsh2119
Kenya	KSh100	Tsh2225
New Zealand	NZ$1	Tsh1637
South Africa	R10	Tsh1892
UK	UK£1	Tsh3138
US	US$1	Tsh2252

For current exchange rates, see www.xe.com.

Tanzania Highlights

1 **Serengeti National Park** (p123) Marvelling at nature's rhythms on the Serengeti Plains during the Great Migration.

2 **Mt Kilimanjaro** (p134) Scaling the summit of Africa or hiking the lower slopes.

3 **Ngorongoro Crater** (p122) Descending into a lost world of wildlife and great beauty.

4 **Zanzibar Archipelago** (p64) Watching an Indian Ocean moonrise, then losing yourself in Zanzibar's Stone Town.

5 **Southern Highlands** (p167) Discovering colourful markets, hiking through rolling hills and seeing elephants in Ruaha National Park.

6 **Lake Victoria** (p143) Enjoying fine birdwatching and exploring tranquil Rubondo Island National Park.

7 **Northeastern Tanzania** (p91) Hiking in the Usambaras or relaxing along the beautiful coast.

8 **Southeastern Tanzania** (p185) Immersing yourself in Swahili culture, boating past grunting hippos, and diving and snorkelling.

9 **Selous Game Reserve** (p190) Tracking down Afria's largest lion population in a vast wilderness area.

10 **Western Tanzania** (p153) Seeing chimpanzees up close, watching wildlife in Katavi and exploring Lake Tanganyika's shoreline.

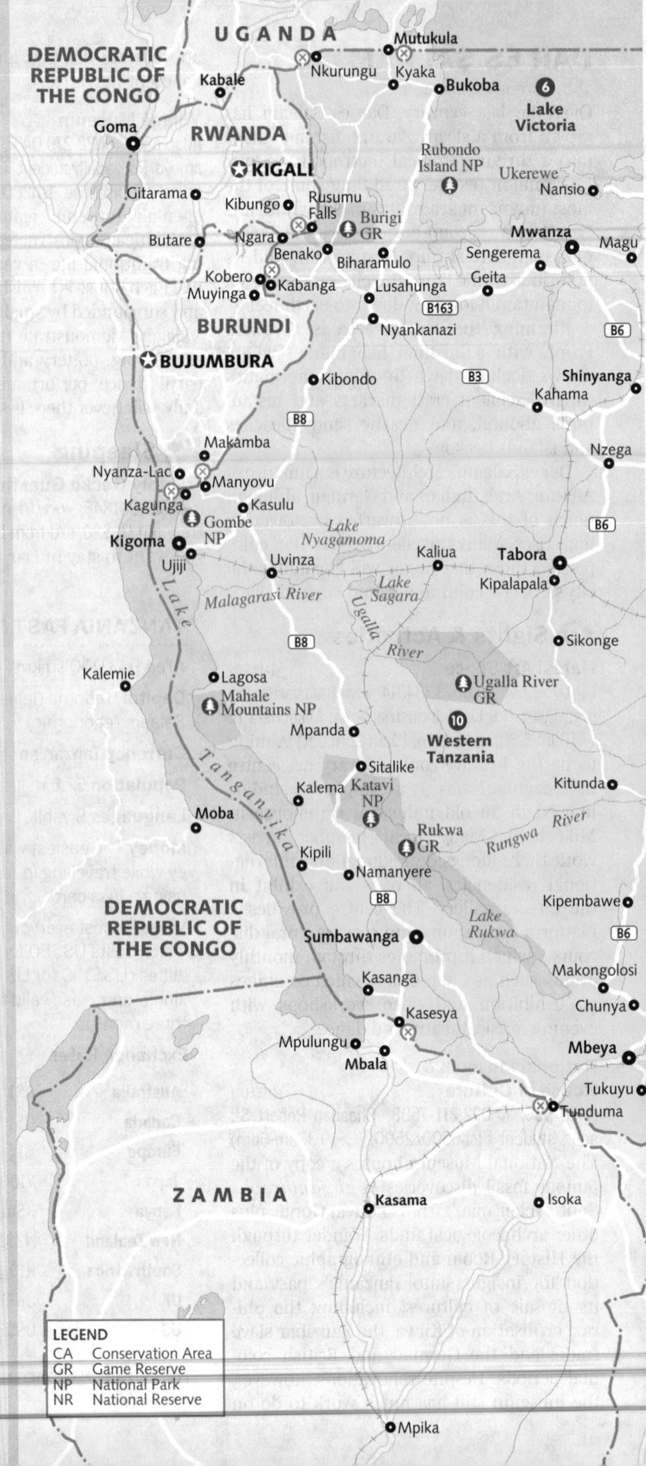

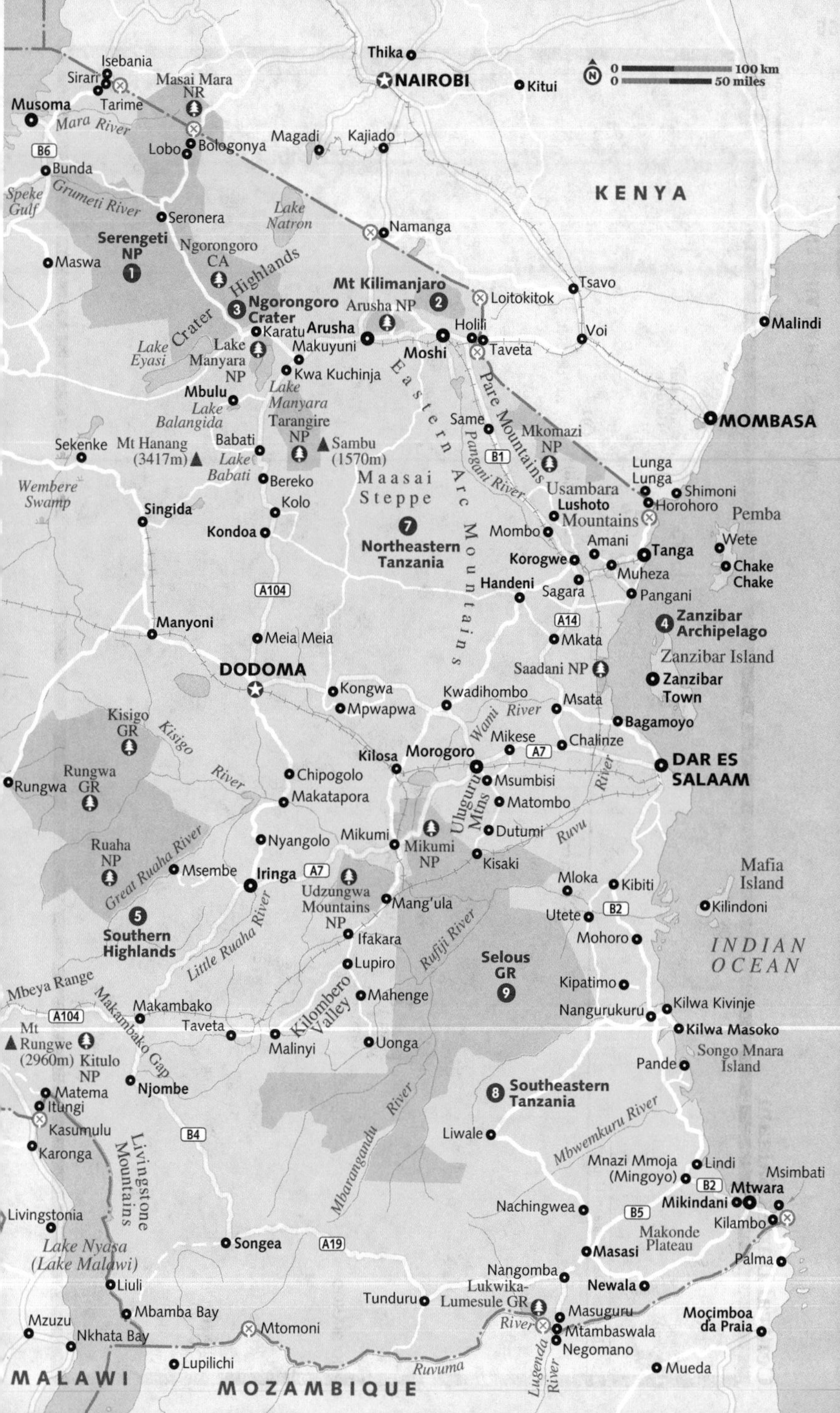

100 km
50 miles
NAIROBI
Thika
Kitui
KENYA
Isebania
Sirari
Tarime
Musoma
Mara River
Masai Mara NR
Lobo
Bologonya
Magadi
Kajiado
B6
Bunda
Speke Gulf
Grumeti River
Seronera
Lake Natron
Namanga
Serengeti NP
1
Maswa
Ngorongoro CA
Crater Highlands
Ngorongoro Crater
3
Mt Kilimanjaro
2
Arusha NP
Loitokitok
Tsavo
Malindi
Karatu
Arusha
Moshi
Holili
Taveta
Voi
Lake Eyasi
Lake Manyara NP
Makuyuni
Kwa Kuchinja
Eastern Arc Mountains
Pare Mountains
MOMBASA
Mbulu
Lake Manyara
Lake Balangida
Tarangire NP
Same
Mkomazi NP
Sekenke
Mt Hanang (3417m)
Babati
Lake Babati
Sambu (1570m)
B1
Pangani River
Lunga Lunga
Shimoni
Horohoro
Wembere Swamp
Bereko
Maasai Steppe
Usambara Mountains
Lushoto
Pemba
Singida
Kolo
Kondoa
7
Northeastern Tanzania
Mombo
Amani
Tanga
Wete
Korogwe
Muheza
Chake Chake
A104
Handeni
Sagara
Pangani
A14
4
Zanzibar Archipelago
Manyoni
Meia Meia
Mkata
Zanzibar Island
DODOMA
Saadani NP
Zanzibar Town
Kongwa
Mpwapwa
Kwadihombo
Msata
Wami River
Bagamoyo
Kisigo GR
Kisigo River
Mikese
A7
Chalinze
Rungwa GR
Rungwa
Kilosa
Morogoro
DAR ES SALAAM
Chipogolo
Msumbisi
Makatapora
Matombo
Uluguru Mtns
Ruvu River
Dutumi
Nyangolo
Mikumi
Mikumi NP
Ruaha NP
Great Ruaha River
Msembe
Iringa
Kisaki
Mafia Island
Udzungwa Mountains NP
Mloka
Kibiti
Mang'ula
Kilindoni
5
Southern Highlands
Little Ruaha River
Utete
B2
Ifakara
Rufiji River
Mohoro
INDIAN OCEAN
Lupiro
Selous GR
9
Mbeya Range
Makambako Gap
Kipatimo
Mahenge
Kilombero Valley
Nangurukuru
Kilwa Kivinje
Makambako
A104
Taveta
Kilwa Masoko
Mt Rungwe (2960m)
Malinyi
Uonga
Kitulo NP
Songo Mnara Island
Pande
Matema
Njombe
8
Southeastern Tanzania
Itungi
Kasumulu
Mbarangandu River
Liwale
B4
Karonga
Livingstone Mountains
Mbwemkuru River
Lindi
Mnazi Mmoja (Mingoyo)
B2
Msimbati
Mtwara
Mikindani
Livingstonia
Nachingwea
B5
Kilambo
Makonde Plateau
Lake Nyasa (Lake Malawi)
Songea
A19
Masasi
Palma
Nangomba
Liuli
Newala
Tunduru
Lukwika-Lumesule GR
Masuguru
Mbamba Bay
River
Mtambaswala
Moçimboa da Praia
Mzuzu
Mtomoni
Nkhata Bay
Negomano
Lupilichi
Ruvuma
Lugenda River
Mueda
MALAWI
MOZAMBIQUE

Central Dar es Salaam

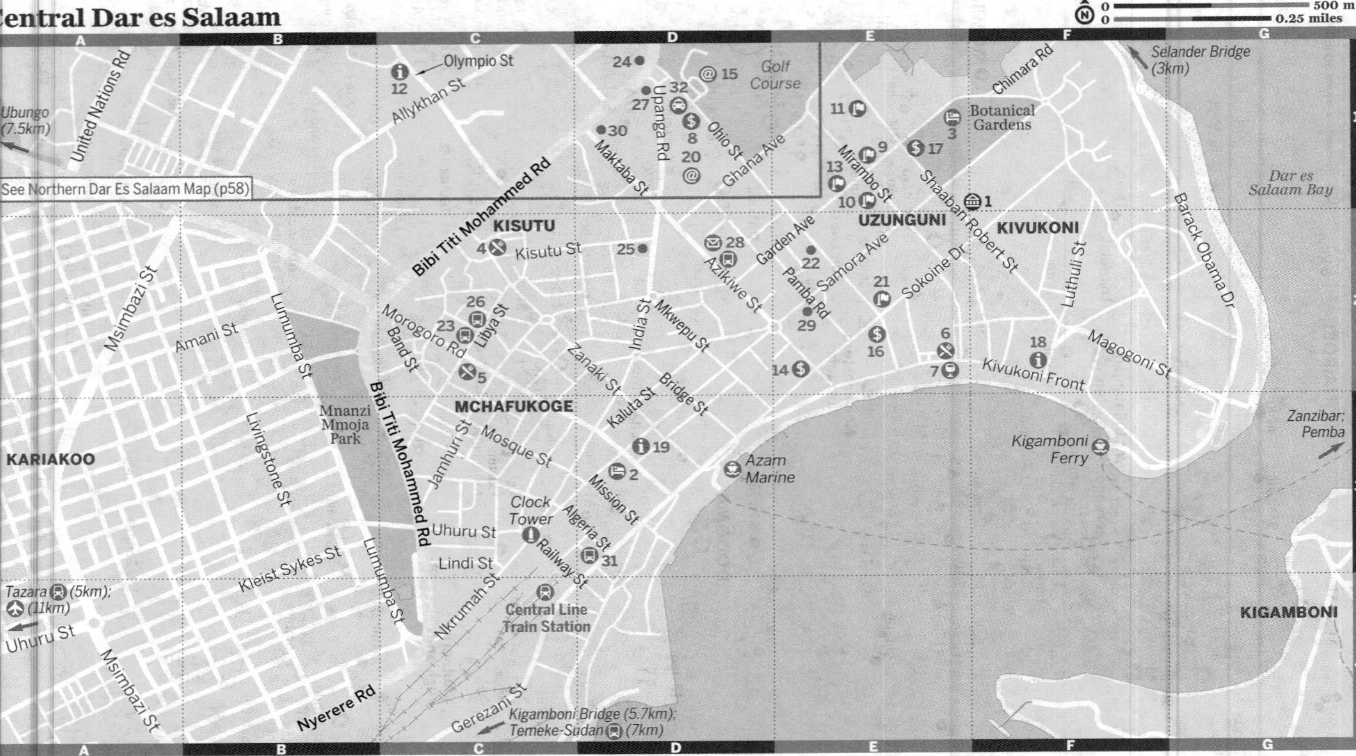

Central Dar es Salaam

Sights
1 National Museum & House of Culture ... F1

Sleeping
2 Harbour View Suites ... D3
3 Southern Sun ... E1

Eating
4 Chapan Bhog ... C2
5 Mamboz Corner BBQ ... C2
6 Oriental ... E2

Drinking & Nightlife
Level 8 Bar ... (see 6)
7 Rouge ... E2

Information
8 Barclays ... D1
9 British High Commission ... E1
10 Canadian High Commission ... E1
German Embassy ... (see 9)
11 Indian High Commission ... E1
12 Marine Parks & Reserves Unit ... C1
13 Mozambique High Commission ... E1
14 National Bank of Commerce ... E2
Netherlands Embassy ... (see 9)
15 Serena Hotel Business Centre ... D1
Standard Chartered ... (see 2)
16 Standard Chartered ... E2
17 Standard Chartered ... E1
18 Surveys & Mapping Division Map Sales Office ... F2
19 Tanzania Tourist Board Information Centre ... D3
20 YMCA Internet Café ... D1
21 Zambian High Commission ... E2

Transport
22 Air Tanzania ... E2
23 Dar Express ... C2
24 Egyptair ... D1
25 Emirates Airlines ... D2
Ethiopian Airlines ... (see 8)
Fastjet ... (see 2)
Jumanne Mastoka ... (see 8)
Kenya Airways ... (see 24)
26 Kilimanjaro Express ... C2
KLM ... (see 24)
27 Linhas Aéreas de Moçambique ... D1
Malawi Airlines ... (see 27)
28 New Posta Transport Stand ... D2
29 Precision Air ... E2
RwandAir ... (see 24)
30 South African Airways ... D1
31 Stesheni Transport Stand ... D3
32 Taxi Stand ... D1

connect with an interesting project, consider checking into Friendly Gecko Guesthouse, 20km north of the city centre off New Bagamoyo Rd. The guesthouse has a mixture of simple rooms in a large, private house with a garden and kitchen, and all profits go to support affiliated community programs.

Taste of Mexico B&B $
(CEFA; 022-278 0425; www.tasteofmexico.co.tz; off Old Bagamoyo Rd, Mikocheni B; s/d/tr/q Tsh50,000/70,000/100,000/120,000; P) This place offers simple, spacious rooms in an attractive, Mediterranean-style building. There's also a breezy rooftop bar and restaurant featuring Mexican dishes. The property is signposted and is one block in from Old Bagamoyo Rd (the turn-off is three blocks north of Bima Rd and about 2km north of Mikocheni B cemetery).

Harbour View Suites BUSINESS HOTEL $$
(Map p56; 0784 564848, 022-212 4040; www.harbourview-suites.com; Samora Ave; r US$125-175;) Well-equipped, centrally located business traveller apartments with views over the city or the harbour. Some rooms have mosquito nets, and all have modern furnishings and a kitchenette. There's a business centre, a fitness centre, a restaurant and a blues bar. Very popular and often full. Underneath is JM Mall shopping centre, with an ATM and supermarket.

Triniti Guesthouse GUESTHOUSE $$
(Map p58; 0755 963686, 0769 628328; www.triniti.co.tz; 26 Msasani Rd; s/d from US$70/80; P) Triniti offers informal lodge-like accommodation in detached wooden bungalows set in a mature garden. While rooms are small, they are painted spotlessly white and are decorated with local artworks and colourful furnishings. Breakfast is a communal affair with homebaked doughnuts, fruit and eggs to order. On Friday night the bar hosts a live band and DJ.

Hotel Slipway HOTEL $$
(Map p58; 0713 888301, 022-260 0893; www.hotelslipway.com; Slipway, Msasani; s US$120-260, d US$135-275, tr US$170-290; P) Integrated into the seafront Slipway shopping complex, this apart-hotel offers good-value accommodation. Rooms and apartments are bright and breezy, with handcrafted wooden furniture, bright Indian bed throws,

Northern Dar Es Salaam

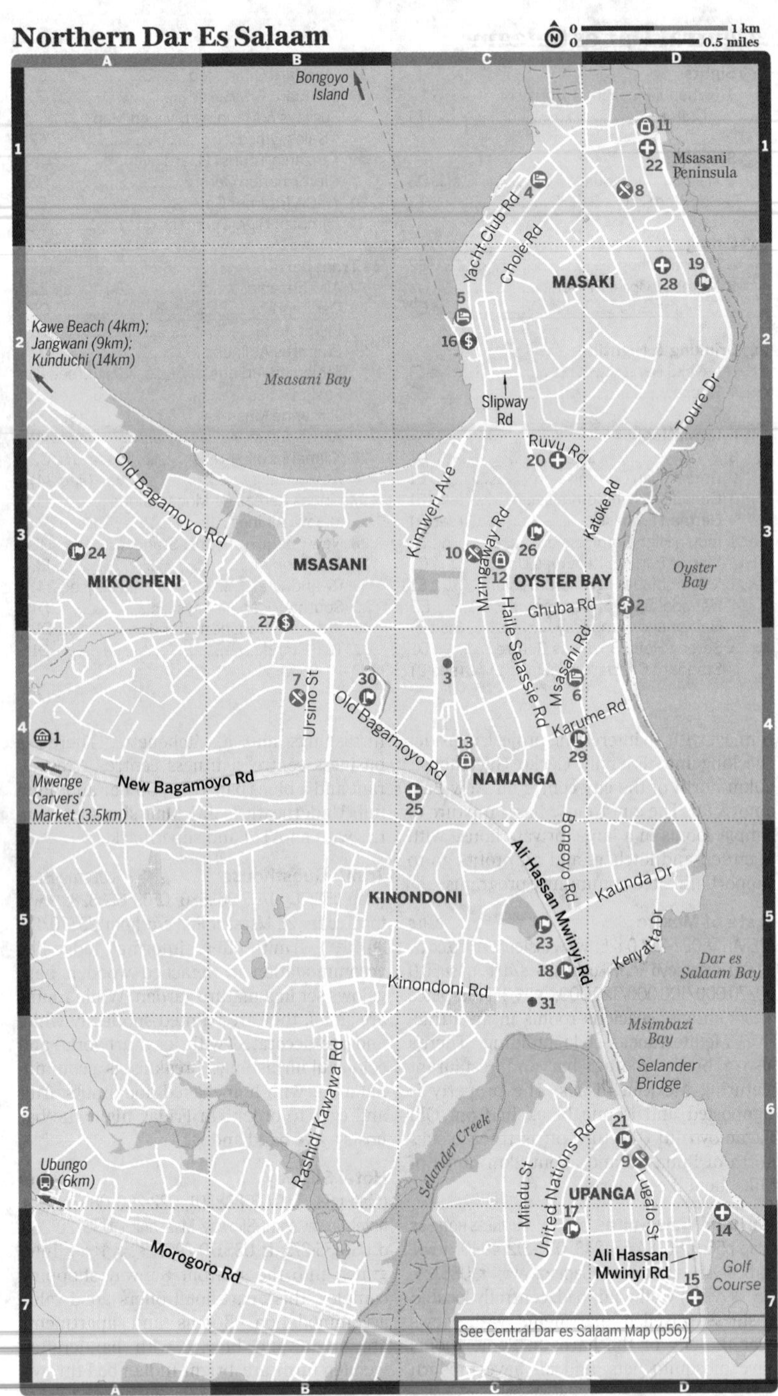

Northern Dar Es Salaam

Sights
1 Village Museum A4

Activities, Courses & Tours
2 Coco Beach D3
3 KIU Ltd C4

Sleeping
4 Alexander's Hotel C1
5 Hotel Slipway C2
6 Triniti Guesthouse C4

Eating
7 Addis in Dar B4
8 Ristorante Bella Napoli D1
9 Under the Mango Tree D6
Waterfront .... (see 5)
10 Zuane Trattoria & Pizzeria C3

Shopping
11 Sea Cliff Village D1
Slipway .... (see 5)
12 Tingatinga Centre C3
13 Wonder Workshop C4

Information
14 Aga Khan Hospital D7
15 Amref Flying Doctors D7
16 Barclays C2
Burundian Embassy .... (see 21)
17 Democratic Republic of the Congo (formerly Zaïre) Embassy C7
18 French Embassy C5
19 Irish Embassy D2
20 IST Clinic C3
21 Italian Embassy D6
22 JD Pharmacy D1
23 Kenya High Commission C5
24 Malawian High Commission A3
25 Premier Care Clinic C4
26 Rwandan Embassy C3
27 Standard Chartered B3
28 The Pharmacy D2
29 Ugandan Embassy C4
30 US Embassy B4

Transport
Coastal Aviation .... (see 5)
31 Swiss International Airlines C5

sea-facing balconies and, in the apartments, well-equipped kitchenettes. On your doorstep you also have three standout restaurants, including the popular **Waterfront** (Map p58; ☎0762 883321; www.hotelslipway.com; Slipway, Slipway Rd, Msasani; meals Tsh15,000-35,000; ⊙noon-midnight;).

★Southern Sun HOTEL $$$
(Map p56; ☎0757 700000, 022-213 7575; www.tsogosunhotels.com; Garden Ave; s/d from US$202/228;) With its Afro-Islamic decor, popular restaurant and professional service, the Southern Sun punches way above its weight. Rooms are furnished with plush, comfortable beds and all mod-cons, while the generous buffet breakfast can be enjoyed on a terrace overlooking the Botanical Gardens. Modest rate reductions are available on weekends.

★Alexander's Hotel BOUTIQUE HOTEL $$$
(Map p58; ☎0754 343834; www.alexanders-tz.com; Maryknoll Lane; s/d from US$150/185;) With its Le Corbusier–style modernist lines, spacious rooftop terrace and shady courtyard, family-run Alexander's is a true boutique hotel. Its 17 stylish rooms have comfortable beds, plump pillows and bright *kikoi* throws, and all front a shaded pool. Breakfast is served in the art- and book-filled dining room, while sundowners and dinners are enjoyed on the upstairs terrace.

Eating

★Chapan Bhog INDIAN $
(56 Bhog; Map p56; ☎0685 401417; www.facebook.com/56Bhog; Kisutu St; meals Tsh6000-15,000; ⊙7am-10pm;) Chapan Bhog's Gujurati *dhoklas* (savoury steamed chickpea cakes), South Indian dosas (fermented crêpes) and thalis are a vegetarian nirvana in a sea of *nyama choma* (roasted meat). The all-vegetarian menu is extensive, and the restaurant has a prime position on temple-lined Kisutu St.

Mamboz Corner BBQ BARBECUE $
(Map p56; ☎0784 243734; cnr Morogoro Rd & Libya St; mains Tsh5000-12,000; ⊙6.30-11.30pm Wed-Mon) This streetside place is home to what many claim is Dar's best grilled chicken, including spicy gujarr chicken, lemon chicken and chicken *sekela* (with tamarind sauce), as well as dry fried fish and bowls of *urojo* (Zanzibar mix).

★Addis in Dar ETHIOPIAN $$
(Map p58; ☎0713 266299; www.addisindar.com; 35 Ursino St; meals Tsh10,000-25,000; ⊙5.30-10.30pm Mon-Sat;) Addis in Dar is decorated with embroidered umbrella lampshades, hand-carved seats and woven tables where food is served communally. Try a combination meal to sample a range of flavours. Everything is served on a large

platter covered with *injera* (sourdough flatbread made of fermented teff flour); tear it off in pieces and use it to scoop up the spicy curries.

Under the Mango Tree EUROPEAN $$
(Map p58; ☎0788 512322, 022-213 1406; www.facebook.com/umtdar; off Ali Hassan Mwinyi Rd, at Alliance Française; meals US$8-20; ⏲9am-6pm Mon-Fri) This bright courtyard-style place serves well-prepared crêpes, burgers, pasta and other light meals. It's worth checking its Facebook page for announcements about frequent evening special events.

Ristorante Bella Napoli ITALIAN $$
(Map p58; ☎022-260 0326, 0778 497776; www.bellanapolitz.com; 530 Haile Selassie Rd; mains Tsh12,000-25,000; ⏲6-10pm Tue-Fri, noon-10pm Sat & Sun; 📶👪) Delicious pizzas and Italian food served in a pleasant garden setting or in the air-con dining room, plus a children's playground.

★**Oriental** ASIAN $$$
(Map p56; ☎0764 701234; 24 Kivukoni Front, Hyatt Regency Dar es Salaam; meals from US$30; ⏲6-10.30pm; 📶) From the high sheen of the marble-tiled floors to the elegant Asian-inspired furnishings, gloved waiters and immaculate sushi bar, the Hyatt's gourmet Asian restaurant aims to seduce and impress. Fortunately the expertly prepared sushi, bright papaya salads and intensely spiced curries and seafood live up to the opulent surroundings. Bookings recommended.

Zuane Trattoria & Pizzeria ITALIAN $$$
(Map p58; ☎0766 679600; www.zuanetrattoriapizzeria.com; Mzingaway Rd; meals Tsh20,000-50,000; ⏲noon-2.30pm & 6-10.30pm Mon-Sat; 👪) With its luxuriant garden setting this Italian trattoria housed in an old colonial villa is one of Dar's most atmospheric dining options. The menu features classics such as wood-fired pizzas, *melanzana parmigiana* (an aubergine- and Parmesan-layered bake), pastas, seafood and grilled fillet steak. There's also a children's playground in the garden. Book ahead; it's very popular.

Drinking & Nightlife

Dar's biggest party nights are Friday and Saturday, with most bars staying open until the wee hours. Upmarket places usually charge a cover (Tsh5000 to Tsh15,000). On Saturday and Sunday, **Coco Beach** (Map p58; Toure Dr) is a popular late-afternoon party venue with local vendors supplying inexpensive beers and snacks. If you decide to hang out here, stay with the crowd and avoid isolated areas of the beach.

Level 8 Bar BAR
(Map p56; ☎0764 701234; 8th fl, Hyatt Regency Dar es Salaam, Kivukoni Front; ⏲5pm-1am) The Hyatt's chic rooftop bar has wonderful views over the harbour, lounge seating and live music some evenings.

Rouge CLUB
(Map p56; ☎0764 701234; Hyatt Regency Dar es Salaam, Kivukoni Front; ⏲10pm-4am Fri & Sat) This upmarket nightclub (entry Tsh15,000) with DJ is on the rooftop of the Hyatt Regency, and attracts a mixed crowd of locals and foreigners.

Shopping

★**Wonder Workshop** ARTS & CRAFTS
(Map p58; ☎0754 051417; info@wonder-workshop.org; 1372 Karume Rd, Msasani; ⏲8.30am-6pm Mon-Fri, 10am-6pm Sat) At this excellent workshop, artists with disabilities create world-class jewellery, sculptures, candles, stationery and other crafts from old glass, metal, car parts and other recycled materials. There's a small shop on the grounds. Crafts can also be commissioned (and sent abroad), and Monday through Friday you can watch the artists at work.

Tingatinga Centre ARTS & CRAFTS
(Map p58; www.tingatinga.org; Morogoro Stores, off Haile Selassie Rd; ⏲9am-6pm) This excellent centre is at the spot where Edward Saidi Tingatinga originally marketed his designs, and it's still one of the best places to buy Tingatinga paintings and to watch the artists at work.

Information

DANGERS & ANNOYANCES

Take the usual precautions in Dar es Salaam:

- Watch out for pickpocketing in crowded areas, and for bag snatching through vehicle windows.
- Stay aware of your surroundings and leave your valuables in a reliable hotel safe.
- At night, always catch a taxi rather than taking a dalla-dalla or walking.
- Avoid walking alone along the path paralleling Barack Obama Dr, on Coco Beach, and at night along Chole Rd.
- Only use taxis from reliable hotels or established taxi stands. Avoid taxis cruising the streets, and never get in a taxi that has a 'friend' of the driver or anyone else already in it.

INTERNET ACCESS

Most hotels, even budget ones, now have either a fixed internet point or wi-fi. Internet cafes abound in the city centre; the more professional ones are tucked away in commercial centres such as Harbour View and Osman Towers. Most charge between Tsh1000 and Tsh2000 per hour.

Main Post Office (Map p56; Azikiwe St; ⌚8am-4.30pm Mon-Fri, 9am-noon Sat) Has terminals (Tsh1500 per hour).

Serena Hotel Business Centre (Map p56; Dar es Salaam Serena Hotel, Ohio St; per 10min Tsh1000; ⌚7.30am-7pm Mon-Fri, 8.30am-4pm Sat, 9am-1pm Sun)

YMCA Internet Café (Map p56; Upanga Rd; per hour Tsh1000; ⌚8am-7.30pm Mon-Fri, to 2pm Sat)

MEDICAL SERVICES

There are good pharmacies at all the main shopping centres, including the **Slipway** (Map p58; www.slipway.net; Slipway Rd, Msasani; ⌚9.30am-6pm) and **Sea Cliff Village** (Map p58; Toure Dr; ⌚9.30am-6pm).

Aga Khan Hospital (Map p58; ☎022-211 5151, 022-211 5153; www.agakhanhospitals.org; Barack Obama Dr) A multi-speciality hospital with internationally qualified doctors offering general medical services and specialist clinics.

Amref Flying Doctors (Map p58; ☎0719 881887, 0784 240500; www.flydoc.org; Ali Hassan Mwinyi Rd) For emergency air evacuations.

IST Clinic (Map p58; ☎022-260 1307, 24hr emergency 0754 783393; www.istclinic.com; Ruvu Rd, Msasani; ⌚8am-6pm Mon-Thu, 8am-5pm Fri, 9am-noon Sat) Fully equipped Western-run clinic, with a doctor on call 24 hours.

JD Pharmacy (Map p58; ☎022-286 3663, 022-211 1049; www.jdpharmacy.co.tz; opposite Sea Cliff Village, cnr Toure Dr & Mhando St; ⌚9am-8pm Mon-Sat, 9am-2pm Sun) Well-stocked pharmacy, with several branches.

Premier Care Clinic (Map p58; ☎0752 254642, 0715 254642; www.premiercareclinic.com; 259 Ali Hassan Mwinyi Rd, Namanga; ⌚8am-5pm Mon-Fri, to noon Sat) Western standards and facilities; also has a branch in Masaki.

The Pharmacy (Map p58; ☎0782 994709; www.thepharmacy.co.tz; Haile Selassie Rd, Shoppers Plaza, Masaki; ⌚9am-9pm) Well-stocked pharmacy; also has a number of other branches around town.

MONEY

There are ATMs all over the city, and in all the major shopping centres.

ATMs

Barclays (Map p58; Slipway, Msasani)

Barclays (Map p56; Ohio St)

National Bank of Commerce (Map p56; cnr Azikiwe St & Sokoine Dr)

Standard Chartered (Map p56; cnr Garden Ave & Shaaban Robert St) City centre.

Standard Chartered (Map p56; Samora Ave) At JM Mall.

Standard Chartered (Map p58; Old Bagamoyo Rd) In Shopper's Plaza.

Standard Chartered (Map p56; cnr Ohio St & Sokoine Dr, NIC Life House)

TOURIST INFORMATION

Marine Parks & Reserves Unit (Map p56; ☎022-215 0621; www.marineparks.go.tz; Olympio St, Upanga; ⌚8am-4.30pm Mon-Fri) Oversees Tanzania's marine parks and reserves.

Surveys & Mapping Division Map Sales Office (Map p56; cnr Kivukoni Front & Luthuli St; ⌚8am-2pm Mon-Fri) Sells dated topographical maps (1:50,000) for mainland Tanzania.

Tanzania Tourist Board Information Centre (Map p56; ☎022-213 1555, 022-212 8472; www.tanzaniatourism.com; Samora Ave; ⌚8.30am-4pm Mon-Fri, to noon Sat) Free tourist maps and brochures, and limited city information.

ℹ Getting There & Away

AIR

Julius Nyerere International Airport (p211) is Tanzania's hub airport. It has two terminals, with domestic and international flights departing from Terminal Two, and charters and light aircraft departing from Terminal One ('old terminal'). Verify the departure terminal when purchasing your ticket.

A third terminal is being constructed to increase capacity to six million arrivals per year. Once completed, all international flights will move to Terminal Three, while Terminal Two will serve domestic routes.

Airlines connecting Dar es Salaam with elsewhere in Tanzania include:

Air Tanzania (TC; Map p56; ☎022-211 3248; www.airtanzania.co.tz; Ohio St, 1st fl, ATC House; ⌚8am-5pm Mon-Fri, 9am-2pm Sat)

Coastal Aviation (Map p58; ☎0713 325673, reservations 022-284 2700; www.coastal.co.tz; Slipway, Slipway Rd, Msasani; ⌚9am-5pm Mon-Fri, 9am-3pm Sat)

Fastjet (Map p56; ☎0784 108900; www.fastjet.com; Samora Ave; ⌚8am-4.30pm Mon-Fri, 8.30am-1pm Sat)

Precision Air (Map p56; ☎0787 888417, 022-213 0800; www.precisionairtz.com; cnr Samora Ave & Pamba Rd; ⊙8am-5pm Mon-Fri, 9am-1pm Sat)

Tropical Air (☎024-223 2511, 0687 527511; www.tropicalair.co.tz; Terminal One, Airport)

ZanAir (☎0716 863857, 024-223 3670; www.zanair.com; Terminal One, Airport)

International arlines flying into Dar es Salaam include:

Egyptair (p212)

Emirates Airlines (p212)

Ethiopian Airlines (p212)

Kenya Airways (p212)

KLM (p212)

Linhas Aéreas de Moçambique (p212)

Malawi Airlines (p212)

RwandAir (p212)

South African Airways (p212)

Swiss International Airlines (p212)

BOAT

Four fast **Azam Marine** (Map p56; ☎022-212 3324; www.azammarine.com; Kivukoni Front) catamarans operate daily between Dar and Zanzibar Island (economy/VIP US$35/50, economy child US$25), leaving between about 7am and 4pm. All take about two hours, with a luggage allowance of 25kg per person. VIP tickets get you a seat in the air-con hold, but arrive early if you want to sit together.

The only place at the port to buy legitimate ferry tickets is the tall, blue-glass building at the southern end of the ferry terminal on Kivukoni Front. The building is marked 'Azam Marine – Coastal Fast Ferries'. It's also possible to purchase tickets online through Azam Marine's website.

The large *Azam Sealink I* ferry to Pemba (adult/child US$70/50, 18 hours including a stop at Zanzibar Island) departs Dar twice weekly. This ferry also takes vehicles. There is also a weekly connection on Sealink between Tanga and Pemba (US$35, four hours).

BUS

Except as noted, at the time of research all buses were departing from and arriving at the main **Ubungo Bus Terminal** (Morogoro Rd), 8km west of the city centre on Morogoro Rd, from where you can connect on the new Dar Rapid Transit (DART) bus network to the city centre (Tsh650, about 20 minutes), or take a taxi (from Tsh30,000, about one hour, more with heavy traffic). Some lines terminate about 500m east along Morogoro Rd, at the junction of Sheikilango Rd ('Ubungo-Sheikilango'). However, a lot is due to change with full implementation of the new DART bus network, when all upcountry transport will be switched to Mbezi (past Ubungo on the Morogoro Rd). Ubungo itself will also benefit from a new terminal, which will replace the current sprawling lot and hopefully tame its notorious touts and hustlers.

As always keep an eye on your luggage and your wallet and try to avoid arriving at night. If you arrive at Ubungo via taxi, ask your taxi driver to take you directly to the ticket office window for the line you want to travel with. Avoid dealing with touts.

Bus tickets can be purchased at Ubungo and – for Dar Express and Kilimanjaro Express – at their city offices on Libya St. Only buy tickets inside the bus offices.

Buses to Kilwa Masoko, Lindi and Mtwara depart from south of the city, at **Temeke–Sudan Market Area** (Temeke Sudani; cnr Mbagala & Temeke Rds) and **Mbagala–Rangi Tatu**.

Dar Express (Map p56; Libya St, Kisutu; ⊙6am-6pm) has daily buses to Moshi (Tsh30,000 to Tsh36,000, 8½ hours) and Arusha (Tsh30,000 to Tsh36,000, 10 hours) departing between 5.30am and 8am from Ubungo bus station. There's also a daily bus to Nairobi (Tsh65,000, 15 hours) at 5.45am.

Kilimanjaro Express (Map p56; Libya St, Kisutu; ⊙4.30am-7pm) runs two daily buses to Moshi (Tsh33,000 to Tsh36,000, 8½ hours) and Arusha (Tsh33,000 to Tsh36,000, 10 hours), departing at 6am and 7am from outside the Kilimanjaro Express office on Libya St, and then about 45 minutes later from Ubungo. Arriving in Dar es Salaam, the buses terminate at Ubungo-Sheikilango bus stop. From Ubungo-Sheikilango, catch a BRT bus into town (Tsh650, 20 minutes).

TRAIN

The train station for **Tazara** (Tanzanian-Zambia Railway Authority; ☎0713 354648, 0732 998855, 022-286 5187; www.tazarasite.com; cnr Nyerere & Nelson Mandela Rds; ⊙ticket office 7.30am-noon & 2-4.30pm Mon-Fri, 9am-noon Sat) is 6km southwest of the city centre (Tsh15,000 to Tsh20,000 in a taxi). Dalla-dallas to the station leave from the New Posta transport stand, and are marked Vigunguti, U/Ndege or Buguruni. Train services run between Dar es Salaam, Mbeya and Kapiri Mposhi (Zambia).

The train station for **Tanzania Railways Limited 'Central Line' trains** (Tanzania Railways Limited; ☎0754 460907, 022-211 6213, 022-211 7833; www.trl.co.tz; cnr Railway St & Sokoine Dr) is just southwest of the ferry terminal in the city centre. 'Central Line' services connect Dar es Salaam with Kigoma and Mwanza via Tabora.

Getting Around

DALLA-DALLAS

Dalla-dallas (minibuses and 30-seater buses) have long been the mainstay of Dar's public transport system, servicing many city destinations for an average price of Tsh400 per ride. They are invariably packed to overflowing, and are difficult to board with luggage. First and last stops are shown in the front window, but routes vary, so confirm with the conductor that the driver is going to your destination.

As DART buses take over, dalla-dallas are being gradually phased out, especially in the city centre, where their numbers have already been greatly reduced. City-centre dalla-dalla terminals still operational at the time of research include the following:

New Posta Transport Stand (Posta Mpya; Map p56; Azikiwe St) At the main post office.

Stesheni Transport Stand (Map p56; Algeria St) Near the Central Line Train Station. Dalla-dallas to Temeke also leave from here; ask for 'Temeke *mwisho*'.

FERRY

The passenger and vehicle **Kigamboni Ferry** (Map p56; per person/vehicle Tsh200/2000; ⏲5am-midnight) operates daily from early morning until late evening between Kivukoni Front and Kigamboni, just across the channel, and the gateway to Dar es Salaam's southern beaches.

TAXI

Taxis don't have meters. Short rides within the city centre cost from Tsh5000. Fares from the city centre to Msasani Peninsula start at Tsh15,000. Never get into a taxi that has other people already in it, and always use taxis affiliated with hotels, or operating from a fixed stand and known by the other drivers at the stand. A convenient **taxi stand** (Map p56; Ohio St) is the one opposite the Dar es Salaam Serena Hotel.

An option for longer trips is to negotiate a daily or half-day rate with a reliable taxi driver such as **Taxi Sultani** (☎0688 364767), for city trips within Dar es Salaam, or **Jumanne Mastoka** (Map p56; ☎0659 339735, 0784 339735; mjumanne@yahoo.com), which is highly recommended also for airport pick-ups and for travel elsewhere in Tanzania.

AROUND DAR ES SALAAM

Jangwani & Kunduchi Beaches

The beaches, resorts and water parks 25km north of Dar es Salaam are popular weekend getaways for families. They are close enough to Dar es Salaam that you can also visit for the day (though leave early to avoid heavy traffic). The southern section of coast around Jangwani Beach is broken up by frequent stone jetties.

Sleeping & Eating

White Sands Hotel RESORT $$$

(☎0758 818696; www.hotelwhitesands.com; Jangwani Beach; s/d/apt from US$180/200/230; P ❄ 🛜 🏊) This large resort has rooms in two-storey rondavels lined up along the waterfront, all with TV, minifridge and sea views. In addition, there are 28 self-catering apartments – some directly overlooking the beach, others just behind overlooking a well-tended lawn. There's also a gym and a business centre, and the restaurant serves popular weekend buffets.

Getting There & Away

Hotels on Jangwani Beach are reached via the signposted White Sands turn-off from New Bagamoyo Rd.

Via public transport, take a dalla-dalla from **New Posta transport stand** in Dar es Salaam to Mwenge (Tsh400). Once at Mwenge, for Jangwani Beach, take a 'Tegeta' dalla-dalla to Africana Junction (Tsh200), and from there a bajaji (tuk-tuk; Tsh2000) or taxi (Tsh3000 to Tsh5000) the remaining couple of kilometres to the hotels.

Taxis from Dar es Salaam cost from about Tsh60,000 one way.

Dar es Salaam's Southern Beaches

The coastline south of Dar es Salaam gets more attractive, tropical and rural the further south you go, and makes an easily accessible getaway, far removed – in ambience, if not in distance – from the city. The beach begins just south of Kigamboni, which is opposite Kivukoni Front and reached in five minutes by the Kigamboni ferry or with your own vehicle via Kilwa Rd and the Nyerere Bridge. About 25km further south, near Ras Kutani, are several exclusive resorts.

Activities

Dekeza Dhows SNORKELLING, KAYAKING

(☎0787 217040, 0754 276178; www.dekezadhows.com; Kipepeo Beach) Dekeza's daily dhow trips (US$35 per person) depart from Kipepeo Beach to Sinda Island. Boats set off at 10am, tracing the edge of nearby coral reefs for an hour or so of snorkelling before set-

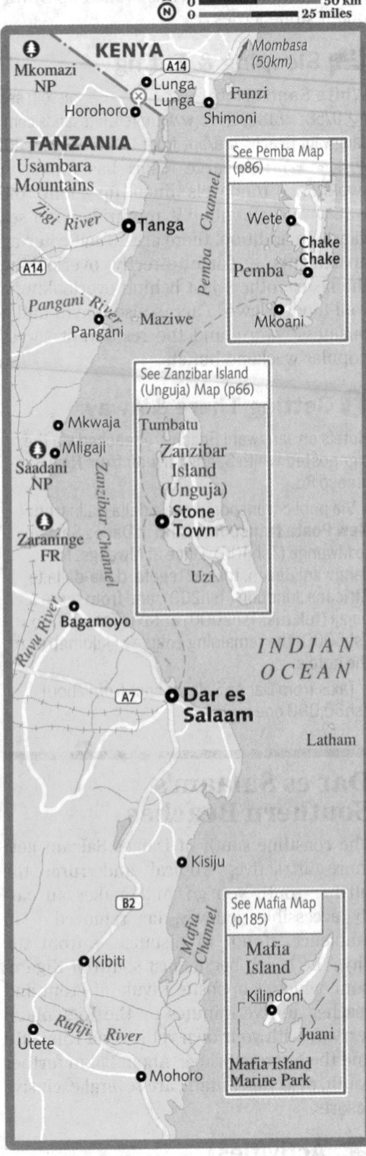

ting up lunch on a deserted beach. Fishing trips aboard the dhows are also possible (US$250 for four people), as are sunset cruises.

Sleeping & Eating

Kipepeo Beach & Village LODGE $$
(☎0754 276178; www.kipepeobeach.com; Kipepeo Village; camping US$10, s/d/tr banda US$20/30/40, s/d/tr chalet US$65/85/115; P) Laid-back Kipepeo, 8km south of the ferry dock, has raised chalets with balconies just back from the beach. Closer to the water, but behind a fence and a bit of a walk to the nearest bathroom, are thatched beach huts without windows, and a camping area. It's a sand-in-the-toes kind of place and has a beachside restaurant-bar.

Ras Kutani RESORT $$$
(☎022-212 8485; www.selous.com; Ras Kutani; per person with full board bungalow/ste from US$390/440; ⊙Jun–mid-Mar;) Set between the sea and a small lagoon on a wonderful stretch of beach, this lovely, barefoot luxury resort has spacious natural-style bungalows with beach-facing verandahs. On a rise away from the main lodge are several suites, each with their own plunge pool. Birdwatching, forest walks, canoeing in the lagoon and snorkelling can be arranged.

Getting There & Away

The main ways to reach Ras Kutani are with your own vehicle or charter taxi. Expect to pay about Tsh100,000 from Dar es Salaam for a drop-off. The hotels can also help you to arrange transport. The Ras Kutani resort has its own airstrip for charter flights.

ZANZIBAR ARCHIPELAGO

POP 1.4 MILLION

Step off the boat or plane onto the Zanzibar Archipelago and you're transported through time and place. This is one of the world's great cultural crossroads, where Africa meets Arabia meets the Indian Ocean.

In Zanzibar Town, the narrow alleys of historic Stone Town meander between ancient buildings decorated with balconies and gigantic carved doors. Meanwhile, on the coast, fishing boats set sail, and in the countryside farmers tend fields of rice or the clove plantations that give Zanzibar its 'Spice Islands' moniker.

Beyond these little-changed traditions, visitors see a very different landscape. The idyllic beaches are dotted with hotels, and the ocean becomes a playground for diving, snorkelling and kitesurfing.

With its tropical tableau and unique culture, plus an active beach-party scene for those that want it, the Zanzibar Archipelago offers a fascinating and highly enjoyable East African Indian Ocean experience.

Zanzibar Island

Zanzibar Island is a jewel in the ocean, surrounded by beaches that rate among the finest in the world. Here you can swim, snorkel or just lounge the hours away, while shoals of luminous fish graze over nearby coral gardens and pods of dolphins frolic offshore.

In the island's capital, Zanzibar Town, sits the historic quarter of Stone Town, with a mesmerising mix of influences from Africa, Arabia, India and Europe.

For these reasons and more, Zanzibar Island (officially called Unguja) is the archipelago's focal point, and the most popular destination for visitors, but choose your spot carefully. While it's easy to find tranquil beauty or party buzz (or both), increasing development threatens the island's ineluctable magic and fragile community resources.

Zanzibar Town

☎024 / POP 400,000

For most visitors Zanzibar Town means Stone Town, the historic quarter where you can wander for hours through a maze of narrow streets, easily losing yourself in centuries of history.

Each twist and turn brings something new – a former palace, a Persian bathhouse, a tumbledown ruin, a coral-stone mansion with carved doors and latticework balconies, or a school full of children chanting verses from the Quran.

Today Zanzibar Town (sometimes designated Zanzibar City) is the capital of the state of Zanzibar, and by far the biggest settlement on Zanzibar Island. It's divided into two unequal parts, separated by Creek Rd: to the west is Stone Town, while to the east are the more recently built areas known as Ng'ambo (literally, 'The Other Side'), with other suburbs such as Amaani, Mazizini, Magomeni and Mwanakwerekwe, an urban sprawl of shops, markets, offices, apartment blocks, crowded slums and middle-class neighbourhoods.

Sights

Shaped like a triangle, Stone Town is bounded on two sides by the sea, and along the third by Creek Rd (officially renamed Benjamin Mkapa Rd). Most sights are on the northern seafront (Mizingani Rd) or hidden away in the narrow streets.

House of Wonders HISTORIC BUILDING
(Beit el-Ajaib; Mizingani Rd) An icon of Stone Town, the House of Wonders rises in impressive tiers of slender steel pillars and balconies overlooking the waterfront. Its enormous carved doors are said to be the largest in East Africa, fronted by two bronze cannon with Portuguese inscriptions dating them to the 16th century. Inside, the National Museum of History & Culture has exhibits on Swahili civilisation and the peoples of the Indian Ocean.

Old Fort HISTORIC BUILDING
(Ngome Kongwe; Mzingani Rd; ⏲9am-10pm) FREE With its pale-orange ramparts overlooking Forodhani Gardens and the ocean beyond, the fort was built by Omani Arabs when they seized the island from the Portuguese in 1698, and over the centuries it's had various uses, from prison to tennis club. Today the scale of the fortifications is still impressive, although there has been some modernisation inside, notably a line of souvenir shops and a pleasant cafe that turns into a bar in the evening.

Forodhani Gardens GARDENS
(Jamituri Gardens) One of the best ways to ease into Zanzibar life is to stop by this waterfront public space. It's a social hub for tourists and locals alike; there's a large restaurant jutting into the sea, two small cafes with outside seating, benches under shady trees, a children's play park, and food stalls in the evening.

Catholic Cathedral CATHEDRAL
(St Joseph's Catholic Cathedral; Cathedral St) One of the first sights travellers see when arriving by ferry are the twin spires of the Roman Catholic cathedral. Serving the local Catholic community, including Goans, Europeans and Tanzanians from Zanzibar and the mainland, it was designed by French architect Berange, whose other work includes the cathedral in Marseilles, and built by French missionaries between 1893 and 1897. Entrance is free but a donation is requested. Mass times are posted on the porch.

Zanzibar Island (Unguja)

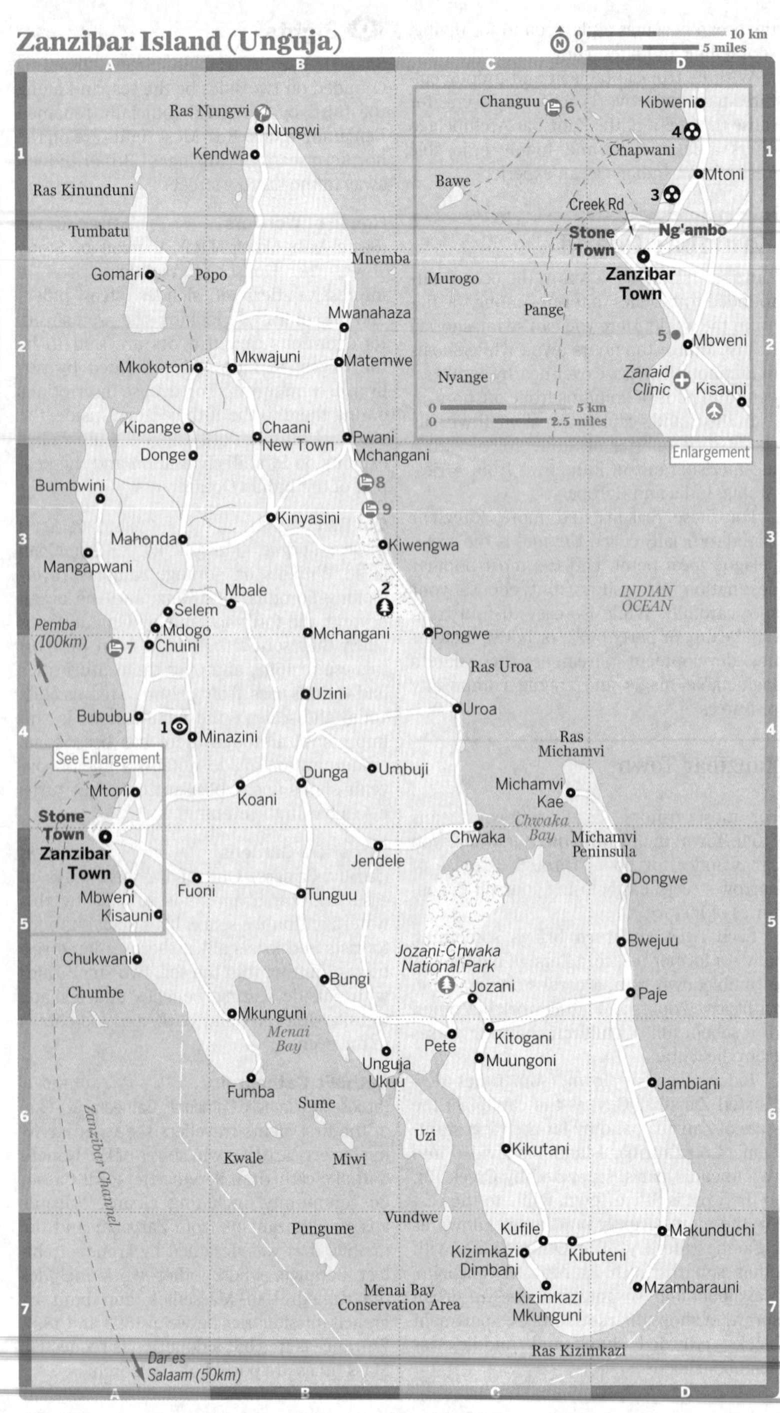

Zanzibar Island (Unguja)

Sights

1 Kidichi Persian Baths.......... A4
2 Kiwengwa-Pongwe Forest Reserve... B3
3 Maruhubi Palace.......... D1
4 Mtoni Palace.......... D1

Activities, Courses & Tours

5 Gallery Tours & Safaris.......... D2

Sleeping

6 Changuu Private Island Paradise........ C1
7 Mangrove Lodge.......... A4
8 Shooting Star Lodge.......... B3
9 Zan View Hotel.......... B3

Anglican Cathedral CATHEDRAL

(Christ Church Anglican Cathedral; www.zanzibaranglican.or.tz; New Mkunazini Rd; with guide, incl slave chambers & slavery exhibit US$5; ⌚9am-6pm Mon-Sat, noon-6pm Sun) The tall spire and grey-yellow walls of the Anglican cathedral dominate the surrounding streets in this part of Stone Town, while the dark-wood pews and stained-glass windows will remind British visitors of churches back home. This was the first Anglican cathedral in East Africa, constructed in the 1870s by the Universities Mission to Central Africa (UMCA) on the site of the former slave market after slavery was officially abolished.

Old Dispensary HISTORIC BUILDING

(Mizingani Rd) With its peppermint-green latticework balconies and sculpted clock tower, this 19th-century charitable dispensary is one of the most attractive landmarks on the waterfront. It was built by Tharia Topan, a prominent Ismaili Indian merchant who also acted as financial adviser to the sultan and as banker to Tippu Tip, Zanzibar's most notorious slave trader. You're free to wander through the interior, which now accommodates offices. In the airy courtyard on the ground floor is the **Abyssinian's Steakhouse** (☎0772 940566; mains Tsh10,000-17,000; ⌚11am-10pm) restaurant.

Darajani Market MARKET

(Creek Rd; ⌚6am-4pm) Zanzibar's main market is a hive of activity, with everything – from spices, fresh fish, slabs of meat and huge baskets full of live chickens to sandals, plastic buckets and mobile phones – all set out in a series of covered halls and overflowing into the surrounding streets. If you're buying food, come in the morning when stuff is fresh, although it's much busier then. For a slightly less crowded and chaotic experience come in the afternoon.

Hamamni Persian Baths HISTORIC BUILDING

(Hamamni St; Tsh1500) Built by Sultan Barghash in the late 19th century, these were the first public baths on Zanzibar. The various rooms were renovated in 2017 and, although there's no longer water inside, it's easy to imagine them in use in bygone days. If the entrance door is closed, ask at the Cultural Arts Centre opposite.

Maruhubi Palace RUINS

(Tsh5000) Maruhubi Palace was built outside Zanzibar Town in 1882 for Sultan Barghash to house his impressively large harem. A few years later it was destroyed by fire, although the remaining walls and arches, and the large columns that once supported an upper balcony, hint at its previous scale. The entrance is 4km north of Zanzibar Town, on the left (west) of the main road towards Bububu.

Kidichi Persian Baths HISTORIC SITE

Sultan Seyyid Said built this bathhouse at Kidichi (11km northeast of Zanzibar Town) in 1850 for his Persian wife, Scheherezade. The royal couple would come here after hunting to refresh themselves in the stylised stucco interiors. Although poorly maintained, you can still make out much of the carving and see the bathing pool and massage tables. Situated among some of Zanzibar's famous spice plantations, Kidichi Persian Baths is usually visited as part of a spice tour.

Mtoni Palace RUINS

Overlooking the coast, away from the heat and hustle of Zanzibar Town, Mtoni Palace was built for Sultan Seyyid Said in 1828. It was home to the sultan's only legitimate wife, many secondary wives and hundreds of children. According to contemporary descriptions, it was a beautiful building with a balconied exterior and a large garden courtyard complete with peacocks and gazelles. Now only a ruin remains with roofless halls and arabesque arches framing glimpses of tropical foliage and an azure sea.

Princess Salme Museum MUSEUM

(☎0779 093066; selgpsm@gmail.com; Emerson on Hurumzi hotel, Hurumzi St; US$5; ⌚10am-5pm Mon-Sun) Carefully curated by the renowned historian Said al Gheithy, this delightful

Stone Town

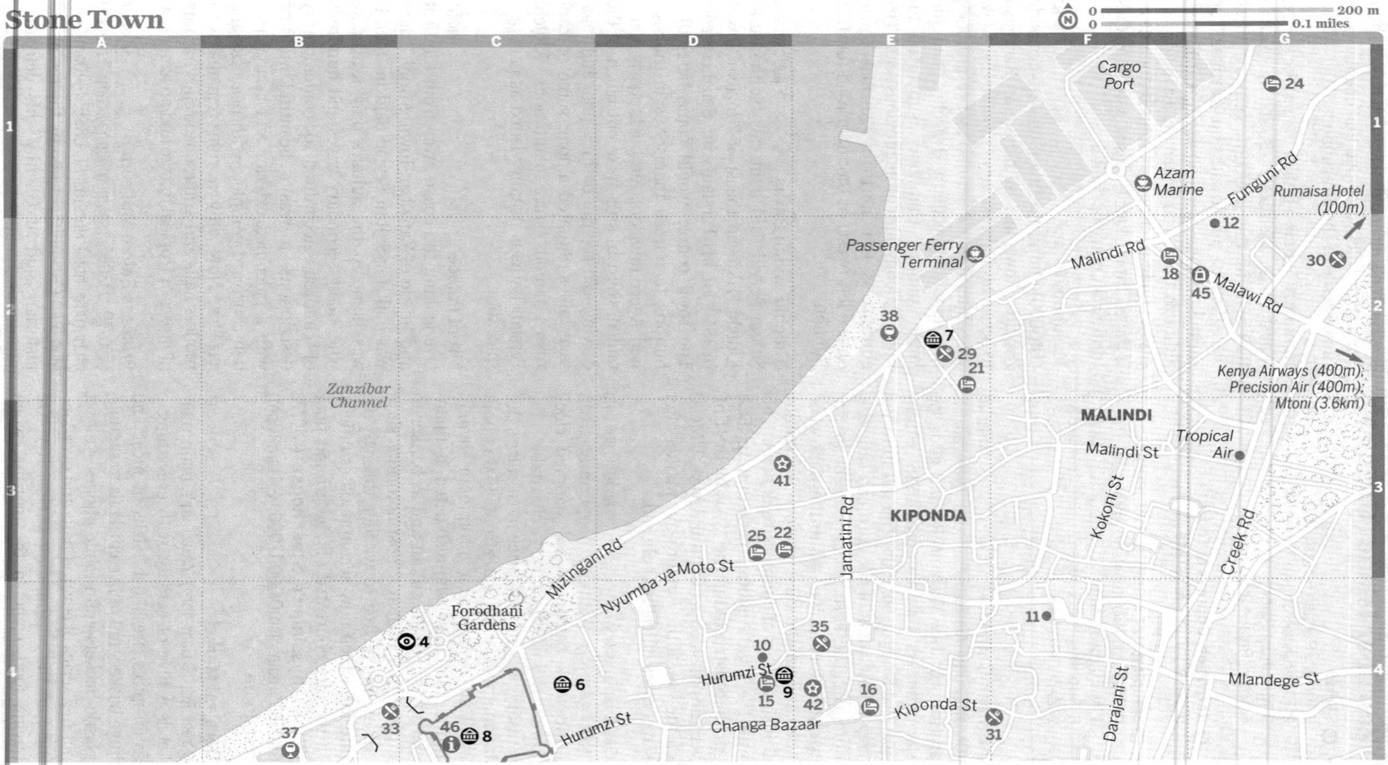

0 — 200 m
0 — 0.1 miles

A B C D E F G
1 2 3 4

Cargo Port
24
Azam Marine
Funguni Rd
Rumaisa Hotel (100m)
12
Passenger Ferry Terminal
Malindi Rd
18
45
Malawi Rd
30
38
7
29
21
Kenya Airways (400m); Precision Air (400m); Mtoni (3.6km)
Zanzibar Channel
MALINDI
Tropical Air
Malindi St
41
KIPONDA
Jamatini Rd
Kokoni St
Creek Rd
25
22
Mizingani Rd
Nyumba ya Moto St
Forodhani Gardens
11
35
10
4
Hurumzi St
9
15
42
16
6
Kiponda St
Darajani St
Mlandege St
31
33
46
8
37
Hurumzi St
Changa Bazaar

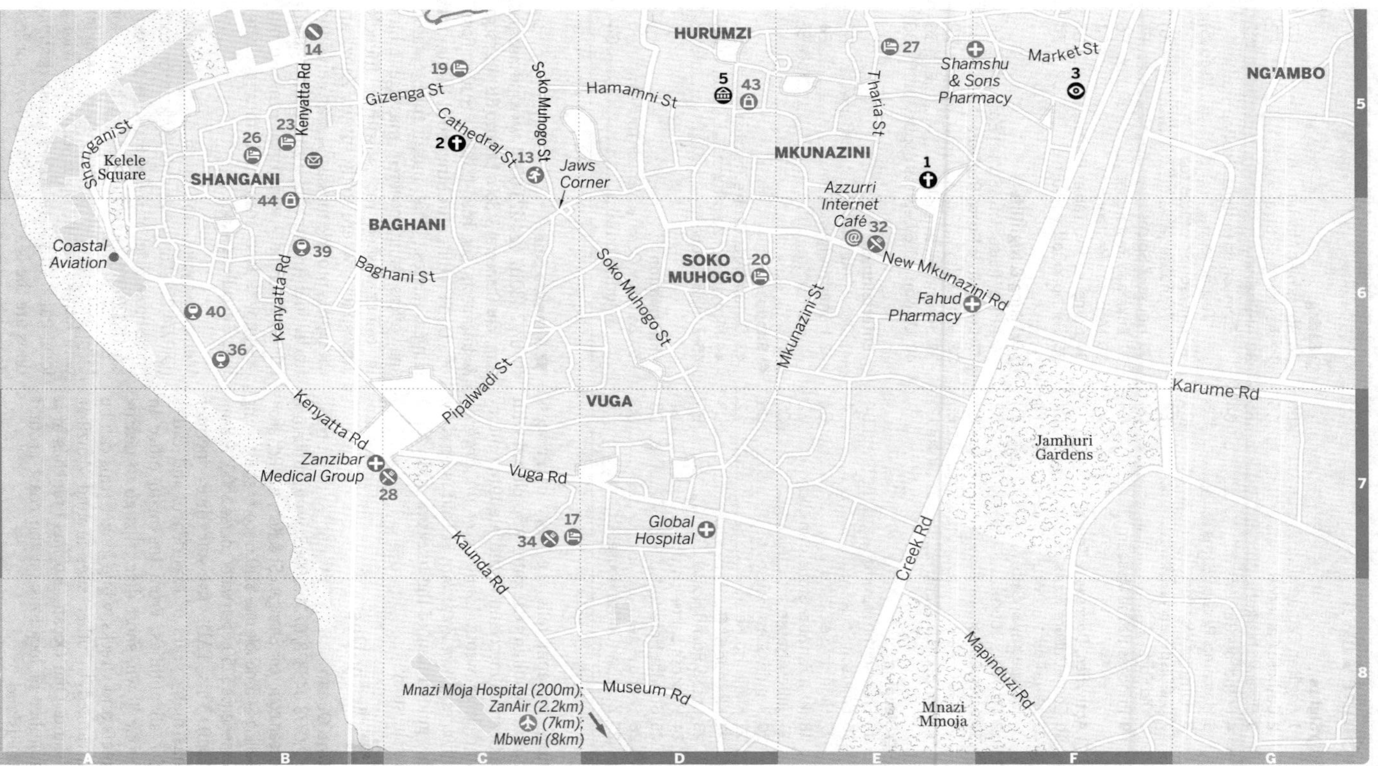
HURUMZI
NG'AMBO
MKUNAZINI
SHANGANI
BAGHANI
SOKO MUHOGO
VUGA
Shangani St
Kelele Square
Kenyatta Rd
Gizenga St
Cathedral St
Soko Muhogo St
Jaws Corner
Hamamni St
Tharia St
Shamshu & Sons Pharmacy
Market St
Azzurri Internet Café
New Mkunazini Rd
Fahud Pharmacy
Coastal Aviation
Baghani St
Mkunazini St
Pipalwadi St
Karume Rd
Zanzibar Medical Group
Vuga Rd
Jamhuri Gardens
Global Hospital
Creek Rd
Kaunda Rd
Mapinduzi Rd
Mnazi Moja Hospital (200m); ZanAir (2.2km); (7km); Mbweni (8km)
Museum Rd
Mnazi Mmoja
1
2
3
5
13
14
17
19
20
23
26
27
28
32
34
36
39
40
43
44
A
B
C
D
E
F
G
5
6
7
8

Stone Town

Sights

1 Anglican Cathedral E5
2 Catholic Cathedral C5
3 Darajani Market F5
4 Forodhani Gardens C4
5 Hamamni Persian Baths D5
6 House of Wonders C4
7 Old Dispensary E2
8 Old Fort C4
9 Princess Salme Museum D4

Activities, Courses & Tours

10 Eco + Culture Tours D4
11 Kawa Tours F4
Membe Kayak Club .... (see 21)
12 Mr Mitu's Tours G2
13 Mrembo Spa C5
14 One Ocean B5
Zanzibar Different .... (see 13)

Sleeping

15 Emerson on Hurumzi D4
16 Emerson Spice E4
17 Hiliki House C7
18 Ikala Zanzibar Stonetown Lodge F2
19 Jafferji House C5
20 Jambo Guest House D6
21 Kholle House E2
22 Kiponda B&B D3
23 Lost & Found Hostel B5
24 Princess Salme Inn G1
25 Seyyida Hotel D3
26 Shaba Hotel B5
27 Zanzibar Coffee House E5

Eating

28 Abyssinian Maritim C7
29 Abyssinian's Steakhouse E2
30 Al-Shabany G2
Emerson on Hurumzi Rooftop Teahouse .... (see 15)
Emerson Spice Rooftop Teahouse .... (see 16)
31 House of Spices F4
32 Lukmaan Restaurant E6
33 Monsoon Restaurant B4
34 Sambusa Two Tables Restaurant C7
35 Zanzibar Coffee House E4

Drinking & Nightlife

36 Africa House Hotel Sunset Bar B6
37 Livingstone Beach Restaurant B4
38 Mercury's E2
39 Sunrise Restaurant B6
40 Up North @ 6 Degrees South B6

Entertainment

41 Dhow Countries Music Academy D3
42 Hurumzini Movie Café E4
Old Fort .... (see 8)

Shopping

43 Cultural Arts Centre Zanzibar D5
44 Memories of Zanzibar B6
45 Zenji Boutique G2

Information

46 Zanzibar Commission for Tourism Information Desk C4

little museum tells the story of Princess Salme, a sultan's daughter who eloped with a German merchant in the late 19th century and later wrote *Memoirs of an Arabian Princess from Zanzibar*. If Said is on duty, his guided tour of the museum adds depth to the story.

Activities

One Ocean DIVING
(☎0773 048828, 0774 310003; www.zanzibaroneocean.com; cnr Shangani St & Kenyatta Rd; snorkelling $45, double dive $110, discover scuba diving experience $150, open water course $500; ⊙8am-6pm) This PADI five-star dive operator has many years of experience, and caters for all abilities. From the main office in Stone Town, short dive trips go to nearby reefs and wrecks, while longer trips can be arranged to other sites around Zanzibar Island. One Ocean also has branches at a number of locations on the coast around the island.

★ **Mrembo Spa** SPA
(☎0777 430117, 024-223 0004; www.mrembospa.com; cnr Cathedral & Soko Muhogo Sts; massage & treatments per hour US$30; ⊙10am-6pm) Don't come to Mrembo looking for clinical suites. This imaginative Swahili spa offers kanga-covered massage tables in colour-washed rooms with a friendly atmosphere, where softly spoken Zanzibari therapists provide massages, manicures and traditional treatments using handcrafted oils and scrubs – which you can also buy (along with local soaps and other products) in the excellent shop.

Membe Kayak Club KAYAKING
(☎0774 228205; www.membekayakzanzibar.com; Kholle House Hotel, off Malindi Rd; kayak per hour/day US$10/30) Good-quality sea kayaks for rent; you can 'self-drive' (if you're familiar with kayaks on the open sea) or go with a local guide (if you're not). Popular destinations are the islands off Stone Town, or less demanding trips along the waterfront.

Tours

Guided tours can be organised with one of the many local tour companies in Zanzibar Town. Popular excursions include dhow cruises (especially popular at sunset), city walking tours (focusing on historical sites in Stone Town), boat trips (usually with snorkelling, swimming and lunch on an island) and spice tours (you guessed it, to nearby spice plantations). Spice tours usually include some out-of-town historical sites as well.

Longer excursions from Zanzibar Town include cruises in Menai Bay or to see dolphins at Kizimkazi. If you choose to take a dolphin tour, use a reputable tour operator that has ethical practices on viewing dolphins (and especially on swimming with dolphins – which we don't recommend).

Look out for guides belonging to the Heritage Guide Association; accredited members specialise in Stone Town history and culture.

Zanzibar Different CULTURAL

(024-223 0004, 0777 430117; www.zanzibardifferent.com; Mrembo Spa, Baghani St;) As the name implies, this company offers unusual excursions and well-known tours with a culturally engaging twist. Stone Town tours focus on marriage roles, children's education and mourning rituals, and a plethora of handicraft traditions. Options further afield include the Princess Salme Tour, retracing the fascinating history of this Zanzibari princess by dhow and flower-fringed donkey chariot.

Kawa Tours CULTURAL

(0777 957995, 0773 795758; www.zanzibarkawatours.com;) This company covers unusual ground. For example, the Ghost Tour takes you to reputedly haunted locations as a way of understanding the history of the slave trade; the Cooking Workshop includes market shopping followed by hands-on learning in a local kitchen; and various Heritage Tours focus on Stone Town's history, culture, architecture, religious buildings and so on.

Eco + Culture Tours TOURS

(024-223 3731, 0755 873066; www.ecoculture-zanzibar.org; Hurumzi St; 10am-5pm) Standard spice/city/dhow tours are offered, plus some longer excursions with an environmental and cultural focus. Guides speak English, French, Spanish, Italian and German. A speciality is the off-the-beaten-track trip to the village of Unguja Ukuu, with a dhow cruise in Menai Bay stopping at tiny remote islands for snorkelling and lunch (US$65 per person for four people).

Mr Mitu's Tours TOURS

(0773 167620; Funguni Rd, off Malawi Rd; tours US$10-20) Mr Mitu's budget-priced spice tours have been famous for decades, so much that the company is now run by his son (also called Mr Mitu). Prices for a half-day tour cost US$10 to US$20 depending on group size, including lunch. Day trips are also available, including the caves and historic sites at Mangapwani, plus a swim at the beach.

Gallery Tours & Safaris TOURS

(0772 077090, 0774 305165; www.gallerytours.net; 9am-5pm) Specialising in top-of-the-line tours and excursions, Gallery Tours can also arrange Zanzibar weddings, honeymoon itineraries and exclusive dhow cruises.

Grassroots Traveller CULTURAL

(0772 821725; www.grassroots-traveller.com) Working closely with community-based projects, NGOs and organisations striving for sustainable development, this forward-thinking company helps travellers craft interesting itineraries blending adventure with community engagement to discover that there's more to Zanzibar than sun, sand and sea. It also helps volunteers hook up successful short- and long-term projects.

Festivals & Events

★ Sauti za Busara MUSIC

(Voices of Wisdom; www.busaramusic.org; festival pass visitors/locals US$120/10; early–mid-Feb) A cultural landmark in Zanzibar since 2003, Sauti za Busara is one of the biggest festivals of its sort in East Africa, showcasing music and musicians of all genres – *taarab,* jazz, Afro-pop or bongo flava – from across Zanzibar, Africa and the world. Performances take place over three days, with venues in the Old Fort and across Stone Town plus some other parts of Zanzibar Island.

Zanzibar International Film Festival CULTURAL

(Festival of the Dhow Countries; www.ziff.or.tz; festival pass US$50; Jul) Zanzibar's film festival celebrates and nurtures arts from East Africa and Indian Ocean countries as diverse as India, Iran and Madagascar. For 16 days venues around Zanzibar Town host a wide range of screenings, plus performances, media-related workshops and musical master classes.

Jahazi Literary & Jazz Festival CULTURAL
(www.jahazifestival.com; weekend pass visitors US$40, locals Tsh25,000; ⏲late Aug-early Sep) A long weekend of words and music – jazz, blues, poetry and storytelling – every year, with performances at the Old Fort and Livingstone Beach Restaurant in Zanzibar Town.

Sleeping

★**Jambo Guest House** GUESTHOUSE $
(☎024-223 3779, 0776 686239; www.jamboguest.com; off Mkunazini St; s/d with shared bathroom US$30/40; ❄📶) Probably the best-value budget accommodation in town and extremely popular with backpackers, Jambo runs like clockwork. Nine spick-and-span rooms with Zanzibari beds share four bathrooms, there's complimentary tea and coffee, and it's within easy reach of several good-value eateries. Local tours and transfers to the east-coast beaches can be arranged.

★**Lost & Found Hostel** HOSTEL $
(☎0684 320699; www.lost57.com; 57 Kenyatta Rd; dm from US$20; ❄📶) Zanzibar's first dedicated backpackers hostel, Lost & Found is perfect for travellers on a tight budget. It's clean, modern, safe, friendly and well located. Guests sleep in comfortable 'pods' (single or double), with curtains for privacy, in two dorms (mixed gender and female only). The shared bathrooms are spotless. There's funky decor and a small balcony overlooking the street.

Kiponda B&B HOTEL $
(Kiponda Hotel; ☎0777 431665, 024-223 3052; www.kiponda.com; Nyumba ya Moto St; s/d US$30/50; ❄📶) A long-standing and popular place with friendly and relaxed staff, the Kiponda has simple but clean rooms (all with fan, some with air-con) on three floors. Breakfast is served on the top-floor terrace, which is also a great place to relax during the day (it's got wi-fi too). Free transfers from the ferry or airport.

Princess Salme Inn HOTEL $
(☎0777-435303; www.princesssalmeinn.com; off Funguni Rd; s/d from US$47/67, with shared bathroom US$35/50; ❄@) In the scruffy but authentic part of town near the dhow harbour, this friendly place has clean and simple rooms with Zanzibar beds and mosquito nets, plus a rooftop breakfast room that catches the breeze. Some cheaper rooms have fan but no air-con. Transport to the east coast and no-hassle boat rides to the nearby islands can be arranged.

★**Mangrove Lodge** LODGE $$
(☎0777 691790, 0773 516213; www.mangrovelodge.com; Chiuni; s US$40-60, d US$80-120; P📶) 🍃 The delightful Mangrove Lodge is owned by a Zanzibari-Italian couple; their gentle style imbues the whole place, from the palm-thatched lounge overlooking the bay to the spacious bungalow rooms in the lush garden. The lodge is at Chuini, about 15km from Stone Town, so it's an ideal place to come to relax after a few days of arduous historical sightseeing.

Kholle House BOUTIQUE HOTEL $$
(☎0772 161033; www.khollehouse.com; off Malindi Rd, behind Old Dispensary; d US$100-140; ❄📶🏊) This hotel was once a palace, built in 1860 for Princess Kholle, favoured daughter of Sultan Said. After meticulous renovation, it now offers bright and luxurious (if slightly compact) rooms, decorated with Zanzibari and art deco furniture. The staff are friendly, the small garden has a plunge pool and the rooftop 'teahouse' has great views over this part of Stone Town.

Shaba Hotel BOUTIQUE HOTEL $$
(☎024-223 8021; www.shaba-zanzibar.com; s/d US$60/75) Hidden in the back streets in a quiet part of Stone Town, but within a short walk of busy Kenyatta Rd, this small hotel is well located, with welcoming staff and rooms combining contemporary design, dhow-wood furniture and African fabrics. There's no restaurant; breakfast is taken in the leafy garden, and there's also a rooftop terrace.

Seyyida Hotel BOUTIQUE HOTEL $$
(☎024-223 8352; www.theseyyida-zanzibar.com; Nyumba Ya Moto St; d from US$110; ❄📶🏊) Lighter and brighter than many Stone Town hotels, the Seyyida eschews dark wood in favour of white tiles. Rooms are modern and styled in neutral tones, reached off open corridors decorated with antique photos and arranged around a verdant courtyard; some have balconies but only one has sea views. There's also a rooftop restaurant, small swimming pool and spa.

Ikala Zanzibar Stonetown Lodge HOTEL $$
(☎0628 001520; www.ikalalodges.com; s/d US$49/79; ❄📶) Bright and cheerful in an

unashamed 'economy' model, the Ikala is ideal if all you need is a clean room, friendly staff and efficient service. Extras (breakfast, air-con, luxury linen, TV, bathroom amenities) are optional for a small fee. Another plus is the neat little bar-restaurant on the roof.

Rumaisa Hotel HOTEL **$$**

(☎0777 752777, 0777 410695; http://rumaisahotel.info; off Malawi Rd; d US$55-70; P) Slightly off the beaten track, the Rumaisa Hotel is worth the journey. Stairs with bamboo bannisters lead to rooms with Zanzibari beds, fridge and TV, with ochre-painted walls giving a vaguely North Africa touch. Staff are very friendly and breakfast is served in the rooftop restaurant.

It's next to the Zancinema on the continuation of Creek Rd beyond the crossroads with Malawi Rd.

Hiliki House GUESTHOUSE **$$**

(☎0777 410131; www.hilikihouse-zanzibar.com; Victoria St; d from US$90; ❄📶) Covering two houses side by side – the original in colonial style, the other in 1950s retro – this small family-run hotel offers peaceful and elegant rooms on a quiet street on the edge of Stone Town, overlooking Victoria Gardens.

★**Emerson Spice** BOUTIQUE HOTEL **$$$**

(☎0775 046395, 024-223 2776; www.emersonspice.com; Tharia St; d US$150-300; ❄📶) With its stained-glass windows, wooden latticework balustrades, tinkling fountains and soft-hued colour scheme, Emerson Spice is one of the most stylish and atmospheric hotels in Stone Town. Created from a 19th-century mansion with wide steps leading down to a small square in the narrow street outside, it has 11 rooms filled with antiques, quirky decorations, rich textiles and deep bathtubs.

Jafferji House BOUTIQUE HOTEL **$$$**

(☎0774 078441; www.jafferjihouse.net; 120 Gizenga St; d US$180-225; ❄📶) The historic former home of the Jafferji family, this beautifully decorated hotel is packed with traditional, modern and colonial artefacts, plus stunning images by well-known photographer Javed Jafferji. You can choose standard or luxury rooms and enjoy the rooftop restaurant with uninterrupted 360-degree views across Stone Town. And if it all gets too much, you can relax in the spa.

Emerson on Hurumzi BOUTIQUE HOTEL **$$$**

(☎0779 854225, 024-223 2784; www.emersononhurumzi.com; 236 Hurumzi St; r/ste US$175/225; 📶) This hotel is simply brimming with character. Two adjacent historic buildings have been restored in a fantastical *Arabian Nights* style; each of the 15 rooms is uniquely and decadently decorated, with traditional Swahili and contemporary design combined perfectly (some might say

STONE TOWN'S ARCHITECTURE

Stone Town's architecture is a fusion of Arabic, Indian, European and African influences. Arab buildings are often square, with two or three storeys. Rooms line the outer walls, allowing space for an inner courtyard and verandas, and cooling air circulation. Indian buildings, also several storeys high, generally include a shop on the ground floor and living quarters above, with ornate facades and balconies. A common feature is the *baraza*, a stone bench facing onto the street that serves as a focal point around which townspeople meet and chat.

The most famous feature of Zanzibari architecture is the carved wooden door, a symbol of wealth and status, and often the first part of a house to be built (or sometimes older than the house, having been moved from a previous location).

Some Zanzibari doors are centuries old, others simply decades old, while others are relatively recent; there's still a thriving door-carving industry today.

Generally, Arabian-styled doors have a square frame with a geometrical shape, and 'newer' doors – many of which were built towards the end of the 19th century and incorporate Indian influences – often have semicircular tops and intricate floral decorations.

Doors may be decorated with carvings of passages from the Quran, and other commonly seen motifs include images representing items desired in the household, such as a fish (expressing the hope for many children) or the date tree (a symbol of prosperity). Some doors have large brass spikes, which are a tradition from India, where spikes protected doors from being battered down by elephants.

CATCHING SUNSET

One of the best ways to start an evening in Stone Town is sipping a drink while watching the sun set over the ocean. But if you want a genuine sundowner, choose your spot carefully as the sun's position changes through the year. Locations on the southwest side of Stone Town, like **Africa House Hotel** (p75), get the best sunset views from October to March, while for locations on the northwest side, like **Mercury's** (☎024-223 3076; Mizingani Rd; ⏲noon-midnight), it's best from April to September.

outrageously). The popular rooftop teahouse restaurant (p75) is open to nonguests for lunch and dinner.

Eating

For traditional Zanzibari food, you can't beat Stone Town. Being near the coast, seafood unsurprisingly features on most menus, often seasoned with flavours from around the Indian Ocean. For those with deep pockets, luxury rooftop restaurants are a must, while markets and street-food options abound for those on lower budgets.

★Lukmaan Restaurant ZANZIBARI **$**
(New Mkunazini Rd; meals Tsh5000-7000; ⏲7am-9pm) Probably the best local restaurant for quality Zanzibari food. There's no menu: just make your way inside to the 1950s counter and see what's on offer. Servings are enormous and include various biryanis, fried fish, coconut curries and freshly made naan.

Al-Shabany ZANZIBARI **$**
(off Malawi Rd; meals from Tsh3500; ⏲10am-2pm) For no-nonsense food at budget prices, it's worth searching out this place in the small side streets off Malawi Rd. Expect pilau and biryani, plus chicken and chips. Takeaway also available.

★Zanzibar Coffee House CAFE **$**
(☎024-223 9319; www.riftvalley-zanzibar.com; Tharia St, Mkunazini; snacks Tsh5000-12,000; ⏲8am-6pm; ❄📶) The top spot in Zanzibar for a serious cup of genuine East African Rift Valley coffee is undoubtedly this charming cafe. Alongside espressos and cappuccinos are milkshakes, crêpes, salads, sandwiches and toasted bruschetta. Tours of the roasting area can be arranged. Upstairs are eight **guestrooms** (☎024-223 9319, 0773 061532; d US$110-170; ❄@), decorated in traditional Zanzibar style.

Monsoon Restaurant ZANZIBARI **$$**
(☎0777 410410; Forodhani; mains Tsh17,000-30,000; ⏲noon-10pm) Something slightly different: Monsoon has traditional-style dining, so you eat at low tables lounging on cushions (shoes off at the door, naturally). The menu is well-prepared Swahili cuisine with a modern twist. It's very atmospheric, further enhanced by the gentle backdrop of live *taarab* music on Wednesday and Saturday evenings. There's also conventional table seating on the terrace outside.

Sambusa Two Tables Restaurant ZANZIBARI **$$**
(☎0774 881921, 024-223 1979; Victoria St; meals Tsh25,000) This simple place did indeed start with just two small tables, but now caters for larger numbers – although it's still in the family house. Here's the routine: visit first to ask what's on offer; if you like it make a reservation, then come along later to sample numerous Zanzibari dishes.

House of Spices MEDITERRANEAN **$$**
(☎0773 573727, 024-223 1264; www.houseofspiceszanzibar.com; Kiponda St; meals Tsh12,000-15,000; ⏲10am-11pm Mon-Sat; 📶) With its lantern-lit rooftop terrace this Mediterranean restaurant has well-executed seafood and wood-fired pizzas. Fish dishes come with a choice of five spiced sauces, there's a good wine list and you can round off your meal with a special spiced digestif. For a lighter evening, there's also a tapas bar. A bonus is the attached small and stylish guesthouse.

True to its name, the building was once the home of a spice trader – the top-floor terraces were used for drying spices.

Abyssinian Maritim ETHIOPIAN **$$**
(☎0772 940556; Vuga Rd; mains Tsh20,000-25,000; ⏲noon-3pm & 6-10pm Wed-Mon) Sit on the airy terrace underneath the pergola of exuberant bougainvillea and wait for enormous platters of *tibs* (grilled meat), *injera* (flatbread) and other specialities at this great little Ethiopian place. Spectacular multicoloured fruit smoothies, *tej* (honey beer) and freshly ground coffee complete the feast.

★ Emerson Spice Rooftop Teahouse FUSION $$$

(☎024-223 2776; www.emersonspice.com; Tharia St; dinner set menu US$40; ⏲7-11pm Fri-Wed) Perched on top of the Emerson Spice hotel (p73), the 'teahouse' (open-sided room) offers 360-degree views and some of the finest food in Stone Town. Many guests come for pre-dinner sundowner cocktails before enjoying five courses of Zanzibar specialities. Mains are mostly seafood-based, such as lemongrass calamari or prawns with grilled mango. Reservations are essential.

Emerson on Hurumzi Rooftop Teahouse ZANZIBARI $$$

(☎024-223 2784, 0779 854225; www.emersononhurumzi.com; Hurumzi St; set menu Tsh40,000; ⏲noon-4pm & 5-11pm) Part of the well-known Emerson on Hurumzi hotel (p73), the rooftop teahouse restaurant is open to nonguests. The food is excellent, and the view simply stunning. Lunch is served from noon to 4pm, or come early for sunset drinks followed by three-course dinners that feature vintage Zanzibari recipes. There's often a live *taarab* music performance too. Reservations are usually required.

Drinking & Nightlife

Most bars in Zanzibar Town are connected to hotels, with a few notable stand-alone exceptions. They all serve local and international brands of beer and other drinks, and several offer cocktails or mocktails involving local fruits and spices. Many hotels also have a 'teahouse' (traditional open-sided room at the top of a building) where you can enjoy a drink with spectacular views.

Livingstone Beach Restaurant BAR

(off Shangani St; ⏲10am-2am) This worn but popular place in the old British consulate building has seating inside and outside on a deck under trees directly on the beach. Food is available lunchtime and evening, but mainly this is the place to come for drinks, especially at sunset or after dark when the setting is delightful by candlelight. There's often live music too.

Africa House Hotel Sunset Bar BAR

(www.africahousehotel.co.tz; Shangani St; ⏲5pm-midnight) With a front-row view of the ocean, the Sunset Bar at the Africa House Hotel – once the British Club – has a wide terrace and steady supply of cold beer, making it a perennially popular place for sundowners.

Sunrise Restaurant BAR

(Kenyatta Rd, cnr Kenyatta Rd & Baghani St; ⏲10am-10pm) The no-frills Sunrise is frequented by locals and budget travellers, and despite the name it's as much a bar as a restaurant, although basic meals (around Tsh10,000) are available. Sit inside to watch TV or out in the garden to catch the breeze.

Up North @ 6 Degrees South BAR

(☎062-064 4611; www.6degreessouth.co.tz; Shangani St; ⏲5-11pm; 📶) Enjoy sundowners and sea views from this rooftop bar above 6 Degrees South restaurant on the southwest-facing side of Stone Town.

☆ Entertainment

Entertainment Zanzibar-style centres on traditional music and dance performances.

★ Dhow Countries Music Academy LIVE MUSIC

(☎0777 416529; www.zanzibarmusic.org; Old Customs House, Mizingani Rd; concerts Tsh10,000; ⏲9am-6pm) Many music genres are studied at this academy and regular evening concerts showcase students' work, from Afro-jazz and fusion to *taarab* – Zanzibar's celebrated sung poetry. For a more hands-on experience, workshops are also available. Check the notice board in the lobby for performance times here and at other venues around town.

Old Fort DANCE

(Tsh5000-10,000) Performances of local music, dance and drumming are often held at the Old Fort, but the schedule is variable. Stop by the information desk at the entrance during the day to check what's on in the evening.

Hurumzini Movie Café CINEMA

(Hurumciné; ☎0628 014454; www.facebook.com/hurumzini; off Hurumzini St; ⏲10am-9pm) Come for coffee, a meal or a movie – or all three. With comfortable sofas, funky decor and an imaginative menu (snacks from Tsh3000;

WHERE TO SHOP

Stone Town's best-known shopping areas include Gizenga St, Hurumzi St, Kenyatta Rd and the streets around Darajani Market. If Tanzanite jewellery is your thing, there are several specialist shops along Kenyatta Rd.

meals Tsh9000 to Tsh15,000), this is a great little place. Swing by during the day to see what's showing in the evening; between 10am and 5pm customers can choose the film, or just enjoy the food and friendly ambience.

Shopping

★Cultural Arts Centre Zanzibar ART
(☎0773 612551; hamadcac.z@gmail.com; Hamamni St; ⏲10am-6.30pm) Organised by the dedicated Hamad and other local artists, with an emphasis on quality and distinctiveness, this arts centre and shop provide a refreshing change from the wooden animals and *tinga-tinga* art found elsewhere in Stone Town. On sale are stunning paintings in traditional and contemporary styles, plus jewellery, candles, soaps and craftware items, mostly made by local cooperatives around Zanzibar.

Zenji Boutique ARTS & CRAFTS
(☎0777 247243; www.zenjicafeboutique.com; Malawi Rd; ⏲8am-8pm) A well-curated showcase of eclectic Zanzibari and Tanzanian crafts displayed with details of their provenance and production. Kit yourself out with upcycled beach bags made from rice sacks or dhow sails, or choose from metalwork sculpture, pretty jewellery made from recycled plastics, and much more. It's all beautifully displayed in a dedicated shop area inside the Zenji Cafe.

Memories of Zanzibar GIFTS & SOUVENIRS
(Kenyatta Rd; ⏲8am-6pm Mon-Sun) This place calls itself an emporium, and it does indeed have a massive range of souvenirs: carvings, clothing, books, ornaments, furnishings, jewellery, fabrics, toys and more, all in a modern environment. Everything has a price label, so there's no haggling, and absolutely no pressure as you browse.

ℹ Information

DANGERS & ANNOYANCES

While Zanzibar is relatively safe, Zanzibar Town does see occasional robberies and muggings.

➡ Keep your money and valuables out of sight (and reach), especially in crowded areas like Darajani Market.

➡ Avoid isolated areas, such as the beaches to the north or south of Stone Town.

➡ At night in Stone Town, especially in the port area, take a taxi or walk in a group.

➡ If you leave Zanzibar Town on the night ferry, take care with your valuables, especially when arriving in Dar es Salaam.

INTERNET ACCESS

Most hotels in Stone Town (and many cafes and restaurants) offer wi-fi, either in the lobby/bar/restaurant or in all rooms – although this can be sketchy in historic buildings due to the thick walls.

Some hotels also have an internet-enabled computer for guest use.

Public internet is available at **Shangani Post Office** (Kenyatta Rd; ⏲8am-12.30pm & 2-4.30pm Mon-Fri, to 12.30pm Sat) and **Azzurri Internet Café** (New Mkunazini Rd; ⏲8.30am-8.30pm); both charge Tsh1000 per hour.

MEDICAL SERVICES

Zanzibar Town has the large state-run **Mnazi Moja Hospital** (Kaunda Rd), but most visitors (and most locals, if they can afford it) use a private facility. Options include **Zanzibar Medical Group** (☎024-223 3134; Kenyatta Rd), a small private clinic, and **Zanaid Clinic** (☎0777 777112; www.zanaid.org; Chukwani Rd, Mbweni; ⏲1-5pm Mon Fri), where the two European-trained doctors have experience in tropical illness and diving injuries. There's also **Global Hospital** (Tasakhtaa Global Hospital; ☎024-223 2341; www.tasakhtaahospital.co.tz; Victoria St, Vuga), a large medical centre where facilities include casualty/emergency room (with ambulance), surgery, dentist, general physician/practitioner (GP) and pharmacy.

For small-scale medical problems, pharmacists can advise; reputable and well-stocked pharmacists include **Shamshu & Sons Pharmacy** (☎0715 411480, 024-223 2199; Market St; ⏲9am-8.30pm Mon-Thu & Sat, 9am-noon & 4-8.30pm Fri, 9am-1.30pm Sun) and **Fahud Pharmacy** (New Mkunazini Rd).

MONEY

Zanzibar Town has a few banks with ATMs, although not all function with non-Tanzanian bank accounts. For changing cash, it's best to use licensed bureaus.

TOURIST INFORMATION

The official Zanzibar Commission for Tourism has a **tourist information desk** (ZCT; Mzingani Rd; ⏲9am-6pm) just inside the entrance to the Old Fort. It's worth stopping to pick up leaflets or get information on upcoming festivals and events. For advice on anything else, the staff's knowledge is limited.

Also be aware that many local tour companies around Zanzibar Town display signs claiming to offer 'tourist information' – but mainly they want to sell you stuff.

Getting There & Away

AIR

Airlines flying in and out of **Zanzibar International Airport** (p211) include the following:

Coastal Aviation (☎024-223 3489, airport 024-223 3112; www.coastal.co.tz; Zancos Tours & Travel, Shangani St) Numerous daily flights connecting Zanzibar with Dar es Salaam, Arusha, Pemba, Tanga and elsewhere in Tanzania and East Africa.

Kenya Airways (☎0786 390004, 024-223 4520/1; www.kenya-airways.com; Muzammil Centre, Malawi Rd) At least two flights daily to/from Nairobi (Kenya), with connections to other cities in Africa and beyond.

Precision Air (☎024-223 5126, 0786 300418; www.precisionairtz.com; Muzammil Centre, Malawi Rd, cnr Malawi & Mlandege Rds) Several flights to/from Dar es Salaam daily, with connections to Kilimanjaro and other destinations in Tanzania and East Africa.

Tropical Air (☎0777 431431, 024-223 2511; www.tropicalair.co.tz; Creek Rd) Daily flights connecting Zanzibar with Dar es Salaam, Pemba, Mafia and Arusha.

ZanAir (☎024-223 3678, 024-223 3670; www.zanair.com; Muzammil Centre, Malawi Rd) Daily flights to/from Dar es Salaam, Pemba and Arusha.

Costs of flights to destinations within Tanzania are similar on all the airlines, although departure days and times vary, and special offers are sometimes available. Some sample destinations and standard one-way fares:

- Arusha/Moshi/Kilimanjaro US$250
- Dar es Salaam US$75
- Pemba US$100

At Zanzibar International Airport, there is no reliable phone number for the public to use for flight (or any) information; you're better off contacting a local airline office or travel agent.

BOAT

Many visitors to Zanzibar travel on one of the regular and reliable services:

Zanzibar to/from Dar es Salaam Kilimanjaro Fast Ferries; high-speed passenger catamarans (standard adult fare US$35, two hours, four services each way daily).

Zanzibar to/from Pemba Sealink Ferries; roll-on, roll-off car and passenger ships (standard adult fare US$35, approximately six hours, two services each way weekly). This ferry also goes to/from Dar, and once weekly to/from Tanga.

Other ferries are *Mandeleo, Serengeti* and *Flying Horse*, but services are unreliable.

All ferries arrive in Zanzibar Town; the **passenger ferry terminal** gate is on Mizingani Rd. There is no reliable phone number for the public to use for ferry information; it is better to contact **Azam Marine** (☎024-223 1655; www.azammarine.com; cnr Malawi & Mizingani Rds), the main ferry operator.

Getting Around

For getting around Stone Town, most people (locals and foreigners) simply walk. It's a compact area and many of the narrow streets are impassible for cars.

TO/FROM THE AIRPORT & FERRY PORT

Zanzibar International Airport (7km southeast of Zanzibar Town) Taxis between the airport and Stone Town charge US$10 to US$20. It generally costs more going *from* the airport, especially at night (expect to pay US$30). Or you can take dalla-dalla 505 (Tsh300, 30 minutes).

Ferry Terminal (Stone Town) Taxis wait outside the gates of the passenger ferry terminal, and charge Tsh5000 to Stone Town hotels (recommended after dark), although nowhere is too far to walk in Stone Town (if you know where you're going).

Many hotels in Stone Town offer airport and ferry port pick-ups for confirmed bookings, sometimes free, sometimes for a small charge; arrange this in advance if required.

Offshore Islands

For clean-water swimming, incredible snorkelling or hassle-free sunbathing, several islands sit within reach of Zanzibar Town, all with stunning beaches and surrounded by reefs.

Bawe, Changuu, Chapwani and Chumbe are 'proper' islands, while others such as Nyange, Pange and Murogo are just sandbanks that partially disappear at high tide.

CHANGUU

Commonly known as Prison Island, the main attractions here are the delightful beach, plus clean water for swimming and snorkelling within easy reach of Zanzibar Town.

You can also admire the giant tortoises, whose ancestors were brought here from the Seychelles over a century ago. History fans may like to know the island was once used to detain slaves and later was the site of a prison and quarantine station. Also on the island is the former house of the British governor, General Lloyd Matthews.

Beyond the main beach, day visitors cannot explore at will, as much of the island is only for guests at **Changuu Private Island**

WORTH A TRIP

CHUMBE ISLAND CORAL PARK

The uninhabited island of Chumbe, about 12km south of Zanzibar Town, has an exceptional shallow-water coral reef along its western shore that abounds with life. The island and reef are protected as Chumbe Island Coral Park, a privately managed nature reserve and ecotourism project.

The reef is in such good condition mainly because it was part of a military zone, off-limits to locals and visitors, until becoming Chumbe Island Coral Park in the 1990s. There are nearly 200 species of coral and about 370 species of fish. The island is also a haven for hawksbill turtles, and dolphins are often seen. Meanwhile, more than 50 species of birds have been recorded here, including the endangered roseate tern.

Overlooked by its landmark historic lighthouse, about 12km south of Zanzibar Town, **Chumbe Island Coral Park Lodge** (☎0777 413232, 024-223 1040; www.chumbeisland.com; Chumbe Island; full board per person US$280; 📶) is a real island getaway combining style, exclusivity and environmental benefits. Accommodation is in 'eco-bungalows' with local decor, solar power, rainwater collection, ocean views and a loft sleeping area that opens to the stars. Activities include forest walks, diving or snorkelling on the reef, and just lounging.

Getting There & Away

Day visits cost US$90 per person and must be arranged in advance, via hotels and tour companies in Zanzibar Town. Boats to Chumbe leave from Mbweni Ruins Hotel; you can make your own way here by taxi or a combination of bus and walking, or have transport included in your tour for US$15 per person each way.

Paradise (☎central reservations 027-254 4595; www.hotelsandlodges-tanzania.com; Changuu Island; 🏊), which was closed for renovation at the time of research.

Getting There & Away

Changuu Island lies about 5km northwest of Zanzibar Town. Trips by boat are organised by most hotels and tour companies in Zanzibar Town and cost around US$25 to US$30 per person.

Nungwi

☎024 / POP 10,000

This large village at Zanzibar Island's northernmost tip was once best known as a dhow-building centre. Today it's a major tourist destination, thanks in part to the beautiful beach and stunning sunsets. The result: a place where traditional and modern knock against each other with full force. Fishing boats still launch from the beach – a scene unchanged for centuries – but they're overlooked by a long line of hotels. Some travellers say Nungwi is a definite highlight; others are happy giving it a miss.

Sights & Activities

Diving, snorkelling, fishing and other water sports are unsurprisingly the main draw here. From Nungwi, frequented dive sites are mainly down the east coast or to Mnemba Island and reefs near Tumbatu Island.

For swimmers, Nungwi's local geography and tidal pattern mean swimming is possible at any time. Other activities available include yoga, cycling and guided tours of the village.

Mnarani Marine Turtle Conservation Pond ANIMAL SANCTUARY
(Mnarani Aquarium; www.mnarani.org; US$5; ⏲9am-6pm) In 1993 the villagers of Nungwi opened this turtle sanctuary in a large natural tidal pool near the lighthouse and since then these sea creatures have enjoyed a degree of protection from being hunted and eaten. You can see turtles of various species and sizes, and proceeds from entrance fees fund an education project for local children, hopefully demonstrating the benefits of turtle conservation.

ZanziYoga YOGA
(☎0776 310227; www.yogazanzibar.com; 6-day retreat with accommodation s/d US$1295/1970) Centre yourself with yoga under the skillful guidance of Marisa van Vuuren. On offer are six-day retreats, including morning and evening yoga sessions plus accommodation at **Flame Tree Cottages** (☎0777 479429, 0737 202161; www.flametreecottages.com; west Nungwi; s/d US$130/170; ❄📶🏊); budget and luxury retreats use other Nungwi hotels.

Divine Diving DIVING
(www.scubazanzibar.com; Amaan Bungalows Beach Resort) Divine Diving, on Nungwi's west beach, is a five-star PADI centre offering small-group dives, Mares equipment and (uniquely) courses in efficient breathing using yoga techniques.

Zanzibar Watersports DIVING
(☎0773 235030; www.zanzibarwatersports.com; Paradise Beach Bungalows; 2/6 dives US$115/310) This company is based at Kendwa with a branch at Paradise Beach Bungalows in west Nungwi. Snorkelling, kayaking, fishing, wakeboarding and dhow cruises are also offered, including an all-day 'seafari' (dhow cruise, snorkelling and lunch on a beach).

East Africa Diving & Water Sport Centre DIVING
(☎0777 420588; www.diving-zanzibar.com; 2/6 dives US$100/280) This is Nungwi's oldest diving outfit, located on the beach near Jambo Brothers Guesthouse. It's five-star PADI accredited, and has boats to carry clients to dive sites, as well as tanks, wetsuits and other kit in various sizes.

Kiteboarding Zanzibar KITESURFING
(☎0779 720259; www.kiteboardingzanzibar.com; 3/9hr lessons US$165/495, rental per day US$90) Kiteboarding Zanzibar is IKO certified and equipped with modern kit. Its Nungwi base is linked to its centre at Pwani Mchangani (where clients are taken if conditions aren't good at Nungwi). If you know what you're doing, and have certification, you can rent gear. For everyone else, lessons are available.

Tours

Nungwi Cycling Adventures CULTURAL
(☎0778 677662, 0777 560352; www.zanzibarcyclingadventures.com; per person US$25-40) Explore the world beyond Nungwi on bike tours to rural villages, ancient ruins, coral caves, traditional blacksmiths, farms and plantations or secret beaches. Trips are led by the mild-mannered and knowledgeable Machano; a Nungwi local and freelance guide, he can also be hired for any other local tours by bike, foot or car.

Cultural Village Tour CULTURAL
(2hr per person US$15) At the Mnarani Marine Turtle Conservation Pond you can arrange village tours that are a great way to see local life beyond the hotel strip. Most fascinating are the dhow-builders; your guide will introduce you, so you can ask questions or simply observe their skills. Note, however, that the dhow-builders don't like being photographed so always ask permission first.

Sleeping & Eating

Mabwe Roots Bungalows BUNGALOW $
(east Nungwi; s US$40) Rustic and relaxed with a reggae vibe, this locally run place has a handful of simple rooms with small bathrooms in a garden set back from the beach behind a couple of larger hotels. It's on Nungwi's quieter eastern side, about 2km from the village centre.

Nungwi Guest House GUESTHOUSE $
(☎0777 777708; www.nungwihouse.com; Nungwi village; d US$50) It's not on the beach, but this local-style guesthouse is just a short walk away in the village centre, and a good budget option. You get simple and clean rooms, all with fans and mosquito nets, in a small garden courtyard, plus a friendly welcome.

Mnarani Beach Cottages LODGE $$
(☎0777 415551, 024-224 0494; www.lighthousezanzibar.com; east Nungwi; d US$80-200; ❄ 📶 🏊) On Nungwi's quieter eastern side, near the lighthouse, Mnarani is on a low cliff with a lovely waterside terrace with the beach just below. It's relaxed and efficient, with friendly staff and small rooms in ochre-painted cottages on spacious grounds overlooking the sea. Also available are large superior rooms, a honeymoon suite and apartments for families or groups of friends.

Warere Beach Hotel HOTEL $$
(☎0782 234564; www.warere.com; east Nungwi; d US$80-110; ❄ 📶) Small, peaceful and relaxed, the Warere is 2.5km outside town on Nungwi's east beach. Two rows of cottages have an angular style, but the design ensures all have a beautiful sea view (and also provides 'natural air-con'). Lush gardens, sandy pathways and an infinity pool complete the picture. There's a restaurant, and tours or activities can be arranged.

Z Hotel HOTEL $$$
(☎0774 266266; www.thezhotel.com; west Nungwi; d US$230-260; ❄ 📶 🏊) The Z has luxurious rooms with contemporary decor in two large four-storey blocks overlooking the sea towards the southern end of Nungwi's west beach. There's also a bar, restaurant,

swimming pool, spa and dive centre. While everything is very comfortable, the hotel and grounds lack a feeling of space.

Double Tree RESORT **$$$**
(Double Tree Resort by Hilton Hotel; ☎0779 000008; www.doubletree.hilton.com; west Nungwi; d US$220-280;) A luxurious hotel complex, with rooms in several two- and three-storey buildings, some with sea views, others overlooking the large swimming pool and manicured gardens, and all with balconies and TV. There's a restaurant, and a bar on a deck overlooking the public beach, plus (should you overindulge in the bar or restaurant) a fitness room.

Information

DANGERS & ANNOYANCES

There have been occasional robberies on quiet sections of the beach; don't walk here alone or with valuables, particularly at night.

ETIQUETTE

Because of the large number of tourists in Nungwi, it's easy to overlook the fact that you're in a traditional, conservative environment. When walking in the village, be respectful, especially with your dress and your interactions with locals, and ask permission before snapping photos.

MONEY

There's no ATM, but most hotels can help you change US dollars into local currency, and there's a forex desk at **Amaan Bungalows Beach Resort** (☎0777 318112; www.amaanbungalows.com; west Nungwi; d US$100-150;).

Getting There & Away

Buses and dalla-dallas (route 116) run throughout the day between Nungwi and Zanzibar Town. It's tarmac road all the way. The public transport stand is near the roundabout in the town centre; taxis and private tourist minibuses will drop you at your hotel.

Kendwa

☎024

Kendwa Beach is a long stretch of sand extending down the west coast about 3km south of the tip of Zanzibar Island. Not surprisingly, this idyllic location means a string of resorts, hotels and guesthouses, but there is still lots of space on the beach. Other attractions include a range of water-based activities, and favourable tidal patterns that ensure swimming at all hours.

Activities

The scene in Kendwa is all about the beach and the ocean, with volleyball nets and dive outlets dotted along the sand. Other energetic water sports or more relaxing dhow cruises can also be arranged.

Most hotels have private areas of beach roped off from public beach, so you can choose when to chat to the local guys selling souvenirs – and when to avoid them and relax in peace.

★**Scuba Do** DIVING
(☎0777 417157; www.scuba-do-zanzibar.com; 2/6 dives US$120/330) Based at Sunset Kendwa, this long-standing and highly experienced Gold Palm and Green Star dive centre is one of the most professional outfits on Zanzibar. The owners, Tammy and Christian, and their well-trained crew of instructors offer excellent courses. Small groups are preferred, with families and kids a speciality. Popular and less well-known dive sites can be reached using high-speed boats.

Kendwa Community Tours TOURS
(☎0778 883306; http://kendwa-communitytours.com) This organisation is run by local people. On offer are tours to Stone Town and other parts of Zanzibar Island, but most interesting are the tours of Kendwa village itself, offering a chance for visitors to leave the beach for a while and see how Zanzibaris live day-to-day. Be prepared for arrangements to be a little relaxed.

Zanzibar Parasailing WATER SPORTS
(☎0779 073078; www.zanzibarparasailing.com; solo/tandem flights US$100/130) Solo and tandem flights along with other motor-powered activities, such as jet skiing, waterskiing, wakeboarding and banana-boating.

Sleeping & Eating

Kendwa Rocks BUNGALOW **$$**
(☎024-294 1113, 0777 415475; www.kendwarocks.com; s/d banda with shared bathroom US$40/50, d bungalow US$60-170;) This long-standing Kendwa classic has something for everyone, from basic *bandas* (thatched-roof huts) with shared bathrooms to luxurious bungalows with private plunge pool right on the beach, via several accommodation options in-between, all set in gardens covering a gently sloping cliff. Rooms set back from the sea may not have views, but they're quieter and more private.

Diamonds La Gemma dell'Est RESORT $$$
(☎024-224 0125; http://lagemmadellest.diamondsresorts.com; s/d with full board from US$350/500; ❄📶🏊) On the northern end of Kendwa beach, this is a very large and luxurious all-inclusive resort (called simply 'Gemma' by the locals) with around 130 rooms all with private veranda and sea view. Facilities include huge swimming pool, beautiful (maintained) beach, several restaurant-bars (including one on a jetty over the water), tennis courts, dive centre, gym and spa.

Fisherman Local Restaurant SEAFOOD $
(mains Tsh7000-10,000) True to its name, this place is run by an enthusiastic group of locals and specialises in seafood. Drinks and other meals are also available. It's on a small terrace under a thatched roof, on the dirt road that runs behind the hotels at the southern end of the beach.

Varadero Zanzibar House LEBANESE $
(meals Tsh8000-10,000; 📶) Serving up Lebanese and Zanzibari meals in neat but simple surroundings, this place is on the dirt road that runs behind the hotels at the southern end of the beach.

Getting There & Away

Kendwa can be reached via any bus or dalla-dalla (route 116) that runs between Zanzibar Town and Nungwi. The fare is TSh3000. Get off at the main Kendwa turn-off, from where it's about 2km along a dirt road to the village and main cluster of beach hotels. If you're driving, this access road is passable in 2WD, with some care needed over the rocky patches.

Matemwe

☎024 / POP 5000

The idyllic beach at Matemwe has some of the finest sand on Zanzibar, and in this sleepy village life still moves at its own pace, despite the hotels and guesthouses nearby. Of all the coastal destinations on Zanzibar Island, this area seems to have the most 'local' atmosphere. For tourists, this tranquil unhurried ambience means Matemwe is definitely a place where it's easy to switch off.

Courses & Activities

Dada COOKING
(☎0777 466304; https://dadazanzibar.wordpress.com; per person around US$25, depending on group size) Bestir yourself from the sunbed and head out to meet local women and learn how they cook. On the menu could be baobab jam or coconut and cassava leaves. This activity is run by Dada, a local development project, just outside Matemwe village. You can book direct with Dada or via most Matemwe hotels.

One Ocean DIVING
(www.zanzibaroneocean.com; Matemwe Beach Village; 2/6 dives US$110/305) One Ocean is an experienced five-star PADI dive outfit with bases in Zanzibar Town and on the east coast, including **Matemwe Beach Village** (☎0777 417250; www.matemwebeach.net; d with half board US$220-300; 📶🏊) guesthouse. On offer are diving courses and trips to Mnemba Island and other local dive sites. Snorkelling trips are also available for US$45 per person.

DIVING AT MNEMBA

Mnemba Island (also called Mnemba Atoll) is one of the best-known and most popular dive sites in Zanzibar, and on the whole coast of East Africa. Here you can see a wonderful variety of marine life, including tuna, barracuda, moray eels, reef sharks, turtles, dolphins, and shoals of batfish, trigger fish and humpback snappers. During the migration season, it's even possible to spot humpback whales.

While the island itself is privately owned, with access restricted to guests of Mnemba Lodge, the surrounding coral reef can be visited by anyone.

As Mnemba is so popular (it's been dubbed the 'Ngorongoro of Zanzibar'), in some areas the sheer number of boats and divers is causing damage to the reef. Experienced dive companies will be delighted to take you to quieter, less crowded sites.

Sleeping & Eating

★**Sele's Bungalows** BUNGALOW $$
(☎0776 931690; www.selesbungalows.wix.com/zanzibar; d US$80-100; ⊙May-Feb; ❄📶) This is a great little place, with friendly owners and just seven impeccably maintained rooms. There's a small swimming pool and convivial bar-restaurant, all set in a lush garden just a few steps from the beach. Most rooms

WORTH A TRIP

JOZANI-CHWAKA NATIONAL PARK

Jozani Forest is the largest area of indigenous forest on Zanzibar Island. Situated south of **Chwaka Bay** on low-lying land, the area is prone to flooding, which nurtures a lush swamplike environment of moisture-loving trees and ferns. The whole area is protected as **Jozani-Chwaka National Park** (adult/child with guide US$10/5; ⌚7.30am-5pm), and is famously home to populations of Zanzibar red colobus monkey (an endangered species found only on Zanzibar) as well as other monkey species, bushbabies, duikers and more than 40 species of birds.

are large and with balcony, and there's a couple of smaller (and cheaper) ones tucked away downstairs.

★**Zanzibar Bandas** BUNGALOW **$$$**
(☎0773 434113; www.zanzibarbandas.com; d US$150-300;) With a small collection of palm-thatched huts and bungalows in a garden on the beach, this place has a laid-back and welcoming atmosphere. Although simply built, accommodation is spotless and good quality. There's also a small swimming pool and bar-restaurant, and the management are keen musicians so performances or informal jamming sessions are common.

Getting There & Away

Matemwe village is on the northeast coast of Zanzibar Island. Dalla-dallas (route 118) travel daily to/from Zanzibar Town (Tsh2500). Early in the day the terminus is the fish market in the centre of the village at the northern end of the beach; later in the day the terminus is the main junction where the main tarmac road meets the dirt road that runs parallel to the coast.

Kiwengwa

☎024 / POP 4000

The spectacularly beautiful beach at Kiwengwa is popular with large hotels and resorts, mostly hidden behind high walls and mostly all-inclusive, with guests seldom leaving the lush grounds. By contrast, just back from the beach, Kiwengwa village appears poor and dusty, highlighting an uncomfortable contrast.

Activities

Kiwengwa's position on a beautiful stretch of coast means it's ideal for swimming and snorkelling, while hotels can arrange diving and all the usual marine-based activities. On-land options include quad biking. For a much more low-key experience, some hotels arrange tours to **Kiwengwa-Pongwe Forest Reserve** ($5).

Zanzibar Quad Adventure ADVENTURE SPORTS
(☎0774087597; www.facebook.com/ZanzibarQuadAdventure; half day with quad bike 1 or 2 people US$120) Trips by quad bike take you away from the coast through farms and plantations to visit a village and see 'the real Zanzibar'. Some visitors may be uncomfortable riding expensive machines through poor areas; others find it enlightening and enjoyable.

Sleeping & Eating

Zan View Hotel HOTEL **$$**
(☎0774 141803; www.zan-view.com; d US$100-150, with sea view US$175-195;) An unexpected find among the large resorts along this stretch of coast, Zan View is a friendly little place with spotless rooms in a house overlooking a small pool and two-storey Robinson Crusoe–style bar, with the ocean beyond. It's not on the beach; to get there is a short walk past a couple of beachfront properties.

Shooting Star Lodge BOUTIQUE HOTEL **$$$**
(☎0777 414166; www.shootingstarlodge.com; d US$200-315;) This small lodge has a beautiful location on a low cliff overlooking a quiet stretch of sand. It also has excellent service and cuisine. The impeccably decorated accommodation ranges from garden rooms to spacious sea-view cottages, and from beside the curved salt-water infinity pool steps lead straight down to the beach.

Getting There & Away

Buses and dalla-dallas (route 117) run between Kiwengwa village and Zanzibar Town (Tsh 2500).

Pongwe

☎024 / POP 1000

Pongwe's arc of sand is dotted with palm trees and about as close to the quintessential tropical paradise as you can get – it's at the far southern end of the more famous Kiwengwa beach.

Sleeping & Eating

★Pongwe Beach Hotel HOTEL $$$
(0784 336181; www.pongwe.com; d US$210-230; P@) The unassuming Pongwe Beach Hotel has 20 bungalows among the palms on a deep arc of bleached white sand. Most rooms are sea facing (three are garden view), spacious and breezy, and deliberately have no air-con, no TV and not even glass in the windows to ensure you fully immerse yourself in this idyllic location.

Seasons Lodge LODGE $$$
(0776 107225; www.seasonszanzibar.com; s/d US$118/235;) This delightful place has 10 rooms, with breezy coral stone bungalows set in a small patch of natural vegetation, each with louvre doors that open onto a deck overlooking the beach. The friendly (and slightly eccentric) owner ensures materials and supplies used are locally made, and only staff from the area are employed, which adds to the relaxed and welcoming atmosphere.

★Upendo HOTEL $$$
(0777 244492, 0777 770667; www.upendozanzibar.com; villa from US$250) Upendo offers luxurious villas and an excellent bar-restaurant (meals US$8 to US$25) that's also open to nonguests. Villas have between one and four bedrooms, with nice touches like coffee machines and fans inside large mosquito nets. Some villas are aimed at honeymooners, and there's an extra-large one for families. Also available are some simple *bandas* (thatched-roof huts).

★The Rock SEAFOOD $$$
(0776 591360; www.therockrestaurantzanzibar.com; meals Tsh15,000-30,000; 10am-10pm) Zanzibar's most photogenic restaurant is perched on a coral outcrop in a stunning location surrounded by sea. At low tide you can walk to it; at other times (maybe after a long lunch) boats are provided. Of course, you're paying for the location, but the food is good and unsurprisingly includes prawns, lobster, crab, fish and other seafood.

Getting There & Away

Most buses and dalla-dallas between Zanzibar Town and Kiwengwa go via Pongwe. Dalla-dallas also run along the coast road between Matemwe and Chwaka via Pongwe and Kiwengwa.

Michamvi Peninsula

024 / POP 2000

Lined with some of the most beautiful beaches on Zanzibar, this long bony finger of a peninsula stretches 10km north from the popular coastal villages of Paje and Bwejuu, separating the mangrove creeks of Chwaka Bay from the turquoise waters of the Indian Ocean.

Sleeping & Eating

Kae Funk BUNGALOW $$
(0774 361768, 0777 021547; www.kaefunk.com; d US$70-100; @) This relaxed place has eight double rooms perched on a small cliff overlooking Chwaka Bay, with a breezy lounge-restaurant down on the sand below, imaginatively decorated with driftwood and flotsam. A large development next door means you can't see the sea, but Kae Funk's own beach bar a short walk away has excellent views, especially at sunset.

Getting There & Away

Dalla-dallas and buses (route 340) travel regularly between Zanzibar Town and Michamvi Kae village (at the tip of the peninsula) via Paje and Bwejuu. There's also at least one dalla-dalla daily between Michamvi Kae and Makunduchi, via Jambiani.

Paje

024 / POP 3500

Thanks to its wonderful beach of white sand and shallow waters, Paje has changed from a sleepy fishing village to a busy resort town with plenty of places to stay and a lively atmosphere. In recent years it has become very popular as a kitesurfing destination, to such an extent that it's sometimes hard to go for a swim.

Activities

Paje is Zanzibar's main kitesurfing centre. In fact it's one of Africa's best spots, attracting enthusiasts and beginners from all around the world. Reasons for this include the constant and predictable onshore winds, the large flat-water lagoon between the beach and the reef, a shallow and sandy sea bed (ideal for beginners), big waves on the reef (for experts), warm water and the relative lack of seaweed farming. Oh yes, and because it's simply beautiful.

Most kite centres rent equipment from around US$15 per hour or US$50 to US$100 per day, and offer a wide range of courses from around US$100 for a half-day beginner's intro to around US$300 for a full-day's advanced training. There are also freelancing locals on the beach who rent out kit at bargain prices, which is fine if you know what you're doing.

Kite Centre Zanzibar KITESURFING
(www.kitecentrezanzibar.com) This IKO-accredited outfit has been operating in Paje since 2006, with experienced instructors offering excellent courses catering to all abilities, as well as kite rental and sales. Also available are downwinders and longer trips, plus week-long package deals combining kiting with accommodation in a nearby hotel or the affiliated **Bellevue Guesthouse** (0777 209576; www.bellevuezanzibar.com; d from US$80;) 5km up the coast (free transfers).

Airborne Kite Centre KITESURFING
(0715 548464; www.airbornekitecentre.com) Friendly and professional outfit offering IKO-accredited courses and private tuition for beginners to would-be instructors. Equipment sales and rental. Full-moon and sundowner trips (followed by a beach party) and downwinders are also available. Guests can stay in the associated Airborne Kite & Surf Village.

Tours

★ Seaweed Center CULTURAL
(0777 107248; www.seaweedcenter.com; tour US$10) The Seaweed Centre is the HQ of a local social enterprise that enables the women of Paje to harvest seaweed and then make a living by transforming it into desirable organic soaps, scrubs and essential oils (also involving cloves, coconut and local honey). Come here to shop or arrange a fascinating tour of the seaweed farms and processing centre.

Sleeping & Eating

★ Demani Lodge LODGE $
(0772 263115; www.demanilodge.com; dm/s/d US$20/38/50;) Demani Lodge is a delightful budget option with neatly constructed cabins and bungalows. There's a seven-bed dorm and double rooms; some have private bathroom, others share a spotless shower block. Friendly management, clean rooms, big garden, hammocks, laundry, small pool and sociable bar make for instant success. The beach is a short walk away along a footpath.

★ Airborne Kite & Surf Village TENTED CAMP $$
(0776 687357, 0715 548464; www.airbornekitecentre.com; d from US$100, tented d from US$90;) Closely linked to Airborne Kite Centre, this delightful place has rooms in a large house and safari tents (with private bathroom), plus a tree house, all in a large garden under shady trees. There's a very friendly atmosphere, and evening parties and barbecues are frequently arranged to polish off a day's kiting.

★ Mr Kahawa CAFE $$
(www.facebook.com/mr.kahawa; snacks & lunches Tsh8000-14,000; 8.30am-5pm;) After a hard morning's kitesurfing, or maybe after a hard night's partying, this is the place for a top-notch espresso or cappuccino, accompanied by a sweet pancake, savoury wrap, panini, juice or salad. It's cool, stylish and in a fantastic position on the beach, so is understandably popular, meaning service can be a little slow at busy times.

Getting There & Away

Paje is located at the junction of the main road along the southeast coast and the road to/from Zanzibar Town.

Dalla-dallas and buses (Tsh2500) run several times daily between Paje and Zanzibar Town. Those between Zanzibar Town and Jambiani or Bwejuu stop here, too. Paje is also on the bus route between Makunduchi and Michamvi.

Private taxis between Zanzibar Town and Paje cost about US$30, and it's around US$10 in a private shared minibus.

Jambiani

024 / POP 8000

Jambiani is a long village stretching over several kilometres on a stunning stretch of coastline and one of the best places on the island to gain an insight into local life. The village itself (actually several villages grouped together as Jambiani) is a sun-baked collection of palm-thatch huts and the sea is an ethereal shade of turquoise – even by Zanzibar standards – dotted with fishing boats, while on the beach women tend seaweed farms.

Sleeping & Eating

★Mango Beach House GUESTHOUSE $
(☎0773 827617, 0773 498949; www.mango-beachhouse.com; s/d from US$35/50;) With only three bedrooms and an open-plan living area like a lounge on the beach, Mango Beach House is a small and sociable place. Rooms are simple but neat with artful decor and colourful fabrics, while the garden has daybeds and driftwood furniture. The attached **Kiddo's Cafe** is excellent (though meals need advance ordering) and attracts nonguests from nearby hotels.

★Red Monkey Lodge HOTEL $$
(☎0777 713366; www.redmonkeylodge.com; d US$95-130;) At the far southern end of Jambiani village, Red Monkey is a small hotel with around 10 spacious rooms – some in bungalows, others in a two-storey building – overlooking the beautiful beach. If you're feeling lazy, there are hammocks dotted about and a shady outdoor bar-restaurant. If you're feeling energetic, bike hire, kitesurfing and other activities can be arranged.

★Zanzistar Guesthouse GUESTHOUSE $$
(☎0774 440792; www.zanzi-star.com; d US$70-80, family house US$220;) A new addition to Jambiani's hotel scene, Zanzistar is simply delightful. Its small size and attentive management makes it feel homey and exclusive at the same time. Rooms have cool and uncluttered decor, and some have their own small private garden shaded by palms and banana trees, while the cheerful restaurant-bar (with occasional live music) attracts guests from nearby hotels.

Getting There & Away

Dalla-dalla 309 runs several times daily between Zanzibar Town and Jambiani (Tsh2500). Buses between Makunduchi and Michamvi also stop here. Jambiani village sits between the tarmac road and the sea; all public transport uses the tarmac road, from where it's about 500m to 1km down to the beach.

Kizimkazi

☎024 / POP 5000

At the southern tip of Zanzibar Island, Kizimkazi would be just another sleepy fishing village if it weren't for the local dolphins that frolic offshore becoming a major tourist attraction. Most days visitors from all over Zanzibar come here to take a boat ride across the clear blue waters of Menai Bay to see the dolphins.

Activities

Although most Kizimkazi hotels offer diving and other activities, the most popular activity is dolphin-watching trips. Arranged via local hotels, prices start from US$25 per person with reputable operators. Local beach boys and taxi drivers also organise boat trips, but we recommend using responsible operators who follow appropriate codes of conduct, both for your safety and the dolphins' well-being.

Sleeping & Eating

Dolphin Safari Lodge LODGE $$
(☎0774 007360; www.dolphin-safari-lodge.com; Kizimkazi Mkunguni; d from US$50;) Low-key, peaceful, friendly and well managed, this small lodge overlooks a quiet beach about 1km southeast of Kizimkazi Mkunguni. Rooms are in bungalows or palm-thatch huts with safari-tent-style zipped doors. There's a simple bar-restaurant with beautiful sea views. The owners hire and train local people to work in the hotel, and operate responsible dolphin- and whale-spotting trips.

★Unguja Lodge LODGE $$$
(☎0774 477477; www.ungujalodge.com; Kizimkazi Mkunguni; s/d with half board from US$280/500;) Set in a patch of forest, this secluded luxury lodge has 10 villas with high thatched roofs and curved walls reminiscent of seashells. They're impeccably decorated and many have sea views (including from the shower). Add the private beach, infinity pool, dive centre and excellent restaurant, and it's easy to see why this place is regularly booked out.

Getting There & Away

To reach Kizimkazi from Zanzibar Town take bus or dalla-dalla 326. The fare is Tsh2500. Alternatively, take Makunduchi bus 310 as far as Kufile junction, then wait for another vehicle or walk to Kizimkazi (about 5km). At the next fork, go right to Kizimkazi Dimbani or left to Kizimkazi Mkunguni.

Pemba

☎024 / POP 450,000

Pemba's terrain is hilly and lushly vegetated, while much of the coast is lined with mangroves and lagoons, interspersed with idyllic beaches and islets. Offshore, coral reefs offer some of East Africa's best diving.

Throughout, Pemba remains largely 'undiscovered', and you'll still have most things to yourself, which is a big part of the island's appeal.

For much of its history, Pemba has been overshadowed by Zanzibar Island, its larger neighbour to the south. Although the islands are separated by only 50km of sea, relatively few tourists cross the channel. Those who do, however, are seldom disappointed.

Getting There & Away

AIR

Pemba's main airport is **Pemba-Karume Airport** (PMA; Chake Chake), 6km east of Chake Chake. ZanAir (www.zanair.com), Coastal Aviation (www.coastal.co.tz) and Auric Air (www.auricair.com) offer daily flights to/from Dar es Salaam (US$140) via Zanzibar Island (US$95). Flights to/from Tanga are also possible with Coastal (US$100) and Auric (US$65).

BOAT

Pemba's main port is at Mkoani, at the southern end of the island. All ferries to/from Zanzibar and Dar es Salaam dock here. Most reliable are

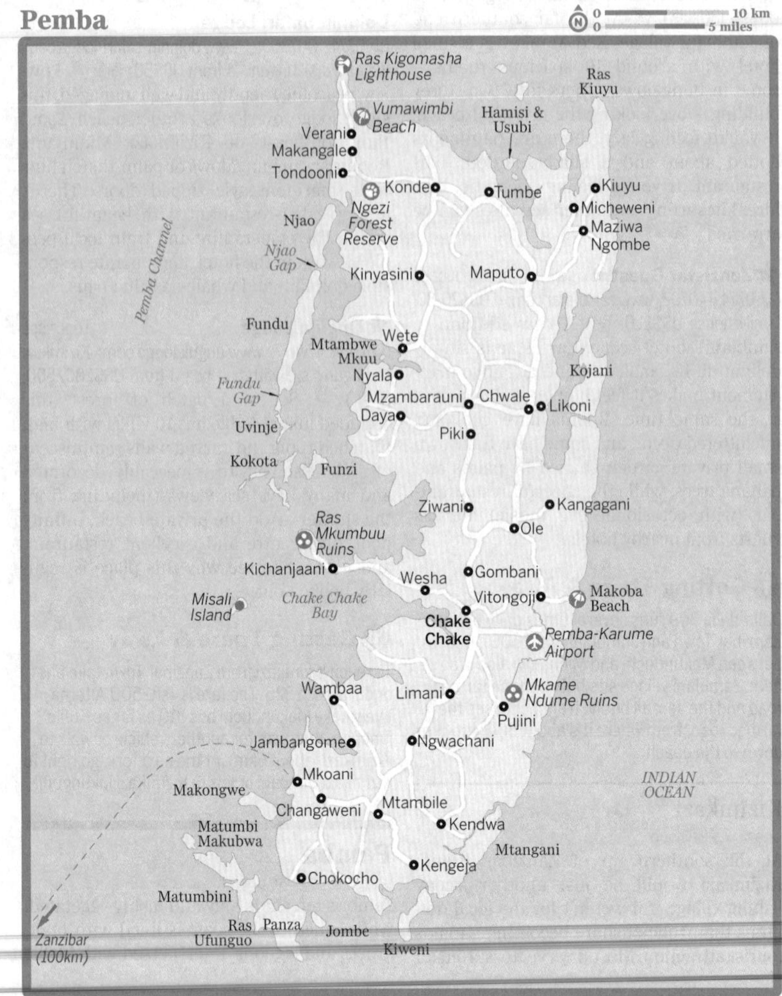

the Sealink roll-on, roll-off car and passenger ferries, operated by **Azam Marine** (p77).

On Pemba, tickets can be purchased at Azam Marine's office at the port in Mkoani, as well as at various travel agents in Chake Chake and Wete.

Another option is the government-operated *Mapinduzi* ferry, which goes twice weekly in each direction between Pemba and Zanzibar. The fare is US$25, but the service is slow and unreliable.

Dhows sail between Wete (in the northwest of Pemba) and Tanga and Mombasa, but foreigners are prohibited.

If you come by boat from Zanzibar Island, mainland Tanzania or Kenya, you'll need to go to the immigration office at the port to get your passport and visa checked.

Getting Around

Buses and dalla-dallas (pick-up truck or minibus) cover the main routes between towns and villages. Over the past few years, many of Pemba's roads have been tarred, and some completely new roads constructed, which has improved comfort if not journey times. Sample routes, fares and durations include Chake Chake to Mkoani (Tsh2000, one to 1½ hours) and Chake Chake to Wete (Tsh2000, 1½ to two hours).

Chake Chake

024 / POP 30,000

Chake Chake is the capital of Pemba. Often called simply 'Chake', it's an appealingly scruffy place with a busy centre of shops and market stalls. Sights are limited, and the nearest beach is at Makoba (7km to the east), so Chake Chake is mainly used by visitors as a transport hub and starting block for deeper exploration on Pemba.

Sights & Activities

★ Misali Island ISLAND

(US$5) Surrounded by crystal waters and stunning coral reefs, Misali offers some of the best diving in East Africa, while snorkelling is spectacular and easily reached from the beach. Around the island, nesting turtles favour beaches on the western side, while on the northeast coast is **Baobab Beach**, with fine sand and a small ranger centre (although information here is limited).

Mkame Ndume Ruins RUINS

The ruined palace of Mohammed bin Abdul Rahman, who ruled Pemba prior to the arrival of the Portuguese (late 15th to early 16th centuries), is an evocative spot. Rahman had a reputation for cruelty and was known as Mkame Ndume (Milker of Men). Today the ruins' primary feature is a large stone staircase that led from the kilometre-long channel (now dry) connecting this site to the ocean.

Ras Mkumbuu Ruins RUINS

(adult/student US$5/3) Ras Mkumbuu is the headland at the end of the thin strip of land jutting into the sea northwest of Chake Chake. It's also the name given to the ruins of an ancient settlement, once called Qanbalu, dating from the 8th century, which by the early 10th century had become one of the major cities along the East African coast. The main ruins, consisting of a large mosque, some tombs and houses, date from around the 14th century, and several walls are still standing.

ZSTC Clove Oil Distillery FACTORY

(tours Tsh5000; 8am-3.30pm Mon-Fri) Pemba is well known for its clove industry, and this distillery is where the clove stems are turned into essential oil. It's operated by the Zanzibar State Trading Corporation (ZSTC) and also here on occasion are cinnamon leaves, eucalyptus leaves, lemongrass and sweet basil. The tour may be a little lackadaisical, but the process is fascinating. Go first to the office and small shop selling the finished product (yes, enter through the gift shop) and arrange a guide.

Tours

Coral Tours TOUR

(0777 437397; tours_travelpemba@yahoo.com; Main Rd; tours for 2 people half-/full-day from US$50/100; 8am-5pm) Headed up by Nassor Haji, the charming and energetic manager, Coral Tours can fix you up with rental bikes (US$10 per day) or cars (US$50), or supply a vehicle and knowledgeable guide for tours (to nearby ruins, Misali Island, Ngezi Forest Reserve or just about anywhere else on Pemba). Also on sale are ferry and plane tickets.

Sleeping & Eating

Hotel Archipelago HOTEL $$

(formerly Hifadhi Hotel; 0777 254777; www.hotelarchipelagopemba.com; Wesha Rd; s/d US$50/70;) With its austere stairwells and utilitarian furniture (including inventory numbers) the Archipelago has the air of a government rest house – which it was – but now it's privately run and the best hotel in town. Rooms are clean

Chake Chake

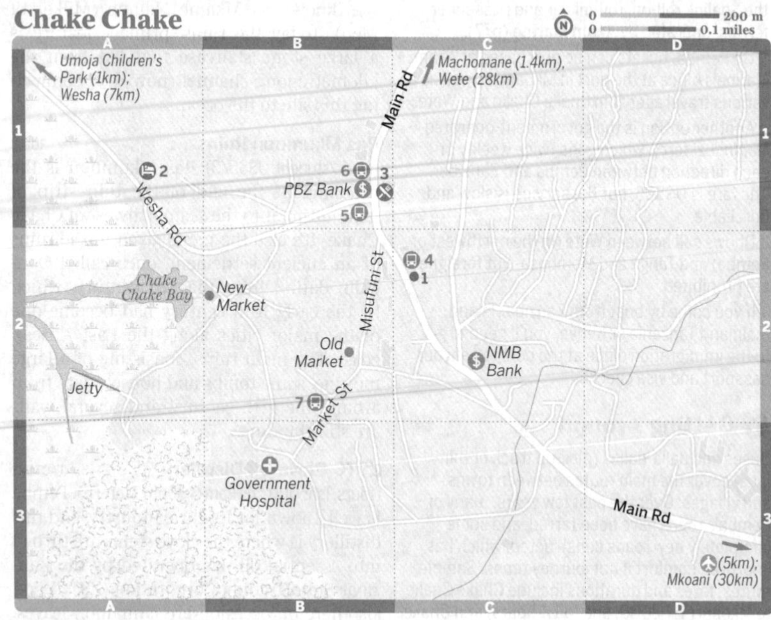

Chake Chake

Activities, Courses & Tours
1 Coral Tours C2

Sleeping
2 Hotel Archipelago A1

Eating
3 Ahaabna B1

Transport
4 Dalla-dallas to Mkoani C2
5 Dalla-dallas to Wesha B1
6 Dalla-dallas to Wete & Konde B1
7 Transport Stand B2

and tidy with fridge, TV and tea-/coffee-making facilities, while staff are friendly and efficient.

Pemba Misali Beach RESORT **$$**
(central reservations 0777 470278; www.oceangrouphotel.com; Wesha Rd; s/d US$80/120;) Out amid the mangroves, 7km from Chake Chake and reached by an impressively long jetty, this resort has functional rooms in a row of bungalows on a small white-sand beach. On a small pier, the restaurant serves international and local food (mains Tsh8000 to Tsh16,000), with a great view over the water towards the eponymous Misali Island in the distance.

Ahaabna TANZANIAN **$**
(Main Rd; meals Tsh5000-6000; 6-8pm) Located on the top floor of a modern concrete building, reached by an anonymous staircase, this no-frills restaurant serves evening meals, usually with just one option on the menu, such as rice with chicken or fish. If you plan to eat here, it's worth checking in advance during the day.

Information

MEDICAL SERVICES

For medical emergencies, the main **government hospital** is next to the museum at the end of Market St, although conditions are basic. The privately run **Dira Hospital** (0777 424418; Wete Rd, Machomane; 7am-9pm) is out in the suburb of Machomane.

MONEY

The main banks in Chake Chake are **NMB** (Main Rd) and **PBZ** (Main Rd); both have ATMs but these don't accept non-Tanzanian cards, and changing money inside the bank itself is a very slow process.

You can change US dollars into local currency at a large hotel, or ask at large shops selling imported (especially electrical) items.

Getting There & Away

There's a transport stand near the old market, but most people go to the main junction near the petrol station and wait there for a dalla-dalla going in the right direction.

Dalla-dallas to Mkoani (Tsh2000, 1½ hours) leave from near Coral Tours. Dalla-dallas to Wete (Tsh1500, 1½ hours) and Konde (Tsh2000, two hours) depart from near PBZ bank, while to Wesha (Tsh500, 30 minutes) they go from the top of Wesha Rd.

A taxi between town and the airport costs about US$10. For longer trips, expect to pay around US$40 to Mkoani and US$70 to the hotels on the Kigomasha Peninsula.

Kiweni

024

This remote and tranquil island just off Pemba's southeastern coast is surrounded by mangroves and long stretches of sand. At its southern end is Pemba Lodge, which provides a truly off-the-beaten-track experience. At the other end of the island is the village of Kiweni, separated from mainland Pemba by a 2km stretch of water.

The island is occasionally marked as Shamiani on some maps.

Sleeping

★Pemba Lodge LODGE $$

(0777 415551, reservations 024-224 0494; www.pembalodge.com; Kiweni (Shamiani) Island; per person full board US$120;) In a quiet spot on a small island off the coast of Pemba this lodge epitomises the word 'remote'. Overlooking the empty beach and ocean beyond are just five rooms in bungalows raised on wooden decks. There's also a restaurant-lounge where friendly staff serve meals, including seafood brought by local fishermen. Activities include kayaking, snorkelling and walks to the village.

Getting There & Away

Locals reach Kiweni village by boat from a landing point about 2km south of the village of Kengeja, which is about 15km directly south of Chake Chake. Guests at Pemba Lodge are transferred by private boat from a tiny beach, hidden among the mangroves, about 1km south of Kengeja.

Mkoani & Around

024 / POP 20,000

Although it's Pemba's major port, Mkoani has eschewed all attempts at development and remains a small and uneventful town. Many visitors arrive here on the boat from Zanzibar Island.

Sleeping

Lala Lodge GUESTHOUSE $$

(0777 111624; www.lalalodgepemba.com; d US$60;) This delightful place has an airy upstairs seating area with views across the bay, and just two rooms available. It's clean, neat and tidy, and right on the beach in the part of town by the fish market, which is either scruffy or authentic depending on your attitude. Kayaks are available for guests (free), and boat trips and diving can be arranged.

Fundu Lagoon LODGE $$$

(reception 0774 438668, reservations +44 7561 366593; www.fundulagoon.com; d full board US$880-980; Jun-Apr;) Luxurious and exclusive, Fundu has rooms in large tents under palm-thatch roofs to create a beach lodge with a safari feel. Rooms are on the hillside with a great view, or on the beach with a small private deck. The restaurant overlooks the infinity pool with the ocean beyond, and the jetty bar is the obvious place for sundowners.

Information

If you come by boat from Zanzibar Island, mainland Tanzania or Kenya, you'll need to go to the immigration office at the port to get your passport and visa checked.

There is a bank in Mkoani, but the ATM doesn't accept non-Tanzanian cards. To change US dollars into local currency, ask discreetly at any shop selling imported goods.

Getting There & Away

Buses and dalla-dallas run regularly to Chake Chake (Tsh1500, one hour) from in front of the port. You can also get buses to Wete (Tsh3000, two hours) and Konde (Tsh3500, 2½ hours) via Chake Chake, but these run more occasionally. To save waiting you're usually better off getting something to Chake and changing there for your onward journey.

Wete

024 / POP 20,000

The sleepy town of Wete is on the northwest coast of Pemba and is a good base for travellers to explore the north of the island. For locals, it's a port for boats to Kenya.

WORTH A TRIP

NGEZI FOREST RESERVE

Ngezi Forest Reserve (Ngezi Vumawimbi Forest Reserve; ☎0773 885777; adult/child US$5/2; ⏰7.30am-3.30pm) In far northeastern Pemba, dense and wonderfully lush Ngezi is one of the last remaining areas of indigenous forest that once covered much of the island, and as close to rainforest that you'll get anywhere on Zanzibar. Protected by a 1476-hectare reserve, the forest is a true double canopy, complete with vines providing swings for raucous vervet monkeys. The entrance gate and visitor centre is 5km west of Konde, on the main dirt road to the Kigomasha Peninsula.

Sleeping & Eating

Hill View Inn GUESTHOUSE $
(☎0776 338366; hillviewinn@gmail.com; s/d US$20/35) This place is a little gem: simple but clean rooms with TV in the lounge, and a nice walled garden with banana trees and a couple of shaded seats. Meals and hot water are available, but both need to be arranged in advance. It's on the edge of the town centre, opposite the grim Soviet-style apartment blocks.

Pemba Crown Hotel HOTEL $
(☎0777 493667, 0773 336867; www.pembacrown.com; Bomani Ave; s/d from US$30/50; ❄📶) With balconies overlooking the main street, very near the market, mosque and bus station, you're certainly in the heart of things at the Crown. Rooms are fairly clean if dull, with mosquito nets. There's no restaurant, but a simple breakfast is provided.

Times Restaurant TANZANIAN, EUROPEAN $
(Bomani Ave; meals Tsh6000; ❄) A step up from the standard basic eating house, the Times' menu promises pizza and chicken curry, as well as staples like fish and rice. If you plan to eat in the evening, call during the day to check availability.

Information

Wete has a bank, but the ATM does not accept non-Tanzanian cards. You can change money at **Allisha Bureau de Change** (Bomani Ave; ⏰8.30am-3.45pm Mon-Sat, 8.45am-12.30pm Sun).

Getting There & Away

There are two dalla-dalla routes between Wete and Chake Chake (Tsh1500, one to 1½ hours): route 606 uses the old road via Ziwani; route 607 uses the new road via Chwale. There are also frequent dalla-dallas between Wete and Konde (route 601; Tsh1500, one hour).

There's a direct bus from Wete via Chake to Mkoani (Tsh3000) timed to connect with the main ferry to/from Zanzibar Island. Departure times vary, so check in advance at the bus station.

All public transport leaves from the bus and dalla-dalla station next to the market in the town centre.

Tumbe

☎024 / POP 4000

The large village of Tumbe lies on a sandy cove on the northern coast fringed by dense mangroves. On the edge of the village is a beach, but forget about parasols and pina coladas here; this is the site of Pemba's largest fish market, while nearby are the ancient Chwaka Ruins.

Getting There & Away

Dalla-dallas travel on two routes between Chake Chake and Konde; those on the main road that runs up the east side of the island go past the junction for Tumbe (Tsh2000, two hours), from where it's a 1km walk through the village to the fish market.

If you're coming from Wete, get a dalla-dalla to Konde, then any vehicle heading west towards Chake, and get off at the Tumbe junction.

Kigomasha Peninsula

☎024

Spectacular beaches sweep along the shores of the Kigomasha Peninsula and this, along with some of the best diving in the whole Zanzibar Archipelago, attracts adventurous visitors. The remote location, in the far northwest of Pemba Island, is another key draw.

Away from the sea and the sand, several traditional villages collectively known as Makangale are dotted along the peninsula's length. Some hotels arrange cultural visits here, although with a sense of exploration (and a sense of direction) you can easily take a stroll in this area and see a slice of local life.

Sights & Activities

Spectacular dive sites include the Njao Gap, the Swiss Reef sea mountains and the sponge-covered Edge, which plunges into the Pemba Channel. As well as the spectacular coral and small marine life, dolphins, manta rays and whales are also regular visitors.

Vumawimbi Beach BEACH

Stepping onto Vumawimbi, you may need to rub your eyes to check you haven't gone to heaven, so idyllic is the view. Stretching along the east side of the Kigomasha Peninsula, and north of Ngezi Forest Reserve, not many outsiders come here, as all the hotels are on the west side, but it's sometimes visited if the wind is from the west, as it's more sheltered. It's an isolated spot, so come with company and a picnic.

Ras Kigomasha Lighthouse LIGHTHOUSE

(US$5) Located on the headland *(ras)* at the far northern tip of the Kigomasha Peninsula, this lighthouse was built by the British in 1900 and is still actively maintained by its keeper. Unlike many lighthouses on Zanzibar it's built of iron, rather than stone. Scale the tiny staircase (95 steps) for wonderful views out to sea and back across the island.

Swahili Divers DIVING

(https://swahiligecko.com; 2 dives US$170) Located at Gecko Nature Lodge and run by the same friendly team, this five-star PADI Dive Centre offers dives for all levels at various sites off the Kigomasha Peninsula. Check the website for combined dive and accommodation deals.

Sleeping & Eating

Verani Beach Lodge CABIN $

(cabins per person US$30) This very basic, locally run place has a couple of simple cabins on the beach. The friendly staff can cook meals with enough advance notice, but most guests here come with their own stoves and supplies. There's no way to book in advance, so turn up and try your luck.

Pemba Paradise HOTEL $$

(0777 800773; www.pembaparadise.com; d US$65-80) This low-key hotel has 16 rooms, white-painted with minimal decor, in a row of double-storey buildings set back slightly from the beach; the upstairs rooms have a better view. The bar-restaurant is set further back, behind the rooms, although there are seats and parasols on the beach so you can still enjoy a sundowner.

Gecko Nature Lodge LODGE $$$

(formerly Kervan Saray; 0773 176737; https://swahiligecko.com; dm/s/d with full board US$80/180/220;) This lodge is a wonderfully relaxing place, under new management since 2016, with double rooms in high-roof bungalows, plus a six-bunk dorm. The restaurant serves a set menu (nonguests US$15) and the beach deck is perfect for a beer at sunset. The same team runs Swahili Divers; other activities include fishing, snorkelling and kayaking, and bike rental is available.

Getting There & Away

Most of the hotels on the Kigomasha Peninsula arrange transfers for guests, usually from the airport at Chake Chake, but collection from Wete or Konde can also be arranged.

If you're on public transport, from Wete there are frequent dalla-dallas to Konde (a surprisingly lively junction village with a couple of shops and cafes), from where you can usually find local dalla-dallas heading up the peninsula as far as the village of Makangale, although you may need to wait several hours; if you're in a rush, you can use a *boda-boda* (motorbike taxi).

NORTHEASTERN TANZANIA

Northeastern Tanzania's highlights are its coastline, its mountains and its cultures. These, combined with the area's long history, easy access and lack of crowds, make it an appealing focal point for a Tanzanian sojourn.

Visit the atmospheric ruins at Kaole and Tongoni, step back to the days of Livingstone in Bagamoyo, relax on palm- and baobab-fringed beaches north and south of Pangani, or explore Saadani National Park. Inland, hike forested footpaths in the Usambaras while following the cycle of market days of the local Sambaa people. Learn about the rich traditions of the Pare Mountains, and experience the bush in seldom-visited Mkomazi National Park.

Most of the northeast is within a half-day's drive or bus ride from both Dar es Salaam and Arusha, and there are good connections to the Zanzibar Archipelago. Main roads are in decent condition and there is a wide range of accommodation.

Northeastern Tanzania

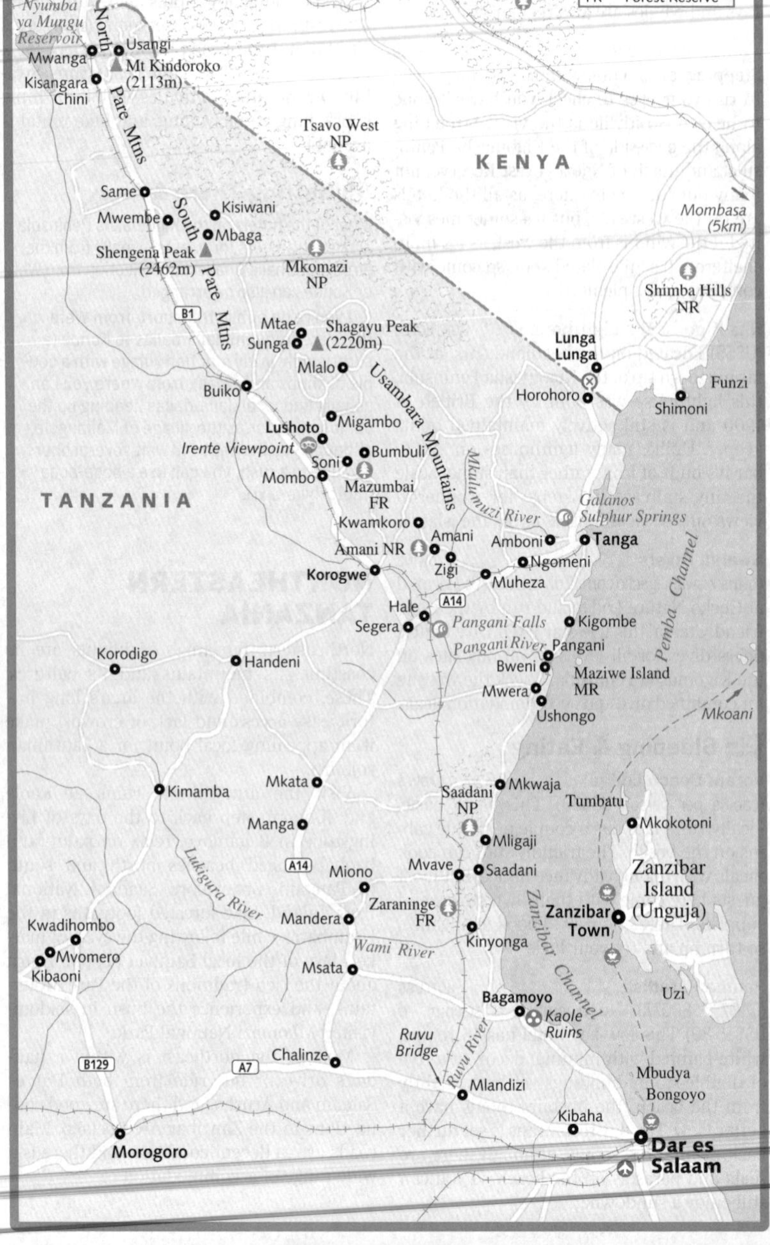

Bagamoyo

☎023 / POP 14,500

Strolling through Bagamoyo's narrow, unpaved streets takes you back to the mid-19th century, when the town was one of the most important settlements along the East African coast and the terminus of the trade caravan route linking Lake Tanganyika with the sea. Slaves, ivory, salt and copra were unloaded here before being shipped to Zanzibar Island and elsewhere, and many European explorers, including Richard Burton, Henry Morton Stanley and David Livingstone, began and ended their trips here. In 1868 French missionaries established Freedom Village at Bagamoyo as a shelter for ransomed slaves, and for the remainder of the century the town served as a way station for missionaries travelling from Zanzibar Island to the interior.

Bagamoyo's unhurried pace and fascinating history make it an agreeable day or weekend excursion from Dar es Salaam.

Sights & Activities

Bagamoyo Town HISTORIC SITE

(adult/child Tsh20,000/10,000) With its cobwebbed portals and crumbling German-era colonial buildings, central Bagamoyo, or Mji Mkongwe (Stone Town) as it's known locally, is well worth exploration. The most interesting area is along Ocean Rd. Here you'll find the old German **boma**, built in 1897, and **Liku House**, which served as the German administrative headquarters.

There is also a school, which dates from the late 19th century and was the first multiracial school in what is now Tanzania. On the beach is the German **customs house** (1895); Bagamoyo's **port**, where you can watch boat builders at work; and a busy **fish market** (on the site of the old slave market), with lively auctions most afternoons. Northwest of here are several small streets lined with carved doors similar to those found elsewhere along the coast. Further south is the mid-19th-century **Old Fort**.

The ridiculously steep fee levied to walk around the old town (required if you want to take photos or enter any of the buildings) is payable at the **Antiquities Branch Office** at the Old Fort, where you can also get a guide.

Kaole Ruins RUINS

(adult/child Tsh20,000/10,000; ⏲8am-4pm Mon-Fri, 9am-5pm Sat & Sun) Just southeast of Bagamoyo are these atmospheric ruins. At their centre are the remains of a 13th-century mosque, which is one of the oldest in mainland Tanzania and also one of the oldest in East Africa. It was built in the days when the Sultan of Kilwa held sway over coastal trade, and long before Bagamoyo had assumed any significance.

Nearby is a second mosque, dating from the 15th century, and about 22 graves, many dating from the same period. Among the graves are several Shirazi pillar-style tombs reminiscent of those at Tongoni, but in somewhat better condition, and a small museum housing Chinese pottery fragments and other remnants. Just east of the ruins, past a dense stand of mangroves, is the old harbour, now silted, that was in use during Kaole's heyday.

The easiest way to reach the ruins on foot is by heading south for about 5km along the road running past Chuo cha Sanaa to the signposted Kaole turn-off at the southern end of Kaole village. A *bajaji* (tuk-tuk) from town costs around Tsh5000 (Tsh10,000 for a taxi).

College of Arts ARTS CENTRE

(Chuo cha Sanaa; www.tasuba.ac.tz) Located about 500m southeast of Bagamoyo along the road to Dar es Salaam is this renowned theatre and arts college, home of the national dance company. When school is in session there are occasional performances, and it's usually possible to arrange drumming or dancing lessons.

The annual highlight is the **Bagamoyo Arts Festival**, usually held around late September or October. The festival features traditional dance and drumming performances, acrobatics displays, drumming workshops and much more.

The festival is not the most organised – advance information on schedules is rarely available – but it is a good way to meet Tanzania's up-and-coming artists and performers, and to get introduced to local talent and culture.

Catholic Museum MUSEUM

(☎023-244 0010; adult/child Tsh10,000/5000; ⏲10am-5pm) About 2km northwest of town and reached via a long, mango-tree-shaded avenue is the Catholic mission and museum, one of Bagamoyo's highlights, with well-labelled displays from Bagamoyo's heyday. In the same compound is the chapel where Livingstone's body was laid before being taken to Zanzibar Town en route to Westminster Abbey. The mission dates from the 1868 establishment of Freedom Village and is the oldest in Tanzania.

Sleeping & Eating

Travellers Lodge LODGE **$$**
(☎023-244 0077, 0754 855485; www.travellers-lodge.com; camping US$8, cottages s US$60-70, d US$80-90; ❄📶) With its relaxed atmosphere and reasonable prices, this is among the best value of the beach places. Accommodation is in clean, pleasant cottages, some with two large beds, scattered around expansive grounds. There's a restaurant and a children's play area. It's just south of the entrance to the Catholic mission and museum.

Firefly HISTORIC HOTEL **$$**
(☎0759 177393; www.fireflybagamoyo.com; India St; camping/dm/r US$10/15/60; 📶🏊) This is a fine choice, with camping on a large lawn sloping down towards the sea (although there's no beach access). Rooms – in an old Arab merchant's house – are no-frills but spacious and atmospheric. There's a small restaurant and an outdoor poolside lounge. The location on the edge of the old town is excellent.

Nashe's Cafe CAFE **$**
(☎023-244 0171, 0676 506705; mains Tsh6000-15,000; ⏰9am-10pm Mon-Sat, 10am-10pm Sun; 📶) Tasty seafood and meat grills are served on a nice rooftop terrace in the centre of the old town. It also does good coffees.

Funky Squids Beach Bar & Grill TANZANIAN, EUROPEAN **$$**
(☎0755 047802; the.funky.squids@gmail.com; meals Tsh10,000-20,000; ⏰11am-10pm; 📶) This bar-restaurant serves a good selection of appetising meat and seafood grills on a large beachfront terrace.

Information

MONEY

CRDB At the town entrance; has an ATM.

National Microfinance Bank At the town entrance; with ATM.

NBC At the petrol station 500m before town along the Dar es Salaam road; has an ATM.

TOURIST INFORMATION

Tourist Information Office (⏰8.30am-4.30pm) This office at the town entrance can set you up with guides for walking tours of the old town, as well as for excursions to the Kaole Ruins and further afield.

The **Catholic Museum** (p93) also offers tourist information.

Getting There & Away

BOAT

Nonmotorised dhows to Zanzibar Island cost around Tsh5000 (around Tsh10,000 to Tsh15,000 for motorised boats) and take around four hours with a good wind. Foreigners are discouraged from taking these, however, and you'll need to register first with the immigration officer in the old customs building, which is also the departure point. Departure times vary, and are often around 1am, arriving at Zanzibar Island sometime the next morning if all goes well. There is no regular dhow traffic to Saadani or Pangani.

BUS

Dalla-dallas (minibuses) from Makumbusho (north of Dar es Salaam along the New Bagamoyo Rd, and accessed via dalla-dalla from New Posta; Tsh500) head to Bagamoyo (Tsh2000, two hours) throughout the day. The transport stand in Bagamoyo is about 700m from the town centre, just off the road heading to Dar es Salaam. Taxis to the beach hotels charge from Tsh3000, and *bajajis* (tuk-tuks) slightly less. There is also a daily dalla-dalla to Saadani village via Msata on the main Arusha highway, departing Bagamoyo at about 10am (Tsh10,000, three hours).

Saadani National Park

About 70km north of Bagamoyo along a lovely stretch of coastline, and directly opposite Zanzibar Island, is tiny **Saadani National Park** (www.saadanipark.org; adult/child US$35.40/11.80), a 1000-sq-km patch of coastal wilderness. Unpretentious and relaxing, it bills itself as one of the few spots in the country where you can enjoy the beach and watch wildlife at the same time.

While terrestrial wildlife-watching opportunities are modest, animals are definitely present. In addition to hippos and crocodiles, it's quite likely that you'll see giraffes, and elephant sightings are increasingly common. With luck, you may also see Lichtenstein's hartebeests, and even lions, although these are more difficult to spot. Birding is very good.

SAADANI NATIONAL PARK

Why Go To enjoy the long, mostly deserted coastline plus some wildlife; ease of access from Dar es Salaam for those without much time.

When to Go June to February; black cotton soil is a problem in many areas during the heavy rains from March to May.

Practicalities Drive, bus or fly in from Dar es Salaam; bus from Bagamoyo; drive from Pangani. Entry points are Mvave gate (at the end of the Mandera road, for visitors from Dar es Salaam); Madete gate (for those coming from Pangani along the coastal road); and Wami gate (for those coming from Bagamoyo). Entry fees are valid for 24 hours, single entry only. All fees are paid with Visa or MasterCard only at the **Saadani Tourist Information office** at Mvave gate. All entry gates are open from 6am to 6pm; exiting the park is permitted up to 7pm. **Saadani National Park Headquarters** (www.tanzaniaparks.go.tz; ⌚8am-5pm) are at Mkwaja, at the northern edge of the park.

Budget Tips There's no vehicle rental at the park. Your best budget bet is to get a group together and arrange a day safari with one of the lodges outside Saadani.

Sights & Activities

Boat trips along the Wami River, wildlife drives (in open-sided vehicles), bush walks and village tours can be arranged through most camps and lodges. Guides (optional for vehicle safaris, but required for walking safaris) cost US$23.60 per day, per group. The **Saadani Tourist Information office** (☎0689 062346; saadani.tourism@tanzaniaparks.go.tz; ⌚6am-6pm) can arrange walking tours of Saadani village.

Sleeping & Eating

Saadani Park Campsite CAMPGROUND $

(camping US$35.40) Saadani's main public campsite is in a good location directly on the beach just north of Saadani village, with basic ablution facilities but no food or drink available.

Kisampa TENTED CAMP $$$

(☎0679 443330; https://kisampa.com; per person full board US$180) For genuine bush adventure, it's difficult to beat this unique and warmly recommended camp. Set about a two-hour drive from Saadani in a private nature reserve, Kisampa is integrated with the surrounding community, and offers many ways for guests to get involved. Accommodation is in open-style bungalows. Saadani safaris, bush walks, beach camping and other activities fill the days.

Simply Saadani LODGE $$$

(Tent With A View; ☎0737 226398, 0713 323318; www.saadani.com; s/d full board from US$355/550, s/d incl full board & wildlife excursions US$475/790; P) This hideaway has raised tree-house-style *bandas* on a lovely stretch of deserted, driftwood-strewn beach, just northeast of the Saadani park boundary. All have verandahs and hammocks. Excursions include safaris in the park and boat trips on the Wami River. The same management runs a lodge in Selous Game Reserve and another camp in Saadani, and combination itineraries can be arranged.

Getting There & Away

Saadani is easily accessed from both Dar es Salaam and Zanzibar as an overnight or weekend excursion. It is a good choice if you don't have time to explore further afield, although it cannot compare with Tanzania's better-known parks and reserves.

Pangani

☎027 / POP 3000

About 55km south of Tanga is the small Swahili outpost of Pangani. It rose from obscure beginnings as just one of many coastal dhow ports to become a terminus of the caravan route from Lake Tanganyika, a major export point for slaves and ivory, and one of the largest ports between Bagamoyo and Mombasa. Sisal and copra plantations were established in the area, and several European missions and exploratory journeys to the interior began from here. By the end of the 19th century, the focus had shifted to Tanga and Dar es Salaam, and Pangani again faded into anonymity. Today the sleepy, dilapidated town makes for an intriguing step back into history.

Tanga

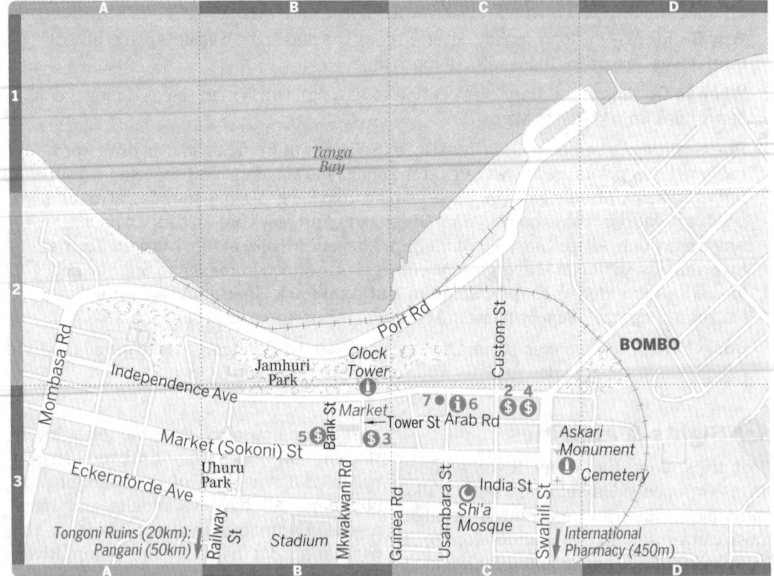

Tours

Staff at the **Pangani Cultural Tourism Program Office** (Pangani bus stand; 8am-5pm) organise various tours. The hotels south of Pangani also organise Maziwe trips and other activities around Pangani, often more reliably and at more economical rates than the cultural tourism program office.

Meandering along the southern edge of town, the muddy Pangani River attracts waterbirds, crocodiles and other animals. It's best explored on a cruise via local dhow, which can be arranged with any of the hotels. Expect to pay about US$70 for up to three people.

Sleeping & Eating

Seaside Community Centre Hostel GUESTHOUSE $
(0755 276422, 0756 655308; s/d/tr Tsh30,000/40,000/75,000, with air-con Tsh40,000/60,000/85,000; P) This church-run place has simple but spotless and pleasant rooms with fans and verandahs, and meals on order. It's just back from the sea, and about 1km from the bus stand (Tsh2000 in a taxi). From the bus stand head straight towards the coast, cross the tarmac Pangani road and follow the signs, bearing right at the fork.

★Tembo Kijani LODGE, BANDA $$
(0785 117098, 0687 027454; www.tembokijani.com; s/d tree-house banda US$105/160, s/d bungalow US$155/240, all incl half board; P) This small ecolodge on a wonderful stretch of beach has four open-sided tree-house *bandas* nestled into the bush just back from the sea, plus comfortable ground-level beach bungalows and tasty, healthy cuisine. The owners have made great efforts to minimise the lodge's footprint and maximise sustainability. The overall results are impressive, with the lodge running on solar and wind power.

★Tides LODGE $$$
(0713 325812, 0756 328393; www.thetideslodge.com; s/d half board from US$265/380; P) The beautiful Tides has a prime beachside location, plus spacious upmarket cottages on the sand and excellent cuisine. The cottages have huge beds surrounded by billowing mosquito nets, large bathrooms and stylish decor. There are also several family cottages and a private honeymooners' luxury suite, plus a beachside bar and restaurant.

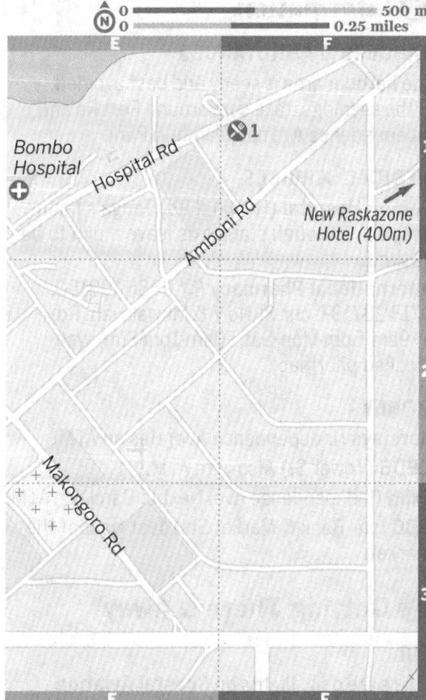

Tanga

Eating

1 Pizzeria d'Amore F1

Information

2 Barclays C3
3 CRDB B3
4 Exim C3
5 NBC B3
6 Tanga Cultural Tourism Enterprise C3

Transport

Azam Marine Booking Office.......(see 2)
7 Coastal Aviation C3

Information

National Microfinance Bank (Boma Rd) ATM that accepts Visa and MasterCard.

Getting There & Away

AIR

Coastal Aviation (p216) has daily flights connecting Mashado airstrip (just south of Pangani town, on the south side of the river) with Dar es Salaam (US$185 one way), Zanzibar Island (US$110), Kilimanjaro airport (US$250) and Arusha (US$250).

BOAT

Dhows sail regularly between Pangani and Mkokotoni, on the northwestern coast of Zanzibar, but these are officially off-limits for foreigners and not recommended. Better and safer is the faster **MV Ali Choba** (0782 457668, 0784 134056; ttozonc@gmail.com), which sails several times weekly between Ushongo (south of Pangani), Pangani and Zanzibar Island (Kendwa). The trip takes about two hours and costs US$335 per boat for up to five passengers, or US$65 per person for six or more passengers between Ushongo and Zanzibar Island (US$355 per boat or US$70 per person between Pangani and Zanzibar). Book directly with them, or through **Emayani Beach Lodge** (0782 457668; www.emayanilodge.com; s/d half board US$115/180; P). Another option is to contact **Mr Wahidi** (0784 489193), who offers motorised dhow transfers between Pangani town and either Nungwi or Kendwa on Zanzibar Island for US$140 per boat for up to four people, or US$35 per person for five or more passengers. Allow about four hours for the trip.

BUS

The best connections between Pangani and Tanga are via the rehabilitated coastal road, with about five buses daily (Tsh2500, 1½ hours). The first departure from Pangani is at about 6.30am, so you can connect with a Tanga–Arusha bus. There's at least one daily direct bus between Pangani and Dar es Salaam (Tsh15,000). Pangani is also connected by dalla-dalla with Muheza (Tsh2500), from where there are connections to Tanga or Korogwe, but the road is worse than the coastal one and transport is sporadic.

There's also a daily bus between Tanga and Mkwaja (at the northern edge of Saadani National Park) that passes Mwera village (6km from Ushongo) daily at about 7am going north and 3.30pm going south. It's then usually possible to hire a motorcycle to take you from Mwera to Ushongo.

Tanga

027 / POP 273,300

Tanga, a major industrial centre until the collapse of the sisal market, is Tanzania's second-largest seaport and its fourth-largest town behind Dar es Salaam, Mwanza and Arusha. Despite its size, it's an agreeable place with a sleepy, semicolonial atmosphere, wide streets filled with cyclists and motorcycles, intriguing architecture and faded charm. It makes a pleasant stop en route to or from Mombasa, and is a springboard to the beaches around Pangani, about 50km south.

Sights

Toten Island ISLAND, HISTORIC SITE

Directly offshore from Tanga is small, mangrove-ringed island Toten Island ('Island of the Dead'), with the overgrown ruins of a mosque dating from at least the 17th century and some 18th- and 19th-century gravestones. Pottery fragments from the 15th century have also been found, indicating that the island may have been settled during the Shirazi era. Toten Island's apparently long history ended in the late 19th century, when its inhabitants moved to the mainland.

While the ruins are less accessible and less atmospheric than those at nearby Tongoni, the island is worth a look if you have extra time. Excursions can be organised through the **Tanga Cultural Tourism Enterprise** (☎027-264 5254, 0765 162875, 0713 375367; www.tangatourismcoalition.com; ⊙8.30am-4pm Mon-Fri, to 1pm Sat) for about US$60 per person including motorboat transfer and guided tour.

Sleeping & Eating

New Raskazone Hotel HOTEL $

(☎0745 643157, 0717 860058, 0756 444529; www.newraskazonehotel.com; Ras Kazone; r without/with air-con Tsh40,000/50,000; ❄) This reliable, good-value place has tidy gardens, quiet, spotless rooms with hot water, TV and window screens, plus a restaurant (meals Tsh6000 to Tsh10,000). The air-con rooms are slightly larger, and worth the extra money. It's in the Ras Kazone residential section of town, and is Tsh5000 in a taxi from the bus stand.

★**Fish Eagle Point** LODGE $$

(☎0784 346006, 0687 680494; www.fisheaglepoint.com; per person full board US$75-130; P 📶 🌊) This lovely lodge has spacious, open-style beachfront cottages in varying sizes, all set around a mangrove-fringed cove. There's a dhow, snorkelling, sea kayaking, fishing and birding. It's ideal for families. Follow the tarmac Horohoro road north from Tanga for 38km to the signposted right-hand turn-off, from where it's 10km further along a dirt track.

Pizzeria d'Amore ITALIAN $$

(☎0715 395391, 0784 395391; Hospital Rd; meals Tsh15,000-20,000; ⊙11.30am-2pm & 6.30-10pm Tue-Sun) A small garden restaurant with tasty pizzas, pasta, seafood and continental fare. It has a breezy upstairs dining terrace and a bar.

Information

DANGERS & ANNOYANCES

The harbour area is seedy and best avoided. In the evenings, take care around Port Rd and Independence Ave near Jamhuri Park.

MEDICAL SERVICES

Bombo Hospital (Hospital Rd) Tanga's main hospital, although standards leave much to be desired.

International Pharmacy (☎0686 108160, 0713 237137; cnr St No 7 & Mkwakwani Rd; ⊙9am-5pm Mon-Sat, 10am-1pm Sun) Well-stocked pharmacy.

MONEY

Barclays (Independence Ave) Has an ATM.

CRDB (Tower St) Also with ATM.

Exim (Independence Ave) Next to Barclays; ATM.

NBC (cnr Bank & Market Sts) Just west of the market.

Getting There & Away

AIR

There are daily flights on **Coastal Aviation** (☎0713 596075, 0713 325673; www.coastal.co.tz; cnr Independence Ave & Usambara St; ⊙8am-4pm Mon-Sat) and **Auric Air** (☎0757 466648; www.auricair.com) between Tanga, Dar es Salaam, Zanzibar Island and Pemba (one way between Tanga and Pemba/Zanzibar Island/Dar es Salaam approximately US$95/130/195). Auric Air's Tanga representative is at the airfield, which is about 3km west of the town centre, just off the Korogwe road (Tsh5000 by taxi).

BOAT

Azam Marine's Sealink ferry goes weekly between Tanga and Pemba (four hours, US$35), with connections on to Zanzibar Island. Departures from Tanga are on Tuesday, and from Pemba on Sunday. Tickets can be bought online or at the **Azam Marine Booking Office** (www.azammarine.com; Custom St; ⊙ hours vary).

BUS

Ratco and other buses for Dar es Salaam depart daily every few hours from 6am to 2pm in each direction (Tsh15,000 to Tsh17,000, six hours).

To Arusha there are at least three departures daily between about 6am and 11am (Tsh17,000 to Tsh19,000, seven to eight hours). To Lushoto there are several direct buses departing daily from 7am (Tsh7000 to Tsh8000, four hours).

To Pangani (Tsh2500, 1½ hours) there are several larger buses and many dalla-dallas throughout the day along the coastal road.

All transport leaves from the main bus stand on Taifa Rd ('Double Rd'), at the corner of Street No 12. It's about 1.5km south of the town centre (Tsh5000 in a taxi), and south of the railway tracks in the Ngamiani section.

Usambara Mountains

With their wide vistas, cool climate, winding paths and picturesque villages, the Usambaras are one of northeastern Tanzania's delights. Rural life revolves around a cycle of colourful, bustling market days that rotate from one village to the next, and is largely untouched by the booming safari scene and influx of 4WDs in nearby Arusha. It's easily possible to spend at least a week trekking from village to village or exploring with day walks.

The Usambaras, which are part of the ancient Eastern Arc chain, are divided into two ranges separated by a 4km-wide valley. The western Usambaras, around Lushoto, are the most accessible. The eastern Usambaras, around Amani, are less developed. Both ranges are densely populated, with an average of more than 300 people per sq km. The main tribes are the Sambaa, Kilindi, Zigua and Mbugu.

Getting There & Away

The Usambaras are easily reached by private vehicle, and by daily bus links from Arusha, Tanga and Dar es Salaam. While the main route in the western Usambaras to Lushoto is tarmac, most other roads are unpaved.

Amani Nature Reserve

The **Amani Nature Reserve** (per visit adult/child US$10/5, per visit Tanzania-registered/foreign vehicle Tsh10,000/US$25) is located west of Tanga in the heart of the eastern Usambaras. Often overlooked, it's a peaceful, lush patch of montane forest humming with the sounds of rushing water, chirping insects and singing birds. It is also exceptionally rich in unique plant and bird species – a highly worthwhile detour for those ornithologically or botanically inclined. Among the unique bird species you may see are Amani sunbirds, banded green sunbirds and green-headed orioles.

Activities

There's a network of short walks along shaded forest paths that can be done alone or with a guide (US$15 per person per day).

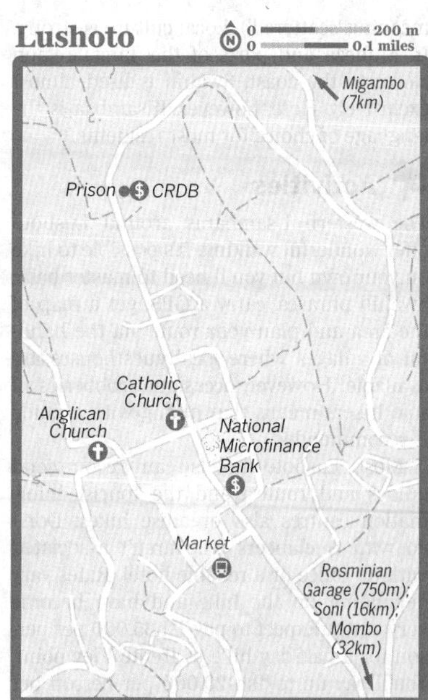

They are detailed in the booklet *A Guide to Trails and Drive Routes in Amani Nature Reserve*, which is sometimes available at the **Zigi Information Centre** (8am-5pm).

Getting There & Away

Amani is 32km northwest of Muheza along a dirt road, which is in fair to good condition the entire way, except for the last 7km, where the road is rocky and in bad shape (4WD only). There's at least one truck daily between Muheza and Amani (Tsh3500, two hours), continuing on to Kwamkoro, 9km beyond Amani. Departures from Muheza are between about 1pm and 2pm. Going in the other direction, transport passes Amani (stopping near the conservation centre office) from about 6am.

Lushoto

027 / POP 500,000

This leafy highland town is nestled in a fertile valley at about 1200m, surrounded by pines and eucalyptus mixed with banana plants and other tropical foliage. It's the centre of the western Usambaras and makes a convenient base for hikes into the surrounding hills.

Lushoto is also the heartland of the Wasambaa people (the name 'Usambara' is a corruption of Wasambaa or Washambala, meaning 'scattered'). Local culture is strong. In Muheza and parts of the Tanga region closer to the coast, Swahili is used almost exclusively. Here, however, Kisambaa is the language of choice for most residents.

Activities

The western Usambaras around Lushoto offer wonderful walking. It's possible to hike on your own but you'll need to master basic Swahili phrases, carry a GPS, get a map of the area and plan your route via the handful of villages where local guesthouses are available. However, occasional robberies of solo hikers means that hiking with a guide is recommended.

Most Lushoto hotels can recommend guides and routes, and the tourist information centres also organise hikes. Don't go with freelancers who aren't associated with an office or a reliable hotel. Rates vary depending on the hike and have become very costly. Expect to pay Tsh35,000 per person for a half-day hike to Irente Viewpoint. You'll pay up to Tsh120,000 per person per day on multiday hikes, including camping or accommodation in very basic guesthouses, guide fees, forest fees for any hikes that enter forest reserves (which includes most hikes from Lushoto) and food.

Information

CRDB (Main Rd) Visa and MasterCard; at the Western Union building, diagonally opposite the prison, at the northern (uphill) end of the main road.

National Microfinance Bank (Main Rd; 8.30am-3.30pm Mon-Fri) ATM accepting Visa and MasterCard.

MARKET DAYS

Local villages are especially colourful on market days, when traders come on foot from miles around to peddle their wares:

Bumbuli Saturday, with a smaller market on Tuesday

Lushoto Sunday, with a smaller market on Thursday

Mlalo Wednesday

Soni Tuesday, with a smaller market on Friday

Sunga Wednesday, very colourful

Getting There & Away

Dalla-dallas go throughout the day between Lushoto and Mombo (Tsh4000, one hour), the junction town on the main highway.

Daily direct buses travel from Lushoto to Tanga (Tsh7000, four hours), Dar es Salaam (Tsh15,000 to Tsh17,000, six to seven hours) and Arusha (Tsh15,000, six hours), with most departures from 7am.

The main bus stand is near the market, with some lines also beginning about 2km below town along the main road opposite the hospital turnoff.

About 1.5km before town on the Mombo road, Rosmini Garage is worth a try if you need vehicle repairs.

Mtae

027 / POP 12,850

Tiny Mtae is perched on a cliff about 55km northwest of Lushoto, with fantastic 270-degree views over the Tsavo Plains and down to Mkomazi National Park. The area makes a fine destination if you only have time for one hike from Lushoto. En route is Sunga village, with a colourful market on Wednesdays. Just to the southeast is **Shagayu Peak** (2220m), one of the highest in the Usambara Mountains. In addition to its many walking paths, the area is also known for its traditional healers.

Sleeping

Mambo Cliff Inn COTTAGE $
(0784 734545; www.mambocliffinn.com; camping/dm/d US$15/25/35-70) This good place perched at 1900m has wonderful views, plus camping, dorm rooms and cottages. Tasty local-style meals are available, and guides can be arranged for hikes and other excursions. It's a fine budget base for exploring the Usambaras.

Mambo Viewpoint Eco Lodge LODGE, CAMPGROUND $$
(0769 522420, 0785 272150; www.mamboviewpoint.org; camping US$8-10, s US$50-90, d US$75-130; P) This place, set at about 1900m and reached via the signposted left-hand fork at the junction 3km before Mtae, has stunning views, plus pleasant cottages and permanent tents. The owners offer information on the area, and can organise hikes, village stays and more. It's a recommended base for exploring the Usambaras.

OFF THE BEATEN TRACK

CULTURAL TOURISM PROGRAMS

Numerous villages around Arusha (and elsewhere in the country) run 'Cultural Tourism Programs' that offer an alternative to the safari scene. Most centre on light hikes and village activities.

Although the line is sometimes blurred in these programs between community empowerment and empowering the enterprising individuals who run them, they nevertheless provide employment for locals and offer an excellent chance to experience Tanzania at the local level. Most have various 'modules' available, from half a day to several nights. Transport, sometimes by dalla-dalla (minibus) and sometimes by private vehicle, is extra. Overnight tours involve camping or homestays; expect conditions to be basic. Payment should be made on-site; always ask for a receipt.

All tours in the Arusha area (and elsewhere) can be booked through the **Tanzania Tourist Board Tourist Information Centre** (p61), which has brochures and a thick binder with detailed information (including prices) about most of them. The office can also outline the best transport options. Most tours should be booked a day in advance, but some guides wait at the TTB office on standby each morning.

If you have further questions, the **Cultural Tourism Program office** (027-205 0025, 0786 703010; www.tanzaniaculturaltourism.com; Natural History Museum, Boma Rd) at the back of the Natural History Museum in Arusha may be able to assist. Be sure to check out its website. You can also contact many of the places directly to make arrangements.

Getting There & Away

The road between Lushoto and Mtae is full of turns and hills, and is particularly beautiful as it winds its way up the final 7km to Mtae. Buses depart Lushoto (Tsh5000, three hours) about 10am. There are also direct daily buses to Mtae from Arusha (Tsh17,000, nine hours), Dar es Salaam (Tsh17,000, nine hours) and Tanga (Tsh15,000, six to seven hours). Taxis from Lushoto charge from about Tsh70,000. For those staying in Mambo, negotiate with the driver to take you all the way or ask to get dropped at the Mtae–Mambo junction, from where it's about 2km further on foot to Mambo village, Mambo Cliff Inn and Mambo Viewpoint Eco Lodge.

Soni

027 / POP 12,840

Tiny Soni is ideal for those seeking a quieter alternative in the Usambaras than the increasingly crowded base of nearby Lushoto (p99). While there is no tourist infrastructure, there is plenty of local character and activity, especially in the market area at the main junction.

Activities

The best place to base yourself and organise hikes is at Maweni Farm, from where you can explore Soni's many attractions. These include **Kwa Mungu Mountain**, about 30 minutes on foot from Soni village centre, and **Ndelemai Forest**. Soni is also the starting point for several wonderful walks, including a two- to three-day hike to the **Mazumbai Forest Reserve** and Bumbuli town, and a three- to five-hour return walk to pine-clad **Sakharani**, a Benedictine mission that sells locally produced wine. There's also a lovely longer walk from Maweni Farm up to **Gare Mission** and on to Lushoto. The area around Gare (one of the first missions in the area) was reforested as part of erosion-control efforts, and it's interesting to see the contrast with some of the treeless, more eroded surrounding areas. After Gare, and as a detour en route to Lushoto, stop at the village of **Kwai**, where there's a women's pottery project. Kwai was also an early research post for soil science and erosion control.

Sleeping

Maweni Farm LODGE **$$**
(0713 417858, 0713 565056, 0787 279371; www.maweni.com; s US$30, d US$50-80, f US$80; P wi-fi)
This atmospheric old farmhouse is set in lovely rambling grounds against a backdrop of twittering birds, flowering gardens and a water-lily-covered pond, with Kwa Mungu mountain rising up behind. Rooms are straightforward and spacious, and meals are healthy and excellent. Knowledgable guides

Northern Tanzania

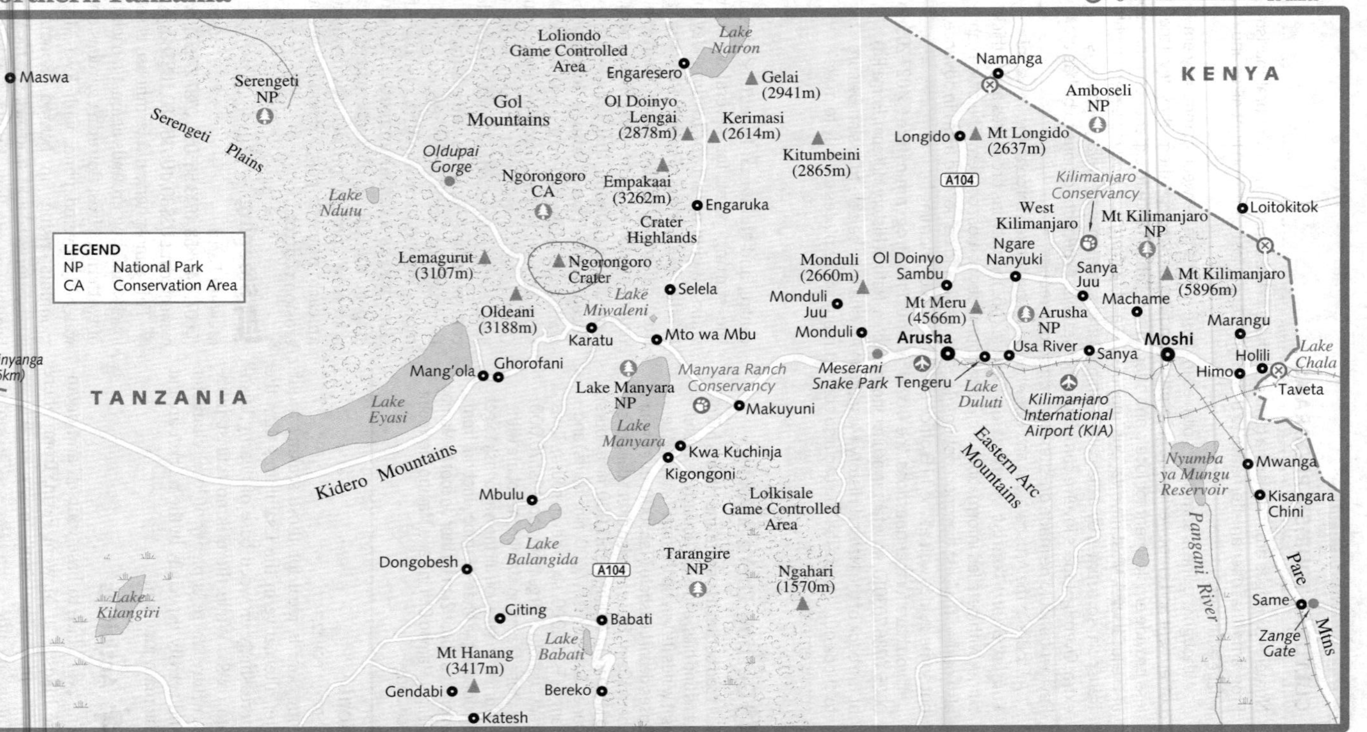

are available, and the property makes a wonderful and quiet base for exploring the Usambaras.

Getting There & Away

Soni is about 20km uphill from Mombo along the road to Lushoto (which is 12km further on). It's easy to reach via dalla-dalla from either destination (Tsh1500 from either Lushoto or Mombo).

NORTHERN TANZANIA

To paraphrase that well-known quote about Africa, those of you who've never been to northern Tanzania are to be envied, because you still have so much to look forward to. Northern Tanzania is a land of superlatives, from Africa's highest mountain to one of the greatest wildlife spectacles on the planet. But Kilimanjaro and the Serengeti are mere starting points to so many journeys of a lifetime. Mt Meru is Kilimanjaro's rival in both beauty and the challenge of climbing it, while the Crater Highlands could be Africa's most haunting landscape. When it comes to wildlife, there's Tarangire's baobab-and-elephant kingdom, Lake Manyara's tree-climbing lions and the flamingos of Lake Natron. And venturing down into Ngorongoro's crater can feel like returning to earth's first morning.

But this is also a journey among the Maasai, the Hadzabe and others whose presence here makes this one of Africa's most stirring and soulful destinations.

Arusha

027 / POP 416,500

Arusha is Tanzania's gateway to the northern circuit of stellar national parks and the starting point of many a memorable safari. It's also a large, sprawling city with all the contradictions that brings.

The town offers a nice break from the rigours of life on the African road – it has excellent places to stay and eat and, for the most part, it's lush and green and enjoys a temperate climate throughout the year, thanks to its altitude (about 1300m) and its location near the foot of Mt Meru.

As the safari capital of northern Tanzania, though, Arusha is also where you're most likely to encounter touts offering safaris, souvenirs and all manner of deals, some genuine, many of them not. Their main haunts are the bus stations and along Boma Rd. The city's downtown area and the main road towards Dodoma are noisy and packed with people and traffic.

Tours

★Via Via Cultural Tours CULTURAL
(0767 562651; www.viaviacafe.com; Boma Rd; 9am-4pm) Run out of the **Via Via cafe** (0782 434845; mains Tsh10,000-18,000; 9am-10pm Mon-Sat) just off the back of the Natural History Museum, this place offers drum lessons (including one hour classes for US$20 and an all-day version for US$50 in which you learn to make your own drum), two-hour city tours (US$30), three-hour 'Maasai Market Tours' (US$30), and cooking classes (US$30).

★Weaving & Walking Tour CULTURAL, WALKING
(0624 235886; per person Tsh10,000) A wonderful way to get under the skin of local life, these tours run by Reda and Flora take you into the heart of Arusha as locals experience it, ending up at Flora's weaving workshop, where she uses recycled textiles to create innovative new fabrics. Tours last between two and four hours. Ring ahead to be picked up from your hotel.

Sleeping

Flamingo Inn GUESTHOUSE $
(0754 260309; flamingoarusha@yahoo.com; Kikuyu St; s/tw US$20/25;) This low-key place has sparse but spotlessly clean rooms with fans and nets, a convenient central location, decent breakfasts and friendly staff.

★Karama Lodge LODGE $$
(0754 475188; www.karama-lodge.com; s/d/tr US$115/150/215;) Truly something different, off Onsea–Moivaro Rd on a forested hillside in the Suye Hill area just southeast of town, Karama offers 22 rustic and rather lovely stilt bungalows, each with a verandah and views to both Kilimanjaro and Meru on clear days. It's signposted north of Old Moshi Rd.

Mvuli Hotels Arusha HOTEL $$
(0786 287761; www.mvulihotels.co.tz; Kundayo Rd; r from US$65;) Not far from the centre, but set in quiet and pretty gardens, Mvuli offers some of Arusha's best

Arusha

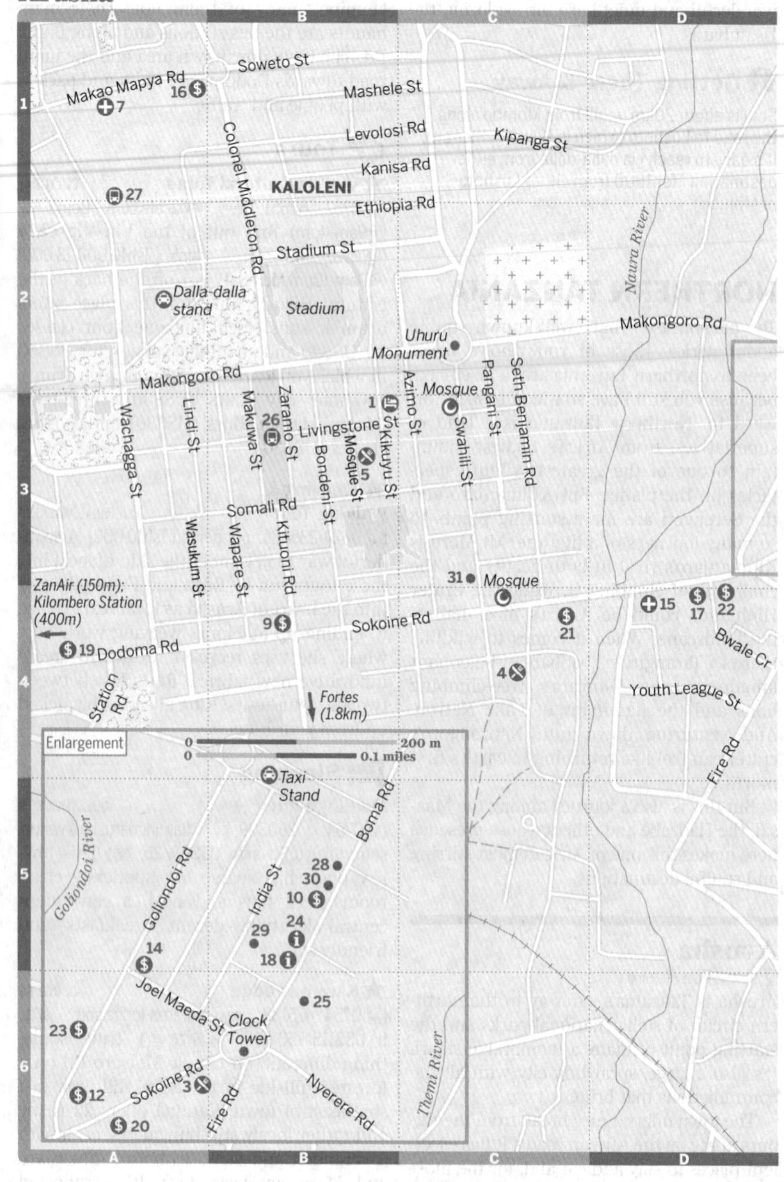

midrange accommodation. Rooms are large and comfortable and come with mosquito nets. There's nothing too remarkable afoot here; it's just that the price-to-quality ratio is rare in these parts for midrange places.

★ **Arusha Coffee Lodge** LODGE **$$$**
(☎027-250 0630; www.elewana.com; Dodoma Rd; s US$193-413, d US$386-550, ste US$325-770; P@🛜🏊) Set smack in the middle of a shade-grown coffee plantation and elegant through and through, this is one of the most

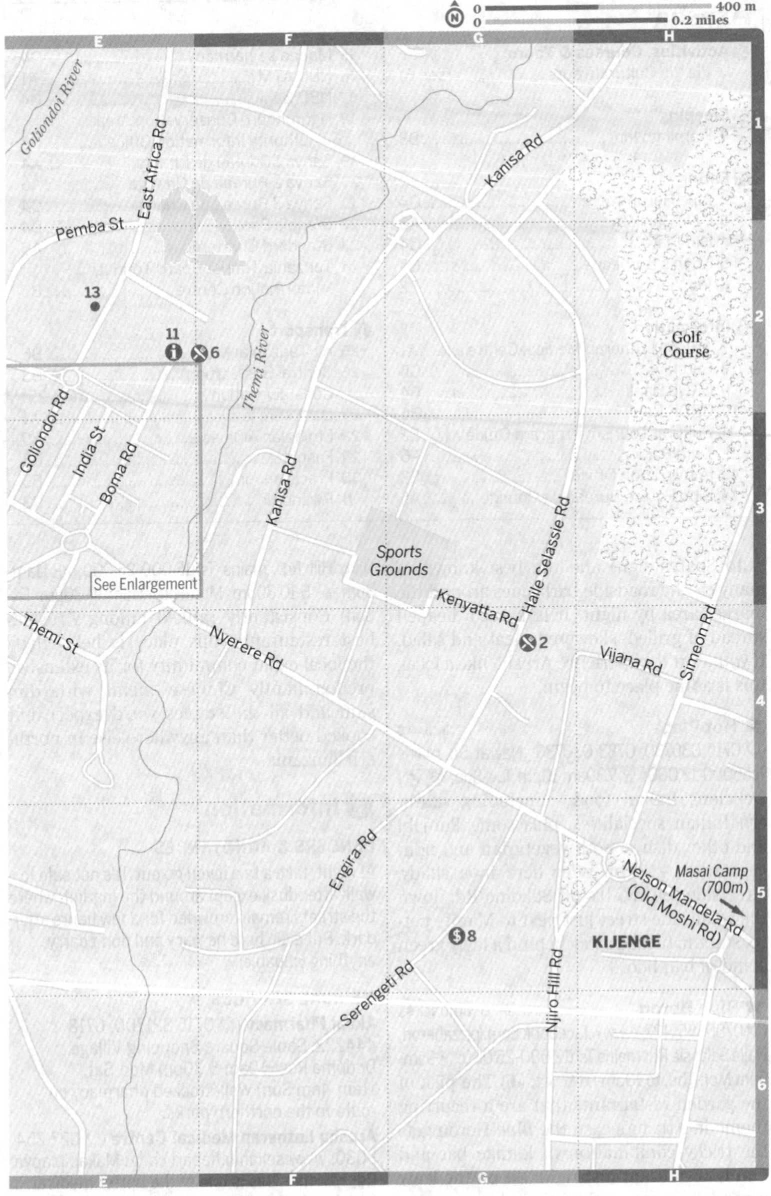

talked-about properties in Arusha. The gorgeous standard rooms have split-level floors, making them feel like suites, and the restaurant has few peers. The only downside is that traffic noise is loud. It's along the highway just west of town.

Eating

★Khan's Barbecue BARBECUE $

(Mosque St; meals Tsh9000-10,000, mixed grill Tsh13,000; ⏲6.30-11pm Mon-Fri, 5-11pm Sat & Sun) This Arusha institution is an auto-spares shop by day (look for the Zubeda

Arusha

Activities, Courses & Tours
Via Via Cultural Tours .... (see 6)

Sleeping
1 Flamingo Inn B3

Eating
2 Blue Heron G4
3 Cafe Barrista A6
4 Hot Plate C4
5 Khan's Barbecue B3
6 Via Via F2

Information
7 Arusha Lutheran Medical Centre A1
8 Barclays G5
9 CRDB Bank B4
10 CRDB Bank B5
11 Cultural Tourism Program Office E2
12 Exim Bank A6
13 Immigration Office E2
14 Kibo Palace Bureau de Change A5
15 Moona's Pharmacy D4
16 NBC ATM A1
17 NBC Bank D4
18 Ngorongoro Conservation Area Authority Information Office B5
19 Sanya 1 Bureau de Change A4
20 Sanya 2 Bureau de Change A6
21 Sanya 3 Bureau de Change C4
22 Stanbic Bank D4
23 Standard Chartered A6
24 Tanzania Tourist Board Tourist Information Centre B5

Transport
25 Air Tanzania B6
26 Central Bus Station B3
Coastal Aviation .... (see 25)
27 Dar Express A1
28 Ethiopian Airlines B5
29 Fastjet B5
30 Precision Air B5
31 RwandAir C3

Auto Spares sign) and the best known of many earthy roadside barbecues around the market area by night. It lays out a heaped spread of grilled, skewered meat and salad. If you want to experience Arusha like a local, this is a fine place to begin.

★ Hot Plate INDIAN $
(☎0715 030730, 0783 030730; Navrat St; mains Tsh6000-12,000; ⊙7.30am-10pm Tue-Sun; 📶✎) Delicious Indian food – including southern Indian specialities, plus some Punjabi and other dishes, both vegetarian and non-vegetarian – is on offer here in a shady, streetside setting. It's off Sokoine Rd, down the small side street just next to Manji's petrol station, tucked away behind a leafy green stand of bamboo.

★ Blue Heron INTERNATIONAL $$
(☎0785 555127; www.facebook.com/pizzaheron; Haile Selassie Rd; mains Tsh12,000-25,000; ⊙9am-5pm Mon-Thu, to 10pm Fri & Sat; 👪) The pick of the garden restaurants that are a recurring theme in Arusha's east, the Blue Heron gets the tricky combination of lounge bar and family restaurant just right. Sit on the leafy verandah or out on the lawn tables to enjoy a menu ranging from paninis and soups to beef tenderloin and various creative specials. The smoothies are divine.

Chinese Whispers ASIAN $$
(☎0688 969669; www.facebook.com/chinesewhispersarusha; 1st fl, Njiro Shopping Complex, Njiro Hill Rd; mains Tsh15,000-26,000; ⊙11am-3pm & 6-10.30pm Mon-Thu, 11am-10.30pm Fri-Sun) Consistently ranked among Arusha's best restaurants, this place is beloved by the local expat community for its extensive, predominantly Chinese menu with dim sum and all the staples you'd expect, but cooked better than anywhere else in northern Tanzania.

Information

DANGERS & ANNOYANCES

At night, take a taxi if you go out. It's not safe to walk after dusk except around the market, where the streets remain crowded for a few hours after dark. But even here be wary and don't carry anything valuable.

MEDICAL SERVICES

Akaal Pharmacy (☎0715 821700, 0718 444222; Sable Square Shopping Village, Dodoma Rd; ⊙9am-5.30pm Mon-Sat, 11am-4pm Sun) Well-stocked pharmacy en route to the northern parks.

Arusha Lutheran Medical Centre (☎027-254 8030; www.selianlh.habari.co.tz; Makao Mapya Rd; ⊙24hr) This is one of the better medical facilities in the region, but for anything truly serious, go to Nairobi (Kenya).

Moona's Pharmacy (☎027-254 5909, 0754 309052; moonas_pharmacy@cybernet.co.tz; Sokoine Rd; ⊙8.45am-5.30pm Mon-Fri, to 2pm Sat) Well-stocked pharmacy west of NBC bank.

MONEY

Forex bureaus are clustered along Joel Maeda St, India St, and Sokoine Rd near the Clock Tower. Most are open 8am to 6pm, including public holidays. ATMs are scattered around the city centre and easy to find, but be prepared for long waits, especially on Friday afternoon.

Foreign-exchange offices include **Kibo Palace** (Joel Maeda St; ⌚7am-5pm), and **Sanya 1** (Dodoma Rd; ⌚7am-7pm), **Sanya 2** (Sokoine Rd; ⌚7am-7pm) and **Sanya 3** (Sokoine Rd; ⌚7am-7pm).

Barclays (Sopa Lodges Bldg, Serengeti Rd; ⌚9.30am-4pm Mon-Fri, 9am-noon Sat)

CRDB Bank (Boma Rd; ⌚8am-4pm Mon-Fri)

CRDB Bank (Sokoine Rd; ⌚8am-4pm Mon-Fri)

Exim Bank (cnr Sokoine & Goliondoi Rds)

NBC ATM (Father Babu Rd; ⌚24hr)

NBC Bank (Sokoine Rd; ⌚8.30am-4pm Mon-Fri, 9am-noon Sat)

Stanbic Bank (Sokoine Rd; ⌚8.30am-3.30pm Mon-Fri)

Standard Chartered (Goliondoi Rd; ⌚24hr)

TOURIST INFORMATION

The bulletin boards at the tourist-board info centre and at **Cafe Barrista** (☎027-254 5677, 0754 288771; www.cafebarrista.com; Sokoine Rd; meals Tsh9000-14,000; ⌚7am-6.30pm Mon-Sat, to 2.30pm Sun; 📶✍) are good spots to find safari mates.

Ngorongoro Conservation Area Authority (NCAA) Information Office (☎027-254 4625; www.ngorongorocrater.go.tz; Boma Rd; ⌚8am-4pm Mon-Fri, 9am-1pm Sat, 10am-1pm Sun) Has free Ngorongoro booklets and a relief map of the conservation area. If you're not paying by credit card at the gate, you'll need to stop here to arrange payment of your entry fees prior to heading out to the crater.

Tanzania National Parks Authority (Tanapa; ☎027-250 3471; www.tanzaniaparks.go.tz; Dodoma Rd; ⌚8am-4pm Mon-Fri) Just west of town, this office has info on Tanzania's national parks and can help with general information and bookings for park accommodation.

Tanzania Tourist Board Tourist Information Centre (p61) Knowledgeable and helpful staff have information on Arusha, northern-circuit parks and other area attractions. They can book Cultural Tourism Program tours (p101) and provide a good free map of Arusha and Moshi. The office also keeps a 'blacklist' of tour operators and a list of registered tour companies.

ℹ Getting There & Away

AIR

Kilimanjaro International Airport, between Arusha and Moshi, handles both domestic and international flights, and is the best option for itineraries in Arusha and the northern safari circuit. It has a currency-exchange desk and an internet connection.

Confirm whether your flight will leave from Kilimanjaro International Airport or Arusha Airport when you buy your ticket.

Air Excel (☎027-297 0248, 027-297 0249; www.airexcelonline.com; Arusha Airport) Flights from Arusha Airport to various Serengeti airstrips and Lake Manyara National Park.

Air Tanzania (☎0784 275384, 0754 282727; www.airtanzania.co.tz; Boma Rd; ⌚8.30am-5pm Mon-Sat) Flights five times weekly between Arusha Airport, Dar es Salaam and Zanzibar Island.

Coastal Aviation (☎027-250 0343; www.coastal.co.tz; Boma Rd; ⌚7am-6pm) Arusha to Lake Manyara, Serengeti and Ruaha National Parks, West Kilimanjaro and Zanzibar.

Ethiopian Airlines (☎027-250 4231; www.ethiopianairlines.com; Boma Rd; ⌚8.30am-12.30pm & 2-5pm Mon-Fri, 8.30am-1pm Sat) International services to Kilimanjaro International Airport from Addis Ababa (Ethiopia).

Fastjet (☎0783 540540; www.fastjet.com; 2nd fl, Blue Plaza, India St; ⌚8am-6pm Mon-Sat) Good for low-cost flights to domestic and other African destinations, with direct Kilimanjaro International Airport to Dar es Salaam flights and onward connections.

Precision Air (☎0756 979490; www.precisionairtz.com; Boma Rd) Flies to Dar es Salaam, Mwanza and Zanzibar Island from Kili International and Arusha Airports. Also handles Kenya Airways bookings.

Regional Air (☎0754 285754, 0784 285753; www.regionaltanzania.com; Sable Square Shopping Village, Dodoma Rd) Connects Arusha Airport with Serengeti and Lake Manyara airstrips, as well as Zanzibar Island.

RwandAir (☎0732 978558; www.rwandair.com; Swahili St) Twice-weekly Kigali to Kili International service.

ZanAir (☎027-254 8877; www.zanair.com; Summit Centre, Dodoma Rd) Connects Arusha Airport with Dar es Salaam, Pemba and Zanzibar Island.

BUS

Arusha has several bus stations, but if you want to avoid them, most buses make a stop on the edge of town before going to the stations. Taxis will be waiting at that location.

Most buses leave early to mid-morning. When leaving Arusha, the best thing to do is book your ticket the day before, so that in the morning when you arrive with your luggage you can get straight on your bus. For pre-dawn buses, take a taxi to the station and ask the driver to drop you directly at your bus.

Arusha National Park

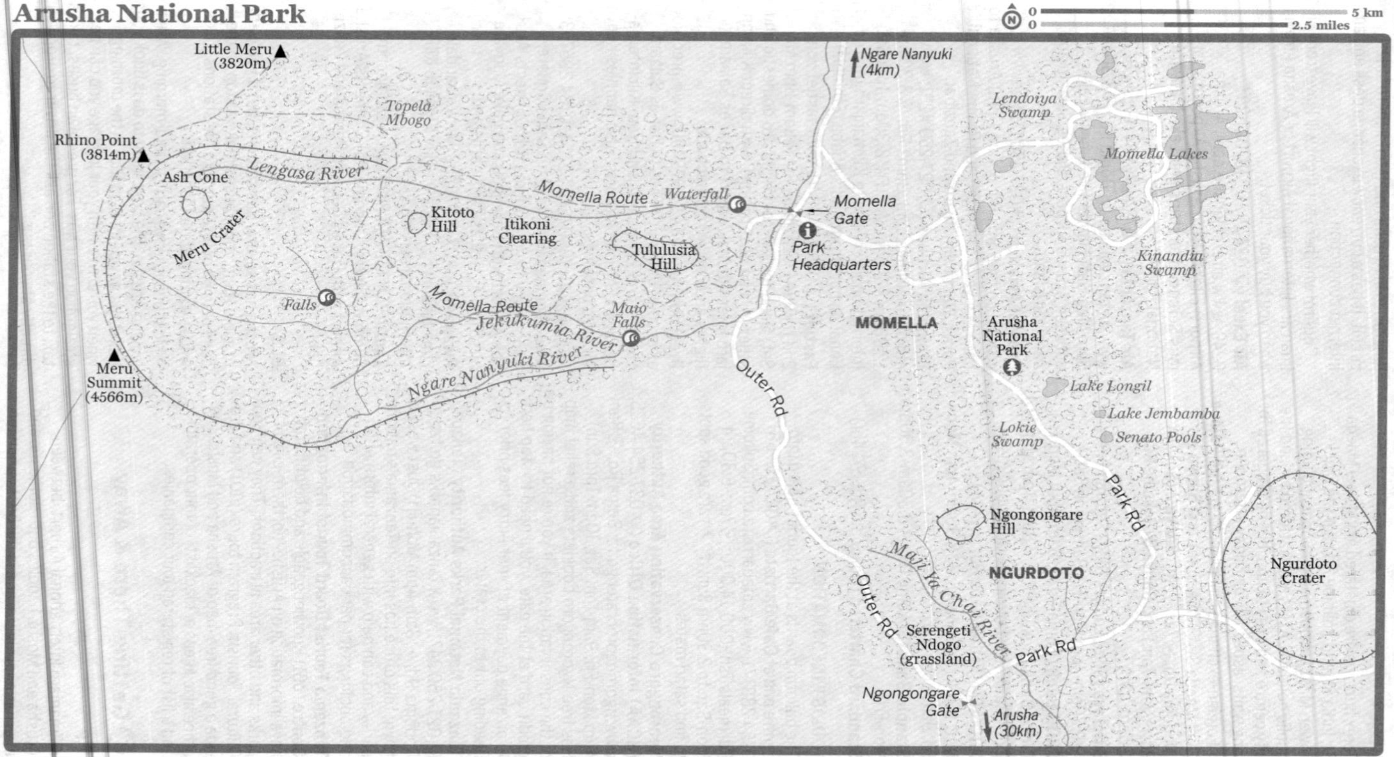

0 5 km
0 2.5 miles
Little Meru (3820m)
Rhino Point (3814m)
Meru Summit (4566m)
Ash Cone
Meru Crater
Topela Mbogo
Lengasa River
Falls
Kitoto Hill
Itikoni Clearing
Momella Route
Waterfall
Tululusia Hill
Momella Route
Jekukumia River
Maio Falls
Ngare Nanyuki River
Ngare Nanyuki (4km)
Momella Gate
Park Headquarters
Outer Rd
MOMELLA
Lendoiya Swamp
Momella Lakes
Kinandia Swamp
Arusha National Park
Lake Longil
Lake Jembamba
Lokie Swamp
Senato Pools
Park Rd
Ngongongare Hill
NGURDOTO
Maji Ya Chai River
Outer Rd
Serengeti Ndogo (grassland)
Park Rd
Ngongongare Gate
Arusha (30km)
Ngurdoto Crater

Despite what you may hear, there are no luggage fees (unless you have an *extraordinarily* large pack).

Central Bus Station (cnr Somali Rd & Zaramo St) Arusha's biggest bus station is intimidatingly chaotic in the morning and popular with touts. If you get overwhelmed, head straight for a taxi, or duck into the lobby of one of the hotels across the street to get your bearings.

Dar Express Bus Station (Makao Mapya Bus Station; Wachagga St) Most of the luxury buses to Dar es Salaam depart from here, including Dar Express and Kilimanjaro Express.

Kilombero Station (Makao Mapya Rd) Several companies serving Babati, Singida, Mwanza and other points generally west, including Mtei Express, have their offices and departure points here, near Kilombero market.

Getting Around

Dalla-dallas (minibuses; Tsh400) run along major roads from early until late; there's a big dalla-dalla stand west of the stadium, off Stadium St. There are taxi stands all around the city centre, including on **Makongoro Rd** (24hr), and some park in front of most hotels, even many budget ones. A ride across town, from the Clock Tower to Makao Mapya bus station, for example, shouldn't cost more than Tsh5000. The usual asking price for both motorcycle taxis and *bajajis* (tuk-tuks) is Tsh2000 for a ride in the city centre.

Arusha National Park

The transition between unappealing urban chaos and pristine mountain hiking trails is rarely so abrupt as it is in **Arusha National Park** (027-255 3995, 0767 536136; www.tanzaniaparks.go.tz; adult/child US$53.10/17.70; 6.30am-6.30pm). One of Tanzania's most beautiful and topographically varied protected areas, the park is dominated by **Mt Meru**, an almost perfect volcanic cone with a spectacular crater. It also shelters **Ngurdoto Crater** (often dubbed Little Ngorongoro), with its swamp-filled floor and lost-world feel.

At 552 sq km, it's a small park and, while there is wildlife here, it's nothing compared to that of other northern-circuit parks. But these minor details can be quickly forgotten when you're walking amid the soul-stirring scenery and exploring the meaningful trekking possibilities.

ARUSHA NATIONAL PARK

Why Go Climbing Mt Meru; canoe and walking safaris; fine birding; easy access (even a day trip) from Arusha.

When to Go Year-round.

Practicalities Drive in from Arusha or Moshi. The main park entrance is at the southern Ngongongare gate. The northern Momella gate is 12km further north near the **park headquarters** (p112), which is the main contact for making campsite reservations. Entrance fees can be paid by credit card at the main Ngongongare gate.

Budget Tips Join a pre-arranged safari or charter a dalla-dalla for the day with other travellers in Arusha; if you're not climbing Mt Meru, visit on a day trip to avoid camping fees.

Activities

Walking safaris (US$25 per person per half-day) are popular. Several trails pass below Mt Meru and another follows the Ngurdoto Crater rim trail (descending into the crater is not permitted). The walk to Njeku Viewpoint in the Meru Crater floor, which follows Stage 1 (p110) of the climb up Mt Meru, is an excellent day hike.

Sleeping & Eating

Momella Gate Public Campsite CAMPGROUND $
(camping US$35.40) In the vicinity of Momella gate are three areas of public campsites, including one with a shower. There are pretty views from here, but the sites can get very busy at weekends.

Kiboko Lodge LODGE $$
(0765 688550; www.kibokolodge.nl; s/d with half board from US$83/146;) Most employees at this nonprofit, charity-run lodge are former street kids who received training at the Watoto Foundation's vocational training school, and a stay here supports the project. The slightly worn but spacious stone cottages have fireplaces, hot water and safes, and the thatched-roof lounge is almost homey. It's 5km down a 4WD-only road east of Ngongongare gate.

★**Hatari Lodge** LODGE $$$
(027-255 3456/7, 0752 553456; www.hatarilodge.com; s/d with full board & incl all activities

TREKKING MT MERU

At 4566m, Mt Meru is Tanzania's second-highest mountain. Although overshadowed by Kilimanjaro in the eyes of trekkers, it's a spectacular volcanic cone with one of East Africa's most scenic and rewarding climbs, involving a dramatic walk along the knife edge of the crater rim.

Mt Meru starts its steep rise from a circular base some 20km across at 2000m. At about 2500m some of the wall has broken away, so the top half of the mountain is shaped like a giant horseshoe. The cliffs of the inner wall below the summit are more than 1500m high, making them among the tallest in Africa. Inside the crater, more recent volcanic eruptions have created a subsidiary peak called the Ash Cone that adds to the scenic splendour.

Practicalities

Costs Trekking companies in both Arusha and Moshi organise treks on Mt Meru. Most charge from US$450 to US$800 for four days. That said, you can do things quite easily on your own for around US$400 for a four-day, three-night trek. You'll also need to add in the costs of food (which you should get in Arusha, as there's nowhere to stock up near the park), and of transport to and from the park.

The following are the minimum per-person costs:

- park entrance fee US$53.10
- hut fees per day US$35.40
- rescue fee per day US$23.60
- guide fees per trip US$17.70 per day

Tipping Park rangers receive a fixed monthly salary for their work and get no additional payment from the park for guiding, which means that tips are much appreciated. It happens rarely, but rangers and porters here occasionally expect the big tips demanded by their Kilimanjaro counterparts. If this happens and you're already on the trail, work out an arrangement to keep going, and then report them to headquarters when you get down the mountain.

For a good guide who has completed the full trek with you, plan on a tip of about US$50 per group. Cook and porter tips should be around US$30 and US$20 respectively. Tip more with top-end companies.

Guides and porters A ranger-guide is mandatory and can be arranged at Momella gate. Unlike on Kilimanjaro, guides on Meru are regular park rangers whose purpose is to assist (and protect) you in case you meet some of the park's buffaloes or elephants, rather than to show you the way, although they do know the route. If there's a shortage of rangers, which is often, you may end up in a larger group than you hoped for.

Optional porters are also available at Momella gate. The charge is US$10 per porter per day and this is paid directly to them at the end of the trek. They come from one of the nearby villages and are not park employees, so you'll also need to pay their park-entrance (Tsh1500 per day) and hut (Tsh2000 per night) fees at Momella gate before starting to trek. Porters will carry rucksacks weighing up to 20kg (excluding their own food and clothing).

Accommodation There are two blocks of four-bed bunkhouses ('huts') spaced for a four-day trek. Especially during the July–August and December–January high seasons, they're often full, so book ahead. It's also a good idea to carry a tent (though if you camp, you'll still need to pay hut fees). Each bunkhouse has a cooking and eating area; bring your own stove and fuel.

Momella Route

The Momella route is the only route up Mt Meru. It starts at Momella gate on the eastern side of the mountain and goes to the summit along the northern arm of the horseshoe crater. The route can be done comfortably in four days (three nights). Trekkers aren't allowed to begin after 3pm, which means that if you travel to the park by bus you'll almost certainly have to camp and wait until the next day to start climbing.

While Meru is small compared to Kilimanjaro, don't underestimate it: because of the steepness, many have found that Meru is almost as difficult a climb. And it's still high enough for you to feel the effects of altitude, so don't try to rush up if you're not properly acclimatised.

Stage 1: Momella gate to Miriakamba Hut (10km, four to five hours, 1000m ascent) There are two routes, one long and one short, at the start of the climb. Most people prefer taking the mostly forested long route up and the short route down, so that's how the trek is described here. And do watch out for buffaloes…

From Momella gate, the road winds uphill for an hour to **Fig Tree Arch**, a parasitic wild fig that originally grew around two other trees, eventually strangling them. Now only the fig tree remains, with its distinctive arch large enough to drive a car through. After another hour the track crosses a large stream, just above Maio Falls, and one hour further you'll reach Kitoto Camp, with excellent views over the Momella Lakes and out to Kilimanjaro in the distance. It's then one final hour to Miriakamba Hut (2514m). From Miriakamba you can walk to the **Meru Crater floor** (a two- to three-hour return trip) either in the afternoon of Stage 1 or during Stage 4 (there is time to do it on the morning of Stage 2, but this is a bad idea as it reduces your time for acclimatisation), but you need to let your guide know you want to do this before starting the climb. The path across the floor leads to Njeku Viewpoint on a high cliff overlooking a waterfall, with excellent views of the Ash Cone and the entire extent of the crater.

Stage 2: Miriakamba Hut to Saddle Hut (4km, three to five hours, 1250m ascent) From Miriakamba the path climbs steeply up through pleasant glades to reach **Topela Mbogo** (Buffalo Swamp) after 45 minutes and **Mgongo Wa Tembo** (Elephant Ridge) after another 30 minutes. From the top of Mgongo Wa Tembo there are great views down into the crater and up to the main cliffs below the summit. Continue through some open grassy clearings and over several stream beds (usually dry) to **Saddle Hut** (3570m).

From Saddle Hut a side trip to the summit of **Little Meru** (3820m) takes about an hour and gives impressive views of Meru's summit, the horseshoe crater, the top of the Ash Cone and the sheer cliffs of the crater's inner wall. As the sun sets behind Meru, casting huge jagged shadows across the clouds, the snows on Kili turn orange and then pink as the light fades.

Stage 3: Saddle Hut to Meru Summit and return (5km, four to five hours, 816m ascent, plus 5km, two to three hours, 816m descent) This stage, along a very narrow ridge between the outer slopes of the mountain and the sheer cliffs of the inner crater, promises some of the most dramatic and exhilarating trekking anywhere in East Africa. During the rainy season, ice and snow can occur on this section of the route, so take care. If there's no mist, the views from the summit are spectacular.

If you're looking forward to watching the sun rise behind Kilimanjaro, but you're not keen on attempting this section in the dark, the views at dawn are just as impressive from **Rhino Point** (3814m), about an hour from Saddle Hut, as they are from the summit, perhaps even more so because you'll also see the main cliffs of the crater's inner wall being illuminated by the rising sun.

Stage 4: Saddle Hut to Momella gate (5km, three to five hours, 2250m descent) From Saddle Hut, retrace the Stage 2 route to Miriakamba. From Miriakamba, the short path descends gradually down the ridge directly to Momella gate. It goes through forest some of the way, then open grassland, where giraffes and zebras are often seen.

US$558/944; P 📶) The most atmospheric and upmarket of the park lodges has tasteful 'modern-retro' rooms filled with personality, a prime location on large lawns frequented by giraffes, and views of Meru and Kilimanjaro on clear days. Rooms are spacious, boasting large windows, and there's a fireplace and top-notch cuisine. It's on the edge of the park, about 2km north of Momella gate.

Rivertrees Country Inn LODGE $$$
(☎0732 971667, 0713 339873; www.rivertrees.com; s/d from US$199/262, 2-room River House US$1000; P @ 📶 🏊) With a genteel old-world ambience and excellent cuisine served family style around a large wooden table, Rivertrees is a perfect post-national-park stop. A variety of rooms and cottages, some wheelchair accessible, are spread throughout vast natural gardens with huge trees along the Usa River. It's east of Usa River Village, set back off the Moshi Hwy.

Meals are superb, as are the cultural tours (to local villages and coffee farms) and spa treatments.

Information

MAPS

The best map of the park is Maco's *Arusha National Park* (1:35,000), widely available in Arusha, although scaling is not always entirely accurate. The Veronica Roodt *Arusha National Park – The Tourist Map* (1:44,000) is also reasonable.

TOURIST INFORMATION

The **park headquarters** (www.tanzaniaparks.go.tz) at Momella gate is the main contact for making campsite reservations.

Getting There & Away

The entrance to Arusha National Park is about 35km northeast of Arusha. Take the main road between Arusha and Moshi to the signposted turn-off, from where it's about 10km north to **Ngongongare gate**, where you pay your entry fees. **Momella gate** – the location of the park headquarters – is about 14km further on. From Momella gate, it's possible to continue along a rough track to Lariboro, on the main Nairobi highway, passing Ngare Nanyuki village (6km north of Momella gate) en route.

There are several buses daily between Arusha and Ngare Nanyuki village, departing Arusha between 1.30pm and 4pm and Ngare Nanyuki between 7am and 8am. Buses stop at Ngongongare gate (Tsh6000, 1½ hours). A taxi from Arusha should cost from Tsh50,000.

Tarangire National Park

> **TARANGIRE NATIONAL PARK**
>
> **Why Go** Excellent dry-season wildlife watching, especially elephants and lions; evocative baobab-studded landscapes.
>
> **When to go** June to October.
>
> **Practicalities** Drive in from Arusha; entrance fees can be paid in cash or by credit card at both the main gate and the Boundary Hill gate.
>
> **Budget Tips** Join a pre-arranged safari or charter a dalla-dalla (minibus) with other travellers; stay outside the park to avoid camping fees.

Welcome to one of Africa's most underrated parks. Thanks to its proximity to Serengeti National Park and Ngorongoro Crater, **Tarangire National Park** (☎0767 536139, 0689 062248; www.tanzaniaparks.go.tz; adult/child US$53.10/17.70; ⏰6am-6.30pm) is usually assigned only a day visit as part of a larger northern-circuit itinerary. Yet it deserves much more, at least in the dry season (July to October). It's a place where elephants dot the plains like cattle, and where lion roars and zebra barks fill the night.

But here the wildlife tells only half the story. Dominating the park's 2850 sq km, Tarangire's great stands of epic baobabs should be reason enough to visit. There are also sun-blistered termite mounds in abundance, as well as grassy savannah plains and vast swamps. And cleaving the park in two is the Tarangire River, its meandering course and (in some places) steep banks providing a dry-season lure for animals and thus many stirring wildlife encounters for visitors.

Sights

The **northern triangle**, bordered by the park boundaries to the northeast and west, and by the Tarangire River and Tarangire Safari Lodge to the south, offers the most easily accessible as well as some of the most rewarding wildlife areas of the park. Amid a varied habitat of open plains and light woodland, you'll find elephants, zebras and wildebeest in abundance in this baobab-rich region, with predators, particularly lions, also a possibility.

Further south, wildlife draws near to the water all along the **Tarangire River valley** that cuts the park in two, while the swamps of **Silale**, **Lormakau** and **Ngusero Oloirobi** are alive with possibility, as predators lie in wait in the shallows whenever herbivores come to drink. This chain of swamps runs north–south through the park, beginning just west of the Tarangire Sopa Lodge. **Gurusi Swamp**, in the park's southwestern bulge, is another area rich in wildlife.

Activities

Walking Safaris

Three-hour walking safaris (US$23.60 per person plus US$23.60 per group) can be organised from the park gate (though the armed rangers are simply security and haven't had much training about wildlife). Most of the lodges can organise walks with their own trained guides, but only for their guests.

Night Drives

Inside the park, Tarangire Safari Lodge can arrange night drives for guests for US$80 per person, plus a US$23.60 ranger fee per group; expect other lodges to follow suit in the not-too-distant future. All of the camps and lodges outside the park boundaries offer night drives in the conservancies and range lands beyond the park. Ask at the gate about the park's own night drives (adult/child US$59/29.50).

Sleeping

Inside the Park

★Tarangire Safari Lodge LODGE $$$
(☎0756 914663, 027-254 4752; www.tarangiresafarilodge.com; s/d with full board US$270/440; P) A fabulous location high above the Tarangire River, good food and service, and well-priced accommodation make this lodge the pick of the in-park options. The sweeping vistas mean that there's no need to go elsewhere for a sundowner. Accommodation includes stone bungalows and standard en suite safari tents; the latter have good views from their doorsteps. It's 10km inside the park gate.

★Oliver's Camp TENTED CAMP $$$
(www.asiliaafrica.com; per person all-inclusive Jul & Aug US$959, rest of year US$689-889; closed Apr & May; P) Oliver's is notable for its fine location near Silale Swamp deep in the park's heart. The 10 comfortable, spacious tents have an agreeably rustic style and the whole camp has an intimate ambience. Excellent guides lead walking safaris, night drives (sometimes using night-vision equipment) and fly camping, making this place ideal for adventurous travellers. Tents have leather armchairs and mahogany headboards.

Sanctuary Swala TENTED CAMP $$$
(☎027-250 9817; www.sanctuaryretreats.com; per person full board & incl all activities Jun-Oct US$775, rest of year rates vary; Jun-Mar; P@) Arguably the most refined safari experience inside Tarangire, this premier-class camp nestles in a grove of acacia trees and overlooks a busy waterhole in the southwestern part of the park near Gurusi Swamp. Each of the 12 lovely tents has a big deck and its own butler. The camp's in a great wildlife-watching location with lots of lions.

Boundary Hill Lodge LODGE $$$
(☎0787 293727; www.tarangireconservation.com; per person with full board US$575; P@) Widely praised for its commitment to the environment and the Maasai community (the community owns a 50% stake in the lodge), Boundary Hill has eight large, individually designed hilltop rooms with balconies peering out over Silale Swamp in the park.

Outside the Park

Zion Campsite CAMPGROUND $
(☎0754 460539; camping US$10; P) A bare and unkempt compound 6km before the park gate it may be, but it's cheaper than camping inside the park, and the showers are warm. Bring your own food.

★Tarangire Treetops Lodge TENTED CAMP $$$
(☎027-250 0630; www.elewana.com; s/d with full board Jun-Oct US$1268/1690, rest of year rates vary; P@) Not your ordinary tented camp, this pampered place has 20 huge suites set on stilts or built tree-house style around the baobabs. It's almost an hour's drive from here to the Boundary Hill gate, but it's ideal if you're looking for more of a luxury-in-the-wilderness experience.

Information

MAPS

Maco puts out the best Tarangire map, available in Arusha and at the park gate. The hand-drawn

New Map of Tarangire National Park, available in Arusha and elsewhere, is outstanding, with different versions for wet and dry seasons.

TOURIST INFORMATION

Main Park Gate & Headquarters (tnp@tanzaniaparks.com; ⏲6am-6.30pm) Basic information about the park, as well as free maps.

Getting There & Away

Tarangire is 130km from Arusha via Makuyuni (which is the last place for petrol and basic supplies). At Kigongoni village, there's a signposted turn-off to the main park gate, which is 7km further down a good dirt access road. The only other entrance is Boundary Hill gate along the northeastern border, which provides access to some lodges located in the area. The park doesn't rent out vehicles.

Coastal Aviation (p107) and Air Excel (p107) sometimes stop at Tarangire's Kuro airstrip on request on their flights between Arusha and Lake Manyara.

Mto wa Mbu

☎027 / POP 11,400

Mto wa Mbu is the busy gateway to Lake Manyara, which is fed by the town's eponymous 'River of Mosquitoes', and you'll pass through here en route between Arusha and Ngorongoro. Over the years, this diverse place – by some estimates, all of Tanzania's 120 tribal groups are present here – has evolved into something of a travellers centre, with plenty of lodges, campsites, hole-in-the-wall eateries, petrol stations, money changers, souvenir stalls and just about anything else that could tempt a passing safari vehicle to disgorge its inhabitants.

Activities

Mto wa Mbu Cultural Tourism Program CULTURAL
(☎027-253 9303, 0784 606654; http://mtoculturalprogramme.tripod.com; day trip from US$30; ⏲8am-6.30pm) The well-organised Cultural Tourism Program offers walking and cycling tours to surrounding villages, markets and a nearby waterfall, with an emphasis on farming, and hiking along the escarpment. Homestays and meals with local families can also be arranged. The office is at the back of the Red Banana Cafe, close to the bus stop on the main road.

Sleeping & Eating

Njake Jambo Lodge & Campsite CAMPGROUND $$
(☎027-250 5553; www.njake.com; Arusha-Karatu Rd; camping/s/d US$10/95/130;) A base for both independent travellers and large overland trucks, Njake Jambo has a shaded and well-maintained grassy camping area, plus 16 good rooms in double-storey chalet blocks.

Twiga Campsite & Lodge HOSTEL $$
(☎0784 901479, 0758 510000; www.twigalodgecampsite.com; Arusha-Karatu Rd; camping US$10, r US$50-100; P@) This popular place is a real travellers hub, with simple but well-kept standard rooms, bungalows and a decent campsite. It's a good place to hook up with other safari-goers, and bike and vehicle hire is available.

Blue Turaco Pizza Point PIZZA $$
(Arusha-Karatu Rd; pizzas Tsh12,000-16,000; ⏲noon-9pm) The Blue Turaco Pizza Point, unmissable along the south side of the main road, makes good wood-fired pizzas. Seating is in a small courtyard area just behind.

Information

MONEY

CRDB (⏲8am-4pm Mon-Fri, to noon Sat) On the main road. Has a sometimes-functional ATM.

TOURIST INFORMATION

The Mto wa Mbu Cultural Tourism Program is the best source of tourist information.

Getting There & Away

BUS

Buses and dalla-dallas run all day from Arusha (Tsh7000, two hours) and Karatu (Tsh2500, one hour) to Mto wa Mbu. You can also come from Arusha on the minibuses that run to Karatu. All vehicles stop along the main road in the town centre.

CAR

Car hire for trips to Lake Manyara and Tarangire National Parks (including fuel and driver US$150 to US$200) and to Ngorongoro Crater (US$200 to US$250) is available in Mto wa Mbu through the Cultural Tourism Program office and Twiga and Njake Jambo campsites.

The track north to Lake Natron begins here.

Lake Manyara National Park

Lake Manyara National Park (027-253 9112, 0767 536137; www.tanzaniaparks.go.tz; adult/child US$53.10/17.70; 6am-6pm) is one of Tanzania's smaller and most underrated parks. While it may lack the size and variety of other northern-circuit destinations (there's pretty much one main north–south route through the park), its vegetation is diverse, ranging from savannah to marsh to evergreen forest (11 ecosystems in all) and it supports one of the highest biomass densities of large mammals in the world. The chance to see elephant families moving through the forest or Lake Manyara's famous population of tree-climbing lions (although sighting them is becoming increasingly rare) are alone reason enough to come.

The dramatic western escarpment of the Rift Valley forms the park's western border. To the east is the alkaline Lake Manyara, which covers one-third of the park but shrinks considerably in the dry season. During the rains, the lake hosts millions of flamingos and other bird life.

Sights

Just inside the park's main gate, the northern woodland is dense, green and overrun by baboon troops; sightings of blue monkeys are also possible. There's a hippo pool at the lake's northernmost tip. Between the water's edge and the steep Rift Valley walls, the floodplains host wildebeest, buffaloes, zebras and Lake Manyara's much-studied elephants, while the thin acacia belt that shadows the lakeshore is where you're most likely to see arboreal lions.

★Lake Manyara Treetop Walkway VIEWPOINT

(0756 977384; www.wayoafrica.com/treetop-walkway; US$35.40, plus treetop park fee US$17.70; 6.30am-5pm) Enjoy a guided bird's-eye view of Manyara on Tanzania's first treetop walkway (370m). It begins at ground level and climbs gently into the canopy, reaching a maximum height of 18m above the forest floor. Given the importance of the trees in Lake Manyara (and the lions that famously climb them), there's a certain magic in climbing up into the canopy.

> **LAKE MANYARA NATIONAL PARK**
>
> **Why Go** Excellent birding; tree-climbing lions; dramatic Rift Valley Escarpment scenery.
>
> **When to Go** Year-round. June to October is best for large mammals; November to June is best for birds.
>
> **Practicalities** Stay in Mto wa Mbu, atop the escarpment or inside the park; bring binoculars, as flamingos can be distant, depending on the day. Entrance fees are paid by credit card at the main gate.
>
> **Budget Tips** Stay in Mto wa Mbu to avoid camping fees; charter a dalla-dalla for the day.

Activities

Night Drives

This is the only northern-circuit park where *anybody* can do night drives. They're run by **Wayo Africa** (Green Footprint Adventures; 0784 203000, 0783 141119; www.wayoafrica.com) from 8pm to roughly 11pm (US$50 per person, plus the park fee of US$59/23.60 per adult/child). Park fees must be paid directly to the park before 5pm. Advance booking (and usually advance payment) is required.

Walking Safaris

The park allows two- to three-hour walking safaris (US$23.60 per person, plus US$23.60 per group of up to eight) with an armed ranger along three trails. Reservations are required and the park has no vehicles to take hikers to the trailheads.

The **Msara Trail**, the nearest path to the gate (11km away), follows its namesake river along the Rift Valley Escarpment through great birdwatching territory up to a viewpoint. The **Lake Shore Trail** starts 38km into the park near the *maji moto* (hot springs). It crosses acacia woodland and savannah and is the path where walkers are most likely to meet large mammals and find flamingos. The **Iyambi River Trail**, 50km from the gate, is wooded and rocky with good birdwatching and a chance to see mammals.

Wayo Africa has three walking options (US$18 to US$35 per person) in the area: a nature walk along the escarpment, a forest walk down the escarpment, and a village walk in Mto wa Mbu (p114). All start from the Lake Manyara Serena Safari Lodge or a pre-arranged point in Mto wa Mbu.

Sleeping

In the Park

Park Bandas BANDA $
(www.tanzaniaparks.go.tz; bandas per person US$35.40) The park has 10 double en suite *bandas* (thatched-roof huts) with hot water, bedding and a cooking area, located just inside the park gate.

★**Lake Manyara Tree Lodge** LODGE $$$
(☎028-262 1267; www.andbeyond.com; per person full board & incl all activities Jun-Sep US$1340, rest of year rates vary; ⊙closed Apr; P 📶 🏊) This lovely, luxurious place is one of the most exclusive lodges in all of Tanzania. The gorgeous stilted tree-house suites with private decks and views from the bathtubs and outdoor showers are set in a mahogany forest at the remote southern end of the park. The food is excellent and the rooms have butler service.

FLAMINGOS & THE ART OF STANDING ON ONE LEG

From Lake Natron to Lake Bogoria in Kenya, it's the classic Rift Valley image: the flamingo – or, rather, massed ranks of flamingos – standing completely still on one leg. Why they do so has baffled scientists for decades.

Finally a 2017 study found that this pose has a very strong scientific reason: flamingos, it seems, expend less energy by standing on one leg than they do standing on two. More specifically, flamingos do not actively use their muscles in any way in this one-legged position. Closer examination of the pose revealed that the standing foot sits directly beneath the body, meaning that the leg angles inwards, enabling the bird to assume the position and remain almost entirely motionless for significant periods.

So easy and perfectly balanced is the pose that flamingos can sleep while standing like this. And the scientists who carried out the study discovered that even dead flamingos could remain on one leg (but not two) without any means of support!

Atop the Escarpment

★**Escarpment Luxury Lodge** LODGE $$$
(☎0767 804864; www.escarpmentluxurylodge.com; s/d full board & incl all activities US$850/1100; P @ 🏊) The wood-floored chalets at this attractive place are the height of luxury – plenty of space, wonderfully deep bathtubs, leather sofas, tasteful recycled furnishings, wide verandahs, the finest linens and big windows. Views of the lake are as expansive as you'd expect from up here on the escarpment.

Lake Manyara Serena Safari Lodge LODGE $$$
(☎027-254 5555; www.serenahotels.com; s/d full board Jul-Oct US$301/509, Nov-Jun s US$114-256, d US$228-433; P @ 📶 🏊) The 67 well-appointed rooms in this large complex occupy appealing two-storey conical thatched bungalows in shady grounds. Nature walks and village visits are available, as is massage. There's no extra cost for the fine views (the best are from the swimming pool). It lacks the intimacy and naturalness of other escarpment properties but is nevertheless a justifiably popular choice.

Below the Escarpment

Migunga Tented Camp TENTED CAMP $$$
(☎0754 324193; www.moivaro.com; camping US$10, s/d/tr full board US$247/348/450; P @) The main attraction of this place (still often known by its previous name, Lake Manyara Tented Camp) is its setting in a grove of enormous fever trees (*migunga* in Swahili) that echoes with bird calls. The 21 tents ringing large, grassy grounds are small but adequate, and they're fairly priced. The camp is 2km south of the main road.

Information

The hand-drawn *New Map of Lake Manyara National Park*, available in Arusha and elsewhere, has different versions for wet and dry seasons but doesn't include the **Marang Forest Reserve** that has recently been added to the park.

Getting There & Away

AIR

Air Excel (p107), Coastal Aviation (p107) and Regional Air (p107) offer daily flights between Arusha and Lake Manyara.

CLIMBING OL DOINYO LENGAI

As one of the best climbs in East Africa, Ol Doinyo Lengai is at once challenging and extremely beautiful.

With a midnight start, a trek from the base village of Engaresero at Lake Natron is possible in one long haul. You'll usually be back down by mid-morning. The climb is not for the faint-hearted, but the rewards are considerable: the sunrise views out over Lake Natron, the escarpment and beyond are among the best in Tanzania.

There are, however, some things to take into account when preparing your ascent. It's strongly recommended that you take a helmet – there are often baboons on the higher slopes and they frequently dislodge gravel and sometimes larger stones; other wildlife to watch out for includes leopards and klipspringers. It's also extremely steep near the summit – although it's a trek rather than a technical climb, in places you'll be close to vertical. And throughout the climb, the loose ash along most of the path makes it difficult going when ascending, and it can be an even tougher, often painful, descent.

Climbing Ol Doinyo Lengai costs between US$60 and US$100 per person, depending on how many are in the party. Guides can be arranged through your lodging or through the community-run Engaresero Tourism Office (p118) at the southeastern entrance to Engaresero.

BUS

Buses and dalla-dallas run frequently from Arusha (Tsh7500, two hours) and Karatu (Tsh3500, one hour) to Mto wa Mbu, the gateway village for Lake Manyara National Park. Once you're at Mto wa Mbu, it's straightforward to get onward transport to Lake Manyara lodges and camps or to hire a vehicle (from USS$150 including fuel and driver) to explore the park.

Lake Natron

Shimmering amid the sun-scorched Kenyan border northeast of Ngorongoro Conservation Area, this 58km-long but just 50cm-deep alkaline lake should be on every adventurer's itinerary. The drives from Mto wa Mbu or the northern Serengeti are remote, with a desolate, other-worldly beauty and an incomparable feeling of space and antiquity. The roads pass through untrammelled Maasai land, with small *bomas* (fortified compounds) and big mountains often in view in a wild, cauterised landscape. From June to November at the lake itself, upwards of three million flamingos gather – it's one of East Africa's most stirring wildlife spectacles. And close to the southern end of the lake, the views of Ol Doinyo Lengai volcano are splendid.

The base for visits is the small oasis of Engaresero (also spelled Ngare Sero; 'impermanent water' in Maasai) on the lake's southwestern shore.

Sleeping

Lengai Safari Lodge LODGE $$$
(☎0754 550542, 0768 210091; www.lengaisafarilodge.com; camping US$10, per person with full board US$120; P 📶 ✈) A few kilometres south of town along the escarpment, this lodge offers unbeatable views of Ol Doinyo Lengai, and good ones of the lake too, including from some rooms. The newly constructed rooms and tents are comfortable rather than luxurious; more were being built at the time of research. It's easily the best location of any of the area's accommodation options.

Lake Natron Tented Camp TENTED CAMP $$$
(☎0754 324193; www.moivaro.com; camping US$10, half board s US$140-250, d US$200-350; P ✈) At the southern end of Engaresero in a grove of trees, this tented camp is a little rundown and the tents are a tad dated, but it's comfortable enough. There's a large and sometimes busy campground with good facilities next door. Strangely, given the proximity, you'll need to step beyond the property for a view of Ol Doinyo Lengai volcano.

Ngare Sero Lake Natron Camp TENTED CAMP $$$
(www.lake-natron-camp.com; per person full board from US$275; P) 🍃 As close as you can sleep to the lake, Lake Natron Camp is wonderfully sited, with tents just back from the shore. The tents are excellent and often strategically placed around natural

plunge pools, and there's a range of activities on offer. The place is at its best when the sun goes down and silence envelopes the lake.

Information

Engaresero Tourism Office (0784 769795; www.engaresero.org; 6am-6.30pm) This community-run tourism office is less about information than organising activities through its **Engaresero Cultural Tourism Program** (0784 769795, 027-205 0025; www.engaresero.org).

Getting There & Away

The road from Mto wa Mbu is partly sandy and partly rocky. During the rainy season you may have to wait a few hours at some of the seasonal rivers before you're able to cross. The road past the lake to Loliondo and into the Serengeti is in better shape because it's used far less. Those continuing this way should carry extra supplies of petrol, since the last proper station is in Mto wa Mbu, though some people sell (expensive) petrol from their homes.

A rickety, crowded bus runs between Arusha and Loliondo, stopping in Engaresero (Tsh27,000, nine hours). It departs Arusha at 6.30am on Sunday and passes back through Engaresero on Thursday around 10am. Trucks (and sometimes 4WDs operating as public transport) run between Mto wa Mbu and Engaresero pretty much daily, but it's not unheard of to have to wait two days to find a ride, especially in the rainy season.

If you're driving from Ngorongoro, you'll need to set out early and count on an entire day to reach Lake Natron – ask at the **Ngorongoro Conservation Area Authority headquarters** (p122) and Nainokanoka ranger post about track conditions.

Karatu

027 / POP 26,600

Roughly halfway between Lake Manyara National Park and Ngorongoro (it's 14km southeast of Lodoare gate), this charmless town set in a beautiful surrounding area makes a convenient base for visiting both. Indeed, many camping safaris out of Arusha overnight here to avoid paying the camping fees in Ngorongoro. Services are basic but include banks that change cash and have ATMs, petrol stations, and several mini supermarkets (although it's better to stock up in Arusha).

Sleeping

Eileen's Trees Inn LODGE $$

(0754 834725, 0783 379526; www.eileenstrees.com; s/d half board from US$75/110; P) This consistently popular place offers accommodation in comfortable adjoining cottages. The rooms are large and come with wooden four-poster beds with mosquito nets, and wrought-iron furnishings in some bathrooms, and the food in the restaurant is well prepared and tasty. The real highlight is the lovely garden – wonderfully silent at night, and filled with birdsong by day.

★ **Manor at Ngorongoro** LODGE $$$

(www.elewanacollection.com; s/d with full board & incl all activities US$1268/1690; P) This exceptional place up in the Ngorongoro foothills north of Karatu has 18 immaculate and classy suites in nine cottages arrayed around leafy, perfectly manicured grounds, with claw-foot bathtubs and furnishings straight from a safari design magazine. It's a beautiful, sophisticated place to spend a few days unwinding in conditions of pure luxury.

★ **Gibb's Farm** LODGE $$$

(027-253 4397; www.gibbsfarm.net; s/d/tr half board US$580/925/1275; P@) The long-standing Gibb's Farm, filling a 1920s farmstead, has a rustic highland ambience, a wonderful setting with views over the nearby coffee plantations, a spa, and beautiful cottages (and a few standard rooms) set around the gardens. The cuisine is made with home-grown organic produce. It's about 5km north of the main road.

Information

MONEY

CRDB, **Exim** and **NBC** banks on the main road have 24-hour ATMs.

TOURIST INFORMATION

The **Ngorongoro Conservation Area Authority Information Office** (www.ngorongorocrater.go.tz; 7.30am-4.30pm Mon-Fri, to 12.30pm Sat & Sun) – about 2km west of Karatu centre in the small complex of shops next to the Bougainvillea petrol station – is the place to go to make arrangements to visit Ngorongoro Crater or elsewhere in the Ngorongoro Conservation Area (NCA), if you don't have a credit card to pay for your entry into the NCA 14km up the road.

Getting There & Away

There are several morning buses between Karatu and Arusha (Tsh7500, three hours), some continuing to Moshi (Tsh11,000, 4½ hours). There are also more comfortable nine-seater minivans to/from Arusha (Tsh8500, three hours) that depart throughout the day. Transport leaves from several spots along the main road.

Lake Eyasi

Uniquely beautiful Lake Eyasi lies at 1030m between the Eyasi escarpment in the north and the Kidero Mountains in the south. Like Lake Natron far to the northeast, Eyasi makes a rewarding detour on a Ngorongoro trip for anyone looking for something remote and different. The lake itself varies considerably in size depending on the rains, and supports a mix of waterbirds including huge breeding-season (June to November) populations of flamingos and pelicans. In the dry season it's little more than a parched lake bed, adding to the rather other-worldly, primeval ambience of the area.

The traditional Hadzabe lend a soulful human presence to the region. Also in the area are the Iraqw (Mbulu), a people of Cushitic origin who arrived about 2000 years ago, and the Datoga, noted metalsmiths whose dress and culture is quite similar to those of the Maasai.

Activities

Lake Eyasi Cultural Tourism Program CULTURAL

(0764 295280; www.tanzaniaculturaltourism.com/dumbe.htm; 8am-6pm) This Cultural Tourism Program, centred on Lake Eyasi, is at the entrance to Ghorofani. Here you can hire English-speaking guides (US$30 per group of up to 10) to visit nearby Hadzabe (an extra US$20 per group) and Datoga communities or the lake. One option is to join the Hadzabe on a hunting trip, for which you'll need to depart before dawn.

Sleeping

Accommodation here is getting better all the time – as more places spring up, the increasingly crowded northeastern shore of the lake may lose a little of its remote feel. There are two tented camps and two lodges, all excellent, along or just back from the shore close to Ghorofani. For budget travellers, there are three very basic guesthouses in Ghorofani and some simple campsites in the area.

★Ziwani Lodge LODGE $$$

(0784 400507; www.ziwanilodge.com; P) Worth every one of its four stars, Ziwani combines faux-Moroccan style with local building materials and the results are stunning. The seven stone-built cottages are stylish, with whitewashed walls, perfectly placed wooden chests and wall decorations. With strong community roots, the lodge offers plenty of opportunities to spend time with the Hadzabe, whether out hunting or on a nature walk.

★Kisima Ngeda TENTED CAMP $$$

(027-254 8715; www.anasasafari.com/kisima-ngeda; camping US$10, s/d half board US$350/475; P) Kisima Ngeda roughly translates as 'spring surrounded by trees': there's a natural spring at the heart of this lakeside property, creating an unexpectedly green and lush oasis of fever trees and doum palms. The seven tents are very comfortable and the cuisine (much of it locally produced, including dairy from the camp's own cows) is excellent. It's signposted 7.5km from Ghorofani.

Tindiga Tented Camp TENTED CAMP $$$

(027-250 6315, 0754 324193; www.moivaro.com; s/d full board US$258/360) Just under 2km from the lakeshore, Tindiga Tented Camp has rustic tents that fit nicely with the overall Lake Eyasi experience – comfortable, but with a sense of being far away from it all.

Getting There & Away

Two daily buses connect Arusha to Barazani, passing Ghorofani (Tsh13,000, 4½ to five hours) on the way. They leave Arusha about 5am and head back about 2pm; you can also catch them in Karatu (Tsh5000, 1½ hours to Ghorofani). There are several passenger-carrying 4WDs to Karatu (Tsh6500; they park at Mbulu junction), departing Ghorofani and other lake towns during the morning and returning throughout the afternoon.

Ngorongoro Conservation Area

Ngorongoro is one of the true wonders of Africa, a lost world of wildlife and singular beauty in the near-perfect crater of a long-extinct volcano. This is one of the most

Ngorongoro Conservation Area

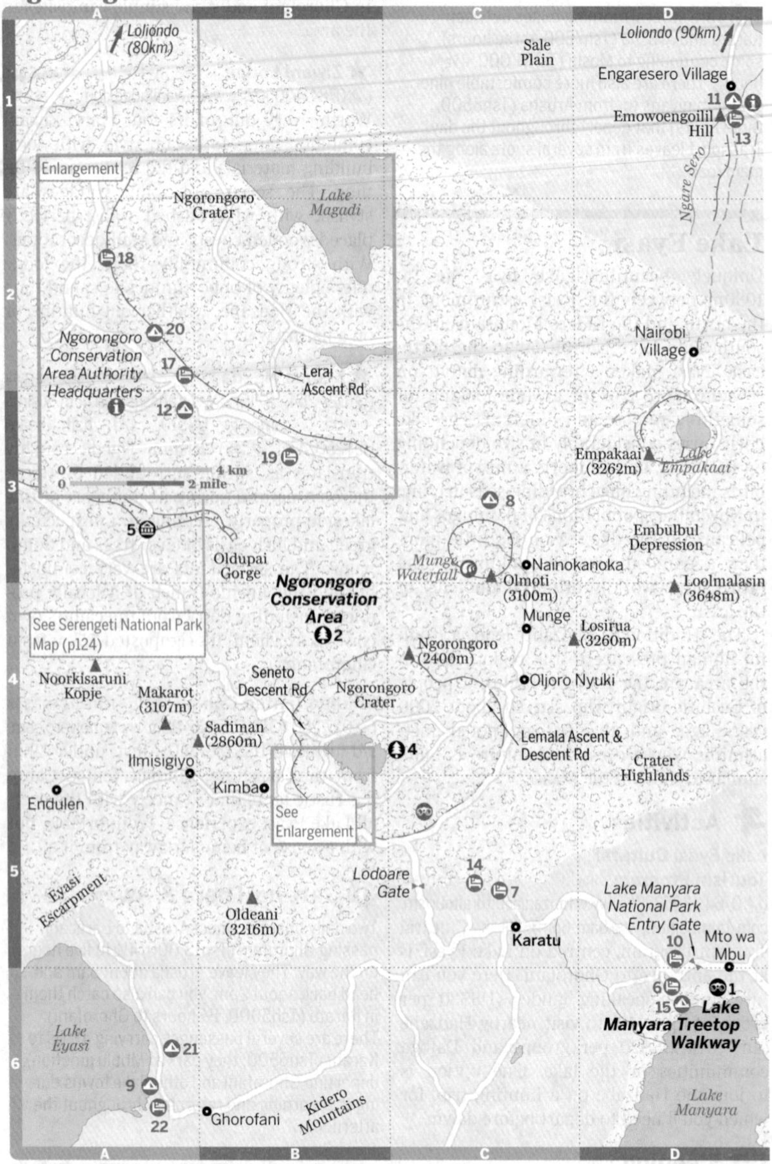

extraordinary places in northern Tanzania and should on no account be missed.

And apart from Ngorongoro Crater, lying within the boundaries of the 8292-sq-km **Ngorongoro Conservation Area** (NCA; ☎027-253 7046, 027-253 7019; www.ngorongorocrater.go.tz; adult/child US$70.80/23.60, crater services fee per vehicle per 24hr US$295; ⏲6am-6pm) are some of northern Tanzania's greatest sights, including Oldupai Gorge and much of the Crater Highlands (although not Ol Doinyo Lengai and Lake Natron).

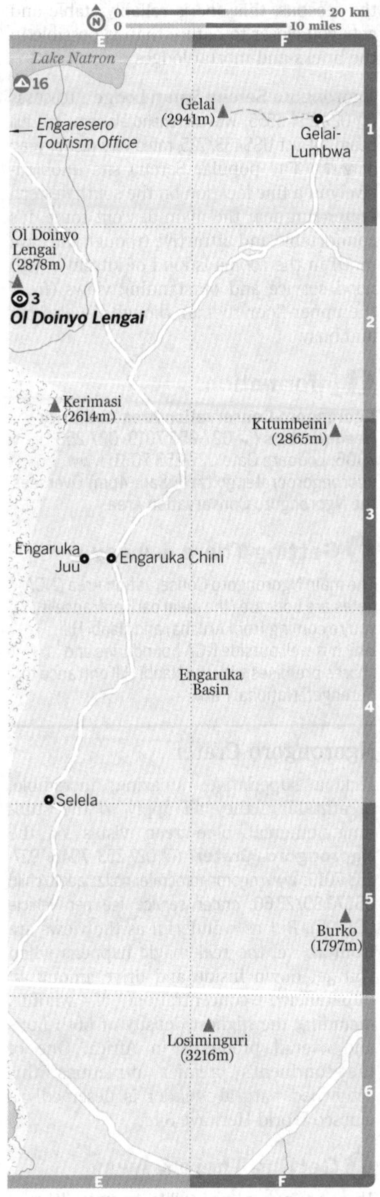

Ngorongoro Conservation Area

Top Sights

1 Lake Manyara Treetop Walkway........ D6
2 Ngorongoro Conservation Area......... B4
3 Ol Doinyo Lengai E2

Sights

Lake Manyara National Park .... (see 1)
4 Ngorongoro Crater C4
5 Oldupai Museum A3

Activities, Courses & Tours

Engaresero Cultural Tourism Program ....(see 11)

Sleeping

6 Escarpment Luxury Lodge................. D6
7 Gibb's Farm...................................... C5
8 Highlands C3
9 Kisima Ngeda................................... A6
10 Lake Manyara Serena Safari Lodge D5
11 Lake Natron Tented Camp D1
12 Lemala Ngorongoro Tented Camp A3
13 Lengai Safari Lodge D1
14 Manor at Ngorongoro C5
15 Migunga Tented Camp D6
16 Ngare Sero Lake Natron Camp E1
17 Ngorongoro Crater Lodge A2
18 Ngorongoro Serena Safari Lodge...... A2
19 Rhino Lodge...................................... B3
20 Simba A Public Campsite A2
21 Tindiga Tented Camp A6
22 Ziwani Lodge..................................... A6

Sleeping & Eating

Simba A Public Campsite CAMPGROUND $

(☎027-253 7019; www.ngorongorocrater.go.tz; camping US$47.20) Ngorongoro's only public campsite is Simba A, up on the crater rim not far from headquarters (p122). It has basic facilities and can get very crowded, so the hot water sometimes runs out. Even so, it's a fine location and by far the cheapest place to stay up on the rim.

Rhino Lodge LODGE $$$

(☎0785 500005; www.ngorongoro.cc; s/d half board US$145/260;) This small, friendly lodge, run by Italians in conjunction with the Maasai community, is one of the cheapest places in the Ngorongoro Conservation Area. The rooms are simple and tidy, and the balconies have fine forest views, often with bushbucks or elephants wandering past. It's arguably the best-value place up here, as long as you don't need a crater view.

★ **Ngorongoro Crater Lodge** LODGE $$$

(☎028-262 1267; www.andbeyond.com; r per person all-inclusive Dec-Feb & Jun-Sep US$1715, rates vary rest of year; P@) Self-described as 'Versailles meets Maasai', this eclectic rim-top lodge (actually three separate lodges) has every luxury you could want. Few spaces lack crater views (even the toilets have them), and the rooms are sophisticated and intimate, with abundant use of wood. This is the place to go for the full Ngorongoro experience of knock-out views and no-expense-spared indulgence.

★**Highlands** TENTED CAMP **$$$**
(www.asiliaafrica.com; per person full board US$359-824) Claiming to be the highest tented camp in the region and with some of the most original tented accommodation in Tanzania, the Highlands is a real treat, combining sweeping Crater Highlands views with blissful isolation. It's a luxurious variation of the dome tent and sits high above Olmoti Crater.

Lemala Ngorongoro Tented Camp TENTED CAMP **$$$**
(☎027-254 8966, 027-254 8952; www.lemalacamp.com; s/d full board Feb & Jun-Oct US$669/978, rates vary rest of year) Beautiful wood-floored safari tents and an attractive bush setting close to the Lemala ascent-descent road make this place an excellent choice. Although some of the other mobile tented camps move with the seasons, this one is reliably stable and gets you closer to nature than is possible in the bricks-and-mortar lodges.

Ngorongoro Serena Safari Lodge LODGE **$$$**
(☎027-254 5555; www.serenahotels.com; s/d full board Jul-Oct US$433/725, rates vary rest of year; P @ ☎) The popular Serena sits unobtrusively in a fine location on the southwestern crater rim near the main descent route. It's comfortable and attractive (though the cave motif in the rooms is kind of kitschy), with good service and outstanding views (from the upper-floor rooms), though it's also big and busy.

ℹ NGORONGORO CONSERVATION AREA

Why Go Extraordinary scenery and fabulous wildlife watching.

When to Go Year-round.

Practicalities Usually visited en route to the Serengeti from Arusha via Karatu. It can get *very* cold on the crater rim, so come prepared. All fees, including those for the crater, are paid at **Lodoare gate**, just south of Ngorongoro Crater on the road from Arusha, or **Naabi Hill gate** on the border with Serengeti National Park. Should you wish to add days or activities to your visit, you can pay fees at the headquarters.

Budget Tips Stay outside the park to avoid camping fees: visit as part of a larger group to reduce your portion of the crater services fee. Even though the US$295 fee to enter the crater is per vehicle, the guards check the number of passengers against the permit, so it's not possible to join up with people you meet at your campsite or lodge once you're inside the Ngorongoro Conservation Area.

ℹ Information

Ngorongoro Conservation Area Authority Headquarters (☎027-253 7019, 027-253 7006, Lodoare Gate 027-253 7031; www.ngorongorocrater.go.tz; ⏲8am-4pm) Oversees the Ngorongoro Conservation Area.

ℹ Getting There & Away

The main Ngorongoro Conservation Area (NCA) gates are Lodoare (the main park entrance if you're coming from Arusha) and Naabi Hill, which is well outside NCA boundaries and shares premises with the Naabi Hill entrance to Serengeti National Park.

Ngorongoro Crater

Pick a superlative: amazing, incredible, breathtaking...they all apply to the stunning, ethereal blue-green vistas of the **Ngorongoro Crater** (☎027-253 7046, 027-253 7019; www.ngorongorocrater.go.tz; adult/child US$70.80/23.60, crater service fee per vehicle US$295). But as wonderful as the views are from above, the real magic happens when you get down inside and drive among an unparalleled concentration of wildlife, including the highest density of both lions and overall predators in Africa. One of the continent's premier attractions, this renowned natural wonder is deservedly a Unesco World Heritage Site.

ℹ Getting There & Away

There's no public transport to the crater. If you aren't travelling on an organised safari and don't have your own vehicle, the easiest thing to do is hire one in Karatu, where most lodges charge from US$160 per day for a 4WD with a pop-up top, including fuel and driver but excluding entry and vehicle fees. Vehicle rental from Mto wa Mbu costs from US$220 per day, including fuel and driver. Note that vehicles with a pop-up top or safari companies without an official licence will not be permitted to enter the Ngorongoro Conservation Area; this usually affects Kenyan companies in particular. Be sure to verify this before making any payments.

Crater access roads:

Seneto Descent only (at the western end of the crater)

Lerai Ascent only (along the crater's southern rim)

Lemala (Sopa) Descent and ascent (eastern end of crater rim)

Getting Around

Only 4WDs are allowed into the crater. The gates open at 6am and close for descent at 4pm; all vehicles must be out of the crater before 6pm. Officially you're only allowed to stay in the crater for a maximum of six hours, but this is rarely enforced. Self-drivers are supposed to hire a park ranger (US$23.60 per vehicle) for the crater where the descent begins, but are sometimes let in without one; note, though, that rangers are getting stricter about enforcing this rule. Petrol is sold at headquarters, but it's cheaper in Karatu.

Oldupai Gorge

Standing near the western rim of the Ngorongoro Crater and looking out towards the west is like contemplating eternity. Table-flat plains stretch towards the Serengeti, with the forbidding Gol Mountains away to the north. Within this landscape, Maasai eke out an existence from the dust of plains where wildlife is wary but present nonetheless – wildebeest, eland, topi, gazelle and zebra herds come here between January and March on the southern stretch of their migration.

But there's more to these plains than meets the eye. Slicing its way through up to 90m of rock and two million years of history, Oldupai (Olduvai) Gorge on the plains northwest of Ngorongoro Crater is a dusty, 48km-long ravine sometimes referred to as the cradle of humankind.

Its unique geological history provides remarkable documentation of ancient life, allowing us to look back to the days of our earliest ancestors.

Sights

Oldupai Museum MUSEUM

(adult/child US$20/10; 7.30am-4.30pm) The small Oldupai Museum on the rim of Oldupai Gorge stands on one of the most significant archaeological sites on earth. It was here in 1959 that Mary Leakey discovered a 1.8-million-year-old ape-like skull from an early hominin (human-like being) now known as *Australopithecus boisei*. This discovery, along with that of fossils of over 60 early hominids (including *Homo habilis* and *Homo erectus*) forever changed the way we understood the dawn of human history. Sadly, the museum is a work in progress.

Getting There & Away

There's no public transport to the site – indeed, you'll often see locals hitchhiking in the area due to the dearth of reliable transport. The gorge is 27km from Ngorongoro Crater's Seneto descent road and 141km from the Serengeti.

> **NGORONGORO FEES**
>
> ➡ If you're transiting through Ngorongoro en route to the Serengeti, you still have to pay the Ngorongoro Conservation Area (NCA) entrance fee.
>
> ➡ Entry fees apply for a 24-hour period. If you enter the NCA at, for example, 10am and you're staying overnight, you must then leave before 10am the next morning to avoid incurring an additional day's fee.
>
> ➡ All entry, camping and crater fees can be paid by credit card at the park gate.

Serengeti National Park

Few people forget their first encounter with the **Serengeti** (028-262 1515, 0767 536125, 0689 062243; www.tanzaniaparks.go.tz; adult/child US$70.80/23.60; 6am-6pm). Perhaps it's the view from Naabi Hill at the park's entrance, from where the grasslands appear to stretch to the ends of the earth. Or maybe it's a coalition of lions stalking across open plains, their manes catching the breeze. Or it could be wildebeest and zebra migrating in their millions, following the ancient rhythm of Africa's seasons. Whatever it is, welcome to one of the greatest wildlife-watching destinations on earth.

At 14,763 sq km, the Serengeti is an epic place, and it's renowned for its predators, especially lions, leopards and cheetahs, with plenty of elephants in residence, too. A few black rhinos around Moru Kopjes

Serengeti National Park

A B C D
1 2 3 4 5 6
Musoma
Lake Victoria
Isuria Escarpment
Ikorongo Hills
Ikorongo Game Reserve
8
2
Grumeti Game Reserve
Bunda
Ruwana River
Ruwana Plain
Sabora Plain
Ndabaka Gate
Ndabaka Plains
3
Kitunge Hills
Grumeti River
Speke Gulf
Handajega Gate
4
Western Corridor
Simiti Hills
Varicho Hills
Musabi Plain
Mwanza (120km)
Dutwa Plains
Serengeti National Park
1
Nyamuma Hills
Kamuyo Hills
10
Makoma Hill
Seronera
Ndoha Plain
Mbalageti River
Serengeti Visitor Centre
Nyaraboro Hills
Maswa
Duma River
Itonjo Hills
Moru Kopjes
Simiyu River

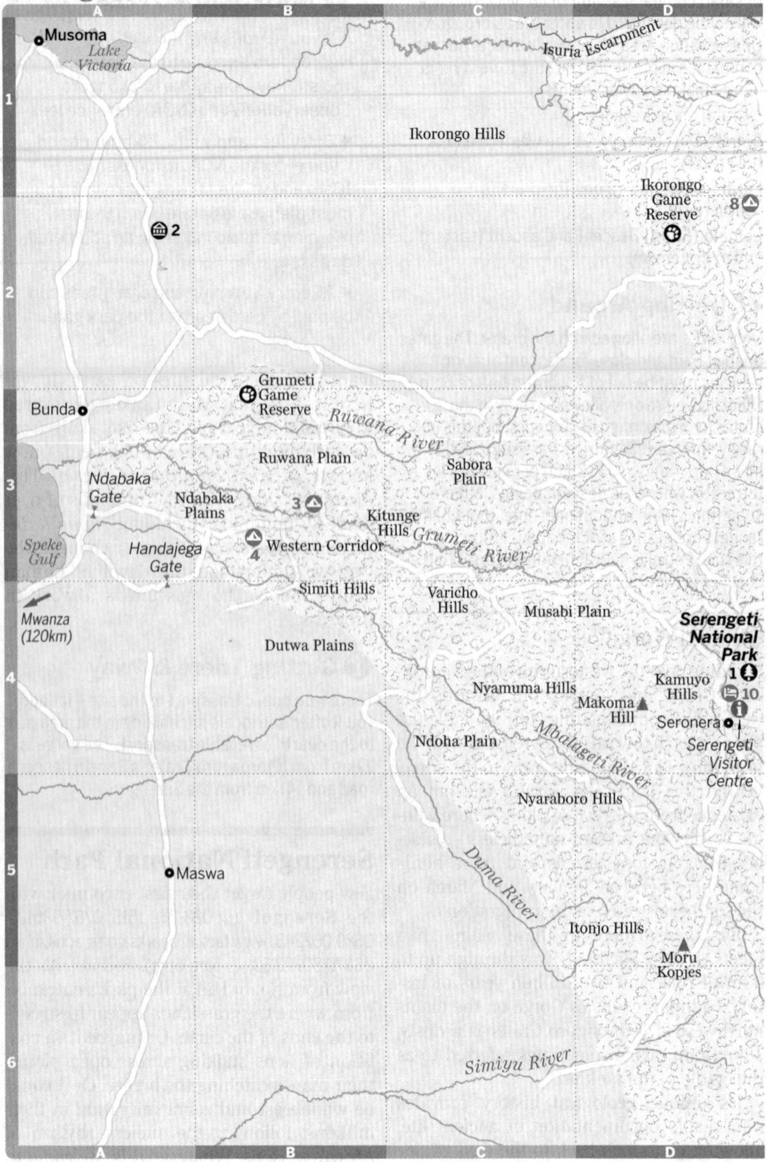

offer a chance to glimpse all of the Big Five (lion, elephant, rhino, leopard and buffalo), although the rhinos are very rarely seen. It's also an incredible birdwatching destination, with over 500 species to spot.

Sights

Seronera & the South

Visiting or staying in Seronera, in the heart of the park and readily accessed from both

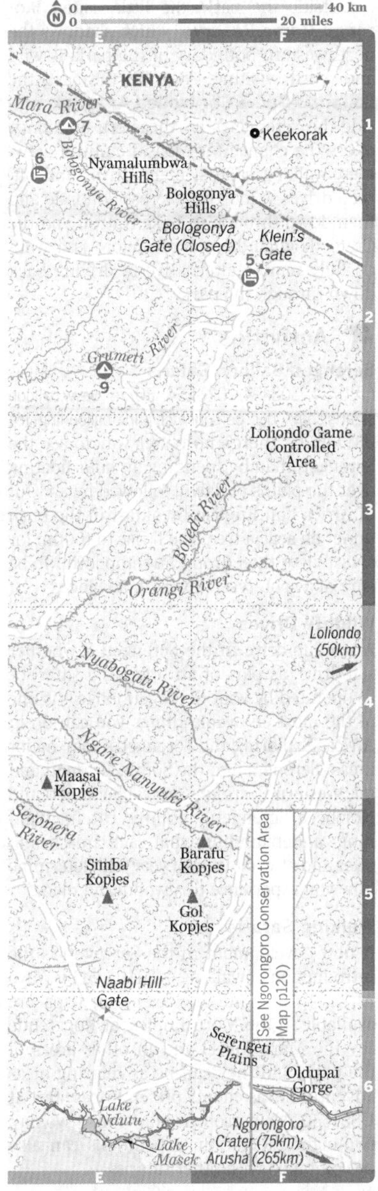

Serengeti National Park

Top Sights
1 Serengeti National Park D4

Sights
2 Mwalimu Julius K Nyerere Museum A2

Activities, Courses & Tours
Serengeti Balloon Safaris ....(see 10)

Sleeping
3 Grumeti Serengeti Tented Camp....... B3
4 Kirawira Camp B3
5 Klein's Camp.......................................F2
6 Lamai Serengeti E1
7 Olakira Camp E1
8 Serengeti Bushtops Camp................. D2
9 Serengeti Migration Camp..................E2
10 Twiga Resthouse D4

Arusha and Mwanza, involves something of a trade-off. On the one hand, this is wildlife central, with sightings of lions (around 300 live in the park's south alone), leopards and cheetahs almost guaranteed. On the other, such abundance comes at a price: you may find yourself among a pack of 20 vehicles jostling in unlovely fashion to look at a single lion.

Southeast of Seronera is a prime base for wildlife watching during the December–April wet season, when it's full of wildebeest. This corner of the Serengeti also has year-round water and a good mix of habitats. Most Seronera safaris concentrate on the **Seronera River** and with good reason: the trees along the riverbank are home to one of the world's densest concentrations of leopards, while lion sightings are common. Lion sightings are also probable around the **Maasai Kopjes**, **Simba Kopjes**, **Moru Kopjes**, **Gol Kopjes** and **Barafu Kopjes**, and around **Makoma Hill**. The vast plains south of the Seronera River, often known simply as the **Serengeti Plains**, are particularly good for cheetahs. The plains that rise towards the **Kamuyo Hills** west of the Seronera River (draw a line west of the Seronera Wildlife Lodge) are particularly good for elephants, spotted hyenas and cheetahs.

Grumeti & the West

The herd migration (p128) usually passes through the Serengeti's Western Corridor, and the contiguous **Grumeti Game Reserve**, sometime between late May and early July. The crossing of the **Grumeti River** may not rival that of the Mara River further north – there are few vantage points and the river is much narrower and easy to cross here – but it's still one of the migration's great spectacles.

SERENGETI NATIONAL PARK

Why Go Wildebeest migration; excellent chance of seeing predators; overall high wildlife density; fine birdwatching; stunning savannah scenery.

When to Go Year-round; July and August for wildebeest migration across the Mara River; February for wildebeest calving; February–May for birdwatching.

Practicalities Drive in from Arusha or Mwanza, or fly in. To avoid congestion, spend some time outside the central Serengeti/Seronera area. Entrance fees can be paid in cash or by credit card at the Naabi Hill, Ndabaka and Klein's gates.

Budget Tips Catch the Arusha–Musoma bus and hope to see something along the way; stay in the public campsites; book a budget safari from Arusha.

During the rest of the year, lions and leopards are prevalent along the forest-fringed Grumeti River, which also has hippos and giant crocodiles. North of the river, try the **Kitunge Hills**, **Ruana Plain** and just about anywhere in the Grumeti Game Reserve, while south of the river concentrate on the **Ndabaka Plains**, **Simiti Hills**, **Dutwa Plains**, **Varicho Hills** and down to the **Mbalageti River**.

These western reaches of the Serengeti are most easily reached from Mwanza. If driving from the Ndabaka gate, count on at least half a day to reach Seronera, at the centre of the park, and more if you stop along the way.

Mara River & the North

Compared with Seronera and the south, the Serengeti's north receives relatively few visitors. It begins with acacia woodlands, where elephants congregate in the dry season, then north of Lobo stretches into vast open plains. The herd migration (p128) usually passes through the western side during August and September and comes down the eastern flank in November.

North of the Grumeti River, the **Bologonya Hills**, **Bologonya River**, **Nyamalumbwa Hills** and **Mara River** are all outstanding. If you're driving from the Mara River to Seronera, allow the best part of a day.

Outside the park, the little-visited **Ikorongo Game Reserve**, which shadows the northwestern boundary of the park, is wild and worth visiting. Away to the east, the **Loliondo Game Controlled Area**, just outside the Serengeti's northeastern boundary, offers the chance for Maasai cultural activities, walking safaris, night drives and off-road drives. A loop east across Loliondo and then down through to Lake Natron and the Crater Highlands or Ngorongoro is a wonderfully remote alternative to driving back down through the park.

Activities

Serengeti Balloon Safaris SAFARI
(☎0784 308494, 027-254 8077; www.balloonsafaris.com; per person incl park ballooning fee US$546.20) There's no better way to see the Serengeti than by spending an hour floating over the plains at dawn, followed by an 'Out of Africa' full English breakfast in the bush under an acacia tree. You'll rise to 1000m for a vast view, then drop to treetop level. To be sure of a spot, reserve well in advance.

Wildlife Drives

A wildlife drive in the Serengeti – whether self-drive, as part of an organised safari or as operated by your Serengeti lodge – is one of the most enjoyable things you can do in Africa. Exploring the Serengeti's four major areas (Seronera and the South, Grumeti and the Western Corridor, Central Serengeti and Northern Serengeti) requires careful planning; understanding what each area has to offer and at what time of year will determine how you experience this wonderful place.

Walking Safaris

A new development in the Serengeti is the introduction of walking safaris. Led by Wayo Africa (p115), multiday camping trips are available in the Moru Kopjes, at Kogatende (by the Mara River) and in other areas of the park, and they can be as relaxing or as adventurous as clients prefer. Prices start at US$1650 per person per day for a two-day, two-night expedition; expeditions can also be combined with other safaris.

Sleeping & Eating

The Serengeti has a full range of sleeping options, from basic campsites with no amenities to top-end luxury lodges and mobile camps that follow the herd migration (p128). Most places within the park are top end, but there are a few more reasonably priced choices, plus several lower-midrange places just outside the park borders.

Twiga Resthouse GUESTHOUSE $$
(☎028-262 1510; www.tanzaniaparks.go.tz; Central Serengeti; r per person US$35.40; P) Twiga offers simple but decent rooms with electricity and hot showers, and satellite TV in the lounge. Guests can use the kitchen, or meals can be cooked for you if you order way in advance. There's a well-stocked little bar and a bonfire at night.

★**Lamai Serengeti** LODGE $$$
(☎0784 208343; www.nomad-tanzania.com; Northern Serengeti; s/d with full board & incl all activities US$1570/2150; ⏲Jun–mid-Mar; P) Built on a kopje near the Mara River in the far-northern Serengeti, Lamai blends into its surroundings so well it's nearly invisible. There are two lodges, one with eight rooms and another with four, each with its own dining areas and swimming pools. All rooms have African-themed decor and soothing earth tones and are open-fronted, with great views.

★**Grumeti Serengeti Tented Camp** TENTED CAMP $$$
(☎028-262 1267; www.andbeyond.com; Western Serengeti; per person with full board & incl all activities US$740-1340; ⏲closed Apr; P) This is one of the best and most luxurious camps in the Serengeti. It mixes its wild location with chic pan-Africa decor and the 10 tents are superluxe. Only three tents have unobstructed views of the Kanyanja River, a prime spot during the herd migration; at other times watch hippos while you lounge in the swimming pool.

Kirawira Camp TENTED CAMP $$$
(☎027-254 5555; www.serenahotels.com; Western Serengeti; s/d with full board Jul-Oct US$636/916, rest of year rates vary; P@) A rare foray by Serena into the world of tented camps, Kirawira makes you wonder why it doesn't do it more often. The camp, ringing a low hill, works a colonial theme with plenty of antiques and polished-wood floors. The tents have big porches and very un-tent-like bathrooms. Guests rave about the food.

THE SERENGETI LION PROJECT

The Serengeti Lion Project is widely considered to be the second-longest-running continuous scientific study of a species in Africa; Jane Goodall's study of chimpanzees in Gombe Stream National Park is the only study to have lasted longer.

And it is from the Serengeti Lion Project that we have learned much of what we know about lions – why they form prides, why they roar, and so on. It all began back in 1966 with Dr George Schaller, now one of the world's most respected wildlife scientists, who wrote what remains the seminal text on lion behaviour: *The Serengeti Lion*.

All the subsequent heads of the project have written books, and it is one of these, Craig Packer's *Lions in the Balance*, that almost sounded the project's death knell. Packer's ongoing criticism of the relationship between the Tanzanian government and the trophy-hunting industry would ultimately lead to Packer's expulsion from the country. For three years, the Serengeti Lion Project barely functioned, and there were fears that the project would fall into the wrong hands or perhaps even come under the aegis of the trophy-hunting industry itself. In the end, in June 2017 responsibility for the project was handed to respected lion scientists Bernard Kissui and Mike Anderson. It now appears likely that the project will continue, at least for the foreseeable future.

The heads of the project and the books they wrote about their experiences are as follows:

George Schaller (1966–69) *The Serengeti Lion* (1972)

Brian Bertram (1969–74) *Pride of Lions* (1978)

Jeannette Hanby and David Bygott (1974–78) *Lion's Share: The Story of a Serengeti Pride* (1982)

Craig Packer (1978–2014) *Into Africa* (1994) and *Lions in the Balance: Man-Eaters, Manes, and Men With Guns* (2015)

Although not specifically relating to lions, Anthony Sinclair's *Serengeti Story: Life and Science in the World's Greatest Wildlife Region* (2012) is also worth tracking down.

FOLLOW THE MIGRATION

You've come to see the wildebeest migration, but how can you be sure to be there when it happens? The short answer is that you can't, and making the decision of when to go where always involves some element of risk. What follows is a general overview of what usually happens, but it's a guide only:

January–March During the rains, the wildebeest are widely scattered over the southern and southwestern section of the Serengeti and the western side of Ngorongoro Conservation Area.

April Most streams dry out quickly when the rains cease, nudging the wildebeest to concentrate on the few remaining green areas, and to form thousands-strong herds that begin to migrate northwest in search of food.

May–early July In early May, the herds cross northwest towards the Western Corridor, and the crossing of the crocodile-filled Grumeti River usually takes place between late May and early July, and lasts only about a week.

Mid-July–August By the second half of July, the herds are moving north and northwest into the northern Serengeti and Kenya's Masai Mara. As part of this northwards push, they make an even more incredible crossing of the Mara River.

September and October In early September, the last stragglers leave the Serengeti and most will remain in the Masai Mara throughout October.

November and December The herds usually begin moving south again in November in anticipation of the rains, crossing down through the heart of the Serengeti and to the south in December.

Exceptions to these general guidelines are common. In November 2013, for example, it began raining in the Masai Mara when the herds had already crossed back into Tanzania, prompting the wildebeest to return en masse to the Mara. There they remained for three weeks before resuming their southwards push. And in June 2014, unseasonal rains in the southern Serengeti prompted the herd to split in two – most continued north as usual, but a significant number of zebras and wildebeest occupied the plains south of Seronera into July.

Indeed, it's becoming increasingly rare for the herd to remain in one group. In 2017 the herds were still in the far south well into April. When they did finally move north, one group headed all the way up to Kenya and were already crossing the Sand River into Kenya's Masai Mara in early June. The remainder followed a more traditional path into the Western Corridor, but even this group was beginning to gather in the Serengeti's north by late June.

★ **Olakira Camp** TENTED CAMP **$$$**
(☎0736 500156; www.asiliaafrica.com; Northern Serengeti; per person with full board & incl all activities Jul & Aug US$929, rest of year rates vary; ⏱Jun–mid-Nov; P 📶) 🍃 Olakira's northern location is one of the Serengeti's finest, with long-distance views down towards Mara River crossing 8, 500m away – one of the busiest during the herd migration – and close to the lively junction between the Mara and Bologonya Rivers. The nine tents are large and beautifully set up and the whole place runs on solar power.

★ **Serengeti Bushtops Camp** TENTED CAMP **$$$**
(www.bushtopscamps.com; Northern Serengeti; s/d with full board & incl all activities US$1250/1800; P @ 📶 🏊) In a remote corner of the northern Serengeti, close to the boundary with the Ikorongo Game Reserve, this remarkable camp has large permanent tents with expansive wooden floors, decks with a spa bath, perfectly placed sofas and fabulous views. Many Serengeti lodges are luxurious, but this place is simply magnificent. The food is similarly excellent.

★ **Serengeti Migration Camp** TENTED CAMP **$$$**
(☎027-250 0630; www.elewanacollection.com; Northern Serengeti; s/d with full board Jul-Oct US$1268/1690, rest of year rates vary; P 📶 🏊) One of the most highly regarded places in the Serengeti, this camp has 20 large, stunning tents with decks, set around a kopje by

the Grumeti River where it passes through the north (not the Western Corridor). A tent's immersion in its surroundings is perfectly blended with the luxury of permanence here. You'll have front-row seats when the herd migration passes through.

Lemala Serengeti TENTED CAMP **$$$**
(www.lemalacamp.com; s/d with full board & incl all activities US$1110/1700) Another leader in mobile-camp comforts in the Serengeti, Lemala has a camp in Ndutu from December to March and one close to the Mara River from July to October. Its formula is simple and compelling – make the camps look as permanent as possible, but with the flexibility to move them when the time is right. Expect luxury and high service standards.

Klein's Camp LODGE **$$$**
(☎028-262 1267; www.andbeyond.com; Northern Serengeti; per person with full board & incl all activities US$840-1340; P 📶 🏊) This classic Serengeti lodge is exclusive and strikingly situated (the views are awesome) on a private concession just outside the northeastern park boundary. There are 10 luxurious stone-and-thatch cottages, and the chance to enjoy bushwalks, night wildlife drives or a relaxing massage.

ℹ Information

Serengeti Visitor Centre (serengeti@tanzaniaparks.go.tz; ⏲8am-5pm) This office at Seronera has a self-guided walk through the Serengeti's history and ecosystems, and it's well worth spending time here before exploring the park. The gift shop sells various basic booklets and maps, and there's a coffee shop with snacks and cold drinks. A new media centre was under construction in mid-2017.

ℹ Getting There & Away

The park has three main entry and exit points, plus two lesser-used gates at Handajega and Fort Ikoma, and the disused Bologonya gate; this gate would be on the route to/from Kenya's Masai Mara National Reserve, but the border is closed and unlikely to open any time soon.

Naabi Hill gate The main (and most heavily trafficked) access gate if you're coming from Arusha; 45km from Seronera, in the central Serengeti.

Ndabaka gate Main gate for the Western Corridor; a 1½-hour drive from Mwanza and 145km from Seronera. Last entry at 4pm.

Klein's gate In the far northeast, Klein's gate allows a loop trip combining the Serengeti, Ngorongoro and Lake Natron, the latter just two to three hours from the park. Last entry at 4pm.

AIR

Air Excel (p107), Coastal Aviation (p107) and Regional Air (p107) have daily flights from Arusha to the park's seven airstrips, including Seronera and Grumeti.

BUS

Although it's not ideal, shoestring travellers can do their wildlife watching through the window of the Arusha–Musoma buses that cross the park, but you'll need to pay entrance fees for Serengeti and Ngorongoro. The buses stop at the staff village at Seronera, but you're not allowed to walk or hitchhike to the campsites or rest houses, and the park has no vehicles for hire, so unless you've made prior transport arrangements it's nearly pointless to get off here.

CAR & MOTORCYCLE

Driving is not permitted in the park after 7pm, except in the visitor-centre area, where the cut-off is 9pm. Petrol is sold at Seronera. Almost everyone explores the park in a 4WD, but except during the heaviest rains 2WDs will have no problems on the main roads and can even manage some of the secondary ones.

Moshi

☎027 / POP 184,300

The noticeably clean capital of the densely populated Kilimanjaro region sits at the foot of Mt Kilimanjaro and makes a good introduction to the splendours of the north. It's a low-key place with an appealing blend of African and Asian influences and a self-sufficient, prosperous feel, due in large part to its being the centre of one of Tanzania's major coffee-growing regions. Virtually all visitors are here to climb Mt Kilimanjaro or to recover after having done so. Yet there's much more to do, including cultural tours and hikes on the mountain's lower slopes.

Activities & Tours

The main activity is preparing for your Kilimanjaro ascent, but to take the easy way out – and for superlative views – try a scenic flight that gets you up close and personal with the mountain from the air. Look for flyers, ask at your hotel, or try **Coastal Aviation** (☎0785 500729, 0785 500445; www.coastal.co.tz; Arusha Rd; ⏲8.30am-5pm Mon-Fri, to noon Sat).

Moshi

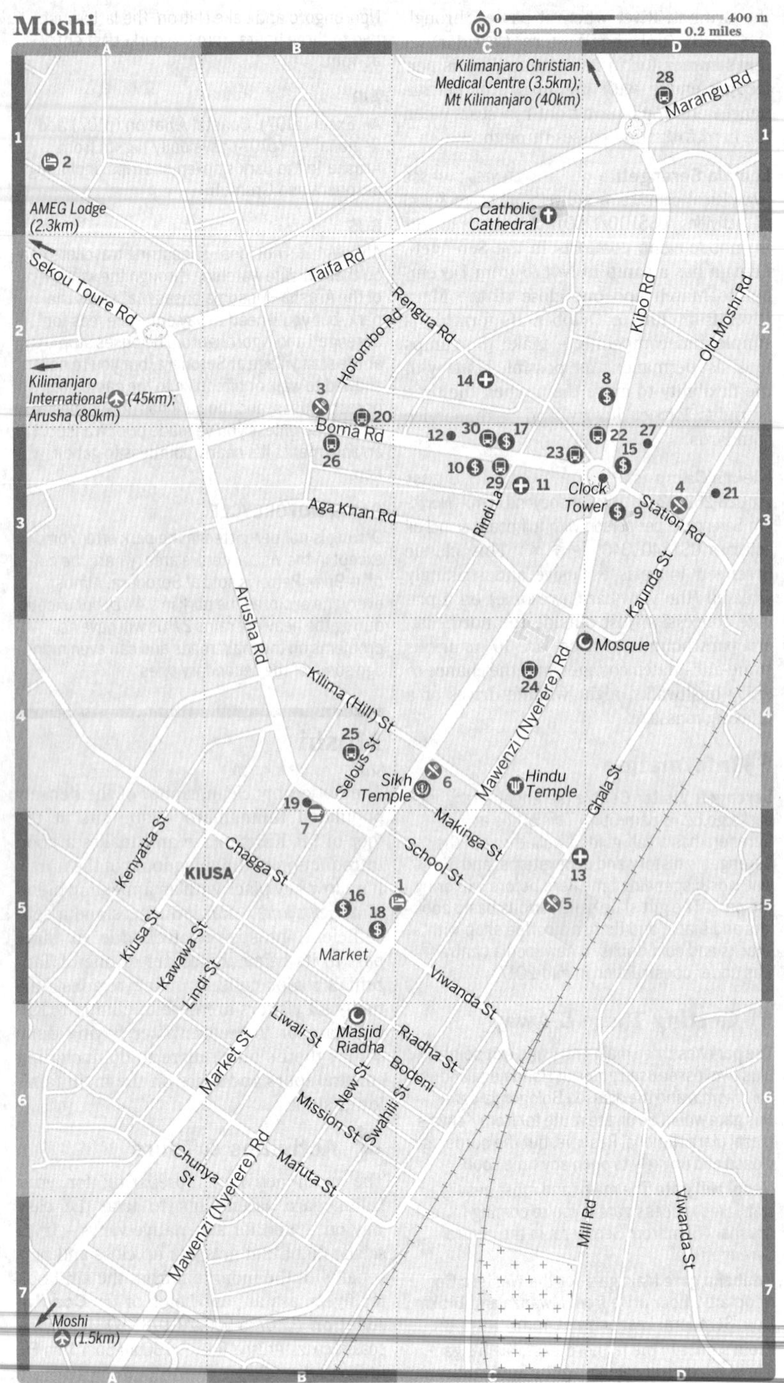
0 400 m
0 0.2 miles
Kilimanjaro Christian Medical Centre (3.5km); Mt Kilimanjaro (40km)
AMEG Lodge (2.3km)
Kilimanjaro International (45km); Arusha (80km)
Moshi (1.5km)
Marangu Rd
Catholic Cathedral
Taifa Rd
Sekou Toure Rd
Rengua Rd
Horombo Rd
Kibo Rd
Old Moshi Rd
Boma Rd
Aga Khan Rd
Rindi La
Clock Tower
Station Rd
Kaunda St
Mosque
Arusha Rd
Kilima (Hill) St
Mawenzi (Nyerere) Rd
Selous St
Sikh Temple
Hindu Temple
Ghala St
Makinga St
School St
Kenyatta St
KIUSA
Chagga St
Kiusa St
Kawawa St
Lindi St
Market
Viwanda St
Liwali St
Masjid Riadha
Riadha St
Bodeni
Market St
New St
Swahili St
Mission St
Chunya St
Mafuta St
Mill Rd
Viwanda St
Mawenzi (Nyerere) Rd

Moshi

Sleeping
1 Haria Hotel ... C5
2 Hibiscus ... A1

Eating
3 Jay's Kitchen ... B2
4 Kilimanjaro Coffee Lounge ... D3
5 Peppers ... C5
6 The Coffee Shop ... C4

Drinking & Nightlife
7 Union Café ... B5

Information
8 Classic Bureau de Change ... D2
9 CRDB Bank ... D3
10 Exim Bank ... C3
11 First Health CRCT Hospital ... C3
12 Immigration Office ... C3
13 Jaffery Charitable Medical Services ... C5
14 Kemi Pharmacy ... C2
15 NBC Bank ATM ... D3
16 NBC Bank ATM ... B5
17 Stanbic Bank ... C3
18 Trast Bureau de Change ... B5

Transport
19 Coastal Aviation ... B4
20 Dar Express ... B2
21 Fastjet ... D3
22 Impala Shuttle ... D3
23 Kilimanjaro Express ... C3
24 Main Bus Station ... C4
25 Metro Express ... B4
26 Mtei Express ... B3
27 Precision Air ... D3
28 Rainbow Shuttle ... D1
29 Riverside Shuttle ... C3
30 Tahmeed Coach ... C3

★ Kahawa Shambani Coffee Tours TOURS
(☎0782 324121; www.kilimanculturaltourism.com/coffee-tour; per person Tsh40,000, transport from Moshi Tsh60,000) With the most popular coffee tour in town, Kahawa Shambani is a laudable community-run venture that not only shows you how beans are grown, picked and roasted but also offers insight into the lives of the Chagga coffee farmers who live on Kilimanjaro's lower slopes. Meals with local families can be arranged, as can additional village and waterfall walks.

Sleeping

★ Hibiscus B&B $
(☎0766 312516; www.thehibiscusmoshi.com; Paris St; s/tw US$30/40;) This cosy B&B has spotless, nicely decorated rooms, all with fan and most with private bathroom, plus a pleasant garden and meals on request. It's in a quiet residential area just northwest of the town centre off Arusha Rd.

★ Haria Hotel HOTEL $
(☎0656 318841; www.hariahotel.com; Mawenzi Rd; r US$35, dm/d with shared bathroom US$10/25;) This laid-back, switched-on place has simple, spacious rooms and a friendly overall feel. The rooftop restaurant-bar serves a good menu of local meals at fair prices with Kili views. It's run by Team Vista (www.teamvista.com.au), and profits go to support its work in the community.

★ AMEG Lodge LODGE $$
(☎027-275 0175, 0754 058268; www.ameglodge.com; s/d from US$82/106, s/d ste US$135/159;) This friendly place wins plaudits from travellers for its lovely setting in 2 hectares of manicured gardens with palm trees and frangipanis, 4km northwest of the centre, off Lema Rd. Attractive rooms with broad verandahs and plenty of space lie dotted around the compound, service is friendly, and the feel is that of a rural oasis on the city fringe.

Eating

★ Kilimanjaro Coffee Lounge CAFE $$
(☎0754 610892; Station Rd; meals Tsh8000-16,000; 8am-9pm Mon-Sat, 10am-8pm Sun;) This cafe's semi-garden setting is back a bit from the road, bringing a semblance of peace, and the food ranges from pizza and Mexican dishes to salads, sandwiches, burgers and steaks, alongside excellent milkshakes and juices. There are the makings of a travellers' classic here, although hopefully it's stopped charging for wi-fi by the time you arrive.

★ Peppers INDIAN $$
(☎0754 058268, 027-275 2473; Ghala St; mains Tsh12,000-16,000; noon-3pm & 6-10pm Tue-Sun;) Changes of ownership and name (it used to be called the Sikh Club) have done this place the world of good. It's part restaurant serving excellent Indian food

(which gets the nod from the local Indian community) and part sports bar for those who like their action on the high screen. There's a pleasant terrace overlooking the football pitch.

Jay's Kitchen KOREAN **$$**
(☎0765 311618, 0768 607456; www.facebook.com/JaysAdventureTanzania; Boma Rd; meals Tsh8000-20,000; ⊙11am-9pm Wed-Mon) Jay's boasts tasty Korean food and sushi, a central location and good garden seating. Also offers takeaway.

ℹ Information

MEDICAL SERVICES

First Health CRCT Hospital (☎027-54051; Rindi Lane) City-centre hospital; no emergency department.

Jaffery Charitable Medical Services (☎027-275 1843; Ghala St; ⊙8am-7pm Mon-Fri, to 6pm Sat, 9am-noon Sun) Medical clinic with Moshi's most reliable laboratory.

Kemi Pharmacy (☎027-275 1560; Rengua Rd; ⊙7.30am-7.30pm Mon-Sat, 11am-4pm Sun) One of numerous pharmacies dotted around the city centre.

Kilimanjaro Christian Medical Centre (☎027-275 4377/80; www.kcmc.ac.tz; ⊙24hr) Around 4.5km north of the centre, off Sokoine Rd.

MONEY

There are numerous ATMs scattered around the central part of Moshi, including several along Boma Rd. **Exim Bank** and **Stanbic Bank** (⊙8.30am-3.30pm Mon-Fri, to noon Sat) both have ATMs on Boma Rd; NBC Bank has 24-hour ATMs, including on **Market St** and the **Clock Tower roundabout**.

CRDB (⊙8.30am-4pm Mon-Fri, to 1pm Sat), also on the roundabout, has an efficient exchange counter. Private exchange bureaus include **Classic** (Kibo Rd; ⊙8am-4pm) and **Trast** (Chagga St; ⊙9am-5pm Mon-Sat, to 2pm Sun).

TOURIST INFORMATION

There's no tourist office in Moshi. **The Coffee Shop** (☎027-275 2707; Kilima St; mains Tsh5000-7000; ⊙7.30am-9.30pm Mon-Sat; 📶), **Kilimanjaro Coffee Lounge** (p131) and **Union Café** (☎027-275 2785, 0784 590184; Arusha Rd; ⊙7.30am-8.30pm; 📶) have message boards, and people seeking climbing partners sometimes post requests on them. **Kiliweb** (www.kiliweb.com) is another info option.

ℹ Getting There & Away

AIR

Kilimanjaro International Airport (KIA) is 50km west of town, halfway to Arusha. The standard taxi fare to/from Moshi is Tsh50,000, although drivers will often request more. There's also the small Moshi airport just southwest of town along the extension of Market St (Tsh5000 by taxi to central hotels), which handles Coastal Aviation flights and occasional charters.

Coastal Aviation (p129) Flies daily to and from Moshi airport (if there are enough passengers) on the Arusha–Tanga–Pangani–Pemba–Zanzibar–Dar es Salaam circuit, with links also possible to the northern national parks.

Fastjet (☎0784 108900; www.fastjet.com; Kaunda St) Daily flights between KIA and Dar es Salaam, with onward connections across Tanzania and East Africa.

Precision Air (☎027-275 3495, 0787 800820; www.precisionairtz.com; Old Moshi Rd; ⊙8am-5pm Mon-Fri, 9am-1pm Sat & Sun) Flies from KIA to Dar es Salaam, Zanzibar Island and Mwanza.

BUS

Buses and minibuses run throughout the day to Arusha (Tsh3000, two hours) and Marangu (Tsh1500 to Tsh2200, 1½ hours).

The **bus station** (Market St) is conveniently located in the middle of the city. There are many touts, and arrivals can be quite annoying if you're new to this sort of thing. This is one good reason to travel with bus companies that have their own offices (many are located along Boma Rd and near the Clock Tower roundabout). It's best to buy tickets the day before you plan to travel.

All of the following buses use their own offices rather than the bus station. Ordinary buses and a few less-reliable luxury companies use the bus station.

Dar Express (Boma Rd) Daily departures to Dar es Salaam (Tsh36,000, seven to eight hours) from 7am to noon aboard full luxury buses (with air-con and toilets). The 7am bus sometimes arrives early enough for you to catch the afternoon ferry to Zanzibar, but don't count on it.

Kilimanjaro Express (Rengua Rd) Morning luxury departures to Dar (from Tsh33,000).

Metro Express (☎0715 113344; Selous St) Two daily departures (luxury/full luxury Tsh33,000/36,000) for Dar at 8am.

Mtei Express (Boma Rd) Buses to Babati (Tsh10,000, four to five hours), Singida (Tsh20,000, nine hours) and Dodoma (Tsh28,000, 12 to 14 hours) via Arusha.

Tahmeed Coach (www.tahmeedcoach.co.ke; Boma Rd) One bus daily to Mombasa (Tsh20,000, eight hours).

There are also several shuttle companies with daily services to and from Nairobi (Kenya) via Arusha for around US$40 per person. These include the reliable **Impala Shuttle** (0754 293119, 0754 360658; Kibo Rd; 6.30am & 11.30am), as well as **Riverside Shuttle** (027-275 0093; www.riverside-shuttle.com; YWCA Bldg, Boma Rd; 6am & 11.30am) and **Rainbow Shuttle** (0784 204025; 6am & 11am).

Marangu

027 / POP 23,000

Nestled on the lower slopes of Mt Kilimanjaro, 40km northeast of Moshi amid dense stands of banana and coffee plants, is the lively, leafy market town of Marangu. It has an agreeable highland ambience, a cool climate and a good selection of hotels, all of which organise treks. While you'll sometimes get slightly better budget deals in Moshi, Marangu makes a convenient launch pad for Kili climbs using the Marangu or Rongai routes, and it's an enjoyable stop in its own right. Apart from anything else, there's a real sense of being up in the foothills here, which adds to the pre-Kili excitement and aids psychological preparation.

Marangu is also the heartland of the Chagga people, and there are many possibilities for walks and cultural activities. *Marangu* means 'place of water', and the surrounding area is laced with small streams and waterfalls (most with a small entry charge for visitors).

Sights & Activities

Both **Banana Jungle Lodge** (0713 780464, 027-275 6565; camping per student/nonstudent US$5/10, s/d/tr US$55/65/80; P) and **Kilimanjaro Mountain Resort** (0754 693461; www.kilimountresort.com; camping with own/hired tents US$20/35, s/d/tr half board US$172/260/398; P@) have authentic scale models of traditional Chagga houses. About 6km southwest of Marangu is Ngangu Hill, with views and the small, old Kilema mission church nearby.

Day hikes as far as Mandara Hut (10km one way; allow around three hours up and 1½ hours back) in Mt Kilimanjaro National Park can be arranged with Marangu-area hotels and trekking operators.

Sleeping & Eating

Babylon Lodge LODGE $$
(0762 016016, 027-275 6355; www.babylonlodge.com; s/d/tr US$50/70/80; P@) Friendly Babylon has straightforward, clean twin- and double-bedded rooms clustered around small, attractive gardens. It's often somewhat more flexible than other properties about negotiating Kilimanjaro trek packages, and staff are very helpful as you sort out arrivals and departures via public transport. It's 700m east of the town's main junction.

Lake Chala Safari Lodge & Campsite CAMPGROUND, LODGE $$$
(Map p306; 0786 111177, 0753 641087; www.lakechalasafarilodge.com; camping with own/hired tents US$10/30, s/d half board US$140/200, day visit US$5; P) If you're looking for something remote and relaxing, this eco-camp overlooking its namesake caldera lake by the Kenyan border could be perfect. It has attractive facilities (including a restaurant and cooking area) and a lovely location, ideal for walks, birdwatching or just chilling. The roomy tents are warm and luxurious, and the vantage point on a rise above the lake is terrific.

Lake Chala lies about 30km southeast of Marangu; continue east past the Marangu turn-off, then go left at the Lake Chala signpost.

Marangu Hotel LODGE $$$
(027-275 6594, 0754 886092; www.maranguhotel.com; camping US$10, s/d/tr half board US$120/200/275;) This long-standing hotel is the first place you reach as you come from Moshi. It has a cosy and appealing old-world ambience, pleasant rooms in expansive, flowering grounds, lovely gardens, and a campground with hot-water showers. Room prices are discounted if you join one of the hotel's fully equipped climbs.

Information

CRDB (8am-4pm Mon-Fri, to midnight Sat) ATM; about 20m south of the main Marangu junction.

NBC (8.30am-4pm Mon-Fri, to midnight Sat) ATM; just uphill from the main junction.

Getting There & Away

Minibuses run throughout the day between Moshi and Marangu's main junction (Marangu Mtoni; Tsh1500 to Tsh2200, 1½ hours). Once you're in Marangu, there are sporadic pick-ups

TREKKING MT KILIMANJARO

When to Climb

Mt Kilimanjaro can be climbed at any time of year, though weather patterns are notoriously erratic and difficult to predict. Overall, the best time for climbing the mountain is in the dry season, from late June to October, and from late December to February or early March, just after the short rains and before the long rains. During November and March/April, it's more likely that paths through the forest will be slippery, and that routes up to the summit, especially the Western Breach, will be covered by snow. That said, you can also have a streak of beautiful sunny days during these times.

Climbing Conditions & Equipment

Conditions on the mountain are frequently very cold and wet, and you'll need a full range of waterproof cold-weather clothing and gear, including a good-quality sleeping bag. It's also worth carrying some additional sturdy water bottles. No matter what the time of year, waterproof everything, especially your sleeping bag, as things rarely dry on the mountain. It's often possible to rent sleeping bags and gear from trekking operators. For the Marangu route, you can also rent gear from the Kilimanjaro Guides Cooperative Society stand just inside Marangu gate, or from a small no-name shop just before the gate. However, especially at the budget level, quality and availability can't be counted on, and it's best to bring your own.

Apart from a small shop at Marangu gate selling a limited range of chocolate bars and tinned items, there are no shops inside the park. You can buy (steeply priced) beer and soft drinks at huts on the Marangu route.

Costs

Kilimanjaro can only be climbed with a licensed guide, and it's recommended that you organise your climb through a tour company. No-frills four-night/five-day treks up the Marangu route start at about US$1500, including park fees and taxes, and no-frills six-day budget treks on the Machame route start at around US$1900. Prices start at about US$1500 on the Rongai route, and about US$2000 for a seven-day trek on the Shira Plateau route. For other routes, the starting points are further from Moshi and transport costs can be significant, so clarify whether they're included in the price.

Most of the better companies provide dining tents, decent-to-good cuisine and various other extras to make the experience more enjoyable and to maximise your chances of getting to the top. If you choose a really cheap trip, you risk inadequate meals, mediocre guides, few comforts, and problems with hut bookings and park fees. Try not to skimp on supplies and other essential elements, as this may compromise your safety. Also remember that an environmentally responsible trek usually costs more.

from the main junction to the Kilimanjaro park gate (Tsh1600), 5km further. For the Holili border crossing to Kenya, change at Himo junction.

If you're travelling to Marangu via public bus from Arusha or Dar es Salaam, ask the driver to drop you at Himo junction, from where frequent dalla-dallas go to Marangu junction (Tsh1200).

Mt Kilimanjaro National Park

Whether you come to climb it or simply to gaze in awe at this remarkable, snowcapped equatorial mountain, drawing near to Mt Kilimanjaro is one of *the* great experiences of African travel. And for once in Tanzania, visiting **Mt Kilimanjaro National Park** (☎027-275 6602; www.tanzaniaparks.go.tz; adult/child US$82.60/23.60; ⏰gates 6.30am-6.30pm, headquarters 8am-5pm), the protected area that surrounds the mountain, is not about the wildlife.

At the heart of the park is the 5896m Mt Kilimanjaro, Africa's highest mountain and one of the continent's most magnificent sights. It's also one of the world's highest volcanoes, and the highest free-standing mountain on earth, rising from cultivated farmlands on the lower slopes, through lush rainforest to alpine meadows, and finally across a lunar landscape to the twin summits of Kibo and Mawenzi.

Whatever you pay for your trek, remember that the following park fees are not negotiable and should be part of any quote from your operator:

National Park entry fees US$82.60 per adult per day

Hut/camping fees US$70.80/59 per person per night

Rescue fee US$23.60 per person per trip

Other costs vary depending on the company, which should handle food, tents (if required), guides and porters, and transport to/from the trailhead; tips are additional.

Practicalities

Park entry gates include Machame, Marangu (the site of park headquarters), Londorosi and several other points; trekkers using the Rongai route should pay their fees at Marangu gate. You must pay at least six days' worth of park fees for all routes except Marangu (five-day minimum).

Tipping

Most guides and porters receive only minimal wages from the trekking companies and depend on tips as their major source of income. As a guideline, plan on tipping about 10% of the total amount you've paid for the trek, divided up among the guides and porters. Common tips for satisfactory service are from about US$10 to US$15 per group per day for the guide, US$8 to US$10 per group per day for the cook and US$5 to US$10 per group per day for each porter.

Guides & Porters

Guides, and at least one porter (for the guide), are obligatory and are provided by your trekking company. You can carry your own gear on the Marangu route, although porters are generally used, but one or two porters per trekker are essential on all other routes.

All guides must be registered with the national-park authorities. If in doubt, check that your guide's permit is up to date. On Kili, the guide's job is to show you the way and that's it. Only the best guides, working for reputable companies, will be able to tell you about wildlife, flowers or other features on the mountain.

Porters will carry bags weighing up to 15kg (not including their own food and clothing, which they strap to the outside of your bag), and your bags will be weighed before you set off.

Maps

Topographical maps include *Map & Guide to Kilimanjaro* by Andrew Wielochowski and *Kilimanjaro Map & Guide* by Mark Savage. The hand-drawn *New Map of the Kilimanjaro National Park* is evocative for an overview but of no real use for trekking detail.

Kilimanjaro's third volcanic cone, Shira, is on the mountain's western side. The lower rainforest is home to many animals, including buffaloes, elephants, leopards and monkeys, and elands are occasionally seen in the saddle area between Kibo and Mawenzi.

A hike up Kili lures around 25,000 trekkers each year, in part because it's possible to walk to the summit without ropes or technical climbing experience. Non-technical, however, does not mean easy. The climb is a serious (and expensive) undertaking, and only worth doing with the right preparation. There are also many opportunities to explore the mountain's lower slopes and to learn about the Maasai and the Chagga, two of the main tribes in the area.

If you're interested in reaching the top, seriously consider adding at least one extra day on to the 'standard' climb itineraries. Although the extra US$150 to US$300 may seem a lot when you're planning your trip, it will seem insignificant later on if you've gone to the expense and effort of starting a trek and then can't reach the top. Don't feel bad about insisting on an extra day with the trekking companies: standard medical advice is to increase sleeping altitude by only 300m per day once you're above 3000m; this is about a third of the

Kilimanjaro Area

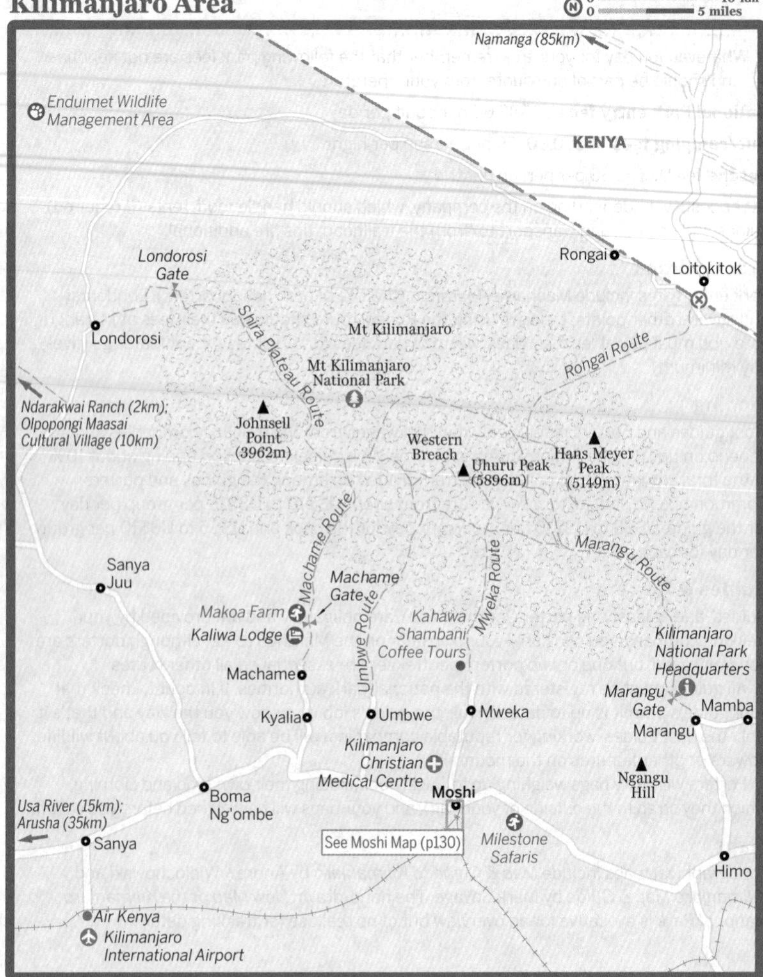

daily altitude gains above 3000m on the standard Kili-climb routes offered by most operators. Also keep in mind that trekkers spend about eight to nine days reaching Mt Everest base camp, which is approximately 500m lower than the summit of Mt Kilimanjaro.

Activities

There are seven main trekking routes to the summit. Trekkers on all but the Marangu route must use tents.

Officially, a limit of 60 climbers per route per day is in effect on Kilimanjaro. It's not always enforced, except on the Marangu route, which is self-limiting because of maximum hut capacities.

Marangu Route

A trek on this route is typically sold as a four-night, five-day return package, although at least one extra night is highly recommended to help you acclimatise, especially if you've just flown into Tanzania or arrived from the lowlands.

Machame Route

This increasingly popular route has a gradual ascent, including a spectacular

WARNING: PARK-FEE SCAMS & DISREPUTABLE GUIDES

Paying park fees For anyone paying directly at the gate, all entry, hut, camping and other park fees must be paid with Visa or MasterCard and your PIN. One scam involves the relevant officer billing you for less than you owe (eg Tsh100 instead of US$100). As you exit the park after your trek, they point this out to you and ask you to pay the difference in cash. The cash, of course, goes into the pocket of whoever is collecting it. Carefully check the amount (*and* currency) before entering your PIN and keep all receipts at least until after you've left the park.

Disreputable guides While most guides are dedicated, professional, properly trained and genuinely concerned to make your trip safe and successful, there are exceptions. Although it doesn't happen often, some guides leave the last hut deliberately late on the summit day to avoid going all the way to the top. Going with a reputable company – preferably one that hires full-time guides (most don't) – is one way to avoid a bad experience. Insist on meeting the guide before you sign up for a trip, familiarise yourself with all aspects of the route, and when on the mountain have morning and evening briefings so you know what to expect each day. The night before summitting, talk to other climbers to be sure your departure time seems realistic (though note that not everyone leaves at the same time); if it doesn't, get an explanation from your guide. Should problems arise, be polite but firm.

day contouring the southern slopes before approaching the summit via the top section of the Mweka route. Usually a six- or seven-day return.

Umbwe Route

Steeper and with a more direct way to the summit than the other routes; very enjoyable if you can resist the temptation to gain altitude too quickly (aim for at least a six-day return). Although this route is direct, the top, very steep section up the Western Breach is often covered in ice or snow, which makes it impassable or extremely dangerous. Many trekkers who attempt it without proper acclimatisation are forced to turn back. An indication of its seriousness is that until fairly recently the Western Breach was considered a technical mountaineering route. Only consider this route if you're experienced, properly equipped and travelling with a reputable operator.

Rongai Route

This popular route starts near the Kenyan border and goes up the northern side of the mountain.

Shira Plateau route

This route is scenic and good for avoiding crowds, but can be challenging for acclimatisation as it begins at 3600m at the Shira Track trailhead. To counteract this, an extra day at Shira Hut is recommended. Better – choose the Lemosho Route, which is essentially the same, but with the advantage that it starts lower at Londorosi gate and is normally done in eight days (rather than six or seven for Shira Plateau).

Lemosho Route

On the western side of the mountain, this is arguably the best all-round route for scenery and acclimatisation. It starts with two days in the forest before crossing the Shira Plateau and then joining up with the Machame route.

Northern Circuit Route

This route – the longest (eight to 10 days) – initially follows the same path as the Shira Plateau route before turning north near Lava Tower and then continuing around the northern ('back') side of Kilimanjaro before tackling the summit via Gilman's Point.

Machame

☎027 / POP 23,300

The rather ill-defined and spread-out village of Machame lies 25km northwest of Moshi on Mt Kilimanjaro's lower slopes, surrounded by dense vegetation and stands of banana. Most visitors only pass through briefly on their way to the trailhead for the popular Machame route up the mountain. As such, it's a last outpost of clamour before your ascent into the clouds.

Sleeping & Eating

Hotel Aishi Machame HOTEL $$

(☎0758 170254; www.aishi-machame.com; Machame Rd; s/d/tr US$60/80/100; P wifi pool) Arguably the most upmarket option in the Machame/Moshi area, this former outpost of the South African Protea chain has good midrange rooms with comfortable beds and plenty of space.

★**Kaliwa Lodge** LODGE $$$

(☎0762 620707; www.kaliwalodge.com; s/d US$99/198; P) At an altitude of 1300m and close to Kilimanjaro's Machame gate, this German-run place opened in 2012 and has a refreshingly contemporary Bauhaus architectural style, comprising restful grey cube-like structures. Rooms have abundant glass, the colour scheme is muted but very modern, and the setting amid palm trees and lush gardens is as lovely as the rest of the place.

Getting There & Away

A handful of daily minibuses connects Machame and Moshi (TSh2500, two hours).

West Kilimanjaro

In a remote corner of northern Tanzania, West Kilimanjaro is a gem. With a couple of terrific tented camps, a fabulous pre-Kilimanjaro world of Amboseli-like plains and light woodlands, and a sprinkling of Maasai manyattas, it's difficult to understand why so few travellers make it out here. You have to work a little harder for your wildlife, it's true, but this is an important dispersal area for lions from southern Kenya, and it's part of an elephant corridor linking Kenya's Amboseli National Park with Mt Kilimanjaro National Park. Climb any hill out here, too, and the views are extraordinary.

A destination in its own right, West Kilimanjaro (from Sanya Juu village to the Kenyan border, and from the Arusha–Namanga road to Mt Kilimanjaro) is also the missing link on the northern safari circuit, enabling you to travel from Lake Natron to Kilimanjaro International Airport without ever having to see Arusha.

Sleeping

★**Shu'mata Camp** TENTED CAMP $$$

(☎0752 553456; www.shumatacamp.de; s/d with full board & incl all activities US$666/1160) This tented camp is a wonderful escape from the safari circuit. Set on a steep hillside, the seven tents have splendid views of Kilimanjaro and down into the Amboseli ecosystem of southern Kenya. The camp's decor is inspired by Hemingway's love for a classic safari camp, and the sense of luxury and blissful isolation make this a fabulous experience.

★**Ndarakwai Ranch** TENTED CAMP $$$

(☎027-250 2713, 0754 333550, 0784 550331; www.ndarakwai.com; s/d with half board & incl wildlife drives US$600/850; P wifi) Ndarakwai Ranch, a lovely 15-tent camp run by the Kili Conservancy, makes a comfortable base for safaris and walks. The sophisticated and spacious permanent tents occupy a lovely woodland area close to the banks of the Ngare Nairobi River amid stands of yellow-barked acacias. Accommodation rates include US$35 per person per night in conservancy fees.

Getting There & Away

There's no public transport to anywhere out here, although Shu'mata Camp, Ndarakwai Ranch and Olpopongi Maasai Cultural Village can all arrange pick-ups from Moshi and elsewhere (for a fee, of course).

CENTRAL TANZANIA

Central Tanzania lies well off most tourist itineraries, and that's just the way we like it. Exceptional and enigmatic, the Unesco World Heritage–listed Kondoa Rock-Art Sites, scattered across remote hills along the Rift Valley Escarpment, are the region's premier attraction. Not far away, Mt Hanang soars to 3417m and is a worthy climb, both for its own sake and for the chance to summit all by yourself. Both attractions also serve as gateways to the world of the colourful Barabaig and other tribes whose traditional lifestyles remain little touched by the modern world.

And then there's Dodoma, Tanzania's legislative capital, an intriguing relic of nationalist ambition with interesting architecture and the region's best facilities. Travel here isn't always easy – transport and accommodation can be a little rough around the edges – but it's a window on a Tanzania few visitors ever get to see.

Dodoma

☎026 / POP 465,000

Dodoma was a nice idea at the time. Like all custom-built capitals – think Abuja or Yamoussoukro in Africa, Brasilia or Canberra elsewhere – Dodoma never really caught on and lacks a certain authenticity and the atmosphere that goes with it, though that may be set to change as President Magufuli is keen to accelerate the capital's role.

In the meantime, the grandiose street layout and the imposing architecture of many places of worship and government buildings sharply contrasts with the humdrum reality of daily life, and makes Dodoma feel as though it's dressed in clothes that are several sizes too big.

Because Dodoma has so many government buildings, be careful taking photos.

Sleeping & Eating

Kidia Vision Hotel HOTEL $

(☎0784 210766; Ninth St; d Tsh30,000-45,000, ste Tsh70,000-80,000; P 📶) Well managed and, unlike most other hotels in its class, well maintained, this is a very solid choice at this level. Rooms are comfy and clean, though you don't get much extra as the price rises. Located on a dusty unpaved section of the street, but don't be put off by that.

★ **New Dodoma Hotel** HOTEL $$

(☎026-232 1641; www.newdodomahotel.com; Railway Rd; s/d with fan US$50/70, with air-con from US$70/95; P ❄ @ 📶 🏊) The former Railway Hotel's tree-filled courtyard is a lovely oasis and the rooms have some style. Suites face the main street and are noisier than the standard rooms. It has a gym, a small swimming pool and three restaurants. Visitors can pay Tsh5000 to use the pool and gym.

Central Tanzania

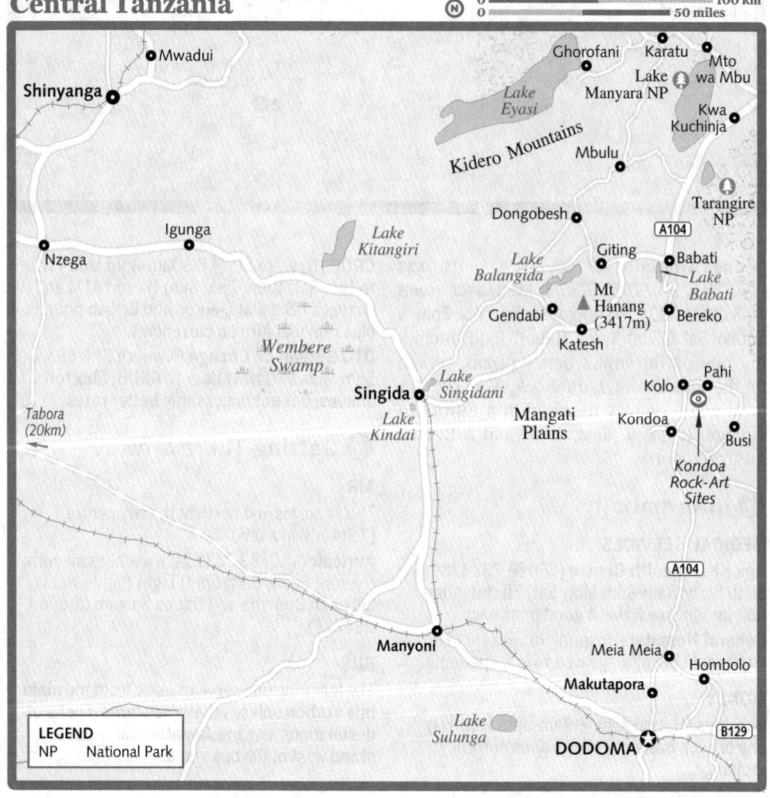

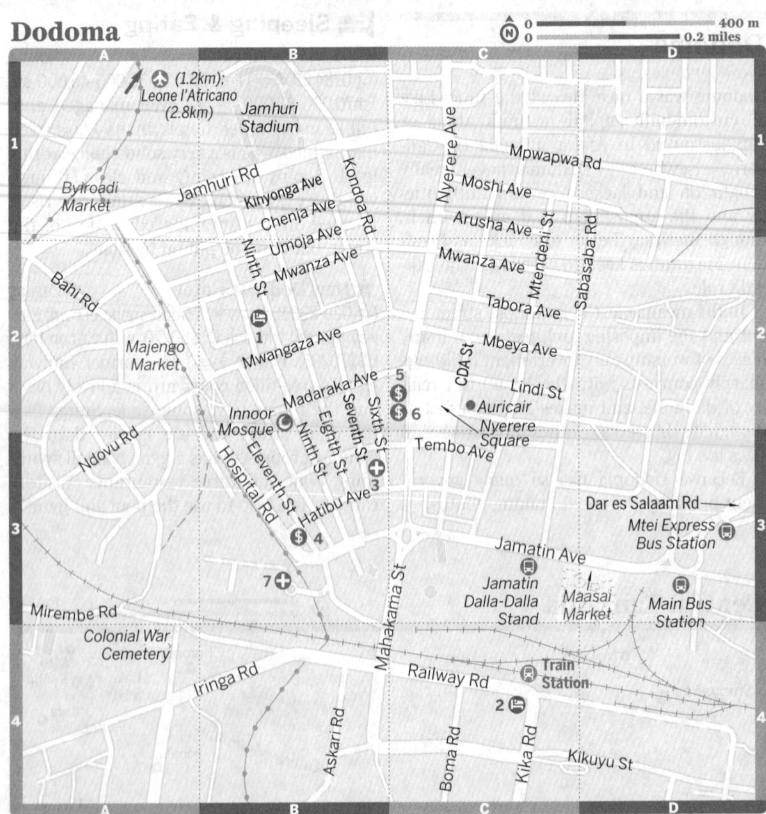

Leone l'Africano ITALIAN $$
(☎0788 629797, 0754 073573; Mlimwa Rd; mains Tsh8500-14,000; ⏲5-10pm Tue-Fri, noon-3pm & 5-10pm Sat & Sun) Tasty Italian food, including one of Tanzania's better pizzas, served in the shadow of Lion Rock. You can try local wines or play it safe with a European vintage. It has a playground and a 12-hole minigolf course.

Information

MEDICAL SERVICES

Aga Khan Health Centre (☎026-232 1789; Sixth St; ⏲8am-8pm Mon-Sat) First destination for illnesses. Has a good pharmacy.

General Hospital (Hospital Rd; ⏲24hr) The city's main hospital, geared to local patients.

MONEY

Barclays (Hatibu Ave; ⏲9am-5pm Mon-Fri) The branch has an ATM and does currency exchange.

CRDB (Nyerere St; ⏲8.30am-4pm Mon-Fri, to 1pm Sat, 10am-2pm Sun) Has an ATM and changes US dollars, euros and British pounds plus regional African currencies.

DTC Bureau de Change (Nyerere St; ⏲9am-5pm Mon-Sat) Next door to CRDB. Shorter queues, but not necessarily better rates.

Getting There & Away

AIR

The airport is just north of the city centre (Tsh4000 in a taxi).

Auricair (☎0783 233334; www.auricair.com; Nyerere Sq; ⏲8am-6pm) Eight flights weekly between Dodoma and Dar es Salaam (around US$225).

BUS

The following bus services leave from the **main bus station** unless otherwise stated. For local destinations, use the **Jamatini dalla-dalla stand** west of the bus stand.

Dodoma

Sleeping

1 Kidia Vision Hotel B2
2 New Dodoma Hotel C4

Information

3 Aga Khan Health Centre B3
4 Barclays B3
5 CRDB C2
6 DTC Bureau de Change C2
7 General Hospital B3

Arusha and Moshi Shabiby and Mtei Express have the best buses to Arusha (from Ts25,000, seven hours) and Moshi (Tsh30,000, 10 to 12 hours). All leave at 6am. Mtei buses leave from their **terminal** by the main bus station.

Dar es Salaam Shabiby has 'full luxury' buses (Tsh26,000, six to seven hours), which means four-across seating and toilets; they leave from the main bus terminal. Other buses (Tsh12,000 to Tsh20,000) depart Dodoma frequently from 6am to 1pm. Buses that started their trip to Dar in Mwanza pass through in the afternoon, and you can usually get a seat on them.

Iringa The route to Iringa (Tsh12,000, three hours) is now paved.

Kondoa and Babati Buses (Tsh7000/12,000, 2½ hours/four hours) depart 6am, 6.30am, 10.30am and noon.

Mwanza Buses (Tsh38,000, eight hours) via Singida (Tsh18,000, three hours) leave Dodoma between 6am and 7.30am, and Mwanza-bound buses from Dar es Salaam pass through around midday.

Kondoa Rock-Art Sites

The district of Kondoa, especially around the tiny village of Kolo, lies at the centre of one of the most impressive collections of ancient rock art on the African continent. The overhanging rocks in the surrounding hills shelter two thousand years' worth of artistic expression, with some sites being still actively in use for animist worship. It's one of Tanzania's least-known and most underrated attractions and, if you can tolerate a bit of rugged travel, makes an intriguing and worthwhile detour.

To visit independently, stop at the **Antiquities Department Office** (☎0752 575096; Kolo; ⌚7.30am-6pm) along Kolo's main road to arrange a permit (Tsh27,000/13,000 per adult/child) and mandatory guide (free, but tips expected), some of whom speak English. There's a good little museum here covering not only archaeology, but also the culture of the Irangi people.

Sights

There are 186 known rock-art sites (but perhaps as many as 450 in total), of which only a portion have been properly documented. If you base yourself in Kolo or Kondoa, you can comfortably see three of the best sites in a day.

Fenga Rock-Art Complex ROCK ART

One of the most impressive of the Kondoa Rock-Art Sites is the excellent Fenga complex, with its dense and lively images. The dominant feature is a painting of people with wild headdresses who appear to be trapping an elephant. It's around 20km north of Kolo and just west off the Arusha–Dodoma Rd, followed by a hilly 1km walk.

Thawi Rock-Art Site ROCK ART

The most varied, and thus the best, overall collection of rock paintings in the Kondoa area is at Thawi, about 15km northwest of Kolo and reachable only by 4WD.

Kolo Rock-Art Site ROCK ART

The most visited, though not the best, Kolo sites (B1, B2 and B3) are 9km east of Kolo village and a 4WD is required. You'll need to climb a steep hill at the end of the road to see them. The most interesting images here are the elongated human figures with what are either wild hairstyles or masks; one scene has been interpreted as the abduction of a woman. You'll also see depictions of rhinos, giraffes and leopards.

Activities

★Kondoa Irangi Cultural Tourism Program CULTURAL

(☎0784 948858, 0715 948858; www.tanzaniaculturaltours.com; Kondoa; per person US$80, minimum 2 people) The Kondoa Rock-Art Sites are the bread and butter of this recommended company in Kondoa town, but director Moshi Changai also leads Barabaig, Sandawe and Irangi village visits by bicycle or car. Overnights in local homes are possible.

Information

There are no banking services for travellers.

Getting There & Away

Kolo is 80km south of Babati. Buses to Kolo (Tsh7500, 2½ hours) depart Babati at 7am and 8.30am. From Arusha, Mtei Express buses to Kondoa, leaving at 6am, pass Kolo (Tsh11,500, five hours). The last bus north from Kondoa leaves at 9am. There are only buses to Dodoma (Tsh8500, three hours) from Kondoa, not Kolo. They leave at 6am, 10am and 12.30pm. Catching a north-bound bus in Kondoa means you'll get a seat; wait for it to pass Kolo and you'll need to stand.

It could be possible to visit as a day trip from Babati (or as a stop en route to Dodoma) using public transport if you're willing to hitch-hike after visiting the Kolo sites; there are usually some trucks travelling this road in the afternoon.

Babati

027 / POP 105,000

The scruffy market town of Babati, about 175km southwest of Arusha in a fertile spot along the edge of the Rift Valley Escarpment, has a frontier feel despite the construction of a smooth new road. It's notable as a jumping-off point for Mt Hanang, 75km southwest, and for a long-running programme of cultural tours, but otherwise it has little to detain you. Stretching south from the city is tranquil Lake Babati, fringed by tall reeds and home to hippos and water birds. If you're here on the 17th of the month, don't miss Babati's monthly *mnada* (market), about 5km south of town.

Sights & Activities

Lake Babati LAKE

This expansive reed-fringed lake south of town is home to hippos; you can explore by dugout with Kahembe's Culture & Wildlife Safaris or the folk at the **Royal Beach Hotel** (0785 125070; camping with own/hired tent Tsh15,000/18,000, bandas Tsh35,000; P).

★ **Kahembe's Culture & Wildlife Safaris** HIKING, CULTURAL

(0784 397477; www.kahembeculturalsafaris.com; Sokoine Rd) This reliable and knowledgeable outfit in Babati have been offering cultural tours in the region since 1992. Besides cycling trips and village visits where you might join in with honey harvesting or maize pounding, it's the main operator organising Mt Hanang climbs. The volunteer programmes incorporate game viewing and cultural exchange with school-building projects.

Sleeping & Eating

Kahembe's Modern Guest House GUESTHOUSE $

(0784 397477; www.kahembeculturalsafaris.com; Sokoine Rd; s/d incl full breakfast Tsh25,000/30,000;) Home of Kahembe's Culture & Wildlife Safaris, this plain and friendly place just northwest of the bus stand has decent twin- and double-bedded rooms with TVs and hot-water showers. The breakfast with sausages, cornflakes, fruit, toast and eggs is included in the price. Pop next door to book a cultural tour with owner Joas.

Ango Bar & Restaurant TANZANIAN $

(Arusha-Dodoma Rd; buffet breakfast Tsh6000, lunch or dinner Tsh8000; 7am-9.30pm) Behind a small petrol station opposite the exit from the bus station, this unexpectedly attractive place offers local fare, always including a veggie dish. Paintings line the walls, pots hang from the wood-beamed ceiling and lively music plays. It's also the best spot for an evening beer.

Information

INTERNET ACCESS

There are internet connections at a couple of places around town.

Manyara Internet Café (Mandela Rd; per hour Tsh2000; 7.30am-7pm Mon-Sat, 10am-2pm Sun)

Rainbow Communication (Mandela Rd; per hour Tsh2000; 8am-6.30pm Mon-Sat)

MONEY

NBC (Arusha-Dodoma Rd) Changes cash and has an ATM.

Getting There & Away

The football-pitch-sized **bus station** is packed with buses, travellers and touts from dawn to dusk. If travelling from Babati to Arusha (Tsh9000, four hours), the first departures in both directions are at 5.30am and the last leave at 4pm, though dalla-dallas go until 6pm. Other destinations include Dodoma (Tsh12,000, four hours), Kondoa (Tsh8500, three hours), Mwanza (Tsh29,000 to Tsh36,000, eight hours) and Singida (Tsh9000, three hours; last departure from Babati around 10am). The Shabiby 'full luxury' buses serving these routes cost Tsh5000 to Tsh10,000 more than the prices quoted, but are well worth it for increased comfort and safety.

LAKE VICTORIA

Tanzania's half of Africa's largest lake sees few visitors, but the region holds many attractions for those with a bent for the offbeat and a desire to immerse themselves in the rhythms of local life beyond the tourist trail. The cities of Musoma and Bukoba have a quiet waterside charm, while most villagers on Ukerewe Island follow a subsistence lifestyle with little connection to the world beyond the shore.

Mwanza, Tanzania's second-largest city, is appealing in its own way and is the perfect launching pad for a Serengeti–Lake Natron–Ngorongoro loop. Add the forests of idyllic Rubondo Island National Park, deep in the lake's southwest reaches, for a well-rounded safari experience.

LAKE VICTORIA FACTS

- Area: 69,484 sq km, about half of which is in Tanzania
- The world's second-largest freshwater lake by surface area after Lake Superior in North America
- Infested with bilharzia in many shoreline areas (swimming isn't recommended)
- Once home to some 500 cichlid species. Populations started to crash in the 1960s due to pollution, overfishing and the introduction of ever-hungry Nile perch. Today there are signs that the cichlid population is recovering. New species and hybrid species, perhaps better able to withstand the modern pressures placed on them, are now emerging.

Musoma

☎028 / POP 134,000

Little Musoma, capital of the Mara region, sits serenely on a Lake Victoria peninsula with both sunrise and sunset views over the water. It's one of those African towns with nothing special on offer other than an addictive appeal.

There are banks and internet cafes along and just off Mukendo Rd.

Sights

★Matvilla Beach BEACH

The best thing to do in Musoma is visit Matvilla Beach at the tip of the peninsula, with its pinky-grey granite boulders. It's prime sunset-watching-with-a-beer territory – and there are bars here to help you with that. To get here, follow Mukendo Rd, Musoma's main street, north of downtown for 1.5km.

Mwigobero Market MARKET

Mwigobero Market is on the city's eastern shore. Small lake boats to nearby islands and villages load and unload passengers and cargo here.

Mwalimu Julius K Nyerere Museum MUSEUM

(☎0769 363590, 0768 872205; Butiama; museum Tsh6500, homes Tsh4000; ⏱8am-5.30pm) Julius Nyerere, the first President of Tanzania, was born in the otherwise insignificant little town of Butiama. This small museum inside the family compound celebrates his life and work. It contains a few stools, shields and other gifts he was given. Boxes of Nyerere's personal effects, including his diaries, a handwritten Swahili translation of part of Plato's *Republic* and collections of his poetry, are also here. Although these are not on display, you can ask the staff to see them.

Sleeping & Eating

★Afrilux Hotel HOTEL $

(☎028-262 0031; Mwigobero Rd; s/d Tsh60,000/80,000; P❄📶) Something of a Musoma institution, the Afrilux has decent hot showers, helpful staff, good wi-fi and a relaxed courtyard bar-restaurant. On the negative side there's zero sound insulation in the rooms.

★Tembo Beach Club CAMPGROUND, GUESTHOUSE $

(☎028-262 2887; camping/r Tsh23,000/66,000; ⏱bar-restaurant 6.30am-10pm; P📶) There's a sociable bar-restaurant (mains Tsh6500) here and a reasonable camping area that's often busy with the clients of overland truck tours. Some rooms have African art on the walls; they are far enough away from the bar that you can be lulled to sleep by waves rather than kept awake by music.

★Matvilla Beach & Lodge CAMPGROUND, BUNGALOW $$

(☎0684 964654; www.matvillabeach.co.tz; Matvilla Beach; camping US$20, bungalows s/d/t

Lake Victoria

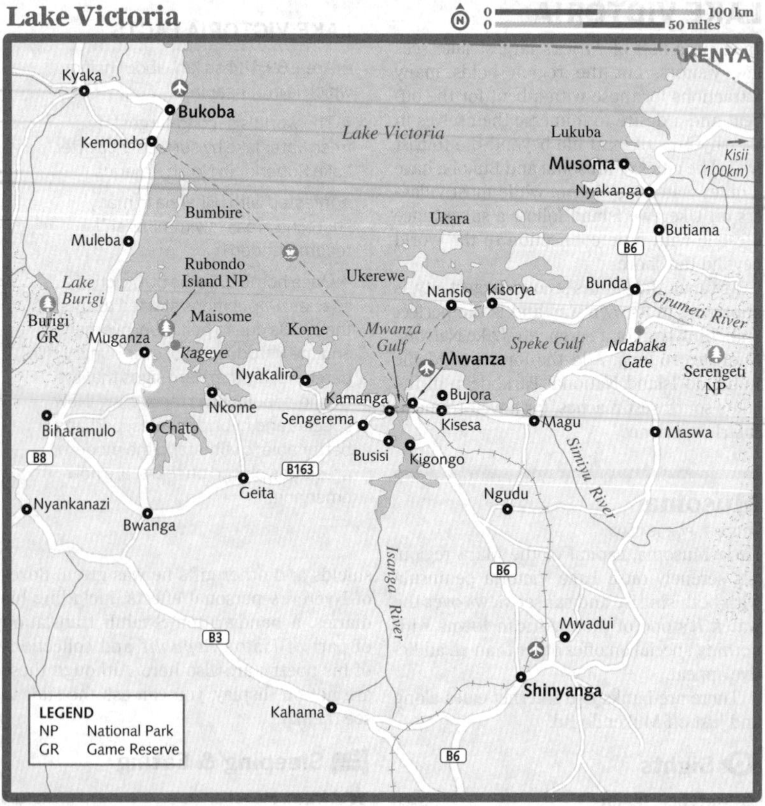

US$25/50/80; P) Out at the tip of the peninsula, 1.5km from the centre, this is a gorgeous multipurpose spot amid the rocks. There are hot showers for campers and stone bungalows that are calm and quiet, and blend into giant, granite boulders.

There's a very popular **bar-restaurant** (0684 964654; www.matvillabeach.co.tz; meals Tsh5000-7000; 6am-11pm) here, everyone's favourite place for fried fish or chicken and a beer. Staff will arrange taxis to take you back to town.

Getting There & Away

AIR

The airport is a five-minute walk from the city centre. **Precision Air** (028-262 0713; www.precisionairtz.com; Kivukoni St; 8am-4.30pm Mon-Fri, to noon Sat) flies four times weekly from Dar es Salaam (Tsh126,000) via Mwanza. The booking office is in the town centre.

BUS

The bus terminal is 6km out of town at Bweri, though booking offices remain in the town centre. Dalla-dallas go frequently to/from the city centre (Tsh4000, 20 minutes) and a taxi costs Tsh10,000. Frequent buses connect Musoma and Mwanza (Tsh10,000, four hours).

To get to Ukerewe Island, take a dalla-dalla to Bunda (Tsh4000, one hour, 5.30am to 4pm) and from there take a bus or dalla-dalla to Kisorya. A ferry (Tsh6000) connects Kisorya and Ukerewe; once on the island, it's another 20 minutes by bus or dalla-dalla to Nansio (the island's largest town).

There's a direct bus to Arusha daily (Tsh35,000, 11 to 12 hours) at 6am, passing through Serengeti National Park (using Ikoma gate) and Ngorongoro Conservation Area. However, you have to pay US$110 in park fees to ride this route, as it enters the park. The drive is pretty and can offer nice animal viewing on the way, but you'll not get the chance to stop for photos. Some people find it's better value to fly.

Mwanza

☎028 / POP 706,500

Tanzania's second-largest city, and the lake region's economic heart, Mwanza is set on Lake Victoria's shore, surrounded by hills strewn with enormous boulders. It is notable for its strong Indian influences, as well as for being a major industrial centre and a busy port. Yet despite its rapidly rising skyline, Mwanza manages to retain a casual feel. In addition to being a stop on the way to Rubondo Island National Park, Mwanza is a great starting or finishing point for safaris through Ngorongoro and the Serengeti, ideally as a loop by adding in Lake Natron.

Sights

Bismarck Rock LANDMARK

Mwanza's icon, Bismarck Rock, is a precariously balanced boulder atop the lovely jumble of rocks in the lake next to the Kamanga ferry pier. The little park here is a brilliant sunset spot.

Jiwe Kuu LANDMARK

(Big Rock, Dancing Rocks) One of the more interesting rock formations around Mwanza is Jiwe Kuu (Big Rock), which some people call the Dancing Rocks. Many round boulders sit atop this rocky outcrop north of town and have managed to last for aeons without rolling off. Dalla-dallas to Bwiru run west down Nyerere Rd; their final stop leaves you within a 1.5km walk of the rocks.

Robert Koch Hill HILL

Smack in the city centre is Robert Koch Hill, with an attractively decrepit German-built mansion at the top. To get here, push through the bustling market, and take the trail through the beer garden and past all the piles of rubbish. You shouldn't go up here late in the day and single women shouldn't go alone.

Mwaloni Market MARKET

(⏲6am-3pm) Mwaloni Market, under the roof with the giant Balimi ad, is quite a spectacle. The city's main fish market, it also has lots of fruits and vegetables, most shipped in on small boats from surrounding villages, and there are almost as many marabou storks as vendors. Photography is currently prohibited because some scenes in the controversial documentary film *Darwin's Nightmare* (2004) were shot here.

Tours

Several travel agencies in town hire out 4WDs and can organise complete safaris to Serengeti and Rubondo Island National Parks. While Mwanza's operators may not be as good as the best agencies in Arusha, they provide solid service and we're unaware of any in town that will blatantly rip you off. It's not easy to meet other travellers in Mwanza, but you can ask the agencies whether they have other clients interested in combining groups to save money, or try posting a notice at **Kuleana Pizzeria** (☎028-250 0955; Post St; snacks Tsh3000-6000, pizzas Tsh14,200-17,700; ⏲7am-9pm; 🖉) 🌿.

Fortes Africa SAFARI

(☎028-250 0561; www.fortes-africa.com; Station Rd) A reputable, reliable and professional company.

Sleeping

★ **Isamilo Lodge & Spa** HOTEL **$$**

(☎0756 771111, 0736 200903; www.isamilolodge.com; 402 Block D, Isamilo; s/d new wing from US$60/80, old wing US$40/70; P❄📶🏊) This hotel has been renovated, and is very good value, especially if you like being away from the town centre. Rooms in the new wing are spacious, and many have wonderful views down to the lake. There's also a spa, large pool and a good Indian restaurant. Travellers usually get the lower resident rates, which makes it much more tempting.

Ryan's Bay RESORT **$$**

(☎0784 699393, 028-254 1702; www.ryansbay.com; Station Rd, Capri Point; s/d from US$110/140; P🚭❄📶🏊) The flashiest place in Mwanza has lake views and large, well-appointed rooms with acacia-tree murals on the walls. There's a good pool, and one of the best Indian restaurants in town (mains Tsh12,000 to Tsh20,000). Larger groups or families can ask about the adjoining rooms that make suites. Smoking allowed on the balconies only.

Wag Hill Lodge LODGE **$$$**

(☎0773 284084; www.waghill.co.tz; s/d bungalow US$105/150, tent US$154/220, villa US$700; P🏊) The intimate and beautiful Wag Hill, on a small wooded peninsula outside Mwanza, is an excellent post-safari cool down. It has bungalows with screened walls and great wooden furniture, luxury tents and villas; almost all have great lake views.

Mwanza

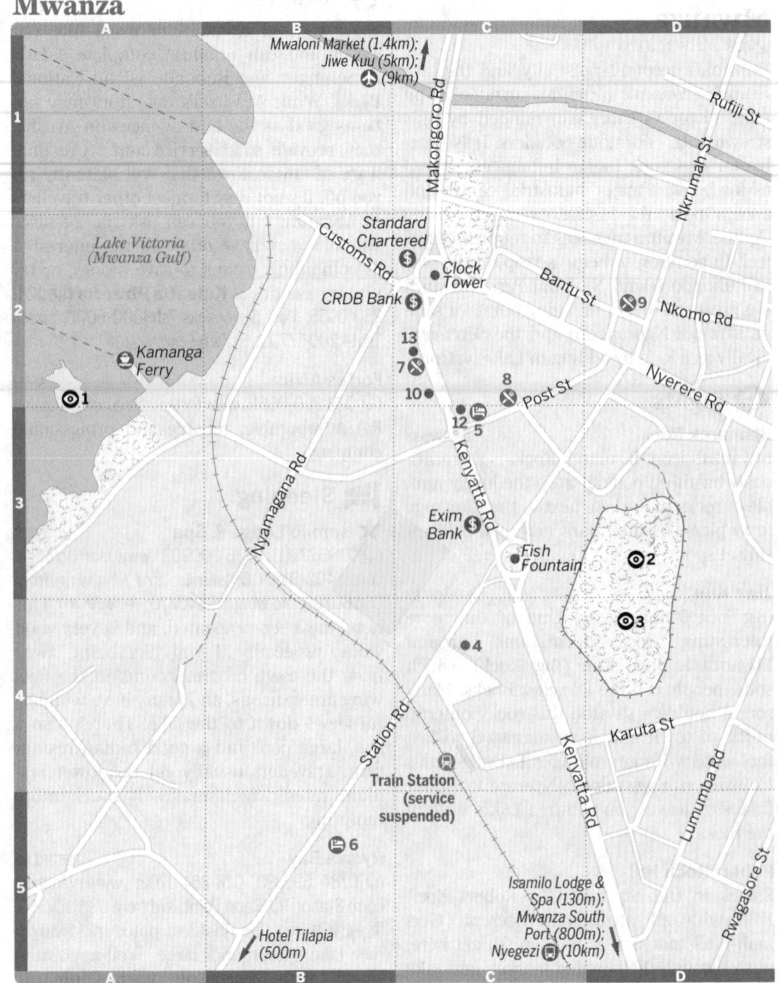

Note that some of the rooms require walking up rock stairs. There's even activities for kids and a special playground.

Eating

Salma Cone STREET FOOD $
(☎0752 661939; Bantu St; ice cream Tsh2000-4000, kebabs Tsh4000; ⏲9am-10pm) *Sambusas* (Indian pastry snacks stuffed with curried meat or vegetables), soft-serve ice cream and juice are all pleasers here, but it's the smell of barbecuing meat that will draw you in for a kebab. With plastic outdoor tables, this is a fun corner to lounge during the evening.

Diners INDIAN $$
(☎028-250 0682; Kenyatta Rd; meals Tsh6000-15,000; ⏲noon-3pm & 6-11pm;) This odd time warp serves some of Mwanza's best Indian food, though oriental decorations and menu items are holdovers from its previous incarnation as a Chinese restaurant.

Hotel Tilapia INTERNATIONAL $$$
(☎028-250 0617; www.hoteltilapia.com; Capri Point; meals Tsh19,000-22,000; ⏲7am-11pm;) The hub of Mwanza's expat population and a magnet to passing tourists, the restaurant of the **Hotel Tilapia** (☎0784 700500; s/d/ste US$100/120/150;)

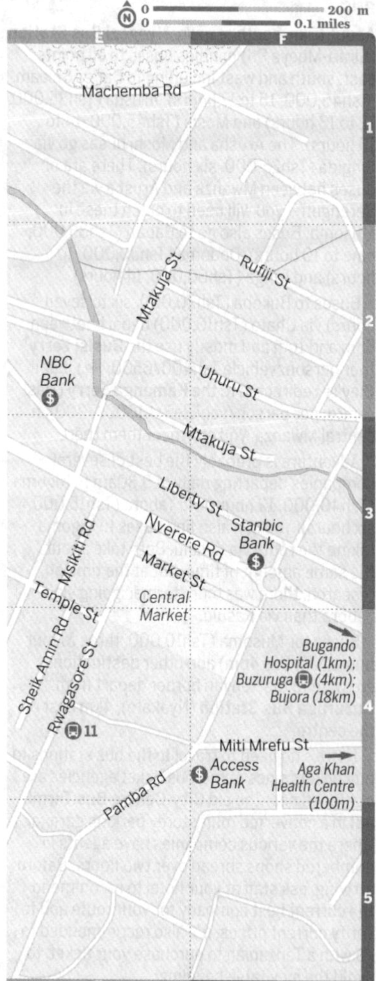

Mwanza

Sights

1 Bismarck Rock A2
2 Old German Mansion D3
3 Robert Koch Hill D4

Activities, Courses & Tours

4 Fortes Africa C4

Sleeping

5 New Mwanza Hotel C3
6 Ryan's Bay B5

Eating

7 Diners C2
8 Kuleana Pizzeria C2
9 Salma Cone D2

Information

Tanzania Tourist Board Tourist Information Centre ....(see 5)

Transport

10 Air Tanzania C2
11 Bus Company Ticket Offices E4
12 Fastjet C3
13 Precision Air C2

has an attractive terrace overlooking the lake. Pied kingfishers chatter and squabble as you choose anything from Japanese teppanyaki and Indian to continental. The kitchen is slow, so expect to take your time.

Information

DANGERS & ANNOYANCES

Mwanza is generally a fairly safe city to stroll about, with few touts or security issues, but be as aware as you would at home. Street begging can be aggressive at times and after 9pm dark side streets should be walked with caution. Bantu St, with its *mishikaki* grills, is loud and boisterous, and gets dicey in the wee hours when many people – often drunk – are heading home.

MEDICAL SERVICES

Aga Khan Health Centre (☎0686 364540, 028-250 2474; www.agakhanhospitals.org; Miti Mrefu St; ⌚24hr) For minor illnesses.

Bugando Hospital (☎028-250 0513; www.bugandomedicalcentre.go.tz; Wurzburg Rd) The government hospital has a 24-hour casualty department.

MONEY

Access Bank (www.accessbank.co.tz; Pamba Rd; ⌚8am-7pm Mon-Fri, to 3pm Sat), **CRDB Bank** (Kenyatta Rd; ⌚9am-3pm Mon-Fri, to 12.30pm Sat), **Exim Bank** (www.eximbank-tz.com; Kenyatta Rd; ⌚9am-5pm Mon-Fri), **NBC Bank** (Liberty St; ⌚8am-7pm Mon-Fri, to 3pm Sat), **Stanbic Bank** (www.stanbicbank.co.tz; Nyerere Rd; ⌚8.30am-3.30pm Mon-Fri, to 12.30pm Sat), **Standard Chartered** (www.sc.com; Makongoro Rd; ⌚9am-5pm Mon-Fri) and other major banks have 24-hour ATMs, with branches scattered throughout the city centre. Most branches also change cash for major currencies.

TOURIST INFORMATION

There's a small **tourist office branch** (☎0766 237967, 028-250 0818; www.tanzaniatourism.com/en; New Mwanza Hotel, Post St; ⌚8am-5pm

WORTH A TRIP

SUKUMA MUSEUM

Sukuma Museum (☎0765 667661; www.sukumamuseum.org; Bujora; Tsh15,000, video Tsh200,000; ⌚9am-6pm Mon-Sat, 10am-6pm Sun) The Sukuma Museum in Bujora village is an open-air museum where, among other things, you'll see traditional Sukuma dwellings, the grass house of a traditional healer, blacksmith's tools and a rotating cylinder illustrating different Sukuma words for counting from one to 10. It is the site of the well-known **Bulabo Dance Festival** in June, where dancers compete using a variety of animals as props.

Mon-Fri, to 1pm Sat) inside the lobby of the **New Mwanza Hotel** (☎028-250 1070, 028-252 1071; www.newmwanzahotel.com; Post St; s/d/ste Tsh123,050/179,000/223,745; P❄️📶🏊). It can give general advice about organising Serengeti safaris and other excursions from Mwanza, but don't expect overly knowledgeable staff.

The Mwanza Guide website (www.mwanza-guide.com) has dated but useful tourist information.

Getting There & Away

AIR

The **airport** (p212) is 10km north of the centre; taxis should cost between Tsh15,000 and Tsh20,000.

Auric Air (☎0783 233334; www.auricair.com; Mwanza Airport) and **Air Tanzania** (☎0756 067783; www.airtanzania.co.tz; Kenyatta Rd) fly daily to Bukoba. Air Tanzania also has at least five flights weekly to Dar es Salaam.

Coastal Aviation (☎0736 200840; www.coastal.co.tz; Mwanza Airport) has a daily flight to Arusha airport stopping at various Serengeti National Park airfields. It also flies to Dar es Salaam and Zanzibar.

Fastjet (☎0784 108900; www.fastjet.com; Kenyatta Rd) flies daily to Dar. One-way fares to Bukoba/Dar average Tsh140,000/200,000.

Precision Air (☎028-250 0819; www.precisionairtz.com; Kenyatta Rd) flies daily to Dar es Salaam, Zanzibar and Kilimanjaro.

Flight schedules and destinations constantly change so it pays to check each airline's website for the latest. There are instances when a flight is cancelled due to lack of customers, so be prepared to make alternative plans at inconvenient times.

BUS

About 10km south of town, **Nyegezi Bus Station** (Sirari-Mbeya Rd) handles buses to all points east, south and west including to Dar es Salaam (Tsh45,000, 15 to 17 hours), Arusha (Tsh35,000, 12 to 13 hours) and Moshi (Tsh45,000, 14 to 15 hours). The Arusha and Moshi buses go via Singida (Tsh25,000, six hours). There are no buses between Mwanza and Arusha via the Serengeti – you will need to catch these in Musoma. Buses also go to Babati (Tsh35,000, nine to 10 hours), Dodoma (Tsh30,000, 10 hours) and Iringa (Tsh60,000, 14 hours).

Buses to Bukoba (Tsh20,000, six to seven hours) via Chato (Tsh10,000) depart between 6am and 1pm and mostly use the **Busisi Ferry** (per person/vehicle Tsh400/6500; 📶), but if they're redirected to the **Kamanga Ferry** (Nasser Rd; per person/vehicle Tsh1000/7200) in central Mwanza, you can meet them there.

Adventure is probably the best of several companies departing daily at 5.30am to Kigoma (Tsh40,000, 12 hours) via Tabora (Tsh15,000, six hours). You can also find buses to Kigoma taking the route via Kasulu. Both take about the same amount of time, but at the time of research, there was more tarmac going via Tabora than via Kasulu.

Buses for Musoma (Tsh10,000, three to four hours, last bus 4pm) and other destinations en route to the Kenyan border depart from **Buzuruga Bus Station** (Nyakato), 4km east of the centre.

There's no need to travel to the bus stations to buy tickets since numerous ticket agencies are stationed near the old **City-Centre Bus Terminal** in a converted multistorey parking garage, where the various companies have agents in numbered shops spread over two floors. Before arriving, ask staff at your hotel to recommend the current best company for your route and to verify current prices. It's also recommended to go with a Tanzanian to purchase your ticket, to avoid the inevitable haggling.

TRAIN

Mwanza is the terminus of a branch of the **Central Line** (Tanzania Railways Limited; ☎022-211 6213, 0754 460907; www.trl.co.tz; cnr Railway St & Sokoine Dr, Dar es Salaam) and trains run to Tabora (1st-class sleeping/2nd-class sleeping/economy Tsh29,600/22,700/11,800, 12 hours) on Sunday, Tuesday and Thursday at 5pm. From Tabora, you can connect to Kigoma (Tsh31,700/24,200/12,500 from Tabora) or continue on to Dar es Salaam (Tsh76,100/54,800/25,000 from Mwanza). If travelling to Kigoma, you'll need to disembark in Tabora (arrivals are in the morning) and spend the day there before boarding the train to Kigoma in the evening. For Dar es Salaam, just stay on the same train.

Around Mwanza

Ukerewe Island

With its simple lifestyle and rocky terrain broken up by lake vistas and tiny patches of forest, Ukerewe Island, 50km north of Mwanza, makes an intriguing, offbeat diversion. **Ikulu** ('White House') is the modest 1928 European-style palace of the island's former king, signposted just behind the market in Bukindo. The real attraction, however, is the deeply rural life of the island. Ukerewe is unusual in its highly successful farming techniques, centuries of stable population, and the fact that every patch of land and every tree is individually owned. There's a fascinating account of how this all works in John Reader's brilliant book *Africa: A Biography of the Continent*.

Nansio, the main town, has internet access (when the island's electricity is working) and only one internationally linked ATM. Shared taxis and dalla-dallas connect Ukerewe's few sizeable villages.

Activities

Visit Ukerewe Island TOURS
(0763 480134; www.facebook.com/visitukereweisland; half-/full-day bike tour Tsh40,000/60,000; 7am-7pm) What could be better than taking in the sights of gorgeous Ukerewe Island on a private bicycle tour? Join local guide Paschal Phares for a trip around the island. Stops are tailored to your interests, but can include scenic viewing spots, a sunset photo op, the Chief's Palace, caves and more. Phares can also arrange walking or canoe/kayaking expeditions.

Sleeping

There are a few low-budget guesthouses and hotels that change ownership frequently, never quite holding on long enough to be the place to go, partly because tourists rarely stay here. But that's the very thing that makes it a destination worth visiting.

La Bima Hotel GUESTHOUSE $
(0752 179055; Nansio; s/tw Tsh18,000/20,000; P) Despite cramped rooms (some with hot water) and peeling paint, this OK place is Nansio's best lodging. It has the top restaurant, too.

Information

Paulo Faustine runs a small **info booth** (0783 864006; guidemwala@gmail.com; Nansio) out of his computer/phone-repair shop.

Getting There & Away

The passenger ferry MV *Clarius* has been undergoing repairs but usually sails daily from Mwanza North Port to Nansio (adult/child Tsh5000/3050, 3½ hours) at 8am; it leaves Nansio for Mwanza at 2pm.

Two other ferries dock at Kirumba, north of Mwanza's centre near the giant Balimi ad. The MV *Nyehunge I* (1st/2nd/3rd class Tsh15,000/7000/6000) departs Mwanza at 9am and Nansio at 2pm for a 3½-hour journey. Its sister, the MV *Nyehunge II* (2nd/3rd class Tsh7000/6000), leaves from Mwanza at 2pm, arriving at 6pm, and leaves Nansio at 7.30am the next morning.

Rubondo Island National Park

Alluring for its tranquillity and sublime lakeshore scenery, **Rubondo Island National Park** (adult/child US$35.40/11.80) is one of Tanzania's best-kept secrets. There may be days when you're the only guests on the 256-sq-km island. Elephants, giraffes, black-and-white colobus, and chimpanzees were long ago introduced alongside the island's native hippo, bushbuck and sitatunga, an amphibious antelope that hides among the marshes and reeds along the shoreline (Rubondo is the best place in Tanzania to see it).

Sleeping

Rubondo Park Bandas & Resthouse CAMPGROUND, BANDA $
(camping & r per person US$35.40) The *bandas* facing the beach at Kageye on Rubondo's eastern shore are some of the better national-park-run *bandas* in Tanzania. Each has a comfortable double and single bed, hot-water bathroom, and privacy afforded by surrounding jungle trees. There's also a resthouse in the same location with similar quality rooms, but with TVs.

★ **Rubondo Island Camp** TENTED CAMP $$$
(0736 500515; www.rubondo.asiliaafrica.com; s/d all-inclusive US$884/1351; closed Apr & May;) Run by the very upmarket Asilia group, this is a wonderful lakeside perch with stunning safari tents. Well, we say tents, but these 'tents' have three solid walls,

fine furnishings, bathrooms to splash in and deliciously comfortable beds. There's a restaurant area hanging onto a low cliff with lake views.

Getting There & Away

AIR

Auric Air (p148) makes a Rubondo diversion on its Mwanza–Bukoba flights (one way US$72). This requires a two-night stay if flying return out of Mwanza since arrival is in the late afternoon and departure in the early morning. **Coastal Aviation** (0752 627825; www.coastal.co.tz) also flies to the park by request. A charter flight with Auric costs around US$3000.

BOAT

There are two ways to reach Rubondo by park boat (up to seven passengers); both should be arranged in advance. Fishermen are prohibited from delivering people to the island.

The park recommends using Kasenda, a small port about 5km from Muganza (Tsh1500 on a motorcycle taxi or Tsh5000 in a taxi). From here it's 20 to 30 minutes by boat to Rubondo Island and another 15 minutes by park vehicle to drive across the island to Kageye. This costs US$118 return per boat. Muganza is just off the main Mwanza–Bukoba road. Public transport is frequent but buses normally drop you at the junction on the main road where the turn-off for Muganza is. There are plenty of motorbikes willing to whizz you into the town or Kasenda. All buses between Bukoba (Tsh12,000, two hours) and Mwanza (Tsh12,000, four hours) pass through, as do Bukoba–Dar es Salaam buses. Dalla-dallas run to nearby destinations such as Biharamulo (Tsh5000, two hours).

The second option is Nkome, at the end of a rough road north of Geita, where the boat costs US$118 to Kageye and takes about two hours. Expect choppy water on this crossing. The warden's office, where you get the boat, is located outside Nkome, Tsh1000 by *piki-piki* (motorbike) or Tsh5000 by taxi from where the final dalla-dalla stops. Two buses go direct from Mwanza to Nkome (Tsh12,000, four to five hours). They leave Mwanza at 10am, but you can meet them at the Kamanga ferry. Alternatively, it is possible to take a bus to Geita, from where there are frequent dalla-dallas to Nkome (Tsh5000, two hours).

> **RUBONDO ISLAND NATIONAL PARK**
>
> **Why Go** The island has a Hollywood movie set feel about it, with thick jungle, tall forests and a wide variety of plants, animals and birds to see. It's easy to get close to wildlife and you'll likely have it all to yourself, too, making for a quiet, peaceful getaway.
>
> **When to Go** June to early November.
>
> **Practicalities** Start from Bukoba or Mwanza, travel to the nearest port (Muganza or Nkome) and continue by park boat. Alternatively, arrive by charter flight. Book accommodation and transport through **park headquarters** (028-252 0720, Saa Nane/Tanapa office, Mwanza 028-254 1819). If the phones are down, staff at the Saa Nane/Tanapa office in Mwanza (028-254 1819, on Capri Point) can help.
>
> **Budget Tips** This is generally a good park for budget travellers. Taking a boat ride from Muganza or Nkome costs US$118. Once there the park *bandas* offer excellent cheap accommodation and self-catering possibilities. Safaris are taken on foot.

Bukoba

028 / POP 128,800

Bustling, green-leafed Bukoba has an attractive waterside setting and a pleasing small-town feel. Everyone who comes to visit here seems to like it, even though it's a little hard to put your finger on exactly why. The town traces its roots to 1890, when Emin Pasha (Eduard Schnitzer), a German doctor and inveterate wanderer, arrived on the western shores of Lake Victoria as part of efforts to establish a German foothold in the region. Since then, the second-largest port on the Tanzanian lakeshore has quietly prospered, thanks to the income generated by coffee, tea and vanilla farming.

In September 2016, the area was hit by a magnitude 5.7 earthquake, which levelled many of the earthen-brick dwellings. Shortly afterwards, extremely heavy rains caused floods and more devastation. The city has now bounced back from these disasters though, and has returned to being a great spot to visit any time of year.

Sights

Most colonial-era buildings are at the lake end of town. When filming *Mogambo* in the Kagera area, Clark Gable, Grace Kelly, Ava Gardner and Frank Sinatra (not in the

Bukoba

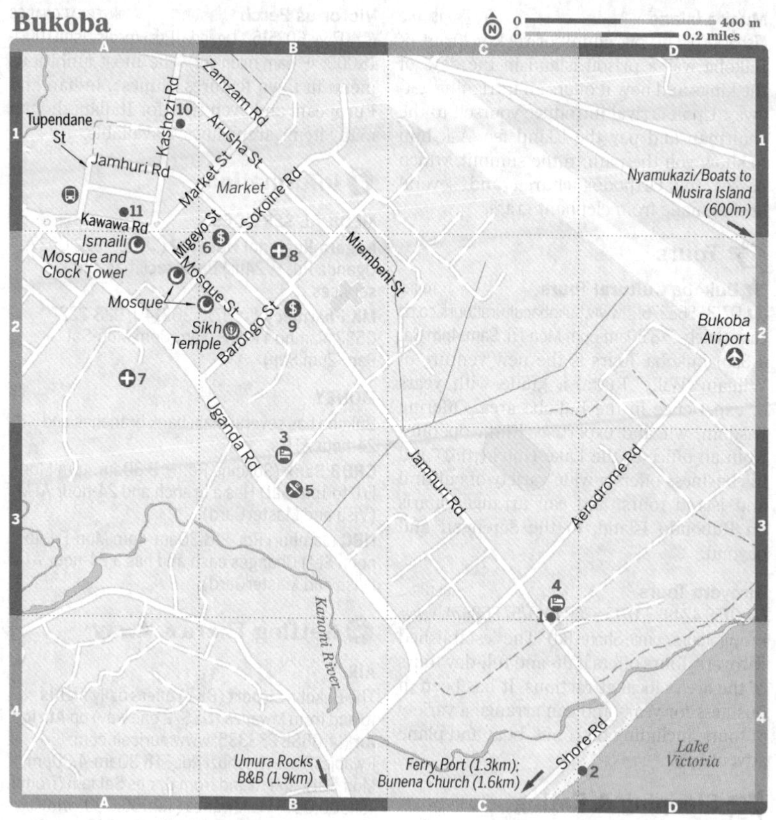

Bukoba

Activities, Courses & Tours

1	Bukoba Cultural Tours	C3
2	Kiroyera Tours	D4

Sleeping

3	CMK Lodge	B3
4	Lake Hotel	C3

Eating

5	Victorius Perch	B3

Information

6	CRDB Bank	B2
7	Kagera Regional Hospital	A2
8	MK Pharmacy	B2
9	NBC	B2

Transport

10	Auric Air	A1
11	Precision Air	A1

movie, but accompanying Gardner, his then wife) enjoyed many a drink at the **Lake Hotel** (☎0754 407860; r Tsh25,000, with shared bathroom Tsh10,000; P), built by the Germans in 1901.

Katuruka Heritage Site ARCHAEOLOGICAL SITE
(adult/child Tsh10,000/3000; ⊙9am-5pm) A stop on the Bukoba Tours (p152) circuit, this site preserves the oldest-known iron-smelting furnace in east, central and southern Africa (from 500 BC; long before equivalent techniques were known in Europe). While the site itself is essentially just old bricks and some small nuggets, there are interesting shrines to King Rugomora (r AD 1650–75) and Mugasha, the god of storms and water. Your guide will tell you some fascinating legends about them.

Musira Island ISLAND

(Tsh3000) The big chunk of rock in front of Bukoba was a prison island in the days of the kings and now it offers an intriguing getaway. Upon arrival introduce yourself to the chairman and pay the island fee. Ask him to show you the path to the summit, which passes the Orthodox church and several homes made from elephant grass.

Tours

★**Bukoba Cultural Tours** TOURS

(☎0713 568276; www.bukobaculturaltours.co.tz; Lake Hotel; ⊙8.30am-6pm Mon-Fri, 9am-4pm Sat & Sun) Bukoba Tours is the new venture of William 'Willy' Rutta, a guide with years of experience in the Bukoba area. Offering wisdom, wit and expertise, Rutta operates from an office at the Lake Hotel (p151) and his business offers a wide variety of cultural and island tours, and can arrange safaris on Rubondo Island, in the Serengeti and beyond.

Kiroyera Tours CULTURAL

(☎0759 424933, 0713 526649, 0757 868974; www.kiroyeratours.com; Shore Rd) The established Kiroyera Tours offers half- and full-day tours of the area's local attractions. It has been in business for years and can arrange a variety of tours, including bike, bus, boat and plane adventures.

Sleeping & Eating

★**Umura Rocks B&B** B&B $

(☎0783 828583; www.umurarocks.com; Umura Rocks, Busimbe A; s/d Tsh70,000/85,000; P⊝❄🛜) This is a lovely B&B with views of Lake Victoria and Musira Island, located just outside Bukoba proper on a high hill. Getting here requires a 4WD vehicle, so call ahead if you don't have one to arrange for pick-up. In addition to serving breakfast, staff can also cook any fish you catch during your stay.

CMK Lodge HOTEL $

(☎0682 265028; off Uganda Rd; r Tsh25,000-35,000; P⊝) Plain but sparkling rooms and a quiet side-road location make this near-downtown hotel one of Bukoba's best in terms of value. Rooms come with a simple breakfast, hot water and mosquito nets on the beds. On top of that you get a warm welcome for free!

Victorius Perch INTERNATIONAL $$

(☎0754 603515; Uganda Rd; meals Tsh10,000-16,000; ⊙6am-midnight) The most ambitious menu in town features Chinese, Indian and European, and even tries for Italian, though many items aren't always available.

Information

MEDICAL SERVICES

Kagera Regional Hospital (☎028-222 0927; Uganda Rd; ⊙24hr) Basic facilities and services.

MK Pharmacy (☎0713 302140, 028-222 0582; Jamhuri Rd; ⊙8am-8pm Mon-Sat, 9am-2pm Sun)

MONEY

Bukoba has several main bank branches and 24-hour ATMs.

CRDB Bank (Sokoine Rd; ⊙8.30am-4pm Mon-Fri, to 1pm Sat) Has a branch and 24-hour ATM (Visa and MasterCard).

NBC (Jamhuri Rd; ⊙8.30am-4pm Mon-Fri, to noon Sat) Changes cash and has a 24-hour ATM (Visa and MasterCard).

Getting There & Away

AIR

The Bukoba **airport** (BKZ) offers daily flights to and from Mwanza (US$72 one way) on **Auric Air** (☎0688 233335; www.auricair.com; Rwabizi Plaza, Kashozi Rd; ⊙8.30am-4.30pm Mon-Sat), and to and from Dar es Salaam (from Tsh360,000) via Mwanza (Tsh165,000) with **Precision Air** (☎028-222 0545, 0782 351136; www.precisionairtz.com; Kawawa Rd).

BOAT

At the time of writing, the ferry service between Bukoba and Mwanza had stopped operating, and restarting it is taking some time. Hopefully the service will begin again in 2018.

BUS

All bus companies have ticket offices at or near the **bus station** (Tupendane St; ⊙5am-6pm). If you prefer to leave the haggling to an expert, the staff at **Bukoba Tours** can also buy tickets for you, for a US$3 fee.

Among the options are buses to the following:

Kampala, Uganda (Tsh20,000, six to eight hours) Two departures daily at 6am and 12.30pm. Visas can be issued at the border.

Kigoma (Tsh28,000, 13 to 14 hours) Every Monday, Wednesday and Friday at 6am.

Mwanza (Tsh20,000, eight hours) Frequent departures between 6am and 12.30pm.

WESTERN TANZANIA

Western Tanzania is rough, remote frontier land, with vast trackless expanses, minimal infrastructure and few visitors: not much different from when Stanley found Livingstone here. The west offers a sense of adventure now missing elsewhere in the country. This is precisely what attracts a trickle of travellers, many of whom plan their itineraries around the schedules of the MV *Liemba,* which sails down Lake Tanganyika, and the Central Line train, which crosses the country.

Western Tanzania

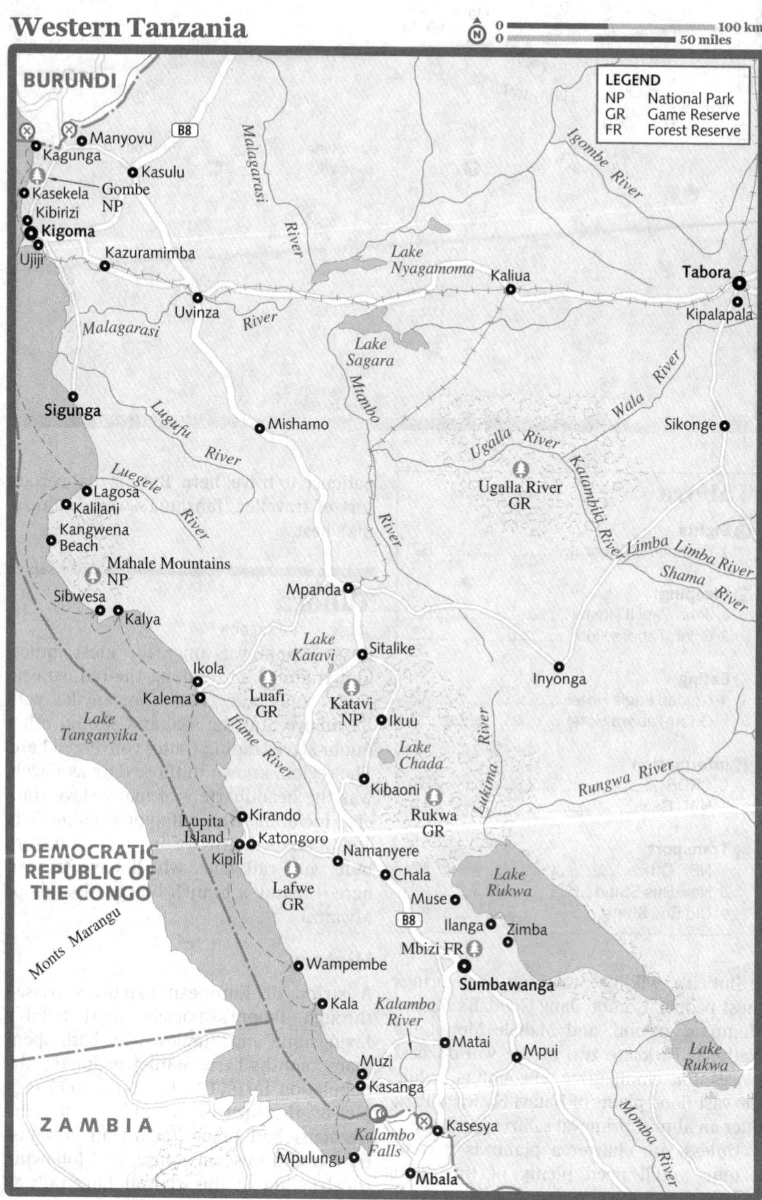

Tabora

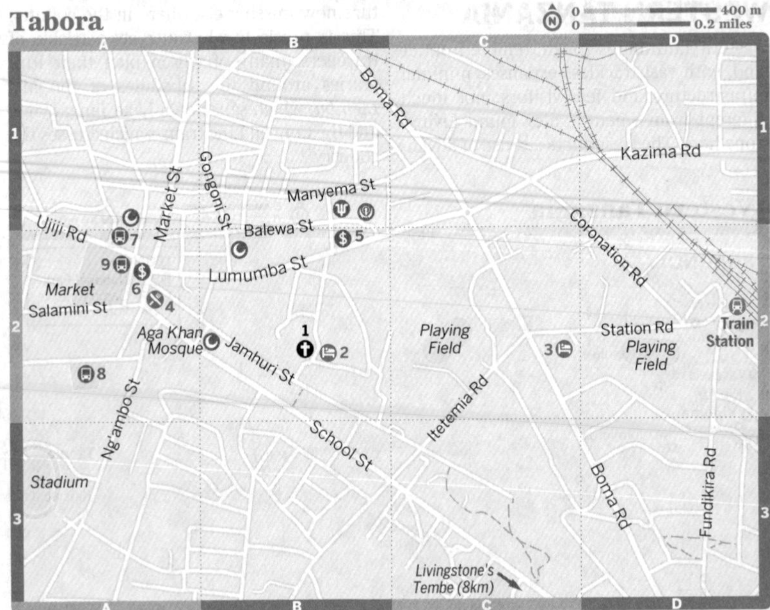

Tabora

Sights
1 Catholic Cathedral B2

Sleeping
2 John Paul II Hostel B2
3 Orion Tabora Hotel C2

Eating
4 Golden Eagle Hotel A2
Orion Tabora Hotel .... (see 3)

Information
5 CRDB B2
6 NBC Bank A2

Transport
7 NBS Office A2
8 New Bus Stand A2
9 Old Bus Stand A2

But it's wildlife watching that brings most people. Gombe, Jane Goodall's former stomping ground, and Mahale Mountains National Park are two of the world's best places for chimpanzee encounters, while the vast flood plains of Katavi National Park offer an almost primeval safari experience.

Unless you charter a plane as part of a tour, you'll need plenty of time and patience to travel here. But for that certain sort of traveller, Tanzania's west is Tanzania's best.

Tabora

026 / POP 227,000

Leafy Tabora was once the most important trading centre along the old caravan route connecting Lake Tanganyika with Bagamoyo and the sea, and several other minor slave-trading routes converged here. The region, known in those days as Kazeh, was the headquarters of many slave traders, including the infamous Tippu Tib. Today it's primarily of interest to history buffs and rail fans, who'll have to wait here if taking a branch line to Mpanda or Mwanza.

History

A string of European explorers passed through Tabora's portals, most notably Livingstone and Stanley, who both spent many months here. Stanley estimated the population in 1871 to be about 5000 people. By the turn of the 19th century the Germans had made Tabora an administration and mission centre, and following construction of the Central Line railway

Tabora became the largest town in German East Africa. It also became a regional education centre and many large schools are still located here.

Sights

Livingstone's Tembe HISTORIC SITE
(☎0754 619627, 0787 281960; Kwihara; Tsh10,000, guide Tsh5000; ⊗8am-4pm) This deep-maroon-coloured, flat-roofed Arabic-style home, built in 1857, is the main attraction in these parts. It was Livingstone's residence for part of 1871. Later that year Stanley waited three months here hoping that the Arabs would defeat Mirambo, famed king of the Nyamwezi (People of the Moon) tribe, and reopen the trail to Lake Tanganyika. When Mirambo was victorious, Stanley had to travel to Ujiji via Mpanda. Stanley and Livingstone returned here together the next year.

Catholic Cathedral CATHEDRAL
This notable and attractive Catholic cathedral has concrete inner walls painted to look like wood and marble.

Sleeping & Eating

John Paul II Hostel GUESTHOUSE $
(☎0717 728515, 0789 812224, 0758 317020; Jamhuri St; s/d/ste Tsh15,000/20,000/50,000; P) Spotless, quiet, secure and cheap. You can't really go wrong at this church-run place where the foundation stone was laid by John Paul II himself. The entrance to the compound is at the back. If the cathedral gate is closed, walk around to the east; it's at the back of the big yellow building. Enter through the attached Nazareth Canteen.

★**Orion Tabora Hotel** HISTORIC HOTEL $$
(☎026-260 4369; oriontbrhotel@yahoo.com; Station Rd; camping Tsh25,000, s Tsh65,000-150,000, d Tsh80,000-175,000; P) The old railway hotel, originally built in 1914 by a German baron as a hunting lodge, has been restored and provides unexpected class in this out-of-the-way region. Ask for a room in the Kaiser Wing, with screened porches looking out onto the gardens.

Golden Eagle Hotel INDIAN, TANZANIAN $
(☎026-260 4623; Market St; meals Tsh8500-15,000; ⊗6am-midnight) Good food and low prices; the Jeera chicken and veggie curry are just Tsh5000. Fish and chips is Tsh14,000. It also serves mocktails, beer and wine.

★**Orion Tabora Hotel** TANZANIAN, EUROPEAN $$
(☎026-260 4369 ext 117; Station Rd; meals Tsh6000-15,000; ⊗6am-midnight) Tabora's top dining spot has a mix of local and continental food, with pizza and Indian available during dinner. There's dining indoors and in the outside bar area, which has a pool table, and live bands play on Friday, Saturday and Sunday. Even more vital, the bar has the skills, technology and ingredients to make a margarita!

Information

CRDB (Lumumba St; ⊗8am-4.30pm Mon-Fri)

NBC Bank (cnr Market St & Ujiji Rd; ⊗8.30am-4pm Mon-Fri, to noon Sat)

Getting There & Away

AIR

Air Tanzania (☎026-260 4401; www.airtanzania.co.tz) flies to both Kigoma (Tsh140,000, Wednesday) and Dar es Salaam (Tsh285,000, Sunday).

BUS

NBS (Ujiji Rd), mostly offering four-across seating, is the top company operating out of Tabora. Some NBS buses depart from its office at the **old bus stand**. All other buses use the nearby **new bus stand**. Several buses depart daily between 6am and 10am to Mwanza (Tsh15,000, six hours). Buses also go to the following:

Arusha (Tsh30,000, 10 to 11 hours, 6am) Goes via Singida (Tsh20,000, four hours) and Babati (Tsh25,000, six to seven hours).

Dodoma (Tsh30,000, 10 hours, 6am)

Kigoma (Tsh15,000, seven hours, 7am)

Mbeya (Tsh45,000, 14 hours, 6am) Sasebossa and Sabena have departures several times a week.

Mpanda (Tsh23,000, 12 hours, 7am)

For all buses, arrive 30 minutes before departure.

TRAIN

Tabora is an important train junction. Trains go to the following:

Dar es Salaam (1st-class sleeping/2nd-class sleeping/economy class Tsh56,500/33,900/25,400, 24 hours, 6.40am Monday, Wednesday and Friday for ordinary trains)

Kigoma (1st/2nd/3rd class Tsh35,700/21,400/16,100, nine to 10 hours, 5.30pm Monday, Wednesday and Saturday)

Mpanda (1st/2nd/3rd class Tsh27,500/21,200/11,100, 10 hours, 5pm Monday, Wednesday and Saturday)

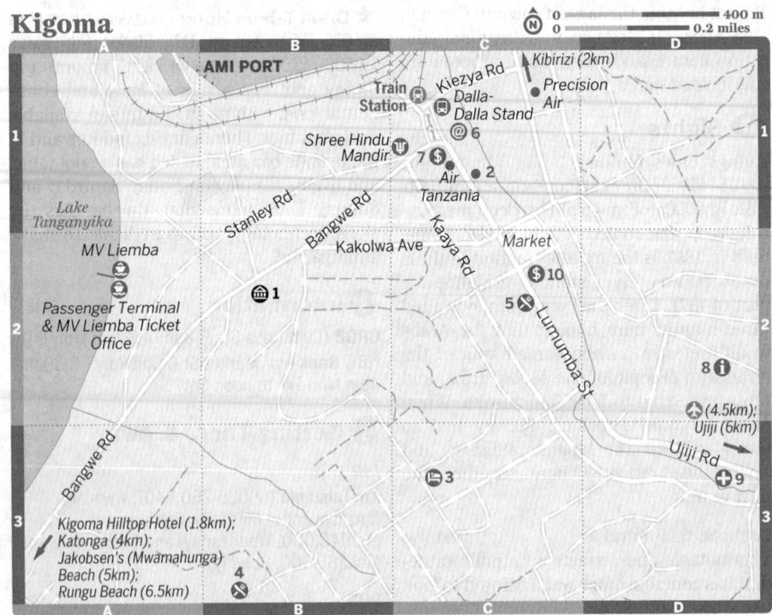

Kigoma

Sights
1 Kaiser House B2

Activities, Courses & Tours
2 Gombe Track Safaris & Tours Tanzania C1

Sleeping
3 Green View Hotel C3

Eating
4 Coast View Resort B3
5 Kigoma Catering C2

Information
6 Baby Come & C@ll C1
7 CRDB C1
8 Gombe/Mahale Visitor Information Centre D2
9 Kigoma International Health Clinic D3
10 NBC C2

Mwanza (1st/2nd/economy class Tsh29,600/22,700/11,800, nine to 10 hours, 7pm Monday, Wednesday and Saturday)

A deluxe train also runs to Dar es Salaam (Tsh56,500/33,900/25,400, 24 hours, 7.20pm Saturday) and Kigoma (Tsh35,700/21,400/16,100, nine to 10 hours, 6am Saturday).

Kigoma

☎028 / POP 135,000

This agreeable little town is the regional capital and only large Tanzanian port on Lake Tanganyika. It's also the end of the line for the Central Line train and a starting point for the MV *Liemba* and visits to Gombe National Park. It's hardly a bustling metropolis, but it feels that way if you've spent any time in other parts of western Tanzania.

Other than a few scattered buildings dating from the German colonial era, including the train station and what some call **Kaiser House** (Bangwe Rd), now the home of the regional commissioner, Kigoma has no real attractions, but the pleasant ambience, some good restaurants and a lively market, plus nearby villages and beaches, make it a nice spot to spend a few days.

Sights & Activities

Katonga VILLAGE

This large and colourful fishing village is quite a spectacle when the 200-plus wooden boats pull in with their catch. During the darkest half of the moon's cycle they come back around 8am after they've spent the night on the lake fishing by the light of lanterns. Dalla-dallas (Tsh400) come here frequently.

Jakobsen's (Mwamahunga) Beach BEACH
(Tsh7000) Jakobsen's is actually two tiny, beautiful sandy coves below a wooded hillside. The overall setting is idyllic, especially if you visit during the week when few people are around. There are some *bandas* for shade, and soft drinks and water are sold at the guesthouse. Watch your belongings, as kleptomaniac baboons roam freely.

Kibirizi VILLAGE
There are many fishermen at Kibirizi, 2km north of town by the oil depots. The early-afternoon loading of the lake taxis is impressive in a noisy, colourful and rather chaotic kind of way. You can walk here by following the railway tracks or the road around the bay.

Gombe Track Safaris & Tours Tanzania TOURS
(☎0756 086577; www.gombesafari.com; Lumumba St; 1-day tour US$395; ⏰9am-5pm Mon-Fri, to 1pm Sat) If taking a lake taxi for four hours to reach Gombe (p159) strikes you as inconvenient, contact Gombe Track Safaris for alternative (albeit more expensive) options. Though an overnight stay is highly recommended, it can even put together a one-day excursion that includes pick-up (at 6am!) right from your hotel.

Gombe Track Safaris & Tours SAFARI
(☎0756 086577; www.gombesafari.com; Lumumba Rd, opposite TRA Bldg) This Kigoma-based company does tours of the western parks, as well as Burundi itineraries (if safe to venture there) and itineraries elsewhere in Tanzania.

Sleeping & Eating

★**Jakobsen's Guesthouse** GUESTHOUSE $
(☎0789 231215, 0753 768434; www.kigomabeach.com; camping per person Tsh20,000, tent or r per person without breakfast Tsh30,000-75,000; P) This comfortable place has a guesthouse with a lovely clifftop perch above Jakobsen's Beach, two cottages and some standing tents, plus two shady campsites with bathrooms, lanterns and grills closer down near the lake. It's good value and a wonderful spot for a respite, but there is no food available so you'll need to self-cater.

★**Green View Hotel** HOTEL $
(☎028-280 4055, 0744 969681; www.greenviewhotel.co.tz; s/d/ste Tsh50,000/70,000/80,000; P ❄ 📶) Despite the lack of a view, Green View offers everything a traveller could need: spotless rooms, good air-con, hot showers and friendly, English-speaking staff, all in a rather Escher-esque building with odd stairs that lead up then down, and a variety of life-sized African animals as decor (fun for kids!). It's up a hill away from the town centre.

Kigoma Hilltop Hotel HOTEL $$
(☎0757 349187; www.mbalimbali.com; s/d/ste US$92/143/225; ❄📶) This hotel is atop an escarpment overlooking the lake. The double and twin cottages are within a large walled compound roamed by zebras. Rooms are reasonably well appointed, there are lovely views from the gardens and there's an expensive restaurant. The pool (nonguests Tsh10,000) is large and well maintained.

Kigoma Catering INTERNATIONAL $
(☎0713 492381; Lumumba St; mains Tsh3000-6000; ⏰8am-5pm) The biggest and broadest menu in town, with primarily local dishes. Though it won't wow you, the food is pretty good.

★**Coast View Resort** TANZANIAN, ITALIAN $$
(mains Tsh10,000-13,000; ⏰7am-9pm, bar to 11pm) Assuming you can score a table with a view (up on the gazebo), it's worth the trip up here for dinner or sundowners. The menu is mostly local, but has some Italian too.

Information

INTERNET ACCESS

Baby Come & C@ll (☎028-280 4702; Lumumba St; per hour Tsh1500; ⏰7.30am-8pm Mon-Sat) Internet access just up from the train station.

MEDICAL SERVICES

Kigoma International Health Clinic (☎0715 491995; Ujiji Rd; ⏰24hr) For minor medical issues. It's 1km beyond Bero petrol station.

MONEY

CRDB (Lumumba St; ⏰8.30am-4pm Mon-Fri, to 1pm Sat, ATM 24hr) Changes US dollars, euros and British pounds. ATM accepts MasterCard and Visa.

NBC (Lumumba St; ⏰8.30am-4pm Mon-Fri, to noon Sat, ATM 24hr) ATM accepts MasterCard and Visa.

TOURIST INFORMATION

Gombe/Mahale Visitor Information Centre (☎0689 062303, 028-280 4009; www.tanzaniaparks.co.tz; ⏰9am-4pm) This helpful

LAKE TANGANYIKA

Lake Tanganyika is the world's longest (660km), second-deepest (more than 1436m) and second-largest (by volume) freshwater lake. At somewhere between nine and 13 million years old, it's also one of the oldest. Thanks to its age and ecological isolation it's home to an exceptional number of endemic fish, including 98% of the 250-plus known species of cichlids. Cichlids are popular aquarium fish due to their bright colours, and they make Tanganyika an outstanding snorkelling and diving destination. Not all of the lake is bilharzia free, so it's best to check locally before diving in.

Kigoma is the only proper town, with the rest of the Tanzanian shoreline dotted by small, rarely visited settlements and a lovely **ecolodge** (p164). Travelling here offers a fascinating look at local life. The rolling countryside around the villages is beautiful, and inviting for hiking.

Besides the services of the historic MV *Liemba*, lake taxis travel the shoreline at least every two or three days. Getting around can be difficult, and sometimes expensive, but with perseverance you can, eventually, get to all lakeside towns and villages overland by a mix of some of the world's most overcrowded buses and trucks, or along the lake via a variety of boats.

office for general information and for booking park-run accommodation is signposted off Ujiji Rd near the top of the hill; turn left at the T-junction.

Getting There & Away

AIR

Air Tanzania (☎0756 530154; www.airtanzania.co.tz; CRDB Bldg, Lumumba St; ⏲8am-5pm Mon-Fri, 9am-2pm Sat & Sun) flies four times weekly between Kigoma and Dar es Salaam (US$200). **Precision Air** (☎0784 298929; www.precisionairtz.com; Kibirizi road; ⏲9am-4pm Mon-Fri, to 2pm Sat) flies five times weekly between Kigoma and Dar es Salaam via Tabora (US$226). Both airlines accept cash only. Air travel to Kigoma is in a constant state of flux, so expect this information to change.

The **airport** (TKQ) is about 5km east of the town centre (about Tsh5000 in a taxi).

BOAT

Ferry

The **MV Liemba** (☎0766 633830, 028-280 2811; ⏲office 8am-4pm Mon-Fri) between Kigoma and Mpulungu (Zambia) via Lagosa (for Mahale Mountains National Park) and other lakeshore towns departs from the passenger terminal at the southern edge of town. Services are on alternate weeks. The **ticket office** (⏲ticket office 8am-4pm Mon-Fri) near the dock is open several hours in advance of departure.

Cargo ships to Burundi and the DRC also take passengers. They depart from Ami Port near the train station.

Lake Taxi

Lake taxis are small, wooden motorised boats, piled high with people and produce, that connect villages along the Tanzanian side of Lake Tanganyika. They're inexpensive, but offer no toilets or other creature comforts, little if any shade, and can be dangerous when the lake gets rough. Nights are very cold. Lake taxis going north depart from Kibirizi village, about 2km north of Kigoma town. Boats to the south leave from Ujiji.

BUS

All buses depart from the dusty streets behind Bero petrol station (coming from Kigoma, look for the large, white petrol station with an NBC ATM). The bus station is surprisingly organised with all the bus companies having little ticket offices with destinations clearly signed in a long row. Other bus ticket offices are scattered around the Mwanga area, just to the west.

Buses go to the following places:

Arusha (Tsh60,000, 20 hours)
Bukoba (Tsh30,000, 12 hours, 6am), via Biharamulo (Tsh27,000, eight hours)
Burundi (Tsh15,000, seven hours)
Mpanda (Tsh23,000, eight hours, 6am)
Mwanza (Tsh40,000, 10 to 12 hours, 6am), via Nyakanazi (Tsh22,000, seven hours)
Tabora (Tsh23,000, eight hours, 6am)
Uvinza (Tsh5000, four hours) All buses to Tabora or Mpanda pass through Uvinza.

TRAIN

Kigoma station is the final stop for the Tanzania Railways Limited Central Line Train (p148) from Dar es Salaam and from Mwanza. Trains depart from Kigoma to Tabora (1st/2nd/3rd class Tsh31,700/24,200/12,500) and Dar es Salaam (Tsh76,100/55,600/27,000) at 4pm on Tuesday, Thursday and Sunday. There is also a weekly express train to Dar departing Kigoma at 8am on Saturday (Tsh79,400/47,600/35,700), stopping at Tabora (Tsh35,700/21,400/16,100).

Getting Around

Dalla-dallas (Tsh400) park in front of the train station and run along the main roads to Bera bus stand, Kibirizi, Katonga and Ujiji. Taxis between the town centre and Bera bus stand or Kibirizi charge Tsh3000 to Tsh4000. Don't pay more than Tsh1000 for a motorcycle taxi anywhere within the city.

Gombe National Park

With an area of only 56 sq km, **Gombe National Park** (☎0689 062303; www.tanzaniaparks.go.tz; adult/child US$118/23.60, trekking fee US$23.60; ⏱6.30am-6.30pm, chimp viewing 8am-4pm) is Tanzania's smallest national park, but its famous primate inhabitants and its connection to Jane Goodall have given it worldwide renown. Many of Gombe's 100-plus chimps are well habituated, and though it can be difficult, sweaty work traversing steep hills and valleys, if you head out early in the morning sightings are nearly guaranteed.

As well as chimp tracking, you can take walks along the lakeshore, and go and see Jane's old chimp-feeding station, the viewpoint on Jane's Peak and Kakombe Waterfall.

Activities

While chimp trekking is the main draw, you can walk along the shoreline and get close to the resident baboons, see waterfowl, hike in the forest and swim in the lake. There are no roads.

Chimpanzee Tracking

Rewarding encounters with chimpanzees is the premier attraction at this park. Visitors are limited to one hour with each group of chimps, but you are allowed to go and find another group after your hour is up for no extra cost. A guide costs US$23.60 per group. Children under age 15 are not permitted to enter the forest, although they can stay at the resthouse.

Sleeping

The park-run accommodation (huts or luxury tents) in Gombe rarely fills up completely, but it's best to book rooms in advance through the visitor information centre (p157) in Kigoma or directly with the park at gombe@tanzaniaparks.go.tz. If you want a more refined experience, opt for the only luxury camp available – tents on raised platforms at the Gombe Forest Lodge (p160).

Tanapa Resthouse GUESTHOUSE $
(☎0689 062303; r per person US$23.60, special tent with shower US$59) Next to the visitor centre at Kasekela, this amenable place has six simple rooms with electricity mornings and evenings. Two overflow facilities have

GOMBE NATIONAL PARK

Why Go Thanks to the work of Dr Jane Goodall, this is arguably the most famous chimpanzee reserve in the world – and one of the best places to see chimps up close.

When to Go Plan your visit for any time other than March and April, when the lodge is closed and rains can make walking the trails hard work. June through October are the easiest (driest) months for chimpanzee tracking.

Practicalities The chimps can be a long walk from the two accommodation options, so be aware you may need to hike for more than an hour depending on where they happen to be. All activities are organised and paid for at Kasekela, on the beach near the centre of the park (this is where lake taxis drop you).

Budget Tips Apart from the high entry fees, it is possible to visit Gombe on a budget: take a lake taxi to and from the park, stay in the Tanapa Resthouse and self-cater. The clock on your entry fee starts the moment you arrive, so wise chimp trekkers arrive at noon on day one, with time for an afternoon trek, then leave by noon the following day after an additional morning trek. This enables two chimp-trekking trips while paying only one 24-hour park-entry fee; however, you will need to pay a guiding fee for each trek. If you stay past the 24-hour mark you will be charged for another full 24 hours even if you only stay a few hours...or minutes.

rooms of lesser quality, and toilets at the back. There are also four 'special' glamping-style tents. Breakfast/lunch/dinner costs US$5/10/10, but you can bring your own food and use the kitchen for a modest fee.

Gombe Forest Lodge TENTED CAMP **$$$**
(☎0732 978879; www.mbalimbali.com; s/d all-inclusive except drinks US$875/1350; ⏲May-Feb) Gombe's only private lodge has a shady, waterside location with just seven tents that offer a certain class and sophistication in the jungle. The tents are luxurious without being ostentatious, and staff do their best to meet your needs during your stay.

Getting There & Away

Gombe is 26km north of Kigoma and the only way there is by boat.

At least one lake taxi to the park (Tsh4000, three to four hours) departs from Kibirizi village, just north of Kigoma, around noon. Returning, it passes Kasekela as early as 7am.

You can also hire boats at Kibirizi; hiring requires hard bargaining, but the price will be a little cheaper than the charter options (around US$250 return to charter a fishing or cargo boat). You may have to pay in advance for petrol, but don't pay the full amount until you've arrived back in Kigoma. Some boat owners may try to tell you there are no lake taxis in an effort to get business.

It's safer and more comfortable (in part because there will be sun shade) to arrange a charter with an established company. Chartering the Tanapa boat costs US$354 return plus US$20 for each night you spend at Gombe. Organise it through the visitor information centre (p157) in Kigoma. Mbali Mbali, also in Kigoma, charges US$773 return for those not staying at the lodge in Gombe and US$413 return for lodge guests (there's no overnight charge). These boats take 1½ to two hours.

Day trips are possible on a chartered boat, but you should leave very early, as late starts reduce your chances of meeting the chimps. Gombe Track Safaris & Tours (p157) can set this up for US$395.

Mahale Mountains National Park

Plain breathtaking is the only way to describe **Mahale Mountains National Park** (www.mahalepark.org; per day adult/child US$94.40/23.60, guiding fee US$23.60; ⏲6am-6pm), with its clear blue waters and white-sand beaches backed by lushly forested mountains soaring straight out of Lake Tanganyika, plus some of the continent's most intriguing wildlife. And, because of its unrivalled remoteness, visitor numbers are low, adding to the allure.

The rainforest blanketing Mahale's western half is, in essence, a small strip of the Congo that got orphaned by the rift that became Lake Tanganyika. It's most notable as a chimpanzee sanctuary, and there are around 900 of our primate relatives residing in and around the park, along with leopards, blue duikers, red-tailed monkeys, red colobus monkeys, giant pangolins and many Rift Valley bird species not found elsewhere in Tanzania. There are also hippos, crocodiles and otters in the lake, and lions, elephants, buffaloes and giraffes roaming the savannah of the mountains' difficult-to-reach eastern side.

Activities

Most come here to get personal with wild chimpanzees, but the area also has amazing hiking opportunities, snorkelling and chances for seeing other wildlife. Whether or not you look for chimps, guide fees are US$23.60/29.50 per group (up to six people; the higher fee is for full-day excursions).

Chimpanzee Tracking

The main reason most people make the considerable effort to visit Mahale is to see chimps. Kyoto University researchers have been studying chimps here since 1965 and their 'M' group is well habituated to people. Mahale's size and terrain mean chimp tracking can take time, and it requires steep, strenuous walking, but almost everyone who visits has a successful sighting. Mahale is widely regarded as one of the best places in the world to see wild chimpanzees.

Only one group of up to six people are allowed with the chimps at any one time. This means that you might have to wait several hundred metres back from the chimps before you get a turn. Each group is allowed only one hour a day with the chimps and this is strictly enforced (with calls of '10 minutes remaining', 'five minutes remaining'). If one hour is not enough (and most people find it is) then it's possible to pay an extra US$100 for a 'photographer's experience' and get three hours with the chimps. You'll also have to pay a negotiable extra fee to your guide.

Face masks (provided) must be worn at all times when in the presence of the chimps. Children under the age of 12 and

MAHALE MOUNTAINS NATIONAL PARK

Why Go Up-close encounters with chimpanzees; stunning scenery with mountains rising up from the lakeshore.

When to Go Open year-round, but March to mid-May is too wet to enjoy it. June through October are the easiest (driest) months for hiking up the steep slopes.

Practicalities There are no roads to the park. Most visitors fly here, but a variety of boats, including the historic MV Liemba (p158), go from Kigoma, Kipili and other lakeshore towns. Entry to Mahale Mountains National Park is at Bilenge, in the park's northwestern corner, and about 10km north of Kasiha, where the park-run *bandas* and several top-end camps are located. Unless you have made other arrangements with one of the lodges, you will need to stop at **park headquarters** (www.tanzaniaparks.go.tz; ⏰7am-6pm) to pay your park fees.

Budget Tips By catching the MV *Liemba* ferry to Mahale, staying in the park *bandas* and self-catering you can have a cheap and fun chimpanzee experience. If your schedule doesn't match the *Liemba*'s you can also get there via lake taxis. Keep in mind that these are very slow, very uncomfortable and not all that safe.

anyone suffering from a cold, flu or other illness are not allowed to visit the chimps, as some have died in the past after they caught the flu from a park visitor.

During June and July the chimps come down to feed around the lodges almost daily.

Hiking

Climbs of **Mt Nkungwe** (2462m), Mahale's highest peak, must be accompanied by an armed ranger. The usual arrangement is two days up and one down, camping midway and again near the peak. Trekkers must bring their own camping gear and food. The climb requires a reasonable degree of fitness, but the trail is in decent shape. A two-day option requires a willingness to scramble and hack your way through the bush.

Swimming

Mahale has fine snorkelling and swimming off its powder-white beaches, but unfortunately humans aren't the only ones to enjoy such beachside beauty – a large crocodile population here means that swimming and snorkelling are only allowed in certain places, and may be banned at times.

Sleeping

Mango Tree Bandas BUNGALOW $
(sokwe@tanzaniaparks.go.tz; Kasiha; bandas per person US$47.20) The cosy Mango Tree *bandas* are set in the forest about 100m from the shore in Kasiha, about 10km south of park headquarters. While they lack lake views, the night sounds are wonderful. You will need to be completely self-sufficient with food and drink, and bring everything you might need with you. The kitchen is well equipped.

Kungwe Beach Lodge TENTED CAMP $$$
(☎0737 206420; www.mbalimbali.com; s/d incl full board & chimpanzee tracking US$1052/1764; ⏰mid-May–mid-Feb; 📶) This is a low-key and enjoyable luxury camp with well-appointed safari tents that boast big four-poster beds, weathered storage chests and piping-hot showers, all hidden under the trees fringing a lovely beach. The centrepiece of the camp is the dhow-shaped dining area. The price includes daily chimp tracking and a boat safari.

Greystoke Mahale LODGE $$$
(☎0787 595908; www.nomad-tanzania.com; s/d all-inclusive US$1885/2730; ⏰Jun-Mar) Situated on a beautiful sandy bay, this is a real Robinson-Crusoe-in-his-hippie-years kind of place where all the rooms are made of knocked-together, weathered, old ship timber. There's a gorgeous multilevel clifftop bar for the essential evening drinks and a tame pelican.

Getting There & Away

AIR

Zantas Air (p216) flies to Mahale twice weekly (assuming there are enough passengers to cover costs – normally four) on Mondays and Thursdays. Usually these are Mbali Mbali customers, but nonguests are accepted to fill the plane. Flights may start from Arusha, Dar es Salaam or Zanzibar (via Dar). Flights sometimes also stop in Kigoma.

All flights stop at Katavi National Park (p163) en route, and thus the parks are frequently visited as a combination package. Expect to pay more than US$970 one way from Arusha, US$770 one way from Ruaha and US$450 to US$530 one way between Mahale and Katavi National Parks.

If you've booked with one of the lodges, a boat will meet your flight. Otherwise arrange a boat in advance with park headquarters (p161).

BOAT

Lake Taxi

Lake taxis head south from Ujiji to Kalilani (Tsh12,000), 2km north of park headquarters (p161), on most days anytime from 5pm to 6pm (sometimes later). The trip often takes more than a day. Generally they depart from Kalilani around noon. Park staff know what's happening with the boats, so they can advise you on days and times.

One option to make the journey more bearable is to take a Saratoga bus from Kigoma to Sigunga (Tsh15,000, six to seven hours, 11am) and wait for the lake taxi there. Sigunga to Kalilani usually takes seven to eight hours. You could also have the park boat pick you up in Sigunga; it's two hours to headquarters. Sigunga has a basic guesthouse.

A couple of weekly boats head north from Kalema (Tsh25,000 or more) or nearby Ikola each evening for an even choppier journey than the one from Kigoma. It can take anywhere from 12 to 36 hours depending on the winds. They head south from Kalilani at around 3pm.

Ferry

It's hard to beat the satisfyingly relaxing journey to Mahale via ferry. The **MV Liemba** (☎028-280 2811) stops at Lagosa (also called Mugambo) to the north of the park (1st/2nd/economy class US$40/35/30), about 10 hours from Kigoma. Under normal scheduling, it reaches Lagosa around 3am whether coming from the north (Thursday) or south (Sunday), but with the frequent delays, southern arrivals present a good chance of passing the park during daylight, which makes for a very beautiful trip. Services are on alternate weeks, but keep in mind the ferry is undergoing major restoration in 2017–18 and may be out of service for some time.

You can arrange in advance at the Gombe/Mahale Visitor Information Centre (p157) in Kigoma or through Mahale park headquarters (p161) for a park boat (holding eight people with luggage) to meet the *Liemba*. It's one hour from the MV *Liemba* to the *bandas*, including a stop to register and pay at Mahale's park headquarters, and costs US$192 return. Lagosa has a basic guesthouse where you can wait for the *Liemba* after leaving the park.

Tanapa Boat

With a bit of luck you can travel for free on the park boat. Park staff travel to Kigoma several times a month and if space is available they'll take passengers. This is usually only possible when leaving the park as on the return trip from Kigoma the boat carries supplies. The Gombe/Mahale Visitor Information Centre (p157) in Kigoma knows when boats are travelling.

ROAD

Saying you can get to Mahale by 'road' is a bit misleading, because there is no road and certainly no public transport – for the moment. However, it is possible to get to Lagosa and the park airstrip by private 4WD (and it has to be a serious 4WD) from both Kigoma and Katavi National Park. The easier route is from Kigoma. A reasonable road runs from Kigoma to Sigunga, leading to a very bumpy track on to Lagosa. Allow six to seven hours for this journey. The route from Katavi is one of the roughest, slowest and most jarringly painful you can make in East Africa. Allow 10 to 12 hours. If you arrive in Lagosa after dark you'll have to overnight there. A jeep hired in either Kigoma or the Katavi area will cost around US$300 with fuel per day (and remember it will take the driver a day to get back home again).

At the time of research, both routes were under construction. In the future, overland access might become easier and cheaper.

Getting Around

There are no roads in Mahale; walking and boating along the shoreline are the only ways to get around.

Mpanda

☎028 / POP 102,000

This small and somewhat scruffy town is a major transit point. Historically it was a significant trade hub and there are still many Arab businessmen living here.

Sleeping & Eating

Mpanda has many hotels, but few good ones, and theft has been reported at the super-cheap ones. Be sure to hide (or not bring!) valuables and split up your cash so if some gets swiped you won't be losing all of it.

There's a row of inexpensive restaurants on 21st St. Otherwise, consider arranging a meal with your hotel.

Moravian Hostel GUESTHOUSE $
(☎0785 006944; s/tw without bathroom or breakfast Tsh7000/9000; P) Tucked behind the

bright white Moravian church, this church-run place is friendly and good enough for the price, quieter than the competition (most other cheapies have attached bars) and convenient for early-morning buses. The common bathrooms won't win any awards, but are functional.

Baraka Guesthouse GUESTHOUSE $
(☎025-282 0485; r Tsh25,000, with shared bathroom Tsh10,000; P) This quiet place west of the centre has tidy rooms with TV and occasional hot water. It's nothing special, but Mpanda being what it is, Baraka's rooms are up there with the best. The bright-blue gate is much easier to spot than the sign.

Shinaz TANZANIAN $
(21st St; set meals Tsh3000; ⏲7-10pm) If you are willing to exercise your Swahili to its fullest and don't mind if things get lost in translation, this no-name eatery has delicious cheap set meals. Look for the blue tarp on the north side of the street just after the bars on the south side. As local as it gets.

Information

INTERNET ACCESS

The post office has reliable internet.

MONEY

CRDB bank has an internationally linked ATM.

Getting There & Away

AIR

Auric Air (www.auricair.com) flies on Thursday afternoons to Mwanza.

BUS

Mpanda's bus station is east of the Sumbawanga road near the southern roundabout. Most companies have ticket offices near the half-built Moravian church in the town centre, and their buses actually start there before going to the station.

Sumry serves Sumbawanga (Tsh14,000, five to six hours, 6am, 8am and 2pm) via Sitalike (Tsh3000, 45 minutes). If you're going to Sitalike the company may try to charge you the full fare to Sumbawanga. Whether or not you pay the lower fare depends on the mood of the people in the ticket office.

NBS and Air Bus go to Tabora (Tsh23,000, eight hours, 6am).

Adventure goes to Kigoma (Tsh23,000, eight to 10 hours, 6am and 3pm) via Uvinza (Tsh20,000, four to five hours).

TRAIN

A branch of the Central Line connects Mpanda with Tabora (2nd/economy class Tsh21,200/11,100, 12 hours) via Kaliua at 3pm on Tuesdays and Sundays.

Katavi National Park

Katavi National Park (☎025-282 9213, 0689 062314; www.tanzaniaparks.go.tz; per day adult/child US$35.40/11.80; ⏲6am-6pm), 35km southwest of Mpanda, is Tanzania's third-largest national park (together with two contiguous game reserves the conservation area encompasses 12,500 sq km) and one of its most unspoiled wilderness areas. Though it's an isolated alternative to more popular destinations elsewhere in Tanzania (Serengeti National Park receives more visitors per day than Katavi does all year), the lodges are just as luxurious as anywhere else. For backpackers it's one of the cheapest and easiest parks to visit, if you're willing to take the time and effort to get there.

KATAVI NATIONAL PARK

Why Go Outstanding dry-season wildlife watching. Rugged and remote wilderness ambience.

When to Go August through October is best for seeing large herds of wildlife. From February to May it's very wet, so getting around the park can be almost impossible and all the top-end camps close. It's a good time for birdwatching though.

Practicalities Drive in or bus from Mpanda or Sumbawanga; fly in from Ruaha National Park or Arusha. All park payments must be made with a credit card (no cash!) at the **park headquarters** (☎025-282 9213, 025-282 0213; katavi@tananiaparks.go.tz) located 1km south of Sitalike or the Ikuu Ranger Post near the main airstrip.

Budget Tips Katavi is one of the more budget-friendly parks. By taking a bus to Sitalike, staying in one of the cheap options there and then setting out on a walking safari you can see Katavi cheaply, though walking safaris often don't see much wildlife. You can also camp in the park.

WORTH A TRIP

LAKE SHORE LODGE & CAMPSITE

The universally praised **Lake Shore Lodge & Campsite** (0752 540792, 0684 540792, 0783 993166; www.lakeshoretz.com; camping US$14, banda s/d full board US$165/250, chalet s/d full board US$350/500; P) has beach chalets with a lovely open 'African Zen' design incorporating shells, sand, ropes, flowers and sun-bleached wood – it's an oasis of barefoot luxury. If this is outside your budget it also has garden *bandas*, which are a low-key version of the chalets, and camping with spotless bathrooms – something, indeed, for everyone.

Sights

Katavi's dominant feature is the 425-sq-km **Katisunga Plain**, a vast grassy expanse at the heart of the park. This and other flood plains yield to vast tracts of brush and woodland (more southern African than eastern), which are the best areas for sighting roan and sable antelopes (together with Ruaha National Park, Katavi is one of the few places you have a decent chance of spotting both). Small rivers and large swamps support huge populations of hippos and crocodiles and Katavi has more than 400 bird species.

The park really comes to life in the dry season, when the flood plains dry up and elephants, lions, zebras, giraffes, elands, topis and many more gather at the remaining waters. The park really stands out for its hippos – up to a thousand at a time can gather in a single, muddy pool at the end of the dry season (late September to early October is the best time) – and its buffaloes. Katavi is home to some of the largest remaining buffalo herds in Africa and it's not unusual to see over a thousand of these steroid-fuelled bovines at any one time.

Activities

Walking Safaris

Walking safaris with an armed ranger and bush camping (US$59 per person, plus a guided walking fee per group of US$23.60 for a short walk or US$29.50 for a long walk) are permitted throughout the park. This makes it a great park for budget travellers. The road to Lake Katavi, a seasonal flood plain, is a good walking route; it begins at the headquarters so a vehicle is not needed.

Some top-end camps no longer allow their guests to go on walking safaris. In part that's because your chance of seeing the park's variety of wildlife is greatly reduced. But there have been reports of some serious incidents involving undertrained park staff leading walking safaris resulting in injury to the tourists. This is also one of the most tsetse-fly-infested parks in Africa.

Self-Drive Safaris

The park no longer hires out vehicles, but Riverside Camp (p165) in Sitalike charges US$200 per day for a 4WD, some with a pop-up roof. A guide or driver (US$20) is highly recommended, both for safety and to make the most of your viewing experience.

Sleeping & Eating

Sleeping options run either top-end or budget here. You can stay in the ultra-luxury tented camps or the super-basic *bandas*. Both are good value for what they offer. Anyone staying in the park has to pay the camping fee, but this will be included in the overall package if staying at one of the top-end camps.

In the Park

Besides bush camping, there are two public campsites (US$35.40): one at Ikuu near Katisunga Plain and the other 2km south of Sitalike. Both have a lot of wildlife passing through. Bring all your food and drink with you.

All park lodges are located around the Katisunga Plain in the vicinity of the Ikuu Airstrip.

Katavi Park Bandas BUNGALOW $
(025-282 9213; www.tanzaniaparks.go.tz; r per person US$35.40; P) This is 2km south of the village and within park boundaries (so you need to pay park entry fees when staying here). The rooms are big, bright and surprisingly good. Zebras, giraffes and other animals are frequent visitors.

★ **Katavi Wildlife Camp** TENTED CAMP $$$
(Foxes; 0754 237422; www.kataviwildlifecamp.com; s/d all-inclusive except drinks US$685/1170; Jun-Feb; P) This comfortable, well-run camp has a prime setting overlooking Katisunga, making it the best place for in-camp wildlife watching. The six tents have large

porches with hammocks and are down-to-earth comfortable without being over the top. The quality guides round out the experience. It's owned by Foxes African Safaris, which offers some excellent combination itineraries with southern parks.

Katuma Bush Lodge TENTED CAMP $$$
(0732 978879; www.mbalimbali.com; s/d all-inclusive except drinks US$767/1184; mid-May–mid-Feb; P) With stunning views over the grasslands, the large safari tents here have four-poster beds, carved wooden showers and plenty of privacy. The defining feature is the relaxing lounge fronted by a deck with a small swimming pool. The price includes a wildlife drive.

Chada Katavi TENTED CAMP $$$
(0787 595908; www.nomad-tanzania.com; s/d all-inclusive US$1260/1800; Jun-Jan; P) Set under big trees in a prime location overlooking the Chada flood plain, this place promotes a classic safari ambience. It's at its most Hemingway-esque in the dining tent. This is a good spot for walking safaris – it has excellent guides – and fly camping can be arranged with advance notice. The price includes a wildlife drive.

Sitalike

Most backpackers stay at this little village on the northern edge of the park.

Riverside Camp BUNGALOW, CAMPGROUND $
(0785 860981, 0784 754740, 0767 754740; camping/s/d US$10/25/50; P) Riverside Camp has a prime setting just above a hippo-filled river. The *bandas* are simple, but the location is worth it. Mr Juma, the owner, is very helpful with arranging vehicle rental for a Katavi safari. Meals can be arranged (dinner/breakfast US$10/5 per person). Vervet monkeys and a host of birds are easy to see here.

Getting There & Away

Safari Airlink (p216) and Zantas Air (p216) fly twice a week to Ikuu Airstrip and the lodges will often let nonguests fly on their planes if space is available. All lodges provide free pick-up at Ikuu Airstrip for their guests. If you aren't staying at a lodge, arrange a vehicle or a ranger for walking *before* you arrive. If you are flying in, it is good to combine a trip to Katavi with a trip to Mahale Mountains National Park. Rangers will be waiting at the airstrip to collect park admission fees from those flying in.

Buses and trucks between Mpanda (Tsh3000, 45 minutes) and Sumbawanga (Tsh15,000, four hours) can pick you up and drop you off in Sitalike or at **park headquarters** (p163). Transport is frequent in the mornings, but after lunch you may have to wait several hours for a vehicle to pass.

Dalla-dallas and taxis depart Sitalike for Mpanda (Tsh3000, 45 minutes) from 7am to 8pm once they have enough people to make it worth the ride. You can hire one directly for Tsh90,000 if there's an emergency.

If you're driving, the only petrol stations are in Mpanda and Sumbawanga.

Vehicle safaris including transport to Katavi and a safari inside the park can be arranged with Riverside Camp in Sitalike and Lake Shore Lodge & Campsite (p164) in Kipili.

Sumbawanga

025 / POP 210,000

Sumbawanga is small and scruffy and not much of a tourist destination in itself, but it provides a great hub for beautiful day trips and overnights around the region, so it's well worth spending a couple of days here. It's large enough to have a solid variety of hotels, restaurants and shops, and is the last stocking-up spot for those headed north to Katavi National Park (p163).

The surrounding Ufipa Plateau, which lies at an invigorating 2000m, is home to many important endemic plants. It has also been declared an 'Important Bird Area' by BirdLife International. The **Mbizi Forest Reserve** (US$10), a couple of hours' walk from Sumbawanga, is a closer place to meet feathered friends.

Also nearby is the shallow **Lake Rukwa**, a birding paradise, which is accessed from many villages near its meandering shoreline. Ilanga, served by frequent 4WDs (Tsh5000, two hours) throughout the day, provides the easiest access.

Activities

★Rukaki Adventure Tours and Safaris TOURS
(0784 704343; Mbeya Rd; walking tours US$10, hiking US$20, Kalambo Falls Tsh20,000 plus US$20; 7am-10pm) A tourism venture headed by the ever-entrepreneurial Charles, Rukaki Adventure Tours can take you to a variety of places: Lake Ruaha, Kalambo Falls, or for hikes and walks in the beautiful hills of the region. Safaris to Katavi (p163) can also be arranged. Private guiding is available (you'll need to negotiate a fee).

Southern Highlands

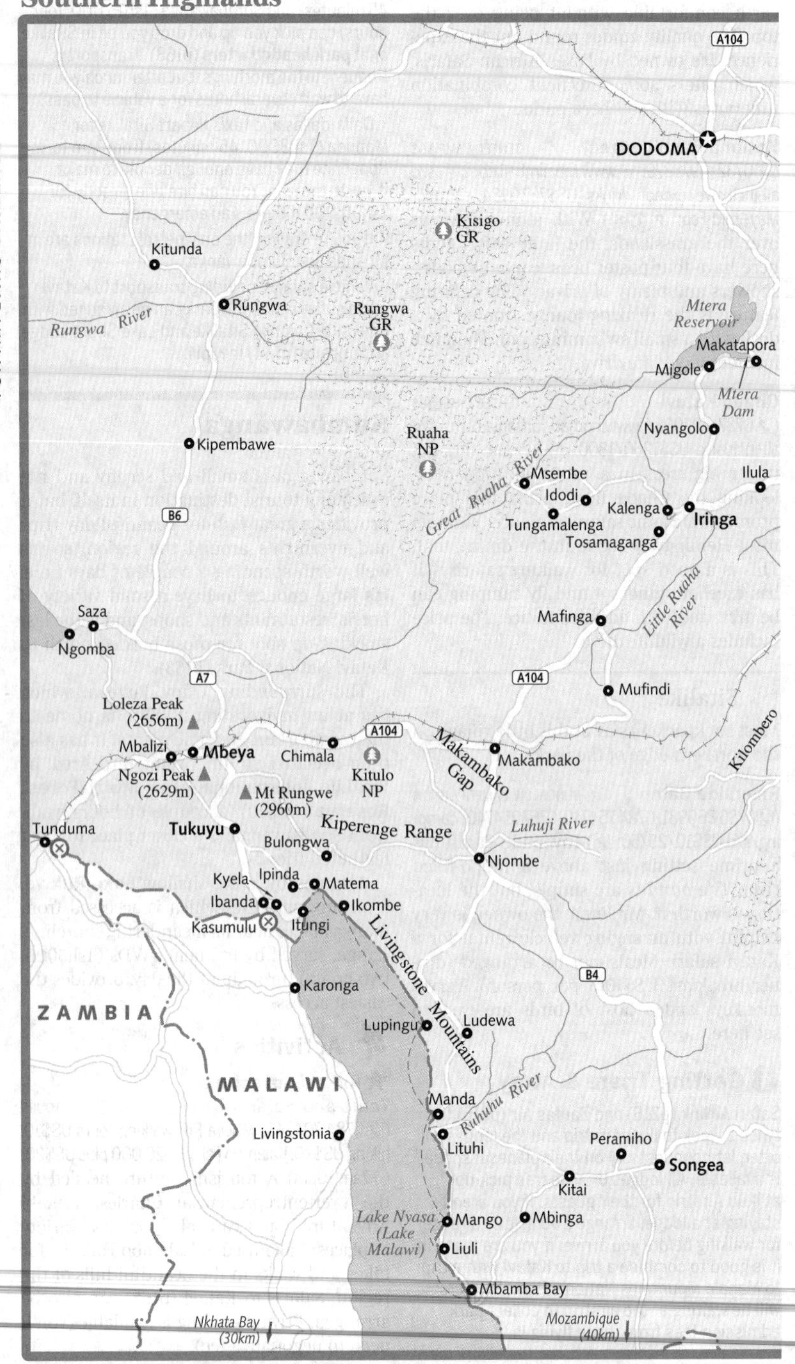

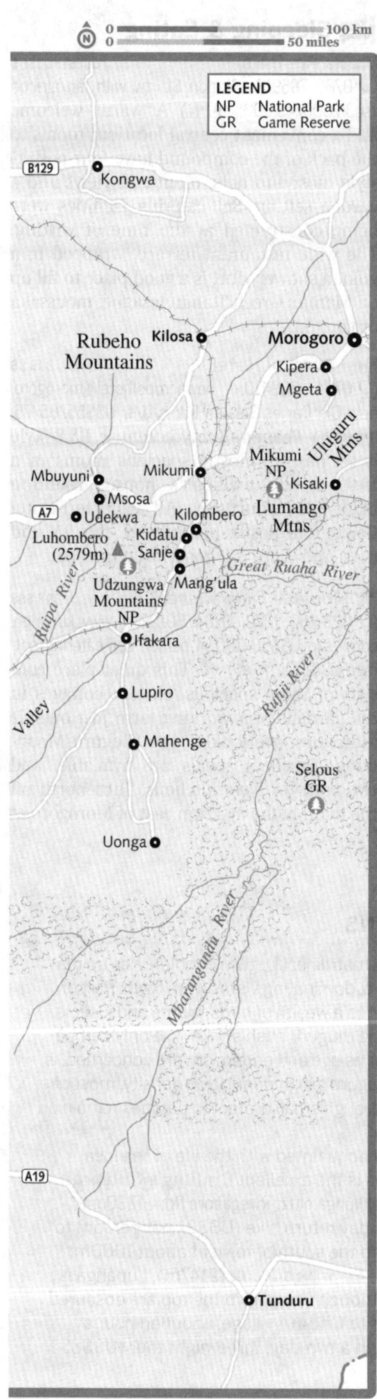

Sleeping & Eating

Ikuwo Lodge HOTEL $

(☎0754 647479, 025-280 2393; Mazwi Rd; r Tsh30,000-40,000; ⊜) If all you want is a place to crash in the centre of the market district, then this aquarium-blue, all-glass block will do nicely. There are instant hot showers and plenty of street noise. The rooms have fridges and include bottled water. No English is spoken though.

Kalambo Falls Lodge HOTEL $

(☎0757 381400, 0754 931336; Katandala St; r Tsh70,000-120,000; P⊜☎) Kalambo Falls Lodge has spacious rooms with large tubs, fridges and in-room wi-fi. It's also got a professional chef and a full bar, making an all-in-one stop if you're staying overnight in Sumbawanga. An additional plus is that it's a fair way from the noisy town centre.

Information

Bethlehem Tourism Information Centre
(☎0753 807593, 0753 807593, 0784 704343; charlesnkuba450@hotmail.com; Mbeya Rd; ⊙7am-10pm) A one-stop tourist information and local tour service operated by the enthusiastic and helpful Charles. He can help with onward transport, and organises local walking tours and trips further afield to destinations such as Lake Rukwa.

Getting There & Away

Numerous bus companies operate out of Sumbawanga and most ticket offices are located just outside the bus stand. Most buses depart between 7am and 9.30am. Buses go to the following:

Kasesya (Tsh 6000, four to five hours)

Mbeya (Tsh15,000 to Tsh20,000, seven hours) via Tunduma (Tsh10,000)

Mpanda (Tsh14,000, four to six hours)

To get to Kasesya on the Zambian border there's also a dalla-dalla (Tsh3000, four to five hours) at 8am and 4pm.

SOUTHERN HIGHLANDS

Tanzania's Southern Highlands officially begin at Makambako Gap, about halfway between Iringa and Mbeya, and extend southwards into Malawi. Here the term encompasses the entire region along the mountainous chain running between Morogoro in the east and Lake Nyasa and the Zambian border in the west.

The highlands are a major transit route for travellers to Malawi or Zambia, and an important agricultural area. They are also wonderfully scenic and a delight to explore, with rolling hills, lively markets, jacaranda-lined streets, lovely lodges and plenty of wildlife. Hike in the Udzungwa Mountains, watch wildlife in Mikumi or Ruaha National Parks, get to know the matrilineal Luguru people in the Uluguru Mountains, or head well off the beaten track to the heart of the Southern Highlands in Tanzania's southwesternmost corner. Here wild orchids carpet sections of Kitulo National Park and verdant mountains cascade down to the idyllic shores of Lake Nyasa.

Morogoro

223 / POP 315,000

Morogoro would be a fairly scruffy town were it not for its verdant setting at the foot of the often cloud-shrouded Uluguru Mountains, which brood over the landscape from the south. The surrounding area is one of the country's breadbaskets and is home to the prestigious Sokoine University (Tanzania's national agricultural institute) and a major educational and mission station. While there are few attractions, Morogoro offers a good and warm introduction to Tanzanian life outside Dar es Salaam, plus the chance for cultural tours and hikes in the nearby Ulugurus.

Sleeping & Eating

Mama Pierina's GUESTHOUSE $
(0786 786913; Station St; tw with fan/air-con Tsh35,000/45,000; P ✱) A warm welcome and a convenient central location; rooms to the back of the compound have four-poster-style mosquito nets, mountain views and a garden setting. Self-catering facilities were being constructed at the time of writing. The wide restaurant terrace, wrapped in a golden shower vine, is a good place to fill up on Mama's Greek/Italian lasagne, moussaka or tzatziki.

New Acropol Hotel B&B $$
(0754 309410; newacropolhotel@morogoro.net; Old Dar es Salaam Rd; s/d/tr US$55/65/75; P ✱) This enjoyably eccentric B&B-style hotel has six mostly spacious rooms in a 1940s estate manager's house around a plant-filled courtyard. All have terracotta floors, four-poster beds, fridge, fan, TV and nets, and there is a good restaurant-bar.

★ **Mbuyuni Farm Retreat** B&B $$$
(023-260 1220, 0784 601220; www.kimango.com; s/d US$90/180, 4-person self-catering cottage US$130; P) This quiet place consists of three spacious, elegant cottages in the gardens of a working farm just outside Morogoro, overlooking the Uluguru Mountains. Excellent meals are available, and two cottages have kitchens. Turn north off the main highway 12km east of Morogoro at

HIKING IN THE ULUGURU MOUNTAINS

The verdant Uluguru Mountains – home to the matrilineal Luguru people – rise up majestically from the plains just south of Morogoro, dominating vistas from town. Part of the Eastern Arc chain, the mountains are home to a wealth of birds, plants and insects. These include many unique species, such as the Uluguru bush shrike. The only comparable mountain-forest area in East Africa, as far as age and endemism are concerned, is the Usambara Mountains. Sadly, due to the Uluguru's high population density, most of the original forest cover has been depleted, although small protected patches remain on the upper slopes.

Hiking is the best way to explore and to get acquainted with the life of the local Luguru. The best contact for organising things is the excellent **Chilunga Cultural Tourism** (0754 477582, 023-261 3323; www.chilunga.or.tz; Rwegasore Rd; 7.30am-6pm) in Morogoro town. Routes include a half-day return hike (US$27 per person) to **Morningside**, an old German mountain hut to the south of town at about 1000m; and a day's return hike (US$45 per person) to **Lupanga Peak** (2147m). Lupanga is the highest point in the immediate vicinity, although views from the top are obscured by the forest. A recommended cultural walk is to **Choma** village, about an hour's walk beyond Morningside, and often included in a two-day, three-night tour (US$85 per person).

Morogoro

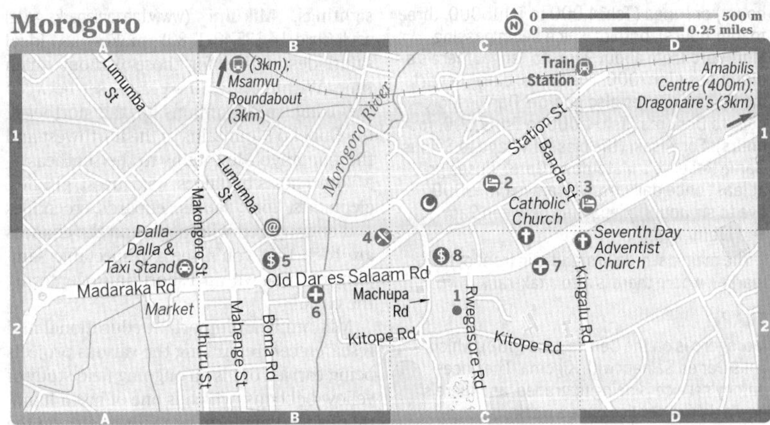

the end of Kingolwira village onto a mango-tree-lined lane and continue over a bridge to the farm.

Red Chilli Restaurant INDIAN, CHINESE $
(New Green Restaurant; ☎0784 498874; Station St; mains Tsh7000-10,000; ⏰9am-11pm; ✎) This long-standing place features functional decor but great grub. The menu has a large selection of Indian dishes, plus Chinese options and grilled chicken or fish and chips.

Information

INTERNET ACCESS

Amabilis Centre (☎0719 348959, 0716 880717; amabilis.conferencecentre@yahoo.com; Old Dar es Salaam Rd; s Tsh25,000, tw without bathroom Tsh20,000; P) There are a few computer terminals here.

Internet Cafe (off Lumumba St; per hour Tsh2000; ⏰8am-10pm Sun-Fri, 7am-10pm Sat) Ask for Pira's Supermarket; this tiny internet cafe is just around the corner.

MEDICAL SERVICES

Marhaba Pharmacy (☎023-261 3304; Old Dar es Salaam Rd; ⏰7.30am-5pm Mon-Sat) Morogoro's best-stocked pharmacy is just east of the dalla-dalla stand and just west of the small footbridge.

Morogoro Regional Hospital (☎0758 170037; Old Dar es Salaam Rd) Basic local medical services.

MONEY

Exim Bank (Lumumba St; ⏰9am-5pm Mon-Fri) ATM.

NBC (Old Dar es Salaam Rd; ⏰9am-5pm Mon-Fri) ATM.

Morogoro

Activities, Courses & Tours
1 Chilunga Cultural Tourism C2

Sleeping
2 Mama Pierina's C1
3 New Acropol Hotel D1

Eating
4 Red Chilli Restaurant B2

Information
5 Exim Bank B2
6 Marhaba Pharmacy B2
7 Morogoro Regional Hospital C2
8 NBC C2

Getting There & Away

AIR

Due to increasing road congestion getting out of Dar es Salaam, the five weekly flights to/from Morogoro (US$160 one way) by Auric Air (www.auricair.com) are an increasingly attractive alternative to the bus for travellers in a hurry.

BUS

The main bus station is 3km north of town on the main Dar es Salaam road, about 300m east of Msamvu roundabout (Tsh6000 in a taxi and Tsh400 in a dalla-dalla; look for vehicles marked 'Kihonda', and confirm that they are going to Msamvu). It's chaotic, with no real order to things; you'll need to ask where to find buses to your destination. Allow at least an hour to catch a dalla-dalla and get yourself sorted at Msamvu.

For all destinations, no larger buses originate in Morogoro. It's best to wait for buses from Dar es Salaam (Tsh7000 to Tsh8000, four hours) or Iringa (Tsh14,000 to Tsh15000, three to four hours), both of which begin passing Morogoro from about 9am. To Tanga, there's a direct bus (Tsh7000, five hours, daily) departing by 8am. Buses also go from Dar via Morogoro to Dodoma (Tsh14,000 to Tsh17,000, four hours). For Kisaki (the closest village to Selous Game Reserve's Matambwe Gate), buses go at least once daily from Msamvu (Tsh9000, five to six hours), departing between 9am and 11am.

The main dalla-dalla stand is in front of the market, where there is also a taxi rank.

TRAIN

Morogoro is on the Central Line (p62), which links Dar es Salaam with Kigoma. The once-patchy service is being upgraded, and there's now a deluxe service once a week.

Mikumi National Park

This is Tanzania's fourth-largest national park, with a landscape of baobabs, black hardwood trees and grassy plains, and the most accessible from Dar es Salaam. With almost guaranteed year-round wildlife sightings, **Mikumi** (www.tanzaniaparks.go.tz; adult/child US$35.40/11.80) makes an ideal safari destination for those without much time. Within its 3230 sq km – set between the Uluguru Mountains to the northeast, the Rubeho Mountains to the northwest and the Lumango Mountains to the southeast – Mikumi hosts buffaloes, wildebeest, giraffes, elephants, lions, zebras, leopards, crocodiles and endangered wild dogs, and the chances are high that you'll see a respectable sampling of these within a short time of entering the park.

Mikumi is an important educational and research centre. Among the various projects being carried out is an ongoing field study of yellow baboons, which is one of just a handful of such long-term primate studies on the continent.

To the south, Mikumi is contiguous with Selous Game Reserve (p190).

MIKUMI NATIONAL PARK

Why Go Easy access from Dar es Salaam; rewarding year-round wildlife watching and birding; giraffes, zebras, buffaloes, wild dogs and sometimes honey badgers.

When to Go Year-round.

Practicalities Drive or bus from Dar es Salaam. Entry fees (valid for 24 hours, single entry only) are payable only with Visa or MasterCard. Driving hours inside the park (off the main highway) are 6.30am to 6.30pm.

Budget Tips Any bus along the highway will drop you at the gate. The park doesn't hire vehicles, but staff sometimes rent their own. Arrange at the gate and be prepared to bargain. For sleeping, the park cottages are cheap and pleasant, with a dining room for meals. Post-safari: flag down an Iringa- or Dar-bound bus to continue your travels. More reliable: hire a safari vehicle through one of the hotels listed under Mikumi town (about US$200 per five-person vehicle for a full-day safari); bring your own lunch and drinks.

Activities

The most reliable wildlife watching is around the Mkata floodplain, to the northwest of the main road, with the open vistas of the small but lovely Millennium ('Little Serengeti') area a highlight. This area is especially good for spotting buffaloes – often quite near the roadside – as well as giraffes, elephants and zebras. Another attraction: the Hippo Pools, just northwest of the main entry gate, where you can watch hippos wallowing and snorting at close range, plus do some fine birding.

Throughout the park there are wonderful birding opportunities: look out for marabou storks and malachite kingfishers.

Sleeping & Eating

Mikumi Park Campsite CAMPGROUND $
(☎0767 536135, 0689 062334; mikumi@tanzaniaparks.go.tz; camping adult/child US$35.40/5.90) Of the park's four ordinary campsites, the one closest to the park headquarters is reasonably well equipped with toilet facilities and a shower.

★**Camp Bastian Mikumi** LODGE $$
(☎0718 244 507, 0782 547 448; www.campbastian.com; b&b s from US$40, d US$60-150, camping US$10-15; wifi) Located 10km west of the main gate, Camp Bastian is a harmoniously beautiful and good-value choice, with quality food and good drivers/guides on hand. There are six stone-floored cottages with wide verandahs, decorated with local fabric

and furniture, as well as a campsite. There are options for half or full board too, also available to campers.

Mikumi Park Cottages & Resthouse COTTAGE $$
(☎0689 062334, 0767 536135; mikumi@tanzaniaparks.go.tz; s/d/tr US$59/88.50/106.20; P ❄) About 3km from the gate, the park cottages and resthouse offer rooms in attached brick bungalows, all with bathroom, fan and air-con, and meals on order (Tsh10,000 per plate) at the nearby dining hall. The resthouse, which consists of two double rooms sharing an entrance, also has a kitchen (bring your own gas). Animals frequently wander just in front.

Vuma Hills TENTED CAMP $$$
(☎0754 237422; www.vumahills.com; s/d incl full board & wildlife drives from US$365/570; P ≋) This pleasant camp is set on a rise about 7km south of the main road, with views over the distant plains. The 16 elegant tented en suite cottages each have a double and a single bed. The mood is relaxed, the cuisine good and the pool makes a nice post-safari treat. The turn-off is diagonally opposite the park entry gate.

Getting There & Away

BUS

All through buses on the Dar–Mbeya highway will drop you at the park gate. Pick-ups can also be arranged from here to continue your onward journey. While vehicle rental can sometimes be arranged privately with park staff, it's better to arrive with your own vehicle or hire one through a Mikumi town hotel.

CAR & MOTORCYCLE

The park gate is about a five-hour drive from Dar es Salaam; speed limits on the section of main highway inside the park are controlled (70km/h during the day and 50km/h at night). A network of generally well-maintained roads in Mikumi's northern section is accessible with a 2WD during most of the year; the south is strictly 4WD, except the road to Vuma Hills Tented Camp.

For combining Mikumi with Selous, the 145km road linking Mikumi's main gate with Kisaki village (21km west of Selous' Matambwe Gate) is now open year-round except during the heavy rains, and makes a scenic 4WD alternative; allow about five hours between the two. Alternatively, you can go via Morogoro (140km and five to six hours between Morogoro and Kisaki).

Iringa

☎026 / POP 175,000

Perched at a cool 1600m on a cliff overlooking the valley of the Little Ruaha River, Iringa was initially built up by the Germans in the late 19th century as a bastion against the local Hehe people. Now it's a district capital, an important agricultural centre and the gateway for visiting Ruaha National Park. Once away from the main street, with its congestion and hustlers, it's also an extremely likeable place, with an attractive bluff-top setting, healthy climate and bracing highland feel.

The new Boma museum of local culture and the Neema Crafts centre are enticing, and there are a couple of outstanding historical sites within easy reach: ancient rock art at Igeleke, and even more ancient Isimila, where you can see Stone Age flints and hammerstones, as well as an extraordinary landscape of earth pillars.

Sights

★Neema Crafts ARTS CENTRE
(☎0783 760945; www.neemacrafts.com; Hakimu St; ⊙8.30am-6.30pm Mon-Sat) This acclaimed vocational training centre for young deaf and disabled people sits just southeast of the Clock Tower roundabout. Operated by the Anglican church, it sells paper and cards made from elephant dung, jewellery, quilts, clothing, batiks and more. Behind the craft shop is a weaving workshop, and adjoining is a popular cafe (p173) and guesthouse (p173). Free workshop tours form part of the centre's remit to change perceptions of people with disabilities. Volunteer opportunities are occasionally available.

★Iringa Boma MUSEUM
(☎026-270 2160, 0762 424642; www.fahariyetu.net; Tsh10,000; ⊙9.30am-5pm) This excellent EU-funded museum is a great new development, as is its small **cafe** (www.fahariyetu.net; mains Tsh8000-10,000; ⊙9.30am-5pm) and quality gift shop (p174). Located between Uhuru Park and Neema, Boma is housed in a 1900 German colonial building. Artfully displayed objects, including an embroidered chief's robe, wooden ceremonial stool and gleaming calabashes, are illuminated by extended captions exploring the ancient and colonial history of the area, tribal traditions

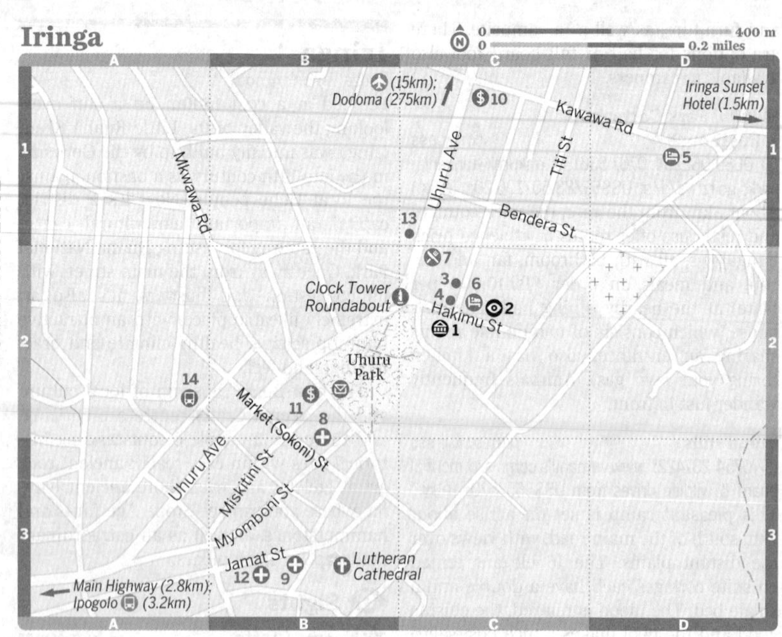

Iringa

Sights
1 Iringa Boma C2
2 Neema Crafts C2

Activities, Courses & Tours
3 Bateleur Safaris & Tours C2
4 Chabo Africa C2

Sleeping
5 Iringa Lutheran Centre D1
6 Neema Umaki Guest House C2

Eating
Boma Café .... (see 1)
7 Hasty Tasty Too C2
Neema Crafts Centre Cafe .... (see 2)

Shopping
Boma .... (see 1)

Information
8 Acacia Pharmacy B2
9 Aga Khan Health Centre B3
10 Barclays C1
11 CRDB B2
12 Myomboni Pharmacy B3
Neema Crafts Centre Internet Cafe .... (see 2)

Transport
13 Auric Air C1
14 Bus Station A2

and clothing and nearby attractions. It's the perfect place to start your explorations of the town.

★Igeleke Rock Art HISTORIC SITE
(off Dodoma road; adult/student & child Tsh10,000/5000; ⌚8am-5.30pm) A large prehistoric frieze, similar in style to the Kondoa rock paintings, located at a spectacular site on the edge of town just west of the Dodoma road. The ochre drawings depict human figures, an elephant, jumping eland and giraffe hiding in long grass. It's an easy and worthwhile excursion from town involving a short but steep walk from the car park. A guide can be arranged on-site (about Tsh10,000 per group) or in advance with Iringa-based tour operators.

Isimila Stone Age Site HISTORIC SITE
(adult/child Tsh20,000/10,000, plus guide fee per group Tsh10,000; ⌚8am-6pm) Here, in the late 1950s, amid a dramatic landscape of eroded sandstone pillars, archaeologists unearthed

one of the most significant Stone Age finds ever identified. Tools found at the site – hammerstones, axeheads, flints and scrapers – are estimated to be between 60,000 and 100,000 years old. There's a museum with small, well-captioned displays highlighting some of the discoveries. Isimila is signposted off the Mbeya road to the left, about 21km southwest of Iringa.

Activities

★Bateleur Safaris & Tours SAFARI
(☎0765 735261, 0762 921825; www.bateleursafaris.co.tz; ⌚8am-7pm) An efficient and welcoming locally run operation located round the corner from Neema Crafts centre. Staff create tailor-made trips to Ruaha (including night safaris) and Mikumi National Parks, as well as short excursions to Igeleke Rock and other local attractions. Bike tours and wildlife are specialities, and it will book accommodation according to your budget.

Chabo Africa SAFARI
(☎0784 893717, 0754 893717; www.chaboafricasafari.com; Hakimu St; ⌚8.30am-5pm Mon-Fri, to 2pm Sat) Offers Ruaha safaris (from about US$450 for a one-night safari), visits to the Igeleke Rock Art and other excursions in and around Iringa.

Sleeping

★Neema Umaki Guest House GUESTHOUSE $
(☎0683 380492, 0768 027991; www.neemacrafts.com; Hakimu St; s/d/f Tsh25,000/45,000/65,000; Wi-Fi) This centrally located guesthouse has an array of clean, comfortable rooms, all with nets and TV. It adjoins Neema Crafts centre, but rooms are in a quieter section towards the back of the complex. Turn east off Uhuru Ave at the clock tower and go down about 100m. The guesthouse entrance is around the corner.

Iringa Sunset Hotel HOTEL $
(☎0754 469 854; Gangilonga Hills; d Tsh60,000-100,000; air-con, Wi-Fi) This new hotel enjoys one of the best locations in Iringa, with an eagle-eye view of the town and surrounding plains. There's a wonderful central dining hall with an open fire in the evenings, and accommodation is in an attractive cluster of stone *bandas* and wooden chalets. The chalets with a view are recommended, and are less expensive.

★Kisolanza – The Old Farm House CAMPGROUND, COTTAGES $$
(☎0754 306144; www.kisolanza.com; Ifunda; camping from US$9, s/d/tr cottages with half board from US$100/160/200, tw without bathroom US$50; P) This gracious 1930s farm homestead 50km southwest of Iringa is fringed by stands of pine and rolling hill country and recommended for its accommodation and outstanding cuisine. There are two camping grounds (overlanders and private vehicles), twin-bedded rooms, cosy wooden chalets, family cottages with fireplace, two luxury garden cottages and a spa. All are spotless, impeccably furnished and excellent value.

Eating

★Hasty Tasty Too TANZANIAN, INTERNATIONAL $
(☎026-270 2061; Uhuru Ave; mains Tsh6000-13,000; ⌚8.30am-8pm Mon-Sat; P) This long-standing Iringa classic has good breakfasts, yoghurt, samosas, shakes and reasonably priced main dishes, including a divine chickpea curry. It's popular with local and expat clientele. You can get toasted sandwiches packed to go and arrange food for Ruaha camping safaris.

★Neema Crafts Centre Cafe CAFE $
(☎0783 760945; www.neemacrafts.com; Hakimu St; mains Tsh3000-13,000; ⌚8am-6.30pm Mon-Fri; Wi-Fi) Located upstairs at Neema Crafts (p171), this cafe is justifiably popular, with local coffees and teas, homemade cookies, excellent cinnamon buns, cakes, soups, and a selection of sandwiches and light meals. The noticeboard is great for finding out about safaris and Swahili classes, and the breezy terrace hung with bunting is one of the town's best hang-outs.

★Mama Iringa Pizzeria & Italian Restaurant ITALIAN $$
(☎0753 757007; mama.iringa@yahoo.com; Don Bosco area; mains Tsh9000-15,000; ⌚noon-2.30pm & 5-9pm Tue-Sun; P) Delicious Italian food – pizzas, gnocchi, lasagne and more, plus salads – are served in the quiet courtyard of a former convent. It's about 3km from the town centre (Tsh5000 in a taxi). Take Mkwawa Rd to the Danish School junction and follow the signposts.

Shopping

★**Boma** ARTS & CRAFTS

(www.fahariyetu.net; ⊙9.30am-5pm) The craft store at the Boma museum has a terrific selection of gifts and crafts, with a specialism in quality handwoven fabrics. This is the place to buy special scarves and wraps; it also sells kids' clothes and soft toys, fabric-hanging storage, notepads and books.

Information

INTERNET ACCESS

Neema Crafts Centre Internet Cafe (Hakimu St; per hour Tsh2000; ⊙8am-6.30pm Mon-Sat) Wi-fi only.

Post office (⊙7.30am-4.30pm Mon-Fri, 8am-noon Sat) Has an attached internet cafe.

MEDICAL SERVICES

Acacia Pharmacy (☎026-270 2335, 0754 943243; cnr Market & Myomboni Sts; ⊙7.30am-7.30pm Mon-Sat, 9am-7pm Sun) Near the market.

Aga Khan Health Centre (☎026-270 2277; Jamat St; ⊙8am-6pm Mon-Fri, to 2pm Sat & Sun) Next to the Lutheran cathedral and near the market.

Myomboni Pharmacy (☎026-270 2617, 026-270 2277; Jamat St; ⊙7.30am-7.30pm) Just downhill from the Aga Khan Health Centre.

MONEY

Barclays (Uhuru Ave; ⊙9am-5pm Mon-Fri) Money changing and an ATM.

CRDB (Uhuru Ave; ⊙8.30am-4.30pm Mon-Fri, to 12.30pm Sat) Offers currency exchange and an ATM.

TOURIST INFORMATION

The bulletin boards at **Hasty Tasty Too** (p173), **Neema Crafts Centre Cafe** (p173) and **Iringa Lutheran Centre** (☎026-270 0722, 0755 517445; www.iringalutherancentre.com; Kawawa Rd; s/d/tr incl full breakfast US$25/45/55; P 📶) are well worth checking, especially to find travel companions for sharing costs on Ruaha safaris. These places can also help you find reliable guides for local excursions and tours.

Getting There & Away

AIR

Auric Air (☎0755 413090; www.auricair.com; Uhuru Ave; ⊙7.30am-4pm Mon-Fri, 8.30am-1pm Sat) has daily flights connecting Iringa with Dar es Salaam (US$180 one way). Iringa's Nduli Airfield is about 12km out of town along the Dodoma road.

BUS

Most buses arrive and depart from the hectic bus station just west of the main street. Ticket offices for all companies can be found here. Book ahead for Shabiby luxury buses to be sure of getting a seat.

If you're arriving on a bus continuing towards Morogoro or Mbeya, you may be dropped off at Ipogoro, 3km southeast of town below the escarpment where the Morogoro–Mbeya highway bypasses Iringa (Tsh5000 for a taxi to/from town, though initial quotes are usually much higher).

Numerous lines go daily to Dar es Salaam (Tsh19,000 to Tsh28,000, nine to 10 hours), leaving from 6am onwards. To Mbeya (Tsh14,000 to Tsh18,000, five to eight hours), Shabiby, Chaula Express and others depart daily between 6am and 10am; Shabiby is recommended for this route, which can otherwise be very slow. Otherwise you can try to get a seat on one of the through buses from Dar es Salaam that pass Iringa (Ipogoro bus station) from about 1pm. To Njombe (Tsh11,000, 3½ hours) and Songea (Tsh19,000, nine hours), Super Feo departs at 6am from the town bus station. To Dodoma (Tsh14,000, four hours), Kimotco and several other companies depart daily from 6am, going via Nyangolo and Makatapora. Some Dodoma buses continue on to Singida (Tsh24,000, seven hours) and Arusha (Tsh40,000, 13 hours).

Ruaha National Park

Ruaha National Park (www.tanzaniaparks.go.tz; adult/child US$35.40/11.80) forms the core of a wild extended ecosystem covering about 40,000 sq km and provides home to Tanzania's largest elephant population, estimated at 12,000. In addition, Tanzania's largest national park hosts buffaloes, greater and lesser kudus, Grant's gazelles, wild dogs, ostriches, cheetahs, roan and sable antelope, and more than 400 types of birds.

Ruaha is notable for its wild and striking topography, especially around the Great Ruaha River, which is its heart, and which is home to crocodiles, hippos and wading birds. Much of it is undulating plateau averaging about 900m in height with occasional rocky outcrops and stands of baobabs. Mountains in the south and west reach to about 1600m and 1900m respectively. Running through the park are several 'sand' rivers, most of which dry up during the dry season, when they are used by wildlife as corridors to reach areas where water remains.

RUAHA NATIONAL PARK

Why Go Outstanding dry-season wildlife watching, especially elephants, hippos, lions and endangered wild dogs; excellent birding; rugged scenery.

When to Go The driest season is between June and November, and this is when it's easiest to spot wildlife along the river beds. During the rainy season, some areas become impassable and wildlife is difficult to locate, but green panoramas, lavender-coloured flowers and rewarding birding compensate.

Practicalities Drive in from Iringa; fly in from Arusha or Dar es Salaam. Entry fees are per 24-hour period, single-entry only, and are payable with Visa or MasterCard only. The main gate (open 7am to 6pm) is about 8km inside the park boundary on its eastern side, near the park's Msembe headquarters. Driving is permitted within the park from 6am to 6.30pm.

Budget Tips Ruaha has no true budget options. Your best bet: get a group of four or five, hire a vehicle in Iringa for an overnight safari and sleep at the old park *bandas*. Meals are available, but bring your own drinks. It's also possible to take the bus from Iringa to Tungamalenga, and arrange car hire there for a safari (about US$250 per day). But confirm vehicle availability in advance, and remember park fees are single-entry only. Car hire from Iringa and sleeping inside the park usually works out to be better value.

Sights

Ruaha is notable as it straddles a transition zone between East African savannah lands and the miombo woodlands more common further south, thus offering a mix of plant and animal species from both regions.

The best place to experience the park is along the river, especially the circuit that runs northeast, following the riverbanks, before turning inwards towards the area around Mwagusi Safari Camp. Birding here is especially fine and sightings of hippos, crocodiles and elephants are almost guaranteed. Try not to miss sunrise and sunset, when the large rocks dotting the river's channel are illuminated and the bordering vegetation and flatlands come alive. Bat-eared foxes and jackals are common around the Msembe area. Lions aren't as readily seen as in the Serengeti, but they are definitely present, with the area just north of the river towards Mwagusi a good bet.

Although the area around the camps on the eastern side of the park fills up during the August to October high (dry) season, Ruaha receives relatively few visitors in comparison with the northern parks. Large sections are unexplored, and for much of the year you're likely to have things to yourself. Whenever you visit, set aside as much time as you can spare; it's not a place to be discovered on a quick in-and-out trip.

Activities

Besides wildlife drives, it's possible to organise two- to three-hour walking safaris (park walking fee US$23.60 per group) from June to January. Bateleur (p173), based in Iringa, organises thrilling night safaris here.

Ruaha Cultural Tourism Program CULTURAL
(☎0788 354286, 0752 142195; www.ruahaculturaltours.com; half-/full-day tour US$20/40, per person full board in Maasai village US$27) Cultural tours of a Maasai village, known as a *boma* (including the chance to spend the night), traditional cooking lessons, nature walks and more. Recommended stop en route to or from Ruaha.

Sleeping & Eating

Inside the Park

Inside the park there are both public and special campsites, as well as park *bandas*. The special campsites have no facilities, and are scattered in the bush well away from park headquarters. All park-run accommodation can be booked at the gate on arrival, or through tour operators in Iringa (p171). Payment must be made at the park gate with Visa or MasterCard.

Ruaha Park Bandas & Cottages COTTAGE $$
(☎0756 144400; ruaha@tanzaniaparks.go.tz; s/d bandas with shared bathroom US$35.40/70.80, s/d/f cottages US$59/118/118) Ruaha's 'old'

park *bandas,* in a fine setting directly on the river near park headquarters, have been partially upgraded. Several have private bathroom, and meals can be arranged or cooked yourself. About 3km beyond here, on a rise overlooking the river in the distance, are the 'new' tidy cement cottages (all with private bathroom). There's a dining hall next door with inexpensive meals.

Accommodation must be paid for at the entry gate with credit card.

★Mwagusi Safari Camp TENTED CAMP **$$$**
(☎UK +44 18226 15721; www.mwagusicamp.com; s/d all-inclusive US$700/1225; ⊙Jun-Mar; P) This highly regarded 16-bed owner-managed camp is set in a prime wildlife-viewing location on the Mwagusi Sand River 20km inside the park gate – animals are more prolific at this spot once the rains have started. The atmosphere is intimate and the guiding is top-notch. Highlights are the spacious tented *bandas,* the rustic, natural feel and the romantic evening ambience.

★Mdonya Old River Camp TENTED CAMP **$$$**
(☎022-260 1747; www.ed.co.tz; per person incl full board & excursions from US$390; ⊙Jun-Mar; P) The relaxed Mdonya Old River Camp, about 1½ hours' drive from park headquarters, has 12 tents on the banks of the Mdonya Sand River, with elephants occasionally wandering through camp. It's a straightforward, unpretentious place with the necessary comforts tempered by a bush feel. If you take advantage of Coastal Travel's special fly-in offers, it offers good value for a Ruaha safari.

★Ruaha River Lodge LODGE **$$$**
(☎0754 237422; www.tanzaniasafaris.info; s/d incl full board & wildlife drives US$425/660; P) This unpretentious, beautifully situated 28-room lodge was the first in the park and is the only place on the river. It's divided into two separate sections, each with its own dining area. The stone cottages directly overlook the river – sit on your verandah and look out for elephants and hippos – and there's a treetop-level bar-terrace with stunning riverine panoramas.

It's about 15km inside the gate, southwest of park headquarters.

Outside the Park

There are several lodges and campsites just outside Ruaha park boundaries along the Tungamalenga village road (take the left fork at the junction when coming from Iringa). If staying here, remember that park entry fees are valid for a single entry only per 24-hour period.

Chogela Campsite CAMPGROUND **$**
(☎0757 151349, 0782 032025; www.chogelasafaricamp.wix.com/chogelasafaricamp; off Tungamalenga village road; camping US$10, s/d safari tents US$30/50; P) Shaded grounds, a large cooking-dining area and hot-water showers make this a popular budget choice. There are also twin-bedded safari-style tents. Vehicle rental can be arranged (US$250 for a full-day safari, with advance notice required; US$350 including pick-up and drop-off in Iringa), as can meals. The camp is about 34km from the park gate along the Tungamalenga road.

Ruaha Cultural Tourism Program (p175) also has a base here, for arranging nature walks, village tours and day or overnight visits to a nearby Maasai community.

Tandala Tented Camp TENTED CAMP **$$$**
(☎0757 183420, 0755 680220; www.tandalacamp.com; off Tungamalenga village road; s/d full board US$250/440; ⊙Jun-Mar; P ≋) Lovely Tandala sits just outside the park boundary, 12km from the gate. Eleven raised tents are scattered around shaded grounds with a bush feel (elephants and other animals are frequent visitors). Staff can organise vehicle rental to Ruaha, and guided walks and night drives in park border areas. The swimming pool and low-key ambience make it a good family choice.

ℹ Getting There & Away

AIR

There is an airstrip at Msembe.

Coastal Aviation (p216) flies from Dar es Salaam and Zanzibar to Ruaha via Selous Game Reserve (one way US$365 from Dar es Salaam, US$425 from Zanzibar) and between Ruaha and Arusha (US$365). Safari Airlink (p216) has similarly priced flights connecting Ruaha with Dar es Salaam, Selous and Arusha, and also with Katavi and Mikumi.

BUS

There's a daily bus between Iringa and Tungamalenga village (Tsh7000, five hours), departing Iringa's Mwangata bus stand (on the southwestern edge of town at the start of the Ruaha road) at 1pm. Look for the vehicle marked 'Idodi-Tungamalenga'. Departures from Tungamalenga's village bus stand (along the

Tungamalenga road, just before Tungamalenga Camp) are at 6am. From Tungamalenga, there's no onward transport to the park, other than rental vehicles arranged in advance through the Tungamalenga road camps (prices start at US$250 per day). There's no vehicle rental once at Ruaha, except what you've arranged in advance with the lodges.

CAR

Ruaha is 115km from Iringa along an unsealed road. About 58km before the park, the road forks; both sides go to Ruaha and the distance is about the same each way, but it's best to take the more travelled and more populated Tungamalenga road (left fork). The closest petrol is in Iringa. Ask at Neema Umaki Guest House (p173) in Iringa about vehicle rental to Ruaha for around US$300 per vehicle for the first day, then US$200 per vehicle for each subsequent day. Neema is a good contact for finding other travellers interested in joining a group.

Makambako

026 / POP 120,000

Makambako (a stop on the Tazara railway line) is a windy highland town where the road from Songea and Njombe meets the Dar es Salaam–Mbeya highway. Geographically the area marks the end of the Eastern Arc mountain range and the start of the Southern Highlands. Makambako, dominated by Bena people, is also notable for its large market, which includes an extensive used-clothes section. Otherwise there's no real reason to stop here other than as a lunch stop if you are driving, or to get off the train and onto the bus to head south to Njombe and Songea.

Sleeping & Eating

Shinkansen Lodge HOTEL $

(Njombe road; s/d Tsh35,000/45,000; P) This small compound has double- and twin-bedded rooms (some with interior windows only) accessed via an imposing Japanese-style entry gate and a well-fortified parking compound. Inside, the rooms are clean, albeit slightly gloomy. There's no food. It's conveniently located about 1km south of the main junction, and about 500m north of the bus stand.

Kondoa AFRICAN $

(Njombe road; mains Tsh5000-8000) This busy local eatery is as good a spot as any to get a meal in Makambako. It's just south of the main highway.

Information

NBC (Njombe road) Has an ATM.

Getting There & Away

The bus stand is about 1.5km south of the main junction along the Njombe road. The first bus to Mbeya (Tsh9000, three hours) leaves at 6am, with another bus at 7am. The first buses (all smaller Coastals) to Njombe (Tsh4000, one hour) and Songea (Tsh14,000, five hours) depart about 6.30am, and there's a larger bus departing at 6.30am for Iringa (Tsh9000, three to four hours), continuing on to Dar es Salaam (around Tsh30,000).

Njombe

026 / POP 150,200

Njombe, about 60km south of Makambako and 235km north of Songea, is a district capital, regional agricultural centre and home of the Bena people. It would be unmemorable but for its highly scenic setting on the eastern edge of the Kipengere Range at almost 2000m. The town hosts a good market, selling wicker baskets coloured with natural dyes.

In addition to giving it the reputation of being Tanzania's coldest town, this perch provides wide vistas over hills that seem to roll endlessly to the horizon. The surrounding area, dotted with tea plantations and fields of wildflowers, is ideal for walking and cycling. As there is no tourism infrastructure, anything you undertake will need to be under your own steam. At the northern edge of town, visible from the main road and an easy walk, are the **Luhuji Falls**.

Sleeping & Eating

Hill Side Hotel HOTEL $

(Chani Motel; 0752 910068, 026-278 2357; chanihotel@yahoo.com; r Tsh30,000-55,000; P) This cosy place has modest twin- and double-bedded rooms, hot water (usually), small but lovely poinsettia-studded gardens, and a good restaurant with TV and filling meals. Turn off the main road onto the dirt lane next to the courthouse (Mahakamani); it's just downhill and diagonally opposite the police station.

FM Hotel HOTEL $

(0786 513321; Main St; s/d/ste Tsh35,000-45,000/55,000/75,000; P) This large, soulless multistorey place bills itself as

Njombe's sleekest option, with modern rooms boasting nets and TV. Some face the highway, with views over Njombe, while others overlook an interior courtyard. There's a restaurant. It's on the main road 1km south of and diagonally opposite the bus stand.

Getting There & Away

It's possible to go from Njombe via public transport or private vehicle along scenic highland backroads to the Kitulo Plateau, and down to the shores of Lake Nyasa.

The bus stand (Main St) is on the west side of the main road, about 600m south of the large grey-water tank.

Buses go daily to Songea (Tsh10000 to Tsh13,000, four hours), Makambako (Tsh4000, one hour), Iringa (Tsh9000, 3½ hours) and Mbeya (Tsh10,000, four hours), with the first departures at 6.30am.

For hikers, there are daily vehicles to Bulongwa (departing Njombe about 10am) and Ludewa (departing by 8am), from where you can walk down to Matema and Lupingu respectively, both on the Lake Nyasa shoreline. You can also catch transport towards Bulongwa at the start of the Makete Rd at the northern end of town, just downhill from the Chani Motel turn-off. This road, which continues past Kitulo National Park and on to Isyonje and the junction with the Tukuyu road, is easily passable during the dry season, though somewhat slower during the rains. A small section near Makete is tarmac.

Mbeya

025 / POP 450,000

The thriving town of Mbeya sprawls at about 1700m in the shadow of Loleza Peak (2656m), in a gap between the verdant Mbeya Range to the north and the Poroto Mountains to the southeast. It was founded in 1927 as a supply centre for the gold rush at Lupa, to the north, but today owes its existence to its position on the Tazara railway line and the Tanzam Hwy, and its status as a major trade and transit junction between Tanzania, Zambia and Malawi.

The surrounding area is lush, mountainous and scenic. It's also a major farming region for coffee, tea, bananas and cocoa. While central Mbeya is on the scruffy side (especially around the bus station), the cool climate, jacaranda trees and views of the hills compensate, and there are many nearby excursions.

Sights & Activities

Amelia at Maua Café & Tours (p179) arranges safaris, horseriding and hikes in the area (from US$70 per day, and US$200 per day with accommodation). She also leads trips to Ngozi Peak and Crater (p181) and many other destinations.

Mbeya Peak MOUNTAIN

Just northwest of Mbeya is Mbeya Peak (2820m). It's the highest point in the Mbeya Range and makes an enjoyable day hike, best done by arranging a local guide through your hotel or a Mbeya travel agency.

Sleeping

Ifisi Community Centre HOTEL, GUESTHOUSE $

(025-256 1021, 0753 011622; www.mec-tanzania.ch; s Tsh30,000, guesthouse r Tsh50,000-60,000, hotel r Tsh60,000-80,000, camping Tsh10,000; P) A very good option for self-drivers en route to/from the Zambian border or points west. There are smallish but spotless guesthouse rooms in this church-run place, plus lovely, spacious, good-value hotel rooms, most with verandahs overlooking a private wildlife sanctuary. It has an inexpensive restaurant and a children's playground. On the north side of the main highway, 18km west of Mbeya.

Mbeya Hotel HOTEL $

(0788 760818, 025-250 2575, 025-250 2224; www.mbeyahotel.com; Kaunda Ave; s/d/tw/ste Tsh 60,000/80,000/90,000/120,000; P) The former East African Railways & Harbours Hotel has a faded colonial charm – check out the marble floor – and African art on the walls. Rooms are straightforward twins and doubles. The better ones (all doubles) are in an extension attached to the main building. More cramped rooms are in separate bungalows out the back. Small shaded gardens and a restaurant.

★ **Utengule Coffee Lodge** LODGE $$

(0786 481902, 0753 020901; www.riftvalley-zanzibar.com; camping US$11.50, s US$70-145, d US$110-195, f from US$180; P) This lovely lodge is set in expansive grounds on a hilly coffee plantation 20km west of Mbeya. Tasteful accommodation includes spacious standard rooms, nicer two-storey balconied suites, and a large, rustic family room. The cafe and restaurant are excellent. From Mbeya, follow the highway

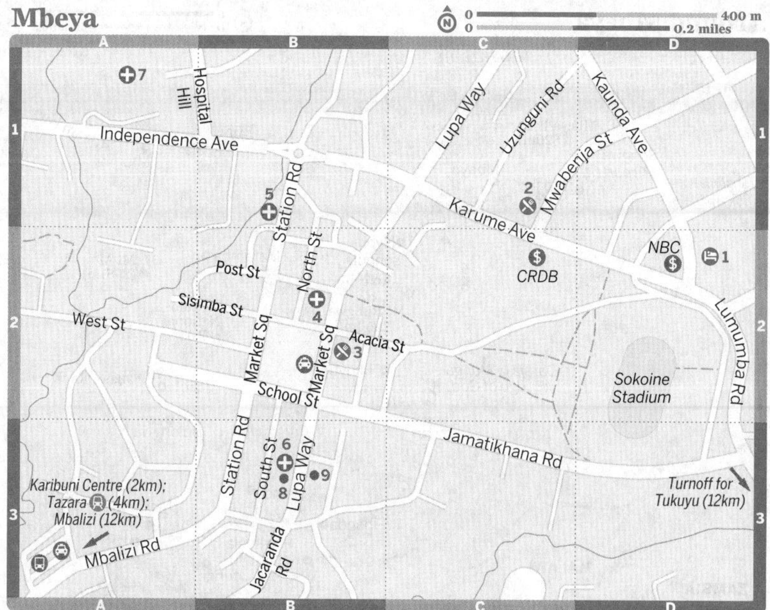

12km west to Mbalizi junction. Turn right and continue 8.5km to the entrance, on your right.

Eating

★Maua Café & Tours CAFE $

(☎0786 248199; 13 Mwabenja St; mains Tsh7000; ⏰8am-5pm Mon, Wed & Thu, to 9pm Tue, Fri & Sat) A brick homestead turned cafe serving big breakfasts, including granola and fresh coffee (Tsh10,000); wraps, burgers and toasties for lunch (from Tsh5000); and pizza, fish and salads for dinner. Sit outside by the hibiscus bush on benches with bright fabric cushions. It has an excellent ethical craft shop and a small backyard campground (US$10), and owner Amelia organises a range of tours.

★Ridge Cafe CAFE $

(1st fl, Business Centre Bldg, cnr Market Sq & Acacia St; drinks & snacks Tsh3000-5000; ⏰7am-8pm Mon-Fri, 9am-9pm Sat, to 3pm Sun; 📶) If you're missing Western culture, stop by this sleek place, stylishly hung with local fabrics, for smoothies, fresh juices, locally sourced gourmet coffees, great baking and other delicacies. It also sells a few crafts and Mbeya coffee beans. It's a good place to connect with travellers and volunteers.

Mbeya

Sleeping

1 Mbeya Hotel D2

Eating

2 Maua Café & Tours C1
3 Ridge Cafe B2

Information

4 Aga Khan Medical Centre B2
5 Babito Pharmacy B1
6 Bhojani Chemists B3
7 General Hospital A1

Transport

8 Fastlink Safaris B3
9 Kipunji Heritage B3

★Utengule Coffee Lodge EUROPEAN $$$

(☎0753 020901, 025-256 0100; www.riftvalley-zanzibar.com; mains Tsh15,000-25,000; ⏰7am-10pm; 📶) If you have your own transport, this spot, 20km west of Mbeya, is the place to go for fine dining, with both a daily set menu and à la carte, and a bar. Speciality coffees (including to take home) are a feature. It also has a swimming pool and a pool table, meaning you can spend a good chunk of your day here.

Around Mbeya

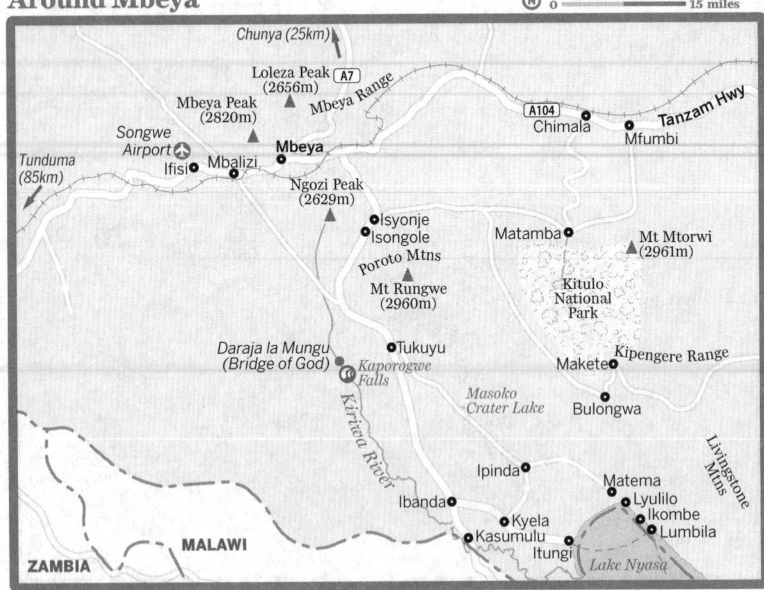

Information

DANGERS & ANNOYANCES

As a major transport junction, Mbeya attracts many transients, particularly in the area around the bus station. Watch your luggage, don't change money with anyone, and only buy bus tickets in the bus-company offices. Also be very wary of anyone presenting themselves as a tourist guide and don't make tourist arrangements with anyone outside of an office. Bus ticketing scams abound, especially for cross-border connections. Ignore all touts, no matter how apparently legitimate, trying to sell you through-tickets to Malawi (especially) or Zambia. Pay the fare only to the border, and then arrange onward transport from there.

Due to road building and spurious police checks, at the time of writing trips to the airport were suffering severe delays. Allow at least an hour.

MEDICAL SERVICES

Aga Khan Medical Centre (☎025-250 2043; cnr North & Post Sts; ⏰8am-8pm Mon-Sat, 9am-2pm Sun) Just north of the market.

Babito Pharmacy (☎0754 376808, 025-250 0965; Station Rd; ⏰7.30am-6.30pm Mon-Fri, 8am-5pm Sat) Located at the north end of Station Rd.

Bhojani Chemists (☎0715 622999, 0688 617999; Jacaranda Rd; ⏰8.30am-5.30pm Mon-Sat) Well-stocked pharmacy.

General Hospital (☎025-250 3456) Serves Mbeya and the surrounding region.

MONEY

CRDB (Karume Ave; ⏰9am-5pm Mon-Sat) ATM.

NBC (cnr Karume & Kaunda Aves; ⏰9am-5pm Mon-Fri, to noon Sat) Changes cash; ATM.

Getting There & Away

AIR

Air Tanzania (p216) and Fastjet (p216) fly around five times weekly between Mbeya and Dar es Salaam (from about Tsh180,000 one way). Air Tanzania is cheaper if you're booking with little notice, while Fastjet have some bargains if you're booking ahead. If you can't get online, book Air Tanzania through **Fastlink Safaris** (☎0752 111102, 0746 650750; Lupa Way; ⏰8.30am-5.30pm Mon-Fri, to noon Sat), and Fastjet through **Kipunji Heritage** (☎0754 457760; www.kipunjiheritage-tours.org; Lupa Way).

Songwe Airport (MBI) lies 22km southwest of Mbeya, just north of the Tanzam Hwy (about Tsh25,000 in a taxi); allow at least an hour, and don't rely on the appearance of the 'shuttle service'.

BUS

Arriving in Mbeya, your bus may arrive at the hectic **Nane Nane** terminal on the edge of town, in which case you'll need to switch to a dalla-dalla (Tsh400) to get to the centre.

Rungwe Express and other lines depart daily from Mbeya's main **bus station** to Dar es Salaam (Tsh45,000, 12 to 14 hours) from 6am, via Iringa (Tsh22,000, five to seven hours) and Morogoro (Tsh35,000, eight to nine hours).

To Njombe (Tsh10,000, four hours) and Songea (Tsh17,500 to Tsh25,000, eight hours), Super Feo departs daily at 6am, with one to two later departures as well.

To Tukuyu (Tsh2500, one to 1½ hours), Kyela (Tsh5000, two to 2½ hours) and the Malawi border (Tsh5000, two to 2½ hours; take the Kyela bus), there are several smaller Coastal buses daily leaving from the Nane Nane bus station about 10km east of Mbeya along the main highway. It's also possible to get to the Malawi border via dalla-dalla, but you'll need to change vehicles in Tukuyu. Note that there are no direct buses from Mbeya into Malawi, though touts at the Mbeya bus station may try to convince you otherwise. Dalla-dallas marked Igawilo or Uyole will drop you at Nane Nane bus station (Tsh400); taxis from town charge about Tsh10,000.

To Matema (Tsh12,000, six hours), there are two direct buses daily, departing Mbeya's Nane Nane bus station between 9am and 10am. Otherwise you'll need to take transport via Tukuyu to Kyela, from there to Ipinda, and then on to Matema.

To Tunduma (Tsh5000, two hours), on the Zambian border, there are daily minibuses. Once across, there's Zambian transport.

To Sumbawanga (Tsh18,000, five to six hours), Sumry goes daily beginning at 6am, with the last bus at 3pm, with some of the early buses continuing on to Mpanda (Tsh32,000, 12 to 14 hours).

To Tabora (Tsh37,000, 13 to 15 hours), there are a few vehicles weekly during the dry season, going via Chunya, and departing from the main Tanzam Hwy just east of central Mbeya.

To Moshi (Tsh55,000, 16 hours) and Arusha (Tsh58,000, 18 hours), Sumry departs daily at 5am.

To Dodoma (Tsh28,000, 10 hours) and Singida (Tsh40,000, 13 hours), there is at least one bus daily via Iringa (Tsh14,000 to Tsh18,000, five to eight hours).

TRAIN

Book tickets at least several days in advance (although sometimes cabins are available at the last minute) at **Tazara train station** (⏲ 8am-noon & 2-5pm Mon-Fri, 10am-noon Sat). It's about 4km west of town just off the main highway (Tsh8000 in a taxi).

ℹ Getting Around

Taxis park at the bus station and near Market Sq. Fares from the bus station to central hotels start at Tsh3000. Dalla-dallas from the road in front of New Millennium Hotel run to the train station and to Mbalizi, but the ones to the train station often don't have room for luggage; taxis are a safer option.

Tukuyu

☎025 / POP 29,500

The small, peppy town of Tukuyu is set in the heart of a beautiful area of hills and orchards near Lake Nyasa. There are many hikes and natural attractions nearby, but only the most basic tourist infrastructure; for all excursions you'll need to rough it. There's compensation, though, in the lush surrounding hills, swathed in tea plantations and dotted with banana-palm groves, and the town itself has a lively daily market selling fruit, veg and clothes.

Sights

Daraja la Mungu (Bridge of God) BRIDGE

South of Ngozi Peak and west of the main road, this natural bridge 22km west of Tukuyu is estimated to have been formed around 1800 million years ago by water flowing through cooling lava that spewed out from the nearby Rungwe volcano. The bridge spans a small waterfall.

Activities

Hiking opportunities abound, with Rungwe Tea & Tours (p182) and Bongo Camping (p182) the main options for organising something. **Afriroots** (☎0732 926350, 0713 652642, 0787 459887; www.afriroots.co.tz; Dar es Salaam tours per person US$40-50) also does tours here. Expect to pay between Tsh20,000 and Tsh35,000 for most tours.

Ngozi Peak & Crater Lake HIKING

This lushly vegetated 2629m-high volcanic peak has a deep-blue lake – the subject of local legends – about 200m below the crater rim. It is about 7km west of the main road north of Tukuyu. To get here via public transport, take any dalla-dalla travelling between Mbeya and Tukuyu and ask to be dropped off; there's a small sign for Ngozi at the turn-off.

Rungwe Tea & Tours HIKING
(☎0754 767389, 025-255 2489; rungweteatours@gmail.com) This is an energetic one-man-show type of place, supported by Rungwe Fairtrade tea growers, where you can organise guides for hikes in the surrounding area. Prices start about Tsh15,000 per day including a guide and local community fee. It's in the Ujenzi area at the 'Umoja wa Wakulima Wadogo wa Chai Rungwe' building, behind the Landmark Hotel.

Mt Rungwe HIKING
(US$10) This 2960m dormant volcano, much of which is protected as the Rungwe Forest Reserve, rises up to the east of the main road north of Tukuyu, adjoining Kitulo National Park. It marks the point where the eastern and western arms of the Rift Valley meet, and is an important centre of endemism.

Sleeping & Eating

Bongo Camping CAMPGROUND $
(☎0732 951763; www.bongocamping.com; camping with own/hired tent Tsh6000/8000; Ⓟ) A backpacker-friendly place with a large, grassy area to pitch your tent, basic cooking facilities, hot-bucket showers, tents for hire and meals on order. It's at Kibisi village, 3.5km north of Tukuyu, and 800m off the main road (Tsh1000 in a taxi from Tukuyu bus stand).

Landmark Hotel HOTEL $
(☎0782 164160, 025-255 2400; camping/s/d US$5/40/45; Ⓟ) Spacious, good-value rooms, all with TV and hot water, a small lawn where it's sometimes permitted to pitch a tent, and a slow but good restaurant. Doubles have two large beds. It's the large multi-storey building at the main junction just up from NBC bank; the street is noisy, so ask for a room at the back.

Kivanga Lounge TANZANIAN $
(lunch Tsh5000; ⏲10am-9pm) Look out for this pinky-orange building with an open-air counter. It serves tasty and filling lunches: beef, chicken or fish with ugali or pilau rice and greens. Nothing fancy, but it's satisfying.

Information

NBC (Main Rd; ⏲9am-4pm Mon-Fri) In the town centre and has an ATM.

Getting There & Away

Minibuses run several times daily between Tukuyu **bus station** (off Main St) and both Mbeya (Tsh2500, one to 1½ hours) and Kyela (Tsh2000, one hour).

Two roads connect Tukuyu with the northern end of Lake Nyasa. The main tarmac road heads southwest and splits at Ibanda, with the western fork going to Songwe River Bridge and into Malawi, and the newly paved eastern fork to Kyela and Itungi port. A secondary rough dirt road heads southeast from Tukuyu to Ipinda and then east towards Matema – only attempt this if you're in a 4WD.

Lake Nyasa

Picturesque and unspoilt Lake Nyasa (also known as Lake Malawi) is Africa's third-largest lake after Lake Victoria and Lake Tanganyika. It's more than 550km long, up to 75km wide and as deep as 700m in parts. It also has a high level of biodiversity, containing close to one-third of the world's known cichlid species. The lake is bordered by Tanzania, Malawi and Mozambique. The Tanzanian side is rimmed to the east by the Livingstone Mountains, whose green, misty slopes form a stunning backdrop as they cascade down to the sandy shoreline. Few roads reach the towns strung out between the mountains and the shore along the lake's eastern side. To the north and east, the mountains lead on to the Kitulo Plateau.

Places of interest around the Tanzanian side of the lake include (from north to south) Kyela, Itungi, Matema, Ikombe, Liuli and Mbamba Bay.

Matema

☎025 / POP 20,000

This quiet lakeside settlement is the only spot on northern Lake Nyasa that has any sort of tourist infrastructure, and with its stunning beachside setting backed by the Livingstone Mountains rising steeply up from the water, it makes an ideal and very family-friendly place to relax for a few days.

Here you can arrange walks and dugout canoe rides through your accommodation or simply lounge on the beach. On Saturdays, there's a **pottery market** at Lyulilo village, about 2km east of Matema village centre along the lakeshore, where Kisi pots from Ikombe are sold.

Sleeping & Eating

★Blue Canoe Safari Camp CAMPGROUND, COTTAGES $

(☎0783 575451; www.bluecanoelodge.com; camping US$9, s bungalows US$40-70, d bungalows US$60-90; P @) This lovely beachfront place has camping with spotless ablution blocks, and luxury bungalows with verandahs overlooking the lake, polished wood floors and comfortable beds with spacious mosquito netting. There are also less-expensive standard bungalows. The bar is well stocked and the cuisine tasty. The operators arrange snorkelling, kayaking and birding excursions. It's 3.5km from Matema; pick-ups are possible with advance notice.

Matema Lake Shore Resort COTTAGE $

(☎0754 487267, 0782 179444; www.mec-tanzania.ch; camping Tsh15,000, s/d/tr/f from Tsh30,000/40,000/75,000/80,000; P) This recommended Swiss-built place has several spacious, breezy, comfortable two-storey beachfront family chalets; some smaller, equally nice double and triple cottages; and a four-bed option. All rooms front directly onto the lake – with lovely views – except the cheaper back ones. The restaurant serves decent, reasonably priced meals, and all self-contained rooms have minifridge and fan.

Information

There's talk of an ATM, but at the time of writing there was nowhere in Matema to withdraw or change money, so bring enough cash with you.

Getting There & Away

BOAT

There is currently no reliable passenger ferry service on the eastern side of Lake Nyasa. Once it resumes, the boat stop for Matema is actually at Lyulilo village, about 25 minutes on foot from the main Matema junction. Just follow the main 'road' going southeast from the junction, paralleling the lakeshore, and ask for the *bandari* (harbour).

BUS

From Tukuyu, pick-ups to Ipinda via Ibanda and Kyela (Tsh2500, three hours) leave around 8am most mornings from the roundabout by the NBC bank. Although drivers sometimes say they are going all the way to Matema, generally they go only as far as Ipinda. Once in Ipinda, pick-ups run onwards to Matema (Tsh300, one hour, 35km). Returning from Matema, departures are in the morning. The only direct buses to Mbeya depart before dawn.

From Kyela, there are several vehicles daily from about 1pm onwards to Ipinda (Tsh1500), a few of which continue on to Matema (Tsh3000, two hours). Departures from Matema back to Kyela run in the morning. From Kyela, it's also fairly easy to hire a vehicle to drop you off at Matema (from about Tsh70,000).

There are also usually two direct buses daily between Mbeya's Nane Nane bus stand and Matema (Tsh10,000, six hours), departing Mbeya between 9am and 10am. All transport in Matema departs from the main junction near the hospital.

Mbamba Bay

☎025 / POP 9500

The relaxing outpost of Mbamba Bay is the southernmost Tanzanian port on Lake Nyasa. With its low-key ambience and attractive beach fringed by palm, banana and mango trees, it makes a good spot to spend a few days waiting for a ferry across Lake Nyasa (once service resumes) or as a change of pace if you've been travelling inland around Songea or Tunduru.

Sleeping & Eating

Mbamba Bay Bio Camp Lodge BANDA, CAMPGROUND $

(☎0765 925255; www.mbambabay-biocamp.com; camping per tent Tsh20,000, s/d permanent tent Tsh30,000/75,000, s/d/q banda Tsh75,000/80,000/135,000) Comfortable stone and thatch bungalows with bathrooms, plus some permanent tents on the beach under *makuti* (thatched palm leaf) roofing. You can also pitch your own tent. Local-style meals are available. It's on the beach about 5km north of Mbamba Bay. Walk, or hire a motorbike at the Mbamba Bay bus stand to bring you there.

St Benadetta Guest House HOSTEL $

(r Tsh25,000) This two-storey church-run place is set on a small rise overlooking the lake. It has simple rooms, a pleasant garden and meals on order.

Getting There & Away

BOAT

The lake **ferries** (☎0766 820382) travel weekly between Mbamba Bay and Matema, departing Mbamba Bay on Sunday (arriving Monday in Matema), and departing Matema on Thursday (arriving Friday in Mbamba Bay). Check this information in advance, as the new ferries hadn't started running at the time of writing.

BUS

There's at least one direct vehicle daily from Songea (Tsh8000, five hours). Otherwise you will need to change vehicles at Mbinga.

Songea

☎025 / POP 235,300

The sprawling town of Songea, situated at an altitude of just over 1000m, is capital of the surrounding Ruvuma region and will probably seem like a major metropolis if you've just come from Tunduru or Mbamba Bay. Away from the scruffy and crowded central market and bus stand area, it's a pleasant, attractive place, with shaded leafy streets, surrounded by rolling hill country dotted with yellow sunflowers and grazing cattle. The main ethnic group here is the Ngoni, who migrated into the area from South Africa during the 19th century, subduing many smaller tribes along the way. Songea takes its name from one of their greatest chiefs, who was killed following the Maji Maji rebellion (p202).

Sights

Songea's colourful **market** (Soko Kuu) along the main road is worth a visit.

The impressive carved wooden doors on the **Catholic cathedral** diagonally opposite the bus stand are also worth a look, as are the bright painted wall paintings inside.

Maji Maji Museum MUSEUM

(Tsh10,000; ⏲8am-4pm) About 1km from the town centre, off the Njombe road, is this small museum commemorating the Maji Maji uprising. Behind it is Chief Songea's tomb. Unmissable sights are the statues of 12 chiefs captured and killed by the Germans, which locals still hang with garlands. From town, take the first tarmac road to the right after passing CRDB bank and continue about 200m. The museum entrance is on the left with a pale-blue archway.

Sleeping & Eating

Heritage Cottage HOTEL $

(☎0754 355306; www.heritage-cottage.com; Njombe Rd; s/d Tsh75,000/90,000; P ❄) This hotel has modern, clean rooms with TV (some with minifridge), a popular bar-restaurant, a large lawn area behind, and a playground for children. It's located 3km north of town along the Njombe Rd.

Seed Farm Villa B&B $

(☎025-260 2500, 0752 842086; www.seedfarmvilla.com; s/d from Tsh75,000/85,000; P ❄ ☎) This place has modern, quiet rooms with TV set in tranquil garden surroundings away from the town centre in the Seed Farm area. It has a sitting room with TV, and a restaurant (advance order necessary). Head out of town along Tunduru Rd for 2.5km to the signposted turn-off, from where it's 200m further on.

Heritage Cottage INTERNATIONAL, INDIAN $

(☎0754 355306; Njombe Rd; mains Tsh12,000-15,000; ⏲7am-10pm) This hotel restaurant has slow service, but provides tasty continental and Indian cuisine and a pleasant covered open-air dining area.

Information

ENTRY & EXIT FORMALITIES

Immigration Office (Uhamiaji; Tunduru Rd; ⏲8am-4pm Mon-Fri) At the beginning of the Tunduru Rd. Get your passport stamped here if you are travelling to/from Mozambique.

INTERNET ACCESS

Amani Internet Café (off Main Rd; per hour Tsh1000; ⏲8.30am-6pm Mon-Sat) A couple of computer terminals and a decent connection.

MEDICAL SERVICES

Should you fall ill, there's a large Benedictine monastery with an affiliated hospital about 30km west of town, in Peramiho.

MONEY

CRDB (Njombe Rd; ⏲9am-5pm Mon-Fri) ATM.

NBC (⏲8.30am-4pm Mon-Fri, to 1pm Sat) Behind the market; ATM.

Getting There & Away

Super Feo departs the bus stand daily from 5am to Iringa (Tsh19,000, eight hours) and Dar es Salaam (Tsh42,000, 13 hours), and at 6am to Mbeya (Tsh19,000 to Tsh24,000, eight hours) via Njombe (Tsh10,000, four hours). There are also departures to Njombe at 9.30am and 11am.

For Mbamba Bay, there's one direct vehicle departing daily by 7am (Tsh8000, five hours). Otherwise get transport to Mbinga and from there on to Mbamba Bay.

To Tunduru (Tsh10,000, four hours), there's a daily bus departing by 7am. There's also one bus daily direct to Masasi (Tsh20,000 to Tsh21,000, six to seven hours), departing by 6am.

Transport to Mozambique departs from the Majengo C area, southwest of the bus stand and about 600m in from the main road; ask locals to point out the way through the back streets. If you're driving to Mozambique, head west 18km from Songea along the Mbinga road to the signposted turn-off, from where it's 120km further on an unpaved but decent road to the Mozambique border.

Tunduru

☎025 / POP 38,000

Tunduru, halfway between Masasi and Songea, is in the centre of an important gemstone-mining region, with a bit of a Wild West feel. The town is also a truck and transit stop, and you're likely to need to spend the night here if travelling between Masasi and Songea.

The route between the two towns passes through the southern reaches of the forested Selous-Niassa Wildlife Corridor, which connects the Selous Game Reserve with the Niassa Reserve in Mozambique. This vital wildlife link has been the cause of a number of infamous man-eating lion incidents around Tunduru over the years.

Sleeping

Namwinyu Guest House GUESTHOUSE $
(☎0655 447225, 0786 447225; Songea Rd; r Tsh30,000; P ❄) This is Tunduru's best accommodation, with clean, pleasant double-bedded rooms (no same-gender sharing) and tasty, inexpensive meals on order. It's along the north side of the main road at the western edge of town, and an easy 10-minute walk from the bus stand.

Getting There & Away

There's at least one bus daily between Tunduru and Masasi, departing by 6am (Tsh8000 to Tsh9000, three to four hours) and also between Tunduru and Songea (Tsh10,000, four hours).

SOUTHEASTERN TANZANIA

Time seems to have stood still in Tanzania's sparsely populated southeast. It lacks the development and bustle of the north, and tourist numbers are a relative trickle. Yet, for safari enthusiasts and divers, and for adventurous travellers seeking to learn about traditional local life, the southeast makes an ideal destination.

Among the southeast's highlights: Selous Game Reserve, with its top-notch wildlife watching; white-sand beaches and stunning corals around Mafia island; and the Kilwa Kisiwani ruins, harking back to days when the East African coast was the centre of trading networks stretching to the Far East.

Mafia and the Selous offer a good selection of comfortable accommodation and Western amenities. Elsewhere tourist infrastructure is more limited, although there are some real gems to be found.

Mafia

POP 46,400

The green islands of the Mafia archipelago are strewn along the coast southeast of Dar es Salaam, surrounded by turquoise waters and glinting white sandbanks. Historically the archipelago lay at a trade crossroads, with visitors from Kilwa and elsewhere on the mainland, as well as from the Zanzibar Archipelago, Comoros and Madagascar.

This rich melting pot of historical influences, together with the archipelago's strong traditional culture, are among Mafia's

Southeastern Tanzania

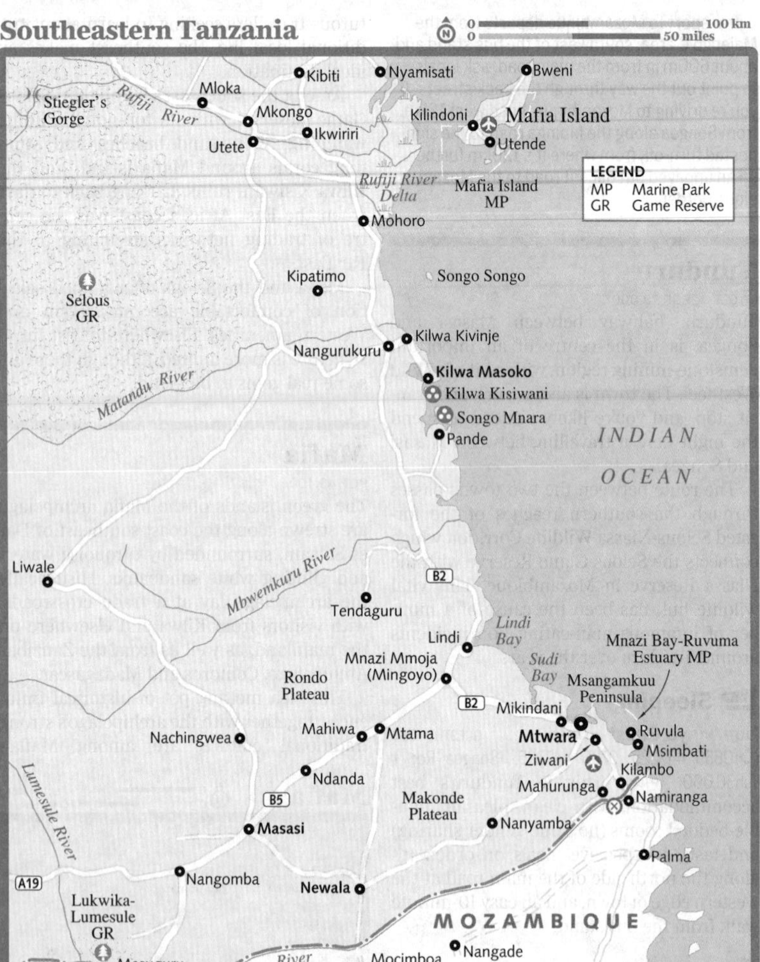

highlights. Other draws include the archipelago's natural beauty, its outstanding marine environment, its tranquil pace and its fine collection of upmarket lodges.

History

In addition to Mafia island, the Mafia archipelago includes Juani (southeast of Mafia), Chole (between Mafia and Juani), Jibondo (south of Juani) and at least a dozen other islets and sandbars. The archipelago first rose to prominence between the 11th and 13th centuries in the days when the Shirazis controlled much of the East African shoreline. Thanks to its central buffer position between the Rufiji River delta and the high seas of the Indian Ocean, it made an amenable trading base, and the local economy soon began to thrive. One of the first settlements was built during this era at Ras Kisimani, on Mafia's southwestern corner, followed by another at Kua on Juani.

By the time the Portuguese arrived in the early 16th century, Mafia had lost much of its significance and had come under the sway of the Sultan of Kilwa. In the early 18th century the island's fortunes revived, and by the mid-19th century it had come within the domain of the powerful Omani sultanate, under which it flourished as a trade centre linking Kilwa to the south and the Zanzibar Archipelago to the north. It was during this era that the coconut palm and cashew plantations that now cover much of the island were established.

Following an attack by the Sakalava people from Madagascar, Mafia's capital was moved from Kua to the nearby tiny island of Chole. Chole's star ascended to the point where it became known as Chole Mjini (Chole City), while the now-main island of Mafia was referred to as Chole Shamba (the Chole hinterlands). Mafia's administrative seat continued on Chole throughout the German colonial era. It was moved to Kilindoni on the main island by the British, who used Mafia as a naval and air base.

Today farming and fishing are the primary sources of livelihood for Mafia's approximately 46,000 residents, most of whom live on the main island. While shopping in the markets, you'll find cassavas, cashews and coconuts in abundance.

Sights

It doesn't take too much imagination to step back in time in the Mafia archipelago, with village life here much the same as during the island's Shirazi-era heyday. On Mafia island itself there are small **beaches** interspersed with the mangroves around Chole Bay, and some idyllic nearby sandbanks; all the lodges arrange excursions. One of the closest is **Marimbani**, a popular picnic stop for snorkelling excursions. Further away is **Mange**, with beautiful white sand populated only by crabs and sea birds, and surrounded by crystal-clear aqua waters. At **Ras Mkumbi**, Mafia's windswept northernmost point, there's a lighthouse dating from 1892, as well as **Kanga beach**, and a forest that's home to monkeys, blue duikers and many birds.

There are **green and hawksbill turtle breeding sites** along Mafia island's eastern shores and on the nearby islands of Juani and Jibondo. To protect these and other local ecosystems, the southeastern part of the island, together with offshore islets and waters, has been gazetted as a national marine park. **Whale sharks** (*potwe* in Swahili) visit Mafia between about November and February, and are best seen offshore near Kilindoni.

Away from Mafia island, intriguing destinations to explore include Chole, Juani and Jibondo islands.

Mafia Island Marine Park PARK
(www.marineparks.go.tz; adult/child US$23.60/11.80) At around 822 sq km, Mafia Island Marine Park is the largest marine protected area in the Indian Ocean, sheltering a unique complex of estuarine, mangrove, coral reef and marine channel ecosystems. These include the only natural forest on the island and almost 400 fish species. There are also about 10 villages within the park's boundaries with an estimated 15,000 to 17,000 inhabitants, all of whom depend on its natural resources for their livelihoods.

Jibondo ISLAND
Sparsely vegetated Jibondo is less aesthetically appealing than Mafia's other islands, and its inhabitants are traditionally unwelcoming towards visitors. However, it is intriguing in that it supports a population of about 3000 people despite having no natural water sources. Jibondo is renowned as a boat-building centre, with much of the wood coming from forests around mainland Kilwa. In Jibondo's village centre, look for the carved door frame on the mosque, said to come from the old settlement at Kua on Juani.

Juani ISLAND, HISTORIC SITE
The large and heavily vegetated island of Juani, southeast of Mafia, has overgrown but evocative ruins at Kua. This includes the remains of several mosques dating from a Shirazi settlement during the 18th and 19th centuries, and crumbling palace walls. Also note the ablutions area just to the right of the main entrance to the settlement. Access to the ruins is only possible at high tide. South of here is a channel and a nearby lagoon for birding and swimming.

Chole ISLAND, HISTORIC SITE
(day visit per person US$4) A good place to start exploring in the Mafia archipelago, especially around the crumbling but atmospheric ruins, dating from the 19th century. Also on Chole is what's probably East Africa's only **Fruit Bat Sanctuary** (Comoros lesser fruit bat), thanks to the efforts of a local women's group who bought the area where an important nesting tree is located.

Activities

Diving & Snorkelling

Mafia offers divers fine corals, a variety of fish, including numerous pelagics, and relaxing, uncrowded diving, usually done from motorised dhows. You can dive year-round in Chole Bay at various sites for all levels, plus there is seasonal diving (October to February) outside the bay for experienced divers. The best month is generally October, and the least favourable months are April, May and early June, when everything shuts down due to the rains. Diver operators include **Big Blu** (0654 089659, 0787 474108; www.bigblumafia.com; Chole Bay), **Mafia Island Diving** (0688 218569; www.mafiadiving.com; Mafia Island Lodge, Chole Bay) and the in-house dive instructors at **Shamba Kilole Eco Lodge** (0753 903752, 0786 903752; www.shambakilolelodge.com; Utende; per person full board in chalet/ste from US$170/220;).

Fishing

Long popular in deep-sea fishing circles, Mafia is known especially for its marlin, sailfish, tuna and other big-game fish. Conditions are best between September and March, with June and July the least-appealing months due to strong winds. Contact Big Blu or **Kinasi Lodge** (0715 669145, 0777 424588; www.kinasilodge.com; Chole Bay; s/d full board from US$180/320; Jun-Mar;). Licences can be arranged through Mafia Island Marine Park Headquarters (p189) in Utende.

Sleeping & Eating

Most dining on Mafia centres on seafood, coconuts and other local ingredients. The island's upmarket hotels offer a mix of local and continental cuisine. Inexpensive local-style snacks and street food are available in Kilindoni.

Chole Foxes Guesthouse GUESTHOUSE $
(0787 877393, 0715 877393; Chole Island; r per person US$35) Chole's only budget accommodation, this small, tranquil guesthouse has a lovely location on the southwestern edge of the island directly overlooking Chole Bay and Mafia island. The three rooms are simple but adequate – all opening onto the mangroves and water – and delicious local-style meals are available for about US$10.

Meremeta Guest House & Apartment GUESTHOUSE $
(0715 345460, 0787 345460; www.meremetalodge.com; Utende; s/d/tr US$40/50/75) This well-priced place has clean and pleasant budget rooms with fan, delicious meals (US$10 to US$15), and free coffee and tea. The helpful owner makes every effort to ensure his guests have a comfortable stay, and also offers bicycle rental and good island excursions. Look for the pink building and local artwork.

Bustani Bed & Breakfast B&B $$
(0682 982165, 0675 168893; www.bustanimafia.com; s/d incl airport transfers US$60/100;) This good-value place on the outskirts of Kilindoni has attractive, tastefully decorated twin- and double-bedded rooms, a pool, a good restaurant and views to the water in the distance. It's under the same management as Butiama Beach and **Big Blu** (0654 089659, 0787 474108; www.bigblumafia.com; Chole Bay; s/d tent US$30/50, s/d r from US$60/100; Jun-Mar;), and is ideal for travellers looking to save some money while enjoying simple comforts and having easy access to excursions.

★ **Butiama Beach** LODGE $$$
(0787 474084; www.butiamabeach.com; s/d half board US$180/300; Jun-Mar;) This lovely 15-room place is spread out in palm-tree-studded grounds on a fine stretch of beach near Kilindoni, about 2km south of the small harbour. Accommodation is in spacious, breezy, appealingly decorated cottages. It has delicious Italian-style dining, sea kayaks for exploring the birdlife in nearby creeks, sunset views and a warm, classy ambience. Very good value for money.

★ **Pole Pole Bungalow Resort** LODGE $$$
(www.polepole.com; Chole Bay; s/d full board plus daily excursion US$384/590; Jun-Mar;) This beautiful, low-key hideaway is set amid the palm trees and tropical vegetation on a long hillside overlooking Chole Bay. It strikes an excellent balance between luxury and lack of pretension with its quiet style, impeccable service, excellent cuisine and comfortable bungalows. Children under 10 years of age are not allowed.

★ **Chole Mjini** TREEHOUSE $$$
(0784 520799, 0787 712427; www.cholemjini.com; Chole Island; s/d full board US$265/420; Jun-Easter) Chole Mjini is an upmar-

ket bush adventure in synchrony with the local community and environment. Sleep in spacious, rustic and fantastic treehouses, eat fresh seafood, experience the real darkness of an African night without electricity, and take advantage of diving excursions, all while supporting Chole Mjini's work with the local community.

Information

INTERNET ACCESS

Internet Café (Kilindoni; per hour Tsh3000; ⌚8am-6pm) At New Lizu Hotel.

MEDICAL SERVICES

For malaria tests, there's a village clinic on Chole island. For treatment or anything serious, go to Dar es Salaam.

MONEY

National Microfinance Bank (Kilindoni) Just off the airport road, and near the main junction in Kilindoni; has an ATM that takes Visa and MasterCard.

TOURIST INFORMATION

General tourist information concerning Mafia Island Marine Park is available at the entry gate along the main road into Utende. For more detailed technical information, **Mafia Island Marine Park Headquarters** (☎023-240 2690; ⌚8am-5pm Mon-Fri) is located about 1km further on next to Mafia Island Lodge.

Getting There & Away

AIR

Coastal Aviation (☎0713 325673, 0785 500229, 022-284 2700; www.coastal.co.tz; Mafia airport; ⌚approx 8am-5pm, depending on flight schedules) flies daily between Mafia and Dar es Salaam (US$125), Songo Songo (US$150, minimum two passengers), Zanzibar Island (US$175) and Kilwa Masoko (US$190, minimum four passengers), with connections also to Selous Game Reserve and Arusha.

Tropical Air (☎024-223 2511, 0687 527511, 0715 364396; www.tropicalair.co.tz; Mafia airport; ⌚approx 8am-5pm, depending on flight schedules) has a slightly cheaper daily flight between Mafia and Dar es Salaam with connections to Zanzibar.

All the Chole Bay hotels arrange airfield transfers for their guests (included in the room price at some; otherwise about US$15 to US$30 per person; enquire when booking).

SEA

A small ferry sails daily in each direction between Mafia (Kilindoni port) and Nyamisati village on the mainland south of Dar es Salaam. Departures from Nyamisati are at 4am and from Kilindoni at 6am (Tsh16,000, about four hours). In Kilindoni, the ticketing office is at the top of the hill leading down to the port; buy tickets the afternoon before. In Nyamisati, buy tickets at the port on arrival. While a trickle of budget travellers reach Mafia this way, remember that there is no safety equipment on any of the boats. They are often crowded, and the ride can be windy and extremely choppy in the middle of the channel. Many boats have capsized on this route. If you want to try, it works better from Mafia to the mainland, as the entire journey is done in the daylight, and your hotel can help you get things sorted with the boat.

To reach Nyamisati, get a southbound dalla-dalla from Mbagala Rangi Tatu (Tsh5500), which is along the Kilwa road and reached via dalla-dalla from Dar es Salaam's Posta (Tsh400); allow up to four hours from central Dar to Nyamisati

To get to Kilndoni's town centre from the port, walk straight up the hill for about 300m. When arriving at Nyamisati, it's easy to find dalla-dallas north to Mbagala and central Dar es Salaam. Heading south from Nyamisati, you'll need to first get a vehicle to Bungu (Tsh3000) along the main Dar es Salaam–Mtwara road. Once in Bungu, you can get onward transport south to Nangurukuru (for Kilwa) and Mtwara. If you get stuck overnight in Nyamisati, ask for the 'mission', where you can sleep for Tsh10,000 per person.

Getting Around

Dalla-dallas connect Kilindoni with Utende (Tsh1000, 30 minutes) several times daily, and at least once daily with Bweni (Tsh4000, four to five hours). On the Kilindoni–Utende route, vehicles depart Kilindoni at about 1pm and Utende at about 7am; the last departure from Utende is about 4.30pm. Departures from Kilindoni to Bweni are at about 1pm, and from Bweni at about 7am. In Kilindoni, the transport stand is in the central 'plaza' near the market. In Utende, the start and end of the dalla-dalla route is at the tiny loading jetty between **Mafia Island Lodge** (☎0763 527619, 0655 378886; www.mafialodge.com; Chole Bay; per person half board US$115-135; ⌚Jun-Apr; ❄📶) and **Big Blu** (p188).

It's also possible to hire taxis or *bajaji* (tuk-tuks) in Kilindoni to take you around the island. Bargain hard, and expect to pay from Tsh15,000 between Kilindoni and Utende for a vehicle (Tsh10,000 for a *bajaji*).

The other option is bicycle, either your own (bring a mountain bike) or a rental (from about Tsh500 per hour for a heavy single-speed; ask around at the Kilindoni market).

To get between Utende and Chole island, most of the Chole Bay hotels provide boat transport for their guests, and transfers can be arranged with **Mafia Island Diving** (p188) and **Big Blu** (p188). Otherwise local boats sail throughout the day from the beach in front of **Mafia Island Lodge** (☎0763 527619, 0655 378886; www.mafialodge.com; Chole Bay; per person half board US$115-135; ⏱Jun-Apr; ❄📶) (Tsh500). Boats also leave from here to Juani, and from Chole it's possible to walk to Juani at low tide. To Jibondo, you can usually catch a lift on one of the water transport boats leaving from the beach near **Pole Pole Bungalow Resort** (p188).

Selous Game Reserve

Selous Game Reserve (mtbutalii@gmail.com; adult/child US$59/35.40, plus daily conservation fee US$17.70-$29.50) is a vast, 48,000-sq-km wilderness area lying at the heart of southern Tanzania. It is Africa's largest wildlife reserve, and home to large herds of elephants, plus buffaloes, crocodiles, hippos, wild dogs, many bird species and some of Tanzania's last remaining black rhinos. Bisecting it is the Rufiji River, which cuts a path past woodlands, grasslands and stands of borassus palm, and provides unparalleled water-based wildlife watching.

Only the section of the reserve north from the Rufiji River is open for tourism; large areas of the south are zoned as hunting concessions. Yet the wealth of Selous' wildlife and its stunning riverine scenery rarely fail to impress. Another draw is the Selous' relative lack of congestion in comparison with Tanzania's northern parks.

Visit soon, however: much of Selous' wealth is under threat from poaching, a uranium mining project and a planned hydroelectric power project along the Rufiji River.

Selous Game Reserve (Northern Section)

Selous Game Reserve (Northern Section)

Top Sights
1 Selous Game Reserve B3

Sights
2 Selous Grave C2
3 Stiegler's Gorge B3

Sleeping
4 Lake Tagalala Public Campsite C2
5 Rufiji River Camp D2
6 Sand Rivers Selous C3
7 Selous Impala Camp C2
8 Selous River Camp D3
9 Siwandu C2

History

Parts of Selous Game Reserve were set aside as early as 1896. However, it was not until 1922 that it was expanded and given its present name (after Frederick Courteney Selous, the British explorer who was killed and buried in the reserve during WWI, and whose grave can still be visited). The area continued to be extended until 1975 when it assumed its current boundaries.

During the 1990s and thereafter, efforts were initiated to link Selous Game Reserve with the Niassa Reserve in Mozambique, with the first stages of the project – including establishment of a wildlife corridor – already functional.

Much of this progress is gradually being reversed by more recent developments within the reserve. These include poaching, uranium mining in the southern part of the Selous (leading to a redrawing of reserve boundaries) and government confirmation in mid-2017 that the Rufiji River – the heart and lifeblood of the Selous – will be dammed near Stiegler's Gorge, in the northwestern part of the reserve, in connection with a planned hydroelectric project.

In 2014 Unesco placed the Selous on its World Heritage in Danger list, and it reconfirmed this decision in 2017. If the dam project moves forward, complete delisting in the near future is a very real possibility. The Selous' only hope for survival now rests in the ability of concerned environmentalists in Tanzania and beyond to convince the government that it can achieve its goals of increasing Tanzania's electrical grid capacity and overall economic health through means other than exploiting one of its greatest natural treasures.

Sights & Activities

Boat safaris on the Rufiji or the reserve's lakes are offered by most camps and lodges. Most also organise walking safaris, usually three-hour hikes near the camps, with a night at a fly camp. Vehicle safaris are permitted in open safari vehicles – a welcome change from Tanzania's northern safari circuit. Self-drive safaris are also possible.

Stiegler's Gorge GORGE

Stiegler's Gorge, which averages 100m in depth, is named after a Swiss explorer who was killed here by an elephant in 1907. It has more recently gained attention as the site of a planned massive hydroelectric power station.

SELOUS GAME RESERVE

Why Go Rewarding wildlife watching against a backdrop of stunning riverine scenery; wonderful, small camps; excellent boat safaris and the chance for walking safaris.

When to Go The Selous is best visited from June through December. Many camps close from March through May, during the heavy rains.

Practicalities Fly or drive in from Dar es Salaam; drive in from Morogoro or Mikumi. Both Mtemere and Matambwe gates are open from 6.30am to 6pm. **Selous Game Reserve Headquarters** (mtbutalii@gmail.com; Matambwe gate; ⏲6.30am-6pm) is at Matambwe on the Selous' northwestern edge.

Budget Tip Travel by bus from Dar es Salaam to Mloka village, and base yourself outside Selous' boundaries, paying park fees only when you enter the reserve.

Self-Drive Safaris

It's 75km through the Selous between Mtemere and Matambwe gates. Spending a few days on each side, linked by a full day's wildlife drive in between, is a rewarding option, although wildlife concentrations in the Matambwe area cannot compare with those deeper inside the reserve towards Mtemere. If you can only explore one area, eastern Selous is the best bet.

Sleeping & Eating

Lake Tagalala Public Campsite CAMPGROUND $

(mtbutalii@gmail.com; per adult/child US$35.40/23.60) Lake Tagalala campsite has basic but good facilities, including cold-water showers and covered cooking areas. There is usually water, but it is worth also filling up a container when entering the reserve. The campsite is located roughly midway between Mtemere and Matambwe gates on a low rise near Lake Tagalala.

★ **Selous River Camp** TENTED CAMP $$

(☎0784 237525; www.selousrivercamp.com; camping US$10, s/d tent full board US$100/155, s/d/tr mud hut full board US$230/300/348;

Jun-Feb) This friendly place is the closest camp to Mtemere gate. It has cosy, river-facing 'mud huts' with bathrooms, plus small standing tents surrounded by forest with cots and shared facilities. The bar-restaurant area is lovely, directly overlooking the river at a particularly scenic spot. Overall it's a great choice for budget travellers.

Boat safaris, wildlife drives and village tours can be arranged.

★Sand Rivers Selous LODGE $$$
(0787 595908; www.nomad-tanzania.com; s/d full board & wildlife excursions US$1365/2040; Jun-Mar; P) Set splendidly on its own on the Rufiji south of Lake Tagalala, this is one of the Selous' most exclusive options, with some of Tanzania's most renowned wildlife guides. The eight luxurious stone cottages have full river views.

★Rufiji River Camp TENTED CAMP $$$
(0784 237422; www.rufijirivercamp.com; per person full board & activities from US$410; Jun-Mar; P) This long-standing, unpretentious camp is run by the Fox family who own camps throughout southern Tanzania. Set in a fine location on a wide bend in the Rufiji River about 1km inside Mtemere gate, it has tents with river views and a sunset terrace. Activities include boat safaris and overnight walking safaris.

★Selous Impala Camp TENTED CAMP $$$
(0753 115908, 0787 817591; www.selousimpalacamp.com; per person with full board & excursions from US$670; Jun-Mar; P) Impala Camp has eight well-spaced, nicely appointed tents in a prime setting on the river near Lake Mzizimia. Its restaurant overlooks the river and has an adjoining bar area on a deck jutting out towards the water, and the surrounding area is rich in wildlife.

Siwandu TENTED CAMP $$$
(Selous Safari Camp; 022-212 8485; www.selous.com; per person all-inclusive US$1014; Jun-Mar; P@) This upmarket camp is set on a side arm of the Rufiji in a lush, beautiful setting overlooking Lake Nzelekela. It's divided into separate camps, each with a half dozen spacious tents, giving a more intimate, exclusive feel. There's a raised dining and lounge area on one side, excellent cuisine and impeccable service throughout. No children under six years of age.

SELOUS GAME RESERVE FEES

All fees are per 24-hour period and for single entry only. At the time of research, neither cash nor credit card were accepted at the reserve gates, although check before travelling as credit card payment at the reserve gates should be implemented in 2018. Meanwhile, payment of all reserve fees (including camping fees, if staying at reserve-run campsites) *must* be made in advance at any NBC bank branch into the following accounts:

US dollar (US$) account: 012105021353

Tanzanian shilling (Tsh) account: 012103011903

You will then need to present the bank receipt at either Mtemere gate or at **Selous Game Reserve Headquarters** (p191) at Matambwe gate in order to be permitted to enter Selous. The above is mainly applicable to self-drive campers or to those arriving at Selous without an advance booking. If you are staying in a lodge or tented camp, whether inside or outside the reserve, you can make payment arrangements in advance with them.

Admission US$59 per adult (US$35.40 per child aged five to 17 years)

Conservation fee US$29.50 per person for those staying at camps inside the Selous; US$17.70 per person for those staying at camps outside the Selous' boundaries.

Vehicle fee Tsh23,600 for Tanzania-registered vehicles

Camping at ordinary campsite US$35.40 per adult (US$23.60 per child)

Camping at special campsite US$59 per adult (US$35.40 per child)

Wildlife guard (mandatory in camping areas) US$29.50

Guide US$47.20 (US$29.50 for walking- or boat-safari guides)

DON'T MISS

THE SELOUS-NIASSA WILDLIFE CORRIDOR

The **Selous-Niassa Wildlife Corridor** (www.selous-niassa-corridor.org) – 'Ushoroba' in Swahili – joins the Selous Game Reserve with Mozambique's Niassa Reserve, forming a vast conservation area of about 120,000 sq km, and ensuring protection of one of the world's largest elephant ranges. In addition to the elephants, estimated to number about 85,000, the area is home to one of the continent's largest buffalo herds, more than half of its remaining wild dog population, a substantial number of lions, and resting and nesting migratory birds.

The area also encompasses large areas of both the Rufiji and Ruvuma river basins, with the watershed running roughly parallel to the Songea–Tunduru road. Local communities in the area are the Undendeule, the Ngoni and the Yao, who have formed various village-based wildlife management areas to support the corridor. Several of these communities have started small ecotourism ventures, including Marumba, southwest of Tunduru. At the Chingoli Society office in the village centre, guides can be arranged for village tours and to visit **Jiwe La Bwana** (with views across the border into Mozambique) and **Chingoli Table Mountain and caves**, used by locals as a hiding place during the Maji Maji rebellion. Tourist infrastructure ranges from basic to non-existent, with a basic campsite just outside the village.

Getting There & Away

AIR

Coastal Aviation (p216) has daily flights linking Selous Game Reserve with Dar es Salaam (US$165 to US$195 one way), Zanzibar Island (US$210 to US$240 one way), Mafia (via Dar, US$275 to US$305 one way) and Arusha (via Dar, US$410 to US$440 one way), with connections to other northern-circuit airstrips. Coastal also flies between the Selous and Ruaha National Park (US$320 to US$350 one way).

Other airlines flying these routes for similar prices include ZanAir (p62) and Safari Airlink (p216). Flights into the Selous are generally suspended during the wet season from mid-March to May. All lodges provide airfield transfers.

BUS

Tokyo Bus Line runs a daily bus between Temeke's Sudan Market (Majaribiwa area) and Mloka village (Tsh12,000, seven to nine hours), which is about 10km east of Mtemere gate. Departures in both directions are between 5.30am and 6.30am. From Mloka, you'll need to arrange a pick-up in advance with one of the camps. Hitching within the Selous isn't permitted, and there are no vehicles to rent in Mloka.

If you are continuing from the Selous to Kilwa, Lindi or Mtwara, there's usually a daily dalla-dalla from Mloka to Kibiti junction, on the main road. It departs Mloka anywhere between 3am and 5am (four to six hours). Once at Kibiti, you'll need to flag down one of the passing buses coming from Dar es Salaam to take you to Nangurukuru junction (for Kilwa) or on to Lindi or Mtwara.

Coming from Morogoro: Tokyo Bus Line goes at least once daily between Morogoro's Msamvu transport stand and Kisaki village (Tsh9000, seven hours), departing in each direction between about 9am and 11am. From Kisaki, you'll need to arrange a pick-up in advance with the lodges to reach Matambwe gate, 21km further on. It's about 180km between Matambwe gate and Morogoro.

CAR

You'll need a 4WD with high clearance in the Selous. There's no vehicle rental at the reserve and motorcycles aren't permitted.

To get here via road, there are two options. The first: take the main tarmac road from Dar es Salaam to Kibiti, where you then branch southwestwards on a mostly decent dirt and sand track to Mkongo, Mloka and on to Mtemere gate (240km). The road's condition is reasonable to good, as far as Mkongo. Mkongo to Mtemere (75km) is sometimes impassable during heavy rains. Allow six hours from Dar es Salaam.

Alternatively, you can go from Dar es Salaam to Kisaki via Morogoro and then on to Matambwe gate (about 350km) via a scenic but rough route through the Uluguru Mountains. It's 141km from Morogoro to Kisaki and 21km from Kisaki on to Matambwe gate. This route has improved considerably in recent times, but is still adventurous. From Dar es Salaam, the road is good tarmac as far as Morogoro. Once in Morogoro, take the Old Dar es Salaam road towards Bigwa. About 3km or 4km from the centre of town, past the Teachers' College Morogoro and before reaching Bigwa, you will come to a fork in the road, where you bear right. From here, the road becomes steep and scenic as it winds its way through the dense forests of the Uluguru Mountains onto a flat plain. Allow five to six hours for the stretch from Morogoro to Matambwe, depending on the season. If you are coming from Dar es Salaam and want to bypass Morogoro, take the unsignposted left-hand turn-off via Mikese, about 25km east of Morogoro on the main Dar es Salaam road that meets up with the Kisaki road at Msumbisi.

Driving from Dar es Salaam, the last petrol station is at Kibiti (about 100km northeast of Mtemere gate), where you should top up. Otherwise try Ikwiriri, from where there is also an access road joining the Mloka track. There is no fuel thereafter. Coming from the other direction, the last reliable petrol station is at Morogoro (about 160km from the Matambwe ranger post). Occasionally you may find both petrol and diesel sold on the roadside at Matombo, 50km south of Morogoro, and at several other villages, although quality isn't reliable. If you plan to drive around the Selous, bring sufficient petrol supplies with you as there are none available at any of the lodges, nor anywhere close to the reserve.

Expect to pay from US$250 to US$300 per vehicle for a one-way transfer from Dar es Salaam via Mloka.

TRAIN

Train is an option for the adventurous, especially if you're staying on the northwestern side of the reserve. With luck, you may even get a preview of the wildlife from the train window. All **Tazara** (p62) trains stop at Kisaki, which is about five to six hours from Dar es Salaam, the first stop for the express train, and the main station of interest. Ordinary trains also stop at Matambwe, near the Selous headquarters, as well as at Kinyanguru and Fuga stations.

It works best to take the train from Dar es Salaam to the Selous, though be sure you have a pick-up confirmed in advance, as the train generally arrives after nightfall. As it is not permitted to drive inside the Selous at night, this will only work for lodges based outside the reserve boundaries. Going the other way, delays are more common, and most lodges are therefore unwilling to collect travellers coming from the Mbeya side. There are several basic and unappealing local guesthouses in Kisaki, should you get stuck.

Kilwa Masoko

☎023 / POP 13,600

Kilwa Masoko (Kilwa of the Market) is a sleepy coastal town nestled amid dense coastal vegetation and several fine stretches of beach about halfway between Dar es Salaam and Mtwara. It's the springboard for visiting the ruins of the 15th-century Arab settlements at Kilwa Kisiwani and Songo Mnara, and, as such, is the gateway into one of the most significant eras in East African coastal history. The town itself is a relatively modern creation, with minimal historical appeal.

Sights & Activities

On the eastern edge of town is **Jimbizi Beach**, a short stretch of sand in a partially sheltered cove dotted with the occasional baobab tree. The best coastline is the long, idyllic palm-fringed open-ocean beach at **Masoko Pwani**, 5km northeast of town, and best reached by bicycle or *bajaji* (tuk-tuk; Tsh5000 one way). This is also where Kilwa Masoko gets its fish, and the colourful harbour area is worth a look, especially in the late afternoon.

Dhow excursions through the mangrove swamps on the outskirts of Kilwa – interesting for their birdlife and resident hippos – can be arranged with Kilwa hotels and with the Kilwa Islands Tour Guides Association, as can a variety of other excursions. These include visits to the extensive limestone caves about 85km northwest of Kilwa at Kipatimo.

Sleeping & Eating

Kilwa Bandari Lodge GUESTHOUSE $
(☎0689 440557, 0717 397814; www.kilwabandarilodge.com; camping Tsh20,000, s Tsh39,000-49,000, d or tw Tsh49,000-59,000; P ❄ ᯤ) Six tidy, modern rooms in the main building, plus several smaller but equally nice rooms in a back annex, make this a great budget bet. All rooms have fan, mosquito net and window screens, and tasty meals are available in the garden restaurant (meals from Tsh8000). It's about 1.5km south of the bus stand along the main road, shortly before the port gates.

Kilwa Seaview Resort LODGE $$
(☎0784 624664, 0784 613335; www.kilwa.net; Jimbizi Beach; camping/s/d/tr/q US$10/90/110/130/150; P ❄) This family-friendly place has spacious A-frame cottages perched along a rocky escarpment overlooking the eastern end of Jimbizi Beach. There's a restaurant, built around a huge baobab tree, serving tasty meals, and the swimming beach is just a short walk away.

Kimbilio Lodge LODGE $$
(☎0713 975807, 0656 022166; www.kimbiliolodges.com; s/d US$80/120; P 📶) This pleasant place has a good beachside setting on Jimbizi Beach. Accommodation is in six, spacious, tastefully decorated bungalows directly on the sand. It's warmly recommended. There's good Italian cuisine and, with advance notice, diving (no instruction). Snorkelling excursions and visits to the hippos and mangrove swamps can be arranged.

Mwangaza Hideaway LODGE $$$
(☎0757 029244, 0765 289538; www.kilwa-mwangaza.com; dm US$25, d/q full board in bungalow/dhow house US$140/200; P ❄) Tranquil Mwangaza has good-value dorm accommodation (with breakfast included) in a refurbished six-bed house, plus a handful of open-style bungalows directly overlooking the mangroves, and a lovely four-person 'dhow house'. The restaurant serves excellent meals. It's on the western side of the peninsula and about 1km off the main road, reached via a signposted turn-off opposite the airfield.

Night Market MARKET $
(off Main Rd, behind bus stand; snacks Tsh500-2000; ⏲6-11pm) Kilwa's lively night market gets going each evening from around 6pm, with grilled *pweza* (octopus), *mishikaki* (grilled meat skewers) and other snacks.

ℹ Information

MONEY

National Microfinance Bank (Main Rd) ATM accepting Visa and MasterCard.

TOURIST INFORMATION

Kilwa Islands Tour Guides Association (Main Rd; ⏲8am-8pm) This small office at the bus stand is the hub of Kilwa's tourism scene. You'll need to stop here to arrange visits to Kilwa Kisiwani and Songo Mnara. It also provides assistance finding accommodation, and offers a range of excursions in the Kilwa area. Prices for most excursions start at about US$25 per person for a guide and transport (less with larger groups).

Antiquities Office (Idara ya Mambo ya Kale; Main Rd; ⏲7.30am-3.30pm Mon-Fri) This is where you get permits to visit Kilwa Kisiwani and Songo Mnara, though as you need to arrange everything through the Kilwa Islands Tour Guides Association anyway, it's easier to stop there first.

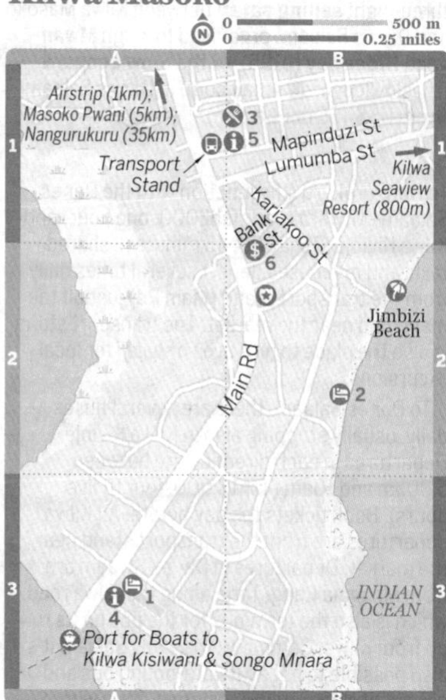

Kilwa Masoko

Sleeping
1 Kilwa Bandari Lodge A3
2 Kimbilio Lodge B2

Eating
3 Night Market B1

Information
4 Antiquities Office A3
5 Kilwa Islands Tour Guides Association B1
6 National Microfinance Bank B2

ℹ Getting There & Away

AIR

Coastal Aviation flies daily on demand between Kilwa and Dar es Salaam (US$275 one way), Zanzibar Island (US$330 one way) and Mafia (US$190 one way). All flights require a minimum of four passengers. Book through the Coastal Aviation office (p61) in Dar es Salaam. Kilwa Masoko's airstrip is about 2km north of town along the main road.

BOAT

Dhows to Songo Songo and other nearby islands are best arranged in Kilwa Kivinje. Boats to Kilwa Kisiwani and Songo Mnara depart from the small **port** (Main Rd) at the southern end of town. An intriguing option for those with time is the three-night **sailing safari** between Kilwa Masoko and Dar es Salaam, organised through **Mwangaza Hideaway** (p195), or the **Slow Leopard** (theslowleopard@gmail.com) in Dar es Salaam (from US$485 per person).

BUS

To Nangurukuru (the junction with the Dar es Salaam–Mtwara road; Tsh2000, one hour) and Kilwa Kivinje (Tsh2000, 45 minutes), shared taxis and minibuses depart several times daily from the transport stand (Main Rd) just off the main road near the market. The transport stand is also the place to hire taxis or *bajaji* for local excursions.

To Dar es Salaam, there are several buses daily, usually stopping also in Kilwa Kivinje. Departures in each direction are between 5.30am and 10am (Tsh13,000, four to five hours). Book tickets the day before. All Kilwa departures are from the transport stand near the market. Departures in Dar es Salaam are from Mbagala Rangi Tatu, along the Kilwa road, which is also the terminus for the bus on its run up from Kilwa. Coming from Dar es Salaam it's also possible to get a Mtwara-bound bus and get out at Nangurukuru junction, from where you can get local transport to Kilwa Kivinje (Tsh1000, 11km) or Kilwa Masoko (Tsh2000, 35km), although you'll usually be charged the full Dar es Salaam–Mtwara fare. This doesn't work as well leaving Kilwa, as buses are often full when they pass Nangurukuru (from about 11am). The best place to wait is at the large Starcom rest stop, along the main road about 200m north of Nangurukuru junction; most through buses stop here.

To Lindi, there's at least one direct bus daily (Tsh7000, four hours), departing Kilwa between 5am and 6am from the transport stand near the market; book a day in advance. There are no direct connections to Mtwara. Either get a shared taxi to Nangurukuru junction, and then try your luck catching a Mtwara-bound bus from there (wait at Starcom rest stop north of Nangurukuru junction) for the full Dar es Salaam–Mtwara fare. Otherwise, go first to Lindi, and take a minivan from there.

Kilwa Kisiwani

POP 1000

Kilwa Kisiwani ('Kilwa on the Island') is a quiet fishing village baking in the sun just offshore from Kilwa Masoko. In its heyday it was the seat of sultans and centre of a vast trading network linking the old Shona kingdoms and the goldfields of Zimbabwe with Persia, India and China. Ibn Battuta, the famed traveller and chronicler of the ancient world, visited Kilwa in the early 14th century and described the town as being exceptionally beautiful and well constructed. At its height, Kilwa's influence extended north past the Zanzibar Archipelago and south as far as Sofala on the central Mozambican coast.

While these glory days are now well in the past, the **ruins of the settlement** (adult/student Tsh27,000/13,000) – together with the ruins on nearby Songo Mnara (p197) island – are among the most significant groups of Swahili buildings on the East African coast and a Unesco World Heritage Site.

Sights

The ruins at Kilwa Kisiwani are in two groups. When approaching Kilwa Kisiwani, the first building you'll find is the **Arabic Fort** *(gereza)*. It was built in the early 19th century by the Omani Arabs, on the site of a Portuguese fort dating from the early 16th century. To the southwest of the fort are the ruins of the beautiful **Great Mosque**, with its columns and graceful vaulted roofing, much of which has been impressively restored. Some sections of the mosque date from the late 13th century, although most are from additions made to the building in the 15th century. In its day, this was the largest mosque on the East African coast. Further southwest and behind the Great Mosque is a smaller **mosque** dating from the early 15th century. This is considered to be the best preserved of the buildings at Kilwa and has also been impressively restored. To the west of the small mosque, with large, green lawns and placid views over the water, are the crumbling remains of the **Makutani**. Inside this large, walled enclosure is where some of the sultans of Kilwa lived. It is estimated to date from the mid-18th century.

Almost 1.5km from the fort along the coast is **Husuni Kubwa**, once a massive complex of buildings covering almost a hectare and, together with nearby **Husuni Ndogo**, the oldest of Kilwa's ruins. The complex, which is estimated to date from the 12th century or earlier, is set on a hill and must have once commanded great views over the bay. Look in particular for the octagonal bathing pool. Husuni Ndogo is smaller than Husuni Kubwa and is thought to date from about the same time, although archaeologists are not yet sure of its original function. To reach these ruins, you can walk along the beach at low tide or follow the slightly longer inland route.

Songo Mnara RUINS

(adult/student Tsh27,000/13,000) The tiny island of Songo Mnara, about 8km south of Kilwa Kisiwani, contains ruins at its northern end – including of a palace, several mosques and numerous houses – that are believed to date from the 14th and 15th centuries. They are considered in some respects to be more significant architecturally than those at Kilwa Kisiwani, with one of the most complete town layouts along the coast, although they're less visually impressive.

Getting There & Away

Local boats go from the port at Kilwa Masoko to Kilwa Kisiwani (Tsh200) whenever there are enough passengers – usually only in the early morning, at about 7am. However, they are not permitted to take tourists. As you are required to go with a guide to the islands, you'll need to pay their prices (US$40 per person including transport, guide fees and entry fee). With a good wind, in a sailing dhow the trip takes about 20 minutes.

Mtwara

023 / POP 108,300

First an obscure fishing village, then an empty shell of a city after the failed East African Groundnut Scheme, sprawling Mtwara is now southeastern Tanzania's major town. The commercialisation of Mtwara's natural gas reserves that started in 2006 sparked a flurry of building and investment. Now, however, with the construction of the gas pipeline to Dar es Salaam, many of the rapidly built high-rises are standing vacant, and the city's somnolent, sunbaked atmosphere is slowly returning. For travellers, Mtwara lacks the historical appeal of nearby Mikindani and other places along the coast. However, with its good infrastructure and easy access, it makes a useful stocking-up point between Tanzania and Mozambique. Mtwara has also become a popular resting point for those travelling between Dar es Salaam and Songea via the newly paved highway between Masasi and Tunduru.

Sights & Activities

The **beach** in Shangani is popular for swimming (high tide only); its gentle currents and general absence of sea urchins and other hazards make it ideal for children. For views over the bay and the white sands of Msangamkuu Peninsula, look for the tiny footpath leading to a viewpoint near the Southern Cross Hotel (p199).

Afri Mak Arts & Crafts Group MUSEUM

(Sinani St; donation; 9am-6pm Mon-Sat, 1-5pm Sun) This tiny museum features masks, spears, tools and other cultural items from the Makonde, Makua and Yao tribes. All displays are labelled in English and Swahili. This is also the best place to get information on the annual **Makuya Festival**. From the small roundabout on Makonde Rd, go one block north, then turn right. It's the second building on the left.

Market MARKET

(Sokoine Rd; 6am-6pm) Mtwara's market is full of colour and activity. You'll find everything here, with the traditional-medicine section and the textile shops particular highlights. It's near the bus stand.

Ayayoru Carvings & Tours TOURS

(0787 194196; www.mtwaratours.com; Sokoine Rd; 8.30am-5.30pm Mon-Sat) Moris Damian and his colleagues offer guided tours in and around Mtwara, including village visits with traditional dancing and drumming. Their small shop downhill from the market has a good selection of woodcarvings and other crafts.

Dhow Port & Fish Market MARKET

Much of Mtwara's fish comes from Msangamkuu on the other side of Mtwara Bay, and this small dhow port and adjoining fish market are particularly colourful in the early morning and late afternoon.

Sleeping & Eating

Drive-In Garden & Cliff Bar GUESTHOUSE $

(0784 503007; Shangani Rd; camping per tent Tsh5000, r without breakfast Tsh20,000-25,000) This friendly place allows campers to pitch their tent in the leafy, bird- and butterfly-filled garden. There are also several simple, good-value rooms, plus a restaurant. It's just across the road from the beach, although for swimming you'll need to walk up to the main Shangani beach area near Shangani junction.

Naf Blue View Hotel GUESTHOUSE $

(023-233 4465, 0656 107990; Sinani St; r Tsh50,000-80,000;) About 400m up (west) from the bus stand, this place is one of the better bets in the busy market area,

Mtwara

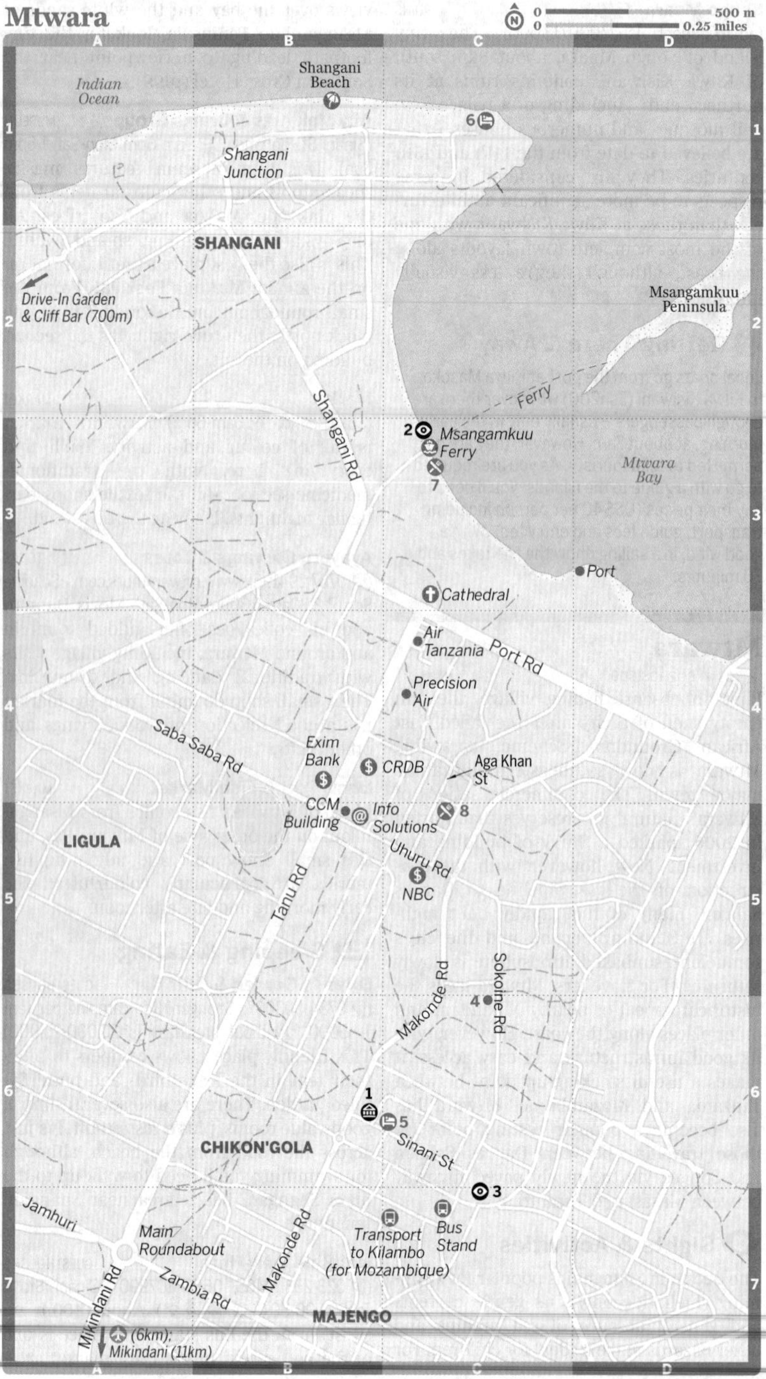

0 500 m
0 0.25 miles
Indian Ocean
Shangani Beach
6
Shangani Junction
SHANGANI
Drive-In Garden & Cliff Bar (700m)
Msangamkuu Peninsula
Ferry
Shangani Rd
2 Msangamkuu Ferry
7
Mtwara Bay
Port
Cathedral
Air Tanzania
Port Rd
Precision Air
Saba Saba Rd
Exim Bank
CRDB
Aga Khan St
CCM Building
Info Solutions
8
LIGULA
Uhuru Rd
NBC
Tanu Rd
Makonde Rd
Sokoine Rd
4
1
5
CHIKON'GOLA
Sinani St
3
Jamhuri
Main Roundabout
Transport to Kilambo (for Mozambique)
Bus Stand
Zambia Rd
Makonde Rd
Mikindani Rd
MAJENGO
(6km); Mikindani (11km)

Mtwara

Sights

1 Afri Mak Arts & Crafts Group B6
2 Dhow Port & Fish Market C3
3 Market C7

Activities, Courses & Tours

4 Ayayoru Carvings & Tours C6

Sleeping

5 Naf Blue View Hotel C6
6 Southern Cross Hotel C1

Eating

7 Fish Market C3
8 Senir Restaurant C5

with small, clean rooms with running hot water, satellite TV and meals on order. There are no mosquito nets.

Southern Cross Hotel HOTEL $
(☎0753 035809, 0712 035809; www.facebook.com/southerncrosshotelmtwara; Shangani waterfront; s/d Tsh60,000/75,000, s/d beach-facing bungalow Tsh120,000/135,000; P 📶) This long-standing Mtwara establishment has a lovely setting, perched on a small, rocky outcrop overlooking the sea at the eastern end of Shangani beach. It has changed ownership and received a complete facelift. The pleasant rooms are either 'standard' (garden view) or sea facing, and there's a deservedly popular waterside restaurant. Breakfast costs Tsh10,000.

Fish Market MARKET $
(off Shangani Rd; ⏰6am-4pm) The fish market at the Msangamkuu ferry dock is good for street food, selling grilled *pweza* (octopus), *vitambua* (rice cakes) and other delicacies. Food is freshest in the early morning.

Senir Restaurant INDIAN $
(☎0682 985678, 0683 045678; Aga Khan St, just off Tanu Rd; mains Tsh5000-14,000; ⏰10.30am-10pm; 🌶) Tasty Indian cuisine (plus some Chinese food) is served inside or on a pleasant, shaded streetside porch. Service is prompt and meals – including a good selection of vegetarian dishes – are well prepared.

Information

INTERNET ACCESS

Info Solutions (Uhuru Rd; per hour Tsh2000; ⏰8am-6pm Mon-Sat) On the side of the CCM building.

MONEY

The following ATMs accept Visa and MasterCard:

CRDB (Tanu Rd)

Exim Bank (Tanu Rd) Also Mtwara's best place to change cash.

NBC (Uhuru Rd; ⏰8am-4pm Mon-Fri, 9am-1pm Sat)

Getting There & Away

AIR

There are five to six flights weekly between Mtwara Airport (p212) and Dar es Salaam (from Tsh330,000 one way) on **Precision Air** (☎023-233 4116, 0782 818442; www.precisionairtz.com; Tanu Rd; ⏰8am-5pm Mon-Fri, 8am-2pm Sat) and three times weekly on **Air Tanzania** (☎0689 737212, 0782 737730; www.airtanzania.co.tz; Tanu Rd; ⏰8am-5pm Mon-Fri, 9am-2pm Sat).

BUS

All long-distance buses depart between about 5am and noon from the main bus stand just off Sokoine Rd near the market.

To Masasi (Tsh7000, four to five hours), there are roughly hourly departures between about 6am and 2pm.

To Songea (Tsh25,000, 10 hours), there is at least one departure daily at 6am.

To Lindi, there are direct buses daily at 6am and again usually at 8am (Tsh7000, three hours).

To Kilwa Masoko, there's no direct bus. You'll need to go first to Lindi and get onward transport from there, or take any Dar es Salaam–bound bus to Nangurukuru junction. For the latter option, you'll usually have to pay the full Dar price.

Direct buses to Newala (Tsh7500, six hours) usually use the southern route via Nanyamba. Departures from Mtwara are between 6am and 8am daily. At the time of research rehabilitation work was starting on this route, so enquire before setting off. It's also possible to reach Newala via Masasi, and via Mtama (en route between Mnazi Mmoja junction and Masasi).

To Dar es Salaam (Tsh23,000, eight hours), there are numerous departures daily in each direction between 6am and 10am, starting and terminating at Temeke's Sudan Market area, on Mbagala Rd, just east of Temeke Rd, where all the southbound bus lines also have booking offices. Book in advance. Some Dar es Salaam–Mtwara buses also start/terminate at Ubungo for approximately the same price.

To Mozambique, there are several pick-ups and at least one minivan daily to Mahurunga and the Tanzanian immigration post at Kilambo (Tsh5000), departing Mtwara between about 6am and 8am. This transport to Kilambo is from in front of Chilindima Guesthouse, one block southwest of the bus stand.

CAR & MOTORCYCLE

If you're driving to or from Dar es Salaam, there are petrol stations in Kibiti, Ikwiriri (unreliable), Nangurukuru, Kilwa Masoko, Lindi and Mtwara. The road is now all paved.

For self-drivers between Mtwara and the Mozambique border at Kilambo, the best places for updated information on the Ruvuma River crossing are Old Boma at Mikindani and Ten Degrees South Lodge, both in Mikindani. At the time of research, Mozambique visas were being issued at the Kilambo border. However, this could change at any time, so get an update before setting your plans. There is no Mozambique consulate in Mtwara; the closest one is in Dar es Salaam (p208).

Getting Around

Taxis can be difficult to find in Mtwara; you'll mostly need to rely on *bajaji* (tuk-tuks), which are everywhere. *Bajaji* 'stands' are at the bus stand, and near the CCM building at the intersection of Tanu and Uhuru roads. To and from the airport (6km southeast of the main roundabout) expect to pay about Tsh10,000 for a taxi and about half that for a *bajaji*. The cost for trips around town in a *bajaji* is Tsh1000 to Tsh2000 (Tsh3000 from the centre to Shangani).

There are a few dalla-dallas running along Tanu Rd to and from the bus stand.

To get to nearby Msangamkuu Peninsula, there is a ferry (off Shangani Rd) that runs daily between sunrise and sunset (Tsh300, about 15 minutes).

Mikindani

☎023

Mikindani – set on a picturesque bay surrounded by coconut groves – is a quiet, charming Swahili town with a long history. Although easily visited as a day trip from the nearby regional travel hub of Mtwara, many travellers prefer Mikindani to its larger neighbour as a base for exploring the surrounding area.

As well as seeing its various historical buildings, it's well worth just strolling through town to soak up the atmosphere and look at the numerous carved Zanzibar-style doors. With more time, make your way up Bismarck Hill, rising up behind the Old Boma, for some views.

Sights & Activities

Walking tours of town and local excursions can be organised at Old Boma at Mikindani and Ten Degrees South Lodge.

Boma HISTORIC BUILDING

The imposing German *boma,* built in 1895 as a fort and administrative centre, has been beautifully renovated as a hotel. Even if you're not staying here, it's worth taking a look and climbing the tower for views over the town. It's just off the B2 (main road).

Slave Market HISTORIC BUILDING

Downhill from the *boma* is the old slave market building, which now houses several craft shops. Unfortunately, it was much less accurately restored than the *boma* and lost much of its architectural interest when its open arches were filled in. The original design is now preserved only on one of Tanzania's postage stamps.

ECO2 DIVING

(☎0783 279446, 0784 855833; www.eco2tz.com; Main Rd) This good outfit offers PADI instruction (with advance reservation) and diving in both Mikindani Bay and at Mnazi Bay-Ruvuma Estuary Marine Park.

Sleeping & Eating

★ **Old Boma at Mikindani** HISTORIC HOTEL $$

(☎023-233 3875, 0757 622000; www.mikindani.com; s US$60-110, d US$110-140; P@令≋) This beautifully restored building is on a breezy hilltop overlooking the town and Mikindani Bay. It offers spacious, atmospheric, high-ceilinged doubles and the closest to top-end standards that you'll find in these parts. There's a sunset terrace with magnificent views, a pool surrounded by bougainvillea bushes and lush gardens, a spa, attentive staff and an excellent restaurant.

Ten Degrees South Lodge LODGE $$

(ECO2; ☎0684 059381, 0766 059380; www.tendegreessouth.com; s/d US$60/70, with shared bathroom US$20/30; @令) This recommended budget travellers' base has four cheaper and simple but spacious and good-value rooms, all with large double beds and shared bathrooms, plus bay views and deckchairs up on the roof. Next door are a handful of newer, self-contained double-bed rooms with hot-water showers. There's also an outdoor restaurant-bar, with tasty wraps, pancakes, coffees and other delicacies from about Tsh15,000.

Getting There & Away

Mikindani is 10km from Mtwara along a sealed road. Minibuses (Tsh500) run between the two towns throughout the day. *Bajajis* (tuk-tuks) from Mtwara charge about Tsh10,000 (it's about Tsh30,000 for a taxi).

Makonde Plateau

This cool and scenic plateau, much of which lies between 700m and 900m above sea level, is home to the Makonde people, famed throughout East Africa for their exotic woodcarvings. With its comparative isolation, scattered settlements and seeming obliviousness to developments elsewhere in the country, it in many ways epitomises inland areas of southeastern Tanzania, and is worth a detour if you're in the area.

Masasi

023 / POP 102,700

Masasi, a district centre and the birthplace of former Tanzanian president Benjamin Mkapa, stretches out along the main road off the edge of the Makonde Plateau against a backdrop of granite hills. It's a potentially useful stop for those travelling to or from Mozambique via the Unity Bridge. The history of the modern settlement dates from the late 19th century, when the Anglican Universities' Mission to Central Africa (UMCA) came from Zanzibar Island to establish a settlement of former slaves here. Today it's notable primarily as a transport hub for onward travel west towards Tunduru, or north to Nachingwea and Liwale. About 40km northeast of Masasi, just off the main road, is the large Benedictine monastery of **Ndanda**, founded by German missionaries in 1906. Adjoining is a hospital, which serves as the major health clinic for the surrounding region.

Information

MONEY

NBC (Main Rd) ATM at the eastern end of town.

TOURIST INFORMATION

Masasi Reserve Warden's Office (0713 311129, 0784 634972, 023-251 0364; Nachingwea Rd; 8am-4pm Mon-Fri) It's essential to stop here first to arrange permits if you're planning to visit Lukwika-Lumesule Game Reserve. The office is in Masasi's Migongo area, about 1km north of the main road en route to Nachingwea, on the left. Ask for Mali Asili (Natural Resources).

Getting There & Away

The bus stand is at the western edge of Masasi at the intersection of the Tunduru, Nachingwea and Newala roads.

The road between Masasi and Mtwara is in generally good condition. Buses travel between the two towns approximately hourly between 6am and 2pm daily (Tsh7000, three to four hours).

Transport leaves several times daily to Newala (Tsh5000, 1½ hours).

UNDERSTAND TANZANIA

History

Tanzania's history begins with the dawn of humankind. Hominid (human-like) footprints unearthed near Oldupai (Olduvai) Gorge, together with archaeological finds from Kenya and Ethiopia, show that our earliest ancestors were likely roaming the Tanzanian plains over three million years ago.

The Independence Struggle

The 1905 Maji Maji rebellion contains the earliest seeds of Tanzanian independence. During the following decades, the nationalist movement in Tanganyika – as what mainland Tanzania was then known – solidified. Farmers' cooperatives began to play an increasingly important political role, as did an up-and-coming group known as the Tanganyika Africa Association (TAA). Soon the TAA came to dominate Tanganyika's political scene, serving as the central channel for grass-roots resentment against colonial policies.

In 1953 the TAA elected an eloquent young teacher named Julius Nyerere as its president. He quickly transformed the group into an effective political organisation. A new internal constitution was introduced on 7 July 1954 (now celebrated as Saba Saba Day) and the TAA became the Tanganyika African National Union (TANU), with the rallying cry of 'uhuru na umoja' (freedom and unity).

Independence was the main item on TANU's agenda. In 1958 and 1959, TANU-supported candidates decisively won general legislative elections, and in 1959 Britain – which at the time held the reins in Tanganyika as governing 'caretaker' – agreed to the establishment of internal self-government. On 9 December 1961 Tanganyika became independent and on 9 December 1962 it was established as a republic, with Nyerere as president.

On the Zanzibar Archipelago, which had been a British protectorate ever since 1890, the predominant push for independence came from the radical Afro-Shirazi Party (ASP). Opposing the ASP were two minority parties, the Zanzibar and Pemba People's Party (ZPPP) and the sultanate-oriented Zanzibar Nationalist Party (ZNP). Both the ZPP and the ZNP parties were favoured by the British. As a result, at Zanzibari independence in December 1963, it was the two minority parties that formed the first government.

This new government did not last long. Within a month, a Ugandan immigrant named John Okello initiated a violent revolution against the ruling ZPPP–ZNP coalition, leading to the toppling of the government and the sultan, and the massacre or expulsion of most of the islands' Arab population. The sultan was replaced by an entity known as the Zanzibar Revolutionary Council, which comprised ASP members and was headed by Abeid Karume.

On 26 April 1964 Nyerere signed an act of union with Karume, thereby creating the United Republic of Tanganyika (renamed the United Republic of Tanzania the following October).

Formation of the union, which was resented by many Zanzibaris from the outset, was motivated in part by the then-prevailing spirit of pan-Africanism, and in part as a Cold War response to the ASP's socialist program.

Karume's government lasted until 1972, when he was assassinated and succeeded by Aboud Jumbe. Shortly thereafter, in an effort to subdue the ongoing unrest resulting from the merger of the islands with the mainland, Nyerere authorised formation of a one-party state and combined TANU and

THE MAJI MAJI REBELLION

The Maji Maji rebellion, which was the strongest local revolt against the colonial government in German East Africa, is considered to contain some of the earliest seeds of Tanzanian nationalism. It began around the turn of the 20th century when colonial administrators set about establishing enormous cotton plantations in the southeast and along the railway line running from Dar es Salaam towards Morogoro. These plantations required large numbers of workers, most of whom were recruited as forced labour and required to work under miserable salary and living conditions. Anger at this harsh treatment and long-simmering resentment of the colonial government combined to ignite a powerful rebellion.

The first outbreak was in 1905 in the area around Kilwa, on the coast. Soon all of southern Tanzania was involved, from Kilwa and Lindi in the southeast to Songea in the southwest. In addition to deaths on the battlefield, thousands died of hunger brought about by the Germans' scorched-earth policy, in which fields and grain silos in many villages were set on fire. Fatalities were undoubtedly exacerbated by a widespread belief among the Africans that enemy bullets would turn to water before reaching them, and so their warriors would not be harmed – hence the name Maji Maji (*maji* means 'water' in Swahili).

By 1907, when the rebellion was finally suppressed, close to 100,000 people had lost their lives. In addition, large areas of the south were left devastated and barren, and malnutrition was widespread. The Ngoni, a tribe of warriors much feared by their neighbours, put up the strongest resistance to the Germans. Following the end of the rebellion, they continued to wage guerrilla-style war until 1908, when the last shreds of their military-based society were destroyed. In order to quell Ngoni resistance once and for all, German troops hanged about 100 of their leaders and beheaded their most famous chief, Songea.

Among the effects of the Maji Maji uprising were temporary liberalisation of colonial rule and the replacement of the military administration with a civilian government. More significantly, the uprising promoted national identity among many ethnic groups and intensified anti-colonial sentiment, kindling the movement for independence.

the ASP into a new party known as Chama Cha Mapinduzi (CCM; Party of the Revolution). This merger, which was ratified in a new union constitution on 27 April 1977, marked the beginning of the CCM's dominance of Tanzanian politics, which endures to this day.

The Great Socialist Experiment

Nyerere took the helm of a country that was economically foundering and politically fragile, its stability plagued in particular by the mainland's lack of control over the Zanzibar Archipelago. Education had also been neglected, and at independence there were only a handful of university graduates in the entire country.

This inauspicious beginning eventually led to the Arusha Declaration of 1967, which committed Tanzania to a policy of socialism and self-reliance. The policy's cornerstone was the *ujamaa* (familyhood) village – an agricultural collective run along traditional African lines, with an emphasis on self-reliance. Basic goods and tools were to be held in common and shared among members, while each individual was obliged to work on the land.

Tanzania's experiment in socialism was acclaimed in the days following independence, and is credited with unifying the country and expanding education and health care. Economically, however, it was a failure. Per capita income plummeted, agricultural production stagnated and industry limped along at less than 50% of capacity. The decline was precipitated by a combination of factors, including steeply rising oil prices, the 1977 break-up of the East African Community (an economic and customs union between Tanzania, Kenya and Uganda), and sharp drops in the value of coffee and sisal exports.

Democracy

Nyerere was re-elected to a fifth term in 1980, amid continuing dissatisfaction with the great socialist experiment in the country. In 1985 he resigned from political office, handing over power to Zanzibari Ali Hassan Mwinyi. Mwinyi tried to distance himself from Nyerere and his policies, and instituted an economic recovery program. Yet the pace of change remained slow, and Mwinyi's presidency was unpopular. The collapse of European communism in the early 1990s and pressure from Western donor nations accelerated the move towards multiparty politics, and in 1992 the constitution was amended to legalise opposition parties.

Since then, five national elections have been held, generally proceeding relatively smoothly on the mainland, but less so on the Zanzibar Archipelago, where tensions between the CCM and the opposition Civic United Front (CUF) are strong. In elections in 2015, Dr John Pombe Magufuli (CCM) was elected president with 58% of the vote in a hotly contested election. His main opposition was former CCM Prime Minister Edward Lowassa of the Party for Democracy and Progress (Chadema), who garnered almost 40% of the vote – the most decisive opposition showing to date in Tanzania's history. Following the elections, Dr Magufuli moved quickly to implement his program, and just over a year into his presidency was receiving considerable acclaim – especially among Tanzania's large rural population – for his stiff anti-corruption measures and his determination to hold government officials accountable to their constituencies. At the same time, he was also receiving criticism for his stifling of open public debate and his stepped-up enforcement of restrictive laws governing freedom of the press. The next elections are scheduled for October 2020.

People

Tanzania is home to about 120 tribal groups, plus relatively small but economically significant numbers of Asians and Arabs, and a tiny European community. Most tribes are very small; almost 100 of them combined account for only one-third of the total population. As a result, none has succeeded in dominating politically or culturally, although groups such as the Chagga and the Haya, who have a long tradition of education, are disproportionately well represented in government and business circles.

About 95% of Tanzanians are of Bantu origin. These include the Sukuma (who live around Mwanza and southern Lake Victoria, and constitute about 16% of the overall population), the Nyamwezi (around Tabora), the Makonde (southeastern Tanzania),

TAARAB MUSIC

No visit to Zanzibar would be complete without spending an evening listening to the evocative strains of *taarab*, the archipelago's most famous musical export. A traditional *taarab* orchestra consists of several dozen musicians using both Western and traditional instruments, including the violin, the *kanun* (similar to a zither), the accordion, the *nay* (an Arabic flute) and drums, plus a singer. There's generally no written music, and songs – often with themes centred on love – are full of puns and double meanings.

Taarab-style music was played in Zanzibar as early as the 1820s at the sultan's palace, where it had been introduced from Arabia. However, it wasn't until the 1900s, when Sultan Seyyid Hamoud bin Muhammed encouraged formation of the first *taarab* clubs, that it became more formalised.

A good time to see taarab performances is during the **Sauti za Busara** (p71) in February.

the Haya (around Bukoba) and the Chagga (around Mt Kilimanjaro). The Maasai and several smaller groups including the Arusha and the Samburu (all in northern Tanzania) are of Nilo-Hamitic or Nilotic origin. The Iraqw, around Karatu and northwest of Lake Manyara, are Cushitic, as are the northern-central tribes of Gorowa and Burungi. The Sandawe and, more distantly, the seminomadic Hadzabe (around Lake Eyasi), belong to the Khoisan ethnolinguistic family.

Tribal structures, however, range from weak to non-existent – a legacy of Julius Nyerere's abolition of local chieftaincies following independence.

About 3% of Tanzania's population lives on the Zanzibar Archipelago, with about one-third of these on Pemba. Most African Zanzibaris belong to one of three groups: the Hadimu, the Tumbatu and the Pemba. Members of the non-African Zanzibari population are primarily Shirazi and consider themselves descendants of immigrants from Shiraz in Persia (Iran).

Religion

About 35% of Tanzanians are Muslim and between 35% and 40% are Christian. The remainder follow traditional religions. There are also small communities of Hindus, Sikhs and Ismailis. Muslims are traditionally found along the coast and in the inland towns that line the old caravan routes. The population of the Zanzibar Archipelago is almost exclusively Sunni Muslim, with tiny Christian and Hindu communities.

Music & Dance

Tanzania has an outstanding music and dance scene, mixing influences from its 100-plus tribal groups, from coastal and inland areas and from traditional and modern. Dar es Salaam is the hub, with the greatest variety of groups and styles, but search around anywhere in the country (asking locals is the best bet) and you'll discover some real gems. Two good contacts are Tumaini University Makumira (www.makumiramusic.org) outside Arusha and Bagamoyo College of Arts (www.tasuba.ac.tz) in Bagamoyo.

The greatest influence on Tanzania's modern music scene has been the Congolese bands that began playing in Dar es Salaam in the early 1960s, and the late Remmy Ongala ('Dr Remmy'), who was born in the Democratic Republic of the Congo (DRC: formerly Zaïre), but gained his fame in Tanzania.

On Zanzibar, the music scene has long been dominated by *taarab*.

Visual Arts

Tanzania's Makonde, together with their Mozambican counterparts, are renowned throughout East Africa for their original and highly fanciful carvings. Although originally from the Southeast around the Makonde Plateau, commercial realities lured many Makonde north. Today the country's main carving centre is at Mwenge in Dar es Salaam, where blocks of hard African blackwood (*Dalbergia melanoxylon* or, in Swahili, *mpingo*) come to life under the hands of skilled artists.

Environment

At over 943,000 sq km (almost four times the size of the UK), Tanzania is East Africa's largest country. It is bordered to the east by the Indian Ocean. To the west are the deep lakes of the Western Rift Valley with mountains rising up from their shores. Much of central Tanzania is an arid highland plateau averaging 900m to 1800m in altitude and nestled between the eastern and western branches of the Great Rift Valley.

Tanzania's mountain ranges are grouped into a sharply rising northeastern section (Eastern Arc), and an open, rolling central and southern section (the Southern Highlands or Southern Arc). A range of volcanoes, the Crater Highlands, rises from the side of the Great Rift Valley in northern Tanzania.

The largest river is the Rufiji, which drains the Southern Highlands en route to the coast. The Ruvuma River forms the border with Mozambique.

Wildlife

ANIMALS

Tanzania's fauna is notable for its sheer numbers and its variety, with 430 species and subspecies among the country's more than four million wild animals. These include zebras, elephants, wildebeests, buffaloes, hippos, giraffes, antelopes, dik-diks, gazelles, elands and kudus. Tanzania is known for its predators, with Serengeti National Park one of the best places for spotting lions, cheetahs and leopards. There are also hyenas and wild dogs and, in Gombe and Mahale Mountains National Parks, chimpanzees. Complementing this are over 1000 bird species of birds, including many endemics.

PLANTS

Small patches of tropical rainforest in Tanzania's Eastern Arc mountains provide home to a rich assortment of plants, many found nowhere else in the world. These include the Usambara or African violet *(Saintpaulia)* and *Impatiens,* which are sold as house plants in grocery stores throughout the West. Similar forest patches – remnants of the much larger tropical forest that once extended across the continent – are also found in the Udzungwas, Ulugurus and several other areas. South and west of the Eastern Arc range are stands of baobab.

Away from the mountain ranges, much of the country is covered by miombo ('moist' woodland), where the main vegetation is various types of *Brachystegia* tree. Much of the dry central plateau is covered with savannah, bushland and thickets, while grasslands cover the Serengeti Plain and other areas that lack good drainage.

National Parks & Reserves

Tanzania has 16 mainland national parks, 14 wildlife reserves, the Ngorongoro Conservation Area, three marine parks and several protected marine reserves.

NATIONAL PARKS

Tanzania's national parks are managed by the Tanzania National Parks Authority (p107).

Park entry fees, which are posted on the Tanapa website, range from US$30 to US$100 per adult per single entry per 24-hour period, depending on the park (US$10 to US$20), with Serengeti, Kilimanjaro, Mahale Mountains and Gombe parks the most expensive, and Mkomazi, Saadani, Mikumi, Udzungwa Mountains, Kitulo, Katavi and Rubondo Island parks the least expensive. The single-entry requirement means that it is not possible to exit a park and re-enter within 24 hours unless you pay entry fees again.

Park camping fees are US$30 per adult (US$5 per child) in public campsites and US$50 per adult (US$10 per child) in special campsites. Other costs include guide fees of US$20 to US$25 per group for walking safaris, plus vehicle fees (US$40 per foreign-registered vehicle and Tsh20,000 for Tanzania-registered vehicles). Note that a value-added tax (VAT) of 18% is applied to all park fees, including park entry fees, camping fees, guide fees and vehicle fees.

At all parks, park entry fees and all other park fees must be paid electronically with a Visa card or MasterCard. It is also possible to pay using a 'smart card', available for purchase from CRDB and Exim banks. In any case, it is advisable to bring Visa or MasterCard as well as US dollars cash or the equivalent in Tanzanian shillings (the latter to cover cases where the card machines are not working) whenever visiting Tanzania's parks.

WILDLIFE RESERVES

Wildlife reserves are administered by the **Tanzania Wildlife Management Authority** (TAWA; www.tawa.go.tz). Fees must be paid in advance, either through your lodge or tented camp or at any NBC bank branch. Selous Game Reserve (p190) is the only reserve with tourist infrastructure. Large areas of most others have been leased as hunting concessions, as has the southern Selous.

MARINE PARKS & RESERVES

Mafia Island Marine Park (p187), **Mnazi Bay-Ruvuma Estuary Marine Park** (www.marineparks.go.tz; adult/child US$23.60/11.80; ⏲7am-6pm), **Tanga Coelacanth Marine Park** (www.marineparks.go.tz; adult/child US$23.60/11.80), **Maziwe Marine Reserve** (adult/child US$11.80/5.90) and the **Dar es Salaam Marine Reserves** (www.marineparks.go.tz; adult/child US$11.80/5.90) – Mbudya, Bongoyo, Pangavini and Fungu Yasini islands – are under the jurisdiction of the Ministry of Natural Resources & Tourism's Marine Parks & Reserves Unit (p61). Except for Mafia Island Marine Park, which accepts credit card only, entry fees for marine parks (US$20 per day per adult, US$10 per child) and marine reserves (US$10 per adult, US$5 per child) are payable in cash only.

NGORONGORO CONSERVATION AREA

The Ngorongoro Conservation Area (p120) was established as a multiple-use area to protect wildlife and the pastoralist lifestyle of the Maasai, who had lost other large areas of their traditional territory with the formation of Serengeti National Park. It is administered by the Ngorongoro Conservation Area Authority (p122). It is notable both for its superlative wildlife watching in the Ngorongoro Crater and for its rugged hiking in the surrounding highlands. Payment for entering the Conservation Area (US$60 per adult per day and US$20 per child entry, plus vehicle and crater service fees – all subject to an 18% value-added tax) must be made via Visa or MasterCard, although it is also advisable to bring cash.

SURVIVAL GUIDE

Directory A–Z

ACCOMMODATION

Price Ranges

The following price ranges refer to a standard double room with bathroom in high season. Unless otherwise stated, VAT of 18%, and continental breakfast is included in the price. For midrange and top-end hotels, full breakfast is usually included.

$ less than US$50 (Tsh100,000)

$$ US$50–150 (Tsh100,000–300,000)

$$$ more than US$150 (Tsh300,000)

Camping

Carry a tent to save money and for flexibility off the beaten track. Note that camping in most national parks costs at least US$30 per person per night – as much as sleeping in park-run accommodation.

National Parks

All parks have campsites, designated as either 'public' ('ordinary') or 'special'. Most parks also have simple huts or cottages (sometimes called *bandas*), several have basic resthouses and some northern circuit parks have hostels (for student groups, or for overflow, if the resthouses or cottages are full).

Public campsites These have toilets (usually pit latrines) and, sometimes, a water source, but plan on being self-sufficient. Most sites are in reasonable condition and some are quite pleasant. No booking required.

Special campsites These are smaller, more remote and more expensive than public sites, with no facilities. The idea is that the area remains as close to pristine as possible. Advance booking required; once you make a booking, the special campsite is reserved exclusively for your group.

Elsewhere

- There are campsites situated in or near most major towns, near many of the national parks and in some scenic locations along a few of the main highways (eg Dar es Salaam–Mbeya and Tanga–Moshi).
- Prices average from US$10 per person per night to more than double this for campsites near national parks.
- Camping away from established sites is generally not advisable. In rural areas, seek permission from the village head or elders before pitching your tent.
- Camping is not permitted on Zanzibar Island.

Guesthouses

Almost every town has at least one basic guesthouse. At the bottom end of the scale, expect a cement-block room, often small and poorly ventilated, and not always very clean, with a foam mattress, shared bathroom facilities (often long-drop toilets and bucket showers), a mosquito net and sometimes a fan. Rates average Tsh10,000 to Tsh15,000 per room per night.

The next level up gets you a cleaner, decent room, often with a bathroom (although not always with running or hot water). Prices for a double room with bathroom average from about Tsh25,000 (from Tsh20,000 for a single).

Some tips:

➡ For peace and quiet, guesthouses without bars are the best choice.

➡ In many towns, water is a problem during the dry season, so don't be surprised if your only choice at budget places is a bucket bath. Many of the cheaper places don't have hot water. This is a consideration in cooler areas, especially during winter, although staff will almost always arrange a hot bucket if you ask.

➡ In Swahili, the word *hotel* or *hoteli* does not mean accommodation but rather a place for food and drink. The more common term used for accommodation is *guesti* (guesthouse) or, more formally, *nyumba ya kulala wageni*.

➡ There are many mission hostels and guesthouses, primarily for missionaries and aid-organisation staff, though some are willing to accommodate travellers, space permitting.

➡ In coastal areas, you'll find bungalows or *bandas* (small thatched-roof cottages with wooden or stone walls) ranging from simple huts on the sand to luxurious en suite affairs.

Hotels & Lodges

Larger towns offer from one to several midrange hotels with en suite rooms (widely referred to in Tanzania as 'self-contained' or 'self-containers'), hot water, and a fan and/or an air-conditioner. Facilities range from not so great to quite reasonable value, with prices averaging from US$30 to US$100 per person.

At the top end of the spectrum, there's an array of fine hotels and lodges with all the amenities you would expect at this price level (from US$100 or more per person per night). Especially on the safari circuits there are some wonderful and very luxurious lodges costing from US$150 to US$500 or more per person per night, although at the high end of the spectrum prices are usually all-inclusive. Some park lodges offer discounted accommodation rates for those arriving with their own vehicles.

ACTIVITIES

Tanzania offers its famous wildlife safaris, plus much more, with diving, snorkelling, birdwatching, kitesurfing, chimpanzee tracking, cycling, hiking and trekking just some of the highlights. Plan your holiday around one of these options, or sample several.

Birdwatching

Tanzania is an outstanding birding destination, with well over 1000 species, including numerous endemics. In addition to the national parks and reserves, top birding spots include the eastern Usambara Mountains and Lake Victoria. Useful websites include the Tanzania Bird Atlas (www.tanzaniabirdatlas.net), the Tanzania Hotspots page on www.camacdonald.com/birding/africatanzania.htm and Tanzanian Birds & Butterflies (www.tanzaniabirds.net).

Chimpanzee Tracking

Gombe National Park (p159) and Mahale Mountains National Park (p160) have hosted international research teams for decades, and are outstanding destinations if you are interested in observing chimpanzees at close quarters.

Hiking & Trekking

Tanzania has rugged, varied terrain and a fine collection of peaks, rolling hills and mountain ranges. Landscapes range from the forested slopes of the eastern Udzungwa Mountains to the sheer volcanic cliffs of the inner wall of Mt Meru's crater, the rolling hill landscapes of the Usambaras and the final scree-slope ascent of Mt Kilimanjaro. Treks and hikes range from village-to-village walks to bush hikes.

Throughout the country, almost all trekking can be done without technical equipment, by anyone who is reasonably fit. However, most excursions – and all trekking or hiking in national parks and wildlife areas – require being accompanied by a guide or ranger. This usually also entails adhering to set (sometimes short) daily stages.

Horse Riding

Riding safaris are possible in the West Kilimanjaro and Lake Natron areas. Contacts include **Makoa Farm** (☎ 0625 312896, 0754 312896; www.makoa-farm.com) and **Kaskazi Horse Safaris** (☎ 0766 432792; www.kaskazihorsesafaris.com). At the time of research, horse-riding safaris were also scheduled to begin in 2018 in Kitulo National Park, down to Matema on Lake Nyasa. Contact Maua Café & Tours (p179) in Mbeya.

CUSTOMS REGULATIONS

Exporting seashells, coral, ivory and turtle shells is illegal. There's no limit on the importation or exportation of foreign currency, but amounts over US$10,000 must be declared.

DANGERS & ANNOYANCES

Tanzania is in general a safe, hassle-free country. That said, you do need to take the usual precautions and keep up with government travel advisories.

➡ Avoid isolated areas, especially isolated stretches of beach. In cities and tourist areas take a taxi at night.

➡ Only take taxis from established taxi ranks or hotels. Never enter a taxi that already has someone else in it other than the driver.

- Never pay any money for a safari or trek in advance until you've thoroughly checked out the company, and never pay any money at all outside the company's office.
- When using public transport, don't accept drinks or food from someone you don't know. Be sceptical of anyone who comes up to you on the street asking whether you remember them from the airport, your hotel or wherever. Take requests for donations from 'refugees', 'students' or others with a grain of salt. Contributions to humanitarian causes are best done through an established agency or project.
- Be wary of anyone who approaches you on the street, at the bus station or in your hotel offering safari deals or claiming to know you.
- In western Tanzania, especially along the Burundi border, there are sporadic outbursts of banditry and political unrest. Get an update locally before setting your plans.
- In tourist areas, especially Arusha, Moshi and Zanzibar Island, touts can be quite pushy, especially around bus stations and budget tourist hotels. Do what you can to minimise the impression that you're a newly arrived tourist: walk with purpose, and duck into a shop if you need to get your bearings or look at a map.
- Arriving for the first time at major bus stations, have your luggage as consolidated as possible, with your valuables well hidden under your clothes. Try to spot the taxi area before disembarking and make a beeline for it. It's well worth a few extra dollars for the fare. While looking for a room, leave your bag with a friend or reliable hotel rather than walking around town with it. Buy your bus tickets a day or two in advance (without your luggage).
- Carry your passport, money and other documents in a pouch against your skin, hidden under loose-fitting clothing. Or store valuables in a hotel safe, if there's a reliable one, ideally inside a pouch with a lockable zip to prevent tampering.
- Keep the side windows up in vehicles when stopped in traffic and keep your bags out of sight (eg on the floor behind your legs).
- When bargaining or discussing prices, don't do so with your money or wallet in your hand.

EMBASSIES & CONSULATES

Most embassies and consulates in Dar es Salaam are open from 8.30am to 3pm Monday to Friday, often with a midday break. Visa applications for all countries neighbouring Tanzania should be made in the morning.

British High Commission (Map p56; ☎022-229 0000; www.gov.uk/government/world/tanzania; Umoja House, cnr Mirambo St & Garden Ave)

Burundian Embassy (Map p58; ☎022-212 7008, 022-212 7007; burundiembassydar@yahoo.com; 1007 Lugalo St, Upanga)

Canadian High Commission (Map p56; ☎022-216 3300; www.canadainternational.gc.ca/tanzania-tanzanie; 38 Mirambo St)

Democratic Republic of the Congo Embassy (Formerly Zaïre) (Map p58; ☎022-215 2388; www.ambardc-tz.org; 20 Malik Rd, Upanga)

French Embassy (Map p58; ☎022-219 8800; www.ambafrance-tz.org; 7 Ali Hassan Mwinyi Rd)

German Embassy (Map p56; ☎022-211 7409/15; www.daressalam.diplo.de; Umoja House, cnr Mirambo St & Garden Ave)

Indian High Commission (Map p56; ☎022-211 3094, 022-211 3079; www.hcindiatz.org; Shaaban Robert St)

Irish Embassy (Map p58; ☎022-260 2355, 022-260 0629; www.dfa.ie/irish-embassy/tanzania; 353 Toure Dr)

Italian Embassy (Map p58; ☎022-211 5935; www.ambdaressalaam.esteri.it; 316 Lugalo St, Upanga)

Kenyan High Commission (Map p58; ☎022-266 8286, 022-266 8285; www.kenyahighcomtz.org; cnr Ali Hassan Mwinyi Rd & Kaunda Dr, Oyster Bay)

Malawian High Commission (Map p58; ☎022-277 4220; www.malawihctz.org; Rose Garden Rd, Mikocheni A)

Mozambique High Commission (Map p56; 25 Garden Ave; ⏲9am-3pm Mon-Thu, 9am-noon Fri)

Netherlands Embassy (Map p56; ☎022-219 4000; www.netherlandsworldwide.nl/countries/tanzania; Umoja House, cnr Mirambo St & Garden Ave)

Rwandan Embassy (Map p58; ☎022-260 0500, 0754 787835; www.tanzania.embassy.gov.rw; 452 Haile Selassie Rd)

Ugandan Embassy (Map p58; ☎022-266 7391; www.daressalaam.mofa.go.ug; 25 Msasani Rd)

US Embassy (Map p58; ☎022-229 4000; https://tz.usembassy.gov; 686 Old Bagamoyo Rd)

Zambian High Commission (Map p56; ☎022-212 5529; ground fl, Zambia House, cnr Ohio St & Sokoine Dr; ⏲visa applications 9.30am-3.30pm Mon, Wed & Fri)

ETIQUETTE

Greetings Take time for greetings.

Dining Don't eat or pass things with the left hand.

Dealing with authority Respect authority, avoid impatience; let deference and good humour see you through.

Visits Before entering someone's house, call out *Hodi* (May I enter?), then wait for the inevitable *Karibu* (Welcome).

Gifts Receive gifts with both hands, or with the right hand while touching the left hand to your right elbow.

GAY & LESBIAN TRAVELLERS

Homosexuality is illegal in Tanzania, including the Zanzibar Archipelago, and prosecutions have become more commonplace. In mid-September 2017, 20 people on Zanzibar Island were arrested while attending a HIV/AIDS education session. Public displays of affection, whether between people of the same or opposite sex, are frowned upon, and homosexuality is culturally taboo.

INTERNET ACCESS

There are internet cafes in all major towns, and wi-fi hotspots are widespread, except in rural areas. Prices at internet cafes average Tsh1000 to Tsh2000 per hour. Speed varies greatly; truly fast connections are rare. Almost all midrange and top-end hotels, including on the safari circuits, and some budget places have wireless access points; some are free, but others charge a modest fee. The best way to connect is either with your smartphone or by purchasing a wi-fi hotspot from one of the mobile providers (about Tsh70,000, including 10GB of initial credit). For topping up, various packages are available, averaging about Tsh35,000 for 10GB, valid for one month. Top-up credit vouchers are sold at roadside shops countrywide.

LANGUAGE COURSES

Tanzania is the best place in East Africa to learn Swahili, the country's official language, together with English. Swahili in coastal areas, especially the Zanzibar Archipelago, is generally considered more pure than the Swahili spoken inland. Some schools can arrange home stays.

ELCT Language & Orientation School (www.studyswahili.com; Lutheran Junior Seminary, Morogoro) This is a long-standing mission-run language school on the outskirts of Morogoro town.

KIU Ltd (Map p58; ☎0754 271263; www.swahilicourses.com) At various locations in Dar es Salaam, plus branches in Iringa and on Zanzibar Island.

Meeting Point Tanga (www.meetingpointtanga.net) Just south of Tanga.

MS Training Centre for Development Cooperation (☎027-254 1044, 0754 651715; www.mstcdc.or.tz; Usa River) About 15km outside Arusha, near Usa River.

MAPS

- Good country maps include those published by Nelles and Harms-ic, both available in Tanzania and elsewhere, and both also including Rwanda and Burundi. Harms-ic also publishes maps for Lake Manyara National Park, the Ngorongoro Conservation Area and Zanzibar Island.
- The Surveys and Mapping Division's Map Sales Office (p61) in Dar es Salaam sells dated topographical maps (1:50,000) for mainland Tanzania. Topographical maps for Zanzibar Island and Pemba are available in Stone Town.
- Hand-drawn 'MaCo' maps (www.gtmaps.com) cover Zanzibar Island, Arusha and the northern parks. They're sold in bookshops in Dar es Salaam, Arusha and Zanzibar Town.

MONEY

The easiest way to access money while travelling in Tanzania is at ATMs using a Visa card.

ATMs

ATMs are widespread in major towns, and all are open 24 hours. But they are occasionally out of service or out of cash, so you should have back-up funds. All internationally linked machines allow you to withdraw shillings with a Visa or MasterCard. Withdrawals are usually to a maximum of Tsh300,000 or Tsh400,000 per transaction (ATMs in small towns often have a limit of Tsh200,000 per transaction) and with a daily limit of Tsh1.2 million (less in small towns). Some machines also accept other cards linked to the Cirrus/Maestro/Plus networks.

The main operators:

Barclays Dar es Salaam, Arusha, Moshi, Zanzibar Island, Tanga

CRDB Major towns

Exim Dar es Salaam, Arusha, Moshi, Mwanza, Tanga, Morogoro

National Bank of Commerce Major towns

Stanbic Dar es Salaam, Arusha, Moshi, Mbeya

Standard Chartered Dar es Salaam, Arusha, Moshi, Mwanza

In large cities, queues at ATM machines on Friday afternoons are notoriously long; take care of your banking before then.

If your ATM withdrawal request is rejected (no matter what reason the machine gives), it could be for something as simple as requesting above the allowed transaction amount for that particular machine; it's always worth trying again. Entering your PIN number erroneously three times results in a captured card.

Cash

US dollars, followed by euros, are the most convenient foreign currencies and get the best rates, although other major currencies are readily accepted in major centres. Bring a mix of large and small denominations, but note that US$50 and US$100 bills get better rates of exchange than smaller denominations. Old-style (small head) US bills and US bills dated prior to 2006 are not accepted anywhere.

Credit Cards

Bring a Visa card or MasterCard. These are essential for withdrawing money at ATMs; Visa is the most widely accepted. A Visa or MasterCard is also required for paying park fees at most national parks. Some upmarket hotels and tour operators accept credit cards for payment, often with a commission averaging from 5% to 10%. However, many don't; always confirm in advance.

Exchanging Money

- Change cash at banks or foreign exchange (forex) bureaus in major towns and cities; rates and commissions vary, so shop around.
- Forex bureaus are usually quicker, less bureaucratic and open longer hours than banks, although most smaller towns don't have them. They also tend to accept a wider range of currencies than banks.
- The most useful bank for foreign exchange is NBC, with branches throughout the country. Countrywide, banks and forex bureaus are closed from noon on Saturday until Monday morning.
- To reconvert Tanzanian shillings to hard currency, save at least some of your exchange receipts, although they are seldom checked. The easiest places to reconvert currency are at the airports in Dar es Salaam and Kilimanjaro, or try at forex shops or banks in major towns.
- For after-hours exchange and exchanging in small towns, as well as for reconverting back to dollars or euros, many Indian-owned businesses will change money, although often at unfavourable rates.
- In theory, it's required that foreigners pay for accommodation, park fees, organised tours, upmarket hotels and the Zanzibar ferries in US dollars, although shillings are accepted almost everywhere at the going rate.

Tipping

Restaurants Tipping is generally not practised in small local establishments, especially in rural areas. In major towns and in places frequented by tourists, tips are expected. Some top-end places include a service charge in the bill. Usually, however, either rounding up the bill or adding about 10% to 15% is standard practice.

Safaris and Treks On treks and safaris, it's common practice to tip drivers, guides, porters and other staff.

Taxis Tipping is not common practice, except for longer (full-day or multiday) rentals.

OPENING HOURS

Opening hours are generally as follows:

Banks and government offices 8am to 3.30pm Monday to Friday

Restaurants 7am to 9.30am, noon to 3pm and 6.30pm to 9.30pm; reduced hours low season

Shops 8.30am to 5pm or 6pm Monday to Friday, 9am to 1pm Saturday; often closed Friday afternoon for mosque services

Supermarkets 8.30am to 6pm Monday to Friday, 9am to 4pm Saturday, 10am to 2pm Sunday

PUBLIC HOLIDAYS

The dates of Islamic holidays depend on the moon and are known for certain only a few days in advance. They fall about 11 days earlier each year and include Eid al-Kebir (Eid al-Haji), Eid al-Fitr and Eid al-Moulid (Maulidi).

New Year's Day 1 January

Zanzibar Revolution Day 12 January

Easter March/April – Good Friday and Easter Monday

Karume Day 7 April

Union Day 26 April

Labour Day 1 May

Saba Saba (Peasants' Day) 7 July

Nane Nane (Farmers' Day) 8 August

Nyerere Day 14 October

Independence Day 9 December

Christmas Day 25 December

Boxing Day 26 December

TELEPHONE

The fast-fading Tanzania Telecom (TTCL) usually has its offices at the post office. TTCL ('landline') numbers are seven digits, preceded by a mandatory three-digit area code.

Phone Codes

Tanzania's country code is 255. To make an international call, dial 000 followed by the country code, local area code (without the initial '0') and telephone number.

Mobile Phones

Local SIM cards work in European and Australian phones. Other phones must be set to roaming. All mobile companies sell pre-paid starter packages for about US$2. Top-up cards are widely available from shops and roadside vendors throughout the country.

TIME

Tanzania time is GMT/UTC plus three hours. There is no daylight saving.

TOURIST INFORMATION

Tanzania Tourist Board (www.tanzaniatourist board.com) The official tourism entity.

VISAS

Officially, visas must be obtained in advance by all travellers who come from a country with Tanzania diplomatic representation. Single-entry visas (but not multiple-entry visas) are also currently issued on arrival (no matter what your provenance) at Dar es Salaam, Kilimanjaro and Zanzibar International Airports, at the Namanga border post between Tanzania and Kenya, and at Tunduma border (between Tanzania and Zambia). In practice, visas are currently also readily issued at most other major land borders and ports (US dollars cash only; single-entry only) with a minimum of hassle. Our advice: get your visa in advance if possible. If not possible, it's well worth giving it a try at the border.

When out and about in Tanzania, always carry at least a photocopy of your passport and visa or resident permit, and have the originals readily accessible.

Visa Extensions

One month is the normal visa validity and three months (upon request) is the maximum. For extensions within the three-month limit, there are immigration offices in all major towns, including **Dar es Salaam** (Uhamiaji; ☎022-285 0575/6; www.immigration.go.tz; Uhamiaji House, Loliondo St, Kurasini; ⏰visa applications 8am-noon Mon-Fri, visa collections until 2pm), **Arusha** (East Africa Rd; ⏰7.30am-3.30pm Mon-Fri) and **Moshi** (Boma Rd; ⏰7.30am-3.30pm Mon-Fri); the process is free and generally straightforward. Extensions after three months are difficult; you usually need to leave the country and apply for a new visa.

VOLUNTEERING

Volunteering opportunities (generally teaching, or in environmental or health work) are usually best arranged prior to arriving in Tanzania. Note that the current cost of volunteer (Class C) resident permits is US$200 for three months. Also note that for any volunteering work involving children, you will require a criminal background check from your home country and/or previous countries of residence.

African Initiatives (www.african-initiatives.org.uk) Focuses on girls' education and women's rights, and offers several ways of getting involved, although most opportunities are outside Tanzania.

Frontier (www.frontier.ac.uk) Marine conservation work, primarily on Mafia Island.

Indigenous Education Foundation of Tanzania (www.ieftz.org) Education work in Maasai areas of northern Tanzania.

Kigamboni Community Centre (☎0788 482684, 0753 226662; www.kccdar.com; Kigamboni) Teaching and other volunteer opportunities in a rural community on the outskirts of Dar es Salaam.

Peace Corps (www.peacecorps.gov) US voluntary organisation with placements in various countries, including Tanzania.

Responsible Travel.com (www.responsible travel.com) Matches you up with ecologically and culturally responsible tour operators to plan a volunteer-focused itinerary.

Trade Aid (www.tradeaiduk.org/volunteer.html) Skills training work in Mikindani village in southern Tanzania.

Voluntary Service Overseas (www.vso.org.uk) British voluntary organisation with placements in Tanzania.

ℹ Getting There & Away

Most travellers reach Tanzania via air or travelling overland through one of the country's many land borders.

Flights, cars and tours can be booked online at lonelyplanet.com/bookings.

ENTERING THE COUNTRY

- Provided you have a visa, Tanzania is straightforward to enter.
- Yellow fever vaccination is required if you are arriving from an endemic area (which includes several of Tanzania's neighbours).

AIR

Tanzania has three international airports.

Julius Nyerere International Airport (DAR; ☎022-284 2402; www.taa.go.tz) Dar es Salaam; Tanzania's air hub.

Kilimanjaro International Airport (JRO; ☎027-255 4252; www.kilimanjaroairport.co.tz) Between Arusha and Moshi, and the best option for itineraries in Arusha and the northern safari circuit. Note: it's not to be confused with the smaller Arusha Airport, 8km west of Arusha, which handles domestic flights only.

Zanzibar International Airport (ZNZ, Abeid Amani Karume International Airport) On Zanzibar Island, at the southern edge of Zanzibar

DEPARTURE TAX

Departure tax is included in the price of a ticket.

Town; it handles frequent charter flights from Europe, as well as several international carriers.

Other airports handling regional flights include **Arusha Airport** (☎027-250 5920; www.taa.go.tz; Dodoma Rd), **Mtwara Airport** (MYW; off Mikindani Rd) and **Mwanza International Airport** (MWZ; ☎022-284 2402).

A useful website for researching and booking East African regional flights is www.tripindigo.com. Tanzania's flagship carrier is Air Tanzania (p216), with domestic destinations, plus a small network of regional destinations. Other useful regional and international carriers include the following (all servicing Dar es Salaam, except as noted):

Air Kenya (☎in Kenya 020-391 6000; www.airkenya.com) Flies between Nairobi and Kilimanjaro International Airport (KIA).

Egyptair (Map p56; ☎0789 516482; www.egyptair.com; Ali Hassan Mwinyi Rd, 1st fl, Viva Towers; ⏲9am-5pm Mon-Fri, 9am-1.30pm Sat) Dar es Salaam to Cairo (Egypt) and beyond.

Emirates (Map p56; ☎022-211 6100, 022-211 6101; Haidery Plaza, cnr Kisutu & India Sts; ⏲8am-4.30pm Mon-Fri, 8.30am-12.30pm Sat) Dar es Salaam to Dubai (UAE) and beyond.

Ethiopian Airlines (Map p56; ☎022-211 7063, 0786 285899; www.ethiopianairlines.com; Ohio St, TDFL Bldg; ⏲8.30am-4.30pm Mon-Fri, 8.30am-1pm Sat) Dar es Salaam and KIA to Addis Ababa (Ethiopia), with onward connections to many other destinations.

Fastjet (p216) Johannesburg (South Africa), Harare (Zimbabwe) and Lusaka (Zambia) to Dar es Salaam.

Kenya Airways (Map p56; ☎0683 390008, 0786 390004, 0786 390005; www.kenya-airways.com; Ali Hassan Mwinyi Rd, 1st fl, Viva Towers; ⏲8.30am-5pm Mon-Fri) Nairobi and Mombasa to KIA, Dar es Salaam and Zanzibar Island in partnership with Precision Air.

KLM (Map p56; ☎0653 333446, 0789 777145, 022-213 9791; www.klm.com; Ali Hassan Mwinyi Rd, 1st fl, Viva Towers; ⏲8.30am-5pm Mon-Fri) Daily flights connecting KIA and Dar es Salaam with Amsterdam (Netherlands).

Linhas Aéreas de Moçambique (Map p56; ☎022-213 4600; www.lam.co.mz; Fast Track Tanzania, Bibi Titi Mohammed Rd; ⏲8.30am-5pm Mon-Fri, 8.30am-1pm Sat) Maputo (Mozambique), Pemba (Mozambique) and Nampula (Mozambique) to Dar es Salaam.

Malawi Airlines (Map p56; ☎022-213 6663; www.malawian-airlines.com; Fast Track Tanzania, Bibi Titi Mohammed Rd; ⏲8.30am-5pm Mon-Fri, 8.30am-1pm Sat) Dar es Salaam and Zanzibar Island to Blantyre (Malawi) and Lilongwe (Malawi); all flights are via Addis Ababa (Ethiopia).

Precision Air (☎022-219 1000, 0787 888417; www.precisionairtz.com) Nairobi (Kenya) to Dar es Salaam and KIA.

Rwandair (Map p56; ☎022-210 3435; www.rwandair.com; Ali Hassan Mwinyi Rd, 2nd fl, Viva Towers; ⏲8am-5pm Mon-Fri, 9am-1pm Sat) Kigali (Rwanda) to KIA and Dar es Salaam.

South African Airways (SAA; Map p56; ☎0717 722772, 022-211 7045/7; www.flysaa.com; cnr Bibi Titi Mohammed Rd & Maktaba St; ⏲8.30am-4.30pm Mon-Fri, 8.30am-12.30pm Sat) Daily between Dar es Salaam and Johannesburg (South Africa).

Swiss International Airlines (Map p58; ☎022-551 0020; www.swiss.com; 84 Kinondoni Rd; ⏲8am-4.30pm Mon-Fri, 8.30am-12.30pm Sat) Dar es Salaam to Zurich (Switzerland).

LAND

Tanzania's land borders are generally straightforward to cross. While there are through-buses on major routes, for less-travelled routes it's generally faster (and often necessary) to take one bus to the border, walk across, and then get onward transport on the other side.

Kenya

The main route to/from Kenya is the good sealed road connecting Arusha (Tanzania) and Nairobi (Kenya) via the recently modernised Namanga border post (open 24 hours, with a bank and immigration inside the main building). There are also border crossings at Horohoro (Tanzania), north of Tanga; at Holili (Tanzania), east of Moshi; at Loitokitok (Kenya), northeast of Moshi; and at Sirari (Tanzania), northeast of Musoma. With the exception of the Serengeti–Masai Mara crossing (which is currently closed), there is public transport across all Tanzania–Kenya border posts.

To/From Mombasa Modern Coast Express (www.modern.co.ke) and several other lines run daily between Dar es Salaam and Mombasa via Tanga, departing in the morning in each direction, and departing around 1pm from Tanga (Tsh15,000 to Tsh17,000, four hours Tanga to Mombasa; Tsh25,000, 10 to 11 hours Dar to Mombasa). There's nowhere official to change money at the border. Touts here charge extortionate rates, and it's difficult to get rid of Kenyan shillings once in Tanga, so plan accordingly.

To/From Nairobi The most convenient and comfortable option between Moshi or Arusha and Nairobi is shuttle buses. They depart daily from Arusha and Nairobi at 8am and 2pm (six hours) and from Moshi (eight hours) at 6am and 11am. The non-resident rate is US$30 one way from Arusha (US$35 from Moshi), but with a little prodding it's usually possible to get the resident price (Tsh30,000/35,000). Pick-ups and drop-offs are at their offices and centrally located hotels. Depending on the timing, they may be willing to pick you up or drop you off at Kilimanjaro International Airport (US$15). Confirm locations when booking.

Recommended companies:

Impala Shuttle (☎0754 008448, 0754 678678, 027-254 3082) Leaves from the car park of Arusha's Impala Hotel and from in front of Chrisburger in Moshi.

Rainbow Shuttle (☎0754 204025, 027-254 8442; www.rainbowcarhire.com) Booking office and departure point in Arusha is at New Safari Hotel. Departures in Moshi are from the YMCA.

Riverside Shuttle (www.riverside-shuttle.com) Daily shuttle service between Moshi, Arusha and Nairobi. The Arusha departure point is just north of Hotel Impala. In Moshi, departures are from the YWCA building, just uphill from the Clocktower Roundabout.

To/From Voi Tahmeed Coach (www.tahmeedcoach.co.ke) has a daily bus from Moshi to Mombasa via Voi (Tsh20,000, seven to eight hours). Also, dalla-dallas go frequently between Moshi and the border town of Holili (Tsh2000, one hour). At the border (6am to 8pm) you'll need to hire a *piki-piki* (motorbike; Tsh1000) or bicycle to cross 3km of no man's land before arriving at the Kenyan immigration post at Taveta. From Taveta, sporadic minibuses go to Voi, where you can then find onward transport to Nairobi and Mombasa. If you're arriving/departing with a foreign-registered vehicle, the necessary paperwork is done only during working hours (8am to 1pm and 2pm to 5pm daily).

To/From Kisii There are currently no direct buses over the border. You'll need to take one of the many daily buses between Mwanza and the Sirari–Isebania border post (Tsh15,000, five hours), and then get Kenyan transport on the other side to Kisii. Dalla-dallas also go daily from Musoma to the border (Tsh6000, two hours).

Malawi

The only crossing is at Kasumulu (Songwe River Bridge; 7am to 7pm Tanzanian time, 6am to 6pm Malawi time), southeast of Mbeya (Tanzania).

From Mbeya's Nane Nane bus stand (p181), there are daily minibuses and 30-seater buses (known as 'coastals') to the border (Tsh5000, two hours). Once through the Tanzanian border post, there's a 300m walk to the Malawian side, and minibuses to Karonga. There's also one Malawian bus daily from the Malawi side of the border and Mzuzu (Malawi), departing the border by mid-afternoon and arriving in Mzuzu by evening.

Some tips:

- Look for buses going to Kyela (these detour to the border) and verify that your vehicle is really going all the way to the border ('Kasumulu'), as some that say they are actually stop at Tukuyu (40km north) or at Ibanda (7km before the border). Asking several passengers (rather than the minibus company touts) should get you the straight answer.
- Your chances of getting a direct vehicle are better in the larger 'coastals', which depart from Mbeya two or three times daily and usually go where they say they are going.
- The border buses stop at the Kasumulu (Songwe River) transport stand, about a seven-minute walk from the actual border; there's no real need for the bicycle taxis that will approach you.
- There are currently no cross-border vehicles from Mbeya into Malawi, although touts at Mbeya bus station may try to convince you otherwise. Going in both directions, plan on overnighting in Mbeya or Tukuyu; buses from Mbeya to Dar es Salaam depart between 6am and 7am.

Mozambique

The main vehicle crossing is via Unity Bridge over the Ruvuma at Negomano, reached via Masasi. There is also the Unity 2 bridge across the Ruvuma at Mtomoni village, 120km south of Songea. It's also possible to cross at Kilambo (south of Mtwara) via vehicle ferry. At the time of research, Mozambique tourist visas were being issued at all borders. However, this situation could change at any time; it's essential to get an update before setting your plans, as it's a long way from the border back to the closest consulate.

Bus Vehicles depart daily from Mtwara beginning at about 6am to the Kilambo border post (Tsh6000, one hour) and on to the Ruvuma River, which in theory is crossed daily by the MV *Kilambo* ferry. The ferry, again in theory, takes half a dozen cars plus passengers (Tsh500 per person). However, its passage depends on tides, rains and mechanical condition. There is also a faster, passenger-only motorboat making crossings throughout the day between 7am and 6pm (Tsh1000). If neither of these are operating, you'll need to negotiate a ride in a dugout canoe (about Tsh5000, 10 minutes to over an hour, depending on water levels, and dangerous during heavy rains). Although improved, the border remains a rough one, and it's common for touts to demand up to 10 times the 'real' price for the boat crossing in dugouts. Watch your belongings, especially when getting into and out of the boats, and keep up with the crowd.

Once in Mozambique, several pick-ups go daily to the Mozambique border crossing at Namiranga, 4km further on, and from there to Palma and Moçimboa da Praia (US$10, three hours).

Further west, one or two vehicles daily depart from Songea's Majengo C area by around 11am (Tsh12,000, three to four hours) to Mtomoni village and the Unity 2 bridge. Once across, you can get Mozambique transport on to Lichinga (Tsh30,000, five hours). It's best to pay in stages, rather than paying the entire Tsh40,000 Songea–Lichinga fare in Songea, as is sometimes requested. With an early departure, the entire Songea–Lichinga trip is easily doable in one day via public transport.

Car The main vehicle crossing is via the Unity Bridge at Negomano, southwest of Kilambo, near the confluence of the Lugenda River. From Masasi, go about 35km southwest along the Tunduru road to Nangomba village, from where a 68km good-condition track leads southwest down to Masuguru village. The bridge is 10km further at Mtambaswala. On the other side, there is a decent-in-the-dry-season 160km dirt road to Mueda (slated to be paved by 2019). There are immigration facilities on both sides of the bridge. Entering Tanzania, take care of customs formalities for your vehicle in Mtwara.

The Unity 2 bridge south of Songea is another option. With a private vehicle the Songea to Lichinga stretch should not take more than about eight or nine hours.

At Kilambo, the MV Kilambo (p215) vehicle ferry operates most days around high tide. Enquire at ECO2 (p200) or the Old Boma (p200) in Mikindani to confirm whether the ferry is running.

Rwanda

The main crossing is at Rusumu Falls, southwest of Bukoba (Tanzania).

Trinity Express goes four times weekly between Dar es Salaam and Kigali via Dodoma, Singida and Kahama (Tsh80,000 to Tsh85,000, 30 to 35 hours). It's better to do the trip in stages. From Mwanza, there are daily buses via Kahama to Benaco (Nyakanazi), from where you can get transport to the border. After walking across the border, there is Rwandan transport on the other side to Kigali; reckon on about 12 to 14 hours and Tsh32,000 for the entire journey from Mwanza to Kigali.

For travellers entering Tanzania from Rwanda: in order to purchase a Tanzania visa at the border, you must have US dollars or Tanzanian shillings. Rwandan francs will not be accepted, and they cannot be exchanged for Tanzanian shillings at the border.

Uganda

The main post is at Mutukula (Tanzania), northwest of Bukoba, with good tarmac on both sides. There's another crossing further west at Nkurungu (Tanzania), but the road is sparsely travelled. From Arusha or Moshi, travel to Uganda is via Kenya.

Kampala Coach has a daily bus from Arusha to Kampala via Nairobi (Tsh75,000, 20 hours). The cost to Jinja is the same as Kampala.

Several companies leave Bukoba at 6am and again at 12.30pm for Kampala (Tsh20,000, six to eight hours). Departures from Kampala are at 7am and again at 11am.

From Mwanza to Kampala, there is a daily direct connection via Bukoba (Tsh45,000, 16 hours).

Zambia

The main border crossing (7am to 8.30pm Tanzania time, 6am to 7.30pm Zambia time) is at Tunduma (Tanzania), southwest of Mbeya. There's also a crossing at Kasesya (Tanzania), between Sumbawanga (Tanzania) and Mbala (Zambia).

Bus Minibuses go several times daily between Mbeya and Tunduma (Tsh4000, two to three hours), where you walk across the border for Zambian transport to Lusaka (about US$20, 18 hours).

The Kasesya crossing is mainly of interest for self-drivers as there's no direct transport; at least one truck daily goes to the border from each side (Tsh10,000, four to five hours from Sumbawanga to Kasesya). With luck you can make the full journey in a day, but since departures from both Sumbawanga and Mbala are in the afternoon, and departures from the borders are in the early morning, you'll likely need to sleep in one of the border villages.

Car If driving from Zambia into Tanzania, note that vehicle insurance is now available at the Kasesya border.

Train The Tazara (www.tazarasite.com) train line links Dar es Salaam with Kapiri Mposhi in Zambia twice weekly via Mbeya and Tunduma. The Mukuba express service departs Dar es Salaam at 3.50pm Friday (1st-class sleeping/2nd-class sleeping/super seater/economy class Tsh104,000/84,600/78,700/72,600, about 43 hours). Kilimanjaro ordinary service departs Dar es Salaam at 11am on Tuesday (Tsh86,500/70,600/65,600/60,500, about 59 hours). Departures from Mbeya to Kapiri Mposhi (express 1st/2nd/super seater/economy class Tsh58,000/46,000/44,400/40,900) are at 1.20pm Saturday (Mukuba express, about 24 hours) and 2pm Wednesday (Kilimanjaro ordinary, about 32 hours). Students with ID get a 50% discount. From Kapiri Mposhi to Lusaka, you'll need to continue by bus. Departures from New Kapiri Mposhi are at 4pm Tuesday (express) and 11am Friday (ordinary). Visas are currently available at the border in both directions.

SEA & LAKE

There's a US$5 port tax for travel on all boats and ferries from Tanzanian ports.

DRC

Cargo boats go roughly once weekly from Kigoma's Ami port to Kalemie (about US$10, deck class only, seven hours) or Uvira. Enquire at Ami port, or check with the Congolese embassy in Kigoma about sailing days and times. Bring food and drink with you, and something to spread on the deck for sleeping. Prior to travelling to the DRC, check government travel advisories for a security update, and keep in mind the difficulty of getting a visa.

Kenya

There is currently no passenger ferry service on Lake Victoria between Tanzania and Kenya. Dhows do ply regularly between Mombasa and the Zanzibar Archipelago, but foreigners are prohibited.

Malawi

There are currently no passenger ferries operating between Tanzania's Mbamba Bay and Malawi's Nkhata Bay. Cargo boats (about Tsh10,000 to Tsh15,000, six hours) occasionally accept passengers, but safety standards are minimal and there have been several sinkings. There are no fixed schedules; ask at Immigration for information on the next sailing. Departures are often in the middle of the night to take advantage of calmer waters.

Mozambique

Dhows between Mozambique and Tanzania (12 to 30 or more hours) are best arranged at Msimbati (Tanzania) and Moçimboa da Praia (Mozambique).

There is currently no official ferry service between southwestern Tanzania and Mozambique. The main option is taking a cargo boat between Mbamba Bay and Nkhata Bay, and then the **MV Chambo** (www.malawitourism.com) on its weekly run from Nkhata Bay on to Likoma Island (Malawi), Cóbuè (Mozambique) and Metangula (Mozambique). There are also small boats that sail along the eastern shore of Lake Nyasa between Tanzania and Mozambique. However, Lake Nyasa is notorious for its severe and sudden squalls, and going this way is risky and not recommended.

There's an immigration officer at Mbamba Bay, Mozambique immigration posts in Cóbuè and in Metangula, and Malawi immigration officers on Likoma Island and in Nkhata Bay, although only the Cóbuè post is currently issuing visas.

In southeastern Tanzania, the **MV Kilambo** (per person/vehicle Tsh500/30,000) ferry crosses the Ruvuma River daily (in theory) between Namiranga (Mozambique) and Kilambo. A smaller passenger-only boat also does the trip daily. There are immigration posts at Kilambo and Namiranga.

Zambia

The venerable MV Liemba (p162) has been plying the waters of Lake Tanganyika for more than a century on one of Africa's classic adventure journeys. It connects Kigoma with Mpulungu in Zambia every other week (in theory), with prices for 1st/2nd/economy class costing US$105/95/75 (payment must be in US dollars cash). The trip takes at least 40 hours and stops en route at various lakeshore villages, including Lagosa (for Mahale Mountains National Park; US$40 for 1st class from Kigoma), Kipili (US$75) and Kasanga (southwest of Sumbawanga; US$100). In theory, departures from Kigoma are every second Wednesday at 4pm, reaching Mpulungu Friday morning. Departures from Mpulungu are (again, in theory) on every second Friday afternoon at about 2pm, arriving back in Kigoma on Sunday afternoon. Delays are common.

Food, soft drinks, beer and bottled water are sold on board, but it's a good idea to bring supplements. First class is surprisingly comfortable, with two clean bunks, a window and a fan. Second-class cabins (four bunks) are poorly ventilated and uncomfortable. There are seats for third (economy) class passengers, but it's more comfortable to find deck space for sleeping. Keep watch over your luggage. Booking early is advisable, but not always necessary, as 1st-class cabins are usually available. There are also two VIP cabins, one with private bathroom.

There are docks at a handful of ports, including Kigoma, Kipili, Kasanga and Mpulungu, but at all other stops you'll need to disembark in the middle of the lake, exiting from a door in the side of the boat into small boats that take you to shore. While it may sound adventurous, it can be rather nerve-racking at night, and if the lake is rough.

For those coming from Zambia, there is usually a Tanzanian immigration officer on board to assist with processing visas.

At the time of writing the *Liemba* was scheduled to undergo major renovations, and schedules are likely to be curtailed or changed; enquire first before setting your plans.

Getting Around

AIR

There is a good flight network – much of it on small planes – connecting Dar es Salaam, Arusha, Zanzibar Island and other major centres with each other, and with major national parks. Sample one-way fares: Dar es Salaam to Mbeya from Tsh200,000; Dar to Mwanza from Tsh180,000; Dar to Kigoma about Tsh400,000; Dar to Arusha or Kilimanjaro International Airport (KIA) Tsh200,000 to Tsh600,000.

Air Tanzania (0782 737730, 0782 782732; www.airtanzania.co.tz) Flights connect KIA with Dar es Salaam and Zanzibar Island, and Dar with Mtwara, Tabora, Kigoma, Mbeya, Mwanza and Bukoba.

Air Excel (027-297 0248; www.airexcelonline.com) Arusha, Serengeti National Park, Lake Manyara National Park, Dar es Salaam and Zanzibar Island.

Auric Air (0783 233334; www.auricair.com) Bukoba, Mwanza, Zanzibar Island, Dar es Salaam, Iringa and other towns, plus Katavi and Rubondo Island National Parks.

Coastal Aviation (022-284 2700, 0713 325673; www.coastal.co.tz; Julius Nyerere International Airport, Dar es Salaam, Terminal 1) Flights to many major towns and national parks, including Arusha, Dar es Salaam, Dodoma, Kilwa Masoko, Lake Manyara National Park, Mafia, Mwanza, Pemba, Ruaha National Park, Rubondo Island National Park, Saadani National Park, Selous Game Reserve, Serengeti National Park, Tanga, Tarangire National Park and Zanzibar Island.

Fastjet (0784 108900; www.fastjet.com) Flights link Dar es Salaam with Kilimanjaro, Zanzibar Island, Mbeya and Mwanza.

Flightlink (0782 354450, 0782 354448; www.flightlink.co.tz; Julius Nyerere International Airport, Dar es Salaam, Terminal 1) Flights connecting Dar es Salaam with the Zanzibar Archipelago, Selous, Dodoma, Iringa, Serengeti and Lake Manyara.

Precision Air (p212) Flies from Dar es Salaam to many major towns including Kilimanjaro, Mtwara, Mwanza and Zanzibar Island.

Regional Air Services (0754 285754, 0784 285753; www.regionaltanzania.com; Dodoma Rd) Arusha, Dar es Salaam, Kilimanjaro, Lake Manyara National Park, Ndutu, Serengeti National Park and Zanzibar Island.

Safari Airlink (0783 397235, 0777 723274; www.flysal.com; Julius Nyerere International Airport, Dar es Salaam, Terminal 1) Dar es Salaam, Arusha, Katavi National Park, Mahale Mountains National Park, Pangani, Ruaha National Park, Selous Game Reserve and Zanzibar Island.

Tropical Air (024-223 2511, 0777 431431; www.tropicalair.co.tz) Zanzibari-owned Tropical Air offers frequent services from Dar to Zanzibar Island, Pemba and Mafia as well as occasional service to Tanga and Arusha.

ZanAir (024-223 3670, 024-223 3768; www.zanair.com) Flights link Arusha, Dar es Salaam, Pemba, Saadani National Park, Selous Game Reserve and Zanzibar.

Zantas Air (0688 434343; www.zantasair.com) Regular shared charters connecting Arusha with Katavi National Park, Mahale Mountains National Park and Kigoma.

BOAT

Dhow

Main routes connect Zanzibar Island and Pemba with Dar es Salaam, Tanga, Bagamoyo and Mombasa; Kilwa Kivinje, Lindi, Mikindani, Mtwara and Msimbati with other coastal towns; and Mafia with the mainland. However, foreigners are officially prohibited on nonmotorised dhows, and on any dhow between the Zanzibar Archipelago and the mainland; captains are subject to fines if they're caught, and safety

TANZANIA TRANSPORT TIPS

Distances are long in Tanzania; it's better to focus on one or two areas rather than trying to fit in too much.

Boat & Ferry Tanzania's ferries are scenic and relaxing and a fine way to travel. However, overcrowding happens and conditions in general are basic. The exceptions to this are the modern ferries plying between Zanzibar Island and Dar es Salaam. Book 1st class for lake ferries well in advance.

Bus To maximise comfort and minimise risk, travel earlier in the day and never at night; sit on the shadier side of the bus and keep your luggage with you. Buy tickets the day before for major routes and only from a proper office (not from a tout).

Car There are a number of good, reliable companies. Rentals with driver are most common, although some allow self-drive.

Train Train travel is slow and scenic; delays are common but on the whole the trips are enjoyable and both main lines are working to upgrade their services. It's a good idea to bring water and snacks. For 1st-class cabins, book as far in advance as possible.

is also a concern. A better option is to arrange a charter with a coastal hotel (many have their own dhows) or with **Safari Blue** (☎0777 423162; www.safariblue.net; Fumba; adult/child $US65/35).

Ferry

Ferries operate on Lake Victoria, Lake Tanganyika and Lake Nyasa, although passenger ferry service on Lake Nyasa was temporarily suspended as of late 2017. Ferries also operate between Dar es Salaam, Zanzibar Island and Pemba, and between Pemba and Tanga. There is a US$5 port tax per trip.

BUS

Bus travel is an inevitable part of the Tanzania experience for many travellers. Prices are reasonable for the distances covered, and there's often no other way to reach many destinations.

- On major long-distance routes, there's a choice of express and ordinary buses; price is usually a good indicator of which is which. Express buses make fewer stops, are less crowded and depart on schedule. Some have toilets and air-conditioning, and the nicest ones are called 'luxury' buses. On secondary routes, the only option is ordinary buses, which are often packed to overflowing, stop often and run to a less-rigorous schedule (and often not to any recognisable schedule at all).
- For popular routes, book in advance. You can sometimes get a place by arriving at the bus station an hour prior to departure. Each bus line has its own booking office, at or near the bus station.
- Express buses have a compartment below for luggage. However, it's best to keep your bag with you. Never put it up on the roof.
- Prices are basically fixed, although overcharging happens. Most bus stations are chaotic, and at the ones in Arusha and other tourist areas you'll likely be hounded by touts. Buy your tickets at the office and not from the touts, and don't believe anyone who tries to tell you there's a luggage fee, unless you are carrying an excessively large pack.
- For short stretches along main routes, express buses will drop you on request, though you'll often need to pay the full fare to the next major destination.
- On long routes, expect to sleep either on the bus, pulled off to the side of the road, or at a grubby guesthouse.

CAR & MOTORCYCLE

Unless you have your own vehicle and/or are familiar with driving in East Africa, it's relatively unusual for fly-in travellers to tour mainland Tanzania by car. More common is to focus on a region and arrange local transport through a tour or safari operator. On Zanzibar Island, however, it's easy, though not so common these days, to hire a car with driver or a motorcycle for touring. Self-drive is rare.

Driving Licences

On the mainland you'll need your home driving licence or (preferable) an International Driving Permit (IDP) together with your home licence. On Zanzibar Island, you'll need an IDP plus your home licence, or a permit from Zanzibar, Kenya, Uganda or South Africa.

Fuel & Spare Parts

Petrol and diesel cost about Tsh2100 per litre. Filling and repair stations are found in all major towns, but are scarce elsewhere, so fill up whenever you get the opportunity and carry a range of spares for your vehicle. In remote areas and for longer stays in national parks, it's essential to carry jerry cans with extra fuel. It can happen that petrol or diesel may be diluted with kerosene or water. Check with local residents or business owners before filling up. It's also common for car parts to be switched in garages (substituting inferior versions for the originals). Staying with your car while it's being repaired helps minimise this problem. Also note your odometer and gas gauge readings before having your car serviced.

Hire

In Dar es Salaam, daily rates for a 2WD vehicle start at about US$80, excluding fuel, plus from US$30 for insurance and tax. Prices for 4WDs are US$100 to US$250 per day plus insurance (US$30 to US$45 per day), fuel and driver (US$20 to US$50 per day). There's also an 18% value-added tax.

Outside the city, most companies require you to hire a 4WD. Also, most will not permit self-drive outside of Dar es Salaam, and none currently offers unlimited kilometres. Charges per kilometre are around US$0.50 to US$1.20. Clarify what the company's policy is in the event of a breakdown.

Elsewhere in Tanzania, you can hire 4WD vehicles in Arusha, Karatu, Mwanza, Mbeya, Zanzibar Town and other centres through travel agencies, tour operators and hotels. Most come with driver. Rates average US$100 to US$250 per day plus fuel on the mainland. On Zanzibar Island, expect to pay from US$50 per day plus fuel for a 2WD.

For vehicle hire with driver, contact the Dar es Salaam–based Jumanne Mastoka (p63).

Road Conditions & Hazards

The Tanzanian government has been moving full steam ahead on roadworks, and all major routes plus many secondary roads are now sealed. The condition of unpaved secondary roads ranges from good to impassable, depending on the

PERILS OF THE ROAD

Road accidents are probably your biggest safety risk while travelling in Tanzania, with speeding buses being among the worst offenders. Road conditions are poor and driving standards leave much to be desired. Overtaking blind is a problem, as are high speeds. Your bus driver may, in fact, be at the wheel of an ageing, rickety vehicle with a cracked windshield and marginal brakes on a winding, potholed road. However, he'll invariably be driving as if he were piloting a sleek racing machine coming down the straight – nerve-racking to say the least. Impassioned pleas from passengers to slow down usually have little effect, and pretending you're sick is often counterproductive. Many vehicles have painted slogans such as *Mungu Atubariki* (God Bless Us) or 'In God we Trust' in the hope that a bit of extra help from above will see them safely through the day's runs.

To maximise your chances of a safe arrival, avoid night travel, and ask locals for recommendations of reputable companies. If you have a choice, it's usually better to go with a full-sized bus than a minibus (the worst option) or a 30-seater bus.

season. For most trips outside major towns you'll need a 4WD.

If you aren't used to driving in East Africa, watch out for pedestrians, children and animals on the road or running into the road. Especially in rural areas, many people have not driven themselves and aren't aware of necessary braking distances and similar concepts. Never drive at night, and be particularly alert for vehicles overtaking blind on curves. Tree branches on the road are the local version of flares or hazard lights and mean there's a stopped vehicle, crater-sized pothole or similar calamity ahead.

Road Rules

Driving is on the left (in theory), and traffic already on roundabouts has the right of way. Unless otherwise posted, the speed limit is 80km/h; on some routes, including Dar es Salaam to Arusha, police have radar. Tanzania has a seat-belt law for drivers and front-seat passengers. The standard traffic-fine penalty is Tsh30,000.

Motorcycles aren't permitted in national parks except for the section of the Dar es Salaam to Mbeya highway passing through Mikumi National Park, on the road between Sumbawanga and Mpanda via Katavi National Park and on the Bagamoyo to Pangani road through Saadani National Park.

HITCHING

Hitching is generally slow going. It's prohibited inside national parks, and is usually fruitless around them. That said, in remote areas hitching a lift with truck drivers may be your only option. Expect to pay about the same or a bit less than the bus fare for the same route, with a place in the cab costing about twice that for a place on top of the load. To flag down a vehicle, hold out your hand at about waist level, palm to the ground, and wave it up and down.

Expat workers or well-off locals may also offer you a ride. Payment is usually not expected, but still offer some token of thanks, such as a petrol contribution for longer journeys.

As elsewhere in the world, hitching is never entirely safe, and we don't recommend it. Travellers who hitch should understand that they are taking a small but potentially serious risk. If you do hitch, it's safer doing so in pairs and letting someone know of your plans.

MINIBUS & SHARED TAXI

For shorter trips away from the main routes, the choice is often between 30-seater buses ('coastals') and dalla-dallas or Hiace minivans. Both options come complete with chickens on the roof, bags of produce under the seats, no leg room and schedules only in the most general sense of the word. Dalla-dallas, especially, are invariably filled to overflowing. Shared taxis are rare. Like ordinary buses, dalla-dallas and shared taxis leave when full, and are the least safe transport option.

TRUCK

In remote areas, trucks sometimes operate as buses (for a roughly similar fare), with passengers sitting or standing in the back. Even on routes that have daily bus service, many people still use trucks.

LOCAL TRANSPORT

Dalla-Dalla

Local routes are serviced by dalla-dallas (minibuses) and, in rural areas, by pick-up trucks or old 4WDs. Prices are fixed and inexpensive (Tsh400 for town runs). The vehicles make many stops and are extremely crowded. Accidents are frequent, particularly in minibuses. Many accidents are caused when the drivers race each other to an upcoming station in order to collect new passengers. Destinations are either posted on a board in the front window, or called out by the driver's assistant, who also collects fares. If you have a large backpack, think twice about getting on a dalla-dalla, especially at rush hour, when it will make the already crowded conditions even more uncomfortable for the other passengers.

Taxi

Taxis, which have white plates on the mainland and a *'gari la abiria'* (passenger vehicle) sign on Zanzibar, can be hired in all major towns. None have meters, so agree on the fare with the driver before getting in. Fares for short town trips start at Tsh2000 (Tsh5000 in Dar es Salaam). In major centres, many drivers have an 'official' price list, although rates shown on it are often significantly higher than what is normally paid. If you're unsure of the price, ask locals what it should be and then use this as a base for negotiations. For longer trips away from town, negotiate the fare based on distance, petrol costs and road conditions, plus a fair profit for the driver. Only use taxis from reliable hotels or established taxi stands. Avoid hailing taxis cruising the streets, and never get in a taxi that has a 'friend' of the driver or anyone else already in it.

TRAIN

For those with plenty of time, train travel offers a fine view of the countryside and local life. There are two lines: Tazara (www.tazarasite.com), linking Dar es Salaam with New Kapiri Mposhi in Zambia via Mbeya and Tunduma; and the Tanzania Railways Limited Central Line (p148) linking Dar es Salaam with Kigoma and Mwanza via Tabora. A Central Line branch also links Tabora with Mpanda, and Tazara runs the Udzungwa shuttle twice weekly between the Kilombero/Udzungwa area and Makambako.

In general, Tazara is more comfortable and efficient than the Central Line. However, both lines are currently in the process of upgrading, and there have already been notable improvements. Central Line now has a comfortable weekly deluxe service. If you want to try the train, consider shorter stretches, such as from Dar es Salaam into Selous Game Reserve, or between Tabora and Kigoma. For longer stretches, bring extra food and drinks to supplement the basic meals that are available on board.

Classes

Tazara has four classes: 1st class sleeping (four-bed compartments), 2nd class sleeping (six-bed compartments), 2nd-class sitting (also called 'super seater') and economy (3rd) class (benches, usually very crowded). Men and women can only travel together in the sleeping sections by booking the entire compartment. At night, secure your window with a stick, and don't leave your luggage unattended, even for a moment. Central Line has 1st class (four-bed compartments), 2nd class (six-bed compartments) and economy. There is also deluxe service on the Central Line (suspended temporarily as of mid-2017).

Reservations

Tickets for 1st and 2nd class should be reserved at least several days in advance, although occasionally you'll be able to get a seat on the day of travel. Economy-class tickets can be bought on the spot.

Kenya

☎254 / POP 47.7 MILLION

Includes ➡

Nairobi 221
Masai Mara National Reserve . . . 252
Mt Kenya Region . . . 289
Amboseli National Park 300
Tsavo West National Park 303
Mombasa 312
Lamu 337

Best Places to Eat

- ➡ Sails (p326)
- ➡ Pilipan Restaurant (p331)
- ➡ Baby Marrow (p336)
- ➡ Karen Blixen Coffee Garden (p235)
- ➡ Talisman (p235)
- ➡ Mama Oliech (p234)

Best Places to Stay

- ➡ Ol Donyo (p304)
- ➡ Kobe Suite Resort (p330)
- ➡ Giraffe Manor (p233)
- ➡ Mara Plains (p260)
- ➡ Cottar's 1920s Camp (p262)

Why Go?

When you think of Africa, you're probably thinking of Kenya. It's the lone acacia silhouetted against a horizon stretching into eternity, the lush, palm-fringed coastline of the Indian Ocean, the Great Rift Valley. Peopling that landscape, adding depth and resonance to Kenya's age old story, are some of Africa's best-known peoples, among them the Maasai, the Samburu, the Turkana, Swahili, the Kikuyu. Drawing near to these cultures could just be a highlight of your visit.

Then, of course, there's the wildlife. This is the land of the Masai Mara, of wildebeest and zebras migrating in their millions with the great predators of Africa following in their wake, of the red elephants of Tsavo, of the massed millions of pink flamingos stepping daintily through lake shallows. Africa is the last great wilderness where these creatures survive. And Kenya is the perfect place to answer Africa's call of the wild.

When to Go

Nairobi

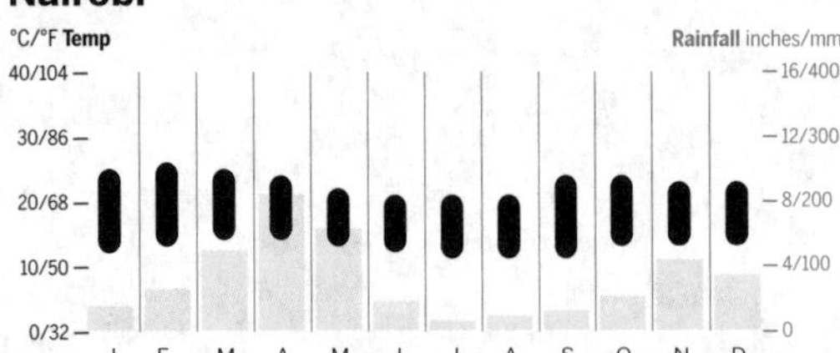

Jul–Oct The annual wildebeest migration arrives in the Masai Mara in all its epic glory.

Jan & Feb Hot, dry weather with high concentrations of wildlife in the major parks.

Nov–Mar Migratory birds present in their millions throughout the country.

NAIROBI

020 / POP 3.915 MILLION / ELEV 1661M

East Africa's most cosmopolitan city, Nairobi is Kenya's beating heart, an exciting, maddening concrete jungle that jarringly counterpoints the untrammelled natural beauty to be found elsewhere in the country.

Nairobi's polarising character ensures that the city is reviled and loved in equal measure, and even those who love it might well admit that it's the kind of place many rave about only once they're away from it. For those who call it home, the city's charms include a vibrant cultural life, fabulous places to eat and exciting nightlife. Its detractors point to its horrendous traffic, poor safety levels ('Nairobbery' is a common expat nickname) and its less-than-gorgeous appearance.

However, with a fabulous national park on its doorstep, some wildlife-centric attractions, the excellent National Museum and a series of quirky sights, Nairobi's reality – like that of so many places with a bad reputation – will often come as a pleasant surprise.

Sights

City Centre

★National Museum MUSEUM

(Map p224; 020-8164134; www.museums.or.ke; Museum Hill Rd; adult/child KSh1200/600, combined ticket with Snake Park KSh1500/1000; 8.30am-5.30pm) Kenya's wonderful National Museum, housed in an imposing building amid lush, leafy grounds just outside the centre, has a good range of cultural and natural-history exhibits. Aside from the exhibits, check out the life-size fibreglass model of pachyderm celebrity Ahmed, the massive elephant that became a symbol of Kenya at the height of the 1980s poaching crisis. He was placed under 24-hour guard by President Jomo Kenyatta; he's in the inner courtyard next to the shop.

Karen & Langata

★Nairobi National Park NATIONAL PARK

(Map p232; 020-2423423; www.kws.go.ke/parks/nairobi-national-park; adult/child US$43/22; 6am-6pm) Welcome to Kenya's most accessible yet incongruous safari experience. Set on the city's southern outskirts, Nairobi National Park (at 117 sq km, one of Africa's smallest) has abundant wildlife that can, in places, be viewed against a backdrop of city skyscrapers and planes coming in to land – it's one of the only national parks on earth bordering a capital city. Remarkably, the animals seem utterly unperturbed by it all.

The park has acquired the nickname 'Kifaru Ark', a testament to its success as a rhinoceros (*kifaru* in Kiswahili) sanctuary. The park is home to the world's densest concentration of black rhinos (more than 50), though even the park's strong antipoaching measures couldn't prevent poachers from killing one of the rhinos in August 2013 and then again in January 2014. They were the first such attacks in six years, and reflect the current sky-high Asian black-market price for rhino horn.

Lions and hyenas are also commonly sighted within the park; rangers at the entrance usually have updates on lion movements. You'll need a bit of patience and a

KENYA FAST FACTS

Area 580,367 sq km

Capital Nairobi

Currency Kenyan shilling (KSh)

Population 47.7 million

Languages English and Swahili; other tribal languages also spoken

Money All banks change US dollars, euros and UK pounds into Kenyan shillings. ATMs can be found in medium-sized towns, so bring cash and a debit or credit card.

Visas Visas, needed by most foreign nationals, are straightforward. An e-visa scheme (www.evisa.go.ke) is the simplest way to apply, pay and receive a visa almost instantly.

Exchange Rates

Australia	A$1	KSh79
Canada	C$1	KSh77
Europe	€1	KSh125
Japan	¥100	KSh95
New Zealand	NZ$1	KSh74
UK	UK£1	KSh141
US	US$1	KSh101

For current exchange rates, see www.xe.com.

Kenya Highlights

1. **Masai Mara National Reserve** (p252) Experiencing expansive savannah and endless wildlife.
2. **Amboseli National Park** (p300) Drawing near to elephants in the shadow of Mt Kilimanjaro for Kenya's most famous picture-postcard views.
3. **Mt Kenya** (p289) Trekking to jagged peaks on the sacred mountain, Kenya's tallest and Africa's second-tallest.
4. **Tsavo West National Park** (p303) Cherishing the rare chance to see the 'Big Five' in one day.

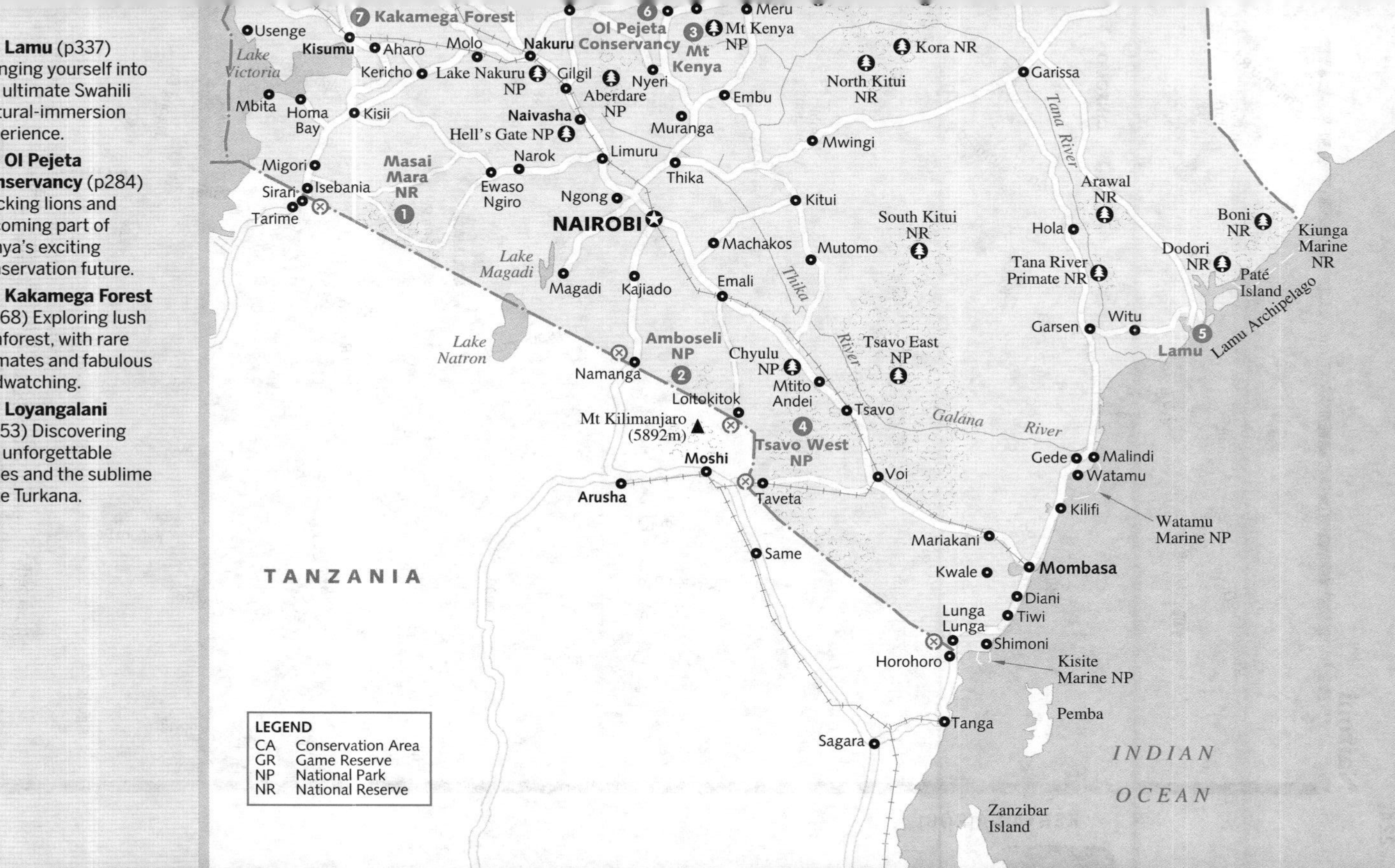

5 Lamu (p337) Plunging yourself into the ultimate Swahili cultural-immersion experience.

6 Ol Pejeta Conservancy (p284) Tracking lions and becoming part of Kenya's exciting conservation future.

7 Kakamega Forest (p268) Exploring lush rainforest, with rare primates and fabulous birdwatching.

8 Loyangalani (p353) Discovering the unforgettable tribes and the sublime Lake Turkana.

Nairobi

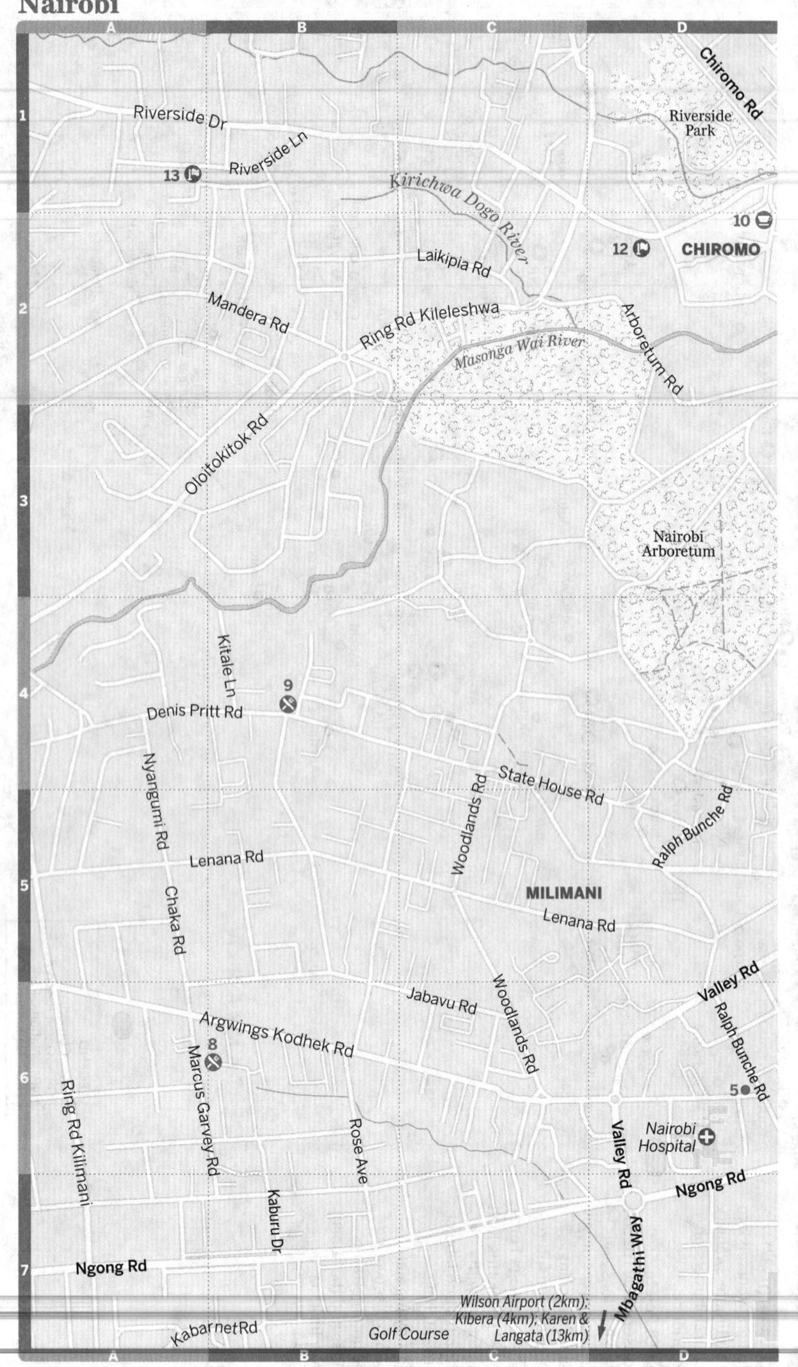
A
B
C
D
1
2
3
4
5
6
7
Riverside Dr
Riverside Ln
13
Chiromo Rd
Riverside Park
Kirichwa Dogo River
10
12
CHIROMO
Laikipia Rd
Mandera Rd
Ring Rd Kileleshwa
Masonga Wai River
Arboretum Rd
Oloitokitok Rd
Nairobi Arboretum
Kitale Ln
9
Denis Pritt Rd
State House Rd
Woodlands Rd
Ralph Bunche Rd
Nyangumi Rd
Lenana Rd
MILIMANI
Lenana Rd
Chaka Rd
Valley Rd
Jabavu Rd
Woodlands Rd
Ralph Bunche Rd
Argwings Kodhek Rd
8
Marcus Garvey Rd
5
Ring Rd Kilimani
Rose Ave
Valley Rd
Nairobi Hospital
Ngong Rd
Kaburu Dr
Mbagathi Way
Ngong Rd
Wilson Airport (2km); Kibera (4km); Karen & Langata (13km)
Kabarnet Rd
Golf Course

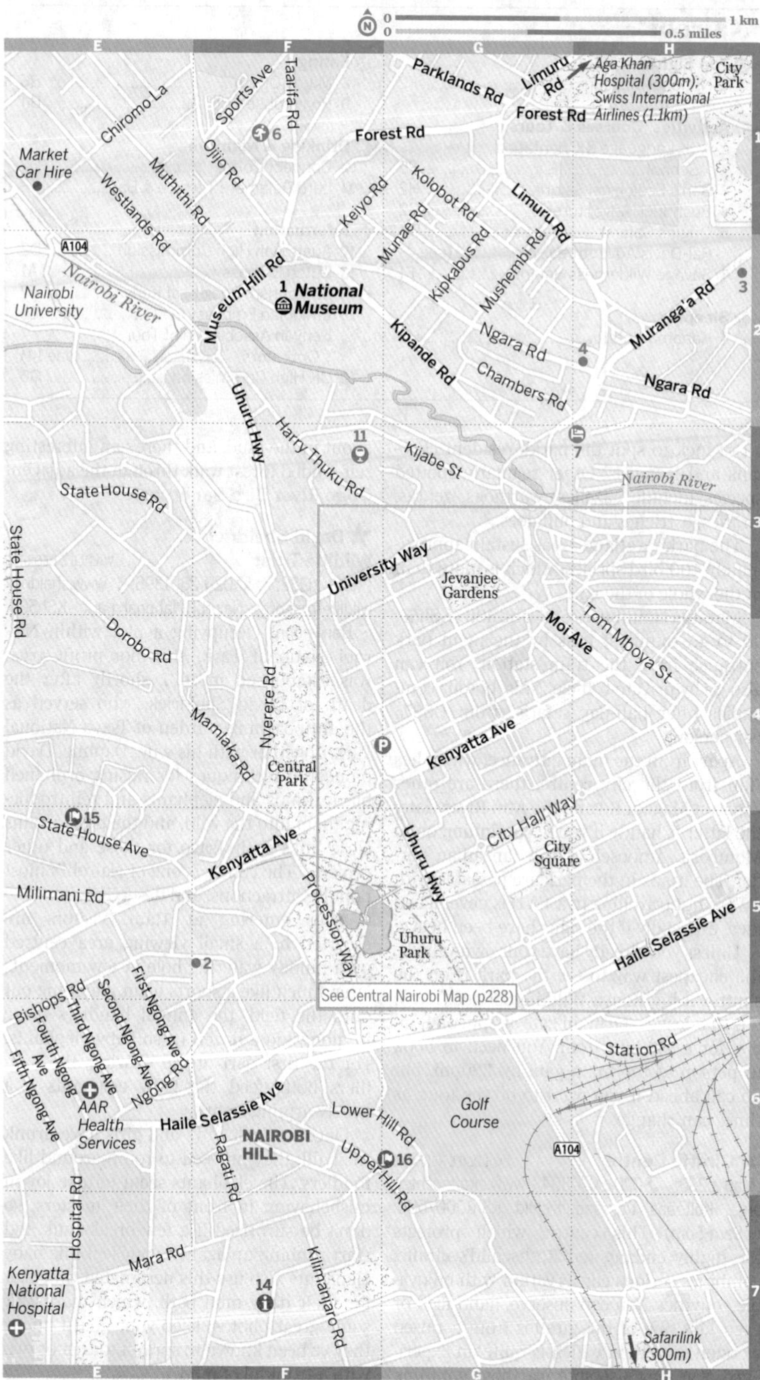
0
1 km
0
0.5 miles
E
F
G
H
Parklands Rd
Limuru Rd
Aga Khan Hospital (300m); Swiss International Airlines (1.1km)
City Park
Forest Rd
Forest Rd
Chiromo La
Sports Ave
Taarifa Rd
6
Market Car Hire
Ojijo Rd
Muthithi Rd
Westlands Rd
Keiyo Rd
Kolobot Rd
Limuru Rd
Munae Rd
Kipkabus Rd
Mushembi Rd
A104
Museum Hill Rd
Nairobi River
Nairobi University
1 National Museum
3
Muranga'a Rd
Kipande Rd
Ngara Rd
4
Chambers Rd
Ngara Rd
Uhuru Hwy
Harry Thuku Rd
11
Kijabe St
7
Nairobi River
State House Rd
State House Rd
University Way
Jevanjee Gardens
Moi Ave
Tom Mboya St
Dorobo Rd
Nyerere Rd
Mamlaka Rd
Kenyatta Ave
Central Park
15
State House Ave
Kenyatta Ave
City Hall Way
City Square
Uhuru Hwy
Procession Way
Milimani Rd
Uhuru Park
Haile Selassie Ave
2
See Central Nairobi Map (p228)
Bishops Rd
Third Ngong Ave
Second Ngong Ave
First Ngong Ave
Fourth Ngong Ave
Fifth Ngong Ave
Ngong Rd
Station Rd
AAR Health Services
Haile Selassie Ave
Lower Hill Rd
Golf Course
NAIROBI HILL
Ragati Rd
Upper Hill Rd
16
A104
Hospital Rd
Mara Rd
Kilimanjaro Rd
Kenyatta National Hospital
14
Safarilink (300m)
1
2
3
4
5
6
7

Nairobi

Top Sights
1 National Museum F2

Activities, Courses & Tours
2 ACK Language & Orientation School F5
3 Ben's Ecological Safaris H2
4 Bushbuck Adventures H2
5 Origins Safaris D6
Pal-Davis Adventures .... (see 4)
6 Savage Wilderness Safaris F1

Sleeping
7 Kahama Hotel H3

Eating
8 Mama Oliech B6
9 Roadhouse Grill B4

Drinking & Nightlife
10 Connect Coffee D2
11 Lord Delamere Terrace & Bar F3

Information
12 Australian High Commission D2
13 Dutch Embassy A1
14 Ecotourism Society of Kenya F7
15 Ethiopian Embassy E5
Kenyan Association of Tour Operators .... (see 14)
16 UK High Commission G6

lot of luck to spot the park's resident cheetahs and leopards. Other regularly spotted species include gazelles, warthogs, zebras, giraffes, ostriches and buffaloes.

The park's wetland areas sustain approximately 400 bird species, which is more than in the whole of the UK.

Matatus (minibuses) 125 and 126 (KSh50, 30 to 45 minutes) pass by the main park entrance from the train station. You can also go by private vehicle. Nairobi tour companies offer half-day safaris (from US$75 per person).

Apart from the main entrance, which lies 7km from the city centre, there are other gates on Magadi Rd and the Athi River Gate; the latter is handy if you're continuing on to Mombasa, Amboseli or the Tanzanian border. The roads in the park are passable with 2WDs, but travelling in a 4WD is never a bad idea, especially if the rains have been heavy.

Unless you already have your own vehicle, the cheapest way to see the park is on the shuttle, a big Kenya Wildlife Service (KWS) bus that leaves the main gate at 2pm on Sunday for a 2½-hour tour. You need to book in person at the main gate by 1.30pm, but do call ahead if you want to do the tour, as times can change.

★Giraffe Centre WILDLIFE RESERVE

(Map p232; ☎020-8070804; www.giraffecenter.org; Koitobos Rd; adult/child KSh1000/500; ⏰9am-5pm) This centre, which protects the highly endangered Rothschild's giraffe, combines serious conservation with enjoyable activities. You can observe, hand-feed or even kiss one of the giraffes from a raised wooden structure, which is quite an experience. You may also spot warthogs snuffling about in the mud, and there's an interesting self-guided forest walk through the adjacent **Gogo River Bird Sanctuary**.

★David Sheldrick Wildlife Trust WILDLIFE RESERVE

(Map p232; ☎020-2301396; www.sheldrickwildlifetrust.org; Nairobi National Park; KSh500; ⏰11am-noon) Occupying a plot within Nairobi National Park, this non-profit trust was established in 1977, shortly after the death of David Sheldrick, who served as the antipoaching warden of Tsavo National Park. Together with his wife, Daphne, David pioneered techniques for raising orphaned black rhinos and elephants and reintroducing them into the wild, and the trust retains close links with Tsavo for these and other projects. The centre is one of Nairobi's most popular attractions, and deservedly so.

After entering at 11am, visitors are escorted to a small viewing area centred on a muddy watering hole. A few moments later, much like a sports team marching out onto the field, the animal handlers come in alongside a dozen or so baby elephants. For the first part of the viewing, the handlers bottle-feed the baby elephants – a heartwarming sight.

Once the little guys and girls have drunk their fill, they proceed to romp around like toddlers. The elephants seem to take joy in misbehaving in front of their masters, so don't be surprised if a few break rank and start rubbing up against your leg! The baby elephants also use this designated time slot for their daily mud bath, which makes for some great photos; keep your guard up, as they've been known to spray a tourist or two with a trunkful of mud.

KENYAN SAFARI COMPANIES

The following companies can organise trips to Kenya's major safari destinations.

Abercrombie & Kent (Map p232; ☎020-6950000; www.abercrombiekent.com; Abercrombie & Kent House, Mombasa Rd) Luxury-travel company with excellent safaris to match.

Basecamp Explorer (Map p232; ☎0733333909; www.basecampexplorer.com/kenya; Gold Rock Bldg) Scandinavian-owned ecotourism operator offering comprehensive and often luxurious camping itineraries with an environmentally sustainable focus. The office is off Mombasa Rd.

Ben's Ecological Safaris (Map p224; ☎0706324970, 0722861072; www.bensecologicalsafaris.com; Muranga'a Rd) This outfit is a birdwatching specialist, but it's good for just about any natural-history or cultural safari across East Africa.

Bushbuck Adventures (Map p224; ☎020-7121505, 0722356838; www.bushbuckadventures.com; 2nd fl, Bhavesh Centre, Ngara Rd) Small company specialising in personalised (including walking) safaris. It has a private semipermanent camp in the Masai Mara.

Eastern & Southern Safaris (Map p228; ☎020-2242828; www.essafari.co.ke; 6th fl, Finance House, Loita St) Classy and reliable outfit aiming at the midrange and upper end of the market, with standards to match. It does all the classic Kenyan trips.

Gametrackers (Map p232; ☎020-2222703; www.gametrackersafaris.com; Masai Lodge Rd, Karen) Long-established and reliable company with a full range of camping and lodge safaris around Kenya; one of the best operators for Lake Turkana and the north. Located off Magadi Rd.

Origins Safaris (Map p224; ☎0724253861, 020-2042695; www.originsafaris.info; 5th fl, Landmark Plaza, Argwings Kodhek Rd) Has a natural-history and cultural focus, with everything from expert birdwatching to traditional ceremonies, as well as other more mainstream safaris.

Pal-Davis Adventures (Map p224; ☎020-2522611, 0733919613; 1st fl, Bhavesh Business Centre, Ngara Rd) Small Kenyan company that gets excellent reports from travellers for its wide range of personalised safaris.

Parading Africa Safaris (☎020-2007378; www.paradingafricasafaris.com; Nyayo Stadium Complex, Block C) An excellent safari company with a full portfolio of Kenyan and wider East African safaris across a range of budgets.

Pollman's Tours & Safaris (Map p232; ☎020-3337234; www.pollmans.com; Pollman's House, Mombasa Rd) Kenyan-based operator that covers all the main national parks, with coastal and Tanzanian trips as well.

Private Safaris (Map p232; ☎020-3607000, Mombasa 0722203780; www.privatesafaris.co.ke; 2nd fl, OiLibya Plaza, Muthaiga) Offering trips that can be highly customised, Private Safaris can book tours throughout sub-Saharan Africa.

Safari Icon Travel (Map p228; ☎0724112227, 020-2242818; www.safariicon.com; 4th fl, Nacico Chambers, cnr Kenyatta & Moi Aves) Well-regarded local company that covers a wide range of safari options in Kenya, Tanzania and Uganda.

Safe Ride Tours & Safaris (Map p228; ☎0722496558, 020-2101162; www.saferidesafaris.com; 2nd fl, Avenue House, Kenyatta Ave) A budget operator recommended for camping excursions around the country.

While the elephants gambol, the keepers talk about the individual orphans and their stories. Explanations are also given about the broader picture of the orphans project and some of the other projects in which the trust is involved. There's also the opportunity to 'adopt' one of the elephants. For those who do, there's a chance to visit when your elephant returns to the stockades around 5pm every evening – advance bookings essential.

Central Nairobi

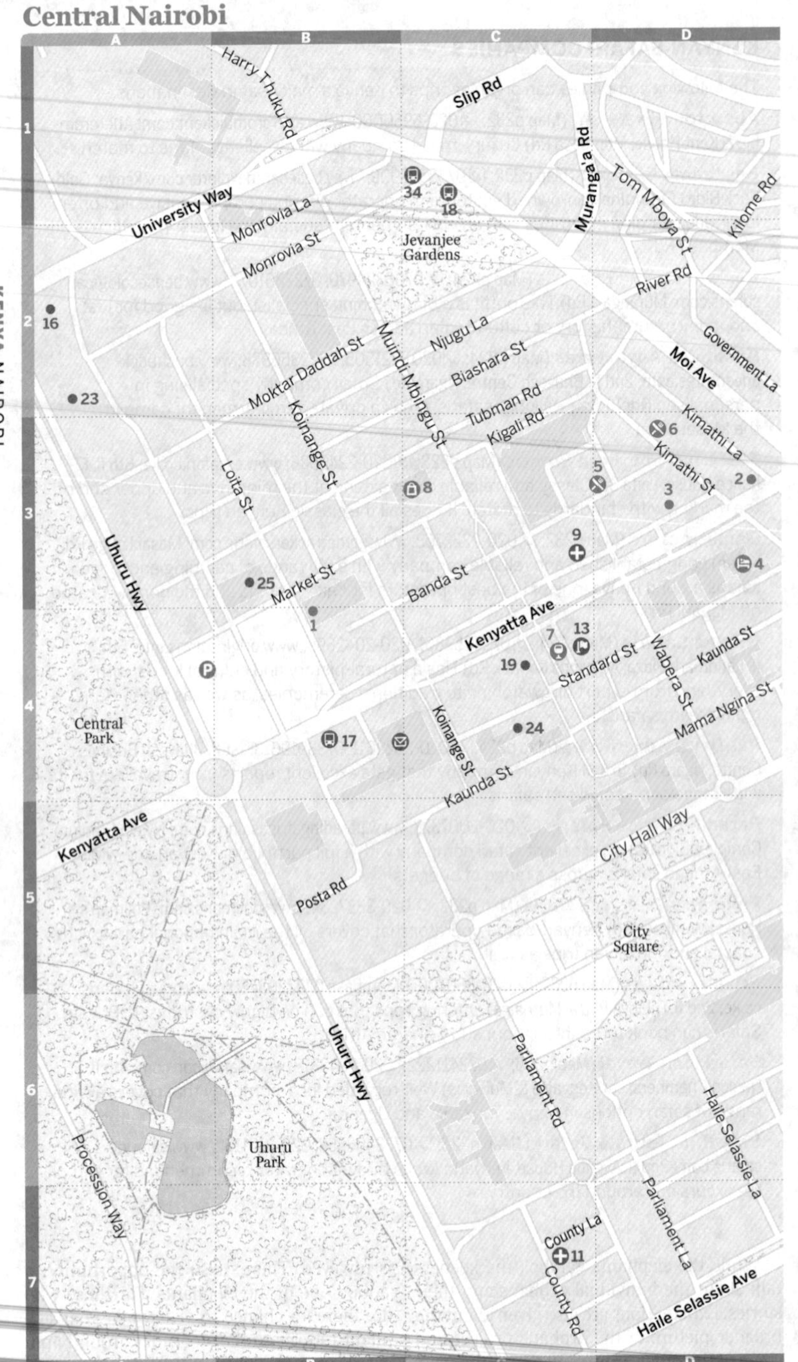

KENYA NAIROBI

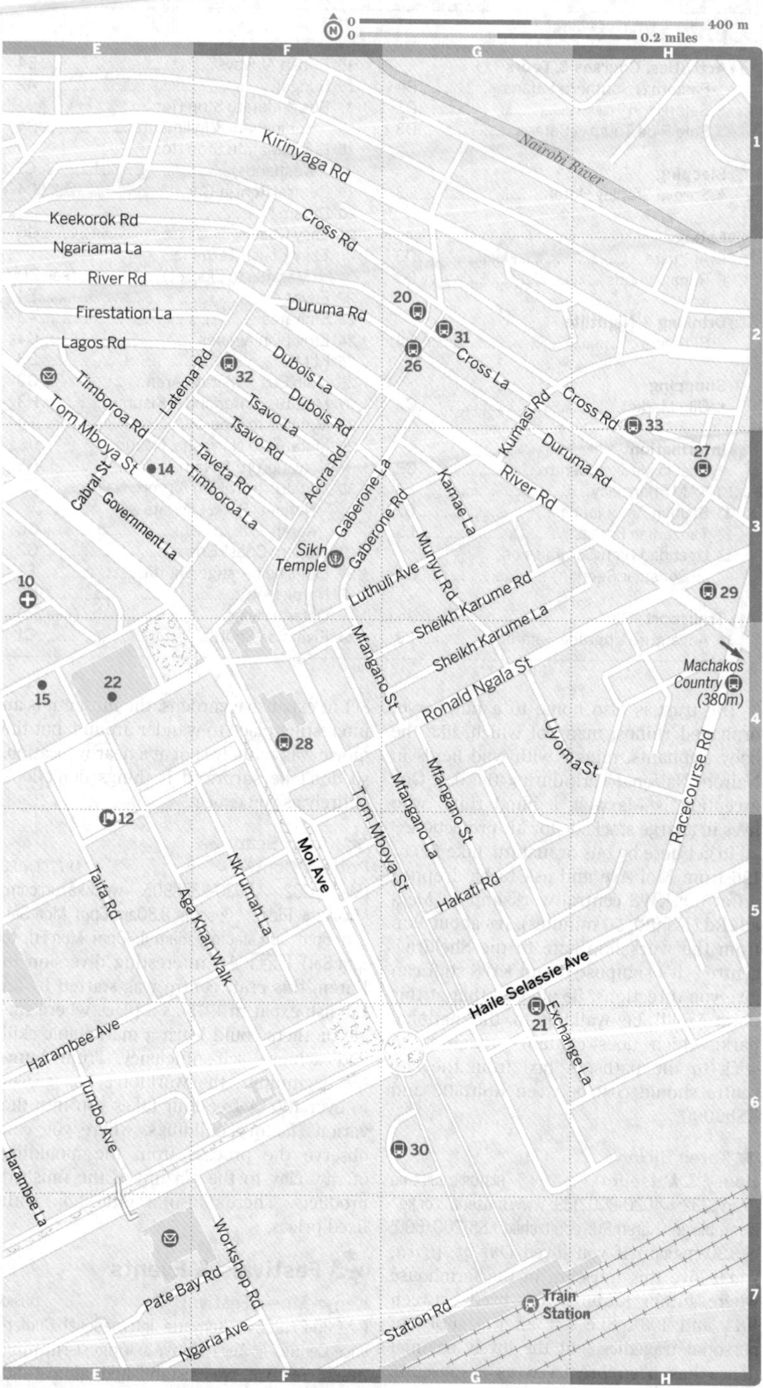

0
400 m
0
0.2 miles
E
F
G
H
1
2
3
4
5
6
7
Nairobi River
Kirinyaga Rd
Keekorok Rd
Ngariama La
River Rd
Firestation La
Lagos Rd
Cross Rd
Duruma Rd
20
31
26
32
Dubois La
Dubois Rd
Cross La
Kumasi Rd
Cross Rd
33
27
Timboroa Rd
Latema Rd
Tsavo La
Tsavo Rd
Tom Mboya St
14
Cabral St
Taveta Rd
Timboroa La
Government La
Accra Rd
Gaberone La
Gaberone Rd
Kamae La
Duruma Rd
River Rd
Munyu Rd
Sikh Temple
Luthuli Ave
10
Sheikh Karume Rd
Sheikh Karume La
29
Machakos Country (380m)
Mfangano St
Ronald Ngala St
15
22
28
Uyoma St
Racecourse Rd
Mfangano St
Mfangano La
Tom Mboya St
12
Moi Ave
Nkrumah La
Hakati Rd
Taifa Rd
Aga Khan Walk
Haile Selassie Ave
21
Exchange La
Harambee Ave
Tumbo Ave
30
Harambee La
Workshop Rd
Pate Bay Rd
Station Rd
Train Station
Ngaria Ave

Central Nairobi

Activities, Courses & Tours
1 Eastern & Southern Safaris B4
2 Safari Icon Travel D3
3 Safe Ride Tours & Safaris D3

Sleeping
4 Sarova Stanley Hotel D3

Eating
5 Al-Yusra D3
6 Ranalo Foods D3

Drinking & Nightlife
7 Simmers C4

Shopping
8 City Market C3

Information
9 Acacia Medical Centre C3
10 KAM Pharmacy E3
11 St John Ambulance C7
12 Tanzanian Embassy E5
13 Ugandan High Commission (Consular Section) C4

Transport
14 Adventure Upgrade Safaris E3
15 British Airways E4
16 Budget A2
17 Bus & Matatu Stop (for Hurlingham & Milimani) B4
18 Bus & Matatu Stop (for Westlands) C1
19 Central Rent-a-Car C4
20 Dream Line G2
21 Easy Coach G6
Easy Coach Terminal (Matatus to Eldoret) .... (see 21)
22 Egypt Air E4
23 Emirates A2
24 Ethiopian Airlines C4
25 KLM B3
26 Main Bus & Matatu Area G2
27 Matatus to Kericho & Kisumu H3
28 Matatus to Kibera F4
29 Matatus to Naivasha, Nakuru, Nyahururu & Namanga H3
30 Matatus to Wilson Airport, Nairobi National Park, Langata & Karen G6
31 Modern Coast Express G2
32 Mololine Prestige Shuttle F2
33 Narok Line H2
Qatar Airways .... (see 25)
34 Riverside Shuttle C1

The trust is also home to a number of orphaned rhinos, many of which, like the baby elephants, mingle with wild herds in Nairobi National Park during the day. One exception is Maxwell, a blind rhino who lives in a large stockade for his protection.

To get here by bus or matatu, take 125 or 126 from Moi Ave and ask to be dropped off at the KWS central workshop on Magadi Rd (KSh80, 50 minutes). It's about 1km from the workshop gate to the Sheldrick centre – it's signposted and KWS staff can give you directions. Be advised that at this point you'll be walking in the national park, which does contain predators, so stick to the paths. A taxi from the city centre should cost between KSh1500 and KSh2000.

★Karen Blixen's House & Museum — HISTORIC BUILDING

(Map p232; 020-8002139; www.museums.or.ke/karen-blixen; Karen Rd; adult/child KSh1200/600; 8.30am-6pm) If you loved *Out of Africa*, you'll love this museum in the farmhouse where author Karen Blixen lived between 1914 and 1931. She left after a series of personal tragedies, but the lovely colonial house has been preserved as a museum. Set in expansive gardens, the museum is an interesting place to wander around, but the movie was actually shot at a nearby location, so don't be surprised if things don't look entirely as you expect!

★Kazuri Beads & Pottery Centre — ARTS CENTRE

(Map p232; 020-2328905; www.kazuri.com; Mbagathi Ridge; shop 8.30am-6pm Mon-Sat, 9am-5pm Sun, factory 8am-4.30pm Mon-Fri, to 1pm Sat) FREE An interesting diversion in Karen, this craft centre was started by an English expat in 1975 as a place where single mothers could learn a marketable skill and achieve self-sufficiency. From humble beginnings, the workforce has grown to over 100. A free tour takes you into the various factory buildings, where you can observe the process from the moulding of raw clay to the glazing of the finished products. There's also a gift shop with fixed prices.

Festivals & Events

Kenya Music Festival — MUSIC

(020-2712964; Kenyatta International Conference Centre; Aug) Kenya's longest-running music festival was established almost 80

DON'T MISS

KIBERA

Kibera (which is derived from a Nubian word, *kibra*, meaning forest) is a sprawling urban jungle of shanty-town housing. Home to as many as a million residents, Kibera is the world's second-largest shanty town (after Soweto in Johannesburg, South Africa). Although it covers 2.5 sq km in area, it's home to somewhere between a quarter and a third of Nairobi's population, and has a density of an estimated 300,000 people per square kilometre. The neighbourhood was thrust into the Western imagination when it featured prominently in the Fernando Meirelles film *The Constant Gardener*, which is based on the book of the same name by John le Carré. With the area heavily polluted by open sewers, and lacking even the most basic infrastructure, residents of Kibera suffer from disease and poor nutrition, not to mention violent crime.

Although it's virtually impossible to collect accurate statistics on shanty towns, as the demographics change almost daily, the rough estimates for Kibera are shocking enough. According to local aid workers, Kibera has one pit toilet for every 100 people; the shanty town's inhabitants suffer from an HIV/AIDS infection rate of more than 20%; and four out of every five people living here are unemployed.

Visiting Kibera

A visit to Kibera is one way to look behind the headlines and, albeit briefly, touch on the daily struggles and triumphs of life in the town; there's nothing quite like the enjoyment of playing a bit of footy with street children aspiring to be the next Didier Drogba. Although you could visit on your own, security is an issue and such visits aren't always appreciated by residents. The best way to visit is on a tour. Two recommended companies are **Explore Kibera** (☎072700517; www.explorekibera.com; per person US$29; ⏰9am & 2pm daily) and **Kibera Tours** (☎0721391630, 0723669218; www.kiberatours.com; per person KSh2500).

Getting There & Away

You can get to Kibera by taking bus 32 or matatu 32c from the Kencom building along Moi Ave. Be advised that this route is notorious for petty theft, so be extremely vigilant and pay attention to your surroundings.

years ago by the colonial regime. African music now predominates, but Western and expat musicians still take part. It's held over 10 days in August.

Tusker Safari Sevens SPORTS
(www.kru.co.ke/safari7s; ⏰Oct & Nov) A high-profile, international seven-a-side rugby tournament, although poor governance issues in recent years have seen its prestige slip a little. Even so, it's always hotly contested and the Kenyan team has a strong record in the tournament, winning most recently in 2013 and 2016. It usually takes place at the Moi International Sport Centre.

Sleeping

City Centre

★Kahama Hotel HOTEL $$
(Map p224; ☎0731430444, 0712379780; www.kahamahotels.co.ke; Murang'a Rd; s/d from US$45/55; P 📶) Almost equidistant between the city centre and the National Museum (p221), this place is a terrific budget choice. Billing itself 'economy with style', it provides just that, with pleasant rooms and comfy beds. The only downside? The new highway passes by the front door – ask for a room at the back.

★Sarova Stanley Hotel HOTEL $$
(Map p228; ☎0719048000; www.sarovahotels.com/stanley-nairobi; cnr Kimathi St & Kenyatta Ave; s/d from US$116/135; P ❄ 📶 🏊) A Nairobi classic. The original Stanley Hotel was established in 1902 – past guests include Ernest Hemingway, Clark Gable, Ava Gardner and Gregory Peck. The latest version boasts large and luxurious rooms and a timeless lobby characterised by plush green leather banquettes, opulent chandeliers and lots of dark-wood trimmings. Rates drop slightly from Friday to Sunday.

Nairobi National Park

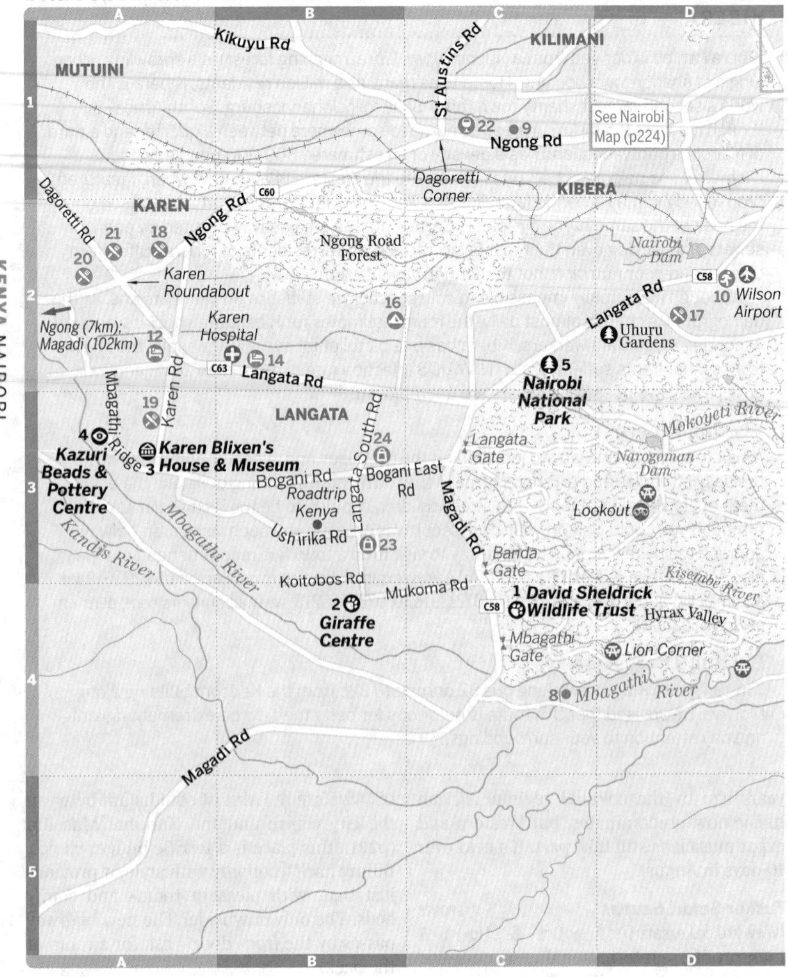

Karen & Langata

★Wildebeest Eco Camp TENTED CAMP $
(☎0734770733; www.wildebeestecocamp.com; 151 Mokoyeti Rd West, Langata; camping from KSh1250, dm tents KSh1750, garden tents s/d from KSh4000/6000, luxury safari tents s/d/tr KSh10,800/13,500/16,000;) This fabulous place is arguably Nairobi's outstanding budget option. The atmosphere is relaxed yet switched on, and the accommodation is spotless and great value, however much you're paying. The deluxe garden tents are as good as those at many exclusive safari places – for a fraction of the price, although the absence of mosquito nets is an issue. A great Nairobi base.

★Milimani Backpackers & Safari Centre HOSTEL $
(☎0722347616, 0718919020; www.milimanibackpackers.com; 57 St Helens Lane, Karen; camping KSh1000, dm KSh1500, cabins s/d KSh3000/3500; @) This terrific place within a very secure gated community is one of the friendliest accommodation options in town, and whether you camp out back, cosy up in the dorms or splurge on your own

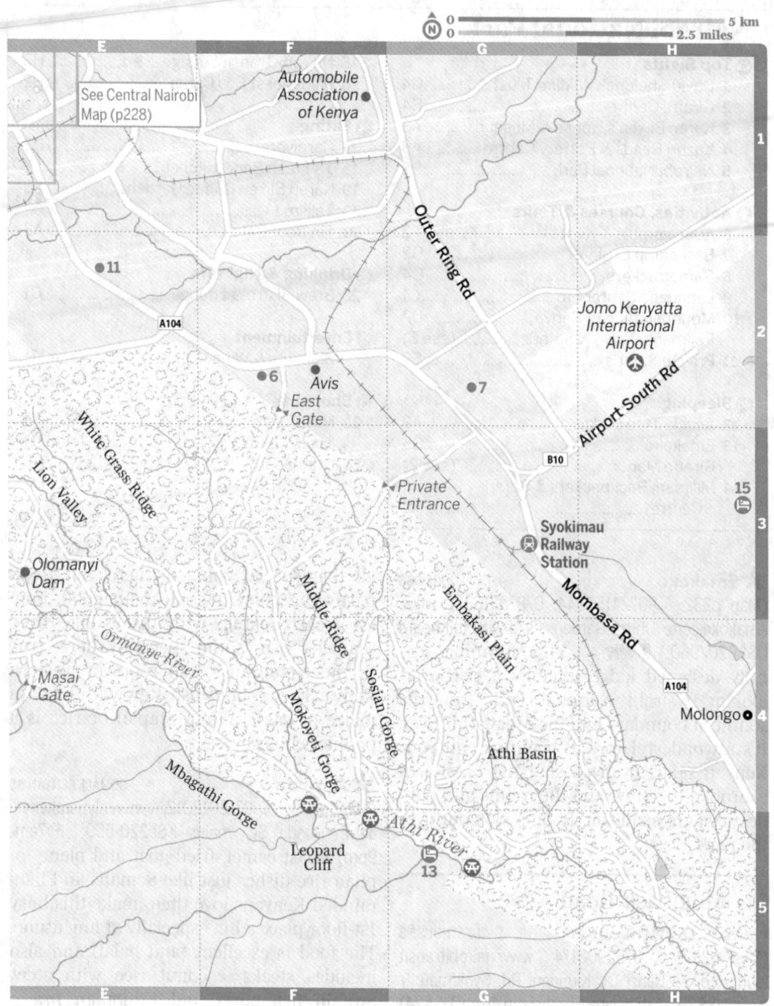

cabin, you'll end up huddled around the fire at night, swapping travel stories and dining on home-cooked meals (from KSh500) with fellow travellers.

★ Acacia Tree Lodge LODGE $$

(☎0702460460; www.acaciatreelodgekenya.com; Marula Lane, Karen; s/d US$80/120; P wi-fi) Stylish decor, attention to detail in everything from the mattresses to the pillows, and a commitment to donating its profits to worthy causes, Acacia Tree Lodge ticks many boxes. The quiet Karen location is another winner. Exceptional value.

★ Giraffe Manor HISTORIC HOTEL $$$

(☎0725675830, 020-8891078; www.thesafaricollection.com; Mukoma Rd, Karen; per person with full board from US$550; P) Built in 1932 in typical English style, this elegant manor is situated on 56 hectares, much of which is given over to the adjacent Giraffe Centre (p226). As a result, you may find a Rothschild's giraffe peering through your bedroom window first thing in the morning. Yet the real appeal here is that you're treated as a personal guest of the owners.

Nairobi National Park

Top Sights
1 David Sheldrick Wildlife Trust C4
2 Giraffe Centre B4
3 Karen Blixen's House & Museum A3
4 Kazuri Beads & Pottery Centre A3
5 Nairobi National Park C2

Activities, Courses & Tours
6 Abercrombie & Kent F2
7 Basecamp Explorer G2
8 Gametrackers C4
9 Language Center Ltd C1
10 Mountain Club of Kenya D2
Pollman's Tours & Safaris .... (see 6)
11 Private Safaris E2

Sleeping
12 Acacia Tree Lodge A2
13 Emakoko G5
Giraffe Manor .... (see 2)
14 Milimani Backpackers & Safari Centre B2
15 Nairobi Transit Lounge H3
16 Wildebeest Eco Camp B2

Eating
17 Carnivore D2
18 J's Fresh Bar & Kitchen A2
19 Karen Blixen Coffee Garden A3
20 Talisman A2
21 Tin Roof Cafe A2

Drinking & Nightlife
22 Brew Bistro & Lounge C1

Entertainment
Blankets & Wine .... (see 17)

Shopping
23 Matbronze B3
Souk .... (see 21)
24 Utamaduni B3

★Emakoko LODGE $$$
(Map p232; ☎0724156044, 0787331632; www.emakoko.com; Uhuru Gardens; s/d with full board US$620/960; P@☎✱) This stunning, artfully designed lodge inhabits a rise overlooking Nairobi National Park from its southern boundary and the Mbagathi River. It's a wonderful way to begin or end your Kenyan safari by bypassing the hassles of Nairobi altogether, and the rooms and public areas are exquisite. Rooms look out over the park.

Mombasa Road

Nairobi Transit Lounge GUESTHOUSE $
(Map p232; ☎0732908174; www.nairobitransitlounge.co.ke; Ulinzi Ct, Kiungani Rd, Syokimau; r from US$29, with shared bathroom from US$24) Handy for Jomo Kenyatta International Airport (6km away) and/or Syokimau railway station, this fine little townhouse has tidy, simple rooms that are outstanding value, even more so once you throw in the friendly and knowledgeable staff.

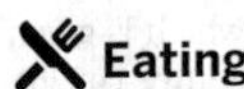

Eating

City Centre

Ranalo Foods AFRICAN $
(Map p228; ☎0770785897; Kimathi St; mains KSh450-800; ⌚8am-11pm) There's nothing all that special going on here, but that's partly the point. It's all about good, honest local cooking, with dishes like fried tilapia – fish is the speciality here, true to the restaurant's Luo roots in western Kenya. The coconut fish stew with ugali (a maize or cassava-flour staple) or rice is a popular choice.

★Al-Yusra SOMALI, KENYAN $$
(Map p228; ☎0712012012; www.alyusrakenya.com; Banda St; mains KSh220-550; ⌚7am-9pm) Roast camel, fried goat and plenty of pilau rice dishes just like Somalis and like-minded Kenyans love them make this busy 1st-floor place a hit, especially at lunchtime. The food is excellent (and halal) and also includes steaks, coconut rice with stew, Swahili fish curry and Ethiopian *injera* bread. Around since 2005, it's already a Nairobi institution.

Karen & Langata

★Mama Oliech KENYAN $$
(Map p224; ☎0723925604; Marcus Garvey Rd; mains KSh700-1350; ⌚11am-11.30pm) Fish dominates the menu here: the whole fried tilapia from Lake Nakuru is the signature dish, especially when ordered with ugali and *kachumbari* (tomato-and-onion salsa). Wildly popular, the restaurant is considered one of Nairobi's best – the sort of place

that locals take first-time visitors to the city (like Facebook founder Mark Zuckerberg in 2016).

★Roadhouse Grill BARBECUE **$$**
(Map p224; ☎0720768663; www.facebook.com/RoadhouseGrillNairobi; Dennis Pritt Rd, Hurlingham; mains from KSh600; ⏲11am-6am Mon-Sat, to midnight Sun) Out beyond Milimani in the west, Roadhouse Grill is widely touted by locals as the best place for *nyama choma* (barbecued meat). The meat (choose the goat) is prepared just as it should be: medium rare and perfectly tender. Order a side of ugali and some *kachumbari*, and you're halfway towards being Kenyan.

★Carnivore GRILL **$$$**
(Map p232; ☎0733611608, 020-5141300; www.tamarind.co.ke/carnivore; Langata Rd, Langata; buffet from KSh4000; ⏲11.30am-11pm; Ⓟ) Love it or hate it, Carnivore serves up Kenya's most famous *nyama choma* – it's been an icon for tourists, expats and wealthier locals for over 25 years. At the entrance is a huge barbecue pit laden with real swords of beef, pork, lamb, chicken and farmed game meats such as crocodile and ostrich. It's a memorable night out.

★Talisman INTERNATIONAL **$$$**
(Map p232; ☎0705999997; www.thetalismanrestaurant.com; 320 Ngong Rd, Karen; mains KSh1400-2350; ⏲8am-midnight Tue-Sun; 📶) This classy cafe-bar-restaurant remains fashionable with the Karen in-crowd, and it rivals any of Kenya's top eateries for imaginative international food. The comfortable lounge-like rooms mix modern African and European styles, the courtyard provides some welcome air, and classics such as feta and coriander samosas and twice-cooked pork belly perk up the palate no end.

★Karen Blixen Coffee Garden INTERNATIONAL, KENYAN **$$$**
(Tamambo; Map p232; ☎0719346349; www.karenblixencoffeegarden.com; Karen Rd, Karen; mains KSh990-2290; ⏲7am-10pm) The Coffee Garden offers diners five areas in which to enjoy its varied menu, including the plush L'Amour dining room, the historic 1901 Swedo House and the recommended main section, a casual restaurant set in a veritable English country garden. Dishes range from gourmet burgers to Swahili curries from the coast. The Sunday lunch buffet (KSh1800) is popular and excellent value.

Westlands

Urban Eatery INTERNATIONAL **$$**
(Map p236; ☎0709815000; www.urbaneatery.co.ke; PWC Tower, Waiyaki Way; mains KSh650-1500; ⏲7am-11pm Mon-Thu, to 1am Fri & Sat, 8am-10pm Sun; 📶) This smart and upmarket place has a huge menu that takes in everything from pizza to sushi, including great salads, sandwiches, burgers and meat grills. Service is attentive and polite, and kids are welcome – there's even a bouncy castle outside.

Mama Rocks at the Alchemist Bar FOOD TRUCK **$$**
(Map p236; ☎0705801230; www.mamarocksburgers.com; Parklands Rd; mains KSh750; ⏲6-11pm Tue, noon-3pm & 6-11pm Wed & Thu, noon-2am Fri & Sat, 1-10pm Sun) Nairobi's first and best food truck is very cool. With an African take on burgers and a location primed and ready for Westlands' night-time crowd, Mama Rocks' highlight is the Mango Masai Mama, a burger topped with mango, chilli-mango sauce and sweet roasted bell peppers. Samantha and Natalie keep things ticking over.

Drinking & Nightlife

★Connect Coffee CAFE
(Map p224; ☎0708790480; www.connectcoffee.net; Prof David Wasawo Dr, Riverfront; ⏲8am-6pm Mon-Fri, 9am-6pm Sat & Sun) One of Nairobi's best and coolest cafes, Connect brings coffee sourced directly from farmers in Kenya, Ethiopia and Uganda to your table, and the barista-prepared offerings range from pour-over filter coffee to a popular cold brew or simply a long black. It's worth asking what's good on the day and then pondering your choices on the rather long menu.

★Alchemist Bar BAR
(The Yard; Map p236; ☎0727591116; www.alchemist.bar; Parklands Rd, Westlands; ⏲noon-11pm Tue & Wed, to 2am Thu, to 5am Fri-Sun) One of Westlands' best nights out, Alchemist is an all-encompassing take on the Nairobi night, with the city's best DJs, terrific food (and a food truck outside) and bar staff (mixologists...) adept at creating perfect cocktails. There's an outdoor lounge area for when the dancing gets too hot and sweaty. Check the website for theme nights and events.

Westlands

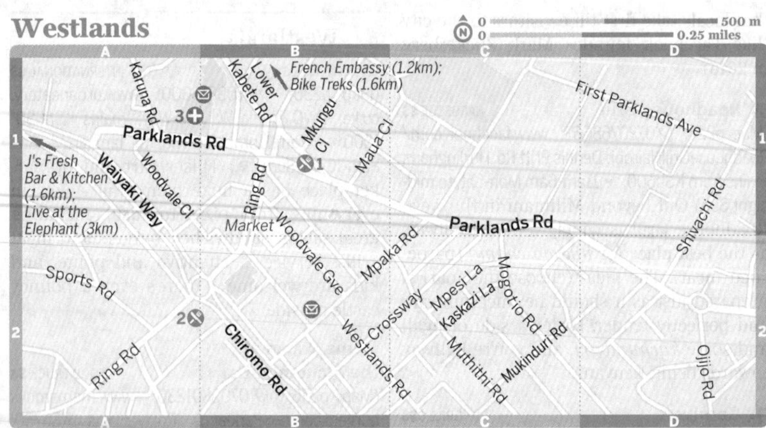

Westlands

Eating
1 Mama Rocks at the Alchemist Bar.....B1
2 Urban Eatery.....A2

Drinking & Nightlife
Alchemist Bar.....(see 1)

Information
3 AAR Health Services Clinic.....A1

★Lord Delamere Terrace & Bar BAR
(Map p224; ☎020-2265000; www.fairmont.com/NorfolkHotel; Norfolk Hotel, Harry Thuku Rd; ⊙noon-3.30pm & 6.30-11pm) Once one of Africa's classic bars, the Lord Delamere Terrace was the starting point of many epic colonial safaris, and the scene of tall tales told by the likes of Ernest Hemingway and the Great White Hunters of the early 20th century. Not much of the former atmosphere remains, but come here as a pilgrimage to the Africa of old.

★Simmers BAR
(Map p228; ☎020-2217632; cnr Kenyatta Ave & Muindi Mbingu St; ⊙8am-1am) If you're tired of having your bum pinched to the strains of limp R&B in darkened discos, Simmers could be your place. The atmosphere at this open-air bar-restaurant is amazing, with enthusiastic crowds turning out to grind the night away to parades of bands playing anything from Congolese rumba to Kenyan benga (contemporary dance).

★J's Fresh Bar & Kitchen BAR, CLUB
(☎0707612585; www.jsfreshbarandkitchen.com; Muthangari Dr, Westlands; ⊙9am-11pm) Building on the winning formula of its sister property (Map p232; ☎0718607197; www.jsfreshbarandkitchen.com; Ngong Rd, Karen; mains KSh750-2100; ⊙noon-midnight) in Karen, J's takes its DJs seriously enough to give them a permanent booth, and the food is so good that you could easily spend a whole night here. Each night's different, but Tuesday is hip hop laced with R&B, while Thursday Night Live is a good way to catch local bands.

★Brew Bistro & Lounge MICROBREWERY, BAR
(Map p232; ☎0719648138; www.thebigfivebreweries.com; Piedmont Plaza, Ngong Rd, West Nairobi; ⊙11am-1am Sun-Wed, to 2am Thu, to 4am Fri & Sat) Craft beers have been slow to take off in Nairobi, but Brew is a lesson in how to do things. The rooftop bar is a beacon of the Nairobi night for its heady mix of German beers, salsa dancing and live music. With five beers emerging from its brewery, great views and good snacks, it's a favourite to head to after dark.

☆ Entertainment

For information on entertainment in Nairobi and for big music venues in the rest of the country, get hold of the *Saturday Nation*, which lists everything from cinema releases to live-music venues. There are also plenty of suggestions in the magazine *Going Out*. Wh@t's On Nairobi (www.whats-on-nairobi.com) is another good resource.

One cool way to tap into what's happening is to rummage around on Kenya Nights Events (www.facebook.com/KenyaNights), where you'll find info on hipster hangouts, the hottest electronica venues, DJ events and entry points into Nairobi's thriving underground music scene. Its Twitter feed (twitter.com/KenyaNights) is also good.

★Blankets & Wine LIVE MUSIC

(Map p232; ☎0736801333, 0720721761; www.blanketsandwine.com; tickets KSh2000-3000; ⏲1st Sun of month) This monthly picnic-concert is one of the best-loved features on Nairobi's live-music circuit. Musicians vary, but the underlying principle is to support local and other East African acts, from acoustic and singer-songwriter to rock and roots. Families are welcome. The site is off Langata Rd.

★Live at the Elephant LIVE MUSIC

(☎0721946710; www.facebook.com/LiveAtTheElephant; Gate 3, Kanjata Rd, Lavington; ⏲from 8pm Fri) This may just be the most appealing live-music venue in town. It draws a trendy, upmarket crowd with its fair share of Nairobi hipsters for the regular programme of up-and-coming artists (mostly

NAIROBI SAFETY

First-time visitors to Nairobi are understandably daunted by the city's reputation. However, don't let fear exile you to your hotel room: the majority of visitors never experience any problems.

- Always hand over valuables if confronted by a thief.
- Exude confidence and don't wear anything flashy.
- Be wary, polite but firm with safari touts and other scammers.
- Always take a taxi from door to door after dark.
- Take particular care with your belongings and bags in the streets east of Moi Ave and at bus stations.
- There's a free helpline (p369) for tourists in trouble.

Theft & Mugging

The most common annoyance for travellers is petty theft, which is most likely to occur at budget hotels and campsites. Take advantage of your hotel's safe and never leave your valuables out in the open. While you're walking around town, don't carry anything that you wouldn't want to lose. As an extra precaution, it's best to only carry money in your wallet, hiding your credit cards and bank cards elsewhere.

In the event that you are mugged, never, ever resist – simply give up your valuables and, more often than not, your assailant will flee the scene rapidly. Remember that a petty thief and a violent aggressor are very different kinds of people, so don't give your assailant any reason to do something rash.

Trouble Spots

Compared to Johannesburg and Lagos – where armed guards, razor-wired compounds and patrol vehicles are the norm – Nairobi's Central Business District (CBD, bounded by Kenyatta Ave, Moi Ave, Haile Selassie Ave and Uhuru Hwy) is quite relaxed and hassle free. Walking around this area by day is rarely a problem. There are also plenty of askaris (security guards) about in case you need assistance.

Once the shops in the CBD have shut, the streets empty rapidly and the whole city centre takes on a deserted and slightly sinister air. After sunset, mugging is a risk anywhere on the streets and you should always take a taxi, even if you're only going a few blocks. This will also keep you safe from the attentions of Nairobi's street prostitutes, who flood into town in force after dark. Uhuru Park is a very pleasant place during daylight hours, but it accumulates all kinds of dodgy characters at night.

There are a few other places where you do need to employ a slightly stronger self-preservation instinct. Potential danger zones include the area around Latema and River Rds (east of Moi Ave), which is a hotspot for petty theft. This area is home to the city's bus terminals, so keep an eye on your bags and personal belongings at all times if passing through here.

Kenyan with some from further afield in Africa). Check out the Facebook page to see what's coming up.

Shopping

★Matbronze ARTS & CRAFTS
(Map p232; ☎0721762855, 0733969165; www.matbronze.com; Kifaru Lane, Karen; ⏲8am-5pm Mon-Thu, to 8pm Fri, to 5.30pm Sat, 9.30am-5.30pm Sun) More than 600 wildlife bronzes by Denis Mathews (from jewellery and small lion-cub-footprint dishes to much larger pieces running into thousands of dollars) make this one of the most appealing places to shop in Kenya. It's all produced at the on-site foundry and every piece is a work of art. There's also a small cafe serving light meals.

★Utamaduni ARTS & CRAFTS
(Map p232; ☎0722205028; http://utamadunishops.com; Bogani East Rd, Karen; ⏲9am-6pm) Utamaduni is a large crafts emporium and easily one of the best places to souvenir shop in Nairobi, with more than a dozen shops selling all kinds of excellent African artworks and souvenirs. Prices start relatively high, but there's *none* of the hard sell you'd get in town. A portion of all proceeds goes to local conservation and other charitable projects.

★Souk ARTS & CRAFTS
(Map p232; ☎0706348215; www.thesoukkenya.com; Dagoretti Rd, Karen; ⏲9.30am-5.30pm Mon-Sat) Some of Kenya's more creative artists, photographers, leatherworkers and other high-quality artisans and artists have come together under one roof – the result is one of Kenya's most discerning shopping experiences. It shares premises with the equally excellent **Tin Roof Cafe** (Map p232; ☎0706348215; www.facebook.com/TinRoofCafe; Dagoretti Rd, Karen; mains KSh950-1100; ⏲8.30am-5.30pm; ᯤ).

City Market MARKET
(Map p228; Muindi Mbingu St; ⏲9am-5pm Mon-Fri, to noon Sat) One of the city's main souvenir businesses is concentrated in this covered market, which has dozens of stalls selling woodcarvings, drums, spears, shields, soapstone, Maasai jewellery and clothing. It's a hectic place and you'll have to bargain hard (and that means *hard*), but there's plenty of good stuff on offer.

It's an interesting place to wander around in its own right, though you generally need to be shopping to make the constant hassle worth the bother.

Information

EMERGENCY

Emergency services	☎999
Police (less-urgent calls)	☎020-240000
St John Ambulance	☎2210000

MEDICAL SERVICES

Nairobi has plenty of health-care facilities that are used to dealing with travellers and expats, which is a good thing. Avoid **Kenyatta National Hospital** (Map p224; ☎0729406939; www.knh.or.ke; Hospital Rd; ⏲24hr) – although it's free, its resources are stretched.

AAR Health Services (Map p224; ☎0734225225, 0725225225; www.aar-healthcare.com/ke; Williamson House, Fourth Ngong Ave; ⏲24hr) Probably the best of a number of private ambulance and emergency air-evacuation companies. It also runs private clinics at various locations around Nairobi, including in **Westlands** (Map p236; ☎0725225225, 0734225225; www.aar-healthcare.com/ke; 4th fl, Sarit Centre Mall, Westlands; ⏲8am-7pm Mon-Fri, to 4pm Sat, 10am-4pm Sun).

Acacia Medical Centre (Map p228; ☎020-2212200; info@acaciamed.co.ke; ICEA Bldg, Kenyatta Ave; ⏲7am-8pm Mon-Fri, to 5pm Sat,

BUSES FROM NAIROBI

DESTINATION	FARE (KSH)	TIME (HR)	COMPANY
Eldoret	1250	7-8	Easy Coach
Kakamega	1450	7½	Easy Coach
Kisumu	1400	7	Easy Coach, Modern Coast Express
Malaba	1400	9-12	Easy Coach
Malindi	1100-2200	10-13	Dream Line, Modern Coast Express
Mombasa	500-2200	6-10	Modern Coast Express, Dream Line

MAJOR MATATU ROUTES

DESTINATION	FARE (KSH)	TIME (HR)	DEPARTURE POINT
Eldoret	800	6	Easy Coach Terminal (Map p66)
Kericho	750	3	Cross Rd (Map p66)
Kisumu	700-1000	5	Cross Rd
Meru	750	4	Main Bus & Matatu Area (Map p66; Accra Rd)
Naivasha	400	2	cnr River Rd & Ronald Ngala St (Map p66)
Nakuru	250-400	3	cnr River Rd & Ronald Ngala St
Namanga	500	2	cnr River Rd & Ronald Ngala St
Nanyuki	500	3	Main Bus & Matatu Area
Narok	500	3	Cross Rd (Narok Line; Map p66; ☎020-2212437)
Nyahururu	500	3½	cnr River Rd & Ronald Ngala St
Nyeri	500	2½	Main Bus & Matatu Area

8am-5pm Sun) Privately-run clinic in the city centre.

Aga Khan Hospital (☎020-3662020; www.agakhanhospitals.org/Nairobi; Third Parklands Ave; ⏲24hr) A reliable hospital with 24-hour emergency services.

KAM Pharmacy (Map p228; ☎020-2227195; www.kampharmacy.com; Executive Tower, IPS Bldg, Kimathi St; ⏲8.30am-6pm Mon-Fri, 9am-2pm Sat) A one-stop shop for medical treatment, with pharmacy, doctor's surgery and laboratory.

Karen Hospital (Map p232; ☎0702222222, 020-6613000; www.karenhospital.org; Langata Rd; ⏲24hr) One of Kenya's best private hospitals.

Nairobi Hospital (Map p224; ☎0702200200, 020-2846000; www.nairobihospital.org; ⏲24hr) One of the city's largest hospitals. It's off Argwings Kodhek Rd.

St John Ambulance (Map p228; ☎020-2210000, 020-340262; www.stjohnkenya.org; County Lane; ⏲24hr) Ambulance services.

MONEY

Money is easily available throughout the city from guarded ATMs accepting international credit and debit cards. There is also no shortage of money-changing offices.

POST

Main Post Office (Map p228; ☎0719072600, 020-243434; Kenyatta Ave; ⏲8am-6pm Mon-Fri, 9am-noon Sat)

Haile Selassie Ave (Map p228; ⏲8.30am-5pm Mon-Fri, 9am-noon Sat)

Tom Mboya St (Map p228; ⏲8.30am-5pm Mon-Fri, 9am-noon Sat)

Sarit Centre (Map p236; Parklands Rd, Westlands; ⏲8.30am-5pm Mon-Fri, 9am-noon Sat)

Mpaka Rd (Map p236; Westlands; ⏲8.30am-5pm Mon-Fri, 9am-noon Sat)

ℹ Getting There & Away

AIR

Nairobi has two airports:

Jomo Kenyatta International Airport (p640) Most international flights to Nairobi arrive at this airport, 15km southeast of the city. There are two international terminals and a smaller domestic terminal; you can easily walk between the terminals.

Wilson Airport (WIL; Map p232; ☎0724255343, 0724256837; www.kaa.go.ke; Langata Rd) Located 6km south of Nairobi's city centre on Langata Rd. It has some flights between Nairobi and Kilimanjaro International Airport or Mwanza in Tanzania, as well as scheduled and charter domestic flights. Note that the check-in time for domestic flights is one to two hours before departure. Also be aware that the baggage allowance is only 15kg, as there isn't much space on the small turboprop aircraft.

BUS

In Nairobi, most long-distance bus-company offices are in the River Rd area, clustered around Accra Rd and the surrounding streets, although some also have offices on Monrovia St for their international services. You should always make your reservation at least 24 hours in advance and check (then double-check) the departure point for the bus.

The **Machakos Country Bus Station** (Landhies Rd) is a hectic, disorganised place with buses heading all over the country; it serves companies without their own departure point. However, if you can avoid coming here, do so as theft is rampant.

Bus Companies

Dream Line (Map p228; ☎070244442, 0729575057; www.facebook.com/DreamlineExpress) A reliable company connecting Nairobi to Mombasa and Malindi.

CLIMBING MT LONGONOT

The one- to 1½-hour hike from the park gate up to the crater rim (2545m) is strenuous but, without question, worth the considerable effort. There are two steep stretches that will challenge those not used to hiking. Your reward is to emerge at the lip of the crater rim for superb views of the 2km- to 3km-wide crater – a little lost world hosting an entirely different forest ecosystem.

It takes between 1½ and 2½ hours to circumnavigate the crater; watch for occasional steam vents rising from the crater floor. A guide to the crater rim and back is KSh1500 (KSh2500 including the summit).

Easy Coach (p376) Long-standing company serving western Kenyan destinations as well as running international buses to Uganda.

Modern Coast Express (p376) With a good safety record, these reliable and slightly more expensive buses link Nairobi to Mombasa, Malindi and Kisumu. There are also international links, including Mombasa–Dar es Salaam and Nairobi–Kampala.

Riverside Shuttle (Map p228; ☎0722328595; www.riverside-shuttle.com; Lagos House, Monrovia St) Mostly international services to Arusha, Moshi and Kilimanjaro International Airport (Tanzania).

MATATU

Most matatus leave from the chaotic Latema, Accra, River and Cross Rds, and fares are similar to those for buses. Most companies are pretty much the same, although some aim for higher standards than others. **Mololine Prestige Shuttle** (Map p228; ☎0711558891; Latema Rd), which operates along the Nairobi–Naivasha–Nakuru–Eldoret route, is one such company.

TRAIN

A brand-new high-speed Nairobi–Mombasa railway line costing US$13.8 billion opened in 2017 and it has begun to revolutionise travel in Kenya, cutting the exhausting journey between Kenya's two biggest cities from 18 hours to just 4½. The line – operated by **Kenya Railways** (☎0728603581, 0709907000; www.krc.co.ke) – will eventually extend to Naivasha as well, and then on to Kampala in Uganda, if all goes to plan.

Services on the *Madaraka Express* are expected to increase over the coming years, but there's currently one 9am departure in each direction every day. In Nairobi, trains depart from and arrive at **Syokimau Railway Station** (Mombasa Rd), 19km southeast of the city centre, and stop at Mtito Andei (one way 2nd/1st class KSh360/1490, 2¼ hours) and Voi (KSh510/2130, 3½ hours) en route to Mombasa (KSh900/3000, 4½ hours). Over time, scheduled stops will also include Emali.

Getting Around

TO/FROM THE AIRPORT & TRAIN STATION

Jomo Kenyatta International Airport Some hotels and most safari companies offer a free airport pick-up service. If not, before leaving the arrivals hall, pay for a pre-booked taxi service (KSh1800 to KSh3000, depending on the time of day and where you're going).

Wilson Airport A taxi to the centre of town will cost at least KSh1200. Alternatively, take bus or matatu 15, 31, 34, 125 or 126 to Moi Ave (KSh50, 15 to 45 minutes depending on traffic).

Syokimau Railway Station Semiregular morning trains (per person KSh120) connect Syokimau with Nairobi's old railway station. A matatu will cost around KSh500 to most points around town, while a taxi could cost up to KSh1500.

MATATU

Nairobi's horde of matatus follows the same routes as buses and displays the same route numbers. For Westlands you can pick up 23 on **Moi Ave** (Map p228) or Latema Rd. Matatu 46 to the Yaya Centre stops in front of the main post office, and 125 and 126 to **Langata** (Map p228) leave from in front of the train station. Buses and matatus for **Milimani** (Map p228) leave from Kenyatta Ave, close to the corner with Posta Rd. There's a central **stop** (Map p228; Moi Ave) for matatus to Kibera. You should keep an eye on your valuables while on all matatus.

TAXI

As people are compelled to use them due to Nairobi's endemic street crime, taxis here are overpriced and undermaintained, but you've little choice, particularly at night. Taxis don't cruise for passengers, but you can find them parked on every other street corner in the city centre – at night they're found outside restaurants, bars and nightclubs.

Fares around town are negotiable but end up pretty standard. Any journey within the city-centre area costs KSh500, from downtown to Milimani Rd costs KSh600, and for longer journeys such as Westlands or the Yaya Centre fares range from KSh750 to KSh1000. From the city centre to Karen and Langata is around KSh1200 one way. It can be much cheaper to hire a taxi for the day if you plan to do a lot of moving around town. Ask at your hotel or simply negotiate with a taxi driver.

SOUTHERN RIFT VALLEY

It's difficult to believe that the geological force that almost broke Africa in two instead created such serene landscapes. But this slice of Africa's Great Rift Valley is, for the most part, cool and calm, swathed in forest and watered by moody mineral lakes that blanch and blush with the movement of pelicans and flamingos. Pretty Naivasha and Elmenteita with its forest halo are the most popular and greenest of the lakes. The altitude peaks and dips all the way from Nairobi to Nakuru, home

Southern Rift Valley

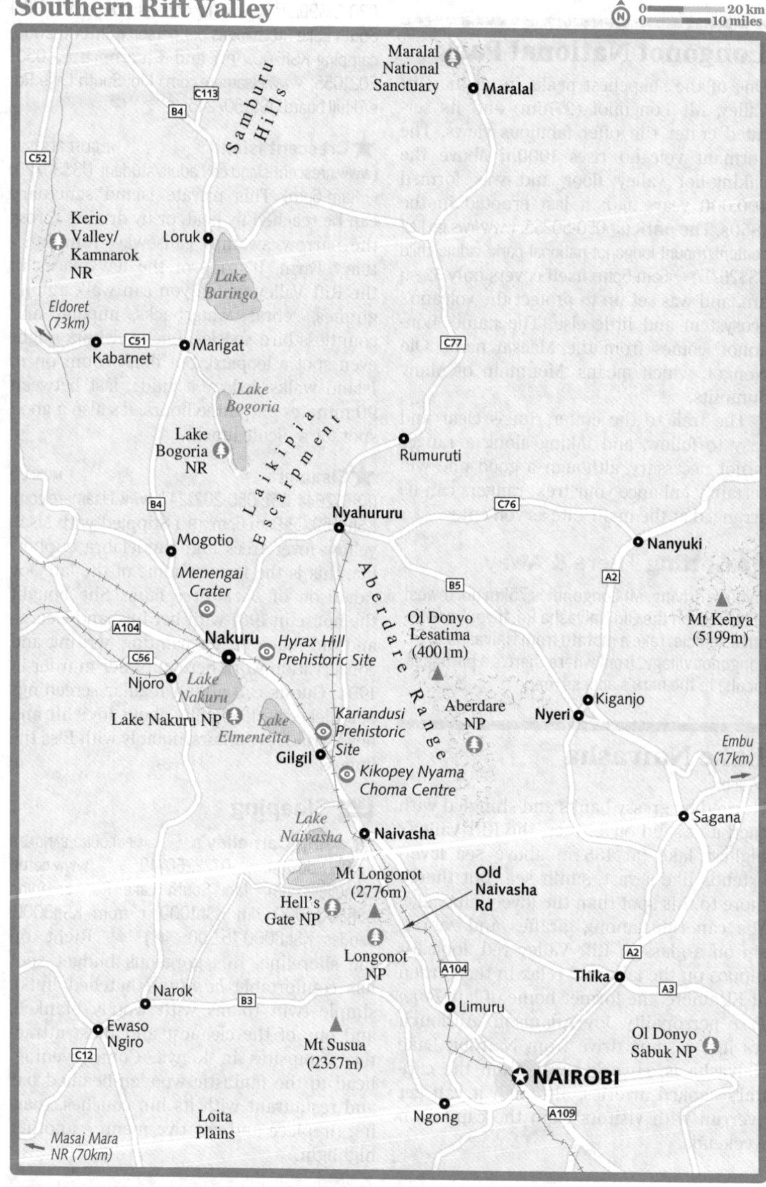

to one of Kenya's premier wildlife parks, and ensuring pleasant weather almost year-round. Lake Baringo, with its hippos, crocodiles and fish eagles, is a place apart, while Lake Magadi, parched and salty, and its surrounds give strong hints of the drama that created this extraordinary corner of the continent.

Longonot National Park

One of the shapeliest peaks in all the Rift Valley, Mt Longonot (2776m) and its serrated crater rim offer fabulous views. The dormant volcano rises 1000m above the baking-hot valley floor and was formed 400,000 years ago; it last erupted in the 1860s. The **park** (☎050-50255; www.kws.go.ke/content/mount-longonot-national-park; adult/child US$26/17; ⏲6am-6pm) itself covers only 52 sq km, and was set up to protect the volcano's ecosystem and little else. The name 'Longonot' comes from the Maasai name Olo Nongot, which means 'Mountain of Many Summits'.

The trail to the crater rim is clear and easy to follow, and taking along a ranger is not necessary, although a good one will certainly enhance your trek; rangers can be arranged at the main gate as you enter.

Getting There & Away

If you're driving, Mt Longonot is 75km northwest of Nairobi on the Old Naivasha Rd. If you're without a vehicle, take a matatu from Naivasha to Longonot village, from where there's a path (ask locals) to the park's access road.

Lake Naivasha

☎050

Hugged by grassy banks and shingled with cacti and sand olive trees, the Rift Valley's highest lake (at 1884m above sea level) extends like a vast, sunlit sea. But there's more to this spot than the lovely blue lake. You can ride among giraffes and zebras, sip on a glass of Rift Valley red, look for hippos on the lake and relax in the garden at Elsamere, the former home of late *Born Free* personality Joy Adamson. Although it's just a short drive from Nairobi, Lake Naivasha is a world away from the capital's choked arteries, although it can get overrun with visitors from the capital on weekends.

Sights & Activities

Most of the camps and lodges along Lake Naivasha's southern shore rent out boats (per boat per hour from KSh3000); most boats have seven seats and come with pilot and lifejackets. Places where nonguests can organise a boat rental include **Fisherman's Camp** (☎0718880634, 0726870590, Nairobi 020-2139922; www.fishermanscamp.com; Moi South Lake Rd; bandas per person KSh1000-2000, camping KSh700; P) and **Elsamere** (☎050-2021055; www.elsamere.com; Moi South Lake Rd; s/d full board US$150/245; P 📶) 🍃.

★Crescent Island WILDLIFE RESERVE

(www.crescentisland.co; adult/student US$30/20; ⏲8am-6pm) This private island sanctuary can be reached by boat, or by driving across the narrow, swampy causeway from Sanctuary Farm. It's one of the few places in the Rift Valley where you can walk among giraffes, zebras, waterbucks, impalas and countless bird species. Lucky visitors might even spot a leopard, but don't count on it. Island walks, led by a guide, last between 90 minutes and three hours. It's also a good spot for a picnic lunch.

★Elsamere MUSEUM

(☎0726443151, 050-2021247; www.elsamere.com; KSh1050; ⏲9am-6pm; P) Stippled with sisal, yellow fever trees and candelabra euphorbia, this is the former home of the late Joy Adamson of *Born Free* fame. She bought the house in 1967 with her husband George and did much of her painting, writing and conservation work here until her murder in 1980. Guests can attend regular screenings of a flickering 1970s film about Joy's life and her myriad love affairs, notably with Elsa the lioness.

Sleeping

★Camp Carnelley's CAMPGROUND, BANDAS $

(☎050-50004, 0722260749; www.campcarnelleys.com; Moi South Lake Rd; camping KSh800-1000, dm KSh1000, r from KSh3000, bandas KSh8000-16,000; P) 🍃 Right on the shoreline, this gorgeous budget spot has comfortable *bandas* (thatched huts), simple twin rooms with woolly blankets and one of the cleanest and most attractive campsites in Kenya. Come evening, head to the fantastic wooden-beamed bar and restaurant with its hip couches, roaring fireplace and creative menu – another highlight.

Lake Naivasha

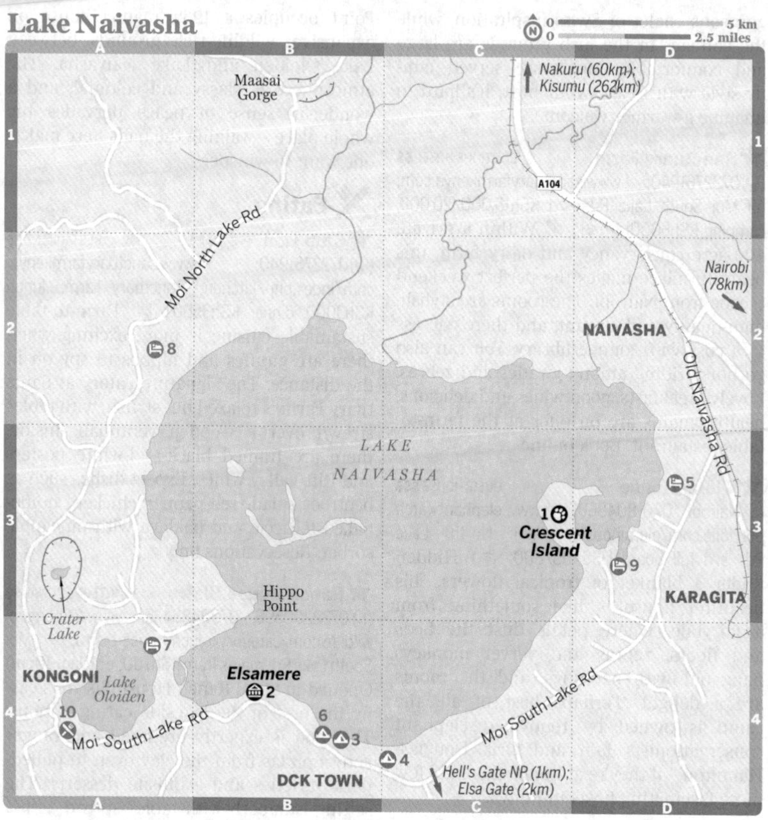

Lake Naivasha

Top Sights
1 Crescent Island C3
2 Elsamere B4

Sleeping
3 Camp Carnelley's B4
4 Crayfish Camp C4
5 Dea's Gardens D3
Elsamere Lodge .... (see 2)
6 Fisherman's Camp B4
7 Hippo Point A4
8 Olerai House A2
9 Sanctuary Farm D3

Eating
Club House .... (see 9)
Lazybones .... (see 3)
10 Ranch House Bistro A4

Crayfish Camp CAMPGROUND $
(☎0720226829; www.crayfishcampnaivasha.com; Moi South Lake Rd; camping per tent KSh2300, s/d KSh4950/7500, fantasy r per person KSh2200; P 📶 🏊) Fancy sleeping in a converted boat with leopard-print curtains? How about a romantic night crammed into a broken-down bus or a toy-sized 4WD? There are 82 rooms ranging from vanilla doubles to fantasy options, plus a theme pub, a kids' play area and a restaurant serving milkshakes. Still, it does feel a bit like a 1980s holiday camp.

★**Dea's Gardens** GUESTHOUSE $$
(☎0734453761, 0733747433; www.deasgardens.com; off Moi South Lake Rd; half board per person KSh9500; 📶 🏊) This charming guesthouse is run by the charismatic and elegant Dea. The main house has three guest rooms and is a

gorgeous chalet of Swiss inspiration, while the cottages in the lush grounds are large and comfortable. Meals are served family style with Dea as your host; it's hard to imagine a warmer welcome.

★ **Sanctuary Farm** BOUTIQUE HOTEL $$
(0722761940; www.sanctuaryfarmkenya.com; off Moi South Lake Rd; s/d KSh15,000/20,000, camping KSh6000;) Within a private 400-acre conservancy and dairy farm, this beautiful place makes the perfect weekend escape from Nairobi. The rooms are stylish, high-quality and elegant, and there's access to a cosy wi-fi lounge/library. You can also go horse riding among giraffes and zebras. Lovely breakfasts, good wines and delicious, healthy mains are on offer at the farm-to-table restaurant. Book online.

★ **Olerai House** GUESTHOUSE $$$
(Nairobi 020-8048602; www.elephantwatchportfolio.com/oleraihouse; Moi North Lake Rd; s/d full board US$495/800;) Hidden under a blanket of tropical flowers, this beautiful house is like something from a fairytale, where petals dust the beds and floors, zebras and vervet monkeys hang out with pet dogs, and the rooms are a delight. Perhaps best of all, the camp is owned by renowned elephant conservationists Iain and Oria Douglas-Hamilton – if they're at home, there are few more fascinating hosts in Kenya.

Hippo Point LODGE $$$
(0733993713; www.hippopointkenya.com; off Moi South Lake Rd; s/d full board US$950/1000) One of the most warmly eclectic places to stay anywhere in the Rift Valley, Hippo Point occupies a 1932 manor house on expansive, wildlife-rich grounds between Lake Oloiden and Lake Naivasha. The atmosphere is classy and colonial, and a wonderful sense of peace pervades the whole place – walking the halls here makes one want to whisper.

HELL'S GATE NATIONAL PARK

Why Go Dramatic volcanic scenery; a chance to walk or cycle through wildlife areas. Rock-climbing is another highlight.

When to Go June to February.

Practicalities There's a small Information Centre at Elsa Gate.

Budget Tips Get any matatu circling Lake Naivasha to drop you at the junction to Elsa Gate, where you can hire a bike for the 2km to the gate itself. Bike rental here runs cheaper than at the Information Centre.

Eating

★ **Club House** RESTAURANT $$
(0722761940; www.sanctuaryfarmkenya.com/index.php/kitchen; Sanctuary Farm; lunch KSh3000, dinner KSh3500) Farm-to-table sustainable cuisine is more exciting when there are giraffes and hippos to spy on in the distance. The signature eatery at Sanctuary Farm is relaxed but stylish, with tables strewn over a wooden verandah. Inside, there are framed black-and-white posters and Rift Valley wines. Expect dishes such as beetroot salad, red-pepper chicken, home-baked focaccia and baklava with pineapple sorbet. Reservations only.

★ **Ranch House Bistro** INTERNATIONAL $$
(0722200596, 0700488475; www.oserengoniwildlife.com/category/ranch-house-bistro; Moi South Lake Rd; mains from KSh700; 10am-10pm) Opened in 2014, Ranch House Bistro is easily the best of the lakeside eating options. The food is expertly prepared and ranges across pizzas from the clay oven to pulled-pork varieties and exquisite desserts. The setting is superb with tables spread across the lawn, but you'll need to book ahead for their Sunday lunch buffet (KSh1300 per person).

★ **Lazybones** INDIAN $$
(050-50004; www.campcarnelleys.com/bar-and-restaurant; Camp Carnelley's, Moi South Lake Rd; mains from KSh500) Camp Carnelley's hip restaurant is popular with NGO workers and other Nairobians at weekends. Grab one of the gorgeous low-slung sofas, or pull up a chair around the roaring fireplace. Co-owner Chrisi's creative menu includes Indian fusion dishes, great salads, fresh fish and even breakfast smoothies. There's also a selection of wines, beers and spirits. Out back, you'll find a pool table.

Getting There & Away

Frequent matatus (KSh100, one hour) run along Moi South Lake Rd between Naivasha town and Kongoni on the lake's western side, passing the turn-offs to Hell's Gate National Park and Fisherman's Camp (KSh70). Taxis charge upwards of KSh2000 for the hop from Naivasha. Contact **Nickson Gatimu** (☎0726797750) if you'd like to arrange a pick-up.

Hell's Gate National Park

Dry, dusty and dramatic but infinitely peaceful, **Hell's Gate** (☎0726610508, Nairobi 020-2379467; www.kws.org; adult/child US$26/17, bike hire KSh500, car entry KSh300; ⏲6am-6pm; Ⓟ) is that rare thing: an adventurous Kenyan park with large animals that's safe to explore by bicycle or on foot. Large carnivores are very rare, so you can cycle to your heart's content past grazing zebras, giraffes, impalas and buffaloes, spot rock hyraxes as they clamber up inclines and chase dust clouds as they swirl in the wind. And if the pedalling isn't enough exercise, hike the gorge or climb Fischer's Tower.

Sights & Activities

Cycling is our favourite way to explore the park, and the main Hell's Gate Gorge is relatively flat; the distance from Elsa Gate to the Lower Gorge is around 7km. Bicycles are available at the park gates for KSh500 per day, or you can pay the KSh215 fee for bringing your own into the park.

Hell's Gate Gorge CANYON

The gorge that runs through the heart of the park is a wide, deep valley hemmed in by sheer, rusty-hued rock walls. Marking its eastern entrance is **Fischer's Tower**, a 25m-high volcanic column which can be climbed with a **guide** (James Maina, ☎0727039388). The tower was named after Gustav Fischer, a German explorer who reached the gorge in 1882. Commissioned to find a route from Mombasa to Lake Victoria, Fischer was stopped by territorial Maasai, who slaughtered almost his entire party.

Lower Gorge CANYON

(Ol Njorowa; guide per hour KSh500) Rising from the main gorge's southern end is the large **Central Tower**, an unusual volcanic plug. A picnic site and ranger's post are close by, from where a walk descends into the Lower Gorge (Ol Njorowa). In some places the riverbed is dry; in others you'll find yourself scrambling down a steep and slippery descent. Some steps have been cut into the rock and some parts may be perilous. We recommend taking a guide.

Sleeping

Naiburta Public Campsite CAMPGROUND $

(camping US$20) 🍃 Naiburta, sitting on a gentle rise on the northern side of the Hell's Gate Gorge and commanding fine views west past Fischer's Tower, is the most scenic site in the area. It has basic toilets, an open *banda* for cooking and freshwater taps.

CLIMBING HELL'S GATE

The sheer rock walls of Hell's Gate are made for climbing and, thankfully, the park has two resident safety-conscious climbing guides (KSh500 per person per hour).

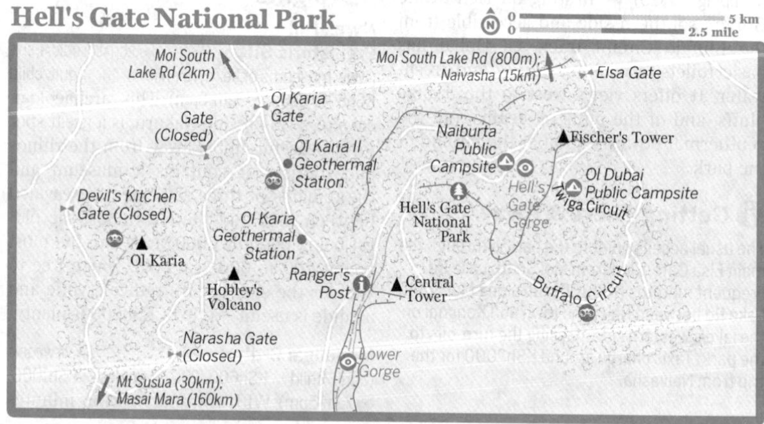

Nakuru

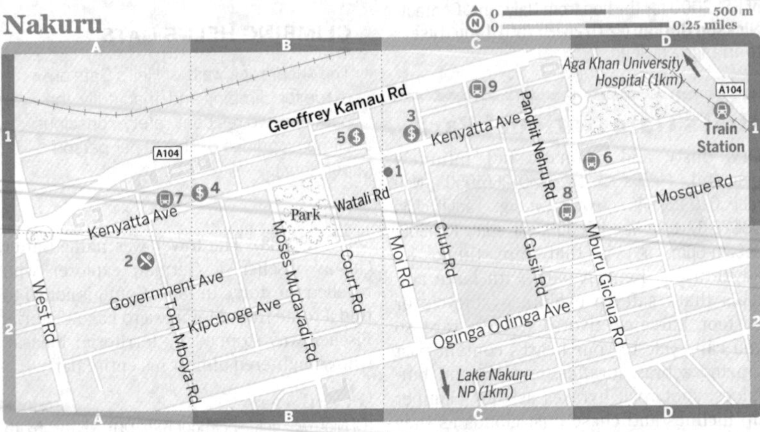

Nakuru

Activities, Courses & Tours
1 Pega Tours C1

Eating
2 Hygienic Butchery A2

Information
3 Barclays C1
4 KCB B1
5 Standard Chartered Bank B1

Transport
6 Bus & Matatu Station D1
7 Easy Coach A1
8 Matatus to Kampi ya Samaki & Marigat C1
9 Molo Line C1

Ol Dubai Public Campsite CAMPGROUND $
(camping US$20) Resting on Hell's Gate Gorge's southern side and accessible from the Buffalo Circuit track, Ol Dubai has basic toilets, a cooking *banda* and freshwater. It offers views west to the orange bluffs, and of the puffs of steam from the geothermal power station at the far end of the park.

Getting There & Away

The usual access point to the park is through the main Elsa Gate, 2km from Moi South Lake Rd. Frequent matatus (KSh100) run along Moi South Lake Rd between Naivasha town and Kongoni on the lake's western side, passing the turn-offs to the park. Taxis charge around KSh2000 for the trip from Naivasha.

Nakuru

051 / POP 308,000

Nakuru is changing fast and, in the process, transforming into one of Kenya's more agreeable towns, gentrifying around the edges and adopting some of the better aspects of Nairobi – minus the stress and the crime. Most travellers speed through the town on their way to the lakes and if that's all you do, you might wonder why anyone would choose to stay here – at first glance, Kenya's fourth-largest city can appear grim and provincial, without much to offer besides a convenient refuel. But stick around longer and we bet you'll start to like it.

If you don't want to fork out to overnight at Lake Nakuru, the city makes a good base for exploring the park and surrounds.

Sights

Hyrax Hill Prehistoric Site ARCHAEOLOGICAL SITE
(www.museums.or.ke/hyrax-hill; adult/child KSh500/250; 9am-6pm) This archaeological site, 4km outside Nakuru, is a great spot for a peaceful amble away from the rhinos and tourists. It contains a museum and the remains of three settlements excavated between 1937 and the late 1980s, the oldest being possibly 3000 years old, the most recent 200 to 300 years old. You're free to wander the site, but it's rather cryptic and a guide is useful – a tip of KSh200 is plenty.

Menengai Crater VIEWPOINT
(adult/child KSh600/200, guides KSh1000; 7am-5pm) With transport and 15 minutes

to play with, you can be out of the grimy streets of Nakuru and standing on the rim of Menengai Crater, a 485m-high natural cauldron and local beauty spot. Outside of weekends, it's a peaceful place that affords striking views down below onto a cushion of lush vegetation. The crater was formed over one million years ago and the last eruption was about 350 years ago.

Sleeping & Eating

★Milimani Guest House GUESTHOUSE $$
(☎0753616263; Maragoli Ave; s/d KSh5500/6600; P 📶) Perched above the town with soaring views towards the lake, this well-run, stylish place is a tranquil escape from the traffic below. Rooms wrap around a living room furnished with sofas and a fireplace, and breakfast is served in the pretty garden. The rooms are bright and clean with hip touches, and the welcome is warm.

Kivu Resort HOTEL $$
(☎0726026894; www.kivuresort.co.ke; off Flamingo Rd; r from US$50; P 📶 🏊) This simple, U-shaped resort sits just 1.5km from Lake Nakuru's main gate. Rooms come without fanfare or pretension but do sport mosquito nets, the price and location are both winners. Residents' rates are cheaper, if you fancy bargaining. There's a tuk-tuk stage 100m away.

Hygienic Butchery KENYAN $
(Tom Mboya Rd; mains KSh180-270; ⏲8am-10pm) Great name, great place. The Kenyan tradition of *nyama choma* is alive and well here. Sidle up to the counter, try a piece of tender mutton or beef and order half a kilo (per person) of whichever takes your fancy, along with chapatis or ugali (no sauce!).

Information

MEDICAL SERVICES

Aga Khan University Hospital (Nakuru Medical Centre; Menengai Dr; ⏲8.30am-5pm Mon-Fri, 9am-1pm Sat) Various lab and other diagnostic services including malaria tests, but no emergency services.

MONEY

Changing cash in Nakuru is easy, with numerous banks and foreign exchange bureaus.

KCB (Kenyatta Ave; ⏲9am-4pm Mon-Fri, to noon Sat) ATM and foreign exchange bureau.

Barclays (Kenyatta Ave; ⏲8am-6pm Mon-Fri, to 2pm Sat) Nakuru's most reliable ATM. Also has a foreign exchange desk.

Standard Chartered Bank (Moi Rd; ⏲9am-5pm Mon-Fri, to 1pm Sat) Bureau de change and an ATM.

Getting There & Away

BUS

Easy Coach (www.easycoach.co.ke; Kenyatta Ave) One of several bus companies offering services to Nairobi (KSh500, three hours), Eldoret (KSh650, 2¾ hours) and Kisumu (KSh750, 3½ hours).

MATATU

Ordinary matatus leave from the chaotic **bus and matatu station** (Mburu Gichua Rd) next to the market. Services include Naivasha (KSh200, 1¼ hours), Eldoret (from KSh350, 2¾ hours), Nairobi (KSh250 to KSh400, three hours) and Kisumu (KSh600, 3½ hours).

Matatus for Lake Baringo (Kampi ya Samaki; KSh250, 2½ hours) or Marigat (for Lake Bogoria; KSh150, two hours) leave from the stand at the southern end of Pandhit Nehru Rd.

Molo Line (☎0722761512; www.mololine prestige.com; Geoffrey Kamau Rd) is the most

LAKE NAKURU NATIONAL PARK

Why Go One of Kenya's best national parks is an easy two-hour drive from Nairobi. You might see tree-climbing lions, flamingos and black and white rhinos.

When to Go Animal viewing is generally good year-round, but avoid the peak of the rainy season, from March to May.

Gateway Town Nakuru

Practicalities Park tickets are valid for 24 hours exactly (or 48 hours, 72 hours etc), so if you enter at 6.30am and plan to sleep in the park, you must leave by the same time the following day. The park's main gate was forced to move back up the hill during the 2014 floods.

Budget Tips Stay outside the park and you'll pay far less for accommodation, and won't risk needing a permit for longer than 24 hours. Pega Tours (p251) offers cheap vehicle hire with guides for those without vehicles.

Lake Nakuru National Park

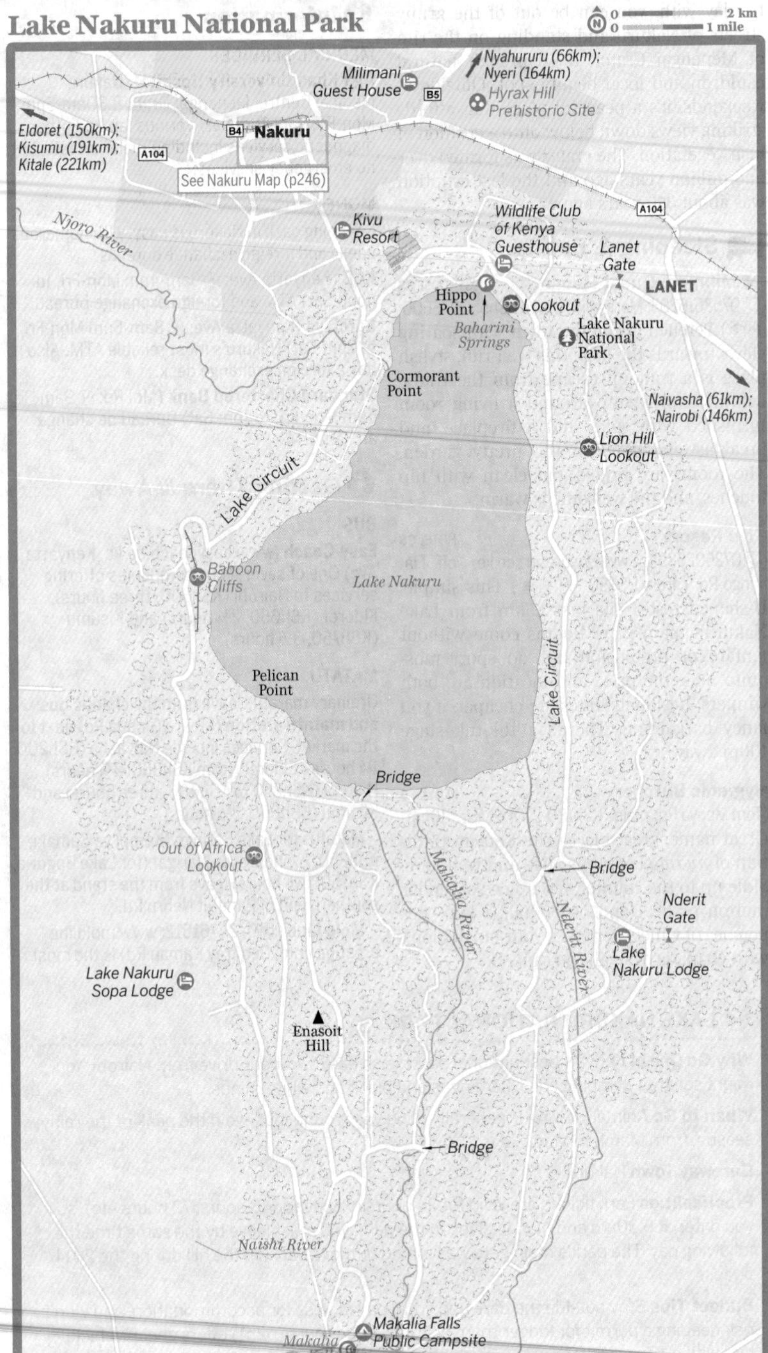

WILDLIFE WATCHING

The park's relatively small size (180 sq km, depending on the reach of the lake) makes it easy to get around the Lake Circuit in a day. The forests anywhere in the park are good for leopards and rare tree-climbing lions imported from eastern Kenya (although sightings of the latter are uncommon). The park's black and white rhinos (around 60 altogether) tend to stick fairly close to the lake shore and sightings are common. The elephant is the only member of the Big Five not present in the park.

The health of the white rhinos in particular is monitored carefully by the rangers; coloured patches on the skin are likely to reflect recent medical treatment. Warthogs are common all over the park, as are waterbucks, elands, zebras and buffaloes, while Thomson's gazelles, impalas and reedbucks can be seen further into the bush. Around the cliffs you may catch sight of hyraxes and birds of prey amid the countless baboons; the latter are by no means shy about enthusiastically reproducing in public.

Since the park's creation in 1961, the population of lesser and greater flamingos has risen and fallen with the soda lake's erratic water levels. When the lake dried up in 1962 (happy first birthday!), the population plummeted, as it later did in the 1970s when heavy rainfall diluted the lake's salinity and affected the blue-green algae – the lesser flamingos' food source. Over much of the last decade healthy water levels have seen flamingo numbers blossom again. If future droughts or flooding make them fly the coop again, you'll probably find them at Lake Bogoria, with smaller populations at Lake Oloiden and Lake Magadi.

reputable of the matatu companies, running services to Nairobi that leave when full from opposite the old Odeon cinema; the first departures of the day are from 4.30am. There are 10 seats, usually with belts, and drivers tend to stick to the speed limit. This prestige shuttle service goes to Nairobi (KSh400), Eldoret (KSh400) and Kisumu (KSh600).

Lake Nakuru National Park

Lake Nakuru (☎0728355267, 0728355207; www.kws.go.ke; adult/child US$60/35; ⏲6.30am-6.30pm) is among Kenya's finest national parks. Flanked by rocky escarpments, pockets of acacia forest and at least one waterfall, the park is gorgeous year-round and is home to both black and white rhinos, lions, leopards, hippos and endangered Rothschild's giraffes. Rising water levels in 2014 forced the park's famous flamingos to flee (although a small number had returned at the time of research), and the lake is now hauntingly surrounded by drowned trees.

The southern end of the lake is the best place to see wildlife. The forested area below Flamingo Hill is a favourite lion-spotting point – lionesses love to sleep in the trees – while leopards frequent the same area, and are also sometimes seen around the Makalia camp.

Sights

Baboon Cliffs VIEWPOINT

This popular viewpoint and one-time lunch spot has superlative views out over the lake, with some fine aerial vistas down onto the flooded lake shore. Baboons, however, are a problem and don't mind raiding vehicles, whether you're inside or not, for food scraps. Visit in the early morning before they've taken over for the day.

Out of Africa Lookout VIEWPOINT

To get the best view that takes in much of the park, head up to the rocky Out of Africa Lookout. Less frequented by tour groups than the lower Baboon Cliff, the incline is steeper but it offers sweeping views out over the lake and fond memories for fans of the film – parts of the movie were filmed in the park, with some shots taken from here.

Sleeping & Eating

Makalia Falls Public Campsite CAMPGROUND $

(camping US$30; P) This campsite has the best facilities of any inside the park, although it's still rather basic – an ablutions block with cold running water is the extent of it. From here you can walk to the **Makalia Falls** and check out the view.

WORTH A TRIP

LAKES BOGORIA & BARINGO

Bogoria

Lake Bogoria (☎Nairobi 020-6000800; www.kws.org; adult/child US$25/15) is backed by the bleak Siracho Escarpment, and moss-green waves roll down its rocky, barren shores. A road that becomes a rough track (and then peters out entirely) runs along the lake's western shore, which is where flamingos gather. About halfway along the lake, **hot springs and geysers** spew boiling fluids from the earth's insides. If you're here early in the morning, you may have the place to yourself.

While the isolated wooded area at the lake's southern end is home to rarely seen leopards, klipspringers, gazelles, caracals and buffaloes, an increase in human activity means that the extravagantly horned greater kudu is increasingly elusive. You can explore on foot or bicycle. If you'd like a guide, enquire at Loboi Gate.

Baringo

Wild and beautiful Lake Baringo is the most remote of the Rift Valley lakes. Steeped in stories, its harsh climate and rocky islets give it a faraway feel; on a hot day, this freshwater lake has more in common with northern Kenya than the rest of the Rift Valley. Birdwatching in Kenya rarely gets better than this, with over 460 species including owls, nightjars, Goliath herons and rare Hemprich's hornbills. Crocs and hippos are also present.

The small village of **Kampi ya Samaki**, on Lake Baringo's shore, is the gateway to the lake. Lake Baringo is not a fee-paying park, but the community charges a toll (KSh200) to access the lake; keep your receipt.

Roberts Camp (☎0717176656; www.robertscamp.com; Kampi ya Samaki; bandas for 2/4 people KSh6000/12,000, d tents KSh2500-4500, camping KSh800; P) A legend in its own right, this atmospheric camp sits right on the lakeshore, wherever that shore may be... The *bandas* are nicely decorated, with eco loos, and there's ample space for camping, plus the Thirsty Goat (mains from KSh750; ⏲7am-10pm) bar-restaurant. The helpful staff can organise boat rides and scorpion- or bird-spotting nature walks. After dark, keep your eyes peeled for hippos, fireflies and the ghosts of old adventurers.

Island Camp (☎0728478638, 0724874661; www.islandcamp.com; Lake Baringo; room/cottage full board incl boat transfers from US$550/740;) Stylish but relaxed, this gorgeous tented camp covers the tip of an island in the middle of Lake Baringo. The lovely tents are a mixture of thatch and canvas, while the superior rooms have private plunge pools and Kenyan art. There's an atmospheric bar, community initiatives, wild gardens made for birdwatching, and a spa tent. Day visitors are welcomed for lunch.

Wildlife Club of Kenya Guesthouse HOSTEL $
(☎0723760970, 0720456546; per person without bathroom KSh1250) Hands down Nakuru's best budget choice, this rather charming cottage inside the park looks out towards the lake and often finds its own gardens frequented by zebras and buffaloes. Inside it's nothing special, but there are six simple rooms with shared bathrooms, as well as a moderately well-equipped kitchen and a comfortable dining room. Self-catering only.

★**Lake Nakuru Sopa Lodge** LODGE $$$
(☎072220632, Nairobi 020-3750235; www.sopalodges.com; s/d full board Jul-Oct US$300/450, rates vary rest of year; P) Unlike Sopa Lodges elsewhere, which are often dated, dark and in obscure locations, this fine new property has light-filled rooms from high on a perch overlooking the lake. The rooms are excellent and take full advantage of the views, while the whole lodge sparkles with impressive service and vantage points at every turn.

Lake Nakuru Lodge LODGE $$$
(☎0720404480, Nairobi 020-2687056; www.lakenakurulodge.com; s/d/tr full board Jul-Mar from US$300/400/500, Apr-Jun from US$200/300/380; P@) The big draw here is the view, stretching outwards from the lodge down into the park. Not all rooms have views – snaffle rooms 101 to 103 if you

want to sit on your terrace and enjoy sweeping vistas of the park. The lodge itself has pleasant garden rooms with wall-to-ceiling balcony windows, and there's a decent buffet restaurant and helpful staff.

Getting There & Away

The park begins on the outskirts of Nakuru (p246), the main gateway town for the park. There is no public transport from the town into the park – contact your accommodation for a transfer (which may or may not be free) from the town, or rent a vehicle in Nakuru.

Getting Around

The park is accessible in a 2WD, though most visitors stay in the park and take hotel-run safaris. You'll need to pay KSh350 per car to bring your own vehicle into the park. You're able to explore the park alone, but guides are available for KSh2500 per four hours. If you don't have your own wheels, **Pega Tours** (0722776094, 0722743440; www.pegatours.co.ke; Utalii Arcade, Kenyatta Ave) in Nakuru is a good bet. Its daily hire rates include a pop-top minibus and a knowledgeable driver/guide from KSh2500 per person (based on four guests).

MASAI MARA & WESTERN KENYA

Narok

050 / POP 40,000

Three hours west of Nairobi, this ramshackle provincial town – the capital of the Mara region – serves as the gateway to the Masai Mara and is the last proper centre before the vast savannahs begin. It's a friendly and surprisingly hassle-free place, but few travellers have reason to stop. Most people roll on in, browse the curio shops while their driver refuels, then roll on out again.

If you stay long enough, however, Narok is worth a few hours of sitting and talking to locals – it's a predominantly Maasai town with an increasingly high number of settlers from elsewhere in the country. The result is a fascinating cultural mix and a good place to take the pulse of the region.

Sleeping & Eating

Seasons Hotel HOTEL $$
(0718323213; www.seasonshotelskenya.com; B3; s US$60-110, d US$100-140;) The largest and most popular place to stop in town, the Seasons Hotel has tired but large, adequate rooms with mosquito nets; the swimming pool is a bonus. If staying overnight, ask for a room on the upper floors at the back to combat street noise.

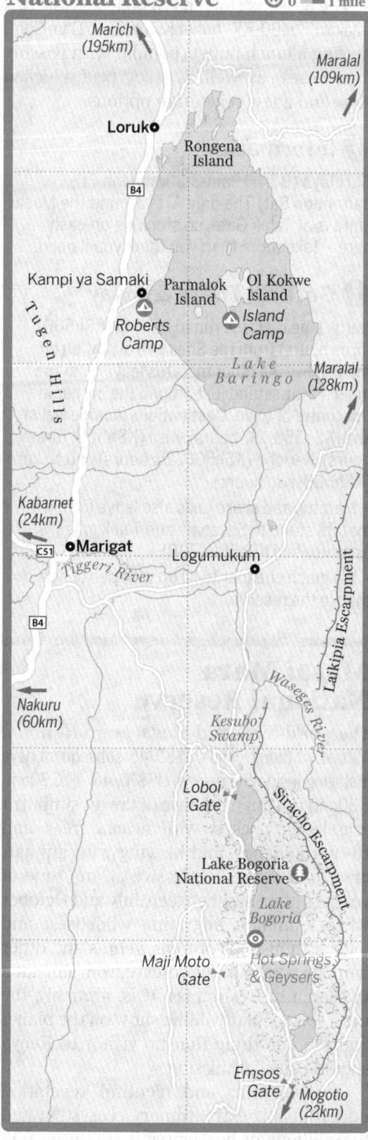

Some of the ground-floor rooms are a little claustrophobic.

The Seasons Hotel has a good **restaurant** (mains KSh400-700, buffet KSh800; ⏲11am-9pm) serving a lunch buffet (popular with passing tour buses) as well as spicy beef, chicken stew and a few vegetarian options.

Information

Barclays (B3; ⏲9am-3.30pm Mon-Fri, 9am-noon Sat) The only ATM around the Masai Mara is at Talek Gate, so stock up on cash here – take more than you think you'll need.

Getting There & Away

Narok Line matatus run to Nairobi (KSh500, three hours) from the Shell petrol station on the B6 Hwy. All other matatus leave from the main matatu stand just around the corner in the centre of town. Destinations include Naivasha (KSh350, 2½ hours), Kisii (KSh500, three hours), Kericho (KSh500, 2½ hours) and Nakuru (KSh500, two hours).

Matatus and share taxis also leave from the matatu stand to Sekenani and Talek gates (matatu/taxi KSh500/700).

It's much cheaper to fill up with petrol here than in the reserve.

Masai Mara National Reserve

The world-renowned **Masai Mara National Reserve** (adult/child US$80/45, subsequent days if staying inside the reserve US$70/40; ⏲6.30am-6.30pm) is a huge expanse of tawny, sunburnt grasslands pocked with acacia trees and river woodlands, and heaving with animals great and small. Impressive at any time of year, it's at its best between July and October when a million migrating wildebeest and tens of thousands of topis, zebras and other animals pour into the reserve from Tanzania in search of fresh grass. It is, arguably, the most spectacular wildlife show on the planet and the one thing that no visitor to Kenya should consider missing.

Reliable rains and plentiful vegetation underpin this extraordinary ecosystem and the millions of herbivores it supports. Wildebeest, zebras, impalas, elands, reedbucks, waterbucks, black rhinos, elephants, Masai giraffes and several species of gazelle all call the Mara home. Predators here include cheetahs, leopards, spotted hyenas, black-backed jackals, bat-eared foxes, caracals and the highest lion density in the world.

Sights

Central Plains

The southeast area of the park, bordered by the Mara and Sand Rivers, is characterised by rolling grasslands and low, isolated hills. With the arrival of the migration, enormous herds of wildebeest and zebras, as well as other plains wildlife, graze here. The riverine forests that border the Mara and Talek Rivers are great places to spot elephants, buffaloes and bushbucks. Leopards are sometimes seen near the Talek and Sand Rivers and around the Keekorok valleys.

Rhino Ridge & Paradise Plains

Rhino Ridge is a good place to see black-backed jackals, as they're known to use the old termitaria here for den sites. Lookout Hill is worth a detour as it offers phenomenal views over the seasonal Olpunyaia Swamp. You may also get lucky and spot one of the few black rhinos that inhabit the reserve anywhere between Lookout Hill and Rhino Ridge and in the vicinity of Roan Hill.

To see lions, the Marsh Pride near Musiara Swamp and the Ridge Pride near Rhino Ridge both starred in the BBC's *Big Cat Diary* so they (as celebrities) are fairly easy to find.

Cheetahs are far more elusive, but are sometimes found hunting gazelles on the Paradise Plains.

Mara River

Pods of hippos can be found in any of the major rivers, with the largest and most permanent concentrations occurring in the Mara River. The river is also home to huge Nile crocodiles and is the scene where wildebeest make their fateful crossings during the migration. The New Mara Bridge in the south is the only all-weather crossing point and another great place to see hippos.

Mara Triangle & Esoit Oloololo (Siria) Escarpment

Unlike the rest of the park, which is under the control of the Narok County Council, the northwest sector of the reserve is managed by the non-profit Mara Conservancy. The only way to reach this part of the park is from either the Oloololo Gate or via the New Mara Bridge. Consequently, this area is less visited than elsewhere, despite having high concentrations of wildlife.

The Olooolo Escarpment, which forms the northwest boundary of the park, was once wooded, but fire and elephant damage mean that it's now mostly grasslands. Rock hyraxes and klipspringers can be readily seen here.

Activities

Wildlife Drives

Virtually all lodges organise wildlife drives through the park. At some cheaper places it will be in a battered old Land Rover or similar, while in the more expensive places

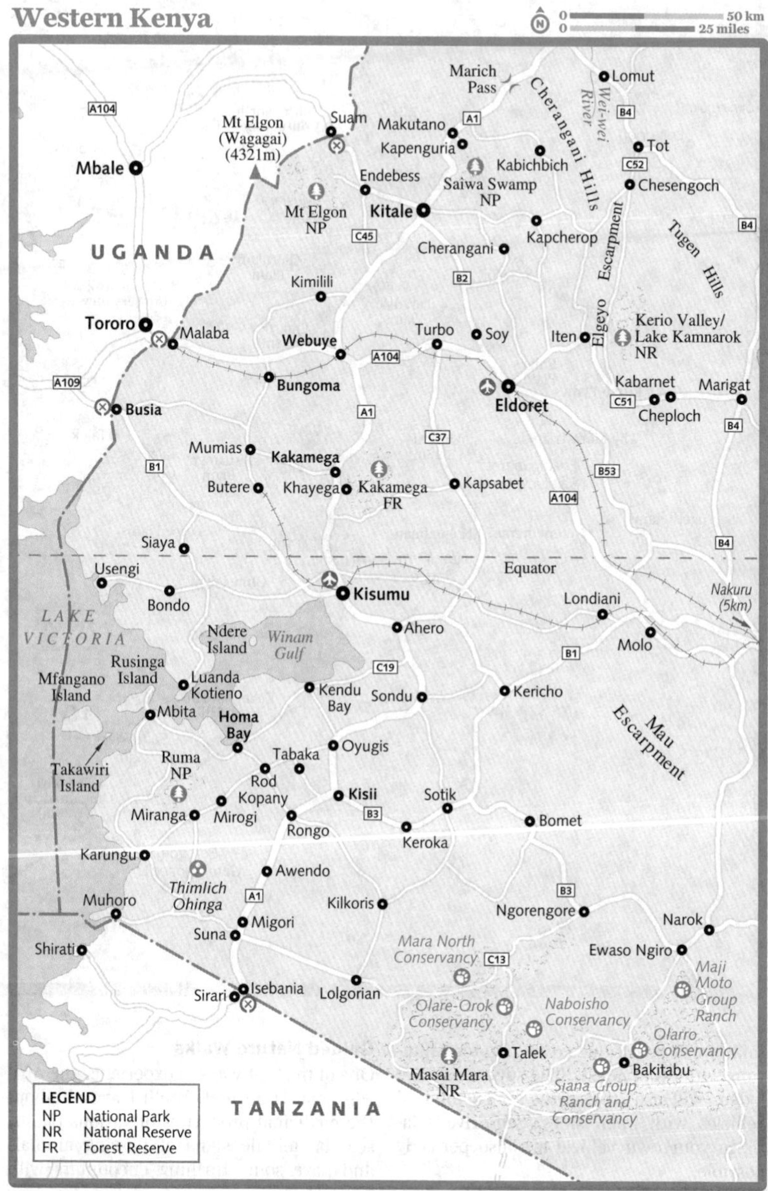

Masai Mara National Reserve

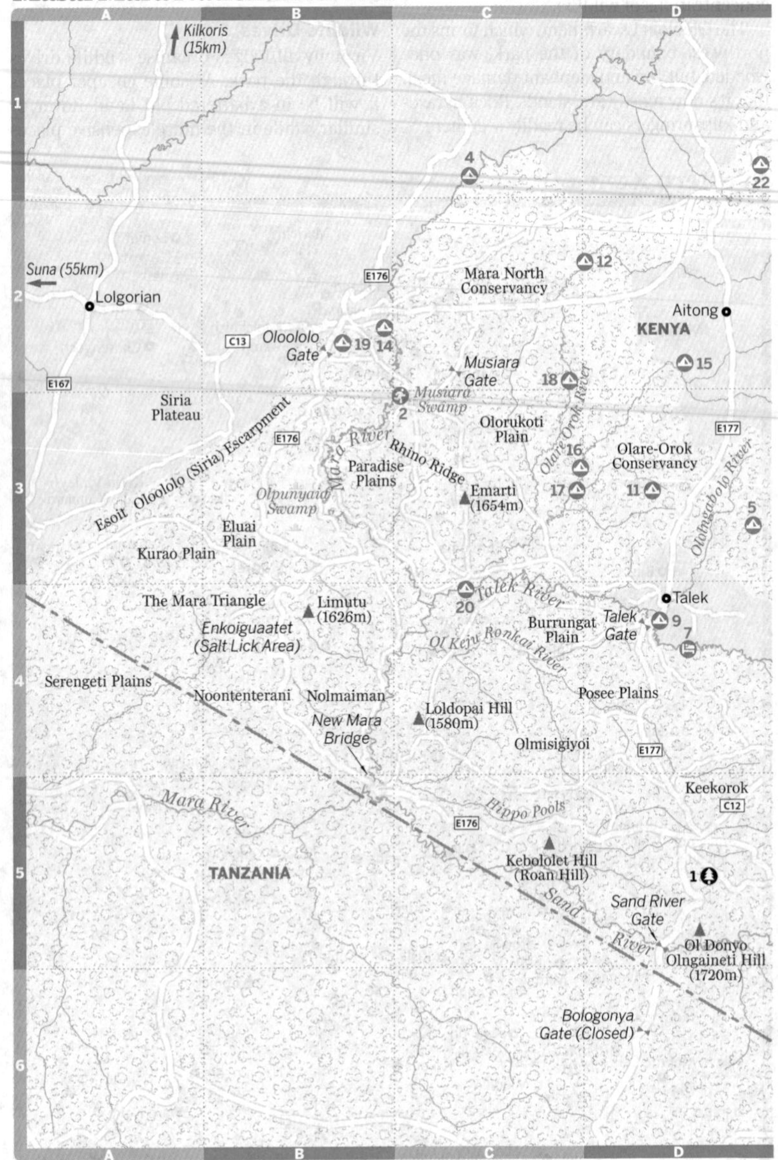

safaris will be conducted in 'pop-top' minivans with other guests. The super-exclusive lodges will use state-of-the-art customised vehicles with open sides. Self-drive safaris in your own vehicle are also perfectly possible.

Guided Nature Walks

One of the best ways to experience the African bush is on foot. You'll learn all about the medicinal properties of various plants, see the telltale signs of passing animals and have some thrilling encounters with

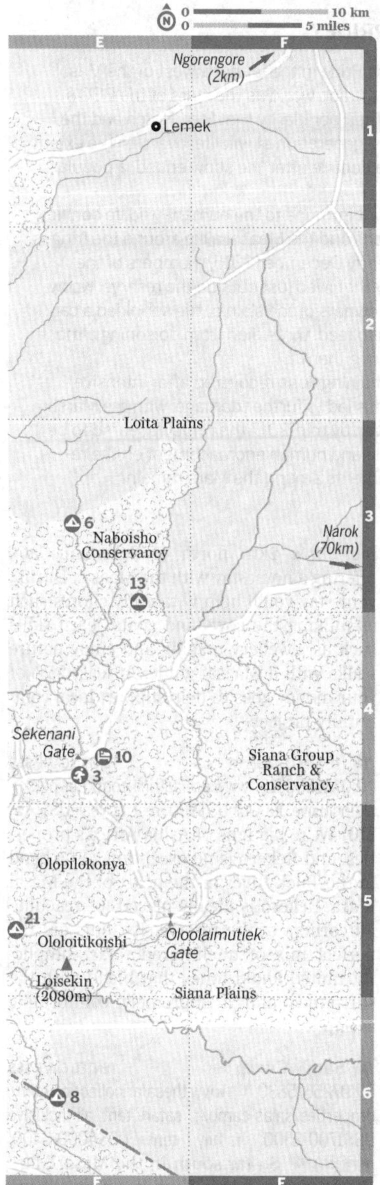

Masai Mara National Reserve

Sights

1 Masai Mara National Reserve............ D5

Activities, Courses & Tours

2 Governors' Balloon Safaris C3
3 Hot Air Safaris E4

Sleeping

4 Alex Walker's Serian C1
5 Asilia Naboisho Camp D3
6 Basecamp Eagle View E3
7 Basecamp Masai Mara......................... D4
8 Cottar's 1920s Camp........................... E6
9 Crocodile Camp Masai Mara D4
10 Ewangan... E4
11 Kicheche Bush..................................... D3
12 Kicheche Mara.................................... D2
13 Kicheche Valley Camp..........................E3
14 Kichwa Tembo Camp B2
15 Mahali Mzuri Camp D2
16 Mara Expedition Camp........................ C3
17 Mara Plains C3
18 Off Beat Mara...................................... C2
19 Public Campsite B2
20 Rekero Camp C4
21 Sala's Camp E5
22 Saruni Mara... D1

wildlife. As it's forbidden to walk within the reserve due to predators, guided walks generally take place in the company of a Maasai *moran* (warrior) outside the park itself, but in the nonetheless wildlife-rich conservancies that surround the reserve to the north and east. Guides can be arranged through your accommodation or safari company.

Balloon Safaris

Several companies operate dawn balloon safaris and there's no better way to start your day than soaring majestically over the rolling grasslands. Flights can be booked at most of the lodges or campsites and include a champagne breakfast, wildlife drive and transport to and from the launch point. Two recommended companies are **Hot Air Safaris** (☎0733300302; www.maraballooning.com; Sekenani; per person US$400-500) and **Governors' Balloon Safaris** (☎0733616204; www.governorsballoonsafaris.com; Governors' Camp; per person US$400-500).

Maasai Manyatta Visits

The Maasai are synonymous with the Masai Mara, and their slender frames, blood-red cloaks, ochre hairstyles and beaded jewellery make them instantly recognisable. Despite their reputation as fearsome warriors with somewhat lofty dispositions, some Maasai *manyattas* (villages) now welcome visitors (around US$20 per person).

Village visits can be organised through any lodge or camp or, if travelling under

WHAT HAPPENED TO THE MARSH PRIDE?

From 1996 until 2008, the lions from the Marsh Pride in the far northwest of the Masai Mara National Reserve were the celebrities of the lion world as the stars of the BBC's wildly popular series *Big Cat Diary*. Such was their popularity that Bibi, Notch and the rest of the pride became household names to a generation of wildlife lovers, to the extent that tracking down the Marsh Pride remains, a decade after the show ended, a popular safari request for visitors to the Masai Mara.

But even lion celebrities such as these are not immune to the human–wildlife conflict that is increasingly complicating the lives of lions and the Maasai alike around the fringes of parks and reserves like the Masai Mara. In early December 2015, members of the pride killed cattle belonging to a Maasai family that lived just outside the reserve. Knowing that the lions would return to their kill, the owners of the slain cattle sprinkled a carcass with pesticide. When eight lions returned to feed, three died from poisoning almost immediately. Seventeen-year-old Bibi was among them.

The perpetrators were arrested and the remaining lions recovered after intensive treatment from the reserve's vets. But the stress led to further damage, with the Marsh Pride splitting into a number of groups. However, by mid-2017 the pride appeared to be once again together, though the issues of cattle and human encroachment on the reserve and the impact of growing human settlements around the Mara remain.

your own steam, you can just turn up at any of the villages (look for the signs saying something along the lines of 'cultural village' – don't just stroll into a proper Maasai *manyatta* unannounced!).

Sleeping & Eating

Public Campsite CAMPGROUND $

(camping per person US$20) The sites are wonderfully open to the elements, with just canvas between you and the nearest predator. You will need to be totally self-sufficient to the point of bringing your own firewood (using the deadwood within the park is prohibited).

★Crocodile Camp Masai Mara TENTED CAMP $$

(☎0772397597, 0721975456; www.crocodilecamp-masaimara.com; camping per person US$6, tent & bedding rental US$15, per person safari tent room only/full board US$40/75; wi-fi) Whether you're camping or looking for a little more comfort in one of their simple safari tents, Crocodile Camp, close to Talek Gate, is an excellent place to stay. With wi-fi in the evenings, a decent bar-restaurant, hot showers and an active safari programme geared towards budget and midrange travellers, it's a good all-round package.

★Ewangan HOMESTAY $$

(☎0721817757; www.maasaimaravillage.com; Sekenani Gate; camping US$20, full board per person US$70, children free) A traditional Maasai *manyatta* 2km north of Sekenani Gate, offering a homestay with the Maasai. During your stay you'll help with daily chores such as milking the cows and goats, learn skills such as jewellery making and enjoy nature walks with a Maasai guide. At least 25% of your money goes to help support local community projects.

★Rekero Camp TENTED CAMP $$$

(☎0736500515; www.asiliaafrica.com; per person all-inclusive Jul-Oct US$930, rest of year US$615-870) We're big fans of Asilia Africa's properties, and Rekero is no exception. On a bend in the Talek River in the heart of the Masai Mara, Rekero is ideally placed for reaching all corners of the reserve. Its tents are the perfect mix of uncluttered safari simplicity, muted khaki tones that blend with the surrounds and a supremely comfortable set-up.

★Sala's Camp TENTED CAMP $$$

(☎0725675830; www.thesafaricollection.com/properties/salas-camp/; safari tent all-inclusive US$1700-2500, family tent US$4000-5400; P wi-fi pool) So far south in the Masai Mara that you're almost in Tanzania, Sala's Camp is a real find. Away from the busier central and northern areas of the reserve, you'll feel like you're in your own private corner of the Mara. That does mean you'll need to drive further to explore, but the remoteness and wonderful tents more than compensate.

★ **Mara Expedition Camp** TENTED CAMP $$$
(☎Nairobi 020-6000457; www.greatplainsconservation.com; s/d full board US$1290/1720; ⏲closed Apr–mid-Jun; 📶) 🌿 A tiny camp that's so well hidden under the riverside trees it's impossible to see until you're pretty much in it. Yet again, Great Plains Conservation has produced a winner that combines clever conservation work with five tents that are the epitome of refined-safari style with leather armchairs, old travellers' trunks and brass bucket showers.

Basecamp Masai Mara LODGE $$$
(☎0733333909; www.basecampexplorer.com/kenya/hotels/basecamp-masai-mara/; tent s/d full board from US$380/600; 📶) 🌿 This upmarket lodge has 16 extremely comfortable tents with large wooden verandahs and smart bathrooms. The camp is very serious about sustainability and recycling, and enjoys a gold eco rating from Ecotourism Kenya. It also has huge grounds and overlooks the river and the Mara beyond. Don't miss the trees planted by the Obama family on their stay here.

Kichwa Tembo Camp TENTED CAMP $$$
(☎Nairobi 020-3688620; www.andbeyond.com; per person full board Jul-Oct US$450-625, rates vary rest of year; 🏊) Just outside the northern boundary of the reserve, Kichwa has been recently renovated and has permanent tents with grass-mat floors, stone bathrooms and tasteful furnishings. Hop in a hammock and take in spectacular savannah views. The camp has an excellent reputation for its food and is well positioned for the migration river-crossing points.

ℹ Information

MONEY

The only ATM in the area is **KCB** (Main Rd, Talek; ⏲8.30am-4pm Mon-Fri, 8.30am-noon Sat) in Talek village (KCB ATMs can be temperamental with foreign cards), so come prepared with cash.

TOURIST INFORMATION

For more on the Masai Mara and surrounding conservancies, see the independent website www.maasaimara.com.

THE 'WHEN' OF THE MARA MIGRATION

While it is easy to make *fairly* reliable predictions about when the migration will arrive in Kenya, there are no guarantees where the herds will be at the time of your visit. As a general rule...

Mid-July–August By the second half of July, the herds are in the northern Serengeti (Tanzania) and heading into the Masai Mara. It is during this stage of the migration that you're most likely to encounter the incredible river crossings of the Mara River.

September–October By early September, the last stragglers should have left the Serengeti and most will remain in the Masai Mara throughout October. It's a time of massive numbers, although river crossings become less common as the year progresses and the wildebeest enjoy the grassy plains they came so far to feed on.

November With the arrival (or in anticipation) of the short rains in November, the herds usually begin to leave the Mara and cross back into Tanzania.

This is what usually happens. But, of course, it doesn't always work out this way. In November 2013, for example, it began raining in the Masai Mara when the herds had already crossed into Tanzania, prompting the wildebeest to return en masse to the Mara. They stayed there for three weeks before resuming their southwards push.

In June 2014, unseasonal rains in the southern Serengeti prompted the herd to split in two – most continued north as usual but a significant number of zebras and wildebeest occupied the plains south of Seronera until well into July, and didn't arrive in Kenya until a month or two later.

In June 2017, the herd again split (which is, according to scientists with whom we spoke, an increasingly common phenomena) and an advance herd crossed the Sand River and into the Masai Mara almost six weeks earlier than usual. The remainder of the herd headed to the Serengeti's western corridor but then moved swiftly north and began crossing into Kenya in early July.

Getting There & Away

AIR

Airkenya (☎020-3916000; www.airkenya.com; Wilson Airport, Nairobi), **Mombasa Air Safari** (☎0734400400; www.mombasaairsafari.com), **Safarilink** (☎020-6690000; www.flysafarilink.com) and **Fly540** (☎0710540540; www.fly540.com; Wilson Airport) each have daily (or more frequent) flights to any of the eight airstrips in and around the Masai Mara.

MATATU, CAR & 4WD

If you're driving to the Mara, be sure to fill up on petrol in Narok, the last chance to fill your vehicle at normal prices on the road from Nairobi. Expensive petrol is available at Mara Sarova, Mara Serena and Keekorok lodges, as well as in Talek village.

The first 50km or so west of Narok on the B3 and C12 are smooth enough, but after the bitumen runs out you'll find yourself on one of Kenya's most notorious roads – a bone-shaking dirt road that many drivers simply dread. Most people drive in the sandy verges of the road, which makes for a far smoother experience, but either way the road is a pain and you might well wonder why you didn't fly. The road is slowly being upgraded: so slowly, in fact, that when they finish they might have to turn around and start again.

That said, having your own wheels in the Mara is a wonderful thing. Even if most safari drives will be done with a guide in their own vehicle, it still means you're free to self-drive through the reserve, which is a huge pleasure in itself, although getting lost is always a slight risk. It's possible to access Talek and Sekenani gates from Narok by matatu (KSh600), after which you'll need to arrange pick-ups from a lodge.

Getting Around

For independent travellers staying outside the reserve, count on paying around US$150 to US$200 per day for a 4WD with a driver-guide and (usually) a picnic lunch. This fee can, of course, be split between as many people as can be comfortably squeezed into the vehicle. There's no public transport within the park.

TROUBLE IN EDEN

In many ways the Masai Mara National Reserve is the epitome of the African dream. Its golden, bleached savannah is covered with unparalleled densities of animals, great and small, and the vast majority of it is untouched by the destructive hand of man. Visitors can't help but be bowled over by its natural riches.

The reality, however, is that not everyone is happy with this wildlife haven. Many local Maasai living in the immediate vicinity of the reserve feel they gain nothing from its presence, despite the sacrifices and hardships they face because of it. The issues they raise include:

- Not being allowed to graze their cattle inside the reserve, which many of them consider to be 'their' land.
- Insufficient and poorly organised compensation when animals kill their cattle outside of the reserve.
- Neglected needs of the Maasai communities. Many communities don't have sufficient access to clean, safe water sources and education and health facilities. Many lodges and camps in and around the reserve advertise their community development projects, but many Maasai dispute that all of this money actually goes to such projects.

Ironically, another problem the reserve faces comes from safari tourism itself. Sightings of big cats tend to attract large numbers of vehicles, and when the lion, cheetah or leopard eventually moves away, many guides (under pressure because their clients want to see such animals up close) break park rules by following the animals off the designated tracks. Such constant attention has caused some animals to change their patterns of behaviour – for instance, cheetahs now frequently attempt to hunt under the midday sun, when most tourists are having lunch in their camp (unfortunately, it's also a time when the chance of a successful kill is radically reduced). Some cheetahs have also been known to use safari vehicles as cover for stalking their prey. Reports are now showing that many animals are spending less time in the reserve itself, choosing to roam in the surrounding conservancies where there are fewer safari vehicles (and, incidentally, where local communities also gain more from tourism).

THE NORTHERN MIGRATION

The Loita Hills are important for what's known as the northern migration, a smaller version of the mass migration of wildebeest from the Serengeti to the Masai Mara. During the northern migration, as many as 250,000 wildebeest and zebras migrate down onto the Mara plains from the Loita Hills, bringing prey in abundance into Mara North, Olare-Orok, Naboisho and the other conservancies, as well as the northern reaches of the reserve itself. The northern migration usually begins with the first rains in March, although in some years these rains – and the migration itself – may not begin until May. The herds generally remain until rains fall in the Loita Hills, which could be in November, but also as late as the following March.

There are concerns that growing human populations in the Loita Hills area and the growing number of fences will seriously threaten the migration's future. The northern version may also lack the drama of the main migration, due to the absence of significant river crossings. But as long as it continues, it can still be quite the spectacle during months otherwise known as the low season.

Mara North Conservancy

Established in 2009, the 300-sq-km Mara North Conservancy (www.maranorth.com) is one of our favourite conservancies in the Mara, ticking all the right boxes for wildlife, classic Mara landscapes and community engagement. Mara North, which abuts the northwestern edge of the Masai Mara National Reserve, is an absolute cliché of what East Africa is supposed to look like: the flat-topped acacias, the long golden grass and animals everywhere. Leopard sightings are common and there are lots of very large lions, as well as some cheetahs and masses of plains wildlife. In fact, during the migration the horizon can be utterly covered in the black dots of wildebeest and seeing lions on a kill is very common.

Sleeping & Eating

★Saruni Mara TENTED CAMP **$$$**
(0735950903, Nairobi 020-2180497; www.saruni.com; s/d all-inclusive Jul-Sep US$930/1560, rest of year s US$560-750, d US$920-1260; wi-fi) Way to the north of any of the other camps, and virtually on the border of the conservancy, this breathtaking camp has around a dozen tents dusted with antique furnishings and colonial bric-a-brac. Some even have open log fires and the decoration in each follows a theme of writer's, photographer's or artist's studio. The setting is in animal-packed, forested hills.

★Kicheche Mara TENTED CAMP **$$$**
(Nairobi 020-2493569; www.kicheche.com; s/d all-inclusive Aug-Oct US$925/1580, per person rest of year US$625-665; wi-fi) Stunningly sited in a lush, intimate valley along a hippo-inhabited stream lined with acacias, Kicheche is a lovely property. The large tents with bucket showers have fine views and are wonderfully strung out along the valley, and there's a lovely mess area with free wi-fi. The safari vehicles have, like all at Kicheche camps, beanbags for photographers – a detail we always appreciate.

★Alex Walker's Serian TENTED CAMP **$$$**
(0718139359, Nairobi 020-2663397; www.serian.com; safari tents US$670-1400; wi-fi) Some of Mara North's most beautiful lodgings, Serian (which means 'serene' in the Maa language) overlooks the Mara River with the Oloololo Escarpment as a backdrop. The tents here, a winning mix of thatch, wood and canvas, are luxurious and they revel in the mystique and nostalgia of the East African safari. The guides here are excellent.

Off Beat Mara TENTED CAMP **$$$**
(0704909355; www.offbeatsafaris.com; s/d all-inclusive US$740/1480; closed Apr, May & Nov; wi-fi) With just six tents on the bend of a tree-lined river, this is one of the smallest and most personable of the Mara North camps, with bush-chic tents filled with heavy wooden furnishings exuding an authentic old-African-safari feel. Wildlife abounds around the camp and this is one place where they've resisted the temptation to manicure the lawn – it *feels* wild.

Getting There & Away

It takes about two hours to drive from Narok to the heart of the conservancy, although it depends where you're going. Self-driving is only permitted in Mara North if driving to/from your camp. Most visitors fly into one of the conservancy's airstrips, where vehicles from the various camps pick up guests.

Naboisho Conservancy

Created in 2011, the 222-sq-km Naboisho Conservancy is one of the Mara's youngest. It's also one of the best, with excellent camps, fabulous predator and other wildlife viewing, as well as picturesque, classic Mara landscapes of whistling thorn, open grasslands, rolling hill country and riverine acacia woodlands. Little wonder, then, that Naboisho won the prestigious Overall Winner of the African Responsible Tourism Awards in 2016, as well as sharing the Wildlife Conservation Prize with Ol Pejeta Conservancy. If you were looking to choose one place for your safari of a lifetime, Naboisho would have to be on the shortlist.

Activities

Most camps offer both wildlife drives and walking safaris – given the number of big cats that call Naboisho home, the latter is guaranteed to get the heart racing.

Wildlife Watching

When it comes to wildlife watching, there are plenty of elephants as well as all the usual plains species. When we last visited, there was one family of five cheetahs and another of three, and the conservancy was home to 60 adult lions spread across three prides. The camps have agreed on a policy of just four vehicles at any viewing – while it can be frustrating waiting if you're in the fifth vehicle on the scene, it's policies like these that help make Naboisho so special and keep its wildlife from being overwhelmed by vehicles.

Sleeping & Eating

★Asilia Naboisho Camp TENTED CAMP **$$$**
(Nairobi 020-2324904; www.asiliaafrica.com; per person all-inclusive Jul-Oct US$895, per person rest of year US$300-635;) So what if the tents, with their huge beds and indoor and outdoor showers, are among the most extravagant around. Why people really stay here is the opportunity to walk over animal-crammed savannah with an expert guide. If that wasn't enough, the wildlife viewing right outside the tents is superb, with big cats frequently passing in front of the camp.

★Kicheche Valley Camp TENTED CAMP **$$$**
(Nairobi 020-2493569; www.kicheche.com; Naboisho; s/d all-inclusive Aug-Oct US$925/1580, per person rest of year US$625-665; closed Apr-May) High in a valley that looks down into the heart of the conservancy – there is not a single light in view at night – Kicheche Valley is a terrific property. Top-level guides, a Gold Eco rating for sustainability and original safari tents with wonderful light floors made from recycled tetrapak, which give them a refreshingly contemporary look, are huge selling points.

Basecamp Eagle View TENTED CAMP **$$$**
(0733333909; www.basecampexplorer.com/kenya/; s/d all-inclusive Jul-Oct US$580/1050, rates vary rest of year;) The most upmarket of the three Basecamp offerings around the Mara. The six tents here are stretched along a ridge with mind-boggling views over a salt lick and miles of savannah. Despite the undisputed luxury, Eagle View still follows the company ethos of uncompromising sustainability. Excellent walking safaris are a highlight of a stay here.

Getting There & Away

Like other Mara conservancies, Naboisho is not open to private vehicles, although you'll generally be allowed to proceed if you're driving directly to/from your lodging – wildlife drives are only possible in vehicles belonging to the conservancy's camps. Most visitors arrive on an air transfer.

Olare-Orok Conservancy

Established in 2006 (as Olare Motorogi), this is now one of the longest established and most successful of the conservancies. It also has one of the highest concentrations of animals, including loads of predators (it has one of the highest lion densities in East Africa) and the lowest densities of tourists – just one tent for every 280 hectares. If you're looking for a Mara conservancy success story, this, along with neighbouring Naboisho, is probably our pick.

Sleeping & Eating

★Mara Plains TENTED CAMP **$$$**
(www.greatplainsconservation.com; s/d all-inclusive mid-Jun–Oct US$2700/3600, per person

US$920-1315;) This utterly captivating camp has a dozen tents with beds and showers carved from old wooden railway sleepers and quality rugs lazing across the floors. The highlight for most, though, are the big, free-standing brass bathtubs overlooking a river of wallowing hippos. In keeping with Great Plains philosophy, the camp's footprint is minimal and could be removed without a trace.

★Kicheche Bush TENTED CAMP **$$$**
(Nairobi 020-2493569; www.kicheche.com; s/d all-inclusive Aug-Oct US$925/1580, per person rest of year US$625-665; P) Considered one of the premier camps in the area, and run with the kind of casual efficiency that brings guests back, Kicheche Bush has well-spaced, enormous tents set within a light fringe of trees, beyond which stretches some of the most reliably impressive wildlife countryside in the whole Mara region. Two resident leopards are sometimes seen close to camp.

Mahali Mzuri Camp TENTED CAMP **$$$**
(www.virginlimitededition.com/en/mahali-mzuri; s/d all-inclusive mid-Jun–mid-Oct US$1620/2400, rest of year US$1100/1660;) Part of Richard Branson's portfolio of exclusive holiday destinations around the world, Mahali Mzuri has large and lovely tents that look out over the plains from an elevated hillside. Rooms are a mix of safari nostalgia (heavy leather sofas and dark-wood furnishings) with contemporary colour splashes and everything designed to maximise the views.

Getting There & Away

Olare-Orok inhabits a triangle between Aitong (in Mara North Conservancy) and the Masai Mara's Talek and Sekenani gates. While many arrive here by chartered air transfer as part of their accommodation package, those coming in their own vehicle should be aware that private vehicles are not allowed in the conservancy, although you should be allowed to continue if driving directly to your camp.

Olderikesi Conservancy

In the far southeast of the Mara region, on the border with Tanzania and the famous Serengeti, the Olderikesi Conservancy covers around 80 sq km. One of the most exclusive of the Mara conservancies, it's also one of the richest in wildlife, including large numbers of lions.

THE LOITA HILLS

To the northeast of the Masai Mara National Reserve are the little-known and spellbindingly beautiful Loita Hills. When accessing them from the Mara area, the hills start out dry and unimpressive, but if you bounce along for enough hours (and we mean hours and hours – the roads here are some of the worst in Kenya), things start to change. The vegetation becomes greener and much more luxuriant, eventually turning into a tangled jungle. The mountains also grow ever bigger, peaking at a respectable 2150m.

This is the most traditional corner of Maasai land and change, though it's coming, is way behind many other parts of the country. Despite the number of Maasai living here, it's also an area of unexpected wildlife – colobus monkeys swing through the trees, turacos light the skies with colour and huge numbers of buffaloes, forest pigs and bushbucks move through the shadows. What makes this area so extraordinary is that it's not covered by any official protection and yet the forests remain fairly untouched. The reason is that there are many places in the forests sacred to the Maasai and the elders tightly control the felling of trees and grazing of cattle. It's a brilliant example of how traditional cultures can thrive alongside wildlife without outside aid.

For the most part, accommodation out here is restricted to a few basic boardings and lodgings in some villages. But there are exceptions. Based in the beautiful and low-key **Jan's Camp** (0718139359; www.maasaitrails.com; s/d 3-night accommodation, hiking & full board package US$2308/4092) , **Maasai Trails** (0717793424, 0718139359; www.maasaitrails.com) organises hiking trips that take you out into some of the more remote reaches of Maasailand where few travellers ever reach, from day hikes out of Jan's Camp to the 12-day Great Maasailand Trail. The longer options take you completely across and over the Loita Hills and down into the Rift Valley near Lake Magadi.

Prices for walks depend on the number of people and length of hike. Stays at Jan's Camp are normally included in the walking package rates.

Kisumu

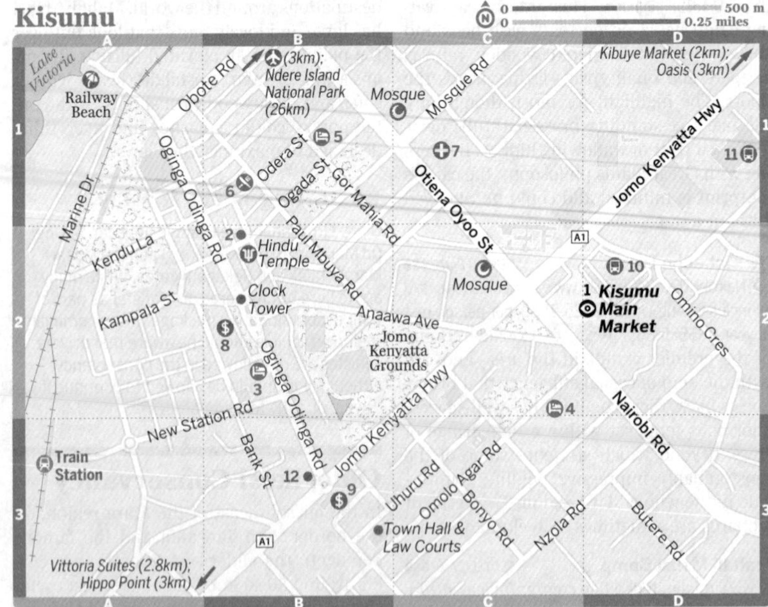

Sleeping & Eating

★Cottar's 1920s Camp TENTED CAMP **$$$**

(☎0700122122, 0733773378; www.cottars.com; s/d all-inclusive Jul-Oct US$1243/2072, rest of year s US$719-1008, d US$1200-1680;) One of the most storied camps in the Mara region, Cottar's, owned by a legendary safari family, induces a misty-eyed sense of longing from those lucky enough to have visited. As the name suggests, the enormous, stunning tents are dressed up like a well-to-do 1920s gentleman's lodging, with all manner of colonial and safari memorabilia.

But there's more to Cottar's than just elegant style. There's some of the best food of any camp, a beautiful pool and a host of activities for children. Get the guides or hosts talking about the camp and family history and you'll spend one of your most memorable evenings out on safari. Guides here are among the best in Kenya.

Getting There & Away

Although you can drive into the conservancy (contact Cottar's in advance for directions), most visitors arrive by air, flying into the airstrip, then exploring in the camp's safari vehicles.

Lake Victoria

Spread over 68,000 sq km, yet never more than 80m deep, Lake Victoria, one of the key water sources of the White Nile, ranks among East Africa's most important geographical features, but is seen by surprisingly few visitors. This is a shame, as its humid shores hide some of the most beautiful and rewarding parts of western Kenya – from untouched national parks to lively cities and tranquil islands.

Kisumu

☎057 / POP 410,000

Set on the sloping shore of Lake Victoria's Winam Gulf, Kisumu might be the third-largest city in Kenya, but its relaxed atmosphere is a world away from that of Nairobi and Mombasa. Until 1977 the port was one of the busiest in Kenya, but decline set in with the collapse of the East African Community (EAC; the common market between Kenya, Tanzania and Uganda) and the port sat virtually idle for two decades. Since the revival of the EAC in 2000, Kisumu has begun to thrive again, and though it was declared a city during its centenary celebrations in 2001, it still doesn't feel like one and

Kisumu

Top Sights

1 Kisumu Main Market D2

Activities, Courses & Tours

Ibrahim Tours Kisumu .... (see 5)
2 Zaira Tours & Travel B2

Sleeping

3 Imperial Hotel Express B2
4 New East View Hotel C2
5 New Victoria Hotel B1

Eating

6 Green Garden Restaurant B1

Information

7 Aga Khan Hospital C1
8 Barclays B2
9 Kenya Commercial Bank B3
Shiva Travels .... (see 3)

Transport

10 Bus & Matatu Station D2
11 Easy Coach D1
12 Kenya Airways B3

remains a pleasant and laid-back place with a number of interesting sights and activities nearby.

Sights & Activities

★Kisumu Main Market MARKET

(off Jomo Kenyatta Hwy; 7am-3pm) Kisumu's main market is one of Kenya's most animated markets and certainly one of its largest – it spills out onto the surrounding roads. If you're curious, or just looking for essentials such as suits or wigs, it's worth a stroll around.

Ndere Island National Park NATIONAL PARK

(www.kws.go.ke/content/ndere-island-national-park; adult/child US$25/15; 6am-6pm) Gazetted as a national park in 1986, this 4.2-sq-km island has never seen tourism take off. It is forested and very beautiful, housing a variety of bird species, plus occasionally sighted hippos, impalas (introduced) and spotted crocodiles, a lesser-known cousin of the larger Nile crocodiles.

Hippo Point Boat Trips BOATING

Hippo Point, sticking into Lake Victoria at Dunga, about 3km south of town, is a beautiful spot at which you're highly unlikely to see any hippos. It is, though, the launch point for pleasant boat rides around the lake. Prices vary among the boats, but expect to pay KSh700 per person, per hour in a group of five.

Ibrahim Tours Kisumu TOURS

(0723083045; www.ibrahimtours.weebly.com) A well-known and trusted tour guide to the many sights and sounds of the Kisumu region. Ibrahim Nandi can arrange boat trips, birdwatching tours, nature walks and excursions to Ndere Island National Park. He can be contacted directly, or through the **New Victoria Hotel** (057-2021067; Gor Mahia Rd; s without bathroom KSh1250, s/d/tr KSh1900/2700/3800).

Sleeping & Eating

New East View Hotel HOTEL $

(0711183017; Omolo Agar Rd; s KSh2000-2750, d KSh2800-3500; P) The town's standout budget option is one of many family homes in the area that have been converted into small hotels. Splashed in bright colours, the rooms have a homely, preloved feel and the welcome is, even for Kenya, unusually warm. Good hot showers with decent water pressure are another plus. Security is also tight.

Imperial Hotel Express HOTEL $$

(0713555365; www.imperialexpress.com; Oginga Odinga Rd; s/d from KSh5900/6900;) Minimalist decor, flat-screen TVs and an overall cool and contemporary look – we very much hope that the Imperial Hotel Express, which opened in 2015, catches on and causes a revolution in urban Kenyan hotels. Pitched at the lower midrange market but with standards that put to shame many much pricier establishments, it's as popular with tourists as with business travellers.

★Vittoria Suites APARTMENT $$

(0791574747; www.vittoriasuites.com/; Ring Rd, off Tom Mboya Rd; s/d US$65/85; P) It may be a touch removed from the centre, but this wonderful place has appealing, brightly painted rooms that are among the best in urban western Kenya. Some have balconies, all have flat-screen TVs and there's a really professional air to the whole place – it wouldn't look out of place in Nairobi.

★Kiboko Bay Resort RESORT $$$

(0711905540; www.kibokobay.com; Dunga Beach; s/d/tr US$140/170/200) At last, a top-end hotel with Lake Victoria frontage. Rooms here have some lovely hardwood furnishings in the safari tents, while the artful use of driftwood brings personality to the deluxe rooms. There's a well-stocked bar (even a sommelier for wine buffs) where you can watch the sunset, a fine restaurant and a classy and sophisticated atmosphere.

★**Green Garden Restaurant** INTERNATIONAL **$**
(Odera St; mains KSh380-500; ⌚8am-11pm) Surrounded by colourful murals and potted palms, the Green Garden is an oasis of culinary delight set in an Italian-themed courtyard. As you would expect, it's an expat hotspot and the word is that the tilapia in spinach and coconut sauce is the way to go. Be prepared to wait a long time for your meal.

Information

MEDICAL SERVICES

Aga Khan Hospital (☎057-2020005; Otiena Oyoo St) A large hospital with modern facilities and 24-hour emergency room.

MONEY

Barclays (Kampala St; ⌚9am-3pm Mon-Fri, 9am-noon Sat) With ATM.

Kenya Commercial Bank (Jomo Kenyatta Hwy; ⌚8am-5pm Mon-Fri, 8am-noon Sat) With ATM (Visa only).

Getting There & Away

AIR

Fly540 (p258), **Jambo Jet** (☎020-3274545; www.jambojet.com) and **Kenya Airways** (☎0711022090; www.kenya-airways.com; Alpha House, Oginga Odinga Rd) offer daily flights to Nairobi (50 minutes). Fly540 also flies to Eldoret.

Shiva Travels (☎057-2022320, 0733635200; Oginga Odinga Rd) and **Zaira Tours & Travel** (☎0722788879; Ogada St) are good for airline ticketing and hotel reservations.

BUS & MATATU

Buses, matatus and Peugeots (shared taxis) to numerous destinations within Kenya battle it out at the large bus and matatu station just north of the main market. Peugeots cost about 25% more than matatus.

Easy Coach (www.easycoach.co.ke; Jomo Kenyatta Hwy) offers the smartest buses out of town. Its booking office and departure point are in the car park just behind (and accessed through) Tusky's Shopping Centre. It has daily buses to Nairobi (KSh1400, seven hours, every couple of hours), Nakuru (KSh800, 4½ hours, every couple of hours) and Kampala (KSh1500, seven hours, 1.30pm, 1.30am and 10.30pm).

Homa Bay

☎059 / POP 60,000

Stretched out across the plains between Mt Homa and Winam Gulf on Lake Victoria, the predominantly Luo town of Homa Bay has a slow, tropical, almost central-African vibe. Not many tourists make it out here – it's a noticeably friendly place, getting about its business without worrying too much about chasing the tourist dollar.

In the town itself, there's little to do beyond wandering the dusty, music-filled streets or strolling down to the lake edge to watch the marabou storks pick through the rubbish as they wait for the fishermen and their morning catch. But there are some interesting walls in the neighbouring hills – the easiest summit to bag is the unmistakable conical mound of **Asego Hill**, which is just beyond the town and takes about an hour to clamber up – and the town makes a great base from which to visit Ruma National Park (p265) and Thimlich Ohinga (p265).

Sleeping

Homa Bay Tourist Hotel HOTEL **$$**
(☎0727112615; s/d from US$62/72; P 📶) This lakeside 'resort' is the town's original hotel, and though the rooms are rather faded they also have character and catch a lake breeze in the evening. The expansive lawns running down to the water's edge are home to many a colourful songbird and there's an outdoor bar with live music on Saturdays (so avoid rooms at the front).

Hippo Buck HOTEL **$$**
(☎0723262000; www.hippobuck.com; Kisii Rd; s US$40-70, d US$60-100; P ❄ 📶) The cheapest standard rooms here, located close to the hills, are sparkling-clean, white-tiled cubes. From there, the more you pay the fancier the rooms become, although the drab colour scheme could do with freshening; there's a fun rondavel bar in the garden. Prices are a little steep for what you get – ask for the resident rates when things are quiet.

Information

Barclays (Off C19; ⌚9am-4pm Mon-Fri, 9am-noon Sat) With ATM.

Getting There & Away

The **Easy Coach office** (www.easycoach.co.ke; C19) is just down the hill from the **bus station**

(C19), in the Total petrol station compound. It has buses to Nairobi (KSh950, eight hours) at 8.45am and 8.45pm. Several other companies and matatus (operating from the neighbouring bus station) ply the routes to Mbita (KSh250, 1½ hours), Kisii (KSh250, 1½ hours) and Kisumu (KSh300, three hours).

Ruma National Park

Bordered by the dramatic **Kanyamaa Escarpment**, and home to Kenya's only population of roans (one of Africa's rarest and largest antelope) is the seldom-visited, 120-sq-km **Ruma National Park** (☎0717176709, 020-35291129; www.kws.go.ke/content/ruma-national-park; adult/child US$25/15, vehicle from KSh300; ⏰6am-6pm). Besides roans, other rarities such as Bohor's reedbucks, Jackson's hartebeests, the tiny oribi antelope and Kenya's largest concentration of endangered Rothschild's giraffes can also be seen here. The most treasured residents are some (very hard to see) rhinos, both black and white, that have been translocated from other parks. Birdlife is also prolific, with 145 different species present, including the migratory blue swallow that arrives between June and August.

You wouldn't make this your first African safari, but it's a chance to track down some species you may not see elsewhere. The park also has an oasis feel to it, so intense is the human settlement and cultivation in this part of the country and surrounding the park.

Sights & Activities

Although dense bush in parts of the park makes wildlife-watching difficult, there's plenty to see in the open savannah areas. In just a short visit you can expect to see masses of giraffes as well as impalas, waterbucks and zebras. The area around the airstrip is particularly rewarding.

Thimlich Ohinga Archaeological Site ARCHAEOLOGICAL SITE
(☎0710236164, Nairobi 020-8164134; www.museums.or.ke/thimlich-ohinga/; KSh1000; ⏰sunrise-sunset) South of Ruma National Park, this is one of East Africa's most important archaeological sites. It holds the remains of a dry-stone enclosure, 150m in diameter and containing another five smaller enclosures, thought to date back as far as the 15th century. Its name translates in Luo as 'frightening dense forest'.

RUMA NATIONAL PARK

Why Go A surprising range of wildlife (roan antelope and Rothschild's giraffes are the pick) and very few visitors.

When to Go Best in the dry season of June to October. During the rains, tracks can become impassable.

Practicalities Easily accessible from Homa Bay, but to be there at dawn when animals are most visible, stay in the park.

Budget Tips The park is set up for those with vehicles, but if you don't have your own wheels, contact the **KWS Warden's Office** (⏰9am-4pm Mon-Fri, 10am-2pm Sat) in Homa Bay, who may be able to arrange a jeep for you.

Sleeping

Oribi Guesthouse COTTAGE $$
(☎0717176709; www.kws.go.ke; cottage excl breakfast US$100; P) This KWS-run guesthouse, near the park headquarters at Kamato Gate, is extortionate if there are only two of you, but quite good value for groups. It has dramatic views over the Lambwe Valley and is well equipped with solar power, hot showers and a fully functioning kitchen, but bring your own food.

Getting There & Away

In your own vehicle, head a couple of kilometres south from Homa Bay and turn right onto the Mbita road. After about 12km you'll come to the main access road, which is signed just as Kenya Wildlife Service (coming from Homa Bay, you might not see the sign as it faces the other way). From there it's another 11km to the park entrance. The park's roads are in decent shape, but require a strong, high-clearance 4WD in the rainy season.

Western Highlands

Despite media impressions depicting a land of undulating savannah stretching to the horizon, the real heart and soul of Kenya, and the area where most people live, are the luminous green highlands. Benefiting from reliable rainfall and fertile soil, the Western Highlands are the agricultural powerhouse of the country; the south is cash-crop country, with vast patchworks of tea plantations covering the region around Kisii and

Kericho; while further north, near Kitale and Eldoret, dense cultivation takes over.

The settlements here are predominantly agricultural service towns, with little of interest unless you need a chainsaw or water barrel. For visitors, the real attractions lie outside these places – the rolling tea fields around Kericho, the tropical beauty of Kakamega Forest, trekking on Mt Elgon, the prolific birdlife in Saiwa Swamp National Park and exploring the dramatic Cherangani Hills.

Kisii

058 / POP 120,000

Kisii is an important transit town for western Kenya and there's a good chance you'll pass through at some point in your explorations here. Some travellers also use it as an access point to the region's renowned soapstone carvings in nearby Tabaka. Important as it may be, Kisii wouldn't win a beauty contest. Actually, that's being kind. Kisii is a noisy, polluted and congested mess and most people (quite sensibly) roll right on through without even stopping.

Sleeping & Eating

St Vincent Guesthouse GUESTHOUSE $
(0733650702; s/d/tw KSh1700/2200/2700; P) This Catholic-run guesthouse off the Moi Hwy isn't the place for a party, but it's hands down the best place to stay in Kisii. Rooms are very clean and cosy, it's quiet and security is good. No alcohol allowed.

Nile Hotel HOTEL $
(0786706089; Hospital Rd; r KSh1000-1600, tw KSh2000) Clean, cheap rooms and a central location make the Nile the best deal in the town centre, although their claim to four stars is, shall we say, aspirational rather than descriptive. The 2nd-floor restaurant (mains KSh250 to KSh400) has a commanding view of the chaos below.

KISII SOAPSTONE

While the feted Kisii soapstone obviously comes from this area, it's not on sale here. Quarrying and carving take place in the Gusii village of **Tabaka**, 23km northwest of Kisii. Soapstone is relatively soft and pliable (as far as rocks go), and with simple hand tools and scraps of sandpaper the sculptors carve chess sets, bowls, animals and the unmistakable abstract figures of embracing couples. Each artisan specialises in one design before passing it on to someone else to be smoothed with wet sandpaper and polished with wax. Most pieces are destined for the curio shops of Nairobi and Mombasa and trade-aid shops around the world. As you would expect, prices are cheaper here than elsewhere. If you're undaunted by adding a few heavy rocks to your backpack, you can save a considerable sum by buying close to the source.

Getting There & Away

The congested matatu terminal in the centre of town is a chaos of loud and often somewhat drunk people trying to bundle you onto the nearest matatu, whether or not you want to go where it's going. If you do manage to pick your own matatu, you'll find regular departures to Homa Bay (KSh250, 1½ hours), Kisumu (KSh300, 2½ hours), Kericho (KSh500, two hours) and Isebania (KSh300, 1¾ hours) on the Tanzanian border.

Tabaka matatus (KSh100, 45 minutes) leave from Cemetery Rd. Returning, it is sometimes easier to catch a *boda-boda* (motorcycle taxi; KSh100) to the 'Tabaka junction' and pick up a Kisii-bound matatu there.

Easy Coach (www.easycoach.co.ke; Moi Hwy) has twice-daily departures to Nairobi (KSh900, eight hours, 10am and 9.30pm). It also has a bus to Narok (KSh500, four hours, 1pm), which is handy for the Mara.

Kericho

052 / POP 180,000

Kericho is a haven of tranquillity and one of Kenya's most agreeable towns. Its surrounds are blanketed by a thick patchwork of manicured tea plantations, each seemingly hemmed in by distant stands of evergreens, and even the town centre seems as orderly as the tea gardens. With a pleasant climate and a number of things to see and do, Kericho makes for a very calming couple of days.

Sights & Activities

Momul Tea Factory TOUR
(KSh500; Mon-Sat) The factory most often visited around Kericho is the Momul Tea Factory, 28km from the town. The factory has 64 collection sites servicing the area's small-scale farmers; it processes a

Kericho

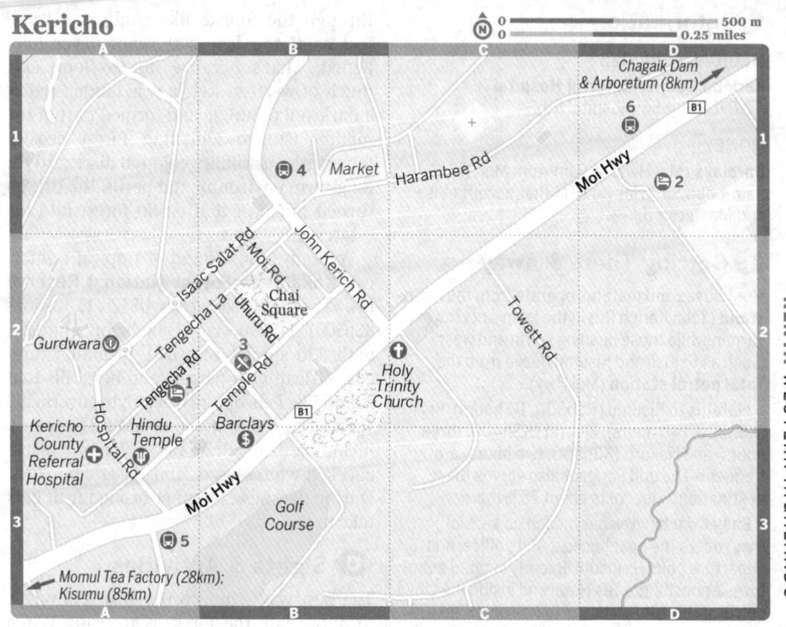

staggering 15 million kilos of green leaf a year. Note: no processing takes place on Mondays.

Harman Kirui TOUR
(☎0721843980; kmtharman@yahoo.com; per person KSh200) Mr Harman Kirui organises fun and informative tea estate and factory tours. Most tours involve walking around the fields and watching the picking (note that the pickers don't work on Sunday). If you want to actually see the process through to the end and visit a factory, you should book at least four days in advance by emailing Harman directly.

Sleeping & Eating

New Sunshine Hotel HOTEL $
(☎052-2030037, 0725146601; Tengecha Rd; s/d/tr KSh2300/3000/3500; 📶) Without doubt the best budget hotel in town (not that the competition is especially stiff). The rooms, while not large, are spotless and the showers are actually hot rather than lukewarm. The attached restaurant (meals KSh350 to KSh550) does a roaring trade.

Tea Hotel HOTEL $$
(☎0714510824; Moi Hwy; camping KSh700, s/d US$70/95; P📶🏊) This grand property was built in the 1950s by the Brooke Bond company and still has a lot of (very faded) period charm. The hotel's most notable features are the vast hallways and dining rooms full of mounted animal heads, and its beautiful gardens with their tea-bush backdrops. Many of the rooms, though, are literally falling to pieces.

Litny's Restaurant KENYAN $
(Temple Rd; mains KSh250-500; ⏲6am-8pm) Along with New Sunshine Hotel, this is regarded as one of the better restaurants in town, though in truth the fried chicken and chips here were no different to the fried chicken and chips we ate elsewhere.

Kericho

Sleeping
1 New Sunshine Hotel A2
2 Tea Hotel D1

Eating
3 Litny's Restaurant B2

Transport
4 Bus & Matatu Stand B1
5 Buses to Kisumu, Kisii & Homa Bay A3
6 Easy Coach D1

Information

MEDICAL SERVICES

Kericho County Referral Hospital (☎0780174556; Hospital Rd)

MONEY

Barclays (Moi Hwy; ⌚9am-4pm Mon-Fri, 9am-noon Sat) Has an ATM that accepts Visa and Mastercard.

Getting There & Away

Most buses and matatus operate from the **main stand** (John Kerich Rd) in the town's northwest corner, while those heading south and west (such as to Kisii and Kisumu) leave from the **Total petrol station** (Moi Hwy).

Matatus to Kisumu (KSh300, 1½ hours), Kisii (KSh300, two hours), Eldoret (KSh400, three hours) and Nakuru (KSh300, two hours) are frequent. The odd Peugeot also serves these destinations, but costs about 25% more.

Easy Coach (www.easycoach.co.ke; Moi Hwy) offers the best buses, but its office, and departure point, is inconveniently located out of town, opposite the Tea Hotel and inside the Libya petrol station. It has buses to Nairobi (KSh1100) throughout the day, as well as frequent buses to Nakuru (KSh550) and Kisumu (KSh500).

Kakamega Forest

☎056

Kakamega Forest, surrounding the town of Kakamega, is like nowhere in Kenya. Indeed, beneath Kakamega's dense, dark canopy – when the monkeys caterwaul through the treetops and birdsong filters through the foliage like sunlight – you'll feel as if the last 200 years never happened. That's because not so long ago, much of western Kenya was hidden under a dark veil of jungle and formed part of the mighty Guineo-Congolian forest ecosystem. With customary colonial disregard for long-term environmental perils, the British turned much of that virgin forest into tea estates.

As Kenya's last stand of tropical rainforest, **Kakamega Forest National Reserve** (www.kws.go.ke; adult/child US$25/15, vehicles KSh300) is especially good for abirders, with 330 species recorded, including turacos, African grey parrots and hornbills that sound like helicopters when flying overhead. Kakamega is also home to several primates, including de Brazza's, colobus, black-cheeked-white-nosed, and Sykes' monkeys. During darkness, hammer-headed fruit bats take to the air.

ANYONE FOR TEA?

Kenya is one of the world's largest tea exporters, along with the likes of India and Sri Lanka, with tea accounting for around 30% of the country's export income. It's unique in that up to 80% of its tea is produced by small landholders.

Tea picking is a great source of employment around Kericho, with mature bushes picked every 17 days and the same worker continually picking the same patch. Good pickers collect their own body weight in tea each day!

Despite Kericho producing some of the planet's best black tea, you will have trouble finding a cup of the finest blends here – most is exported.

Sights & Activities

The best way – indeed the only real way – to appreciate the forest is to walk. While guides are not compulsory, they are well worth the extra expense. Not only do they prevent you from getting lost, but most are walking encyclopaedias and will reel off both the Latin and common names of almost any plant or insect you care to point out, along with any of its medicinal properties.

There are two main patches of forest; confusingly, they often use the same name. The northern Kakamega Forest National Reserve (also known as the Buyangu area) has a variety of habitats, but is generally very dense with considerable areas of primary forest and regenerating secondary forest. The forest here is managed by the KWS. There's a total ban on grazing, wood collection and cultivation in this zone. The southern section (known as Isecheno) forms the Kakamega Forest Reserve. Predominantly forested, this region supports several communities and is under considerable pressure from both farming and illegal logging, but entry fees are lower and it has better accommodation.

Kakamega Forest Reserve PARK

(adult/child KSh600/150) Kakamega Forest Reserve is the more degraded area of the forest, yet it's the more popular area with tourists. The five-hour return hike to

Lirhanda Hill for sunrise or sunset is highly recommended. An interesting short walk (2.6km) to a 35m-high watchtower affords views over the forest canopy and small grassland.

Buyangu Hill Lookout VIEWPOINT

It's a 4km drive or walk from the park entrance to Buyangu Hill, from where there are uninterrupted views east to the Nandi Escarpment.

Lirhanda Hill Lookout VIEWPOINT

Depending on where you're staying, it can be about a five-hour return hike to Lirhanda Hill. Being there for sunrise or sunset is highly recommended.

Kakamega Rainforest Tour Guides WALKING

(KRTG; ☎0726951764; short/long walk per person KSh600/1200) Next to the forest reserve office, KRTG supplies knowledgeable guides to the forest for a variety of walks, including recommended night walks (KSh1500 per person) and sunrise/sunset walks (KSh1000 per person). These are some of the best-value nature walks you'll find in Kenya, with lots of wildlife to spot.

KEEP WALKING

(☎0704851701) The Kakamega Environmental Education Programme (KEEP) is a locally established initiative that aims to educate the local community and visitors on the wonders of the Kakamega Forest and the threats it's under. The organisation also runs various community and conservation programmes and has been credited with much of the success in slowing the pace of destruction of the forest.

Kafkogoa TOUR

(☎0724143064) Guides from this association cost KSh2000 for up to three hours and can be arranged at the park gates.

Sleeping & Eating

Forest Rest House GUESTHOUSE $

(camping KSh650, r per person KSh500) The four rooms of this wooden house, perched on stilts 2m above the ground and with views straight onto a mass of jungle, might be very basic (no electricity, no bedding and cold-water baths that look like they'd crash through the floorboards if you used one), but they'll bring out the inner Tarzan in even the most obstinate city slicker.

Kakamega Forest

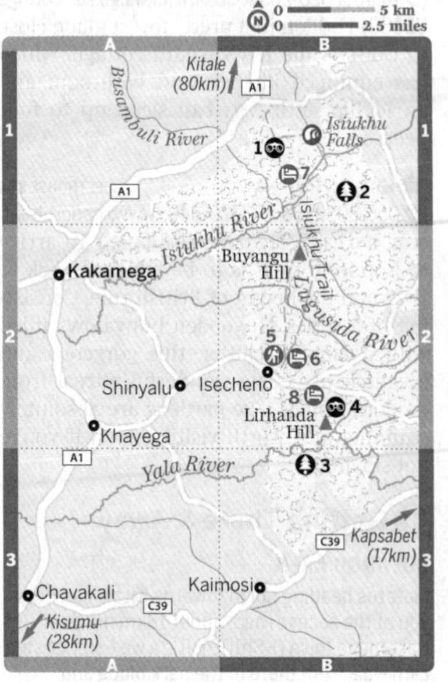

Kakamega Forest

Sights

1	Buyangu Hill Lookout	B1
2	Kakamega Forest National Reserve	B1
3	Kakamega Forest Reserve	B3
4	Lirhanda Hill Lookout	B2

Activities, Courses & Tours

	Kafkogoa	(see 5)
5	Kakamega Rainforest Tour Guides	B2
	KEEP	(see 5)

Sleeping

6	Forest Rest House	B2
7	Isikuti Guesthouse	B1
8	Rondo Retreat	B2
	Udo's Bandas & Campsite	(see 7)

Udo's Bandas & Campsite BANDAS $

(☎Nairobi 020-2654658; www.kws.go.ke; camping adult/child US$20/15, bandas per person US$40) Named after Udo Savalli, a well-known ornithologist, this lovely KWS site is tidy, well maintained and has seven simple thatched *bandas*. Nets are provided, but you will need your own sleeping bag and other supplies. There are long-drop toilets, bucket showers and a communal cooking and dining shelter.

Isikuti Guesthouse GUESTHOUSE **$$**
(☎Nairobi 020-2654658; www.kws.go.ke; cottage US$60) Hidden in a pretty forest glade close to Udo's is the KWS Isikuti cottage, which has equipped kitchen and bathroom and an idyllic setting. It can sleep up to four people.

★ **Rondo Retreat** GUESTHOUSE **$$$**
(☎056-2030268, 0733299149; www.rondoretreat.com; s/d half board US$200/275; P) To arrive at Rondo Retreat is to be whisked back to 1922 and the height of British rule. Consisting of a series of wooden bungalows filled with a family's clutter, this gorgeous and eccentric place is a wonderful retreat from modern Kenya. The gardens are absolutely stunning and worth visiting even if you're not staying.

Getting There & Away

BUYANGU AREA

Matatus heading north towards Kitale can drop you at the access road, about 18km north of Kakamega town (KSh100). It's a well-signposted 2km walk from there to the park office and Udo's (p269).

> ### KAKAMEGA FOREST
>
> **Why Go** This unique rainforest ecosystem has more than 330 species of birds, 400 species of butterflies and seven different primate species, including the rare de Brazza's monkey.
>
> **When to Go** The best viewing months are June, August and October, when many migrant bird species arrive. October also sees many wildflowers bloom, while December to March are the driest months.
>
> **Practicalities** As the northern section of the forest is managed by KWS and the southern section by the Kenyan Forest Department, it is not possible to visit the whole park without paying both sets of admission charges. Both areas have their pros and cons.
>
> **Budget Tips** Entry fees to the southern Kakamega Forest Reserve are lower, and accommodation generally cheaper, than in the northern Kakamega Forest National Reserve, so it makes sense for budget travellers to base themselves there.

ISECHENO AREA

Regular matatus link Kakamega with Shinyalu (KSh90), but few go on to Isecheno. Shinyalu is also accessed by a rare matatu service from Khayega. From Shinyalu you will probably need to take a *boda-boda* to Isecheno (KSh100).

The improved roads are still treacherous after rain and you may prefer to walk once you've seen the trouble vehicles can have. Shinyalu is about 7km from Khayega and 10km from Kakamega. From Shinyalu it's 5km to Isecheno.

The dirt road from Isecheno continues east to Kapsabet, but transport is rare.

Eldoret

☎053 / POP 335,000

The Maasai originally referred to this area as *eldore* (stony river) after the nearby Sosiani River. Today, Eldoret is a thriving service town straddling the Kenya–Uganda highway. It's the principal economic hub of western Kenya, but for the traveller there is little to see and less to do. The highlight is a visit to the **Doinyo Lessos Creameries Cheese Factory** (☎020-2115300, 0726600204; www.doinyolessos.com; Kenyatta St; ⏲8am-6pm) to stock up on any one of 20 different varieties of cheese. It's also a gateway to Iten, the home of long-distance Kenyan running.

Eldoret is a Kalenjin stronghold (the tribe of former president Daniel arap Moi and controversial vice-president William Ruto) and something of a bellweather for the political health of the nation. In 2008, it achieved notoriety when 35 people (mostly Kikuyus) were burnt alive in a church on the outskirts of town. This incident was the largest single loss of life during the 2007 post-election violence.

Sleeping & Eating

Keellu Resort Centre HOTEL **$**
(☎Nairobi 020-2601258; www.keelluresort.com; Iten Kapkoi Rd; s/d from KSh2500/4000; P) Around 36km northeast of Eldoret in high-altitude Iten, Keellu Resort Centre was founded in 2012 by world-renowned athlete Wilson Kipsang. It's a decent base if you're here to visit or train at the High Altitude Training Centre (p272). Rooms are tidy rather than exciting, but come with mosquito nets. The restaurant serves Kenyan, Chinese and Indian dishes.

Eldoret

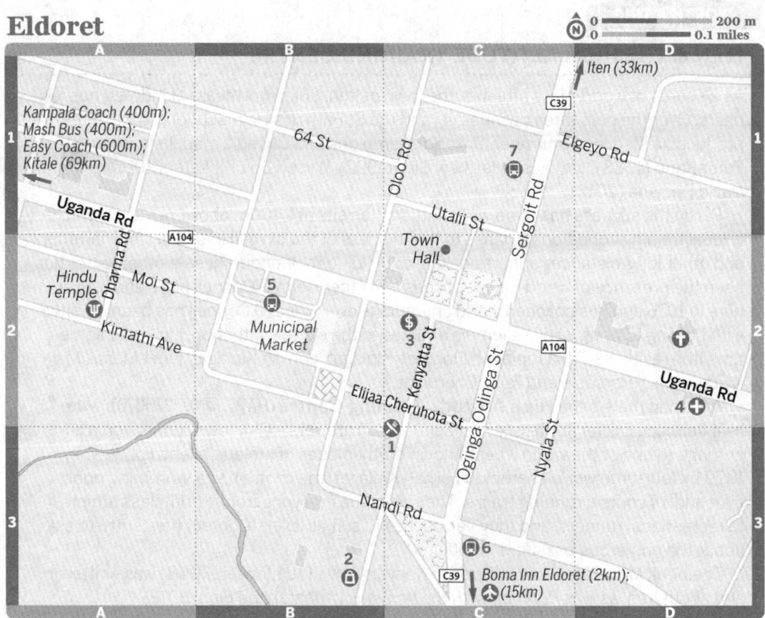

★**Boma Inn Eldoret** HOTEL $$$
(0719025000; www.theboma.co.ke/boma-inn-eldoret/; Ramogi Dr, off Elgon Rd; s/d/ste from US$165/198/330;) This swish business-class hotel, 2km from the city centre, is hands down the best place to stay in Eldoret. The large rooms are smart and stylishly decorated, and they have comfortable beds, big desks to work at and piping-hot showers. There's a decent in-house restaurant as well as a pool and gym. All profits go to the Kenyan Red Cross.

Poa Place Resort HOTEL $$$
(0703129990; www.poaplace.co.ke; off B54; safari tent/cottage US$144/206;) The safari tents on manicured lawns and between high hedgerows are a little incongruous, but the quality of both the tents and lovely cottages is unimpeachable. Colourful furnishings, four-poster beds and hardwood floors make staying here a real pleasure.

★**Sunjeel Palace** INDIAN $$
(0720554747; Kenyatta St; mains KSh400-650; 11am-11pm;) This formal, dark and spicy Indian restaurant serves superb, real-deal curries. Portion sizes are decent and if you mop up all the gravy with a freshly baked butter naan, you'll be as satisfied as Ganesh himself.

Eldoret

Eating
1 Sunjeel Palace C3

Shopping
2 Doinyo Lessos Creameries Cheese Factory B3

Information
3 Barclays C2
4 Eldoret Hospital D2

Transport
5 Bus & Matatu Stand B2
6 Local Matatus C3
7 Matatus to Iten & Kabarnet C1

Information

MEDICAL SERVICES

Barclays (Uganda Rd; 9am-4pm Mon-Fri, 9am-noon Sat) With ATM.

MONEY

Eldoret Hospital (053-2062000; www.eldorethospital.com; Makasembo Rd; 24hr) One of Kenya's best hospitals, with a 24-hour emergency unit. It's off Uganda Rd.

WORTH A TRIP

ITEN & THE HIGH ALTITUDE TRAINING CENTRE

As a source of world-class athletes, the town of Iten, 36km northeast of Eldoret, has few peers. Over the past three decades, it (and the St Patrick's High School in particular) has produced a staggering number of world champions and Olympic medalists, among them Peter Rono (1988 Olympics), Matthew Birir (1992), Wilson Boit Kipketer (2000) and David Rudisha (2012).

Partly the success has to do with altitude: Iten sits at 2400m above sea level, which is ideal training conditions (thanks to the thinness of the oxygen in the air) for marathon and other long-distance runners seeking to build up their endurance. Another factor has been the presence of world-class coaches – Brother Colm O'Connell of Ireland arrived here in 1976 and has coached world champions ever since; O'Connell has been credited with helping to bring Kenya's female athletes to the world's attention, including sometime Iten residents Edna Kiplagat, Florence Kiplagat, Lornah Kiplagat, Linet Masai, Mary Keitany, Sally Barsosio and Rose Cheruiyot.

And then there's the **High Altitude Training Centre** (HATC; ☎0772700701; www.hatc-iten.com; Eldoret Rd, Iten; ⏰8am-8pm), which attracts well-known runners on a pilgrimage to one of the world's best-known mother lodes of athletic talent. Founded in 1999 by four-time world champion Lornah Kiplagat, the centre has a swimming pool, gym and, of course, running tracks. They welcome everyone from world-class athletes to recreational runners, and they've coaches to suit all levels. Contact the centre to ask about the numerous packages on offer.

The book *More Fire: How to Run the Kenyan Way* (Toby Tanser; 2008) was written in and about Iten, as was *Running with the Kenyans* (Adharanand Finn; 2012).

If you don't have your own wheels, matatus (KSh120, one hour) connect Iten with Eldoret's Sergoit Rd.

ℹ Getting There & Away

AIR

Fly540 (p258) has flights that connect Eldoret with Nairobi and (less frequently) Lodwar.

Jambo Jet (p264) This Kenya Airways subsidiary flies to/from Nairobi.

MATATU

The main **matatu stand** is in the centre of town by the municipal market on Uganda Rd, though some local matatus and more Kericho services leave from Nandi Rd. Irregular matatus to Iten and Kabarnet leave from Sergoit Rd. Further west on Uganda Rd, matatus leave for Malaba on the Uganda border.

BUS

A string of bus companies lines Uganda Rd west of the Postbank. Most service Nairobi via Nakuru.

Easy Coach (Uganda Rd) Buses to Nairobi (KSh1250, 9.30am and 10pm, eight hours).

Kampala Coach (Uganda Rd) Noon and midnight buses to Kampala (KSh2000, six hours).

Mash Bus (☎0730889000; www.masheastafrica.com; Uganda Rd) Buses to numerous cities across Kenya.

ℹ Getting Around

A matatu to or from the international airport costs KSh100, and a taxi will cost around KSh1000 to KSh1500. *Boda-bodas* (especially the motorised variety) can be found on most street corners.

Kitale

☎054 / POP 120,000

Agricultural Kitale is a friendly market town with a couple of interesting museums and a bustling market. But we like it best as the gateway to some of the more rewarding excursions in this part of the country. It makes a fine waystation en route to explorations of Mt Elgon and Saiwa Swamp national parks. It also serves as the take-off point for a trip up to the western side of Lake Turkana.

◉ Sights

Treasures of Africa Museum MUSEUM

(☎0722547765; A1 Hwy; KSh500; ⏰9am-12.30pm & 2-5pm Mon-Sat) This private museum is the personal collection of Mr Wilson, a former colonial officer in Uganda and quite a character. Based mainly on his experiences with the Karamojong people of northern Uganda, Mr Wilson's small museum illustrates his theory that a universal worldwide agricultural culture existed as far back as the last ice age.

Kitale Museum MUSEUM
(📞054-30996, Nairobi 020-3742741; www.museums.or.ke/81-2/; A1 Hwy; adult/child KSh500/250; ⏲9.30am-6pm) Founded on the collection of butterflies, birds and ethnographic memorabilia left to the nation in 1967 by the late Lieutenant Colonel Stoneham, this museum has an interesting range of ethnographic displays of the Pokot, Akamba, Marakwet and Turkana peoples. There are also any number of stuffed dead things shot by various colonial types, including a hedgehog and a cheetah with a lopsided face.

Sleeping & Eating

Iroko Twigs Hotel HOTEL $
(📞0773475884; Kenyatta St; s/d KSh3200/3800; 📶) If you can overlook a few missing bathroom tiles and a little wear and tear, this is far and away the smartest hotel in town, although that's not saying a whole lot. The rooms (doubles more than singles) are pleasingly decorated with polished wood and art, and there are coffee- and tea-making facilities and even dressing gowns in the wardrobes.

Alakara Hotel HOTEL $
(📞072280023; Kenyatta St; s/d KSh1600/2200, without bathroom KSh1200/1350; 🅿) The most inviting super cheapie in town is safe, friendly, clean and has comfortable beds and reliable(ish) hot water. It also has a good bar, restaurant and TV room. Or to put it another way: this is as good as it gets.

Iroko Boulevard Restaurant KENYAN $
(Askari Rd; mains KSh150-300; ⏲6.30am-6.30pm) It's got style, it's got glamour, it's got big-city aspirations and it's totally unexpected in Kitale. With cheap dishes and an old Morris car hanging from the ceiling, this is the most popular place to eat in town. The food is reliably good with a few international dishes to vary things a little.

Information

Barclays (Bank St; ⏲9am-4pm Mon-Fri, 9am-noon Sat) With ATM. Other banks are next door.

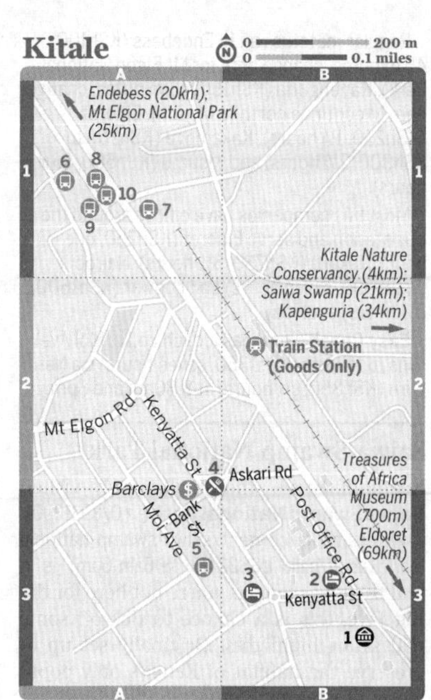

Kitale

Sights
1 Kitale Museum B3

Sleeping
2 Alakara Hotel B3
3 Iroko Twigs Hotel B3

Eating
4 Iroko Boulevard Restaurant A2

Transport
5 Easy Coach A3
6 Main Bus & Matatu Park A1
7 Matatus to Eldoret & Nairobi A1
8 Matatus to Kapenguria A1
9 Matatus to Kisumu & Kakamega A1
10 Matatus to Marich Pass A1

Getting There & Away

Matatus, buses and Peugeots are grouped by destination, and spread in and around the main bus and matatu park. Matatus run from different points in the scrum. Those to Eldoret and Nairobi leave from the other side of the main road, the departure points for Kapenguria and Marich Pass are right next to each other, while those to Kisumu and Kakamega are a further block west.

Regular matatus run to Endebess (KSh100, 45 minutes, change here for Mt Elgon National Park), Kapenguria (KSh150, 45 minutes, change here to continue north to Marich), Eldoret (KSh250, 1¼ hours), Kakamega (KSh250 to KSh300, 2½ hours) and Kisumu (KSh500, four hours).

Most bus companies have offices around the bus station and serve Eldoret (KSh250, one hour), Nakuru (KSh750, 3½ hours), Nairobi (KSh1000, seven hours) and Lodwar (KSh1600, 8½ hours) each day.

Easy Coach (www.easycoach.co.ke; Moi Ave) runs to Nairobi (KSh1350, seven hours) via Nakuru (KSh850, six hours) at 8.30am and 8pm.

Saiwa Swamp National Park

North of Kitale, the small, rarely visited **Saiwa Swamp National Park** (0789312901; www.kws.go.ke/content/saiwa-swamp-national-park; adult/child US$22/13; 6am-6pm) is a real treat – as long as you're not here for the Big Five, this is a chance to tick off some real safari highlights. Originally set up to preserve the habitat of Kenya's only population of sitatunga antelope, the 15.5-sq-km reserve is also home to blue, vervet and de Brazza's monkeys and some 370 species of birds. The fluffy black-and-white colobus monkey and the impressive crowned crane are both present, and you may see Cape clawless and spot-throated otters (watchtower 4 is the best place from which to look for these).

SAIWA SWAMP NATIONAL PARK

Why Go Kenya's smallest national park has great appeal for ornithologists, thanks to its prolific birdlife. It's also the most reliable place to see the semi-aquatic sitatunga antelope.

When to Go The park can be visited at any time, though access roads become very slippery after rain.

Practicalities This is an easy and cheap park for independent travellers to visit. The park is only accessible on foot and walking trails skirt the swamp. Duckboards go right across it, and there are some rickety observation towers. Guides are not compulsory, though your experience will be greatly enhanced by taking one.

Budget Tips Stay in Kitale and catch a matatu to the junction for the park. Walk to the gates and explore the park without the aid of a guide.

Sleeping

Sitatunga Public Campsite CAMPGROUND $
(0789312901; www.kws.go.ke/content/saiwa-swamp-national-park; camping US$20; P) A lovely site with flush toilets, showers, two covered cooking *bandas* and colobus monkeys in the trees above. It's close to the park entrance from where it's signposted, and adjacent to **Sitatunga Treetop House** (0789312901; www.kws.go.ke; tree house US$50; P).

★ **Sirikwa Safaris** GUESTHOUSE $$
(Barnley's Guesthouse; 0723917953; www.sirikwasafaris.com; camping KSh700, tents excl breakfast s/d KSh2500/3000, s/d with shared bathroom excl breakfast KSh3500/6000) Owned and run by the family that started Saiwa, this beautiful old farmhouse is 11km from the swamp. You can choose between camping in the grounds, sleeping in a well-appointed safari tent or, best of all, opting for one of the two bedrooms full of *National Geographic* magazines, old ornaments and antique sinks.

Getting There & Away

The park is 18km northeast of Kitale. Take a matatu towards Kapenguria and get out at the second signposted turn-off (KSh90, 15 minutes), from where it's a 5km walk or KSh100 *moto-taxi* ride.

Mt Elgon National Park

Straddling the Ugandan border and peaking with Koitoboss (4187m), Kenya's third-highest peak, and Uganda's Wagagai (4321m), the slopes of **Mt Elgon** (020-3539903 Nairobi; www.kws.go.ke/content/mount-elgon-national-park; park entrance adult/child US$26/17, vehicles from KSh300; 6am-6pm) are a sight indeed – or at least they would be if they weren't buried under a blanket of mist and drizzle most of the time.

With rainforest at the base, the vegetation ascends through bamboo jungle to alpine moorland featuring giant groundsel and giant lobelia plants.

Common animals include buffaloes, bushbucks (both of which are usually grazing on the airstrip near Cholim Gate), olive baboons, giant forest hogs and duikers. The

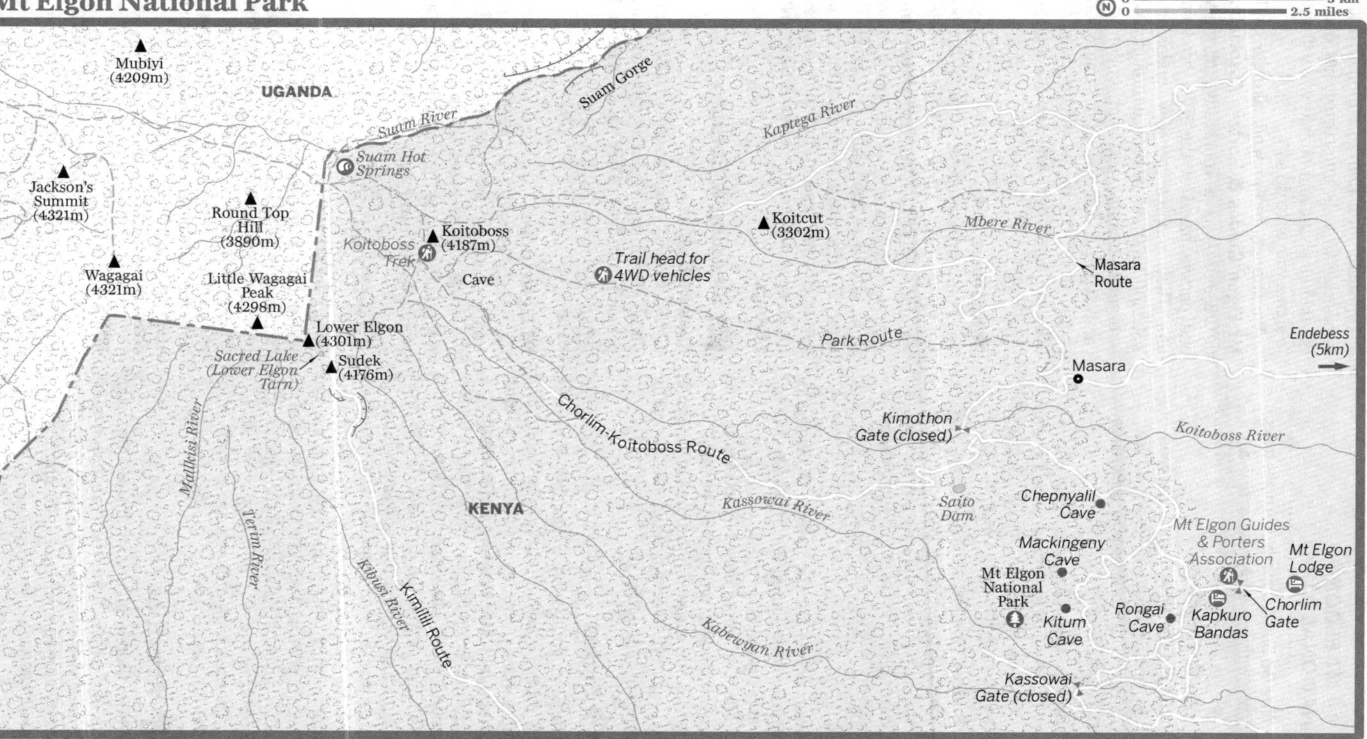

Mt Elgon National Park
0 5 km
0 2.5 miles
Mubiyi (4209m)
UGANDA
Suam Gorge
Suam River
Kaptega River
Suam Hot Springs
Jackson's Summit (4321m)
Round Top Hill (3890m)
Koitoboss (4187m)
Koitoboss Trek
Koitcut (3302m)
Mbere River
Trail head for 4WD vehicles
Masara Route
Wagagai (4321m)
Little Wagagai Peak (4298m)
Cave
Park Route
Endebess (5km)
Lower Elgon (4301m)
Sacred Lake (Lower Elgon Tarn)
Sudek (4176m)
Masara
Kimothon Gate (closed)
Koitoboss River
Chorlim-Koitoboss Route
Mallkisi River
Terim River
KENYA
Kassowai River
Saito Dam
Chepnyalil Cave
Mt Elgon Guides & Porters Association
Mackingeny Cave
Mt Elgon Lodge
Mt Elgon National Park
Kibusi River
Kimililli Route
Kitum Cave
Rongai Cave
Kapkuro Bandas
Chorlim Gate
Kabewyan River
Kassowai Gate (closed)

MT ELGON NATIONAL PARK

Why Go Some superb overnight treks along with some interesting half-day options to caves occasionally visited by salt-loving elephants.

When to Go It's extremely wet most of the year. Serious trekkers should visit between December and February when it's at its driest.

Practicalities Waterproof gear and warm clothing are essential, as the area is as chilly as it is wet. Altitude may also be a problem for some people.

Budget Tips The easiest section of the park to visit is the area accessed through Chorlim Gate, from where you can walk to the caves and surrounding forest.

lower forests are the habitat of black-and-white colobus monkeys and blue and de Brazza's monkeys.

There are more than 240 species of birds here, including red-fronted parrots, Ross's turacos and casqued hornbills. On the peaks you may even see a lammergeier dropping bones from the thin air.

Sights

The Elkony Caves are a highlight of visiting Mt Elgon National Park. Four main lava tubes (caves) are open to visitors: **Kitum**, **Chepnyalil**, **Mackingeny** and **Rongai**.

Kitum extends more than 200m underground, while Mackingeny, with a waterfall cascading across the entrance, is the most spectacular of the caves and has colonies of large fruit bats and smaller horseshoe bats towards the rear. If you plan on entering, be sure to bring whatever kind of footwear you feel will cope well with 100 years of accumulated, dusty bat shit and all the roaches that feed off it.

The caves are a 6km drive or walk from Chorlim Gate.

Activities

While there's plenty of interesting wildlife and plants here, the real reason most people visit Mt Elgon National Park is to stand atop the summit high above Kenya and Uganda.

Unusually for a Kenyan national park, it is possible to walk unescorted, but due to the odd elephant and buffalo you will need to sign a waiver to do so.

We strongly recommend taking a guide. **Mt Elgon Guides & Porters Association** (☎0733919347) is a cooperative of guides and porters based at the KWS headquarters. Their services (per day guide/porter KSh3500/1200) can be booked through KWS.

If you're trekking, your only option is to camp (US$20). The fee is the same whether you drop tent in the official campsites (Chorlim, Nyati, Saito and Rongai) or on any old flat spot during your trek.

★Koitoboss Trek HIKING

The climb up Koitoboss is one of the best Mt Elgon treks. Allow at least four days for any round-trip hikes, and two or three days for any direct ascent of Koitoboss from Chorlim Gate. Once you reach the summit, there are a number of interesting options for the descent, including descending northwest into the crater to **Suam Hot Springs**.

Sleeping & Eating

Kapkuro Bandas BANDAS $

(☎020-3539903; www.kws.go.ke; banda US$40) These decent stone *bandas* can sleep three people in two beds. They have simple bathrooms and small, fully equipped kitchen areas.

Mt Elgon Lodge LODGE $$

(☎0722875768; s/d/tr US$45/70/110) A few hundred metres before the main gate, this very faded lodge is set in grassy grounds with views down to the lowlands. Rooms are plain but clean and meals are available.

Information

ENTRY & EXIT FORMALITIES

With prior arrangement through the KWS it's theoretically possible to walk into Uganda and back again without needing to go through immigration procedures, or to cross into Uganda and complete formalities in the nearest town. Note: these are quite recent developments and we're yet to hear from anyone who's actually done it.

MAPS

KWS produces a 1:35,000 map (KSh450) of the park as well as a guidebook (KSh750), both of which are sold at Chorlim Gate.

Getting There & Away

From Kitale, catch an Endebess-bound matatu to the park junction (KSh100, 45 minutes), from where it's a 15-minute motorbike taxi ride (KSh100 to KSh150) to the park gate. Be sure to grab your driver's phone number so you can contact him for a ride back to Endebess.

CENTRAL HIGHLANDS & LAIKIPIA

The Central Highlands are the spiritual heartland of Kenya's largest tribe, the Kikuyu. This is the land the Mau Mau fought for, that the colonists coveted and whose natural, cyclical patterns define the lives of the country's largest rural population. These highlands form one of the most evocative sections of Africa's Great Rift Valley. It is here that Mt Kenya, Africa's second-highest mountain, rises into the clouds – climbing it is one of the great rites of passage of African travel.

In its shadow lie two of Kenya's most intriguing national parks: rhino- and lion-rich Meru National Park, and Aberdare National Park, home to some of the oldest mountains on the continent. Finally there's Laikipia, fount of so much that's good about modern conservation. It's also the scene for some of the best wildlife watching anywhere in Kenya.

Nyeri

061 / POP 225,357

Nyeri is a welcoming and bustling Kikuyu market town. It's as busy as the Central Highlands get, but unless you have a thing for chaotic open-air bazaars and the restless energy of Kikuyu and white Kenyans selling maize, bananas, arrowroot, coffee and macadamia nuts, there's no real reason to linger for longer than it takes to plot your onward journey.

Central Highlands & Laikipia

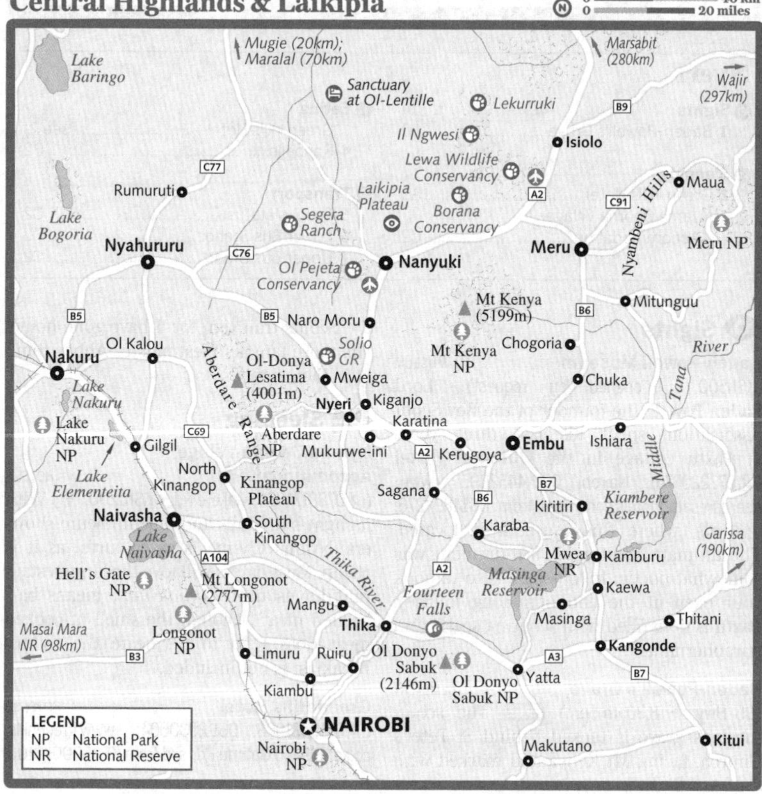

Nyeri

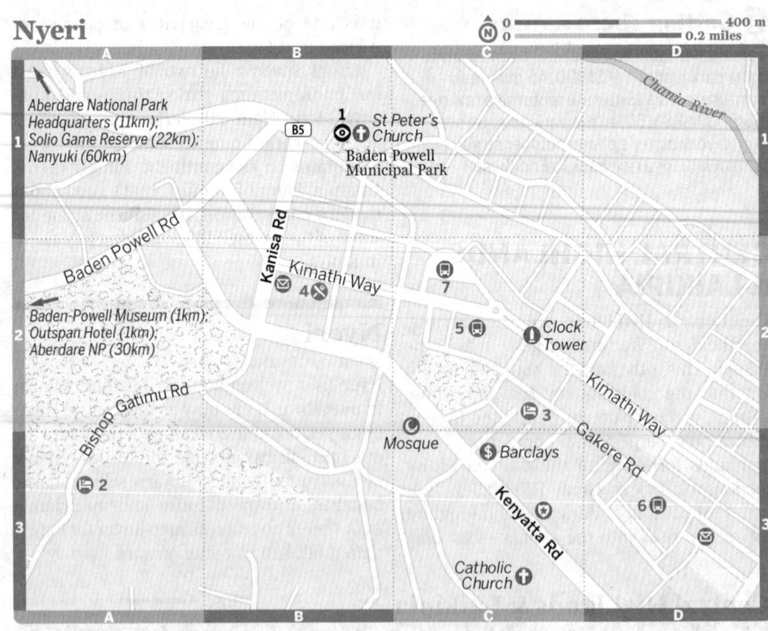

Nyeri

Sights
1 Baden-Powell's Grave B1

Sleeping
2 Green Hills Hotel A3
3 Nyama Choma Village Accommodation C2

Eating
Green Hills Hotel .... (see 2)
4 Raybells B2

Transport
5 Local Matatus C2
6 Lower Bus Stand D3
7 Upper Bus Stand C2

Sights

Baden-Powell Museum MUSEUM

(KSh500; opened on request) Lord Baden-Powell, the founder of the Boy Scout Association, spent his last three years at Paxtu cottage in the **Outspan Hotel** (0722207761, Nairobi 020-4452095; www.aberdaresafarihotels.com; s/d from US$189/276;), where this museum is located. The ultimate scoutmaster's retirement was somewhat poetic: to 'outspan' is to unhook your oxen at the end of a long journey. Paxtu is now filled with scouting scarfs and paraphernalia.

Baden-Powell's Grave CEMETERY

(B5 Hwy; 8.30am-5pm) FREE The scoutmaster's grave is tucked behind St Peter's Church, facing Mt Kenya and marked with the Scouts trail sign for 'I have gone home'. His more famous Westminster Abbey tomb is, in fact, empty.

Sleeping

Nyama Choma Village Accommodation HOTEL $

(0788174384; Gakere Rd; r KSh1200;) With its light-blue walls and blue-linoleum showers, Nyama Choma is as colourful as it is cheap. Meat-eaters will love the large restaurant downstairs (*nyama choma* means 'barbecued meat'), though the smell of cooked meat does tend to permeate the rooms. Breakfast is not included.

Green Hills Hotel HOTEL $$

(0716431988, 061-2030604; www.greenhills.co.ke; Bishop Gatimu Rd; s/d from KSh6000/8100, s/d ste KSh23,000/28,000; P) The best deal in town is actually a little way out of Nyeri. The small drive is worth it for the palm-lined, poolside ambience and general sense of serenity. A few questionable style choices notwithstanding, the rooms are nicely turned out, comfortable and have mosquito nets.

★ **Sandai Farm** GUESTHOUSE $$$
(0721656699; www.africanfootprints.de; camping KSh500, s/d full board US$145/250, cottages from US$80; P@) Fourteen kilometres northwest of town (ask locals for directions), Sandai is run by the effervescent Petra Allmendinger, whose enthusiasm and warm welcome make this a great escape for those looking for something a little more personal than what's on offer elsewhere. Accommodation is either in the extremely cosy lodge or in self-contained cottages that can accommodate up to six.

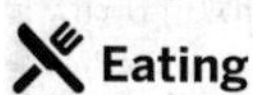

Eating

Raybells INTERNATIONAL $
(020-2370035; Kimathi Way; mains KSh150-500; 6.30am-8pm) Pretty much anything you want to eat (well, anything Kenyan or Western) from pizza to *nyama choma* is available and cooked passably well here. You may want to avoid the fresh juice as it has tap water added to it.

Green Hills Hotel INTERNATIONAL $$
(061-2030604; www.greenhills.co.ke; Bishop Gatimu Rd; mains/buffets KSh750/1650; 6am-11pm; P) The full buffet here (when numbers permit) is an impressive piece of work, with some tasty mixed-grill options done up in a satisfyingly fancy fashion. Steaks are tender and come sizzling on a platter with a good mix of veggies, though the star dish is the *kuku wa kupaka* (chicken in spicy coconut milk).

Information

Barclays (Kenyatta Rd; 9am-4pm Mon-Fri, to noon Sat) One of several banks around town with an ATM; will exchange cash.

Main Post Office (Kanisa Rd; 7.45am-6pm Mon-Fri, 9am-1pm Sat) Send home postcards as well as larger items with the EMS courier service.

Post Office (Gakere Rd; 7.45am-6pm Mon-Fri, 9am-1pm Sat) Good for stamps; near the lower bus stand.

Nyeri Police Station (Kenyatta Rd)

Getting There & Away

The **Upper Bus Stand** deals with sporadic buses and a plethora of matatus to destinations north and west of Nyeri including Nanyuki (KSh250, one hour), Nyahururu (KSh350, 1¼ hours) and Nakuru (KSh550, 2½ hours).

From the **Lower Bus Stand**, matatus head in all directions south and east including Thika (KSh300, two hours) and Nairobi (KSh500, 2½ hours).

If you are without transport and want to explore the area surrounding Nyeri, head to the **local matatu** stand.

Matatu prices are always negotiable, so don't be afraid to shop around if you are on a tight budget.

Aberdare National Park

Boasting a large number of elephants as well as black rhinos, **Aberdare National Park** (0772171247, Nairobi 020-2379407; www.kws.org; adult/child US$52/26; 6am-6pm) lures those who want more than just a safari. With dense forests, 300m-high waterfalls and amazing hikes, this park is as much about the flora as it is the fauna. While trekking, keep an eye open for bush pigs, rare black leopards and buffaloes.

Activities

To trek within the park requires advance permission from the warden at park headquarters, who may (depending on where you plan

ABERDARE NATIONAL PARK

Why Go Two interesting ecosystems to explore: a dense rainforest and high, Afro-alpine moorlands with great trekking possibilities and some spectacular waterfalls.

When to Go The park receives plenty of rain year-round. The driest months are January to February and June to September.

Practicalities During the rains, roads are impassable, and the numbered navigation posts in the Salient are often difficult to follow. The most straightforward route is to drive between the Ruhuruini and Mutubio West gates.

Budget Tips Camp at public campsites or organise a day trip with other travellers from Nyeri.

Aberdare National Park

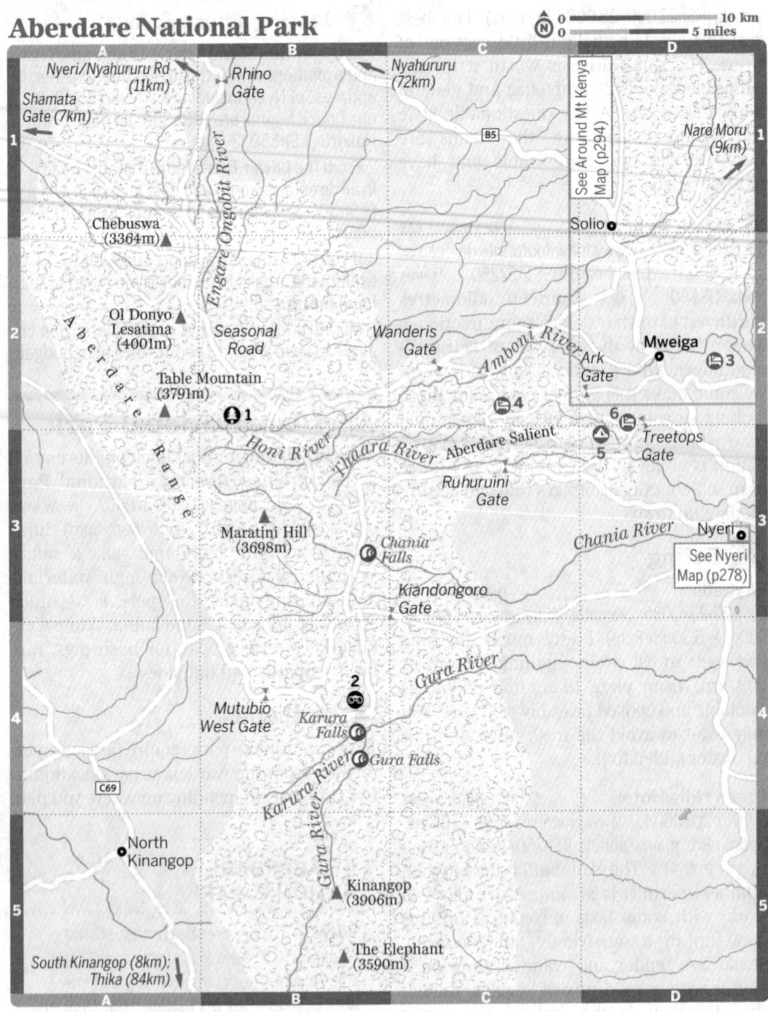

Aberdare National Park

Sights

1 Aberdare National Park....................B2
2 Karura Falls Lookout.......................B4

Sleeping

3 Aberdare Country Club....................D2
4 Ark...C2
5 Prince Charles Campsite..................D3
6 Treetops.....................................D2

to walk) insist on providing an armed ranger to guide and protect you against inquisitive wildlife (KSh2000/4000 per half/full day).

The **Northern Moorland** and its four main peaks (all 3500m to 4000m) are excellent trekking spots; the tallest mountain in the park is **Ol Donyo Lesatima** (4000m), a popular bag for those on the East African mountain circuit. Between Honi Campsite and Elephant Ridge is the site of the **hideout** of Mau Mau leader Dedan Kimathi, who used these mountains as a base; many of his companions learned the ropes of jungle warfare fighting in Burma in WWII.

On the **Kinangop Plateau**, from the dirt track that connects the Ruhuruini and Mutubio West gates, it is possible to walk to

RIGHT ROYAL CONNECTIONS

Trivia for royal-philes: **Treetops** isn't actually the spot where Princess Elizabeth became Queen Elizabeth II. Yes, Liz was sleeping in Treetops when George VI died in 1952, but in 1954 Mau Mau guerrillas blew the original lodge to twigs. Three years later, a much larger rendition was built on the opposite side of the waterhole. 'Every time like the first time', goes the Treetops slogan, and we agree: sleeping here feels like travelling back to the day that the 25-year-old Elizabeth went to bed a princess and awoke a queen.

Fifty-eight years later, another young lady, this time a commoner, answered 'yes' to a question that will eventually see her crowned the Queen of the Commonwealth. On the verandah of a small log cabin, high on the flanks of Mt Kenya, Prince William asked Kate Middleton to be his wife. Under the guise of fishing on Lake Alice, William and Kate travelled to the remote Rutundu cabins, where he popped the big question. And so it is that while the fishing trip was a complete failure, Prince William still managed quite the catch.

the top of **Karura Falls** and watch Karura Stream slide over the rocky lip into the 272m abyss. Weather permitting, you may be able to make out the misty veil of Kenya's tallest cascade, the **Gura Falls** (305m), in the distance. Unfortunately, there are no tracks to Gura Falls or the base of Karura Falls. You can, however, visit the far smaller **Chania Falls** further north.

Sleeping & Eating

Prince Charles Campsite CAMPGROUND $
(☎0774160327; www.kws.go.ke; camping per adult/child US$35/20; P) Prince Charles Campsite is one of six 'special' campsites in Aberdares, which means they have to be reserved ahead of time through KWS. The special campsites have no facilities and, quite frankly, no advantage over the public campsites other than a possible lack of fellow campers.

★**Treetops** HISTORIC HOTEL $$$
(☎0722207761; www.treetops.co.ke; s/d US$234/360, s/d ste US$259/385; P@⑦) Treetops is sold through the Outspan Hotel (p278) in Nyeri, where check-in happens. From here guests must drive themselves to Treetops, where they dine, sleep and have breakfast, after which they leave at their leisure. Although the rooms are small, they are all kitted out with dark-wood floors, ochre feature walls and attractive prints.

Ark HOTEL $$$
(☎0737799990; www.thearkkenya.com; s/d US$195/315) The Ark dates from the 1960s, and has petite rooms and a lounge that overlooks a waterhole. An excellent walkway leads over a particularly dense stretch of the Salient, and from here and the waterhole lounge you can spot elephants, rhinos, buffaloes and hyenas.

Information

Unusually for Kenya, excellent 1:25,000 maps are available at the gates.

Getting There & Away

You'll need your own wheels to visit Aberdare National Park comfortably. Access roads from the B5 Hwy to the Ark and Treetops are in decent shape, though keep in mind that it takes a few hours to get from the Salient to the moorlands and vice versa.

If you don't have your own vehicle, you can book an overnight excursion from the **Aberdare Country Club** (☎0737799990; www.aberdarecountryclub.com; s/d/tr full board US$180/305/434, day entry adult/child KSh1000/500; P⑦≋) in Nyeri.

Laikipia Plateau

Set against the backdrop of Mt Kenya, the Laikipia plateau extends over 9500 sq km of semi-arid plains, dramatic gouges and acacia-thicket-covered hills. This patchwork of privately owned ranches, wildlife conservancies and small-scale farms has become one of the most important areas for biodiversity in the country, boasting wildlife densities second only to those found in the Masai Mara. It's the last refuge of Kenya's African wild dogs and it's here that some of the most effective conservation work in the country is being done. Indeed, these vast plains are home to some of Kenya's highest populations of endangered species, including half of the country's black rhinos and half of the world's Grevy's zebras.

For more information on the region's ecosystems and wildlife, contact the **Laikipia Wildlife Forum** (☎0726500260; www.laikipia.org) and pick up a copy of *Laikipia – A Natural History Guide,* sold at many lodge gift shops across the region.

Nyahururu

☎065 / POP 36,450 / ELEV 2360M

This unexpectedly attractive town leaps out of the northwest corner of the highlands and makes a decent base for exploring the western edge of the Aberdares. Its former namesake, Thomson's Falls, are beautiful in their own right with great trekking potential when the security situation permits.

Sights

Thomson's Falls WATERFALL

(adult/child KSh200/50; ⏰7am-6pm) Set back in an evergreen river valley and studded with sharp rocks and screaming baboons, the white cataracts plummet over 74m. The dramatic experience of looking up at the falls as baboons pad over the surrounding cliffs is worth the drenching you get from the falls' spray. While the vicinity of the falls is generally safe (minus several overbearing vendors), there have been incidents of serious assaults, particularly of women, on the nearby treks.

Sleeping & Eating

Thomson's Falls Lodge HOTEL $$

(☎065-2022006; www.thomsonsfallslodge.org; off B5 Hwy; camping KSh1200, s/d/tr US$80/100/140; P Wi-Fi) While in need of a makeover, the lodge sits right above the falls (p282) and does a great job of instilling that good old 'I'm a colonial aristocrat on a hill-country holiday' vibe. Rooms are spacious but cosy, thanks in no small part to the log fireplaces.

Panari Resort HOTEL $$$

(☎0709070000; www.panariresort.com; off B5 Hwy; s/d/tr KSh15,300/17,100/18,900, cottage s/d/tr KSh17,000/19,000/21,000; P ❄ Wi-Fi Pool) Opened in March 2016, this is the most luxurious spot in Nyahururu. With sprawling grounds, plush grass and loads of activities for the family, this is the place to splurge. The rooms are large, though minimal, with a big fireplace for winter nights. Some cottage rooms have direct views of the falls.

It's also home to the most upscale **restaurant** (mains KSh600-1700, breakfast/lunch/dinner buffet KSh2000/3000/3000; ⏰7am-10pm; P Wi-Fi) in Nyahururu; you can order off the menu though everything is also offered at the buffet. While there is no mistaking that the cold and impersonal restaurant is inside a hotel, the food is tasty and you won't leave hungry.

Club Comfort KENYAN $

(☎065-2022326; mains KSh150-600; ⏰6am-midnight) To eat with the locals, head here and unleash your inner carnivore as you chow down a 1kg plate of *nyama choma.* The food isn't the quickest, so bring a book or brush up on your Swahili with the local crowd.

Information

MEDICAL SERVICES

Nyahururu County Referral Hospital (B5 Hwy, opposite police station; ⏰24hr) The hospital provides a variety of services, from X-rays to vaccinations, though expect a long wait to be seen by a doctor.

MONEY

Barclays (cnr Sulukia & Sharpe Rds; ⏰9am-4pm Mon-Fri, to noon Sat) Full-service bank with 24-hour ATM.

Getting There & Away

There are numerous matatus that run from the **Bus & Matatu Station** (Ol Kalou Rd) to Nakuru (KSh220, 1¼ hours) and Nyeri (KSh350, 1¾ hours) until late afternoon. Less plentiful are services to Naivasha (KSh400, two hours), Nanyuki (KSh420, three hours) and Nairobi (KSh500, 3½ hours). The occasional morning matatu reaches Maralal (KSh600, four hours).

Several early-morning buses also serve Nairobi (KSh450, three hours).

Don't be afraid to haggle or shop around for the best-priced matatu.

Nanyuki

☎062 / POP 49,233

Nanyuki serves as a gateway to the Laikipia plateau, one of Africa's most important wildlife conservation areas. Despite being a market town, it is probably the most cosmopolitan city in the area outside of Nairobi,

Nanyuki

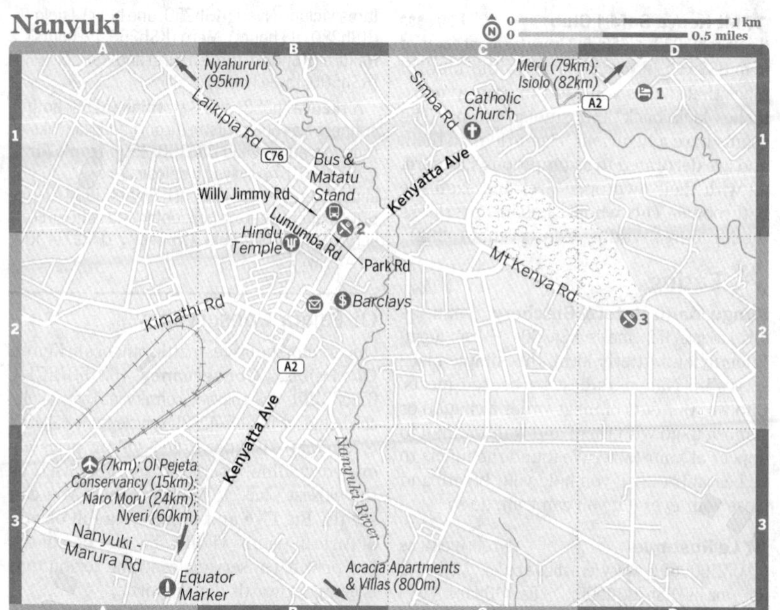

with its share of international tourists (here to climb Mt Kenya or to visit the myriad safari parks), British Army soldiers (there is a training facility nearby) and Kenyan Air Force pilots (this is the site of the country's main air-force base).

Sights & Activities

Mt Kenya Wildlife Conservancy Animal Orphanage ZOO

(Nairobi 020-2330079; www.animalorphanagekenya.org; Mt Kenya Safari Club; per person KSh1500; 10am-5pm;) It may come off a little zoo-like at first but this orphanage is one of the few places in the world to have successfully bred the rare mountain bongo. Its success is such that there are now plans to release some of the captive-bred antelope into the Mt Kenya forests to bolster the current population of around 70. Children, and anyone who wants to have a baby monkey scramble over their head, will love this place.

Sleeping

Acacia Apartments & Villas APARTMENT $

(0722312300, 0713906349; nanyukiacacia@gmail.com; off the A2 Nyeri-Nanyuki Hwy; r from KSh2000; P) Located slightly out of town on the way to Mt Kenya Safari Club (p284), this is the best budget option in the area. Each apartment has two en-suite bedrooms, a full kitchen with microwave and stove, and a lounge with couches and TV. There is also a balcony attached to each room, as well as the lounge.

Nanyuki

Sleeping

1	Kongoni Camp	D1

Eating

	Kongoni Camp	(see 1)
2	Kungu Maitu Hotel & Butchery	B1
3	Le Rustique	D2

★ **Kongoni Camp** BANDAS $$

(062-2031225, 0702868888; www.kongonicamp.com; s/d KSh6700/12,500; P @) Founded by a friendly local-turned-Londoner-turned-local-again, Kongoni has five, concrete circular *bandas* as well as some newer rooms that are simple but designed with a touch of safari flair. It's one of the few genuinely midrange options around town and there's a large restaurant-cum-bar (p284) with a varied menu.

★Mt Kenya Safari Club HOTEL $$$
(☎Nairobi 020-2265555; www.fairmont.com; d from US$533; P@🛜🏊) This is the kind of place that makes you want to grow a moustache, kick back and smoke a pipe. The rooms have a luxurious, classic look to them and are decorated to a sumptuous standard, all with their own open fires and exquisite bathrooms. The whole shebang overlooks the Mt Kenya Wildlife Conservancy (p283).

Eating

Kungu Maitu Hotel & Butchery KENYAN $
(off Laikipia Rd; meals KSh200; ⏲8am-10pm) Friendly and utterly local, this simple place serves up Nanyuki's best barbecued meats. Choose your cuts of meat, order a chapati or samosa to go with them and wait for it all to appear at your table. We found the toilets to be bearable only if you hold your breath and close your eyes – if you can wait, do so.

★Le Rustique INTERNATIONAL $$
(☎0721609601; www.lerustique.co.ke; Mt Kenya Rd; mains KSh700-1500; ⏲8am-10pm; 🛜👪) This one-time Nairobi favourite has upped sticks and headed north to Nanyuki. The fare, overseen to every last detail by owner Maike Potgieter, is superb, with pizzas, crêpes and an excellent wine list. But the atmosphere is as much of a drawcard, with an open fireplace for those cold Laikipia evenings or the quiet garden for warmer days.

Kongoni Camp INDIAN, INTERNATIONAL $$
(☎0702868888; www.kongonicamp.com; mains KSh800-1900; ⏲6am-10pm; 🛜👪) One of the top restaurants in Nanyuki with a large variety of international dishes – hamburgers, steak, pizza – though its speciality is Indian food. With a proper tandoor oven, this place can cure any naan bread and chicken tikka masala cravings you may have! Ask about its 'top shelf' whisky collection for an after-dinner treat.

Information

Barclays (Kenyatta Ave; ⏲9am-4pm Mon-Fri, to noon Sat) Reliable ATMs.

Post Office (Kenyatta Ave; ⏲7.45am-6pm Mon-Fri, 9am-4pm Sat)

Getting There & Away

Nanyuki is well connected to all points north and south as well as most major Rift Valley towns from the **bus and matatu stand**. Sample matatu fares include Nyeri (KSh250, one hour), Isiolo (KSh280, 1½ hours), Meru (KSh250, 1½ hours), Nakuru (KSh650, three hours) and Nairobi (KSh500, three hours).

Airkenya (p258) and **Safarilink** (p258) both connect Nairobi's Wilson Airport and Nanyuki (one way adult/child US$190/150). **Tropic Air** (☎071-5018740; www.tropicairkenya.com; Nanyuki Airport; flights US$470-6000) offers charter-helicopter and light-aircraft services from **Nanyuki Airport** (☎0722714000; off A2 Hwy).

Ol Pejeta Conservancy

Once one of the largest cattle ranches in Kenya, **Ol Pejeta Conservancy** (☎0707187141, 0735801101; www.olpejetaconservancy.org; adult/child/student US$85/42/21, vehicle from KSh400; ⏲7am-7pm) is now a 365-sq-km, privately owned wildlife reserve. It markets itself as the closest place to Nairobi where you can see the Big Five and possesses a full palette of African plains wildlife. It's also one of the few private conservancies in the region that is geared towards day visitors.

It's the rhinos that form the centrepiece of the conservancy effort here – its (at last count) 111 black rhinos form the largest population in East Africa. However, Ol Pejeta's role in the wider ecosystem extends beyond its boundaries thanks to its partner agreements and wildlife corridors with other Laikipia ranches. Ol Pejeta is also extremely active in local community projects including school infrastructure, health care and the provision of clean water.

Sights

★Endangered Species Enclosure ZOO
(adult/child US$40/20) This 283-hectare drive-through enclosure next to the **Morani Information Centre** (⏲7am-6.30pm) FREE is home to the last three remaining northern white rhinos (one male and two females), an ever-so-close-to-being-extinct subspecies. The rhinos were brought here from the Dvur Kralove Zoo in the Czech Republic in 2009, but have not yet bred successfully. Also in the enclosure are the endangered Grevy's zebra and Jackson's hartebeest.

Chimpanzee Sanctuary ZOO
(⏲10am-4.30pm) FREE Home to 39 profoundly damaged chimpanzees rescued from captivity across Africa and further afield, Ol Pejeta's Chimp Sanctuary encompasses two large enclosures cut in two by

the Ewaso Ngiro River. There's an elevated observation post and keepers are usually on hand to explain a little about each chimp's backstory; note the tiny replica cage in which one of the chimps was chained for years on end prior to being brought to the sanctuary.

Activities

The conservancy has many activities, such as **bird walks**, **guided bush walks**, **night wildlife viewing** and **dog tracking**, which you can arrange at the park gate or through your accommodation; each costs US$40/20 per adult/child.

The conservancy is now cashless. You can pre-pay online or via card or bank transfer.

★Lion-tracking WILDLIFE
(adult/child US$40/20) Easily our pick of the activities on offer, this nightly excursion trains you in the art of identifying individual lions and takes you out to find them using radio receivers. The data you gather forms part of the conservancy's database on Ol Pejeta's estimated 65 to 70 resident lions. The rangers will collect you from your accommodation.

Hippo Hide Walk WALKING
(7am-6.30pm) FREE This 20-minute meander along the riverbank happens in the company of a knowledgeable local ranger – hopefully you'll see hippos but it's worth doing even if you don't. Open to day visitors, there is no set schedule for the walks, but you can request one of the standby rangers to take you.

Sleeping & Eating

Ewaso Campsite CAMPGROUND $
(0707187141; www.olpejetaconservancy.org; camping adult/child KSh1000/500) Protected by dense foliage but with good river views, this is probably the pick of the sites in the park centre.

★Kicheche Laikipia TENTED CAMP $$$
(Nairobi 020-2493569; www.kicheche.com; s/d all-inclusive US$700/1400; P) Close to the geographical centre of the park and overlooking a waterhole, this excellent tented camp has six stylishly furnished tents, an overall air of sophistication and impeccable service. It's Ol Pejeta's most exclusive accommodation.

OL PEJETA CONSERVANCY

Why Go East Africa's largest black-rhino population; excellent wildlife viewing and activities; most accessible of the Laikipia conservancies.

When to Go Year-round, although you'll need a 4WD from late March to late May.

Practicalities Only the Serat Gate and main Rongai Gate (both in the conservancy's east) are open to visitors.

Budget Tips Rent a matatu for the day with other travellers in Nanyuki; if staying overnight, stay at one of the campsites.

★Sweetwaters Serena Camp TENTED CAMP $$$
(0732123333; www.serenahotels.com; s/d full board from US$373/506; P) The 56 large and beautifully appointed en-suite tents by the reliable Serena chain are high-end but with prices that are more accessible than those of other properties. The central location is a plus (handy for most of the conservancy) and a minus (things can get busy around here), depending on your perspective.

Morani's Restaurant CAFE $$
(0706160114; www.moranisrestaurant.com; mains KSh750-1000; 8am-5pm) Next to the Morani Information Centre (p284), this terrific little cafe with outdoor tables serves up excellent dishes that range from the Morani burger made from prime Ol Pejeta beef to Kenyan beef stew or a Mediterranean wrap. Fresh juices, fine smoothies and Kenyan coffee round out an excellent package.

Information

Pick up a copy of the *Ol Pejeta Conservancy* map (KSh700) from the entrance gate or download it for free from the website (www.olpejetaconservancy.org).

Getting There & Away

Ol Pejeta is 15km southwest of Nanyuki, which also has the nearest **airport** (p284). It's well signposted. The last 9km is a gravel road, but more than passable without a 4WD.

Segera Ranch

North of Ol Pejeta Conservancy (p284) in southern Laikipia, this 202-sq-km ranch is a perfect example of how Laikipia works. It's a model cattle ranch, but wildlife is also prolific here, including the three big cats, elephants, buffaloes and endangered species such as Grevy's zebra (15 of them at last count), Patas monkey (a small troop lives along the ranch's eastern border) and the reticulated giraffe. The landscape here is classic Laikipia terrain – seemingly endless savannah country cut through with rocky river valleys and riverine woodland.

The ranch is owned by philanthropist Jochen Zeitz, whose **Zeitz Foundation** (www.zeitzfoundation.org) is active in local community projects with local schools, women's groups and the Samuel Eto'o Soccer Academy for budding football stars. The foundation's philosophy is based on the 'Four Cs' – conservation, community, culture and commerce.

Sleeping & Eating

★ **Segera Retreat** LODGE **$$$**
(www.segera.com; s/d all-inclusive US$1190/2100, villas from US$1400; P ❄ 📶 ≋) We can be difficult to impress, but this place left us speechless. Six villas and a couple of houses inhabit an oasis in the heart of the ranch, looking out onto the savannah, yet enclosed within their own natural compound that keeps dangerous animals out. The villas are utterly magnificent – spacious, luxurious in every way and steeped in safari tradition.

Getting There & Away

Segera is roughly 50km from Nanyuki, off the C76 Hwy. **Segera Retreat** can organise a car and driver for you if you do not have your own wheels.

Lewa Wildlife Conservancy

Although technically not a part of Laikipia, **Lewa Wildlife Conservancy** (LWC; ☎064-3131405, 0722203562; www.lewa.org; conservation

THE LEWA STORY

Like so many Laikipia properties that later became wildlife conservancies, Lewa Downs was an expansive cattle ranch owned since colonial times by white settlers. In 1983, the owners, the Craig family, along with pioneering rhino conservationist Anna Merz, set aside 20 sq km of Lewa as the Ngare Sergoi Rhino Sanctuary. They received their first rhino a year later, and the numbers grew to 16 in 1988. The Craigs doubled the sanctuary's size, and by 1994 the entire cattle ranch (along with the adjacent Ngare Ndare Forest Reserve) was enclosed within an electric fence to create a 251-sq-km rhino sanctuary. The Lewa Wildlife Conservancy in its current form was formed in 1995.

True to its origins as a sanctuary to save Kenya's rhinos, Lewa's primary conservation focus continues to be rhinos. Lewa suffered not a single poaching event between 1983 and 2009 – the joke doing the rounds of the conservation community for much of this time was that Lewa was 'State House' (Kenya's presidential palace) for rhinos. Sadly, poaching has been on the rise ever since, with six of Lewa's rhinos killed in 2013, prompting a massive investment in anti-poaching operations. Since the start of these operations, Lewa has not had a single incident of rhino poaching.

At last count, Lewa was home to 83 black rhinos and 74 white rhinos (that's around 15% of the Kenyan total). And despite the poaching, the conservancy is close to its carrying capacity for rhinos. In 2014, the fence that separated Lewa from the 142-sq-km Borana Conservancy (p288) to the west was torn down, effectively increasing the size of the rhino sanctuary by 25%.

Rhinos aside, Lewa's conservation effort has been astounding and 20% of the world's Grevy's zebras call the reserve home.

Central to the Lewa model is a serious commitment to community development, fuelled by a recognition that local people are far more likely to protect wildlife if they have a stake (financial or otherwise) in its survival. Lewa Wildlife Conservancy is a non-profit organisation that invests around 70% of its annual US$2.5-million-plus budget into health care, education and various community projects for surrounding villages.

In 2013, Lewa Wildlife Conservancy was inscribed on Unesco's World Heritage list as an extension to the existing Mt Kenya National Park/Natural Forest site.

fee per adult/child per night US$105/53), a vast region of open savannah grasslands that falls away from the Mt Kenya highlands, is very much a part of Laikipia's story. It was at Lewa that the conservancy idea was pioneered and it remains a leader in all of the elements – serious wildlife protection wedded to innovative community engagement – that have come to define the private conservancies of Laikipia and elsewhere. Apart from anything else, Lewa ranks among the premier wildlife-watching territories anywhere in Kenya. And unlike in Kenya's national parks, where off-road driving is prohibited, Lewa's guides delight in taking visitors to almost within touching distance of rhinos, elephants and other species.

Sights & Activities

The following activities (with sample per-person prices) can be booked through your accommodation.

Excursions to Il Ngwesi US$40, half-day

Tour of Lewa Wildlife Conservancy's HQ Free (US$10 if you visit the tracker dogs), one to two hours

Orphan Rhino Project US$15, 30 minutes (this was where the moving final scene in Sir David Attenborough's *Africa* series was filmed)

Visit to local school US$50 donation

Horse-riding safari US$55, one hour

Walking safari in Ngare Ndare Forest US$30 conservation fee, one to three hours

Quad bike/buggy safari Price on application

Flying safari Price on application

Festivals & Events

Lewa Safaricom Marathon SPORTS
(www.safaricom.co.ke/safaricommarathon; adult/child KSh15,000/3000; late Jun/early Jul) It's one thing to run a marathon to the encouraging screams of people, but it's entirely another to run it sharing the course with elephants, rhinos and the odd lion! Established in 2000 to raise funds for wildlife conservation and community development, the Safaricom Marathon, run within the Lewa Wildlife Conservancy (p286), is renowned as one of the planet's toughest marathons.

LEWA WILDLIFE CONSERVANCY

Why Go For some of the finest wildlife viewing in Kenya; almost guaranteed sightings of all the Big Five; walking safaris and night safaris. No minibus circus.

When to Go Year-round, but the dry season (June to October) is best.

Practicalities Lewa is closed to casual visitors: you must be staying at one of the (very expensive) lodges in order to enter. Most visitors fly in from Nairobi but road access is easy from Isiolo or the Central Highlands.

Budget Tips Not suitable for budget travellers.

Sleeping & Eating

★ **Lewa Safari Camp** TENTED CAMP $$$
(0730127000; www.lewasafaricamp.com; s/d all-inclusive US$921/1228;) This impressive property lies in the northwest corner of the conservancy, about an hour's drive from the main Matunda Gate. Its safari tents are large and have that whole chic-bush-living thing down to a tee; they're arrayed around a shallow valley and large wildlife is kept out so you can walk around freely (although you'll be given an escort at night).

Kifaru LODGE $$$
(Nairobi 020-2127844; www.kifaruhouse.com; per person all-inclusive US$1250;) Luxury hilltop *bandas* with no expense spared, not to mention fine views over the plains and an air of exclusivity with no more than 12 guests in camp at any one time.

Sirikoi LODGE $$$
(0727232445; www.sirikoi.com; s/d tents all-inclusive US$1175/1970, 4-bed cottage US$4665, 6-person house US$7000;) Stunning rooms in luxury tents, cottages and in the main house in the heart of the conservancy.

Getting There & Away

The turn-off to Lewa Wildlife Conservancy is only 12km south of Isiolo (the entrance gate is another 5km on) and is well signposted on the A2 Hwy. Private vehicles are not generally allowed into Lewa. Those arriving by private vehicle will have to leave their car at the entrance gate and change to a lodge-provided jeep.

Airkenya (p258) and Safarilink (p258) provide daily flights between Lewa and Nairobi's Wilson Airport (adult one way US$250), sometimes via Nanyuki.

Il Ngwesi Group Ranch

Il Ngwesi is a fine example of a private conservation project linking wildlife conservation and community development, albeit on a smaller scale than seen elsewhere. The Maasai of Il Ngwesi (the name Il Ngwesi translates as 'people of wildlife'), with help from the neighbouring Lewa Wildlife Conservancy (p286), have transformed this undeveloped land, previously used for subsistence pastoralism, into a prime wildlife conservation area hosting white and black rhinos, waterbucks, giraffes and other plains animals.

The south is quite steeply contoured in places, but the highest point (Sanga, at 1907m) lies on Il Ngwesi's western boundary. The northern lowlands mostly consist of light woodland. Just outside the eastern border of Il Ngwesi, Maasai, Turkana and Samburu villages line the trackside.

Sleeping & Eating

Il Ngwesi Eco Lodge LODGE **$$$**
(0741770540, Nairobi 020-2033122; www.ilngwesi.com; s/d all-inclusive US$500/850;) Il Ngwesi community supplements its herding income with tourist dollars gained from this award-winning ecolodge. The divine open-fronted thatched cottages here boast views over the dramatic escarpment, and at night the beds in some rooms can be pulled out onto the private 'terraces', allowing you to snooze under the Milky Way. Profits go straight to the Maasai community.

Getting There & Away

Il Ngwesi is north of Lewa and accessed off the main Isiolo to Nairobi Rd. Lewa Safari Camp (p287) organises half-day visits to Il Ngwesi from Lewa, which include visits to a Maasai *manyatta*, nature walks and explanations of Maasai tradition.

Borana Conservancy

One of the longest-standing conservancies in the area, the Borana cattle ranch – now the **Borana Conservancy** (0727735578; www.borana.co.ke) – owned by the Dyer family for three generations, turned its focus onto wildlife and community projects in 1992. This beautiful 142-sq-km conservancy suddenly became a whole lot more attractive in 2013, when rhinos from Lewa Wildlife Conservancy (p286) were translocated here. The following year the fence between Borana and Lewa was torn down. What that means is that Borana is now an integral part of one of Kenya's most important rhino sanctuaries. It's perfect rhino habitat (14 rhinos were born on the conservancy in 2016) and seeing African wild dogs (as well as, at last count, 18 lions and other plains species) is also a possibility here.

As it is something of a Laikipia trademark, Borana ploughs its money into anti-poaching operations, community development and grasslands habitat management.

Sleeping & Eating

Borana Lodge LODGE **$$$**
(0721702770, 0727735578; www.borana.co.ke; s/d all-inclusive US$736/1240, conservation fee per adult/child US$105/53;) On a hill and overlooking a waterhole, this appealing, family-run lodge manages a perfect balance between rustic and luxury. The eight thatched cottages have stone floors and walls, and look down over the waterhole where wildlife is common. The main building is wonderfully colonial from its fireplace to its stiff drinks.

Getting There & Away

Located northeast of Nanyuki, the lodge is a 4½-hour drive from Nairobi along the A2 and a 4WD is not necessary. There is also an airstrip for those with larger wallets and less time. Note that you have to be staying at **Borana Lodge** in order to access the conservancy.

Lekurruki Community Ranch

Ranged across almost 120 sq km north of Il Ngwesi and northwest of Lewa Wildlife Conservancy (p286), this community ranch is the homeland of the Mukogodo Maasai. With a good mix of habitats – the bordering Mukogodo Forest is partially on the ranch and is often said to be one of the largest indigenous forests in East Africa, while the remainder of the ranch is made up of open savannah – the ranch has a rich variety of both flora and fauna. Of the latter, you'll find predators and buffalo here, but elephants are the main drawcard with one herd almost 500-strong. More than 200 bird species and over 100 butterfly species have been recorded on the ranch.

Sleeping & Eating

Tassia Lodge LODGE $$$
(☎0790486298; www.tassiasafaris.com; s/d all-inclusive US$810/1180, conservation fee per person per night US$60;) The immensity of African landscapes and the intimacy of the community lodge experience are perfectly combined at Tassia Lodge, high on a rocky bluff on Lekurruki Community Ranch. Rooms are open sided and have an original handmade look with natural wood and stone used throughout. Views are splendid and activities include walking safaris and botanical walks.

Getting There & Away

Lekurruki Community Ranch is located north of Il Ngwesi and northwest of Lewa Wildlife Conservancy (p286). You cannot self-drive to **Tassia Lodge**, but transfers can be arranged from Nanyuki (US$250 per six-seater vehicle, 2½ hours) or the Lewa airstrip (US$250 per six-seater vehicle, two hours). You can also organise a charter flight to the Tassia airstrip from Nairobi, Nanyuki or Gilgil.

Mt Kenya Region

Mt Kenya National Park

Africa's second-highest mountain might just be its most beautiful. Here, mere minutes from the equator, glaciers carve out the throne of Ngai, the old high god of the Kikuyu. To this day the tribe keeps its doors open to the face of the sacred mountain, and some still come to its lower slopes to offer prayers. Besides being venerated by the Kikuyu, Mt Kenya and **Mt Kenya National Park** (☎0712294084, Nairobi 020-3568763; www.kws.go.ke; adult/child US$52/26) have the rare honour of being both a Unesco World Heritage Site and a Unesco Biosphere Reserve.

The highest peaks of Batian (5199m) and Nelion (5188m) can only be reached by mountaineers with technical skills, but Point Lenana (4985m), the third-highest peak, can be reached by trekkers and is the usual goal for most mortals. When the clouds part, the views are simply magnificent.

Climbing Mt Kenya

There are at least seven different routes up Mt Kenya. Of those, we cover Naro Moru, the easiest and most popular, as well as

Mt Kenya National Park

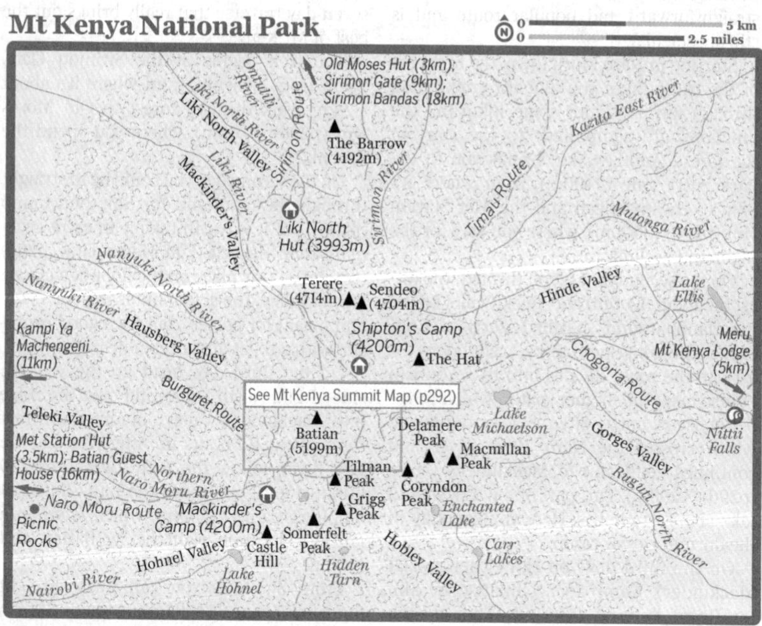

MT KENYA NATIONAL PARK

Why Go Awe-inspiring views from Africa's second-highest mountain; unlike Mt Kilimanjaro, it's possible to take different routes up and down, with arguably better scenery.

When to Go Climb during the driest months: mid-January to late February and late August to September.

Practicalities Don't underestimate the difficulty of this trek. You'd be flirting with death by not taking a guide.

Budget Tips Don't skimp on safety and length of acclimatisation; carry your own gear and cook your own meals; camp instead of staying in the huts.

Sirimon and Chogoria, which are excellent alternatives, and the exciting but demanding Summit Circuit, which circles Batian and Nelion, enabling you to mix and match ascending and descending routes. Other routes include the Timau Route and Burguret Route.

Naro Moru Route

Although the least scenic, this is the most straightforward and popular route and is still spectacular.

Starting in Naro Moru town, the first part of the route takes you along a gravel road through farmlands for some 13km (all the junctions are signposted) to the start of the forest. Another 5km brings you to the park entry gate (2400m), from where it's 8km to the roadhead and the Met Station Hut (p296) (3000m), where you stay for the night and acclimatise.

On the second day, set off through the forest (at about 3200m) and Teleki Valley to the moorland around so-called **Vertical Bog**; expect the going here to be, well, boggy. At a ridge the route divides into two. You can either take the higher path, which gives better views but is often wet, or the lower, which crosses the Naro Moru River and continues gently up to Mackinder's Camp (p296) (4200m). This part of the trek should take about 4½ hours. Here you can stay in the dormitories or camp.

On the third day you can either rest at Mackinder's Camp to acclimatise or aim for **Point Lenana** (4985m). This stretch takes three to six hours, so it is common to leave around 2am to reach the summit in time for sunrise. From the bunk-house, continue past the ranger station to a fork. Keep right and go across a swampy area, followed by a moraine, and then up a long scree slope – this is a long, hard slog. The KWS Austrian Hut (p296) (4790m) is three to four hours from Mackinder's and about one hour below the summit of Lenana, so it's a good place to rest before the final push.

The section of the trek from Austrian Hut up to Point Lenana takes you up a narrow rocky path that traverses the southwest ridge parallel to the Lewis Glacier, which has shrunk more than 100m since the 1960s. Be careful, as the shrinkage has created serious danger of slippage along the path. A final climb or scramble brings you up onto the peak. In good weather it's fairly straightforward, but in bad weather you shouldn't attempt the summit unless you're experienced in mountain conditions or have a guide.

Sirimon Route

A popular alternative to Naro Moru, Sirimon has better scenery, greater flexibility and a gentler rate of ascent, but takes a day longer. It's well worth considering combining it with the Chogoria Route for a six- to seven-day traverse that really brings out the best of Mt Kenya.

The trek begins at the Sirimon Gate, 23km from Nanyuki, from where it's about a 9km walk through forest to Old Moses Hut (p296) (3300m), where you spend the first night.

On the second day you could head straight through the moorland for Shipton's Camp (p296), but it is worth taking an extra acclimatisation day via Liki North Hut (p296) (3993m), a tiny place on the floor of a classic glacial valley. The actual hut is in poor shape and meant for porters, but it's a good campsite with a toilet and stream nearby.

On the third day, head up the western side of Liki North Valley and over the ridge into Mackinder's Valley, joining the direct route about 1½ hours in. After crossing the Liki River, follow the path for another 30 minutes until you reach the bunk-house at Shipton's Camp (4200m), which is set in a fantastic location right below Batian and Nelion.

From Shipton's you can push straight for Point Lenana (4985m), a tough 3½- to five-hour slog via Harris Tarn and the tricky north-face approach, or take the Summit Circuit in either direction around the peaks to reach Austrian Hut (p296) (4790m), about one hour below the summit. The left-hand (east) route past Simba Col (4620m) is shorter but steeper, while the right-hand (west) option takes you on the Harris Tarn trail nearer the main peaks.

From Austrian Hut take the standard southwest traverse up to Point Lenana. If you're spending the night here, it's worth having a wander around to catch the views up to Batian and down the Lewis Glacier into the Teleki Valley.

Chogoria Route

This route crosses some of the most spectacular and varied scenery on Mt Kenya, and is often combined with the Sirimon Route (usually as the descent). The main reason this route is more popular as a descent is the 29km bottom stage. While not overly steep, climbing up that distance is much harder than descending it.

The only disadvantage with this route is the long distance between Chogoria and the park gate. These days most people drive, although it's a beautiful walk through farmland, rainforest and bamboo to the park gate. Most people spend the first night here,

ORGANISED TREKS

If you bargain hard, a package trek may end up costing only a little more than organising each logistical element of the trip separately. If you're keen to save money, think like a wildebeest and join a herd – the larger the group, the cheaper the per-person rate. Prices generally include guides, cooks and porters, park fees, meals and accommodation.

EWP (Executive Wilderness Programmes; ☎UK 1550-721319; www.ewpnet.com/kenya; 3-/7-day trips from US$645/1445; ⏲9am-4.30pm) This UK company employs local guides and may be a good option if you want to book your travel before you arrive in Kenya. Prices get cheaper with more people, so try to get some friends to join you.

IntoAfrica (☎Nairobi 0722511752, UK 0114-2555610; www.intoafrica.co.uk; 7-day treks from US$1695) Highly recommended by readers, IntoAfrica is an environmentally and culturally sensitive company offering both scheduled and exclusive seven-day trips ascending the Sirimon Route and descending Chogoria. All trips are calculated to ensure that local contractors earn a fair living wage from their work.

KG Mountain Expeditions (☎0733606338, Nairobi 020-2033874; www.kenyaexpeditions.com) Run by a highly experienced mountaineer and a team of knowledgeable trekkers, KG offers all-inclusive scheduled treks.

Mountain Rock Safaris Resorts & Trekking Services (Bantu Mountain Lodge; ☎0722511752, Nairobi 020-242133; www.mountainrockkenya.com) Runs the Bantu Mountain Lodge (☎0718136539, 0728057293; www.mountainrockkenya.com; camping US$10, s/d from US$65/100) near Naro Moru. Its popular four-day Naro Moru–Sirimon crossover trek costs US$650 per person.

Mountain View Tour Trekking Safaris (☎0722249439; mountainviewt@yahoo.com; guide per day from US$20) An association of local guides working together; the guides often approach independent travellers as they arrive in Naro Moru.

Mt Kenya Guides & Porters Safari Club (☎0723087042, 0726369611; www.mtkenyaguides.com; per person per day from US$120) The most organised association of guides, cooks and porters in Naro Moru. A full-service tour, including a porter, food, transport and accommodation, will cost US$120 per person per day, though you can also just book a guide (US$20 per day) or a porter (US$15 per day).

Naro Moru River Lodge (☎0708984002, 0708984005; www.naromoruriverlodge.com; 4-day trip per person US$719-1497) Runs a range of all-inclusive trips and operates **Met Station Hut** (p296) and **Mackinder's Camp** (p296) on the Naro Moru Route.

Mt Kenya Chogoria Guides & Porters Association (☎0733676970; anthonytreks@yahoo.com; per person per day from US$120) A small association of guides, cooks and porters based at the Transit Motel (☎0725609151; camping per person KSh300, s/d KSh1500/2000; P), specialising in the Chogoria route up the mountain.

Mt Kenya Summit

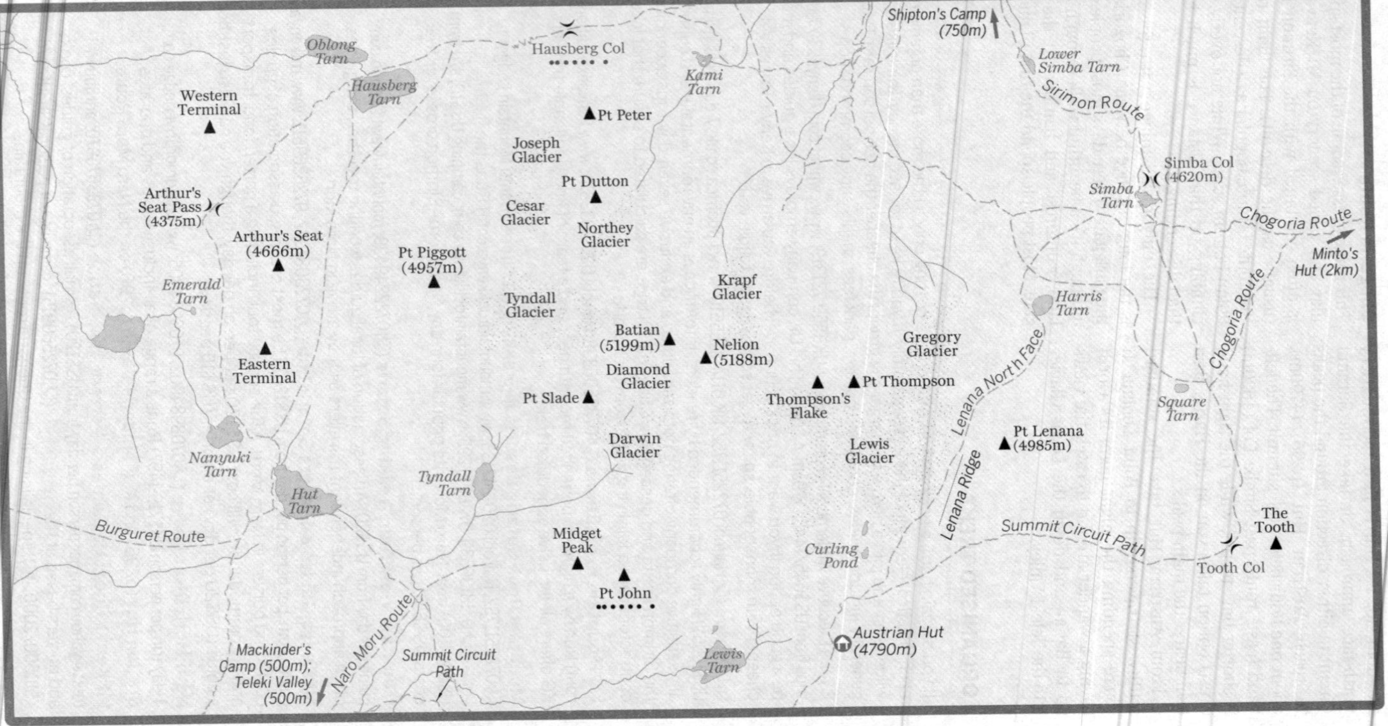

either camping at the gate or staying nearby in Meru Mt Kenya Lodge (p296) (3000m).

On the second day, head up through the forest to the trailhead (camping is possible here). From here it's another 7km over rolling foothills to the Hall Tarns area and **Minto's Hut** (4300m). Like Liki North (p296), this place is only intended for porters, but makes for a decent campsite. Don't use the tarns here to wash anything, as careless trekkers have already polluted them.

From here follow the trail alongside the stunning **Gorges Valley** (another possible descent for the adventurous) and scramble up steep ridges to meet the Summit Circuit. It is possible to go straight for the north face or southwest ridge of Point Lenana, but stopping at Austrian Hut (p296) or detouring to Shipton's Camp (p296) gives you more time to enjoy the scenery.

Allow at least five days for the Chogoria Route, although a full week is better.

Summit Circuit

While everyone who summits Point Lenana gets a small taste of the spectacular Summit Circuit, few trekkers ever grab the beautiful beast by the horns and hike its entire length. The trail encircles the main peaks of Mt Kenya between the 4300m and 4800m contour lines and offers challenging terrain, fabulous views and a splendid opportunity to familiarise yourself with this complex mountain. It is also a fantastic way to acclimatise before bagging Point Lenana.

One of the many highlights along the route is a peek at Mt Kenya's southwest face, with the long, thin Diamond Couloir leading up to the **Gates of the Mists** between the summits of Batian and Nelion.

Depending on your level of fitness, this route can take between four and nine hours. Some fit souls can summit Point Lenana (from Austrian Hut (p296) or Shipton's Camp (p296)) and complete the Summit Circuit in the same day.

The trail can be deceptive at times, especially when fog rolls in, and some trekkers have become seriously lost between Tooth Col and Austrian Hut. It is imperative to take a guide.

What to Take

Consider the following to be a minimum checklist of necessary equipment. If you don't have your own equipment, items can be rented from some guiding associations. Prices vary, but expect to pay in the vicinity of KSh700/300/250/400 for a two-person tent/sleeping bag/pair of boots/stove per day.

- A good sleeping bag and a closed-cell foam mat or Thermarest if you're camping (nightly temperatures near the summit often drop to below -10°C).
- A good set of warm clothes (wool or synthetics – never cotton, as it traps moisture).
- Waterproof clothing (breathable fabric like Gore-Tex is best) as it can rain heavily any time of year.
- A decent pair of boots and sandals or light shoes (for the evening when your boots get wet).
- Sunblock and sunglasses (at this altitude the sun can do some serious damage to your skin and eyes).
- A tent, stove, basic cooking equipment, utensils, a 3L water container (per person) and water-purifying tablets (if you don't intend to stay in the huts along the way). Stove fuel in the form of petrol and

MT KENYA ENVIRONMENT

There are ecosystems on the slopes of Mt Kenya that cannot be found anywhere else in the country.

This extinct volcano hosts, at various elevations, upland forest, bamboo forest (2500m), high-altitude equatorial heath (3000m to 3500m) and lower alpine moorland (3400m to 3800m), which includes several species of bright everlasting flowers. Some truly surreal plant life grows in the Afro-alpine zone (above 3500m) and the upper alpine zone (3800m to 4500m), including hairy carpets of tussock grass, the brushlike giant lobelias, or rosette plants, and the sci-fi-worthy *Senecio brassica*, or giant groundsel, which looks like a cross between an aloe, a cactus and a dwarf. At the summit it's all rock and ice.

Unfortunately, there's more rock than ice these days. Warmer weather has led to disappearing glaciers, and ice climbing in Mt Kenya is largely finished. The impact of reduced snow melt upon the region's rivers – Mt Kenya is the country's most important permanent watershed – is already being felt.

Around Mt Kenya

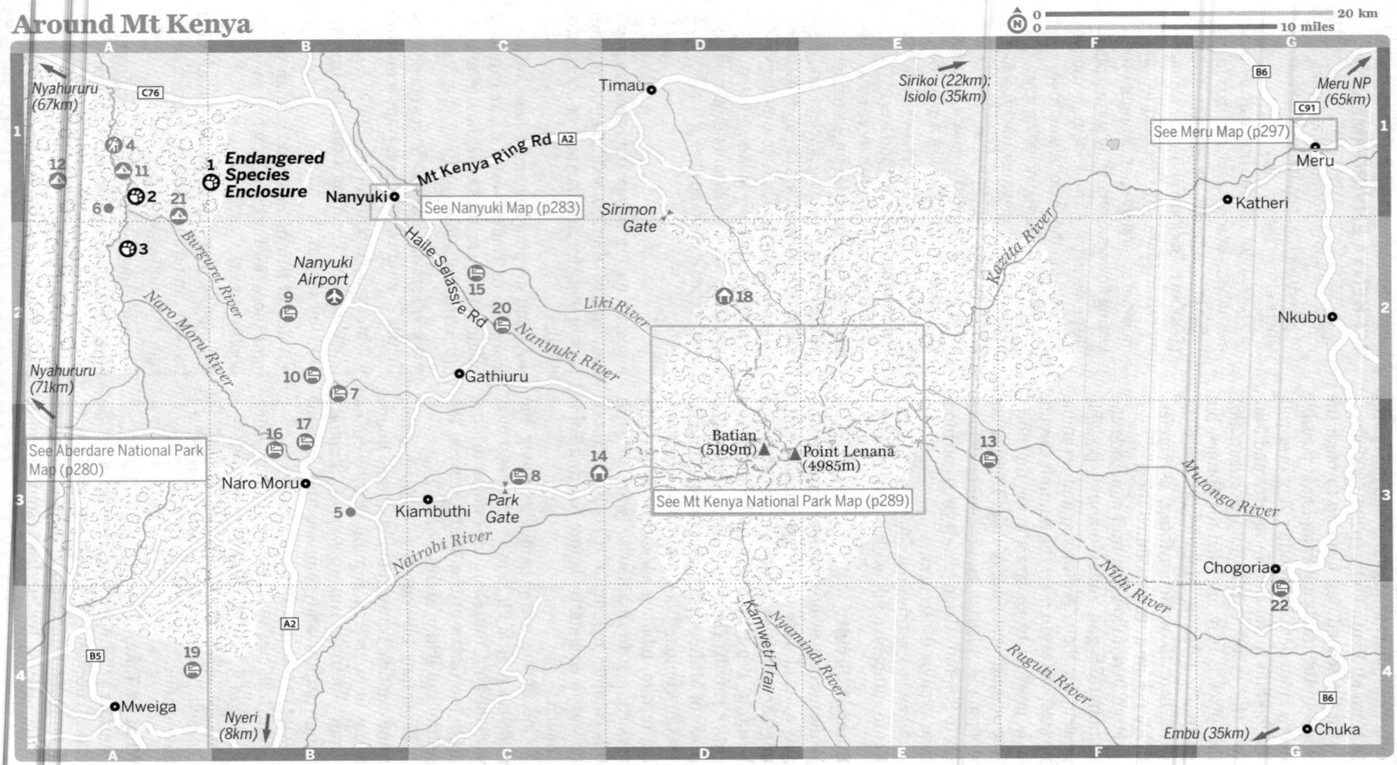

0 — 20 km
0 — 10 miles

1 Endangered Species Enclosure
2
3
4
5
6
7
8
9
10
11
12
13
14
15
16
17
18
19
20
21
22

Nyahururu (67km)
C76
Nanyuki
Mt Kenya Ring Rd
A2
See Nanyuki Map (p283)
Timau
Sirikoi (22km); Isiolo (35km)
B6
Meru NP (65km)
C91
See Meru Map (p297)
Meru
Katheri
Sirimon Gate
Burguret River
Nanyuki Airport
Haile Selassie Rd
Kazita River
Liki River
Nkubu
Naro Moru River
Nanyuki River
Nyahururu (71km)
Gathiuru
See Aberdare National Park Map (p280)
Batian (5199m)
Point Lenana (4985m)
Naro Moru
Park Gate
Kiambuthi
See Mt Kenya National Park Map (p289)
Mutonga River
Nairobi River
Chogoria
Nithi River
Kamweti Trail
Nyamindi River
Ruguti River
B5
Mweiga
Nyeri (8km)
Embu (35km)
Chuka

Around Mt Kenya

Top Sights

1 Endangered Species Enclosure B1

Sights

2 Chimpanzee Sanctuary............A1
Morani Information Centre............(see 1)
Mt Kenya Wildlife Conservancy Animal Orphanage ....(see 15)
3 Ol Pejeta Conservancy............A2

Activities, Courses & Tours

4 Hippo Hide Walk............A1
Mountain Rock Safaris Resorts & Trekking Services.......(see 7)
Mt Kenya Chogoria Guides & Porters Association............(see 22)
5 Mt Kenya Guides & Porters Safari Club............B3
Naro Moru River Lodge............(see 16)
6 Rift Valley Adventures............A1

Sleeping

7 Bantu Mountain Lodge............B2
8 Batian Guest House............C3
9 Colobus Cottages............B2
10 Creaky Cottage............B2
11 Ewaso Campsite............A1
12 Kicheche Laikipia............A1
13 Meru Mt Kenya Lodge............E3
14 Met Station Hut............C3
15 Mt Kenya Safari Club............C2
16 Naro Moru River Lodge............B3
17 Nelion Hotel............B3
18 Old Moses Hut............D2
19 Sandai Farm............A4
20 Sirimon Bandas............C2
21 Sweetwaters Serena Camp............A1
22 Transit Motel............G4

Eating

Morani's Restaurant............(see 1)
Trout Tree Restaurant............(see 10)

kerosene (paraffin) is fairly easily found in towns.

- If you have a mobile phone, take it along; reception on the mountain's higher reaches is actually very good.

- Technical climbers and mountaineers should get a copy of the **Mountain Club of Kenya** (MCK; Map p232; www.mck.or.ke; Langata Rd, Westlands) *Guide to Mt Kenya & Kilimanjaro*. This substantial and comprehensive guide is available in bookshops or from MCK offices; MCK also has reasonably up-to-date mountain information posted on its website.

A few other things to remember:

- If a porter is carrying your backpack, always keep essential clothing (warm- and wet-weather gear) in your day pack because you may become separated for hours at a time.

- Don't sleep in clothes you've worn during the day because the sweat your clothes will have absorbed keeps them moist at night, reducing their heat-retention capabilities.

- Fires are prohibited in the open except in an emergency; in any case, there's no wood once you get beyond 3300m.

Guides, Cooks & Porters

Don't underestimate the difficulty of the trek to Point Lenana. Unless you're a seasoned trekker with high-altitude experience and know how to read maps and use a compass, you'll be flirting with death by not taking a guide – people die on the mountain every year. A good guide will help set a sustainable pace, which should help you avoid headaches, nausea and other (sometimes more serious) effects of altitude sickness. And by spending at least three nights on the ascent, you'll enjoy yourself more too. Your guide should also be on the lookout for signs of hypothermia and dehydration in you (fluids and warm clothing go a long way towards preventing both) and be able to deal with the unpredictable weather. They will also hopefully dispense interesting information about Mt Kenya and its flora and fauna.

Having a porter for your gear is like travelling in a chauffeured Mercedes instead of a matatu. With both a porter and guide on your team, your appreciation of this mountain will be enhanced a hundredfold. If you hire a guide or porter who can also cook, you won't regret it.

The KWS issues vouchers to all registered guides and porters, who should also hold identity cards; they won't be allowed into the park without them.

Costs

Park fees must be factored into the overall cost of climbing Mt Kenya, as well as the costs of guides, food and tips.

Park fees for non-residents are adult/child US$52/26 per day. There is no discount on fees for staying longer. Note that KWS parks no longer accept cash, so you will have to pay at the gate with M-Pesa or a credit card. If you only have cash, you can get a bank deposit slip from any Kenya Commercial Bank or Standard Chartered Bank.

The cost of guides varies depending on the qualifications of the guide, whatever the last party paid and your own negotiating skills. You should expect to pay a minimum of US$30/25/20 per day for a guide/cook/porter.

In addition to the actual cost of hiring guides, cooks and porters, tips are expected but these should only be paid for good service. For a good guide who has completed the full trek with you, plan on a tip of about US$50 per group. Cook and porter tips should be around US$30 and US$20 respectively.

Sleeping

As well as the official sleeping options on each route, it is possible to camp anywhere on the mountain; the cost of camping is included in the four- to six-day park-fee packages payable at any gate. Most people camp near the huts or bunk-houses, as there are often toilets and water nearby.

NARO MORU ROUTE

There are three good bunk-houses along this route: **Met Station Hut** (0708984002; www.naromoruriverlodge.com; dm US$26) is at 3000m, **Mackinder's Camp** (0708984002; www.naromoruriverlodge.com; dm US$34) is at 4200m and **Austrian Hut** (www.kws.go.ke; dm KSh2000) is at 4790m. Beds in Met Station and Mackinder's are harder to find, as they're booked through Naro Moru River Lodge (p297). If you're denied beds, you can still climb this route if you camp and carry all the appropriate equipment.

Those needing more luxury can doss in lovely, KWS-run **Batian Guest House** (www.kws.go.ke/content/batian-guest-house; 8-bed banda US$180), which sleeps eight and is a kilometre from the Naro Moru Gate.

SIRIMON ROUTE

Old Moses Hut (0718136539; www.mountainrockkenya.com; dm US$20) at 3300m and **Shipton's Camp** (0718136539; www.mountainrockkenya.com; dm US$20) at 4200m serve trekkers on this route. They're both booked through the Mountain Rock Lodge (p294). Many trekkers acclimatise by camping at **Liki North Hut** FREE.

If you'd like a little more comfort, book into the excellent KWS **Sirimon Bandas** (www.kws.go.ke/content/sirimon-cottage; banda US$80), which are located 9km from the Sirimon Gate. Each banda sleeps four.

CHOGORIA ROUTE

The only option besides camping on this route is **Meru Mt Kenya Lodge** (per person KSh2000), a group of comfortable cabins administered by **Meru South County Council** (0729390686; Chuka; per person from KSh2000). Ask your guide to reserve these in advance, as during peak season they can be booked out.

Eating

You'll need to be totally self-sufficient if you're climbing Mt Kenya, as none of the lodges or camps on the route offer meals. However, most packages include cooks who both carry and prepare all meals for you on the way. Even if that is the case, take citrus fruits and/or citrus drinks as well as chocolate, sweets or dried fruit to keep your blood-sugar level up.

Getting There & Away

Short of hiring your own helicopter, the only way to reach the summit of Mt Kenya is on foot, and if you're starting your climb in the village of Naro Moru, you can set out directly from there. Naro Moru is a three-hour drive from Nairobi and is accessible in a 2WD car. If you are hiking the Sirimon or Chogoria routes, you may need a 4WD with high clearance to get to the gate.

COOKING AT ALTITUDE

Increased altitude creates unique cooking conditions. The major consideration is that the boiling point of water is considerably reduced. At 4500m, for example, water boils at 85°C; this is too low to sufficiently cook rice or lentils (pasta is better) and you won't be able to brew a good cup of tea (instant coffee is the answer). Cooking times and fuel usage are considerably increased as a result, so plan accordingly.

To avoid severe headaches caused by dehydration or altitude sickness, drink at least 3L of fluid per day and bring rehydration sachets. Water-purification tablets, available at most chemists, aren't a bad idea either (purifying water by boiling at this altitude would take close to 30 minutes).

Meru

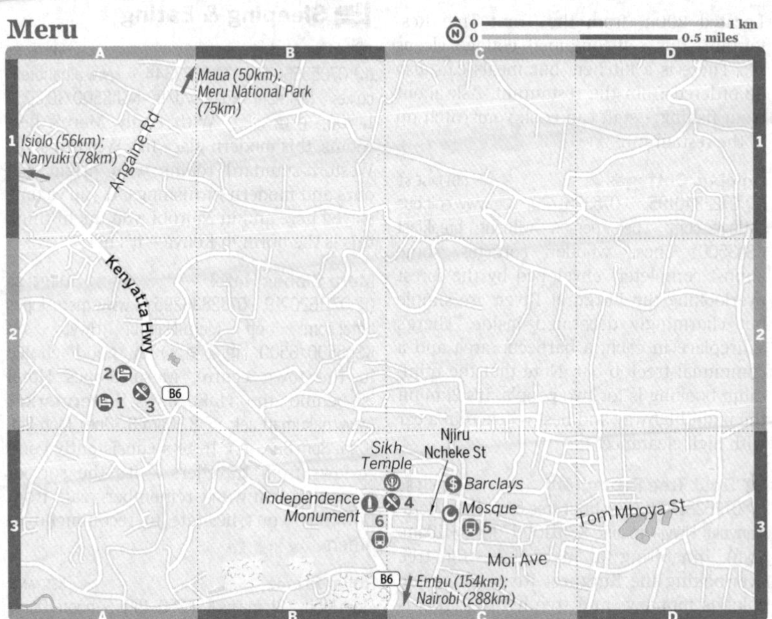

particularly if it has rained recently, though most trekking companies will pick you up from a nearby town for an extra fee.

Naro Moru

☎062 / POP 9000

Naro Moru may be little more than a string of shops and houses, with a couple of very basic hotels and a market, but it's the most popular starting point for treks up Mt Kenya.

Activities

In addition to gazing up at Mt Kenya (best before 6.30am, after which it is usually obscured by clouds) and starting the Naro Moru Route (p290) up to its summit, there are a number of interesting day excursions. Some guide associations can organise **nature walks** on Mt Kenya and hikes to the impressive **Mau Mau caves**.

Sleeping & Eating

★Nelion Hotel HOTEL $$
(☎0714009219; www.the-nelion.co.ke; s/d from KSh10,000/16,000; P 🛜 🏊) Offering 10 wooden log cabins complete with king-size beds, this is the top place to stay in the area. Just under 4km away from Naro Moru, the hotel is still quite tranquil. Families will love the pool and playground.

Naro Moru River Lodge LODGE $$
(☎0724082754; www.naromoruriverlodge.com; campsite/dm US$18/34, s/tw full board US$141/191, cottages from US$96; P 🛜 🏊) A bit like a Swiss chalet, the River Lodge is a lovely collection of dark, cosy cottages and rooms embedded into a sloping hillside that overlooks the rushing Naro Moru River, 3km from town. All three classes of room are lovely, but the middle-of-the-road 'superior' option seems the best value of the lot.

Creaky Cottage COTTAGE $$
(☎0735965636; www.trout-tree.com/accommodation; cottage from KSh12,500)

Meru

Sleeping
1 Alba Hotel A2
2 Meru Slopes Hotel A2

Eating
3 Nakumatt Supermarket A2
4 Royal Prince C3

Transport
5 Bus & Matatu Stand C3
6 Matatu Stand B3

Located 200m from the Trout Tree Restaurant, this self-contained cottage sleeps six. There is a kitchen, but meals can also be ordered from the restaurant. Ask about trout fishing – staff can cook your catch up at the restaurant.

Colobus Cottages COTTAGE $$
(☎0722840195, 0753951720; www.colobuscottages.com; per person without breakfast KSh3500) These wooden cottages, some almost completely enveloped by the forest overlooking the Burguret River, are simple but charmingly decorated inside. There's a fireplace in each, a barbecue area and a communal treetop bar. Note that the minimum booking is for two people. It's 2km off the main highway and best reached in a car with high clearance.

★**Trout Tree Restaurant** SEAFOOD $$$
(☎0726281704; www.trout-tree.com; Naro Moru-Nanyuki Hwy; mains KSh1100-1700; ⊙10am-4pm) Inhabiting a marvellous fig tree overlooking the Burguret River, alongside colobus monkeys and tree hyraxes, this is one of the most original places to eat in Kenya's Central Highlands. It doesn't do much else, but we never tire of the trout combinations – smoked trout and cucumber salad, trout chowder, trout curry, tandoori trout, whole grilled trout…chargrilled is best of all.

Information

There are no banks, and as the KWS no longer accepts cash, make sure you have a credit card or M-Pesa.

Getting There & Away

There are plenty of buses and matatus heading to Nanyuki (KSh80, 30 minutes), Nyeri (KSh180, 45 minutes) and Nairobi (KSh600, three hours) from either the northbound or southbound bus parks.

Meru

☎064 / POP 240,900

Meru is the largest municipality in the Central Highlands and the epicentre of Kenyan production of *miraa,* a mild, leafy stimulant more widely known outside of Kenya as *khat.* The town itself is like a shot of the stuff: a briefly invigorating, slightly confusing head rush but you'll wonder what the point of it all was when the first effects wear off.

Sleeping & Eating

★**Alba Hotel** HOTEL $$
(☎0705556677, 072-8223344; www.albahotels.co.ke; Milimani Rd; s/d/tr KSh8500/10,200/12,700; P@🛜❄) With easily Meru's best rooms, this modern place has Western-style, Western-standard rooms with bright colours and modern furnishings. If you've only stayed here and in Nairobi, you might think this is the norm in Kenya – it's not.

Meru Slopes Hotel HOTEL $$
(☎0711620219, 0738836295; www.meruslopeshotel.com; off Meru-Nairobi Hwy; s/d KSh5500/6500; P@🛜❄) A good choice in the town centre, Meru Slopes Hotel is behind the **Nakumatt Supermarket** (www.nakumatt.net; ⊙8.30am-8.30pm Mon-Sat, 10am-8pm Sun; P). It gets consistently good reviews from travellers – it's the sort of place that you won't remember years from now but won't hesitate to recommend to others.

Royal Prince KENYAN $
(Tom Mboya St; mains KSh250-450; ⊙noon-10pm) There are two storeys of bustling eating goodness at this cheap hotel. The downstairs restaurant specialises in all things fried, while upstairs houses the '*choma* zone', and also doubles as a bar during the day and a club after dark.

Information

Barclays (Tom Mboya St; ⊙9am-4pm Mon-Fri, to noon Sat) Branch with 24-hour ATM.

Getting There & Away

All transport leaves from the area between the main mosque and the market at the eastern end of the town centre.

You'll find regular **bus** departures throughout the day from 6.45am onward to Embu (KSh400, two hours), Thika (KSh400, 3½ hours) and Nairobi (KSh500, five hours). There's also at least one late-afternoon departure to Mombasa (KSh1600, 12 hours).

Regular **matatus** also serve Nairobi (KSh750, four hours), Thika (KSh650, 3½ hours), Embu (KSh450, two hours), Nanyuki (KSh350, 1½ hours) and Isiolo (KSh300, 1½ hours).

Meru National Park

Welcome to one of Kenya's most underrated parks. Marred by serious poaching in the 1980s and the subsequent murder of George Adamson (of *Born Free* fame) in

1989, **Meru National Park** (☎061-2303094, Nairobi 020-2310443; www.kws.org; adult/child US$52/35; ⏰6am-7pm) fell off the tourist map and has never quite managed to get back on. This is a pity, because it has all the essential ingredients for a classic safari destination, with some fine accommodation, excellent prospects for seeing lions and rhinos, and a landscape that incorporates Hemingway-esque green hills, arid, Tsavo-like savannah and fast-flowing streams bordered by riverine forests, baobab trees and doum palms. The advantage of being one of Kenya's best-kept secrets is plain to see – you're likely to have much of it all to yourself.

Sights

Although this is a large park covering 870 sq km, most of the wildlife action is concentrated in the northern sector. The triangle of largely open savannah between **Mururi Swamp**, **Leopard Rock Swamp** and **Mughwango Swamp** is easily the park's happiest hunting ground for lions and the herbivores they stalk.

The park's most significant waterway, **Rojewero River**, is a reliable place to view hippos and crocodiles. To the south you may want to check out **Elsa's Grave**, a stone memorial to the Adamsons' star lioness. Access to the adjacent **Kora National Park** is via the bridge near **Adamson's Falls**.

Rhino Sanctuary NATIONAL PARK
(⏰6am-6pm) FREE A signposted hard right not long after entering Murera Gate takes you to Meru's 48-sq-km Rhino Sanctuary, one of the best places in Kenya to see wild rhinos. At last count, this fenced portion of the park was home to 25 black and 55 white rhinos, many of whom were reintroduced here from Lake Nakuru National Park after the disastrous poaching of the 1980s.

Sleeping & Eating

Kinna Bandas BANDAS $$
(☎061-2303094; www.kws.go.ke; bandas US$80;) These three *bandas* each sleep two and are stocked with kerosene lanterns that add the right romanticism to a star-studded bush night. Located in the heart of the park, you can't get closer to the wildlife without the risk of being eaten by it. There's also a 10-bed guesthouse (US$250) and one four-bed cottage (US$160).

★**iKweta Safari Camp** TENTED CAMP $$
(☎0705200050; www.ikwetasafaricamp.com; s/d full board US$86/143; P) This terrific place is just outside Meru National Park, 2.5km from Murera Gate on the road in

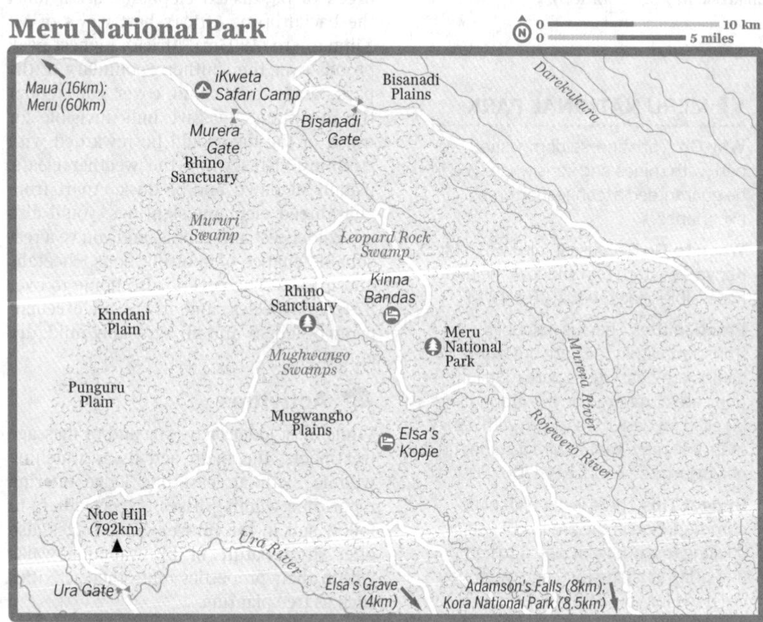

from Meru, so you can be inside the park in minutes. The semi-luxurious tents (with wi-fi) are outrageously good value and put to shame many tented camps that charge so much more for so much less.

★ **Elsa's Kopje** BANDAS $$$
(☎0730127000, 0733333887; www.elsaskopje.com; s/d full board from US$843/1124; 🏊) Plenty of hotels claim to blend into their environment, but Elsa's did so in such a seamless manner that the bar on chic ecosuites was permanently raised. Carved into Mugwangho Hill, these highly individualised 'three-walled' rooms open out onto views that *The Lion King* animators would have killed for.

ℹ Information

The KWS *Meru National Park Map* (KSh500), sometimes sold at the park gates, is helpful if you want to find your way around.

ℹ Getting There & Away

The park is roughly 1½ hours from Meru via the D484 Hwy. If you need a vehicle, **J Kirimi Safaris** (☎0721683700; http://bestkenyasafari.com/meru-national-park-safari) offers full-day safari packages from KSh18,000 per vehicle.

Airkenya (p258) has twice-daily flights connecting Meru to Nairobi's Wilson Airport (adult/child one way US$268/186).

> **ℹ MERU NATIONAL PARK**
>
> **Why Go** A pristine, seldom-visited park with rhinos and lions where you'll be guaranteed a 'congestion-free' experience.
>
> **When to Go** Because it falls within Mt Kenya's eastern rain shadow, the park is accessible year-round with a 4WD.
>
> **Practicalities** There is no public transport within the park but self-drive safaris are possible as park road junctions are numbered on the ground and labelled on park maps. Even with a park map, you may want to hire a guide (under/over three hours KSh1700/3000).
>
> **Budget Tips** There is not a lot of accommodation in the area, so if you are sticking to a budget it's best to camp and bring in all the food and water you will need for your stay.

SOUTHEASTERN KENYA

Southeastern Kenya is one of the great wildlife-watching destinations in Africa. Here you'll find a triumvirate of epic Kenyan parks – Amboseli, Tsavo West and Tsavo East – that are home to the Big Five and so much more. The landscapes, too, are something special, from Amboseli's backdrop of Africa's highest mountain, Mt Kilimanjaro, to the rugged beauty of Tsavo West's Ngulia Hills and the Chyulu Hills, Hemingway's Green Hills of Africa. Down here you'll also find smaller sanctuaries and so many exciting initiatives that combine conservation with community engagement. Many of these ensure that the chances to get to know the Maasai – the soulful human inhabitants of this land – on equal terms rank among the best in Kenya. And with good (if busy) roads and a newly minted rail link, it all adds up to Kenya at its wildest and yet most accessible.

Amboseli National Park

Amboseli (☎0716493335, Nairobi 020-8029705; www.kws.go.ke; adult/child US$60/35; ⏲6am-6pm) belongs in the elite of Kenya's national parks, and it's easy to see why. Its signature attraction is the sight of hundreds of big-tusked elephants set against the backdrop of Africa's best views of Mt Kilimanjaro (5895m). Africa's highest peak broods over the southern boundary of the park, and while cloud cover can render the mountain's massive bulk invisible for much of the day, you'll be rewarded with stunning vistas when the weather clears, usually at dawn and/or dusk. Apart from guaranteed elephant sightings, you'll also see wildebeest and zebras, and you've a reasonable chance of spotting lions, cheetahs and hyenas. The park is also home to over 370 bird species, and it has an excellent array of lodges and an agreeably mild, dry climate.

Activities

While most lodges have spa and/or massage treatments, the main activity is watching wildlife, with at least one lodge offering night-time wildlife drives (expect others to follow suit in the future). Most lodges also offer short nature or birdwatching walks within their properties and other activities such as tree planting.

Southeastern Kenya

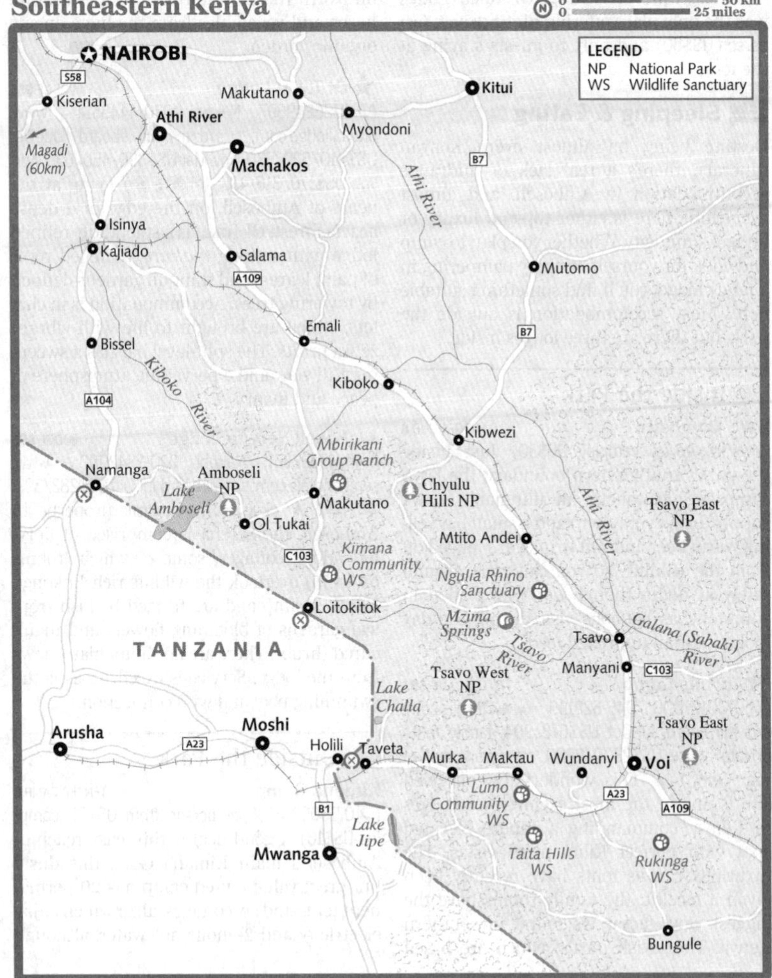

Wildlife Watching

The park's permanent swamps of **Enkongo Narok**, **Olokenya** and **Longinye** create a marshy belt across the middle of the park; this is where you'll encounter the most wildlife. Elephants love to wallow around in the muddy waters and you've a good chance of seeing hippos around the edge. For really close-up elephant encounters, **Sinet Causeway**, which crosses Enkongo Narok near (Normatior) Observation Hill, is often good; climb **Normatior** for fine views. The surrounding grasslands are home to grazing antelope, zebras and wildebeest, with spotted hyenas, cheetahs and lions sometimes lurking nearby; there's a reasonably reliable hyena den signposted northeast of the hill, which all the guides know about.

Birdlife is especially rich in these swamps when the migrants arrive in November.

If you're taking the road that runs east across the park to the Kimana Gate, watch for giraffes in the acacia woodlands; this is the best place inside the park for giraffe-spotting. We've also had excellent luck out here with cheetahs and lions.

At the time of writing, Ol Tukai Lodge was the only place offering **night drives** (per person US$80) and only to guests staying at the lodge.

Sleeping & Eating

Despite being on almost every Kenyan itinerary, there's a real lack of midrange accommodation in Amboseli, and almost everything here is either top-end luxury or budget simplicity. Whether you plan to camp and cook for yourself or enjoy pampering in a fancy lodge, you'll find something suitable here. Most accommodation is outside the park, but there are three lodges inside.

Inside the Park

KWS Campsite CAMPGROUND **$**
(www.kws.go.ke; camping US$30) Just inside the park's southeastern boundary, the KWS campsite has toilets, an unreliable water supply (bring your own) and a small bar selling warm beer and soft drinks. It's fenced off from the wildlife, so you can walk around safely at night, though *don't* keep food in your tent, as baboons visit during the day looking for an uninvited feed.

★Tortilis Camp TENTED CAMP **$$$**
(☎0730127000, 045-622195; www.tortilis.com; s/d full board Jul-Oct US$678/904, family tent/private house US$2300/2800, rates vary rest of year; P 📶) This wonderfully conceived site is one of the most exclusive ecolodges in Kenya, commanding a superb elevated spot with perfect Kilimanjaro vistas. The luxurious canvas tents have recently been given a facelift; the family rooms have the biggest wow factor we found in southern Kenya. The lavish meals, which are based on North Italian traditional recipes, feature herbs and vegetables from the huge on-site organic garden.

★Ol Tukai Lodge LODGE **$$$**
(☎0726249697, Nairobi 020-4445514; www.oltukailodge.com; s/d/tr full board Jul-Oct US$410/520/730, Nov-Mar US$350/450/630, Apr-Jun US$170/315/435; P @ 📶 🏊) Lying at the heart of Amboseli, on the edge of a dense acacia forest, Ol Tukai is a splendidly refined lodge with soaring *makuti* (thatched roofs of palm leaves) and tranquil gardens defined by towering trees. Accommodation is in chalets, which are brought to life with vibrant zebra prints. The split-level bar has a sweeping Kili view and a pervading atmosphere of peace and luxury.

Amboseli Serena Lodge LODGE **$$$**
(☎0735522361, Nairobi 020-2842000; www.serenahotels.com; s/d full board Jul-Oct US$282/392; @ 📶 🏊) A classically elegant property in Amboseli, the Serena is comprised of fiery-red adobe cottages, some of which (rooms 68 to 75) overlook the wildlife-rich Enkongo Narok swamp and are fringed by lush tropical gardens of blooming flowers and manicured shrubs. There are no Kilimanjaro views from the lodge. Service is excellent, as is the swimming pool and wi-fi connection.

Outside the Park

Kimana Camp TENTED CAMP **$**
(☎0715059635; per person from US$31, camping US$10) A good deal within easy reach of Amboseli's main Kimana Gate, this dusty but great-value tented camp has 20 permanent tents and six cottages, all of which enjoy electricity and 24-hour hot water, although

AMBOSELI NATIONAL PARK

Why Go To see big-tusked elephants, Africa's best Mt Kilimanjaro views, lions, cheetahs, hyenas, wildebeest and zebras, and rich birdlife.

When to Go Year-round. The dry season (July to October and January to February) is best for spotting wildlife, while November to March is the best time to see migratory birds. Much of the wildlife moves beyond the park during and immediately after the rains.

Practicalities The two most popular entrance gates are Iremito (accessible from Emali along the Nairobi–Mombasa highway) and Kimana (southeast). The two western approaches (Kitirua and Meshanani gates) are in poor condition. The park is accessible in 2WD, but 4WD is always the best option, particularly after rain.

Budget Tips Camp at a public campsite inside the park, or one of the private camps outside Kimana Gate. If you choose the latter, time your forays into the park carefully to make maximum use of the 24-hour entrance fee.

Amboseli National Park

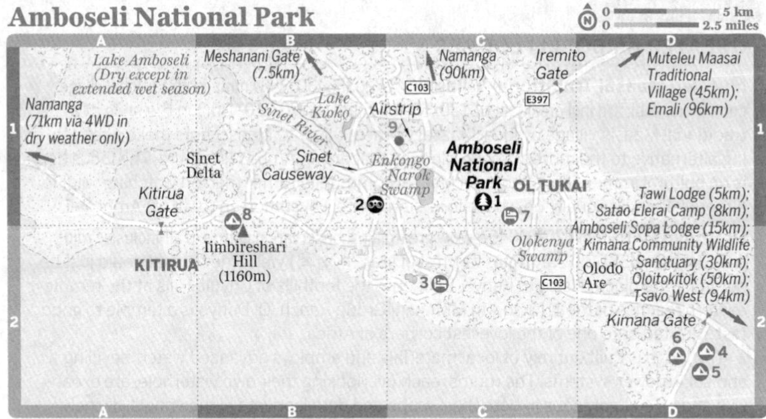

the bathrooms are extremely simple in both cases. There's a restaurant, a kitchen that guests can use and views of Kilimanjaro.

★ **Tawi Lodge** LODGE $$$
(☎Nairobi 020-2660080; www.tawilodge.com; s/d full board Jul-Sep US$530/820, rates vary rest of year; P 📶 ≋) 🌿 Set on its own private 24-sq-km conservancy close to Kimana Gate and with its own airstrip, Tawi Lodge is our pick of the places southeast of the park. You've got the choice of going into Amboseli or exploring Tawi's own wildlife-rich area, while the cottages are refined, beautifully furnished and most come with fine Kili views. There's even an on-site spa, and night drives are possible.

Kibo Safari Camp TENTED CAMP $$$
(☎0721380539; www.kibosafaricamp.com; per person from US$160; P 📶 ≋) Around 2km from Kimana Gate, Kibo Safari Camp gives you the experience of a tented camp without asking the prohibitive fees of the lodges inside the park proper; you can be inside the park soon after sunrise. The 72 tents and expansive grounds are beautifully kept and there are astonishing views of Kilimanjaro to be had, as well as a good restaurant serving high-quality buffet meals.

Getting There & Away

AIR

Airkenya (www.airkenya.com; adult/child one way US$187/138) has daily flights between Nairobi's Wilson Airport (35 minutes) and Amboseli. You'll need to arrange with one of the lodges or a safari company for a vehicle to meet you at the airstrip, which is inside the park proper, near Ol Tukai Lodge (p302). Most lodges within the park charge around US$40 for the transfer from the airstrip.

CAR & 4WD

There are four gates. Approaches to the park from the west (Kitirua and Meshanani gates) are in poor condition; the Iremito (northeast) and Kimana (southeast) gates are in better condition. The park is accessible in 2WD, but 4WD is always the best option, particularly after rain.

Amboseli National Park

Top Sights
1 Amboseli National Park C1

Sights
2 Normatior (Observation Hill) B1

Sleeping
3 Amboseli Serena Lodge C2
4 Kibo Safari Camp D2
5 Kimana Camp D2
6 KWS Campsite D2
7 Ol Tukai Lodge C1
8 Tortilis Camp B1

Transport
9 Airkenya C1

Tsavo West National Park

☎043

Welcome to the wilderness. **Tsavo West** (☎0720968527, Nairobi 0800597000, Nairobi 020-2384417; www.kws.go.ke/tsavo-west-national-park; adult/child US$52/35; ⏰6am-6pm) is one of Kenya's larger national parks (9065 sq km), covering a huge variety of landscapes

DON'T MISS

GREATER AMBOSELI LODGES

Muteleu Maasai Traditional Village (☎0720356430; www.mmaasaitraditionalvillage.com; Merrueshi; s/d incl breakfast US$30/50, full board US$70/120) Built in the style of a traditional Maasai village by local Maasai women, these 10 Maasai huts make a refreshing alternative to the more upmarket lodges that are an Amboseli feature. The focus here is on cultural immersion in the local Maasai community rather than on watching wildlife, although it could equally be a base for visiting (or a waystation en route to) Amboseli.

Ol Donyo (☎Nairobi 020-600457; www.greatplainsconservation.com; s/d all-inclusive mid-Jun–Oct from US$1733/2310, rates vary rest of year; P) Welcome to what could just be our favourite place to stay in Kenya. Built onto the foothills of Chyulu Hills at the remote eastern reaches of the 1113-sq-km Mbirikani Group Ranch, Ol Donyo is a temple to good taste grafted onto one of the loveliest corners of Africa.

The lodge is built entirely of local materials and employs advanced water recycling and solar-power systems. The rooms, each overlooking their own waterhole, are expansive and utterly gorgeous in both their scope and detail: private plunge pools, divinely comfortable four-poster beds with Kilimanjaro views, complete privacy and roof beds are merely the beginning of an overwhelming sensory experience that takes safari chic to a whole new level. The meals are world-class as well.

Day or night wildlife drives are, of course, possible, but so, too, are walking safaris out onto the plains or up onto the Chyulu Hills, horse-riding safaris and even running safaris for those eager not to let their exercise regimen slip.

Campi ya Kanzi (☎0720461300; www.maasai.com; s/d tented cottage US$950/1500, s/d tented suites US$1200/1900, conservation fee per adult/child from US$101/51; P) Campi ya Kanzi is, quite simply, an outstanding place to stay. Set upon the slopes of the Chyulu Hills – these may have been Ernest Hemingway's 'Green Hills of Africa' and that sobriquet means so much more here than it does in Chyulu Hills National Park – accommodation here is in luxury tents scattered around an enormous ranch that is centred on a nostalgically decorated stone lodge.

Wildlife drives (of both the day and night variety), walking safaris up into the Chyulu Hills, transcendental meditation sessions and visits to Maasai villages are all possible, but you'll also be tempted to simply nurse a drink as you gaze out across Maasailand towards Mt Kilimanjaro in all its glory.

Campi ya Kanzi was begun and continues to be overseen by Italians Luca and Antonella. While they bring so much personality to this place, Campi ya Kanzi is very much a Maasai concern. The camp's environmental credentials are also impeccable and the camp directly supports education, health care and environmental conservation in local communities, quite apart from employing dozens of local Maasai staff.

from swamps, natural springs and rocky peaks to extinct volcanic cones, rolling plains and sharp outcrops dusted with greenery.

This is a park with a whiff of legend about it, first for its famous man-eating lions in the late 19th century and then for its devastating levels of poaching in the 1980s. Despite the latter, there's still plenty of wildlife here, although you'll have to work harder and be much more patient than in Amboseli or the Masai Mara; the foliage is generally denser and higher here. Put all of these things together, along with its dramatic scenery, fine lodges and sense of space, and this is one of Kenya's most rewarding parks.

Sights

Chyulu Gate & the West

The plains, rocky outcrops and light woodland between Kilaguni Serena Lodge and the Chyulu Gate are good for zebras and other herbivores, and sustain a healthy population of lions, leopards and spotted hyenas – the epic battle between rival hyena clans that we witnessed here on our last visit remains a favourite Tsavo memory.

★**Shetani Lava Flows** LOOKOUT, VOLCANO

About 4km west of the Chyulu Gate of Tsavo West National Park, on the road to

Amboseli, are the spectacular Shetani lava flows. 'Shetani' means 'devil' in Kiswahili: the flows were formed only a few hundred years ago and local peoples believed that it was the devil himself emerging from the earth. This vast expanse of folded black lava spreads for 50 sq km across the savannah near the Chyulu Hills, looking strangely as if Vesuvius dropped its comfort blanket here.

The last major eruption here is believed to have taken place around 200 years ago, but there are still few plants among the cinders. It's possible to follow the lava flows back from the Amboseli–Tsavo West road to the ruined cinder cone of Shetani. The views are spectacular, but you need to be wary of wildlife in this area, as there are predators about.

Nearby are the **Shetani Caves**, which are also a result of volcanic activity. You'll need a torch (flashlight) if you want to explore, but watch your footing on the razor-sharp rocks and keep an eye out for the local fauna – we've heard rumours that the caves are sometimes inhabited by hyenas, who don't take kindly to being disturbed. Some of the Tsavo West lodges charge US$50 per person for guided excursions out here.

Rhino Valley

This is a highly recommended area for wildlife watching, with plenty of antelope species keeping a careful eye out for the resident lions, leopards and cheetahs. You'll also see elephants, giraffes and, if you're lucky, black rhinos. Birdlife is also particularly diverse here. The signposted 'Rhino Valley Circuit' is a good place to start, and anywhere along the Mukui River's ponds and puddles is a place to watch and wait.

★Ngulia Hills MOUNTAIN

Rising more than 600m above the valley floor and to a height of over 1800m above sea level, this jagged ridgeline ranks among the prettiest of all Tsavo landforms, providing as it does a backdrop to Rhino Valley. The hills can be climbed with permission from the **warden** (☎043-30049; tsavowestnp@kws.go.ke), while the peaks are also a recognised flyway for migrating birds heading south from late September through to November.

Tsavo Gate & the East

Many visitors heading for Tsavo East National Park or Mombasa use this gate. Wildlife spotting in this eastern section of the park is challenging due to the quite dense foliage, but both leopards and lions are known to frequent the area.

★Ngulia Rhino Sanctuary WILDLIFE RESERVE

(⏲4-6pm) At the base of Ngulia Hills, this 90-sq-km area is surrounded by a 1m-high electric fence and provides a measure of security for around 80 of the park's highly endangered black rhinos. There are driving tracks and waterholes within the enclosed area, but the rhinos are mainly nocturnal and the chances of seeing one are slim – black rhinos, apart from being understandably shy and more active at night, are browsers, not grazers, and prefer to pass their time in thick undergrowth.

Tsavo River & the South

Running west–east through the park, this lovely year-round river is green-shaded and surrounded for much of its path by doum palms. Along with Mzima Springs, the river provides aesthetic relief from the vast semi-arid habitats that dominate the park.

TSAVO WEST NATIONAL PARK

Why Go For the dramatic scenery, wilderness and good mix of predators (lions, leopards, cheetahs and hyenas), prey (lesser kudus, gazelles, impalas) and other herbivores (elephants, rhinos, zebras, oryxes and giraffes).

When to Go Year-round. The dry season (May to October and January to March) is best for spotting wildlife. November to March is the best time to see migratory birds.

Practicalities Drive in from Mtito Andei or Tsavo Gate along the Nairobi–Mombasa road. There is a campsite close to the park entrance and lodges throughout the park.

Budget Tips Rent a matatu with other travellers in Mtito Andei; if staying in a lodge, June is much cheaper than July.

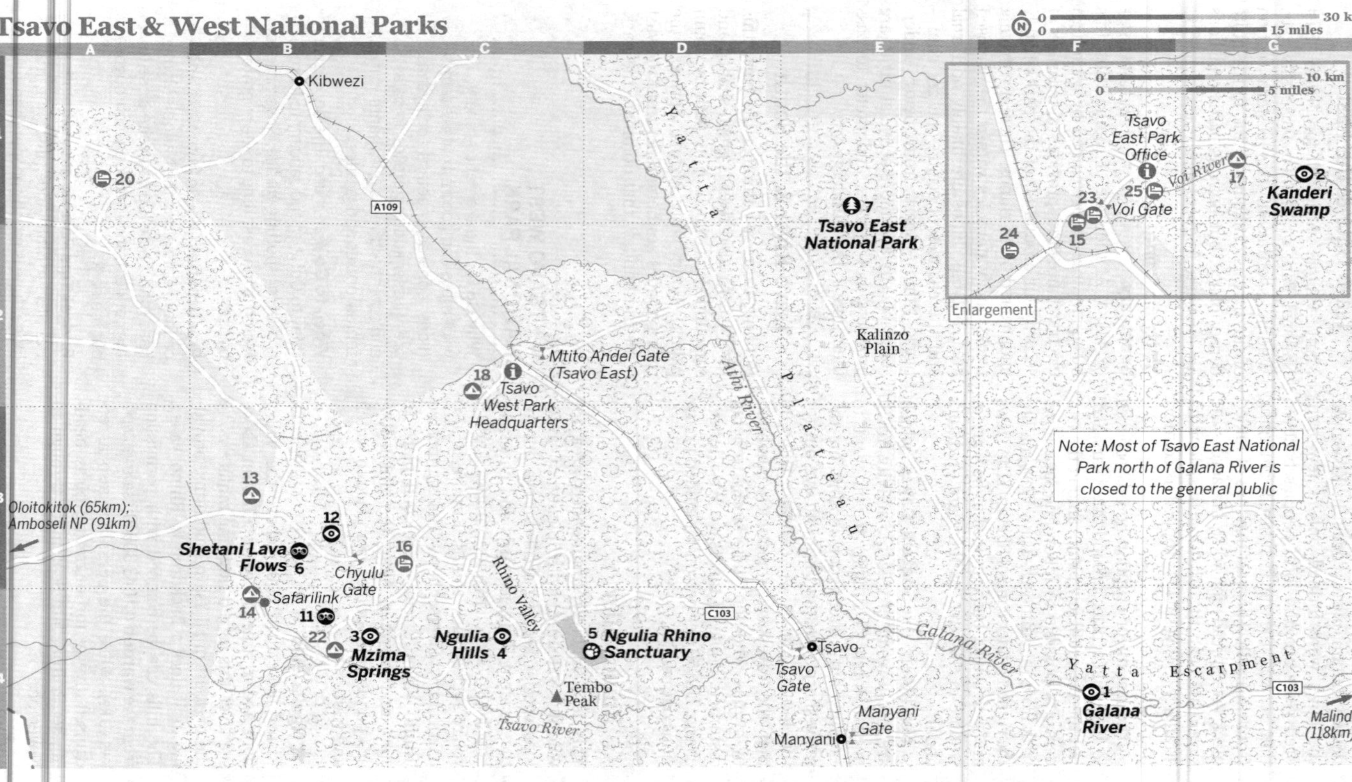
Tsavo East & West National Parks
30 km
15 miles
Kibwezi
20
A109
Yatta Plateau
7
Tsavo East National Park
Tsavo East Park Office
Voi River
17
2
Kanderi Swamp
23
25
Voi Gate
24
15
10 km
5 miles
Enlargement
Kalinzo Plain
Mtito Andei Gate (Tsavo East)
18
Tsavo West Park Headquarters
Athi River
Note: Most of Tsavo East National Park north of Galana River is closed to the general public
13
Oloitokitok (65km); Amboseli NP (91km)
12
Shetani Lava Flows 6
Chyulu Gate
16
Safarilink
14
11
22
3
Mzima Springs
Rhino Valley
Ngulia Hills 4
5 Ngulia Rhino Sanctuary
C103
Tembo Peak
Tsavo River
Tsavo
Tsavo Gate
Manyani Gate
Manyani
Galana River
Yatta Escarpment
1
Galana River
Malindi (118km)

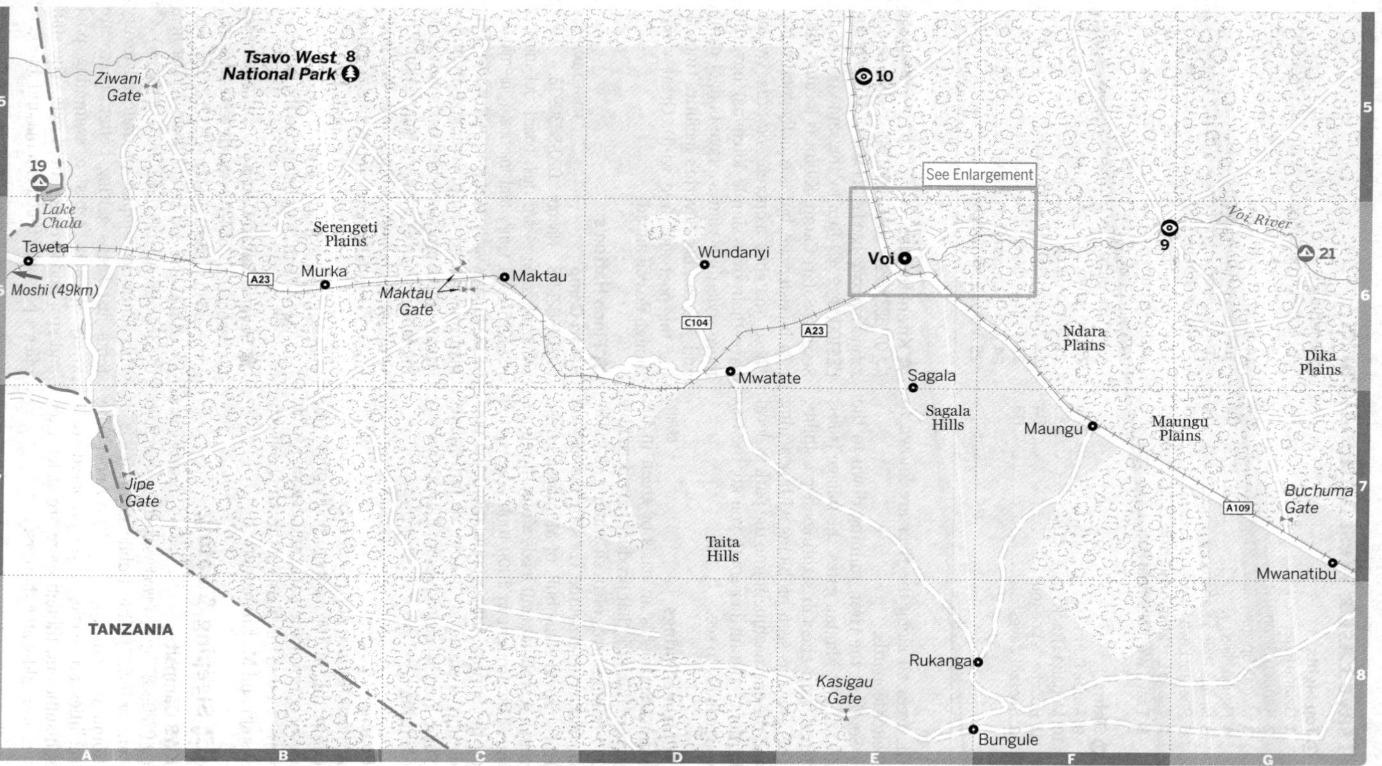

Tsavo West National Park
8
Ziwani Gate
19
Lake Chala
Taveta
Moshi (49km)
A23
Serengeti Plains
Murka
Maktau Gate
Maktau
Wundanyi
C104
Mwatate
10
See Enlargement
Voi
9
Voi River
21
Ndara Plains
Dika Plains
Sagala
Sagala Hills
Maungu
Maungu Plains
Buchuma Gate
A109
Mwanatibu
Jipe Gate
Taita Hills
TANZANIA
Rukanga
Kasigau Gate
Bungule
A
B
C
D
E
F
G
5
6
7
8

Tsavo East & West National Parks

Top Sights

1 Galana River F4
2 Kanderi Swamp G1
3 Mzima Springs B4
4 Ngulia Hills C4
5 Ngulia Rhino Sanctuary D4
6 Shetani Lava Flows B3
7 Tsavo East National Park E1
8 Tsavo West National Park B5

Sights

9 Aruba Dam F6
10 Mudanda Rock E5
11 Poacher's Lookout B4
12 Shetani Caves B3

Sleeping

Ashnil Aruba Lodge .... (see 9)
13 Campi ya Kanzi B3
14 Finch Hatton's Safari Camp B4
15 Impala Safari Lodge F2
16 Kilaguni Serena Lodge C3
Kitani Bandas .... (see 22)
17 KWS Campsite G1
18 KWS Campsite C2
19 Lake Chala Safari Lodge & Campsite A5
20 Ol Donyo A1
21 Satao Camp G6
22 Severin Safari Camp B4
23 Tsavo Lodge F1
24 Voi Lutheran Guesthouse F2
25 Voi Wildlife Lodge F1

The trees all along the river are known to shelter leopards.

South of the river, running down to the Ziwani and Maktau gates, the foliage is less dense, with cheetah sightings a possibility. This area has seen problems with poaching and the encroachment into the park by local herders – the further south you go, the less you're likely to see.

★Mzima Springs SPRING

Mzima Springs is an oasis of green in the west of the park that produces an incredible 250 million litres of fresh water a day. The springs, whose source rises in the Chyulu Hills, provides the bulk of Mombasa's fresh water. A walking trail leads along the shoreline. The drought in 2009 took a heavy toll on the springs' hippo population; the population is stable at around 20 individuals. There are also crocodiles and a wide variety of birdlife.

Poacher's Lookout VIEWPOINT

A short distance northwest of Severin Safari Camp, this hilltop vantage point offers fine views out over the park, and especially fine views west to the plains of the Amboseli ecosystem and Mt Kilimanjaro.

Sleeping & Eating

KWS Campsite CAMPGROUND $

(☎0720968527; www.kws.co.ke; Komboyo; camping US$20) This public campsite is at Komboyo, 8km from the Mtito Andei Gate. Facilities are basic, so be prepared to be self-sufficient, though there are at least toilets and cold-water showers.

★Kitani Bandas BANDAS $$

(☎0716833222, 041-2004154; www.severinsafaricamp.com; bandas Jul-Mar US$125, Apr-Jun US$100; P 📶 🏊) Run by the same people as Severin Safari Camp, Kitani is located 2km past its sister site, but is equally good value. These thatched concrete *bandas* (which have their own simple kitchens) have far more style than your average budget camp and you can use Severin's facilities (including the pool and free wi-fi). Great value, though do call ahead.

★Finch Hatton's Safari Camp TENTED CAMP $$$

(☎0716021818, Nairobi 020-8030936; www.finchhattons.com; s/d full board Jul–mid-Oct US$1225/1960, family tent full board Jul–mid-Oct US$3240, rates vary rest of year; P 📶 🏊) This luxurious tented camp, arranged around a stream full of crocs and hippos, is now looking fancier than ever after a renovation. The 17 massive, glamorous tents have vast beds, huge verandahs and incredible outdoor bathrooms complete with copper bathtubs. There's a spa, gym and pool, courteous staff and a wonderfully stylish air to the place.

★Severin Safari Camp TENTED CAMP $$$

(☎Nairobi 020-2684247; www.severinsafaricamp.com; s/d full board Jul-Mar US$252/388, Apr-Jun US$143/286, s/d ste full board Jul-Mar from US$379/506, Apr-Jun US$279/372; P 📶 🏊) This fantastic complex of thatched luxury tents just keeps getting better. There are lovely, spacious tents, a swimming pool and spa, and even a tented gym. The staff offer a personal touch (Manja and Juergen, a pastry chef, have been running this place since 2008), the food is outstanding and the tents are large and sumptuous despite costing considerably less than others elsewhere in the park.

Kilaguni Serena Lodge LODGE **$$$**
(☎045-622376; www.serenahotels.com; s/d full board Jul-Oct US$243/342, rates vary rest of year; P@🛜🏊) As you'd expect from the upmarket Serena chain, this lodge is extremely comfortable with semi-luxurious, if slightly dated rooms. The centrepiece here is a splendid bar and restaurant with soaring thatched ceilings, volcanic stone and a panoramic bar overlooking a busy illuminated waterhole – the vista stretches all the way from Mt Kilimanjaro to the Chyulu Hills and has the wow factor upon arrival.

Information

MAPS

Tsavo West National Park map and guidebook is available from Mtito Andei Gate.

TOURIST INFORMATION

Tsavo West Park Headquarters The nearest park entrance to Mtito Andei; there is limited information here and a rather dusty interpretation centre.

Getting There & Away

There are six gates into Tsavo West, but the main access is just off the Nairobi–Mombasa road at Mtito Andei and Tsavo gates. Payment can be made at all gates.

Safarilink (☎Nairobi 020-6690000; www.flysafarilink.com; adult/child one way US$224/170) has daily flights between Nairobi's Wilson Airport and Tsavo West, with airstrips near Finch Hatton's Camp and Kilaguni Serena Lodge. You'll need to arrange with one of the lodges or a safari company for a vehicle to meet you at the airstrip.

Fuel is generally available at Kilaguni Serena Lodge and Severin Safari Camp, but fill up before entering the park.

The newly inaugurated Nairobi–Mombasa railway stops at Mtito Andei – most lodges and tented camps in the park offer transfers from the station.

Tsavo East National Park

☎043

Kenya's largest national park, **Tsavo East** (☎0722290009, 0775563672, Nairobi 020-6000800; www.kws.go.ke/content/tsavo-east-national-park; adult/child US$52/35; ⌚6am-6pm), has an undeniable wild and primordial charm and is a terrific wildlife-watching destination. Although one of Kenya's largest rivers flows through the middle of the park, the landscape here is markedly flatter and drier and lacks the drama of Tsavo West. The flip side is that spotting wildlife is generally easier thanks to the thinly spread foliage.

Despite the size of the park, the area of most wildlife activity is actually quite compact – the northern section of the park is largely closed and can only be visited with advance permission due to the threat of banditry and ongoing campaigns against poachers. The demarcation point is the Galana River.

Sights

Most people come to Tsavo East to see the famous red elephants of Tsavo – their colour comes from bathing in the red Tsavo mud (to keep the skin cool and prevent insect bites). The two Tsavo parks have the largest elephant populations of any Kenyan parks and include a third of the country's total, although herds are quite small. Lion and cheetah sightings are also common; unusually, the male lions are almost maneless.

Tsavo East is also notable as one of few places in southern Kenya where you can tick off some species usually seen only much further north. We've had luck here with the Somali ostrich (notable for its blue neck)

TSAVO EAST NATIONAL PARK

Why Go Wilderness, red elephants and leopards, lions and cheetahs. The park also has close to 500 bird species.

When to Go June to February. Wildlife concentrations are highest in the dry season (September to October and January to early March).

Practicalities Drive in from Voi, Manyani or Tsavo gates along the Nairobi–Mombasa road. The Sala and Buchuma gates are good for Mombasa. There are a small number of lodges and camps throughout the park or close to Voi Gate.

Budget Tips Rent a matatu or organise a budget safari with other travellers in Voi or the coast; use public campsites.

and the gerenuk, an unusual breed of long-necked gazelle that 'browse' by standing on their hind legs and stretching their necks, as if yearning to be giraffes.

Aruba Dam LAKE

Some 30km east of Voi Gate is the Aruba Dam, which spans the Voi River. It also attracts heavy concentrations of diverse wildlife; one of the park's regularly spotted lion prides ranges around here. Away to the east and southeast, all the way down to the Buchuma Gate, the open grasslands provide the perfect habitat for cheetahs and sightings are more common here than almost anywhere else in southeastern Kenya.

★Kanderi Swamp RIVER

Around 10km from Voi Gate, the lovely area of green known as Kanderi Swamp is home to a resident pride of lions, and elephants also congregate near here; this is one of only two water sources in the park during the dry season. The landscape here has a lovely backdrop of distant hills. A number of vehicle tracks also follow the contours of the Voi River; keep an eye on the overhanging branches for leopards.

★Galana River RIVER

Running through the heart of the park and marking the northernmost point in the park that most visitors are allowed to visit, the Galana River, which combines the waters of the Tsavo and Athi Rivers, cuts a green gash across the dusty plains. Surprisingly few visitors make it even this far and sightings of crocs, hippos, lesser kudus, waterbucks, dik-diks and, to a lesser extent, lions and leopards are relatively common. Watch out also for the distinctive Somali ostrich.

Mudanda Rock MOUNTAIN

Towering over a natural dam near the Manyani Gate, this towering natural formation runs for over 1.5km. It attracts elephants in the dry season and is reminiscent of Australia's Uluru (Ayers Rock), albeit on a much smaller scale. Leopards and elephants are among the wildlife to watch out for here.

MAN-EATERS OF TSAVO

The famed 'man-eaters of Tsavo' were among the most dangerous lions to ever roam the planet. During the building of the Kenya–Uganda Railway in 1898, efforts soon came to a halt when railway workers started being dragged from their tents at night and devoured by two maneless male lions.

The surviving workers soon decided that the lions had to be ghosts or devils, which put the future of the railway in jeopardy. Engineer Lt Col John Henry Patterson created a series of ever more ingenious traps, but each time the lions evaded them, striking unerringly at weak points in the camp defences. Patterson was finally able to bag the first man-eater by hiding on a flimsy wooden scaffold baited with the corpse of a donkey. The second man-eater was dispatched a short time later, although it took six bullets to bring the massive beast down.

According to Patterson's calculations, the two lions killed and ate around 135 workers in less than one year. He detailed his experiences in the best-selling book *The Man-Eaters of Tsavo* (1907), which was later rather freely filmed as *Bwana Devil* (1952) and *The Ghost and the Darkness* (1996).

Patterson turned the two man-eaters into floor rugs. In 1924 he finally rid himself of the lions by selling their skins to the Chicago Field Museum for the sum of US$5000. The man-eaters of Tsavo were then stuffed and placed on permanent display, where they remain to this day.

Hypotheses vary as to why these lions became man-eaters. Tsavo lions have noticeably elevated levels of the male sex hormone testosterone. The pair themselves also had badly damaged teeth, which may have driven them to abandon their normal prey and become man-eaters. An outbreak of rinderpest (an infectious viral disease) might have decimated the lions' usual prey, forcing them to find alternative food sources. One final theory is that the man-eaters may have developed their taste for human flesh after growing accustomed to finding human bodies at the Tsavo River crossing, where slave caravans often crossed en route to Zanzibar.

Sleeping & Eating

KWS Campsite CAMPGROUND $

(camping US$20) Decent site with toilets, showers and a communal kitchen. The location is good, as most safari vehicles don't loop down this way and there's some good wildlife-viewing down by the riverbank and in nearby Kanderi Swamp. You'll need to register at the gate and be entirely self-sufficient in food and water to stay here. Limited supplies are available in Voi.

Voi Wildlife Lodge LODGE $$

(0733201240, 0722201240; www.voiwildlifelodge.com; s/d full board from US$117/180; P) Close to Voi Gate, this well-run place is actually a number of places in one. From the main property, there are fine views into the park from some of the recently renovated rooms as well as from the restaurant and viewing platform. At its Manyatta property, the tents have private plunge pools. It's a good deal in a good location just outside the park.

Satao Camp TENTED CAMP $$$

(Nairobi 020-2434610; www.sataocamp.com; s/d full board Jul-Oct US$337/436, rates vary rest of year; P) Located on the banks of the Voi River, this luxury camp was recently renovated and now looks better than ever. There are 20 canopied tents, all of which are perfectly spaced within sight of a waterhole that's known to draw lions, cheetahs and elephants on occasion. The elevated viewing tower and the sense of being far removed from the safari scrum are big selling points here.

Ashnil Aruba Lodge LODGE $$$

(Nairobi 020-4971008; www.ashnilhotels.com; s/d full board US$262/350; P@) A stone's throw from the wildlife-rich Aruba Dam, this lodge has attractively decorated rooms decked out in safari prints, although it's the six luxury tents that are the real stars, with a far stronger sense of light and space than the rooms. In the heart of the park, it's an ideal starting point for most Tsavo East safaris.

Information

MAPS

The *Tsavo East National Park* map and guidebook is available from Voi Gate.

TOURIST INFORMATION

Tsavo East Park Office (0722290009) The park's eastern entrance; good for park information.

Getting There & Away

You'll need your own wheels to explore Tsavo East, and so even though it's perfectly easy to access the park on public transport from the town of Voi on the main road between Nairobi and Mombasa, it's not very useful unless you've got onward transport into the park booked.

A track through the park follows the Galana River from the Tsavo Gate to the Sala Gate; others fan out from Voi Gate. To access the park with your own vehicle use the following park gates.

To/from Nairobi or Tsavo West Voi, Tsavo or Manyani gates.

To/from Mombasa Sala or Buchuma gates.

Fuel is available in Voi; fill up before entering the park.

Voi

043 / POP 45,485

Voi is a key service town at the intersection of the Nairobi–Mombasa road, the road to Moshi in Tanzania and the access road to the main Voi Gate of Tsavo East National Park. As such, much of its activity is designed around trying to catch the monetary crumbs that fall from the pockets of those changing transport, on safari or simply passing through. Think of it more as a place to get directions, fill up on petrol, change money and buy a newspaper or some snacks for the road, than as a place to linger.

Sleeping & Eating

You'll find simple places serving *nyama choma* in numerous places surrounding the main matatu park and market in the centre of town. Wandering traders sell fresh fruits. Of the hotels and lodges in town, Impala Safari Lodge (p312) and **Tsavo Lodge** (0721328567; www.tsavolodgesandcamps.com; s/d/tr full board US$55/90/120; P) both have reasonable restaurants – non-guests should book ahead.

★ **Voi Lutheran Guesthouse** GUESTHOUSE $

(Nairobi 020-2668607; www.voiguesthouse.com; Bogesunds Farm, off Mombasa Rd; s/d incl breakfast KSh2300/3300, full board KSh3300/5300, per person incl breakfast/full board with shared bathroom KSh1500/2500) Easily the pick of the accommodation if you're not staying in the park, the Lutheran Guesthouse occupies a handsome house on a farm 1km west of the Nairobi–Mombasa road. Rooms have some colourful touches, with local basket decor and zebra-print shower curtains, and it's a much quieter choice than anywhere in town. The turn-off is 1km north of the Taveta turn-off along the main highway.

Impala Safari Lodge LODGE $$
(☎0750153694; www.impalasafarilodge.com; Edward Maganga Rd; s/d US$74/88; P 📶 ❄) In Voi but slightly removed from the main-road scrum, Impala Safari Lodge offers attractive safari tents in a secure compound. While the setting is more suburban than wilderness, the price is excellent and you're only a short drive from the national park.

Getting There & Away

Frequent buses and matatus run to/from Mombasa (KSh250 to KSh600, three hours), and buses run to Nairobi (KSh600 to KSh1400, six hours). There are at least daily matatus to Wundanyi (KSh300, one hour) and Taveta (KSh550, two hours), on the Tanzanian border.

Voi also lies along the recently upgraded Nairobi–Mombasa railway line.

MOMBASA & THE SOUTH COAST

Mombasa

☎041 / POP 915,101

Mombasa, a melting pot of languages and cultures from all sides of the Indian Ocean, waits like an exotic dessert for travellers who make it to Kenya's coastline. Having more in common with Dakar or Dar es Salaam than Nairobi, Mombasa's blend of India, Arabia and Africa can be intoxicating, and many visitors find themselves seduced by East Africa's biggest and most cosmopolitan port despite its grime and sleaze, which somehow only adds to the place's considerable charm.

Indeed, the city dubbed in Swahili *Kisiwa Cha Mvita* – the Island of War – has many faces, from the ecstatic passion of the call to prayer over the Old Town, to the waves crashing against the coral beaches below Fort Jesus and the sight of a Zanzibar-bound dhow slipping over the horizon. As the Swahili people themselves say in an old proverb: 'Mombasa is famous, but its waters are dangerously deep. Beware!'

Sights

★Fort Jesus MUSEUM
(Map p314; www.museums.or.ke; Nkrumah Rd; adult/child KSh1200/600; ⏲8am-6pm) This 16th-century fort and Unesco World Heritage treasure is Mombasa's most visited site. The metre-thick walls, frescoed interiors, traces of European graffiti, Arabic inscriptions and Swahili embellishment aren't just evocative, they're a palimpsest of Mombasa's history and the coast writ in stone. You can climb on the battlements and explore its tree-shaded grounds.

The fort was built by the Portuguese in 1593 to serve as both symbol and headquarters of their permanent presence in this corner of the Indian Ocean. It's ironic, then, that the construction of the fort marked the beginning of the end of local Portuguese hegemony. Between Portuguese sailors, Omani soldiers and Swahili rebellions, the fort changed hands at least nine times between 1631 and the early 1870s, when it finally fell under British control and was used as a jail; it opened as a museum in 1960.

The fort was the final project completed by Giovanni Battista Cairati, whose buildings can be found throughout Portugal's eastern colonies, from Old Goa to Old Mombasa. The building is an opus of period military design – assuming the structure was well manned, it would have been impossible to approach its walls without falling under the cone of interlocking fields of fire.

Within the fort compound, the **Mazrui Hall**, where flowery spirals fade across a wall topped with wooden lintels left by the Omani Arabs, is worthy of note. In another room, Portuguese sailors scratched graffiti that illustrates the multicultural naval identity of the Indian Ocean, leaving walls covered with four-pointed European frigates, three-pointed Arabic dhows and the coir-sewn 'camels of the ocean': the elegant Swahili *mtepe* (traditional sailing vessel). The **Omani house**, in the San Felipe bastion in the northwestern corner of the fort, was built in the late 18th century and has a small fishing dhow outside it. Inside there's a small exhibition of Omani jewellery, weaponry and other artefacts. The eastern wall includes an Omani audience hall and the Passage of the Arches, which leads under the pinkish-brown

The Coast

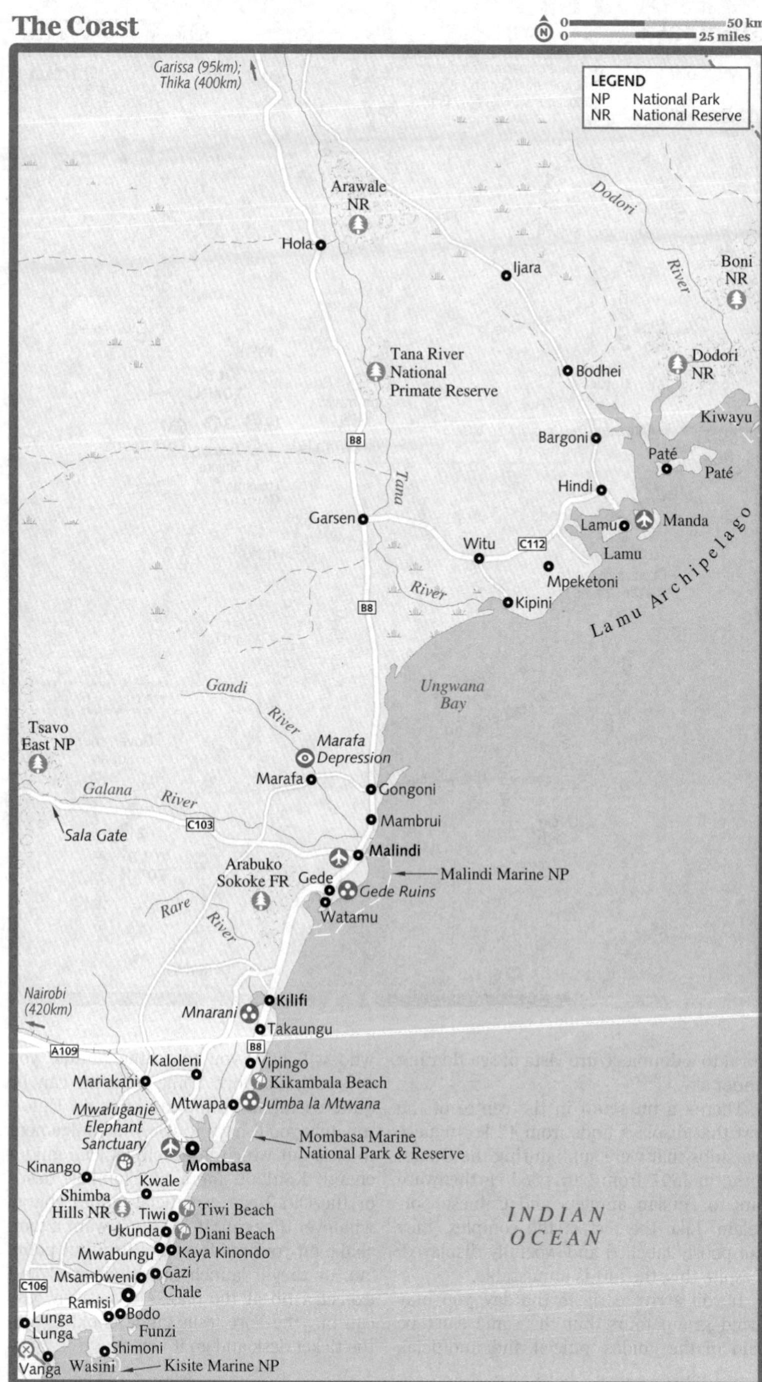

0 50 km
0 25 miles
LEGEND
NP National Park
NR National Reserve
Garissa (95km); Thika (400km)
Arawale NR
Hola
Ijara
Dodori River
Boni NR
Tana River National Primate Reserve
Bodhei
Dodori NR
Kiwayu
Bargoni
Paté
Paté
Hindi
B8
Tana
Garsen
Lamu
Manda
Lamu
Witu
C112
Mpeketoni
River
Kipini
Lamu Archipelago
B8
Ungwana Bay
Gandi River
Tsavo East NP
Marafa Depression
Marafa
Gongoni
Galana River
Sala Gate
C103
Mambrui
Malindi
Malindi Marine NP
Arabuko Sokoke FR
Gede
Gede Ruins
Watamu
Rare River
Nairobi (420km)
Kilifi
Mnarani
Takaungu
A109
B8
Kaloleni
Vipingo
Mariakani
Kikambala Beach
Mwaluganje Elephant Sanctuary
Mtwapa
Jumba la Mtwana
Mombasa Marine National Park & Reserve
Mombasa
Kinango
Kwale
Shimba Hills NR
Tiwi
Tiwi Beach
Ukunda
Diani Beach
INDIAN OCEAN
Mwabungu
Kaya Kinondo
Msambweni
Gazi
C106
Chale
Ramisi
Bodo
Lunga Lunga
Funzi
Shimoni
Vanga
Wasini
Kisite Marine NP

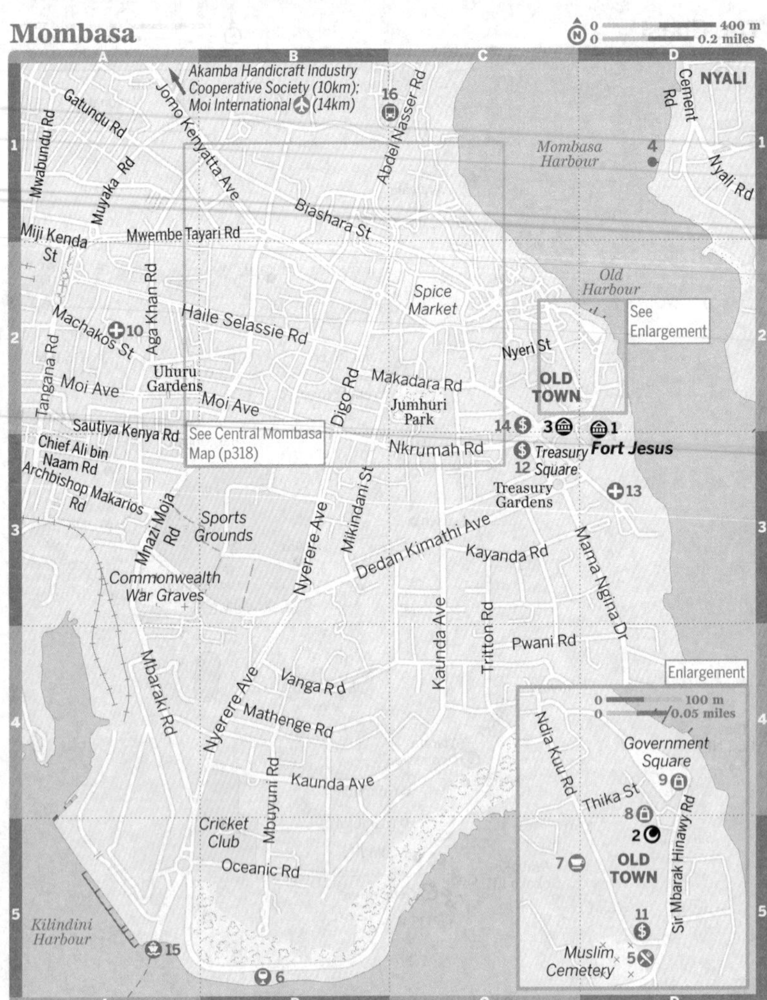

coral to a double-azure vista of sea floating under sky.

There's a **museum** in the centre of the fort that displays finds from 42 Portuguese warships that were sunk during the Omani Siege in 1697, from barnacled earthenware jars to Persian amulets and Chinese porcelain. Like the rest of the complex, they are poorly labelled and woefully displayed. Despite this, the fort is unmissable.

If you arrive early in the day, you may avoid group tours, but the same can't be said of the guides, official and unofficial, who will offer you tours the minute you approach the fort. Some of them can be quite useful and some can be duds. Unfortunately you'll have to use your judgement to suss out which is which. Official guides charge KSh1200 for a tour of Fort Jesus or the Old Town; unofficial guides charge whatever they can. If you don't want a tour, shake off your guide with a firm but polite 'no', or they'll launch into their spiel and expect a tip at the end. Alternatively, you can buy the Fort Jesus guide booklet from the ticket desk and go it alone.

Mombasa

Top Sights
1 Fort Jesus ... D2

Sights
2 Mandhry Mosque ... D5
3 Old Law Courts ... C2

Activities, Courses & Tours
4 Tamarind Dhow ... D1

Eating
5 The Fort ... D5

Drinking & Nightlife
6 Florida Club ... B5
7 Jahazi Coffee House ... C5

Shopping
8 Sandal Shop ... D4
9 Yusufi Antiques & Gallery ... D4

Information
10 AAR Mombasa Health Centre ... A2
11 Fort Jesus Forex Bureau ... D5
12 Kenya Commercial Bank ... C3
13 Mombasa Hospital ... D3
14 Standard Chartered Bank ... C2

Transport
15 Likoni Car Ferry ... A5
16 Tawakal ... C1

Old Law Courts GALLERY

(Map p314; Nkrumah Rd; 8am-6pm) FREE Dating from 1902, the old law courts on Nkrumah Rd have been converted into an informal gallery, with regularly changing displays of local art, Kenyan crafts, school competition pieces and votive objects from various tribal groups.

Spice Market MARKET

(Map p318; Langoni Rd; sunrise to sunset) This market, which stretches along Nehru and Langoni Rds west of the Old Town, is an evocative, sensory overload – expect lots of jostling, yelling, wheeling, dealing and, of course, the exotic scent of stall upon stall of cardamom, pepper, turmeric and curry powders, with stalls along Langoni Rd selling delicious street food.

Mandhry Mosque MOSQUE

(Map p314; Sir Mbarak Hinawy Rd) Founded in 1570, Mandhry Mosque in the Old Town is the city's oldest, and an excellent example of Swahili architecture, which combines the elegant flourishes of Arabic style with the comforting, geometric patterns of African design – note, for example, the gently rounded minaret. Not open to visitors.

Lord Shiva Temple TEMPLE

(Map p318; Mwinyi Ab Rd; 10am-12.30pm) Mombasa's large Hindu population doesn't lack for places of worship. The enormous Lord Shiva Temple is airy, open and set off by an interesting sculpture garden.

Holy Ghost Cathedral CHURCH

(Map p318; Nkrumah Rd) The Christian Holy Ghost Cathedral is a very European hunk of neo-Gothic buttressed architecture, with massive fans in the walls to cool its former colonial congregations.

Activities

Luxury dhow cruises around the harbour are popular in Mombasa and, notwithstanding the price, they are an excellent way to see the harbour, the Old Town and Fort Jesus, and get a slap-up meal at the end of it.

★Tamarind Dhow BOATING

(Map p314; 041-4471747, 0733623583; www.tamarind.co.ke; Cement Silo Rd; lunch/dinner cruise per person US$70/92; departs 1pm/6.30pm) This top-billing cruise is run by the posh Tamarind restaurant chain. It embarks from the jetty below Tamarind restaurant in Nyali and includes a harbour tour and fantastic meal. Prices include a cocktail and transport to and from your hotel. The two Jahazi dhows themselves are beautiful pieces of work.

Suleiman Sabdallah WALKING

(0722478570) Reliable, knowledgeable, licensed tour guide happy to take you around the fort or Old Town.

Festivals & Events

★Mombasa Carnival FESTIVAL

(zainab@africaonline.co.ke; Nov) Street festival, with a month of music, dance and other events.

Sleeping

Mombasa has a number of decent hotels, though in general the more upmarket places tend to be far from the city centre.

TOURS & SAFARIS FROM MOMBASA

A number of tour companies offer standard tours of the Old Town and Fort Jesus (per person from US$60), plus safaris to Shimba Hills National Reserve and Tsavo East and Tsavo West national parks, famed for their easy access to wildlife. Most safaris are expensive lodge-based affairs, but there are a few camping safaris to Tsavo East and West.

The most popular safari is an overnight tour to Tsavo, and though most people enjoy these, be warned that a typical two-day, one-night safari barely gives you time to get there and back, and that your animal-spotting time will be very limited. It's much better to add in at least one extra night. There are several tour companies in Mombasa that receive positive feedback regarding their tours.

Ketty Tours (Map p318; ☎0722209516, 041-2315178; www.kettysafari.com; Ketty Plaza, Moi Ave) Full range of multiday Masai Mara safaris, as well as overnight Tsavo East safaris and day trips to Shimba Hills. Also rents cars and can organise a car and driver.

Natural World Kenya Safaris (Map p318; ☎041-2226715, 0720894288; www.naturaltoursandsafaris.com; Jeneby House, Moi Ave) The hard sell prattled by the company 'representatives' on the street can be a little off-putting, but they have a solid reputation for arranging multiday safaris, as well as Mombasa city tours and trips to Tsavo East, ranging from a day to a week.

Dirt-cheap choices are in the busy area close to the bus stations on Abdel Nasser Rd and Jomo Kenyatta Ave. Lone female travellers might want to opt for something a little further up the price scale and away from the bus station area, which is rather sketchy.

Glory Grand Hotel BUSINESS HOTEL **$**
(Map p318; ☎041-2313564; Kwa Shibu Rd; s/d from KSh3500/4500) Neither glorious nor grand, this hotel is instead excellent value, with spruced-up rooms that hint at business-hotel style – minus the cost. Breakfast is simple, but it's a safe, convenient place to sleep and is located in a quiet(ish) area.

New Palm Tree Hotel HOTEL **$**
(Map p318; ☎0715442017; www.newpalmtreehotel.com; Nkrumah Rd; s/d/tr KSh2500/3500/4500; 📶) If you're looking for central, budget-friendly but reasonably comfortable digs, this place delivers. Rooms are arranged around a courtyard and while the amenities (such as hot water) aren't always reliable, the service is personable and helpful, it's generally well cared for and there's a good vibe about the place, including a Ugandan restaurant downstairs.

Royal Court Hotel BUSINESS HOTEL **$$**
(Map p318; ☎0733412867; www.royalcourtmombasa.co.ke; Haile Selassie Rd; s/d KSh7700/10,500; ❄📶🏊) The swish lobby is the highlight of this stylish business hotel. Still, service and facilities are good, disabled access is a breeze and you get great views and food at the Roof Restaurant (on the roof), which also has a pool, and Malaika Brasserie. It wins points for charging everyone the same rates and for the spa and gym.

Lotus Hotel HOTEL **$$**
(Map p318; ☎041-2313207; www.lotushotelmombasa.com; Cathedral Lane, off Nkrumah Rd; s/d US$50/75; ❄📶) One of the best-value midrange options in Mombasa, the old-world Lotus is central and has clean, compact rooms with hot water and functioning air-conditioning. Staff are especially welcoming, and there are two bars downstairs to boot.

Sentrim Castle Royal Hotel HISTORIC HOTEL **$$**
(Map p318; ☎041-2228790, 0735339920; www.sentrim-hotels.net; Moi Ave; s/d/tr US$75/110/145; ❄📶) With an impressive colonial exterior, Castle Royal harks back to glory days of yore. The service is friendly and helpful. The rooms have good bathrooms and flat-screen TVs, though the cheapest ones are overpriced and nothing special. There's a beautiful terrace looking out over the city. Due to road noise, be sure to get a room at the back.

Eating

Mombasa is good for street food: stalls sell samosas, bhajis, kebabs and the local take on pizza (meat and onions wrapped in soft dough and fried). A few dish out stew and ugali. For dessert, seek out *haluwa* (an Omani version of Turkish delight), fried taro root, sweet baobab seeds and sugared doughnuts.

Island Dishes KENYAN $

(Map p318; ☎0711122221; Kibokoni Rd; mains KSh150-350; ⏰8am-11pm) Once your eyes have adjusted to the dazzling strip lights, feast them on the tasty menu at this very popular Swahili restaurant. *Mishikaki* (marinated, grilled meat kebabs), chicken tikka, fish with coconut, *mkate mayai* (Swahili pizza), fresh juices and all the usual favourites are on offer to eat in or take away, though the biryani is only available at lunchtime.

★ **Shehnai Restaurant** INDIAN $$

(Map p318; ☎0722871111; www.restaurantshehnai.com; Fatemi House, Mwindani Rd; mains KSh700-1500; ⏰noon-2pm & 7-10pm Tue-Sun; ✎) This reputable *mughlai* (North Indian) curry house is popular with the local Indian community and does delicious dishes such as *gosht palakwalla* (lamb with masala and spinach) and a superb chicken biryani. The staff are friendly and the entire place has an air of gentility absent elsewhere in Mombasa. There's no alcohol.

Urban Street Food INTERNATIONAL $$

(Map p318; ☎0700907363; www.urbanstreetfood.co.ke; Nkrumah Rd; mains KSh500-750; ⏰7am-11pm Mon-Sat; 📶) This textbook hip, yellow-walled place with an industrial vibe in central Mombasa does several things few other local establishments do, including great coffee, small plates of hummus, juicy burgers and gorgeous fresh juices. There's a distinct Middle Eastern slant to the otherwise international menu, with shawarma jostling with pizza and a selection of good breakfasts. Delivery is available.

New Recoda Restaurant SWAHILI $$

(Map p318; ☎0720436709; Kibokoni Rd; mains KSh400-700; ⏰6am-11pm) The legendary, decades-old Moi Ave eatery has migrated to a new location, but the shish kebabs are as flavourful as ever. The coconut prawns and fruit juices also get high marks.

The Fort SEAFOOD $$$

(Map p314; ☎0722776399; www.thefort.co.ke; Nkrumah Rd; mains KSh1000-2000; ⏰noon-11pm Tue-Sun; 📶) Right opposite the entrance to Fort Jesus, Mombasa's main sight, this excellent restaurant is an obvious place for a meal after your visit. The speciality here is local seafood cooked in a variety of Swahili sauces, but there's lots of other choices, including seafood risotto and pizzas.

Drinking & Nightlife

Despite the paucity of restaurants selling alcohol in Mombasa, there are plenty of good drinking holes and even a couple of nightclubs. Between security issues after dark and its conservative Muslim population, Mombasa actually does pretty well.

★ **Jahazi Coffee House** CAFE

(Map p314; ☎0738277975; www.jahazicoffeehouse.com; Ndia Kuu Rd; ⏰8am-7pm Mon-Sat) With lashings of sexy Mombasa style, this lounge cafe is the perfect spot to chill out in cushion-strewn, arty surrounds. Did we mention that it has great coffee? The Swahili pot, if you're after something different, turns the grind into a ritual. You won't want to leave.

Florida Club CLUB

(Map p314; ☎0701568746; Mama Ngina Dr; after 7pm KSh300; ⏰6pm-6am) We know why this place was named after the Disney state. Like a theme park for grown-ups, there's all sorts to get into here: an outdoor pool, a 'crazy' blue bar, fluorescent palm trees, small casino, Vegas-style floor shows and DJ sets from 7pm.

Shopping

From spices, wood carvings and antiques to handmade sandals, tailored clothing and woven sarongs, Mombasa is a great place to shop. Bargaining is a must in most places; shop around before you decide what you want and offer a price that you're prepared to pay. If buying several items from the same seller, discounts can be negotiated.

★ **Akamba Handicraft Industry Cooperative Society** ARTS & CRAFTS

(☎Nairobi 020-2654362; www.akambahandicraftcoop.com; Port Reitz Rd; ⏰8am-5pm Mon-Fri, to noon Sun) 🍃 This cooperative employs an incredible 10,000 people from the local area. It's also a non-profit organisation that produces fine woodcarvings, from animal shapes and polished calabash bowls to stick-thin Maasai figures, replica Maasai shields, salad spoons and elaborate masks. Kwa Hola/Magongo matatus run right past the gates from the Kobil petrol station on Jomo Kenyatta Ave. Very fair prices.

Central Mombasa

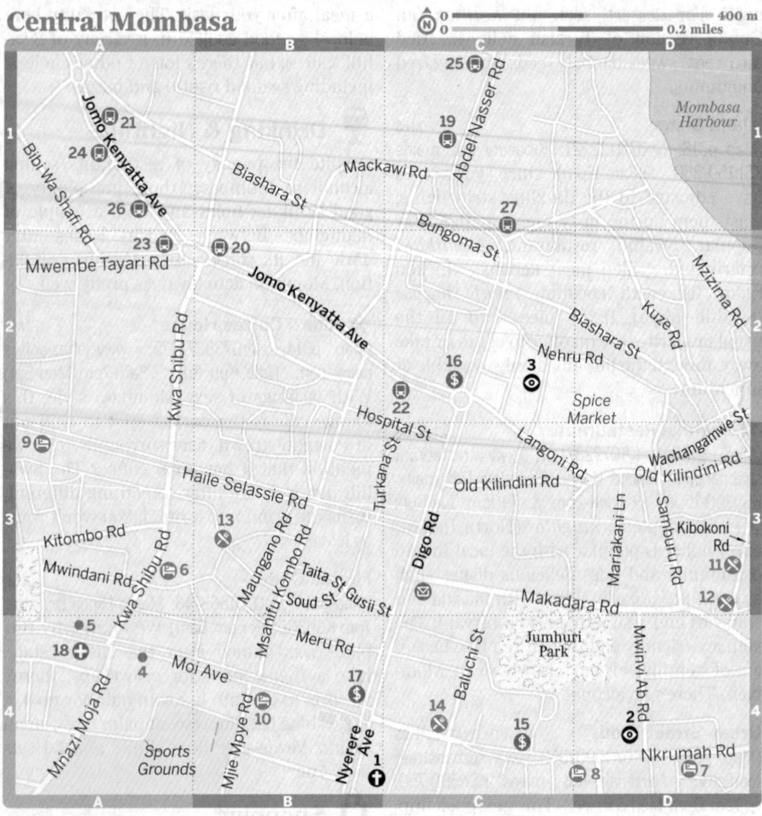

Central Mombasa

Sights

1 Holy Ghost Cathedral B4
2 Lord Shiva Temple D4
3 Spice Market C2

Activities, Courses & Tours

4 Ketty Tours A4
5 Natural World Kenya Safaris A4

Sleeping

6 Glory Grand Hotel A3
7 Lotus Hotel D4
8 New Palm Tree Hotel D4
9 Royal Court Hotel A3
10 Sentrim Castle Royal Hotel B4

Eating

11 Island Dishes D3
12 New Recoda Restaurant D3
13 Shehnai Restaurant B3
14 Urban Street Food C4

Information

15 Barclays C4
16 Barclays C2
17 Kenya Commercial Bank B4
18 Sairose Pharmacy A4

Transport

19 Buses & Matatus to Malindi & Lamu C1
20 Buses to Arusha & Moshi (Mwembe Tayari Health Centre) B2
21 Mash A1
22 Matatus to Nyali C2
23 Matatus to Voi & Wundanyi A2
24 Modern Coast A1
25 Simba Coaches C1
26 Tahmeed A1
27 TSS Express C1

★**Yusufi Antiques & Gallery** ARTS & CRAFTS, ANTIQUES
(Map p314; ☎0723849226; Sir Mbarak Hinawy Rd; ⏰10am-6pm Mon-Sat) A real treasure trove of carvings and masks, particularly from West Africa and the Congo, as well as fetishes, brass lanterns and other goodies. Some amazing Kenyan items as well, including two-faced ceremonial masks embroidered with cowrie shells. One for collectors.

Sandal Shop SHOES
(Map p314; off Sir Mbarak Hinawy Rd; ⏰7am-6pm Mon-Sat) You're likely to see these attractive leather sandals with beading embroidery all over Kenya. Watch them being made at this cobblers shop and buy them for the fairest prices around (from KSh500).

ℹ Information

DANGERS & ANNOYANCES

Sensible precautions should be taken, such as avoiding poorly lit streets after dark and not displaying your valuables. When in doubt, hailing a tuk-tuk is an easy (and cheap) answer. Women may expect a bit more attention if walking alone through the Old Town. Two pickpocketing and bag-snatching hotspots are the junction of Jomo Kenyatta Ave and Mwembe Tayari Rd – the departure point for many buses and matatus – and the Likoni ferry, which tends to get jam-packed.

MEDICAL SERVICES

The following are the best medical services in Mombasa.

AAR Mombasa Health Centre (Map p314; ☎0731191067; www.aar-healthcare.com; Pereira Bldg, Machakos St, off Moi Ave; ⏰24hr) Around-the-clock medical clinic.

Mombasa Hospital (Map p314; ☎0733333655, 041-2312191; www.mombasahospital.com; off Mama Ngina Dr) Best private hospital in the region.

Sairose Pharmacy (Map p318; ☎0733320201; Moi Ave; ⏰7am-10pm Mon-Sat, 9am-10pm Sun) Open late.

MONEY

Outside business hours you can change money at most major hotels, although rates are usually poor. ATMs can be found everywhere and nearly all accept international credit and debit cards.

Kenya Commercial Bank (Map p314; Nkrumah Rd) With ATM. Another on **Moi Ave** (Map p318; Moi Ave).

Barclays (Map p318; Digo Rd) Has an ATM, as does another branch on **Nkrumah Rd** (Map p318; Nkrumah Rd).

SECURITY IN MOMBASA

Although most of the sporadic attacks linked to the al-Qaeda affiliate Al-Shabaab affected sections of Nairobi – the biggest being the attack at Westgate Mall in September 2013 – Mombasa and the south coast have borne the brunt of the effect on tourism. Following two small-scale bomb blasts that killed four people at a bus station and a hotel in May 2014, several countries, including the UK, USA and Australia, issued warnings against travelling to Mombasa island and sections of the coast between Mtwapa Creek in the north and Tiwi in the south. While the warnings had all been rescinded at research time, tourism in Mombasa and along the coast was still affected by the apprehension and fear of violent outbreaks that accompanied the close and bitterly contested national election.

Fort Jesus Forex Bureau (Map p314; ☎041-316717; Ndia Kuu Rd; ⏰9am-5pm Mon-Fri) Currency exchange.

Standard Chartered Bank (Map p314; Treasury Sq, Nkrumah Rd) With ATM.

POST

Post Office (Map p318; ☎041-227705; Digo Rd; ⏰9am-5pm Mon-Fri, to 1pm Sat)

TOURIST INFORMATION

There is currently no tourist information office in Mombasa. Hotels, travel agencies and your fellow travellers are your best bet for up-to-date travel information about the city and its surroundings.

ℹ Getting There & Away

AIR

From **Moi International Airport** (MBA; ☎041-3433211, Nairobi 020-3577058; Airport Rd), around 9km northwest of central Mombasa, there are up to a dozen flights to Nairobi (from US$55) daily with Fly540 (p258) and Kenya Airways (p373). There is also a daily flight to Lamu (US$90) with **Mombasa Air Safari** (p258) (www.skywardexpress.co.ke) and one to Zanzibar (US$140) with Fly540. From a separate terminal, Mombasa Air Safari (www.mombasaairsafari.com) connects Mombasa with airstrips in the Masai Mara.

ARRIVING IN MOMBASA

Moi International Airport (p319) There is no public transport from the airport. Taxi fare to central Mombasa is KSh2000. A tuk-tuk to the airport costs KSh1000, plus parking fee of KSh60.

Mombasa Terminus (Mombasa-Nairobi Rd; ⏲ticket sales 7am-4pm) The *Madaraka Express* train from Nairobi arrives at the newly built Mombasa Terminus, 18km from the city, and is met by taxis and matatus. A taxi into Mombasa costs around KSh2500, while matatus drop passengers off by the former train station in the centre for KSh150. Tuk-tuks are not allowed in the train station car park, but if you walk out to the main road (around 300m), you'll find them waiting at the junction.

BUS & MATATU

To Nairobi

There are dozens of daily departures in both directions (mostly in the early morning and late evening). Daytime services take at least eight hours, and overnight trips take 10 to 12 hours, and are not terribly recommended.

The trip isn't particularly comfortable, although it's not bad for an African bus ride, but note that the Nairobi–Mombasa road is accident prone. Speedometers with an 80km/h limit fitted on buses and matatus have eased the problem somewhat, but some drivers continue to flout rules. Theft is also an issue on this route: as much as it disappoints us to say so, don't accept food and drink from fellow travellers; we've heard too many stories of *wazungu* (white people – both tourists and Kenyans) being drugged and mugged on this route. Most trips, however, are crime and accident free.

Fares vary from KSh700 to KSh2200, with **Modern Coast** (Map p318; ☎0705700888; www.modern.co.ke; Jomo Kenyatta Ave) the swishest (and most expensive) of the lot. **Mash** (Map p318; ☎0730889000; www.masheast africa.com; Jomo Kenyatta Ave) is also a good bet. Most companies have at least four departures daily. Several companies go to Kisumu and Lake Victoria, but all go via Nairobi first.

Matatus to Voi and Wundanyi (Map p318; Mwembe Tayari Rd), towards Nairobi, depart from the junction of Mwembe Tayari Rd and Jomo Kenyatta Ave.

North to Malindi & Lamu

There are numerous daily buses and matatus heading up the coast to Malindi, leaving from in front of the Noor Mosque on Abdel Nasser Rd. Buses take up to three hours (around KSh700) and matatus take about two hours (KSh500 rising to KSh700 during holidays and very busy periods).

Tahmeed (Map p318; ☎0729356561; Jomo Kenyatta Ave), **Tawakal** (Map p314; ☎0722550111; Abdel Nasser Rd), **Simba** (Map p318; ☎0707471410; Abdel Nasser Rd) and **TSS Express** (Map p318; ☎0704137202; Abdel Nasser Rd) have buses to Lamu (KSh800 to KSh1200), most leaving at around 7am (report 30 minutes early) from their offices on Abdel Nasser Rd and Jomo Kenyatta Ave. Tawakal is considered to be the most comfortable and reliable. Buses take around seven hours to reach the Lamu ferry at Mokoke and travel via Malindi. At research time, buses had to join an armed convoy between Garsen and Witu, as that stretch of road north of Malindi is known for intermittent banditry.

Matatus to Nyali (Map p318; Jomo Kenyatta Ave) depart from Jomo Kenyatta Ave.

South to Diani Beach

Regular buses and matatus leave from the far side of the Likoni ferry terminal and travel along the southern coast.

To Tanzania

Mash, **Modern Coast**, **Tahmeed** and **TSS Express** have daily departures to Dar es Salaam (KSh1400 to KSh2200, 10 to 12 hours) via Tanga from their offices on Jomo Kenyatta Ave, near the junction with Mwembe Tayari Rd. Dubious-looking **buses to Arusha and Moshi** (Map p318; Jomo Kenyatta Ave) leave from in front of the Mwembe Tayari Health Centre in the morning or evening.

TRAIN

From the **Mombasa Terminus**, the new high-speed *Madaraka Express* connects Mombasa and Nairobi (economy/1st class KSh700/3000, 4½ hours). Departures from Mombasa are at 9am daily; at research time, tickets could only be purchased at the train station with cash.

Getting Around

BOAT

The **Likoni ferry** (Map p314; www.kenyaferry.co.ke) connects Mombasa island with the southern mainland, so if you want to head to Diani Beach or any points south of there, you have to take the ferry unless you want to travel hours out of your way.

There's a crossing roughly every 15 minutes between 5am and 12.30am, and hourly outside these times. It's free for pedestrians and cyclists, KSh150 per car, KSh190 per 4WD and

KSh270 for a pick-up or big safari jeep. To get to the jetty from the centre of town, take a Likoni matatu from Digo Rd. Do also note that there can be long waits at rush hour on this route, so plan your trip accordingly.

MATATU, TAXI & TUK-TUK

Matatus charge between KSh30 and KSh50 for short trips. There are also plenty of three-wheeled tuk-tuks about, which run from about KSh50 to KSh200 for a bit of open-air transit. These two are the main forms of transport in Mombasa.

Taxis are expensive and hard to find. Ask your hotel to call one for you. Assume it'll cost KSh2500 from the train station to the city centre.

South of Mombasa

From Mombasa to the Tanzanian border there's some serious sand. And not just any sand; these beaches are some of Africa's most splendid. Think vast stretches of white sand, lapped at by cerulean waters and topped with buff kitesurfers. There are far worse places to spend a few days.

And yet, this stretch of Kenya is about more than just beach life. Slip into the sea and lie under those coconut fronds, but, while you're at it, try walking through a 600-year-old sacred forest, scouting for mudskippers in a forest of mangroves, snorkelling in the jewel-box waters of a marine park or feeling the salty wind curl off a dhow's prow as you head to a new island.

Shimba Hills National Reserve

Cool and grassy, this 320-sq-km **national reserve** (☎0704467855; www.kws.org; adult/child US$22/13; ⏰6am-6pm) makes an easy day trip from Diani Beach. Its lush hills are home to sable antelope, elephants, warthogs, baboons, buffaloes and Masai giraffes, as well as 300 species of butterfly. The sable antelope have made a stunning recovery here after their numbers dropped to less than 120 in 1970.

In 2005 the elephant population reached an amazing 600 – far too many for this tiny space. Instead of culling the herds, KWS organised an unprecedented US$3.2 million translocation operation to reduce the pressure on the habitat, capturing no fewer than 400 elephants and moving them to Tsavo East National Park, a wildlife reserve between Mombasa and Nairobi.

There are more than 150km of tracks that criss-cross the reserve.

Sleeping

Shimba Hills Lodge LODGE **$$$**
(☎0711367345; www.shimbalodge.net; Kinango Rd; r from US$160) Entered by a separate park gate from the main entrance, this dark timber lodge features an attractive interior, strewn with numerous Congolese and West African carvings. The rooms are snug, bright and come with welcome splashes of colourful art. The highlight is the wildlife seen from the boardwalk, which looks out over a forest clearing with a small lake.

Getting There & Away

Shimba Hills is 40km south of Mombasa. The majority of the roads inside the park are accessible by city car during the drier months, with only a couple of tracks designated 4WD only. During the rainy season you'll need a 4WD to enter the reserve.

SHIMBA HILLS NATIONAL RESERVE

Why Go It's an easy day trip from the coast, has good elephant spotting and is the only Kenyan home of the sable antelope.

When to Go Year-round, but the dry season (November to March) is best.

Practicalities Diani Beach, 45 minutes' drive away, is the most popular base, and numerous safari companies and hotels there offer trips to Shimba Hills. With good roads, short distances and ease of access, this is a perfect family-friendly park.

Budget Tips Some of the package deals offered by Diani Beach hotels (per person from US$75) actually represent the best value for a trip to Shimba Hills. You'll have to come by tour; or, during the dry months, a cheaper option might be to rent a regular city car in Mombasa for a couple of days and find people to car-share with you.

Best Time of Day For the best chances of seeing wildlife, get to the park early – like 6am early. Alternatively, spend the night.

Every safari company in Mombasa and Diani Beach offers trips to Shimba Hills (half-day tours per person from US$75). If you're travelling with others, renting a car in Mombasa may be the cheapest way to go.

Mwaluganje Elephant Sanctuary

Opened in October 1995 to create a corridor along an elephant migration route between Shimba Hills and Mwaluganje Forest Reserve, and comprising 240 sq km of ruggedly beautiful country along the valley of the Cha Shimba River, this **sanctuary** (☎0721765476; www.elephantmwaluganje.co.ke; adult/child US$15/2, vehicles KSh150-300; ⏲6am-6pm) is home to one of the densest concentrations of pachyderms on the continent (150 or so, to be precise). Sightings of these magnificent beasts are guaranteed, and the reserve's relative remoteness means that you're unlikely to have to share them with many other visitors. All this makes Mwaluganje more suitable for those who've done a few safaris elsewhere and are after a wilder, more pristine experience. The drier country means the wildlife in Mwaluganje differs slightly from that of wetter and greener Shimba Hills, especially so when it comes to the birds.

This sanctuary is a good example of community-based conservation, with local people acting as stakeholders in the project.

Sleeping

Mwaluganje Elephant Camp TENTED CAMP **$$$**
(☎0721765476; camping KSh1000, s/d US$170/245) This rather fine place has very plush safari tents overlooking a waterhole. If you can't afford the fancy-pants tents, then camp in your own tent at the campsite, located near the main gate. The setting is sublime (though rocks make things tricky for tent pegs). It's as genuine an African wilderness experience as you can ask for.

Getting There & Away

The main entrance to the sanctuary is about 13km northeast of Shimba Hills National Reserve, on the road to Kinango. A shorter route runs from Kwale to the Golini gate, passing the Mwaluganje ticket office. It's only 5km but the track is 4WD only. The roads inside the park are pretty rough and a 4WD is the only way to get around. Some Mombasa- and Diani-based operators offer organised tours.

Tiwi Beach

☎040

The sleepy, shaded and secluded antithesis to nearby Diani Beach, Tiwi makes a lovely, quiet, cottage-style escape by the ocean. The wide, white beach is studded with skinny palms and there is very little in the way of beach boys. Tiwi also has a beautiful coral reef, part of which teems with starfish of all shapes and colours. A stable, pool-like area between the shore and the coral is great for swimming and snorkelling.

Sleeping

Coral Cove Cottages COTTAGE **$$**
(☎0722732797; www.coralcove.tiwibeach.com; cottages KSh5500-8600) A good self-catering option, offering simple, colourful cottages within sight of the ocean. Expect a warm welcome – from the menagerie of dogs, cats, ducks and rescued parrots, as well as from host Kerstin – and cottages furnished with everything you might need for a weekend hideaway. The turn-off is next to the one for Twiga.

Sand Island Beach Cottages COTTAGE **$$**
(☎0722395005; www.sandislandbeach.com; cottages US$120-200; 📶) Named after the spit of sand exposed by low tide, Sand Island consists of 10 spacious, airy, self-catering cottages overlooking the sand. Each has its own style – Pweza cottage, for example, features furniture made from salvaged Swahili doors – and all have colourful quilts and shady terraces. It's signposted from the main Tiwi Beach road and lies 3.5km along a dirt track.

Getting There & Away

To get to Tiwi, turn left off the main highway (A14) about 18km south of Mombasa (or right if you're coming from Diani) and follow the track until it terminates at a north–south T-junction.

Buses and matatus on the road between the Likoni ferry crossing and Ukunda can drop you at the start of either track down to Tiwi (KSh100). The **Tiwi bus stop** or the southern turn-off, known locally as Tiwi 'spot', is much easier to find. Although it's only 3.5km to the beach, both access roads are notorious for muggings, so take a *boda-boda* (around KSh200), a taxi (KSh500) or hang around for a lift. If you're heading back to the highway, any of the accommodation places can call ahead for a taxi.

DON'T MISS

THE SACRED FOREST

Kaya Kinondo (0722446916; www.kaya-kinondo-kenya.com; Diani Beach Rd; KSh1000; 8am-5pm) This forest, sacred to the Digo people, is the only one of the area's sacred forests that's open to visitors. Visiting this small grove is a nature walk, historical journey and cultural experience. As you make your way across tangled roots and chunks of ancient coral, the guide points out various plants used in traditional medicine, and there's the chance to transmit your fears and worries to an ancient tree by hugging it. Expect to tip your guide.

Before entering the Kaya Kinondo you have to remove head wear, promise not to kiss anyone inside the grove, wrap a black *kaniki* (sarong) around your waist and go with a guide, who will explain the significance of some of the 187 plant species inside. They include the 'pimple tree', a known cure for acne; a palm believed to be 1050 years old; snatches of coral; and the rather self-explanatory 'Viagra tree'. Enormous liana swings (go on, try it) and strangling fig trees abound.

Many *kaya* (sacred forests) have been identified in this area, all of which were originally home to Mijikenda villages. The Mijikenda (Nine Homesteads) comprises nine subtribes – Chonyi, Digo, Duruma, Giriama, Jibana, Kambe, Kauma, Rabai and Ribe – united, to a degree, by culture, history and language. Yet each of the tribes remains distinct and speaks its own dialect of the Mijikenda language. Still, there's a binding factor between the Nine Homesteads, and between the modern Mijikenda and their ancestors: their shared veneration of the *kaya*.

This historical connection becomes concrete when you enter the woods and realise – and there's no other word that fits here – they simply feel old.

Many trees are about 600 years old, which corresponds to the arrival of the first Mijikenda from Singwaya, their semi-legendary homeland in southern Somalia. Cutting vegetation within the *kaya* is strictly prohibited – visitors may not even take a stray twig or leaf from the forest.

The preserved forests do not just facilitate dialogue with the ancestors, they also provide a direct link to ecosystems that have been clear-felled out of existence elsewhere. Kaya Kinondo contains five possible endemic species, and 140 tree species classified as 'rare', within its 30 hectares – the space of a suburban residential block.

The main purpose of the *kaya* was to house the villages of the Mijikenda, which were located in a large central clearing. Entering the centre of a *kaya* required ritual knowledge to proceed through concentric circles of sacredness surrounding the node of the village. Sacred talismans and spells were supposed to cause hallucinations that disoriented enemies who attacked the forest.

The *kaya* were largely abandoned in the 1940s and conservative strains of Islam and Christianity have denigrated their value to the Mijikenda, but thanks to their Unesco World Heritage status, they will hopefully be preserved for future visitors. The *kaya* have lasted 600 years; with luck, the wind will speak through their branches for much longer.

Diani Beach

040 / POP 62,529

With a flawless, long stretch of white-sand beach hugged by lush forest and kissed by surfable waves, it's no wonder Diani Beach is so popular. This resort town scores points with a diverse crowd: party people, families, honeymooners, backpackers and watersports enthusiasts.

But if that sounds like your typical resort town, think again. Diani has some of the best accommodation in Kenya, from budget party hostels to funky kitesurfing lodges and intimate honeymoon spots. Most places are spread along the beach road, hidden behind a line of forest.

When lazing in a hammock gets tiring, visit the coral mosques with their archways that overlook the open ocean, venture into the sacred forests where guides hug trees that speak in their ancestors' voices, or take in the monkey sanctuary – all are good ways to experience more of the coast than the considerable charms of sun and sand.

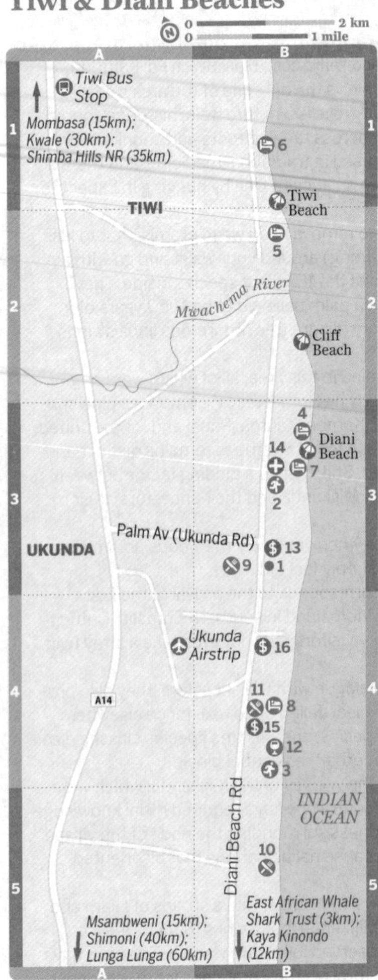

Tiwi & Diani Beaches

Activities, Courses & Tours

1	Coral Spirit	B3
	Diani Bikes	(see 11)
	Diani Marine	(see 12)
2	Pilli Pipa	B3
3	Skydive Diani	B4

Sleeping

4	AfroChic Diani Beach	B3
5	Coral Cove Cottages	B2
6	Sand Island Beach Cottages	B1
7	The Maji	B3
8	Water Lovers	B4

Eating

9	Coast Dishes	B3
10	Nomad	B5
11	Shanshin-Ka	B4

Drinking & Nightlife

12	Forty Thieves Beach Bar	B4

Information

13	Barclays	B3
14	Diani Beach Hospital	B3
15	Forex Bureau	B4
16	Kenya Commercial Bank	B4

Sights

★Colobus Conservation Centre WILDLIFE RESERVE

(☎0711479453; www.colobusconservation.org; Diani Beach Rd; tours adult/child KSh750/250; ⊙8am-4.30pm Mon-Sat) Notice the monkeys clambering on rope ladders over the road? The 'colobridges' are the work of the Colobus Conservation Centre, which aims to protect the Angolan black-and-white colobus monkey, a once-common species now restricted to some 5000 monkeys in a few isolated pockets of forest south of Mombasa. It runs excellent tours of its headquarters, where you'll likely get to see a few orphaned or injured colobus, Sykes' and vervet monkeys undergoing the process of rehabilitation to the wild.

Activities

★Diani Bikes CYCLING

(☎0713959668; www.dianibikes.com; Diani Beach Rd; tours per person €25-35) This cycling outfit gets rave reviews from travellers for their engaging tours that include visiting the Kaya Kinondo and a typical rural Kenyan village, and nature trails good for spotting colobus monkeys. The Beach Ride is the longest (five hours) and includes a canoe trip through mangroves.

★H_2O Extreme KITESURFING

(☎0721495876; www.h2o-extreme.com; Diani Beach Rd, Kenyaways Kite Village) The best-regarded kitesurfing outfit in Diani offers half-day beginner courses for €100, as well as windsurfing and stand up paddle boarding (SUP) lessons (per hour €25). You can also rent SUPs (per hour €10), kitesurfing equipment (per hour €40), single and two-person sea kayaks (per hour €25), and body boards (per hour €10).

★Pilli Pipa WATER SPORTS
(☎0722205120, 0724442555; www.pillipipa.com; Diani Beach Rd, Colliers Centre; from KSh7500) The reputable dive school Pilli Pipa offers excellent dhow safaris, dolphin-spotting trips, whale watching, night dives and snorkelling trips to Kisite Marine National Park (p327).

Diani Marine DIVING
(☎0707629061; www.dianimarine.com; Diani Beach Rd, Diani Marine Village) This highly regarded, German-run centre provides its own accommodation. PADI open-water diving courses cost €495, with single dives from €90.

Skydive Diani ADVENTURE SPORTS
(☎0701300400; www.skydivediani.com; Diani Beach Rd, nr Forty Thieves Beach Bar) Set up by a British Army parachutist and a professional skydiver (among others), this highly professional outfit – the only one of its kind in East Africa – lets you live the most intense 50 seconds of your life by letting you fall 3500m over Kenya's coastal reefs. Go for a tandem jump (US$350), or the Accelerated Freefall course (US$2600).

Sleeping

★Diani Backpackers HOSTEL $
(☎0700713666; www.dianibackpackers.com; off Diani Beach Rd; camping KSh600, dm KSh1300-1500, r KSh2600-4000; P 📶 ≋) Stylish and secure, Diani Backpackers has airy dorms, our favourite being Baobab, with an actual baobab growing through its middle, and comfortable private rooms (one with own bath). Come to party at the 24-hour bar and pool, or chill out in the lush garden.

★Kenyaways Kite Village BOUTIQUE HOTEL $$
(☎0726126204, 0739760733; www.thekenyaway.com; Diani Beach Rd; s/d from US$55/80; 📶 ≋) This small, stylish kitesurfing lodge is one of our favourite places to stay in Diani. The gorgeously rustic rooms are simple but lovely, with painted timber bed frames, whitewashed walls and a sea breeze. Downstairs there's a good beachside bar and restaurant that attracts surfers and a chilled-out crowd. Friendly staff and a superb stretch of beach seal the deal.

★AfroChic Diani Beach BOUTIQUE HOTEL $$$
(☎0730127000; www.afrochicdiani.com; Diani Beach Rd; r per person US$380-637; ❄ 📶 ≋) With just 10 individually decorated rooms and an elegant lobby and common area filled with West African carvings, this intimate hotel is all about attention to detail. We love the hand-carved bed frames and Maasai-beading chairs. The food makes the best of seasonal produce and is served 'anywhere, anytime', be it in your room or by the pool.

★Water Lovers HOTEL $$$
(☎0735790535; www.waterlovers.it; Diani Beach Rd; r €250-569; P 📶 ≋) Beautiful, peaceful and intimate, Water Lovers has eight rooms and one villa, all designed with aesthetics, sustainability and love in mind. The furniture is a mix of Swahili wood and Italian pottery, and the wonderful staff will cater for every need. As you might expect from Italian owners, there's a great private restaurant serving organic fare and homemade pasta.

★The Maji HOTEL $$$
(☎0773178873/4; http://themaji-com; Diani Beach Rd; r US$120-576; P 📶 ≋) Among the loveliest of Diani's beachfront boutique hotels, the Maji – which means 'water' in Swahili – is simply gorgeous. The water feature in the beautiful Swahili lobby is surrounded by West African carvings, with welcome touches of contemporary art throughout. Each of the 15 rooms has its own vibe, but all have enormous beds, high ceilings and lovely bathrooms. Bliss.

Eating

Coast Dishes KENYAN $
(☎0722410745; Palm Ave, Ukunda; mains KSh450; ⏲6am-11pm) Want to give the overpriced tourist restaurants a miss? Want to eat where the locals eat? Coast Dishes ticks both of these boxes and, if you're sensible, you'll opt for a steaming great bowl of biryani, the house special.

★Shanshin-Ka JAPANESE $$
(☎0720747803; Diani Beach Rd; mains KSh400-950; ⏲10am-10pm Tue-Sat, 12.30-10pm Sun) A spartan aesthetic and a full menu of authentic Japanese dishes are Shanshin-Ka's two distinguishing features. The portions of teriyaki, udon, tempura and yakitori dishes are generous, the sushi rolls are excellent (we're particular fans of Dynamite), the fruit juices are terrific and there's even a free palate cleanser in the form of fresh fruit at the end.

★**Sails** SEAFOOD $$$
(☎0716863884; www.almanararesort.com/sails; Diani Beach Rd, Almanara Luxury Villas Resort; mains KSh1200-2700; ⏰noon-2pm & 6.30-10.30pm Wed-Mon; P📶✍) By far the most stylish place to eat in Diani, Sails is gorgeous: a canopy of billowing white canvas separates the restaurant from the stars, while waiters serve up fine dishes, particularly seafood, including Zanzibar-style snapper, steamed ginger crab and smoked Malindi sailfish. Reservations highly recommended in the evening.

★**Nomad** SEAFOOD $$$
(☎0735373888; www.thesandsatnomad.com; Diani Beach Rd, Sands at Nomad; mains KSh690-3590; ⏰7.30am-10.30pm; 📶) One of the best restaurants in Diani, Nomad benefits from stellar sea views from its terrace and a talented chef who cooks up such culinary magic as seared yellowfin tuna with smoked aubergine and ginger and coconut crab. The sushi is among Kenya's best as well.

Drinking & Nightlife

Diani Beach is an enclave of party-goers and has plenty going on after dark, mainly in the shape of busy bars where cocktails are downed. There are also occasional dancing and beach parties. Ask around when you're here; your hotel should be able to point you in the right direction.

★**Forty Thieves Beach Bar** BAR
(☎0712294873; www.facebook.com/40beachbar; Diani Beach Rd; ⏰8am-midnight Sun-Thu, 8am-dawn Fri & Sat; 📶) A legendary beach-side boozer with sand floors and waves crashing onto the shore just metres from the long wooden bar, Forty Thieves is a Diani Beach institution and you'll find it busy with daytime drinkers and football watchers at any time. Come the evenings, it's always full. The Sunday roast is a big hit.

ℹ Information

DANGERS & ANNOYANCES

Take taxis at night and try not to be on the beach by yourself after dark. Beachfront hotels have security guards and if you have to walk a short distance along the beach in the evening, some will oblige you by lighting your way or even walking with you. Souvenir sellers are an everyday nuisance, sex tourism is pretty evident and beach touts can be a bit of a hassle – you'll hear a lot of, 'Hey, one love, one love' Rasta-speak spouted by guys trying to sell you drugs or scam you into supporting fake charities for 'local schools'.

MEDICAL SERVICES

Diani Beach Hospital (☎0700999999; www.dianibeachhospital.com; Diani Beach Rd; ⏰24hr) One of the best private hospitals in Kenya.

MONEY

Barclays (Diani Beach Rd, Barclays Centre) With ATM.

Forex Bureau (Diani Beach Rd; ⏰9am-5pm Mon-Fri) Currency exchange.

Kenya Commercial Bank (Diani Beach Rd) With ATM.

ℹ Getting There & Away

AIR

From **Ukunda Airstrip** (☎0711305051) there are at least three flights per day to Nairobi (from US$48) with Fly540 (p258), **FlySAX** (www.fly-sax.com) and Airkenya (p258). Many hotels along Diani Beach offer free pick-up from the airstrip; otherwise you're looking at a minimum taxi fare of KSh700.

BUS & MATATU

Numerous matatus run south from the Likoni ferry in Mombasa directly to Ukunda (KSh200, 30 minutes), the junction for Diani, and onwards to Msambweni and Lunga Lunga. From Ukunda, matatus run to the beach (KSh70) all day; check before boarding to see if it's a 'Reef' (heading north along the strip, then south) or 'Neptune' (south beach only) service.

TAXI

Taxis, *boda-bodas* and tuk-tuks hang around Ukunda junction and all the main shopping centres, and most hotels and restaurants will also have a couple waiting at night. *Boda-bodas* are the cheapest of the lot, with short hops costing from KSh100; tuk-tuks are a little pricier. Much depends on your negotiating skills.

Shimoni

☎040

The fishing village of Shimoni, the site of alleged slave caves, has a tranquil Swahili vibe. As it is the departure point for boats to Wasini Island, Shimoni is mostly visited as part of a package tour that includes the island and a dhow trip to Kisite Marine National Park (p327). This does mean the chilled nature of the village is disrupted when convoys of tour buses rock up in the mornings during high season. Independent travellers tend to get pounced on by boat captains as soon as they make an appearance.

Activities

Shimoni is the jumping-off point for dhow and boat tours of the Kisite Marine National Park. If you've signed up for an organised dhow trip in Diani, all the fees and paperwork are taken care of. If coming independently, it's up to you to pay the marine park fee at the **office** (0723929766; www.kws.go.ke; 8am-6pm) here and negotiate with one of the local boat captains. They tend to have life jackets and snorkelling gear on board; inspect it before setting off, though.

Sleeping & Eating

Shimoni Gardens BANDAS $
(0722630638; per person KSh2500) This cluster of 15 tiny *bandas* (thatched-roof huts) sits amid tranquil, leafy grounds 2.5km south of Shimoni pier. While there's no room to swing a cat in any of them, you will find either twin beds or a snug double in each one, along with a bathroom that would suit Thumbelina. A *banda* is set aside as a guest kitchen.

Shimoni Reef Lodge LODGE $$
(0722270826, 0725643733; www.shimonireeflodge.com; s/d/ste US$100/130/155;) This waterfront base for deep-sea fishing and diving with a saltwater pool and an average (though beautifully situated) restaurant is a tranquil spot. The whitewashed rooms, although spacious and bright, aren't particularly luxurious – they're best enjoyed after a day on the ocean wave.

Getting There & Away

There are matatus every hour or so between the Likoni ferry crossing and Shimoni (KSh350, 1½ hours) until about 6pm. Matatus heading to the Tanzanian border from Ukunda (for Diani Beach) can drop you at the Shimoni turn-off, where you can catch a *boda-boda* for around KSh150.

Wasini Island

040

The final pearl in the tropical beach necklace that stretches south of Mombasa is the idyllic island of Wasini, located about 76km south of the Likoni ferry crossing. With its faded white alleyways, Swahili fishing vibe and fat, mottled trees, this tiny island (it's only 5km long) feels like a distant relative of Lamu and Zanzibar. It's ripe with the ingredients required for a perfect backpacker beachside hideaway: it has that sit-under-a-mango-tree-and-do-nothing-all-day vibe, a coastline licked with pockets of white sand and Kisite Marine National Park, the most gorgeous snorkelling reef on the coast. In fact, the only things it doesn't have are regular electricity, banana-pancake traveller cafes, backpacker hostels and cars, and it's all the better for it.

Sights

★Kisite Marine National Park NATIONAL PARK
(www.kws.org; adult/child US$25/13) Off the south coast of Wasini, this gorgeous marine park, which also incorporates the Mpunguti Marine National Reserve and the two tiny Penguti islands, is one of the best in Kenya. The park covers 28 sq km of pristine coral reefs and offers colourful diving and snorkelling, with frequent dolphin and turtle sightings. The marine park is accessible by dhow tour from Diani Beach or private boat hired in Wasini (per person from KSh2500 to KSh3000).

Mkwiro VILLAGE
Mkwiro is a small village on the unvisited eastern end of Wasini Island. The gorgeous hour-long walk from Wasini village, through woodlands, past tiny hamlets and along the edge of mangrove forests, is more than reason enough to visit. There are some wonderful, calm swimming spots around the village. Local children are sure to take you by the hand and show you the best swimming places.

Activities

Besides Wasini-based operators, Pilli Pipa (p325) and **Coral Spirit** (0716440223; www.coralspirit.com; Diani Beach Rd, Centrepoint; dhow trips US$115) in Diani Beach also operate snorkelling and diving tours to Kisite Marine National Park.

★Charlie Claw's WATER SPORTS
(0722205155/6; www.wasini.com) This highly regarded outfit offers diving and snorkelling trips to Kisite, as well as to Mako Koko reef a few kilometres west. Dhow sunset cruises are also on offer. Some of the day excursions include lunch at its eponymous restaurant on Wasini Island, where they cook up a seafood feast of grilled crab and seared Swahili beef steaks.

Sleeping & Eating

Blue Monkey Cottages COTTAGE $

(☎0715756952; http://wasini.net/blue-monkey-beach-cottages; s/d/tr KSh2500/3300/3900) Made entirely of local materials – salvaged coral, stone, shells, driftwood, palm-thatched roofs – these rustic cottages on the outskirts of Wasini village are drowning in bougainvillea. The private beach, delicious Swahili food (vegan and seafood meals KSh380 to KSh720) and a feeling of disconnectedness, helped by the relative seclusion and reliance on solar power, are the things that lure travellers here.

★**Paradise Lodge** LODGE $$

(☎0718778372; www.paradisediver.net; per person safari tent €60, r €75-85) This friendly little dive lodge on the eastern side of Wasini has a range of simple but colourful rooms (the most expensive with en suite), plus two furnished safari tents. Diving trips can also be arranged. You can sleep here independently, or as part of a diving tour.

Getting There & Away

Although most people come to Wasini on organised tours, you can cross the channel by motorboat (per person from KSh2000) or by simple wooden vessel with the islanders (KSh350) from the mainland village of Shimoni – head to its pier to assess your options.

LAMU & THE NORTH COAST

Kilifi

☎041 / POP 44,257

A passionate group of Kenyans and expats have transformed Kilifi from a sweet but soporific backwater into a stunning place renowned for its eco-projects and clean, green, joyful living.

Gorgeous beach houses stand atop the creek, yachts dance in the bay and warm waves wash fantasy beaches buttered with lashings of soft white sand. You'll find orange groves and hermit crabs, fresh oysters and pizza ovens, permaculture projects and sailing schools, beach barbecues and night swimming. And you might even spot a whale shark migration from the windy brink of Vuma Cliffs.

The town is also home to a renowned medical research centre, so with a steady stream of doctors, sailors, backpackers, aid workers, artists and yogis passing through, you'll never be short of crew with whom to share those oysters.

Sights

Bofa Beach BEACH

(Bofa Rd) Bofa Beach is a wide slash of white sand, with swaying palms and rolling Indian Ocean surf. It's the stuff of which fantasies are made. A path to the left of **Kilifi Bay Beach Resort** (☎0722202564; www.madahotels.com; Bofa Rd; s/d from €176/221;) takes you there.

Mnarani RUINS

(adult/child KSh500/250; ⏲7am-6pm) The partly excavated, atmospheric ruins of the Swahili city of Mnarani are high on a bluff just west of the old ferry landing stage on the southern bank of Kilifi Creek. The best-preserved ruin is the Great Mosque, with its finely carved inscription around the mihrab (prayer niche showing the direction of Mecca). Under the minaret lies the skeleton of the supposed founder of the town.

Kilifi Creek CREEK

This might be the only place where we wouldn't mind being up the creek without a paddle. It's just gorgeous, from the cliffs jutting up out of the water, to the hermit crabs scooting along the shoreline. Boat hire can easily be arranged, and there are lots of lovely spots for wild, romantic camping.

★**Vuma Cliffs** NATURAL FEATURE

(Takaungu) Just outside the village of Takaungu, you fly on the back of a motorbike down dirt roads, past spiky fields of sisal and giant baobabs towering above maize crops. Abruptly, the land ends in jagged black coral cliffs, pounded relentlessly by the rolling waves of the Indian Ocean. It's a desolate and lonely place that seems like a secret portal into Scotland rather than the Kenyan coast. Motorbikes to the cliffs are organised by Distant Relatives (p329) (KSh1500 for one or two people).

Activities

★**Buccaneer Diving** DIVING

(☎0714757763; www.buccaneerdiving.com; 2-tank dive US$130; ⏲Oct-Apr) The lovely Tim runs this excellent diving centre over at

Mnarani Club (☎Nairobi 020-8070501/2; www.mnarani.co.za; off Mombasa-Malindi Rd; s/d from US$117/196; P❄📶🏊), covering everything from the basics to instructor-level dives and cave and wreck exploration. PADI open water from US$595.

Three Degrees South BOATING
(☎0714783915, 0714757763; www.3degreessouth.co.ke; 3-day course KSh24,500) This British Royal Yachting Association–affiliated sailing school is one of the best places to learn on the East African coast. Expect expert tuition for beginners and advanced sailors, serious attention to safety and a vast expanse of (beautiful) empty space. Windsurfing courses on Kilifi Creek also offered.

Sleeping

★Distant Relatives HOSTEL, LODGE $
(☎0702232323; www.kilifibackpackers.com; camping KSh800, dm/s/d/bandas KSh1500/3500/4500/6000, tents KSh3000; P📶🏊) Both an ecolodge and a backpackers, this place gets it so right. The fantastic owners, staff and guests have created a living, breathing space that's a haven for everyone. Expect good vibes, good people and good conscience. We love the pizza oven and the amazing bamboo showers. Follow the signs for around 2km from opposite Tusky's Supermarket on the main road.

★Takashack COTTAGE $$
(bruceryrie@yahoo.com; Takaungu beach; whole house KSh7500; P) On gorgeous Takaungu beach and off the electricity grid, this eclectic, relaxed three-bedroom house makes a great escape. Catch the sunrise from the top floor, taste the fish curry and ginger prawns cooked by Nickson the caretaker, jump in the ocean and, after dark, watch the house light up from the glow of amber hurricane lanterns. Email bookings only.

Eating

Boatyard SEAFOOD $$
(☎0721590502; www.facebook.com/KilifiBoatyard; mains from KSh700; ⏲7am-7pm) Jetties and boats, fresh crab and fries, salty air…there's nothing better than a long, lazy meal at the Boatyard, especially when it involves fresh oysters (oyster night is Saturday), fish and chips or full English breakfasts for homesick Brits. This is a great place to meet enthusiastic deep-sea fishermen and yachting old sea salts.

★Nautilus SEAFOOD $$$
(☎0713762748; Old Ferry Rd; mains KSh1000-2500; ⏲noon-3pm & 6-11pm Tue-Sun) We're still dining out on our last memory of dinner at Nautilus. This Swiss-owned restaurant offers fine, romantic dining with gorgeous views over the water and a warm welcome. The wine is good, the oysters are even better and the prawns in spicy coconut milk top the lot.

Getting There & Away

All buses and matatus travelling between Mombasa and Malindi stop at Kilifi.

Watamu

☎042 / POP 10,030

Laid-back little Watamu looks out over the Indian Ocean and enjoys a blinding white-sand beach and a soft breeze coming off the water. It's a gorgeous slice of coastline and one that includes its own marine national park. As well as its natural endowments, great dining scene and relaxed village vibe, Watamu makes an excellent base from which to explore the nearby Gede

THE BEST GREEN PROJECTS ON THE COAST

Distant Relatives, a backpackers and ecolodge in Kilifi, is an ecosystem in its own right, with a beautiful garden that serves as the basis for permaculture projects. Beds are made from neem trees, mattresses are stuffed with cotton from kapok trees and coat hangers are made from empty wine bottles. Permaculture design courses, taught by big East African names, are held here frequently, covering everything from grafting to composting toilets. The ecolodge does a great deal to support the local community, offering traditional Swahili meals with local families, supporting local seamstresses and more.

Wild Living (☎0791183312; Mombasa-Malindi Rd; ⏲8am-6pm) conservation centre is a beautiful 53-hectare conservancy on the outskirts of Kilifi. It serves as a training centre for farmers interested in eco-charcoal production and aloe farming. The shop and cafe can arrange tours of the site.

WORTH A TRIP

JUMBA LA MTWANA

These Swahili ruins, just north of Mtwapa Creek, have as much archaeological grandeur as the more famous Gede ruins. **Jumba la Mtwana** (www.museums.or.ke; adult/child KSh500/250; ⏲8am-6pm) means 'Big House of Slaves' and locals believe the town was an important slave port in the 14th or 15th century. There's a small museum on Swahili culture and an excellent restaurant by the sea, and the custodian gives excellent tours for a small gratuity. The ruins are down a 3km access road, 2km north of Mtwapa Creek bridge.

ruins, Arabuko Sokoke Forest Reserve and the mangrove-fringed waterways of Mida Creek.

Sights

★Bio-Ken Snake Farm & Laboratory SERPENTARIUM
(☎emergency snakebite 0718290324; www.bio-ken.com; Jacaranda Rd; adult/child KSh1000/500; ⏲10am-noon & 2-5pm) This humble-looking place is one of the world's most renowned snake research centres. Bio-Ken specialises in antivenin research and acts as an emergency service for snakebite victims throughout the region. Passionate guides lead excellent 45-minute tours (included in the price), during which they introduce you to such deadly beauties as the black spitting cobra, black mamba, horned viper, puff adder, and the innocuous-looking but deadly twig snake for whose venom there's no cure.

★Watamu Turtle Watch WILDLIFE RESERVE
(☎0713759627; www.watamuturtles.com; Turtle Bay Rd; suggested donation KSh300; ⏲2-4pm Mon, 9.30am-noon & 2-4pm Tue-Fri, 9.30am-noon Sat) This excellent organisation protects the approximately 50 hawksbill and green turtles that lay their eggs on Watamu Beach. The centre provides much-needed education in the local community about the fragility of sea turtles, and actively patrols for people selling turtle shell. At the trust's rehabilitation centre you can normally see turtles being treated for injury or illness and learn about these magnificent creatures. It's a very worthwhile visit.

Watamu Marine National Park NATIONAL PARK
(www.kws.go.ke/content/watamu-marine-national-park-reserve; adult/child US$20/15; ⏲8am-6pm) The southern part of Malindi Marine National Park, this reserve includes some magnificent coral reefs, abundant fish life and sea turtles. To get here to snorkel and dive, you'll need a boat, which is easy enough to hire at the KWS office (p331), where you pay the park fees, at the end of the coast road. Boat operators ask anywhere from KSh2500 to KSh5000 for two people for two hours; it's all negotiable. Alternatively, arrange trips with recommended water-sports operators.

Activities

★Aqua Ventures ADVENTURE SPORTS
(☎0733906577, 0703628102; www.diveinkenya.com; Turtle Bay Rd, Ocean Sports Resort; dives from €45) Veteran diving outfit operated by British ex-military. It's the only British Sub-Aqua Club (BSAC) Premier Centre in Kenya and a full range of dives and courses is on offer, from five-day PADI open water (US$590) to night dives and wreck dives.

Tribe Kitesurfing KITESURFING
(☎0718553355; www.tribe-watersports.com; Turtle Bay Rd; ⏲9am-5pm) This excellent outfit is your go-to place for kitesurfing courses (three-day beginner course US$330) and equipment in Watamu. It also offers SUP 'surfaris', and rents boards (US$22 per hour).

Ocean Sports WATER SPORTS
(☎0734195227; www.oceansports.net; Turtle Bay Rd, Ocean Sports) Offers windsurfing courses from €25, which is about as cheap as you'll find in Kenya. Kayaks and SUPs are also available for hire.

Mwamba Field Study Centre WILDLIFE
(☎Nairobi 020-2335865; www.arocha.or.ke; Plot 28, Watamu Beach) This Christian conservation society, based out of the namesake guesthouse, is involved in various worthwhile projects, from ringing endangered bird species and protecting vulnerable coastal ecosystems to sponsoring the education of local children. Guests at their guesthouse are welcome to participate in various conservation-related activities.

Sleeping & Eating

★Kobe Suite Resort BOUTIQUE HOTEL $$
(☎0722658951; www.kobesuiteresort.com; Turtle Bay Rd; s/d US$110/130; ❄📶🏊) With five

rooms facing Kenya's best beach and a further 18 set back around a second saltwater pool, this boutique hotel works a sleek, dreamy vibe. Expect Swahili archways, bougainvillea window frames, brushed concrete surfaces and a minimalist feel. The garden hides intimate coves and a fire pit, there's a beautiful rooftop terrace and the restaurant serves fine Italian food.

★**Watamu Treehouse** BOUTIQUE HOTEL **$$$**
(☎0712810055; www.treehouse.co.ke; Turtle Bay Rd; s/d US$100/200; 📶) A wonder of recycled stained-glass windows, curvy walls of brushed concrete, nooks with sofas for sunset-watching and gnarled railings made of coconut wood, this twin-towered tree-house retreat rises from a sea of greenery. The seven plush, whitewashed rooms with rainhead showers are open to the elements, and this is a tranquil space for relaxation, yoga, paddle boarding and tasty, healthy meals.

★**Pilipan Restaurant** FUSION **$$$**
(☎0736724099; Turtle Bay Rd; mains KSh800-2000; ⏰noon-2.30pm & 6-10pm Tue-Sun; P 📶) Set on a breezy Swahili-style outdoor terrace looking down on mangrove-strewn Prawn Lake, Pilipan turns up Watamu's chic factor, particularly after sunset, when the place is lit with twinkling fairy lights and candles. The mostly-Indian-but-not-quite menu includes sambal squid, Camembert samosas, tuna carpaccio and malabar prawn curry. There's a stylish bar area for aperitifs and sundowners.

ℹ Information

MONEY

Barclays (Jacaranda Rd, Watamu Supermarket)

Kenya Commercial Bank (Beach Way Rd) Has an ATM.

TOURIST INFORMATION

Kenya Marine Park Office (www.kws.go.ke; Turtle Bay Rd; ⏰8am-5pm) Marine park entry fees (US$20/day) payable here.

ℹ Getting There & Away

Watamu is about a two-hour drive north of Mombasa and about a 40-minute drive south of Malindi. Matatus run regularly between the three destinations. Heading north, they depart from the **matatu stand** in Watamu village; southbound vans leave from the **matatu stop** near the Gede ruins. Matatus to Malindi charge KSh150; to Mombasa they charge KSh500 to KSh700.

Arabuko Sokoke Forest Reserve

This 420-sq-km tract of natural forest – the largest indigenous coastal forest remaining in East Africa – is most famous as the home of the golden-rumped elephant shrew. Yes, you read that right – it's a guinea-pig-sized rodent with a long furry trunk and a (mostly) monogamous streak, and the **Arabuko Sokoke Forest Reserve** (☎0729295382; www.kenyaforestservice.org; Mombasa-Malindi Rd; adult/child US$20/10; ⏰6am-6pm) is its only natural habitat.

Besides this marvellous creature, the forest is home to about 240 bird species, including the Amani sunbird, the Clarke's weaver and the Sokoke scops owl – Africa's smallest owl. More than 33 species of snakes slither through the undergrowth and shy waterbucks hide behind mahogany trees. The forest's other denizens include the elephant shrews' largest relative, the elephant, as well as the shy Aders' duiker (miniature antelope), Sykes' monkeys and yellow baboons.

An overnight stay (or very early arrival) greatly increases your chances of spotting wildlife.

Activities

From the four entrances to the park, nature trails and 4WD tracks cut through the forest. There are bird trails at Kararacha Pools and Spinetail Way, located 16km south of the main entrance, accessed via the Kararacha entrance. From the Mida entrance, a trail leads to the Whistling Duck Pools, a favourite gathering place of whistling ducks, open-billed storks and grebes. A short trail leads north from the main entrance to the Treehouse, an excellent vantage point for spotting elephants who come to drink from a nearby lake; you may also spot them along the 4WD Elephant Track.

Sleeping

Treehouse TREEHOUSE **$**
(camping US$15) Pitch your tent on this platform high up in a tree, overlooking an elephant watering hole. No facilities but great wildlife encounters!

Kararacha Camping CAMPGROUND **$**
(camping US$15) Basic campsite near the Kararacha entrance to the reserve, with cold showers and pit toilets.

Getting There & Away

The forest is just off the main Malindi–Mombasa road. The main entrance is about 1.5km west of the turn-off to Gede and Watamu, while the Mida entrance is about 3km further south, and the Kararacha entrance is another 11km or so south of Mida. Buses and matatus between Mombasa and Malindi can drop you at either entrance. From Watamu, matatus to Malindi can drop you at the main junction.

Gede Ruins

If you thought Kenya was all about nature, you're missing an important component of its charm: lost cities. The remains of medieval Swahili towns dot the coast, and many would say the most impressive of the bunch are the **Gede ruins** (☎0723359652; www.museums.or.ke; off Mombasa-Malindi Rd; adult/child KSh500/250; ⏲8am-6pm).

This series of coral palaces, mosques and townhouses, which once housed 3000 people, lies quietly in the jungle's green grip. Here, archaeologists found evidence of the cosmopolitan nature of Swahili society: silver necklaces decorated with Maria Teresa coins (from Europe) and Arabic calligraphy (from the Middle East), vermicelli makers from Asia that would become pasta moulds in the Mediterranean, Persian sabres, Arab coffee pots, Indian lamps, Egyptian or Syrian cobalt glass, Spanish scissors and Ming porcelain.

Entry to the dusty **museum** is included in the site ticket. There's a small collection of excavated Chinese coins, porcelain bowls, weapons, terracotta pots and other items found here.

History

Gede, which reached its peak in the 15th century, was inexplicably abandoned in the 17th or 18th century. Some theories point to disease and famine, others blame guerrilla attacks by Somalian Galla people and cannibalistic Zimba from near Malawi, or punitive expeditions from Mombasa. Or Gede ran out of water – at some stage the water table here dropped rapidly and the 40m-deep wells dried up.

Tours

Guided tours are available from the gate for around KSh500.

Getting There & Away

The ruins lie off the main highway, on the access road to Watamu. The easiest way to get here is on any matatu plying the main highway between Mombasa and Malindi. Get off at the village of Gede and follow the well-signposted dirt road from there – it's about a 10-minute walk. Tuk-tuks from Watamu charge around KSh200 to get you here.

Malindi

☎042 / POP 84,154

Having hosted Vasco da Gama's fleet in 1498, Malindi has been welcoming strangers ever since. It's a bustling town that doesn't quite have the architecture of Lamu or the easy-going charm of Watamu, but it makes up for it with several worthwhile historical sights, its own marine national park and some fantastic stretches of beach. Beloved by Italians – many of whom have settled here (particularly Sicilians back in the 1970s, allegedly fleeing from Interpol) – Malindi has been feeling the pinch lately, with economic depression in Europe impacting on much of its visitor market. Still, it remains a melting pot of local cultures with a rich and fascinating history. Wander through the alleys of the atmospheric old town, dine on terrific Italian food beside the Indian Ocean or take a plunge into the crystal-clear waters of the national park, and you'll discover for yourself that Malindi is quite the charmer.

Sights

Malindi Marine National Park NATIONAL PARK
(www.kws.go.ke; adult/child US$20/15; ⏲6am-6pm) The oldest marine park in Kenya covers 213 sq km of powder-blue fish, organ-pipe coral, green sea turtles and beds of Thalassia seagrass. If you're extremely lucky, you may spot mako and whale sharks. Unfortunately, these reefs have suffered (and continue to suffer) extensive damage, evidenced by the piles of seashells on sale in Malindi. Monsoon-generated waves can reduce visibility from June to September.

Vasco da Gama Pillar LANDMARK
(off Mama Ngina Rd; adult/child KSh500/250; ⏲8am-6pm) More impressive for what it represents (the genesis of the Age of Exploration) than the edifice itself. Erected by the Portuguese explorer Vasco da Gama as a navigational aid in 1498, the coral column is topped by a cross made of Lisbon stone,

DON'T MISS

MIDA CREEK

Hugged by silver-tinged mudflats flowing with tiny ghost and fiddler crabs and long tides, 32-sq-km-Mida Creek is a place where the creeping marriage of land and water is epitomised by a mangrove forest and the salty, fresh scent of wind over an estuary. Eight types of mangroves thrive here, along with dozens of species of birds, including the rare crab plover. Giriama people live next to the creek, maintaining a boardwalk for birdwatchers and offering accommodation to those keen on experiencing a local way of life. Mida Creek is at its best at dawn, sunset, and in the clear evenings when the stars rain down on you. Explore it by stand up paddle board, canoe or boat.

Mida Ecocamp (0729213042; www.midaecocamp.com; camping KSh500, huts per person KSh900-1400) This relaxed ecocamp has *the* most perfect position, between the forest, the creek and the stars. Accommodation is in atmospheric traditional huts – choose from Zanzibar (duplex with a breezy upper terrace), Giriama (haystack with amiable face and raised platform beds) and Swahili (square, with a thatched roof). The eco-credentials stretch to solar panels, renewable materials and a serious Giriama community focus.

Merry Crab Cove (0792295131; www.mcc-guesthouse-backpackers.net; Uyombo; dm KSh1800, d KSh6500-8500;) We challenge you to find a lovelier backpackers' spot on Kenya's north coast! A converted luxury resort, the Merry Crab retains the rain-head showers and sumptuous room design, with a saltwater pool, own beach and sunset-watching terrace. The delightful owners make guests feel like family, and boat transfers to Watamu are organised. By road, follow signs for Rock and Sea.

Rock and Sea (0722658951; ste €400;) This ambitious ecolodge consists of just four rooms – three in plexi 'eco-bubbles' and a brushed concrete one next to a 2000-year-old baobab, crowned with a sunset-watching platform. Its hillock location gives it the best views of Mida Creek and the restaurant is great for sundowners. Speedboat transfers from Watamu are available, or follow the signs from Matasangoni turn-off for 4.5km.

Crab Shack (0725315562; mains KSh800-1200; 10am-8pm) Crab samosas, grilled calamari and steamed fish await at the end of a mangrove boardwalk, overlooking Mida Creek. This lovely Giriama-run spot is a favourite for sunset-watching, too. It's a 3km walk or *boda-boda* ride along the road directly opposite Turtle Bay Hotel. Follow the signs for Mida Creek Community Ecotourism Enterprizes at the crossroads.

Getting There & Away

Any bus travelling between Mombasa and Malindi can drop you on the main road near the turn-offs for Mida Creek boardwalk, and the Mida Ecocamp, from where it's a pleasant, leafy, 20-minute walk to the water.

which almost certainly dates from the explorer's time. There are good views from here down the coast and out over the ocean.

Activities

Malindi is one of the top destinations in the world for kitesurfing, with the best seasons being July to September and January to April. The best place to learn is at Che Shale (p335), the kitesurfing camp/beach retreat north of Malindi, partially responsible for introducing the sport to the area. A three-day course for beginners costs €340.

Aqua Ventures DIVING

(0703628102; www.diveinkenya.com; Mama Ngina Rd, Driftwood Beach Club) Based at the **Driftwood Beach Club** (0721724489; www.driftwoodclub.com; Mama Ngina Rd; s/d from KSh7300/14,500;), Aqua Ventures is one of the best diving outfits in town. Dives start at US$50, but buying a package reduces the cost considerably.

Blue Fin DIVING

(0722261242; www.bluefindiving.com; Mama Ngina Rd) With the marine park just offshore from Malindi, scuba diving is a popular

Malindi

0 500 m
0 0.25 miles

Che Shale (20km); Marafa (30km)
B8
Ngowe Rd
Mtangani Rd
Lamu Rd
Makaburini Rd
INDIAN OCEAN
9
7
8
10
Lamu Rd
Kenyatta Rd
Malindi Bay
Muslim Cemetery
Uluru Park
Jetty
Ngala Rd
C103
Odinga St
Hindu Temple
Jamhuri St
Jumaa Mosque & Palace
11
Tana St
Uhuru Rd
3
Boatyards
Old Market
Casuarina Rd
5
Mombasa Rd
OLD TOWN
6
2
1
Mama Ngina Rd
Malindi (2km); Gede (18km); Arabuko Sokoke Forest Reserve (20km) Watamu (24km); Mombasa (118km)
4
Malindi Marine NP (2.8km)

Malindi

Sights

1 Vasco da Gama Pillar D5

Activities, Courses & Tours

Aqua Ventures .... (see 4)
2 Blue Fin D5

Sleeping

3 Dagama's Inn D5
4 Driftwood Beach Club D7

Eating

5 Baby Marrow D5
6 Dreamland C5

Information

7 Barclays B3
8 Dollar Forex Bureau B3
9 Malindi Tourist Office B2
10 Standard Chartered Bank B3

Transport

11 Simba Coaches B4
Tahmeed .... (see 11)
Tawakal .... (see 11)

activity, although the visibility is greatly reduced by silt between March and June. Blue Fin is reputable and operates out of several resorts in town. Open water courses from €360.

Sleeping

Tourism is the lifeblood of Malindi, and there's an almost-unbroken stretch of hotels and resorts along the town's coastline. Falling visitor numbers in recent years mean that some excellent deals are available, and you can often snag a room at well below the normal rack rate. Some places close or scale-down operations in October and between April and June.

Dagama's Inn INN $

(☎0701864446, 0722357591; Mama Ngina Rd; s/d excl breakfast KSh1200/1400) This friendly little place is a real seaside travellers' inn – that's to say that seamen prop up the bar with mermaid stories, and drunken sailors make eyes at the barmaid. The rooms are spacious but simple. If you can get hot water out of those rusty water-storage tanks, you're a better person than us.

★ **Barefoot Beach Camp** TENTED CAMP $$

(☎0722421351; www.barefootbeachcampkenya.com; camping KSh1000, r with half board KSh6500) Venture 25km from Malindi, and you can have Mambrui North Beach almost to yourselves at this intimate and relaxed camp, run by fantastic hosts. Glamp in one of five luxury safari tents with sumptuous beds and bathrooms, or camp out. Gourmet seafood dishes are served here; book 24 hours in advance if not staying at the camp.

★ **Che Shale** BANDAS $$

(☎0722230931; www.cheshale.com; s €45-180, d €90-180; wi-fi) Three kinds of people make their way to this camp on Mambrui Beach, 25km north of Malindi: kitesurfers, foodies and tranquillity seekers. Choose between three types of *bandas*, all crafted from local materials: basic (shared loo outside), beach-front (king-sized bed, relaxation space on the porch) and luxury (even snazzier). The excellent restaurant's mangrove crab dishes are unique on the coast.

★ **Villa Fortuna Malindi** GUESTHOUSE $$

(☎0735923507; Crocodile Rd; r KSh5650-8400; air-con, wi-fi, pool) Drowning in a riot of bougainvillea, this *makuti* (thatched-roof of palm leaves) guesthouse overlooks a kidney-shaped pool in a secure, gated property. The warm welcome from the owners and their tiny dogs and cats is second to none. It's down an unlit dirt road from Marine Park Rd, so take a *boda-boda* (motorcycle taxi; KSh100) in the evenings.

It's a convenient 10-minute walk from the marine park and a 5-minute walk from the beach.

Eating

With great seafood, strong Italian influences and numerous restaurants, Malindi is one of the best places to eat on the coast and has some of the best pizza, pasta and gelato in Africa. Street-food heaven is Jamhuri St, where stalls line both sides of the road selling deep-fried goodies, bhajis, dates and chapattis.

Dreamland KENYAN $

(Casuarina Rd; mains around KSh400; ⌚noon-10pm Mon-Sat) The outer walls look a bit like the children's ward of a hospital, but there's nothing sterile about this circular roadside lunch spot. Expect friendly service, local banter and a blaring TV. The fresh juice is good.

★ **Rosada** ITALIAN $$$

(☎0700501813; off Casuarina Rd; mains from KSh800; ⌚8am-10pm Nov-Feb, until 5pm Mar-Oct;

) Right on the sand, Rosada is a chilled beach bar with great cocktails and some wonderful views out over the marine park. Monday night is a popular beach party, which sees dancing on the beach once the sun has gone down. The food gets rave reviews, particularly the pizzas.

★ **Baby Marrow** ITALIAN, SEAFOOD $$$

(0700766704; Mama Ngina Rd; mains KSh800-2200; noon-3pm & 7-11pm, evenings only in low season;) This standout restaurant is not only one of the best on the coast, but in the entire country. Think leafy, intimate setting, *makuti* roof, and bold contemporary art, while the charming staff bring you house specialities such as smoked sailfish, pizza bianca, vodka sorbet or Sicilian ice cream. The jungle bar is a good spot for a digestif.

Information

DANGERS & ANNOYANCES

Being on the beach alone at night is asking for trouble, as is walking along any quiet beach back road at night. Avoid the far northern end of the beach, or any deserted patches of sand, as muggings are common. There are lots of guys selling drugs, so remember: everything is illegal. Drug sales often turn into stings, with the collusive druggie getting a cut of whatever fee police demand from you (if they don't throw you in jail).

MONEY

Barclays (Lamu Rd) With ATM.

Dollar Forex Bureau (Lamu Rd; 9am-6pm Mon-Sat) Rates may be slightly better here than at the banks.

Standard Chartered Bank (Lamu Rd, Stanchart Arcade) With ATM.

TOURIST INFORMATION

Malindi Tourist Office (042-2120747; Lamu Rd, Malindi Complex; 8am-12.30pm & 2-4.30pm Mon-Fri) Not a great deal of information on the area, but it's the place to register your complaints if you've had a bad experience with a local tour operator.

Getting There & Away

AIR

Malindi Airport (042-2131201; https://kaa.go.ke/airports/our-airports/malindi-airport; off Mombasa-Malindi Rd) has up to four daily flights to Nairobi (from US$47 one way, one hour) with Airkenya (p258), Fly540 (p258) and **Fly-SAX** (www.fly-sax.com), and a daily flight to Lamu (from US$59 one way, 25 minutes) with Fly540.

WORTH A TRIP

MARAFA

One of the more intriguing sights inland from the north Kenyan coast is Hell's Kitchen or Nyari ('the place broken by itself'). About 30km northeast of Malindi, it's an eroded sandstone gorge where jungle, red rock and cliffs heave themselves into a single stunning Mars-like landscape. You can take an organised tour, take a taxi (KSh9000), drive, or catch a morning matatu from Mombasa Rd in Malindi to Marafa village (KSh200, 2½ hours) and walk for 20 minutes.

Marafa Depression (Hell's Kitchen; KSh800, guide KSh500; 7am-7pm) is currently managed as a local tourism concern by Marafa village, with the steep admission costs going into village programmes. A guide will walk you around the lip of the gorge and into its heart of sandstone spikes and melted-candle-like formations, and tell the story of Hell's Kitchen. Which goes like so: a rich family was so careless with their wealth that they bathed themselves in the valuable milk of their cows. God became angry with this excess and sank the family homestead into the earth. The white and red walls of the depression mark the milk and blood of the family painted over the gorge walls. The more mundane explanation? The depression is a chunk of sandstone that's geologically distinct from the surrounding rock and more susceptible to wind and rain erosion.

There are two very basic places to stay if needed (KSh1000), plus a restaurant right next to the gorge.

If you come by private transport, it's worth making a day trip of it and enjoying the beautiful African countryside, with its fields of maize studded with chunky baobab trees, mud houses with *makuti* roofs and cattle herders tending their beasts.

BUS & MATATU

Bus-company offices are found opposite the old market in the centre of Malindi. The main bus companies are **Tahmeed** (☎ 0711756970; Jamhuri St), **Tawakal** (☎ 0705090122; Jamhuri St) and **Simba Coaches** (☎ 0774471112; Tana St), and they all run services to Lamu, Mombasa and Nairobi (via Mombasa).

Getting Around

You can rent bicycles from most hotels for around KSh700 per day. Tuk-tuks are ubiquitous – a short hop through town should cost around KSh150 to KSh200. *Boda-bodas* are even cheaper – KSh50 to KSh100 for a short hop. A taxi to the airport is around KSh1000 and a tuk-tuk is KSh200. However, these are official prices and you'll need the gift of the gab to actually bargain down to this.

Lamu

☎ 042

Lamu Town seems almost ethereal as you approach it from the water, with the shopfronts and mosques creeping out from behind a forest of dhow masts. Up close, the illusion shatters and the town becomes a hive of activity – from the busy waterfront, with heavy carts wheeled to and fro, to the pungent labyrinth of donkey-wide alleyways, along which women whisper by in full-length *bui-bui* (black cover-all worn by some Islamic women outside the home) and stray cats hunt for scraps. Your nostrils are assaulted with blue smoke from meat grilling over open fires, donkey dung and the organic scent of the cured wooden shutters on houses built of stone and coral. Many visitors call this town – the oldest living town in East Africa, a Unesco World Heritage Site and arguably the most complete Swahili town in existence – one of the highlights of their trip to Kenya.

Sights

★Lamu Museum MUSEUM

(☎ 0721660645; www.museums.or.ke; Harambee Ave, Waterfront; adult/child KSh500/250; ⊙8am-6pm) The best museum in town (and the second best in Kenya) is housed in a grand Swahili warehouse on the waterfront. This is as good a gateway as you'll get into Swahili culture and that of the archipelago in particular. Exhibitions focus on boat-building, domestic life and weddings, the intricate door carvings that you're likely to encounter (from Swahili and Omani to Kijumwa, Swabu and Bajun) and traditional silver jewellery. Don't miss the ceremonial *siwa* (side-blow) horns of ivory and brass.

Donkey Sanctuary WILDLIFE RESERVE

(Harambee Ave; ⊙9am-1pm Mon-Fri) FREE A man without a donkey *is* a donkey, claims one Swahili proverb. Or, as the staff of this sanctuary might tell you, a man who doesn't look after his donkey *is* a donkey. With around 3000 donkeys active on Lamu, *Equus asinus* is the main form of transport here. Visitors are free to visit the sanctuary and learn about its work – donations appreciated.

Swahili House MUSEUM

(www.museums.or.ke; adult/child KSh500/250; ⊙8am-6pm) This preserved 16th-century Swahili house, tucked away to the side of Yumbe Guest House, in a tranquil courtyard with a well, is beautiful. The entry fee for viewing the two sleeping galleries and upstairs kitchen is very hard to justify, though, especially as half the hotels in Lamu are as well preserved.

Lamu Market MARKET

(next to Lamu Fort) Atmospheric and somewhat chaotic, this quintessential Lamu market is best visited early in the morning. Bargain for fresh tuna and sailfish, wade through alleys teeming with stray cats and goats, and experience Lamu at its craziest. If you're sick of seafood, this is the place to find your fruit and veg.

Lamu Fort FORTRESS

(www.museums.or.ke; Main Sq; adult/child KSh500/200; ⊙8am-6pm) This squat castle was built by the Sultan of Paté between 1810 and 1823. From 1910 right up to 1984 it was used as a prison. It now houses the island's

> WORTH A TRIP
>
> **SHELA BEACH**
>
> Most people are here for the beach – a 12km-long, wide sweep of pristine white sand where you're guaranteed an isolated spot (at least if you're prepared to walk some way) to catch some rays. Swimming is possible, but there are places with strong rip currents – particularly around **The Fort hotel** (www.thefortshela.com; d from US$215; ❄📶) – so get some local advice before venturing into the water.

Lamu

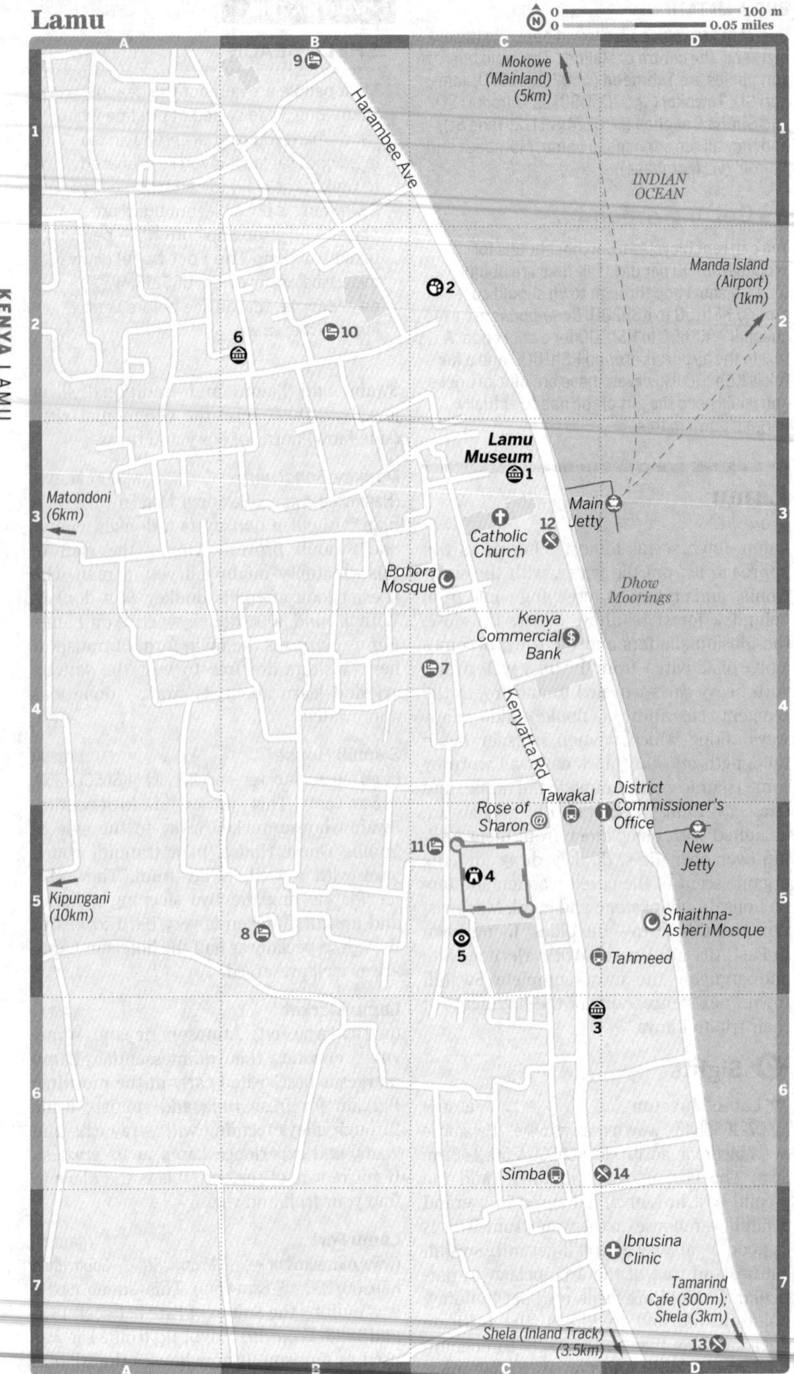

0 100 m
0 0.05 miles
A
B
C
D
1
2
3
4
5
6
7
Mokowe (Mainland) (5km)
Harambee Ave
INDIAN OCEAN
Manda Island (Airport) (1km)
Lamu Museum
Main Jetty
Matondoni (6km)
Catholic Church
Bohora Mosque
Dhow Moorings
Kenya Commercial Bank
Kenyatta Rd
District Commissioner's Office
Tawakal
Rose of Sharon
New Jetty
Kipungani (10km)
Shiaithna-Asheri Mosque
Tahmeed
Simba
Ibnusina Clinic
Tamarind Cafe (300m); Shela (3km)
Shela (Inland Track) (3.5km)
1
2
3
4
5
6
7
8
9
10
11
12
13
14

Lamu

Top Sights

1 Lamu Museum C3

Sights

2 Donkey Sanctuary C2
3 German Post Office Museum C6
4 Lamu Fort C5
5 Lamu Market C5
6 Swahili House B2

Sleeping

7 Amu House C4
8 Jambo House B5
9 Lamu House B1
10 Stone House Hotel B2
11 Subira House C5

Eating

12 Bush Gardens Restaurant C3
Moonrise .... (see 9)
13 Olympic Restaurant D7
14 Whispers Cafe D6

library, which holds one of the best collections of Swahili poetry and Lamu reference work in Kenya, while the upstairs walkway is a gallery space for temporary exhibitions (stunning photos of the Tana River delta, when we visited). Entry is free with a ticket for Lamu Museum (p337).

Festivals & Events

Maulid Festival RELIGIOUS
(www.lamu.org/maulid-celebration.html; Dec/Jan) Marking the birth of the Prophet Mohammed, this festival has been celebrated on the island for over 100 years and much singing, dancing and general jollity takes place around this time. On the final day a procession heads down to the tomb of the man who started it all, Ali Habib Swaleh. Its date shifts according to the Islamic calendar.

Lamu Cultural Festival CULTURAL
(Nov) Exact dates for this colourful carnival vary each year, but it often falls in November. Expect donkey and dhow races, Swahili poets and island dancing.

Sleeping

The alleyways of Lamu offer a full range of beautiful, centuries-old Swahili houses converted into budget digs and boutique hotels alike. Competition means that there's always scope for price negotiation. Touts will invariably try to accompany you to get commission; the best way to avoid this is to book one night in advance, so you know what you'll be paying.

★ Jambo House B&B $
(0713411714; www.jambohouse.com; s/d from KSh1400/1800;) Hands down the best place in town for budget travellers, this friendly guesthouse is owned by German world traveller Arnold, a treasure trove of all things Lamu. He tells guests what they can do in Lamu and how to do it, and dishes out maps of the town. Five snug rooms and a hearty breakfast seal the deal.

Amu House B&B $
(0792558449, 0717308131; www.amuhousekenya.com; s/d/tr KSh2500/3500/2500;) A winner during the hottest months, this beautifully restored 16th-century Swahili house is one of the coolest places on the island. Friendly manager/musician Kesh houses his guests in seven rooms, decked out in traditional style, and there's a breezy rooftop chill-out terrace with hammocks for relaxation. No wi-fi just yet.

Stone House Hotel BOUTIQUE HOTEL $
(0722528377, 0736699417; www.stonehousehotellamu.com; r KSh2000-4500;) This Swahili mansion is set into a tourist-free backstreet and is notable for its fine, whitewashed walls and fantastic rooftop, which includes a good restaurant (no alcohol) with excellent views over the town and waterfront. The rooms are spacious and nicely decorated, and it's easily one of the better-value options in town.

Subira House GUESTHOUSE $$
(0707293832, 0726916686; www.subirahouse.com; s/d from KSh6000/9000;) This Swedish-owned property features graceful arches and twin gardens with wells. The Sultan of Zanzibar knew a thing or two about style when he built the house 200 years ago. As well as seven stylish bedrooms (the ones at the top are smaller but brighter and breezier), there are relaxing common spaces and serious eco-credentials. We rate the restaurant highly.

★ Lamu House BOUTIQUE HOTEL $$$
(0792469577; www.lamuhouse.com; Harambee Ave; r US$150-200;) In a town where every building wants to top the preservation stakes, Lamu House stands out. It consists of two fused Swahili villas. Each of its handful of rooms is individually decorated and

DON'T MISS

DHOW TRIPS

More than the bustle of markets or the call to prayer, the pitch of 'We take dhow trip, see mangroves, eat fish and coconut rice' is the unyielding chorus of Lamu's voices when you first arrive. That said, taking a dhow trip (and seeing the mangroves and eating fish and coconut rice) is generally fun, though this depends to a large degree on your captain. Guesthouses such as Jambo House (p339) work with several reliable captains and it's good to get recommendations from other travellers. There's a real joy to kicking it on the boards under the sunny sky, with the mangroves drifting by in island time while snacking on spiced fish.

Trips include dhow racing excursions (learning how to tack and race these amazingly agile vessels is quite something), sunset sails, adventures to Kipungani and Manda Island, deep-reef fishing and even three-day trips south along the coast to Kilifi (from US$120 per person).

Prices vary, depending on where you want to go, who you go with and how long you go for. With bargaining you could pay around KSh2500 per person in a group of four or five people, on a half-day basis. Don't hand over any money until the day of departure, except perhaps a small advance for food. On long trips, it's best to organise your own drinks. A hat and sunscreen are essential.

comes with a breezy private terrace, while the common spaces are a riot of woodcarvings and art. The excellent Moonrise restaurant serves fine Swahili cuisine.

A free boat service to Manda Island leaves from here every morning at 8am.

Eating

Bush Gardens Restaurant INTERNATIONAL $$
(0714934804; Harambee Ave; mains KSh600-2000; 7am-10pm) This place is a backpacker institution, though food isn't quite as good as it's supposed to be. The large portions of biriyani, grilled fish and other offerings, including 'monster crab' and the inevitable lobster in Swahili sauce, are quantity over quality, washed down with good juices and shakes mixed up in British pint mugs.

Tamarind Cafe SEAFOOD $$
(0710500760; mains KSh600-1400; noon-9pm) Built around a sturdy tamarind tree, this wonky tree house-restaurant overlooks the dhows on the waterfront. Lobster, prawns, squid and catch of the day are all present on the menu and simply prepared, and there's a friendly cat that'll climb all over you.

★ **Whispers Cafe** CAFE $$
(Kenyatta Rd; mains KSh400-950; 9am-2pm & 4-6.30pm Mon-Sat; wi-fi) You know how sometimes you just need that escape into the world of magazines and fresh pastries? Welcome to Whispers. For a real cappuccino, light meals, mega juices and smoothies, or the best desserts in town, this cafe with a garden, set in the same building as the Baraka Gallery, is just the ticket.

Olympic Restaurant AFRICAN $$
(0728667692; Harambee Ave; mains KSh500-1000) The family that runs the Olympic makes you feel as if you've come home every time you enter, and their food, particularly the curries and biriyani, is excellent. There are few better ways to spend a Lamu night than with a cold mug of passion-fruit juice and the noir-ish view of the docks here, at the ramshackle end of town.

★ **Moonrise** FUSION $$$
(0708073164; Harambee Ave, Lamu House; mains KSh900-1550; 7am-10pm; wi-fi) Particularly strong when it comes to seafood dishes and slightly set back from the waterfront, this is the best restaurant in town. Feast on the likes of fish tacos with mango salsa, ginger crab with coconut rice and such crowd pleasers as chicken and chips.

Drinking & Nightlife

As an Islamic town, Lamu has few options for drinkers and local sensibilities should be respected. However, Lamu's fruit juices, which are sold in almost every restaurant, are very good.

Town Walk
Lamu

START LAMU MAIN JETTY
FINISH LAMU MAIN JETTY
LENGTH APPROXIMATELY 4KM; ONE TO 1½ HOURS

The best, indeed only, way to see Lamu Town is on foot. Few experiences compare with exploring the far backstreets, where you can wander amid wafts of cardamom and carbolic and watch the town's agile cats scaling the coral walls. There are so many wonderful Swahili houses that it's pointless for us to recommend specific examples – keep your eyes open wherever you go, and don't forget to look up.

Starting at the **1 main jetty**, head north past the **2 Lamu Museum** (p337) and along the waterfront until you reach the **3 door-carving workshops**.

From here head onto Kenyatta Rd, passing an original Swahili **4 well**, and into the alleys towards the **5 Swahili House museum** (p337). Once you've had your fill of domestic insights, take any route back towards the main street.

After you've hit the main square and the **6 fort** (p337), take a right to see the crumbled remains of the 14th-century **7 Pwani Mosque**, one of Lamu's oldest buildings – an Arabic inscription is still visible on the wall. From here you can head round and browse the covered **8 market** (p337) then negotiate your way towards the bright, Saudi-funded **9 Riyadha Mosque**, the centre of Lamu's religious scene.

Now you can take as long or as short a route as you like back to the waterfront. Stroll along the promenade, diverting for the **10 German Post Office Museum** – the door is another amazing example of Swahili carving. If you're feeling the pace, take a rest and shoot the breeze on the **11 baraza ya wazee** ('old men's bench') outside the stucco minarets of the **12 Shiaithna-Asheri Mosque**.

Carrying on up Harambee Ave will bring you back to the main jetty.

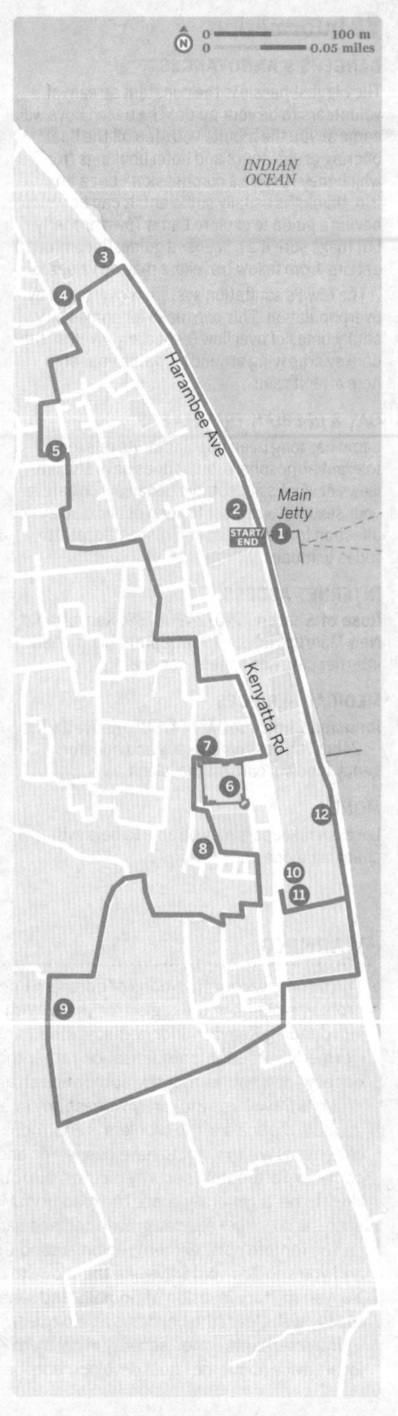

Information

DANGERS & ANNOYANCES

The biggest hassle is the constant stream of volunteers to be your guide. The beach boys will come at you the minute you step off the boat, offering drugs, tours and hotel bookings (for which they receive a commission), but a firm 'No, thanks' is usually sufficient. It can be worth having a guide to explore Lamu Town properly, but make sure it's a licensed guide. Recommendations from fellow travellers may be valuable.

The town's sanitation system is overtaxed by overpopulation. This can make for some hairy, stinky times of overflow (especially given all the donkey crap lying around) – watch your step here after it rains.

GAY & LESBIAN TRAVELLERS

Lamu has long been popular for its relaxed, tolerant atmosphere, but it does have Muslim views of what's acceptable behaviour. Whatever your sexuality, it's best to keep public displays of affection to a minimum and respect local attitudes to modesty.

INTERNET ACCESS

Rose of Sharon (☎0724966799; Kenyatta Rd, New Mahrus Hotel; ⏰9am-9pm) This friendly internet cafe has speedy service.

MEDICAL SERVICES

Ibnusina Clinic (☎0721447985; Kenyatta Rd; ⏰24hr) The best emergency and nonemergency medical care on the island.

MONEY

Local shopkeepers may be able to help with changing money.

Kenya Commercial Bank (Harambee Ave) The main bank on Lamu, with an ATM (Visa only). Several other ATMs along the waterfront.

TOURIST INFORMATION

Rumour has it that a tourist office will open in the not too distant future somewhere along the waterfront. In the meantime, http://lamutourism.org is an excellent source of local info.

WOMEN TRAVELLERS

Female travellers should note that most Lamurians hold strong religious and cultural values and may be deeply offended by revealing clothing. There have been some isolated incidents of rape, which locals say were sparked by tourists refusing to cover up. That may outrage some Western ears, but the fact remains that you risk getting into trouble if you walk around in small shorts and low-cut tops. There are kilometres of deserted beaches on which you can walk around butt naked if you choose, but we urge you to respect cultural norms in built-up areas.

Getting There & Away

AIR

Lamu Airport is on Manda Island, and boats across the channel to Lamu cost KSh100. You'll be met by 'guides' at the airport who will offer to carry your bags to the hotel of your choice for a small consideration (about KSh200). Many double as touts, so be cautious about accepting the first price you're quoted when you get to your hotel.

There are several daily flights to Nairobi (from US$108, two hours) with Fly540 (p258), Airkenya (p258), **Skyward Express** (www.skywardexpress.co.ke) and Safarilink (p258).

WARNING

The strong warrior traditions of northern Kenya's nomadic people have led to security problems plaguing the region for years. With an influx of cheap guns from conflict zones surrounding Kenya, minor conflicts stemming from grazing rights and cattle rustling (formerly settled by compensation rather than violence) have quickly escalated into ongoing gun battles that the authorities struggle to contain.

While travellers, who rarely witness any intertribal conflict, may consider the issue exaggerated, the scale of the problem is enormous and growing. Over the past decade hundreds of Kenyans are thought to have been killed and tens of thousands displaced by intertribal conflicts. Fortunately, security on the main routes in the north, and anywhere a tourist is likely to be, is generally good. The road from Marsabit to Moyale – previously a banditry hotspot – is no longer a jutted gravel road and banditry incidents have dropped dramatically.

The remote northeastern region around Garsen, Wajir and Mandera is still unstable and you should avoid travelling there due to continuing conflicts. Likewise, a full-scale Kenyan military invasion of Somalia and renewed fighting in the region is a strong reason to stay well clear (the border is also closed).

Improvements or not, security in northern Kenya is a fluid entity. Travellers should seek local advice about the latest developments before visiting and never take unnecessary risks.

Safarilink and Airkenya fly to Nairobi Wilson. A single Skyward Express flight serves Mombasa (US$80, 45 minutes, daily) while Fly540 and **Fly-SAX** (www.fly-sax.com) fly daily to Malindi (US$45, 30 minutes).

BUS

There are booking offices for the main bus companies either on Kenyatta Rd or along the waterfront. Buses leave from the jetty on the mainland and dock at Lamu's main jetty. The going rate for a trip to Mombasa (eight to nine hours) is KSh1100 to KSh1300. Most buses leave between 7am and 8am (11am and 1pm departures with Tawakal); the first connecting *mtabotis* (motorboat taxis) leave Lamu Town between 6am and 6.30am. Book bus tickets in advance and be on time; buses leave on the dot and will resell the seats of late-coming passengers further up the line. The most reliable companies are **Simba** (☎0707471110, 0707471111; off Kenyatta Rd), **Tahmeed** (☎0724581015, 0724581004; Kenyatta Rd) and **Tawakal** (☎0705090122; Kenyatta Rd); Tawakal is the fastest.

At the time of writing, armed guards were on every Lamu-bound bus from Mombasa and all vehicles were required to travel in convoy between Witu and Garsen.

Coming from Mombasa to Lamu, buses will drop you at the mainland jetty at Mokowe. From there you can either catch a *mtaboti* (KSh100, 30 minutes) or a speedboat (KSh150, 10 minutes). Don't listen to touts who try to tell you that you need to charter your own *mtaboti*.

Getting Around

Boats to the airstrip on Manda Island (KSh100) leave from the **main jetty** (Harambee Ave) about an hour before the flights leave. In theory, you have to be at the airport an hour before your flight.

Plenty of motorised dhows run to Shela throughout the day until around sunset from the **new jetty** (Harambee Ave); these cost about KSh100 per person if you share a boat with others or KSh500 if you don't. After dark, boat captains charge KSh1500 between Lamu Town and Shela.

There are also daily boats between Lamu and Paté Island (KSh200 to KSh250, two hours).

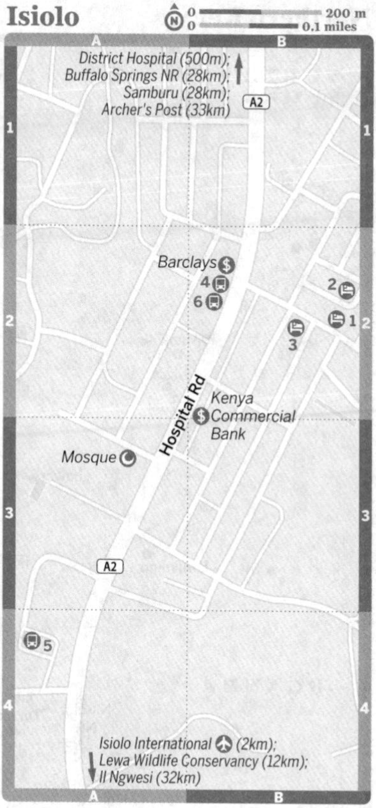

Isiolo

Isiolo

Sleeping

1 Bomen Hotel B2
2 Josera Guest House B2
3 Moti Peal Hotel B2

Eating

Bomen Hotel .... (see 1)

Transport

4 Liban Buses B2
5 Matatu Stand A4
6 Moyale Star Buses B2

NORTHERN KENYA

Calling all explorers! We dare you to challenge yourself against some of the most exciting wilderness in Africa. Step forward only if you're able to withstand appalling roads, searing heat, clouds of dust torn by relentless winds, primitive food and accommodation, vast distances and more than a hint of danger.

The rewards include memories of vast, shattered lava deserts, camel herders walking their animals to lost oases, fog-shrouded mountains full of mysterious creatures, prehistoric islands crawling with massive reptiles, and jokes shared with

Northern Kenya

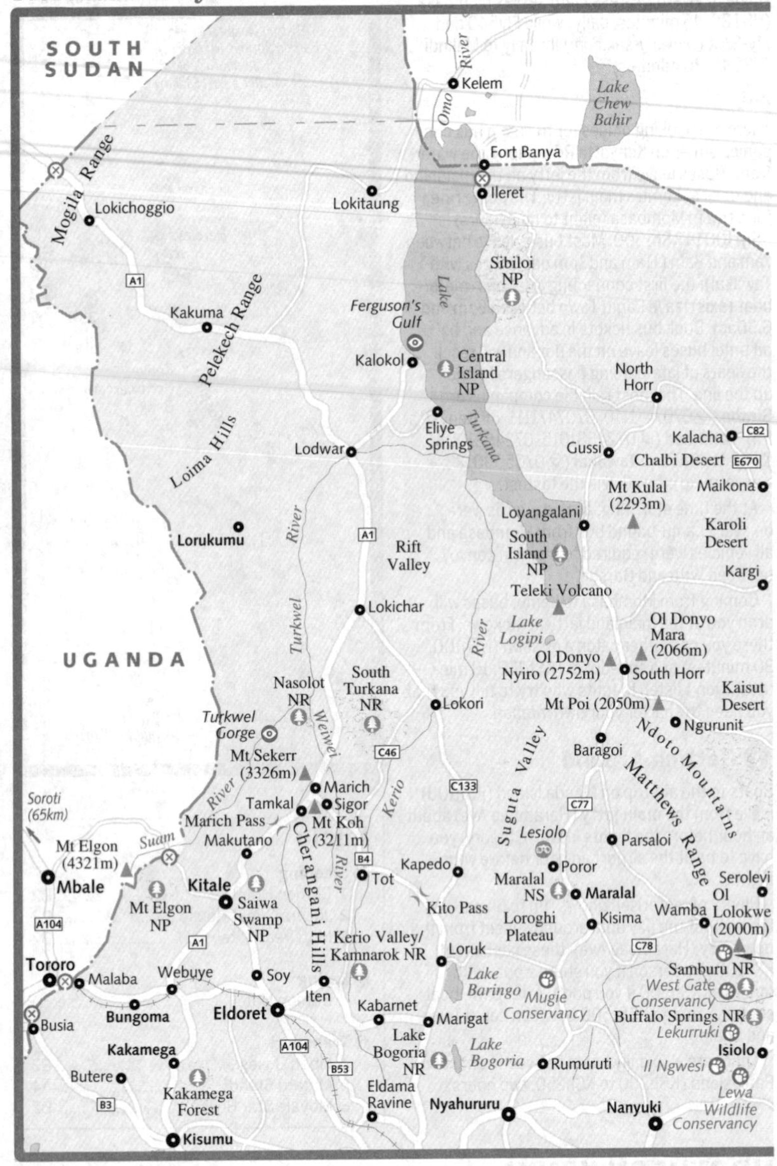

traditionally dressed warriors. Additional perks include camel trekking through piles of peachy dunes, elephant encounters in scrubby acacia woodlands and the chance to walk barefoot along the fabled shores of a sea of jade.

Isiolo to Moyale

For most people this route means one of two things: the wildlife riches of the Samburu ecosystem, or the road to the cultural riches of Ethiopia. But in between and

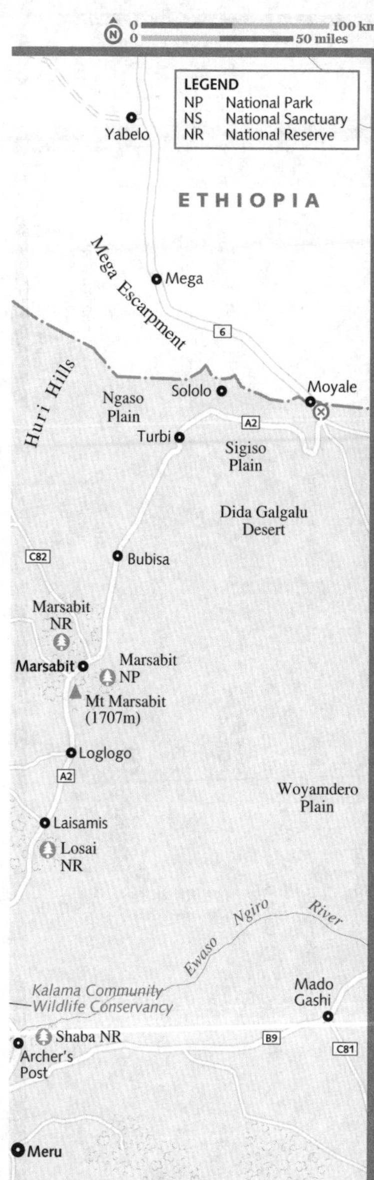

beyond, this area has much more to offer. You can drink tea and track wildlife with the Samburu people, climb mist-shrouded volcanoes in the desert, blaze trails in untrammelled mountains and get so far off the beaten track you'll start to wonder whether you're still on the same planet. All told, this massive wilderness offers something to anyone whose heart sings with adventure.

Isiolo

064 / POP 143,294

Isiolo is where anticipation and excitement first start to send your heart aflutter. This vital pit stop on the long road north to Ethiopia from central Kenya is a true frontier town, a place on the edge, torn between the cool, verdant highlands just to the south and the scorching badlands – home of nomads and bandits – to the north. On a more practical note, it's also the last place with decent facilities until Maralal or Marsabit.

Among the first things you'll undoubtedly notice is the large Somali population (descendants of WWI veterans who settled here) and the striking faces of Boran, Samburu and Turkana people walking the streets. It's this mix of people, cultures and religions that's the most interesting thing about Isiolo. Nowhere is this mixture better illustrated than in the hectic market.

Sleeping & Eating

Moti Peal Hotel HOTEL $
(064-5352400; www.moti.co.ke; s/d KSh2500/3500;) This smart place markets itself as the 'Pearl of Isiolo'. This actually says more about the state of Isiolo than the quality of the hotel, but even so it's shockingly clean, well run and has friendly management. Each room has a large double bed, mosquito net and spacious balcony.

Bomen Hotel HOTEL $
(0721698849; Great North Rd; s/tw KSh2500/3500; P) The NGOs' favourite home, it has the town's most toe-curlingly frilly pink bed sheets! It also has TVs, shared terraces with views and unfailingly polite staff.

The **restaurant** (meals KSh400-650; 6am-10.30pm;) is a rare place serving more than the local usuals, with fried tilapia (Nile perch), pepper steak, goulash and curries up for grabs. Has an attached bar with comfy couches and cheap beer.

Josera Guest House HOTEL $
(0728059274; r KSh1500-2000) Excellent-value sky-blue rooms that range from tiny cubes to those large enough to swing a backpack. All have hot showers and there's a decent in-house restaurant.

Samburu & Buffalo Springs National Reserves

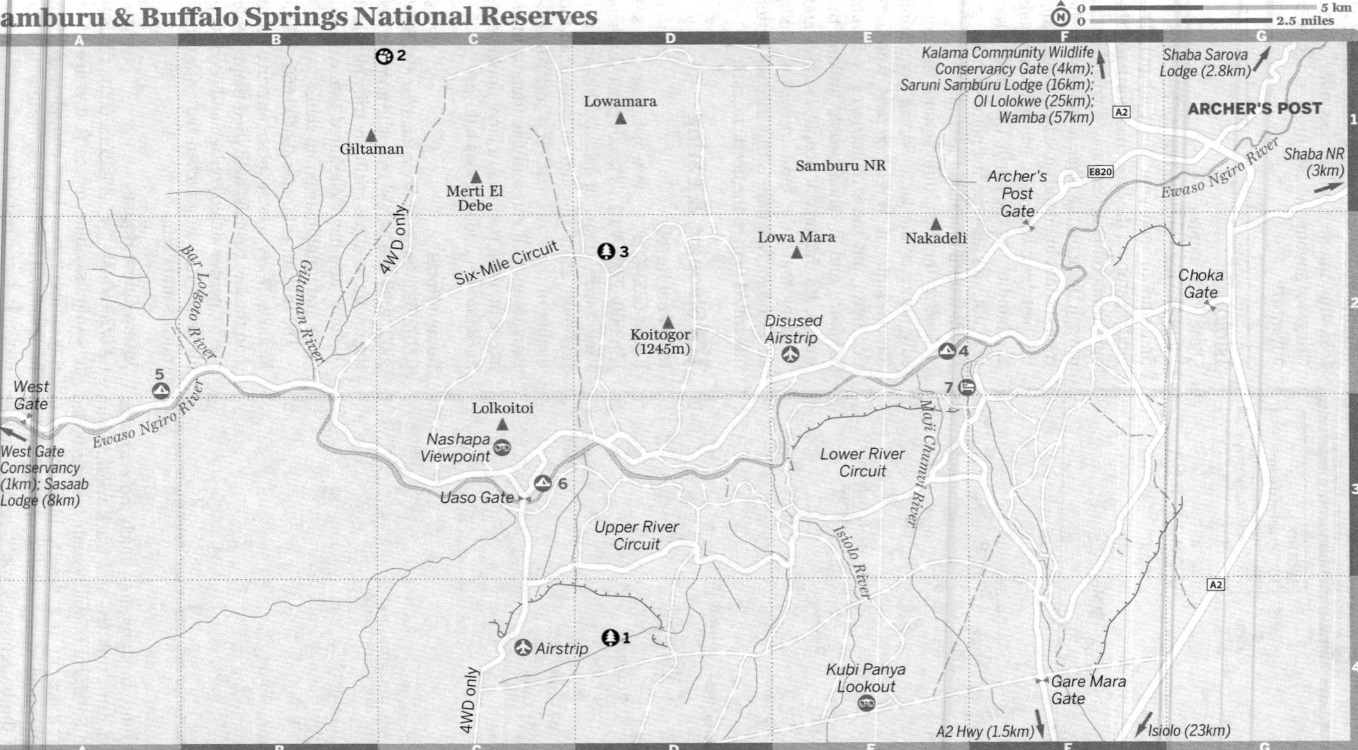

Samburu & Buffalo Springs National Reserves

Sights
1 Buffalo Springs National Reserve ... D4
2 Kalama Community Wildlife Conservancy ... C1
3 Samburu National Reserve ... D2

Sleeping
4 Elephant Bedroom ... E2
5 Elephant Watch Camp ... A2
6 Riverside Camp ... C3
Samburu Public Campsite ... (see 6)
7 Samburu Simba Lodge ... E2

Information

MEDICAL SERVICES

District Hospital (Hospital Rd; 24hr)

MONEY

Banks are scarce in the north, so plan ahead.

Barclays (Hospital Rd; 9am-4pm Mon-Fri, to noon Sat) With an ATM.

Kenya Commercial Bank (Hospital Rd; 8.30am-3pm Mon-Fri, to noon Sat) With an ATM and foreign exchange.

Getting There & Away

AIR

At the time of research, the **Isiolo International Airport** (HKIS; 0728165349) had opened though it was not yet fully operational. Some passenger flights were slated to be available from Nairobi in late 2017. The airport is also supposed to eventually offer international flights to Somalia and South Sudan.

BUS & MATATU

Most of the bus companies serve Nairobi (KSh600, 4½ hours), with buses generally leaving between 5.30am and 6.30am from outside their respective offices on the main road through town. They also stop at the matatu and bus stand just south of the market.

Evening buses operated by **Liban Buses** (0722244847; Hospital Rd) creep north to Marsabit (KSh500, five hours, 4.30pm). **Moyale Star Buses** (0721438454; Hospital Rd) race like the wind – or perhaps a gentle breeze – to Moyale (KSh1500, 10 hours, 1.30pm) via Marsabit (KSh750, five hours).

For Maralal, take an early-morning matatu to Wamba (KSh350, 2½ hours) and then a Maralal-bound matatu (KSh500, 2½ hours) from there. Regular matatus leave from a chaotic **stand** around the market and also serve Archer's Post (KSh130 to KSh150, 25 minutes), Meru (KSh150, 1½ hours) and Nanyuki (KSh250, 1¾ hours).

Samburu, Buffalo Springs & Shaba National Reserves

Blistered with termite skyscrapers, cleaved by the muddy Ewaso Ngiro River and heaving with heavyweight animals, this triumvirate of national reserves has a beauty that is unsurpassed, as well as a population of creatures that occur in no other major Kenyan park. These species include the blue-legged Somali ostrich, endangered Grevy's zebra, beisa oryx, reticulated giraffe and gerenuk – gazelles that dearly wish to be giraffes. Despite covering just 300 sq km, the reserves' variety of landscapes and vegetation is amazing.

Sights

Shaba National Reserve (adult/child US$70/40, vehicle KSh1000; 6am-6pm), with its great rocky kopjes (isolated hills), natural springs and doum palms, is the most physically beautiful of the reserves, and you'll have it almost to yourself, but it often has less visible wildlife. The open savannahs, scrub desert and verdant river foliage in **Samburu** (adult/child US$70/40, vehicle KSh1000; 6am-6pm) and **Buffalo Springs** (adult/child US$70/40, vehicle KSh1000; 6am-6pm) virtually guarantee close encounters with elephants and all the other wildlife. The best wildlife viewing is almost always along the banks of the Ewaso Ngiro in Samburu.

Sleeping & Eating

SAMBURU NATIONAL RESERVE

Riverside Camp TENTED CAMP $
(Edwards Camp; 0721252737, 0721108032; Samburu NR; per person KSh1500, per person full board KSh3000) On the northern bank of the Ewaso Ngiro River, the scrappy (and hot) dark canvas safari tents here might not climb as luxuriously high as some of the big-boy lodges but, let's face it, this is much more authentic Africa. Meals can be prepared on request. It's very close to the park headquarters.

Samburu Public Campsite CAMPGROUND $
(Samburu NR; camping US$35) The main public campsite is close to the park headquarters. It lacks even the most basic facilities and there are lots of baboons with light fingers. Arrange your stay at the park gates.

SAMBURU, BUFFALO SPRINGS & SHABA NATIONAL RESERVES

Why Go To see some of Kenya's most unique creatures in a compelling and beautiful desert landscape. Samburu is also one of the best places in the country to see elephants. Crowds of visitors are non-existent.

When to Go There's little rain in these parts so it's possible to visit year-round, but between November and March animals congregate near the Ewaso Ngiro River.

Practicalities Isiolo is the main gateway town. Conveniently, for the moment at least, Buffalo Springs, Shaba and Samburu entries are interchangeable, so you only pay once, even if you're visiting all three in one day. You must buy your ticket at the gate to the park in which you're staying.

Budget Tips You can camp in any of the reserves (but you mostly need to be self-sufficient). However, you'll still need a vehicle to get around. These can be hired by the half-day in Archer's Post.

★ **Elephant Watch Camp** TENTED CAMP **$$$**
(0713037886, 0731596437; www.elephantwatchportfolio.com; Samburu NR; s/d all-inclusive US$809/1618; closed Apr–10 May & Nov–10 Dec) Undoubtedly the most unique and memorable place to stay in Samburu (p347). Massive thatched roofs cling to crooked acacia branches and tower over cosy, palatial, eight-sided tents and large, grass-mat-clad terraces. Natural materials dominate the exteriors, bright textiles the interiors, and the bathrooms are stunning.

Elephant Bedroom TENTED CAMP **$$$**
(Nairobi 020-4450035; www.atua-enkop.com; Samburu NR; s/d all-inclusive US$395/580;) Twelve absolutely superb riverfront tents that are so luxurious even budding princesses will feel a little overwhelmed by the surroundings. Exactly how luxurious are we talking? Well, when was the last time you saw a tent that came with a private plunge pool?

BUFFALO SPRINGS NATIONAL RESERVE

Samburu Simba Lodge LODGE **$$$**
(0729407162, Nairobi 020-2012243; www.simbalodges.com; s/d full board US$550/630; @) It doesn't exactly blend harmoniously into the countryside, but this large lodge, with accommodation in big rooms scattered over several blocks, is ideal for those who prefer something other than canvas between them and the wildlife. It's one of the few options in Buffalo Springs (p347).

SHABA NATIONAL RESERVE

Joy's Camp TENTED CAMP **$$$**
(0730127000; www.joyscamp.com; Shaba NR; s/d all-inclusive from US$671/894;) Once the home of Joy Adamson, of *Born Free* fame, this is now an outrageously luxurious camp in Shaba's remotest corner. The accommodation is in 'tents', but these tents aren't like others – they come with underfloor lighting, lots of stained glass and giant, walk-in rain showers.

Shaba Sarova Lodge LODGE **$$$**
(0728603590; www.sarovahotels.com; Shaba NR; s/d full board from US$270/315; @) This place nestles on the Ewaso Ngiro River and its pathways intertwine with frog-filled streams and ponds. There's a large pool and natural springs flow through the gorgeous open-air bar. The rooms are very comfortable with lots of Africana-style art. The lodge leaves bait along the river to attract crocodiles, so sightings are guaranteed.

Getting There & Away

Airkenya (p258) and **Safarilink** (p258) have frequent flights from Nairobi's Wilson Airport to **Samburu** (p347). You can also fly into **Kalama** (0721463930; www.nrt-kenya.org/kalama; conservation fee incl in accommodation price), which is roughly 40km north of the parks.

The vehicle-less can try to wangle a 4WD and driver in Archer's Post or Isiolo for about US$100 per half-day.

The bridge between Samburu and Buffalo Springs (p347) has repeatedly collapsed for years due to flooding and mismanagement. Currently, the bridge cannot be crossed so if you want to visit both Samburu and Buffalo Springs, you'll need to make a long detour back to Archer's Post and the main A2 road, which can take up to three hours. Petrol is available in Archer's Post.

Matthews Range

West of the remarkable flat-topped Ol Lolokwe (p274) mountain, and north of Wamba, is the Matthews Range. The name might sound tame but, rest assured, this is real African wilderness, full of 1000 adventures. These forests and dramatic slopes support a wealth of wildlife, including elephants, lions, buffaloes and Kenya's most important wild dog population. With few roads and almost no facilities, the mountains reward only those willing to go the extra kilometre on foot.

In 1995 the local Samburu communities collectively formed a Trust to look after the **Namunyak Wildlife Conservancy**, now one of Kenya's most successful community conservation programmes.

Sleeping

★Kitich Camp TENTED CAMP $$$
(0730127000; www.kitichcamp.com; s/d all-inclusive US$562/936; closed Apr–mid-Jun & Nov–mid-Dec; P wi-fi) One of the remotest camps in Kenya, Kitich falls squarely into the luxury-tented-camp category, but staying here is unquestionably a wild-Africa experience. Elephants pass through the camp almost daily and exploration of the thick forests is done on foot with expert Samburu trackers. This is a unique safari experience and one of the most exciting places to stay in Kenya.

Getting There & Away

Matatus run from Isiolo (KSh350) and Maralal (KSh400) to Wamba, but you'll need your own transport from there to head into the range. The drive from Wamba takes approximately two hours, though in the rainy season this may be much longer if the roads become impassable, in which case you'll need to take an alternative route. Four-wheel drive is essential. **Kitich Camp** can arrange a transfer from Kalama airstrip (KSh20,000 per vehicle).

Marsabit

069 / POP 5000

The small town of Marsabit sits on the side of a 6300-sq-km shield volcano, the surface of which is peppered with 180 cinder cones and 22 volcanic craters, many of which house lakes – or at least they do when the rains have been kind. While the town is less attractive than its surrounds, which also comprise the enormous 1500-sq-km **Marsabit National Reserve** and the smaller Marsabit National Park (p350), it's an interesting and lively place, thanks to colourful nomads passing through and a lively market.

Sleeping & Eating

JeyJey Centre HOTEL $
(0728808801/2; A2 Hwy; camping KSh300, s/d/tw with shared bathroom KSh800/1200/1800, d KSh1350; P) This mud-brick castle bedecked in flowers is something of a travellers' centre and is always bursting with road-hardened souls. Basic rooms with mosquito nets surround a courtyard, and bathrooms (even shared ones) sport on-demand hot water. There's also an unattractive campground.

Nomads Trail Hotel HOTEL $
(0726560846; A2 Hwy; s/d old rooms KSh1800/2700, new rooms KSh2500/3700; P wi-fi) The rooms here are prim and proper and all have attached bathrooms that come with – wait for it – real hot water from a real shower! Upstairs are some newer rooms that, for Marsabit, are surprisingly posh. There is also a restaurant serving decent fare.

Saku Guest House HOTEL $$
(0799189160; www.sakuguesthousemarsabit.com; s/d KSh2200/5000; P wi-fi) Built in 2017, this is the poshest place to stay in Marsabit. The rooms are large and each comes with

WORTH A TRIP

NDOTO MOUNTAINS

Climbing from the Korante Plain's sands are the magnificent rusty bluffs and ridges of the Ndoto Mountains. Kept a virtual secret from the travelling world by their remote location, the Ndotos abound with hiking, climbing and bouldering potential. **Mt Poi** (2050m), which resembles the world's largest bread loaf from some angles, is a technical climber's dream – its sheer 800m north face begs to be bagged. If you're fit and have a whole day to spare, it's a great hike to the summit and the views are extraordinary.

The tiny village of **Ngurunit** is the best base for your adventures and is interesting in its own right, with captivating, traditionally dressed Samburu people living in simple, yet elegantly woven, grass huts.

a clean bed and a TV. If you are looking for a splurge, try the VIP rooms (KSh7000), which have a widescreen TV, lounge and four-poster bed.

The **restaurant** (☎0799189160; www.sakuguesthousemarsabit.com; mains KSh300-700; ⊙6am-10pm; P 📶) on the 2nd floor is spotlessly clean and bright. The menu (yes, there is an actual menu!) is varied and has the most choice of any restaurant in the area. We recommend the King Saku Marsabit, a spicy chicken dish large enough to share.

ℹ Information

Co-operative Bank (A2 Hwy; ⊙8.30am-4pm Mon-Fri, to noon Sat) Has an ATM that works with foreign Visa cards.

Kenya Commercial Bank (off Post Office Rd; ⊙8.30am-4pm Mon-Fri, to noon Sat) With ATM.

Bliss GVS Medical Clinic (☎0730604000; www.blissgvshealthcare.com; Post Office Rd; ⊙9am-6pm Mon-Sat)

ℹ Getting There & Away

Although improved security means convoys and armed guards are no longer being used to Moyale or Isiolo, it's still wise to get the latest security and Ethiopian border information from locals and the **police station** (⊙24hr) before leaving town. As a rule, if buses and trucks travel in a convoy, or take armed soldiers on board, you should too!

There is little public transport to Lake Turkana, but enquire at the larger hotels to catch a lift with a local heading towards North Horr.

BUS

With the completion of the paved road from Moyale to Isiolo, the number of bus companies serving the route has exploded. Most are situated on the main road near the **JeyJey Centre** (A2 Hwy; meals KSh300-500; ⊙11am-7pm). **Moyale Liner Buses** (☎0705614600; www.moyaleliner.co.ke) connect Marsabit to Moyale daily (KSh800, six hours, 5.30pm). Heading south, both Moyale Liner and **Liban Buses** (☎0715099446; A2 Hwy) run to Isiolo (KSh700, six hours) and Nairobi (KSh1700, eight hours).

CAR & MOTORCYCLE

The road north and south of Marsabit is now completely paved and accessible with a normal car. However, if you are looking to venture to **Marsabit National Park** or towards Lake Turkana, a 4WD is a necessity. There are several petrol stations on the main road.

Marsabit National Park

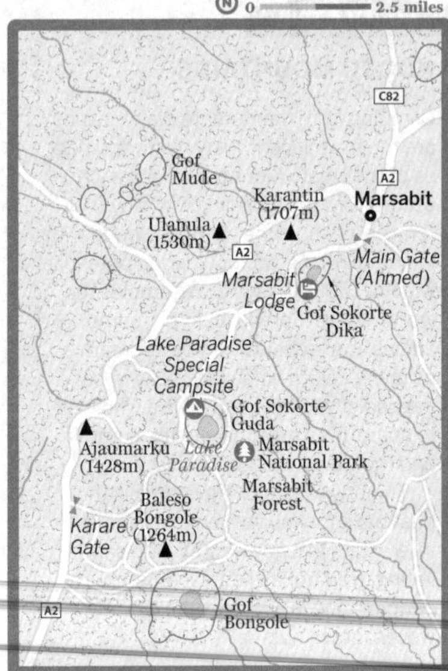

Within the larger national reserve, this small **park** (www.kws.go.ke; adult/child US$30/20; ⊙6am-7pm), nestled on Mt Marsabit's upper slopes, is coated in thick forests and contains a wide variety of wildlife, including leopards, elephants (some with huge tusks) and buffaloes. The park forms a key point on an elephant migration route that extends as far as the slopes of Mt Kenya. The dense forest makes spotting wildlife very difficult, but fortunately help is at hand in the form of a couple of natural clearings with semi-permanent lakes, where animal sightings are almost guaranteed.

This is a very climate-affected park. In the increasingly common years when the rains fail, the park very quickly turns brown, parched and apparently lifeless. In more generous years the vegetation positively glows green, the lakes fill with water and animals seem to reappear from nowhere.

🛏 Sleeping & Eating

Lake Paradise Special Campsite CAMPGROUND $
(www.kws.go.ke; camping US$35) This picturesque site, with nothing but a dried-up lake bed and firewood, is the only place to camp in the park. Due to roaming buffaloes and elephants, a ranger must be present when you camp here.

Marsabit Lodge LODGE $$
(☎0726625477; s/tw KSh6000/7500; P) If you don't mind the rather faded rooms, this basic lodge has a deliciously peaceful setting overlooking the lake known as Gof Sokorte Dika. Expect friendly service and a chef who, no doubt in pleasure at actually having something to do, puts together great meals. Electricity is by generator in the evening only.

Getting There & Away

The Ahmed Gate is closest to Marsabit. Inside the park, a 4WD is a necessity. If you're without transport it's possible to walk to **Marsabit Lodge** from the park gate with an armed ranger (KSh3000 for half a day; organise this through the park office the day before if possible). With luck you'll have some exciting encounters with buffaloes and elephants.

Maralal to Turkana's Eastern Shore

Journeying to a beautiful Jade Sea shouldn't be something that's easy to do, and this route, the ultimate Kenyan adventure, is certainly not easy. Your backside will take a battering, but you'll be rewarded 1000 times over with memories of vibrant tribes, camel caravans running into a red sunset, mesmerising volcanic landscapes and, of course, the north's greatest jewel – Lake Turkana.

Maralal

☎065 / POP 24,612

Maralal is the kind of place where you should spend some time. After all, the town's most famous former resident was one of the greatest explorers of the 20th century, Wilfred Thesiger, and if he decided that Maralal was the perfect place for retirement, then it must be doing something right. Yet, few people choose to take the time to enjoy it, most stopping only for a night en route to Lake Turkana. The lucky ones tend to be those using the erratic public transport, as they end up delayed here for enough time to appreciate the town.

Sleeping & Eating

Sunbird Guest House GUESTHOUSE $
(☎0720654567; s/d KSh1000/2000; P 📶) The single rooms are starting to look a little old and damp but, by and large, this very friendly place has quiet, clean and comfortable rooms with nice linen, mosquito nets and hot water in the bathrooms. The courtyard has a sunny, garden vibe and there's a pleasant restaurant serving healthy fried stuff.

DON'T MISS

MARALAL INTERNATIONAL CAMEL DERBY

Inaugurated in 1990, the annual **Maralal International Camel Derby** is one of the biggest events in Kenya, attracting riders and spectators from around the world in mid- to late August. The derby is now run by Nairobi-based Adventure 360 Africa (www.adventure360africa.com). The parties surrounding the event are justifiably well known, and worth the trip for many visitors.

However, if you'd rather just get involved in some fast-moving camel action, the derby's first race has your name written all over it – it's for amateur camel riders! It's a butt-jarring 11km journey. Don't even start feeling sorry for your backside – the professional riders cover 42km.

★**Samburu Guest House** HOTEL $$
(☎0725363471; www.samburuguesthouse.com; s/d KSh2500/5000; P 📶) With a new wing, this hotel has been modernised, with large beds, mosquito nets and TVs in each room. Request a room in the new wing for extra comfort. There is also a restaurant attached that serves good Kenyan fare.

Coast Dishes KENYAN $
(mains KSh80-300) While the atmosphere is far from coastal, this place, run by a couple from the sultry coast, offers daily dishes such as pilau – it's made with goat rather than fish or chicken, but it will still whet your appetite.

Pop Inn Hotel KENYAN $
(meals KSh150-250; ⏰7am-8pm) This zebra-striped building has decent Kenyan staples and is popular with locals.

Information

Maralal Medical Clinic (Sanctuary Rd; ⏰8am-6pm) Small clinic with dishevelled facilities on Maralal's main road.

Equity Bank (⏰8am-4.30pm Mon-Fri, to noon Sat) A more reliable ATM than that at KCB.

Maralal

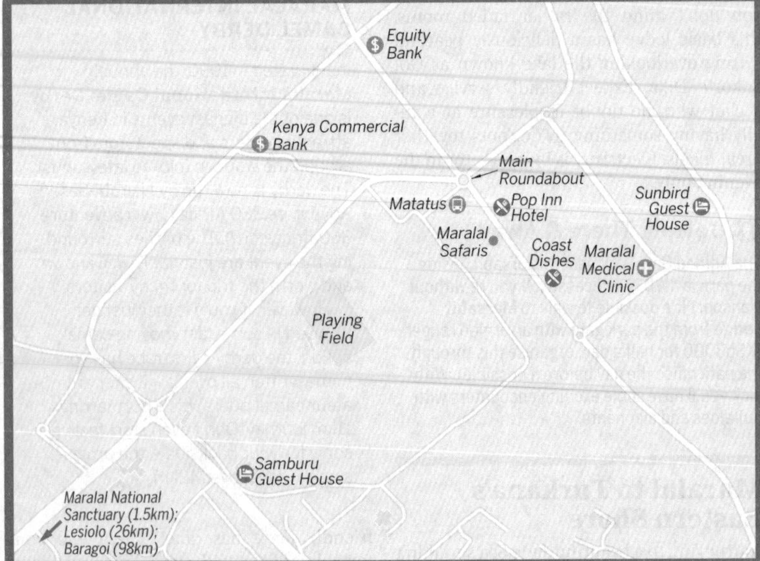

Kenya Commercial Bank (8.30am-4pm Mon-Fri, to noon Sat) Behind the market, with an ATM, but staff can be a bit stroppy when presented with foreign Visa cards.

Getting There & Away

BUS & MATATU

Matatus serve Nyahururu (KSh500, three to four hours), Rumuruti (KSh300 to KSh400, 2½ hours) and Wamba (KSh500, 3½ hours). For Nairobi you need to change in Nyahururu. Reaching Isiolo involves staying overnight in Wamba to catch the early-morning southbound matatu.

There are buses too, which look like they're crossed with a tank, heading to Baragoi (KSh500) at around 11am every morning. As there is still no regular transport north from there, it's more pleasant to wait in Maralal for something heading further north. **Maralal Safaris** (0721808017; 9am-5pm) is able to book onward bus travel and sometimes has connections to trucks heading north.

Most **local transport** (C77 Hwy) leaves from the main roundabout.

TRUCK

Waits for trucks to Loyangalani (KSh1000 to KSh1500, nine to 12 hours), on the shore of Lake Turkana, might last from a few days to a week. Start asking around as soon as you arrive in town and remember that while breaking the truck journey in Baragoi or South Horr may seem like a good idea, you might have to wait for a week before another truck trundles through. After rain you can expect prices for all transport to rise.

Baragoi

065 / POP 20,000

Baragoi is a dusty, diminutive town that is enveloped by some spellbinding surroundings. The long descent off the Loroghi Plateau towards the village serves up some sweet vistas, and for kilometre after gorgeous kilometre you'll literally see nothing but tree-studded grasslands. For years this area looked like it should be wall to wall with grazing antelope, but the reality was that very few things larger than a dik-dik lived here. With wildlife conservancies stretching ever further northward, that's changing, and we've seen herds of Grevy's zebras out here – locals tell us that wildlife numbers are building rapidly.

Sleeping & Eating

Morning Star Guest House HOTEL $
(0790734856; s/d with shared bathroom KSh400/800) The bougainvillea-dressed Morning Star Guest House provides for a

night's kip – though it doesn't supply the peg you'll need to place over your nose before entering the communal toilets.

Getting There & Away

The dirt track from Maralal to Baragoi is very rocky in places, but still one of the better stretches of road in this area. Even so, if there has been any rain it becomes treacherous. The drive takes a minimum of three hours.

There are now daily buses to Maralal (KSh500, three hours); these leave from **Star Station Filling** (6am-8pm), which sells expensive petrol, but it is the only station between South Horr and Maralal.

Approaching the Lake

Travelling north from South Horr, the scrub desert suddenly scatters and you're greeted by vast volcanic armies of shimmering bowling-ball-sized boulders, cinder cones and reddish-purple hues. If this arresting and barren Martian landscape doesn't take your breath away, the first sight of the sparkling Jade Sea a few kilometres north certainly will.

As you descend to the lake, South Island stands proudly before you, while Teleki Volcano's geometrically perfect cone lurks on Turkana's southern shore. Since you've probably pulled over for the moment, looking for your swimming kit, we thought we'd warn you that Turkana has the world's largest crocodile population.

Loyangalani

069 / POP 16,965

Standing in utter contrast to the dour desert shades surrounding it, tiny Loyangalani assaults all your senses in one crazy explosion of clashing colours, feather headdresses and blood-red robes. Overlooking Lake Turkana and surrounded by small ridges of pillow lava (evidence that this area used to be underwater), the sandy streets of this one-camel town are a meeting point of the great northern tribes: Turkana and Samburu, Gabbra and El Molo. It's one of the most exotic corners of Kenya and a fitting reward after the hard journey here.

Sights & Activities

The El Molo tribe, which is one of Africa's smallest, lives on the lake shore just north of Loyangalani in the villages of **Layeni** and **Komote**. Although outwardly similar to the Turkana, the El Molo are linguistically linked to the Somali and Rendille people. Unfortunately, the last speaker of their traditional language died before the turn of the millennium. Visiting their villages (KSh1000 per person, negotiable) is something of a circus and you shouldn't expect to see many people traditionally dressed.

South Island National Park NATIONAL PARK

(adult/child US$22/13) Designated a World Heritage Site by Unesco in 1997, this 39-sq-km purplish volcanic island is completely barren (minus some rock art) and uninhabited, apart from large populations of crocodiles, venomous snakes and feral goats. Spending the night at a **special campsite** (US$35), which is close to the main dock, makes for an even eerier trip. Visit the KWS headquarters (p354) to pay the entry fee and book a boat – boats can also be hired from Palm Shade Camp (p354) and Malabo Resort (p354).

Mt Kulal MOUNTAIN

Mt Kulal (2293m) dominates Lake Turkana's eastern horizon and its forested volcanic flanks offer some serious hiking possibilities. This fertile lost world in the middle of the desert is home to some unique creatures, including the Mt Kulal chameleon, a beautiful lizard first recorded in only 2003.

No matter what the local guides tell you, trekking to the summit from Loyangalani in

GETTING AROUND NORTHERN KENYA

While you can get to the main towns with a normal car, you will need a 4WD if you want to visit the parks or head off the newly paved roads towards Lake Turkana. However, while having your own 4WD gives you flexibility, it comes with its own challenges due to wide-ranging road conditions. For starters, you'll need a large 4WD with high ground clearance and a skid plate to protect the undercarriage (a Toyota RAV4 or Suzuki won't do). You should have a high-rise jack, sand ladders, a shovel, a long strong rope or chain (to hitch up to camels or other vehicles), a tool kit, plus enough fuel, water and spare tyres (one is rarely enough). A compass, GPS and good map are also invaluable.

a day isn't feasible. Plan on several days for a return trip. Guides (KSh1000 per day) and donkeys (KSh500 per day) to carry your gear can be hired in Loyangalani, or you can part with considerable sums of cash (KSh30,000 to KSh40,000) for a lift up Mt Kulal to the villages of Arapal or Gatab. From there you can head for the summit and spend a long day (eight to 10 hours) hiking back down to the base of the mountain.

If you pass by Arapal, be sure to whistle a tune at the **singing wells** where the Samburu gather water (and sing while doing so – hence the name).

Sleeping & Eating

★Malabo Resort BANDAS $
(☎0724705800, 0722381548; www.malaboresort.co.ke; camping KSh750, hut from KSh2000, banda KSh2500; P) For our money, this is the best place to stay in Loyangalani, just a few hundred metres north of the village and with slight lake views. There's a range of decent *bandas* with arty wooden beds and attached bathrooms, or there are thatched huts based on a traditional Turkana design. The bar-restaurant area is a good place to hang out.

Palm Shade Camp BANDAS $
(☎0726714768; camping KSh600, s/tw hut with shared bathroom KSh1000/2000, s/d KSh2400/4800; P) Drop your tent on the grass beneath acacias and doum palms, lie back in one of the clean, tiled, newly constructed rooms, or crash in the tidy domed huts with their unique meshed cut-out walls that let in light and heavenly evening breezes. The manager is an endless source of information on travel in the area.

Cold Drink Hotel KENYAN $
(meals KSh100-300; ⏲7am-8pm) Not just cold drinks but also, according to locals, the finest eating experience in all of Turkana country, which sadly might actually be true. It's a bit of an institution as it was the town's first hotel, so it's well known by travellers and is good for more authentic Loyangalani food (compared to what's offered at the newer hotels).

Information

There are no banking services in Loyangalani.

Naring'oi Women Group Internet Kiosk (per minute KSh5; ⏲open on request) The only option for internet access in town.

KWS Headquarters (☎0727332834; www.kws.go.ke) Located towards the lake and tiny 'port', this office doesn't receive many tourists. But it will try to help with information on local sights and activities, and can arrange boat trips to South Island.

Getting There & Away

Trucks loaded with fish (and soon-to-be-smelly passengers) leave Loyangalani for Maralal (around KSh1000, nine to 12 hours) once or twice a week at best. Trucks heading in any other direction are even rarer and locals talk of waits

DON'T MISS

SIBILOI NATIONAL PARK

A Unesco World Heritage Site, and probably Kenya's most remote national park, **Sibiloi** (www.kws.go.ke; adult/child US$22/13) is located up the eastern shore of Lake Turkana and covers 1570 sq km. It was here that Dr Richard Leakey discovered the skull of a *Homo habilis* believed to be 2.5 million years old, and where others have unearthed evidence of *Homo erectus*.

The National Museums of Kenya (NMK; www.museums.or.ke) maintains a small museum and Koobi Fora (www.kfrp.com) has a research base. Best to contact all of the following before venturing in this direction: the **Loyangalani Desert Museum** (adult/child KSh500/250) staff (you'll have to go in person), the Kenya Wildlife Service (www.kws.go.ke) and NMK.

It's usually possible to sleep in one of Koobi Fora research base's *bandas* (per person KSh1000) or to pitch a tent in one of the campsites (camping per person KSh500).

In the dry season it's a tricky seven-hour drive north from Loyangalani to Sibiloi. You will need a guide from either KWS or the **Loyangalani Desert Museum**. Hiring a jeep in Loyangalani will work out at around KSh40,000 per day. It's also possible to hire a boat (KSh30,000 to KSh40,000 return, with an overnight stop) from Ferguson's Gulf on the western side of the lake.

of between a week and a month for transport to North Horr (around KSh1000). There are buses roughly every other day to Marsabit (KSh1000), but if you are in a hurry, you can try to catch a ride with a truck. When trucks do travel to Marsabit, they tend to take the slightly easier southern route via Kargi and charge a flexible KSh1000. It's better to travel from Loyangalani to North Horr, rather than the other way around, because with buses every other day from North Horr to Marsabit you won't get stuck for more than a night – going from North Horr to Loyangalani could mean waiting in North Horr for a week or more. This would be bad.

If you're travelling in your own vehicle, you have two options to reach Marsabit: continue northeast from Loyangalani across the dark stones of the Chalbi Desert towards North Horr, or head 67km south towards South Horr and take the eastern turn-off via Kargi. The 270km Chalbi route (10 to 12 hours) is hard in the dry season and impossible after rain. It's also wise to ask for directions every chance you get, otherwise it's easy to take the wrong track and not realise until hours later. This would also be bad. The 241km southern route (six to seven hours) via the Karoli Desert and Kargi is composed of compacted sands and is marginally less difficult in the rainy season.

The Catholic mission occasionally sells petrol out of the barrel, but prices are exorbitant.

Marich to Turkana's Western Shore

Despite boasting some of northern Kenya's greatest attributes, such as copious kilometres of Jade Sea shoreline, striking volcanic landscapes, ample wildlife and vivid Turkana tribes, this remote corner of the country has seen relatively few visitors. However, this may change if the highway north of Lokichar is completed, but at the time of research that was not looking likely to happen any time soon.

Marich Pass & Cherangani Hills

The spectacular descent from Marich Pass, north of Kitale, through the lush, cultivated Cherangani Hills leads to arid surroundings, with sisal plants, cactus trees and acacias lining both the road and the chocolate-brown Morun River. Just north, the minuscule village of Marich marks your entrance into northern Kenya. Welcome to adventure!

DON'T MISS

LAKE TURKANA FESTIVAL

Held in mid-June, the **Lake Turkana Festival** (http://laketurkanacultural festival.com) is a jamboree of all that's colourful in the tribes of northern Kenya. Originally organised by the German embassy, it is now run by Kenya's tourism board, KWS and National Museums of Kenya. If you want to see people in their tribal best, there's no better time to be in Loyangalani.

Activities

Cherangani Hills TREKKING

The Cherangani Hills, covered in thick forest, are actually the fourth-highest mountain range in Kenya. There is a plethora of hiking options and several of them are quite gentle slopes through open farmland and sheltered valleys. Many people consider these intensely farmed and deeply forested hills to be one of the most beautiful corners of the country.

Mt Sekerr TREKKING

Although the northern plains may beckon, it's worth heading into the hills for some eye-popping and leg-loving hiking action. Mt Sekerr (3326m), also known as Mt Mtelo, is a few kilometres northwest of Marich and can be climbed comfortably in a three-day round trip via the agricultural plots of the Pokot tribe, passing through forest and open moors.

Sleeping

Marich Pass Field Studies Centre CAMPGROUND, BANDAS $

(www.gg.rhul.ac.uk/MarichPass; camping US$7, dm US$8, s/tw US$26/35, with shared bathroom US$16/21) Just north of Marich village, this is essentially a residential facility for visiting student groups, but it also makes a great base for independent travellers. The centre occupies a beautiful site alongside the misty Morun River and is surrounded by dense bush and woodland. Facilities include a secure campground as well as a tatty dorm and simple, comfortable *bandas*.

The centre can organise guides for walks around the hills (half/full day US$9/14).

Getting There & Away

The stretch of the scenic A1 Hwy from Kitale to the Marich Pass via Makutano is often described as 'Kenya's most spectacular tarmac road'.

Buses plying the A1 between Kitale and Lodwar can drop you anywhere along the route, whether at Marich or the field studies centre (p355). You may be asked to pay the full fare to Lodwar (KSh1500), but a smile and some patient negotiating should reduce the cost.

The road north of the Marich Pass is still a bit of a mess, however, so a 4WD is recommended for trips up-country. Hopefully that won't be necessary forever, as the recent discovery of oil around Lokichar means this section of road is slated to be improved.

Lodwar

☎054 / POP 48,316

Besides Lokichoggio near the South Sudan border, Lodwar is the only town of any size in the northwest. Barren volcanic hills skirted by traditional Turkana dwellings sit north of town and make for impressive sunrise vistas. Lodwar has outgrown its days as just an isolated administrative outpost of the Northern Frontier District and has now become the major service centre for the region. If you're visiting Lake Turkana, you'll find it convenient to stay here for at least one night.

LAKE TURKANA FACTS

- Lake Turkana, the world's largest permanent desert lake, has a shoreline that's longer than Kenya's entire Indian Ocean coast.
- The lake's water level was over 100m higher some 10,000 years ago and used to feed the mighty Nile. Environmentalists have claimed that the Gibe 3 Dam in Ethiopia has caused the lake's water level to drop 1.5m and some shores have receded by almost 2km.
- The first Europeans to reach the lake were Austrian explorers Teleki and von Höhnel in 1888. They proudly named it Lake Rudolf, after the Austrian Crown Prince at the time. It wasn't until the 1970s that the Kiswahili name Turkana was adopted.

Sleeping & Eating

Ceamo Prestige Lodge HOTEL $$
(☎0721555565, 0718999703; www.ceamolodge.com; s/d KSh6500/8500; P❄📶) A short way out of town, this new place is also Lodwar's flashest place to stay, with large, cool, quiet, tiled rooms in a bungalow setting. It might be Lodwar's finest but it's still very overpriced. The attached restaurant/pub is probably your best bet for some *nyama choma* (KSh10,000) and a cold beer.

★**Cradle Tented Camp** TENTED CAMP $$$
(☎0722870214; www.thetentedcradlecamp.comp; tent US$150; P❄📶) When not escaping the Turkana heat in the large swimming pool, you can relax on your balcony in front of your large tent, which comes complete with TV, minibar and luxurious bathroom.

Nawoitorong Guest House KENYAN $
(meals KSh250-450; ⏰7am-8pm) Burgers and toasted sandwiches join local curries and various meaty fried dishes on the menu, all served in an open-air *boma* on the large grounds. It offers the most pleasant dining experience in the region, but give staff time – lots of it – to prepare dinner!

Information

Internet is scarce – the larger hotels, such as the **Cradle Tented Camp** and **Ceamo Prestige Lodge** have wi-fi, but it is hit-and-miss. There is decent reception if you are on a mobile data plan.

Lodwar District Hospital (☎0775996389; ⏰24hr)

Kenya Commercial Bank (⏰8.30am-4pm Mon-Fri, to noon Sat) Has an ATM and changes cash and travellers cheques.

Getting There & Away

Fly540 (p258) runs frequent flights from Nairobi to **Lodwar Airport**, via Eldoret, for around US$150 (two hours).

There are regular buses plying the long route south departing from the **bus station** (☎0727096551). For more local travel, several operators offer services to Kitale (KSh2000, 8½ hours), with departures from close to **Salama Hotel** (meals KSh80-150; ⏰6am-9pm). The use of matatus is unknown here – most operators use bike taxis instead.

To get to Eliye Springs or Ferguson's Gulf, you can ask your hotel to sort out a private car for you (KSh70,000 per day). Your other option is on the back of a bike taxi, which is the cheapest option (KSh30,000) but not the most comforta-

DON'T MISS

CENTRAL ISLAND NATIONAL PARK

Bursting from the depths of Lake Turkana, and home to thousands of living dinosaurs, is the Jurassic world of **Central Island** (www.kws.go.ke; adult/child US$22/13) volcano, last seen belching molten sulphur and steam just over three decades ago. It's one of the most otherworldly places in Kenya. Quiet today, its stormy volcanic history is told by the numerous craters scarring its weathered facade. Several craters have coalesced to form three sizeable lakes, one of which is home to thousands of fish that occur nowhere else.

Both a national park and Unesco World Heritage Site, Central Island is an intriguing place to visit. Budding Crocodile Dundee types will love the 14,000 or so Nile crocodiles, some of which are massive, that flock here at certain times of year (May is the most crocodile-friendly month, but there are some crocs here year-round). The most northerly crater lake, which is saline, attracts blushing pink flocks of flamingos.

Central Island Campsite (☎0800597000; www.kws.go.ke; camping US$20) This is the only accommodation option on the island. Located close to the dock, it is the ideal setting-off point for treks around the island. Unlike at South Island National Park (p353), there are trees to which you can tie your tent.

Getting There & Away

Hiring a boat from Ferguson's Gulf or Eliye Springs is the only option to get here. It's easiest to head to the KWS camp (www.kws.go.ke) in Ferguson's Gulf and ask them to sort out a boat for you (KSh15,000); alternatively, try the **Eliye Springs Resort** (boats KSh18,000).

KWS can also put you in touch with locals who have boats to try to haggle the price down to around KSh10,000. Don't ever think about being cheap and taking a sailboat – the 10km trip and the sudden squalls that terrorise the lake's waters aren't to be taken lightly.

ble. Never accept the first price offered to you – these are negotiable and you are likely to get it cheaper if you have time to shop around.

There are several reliable petrol stations in Lodwar. Note that petrol becomes much more scarce if you venture outside of town, so make sure you stock up.

Eliye Springs

☎054 / POP 5000

Spring water percolates out of crumbling bluffs, and oodles of palms bring a taste of the tropics to the remote sandy shores of Lake Turkana. Down on the slippery shore, children play in the lake's warm waters, while Central Island lurks magically on the distant horizon. Eliye Springs is the best place to get a taste of the lake's western shore.

Sleeping & Eating

Eliye Springs Resort RESORT $$

(☎0703891810; www.eliyespringsresort.com; camping KSh600, hut per person with shared bathroom KSh1800, r/luxury boma per person KSh4200/10,800; P) For many years all that stood on the shores of Eliye Springs was the shell of an abandoned lodge, but it's been brought back to life by a German with a passion for Turkana. The resort has a mixture of self-contained rooms and traditional Turkana huts made of sticks. Camping is also available, as are meals.

The resort offers a variety of activities, such as big-game fishing, boat trips to Central Island or Sibiloi National Park (p354), and aerial flights over Turkana country.

Getting There & Away

The turn-off for Eliye Springs is signposted a short way along the Lodwar–Kalokol road. The gravel is easy to follow until it suddenly peters out and you're faced with a fork in the road – stay left. The rest of the way is a mix of gravel, deep sand and even deeper sand, which can turn into a muddy nightmare in the wet season. Over the really bad sections, locals have constructed a 'road' out of palm fronds, which means that on a good day, normal cars can even make it here (though expect to do a bit of pushing and shoving). There is also a route to Eliye Springs that goes by the Lodwar District Hospital (p356), but only take this route if you are with a local and in a 4WD. Petrol is only available in Lodwar, so make sure you have a good supply before heading to Eliye Springs or Ferguson's Gulf.

There is also an airstrip close to the water. Contact Eliye Springs Resort (p357) for more information on chartering a plane from Lodwar Airport (p356) (US$160 per person).

If you don't have your own vehicle, you can usually arrange a private car and driver in Lodwar for about KSh7000, including waiting time, or hop on the back of a *boda-boda* for KSh1500. If you are staying overnight, you'll have to arrange transport back to Lodwar for roughly the same amount.

UNDERSTAND KENYA

History

The early history of Kenya, from prehistory to independence is covered in the History (p562) chapter.

Mau Mau Rebellion

Kenya was Great Britain's East African heartland and the battle for independence was always going to be one of Africa's more bitter struggles for freedom.

Despite plenty of overt pressure on Kenya's colonial authorities, the real independence movement was underground. Tribal groups of Kikuyu, Maasai and Luo took secret oaths, which bound participants to kill Europeans and their African collaborators. The most famous of these movements was Mau Mau, formed in 1952 by disenchanted Kikuyu people, which aimed to drive the white settlers from Kenya forever.

The first blow was struck early with the killing of a white farmer's entire herd of cattle, followed a few weeks later by the massacre of 21 Kikuyu loyal to the colonial government. The Mau Mau rebellion had started. Within a month, Jomo Kenyatta and several other Kenyan African Movement (KAU) leaders were jailed on spurious evidence, charged with 'masterminding' the plot. The various Mau Mau sects came together under the umbrella of the Kenya Land Freedom Army, led by Dedan Kimathi, and staged frequent attacks against white farms and government outposts. By the time the rebels were defeated in 1956, the death toll stood at more than 13,500 Africans (guerrillas, civilians and troops) and just more than 100 Europeans.

Upon his release in 1959 Kenyatta resumed his campaign for independence. Soon even white Kenyans began to feel the winds of change, and in 1960 the British government officially announced their plan to transfer power to a democratically elected African government. Independence was scheduled for December 1963, accompanied by grants and loans of US$100 million to enable the Kenyan assembly to buy out European farmers in the highlands and restore the land to the tribes.

Independence

With independence scheduled for 1963, the political handover began in earnest in 1962, with the centralist Kenya African National Union (KANU) and the federalist Kenya African Democratic Union (KADU) forming a coalition government.

The run-up to independence was surprisingly smooth, although the redistribution of land wasn't a great success; Kenyans regarded it as too little, too late, while white farmers feared the trickle would become a flood. The immediate effect was to cause a significant decline in agricultural production, from which Kenya has never fully recovered.

The coalition government was abandoned after the first elections in May 1963 and Kikuyu leader, Jomo Kenyatta (formerly of the KANU), became Kenya's first president on 12 December, ruling until his death in 1978. Under Kenyatta's presidency, Kenya developed into one of Africa's most stable and prosperous nations.

While Kenyatta is still seen as one of the few success stories of Britain's withdrawal from empire, he wasn't without his faults. Biggest among these were his excessive bias in favour of his own tribe and escalating paranoia about dissent. Corruption soon became a problem at all levels of the power structure and the political arena contracted.

The 1980s

Kenyatta was succeeded in 1978 by his vice-president, Daniel arap Moi. A Kalenjin, Moi was regarded by establishment power brokers as a suitable frontman for their interests, as his tribe was relatively small and in thrall to the Kikuyu. Moi went on to become one of the most enduring 'Big Men' in Africa, ruling in virtual autocracy for nearly 25 years.

On assumption of power, Moi sought to consolidate his regime by marginalising those who had campaigned to stop him from succeeding Kenyatta. Lacking a capital base of his own, and faced with shrinking economic opportunities, Moi resorted to the politics of exclusion. He reconfigured the financial, legal, political and administrative institutions. For instance, a constitutional amendment in 1982 made Kenya a de jure one-party state, while another in 1986 removed the security of tenure for the attorney general, comptroller, auditor general and High Court judges, making all these positions personally beholden to the president. These developments had the effect of transforming Kenya from an 'imperial state' under Kenyatta to a 'personal state' under Moi.

Winds of Change

By the late 1980s, most Kenyans had had enough. Following the widely contested 1988 elections, things came to a head on 7 July 1990 when the military and police raided an opposition demonstration in Nairobi, killing 20 and arresting politicians, human-rights activists and journalists. The rally, known thereafter as Saba Saba ('seven seven' in Swahili), was a pivotal event in the push for a multiparty Kenya. The resulting pressure led to a change in the constitution that allowed opposition parties to register for the first time.

Faced with a foreign debt of nearly US$9 billion and blanket suspension of foreign aid, Moi was pressured into holding flawed multiparty elections in early 1992. To make matters worse, about 2000 people were killed during tribal clashes in the Rift Valley. Moi was overwhelmingly re-elected.

The 1997 election, too, was accompanied by violence and rioting. European and North American tour companies cancelled their bookings and around 60,000 Kenyans lost their jobs. Moi was able to set himself up as peacemaker, calming the warring factions and gaining 50.4% of the seats for KANU. After the elections, KANU was forced to bow to mounting pressure and initiate some changes: some Draconian colonial laws were repealed, as well as the requirement for licences to hold political rallies.

But Kenya was about to enter an even more difficult period. On 7 August 1998, Islamic extremists bombed the US embassies in Nairobi and Dar es Salaam in Tanzania, killing more than 200 people and bringing al-Qaeda and Osama bin Laden to international attention for the first time. The effect on the Kenyan economy was devastating. It would take four years to rebuild the shattered tourism industry.

Democratic Kenya

Having been beaten twice in the 1992 and 1997 elections due to disunity, 12 opposition groups united to form the National Alliance Rainbow Coalition (NARC). With Moi's presidency due to end in 2002, many feared that he would alter the constitution again to retain his position. This time, though, he announced his intention to retire.

Moi put his weight firmly behind Uhuru Kenyatta, the son of Jomo Kenyatta, as his successor, but the support garnered by NARC ensured a resounding victory for the party, with 62% of the vote. Mwai Kibaki was inaugurated as Kenya's third president on 30 December 2002.

When Kibaki assumed office in January 2003, donors were highly supportive of the new government and its pledges to end corruption. In 2003–04, donors contributed billions of dollars to the fight against corruption, including support for the office of a newly appointed anticorruption 'czar'.

Corruption Continues

Despite initially positive signs, it became clear by mid-2004 that large-scale corruption was still a considerable problem in Kenya. Western diplomats alleged that corruption had cost the treasury US$1 billion since Kibaki took office. In February 2005, the British High Commissioner, Sir Edward Clay, denounced the 'massive looting' of state resources by senior government politicians, including sitting cabinet ministers. Within days, Kibaki's anticorruption 'czar', John Githongo, resigned and went into exile amid rumours of death threats related to his investigation of high-level politicians. With Githongo's release of a damning detailed dossier on corruption in the Kibaki regime in February 2006, Kibaki was forced to relieve three ministers of their cabinet positions.

But the Kibaki government did at least succeed in making primary and secondary education more accessible for ordinary Kenyans, while state control over the economy was loosened.

Things Fall Apart

On 27 December 2007, Kenya held presidential, parliamentary and local elections. While the parliamentary and local-government elections were largely considered credible, the presidential elections were marred by serious irregularities, reported by both Kenyan and international election monitors, and by independent nongovernmental observers. Nonetheless, the Electoral Commission declared Mwai Kibaki the winner, triggering a wave of violence across the country.

The Rift Valley, Western Highlands, Nyanza Province and Mombasa – areas afflicted by years of political machination, previous election violence and large-scale displacement – exploded in ugly ethnic confrontations. The violence left more than 1000 people dead and over 600,000 people homeless.

Fearing for the stability of the most stable linchpin of East Africa, former UN secretary-general Kofi Annan and a panel of 'Eminent African Persons' flew to Kenya to mediate talks. A power-sharing agreement was signed on 28 February 2008 between President Kibaki and Raila Odinga, the leader of the ODM opposition. The coalition provided for the establishment of a prime ministerial position (to be filled by Raila Odinga), as well as a division of cabinet posts according to the parties' representation in parliament.

Rebuilding Confidence

Despite some difficult moments, the fragile coalition government stood the test of time. Arguably its most important success was the progressive 2010 constitution, which was passed in a referendum by 67% of Kenya's voters. Among the key elements of this new constitution are the devolution of powers to Kenya's regions, the introduction of a bill of rights and the separation of judicial, executive and legislative powers.

In 2013 Uhuru Kenyatta won hotly contested presidential elections, claiming 50.07% of the vote and thereby avoiding the need for a run-off election against Raila Odinga. Despite widespread reports of irregularities in the conduct of the elections, the Supreme Court upheld the result and postelection violence was minimal. Kenya breathed a huge sigh of relief. He won again in 2017, and when the opposition challenged the outcome in court, the results were annulled and fresh elections called. The opposition boycotted the election and although President Kenyatta won, voter turnout was low and there was considerable uncertainty about the political road ahead.

Kenya Today

Life in Kenya is as complicated as ever, but there's a lot to suggest that the country is moving in the right direction. High (and consistent) economic growth levels and a muscular democratic scene that seems to have survived yet another fiercely disputed election, along with improving security and a dynamic cultural scene, are all signs that Kenya is an increasingly good place to live. However, age-old problems such as drought, a growing population and conflict over shrinking resources remain.

The Challenges of Democracy

Ever since the widespread political and ethnic violence that followed the disputed 2007 elections, when more than 1000 people were killed, Kenya and its friends hold their collective breath whenever the country goes to the polls. Thankfully, Kenya's hotly contested 2017 elections ended peacefully. And then, in an event unprecedented in African politics, Kenya's highest court ruled in favour of an opposition challenge, the elections were annulled and new elections were scheduled. It was a landmark moment in Kenya's road to democracy. Sadly, however, the rerun was boycotted by the opposition, one of the country's electoral commissioners fled to the US, and barely one-third of Kenyans cast their ballots (compared with 80% in the first round). Although Uhuru Kenyatta was declared the winner, the future appears more uncertain than ever. Just when Kenyans thought they had survived another election...

The Coming Environmental Crisis?

Drought has always stalked East Africa, with some parts of Kenya just one failed rainy season from a major crisis. For all the growth in Kenya's urban middle class, much of the population continues to live at subsistence levels, wholly dependent upon the rains that sustain their crops or provide grazing for their livestock. Often these people live alongside wildlife-rich national parks or private ranches and conservancies that are closed to them despite having what could be prime grazing or agricultural lands within their borders. Failed rains in 2016 and again the following year, especially in the country's north and west, prompted the large-scale movement of armed herders and gangs onto the Laikipia plateau, where many of the ranches are owned by white Kenyans. One prominent conservationist was killed, another was critically injured, and a number of lodges were burned to the ground. Things have quietened down since then, but there are fears that these may be the first shots in a coming war in a country with a rapidly growing population, increasingly unpredictable rains and fiercely contested yet scarce resources.

Daily Life

Traditional cultures are what hold Kenya together. Respect for one's elders, firmly held religious beliefs, traditional gender roles and the tradition of *ujamaa* (familyhood) create a well-defined social structure with stiff moral mores at its core. Extended family provides a further layer of support, while historically, the majority of Kenyans were either farmers or cattle herders with family clans based in small interconnected villages. Even today, as traditional rural life gives way to a frenetic urban pace, this strong sense of community remains.

Kenya is home to over 40 tribal groups. Although most tribal groups have coexisted quite peacefully since independence, the ethnocentric bias of government and civil service appointments has led to escalating unrest and disaffection. During the hotly contested elections of 1992, 1997 and 2007, clashes between two major tribes, the Kikuyu and Luo, bolstered by allegiances with other smaller tribes like the Kalenjin, resulted in death and mass displacement.

Religion

As a result of intense missionary activity, the majority of Kenyans outside the coastal and eastern provinces are Christians (including some home-grown African Christian groups that do not owe any allegiance to the major Western groups). Hardcore evangelism has made some significant inroads and many TV-style groups from the US have a strong following. In the country's east, the majority of Kenyans are Sunni Muslims. They make up about 11% of the population.

Arts

Music

With its diversity of indigenous languages and cultures, Kenya has a rich and exciting music scene. Influences, most notably from the nearby Democratic Republic of Congo and Tanzania, have helped to diversify the sounds. More recently reggae and hip-hop have permeated the pop scene.

The live music scene in Nairobi is excellent and a variety of clubs cater for traditional and contemporary musical tastes. A good reference is the *Daily Nation,* which publishes weekly Top 10 African, international and gospel charts and countrywide gig listings on Saturday. Beyond Nairobi, take what you can get.

Literature

Ngũgĩ wa Thiong'o (1938–), Kenya's best-known writer, is uncompromisingly radical, and his harrowing criticism of the neocolonialist politics of the Kenyan establishment landed him in jail for a year (described in his *Detained: A Prison Writer's Diary*), lost him his job at Nairobi University and forced him into exile. His works include Petals of Blood (1977), Matigari (1987), The River Between (1965), A Grain of Wheat (1967), Devil on the Cross (1980) and Wizard of the Crow (2006), which was shortlisted for the 2007 Commonwealth Writers' Prize. His latest works are memoirs: *Dreams in a Time of War* (2010), *In the House of the Interpreter* (2012) and *Birth of a Dream Weaver: A Memoir of a Writer's Awakening* (2016). All his works, whether fiction or non-fiction, offer insightful portraits of Kenyan life. Ngũgĩ has also written extensively in his native language, Gikuyu.

Another important Kenyan writer is Meja Mwangi (1948–), who sticks more to social issues and urban dislocation but has a mischievous sense of humour. Binyavanga Wainaina (1971–) is one of Kenya's rising stars. Highly regarded female writers include Grace Ogot, Margaret Atieno Ogola, Marjorie Magoye and Hilary Ngweno.

To stay up to date with the contemporary scene, look out for *Kwani?* (kwani.org), Kenya's first literary journal, established by Wainaina in 2003. It hosts an annual literary festival that attracts a growing number of international names.

Environment

Kenya's natural environment is at once inspiring and troubled. The country is home to some of East Africa's most beautiful landscapes, from its signature savannah to palm-fringed coast with sky-high mountains, parched deserts and dense forests in between. But Kenya faces a slew of environmental issues that challenge the very sustainability of its future, with impacts upon everything from food security to the viability of protected areas. Like so many things Kenyan, it's a complicated, fascinating story.

The Land

Kenya straddles the equator and covers an area of some 583,000 sq km, including around 13,600 sq km of Lake Victoria. It is bordered to the north by the arid bushlands of Ethiopia and Sudan, to the east by the Indian Ocean and the deserts of Somalia, to the west by Uganda and Lake Victoria, and to the south by Tanzania.

Kenya is dominated by the Great Rift Valley, a vast range of valleys that follows a 5500km-long crack in the earth's crust. The Rift's path through Kenya can be traced through Lake Turkana, the Cherangani Hills and Lakes Baringo, Bogoria, Nakuru, Elmenteita, Naivasha and Magadi. Within the Rift are numerous 'swells' (raised escarpments) and 'troughs' (deep valleys, often containing lakes), and there are some huge volcanoes, including Mt Kenya, Mt

A KENYAN PLAYLIST

- *Virunga Volcano* (Orchestre Virunga; 1984) Samba, sublime guitar licks, a bubbling bass and rich vocals.
- *Nairobi Beat: Kenyan Pop Music Today* (1989) Regional sounds including Luo, Kikuyu, Akamba, Luhya, Swahili and Congolese.
- *Guitar Paradise of East Africa* (1990) Ranges through Kenya's musical styles including the classic hit 'Shauri Yako'.
- *Journey* (Jabali Afrika; 1996) Stirring acoustic sounds complete with drums, congas, shakers and bells.
- *Amigo* (Les Wanyika; 1998) Classic Swahili rumba from one of Kenya's most influential bands.
- *Nuting but de Stone* (1999) Phenomenally popular compilation combining African lyrics with American urban sounds and Caribbean ragga.
- *Kenyan: The First Chapter* (2000) Kenya's home-grown blend of African lyrics with R&B, house, reggae and dancehall genres.
- *Necessary Noize* (Necessary Noize 2; 2000) Hip-hop, reggae and R&B that produced numerous hits.
- *Nairobbery* (K-South; 2002) The landmark hip-hop album that launched the careers of this popular band.
- *Yahweh* (Esther Wahome; 2003) The hit 'Kuna Dawa' from this album improbably crossed over from gospel song to nightclub hit.
- *Kilio Cha Haki – A Cry for Justice* (2004) Groundbreaking rap in Sheng (a mix of Kiswahili, English and ethnic languages).
- *Mama Africa* (Suzanna Owiyo; 2009) Acoustic Afropop from the Tracy Chapman of Kenya.
- *82* (Just a Band; 2009) Experimental Afro-fusion that Kenya fell in love with.
- *Magic in the Air* (Mayonde; 2015) Debut pop album from a talent to watch.
- *Tusk at Hand* (Parking Lot Grass; 2015) Hard-rock protest songs sung in Swahili.

Elgon and Mt Kilimanjaro (across the border in Tanzania).

The African savannah covers an estimated two-thirds of the African land mass and owes its existence to the Rift Valley when volcanic lava and ash rained down upon the lands surrounding the Rift's volcanoes, covering the landscape in fertile but shallow soils. Grasses flourished as they needed little depth for their roots to grow. The perfectly adapted acacia aside, however, no other plants were able to colonise the savannah, as their roots were starved of space and nourishment. In Kenya, the most famous sweeps of savannah are found in the country's west (particularly in the Masai Mara National Reserve) and south.

Along the coast of East Africa, warm currents in the Indian Ocean provide perfect conditions for coral growth, resulting in beautiful underwater coral reefs. In contrast, much of northern Kenya is extremely arid, with rainfall of less than 100mm a year. A number of contiguous deserts occupy the territory between Lake Turkana's eastern shore and the Ethiopian and Somali borders.

The main rivers in Kenya are the Athi/Galana River, which empties into the Indian Ocean near Malindi, and the Tana River, which hits the coast midway between Malindi and Lamu. Aside from Lake Victoria, Kenya has numerous small volcanic lakes and mighty Lake Turkana, which straddles the Ethiopian border.

Wildlife

Kenya is home to all of the charismatic megafauna that draw so many visitors to Africa, and the daily battle between predators and prey brings so much personality to the Kenyan wilds. The 'Big Five' – lion, buffalo, elephant , leopard and rhino – are relatively easy to spot in a number of places. The birdlife here is equally diverse – Kenya is home to over 1100 species, with millions of migratory birds arriving or passing through the country from November to October.

ENDANGERED SPECIES

Many of Kenya's major predators and herbivores have become endangered over the past few decades, because of poisoning, the ongoing destruction of their natural habitat and merciless poaching for ivory, skins, horn and bushmeat.

The black rhino is probably Kenya's most endangered large mammal. It is also often described as Kenya's indigenous rhino – historically, the white rhino was not found in Kenya. Pursued by heavily armed gangs, the black rhino's numbers fell from an estimated 20,000 in the 1970s to barely 300 a decade later. Numbers are slowly recovering (rhinos are notoriously slow breeders), with an estimated 600 to 700 black rhinos surviving in the wild in Kenya, which represents around one-sixth of Africa's total (or close to 90% of the world population for the eastern subspecies of black rhino). Despite some poaching incidents, Kenya's black rhino population almost doubled in the decade to 2016. **Rhino Ark** (☎020-2136010; www.rhinoark.org) is one organisation that raises funds to create rhino sanctuaries or to build fences around national parks, as they have done in Aberdare National Park, and donations are always appreciated. Your best chance of seeing the black rhino is at Ol Pejeta Conservancy, Lewa Wildlife Conservancy and Solio Game Reserve, as well as in the national parks of Nairobi, Tsavo West, Aberdare, Meru and Lake Nakuru.

While the elephant is not technically endangered, it is still the target of poachers, and a large number are killed every year, especially in the area around Tsavo East National Park. Elephant numbers in Kenya fell from 45,000 in 1976 to just 5400 in 1988. The Great Elephant Census of 2016 (www.greatelephantcensus.com) estimated that there were around 26,000 elephants in Kenya, and the country is one of the few places in Africa where elephant numbers are growing, although admittedly very slowly.

Lions are also considered endangered in Kenya with fewer than 2000 thought to survive, although this is feared to be an overestimate. The only viable lion populations in the long-term are those in Laikipia, Meru National Park and Maasailand (which stretches across southern Kenya from the Masai Mara National Reserve to Tsavo East National Park).

National Parks & Reserves

Kenya's national parks and reserves rate among the best in Africa. Around 10% of the country's land area is protected by law – that means, at least in theory, no human habitation, no grazing and no hunting within park boundaries. The parks range from the

15.5-sq-km Saiwa Swamp National Park to the massive, almost 21,000-sq-km Tsavo East and West national parks. Together they embrace a wide range of habitats and ecosystems and contain an extraordinary repository of Africa's wildlife.

VISITING NATIONAL PARKS & RESERVES

Going on safari is an integral part of the Kenyan experience, and the wildlife and scenery can be extraordinary. Even in more popular parks such as Masai Mara National Reserve and Amboseli National Park, which can become massively overcrowded in high season (July to October and January to February, although KWS maintains high-season prices into March), this natural splendour is likely to be your most enduring memory.

PRIVATE CONSERVANCIES

The widespread conversion of private cattle ranches or community lands into wildlife or community conservancies adds a whole new dimension to your safari experience in Kenya.

In the case of private conservancies, many are open only to those who pay to stay at one of the (usually exclusive) lodges or tented camps within the conservancy's boundaries. Such restrictions sometimes, but don't always, apply to the community conservancies. Most also charge a conservation fee – often around US$100 per person per day – whose proceeds go directly to wildlife conservation or community development projects.

One exception is Ol Pejeta Conservancy (p284), which is open to the public (adult/child US$85/42) – it's the closest conservancy experience to visiting a national park, but with fun activities thrown in.

In all cases, these conservancies are free to set their own rules, and these are invariably far less restrictive than those imposed by the KWS. The two most obvious examples are that both walking safaris (usually accompanied by an armed guide or ranger) and night game drives are permitted on the conservancies. Other activities – including, in some cases, horse riding – are also possible.

Environmental Issues

Kenya faces a daunting slew of environmental issues, among them deforestation, desertification, threats to endangered species and the impacts of tourism. In response, Kenya's private conservation community has taken matters into its own hands with, in many cases, exceptional results.

PARK ENTRY FEES

All KWS entry fees must now be paid by credit card or via the M-Pesa phone app. The rationale behind the move to prohibit the use of cash to pay park entry fees was to eliminate corruption by KWS staff.

KWS CATEGORY	PARK/RESERVE	NONRESIDENT ADULT/CHILD (US$)	CAMPING NON-RESIDENT ADULT/CHILD (US$)
	Masai Mara	80/45	20/15
Premium	Amboseli, Lake Nakuru	60/35	30/25
Wilderness	Meru, Tsavo East, Tsavo West	52/35	20/15
Aberdare National Park	Aberdare	52/26	20/15
Urban Safari	Nairobi National Park	43/22	20/15
Mountain Climbing (Day Trip)	Mt Kenya	52/26	20/15
Mountain Climbing (4-Day Package)	Mt Kenya	208/104	20/15
Scenic & Special Interest A	Hell's Gate, Mt Elgon, Ol Donyo Sabuk, Mt Longonot	26/17	20/15
Scenic & Special Interest B	Chyulu, Marsabit, Arabuko Sokoke, Kakamega, Shimba Hills, all other KWS parks	22/13	20/15
Marine Parks	Kisite, Malindi, Watamu, Mombasa, Kiunga	17/13	n/a

KENYA ENVIRONMENT

BANNING PLASTIC BAGS

At the end of August 2017, Kenya introduced one of the world's strictest laws against the use of plastic carrier bags. The law, which survived a High Court challenge and warnings of 80,000 job losses in the plastic-bag-production industry, allows for those who break the law to be sentenced to four years in prison or face a US$38,000 fine. In practice, in the first months of the law's implementation, police were instructed to warn violators and confiscate the offending bags.

No one who has travelled in Kenya could doubt the need for such a law, with plastic bags filling the countryside and vacant plots of land, especially in Kenyan cities. In addition to being an eyesore, plastic bags have the potential to impact upon public health: for example, according to the United Nations Environment Programme, 20 polythene bags were pulled from the stomach of just one cow in one Nairobi abattoir, as grazing cattle feed on the bags.

The government estimates that before the ban Kenyans used 24 million plastic bags every month. And travellers are certainly not exempt – if you're arriving by air with duty-free plastic shopping bags, the bags will be taken from you before you leave the airport.

Later in 2017, the government announced a further ban, this time on taking plastic water bottles into Nairobi National Park and the nearby Karura Forest. It seems likely that the ban will be extended to cover all national parks in the not-too-distant future.

DEFORESTATION

More than half of Africa's forests have been destroyed over the last century, and forest destruction continues on a large scale in parts of Kenya – today, less than 3% of the country's original forest cover remains. Land grabbing, charcoal burning, agricultural encroachment, the spiralling use of firewood and illegal logging have all taken their toll over the years. However, millions of Kenyans (and the majority of hotels, lodges and restaurants) still rely on wood and charcoal for cooking fuel, so travellers to the country will almost certainly contribute to this deforestation, whether they like it or not.

Native hardwood, such as ebony and mahogany, is often used to make the popular carved wooden statue souvenirs sold in Kenya. Although this industry supports thousands of local families who may otherwise be without an income, it also consumes an estimated 80,000 trees annually. The World Wide Fund for Nature (WWF) and Unesco campaigned to promote the use of common, faster-growing trees, and many handicraft cooperatives now use wood taken from forests managed by the Forest Stewardship Council. If you buy a carving, ask if the wood is sourced from managed forests.

DESERTIFICATION

Northern and eastern Kenya are home to some of the most marginal lands in East Africa. Pastoralists have eked out a similarly marginal existence here for centuries, but recurring droughts have seriously degraded the land, making it increasingly susceptible to creeping desertification and erosion. As a consequence, the UN estimates that the livelihoods of around 3.5 million herders may be under medium- to long-term threat.

And desertification, at least in its early stages, may even begin to encroach upon the most unlikely places. The fertile lands of Kenya's Central Highlands rank among Africa's most agriculturally productive, but therein lies their peril: here, around three-quarters of Kenya's population crowds into just 12% of the land, with the result that soils are being rapidly depleted through overexploitation – one of the early warning signs of desertification.

SURVIVAL GUIDE

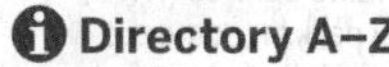

Directory A–Z

ACCOMMODATION

Seasons

- High-season prices usually run from July (sometimes June) to October, from January until February, and include Easter and Christmas, although there may be slight variations in some regions. Sometimes high season is also referred to as peak season. Low season usually covers the rest of the year, although many lodges and top-end hotels also have intermediate shoulder seasons.

- On the coast, peak times tend to be July, August and December to March, and a range of lower rates can apply for the rest of the year.
- During the low season many companies offer excellent deals on accommodation on the coast and in the main wildlife parks, often working with airlines to create packages aimed at the local and expat market.

Prices

All-inclusive & full board It's worth remembering that many places, particularly those in national parks or other remote areas, offer full-board-only rates – prices may, therefore, seem higher than you'd expect, but less so once you factor in three meals a day. Some also offer what are called all-inclusive or 'package rates' that include full board accommodation but also things such as game drives, transfers and other extras.

Dual pricing Kenya also operates on a dual pricing system, particularly in midrange and top-end places – nonresidents pay significantly more (often double or triple the price) than Kenyan (or other East African) residents. When things are quiet, you may be able to get the residents' rate if you ask, but don't count on it.

Currencies Hotels and other places to stay in Kenya quote their prices in a variety of currencies, usually US dollars or Kenyan shillings (KSh). In almost all cases you can pay in dollars, shillings, euros and (sometimes) other foreign currencies.

Price ranges The following price ranges refer to a high-season double room with bathroom. Unless otherwise stated, breakfast is included in the price.

$ less than KSh5000 (US$50)

$$ KSh5000–15,000 (US$50–150)

$$$ more than KSh15,000 (US$150)

Bandas

Bandas are Kenyan-style huts and cottages, usually with some kind of kitchen and bathroom, which offer excellent value. Although there are numerous private examples, there are also Kenya Wildlife Service (KWS) *bandas* at some national parks – some are wooden huts, some are thatched stone huts and some are small brick bungalows with solar-powered lights.

Facilities range from basic dorms and squat toilets to kitchens and hot water provided by wood-burning stoves. In such places, you'll need to bring all your own food, drinking water, bedding and firewood.

Although originally aimed at budget travellers, an increasing variety of places are calling *bandas* huts, which are decidedly midrange in price and quality.

Beach Resorts

Much of the coast, from Diani Beach to Malindi, is taken up by huge luxury beach resorts. Most offer a fairly similar experience, with swimming pools, water sports, bars, restaurants, mobs of souvenir vendors on the beach and 'tribal' dance shows in the evening. They aren't all bad, especially if you want good children's facilities, and a handful of them have been very sensitively designed. Note that many of these places will close in early summer, generally from May to mid-June or July.

Camping

There are many opportunities for camping in Kenya, and although gear can be hired in Nairobi and around Mt Kenya, it's worth considering bringing a tent with you.

Public campsites There are KWS campsites in just about every national park or reserve. These are usually very basic, with a toilet block with a couple of pit toilets, a water tap, perhaps public showers and very little else. They cost US$30/25 per adult/child in Amboseli and Lake Nakuru national parks, begin at US$20 per person in Masai Mara National Reserve and US$20/15 in all other parks.

Special campsites As well as these permanent campsites, KWS also runs so-called 'special' campsites in most national parks. These sites move every year and have even fewer facilities than the standard camps, but cost more because of their wilder locations and set-up costs. They cost US$50/25 per adult/child in Amboseli and Lake Nakuru, US$35/20 elsewhere; a reservation fee of KSh7500 per week is payable on top of the relevant camping fee.

Private campsites Private sites are rare, but they offer more facilities and may hire out tents if you don't have your own. It's sometimes possible to camp in the grounds of some hotels in rural towns, and Nairobi has some good private campsites. Camping in the bush is possible but unless you're doing it with an organised trip or a guide, security is a major concern – don't even think about it on the coast.

Hostels

The only youth hostel affiliated with Hostelling International (HI) is in Nairobi. It has good basic facilities and is a pleasant enough place to stay, but there are plenty of other cheaper choices that are just as good. Other places that call themselves 'youth hostels' are not members of HI, and standards are variable.

Hotels & Guesthouses

Real bottom-end hotels (often known as 'board and lodgings' to distinguish them from *hotelis*, which are often only restaurants) are widely used as brothels, and tend to be very run-down. Security at these places is virtually non-existent, though the better ones are set around courtyards, and are clean if not exactly comfortable.

Proper hotels and guesthouses come in many different shapes and sizes. As well as the top-end Western companies, there are a number of small Kenyan chains offering reliable standards across a handful of properties in particular towns or regions, and also plenty of private, family-run establishments.

Self-catering options are common on the coast, where they're often the only midpriced alternative to the top-end resorts, but not so much in other parts of the country. A few fancier places offer modern kitchens, but more often than not the so-called kitchenettes will be a side room with a small fridge and portable gas stove.

Terms you will come across in Kenya include 'self-contained', which just means a room with its own private bathroom, and 'all-inclusive', which generally means all meals, certain drinks and possibly some activities should be included. 'Full board' accommodation includes three meals a day, while 'half board' generally means breakfast and dinner are included.

Safari Lodges

Hidden away inside or on the edges of national parks and wildlife conservancies are some fantastic safari lodges. These are usually visited as part of organised safaris, and you'll pay much more if you just turn up and ask for a room.

Some of the older places trade heavily on their more glorious past, but the best places feature five-star rooms, soaring *makuti*-roofed bars (with a thatched roof of palm leaves) and restaurants overlooking waterholes full of wildlife. Staying in at least one good safari lodge while you're in Kenya is recommended.

Rates tend to fall significantly in the low season.

Tented Camps

As well as lodges, many parks and conservancies contain some fantastic luxury tented camps. These places tend to occupy wonderfully remote settings, usually by rivers or other natural locations, and feature large, comfortable, semi-permanent safari tents with beds, furniture, bathrooms (usually with hot running water) and often some kind of external roof thatch to keep the rain out; you sleep surrounded by the sounds of the African bush.

Most of the camps are very upmarket and the tents are pretty much hotel rooms under canvas. The really exclusive properties occupy locations so isolated that guests fly in and out on charter planes.

ACTIVITIES

Kenya has a long list of activities that are at once terrific ways to explore Kenya's varied terrain and fabulous experiences in their own right.

Ballooning

Usually includes a 1½-hour flight, champagne breakfast and wildlife drive from around US$400 per person. In the Masai Mara only.

Cycling & Mountain-Biking

Operators **Bike Treks** (☎020-4446371, 020-2141757; www.angelfire.com/sk/biketreks; Kabete Gardens, Westlands) and **Rift Valley Adventures** (☎0707734776; www.riftvalleyadventures.com; half-/full-day cycling tour from US$70/120) offer specialised cycling trips. Many places to stay (particularly campgrounds) can arrange bicycle hire for KSh500 to KSh1200 per day. Good places to go cycling include Masai Mara National Reserve, Ol Pejeta Conservancy and Hell's Gate National Park, although you can only do the first two as part of an organised group.

Diving & Snorkelling

If you aren't certified to dive, almost every hotel and resort on the coast can arrange an open-water diving course. They're not much cheaper (if at all) than anywhere else in the world – a five-day PADI certification course starts at around US$470. Trips for certified divers including two dives go for around US$100. October to March is the best time, but during June, July and August it's often impossible to dive due to the poor visibility caused by heavy silt flow from some rivers. That said, some divers have taken the plunge in July and found visibility to be a very respectable 7m to 10m, although 4m is more common.

Trekking & Climbing

Kenya has some of the best trekking trails in East Africa, ranging from strenuous mountain ascents to rolling hill country and forests. It is, of course, always worth checking out the prevalence of any wild animals you might encounter along the trail. In some instances, it may be advisable to take a local guide, either from the KWS, if they operate in the area, or a local village guide.

Water Sports

Conditions on Kenya's coast are ideal for windsurfing – the country's offshore reefs protect the waters, and the winds are usually reasonably strong and constant. Most resort hotels south and north of Mombasa have sailboards for hire. Diani Beach in particular is good for water sports.

White-Water Rafting

The most exciting times for white-water rafting trips are late October to mid-January and early April to late July, when water levels are highest. The Athi/Galana River in particular has substantial rapids, chutes and waterfalls. The people to talk to are **Savage Wilderness Safaris** (Map p224; ☎ 020-7121590; www.savagewilderness.org).

CUSTOMS REGULATIONS

There are strict laws about taking wildlife products out of Kenya. The export of products made from elephant, rhino and sea turtle are prohibited. The collection of coral is also not allowed. Ostrich eggs will be confiscated unless you can prove you bought them from a certified ostrich farm. Always check to see what permits are required, especially for the export of any plants, insects and shells.

Allowable quantities you can bring into Kenya are:

Alcohol 1L

Cigarettes 200

Cigars 50

Perfume 250mL

Pipe tobacco 250g

DANGERS & ANNOYANCES

While Kenya can be quite a safe destination, there are still plenty of pitfalls for the unwary or inexperienced traveller, from everyday irritations to more serious threats.

- Always take a taxi from door to door after dark in cities, especially Nairobi.
- Avoid deserted beach areas at night.
- Keep all of your valuables locked safely away, especially when out and about in Nairobi, or when spending a day at the beach.
- Never travel major intercity roads at night due to the heightened risk of road accidents.
- Keep a close eye on travel advisories issued by foreign governments.

Banditry

Northeast The ongoing conflict in Somalia has had an effect on the stability and safety of northern and northeastern Kenya – the latter is considered extremely dangerous and has been for years thanks to bandits and poachers. AK-47s have been flowing into the country for many years, and the newspapers are filled with stories of hold-ups, shoot-outs, cattle rustling and general lawlessness. Visitors to Lamu should fly if possible.

Northwest In the northwest, the main problem is armed tribal wars and cattle rustling across the South Sudanese border. There are Kenyan *shiftas* (bandits) too, of course, but cross-border problems seem to account for most of the trouble in the north of the country.

Risk Despite all the headlines, tourists are rarely targeted, as most of the violence and robberies take place far from the main tourist routes. Security has also improved considerably in previously high-risk areas, such as the Isiolo–Marsabit and Marsabit–Moyale routes. However, you should check the situation locally before taking these roads, and should avoid Garissa County altogether.

South Sudan & Ethiopia borders The areas along the South Sudanese and Ethiopian borders are sometimes considered risky – check the situation carefully if you're planning to travel overland between either country and Kenya.

Crime

Even the staunchest Kenyan patriot will readily admit that one of the country's biggest problems is crime. It ranges from petty snatch theft and mugging to violent armed robbery, carjacking and, of course, white-collar crime and corruption. As a visitor you needn't feel paranoid, but you should always keep your wits about you, particularly at night.

Although crime is a fact of life in Kenya, it needn't spoil your trip. Above all, don't make the mistake of distrusting everyone you meet – the honest souls you encounter will far outnumber any crooks who cross your path.

Precautions Perhaps the best advice for when you're walking around cities and towns is not to carry anything valuable with you – that includes jewellery, watches, cameras,

KENYA'S BEST TREKKING

The following places are all good for proper mountain trekking in varying degrees of difficulty:

- **Mt Kenya** (p289)
- **Mt Elgon National Park** (p274)
- **Mt Longonot** (p242)
- **Cherangani Hills** (p355)
- **Loita Hills** (p261)
- **Aberdare National Park** (p279)
- **Ndoto Mountains** (p349)

For forest hiking, we especially like the following:

- **Kakamega Forest Reserve** (p268)
- **Matthews Range** (p349)
- **Arabuko Sokoke Forest Reserve** (p331)

bumbags, daypacks and money. Most hotels provide a safe or secure place for valuables, although you should also be cautious of the security at some budget places.

Mugging While pickpocketing and bag snatching are the most common crimes, armed muggings do occur in Nairobi and on the coast. Always take taxis after dark.

Snatch & run Snatching crimes happen more in crowds. If you suddenly feel there are too many people around you, or think you are being followed, dive straight into a shop and ask for help.

Luggage This is an obvious signal to criminals that you've just arrived. When arriving anywhere by bus, it's sensible to take a 'ship-to-shore' approach, getting a taxi directly from the bus station to your hotel. You'll have plenty of time to explore once you've safely stowed your belongings. Also, don't read a guidebook or look at maps on the street – it attracts unwanted attention.

Reporting crime In the event of a crime, you should report it to the police, but this can be a real procedure. You'll need to get a police report if you intend to make an insurance claim. In the event of a snatch theft, think twice before yelling 'Thief!' It's not unknown for people to administer summary justice on the spot, often with fatal results for the criminal. In Nairobi, the **tourist helpline** (☎020-604767; ⊙24hr) is a free service for tourists in trouble. It is a good nationwide network and works closely with the police and local authorities.

Scams

Expensive stories At some point in Kenya you'll almost certainly come across people who play on the emotions and gullibility of foreigners. Nairobi is a particular hotspot, with 'friendly' approaches a daily, if not hourly, occurrence. People with tales about being refugees or having sick relatives can sound very convincing, but they all end up asking for cash. It's OK to talk to these people if they're not actively hassling you, but you should probably ignore any requests for money.

Over-friendly strangers Be sceptical of strangers who claim to recognise you in the street, especially if they're vague about exactly where they know you from – it's unlikely that any ordinary person is going to be *this* excited by seeing you twice. Anyone who makes a big show of inviting you into the hospitality of their home also probably has ulterior motives. The usual trick is to bestow some kind of gift upon the delighted traveller, who is then emotionally blackmailed into reciprocating.

Car scams Tourists with cars also face potential rip-offs. Don't trust people who gesticulate wildly to indicate that your front wheels are wobbling; if you stop, you'll probably be relieved of your valuables. Another trick is to splash oil on your wheels, then tell you the wheel bearings, differential or something else has failed, and direct you to a nearby garage where their friends will 'fix' the problem – for a substantial fee, of course.

Terrorism

Terrorism is, unfortunately, something you have to consider when visiting Kenya, although the vast majority of the country is safe to visit. Remember that reports of an attack in, for example, Mombasa is likely to have very little impact upon the safety of visiting the Masai Mara or even Tsavo East National Park.

The country has come under major terrorist attack on at least three occasions: in August 1998 the US embassy in Nairobi was bombed; in November 2002 the Paradise Hotel, north of Mombasa, was car-bombed at the same time as a rocket attack on an Israeli jet; and in September 2013 terrorists attacked the upscale Westgate Shopping Mall in Nairobi. Since then, security has been tightened considerably.

EMBASSIES & CONSULATES

Australian High Commission (Map p224; ☎020-4277100; www.kenya.embassy.gov.au; ICIPE House, Riverside Dr, Nairobi; ⊙9-11am Mon-Thu)

Canadian High Commission (☎020-3663000; www.canadainternational.gc.ca/kenya/index.aspx?lang=eng; Limuru Rd, Gigiri, Nairobi; ⊙7.30am-4pm Mon-Thu, to 1pm Fri)

Ethiopian Embassy (Map p224; ☎0722207025, 020-2732050; State House Ave, Nairobi; ⊙9am-noon Mon-Fri)

French Embassy (☎07605555; www.ambafrance-ke.org; Peponi Gardens, Nairobi; ⊙8.30am-1pm & 2-5.30pm Mon-Thu, 8.30am-1pm Fri)

German Embassy (☎020-4262100; www.nairobi.diplo.de; 113 Riverside Dr, Nairobi; ⊙8am-12.30pm Mon-Fri)

Netherlands Embassy (Map p224; ☎020-4288000; www.netherlandsworldwide.nl/countries/kenya; Riverside Lane, Nairobi; ⊙9-10.45am Mon, 8.30-10.45am Tue-Thu)

South Sudan Embassy (☎0729790144; 2nd fl, Senteu Plaza, Galana Rd, Nairobi; ⊙9am-5pm Mon-Thu, to noon Fri)

Tanzanian Embassy (Map p228; ☎020-2311948; www.tanzaniahc.or.ke; Reinsurance Plaza, Aga Khan Walk, Nairobi; ⊙8.30am-2pm Mon-Fri)

Uganda High Commission (Consular Section) (Map p228; ☎020-4445420, 020-311814; www.nairobi.mofa.go.ug; 1st fl, Uganda House, Kenyatta Ave, Nairobi; ⊙9am-noon Mon-Fri)

The consular section is in the city centre. There's also the High Commission office further out.

UK High Commission (Map p224; ☎020-2844000; www.gov.uk/world/organisations/british-high-commission-nairobi; Upper Hill Rd, Nairobi; ⏰7am-4pm Mon-Thu, to 1pm Fri)

US Embassy (☎020-3636000; https://ke.usembassy.gov; United Nations Ave, Nairobi; ⏰8am-4.30pm Mon-Fri)

INTERNET ACCESS

Wi-fi You'll find wi-fi in all but the very cheapest or most remote hotels, though speeds vary enormously. Many wildlife lodges have wi-fi access, but it tends to be highly unreliable. Budget and midrange lodges rarely have internet access at all.

Mobile networks Safaricom, Telkom and Airtel are your best bets for internet access on your phone. Data is cheap and speeds are generally decent, especially compared to other countries in East Africa.

LANGUAGE COURSES

Taking a Swahili-language course (or any course) entitles you to a 'Pupil's Pass', which is an immigration permit allowing continuous stays of up to 12 months. You may have to battle with bureaucracy and the process may take months, but it can be worth it, especially as you will then have resident status in Kenya during your stay.

ACK Language & Orientation School (Map p224; ☎0718233085, 020-2721893; www.acklanguageschool.org; Bishops Rd, Upper Hill) The Anglican Church runs full-time Swahili courses of varying levels lasting 14 weeks and taking up to five hours a day. Private tuition is available on a flexible part-time schedule.

Language Center Ltd (Map p232; ☎020-3870610, 0721495774; www.language-cntr.com/welcome.shtml; Ndemi Close) A good Swahili centre offering a variety of study options ranging from private hourly lessons to daily group courses.

LEGAL MATTERS

All drugs except *miraa* (a leafy shoot chewed as a stimulant) are illegal in Kenya. Marijuana (commonly called *bhang*) is widely available but illegal; possession carries a penalty of up to 10 years in prison. Dealers are common on the beaches north and south of Mombasa and frequently set up travellers for sting operations for real or phoney cops to extort money.

African prisons are unbelievably harsh places – don't take the risk. Note that *miraa* is illegal in Tanzania, so if you do develop a taste for the stuff in Kenya, you should leave it behind when heading south.

LGBT+ TRAVELLERS

Negativity towards homosexuality is widespread in Kenya and recent events ensure that it's a brave gay or lesbian Kenyan who comes out of the closet. Frequent denunciations by those in power have created a toxic atmosphere of homophobia, which sometimes spills over into violence and, more often, into government harassment. In July 2014, for example, 40 people were arrested for 'suspected homosexuality' in a Nairobi nightclub.

Underlying all of this is a penal code that states that homosexual (and attempted homosexual) behaviour is punishable by up to 14 years in prison. Attitudes may be slowly shifting, however – in 2015 Kenya's High Court ruled in favour of the National Gay and Lesbian Coalition of Kenya being able to register as an NGO, something that had previously been rejected multiple times due to homosexuality's illegality in Kenya. This has at least given gay people in Kenya a voice and is the first step on the long path towards legalisation. No law currently prohibits discrimination on the basis of sexual orientation.

The main challenge to the acceptance of gay and lesbian lifestyles in Kenya is religion. Nearly all churches and mosques maintain a vociferously anti-gay position, and this is amplified by the presence of homophobic American churches that actively campaign in Kenya against gay rights. In early 2014 star author Binyavanga Wainaina revealed publicly that he was gay to protest against a resurgence in anti-gay laws and public debate across Africa. A few others have followed suit, but visibility for gay people remains extremely low.

While there are very few prosecutions under the law, it is certainly better to be discreet as a gay foreigner in Kenya. Some local con artists do a good line in blackmail, picking up foreigners then threatening to expose them to the police.

Useful Resources

David Tours (www.davidtravel.com) Can arrange anything from balloon safaris to luxurious coastal hideaways, all with a gay focus.

Gay and Lesbian Coalition of Kenya (GALCK; www.galck.org) Local advocacy group that keeps a low profile but that it exists at all in the public domain represents a scrap of progress.

Global Gayz (www.globalgayz.com/africa/kenya) Links to Kenyan gay issues.

MAPS

Country Maps

➡ The *Tourist Map of Kenya* gives good detail, as does the *Kenya Route Map;* both cost around KSh250.

➡ Marco Polo's 1:1,000,000 *Shell Euro Karte Kenya*, Geocenter's *Kenya* (1:1,000,000) and IGN's *Carte Touristique: Kenya* (1:1,000,000) are useful overview maps that are widely available in Europe. The scale and clarity are very good, but the locations of some minor features are inaccurate.

➡ For those planning a longer trip in southern and East Africa, Michelin's 1:4,000,000 *Map 955 (Africa Central and South)* is very useful.

National Park Maps

Most maps to Kenya's national parks might look a bit flimsy on detail (you won't get much in the way of topographical detail), but they include the numbered junctions in the national parks.

Tourist maps Macmillan publishes a series of maps to the wildlife parks and these are not bad value at around KSh250 each (three are available in Europe: *Amboseli*, *Masai Mara* and *Tsavo East & West*). Tourist Maps also publishes a national park series for roughly the same price. The maps by the KWS are similar.

Survey of Kenya The most detailed and thorough maps are published by the Survey of Kenya, but the majority are out of date and many are also out of print. The better bookshops in Nairobi usually have copies of the most important maps, including *Amboseli National Park* (SK 87), *Masai Mara Game Reserve* (SK 86), *Meru National Park* (SK 65), *Tsavo East National Park* (SK 82) and *Tsavo West National Park* (SK 78).

Kenya Institute of Surveying & Mapping (☎020-8561484; off Thika Rd, Nairobi) It may be worth a visit to this office, but this can take all day and there's no guarantee it will have any more stock than the bookshops.

MONEY

All banks change US dollars, euros and UK pounds into Kenyan shillings. ATMs can be found in medium-sized towns, so bring cash and a debit or credit card.

ATMs

Virtually all banks in Kenya now have ATMs, most of which accept international credit and debit cards. Barclays Bank has easily the most reliable machines for international withdrawals, with ATMs in most larger Kenyan towns. Standard Chartered and Kenya Commercial Bank are also good options. Whichever bank you use, the international data link still goes down occasionally, so don't rely on being able to withdraw money whenever you need it, and always keep a reasonable amount of cash on hand.

Cash

The unit of currency is the Kenyan shilling (KSh), which is made up of 100 cents. Notes in circulation are KSh1000, 500, 200, 100, 50 and 20, and there are also coins of KSh40, 20, 10, five and one. Locally the shilling is commonly known as a 'bob', after the old English term for a one-shilling coin. The shilling has been relatively stable over the last few years, maintaining fairly constant rates against the US dollar, euro and UK pound.

Credit Cards

Credit cards are becoming increasingly popular. Visa and Mastercard are now widely accepted in midrange and top-end hotels, top-end restaurants and some shops.

Moneychangers

The best places to change money are foreign exchange or 'forex' bureaus, which can be found everywhere and usually don't charge commission. The rates for the main bureaus in Nairobi are published in the *Daily Nation* newspaper.

Tipping

Hotel porters Tips expected in upmarket hotels (from KSh200).

Restaurants Service charge of 10% often added to the bill plus 16% VAT and 2% catering levy.

Taxi drivers As fares are negotiated in advance, no need to tip unless they provide you with exceptional service.

Tour guides, safari drivers & cooks Gratuity is expected at the end of your tour/trip. Count on around US$10 to US$15 per day per group.

OPENING HOURS

Opening hours can vary throughout the year, particularly in tourist areas, less so in larger cities. We've provided high-season opening hours; hours will generally decrease in the shoulder and low seasons.

Banks 9am–3pm or 4pm Monday to Friday, 9am–noon Saturday

Post offices 8.30am–5pm Monday to Friday, 9am–noon Saturday

Restaurants 11.30am–2pm or 3pm and 5pm or 6pm–9pm; some remain open between lunch and dinner

Shops 9am–5pm Monday to Friday, 9am–noon Saturday; some stay open later and open on Sundays

Supermarkets 8.30am–8.30pm Monday to Saturday, 10am–8pm Saturday

POST

Service The Kenyan postal system is run by Posta (www.posta.co.ke). Letters sent from Kenya rarely go astray but can take up to two weeks to reach Australia or the USA.

Parcels If sent by surface mail, parcels take three to six months to reach Europe, while airmail parcels take around a week.

Courier Most things arrive eventually, although there is still a problem with theft within the system. Curios, clothes and textiles will be OK, but if your parcel contains anything of obvious value, send it by courier. Posta has its own courier service, EMS, which is considerably cheaper than the big international courier companies. The best place to send parcels from is the main post office in Nairobi.

PUBLIC HOLIDAYS

New Year's Day 1 January
Good Friday and Easter Monday March/April
Labour Day 1 May
Madaraka Day 1 June
Moi Day 10 October
Kenyatta Day 20 October
Independence Day 12 December
Christmas Day 25 December
Boxing Day 26 December

TELEPHONE

Landlines continue to be used by most businesses in Kenya, but otherwise the mobile phone is king. Prices are low, data is fast and coverage is excellent in most towns and cities.

Mobile Phones

Buy a SIM card from one of the Kenyan mobile-phone companies: Safaricom (www.safaricom.co.ke), Airtel (www.africa.airtel.com/kenya) or Telkom (www.telkom.co.ke). SIM cards cost about KSh100 and you can then buy top-up scratch cards and use them either for data or calling credit.

While coverage is excellent in Kenya, you often won't be able to use your phone or data in more remote areas, including many national parks.

Phone Codes

- Kenya's regions have area codes that must be dialled, followed by the local number.
- The international dialling code for Kenya is 254.
- When dialling Kenya from abroad, drop the first zero in the area code.

TIME

Kenya is three hours ahead of Greenwich Mean Time (GMT) year-round.

TOURIST INFORMATION

Considering the extent to which the country relies on tourism, it's incredible to think that there is still no tourist office in Nairobi. There are a tiny handful of information offices elsewhere in the country, ranging from helpful private concerns to underfunded government offices; most can at least provide basic maps of the town and brochures on local businesses and attractions, but precious little else.

TRAVELLERS WITH DISABILITIES

Travelling in Kenya is not easy for people with a physical disability, but it's not impossible. Very few tourist companies and facilities are geared for travellers with disabilities, and those that are tend to be restricted to the expensive hotels and lodges. However, Kenyans are generally very accommodating and willing to offer whatever assistance they can. Visually or hearing-impaired travellers, though, will find it very hard to get by without an able-bodied companion.

In Nairobi, only the ex-London taxi cabs are spacious enough to accommodate a wheelchair, but some safari companies are accustomed to taking people with a disability out on safari.

VISAS

Visa on arrival Tourist visas can still be obtained on arrival at all three international airports and at the country's land borders with Uganda and Tanzania. This applies to Europeans, Australians, New Zealanders, Americans and Canadians, although citizens from a few smaller Commonwealth countries are exempt. Visas cost US$50/€40/£30 and are valid for three months from the date of entry. Tourist visas can be extended for a further three-month period. Check before travelling whether the visa-on-arrival scheme has been replaced by the e-visa, which must be applied for in advance.

E-visa The Kenyan government's online visa portal (www.evisa.go.ke) issues single-entry tourist visas (US$51) valid for up to 90 days from the date of entry, as well as transit visas (US$21). Simply register, apply and pay online, and once it's approved (within two business days) you'll be sent a PDF visa document to print out, which you then present on entry to Kenya.

Single-entry visas Under the East African partnership system, visiting Tanzania or Uganda and returning to Kenya does not invalidate a single-entry Kenyan visa, so there's no need to get a multiple-entry visa unless you plan to go further afield. Always check the latest entry requirements with embassies before travel.

Prearranged visas It's also possible to get visas from Kenyan diplomatic missions overseas, but the only reasons to do so are if you come from a country not eligible for an on-arrival visa, you want to get a multiple-entry visa, or you need longer than three months in the country. If this is the case for you, apply well in advance, especially if you're doing it by mail.

Visas for Onward Travel

Since Nairobi is a common gateway city to East Africa and the city centre is easy to get around, many travellers spend some time here picking up visas for other countries that they intend to visit. But be warned: although officially issuing visas again, the Ethiopian embassy in Nairobi was not issuing tourist visas for a number of years and the situation could change again. Call the embassy to check.

Most embassies will want you to pay visa fees in US dollars, and most open for visa applications from 9am to noon, with visa pick-ups around 3pm or 4pm. Again, contact the embassy in question to check the times as these change regularly in Nairobi.

VOLUNTEERING

There are a large number of volunteers in Kenya, and volunteering can be a great way to reduce the ecological footprint of your trip. As a general rule, volunteering works best for both the traveller and the organisation in question if you treat it as a genuine commitment rather than simply a fun extension of your trip. It's also preferable if you have a particular skill to bring to the experience, especially one that cannot be satisfied by local people.

Keep in mind that there is no such thing as a perfect volunteer placement. Generally speaking, you'll get as much out of a programme as you're willing to put into it; the vast majority of volunteers in Kenya walk away all the better for the experience.

Note that for any volunteering work involving children, you will require a criminal background check from your home country and/or previous countries of residence.

Kenyan Organisations

A Rocha Kenya (☎042-2332023, Nairobi 020-2335865; www.arocha.or.ke) Programmes (including Mida Ecocamp) near the Arabuko Sokoke Forest and Mida Creek. Also operates the Mwamba Field Study Centre at Watamu Beach.

Watamu Turtle Watch (p330) Helps protect the marine turtles that come to Watamu to lay eggs on the beach.

Getting There & Away

Nairobi is a major African hub with numerous African and international airlines connecting Kenya to the world. By African standards, flights between Kenya and the rest of Africa or further afield are common and relatively cheap, and flying is by far the most convenient way to get to Kenya.

Kenya is also a popular and relatively easy waystation for those travelling overland between southern Africa and Egypt. Finding your way here can be tricky – with several war zones in the vicinity – and such journeys should only be considered after serious planning and preparation. But they're certainly possible, and it's rarely Kenya that causes problems.

Flights, cars and tours can be booked online at lonelyplanet.com/bookings.

ENTERING THE COUNTRY

Entering Kenya is generally pleasingly straightforward, particularly at the international airports, which are no different from most Western terminals.

Visas, needed by most foreign nationals, are straightforward. An e-visa scheme (www.evisa.go.ke) has now been rolled out and is the simplest way to apply, pay and receive a visa almost instantly. It is expected to replace the visa-on-arrival scheme soon. Contact your nearest Kenyan diplomatic office to get the most up-to-date information.

AIR

Airports

Kenya has three international airports; check out the website www.kaa.go.ke for further information.

Jomo Kenyatta International Airport (p640) Most international flights to and from Nairobi arrive at this airport, 15km southeast of the city. There are two international terminals and a smaller domestic terminal; you can easily walk between the terminals.

Moi International Airport (p319) In Mombasa, 9km west of the city centre, and Kenya's second-busiest international airport. Apart from flights to Zanzibar, this is mainly used by charter airlines and domestic flights.

Wilson Airport (p239) Located 6km south of Nairobi's city centre on Langata Rd. Has some flights between Nairobi and Kilimanjaro International Airport or Mwanza in Tanzania, as well as scheduled and charter domestic flights.

Airlines

The main national airline carrier is **Kenya Airways** (☎Nairobi 020-3274747; www.kenya-airways.com). It has a generally good safety record, with just one fatal incident since 1977.

Other international airlines flying to Nairobi include the following:

Air Mauritius (☎Nairobi 020-822805; www.airmauritius.com)

British Airways (Map p228; ☎Nairobi 020-3277400; www.britishairways.com; Mama Ngina St)

Daallo Airlines (☎Nairobi 020-317318; www.daallo.com)

DEPARTURE TAX

Departure tax is included in the price of a ticket.

Egypt Air (Map p228; ☎Nairobi 020-2226821; www.egyptair.com.eg; City Hall Way)

Emirates (Map p228; ☎Nairobi 020-7602519; www.emirates.com; Uhuru Hwy)

Ethiopian Airlines (Map p228; ☎Nairobi 020-2296000; www.ethiopianairlines.com; Standard St)

KLM (Map p228; ☎Nairobi 020-2958210; www.klm.com; Loita St)

Precision Air (☎Nairobi 020-3274282; www.precisionairtz.com)

Qatar Airways (Map p228; ☎Nairobi 020-2800000; www.qatarairways.com; Loita St)

Rwandair (☎Nairobi 020-343870; www.rwandair.com)

South African Airways (☎Nairobi 020-2247342; www.flysaa.com)

Swiss International Airlines (☎Nairobi 020-2666967; www.swiss.com; Limuru Rd)

Thomson Airways (www.thomson.co.uk)

Tickets

Seasons It's important to note that flight availability and prices are highly seasonal. Conveniently for Europeans, the cheapest fares usually coincide with the European summer holidays, from June to September.

Charter flights It's also worth checking out cheap charter flights to Mombasa from Europe, although these will probably be part of a package deal to a hotel resort on the coast. Prices are often absurdly cheap and there's no obligation to stay at the resort you're booked into.

Onward tickets If you enter Nairobi with no onward or return ticket you may incur the wrath of immigration, and be forced to buy one on the spot – an uncommon but expensive exercise.

LAND

Ethiopia

Security With ongoing problems in South Sudan and Somalia, Ethiopia offers the only viable overland route into Kenya from the north. The security situation around the main entry point at Moyale is changeable – the border is usually open, but security problems often force its closure. Most foreign governments warn against travel to areas of Kenya bordering Ethiopia and, sometimes, along the highway between Isiolo and Moyale. Even so, cattle- and goat-rustling are rife, triggering frequent cross-border tribal wars, so check the security situation carefully before attempting this crossing.

Visas Theoretically, Ethiopian visas can be issued at the Ethiopian embassy in Nairobi, but expect a number of hurdles, including having to provide a letter of introduction from your own embassy in Nairobi, which is likely to be hard to get. Persistence generally pays off, however, so if you have plenty of time, it should be possible to get an Ethiopian visa eventually.

Cars & Motorcycles Those coming to Kenya with their own vehicle could also enter at Fort Banya, on the northeastern tip of Lake Turkana, but it's a risky route with few fuel stops. There's no border post; you must already possess a Kenyan visa and get it stamped on arrival in Nairobi. Immigration are quite used to this, but not having an Ethiopian exit stamp can be a problem if you want to re-enter Ethiopia.

Public Transport There were no cross-border bus services at the time of writing. If you don't have your own transport from Moyale, there's a daily bus between Moyale and Marsabit (KSh800), while lifts can be arranged with the trucks (KSh500).

From immigration on the Ethiopian side of town it's a 2km walk to the Ethiopian and Kenyan customs posts. A yellow-fever vaccination is required to cross either border at Moyale. Unless you fancy being vaccinated at the border, get your jabs in advance and keep the certificate with your passport. A cholera vaccination may also be required.

Tanzania

The main land borders between Kenya and Tanzania are at Namanga, Loitokitok, Taveta, Isebania and Lunga Lunga, and can be reached by public transport. There are no train services between the two countries.

There are also no border crossings open between the Serengeti and the Masai Mara – the closest crossings are at Sirari to the west and (much further away) Namanga to the east. Reports suggest that Kenya would like to open the crossing, but Tanzania remains resolutely opposed. With that being the case, it is highly unlikely that any of the direct Serengeti–Mara border crossings will open in the foreseeable future.

Although all of the routes may be done in stages using a combination of buses and local matatus (minibuses), there are six main routes to/from Tanzania:

- Mombasa–Tanga/Dar es Salaam
- Mombasa–Arusha/Moshi
- Nairobi–Arusha/Moshi (via Namanga)
- Nairobi–Moshi (via Loitokitok)
- Nairobi–Dar es Salaam
- Nairobi–Mwanza

Uganda

The main border posts between Kenya and Uganda are at Busia and Malaba; the latter is an alternative if you're travelling via Kisumu.

There's plenty of cross-border transport, including long-haul bus services between Nairobi and Kampala.

Trekkers in either the Ugandan or Kenyan national parks on Mt Elgon also have the option of walking over the border.

SEA & LAKE

At the time of writing there were no international ferries operating on the coast or Lake Victoria, although there's been talk for years of a cross-lake ferry service between Kenya, Tanzania and Uganda.

Tanzania

It's theoretically possible to travel by dhow between Mombasa and the Tanzanian islands of Pemba and Zanzibar, but first of all you'll have to find a captain who's making the journey and then you'll have to bargain hard to pay a reasonable amount for the trip. The best place to ask about sailings is at Shimoni. There's a tiny immigration post there, but there's no guarantee they'll stamp your passport so you might have to go back to Mombasa for an exit stamp.

Getting Around

AIR

Including the national carrier, Kenya Airways, a handful of domestic operators of varying sizes run scheduled flights within Kenya. Destinations served are predominantly around the coast and the popular national parks, where the highest density of tourist activity takes place. Most operate small planes and many of the 'airports', especially those in the parks, are dirt airstrips with very few if any facilities.

With all airlines, be sure to book well in advance (this is essential during the tourist high season). You should also remember to reconfirm your return flights 72 hours before departure, especially those that connect with an international flight. Otherwise, you may find that your seat has been reallocated. All of the following airlines fly to Nairobi.

Airkenya (p258) Amboseli, Diani Beach, Lamu, Lewa, Malindi, Masai Mara, Meru, Mombasa, Nakuru, Nanyuki and Samburu.

Fly540 (p258) Eldoret, Kisumu, Lamu, Lodwar, Malindi, Masai Mara and Mombasa.

Jambo Jet (☎ Nairobi 020-3274545; www.jambojet.com) Subsidiary of Kenya Airways that flies to Diani Beach, Eldoret, Kisumu, Lamu, Malindi and Mombasa.

Kenya Airways (p373) Kisumu, Malindi and Mombasa.

Mombasa Air Safari (p258) Amboseli, Diani Beach, Kisumu, Lamu, Malindi, Masai Mara, Meru, Mombasa, Samburu and Tsavo West.

Safarilink (p258) Amboseli, Diani Beach, Kiwayu, Lamu, Lewa Downs, Loisaba, Masai Mara, Naivasha, Nanyuki, Samburu, Shaba and Tsavo West.

BICYCLE

Loads of Kenyans get around by bicycle, and while it can be tough for those who are not used to the roads or climate, plenty of hardy visiting cyclists tour the country every year.

Safety Whatever you do, if you intend to cycle here, do as the locals do and get off the road whenever you hear a car coming. And no matter how experienced you are, it would be tantamount to suicide to attempt the road from Nairobi to Mombasa, or from Nairobi to Nakuru, on a bicycle.

Rural touring Cycling is easier in rural areas, and you'll usually receive a warm welcome in any villages you pass through. Many local people operate *boda-bodas* (bicycle or motorcycle taxis), so repair shops are quite common along the roadside. Be wary of cycling on dirt roads as punctures from thorn trees are a major problem.

Mountain biking The hills of Kenya are not particularly steep but can be long and hard. You can expect to cover around 80km per day in the hills of the Western Highlands, somewhat more where the country is flatter. Hell's Gate National Park, near Naivasha, is particularly popular for mountain biking, but you can also explore on two wheels around Mt Kenya, the Masai Mara and Ol Pejeta Conservancy.

Hire It's possible to hire road and mountain bikes in an increasing number of places, usually for KSh600 to KSh1000 per day. Few places require a deposit, unless their machines are particularly new or sophisticated.

BOAT

The only ferry transport on Lake Victoria at the time of writing is across the Winam Gulf between Mbita Point (near Homa Bay) and Luanda Kotieno, where matatus go to Kisumu. You might also find motorised canoes to Mfangano Island from Mbita Point.

BUS

Services Kenya has an extensive network of long- and short-haul bus routes, with particularly good coverage of the areas around Nairobi, the coast and the western regions. Services thin out the further from the capital you get, particularly in the north, and there are still plenty of places where you'll be reliant on matatus.

Operators Buses are operated by a variety of private companies that offer varying levels of comfort, convenience and roadworthiness. They're considerably cheaper than taking the train or flying and, as a rule, services are frequent, fast and can be quite comfortable.

Facilities In general, if you travel during daylight hours, buses are a fairly safe way to get around – you'll certainly be safer in a bus than in a matatu. The best coaches are saved for long-haul and international routes, and offer DVD movies, drinks, toilets and reclining airline-style seats; some of the newer ones even have wi-fi. On shorter local routes, however, you may find yourself on something resembling a battered school bus.

Seating tips Whatever kind of conveyance you find yourself in, don't sit at the back (you'll be thrown around like a rag doll on Kenyan roads) or right at the front (you'll be the first to die in a head-on collision, plus you'll be able to see the oncoming traffic, which is usually best left to the driver or those with nerves of steel).

Safety There are a few security considerations to think about when taking a bus in Kenya. Some routes, most notably the roads from Malindi to Lamu and Isiolo to Marsabit, have been prone to attacks by *shiftas* (bandits) in the past; check things out locally before you travel. Another possible risk is drugged food and drink: it is best to politely refuse any offers of drinks or snacks from strangers.

The main national bus operators in Kenya:

Busways (☎020-2227650) Western Kenya and the coast.

Coastline Safaris (Coast Bus; ☎0722206446; www.coastbus.com) Western and southern Kenya, and Mombasa.

Dreamline Executive (☎0731777799) Nairobi, Mombasa and Malindi.

Easy Coach (Map p228; ☎0726354301, 0738200301; www.easycoach.co.ke; Haile Selassie Ave) Rift Valley and western Kenya.

Modern Coast Express (Oxygen; Map p228; ☎0737940000, 0705700888; www.modern.co.ke; cnr Cross Lane & Accra Rd) Nairobi, Mombasa, Malindi and western Kenya.

Costs

Kenyan buses are pretty economical, with fares starting at around KSh150 for an hour-long journey between towns, while fares between Nairobi and Mombasa begin at KSh600 for the standard journey and can go as high as KSh2000 for premium services.

Reservations

Most bus companies have offices or ticket agents at important stops along their routes, where you can book a seat. For short trips between towns, reservations aren't generally necessary, but for popular longer routes, particularly Nairobi–Kisumu and Nairobi–Mombasa, buying your ticket at least a day in advance is highly recommended.

CAR & MOTORCYCLE

Many travellers bring their own vehicles into Kenya as part of overland trips and, expense notwithstanding, it's a great way to see the country at your own pace. Otherwise, there are numerous car-hire companies that can rent you anything from a small hatchback to a 4WD, although hire rates are very high.

If you're a seasoned driver in African conditions, hiring a sturdy vehicle can also open up relatively inaccessible corners of the country. However, do be aware that Kenyan drivers are some of the most dangerous in the world, and be prepared to have to pull off the main Nairobi–Mombasa highway in order to avoid collisions with oncoming overtaking trucks in your lane. This is definitely not a place for inexperienced or nervous drivers.

If you don't fancy driving yourself, hiring a vehicle with a driver rarely costs a lot more, but then of course you have to pay for the driver's food and accommodation and that quickly adds up.

Automobile Associations

A useful organisation is the **Automobile Association of Kenya** (Map p232; www.aakenya.co.ke).

MAJOR BUS ROUTES

FROM	TO	PRICE (US$)	DURATION (HR)	COMPANY
Mombasa	Tanga	10	4	Modern Coast Express
Mombasa	Dar es Salaam	15-20	5-8	Modern Coast Express
Nairobi	Moshi	40-45	7½	Riverside Shuttle
Nairobi	Arusha	35	5½	Riverside Shuttle
Nairobi	Kampala	30	10-12	Modern Coast Express
Nakuru	Kampala	25	11-12	Easy Coach

Bribes

Although things have improved, police will still stop you and will most likely ask you for a small 'donation' or, as Kenyans say, the police will let you know that they are 'hungry'. To prevent being taken advantage of, always ask for an official receipt – this goes a long way in stopping corruption. Also, always ask for their police number and check it against their ID card as there are plenty of con artists running about. If you're ever asked to go to court, consider saying yes as you just might call their bluff and save yourself a bit of cash.

Driving Licences

An International Driving Permit (IDP) is not necessary in Kenya as most foreign licences are accepted, but it can be useful. If you have a British photo-card licence, be sure to bring the counterfoil, as the date you passed your driving test (something car-hire companies may want to know) isn't printed on the card itself.

Fuel & Spare Parts

Fuel prices Generally lower outside the capital, but can creep up to frighteningly high prices in remote areas and inside national parks, where petrol stations are scarce and you may end up buying dodgy supplies out of barrels from roadside vendors.

Availability Petrol, spare parts and repair shops are readily available at all border towns, though if you're coming from Ethiopia you should plan your supplies carefully, as stops are few and far between on the rough northern roads.

Parts Even if it's an older-model vehicle, local spare-parts suppliers in Kenya are very unlikely to have every little part you might need, so carry as many such parts as you can. Belt breakages are probably the most common disaster you can expect, so bring several spares.

Fire equipment Note that you can be fined by the police for not having a fire triangle and an extinguisher, although the latter is more often asked for in neighbouring Tanzania.

Hire

Hiring a vehicle to tour Kenya (or at least the national parks) is an expensive way of seeing the country, but it does give you freedom of movement and is sometimes the only way of getting to more remote parts of the country. However, unless you're sharing with a sufficient number of people, it's likely to cost more than you'd pay for an organised camping safari with all meals.

Starting rates for hire almost always sound very reasonable, but once you factor in mileage and the various types of insurance, you'll be lucky to pay less than US$50 per day for a saloon car, US$80 per day for a small 4WD or US$150 per day for a proper 4WD.

Hiring a vehicle with unlimited kilometres is the best way to go. Rates are usually quoted without insurance, with the option of paying a daily rate (usually around KSh1500 to KSh3000) for insurance against collision damage and theft. It would be financial suicide to hire a car in Kenya without both kinds of insurance. Otherwise you'll be responsible for the full value of the vehicle if it's damaged or stolen.

Even if you have collision and theft insurance, you'll still be liable for an excess of anywhere between KSh5000 to KSh150,000 (depending on the company) if something happens to the vehicle; always check this before signing. You can usually reduce the excess to zero by paying another KSh1500 to KSh2500 per day for an excess loss waiver. Note that tyres, damaged windscreens and loss of the tool kit are always the hirer's responsibility.As a last sting in the tail (unless you've been quoted an all-inclusive rate), you'll be charged 16% value added tax (VAT) on top of the total cost of hiring the vehicle.

Unless you're just planning on travelling on the main routes between towns, you'll need a 4WD vehicle. Few of the car-hire companies will let you drive 2WD vehicles on dirt roads, including those in the national parks, and if you ignore this proscription and have an accident you'll be personally liable for any damage to the vehicle.

A minimum age of between 23 and 25 years usually applies for hirers. Some companies require you to have been driving for at least two years. An IDP is not required, but you will need to show your passport.

It's generally true to say that the more you pay for a vehicle, the better its condition will be. The larger companies are usually in a better financial position to keep their fleet in good order. Always be sure to check the brakes, the tyres (including the spare), the windscreen wipers and the lights before you set off.

The other factor to consider is what the company will do for you (if anything) if you have a serious breakdown. The major hire companies *may* deliver a replacement vehicle and make arrangements for recovery of the other vehicle at their expense, but with most companies you'll have to get the vehicle fixed and back on the road yourself, and then try to claim a refund.

If you plan to take the car across international borders, check whether the company allows this – many don't, and those that do charge for the privilege.

And a final warning: always return the vehicle with a full tank of petrol; if you don't, the company will charge you twice the going rate to fill up.

We recommend the following local and international hire companies. Be aware that some places offering car hire in Kenya online are scammers. Never wire money to anyone, and double-check the reputation of a company before entering into a contract.

Adventure Upgrade Safaris (Map p228; ☎020-228725, 0722529228; www.adventureupgradesafaris.co.ke; Tom Mboya St) An excellent local company with a good range of vehicles and drivers.

Avis (Map p232; ☎0703046500, 020-2966500; www.avis.co.ke; Xylon Complex, Mombasa Rd) Has outlets in Nairobi, at Jomo Kenyatta Airport, Mombasa and Mombasa airport.

Budget (Map p228; ☎020-652144; www.budget.co.ke; College House, University Way) Offers car hire at both the airport and downtown Nairobi. Also has an office at Mombasa airport.

Central Rent-a-Car (Map p228; ☎020-2222888; www.carhirekenya.com; ground fl, 680 Hotel Bulding, Muindi Mbingu St) Long-standing car-hire agency with 4WDs, SUVs and normal cars at competitive rates.

Market Car Hire (Map p224; ☎020-225797, 0722515053; www.marketcarhire.com; 6th fl, Tower 2, The Mirage, Chiromo Rd) Local car-hire firm with a solid reputation that has been operating for 40 years.

Roadtrip Kenya (Map p232; ☎0791959998; www.roadtripkenya.com; Jungle Junction, Kongoni Rd, Langata) New arrivals in Nairobi, this long-standing Dutch-run agency has been working in Uganda and Tanzania for years and offers excellent value, local knowledge and support.

Parking

In small towns and villages parking is usually free, but there's a pay-parking system in Nairobi, Mombasa, Nakuru, Nyeri, Nanyuki and other main towns. Attendants issue one-day parking permits for around KSh100, valid anywhere in town. If you don't get a permit, you're liable to be wheel-clamped, and getting your vehicle back will cost you a few thousand shillings. With that said, it's always worth staying in a hotel with secure parking if possible.

Road Conditions

Road conditions vary widely in Kenya, from flat, smooth highways to dirt tracks and steep, rocky pathways. Many roads are severely eroded at the edges, reducing the carriageway to a single lane, which is usually occupied by whichever vehicle is bigger in any given situation.

Trouble spots The roads in the north and east of the country are particularly poor, although the situation is improving. The main Mombasa–Nairobi–Malaba road (A104) is badly worn in places due to the constant flow of traffic, but has improved in recent years. The never-ending stream of trucks along this main route through the country will slow travel times considerably.

National parks Roads in national parks are all made of *murram* (dirt) and many have eroded into bone-shaking corrugations through overuse by safari vehicles. Keep your speed down, slowly increasing until you find a suitable speed (when the rattling stops), and be careful when driving after rain. Although some dirt roads can be negotiated in a 2WD vehicle, you're much safer in a 4WD.

Road Hazards

The slightest breakdown can leave you stranded for hours in the bush, so always carry drinking water, emergency food and, if possible, spare fuel.

Vehicles The biggest hazard on Kenyan roads is simply the other vehicles on them, and driving defensively is essential. Ironically, the most dangerous roads in Kenya are probably the well-maintained ones, which allow drivers to go fast enough to do really serious damage in a crash.

Potholes On poor roads, potholes are a dual problem: driving into them can damage your vehicle or cause you to lose control, and sudden avoidance manoeuvres from other vehicles are a constant threat.

People & livestock On all roads, be very careful of pedestrians and cyclists. Animals are another major hazard in rural areas, be it monkeys, herds of goats and cattle, or lone chickens with a death wish.

Acacia thorns These are a common problem if you're driving in remote areas, as they'll pierce even the toughest tyres.

Bandits Certain routes have a reputation for banditry, particularly the Garsen–Garissa–Thika road, which is still essentially off limits to travellers. The road from Isiolo to Marsabit and Moyale has improved considerably security-wise in the last few years, while some coast roads between Lamu and Malindi remain subject to occasional insecurity. Seek local advice before driving any of these routes.

Road Rules

➡ You'll need your wits about you if you're going to tackle driving in Kenya. Driving practices here are some of the worst in the world and all are carried out at breakneck speed. Indicators, lights, horns and hand signals can mean anything from 'I'm about to overtake' to 'Hello *mzungu* (white person)!' or 'Let's play chicken with that elephant', and should never be taken at face value.

➡ Driving is on the left-hand side of the road, but Kenyans habitually drive on the wrong side of the road whenever they see a pothole, an animal or simply a break in the traffic – flashing your lights at the vehicle hurtling towards you should be enough to persuade the driver to get back into their own lane.

➡ Never drive at night unless you absolutely have to, as few cars have adequate headlights and the roads are full of pedestrians and cyclists. Drunk driving is also very common.

➡ Note that foreign-registered vehicles with a seating capacity of more than six people are not allowed into Kenyan national parks and reserves; jeeps should be fine, but VW Kombis and other campervans may have problems.

HITCHING

Hitchhiking is never entirely safe in any country, and we don't recommend it. Travellers who hitch should understand they are taking a small but potentially serious risk. It's safer to travel in pairs and let someone know where you are planning to go. Also beware of drunken drivers. Although it's risky, many locals have no choice but to hitch, so people will know what you're doing if you try to flag down cars.

Signalling The traditional thumb signal will probably be understood, but locals use a palm-downwards wave to get cars to stop.

Contributions Many Kenyan drivers expect a contribution towards petrol or some kind of gift from foreign passengers, so make it clear from the outset if you are expecting a free ride.

National parks If you're hoping to hitch into the national parks, dream on! You'll get further asking around for travel companions in Nairobi or any of the gateway towns.

Local hitchers On the other side of the wheel, foreign drivers will be approached regularly by Kenyan hitchers demanding free rides – giving a lift to a carload of Maasai is certainly a memorable cultural experience.

LOCAL TRANSPORT

Boda-Boda

Boda-bodas (bicycle or motorcycle taxis) are common in areas where standard taxis are hard to find, and also operate in smaller towns and cities such as Nakuru or Kisumu. There's a particular proliferation on the coast, where the bicycle boys also double as touts, guides and drug dealers in tourist areas. A short ride should cost around KSh100 or so.

Matatu

Local matatus are the main means of getting around for local people, and any reasonably sized city or town will have plenty of services covering every major road and suburb.

Fares These start at around KSh40 and may reach KSh100 for longer routes in Nairobi.

Vehicles The vehicles themselves can be anything from dilapidated Peugeot 504 pickups with a cab on the back to big 20-seater minibuses. The most common are white Nissan minibuses (many local people prefer the name 'Nissans' to matatus).

Shared Taxi

Shared Peugeot taxis are a good alternative to matatus. The vehicles are usually Peugeot 505 station wagons that take seven to nine passengers and leave when full.

Peugeots take less time to reach their destinations than matatus as they fill quicker and go from point to point without stopping, and so are slightly more expensive. Many companies have offices around the Accra, Cross and River Rds area in Nairobi, and serve destinations mostly in the north and west of the country.

Taxi

Even the smallest Kenyan towns generally have at least one banged-up old taxi for easy access to outlying areas or even more remote villages, and you'll find cabs on virtually every corner in the larger cities, especially in Nairobi and Mombasa, where taking a taxi at night is virtually mandatory.

Fares These are invariably negotiable and start around KSh350 to KSh600 for short journeys. Since few taxis in Kenya actually have functioning meters (or drivers who adhere to them), it's advisable that you agree on the fare prior to setting out. This will inevitably save you the time and trouble of arguing with your cabbie over the fare.

Bookings Most people pick up cabs from taxi ranks on the street, but some companies will take phone bookings and most hotels can order you a ride.

Tuk-Tuk

They're an incongruous sight outside southeast Asia, but several Kenyan towns and cities have these distinctive motorised minitaxis. The highest concentration is in Malindi, but they're also in Nairobi, Mombasa, Nakuru, Machakos and Diani Beach; Watamu has a handful of less sophisticated motorised rickshaws. Fares are negotiable, but should be at least KSh100 less than the equivalent taxi rate for a short journey (and you wouldn't want to take them on a long one!).

MATATU

Matatus, usually in the form of minivans, are the workhorses of Kenya's transport system. Apart from in the remote northern areas, where you'll rely on occasional buses or paid lifts on trucks, you can almost always find a matatu going to the next town or further afield, so long as it's not too late in the day. Simply ask around among the drivers at the local matatu stand or 'stage'. Matatus leave when full and the fares are fixed. It's unlikely you will be charged more than other passengers.

Safety Despite a periodic government drive to regulate the matatu industry, matatus remain notorious for dangerous driving, overcrowding and general shady business. A passenger backlash has seen a small but growing trend in more responsible matatu companies offering less crowding, safer driving and generally better security on intercity services. Mololine Prestige Shuttle is one of these plying the route from Nairobi to Kisumu or Nakuru.

Accidents As with buses, roads are usually busy enough for a slight shunt to be the most likely accident, though of course congestion never stops drivers jockeying for position like it's the Kenya Derby. Wherever you go, remember that most matatu crashes are head-on collisions – under no circumstances should you sit in the 'death seat' next to the matatu driver. Play it safe and sit in the middle seats away from the window.

TRAIN

The Uganda Railway was once the main trade artery in East Africa and, after massive investment, will be again. Inaugurated in 2017, the new high-speed Nairobi–Mombasa rail service has cut travelling time from 18 hours (the old train service) to just 4½ hours. It's faster, cheaper and safer than taking the bus. The service stops in Mtito Andei and Voi.

The line – operated by Kenya Railways – will eventually extend to Naivasha as well (with a branch line to Kisumu), and then on to Kampala in Uganda, if all goes to plan.

Classes & Costs

There are two classes on Kenyan trains – as all services are seat only, the difference between the two is all to do with comfort.

Services are likely to increase over the coming years, but for now there's one 9am departure daily in each direction. From Nairobi, services stop at Mtito Andei (one way 2nd/1st class KSh360/1490, 2¼ hours) and Voi (KSh510/2130, 3½ hours) en route to Mombasa (KSh900/3000, 4½ hours).

Reservations

There are booking offices at the train stations in Nairobi (Syokimau Railway Station) and Mombasa, and at present it's recommended that you show up in person; online and phone booking services have been promised, but were not yet operational at the time of writing.

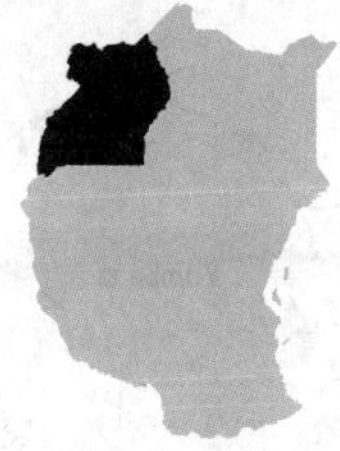

Uganda

☎ 256 / POP 41.5 MILLION

Includes ➡

Kampala........... 384
Entebbe............401
Jinja............. 406
Rwenzori Mountains National Park...... 436
Queen Elizabeth National Park...... 439
Bwindi Impenetrable National Park...... 445
Mgahinga Gorilla National Park.......457
Murchison Falls National Park...... 468

Best Places to Eat

- ➡ Khana Khazana (p395)
- ➡ Prunes (p395)
- ➡ Thai Garden (p405)
- ➡ Elephante (p423)
- ➡ Nurali's Café (p414)
- ➡ Mama Ashanti (p395)

Best Places to Stay

- ➡ Papaya Lake Lodge (p430)
- ➡ Wildwaters Lodge (p412)
- ➡ Fort Murchison (p472)
- ➡ Little Elephant Camp (p443)
- ➡ Bwindi Lodge (p449)

Why Go?

With a tapestry of landscapes, excellent wildlife watching and welcoming locals, Uganda packs a lot into one small country. It's home to Africa's tallest mountain range (the Rwenzoris), the source of the Nile, the world's longest river and the continent's largest lake. Rafting the Nile offers a world-class adrenaline adventure, but the country's most iconic experience is tracking mountain gorillas in their misty habitat. And if you view the Big Five, you'll see that nature – diverse and resplendent – looms large here.

Emerging from the shadows of Uganda's dark history, tourism is returning the sheen to the 'pearl of Africa'. While anti-gay sentiments mar an otherwise positive picture, Uganda remains one of the safest destinations in Africa – save for the odd hippo at your campsite. Don't rush. Here you'll find the best the continent has to offer at a good value and with fewer visitors than in longer-established East African destinations.

When to Go

Kampala

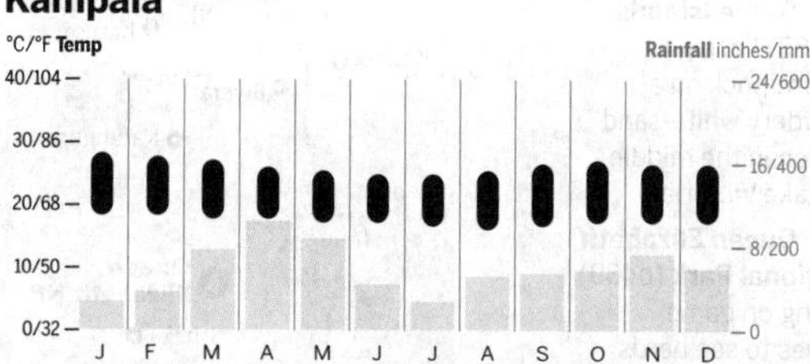

Jun–Sep The best bet weatherwise: not too hot with minimal rainfall.

Jan–Feb Perfect climate to head for the hills to climb the Rwenzoris or Mt Elgon.

Oct–Nov Can be rainy, but fewer travellers means gorilla permits are much easier to obtain.

Uganda Highlights

1. **Bwindi Impenetrable National Park** (p445) Trekking through the jungle to marvel at critically endangered mountain gorillas.
2. **Nile River** (p409) Taking on the wild waters of the Kalagala Falls, some of the best white-water rafting in East Africa.
3. **Murchison Falls** (p468) Gazing upon the world's most powerful waterfall during a boat ride up the Victoria Nile.
4. **Lake Bunyonyi** (p453) Chilling out on a remote island on the most beautiful lake in Uganda.
5. **Kidepo Valley National Park** (p419) Exploring unvarnished Africa at its wild and colourful best.
6. **Rwenzori Mountains** (p436) Tackling the ice-capped peaks of Africa's highest range, evocatively known as the 'Mountains of the Moon'.
7. **Ssese Islands** (p463) Lazing in a hammock on a powdery white-sand beach in the middle of Lake Victoria.
8. **Queen Elizabeth National Park** (p439) Going on game drives to see herds of elephants, hippos, giraffes and lions.

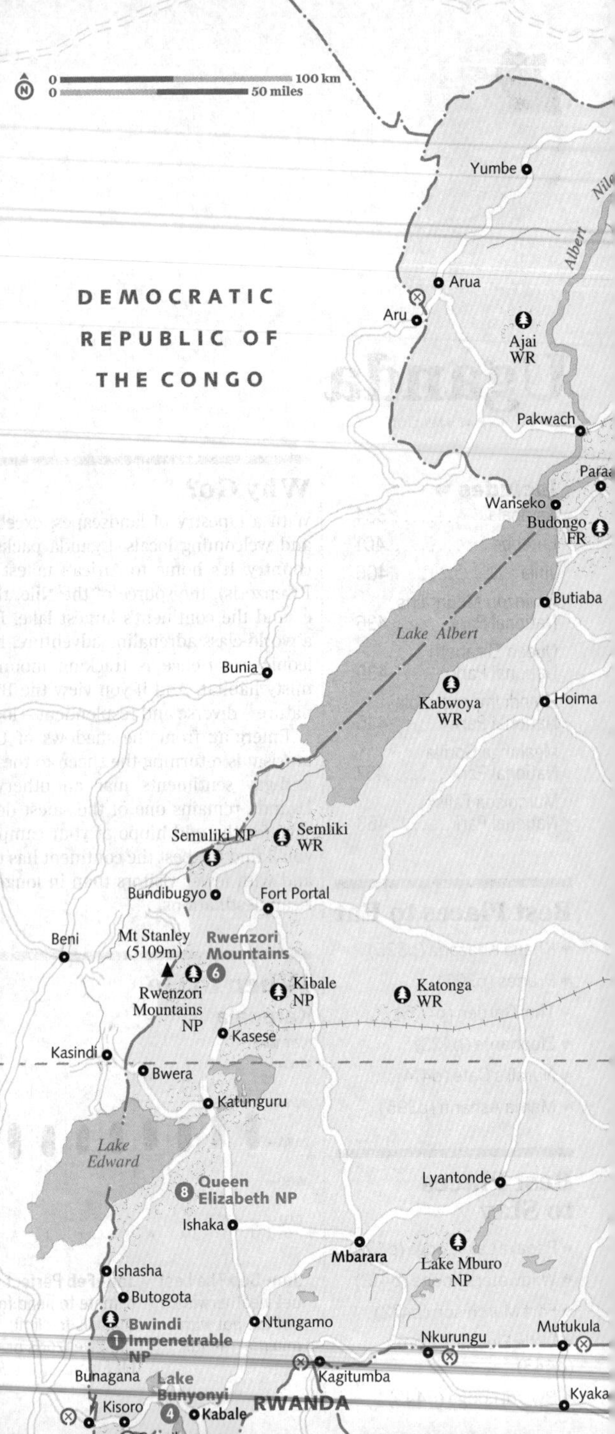

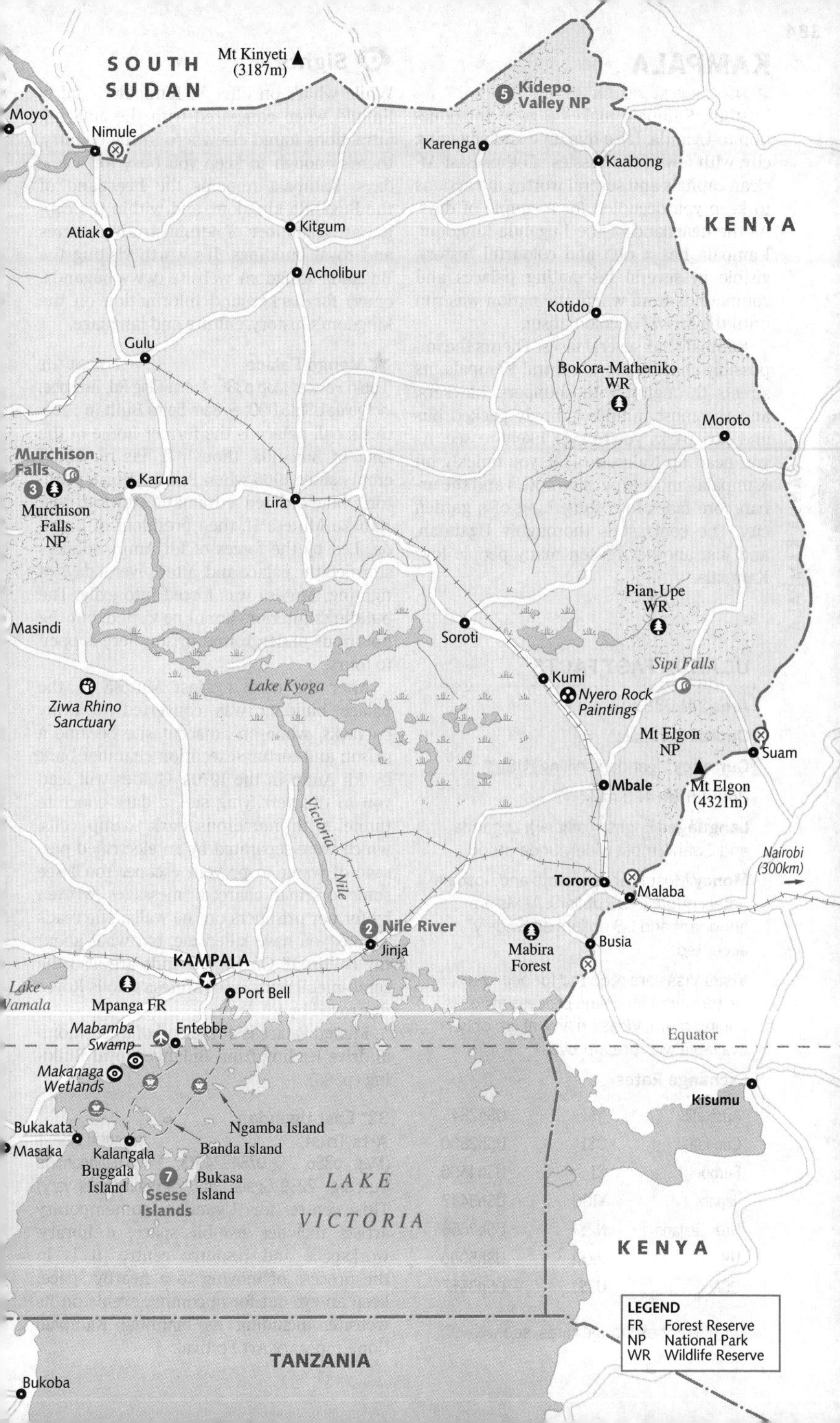

SOUTH SUDAN
Mt Kinyeti (3187m)
Kidepo Valley NP
Moyo
Nimule
Karenga
Kaabong
KENYA
Atiak
Kitgum
Acholibur
Kotido
Gulu
Bokora-Matheniko WR
Moroto
Murchison Falls
Murchison Falls NP
Karuma
Lira
Pian-Upe WR
Masindi
Soroti
Sipi Falls
Lake Kyoga
Kumi
Nyero Rock Paintings
Ziwa Rhino Sanctuary
Mt Elgon NP
Suam
Mbale
Mt Elgon (4321m)
Victoria Nile
Nairobi (300km)
Tororo
Malaba
Nile River
Mabira Forest
Busia
Jinja
KAMPALA
Lake Wamala
Mpanga FR
Port Bell
Mabamba Swamp
Entebbe
Equator
Makanaga Wetlands
Kisumu
Ngamba Island
Bukakata
Masaka
Kalangala
Banda Island
Buggala Island
Ssese Islands
Bukasa Island
LAKE VICTORIA
KENYA
LEGEND
FR Forest Reserve
NP National Park
WR Wildlife Reserve
TANZANIA
Bukoba

KAMPALA

0414 / POP 1.6 MILLION

Bustling Kampala makes a good introduction to Uganda. It's a dynamic and engaging city, with few of the hassles of other East African capitals and several worthy attractions to keep you occupied for a couple of days. As the heartland of the Buganda kingdom, Kampala has a rich and colourful history, visible in several fascinating palaces and compounds from where the nation was run until the arrival of colonialism.

Kampala has several faces. There's the impossibly chaotic jam of central Kampala, its streets thronging with shoppers, hawkers, and the most mind-bogglingly packed bus and taxi parks you're ever likely to see. As you head up Nakasero Hill, you quickly hit Kampala's most expensive hotels and the urban core fades into something of a garden city. The contrast is thoroughly Ugandan, and just another reason many people love Kampala.

UGANDA FAST FACTS

Area 241,038 sq km

Capital Kampala

Currency Ugandan shilling (USh)

Population 41.5 million

Languages English (official), Luganda and Swahili most widely understood

Money Most tour operators and upscale hotels quote in US dollars. ATMs are abundant and US dollars are widely accepted.

Visas Visas are required for nearly all visitors, with an online process for obtaining them. Visas on arrival are only available with preapproval.

Exchange Rates

Australia	A$1	USh2845
Canada	C$1	USh2800
Europe	€1	USh4500
Japan	¥100	USh3442
New Zealand	NZ$1	USh2656
UK	UK£1	USh5096
USA	US$1	USh3657

For current exchange rates, see www.xe.com.

Sights

While what's on offer in Kampala is fairly limited when compared with the amazing attractions found elsewhere in the country, there's enough to keep you busy for a few days. Kampala remains the heartland of the Buganda kingdom, and within the capital are a number of administrative centres and royal buildings. It's worth visiting the Buganda Kingdom website (www.buganda.or.ug) for background information on the kingdom's history, culture and language.

★Mengo Palace HISTORIC SITE

(Lubiri Palace; Map p386; Lubiri Ring Rd, Twekobe; incl guide USh15,000; 8am-5pm) Built in 1922, this small palace is the former home of the king of Buganda, though it has remained empty since 1966 when Prime Minister Milton Obote ordered a dramatic attack to oust Kabaka Mutesa II, then president of Uganda. Led by the forces of Idi Amin, soldiers stormed the palace and, after several days of fighting, Mutesa was forced into exile. The building's interior cannot be visited, but the notorious underground prison here is open to tours.

After the coup against Mutesa II, the palace building was converted to army barracks, while an adjacent site became a prison and torture-execution chamber built by Idi Amin in the 1970s. Guides will lead you to this terrifying site, a dark concrete tunnel with numerous dark, damp cells, which were separated by an electrified passage of water to prevent escape. You'll see some original charcoal messages written by former prisoners on the walls: one reads 'Obote, you have killed me, but what about my children!' On the grounds are also the scrap-metal remains of Mutesa's Rolls Royce destroyed by Idi Amin.

Mengo Palace is at the end of a ceremonial drive leading from Bulange Royal Building (p385).

32° East Ugandan Arts Trust CULTURAL CENTRE

(Map p386; 0784924513; www.ugandanartstrust.org; 2239 Ggaba Rd; exhibit times vary) This centre for Ugandan contemporary artists includes exhibit space, a library, workspace and resource centre. It is in the process of moving to a nearby space; keep an eye out for upcoming events on its website, including its biannual Kampala Contemporary Art Festival.

Kampala Hindu Temple TEMPLE
(Map p388; ☎0414-256036; 8 Snay Bin Amir Rise; ⊙4-7.30pm) Right in the city centre, this temple has elaborate towers and a swastika-emblazoned gate. Peek inside to see the unexpected dome.

Kasubi Tombs MAUSOLEUM
(Map p386; www.kasubitombs.org; Kasubi Hill; USh10,000; ⊙8am-5pm) The Unesco World Heritage–listed Kasubi Tombs are of great significance to the Buganda kingdom as the burial place of its kings and royal family. The huge thatched-roof palace was originally built in 1882 as the palace of Kabaka Mutesa I, before being converted into his tomb following his death two years later. The tombs were destroyed in an arson attack in March 2010, however, and are still being rebuilt, with no end to the work in sight at present.

Outside, forming a ring around the main section of the compound, are the homes (fortunately not damaged by the fire) of the families of the widows of former *kabaka* (kings). Royal family members are buried amid the trees out the back, and the whole place has the distinct feel of a small rural village.

Parliament House NOTABLE BUILDING
(Map p388; Parliament Ave; ⊙8.30am-4.30pm Mon-Fri) Open to the public, a visit to parliament is an interesting way to spend an hour or two. You can either tour the building or see the government in action – during sitting weeks, parliament operates from 2.30pm Tuesday to Thursday and is conducted in English. You need to visit the public-relations department (room 114) to arrange a visit and make a written request to see question time. Usually you can arrange a visit on the spot.

You'll need to bring an identification card and be decently dressed.

In the main lobby look out for the huge wooden cultural map of Uganda featuring the country's flora and fauna.

National Mosque MOSQUE
(Gadaffi Mosque; Map p388; Old Kampala Rd; incl tour USh10,000) One of Kampala's premier sights, the prominent National Mosque (widely known as the Gadaffi Mosque) was begun by Idi Amin in 1972 but only completed in 2007 with a donation from Colonel Gadaffi. The hour-long tour allows you to scale its soaring minaret for the best views of Kampala, and takes you within its gleaming interior. Free entry for Muslims.

Wamala Tombs HISTORIC SITE
(Map p386; Nansana, Wasiko District; incl guide USh10,000; ⊙8am-5pm) A low-key Buganda royal site, Wamala Tombs is 11km north of Kasub. Arrange a guided visit at Kasubi Tombs.

Uganda Martyrs' Shrine HISTORIC SITE
(Map p386; ☎0312-274581; www.ugandamartyrsshrine.org.ug; Namugongo; USh15,000; ⊙9am-6pm) Located in Namugongo, this shrine marks the spot where Kabaka Mwanga II ordered the execution of 14 Catholics who refused to denounce their faith, including church leader Charles Lwanga who was burnt alive on or around 3 June 1886 – which is now celebrated as Martyrs' Day. The shrine represents an African hut but looks more like something built by NASA than the Catholic church.

The shrine is 15km outside Kampala, off Jinja Rd. To get here, take a minibus from Kampala's Old Taxi Park (p400).

Namirembe Cathedral CHURCH
(Map p388; ☎0414-270212; Namirembe Hill) This huge domed Anglican cathedral, finished in 1919, has a distinct Mediterranean feel. In years past the congregation was called to worship by the beating of enormous drums, which can still be seen in a little hut alongside the church.

Uganda Museum MUSEUM
(Map p388; ☎0414-267538; Kira Rd; adult/child USh5000/2500; ⊙10am-5.30pm) There's plenty to interest you here with a varied and well-captioned ethnographic collection covering clothing, hunting, agriculture, medicine, religion and recreation, as well as archaeological and natural-history displays. Highlights include traditional musical instruments, some of which you can play, and the fossil remains of a Napak rhino, a species that became extinct eight million years ago. Head outside to wander through the traditional thatched homes of the various tribes of Uganda; plus get a look at Idi Amin's Mercedes.

Bulange Royal Building NOTABLE BUILDING
(Map p388; www.buganda.or.ug; Kabakanjagala Rd; incl guide US$10; ⊙8am-5pm) A great place to learn about the history and culture of the Buganda Kingdom; guided tours take you inside the parliament building, providing interesting stories and details about the 56 different clans. Buganda Parliament is held twice a month on Monday mornings, though it is conducted in Lugandan. Buy your ticket

Kampala

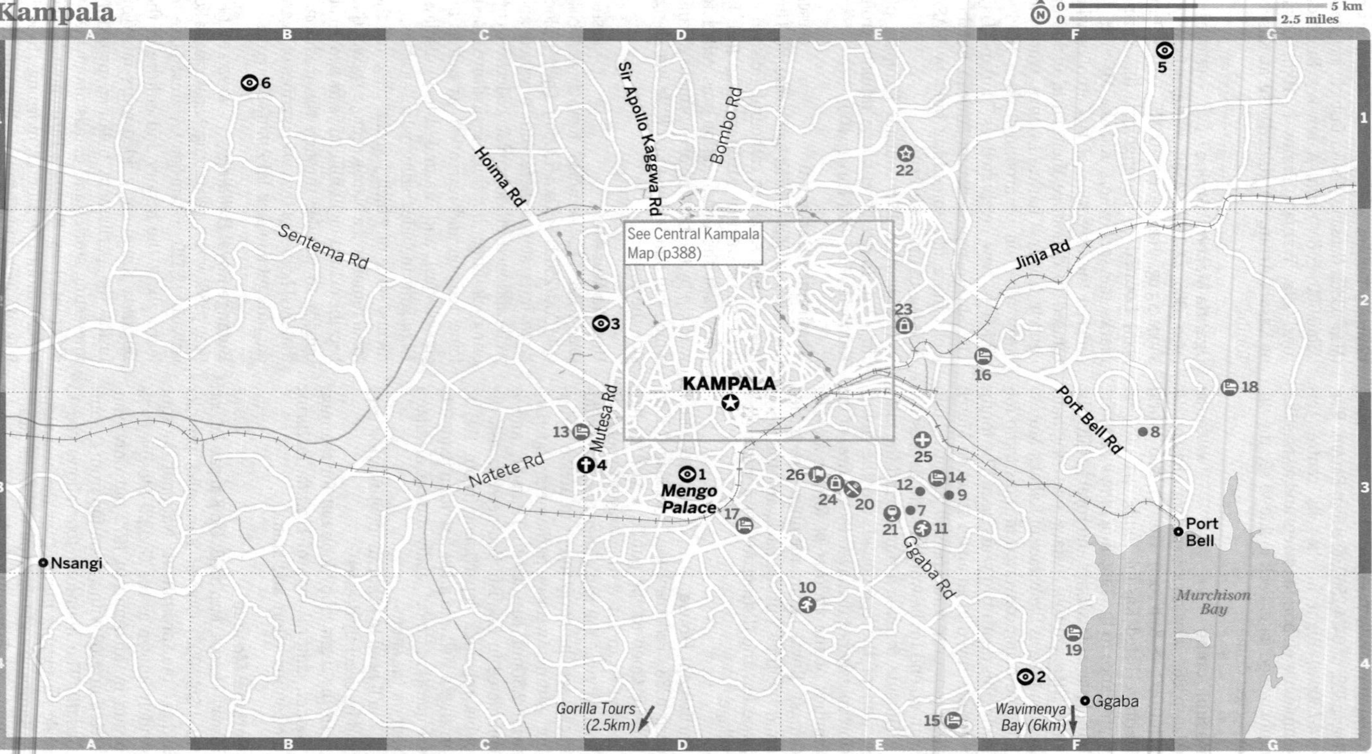
0 5 km
0 2.5 miles
Sir Apollo Kaggwa Rd
Bombo Rd
Hoima Rd
Sentema Rd
See Central Kampala Map (p388)
Jinja Rd
KAMPALA
Port Bell Rd
Mutesa Rd
Natete Rd
Mengo Palace
Ggaba Rd
Port Bell
Nsangi
Murchison Bay
Gorilla Tours (2.5km)
Wavimenya Bay (6km)
Ggaba

Kampala

Top Sights
1 Mengo Palace ... D3

Sights
2 32° East Ugandan Arts Trust ... F4
3 Kasubi Tombs ... D2
4 Rubaga Cathedral ... D3
5 Uganda Martyrs' Shrine ... F1
6 Wamala Tombs ... B1

Activities, Courses & Tours
7 Changing Horizons ... E3
8 Great Lakes Safaris ... F3
9 Matoke Tours ... E3
Red Chilli Hideaway ... (see 18)
10 Red Dirt Mountain Biking ... E4
11 Refuge & Hope ... E3
12 Road Trip Uganda ... E3

Sleeping
13 Backpackers Hostel ... C3
14 Banda Inns ... E3
15 Cassia Lodge ... E4
16 Le Bougainviller ... F2
17 Makindye Country Club ... D3
18 Red Chilli Hideaway ... G2
19 Yellow Haven Lodge ... F4

Eating
20 Le Chateau ... E3
Quality Hill ... (see 24)

Drinking & Nightlife
21 Deuces ... E3

Entertainment
22 Ndere Centre ... E1

Shopping
23 Banana Boat ... E2
Game ... (see 23)
24 Quality Hill ... E3

Information
25 International Hospital Kampala ... E3
26 US Embassy ... E3

at the adjacent Buganda Tourism Centre (p399) which also sells bark-cloth clothing and books on Bugandan culture.

Rubaga Cathedral CHURCH
(Map p386; ☎0414-258112; Rubaga Hill) This twin-towered Roman Catholic cathedral has a memorial to the Uganda Martyrs, with 22 Catholic victims (later declared saints) enshrined in the stained-glass windows. They were among other Ugandan Christians burnt or hacked to death by Kabaka Mwanga II in 1885 and 1886 for refusing to renounce the 'white man's religion'.

Activities

Refuge & Hope VOLUNTEERING
(Map p386; ☎0781699872; www.refugeandhope.org; 1694 Mitala Rd, Kitsana) This nonprofit helps refugees living in Kampala to rebuild their lives through education and personal and professional development.

Red Dirt Mountain Biking MOUNTAIN BIKING
(Map p386; ☎0772458796; www.reddirtuganda.com; 479 Mubuto Rd, Makindye; day tour USh150,000;) Offering jaunts outside Kampala, Jinja rides and original mountain-bike safaris to Lake Mburo, this is the two-wheel tour operator of choice. Day trips (including transport, guide and snack) take a 30-minute boat ride across Lake Victoria to fire roads and single tracks that feel a world away from the city. Also rents out and repairs bikes.

Uganda Charity Trust Fund VOLUNTEERING
(UCTF; Map p388; ☎0782469402; www.uctf.org; Plot 2A Lugogo Lane, Naguru) A charity specialising in youth development offers varied roles for skilled volunteers including teaching and coaching disadvantaged kids. Most programs are run out of Kampala.

Tours

★**Road Trip Uganda** SELF-DRIVE TOURS
(Map p386; ☎0773363012; www.roadtripuganda.com; off Tank Hill Rd, Muyenga) Popular with adventurous travellers, this Dutch-owned company fills a much-needed market by providing an affordable option for self-drive (or guided) tours in fully equipped RAV4s and Land Cruisers. It offers a good selection prebooked self-drive routes, which include accommodation bookings and detailed itineraries. Full camping equipment is available for an extra US$5 per day.

Walter's Boda-Boda Tours TOURS
(☎0791880106; www.walterstours.com; per person US$40) These unique, half-day city tours are taken sitting on the back of a *boda-boda* in a group travelling at a safe pace. Tours take in the main sights, and incorporate local experiences such as sampling Ugandan food and banana beer. It also runs tours further afield. Helmets are provided.

Central Kampala

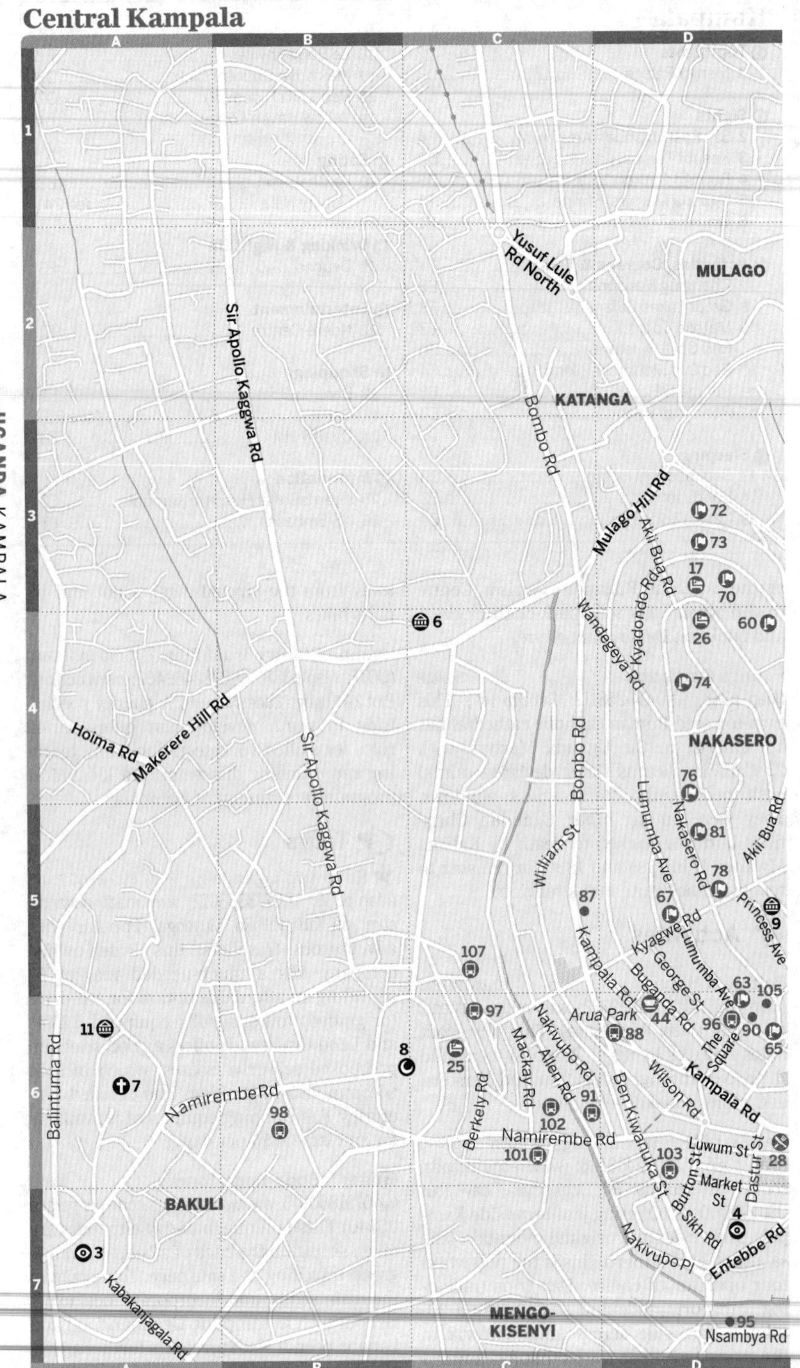

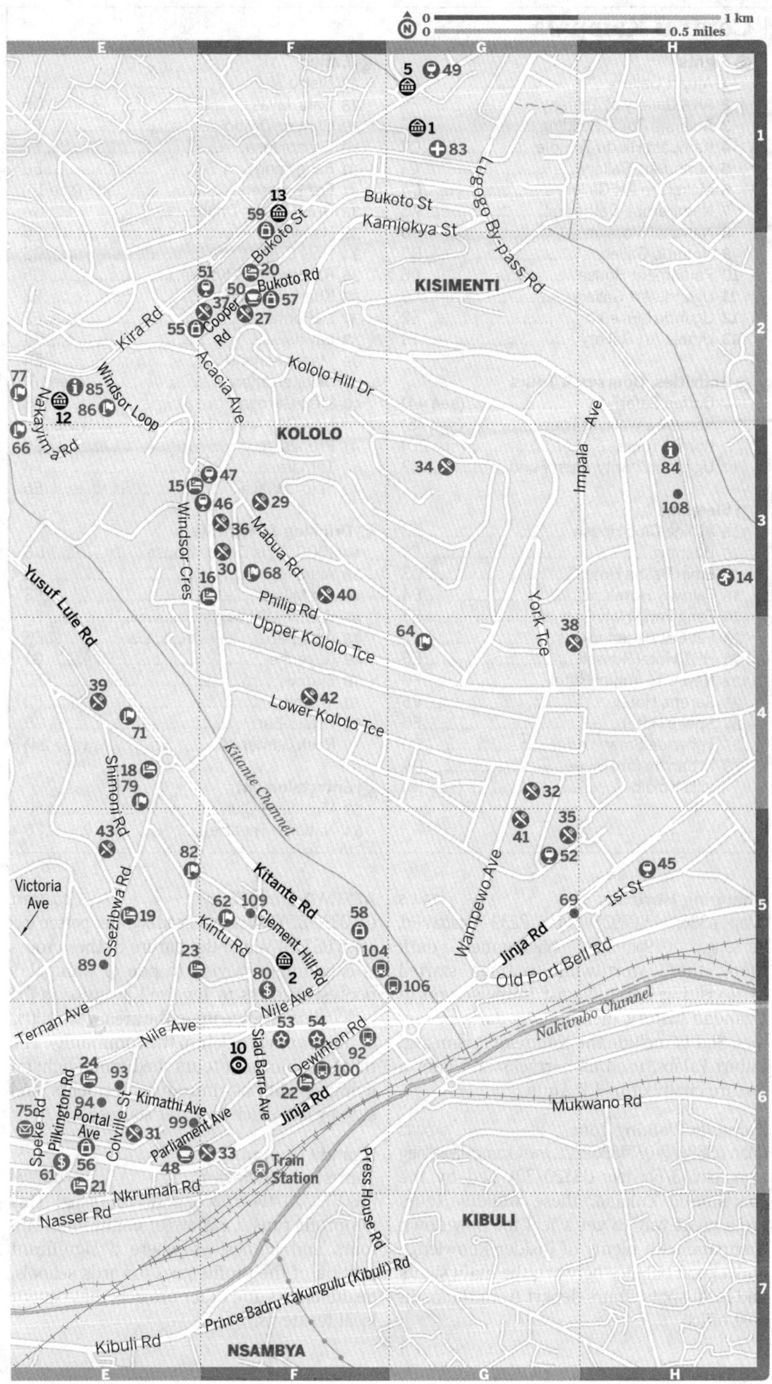
0
1 km
0
0.5 miles
KISIMENTI
KOLOLO
KIBULI
NSAMBYA
Bukoto St
Kamjokya St
Lugogo By-pass Rd
Bukoto Rd
Kira Rd
Cooper Rd
Acacia Ave
Kololo Hill Dr
Windsor Loop
Nakayima Rd
Windsor Cres
Mabua Rd
Philip Rd
Upper Kololo Tce
Lower Kololo Tce
Impala Ave
York Tce
Yusuf Lule Rd
Shimoni Rd
Kitante Channel
Kitante Rd
Ssezibwa Rd
Victoria Ave
Kintu Rd
Clement Hill Rd
Wampewo Ave
Jinja Rd
1st St
Old Port Bell Rd
Nakivubo Channel
Ternan Ave
Nile Ave
Siad Barre Ave
Dewinton Rd
Kimathi Ave
Speke Rd
Pilkington Rd
Portal Ave
Colville St
Parliament Ave
Train Station
Nkrumah Rd
Nasser Rd
Press House Rd
Mukwano Rd
Prince Badru Kakungulu (Kibuli) Rd
Kibuli Rd

Central Kampala

Sights
1 Afriart Gallery G1
2 AKA Gallery at Tulifanya F5
3 Bulange Royal Building A7
4 Kampala Hindu Temple D7
5 Karibu Art Gallery G1
6 Makerere Art Gallery C4
7 Namirembe Cathedral A6
8 National Mosque B6
9 Nommo Gallery D5
10 Parliament House F6
11 Uganda Art Gallery A6
12 Uganda Museum E2
13 Umoja Art Gallery F1

Activities, Courses & Tours
Coffee Safari .... (see 44)
Kampala Walking Tour .... (see 75)
Kombi Tours .... (see 20)
14 Uganda Charity Trust Fund H3

Sleeping
15 Athina Club House E3
16 Bushpig F3
17 Emin Pasha Hotel D3
18 Fairway Hotel E4
19 Fang Fang Hotel E5
20 Fat Cat Backpackers F2
21 HBT Hotel Russell E6
22 New City Annex Hotel F6
23 Serena Hotel E5
24 Speke Hotel E6
25 Tuhende Safari Lodge C6
26 Urban by City Blue D4
Villa Kololo .... (see 16)

Eating
27 Bistro F2
28 Cafe Javas D6
29 Cantine Divino F3
30 Casablanca F3
31 Fang Fang E6
Fez Brasserie .... (see 17)
32 Great Indian Dhaba G4
33 Haandi F6
34 Holy Crêpe G3
35 Kardamom & Koffee G5
36 Khana Khazana F3
37 La Fontaine F2
38 Lawns G4
39 Mama Ashanti E4
Mediterraneo .... (see 16)
40 Miso Garden F3
New City Annex Hotel .... (see 22)
41 Prunes G5
42 Tamarai F4
43 Yujo Izakaya E5

Drinking & Nightlife
44 1000 Cups Coffee House D6
45 Ange Noir H5
46 Big Mike's F3
47 Bubbles O'Learys F3
48 Café Pap E6
49 Cayenne G1
50 Endiro F2
51 Iguana F2
52 Otters Bar G5
Rock Garden .... (see 24)

Entertainment
53 Musicians Club F6
54 National Theatre F6

Changing Horizons TOURS
(Map p386; ☎0793845147; 2239 Ggaba Rd, Kansanga; ⊙9am-5pm) Nicknamed 'dark tours', these worthwhile outings started by a visiting criminologist immerse you in Ugandan history, including its darker chapters. Sights include the Katareke Prison and Lubiri Palace, used as barracks and later a torture chamber by Idi Amin.

Kampala Walking Tour WALKING
(Map p388; ☎0774596222; www.kampalawalkingtours.com; 3/6hr tour US$20/30) Led by the charismatic Zulaika, these walking tours are a great way to get a feel for downtown Kampala, with plenty of insider knowledge and a good balance between the main sights and local spots. Tours depart from the main post office.

AFFCAD Slum Tour CULTURAL
(☎0392-859254; www.affcad.org; per person incl lunch US$25) While the nature of these tours is contentious, a visit to one of Kampala's poorest districts in Bwaise-Kawempe is led by locals who grew up in the area, with 100% of funds going back into the community. The three- to four-hour tours shed brutal light on living conditions, introduce residents and stop by sites such as water sources.

Uganda Community Tourism Association CULTURAL
(UCOTA; ☎0414-501866; www.ucota.or.ug) This nonprofit runs a variety of community-run tours and homestays where a significant portion of the profits goes towards schools, health clinics and other projects that benefit local residents.

Shopping
55 Aristoc ... E2
56 Aristoc ... E6
57 Banana Boat ... F2
Bold ... (see 55)
Def.i.ni.tion ... (see 55)
58 Garden City Complex ... F5
59 Kampala Fair ... F1
Nakumatt ... (see 55)

Information
60 Australian Consulate ... D4
61 Barclays ... E6
Belgium Embassy ... (see 90)
Buganda Tourism Centre ... (see 3)
62 Burundi Embassy ... F5
Canadian Embassy ... (see 99)
63 Danish Embassy ... D6
64 DRC Embassy ... G4
65 Dutch Embassy ... D6
66 Ethiopian Embassy ... E3
67 French Embassy ... D5
68 German Embassy ... F3
69 Immigration Office ... G5
70 Indian Embassy ... D3
71 Irish Embassy ... E4
72 Italian Embassy ... D3
73 Japanese Embassy ... D3
74 Kenyan High Commission ... D4
75 Main Post Office ... E6
76 Nigerian High Commission ... D4
77 Rwandan Embassy ... E2
78 South African High Commission ... D5
79 South Sudan Embassy ... E4
80 Stanbic ... F5
81 Sudan Embassy ... D5
82 Tanzanian High Commission ... E5
83 The Surgery ... G1
84 Tourism Uganda ... H3
85 Uganda Wildlife Authority ... E2
86 UK Embassy ... E2

Transport
87 Alpha Car Rentals ... C5
88 Arua Park ... D6
89 British Airways ... E5
90 Brussels Airlines ... D6
91 Buganda Bus Park ... C6
92 Easy Coach ... F6
93 Emirates ... E6
94 Ethiopian Airlines ... E6
95 Europcar ... D7
96 Falcon ... D6
97 Friends Safari ... C6
Hertz ... (see 31)
98 Jaguar Executive Coaches ... B6
99 Kenya Airways ... E6
KLM ... (see 99)
100 Mash ... F6
101 New Bus Park ... C6
102 New Taxi Park ... C6
103 Old Taxi Park ... D6
104 Pineapple Express ... F5
Post Bus ... (see 75)
105 Qatar Airways ... D6
106 Queens Coach ... G5
RwandAir ... (see 90)
107 Simba (Namayiba Terminal) ... C5
108 South African Airways ... H3
109 Turkish Airlines ... F5

Coffee Safari TOURS
(Map p388; 0772505619; www.1000cupscoffee.com; 18 Buganda Rd; US$100; 7.30am Fri) You can trace your coffee from the cup to the farm on day tours run by 1000 Cups Coffee House (p397). Book before noon on Thursday.

Festivals & Events

Kampala City Festival CULTURAL
(www.kcca.go.ug; 1st week Oct) One of East Africa's biggest street parties is held early each October with floats and performers celebrating Ugandan culture. Traditional and contemporary art, fashion and music are all showcased over multiple stages.

Amakula International Film Festival FILM
(www.amakula.org; Mar) Hosted at the Uganda Museum (p385), the Amakula International Film Festival is one of Africa's oldest independent film festivals, and shows Ugandan and international features and shorts. It's usually in March, but check the website to confirm dates.

LaBa! Street Arts Festival ART
(www.labaartsfestival.wordpress.com; late May or early Jun) An open-air art space where artists sell their works alongside music and dance performances.

Sleeping

Kampala has some excellent budget and top-end accommodation, but is fairly poorly set up for midrange travellers, though a couple of recent additions have improved things somewhat. Wherever you are, you'll need *boda-bodas* (motorcycle taxis) or minibus taxis to get around, so don't worry too much about what neighbourhood you'll be in – though Kololo is best for nightlife and dining.

★**Bushpig** HOSTEL $

(Map p388; ☎0772285234; www.bushpigkampala.com; 31 Acacia Ave, Kololo; d US$45, dm/s/d/tr with shared bathroom US$15/25/40/53; 📶) A slice of luxury by the standards of African hostels, Bushpig is housed in a smart complex that also functions as a posh hotel and restaurant. The staff are exceptionally friendly and the cool vibe in the dorms and spacious doubles makes up for the street noise outside. Best of all is the excellent hostel restaurant and great water pressure.

★**Red Chilli Hideaway** HOSTEL $

(Map p386; ☎0312-202903, 0772509150; www.redchillihideaway.com; 13-23 Bukasa Hill View Rd, Butabika; camping/dm/s/d/tr US$8/12/45/50/55, s/d/tr with shared bathroom from US$30/35/40; @📶🏊) Red Chilli has created its dream hostel on these premises. Drawing upon years of experience, the end results include piping-hot water, comfy beds, a saltwater pool, beach volleyball, a grassy lawn, pizzeria, multiple bars, tasty and cheap meals, free computers and a TV lounge – it's all here. Day visitors (adult/child USh10,000/5000) can use the pool.

Banda Inns GUESTHOUSE $

(Map p386; ☎0759334746, 0751789538; www.bandainns.com; Scops Lane, off Lubbobbo Cl; s/d from €30/45; 📶) A large multiroom house with a breezy terrace and big garden, Banda Inns is rather hidden away at the end of a small side street some way from Kampala's chaotic downtown. A relaxing oasis with kind staff, this relaxed place offers a range of comfortable and well-appointed rooms and a great breakfast.

Fat Cat Backpackers HOSTEL $

(Map p388; ☎0771393892; www.fatcatafrica.com; 13 Bukoto St, Kololo; dm US$15, s/d/tr with shared bathroom incl breakfast US$30/40/50; 📶) In a cool 1950s art-deco building complete with brushed concrete interiors, the Fat Cat is a top budget choice. The Kololo location is particularly prime if you fancy some night-life. Private rooms share bathrooms with the dorms. There's kitchen use, 24-hour reception and laundry services. Two shady courtyards and a rooftop terrace with panoramic views are perfect for chilling.

New City Annex Hotel HOTEL $

(Map p388; ☎0414-254132, 0775958867; ncahotel@gmail.com; 7 Dewinton Rd; r from USh60,000, s/d with shared bathroom from USh18,000/40,000; 📶) Regularly booked out by Peace Corp volunteers and budget travellers, the New City Annex is rather unappealing but it gets the job done with simple, fan-cooled rooms and a handy city-centre location adjacent to a Nairobi bus office. Beware of the street noise. An excellent restaurant downstairs serves all meals and staff are surprisingly delightful.

Tuhende Safari Lodge GUESTHOUSE $

(Map p388; ☎0772468360; www.tuhendesafarilodge.com; 8 Martin Rd, Old Kampala; dm/r US$10/60) Not many travellers stay in Old Kampala, but this place has become a favourite with aid workers on break from up-country due to its large comfortable rooms (no bunk beds here) and great little cafe.

Backpackers Hostel HOSTEL $

(Map p386; ☎0772430587; www.backpackers.co.ug; Natete Rd, Lunguja; camping USh14,000, dm USh25,000-30,000, s/d with shared bathroom USh35,000/55,000, r USh85,000; P@📶) The first hostel to open its doors in Kampala, the Aussie-owned Backpackers is a relaxed escape only a short taxi ride out of the city centre. The facilities are generally good, but could do with some maintenance. The introduction of a boisterous nightclub hasn't worked in its favour. To get here take a Natete/Wakaliga taxi from the New Taxi Park (p400).

This is also the place to get information on trekking in the Rwenzoris, as the owner set up the world-class Rwenzori Trekking Services.

★**Yellow Haven Lodge** BOUTIQUE HOTEL $$

(Map p386; ☎0777609947; http://yellowhaven.com; Musumba Rd; d incl breakfast US$97-177; 📶🏊) 🍃 Haven is the operative word in this boutique lodging on Kampala's outskirts near the airport. On Lake Victoria, the surrounding marshland attracts prolific birdlife. Rooms, including a new tree house, offer lovely simplicity, with canopy beds and no TV. Instead there's an authentic Irish pub, garden lounge area and meandering stone paths to a saltwater pool and pond.

Hosts Joan and Ronald offer a slew of activities, including on-site African cooking classes, hiking trips, biking and boat rides straight off their private dock. There's also a sauna and massage room.

Cassia Lodge HOTEL $$
(Map p386; ☎0755777002; www.cassialodge.com; Buziga Hill; s/d/tr incl breakfast from US$140/160/180; ❄@🛜🏊) A rare patch of tranquillity with spellbinding views of Lake Victoria and hills that seem to never end. The simple yet tasteful rooms face the lake with balconies and patios. There's a good stock of books on Uganda for sale. Day trippers (entry USh10,000) can use the small but pleasant pool. It's a long way from central Kampala, signposted 2.3km off Ggaba Rd.

Makindye Country Club HOTEL $$
(Map p386; ☎0414-510290; www.makindyecountryclub.com; 59 Mobutu Rd, Makindye Hill; s/d incl breakfast from US$85/105, with shared bathroom US$70/85; ❄@🛜🏊) Formerly a members-only club for US embassy staff, Makindye Country Club is now under British management and open for all. The eclectic mix of rooms, all with very '70s decor, are set over huge grounds with plenty of recreational activities: outdoor lap pool, clay tennis courts, gym, squash courts, classes, games room, TV lounge and a huge playground for kids.

It's on the fringes of Kampala, just off the Entebbe Rd.

Fairway Hotel HOTEL $$
(Map p388; ☎0414-257171; www.fairwayhotel.co.ug; 1 Kafu Rd; s/d incl breakfast US$125/145; P❄@🛜🏊) Overlooking a golf course, this older property is midway through major renovations. The lobby betrays some gaudy and glittery roots but refurbished rooms are spot on, with glass showers, flat-screen TVs and safes. It's in a convenient location, with topiary gardens and facilities including pool, gym, and multiple restaurants and bars.

HBT Hotel Russell HOTEL $$
(Map p388; ☎0780255584, 0780255581; www.hbthoteluganda.com; 1 Russell Rd, Namanda Plaza; r from USh182,000; ❄🛜) This place is potentially the best of the very few midrange

UGANDA KAMPALA

KAMPALA ART

With a number of decent galleries, Kampala is home to a healthy and dynamic contemporary-art scene. While it lacks a major museum dedicated to art, many commercial galleries have monthly art shows and a few have permanent exhibitions. START (www.startjournal.org) is an excellent online arts journal that provides good info on Kampala's scene.

Afriart Gallery (Map p388; ☎0712455555, 0414-375455; www.afriartgallery.org; 56 Kenneth Dale Dr; ⏲9am-6pm Mon-Sat) This classy little gallery features works by serious local artists. Downstairs has changing monthly exhibits, while upstairs is a permanent collection, but everything is for sale.

Nommo Gallery (Map p388; ☎0414-234475; www.uncc.co.ug/nommo-gallery; 4 Victoria Ave; ⏲8am-6pm Mon-Fri, 9am-4pm Sat & Sun) Established by the Ugandan Culture Centre in 1964, Nommo is a reliable spot for quality artwork.

Makerere Art Gallery (Map p388; ☎0756116751; www.makerereartgallery.wordpress.com; Makerere University; ⏲9am-5pm Mon-Fri, 10am-4pm Sat, by appointment Sun) Small, but definitely worth a visit, with fascinating monthly exhibitions; check the website for events. There are also some cool sculptures on the grounds.

Karibu Art Gallery (Map p388; ☎0785085698; www.facebook.com/karibuartgallerystudio; Kisasi Rd; ⏲9am-6pm) An artist-run gallery and studio featuring emerging and established Ugandan abstract and contemporary artists.

Umoja Art Gallery (Map p388; ☎0434-660484; www.umojaartgallery.com; 85 Kira Rd; ⏲11am-6.30pm Mon-Sat, by appointment Sun) A small contemporary gallery featuring Ugandan paintings and abstract sculptures in monthly shows.

Uganda Art Gallery (Map p388; ☎0782031244; 651 Willis Rd; ⏲8am-7pm Mon-Fri, 9am-6pm Sat & Sun) Just down from **Namirembe Cathedral** (p385), this small-scale gallery sells quality paintings by local artists at affordable prices.

AKA Gallery at Tulifanya (Afrique Kontemporary Art Gallery; Map p388; ☎0414-254183; www.tulifanyagallery.com; 28 Hannington Rd; ⏲10am-5pm Tue-Fri, to 4pm Sat) Formerly known as Tulifanya, this well-established gallery has knowledgeable owners who can inform you about artists who matter. It features a notable Geoffrey Mukasa collection.

BYO GEAR

Travellers on a tight budget should consider investing in a tent; handy for visiting national parks, and for lodges and backpacker places across Uganda, most of which offer cheap camping. In Kampala, department stores **Game** (Map p386; 0312-350400; Lugogo Bypass Rd, Lugogo Mall; 8am-10pm) and **Nakumatt** (Map p388; www.nakumatt.net; Acacia Ave, Acacia Mall; 24hr) – also in Entebbe – both sell inexpensive, portable tents (two-person from USh125,000) that should last for the duration of your trip, as well as other camping goods such as sleeping bags, chairs and ice coolers.

options in Kampala, though a faulty air-con unit could be a big blow. It's superbly central and has spacious, stylish and impressively clean rooms, a good restaurant that serves all meals (and does room service) and friendly – if not always efficient – staff.

Speke Hotel HOTEL $$
(Map p388; 0414-259221; www.spekehotel.com; Nile Ave; r incl full breakfast US$138;) One of Kampala's oldest hotels, this characterful, refurbished address adds creature comforts to age and grace. All rooms are rather simple, but have wooden floors and many have balconies. It's in a great central location and the terrace bar is a popular meeting place.

There's also a good Italian restaurant, but a heaving bar is right next door so take a room in the back.

Fang Fang Hotel HOTEL $$
(Map p388; 0414-235828; www.fangfang.co.ug; 9 Ssezibwa Rd; s/d from US$89/119;) Just beyond the city centre, this stately 1980s old-timer has seen some wear. Discounts are available. There's a quality Chinese restaurant, not to be confused with its flagship, eponymous one in **Colville St** (Map p388; 0414-235828; Colville St; mains from USh27,000; 11am-midnight;).

Athina Club House GUESTHOUSE $$
(Map p388; 0414-341428; www.athinaclubhouse.com; 30 Windsor Cres; s/d incl breakfast US$50/65;) With mismatched furniture and stained rugs, this old mainstay has seen better days. Rooms have retro fittings and floral curtains, large-sized poster beds and bathrooms with reliable hot water. It's oddly in the well-heeled suburb of Kololo near upmarket bars and restaurants.

★**Emin Pasha Hotel** BOUTIQUE HOTEL $$$
(Map p388; 0414-236977; www.eminpasha.com; 27 Akii Bua Rd; s/d incl breakfast from US$250/270; P) Kampala's finest boutique hotel is housed in an elegant property set in wonderful gardens with rooms that blend lodge atmosphere with luxury. The more expensive ones feature claw-foot bathtubs, while all have classic writing desks, four-poster beds and gorgeous slate bathrooms.

A well-regarded restaurant shares the grounds, as does an impressively luxurious spa if you're up for some more pampering.

★**Villa Kololo** BOUTIQUE HOTEL $$$
(Map p388; 0414-500533; www.villakololo.com/accommodations; 31 Acacia Ave, Kololo; s/d incl breakfast from US$130/180, ste US$250;) With an excellent location in upmarket Kololo, this Italian-owned designer hotel has smart, well-priced rooms that balance tasteful North African decor and Rajasthani motifs with all the mod cons. The suite is a standout with spa bath, zebra-skin rugs and antique furniture. Currently expanding to double its capacity, you might find some growing pains. Downstairs is the popular Mediterraneo (p396) restaurant.

Urban by City Blue BOUTIQUE HOTEL $$$
(Map p388; 0312-563000, 0793000001; www.citybluehotels.com; 22 Akii Bua Rd, Nakasero; s/d incl full breakfast from US$140/170, ste US$250;) In a strikingly modern building, this trendy minimalist hotel features 37 modern yet somewhat sterile rooms around a sparkling pool and inviting lawn. Upstairs rooms are far more spacious and brighter than those poolside. Has a small gym. Breakfast is a feast.

Le Bougainviller BOUTIQUE HOTEL $$$
(Map p386; 0414-220966; www.bougainviller.com; 1-7 Katazamiti Rd, Bugolobi; s/d incl buffet breakfast from US$116/136;) A slice of the Mediterranean in Africa, Le Bougainviller's 20 sleek rooms are split across two gorgeous buildings sharing a courtyard. The best rooms have plush four-poster beds and face a flower-filled garden, while the apartments feature contemporary lofts, kitchens and bathtubs. There's also a sauna, small slate pool and a French restaurant, though the caged songbirds seem rather unnecessary.

Serena Hotel HOTEL $$$
(Map p388; ☎0414-309000; www.serenahotels.com; Kintu Rd; s/d incl breakfast from US$303/323;) Aimed at the business traveller, this sprawling luxury hotel set in 17-acre grounds full of streams and ponds has undergone a massive multimillion-dollar renovation. It often hosts international conferences, hence security is ultratight, which can be a pain for the casual traveller.

Eating

Kampala is packed with quality restaurants and the international population brings considerable variety to the dining scene. Head to Kololo for a smart meal, though street food can be found everywhere. There are plenty of large supermarkets ideal for stocking up before heading up-country.

Prunes INTERNATIONAL $
(Map p388; 8 Wampewo Ave; set brunch USh12,000-17,000, mains USh20,000-32,000; 8am-10pm;) A great spot for brunch, lunch or a laid-back dinner, Prunes is a popular expat hang-out. It does great Ugandan coffee to go with comfort food such as toasties, burgers and healthy salads of beetroot, goat's cheese, apple and nuts. Saturday mornings take on a different feel with its buzzy farmers market. The backyard playground will keep kids busy.

Kardamom & Koffee CAFE $
(Map p388; ☎0755166744; Plot 4, KAR Rd, Kololo; mains USh9000-18,000; 9.30am-6pm Tue-Sat) Come for the relaxed garden setting, strong coffee, spiced tea and carrot cake. Fresh juices, mezze plates and watermelon feta salad are a few of the light offerings. There's also an on-site bookshop and a lovely homegoods shop with Indian imports.

Holy Crêpe CRÊPES $
(Map p388; ☎0754843576; 17 Kololo Hill Lane, Kololo; crêpes USh12,000-32,000; 8am-9pm Mon-Thu, to 10pm Fri-Sun) Billing itself (perhaps unshockingly) as Uganda's first crêperie, this spot perched on top of Kololo Hill has sweeping views of Kampala. The main reason to come here, though, is the excellent crêpes and galettes on offer from its breezy rooftop dining room. There's a full cocktail menu too, making this a perfect place for a sundowner.

La Fontaine INTERNATIONAL $
(Map p388; ☎0772406197; www.lafontaine-kampala.com; Bukoto St, Kisementi; mains USh15,000-22,000; 8am-10.30pm;) While you don't come here for fine dining or lightning-fast service, you do get cheap, tasty food in a laid-back, atmospheric environment. The fish dishes, such as grilled tilapia (Nile perch) with garlic butter, are the pick.

New City Annex Hotel UGANDAN $
(Map p388; 7 Dewinton Rd; mains from USh12,000-18,000; 6am-11pm;) This basic hotel restaurant does Ugandan food, with excellent local flavours (including good vegetarian options) and healthy breakfasts, a rarity in Kampala. It regularly attracts members of parliament and Peace Corps volunteers.

★**Khana Khazana** INDIAN $$
(Map p388; ☎0414-233049; 20 Acacia Ave; mains USh20,000-48,000; noon-3.30pm & 7-11pm Tue-Sun;) Regarded by many as the best Indian in town and even far beyond, classy Khazana is a great place to treat yourself. It features atmospheric Rajasthani-inspired decor, crisp white tablecloths and professional waiters serving a menu full of wonderful tandoori dishes and creamy north Indian curries. Home delivers too.

Mama Ashanti AFRICAN $$
(Map p388; ☎0774542855; www.mamaashanti.com; 20 Kyadondo Rd; mains USh25,000-40,000; 9am-11pm Mon-Sat) West African fare isn't so common here and this is some of the best. Mama Ashanti tempts with *egusi* (minced spinach, pumpkin seed and groundnut) with pounded yam, delicious grilled kebabs in a dry chilli rub, and fragrant stews. The spacious garden setting is a good place for a drink or ginger passionfruit juice.

Miso Garden ASIAN $$
(Map p388; ☎0772741236; 14 Mabua Rd; USh18,000-32,000; noon-3pm & 6.30-10pm;) In a candlelit garden setting under a jackfruit tree, this popular Korean-owned restaurant offers up a selection of Korean and Japanese dishes. Bibimbap (rice with vegetables, meat and fried egg) sizzles in a stone bowl; there's also savoury kimchi pancakes, Korean barbecue and sushi rolls.

Bistro BISTRO $$
(Map p388; ☎0757247876; Kololo Hill Dr; mains USh24,000-36,000; 7.30am-10pm Mon-Fri, to 4.30pm Sat & Sun) With a varied menu, seductive cocktails and good service, this refined bistro is popular with Ugandans and expats alike. Tapas are great, but there are also delicious pastas, crisp onion rings in ginger sauce and burgers, all in a pleasant atmosphere.

Great Indian Dhaba INDIAN $$
(Map p388; 0751903647; 3 Wampewo Ave; USh18,000-22,000; 11am-11pm;) Serving an extensive menu of northern and southern Indian cuisine, this casual garden restaurant delivers. There's sufficient spice and great value in the thali lunch specials, available on weekdays, and even a kids' menu.

Cafe Javas INTERNATIONAL $$
(Map p388; 0393-106502; www.cafejavas.co.ug; Kampala Rd; USh16,500-30,000; 8am-10pm Mon-Sat) It's really hard to fault this place, a bright, spotless and roomy cafe in the middle of downtown Kampala. A huge menu takes in everything from delicious (and vast) breakfasts to excellent coffee, freshly baked pastries, sandwiches, wraps and full meals. Service is attentive and fast, and in the mornings it seems like most of Kampala is brunching here.

Quality Hill DELI $$
(Map p386; Ggaba Rd; mains from USh20,000; 7am-10pm) To pack a gourmet picnic or just hang out, visit this fashionable foodie enclave, home to Quality Cuts Butchery for meat and cheese, the superb La Patisserie bakery and the Cellar wine shop.

Lawns AFRICAN $$
(Map p388; 0756712521; www.thelawns.co.ug; 34 Impala Ave; mains USh20,000-66,000; noon-midnight;) A pretty garden restaurant offering carnivores anything from tender beef steaks to more exotic ostrich burgers, wildebeest steaks and crocodile in garlic-wine sauce. If you're really into the idea, go the game-meat platter or the 1.5kg croc tail that feeds four. Thankfully the cute bunnies roaming the grounds aren't on the menu.

Casablanca ETHIOPIAN $$
(Map p388; 0789566272; 26 Acacia Ave; mains from USh18,000; noon-late) Another big player in Kololo's fantastic multicultural food scene, Casablanca does tasty *injera* (flatbread) dishes in its outdoor candlelit garden restaurant. The perfect place to kick off proceedings for a night out on the town.

★**Mediterraneo** ITALIAN $$$
(Map p388; 0414-500533; www.villakololo.com/menu; 31 Acacia Ave, Kololo; pizzas from USh45,000, mains USh31,000-81,000; noon-10.30pm;) This upmarket open-air Italian restaurant occupies a sprawling wood deck in a tropical garden, lit at night with kerosene lamps. The Italian chef creates fantastic thin-crust pizzas and handmade pastas, such as pappardelle funghi with porcini imported from Italy. You can also dine on steak or grilled rock lobster. Reservations are recommended.

Fez Brasserie INTERNATIONAL $$$
(Map p388; 0414-236977; 27 Akii Bua Rd; mains USh30,000-42,000; 12.30-3pm & 6.30-11pm;) One of Kampala's most renowned restaurants, this gorgeous spot looking out over the leafy grounds of the Emin Pasha hotel has an ever-evolving fusion menu, which respects vegetarians, uniting flavours from five continents. Chilled avocado soup and the tender grilled beef with rocket deliver. Or just come for a drink on the comfy couches in the wine bar.

Yujo Izakaya JAPANESE $$$
(Map p388; 0794289856; www.yujo.ug; 36 Kyadondo Rd, Nakasero Hil; sushi from USh18,000, mains USh19,000-89,000; noon-11pm) In a gorgeous setting, this highly regarded, popular and friendly restaurant offers a slice of traditional Japan. Known primarily for its imported rice wine, excellent sushi and sashimi selection, it also serves tasty homemade ramen and *okonomiyaki* (savoury pancakes).

Cantine Divino ITALIAN $$$
(Map p388; 0700805000; Mabua Rd; mains USh33,000-46,000; 9am-10pm) Doubling as a stylish wine bar, this upmarket Italian grill is a spot to see and be seen. Think steak with rustic potatoes, flame-grilled lamb chops and homemade pastas. There's an extensive (and expensive) wine list prominently featuring bottles from South Africa and Italy, and a deli case of imported chacuterie.

Tamarai THAI $$$
(Map p388; 0755794958; http://tamarai.restaurant.ug; 14 Lower Kololo Tce; mains USh20,000-42,000; 11am-10pm;) Kampala's premier Thai restaurant is a classy affair stylishly set in an immense open-air thatched hut. All your favourite Thai classics (plus a few pan-Asian dishes) are prepared authentically using fresh ingredients and fragrant herbs. Tea lovers will rejoice with 16 varieties to choose from.

Le Chateau BELGIAN $$$
(Map p386; Ggaba Rd; mains USh38,000-60,000; 7am-11pm;) Though popular for its Ugandan beef tenderlion, Le Chateau serves an extensive Belgian menu that includes Flemish stew, crispy fries, snails and a selection of 11 Belgian beers, all served under an enormous thatched roof. Recently renovated, its open-air curtained booths offer cosy ambience and there's top-notch service.

Haandi INDIAN $$$
(Map p388; 0701411221; www.haandikampala.ug; 1st fl, 7 Kampala Rd, Commercial Plaza; mains USh18,000-72,000; 11.30am-11pm;) Always crowded with locals, this restaurant features the best of North Indian frontier cuisine. Experiment a little with the tilapia (Nile perch) curries or the prawns *makhini* (queen prawns cooked in a coconut-milk sauce).

Drinking & Nightlife

Nightlife in Kampala is something to relish with a host of decent bars and clubs throughout the city. Caffeine lovers also have plenty of choice. Be warned that pickpockets are prevalent, and it's not advisable to carry any valuables, especially phones. The presence of prostitutes is another tedious reality in many of Kampala's nightspots.

Otters Bar BAR
(Map p388; 0785201417; www.ottersbar.com; 15 Ngabo Rd, Kololo; noon-5am Wed-Sat, 1.30-11pm Sun) With the most agreeable garden atmosphere thick with ferns and strewn with lights, this is a fine place to get a pint. There are also cocktails, pizza and snacks.

Big Mike's BAR, CLUB
(Map p388; 0778360002; www.bigmikes.biz; 19 Acacia Ave, Kololo; 5pm-late) Whether you're looking for a lively beer garden, a swanky cocktail bar or a pumping club, Big Mike's has it covered – all under one roof. It's popular for good reason, and you can find everything from stand-up comedy nights to sports screenings and quiz nights here; check the website for upcoming events.

Endiro CAFE
(Map p388; 0312-515322; www.endirocoffee.com; 23b Cooper Rd, Kisementi-Kololo; 7am-10pm;) Full of diners plugged into their laptops, this smart, earthy cafe has free wi-fi to go with its strong Ugandan coffee, fresh juices and excellent breakfasts. The thick vegetation surrounding the outdoor seating provides some respite from Kampala's busy streets.

1000 Cups Coffee House CAFE
(Map p388; 0772505619; www.1000cupscoffee.com; 18 Buganda Rd; coffee from USh7000; 8am-9pm Mon-Sat, to 7pm Sun) For espresso, aeropress or cold drip, caffeine aficionados will want to head here. There's a good range of single-origin beans from across East Africa – expect to pay a premium – and a menu of light bites, along with a selection of international newspapers and magazines.

Café Pap CAFE
(Map p388; 0414-254570; www.cafepap.com; 13b Parliament Ave; 7am-11pm Mon-Sat, 9.30am-11pm Sun;) This busy cafe on Parliament Ave is a good spot for Ugandan coffee, farmed on the slopes of Elgon, the Rwenzoris and the Virungas, as well as freshly squeezed juices and breakfasts.

Deuces BAR
(Map p386; Ggaba Rd, Kansanga; 24hr) Taking over from Al's bar, one of Uganda's most famous (although notorious) bars, Deuces keeps the flag flying as the place in Kampala that never sleeps.

Cayenne BAR
(Map p388; www.cayennekampala.com; 1213 Kira Rd, Bukoto; noon-late Tue-Sun, from 4pm Mon;) An attractive outdoor set-up with a sprawling tree, luxurious pool and popular restaurant, Cayenne is a top place to hit night or day. However, the party only truly gets started late night when DJs, live music and multiple bars are in full swing. Dress is smart casual (no shorts or flip-flops) and there's a cover charge after 11pm weekends.

Iguana BAR
(Map p388; 0777020658; 8 Bukoto St, Kisementi; 5pm-late) Heaving with *wazungu* (foreigners) and locals, divey Iguana is a contender for the most popular bar in town. Upstairs is a boozy affair, whether as a spot for after-work drinks or late evenings with DJs spinning anything from house to dance hall or old-school hip-hop. Downstairs has a pool table and live reggae bands.

Rock Garden BAR
(Map p388; Nile Ave, Speke Hotel) One of the definitive stops on the Kampala night shift, this cool place has a covered bar and a huge outdoor area. Be careful here: pickpocketing is often part of the experience.

Bubbles O'Learys PUB

(Map p388; ☎0794441977; http://bubblesolearys.com; 19 Acacia Ave, Kololo; ⊙noon-late; 📶) A Kololo institution, Bubbles is the closest you'll find to a true pub in Kampala. Its bar and furnishings were shipped in from an old Irish boozer back on the Emerald Isle. It's a buzzing spot drawing a fun crowd of expats and locals, and has a great beer garden too.

Ange Noir CLUB

(Map p388; ☎0414-230190; www.angenoir.net; 77a 1st St; ⊙10pm-late Thu-Sun) In an industrial location, the 'black angel' has long held Kampala's most popular dance floor. Events are listed on the website.

☆ Entertainment

★Ndere Centre DANCE

(Map p386; ☎0414-597704; www.ndere.com; Kisaasi Rd; adult/child USh30,000/15,000) If you're interested in traditional dance and music, try to catch a dinner-theatre performance of the Ndere Troupe at Ndere Centre. It showcases dances from many of Uganda's tribal groups with high-energy shows taking place in a 700-seat amphitheatre on Sundays at 6pm and Wednesday at 7pm. On Fridays it's afro-jazz from 7pm. Dinner is mediocre (and optional).

It also offers traditional drumming and dance classes. The troupe has a lovely base way out in Ntinda, which includes a restaurant-bar and guesthouse.

Musicians Club CONCERT VENUE

(Map p388; Siad Barre Ave; ⊙8pm-midnight) FREE Kampala musicians get together every Monday at the National Theatre for informal jams and live performances – a must if you're in the city. The place fills with Ugandans letting off steam after work and the drinks flow. On the second and last Monday of the month, the event shifts outside and becomes a minifestival, with beer tents and a serious sound system.

National Theatre LIVE MUSIC

(UNCC; Map p388; ☎0414-254567; www.uncc.co.ug; 6 Dewinton Rd) There's a quality program of music, film, dance and drama performances in the theatre itself, but most travellers come here for the popular, free nightly outdoor events. Grab a beer and a chair and catch an informal open-stage jam on Monday evenings, African drumming on Tuesdays or comedy night on Thursdays, where the merriment is in English and Luganda.

Shopping

★Kampala Fair CLOTHING

(Map p388; ☎0788405808; 50 Butoko St, Kisementi; ⊙9.30am-6pm) Selling gorgeous women's *kitenge* dresses in traditional patterns, separates, children's clothing and some batik pillows, this fair-trade boutique is a solid choice for keepsake clothing, with craftsmanship superior to that you'd find in the market and a treasure trove of colours and styles. If you are in town a few days they can even do alterations.

Bold CLOTHING

(Map p388; www.boldkla.com; Acacia Ave, 1st fl Acacia Mall; ⊙9am-9pm Mon-Sat, 10am-7pm Sun) A team of local designers produces contemporary styles and accessories using African fabrics and designs.

Def.i.ni.tion CLOTHING

(Map p388; ☎0700914924; 1st fl, Acacia Ave, , Acacia Mall; ⊙9am-9pm) Cool local label selling hip, vibrant accessories, fabrics, designer T-shirts and clothing.

Quality Hill ARTS & CRAFTS

(Map p386; Ggaba Rd; ⊙9am-7pm Mon-Sat) A guy with a great selection of Congolese carvings lays out his wares at this upmarket complex of patisseries and wine shops.

Aristoc BOOKS

(Map p388; ☎0703528214; 23 Kampala Rd; ⊙8.30am-5.30pm Mon-Fri, 9am-4.30pm Sat) This is the best place for English-language publications, with a great selection of books on Uganda, as well as novels. Stock up before a long road trip. There are branches at **Acacia Mall** (Map p388; Acacia Ave; ⊙8.30am-5.30pm) and **Garden City** (Map p388; ☎0414-341382; Yusuf Lule Rd; ⊙8am-9pm).

Banana Boat ARTS & CRAFTS

(Map p388; ☎0414-232885; www.bananaboat.co.ug; 23 Cooper Rd, Kismenti; ⊙9am-7pm) 🍃 A sophisticated craft shop selling smart local items such as excellent batiks, and handmade stuff from all over Africa, including Congolese carvings. There's an outlet with an emphasis on homes and interiors in **Lugogo Mall** (Map p386; ☎0414-222363; Lugogo Bypass Rd; ⊙9am-7pm).

ⓘ Information

DANGERS & ANNOYANCES

Kampala is a largely hassle-free city and is safe as far as Africa's capitals go. However, take care in and around the taxi parks, bus parks and markets, as pickpockets operate. Drive-by bag snatching by motorcyclists has been reported around Tony Acacia Ave. Muggings and robberies can happen as they do anywhere in the world, so follow the ordinary big-city precautions. As with elsewhere in Africa, thieves who are caught red-handed will often face a mob-justice beating, but the Kampala twist is that they'll also be stripped down to their 'Adam suits' before being sent off. Kampala is also notorious for traffic jams – *boda-bodas* are certainly the fastest way to get around the city but they have high rates of accidents.

EMERGENCY & IMPORTANT NUMBERS

Police & Ambulance	999
Police & Ambulance (from a mobile phone)	112

INTERNET ACCESS

Free wi-fi is ubiquitous in hotels, restaurants, bars and cafes. Internet cafes do still exist, but are a dying breed as they are in much of Africa. Prices usually cost from USh3000 per hour.

MEDICAL SERVICES

International Hospital Kampala (IHK; Map p386; 0312-200400, emergency 0772200400; http://ihk.img.co.ug; St Barnabus Rd, Kisugu-Namuwongo; 24hr) Kampala's largest private hospital and one of the best in the country. There is an emergency department for urgent treatment as well as a 100-bed hospital that is the pioneer of Western-standard health care in Uganda.

The Surgery (Map p388; 0312-256001, emergency 0752756003; www.thesurgeryuganda.org; 42 Naggulu Dr, Naguru; 8am-6pm Mon-Sat, emergency 24hr) A highly respected clinic run by Dr Dick Stockley, an expat British GP. Stocks self-test malaria kits.

MONEY

Stanbic (Map p388; 17 Hannington Rd, Crested Towers Bldg; 9am-3pm Mon-Fri, to noon Sat) and **Barclays** (Map p388; Kampala Rd; 8am-4pm Mon-Fri, 9am-2pm Sat) are the most useful banks in Kampala. Both accept international cards and have plenty of ATMs about town.

Most main bank branches and foreign-exchange bureaus are along or near Kampala Rd.

POST

Main Post Office (Map p388; Kampala Rd; 8am-6pm Mon-Fri, 9am-2pm Sat) Offers national and international postal services.

TOURIST INFORMATION

Kampala has no official tourist office, but it does have a number of useful online resources and magazines.

Buganda Tourism Centre (Map p388; 0414-271166; Natete Rd; 7.30am-6pm Mon-Sat, 10am-5pm Sun) Has tourist information and sells tickets to the Bulange Royal Building.

The Eye (www.theeye.co.ug) Free, bimonthly magazine and website with listings and reviews for Kampala and other tourist towns.

Pearl Guide (www.thepearlguide.co.ug) Online and hard-copy magazine with good info on upcoming events, food reviews and features on Uganda. It's aimed more at 'premium travel experiences' – so features pricier lodges, tours and restaurants.

Tourism Uganda (Map p388; 0414-342196; www.visituganda.com; 42 Lugogo Bypass; 8.30am-5pm Mon-Fri, 9am-1pm Sat) More of a marketing office, this tourist office lacks any really useful info, but has a good website.

Visit Kampala (www.visitkampala.net) Handy website with good overview of things to see and do in Kampala, upcoming events and general tourist info.

Getting There & Away

BOAT

For adventure travellers in the tradition of Paul Theroux, cargo ships generally sail a few times per week between Kampala's Port Bell and Mwanza, Tanzania. This isn't a mainstream option and there's no ticket office so you'll need to head to the port to negotiate fares with the captain.

BUS

Destinations are posted in the front windows and buses generally follow the times they tell you, though the later it is in the day, the more likely there are to be delays. Buses leave early if they're full. Fares vary enormously, but we give the average or most common fare.

Destination	Fare (USh)	Duration (hr)
Arua	30,000	7
Fort Portal	20,000	5
Gulu	25,000	5
Hoima	20,000	5
Jinja	10,000	2
Kabale	30,000	8
Kasese	25,000	7
Katunguru	25,000	8
Kisoro	35,000	9
Kitgum	30,000	7
Masaka	18,000	3
Masindi	15,000	4
Mbale	25,000	5
Soroti	25,000	7

Buganda Bus Park (Main Bus Park; Map p388; off Namirembe Rd) Kampala's main bus terminal has the most departures.

New Bus Park (Map p388; off Namirembe Rd) Buses to Kisoro, Kabale, Gulu and Kihihi.

Arua Park (Map p388; Johnston St) Buses to towns around Murchison Falls National Park.

Post Bus

Post Bus (Map p388; ☎0414-255685; www.ugapost.co.ug; Speke Rd) is the most highly recommended means of public transport, having the best safety record and most experienced drivers. Buses depart in various directions between 6am and 8am from the Speke Rd side of the main post office. Information and day-before reservations are in the building behind the post office.

At the time of writing, Post Bus was not running the eastern route, but it is expected to resume.

Destination	Fare (USh)	Duration (hr)
Gulu	25,000	6
Hoima	14,000	6½
Kabale	25,000	8
Masindi	12,000	5
Mbale	20,000	6
Mbarara	16,000	5
Soroti	25,000	7
Tororo	12,000	4

International Buses

Numerous bus companies offer direct daily links from Kampala to Kenya, Tanzania, Rwanda, South Sudan and the DRC.

Pineapple Express Bus Shuttle

A convenient, well-priced and safe alternative to normal public transport between Uganda's three main tourist centres (Entebbe, Kampala and Jinja) is the **Pineapple Express** (Map p388; ☎0787992277; www.entebbejinjashuttle.com; Yusuf Lule Rd, Oasis Mall) bus shuttle. From Kampala it departs Oasis Mall at 1.30am, 10am and 4.15pm for Entebbe (US$12, two hours), and 10.15am and 4.15pm for Jinja (US$14, 1½ hours).

MINIBUS TAXIS

Kampala has two main 'taxi' parks for minibuses, and both serve destinations around the country as well as Kampala itself. Although packed, there's a degree of organisation. Buses to Entebbe leave from both parks.

Old Taxi Park (Map p388) The busier of the two taxi parks serves towns in eastern Uganda.

New Taxi Park (Map p388) Services western and northern destinations.

TRAFFIC-JAM NIGHTMARES

Traffic jams are a major headache in Kampala, so no matter where you're going in the city, plan ahead if you need to get there at an appointed time. Rush hours are particularly bad, usually from 7.30am to 9.30am, 1pm to 2.30pm and 4.30pm to 7.30pm; on Friday it seems to last all day.

It all comes to a head in central Kampala, where you get snared among the chaos of two taxi parks, two bus parks and a bustling market, all within 1 sq km of each other. It's not uncommon for the last few kilometres of your journey to take an hour, which can be demoralising after returning to town from a long ride. If your luggage is easy to reach, jump off and grab a *boda-boda* to clear the mess; if it's in the luggage storage compartment, you have no choice but to wait it out.

Getting Around

TO/FROM THE AIRPORT

The cheapest and most direct option is to take the green bus that heads to Entebbe International Airport (USh3000, one hour) from Nasser Rd (off Nkrumah Rd) in Central Kampala. It departs on the hour from 8am to 6pm – leave plenty of time to get to Entebbe.

BODA-BODAS

Motorbike taxis are the fastest way to get around Kampala since they can weave in and out of traffic jams, though it comes with the catch of their horrendous safety record.

Drivers have imposed an unofficial minimum fare of USh2000 around the city centre and are pretty good about sticking to it. *Boda-bodas* can also be hired by the hour or day, but prices will depend on how big a swath of the city you plan to tackle. If you go this route, buy your driver a newspaper to read while waiting and you'll have a new best friend.

For a more secure ride, **Safe Boda** (☎0800300200; www.safeboda.com; ⏲9am-6pm Mon-Fri) provides helmets and trained drivers.

CAR & MOTORCYCLE

The following offer rental services with 4WD vehicles and drivers.

Road Trip Uganda (p387) A reliable Dutch-run operation with optional camping equipment and travel itineraries.

Ashiraf Mwanje (p493) Ashiraf is a responsible driver with his own 4WD vehicle, available for safari trips or visits around Uganda. His ability to speak a handful of tribal languages can come in handy.

Alpha Car Rentals (p493) Offering SUVs from US$50 to US$160 per day, including safari vehicles.

More standard rental agencies include **Europcar** (Map p388; 0414-237211; www.europcar.com; 11 Nsambya Rd; 8am-6pm) and **Hertz** (Map p388; 0781409430; www.hertz.com; Colville St; 9am-5pm).

MINIBUS TAXIS

The ubiquitous white and blue minibus taxis (charging USh3000 on average) fan out from the city centre to virtually every point in Kampala. Many start in the taxi parks (for most destinations you can use either park), but it's quicker to flag one down on Kampala Rd as they don't need to navigate the nightmare traffic jam around the taxi parks.

SPECIAL-HIRE TAXI

Most 'special-hire' taxis are unmarked to avoid licensing and taxes, but if you see a car with its door open or with the driver sitting behind the wheel while parked, it's probably a special-hire. It's best to grab the number of a recommended driver through your hotel or a trusted local contact.

A standard short-distance fare is around USh15000 to USh25,000. Waiting time is around USh200 per minute. Prices will be higher at night and during rush hour.

For a marked yellow cab, try **Kampala Taxi** (0417-130130, 0712489222; www.kampalataxi.com; per km USh3000).

AROUND KAMPALA

Entebbe

0414 / POP 79,700

On the shores of gorgeous Lake Victoria, Entebbe is an attractive, verdant town that served as the capital city during the early years of the British protectorate. Today it's the relaxed pace of life and nearby natural attractions that give the city its charm rather than any notable colonial relics.

Unless you have reason to rush into Kampala, Entebbe makes a nice, chilled-out introduction to Uganda, and many visitors prefer to base themselves here for a few days rather than in Kampala's traffic-choked streets. It's also the ideal place to end your trip if you're stuck with one of the many early-morning flights out of Uganda's only international airport.

Sights

Ngamba Island Chimpanzee Sanctuary WILDLIFE RESERVE

(0758221880, 0414-320662; www.ngambaisland.org; half-day trip US$168; departure 9am & 12.45pm) Located 23km southeast of Entebbe in Lake Victoria, Ngamba Island Chimpanzee Sanctuary, or 'Chimp Island', is home to over 40 orphaned or rescued chimpanzees who are unable to return to the wild. Humans are confined to one of the 40 hectares while the chimps wander freely through the rest, emerging from the forest twice a day for feeding at 11am and 2.30pm. This coincides with visitor arrival times to the island, with viewings of the chimps via a raised platform.

While it can't compare to the experience of seeing chimps in the wild, especially due to the large electrified fence that separates chimp from human, it still makes for a worthwhile excursion to observe the animals' remarkable behaviour. Guides here are informative, and there are individual profiles for each chimp, detailing both their distinct personalities and history. There are also big monitor lizards in residence and abundant birdlife.

The island is a project of the Chimpanzee Sanctuary & Wildlife Conservation Trust, which arranges bookings for day trips and accommodation.

Rates are based on a minimum group of two, though one individual can go at a higher rate. It's cheaper with larger group sizes. The half-day trip includes entry, guide and boat transport. Two trips depart from Entebbe per day: in the morning at 9am, returning at 12.45pm, or departing at 12.45pm and returning by 4.45pm.

The CSWCT also offers an overnight experience (first night/additional nights US$539/185) in a self-contained, solar-powered safari tent. Rates include lodging, full board, transport, activities and entry, based on two guests. Check the website for add-on activities.

Arrive via speed boat (50 minutes) or motorised canoe (90 minutes) from the Entebbe dock. Those who arrive via their own transport must pay an entry fee (adult/child US$35/15).

Uganda Wildlife Education Centre ZOO

(UWEC; 0414-320520; www.uwec.ug; 56/57 Lugard Ave; US$15; 8am-6pm;) While it functions primarily as a zoo, this centre is

Entebbe

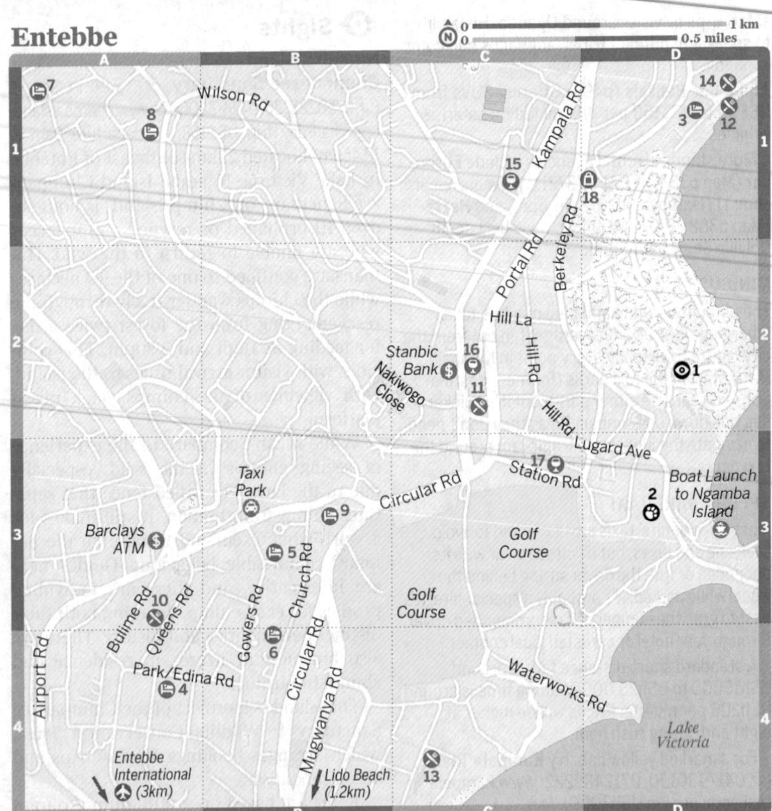

actually a world-class animal refuge that has benefited from international assistance in recent years. Most of the animals on display were once injured or were recovered from poachers and traffickers. Star attractions include chimpanzees (a good alternative to pricier Ngamba Island), southern white rhinos, lions, leopards and shoebill storks. Keep an eye out for the baby elephant wandering about too.

A variety of programs gets you closer to the animals, including chimp encounters (US$200), behind-the-scenes tours (US$70) and zookeeper for the day (adult/child US$100/50); book directly through UWEC for discounts. There are long-term volunteering opportunities and it has on-site lodging.

Uganda Reptiles Village ZOO
(☎0782349583; www.reptiles.ug; Bunono Village; adult/child US$10/5; ⏰8am-6.30pm) Get up close to some of the world's deadliest snakes, including mambas, cobras, puff adders and vipers, as well as chameleons, crocs and lizards, all of which are rescued or injured. It's around 3km off the Entebbe–Kampala road, about a 20-minute drive from Entebbe.

Entebbe Botanical Gardens GARDENS
(☎0414-320638; USh10,000; ⏰9am-7pm) Laid out in 1898, these expansive gardens are perfect for a leisurely stroll. The highlights are its pockets of thick rainforest, which locals claim some of the original *Tarzan* films were made in, and excellent birdwatching with 115 species (USh10,000 per guide). You'll see plenty of monkeys, including black-and-white colobus, and tree squirrels too.

Activities

Uganda Wildlife Education Centre VOLUNTEERING
(UWEC; ☎0414-320520; www.uwec.ug; 56/57 Lugard Ave) Assist rescued and injured ani-

Entebbe

Sights

1 Entebbe Botanical Gardens.................D2
2 Uganda Wildlife Education Centre.................D3

Activities, Courses & Tours

Uganda Wildlife Education Centre.................(see 2)

Sleeping

3 2 Friends Beach Hotel.................D1
4 Airport Guesthouse.................A4
5 Boma.................B3
6 Entebbe Backpackers Hostel & Campsite.................B4
7 Gorilla African Guesthouse.................A1
8 Karibu Guesthouse.................A1
9 Lake Victoria Hotel.................B3
Papyrus Guesthouse.................(see 8)
Uganda Wildlife Education Centre.................(see 2)

Eating

10 Anna's Corner.................A3
11 Gately Inn Entebbe.................C2
12 Goretti's Beachside Pizzeria & Grill.................D1
13 Imperial Resort Beach Hotel.................C4
14 Thai Garden.................D1

Drinking & Nightlife

15 Club Knight Riders.................C1
16 Four Turkeys.................C2
17 O's Bar.................C3

Shopping

18 Victoria Mall.................D1

mals at Uganda Wildlife Education Centre in Entebbe, with month-long stints involving animal keeping and rehabilitation, and staying in a local homestay.

Sleeping

★Via Via Guesthouse GUESTHOUSE $

(0781524991; http://viavia.world/en/africa/entebbe; Kisalu Rd, Katabi; camping/dm US$5/15, s/d from US$40/50;) This new Belgian-run lodging provides superb value, with attractive rooms featuring plush towels and strong showers – for slightly more you can get a room with pond views. There's a waterfront cafe with monkeys and birds traipsing through the canopy at dusk and a cool art gallery on-site. Wi-fi access is at the cafe only.

Gorilla African Guesthouse HOSTEL $

(0781516422; http://gorilla-african-guest-house.weebly.com; 14 Jinja Rd; dm/s/d/tr US$15/30/40/60;) Built around a flower-filled courtyard, this bright backpacker house clad in tangerine paint has simple rooms with nets but without screens. Dorms are rather cramped. The hosts are friendly and there's an on-site restaurant and bar, and bicycles for rent.

Entebbe Backpackers Hostel & Campsite HOSTEL $

(0414-320432; www.entebbebackpackers.com; 33/35 Church Rd; camping/dm/s/d USh10,000/20,000/40,000/50,000, s/d lazy camping USh15,000/20,000;) A popular, colourful and straight-down-the-line backpackers without the whole party scene. The pricier rooms are spacious, while all are spotless. The helpful owners can suggest things to do around town and beyond. It's often full, so book ahead. All rooms come with mosquito nets and there's a guest kitchen – rare in Uganda.

African Roots GUESTHOUSE $$

(0784423207; http://africanrootsgh.com; 8 Left Lane; s/d/tr incl breakfast US$55/70/90;) With a home-like atmosphere, this pleasant midrange option offers 10 smart rooms with canopy beds and an on-site restaurant with a surprisingly good selection of dishes. It's less roomy than other offerings, with no outdoor lounge space, but guests love it.

Airport Guesthouse GUESTHOUSE $$

(0414-370932; www.gorillatours.com; 17 Mugula Rd; s/d/tr incl breakfast US$70/82/115;) One of the best-value options in town, the renovated rooms here maintain a great balance between style and home comfort. Rooms feature verandas looking out to a sprawling manicured garden and huge beds laden with pillows. The delicious three-course dinners served on the lawn are worth trying, by reservation only.

Boma GUESTHOUSE $$

(0772467929; www.boma.co.ug; 20a Gowers Rd; s/d incl breakfast US$147/170;) This verdant guesthouse has an intimate atmosphere thanks to its lovely 1940s decor, a swimming pool and a landscaped, flower-filled yard. There's also solar-heated water and rooms with safes and flat-screen TVs. The food gets rave reviews. Mountain bikes are also available.

Uganda Wildlife Education Centre BANDA $$
(UWEC; ☎0414-320520; www.uwec.ug; 56-57 Lugard Ave; s/d incl breakfast US$50/70) A novel arrangement that allows you to stay on the premises of the wildlife centre and be privy to nightly lion roars and hyena howls from nearby enclosures. The thatched brick *bandas* (thatched-roofed huts) that back on to the giraffe enclosure are the most popular. Rates include entry, plus your money helps fund the centre's rescue activities.

★**Karibu Guesthouse** GUESTHOUSE $$$
(☎0777044984; www.karibuguesthouse.com; 84 Nsamizi Rd; s/d from US$125/145; 📶🏊) A superb boutique guesthouse experience, Karibu has peaceful, shady gardens, a pool with waterfall cascade and a pétanque pit. Stylish rooms, garden-side or in the main house, are decked in African motifs. The fantastic Mediterranean restaurant (open to nonguests with reservation) also serves delicious three-course breakfasts. It's run by a young Corsican-Kiwi couple and friendly and helpful staff.

2 Friends Beach Hotel HOTEL $$$
(☎0772236608; www.2friendshotel.com; 3 Nambi Rd; s/d incl breakfast from US$90/120; 📶🏊) A lovely treat with crisp white linens, glass showers and all the details (robes, safe, minifridge and flat-screen TV). This supremely laid-back and friendly place is also one of the few hotels in Entebbe to make use of Lake Victoria's beaches, with its own private patch of sand, complete with bamboo bar. Upgrade for lake views.

Papyrus Guesthouse GUESTHOUSE $$$
(☎0787778424; www.papyrusguesthouse.com; 2 Uringi Cl; s/d/tr US$85/120/175; 📶) This nine-room guesthouse is a real charmer, channelling a rustic atmosphere with kerosene lamps on the patio and a lovely gazebo on the premises. Large guest rooms have bright African-print bed covers and thoughtful touches.

Lake Victoria Hotel HOTEL $$$
(☎0312-310100; www.laicohotels.com/laico-lake-victoria; Circular Rd; s/d incl full breakfast from US$180/230; ❄@📶🏊) This sprawling hotel has the feel of a conference centre, with well-appointed, business-style rooms. It's worth upgrading for more space. Its massive swimming pool (day pass USh25,000) is the highlight, with a 9.2m diving board, sunloungers and bar. Keep an eye out for the tortoises in the garden.

Protea Hotel HOTEL $$$
(☎0414-323132; www.proteahotels.com; 36-40 Sebugwawo Dr; r incl breakfast from US$203; ❄@📶🏊) Plonked directly on Lake Victoria (and just across from the airport) this smart chain is the best of the upmarket hotels in Entebbe. Business-style rooms have all the mod-cons for a comfortable stay, while its glassed-in lobby has terrific lake views. There's an attractive pool, private beach and small chip-and-putt golf course. Owned by Marriott.

Eating

Goretti's Beachside Pizzeria & Grill PIZZA $
(Nambi Rd; pizzas USh20,000-35,000; ⌚8.30am-10pm; 📶) What could be better than eating a wood-fired pizza on the beach with Lake Victoria lapping at your feet? Not much, actually, and it's the reason why Goretti's is such a consistent favourite with locals and visitors alike.

Faze 3 INTERNATIONAL $$
(Airport Rd; mains USh14,000-30,000; ⌚7am-midnight; 📶) Close to the airport, Faze 3 is a solid choice for dining out. Its outdoor decking is a top spot to catch lake breezes while feasting on anything from roast pork to tilapia (Nile perch) tikka, chicken-schnitzel burger or a good ol' meat pie.

Anna's Corner CAFE $$
(☎0788096893; 12 Queens Rd; mains USh10,000-33,000; ⌚8am-9pm; 📶) In a new location, this wonderful expat institution does wood-fired pizzas and the best coffee in town. Bored with local food? Dig into a Bali burger with mango curry or Thai beef salad. Breakfast is a good bet too. There's also a Congolese craft store, Friday movie nights, Tuesday salsa lessons and regular coffee tastings.

Imperial Resort Beach Hotel INTERNATIONAL $$
(Mpigi Rd; weekend entry USh3000, mains USh18,000-35,000) Good place for fish and chips on the beach (but watch out for scavenging maribou stork), or a choice of meat

dishes or pizza. Alternatively there are garden tables, or those with jet lag can hit the 24-hour restaurant inside the hotel.

★Thai Garden THAI $$$

(☎0786572001; 9 Nambi Rd; mains USh22,000-60,000; ⏰11.30am-10pm; ☑) With a conscientious Thai owner, this restaurant more than delivers with fresh lemongrass in your coconut soup, a red curry both light and spicy, icy beer and fresh green-papaya salad. The lush setting features patio and garden seating surrounded by tropical blooms and sunbirds drinking nectar. It's a delight, though portions are on the small side.

Gately Inn Entebbe INTERNATIONAL $$$

(www.gatelyinn.com/dining; 2 Portal Rd; mains USh28,000; ⏰7am-9pm; 📶) This open-air restaurant, surrounded by a wonderful African garden, serves international foods ranging from burgers to Madras curry. The atmosphere is great, but under new administration the food is somewhat average.

Drinking & Nightlife

Entebbe's large expat population, wealthy locals and small but constant number of travellers mean that the town has a decent number of things going on after dark. Downtown Entebbe has a number of pubs, sweaty clubs and raucous bars to choose from.

O's Bar BAR

(☎0706973757; 9 Station Rd; ⏰4pm-6am Fri-Sun) Across from the golf course, this happening bar has outdoor decking, indoor lounge and sport on the TV.

Four Turkeys PUB

(Kampala Rd; ⏰10am-midnight) A local and NGO hang-out on the main strip with good pub grub and cold beer.

Club Knight Riders CLUB

(☎0776966261; http://knightridersdiscotheque.club; Kampala Rd; ⏰9pm-6am Wed & Fri-Sun) The place to kick on to once you're ready to hit the dance floor. Check its website for special events.

Shopping

Victoria Mall MALL

(Berkeley Rd; ⏰7am-10pm) Love it or loathe it, mall culture has well and truly arrived in Uganda, with this shiny new complex opening in 2013. As well as eateries and shops, there's a Nakumatt supermarket that comes in handy for groceries as well as camping equipment.

Information

Exchange rates at the banks in town are better than those at the airport, but lower than in Kampala. The following banks have ATMs.

Stanbic Bank (Kampala Rd)

Barclays (off Airport Rd)

Getting There & Away

The brand new four-lane Entebbe Express Hwy should debut by 2019 and slash journey times between Entebbe International Airport and Kampala when it opens. At present the journey takes around 1½ hours, though in traffic it can be two hours or more.

BUS

Pineapple Express (p400) shuttle runs daily from the airport and guesthouses to Kampala (US$12, two hours) at 5am, 2.30pm and 11pm. The first two buses also serve Jinja (US$24, four hours).

Minibus taxis run between Entebbe and either taxi park in Kampala (USh2500, 1½ hours) throughout the day. A special-hire from the airport to Kampala will cost you anywhere from USh80,000 to USh100,000.

FERRY

There's boat transport to the Ssese Islands.

A catamaran, the *MV Armani*, connects Entebbe's **Nakiwogo dock** to Kalangala Bay on Buggala Island every day in both directions (per vehicle/person USh25,000/20,000). It leaves the Ssese Islands each morning at 8am from Kalangala Bay, arriving at 11.30am in Entebbe. It then heads back to Kalangala Bay from Entebbe at 2pm, arriving around 5.30pm. Show up two hours early.

There's also a **boat launch to Ngamba Island** for visits to the **chimpanzee sanctuary** (☎0758221880; www.ngambaisland.org; 24 Lugard Ave, Ngamba Island; half-/full-day trip US$50/90, s/d full board US$309/420). Captains charge according to boat size, group size and demand; if you can, arrange travel with the sanctuary directly.

TAXI

Shared-car taxis run very infrequently to the airport (USh2000) from the **taxi park** in Entebbe, so most people use a special-hire taxi (USh20,000).

Mabamba Swamp Wetlands

Mabamba Swamp is one of the most convenient places in Uganda to spot the highly sought-after shoebill in its natural habitat. Regularly featured on tourism brochures, these appealingly grotesque birds look like they've crawled straight out of the swamp (which they literally have), with their out-of-proportion features and massive dirty-yellow bill that resembles an old battered shoe. Birdwatching is mostly via canoe, where you'll navigate waterways comprising lily pads and papyrus swamp. Among the 260 species in the region, other notable birds include the papyrus yellow warbler, pallid harrier and blue swallow.

Activities

There's about an 80% success rate for shoebill sightings here. Guides can be arranged from UWEC (p402) in Entebbe for around USh100,000 (per group of three) including boat hire.

Getting There & Away

While the swamp is 12km away as the crow flies, it's a 40km (one hour) drive from Entebbe. Most visitors come on tour from Entebbe.

To get here on your own, catch a minibus taxi to Kasanje, then a *boda-boda* to the Mabamba jetty. Otherwise a private car will cost around USh100,000 return with wait time.

Mpanga Forest Reserve

The 453-hectare **Mpanga Forest Reserve** (0776949226; USh20,000) offers a decent option to escape the chaos of Kampala for a day or two, though most people visit on a day trip. It's best known for its 181 species of butterfly, while red-tailed monkeys can be seen during the day and bushbabies during guided night walks (USh20,000 per person).

Sleeping

Mpanga Ecotourism Site BANDA $
(camping/dm/s/d USh10,000/10,000/20,000/40,000) This basic lodge has a mix of private and dorm beds in *bandas,* plus camping on the lawn.

Getting There & Away

The reserve is 35km out of Kampala – take a Masaka minibus (USh8000, one hour) and get off at Mpanga, walking the last 800m.

The Equator

The equator crosses the Kampala–Masaka road 65km southwest of Kampala, with the expected monument that springs up in equator-hopping destinations. Two concrete circles mark the spot. If you have a GPS you can get your photo taken on the real equator, about 30m to the south, but it's not nearly as photogenic.

Drop in to **Aidchild's Equation Cafe** (077616861; www.aidchild.org/aidchild-businesses; mains USh8,000-16,000) for a drink, coffee or a meal, and browse the artwork. All profits fund activities to assist HIV/AIDS orphans.

EASTERN UGANDA

Thanks to an intoxicating blend of adrenaline adventures and superb scenery, eastern Uganda is a must on any East African journey. Here the mighty Nile begins its epic journey north. White-water rafting the Nile River is the main draw for adventurers seeking a wild ride, but there's also the subtler, sweatier pleasure of trekking through Mt Elgon National Park or relaxing with a visit to stunning Sipi Falls. The regional capital of Jinja offers a charming and friendly base on the shores of Lake Victoria where travellers can spend a few days or more enjoying the chilled atmosphere and top-notch outdoor activities.

Jinja

0434 / POP 82,800

Famous as the historic source of the Nile River, Jinja is now the adrenaline capital of East Africa. Get your fix of white-water rafting, kayaking, quad biking, mountain biking and horse riding in a gorgeous natural setting with crumbling colonial architecture. The Nile River's world-famous rapids are under threat, however. In 2011 the Bujagali Hydroelectric Project buried around half of the rapids under a giant reservoir. Although the government has pledged to not further dam the river, Uganda still needs energy and so a new hydroelectric plant is planned for Kalagala Falls. Though worker strikes and faulty construction have it behind schedule for now, it's expected that the Isimba Dam will flood

Eastern Uganda

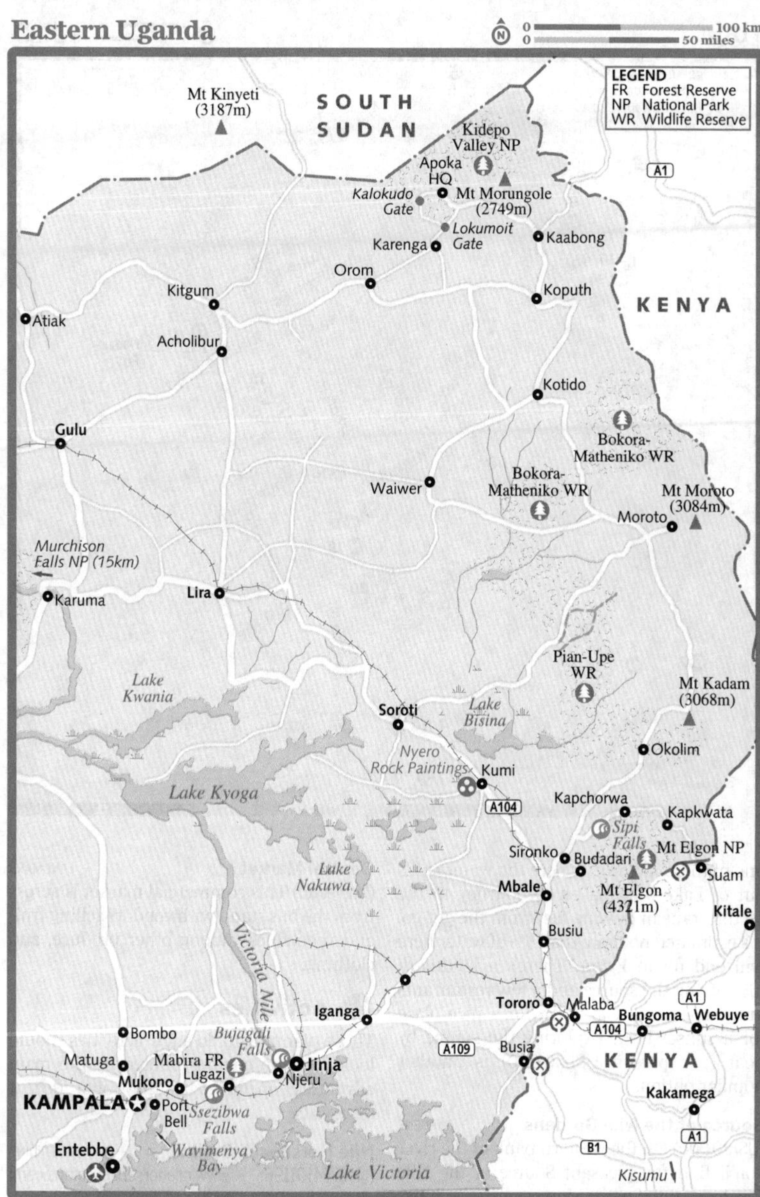

some key rapids and even an island lodging as early as October 2018. It's not the end of rafting though. Meanwhile locals keep pushing to keep Jinja's tourism industry alive with offerings that have wisely begun to diversify.

Sights

Source of the Nile River RIVER

(per person/car/motorcycle USh10,000/2000/500; admission charged 7am-7pm, open 24hr) The birthplace of the mighty Nile river (or

Jinja

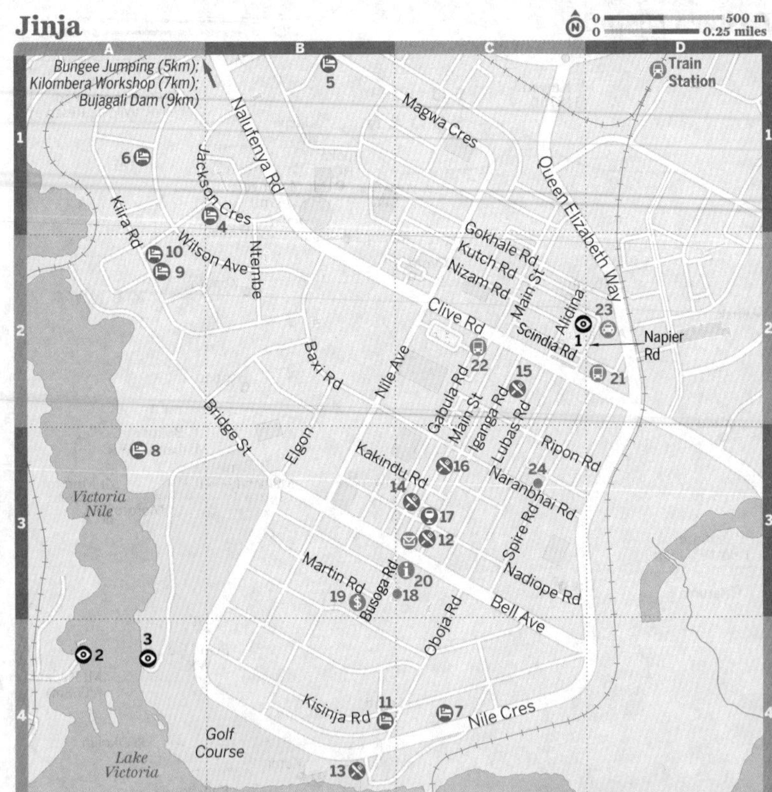

one of them anyway...), here the water spills out of Lake Victoria on its journey to the Mediterranean flowing fast from the get-go. It's estimated no more than 5% of water here will end up in Egypt. There's a landmark identifying the source and a few restaurants and bars, which can make for a nice place for a sunset beer. Exploring the source by boat (per person USh50,000) is another popular option.

Source of the Nile Gardens GARDENS
(USh10,000) On the western bank of the river you'll find the pleasant Source of the Nile Gardens and Speke Monument – a pillar commemorating where the British explorer first laid claim to the historic source of the Nile in 1858. Birders enjoy the 15-minute walking trail. In recent times the source has been traced anywhere from Rwanda to Burundi.

Central Market LANDMARK
(Napier Rd) This commercial market is across from the bus stand with vendors selling fruit and vegetables, among other produce, and clothing.

Activities

Those planning to do a few activities should look into the combos offered by the main adventure operators as they offer decent discounts.

Nile Horseback Safaris HORSE RIDING
(☎0774101196; www.nilehorsebacksafaris.com; off Kayunga Rd; 1/3hr ride US$40/80) Exploring Jinja via horseback is a popular activity, taking you alongside the Nile River and through local villages, tea estates and sugar plantations. There are also sunset rides (US$60) and overnight safaris (from US$265). Riders need to wear long trousers and closed shoes,

Jinja

Sights

1 Central Market C2
2 Source of the Nile Gardens A4
3 Source of the Nile River A4

Activities, Courses & Tours

FABIO .... (see 14)
Nalubale Rafting .... (see 9)
Nile River Explorers .... (see 6)

Sleeping

4 2 Friends Guesthouse B1
5 Busoga Trust Guesthouse B1
6 Explorers Backpackers A1
7 Gately on the Nile C4
8 Jinja Backpackers A3
9 Nalubale Teahouse A2
10 Source of the Smile Guesthouse A2
11 Surjio's B4

Eating

12 Deli C3
Gately on the Nile .... (see 7)
13 Jinja Sailing Club B4
14 Leoz C3
15 Moti Mahal C2
16 Source Café C3

Drinking & Nightlife

Babez .... (see 12)
Bourbon .... (see 8)
17 Spot 6 .... C3

Shopping

A Bernadette .... (see 10)

Information

18 Immigration Office C3
19 Stanbic Bank B3
20 Tourist Centre C3

Transport

21 Bus Station D2
22 Night-time Taxi Stage for Kampala C2
23 Taxi Park D2
24 Wemtec C3

and there's a 90kg weight limit. Trips depart at 10am and 2pm daily.

To get here, cross the bridge over Owen Falls dam and take a right at Kayunga Rd, from where it's 1km; a *boda-boda* from Jinja will cost around Ush12,000 or, better yet, charter a water-taxi from Bujagali Dam.

Feather & Fin BIRDWATCHING, FISHING
(☎0772900451; www.fb.me/featherandfinpursuits; birdwatching half-/full-day US$40/90, fishing half-/full-day US$50/110) Whether you're looking to land a tilapia (Nile perch), or tick off a fishing eagle, kingfisher or stork, Feather & Fin can sort you out for a morning or full-day session of fishing and birdwatching. Longer trips are also available. Check its Facebook page for more information. Trips depart from Bujagali.

All Terrain Adventures ADVENTURE SPORTS
(☎0772377185; www.atadventures.com; Bujagali Falls; 1hr/half-day/full-day US$49/119/195) After a little spin on the practice circuit, quad-bike riders explore the paths and trails criss-crossing the countryside along the banks of the Victoria Nile. There are several options, including a twilight safari that includes dinner in a village. It offers overnight trips and kid-sized rides are also available. Located at the main entrance gate to Bujagali Falls.

White-water Rafting

The source of the Nile is one of the most spectacular white-water rafting destinations in the world and for many visitors to Uganda a rafting trip is the highlight of their visit. Here you can expect long, rollicking strings of Grade IV and V rapids, with plenty of thrills and spills. Despite the intensity of some rapids, most people who venture here are first-time rafters; it's the perfect opportunity to get out of your comfort zone and try something different.

The three most reputable rafting companies are **Nile River Explorers** (NRE; ☎0772422373; http://raftafrica.com; Wilson Ave; rafting combo US$140), **Nalubale Rafting** (☎0782638938; www.nalubalerafting.com; half-/1-/2-day trips US$125/140/255) and **Adrift** (☎0755225587, 0752225587; www.adrift.ug; Kimaka Rd; half-/full-day trips US$125/140), all equal in terms of professionalism and pricing, with an outstanding emphasis on safety (all rafting trips are accompanied by a fleet of rescue kayaks and a safety boat).

They will also shuttle you out from Kampala for free, picking up punters from popular hostels and hotels, and returning in the evening if you just want to make it a day trip. If you want to stick around, they'll give you a free night's accommodation in a dormitory. All offer pick-ups from hotels in Jinja.

GANDHI IN UGANDA

A surprising find at the source of the Nile is a shrine to Mahatma Gandhi. As per his wishes, on his death in 1948 his ashes were divided up to be scattered in several of the world's great rivers, including the Nile in Uganda. This bronze bust, donated by the Indian government, commemorates the act.

Besides the standard big water runs, there's also less-extreme options for those who don't want to be flung into the raging water. Family float trips are offered, which bypass the big waves and are guaranteed to garner squeals of delight from young kids. A full-day family float with Nile River Explorers and Nalubale Rafting costs US$40 per person.

All the companies take on the Big Four – monster Grade V rapids, including Itanda (The Bad Place) – but there is always a safety boat on hand if you decide the rapids are just too big for you. They each also include a host of incentives to lure you over, including meals and beers.

Kayaking

An alternative to rafting is to go solo and kayak through the raging river, or take a more leisurely paddle on flat water. Jinja is mostly known among freestyle kayakers for its epic Nile Special wave.

Kayak the Nile KAYAKING

(☎0772880322; www.kayakthenile.com; kayaking white-water full day from US$25, tandem US$160, flat-water from US$75, SUP from US$30) Run by pro-kayaking husband-wife team Sam and Emily, the main attraction here is white-water kayaking, for both beginners (solo or tandem) and advance freestyle kayakers. White-water SUP (stand-up paddle-boarding) is another thrilling activity. However, it's not all about taming rapids, with relaxing flat-water trips available on sit-on-top kayaks or SUPs. Multiday trips are available too.

It's based at Nile River Explorers Campsite in Bujagali.

Boating

Boat trips can be arranged at Jinja Sailing Club (p412), where individuals pay USh25,000 to go to the source of the Nile, visiting islands along the way. You can also go via boats leaving the east bank of the Nile at Ripon Falls, but there's a parking and entry fee (each USh10,000). Make sure the boat carries life jackets.

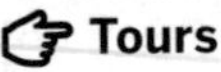

Tours

FABIO CYCLING, TOURS

(First African Bicycle Information Office; ☎0705935030, 0434-121255; www.fabio.or.ug; 9 Main St; 24hr bike hire USh15,000, tours USh50,000) This NGO arranges bike tours around Jinja and Lake Victoria with a focus on discovering its rich history. It also rents out basic single-speed bikes and mountain bikes for those who prefer to go it alone.

Sleeping

Jinja has some wonderful guesthouses in its leafy suburbs away from the dusty city centre, as well as along its gorgeous shoreline on Lake Victoria. There are also some fantastic options further downriver, near Bujagali, around 8km from Jinja. This is where most of the backpacker and activities bases are.

Nile River Explorers Campsite HOSTEL $

(☎0772422373; http://raftafrica.com/site/accommodation/explorers-river-camp.html; Bujagali; camping/dm US$7/12, r from US$50, r with shared bathroom from US$30; @📶) The most popular place to stay at Bujagali, this attractive camp is set on a grassy site with sensational river views. There's a good mix of budget rooms, often full with overland truckers and backpackers, but the tented camps sloped along the terraced hill are the pick of the bunch – they have superb outlooks – as do the showers!

The restaurant and its beer garden also have sensational views (definitely worth a visit, even if you're not staying here), and serve up tasty burgers and other favourites. It's packed to the rafters come evening and is one of Jinja's best places to party.

Busoga Trust Guesthouse GUESTHOUSE $

(☎0434-120490; www.busogatrust.co.uk/busogatrust/guesthouse; 18 Lubogo Lane; incl breakfast dm USh34,000, s/d from USh40,000/55,000; 📶) Usually full of NGO workers, this is the perfect choice for those not into Jinja's backpacker scene. Busoga Trust has a chilled-out vibe with homely lounge, kitchen for self-caterers, fast wi-fi, a patio looking out to its garden and spacious rooms. Proceeds go directly towards water-sanitation projects in rural villages. Reserve online.

Jinja Backpackers HOSTEL $
(☎0774730659; www.jinjabackpackers.com; Bridge Cl; camping/dm US$5/10, s/d with shared bathroom US$25/30, cottage per person US$45;) This unassuming, relaxed backpackers is owned by a Kiwi-Aussie couple who've set up rooms in a large sheep shearing–like shed with dorms and private rooms centred on a ping-pong table. It's conveniently set just back from Bourbon (p412) bar and the waterfront, outside the town centre.

Nalubale Teahouse HOSTEL $
(☎0782638938; www.nalubalerafting.com/rooms.html; 38 Kiira Rd; camping/dm US$5/10) The base for Nalubale rafters (p409), who stay for free, this lively backpacker hangout has clean dorms with hot showers in a colonial house set in a leafy neighbourhood. The ample living room has foosball and resident monkeys keep it interesting.

Nile River Camp CAMPGROUND, BACKPACKERS $
(☎0776900450; www.camponthenile.com; Bujagali; camping/dm US$6/12, d safari tent US$45;) This laid-back site run by Nalubale Rafting (p409) has a scenic river location fringed with eucalyptus trees and an atmospheric thatched-roof restaurant/bar. There are hammocks strung about the place and the swimming pool is a huge draw.

Mountain bikes can be rented (US$35 per day).

Explorers Backpackers HOSTEL $
(☎0434-120236; www.raftafrica.com; 41 Wilson Ave; camping/dm/d incl breakfast US$8/10/40, cottage incl breakfast US$40-50; @) Jinja's original crash pad is still a popular budget choice with attractive murals and open-air lounge spaces. Dorms are decent and the forest cottage with lovely wall murals is equipped with a kitchen. Sunday brunch is a highlight. Overland trucks pop in now and then, but this is a much quieter spot than Bujagali.

★**Source of the Smile Guesthouse** GUESTHOUSE $$
(☎0783842021; www.sourceofthesmile.com; 39 Kiira Rd; s/d/tr from US$80/88/125;) With cool tropical design, a gorgeous garden and pool, this relaxed guesthouse indeed invites smiles. Its Icelandic owner and local staff are helpful and interactive, and the huge buffet breakfast beats most in Uganda. For other meals, there are menus for ordering out. Tiled poolside rooms offer an extra dose of character; otherwise there are cheaper, more conventional rooms out the back.

★**Haven** BANDA $$
(☎0702905959; www.thehaven-uganda.com; camping US$15, lazy camping s/d incl half board US$65/100, bandas s/d incl half board from US$130/210;) Overlooking a wild Class VI rapid, this wonderful, friendly lodge is all about location. With pleasant grounds featuring a play area, bike rentals and sandbox, it's great for families too. There are sensational panoramas from suave *bandas*, tents and bungalows, all with hot water. It boasts numerous ecofriendly credentials, a safari-style restaurant and swimming pool with sunloungers.

★**Gately on the Nile** BOUTIQUE HOTEL $$
(☎0772469638, 0434-122400; www.gatelyonnile.com; 47 Nile Cres; incl breakfast s/d from US$80/106, s/d/tr cottages US$120/160/200; @) Gately's stylish rooms boast high ceilings, mosaic tile floors and batik fabrics. They're split between a lovely garden house and loft apartments and a gigantic villa across the road, all with views of Lake Victoria. The Mediterranean-style house is a great choice for honeymooners and families. Service is attentive and the restaurant (p412) is one of the best in town.

2 Friends Guesthouse GUESTHOUSE $$
(☎0783160804; www.2friends.info; 5 Jackson Cres; s/d incl full breakfast from US$107/124; @) A relaxed guesthouse with smart safari-themed rooms with flat-screen TVs, safes and attractive Ugandan art. Cottages around a lovely bamboo garden and swimming pool go for slightly more. There are bikes for hire (USh15,000 per day), plus free laundry service and a worthwhile on-site restaurant.

Surjio's BOUTIQUE HOTEL $$
(☎0787637637; www.surjios.com; 24 Kisinja Rd; s/d/tr/q incl full breakfast US$80/125/145/160;) Relaxed Surjio's has a pleasant garden set away from town near the edge of the Nile. Pricier rooms are spacious with polished blonde-wood floors, high beds and lovely bathrooms. Go for an upstairs room for a glimpse of the Nile. Staff are friendly, and it has a swimming pool and a popular pizzeria with gluten-free options.

Hairy Lemon BANDA $$
(☎0772828338, 0434-130349; www.hairylemonuganda.com; camping US$35, dm from US$38, bandas US$42-70, all incl full board) Situated 15km downstream from the rafting starting point, Hairy Lemon's isolated location on a small island makes it the perfect getaway

retreat. More rustic than luxurious, dorms and *bandas* are basic and mostly share bathrooms. A short paddle away is Nile Special, a world-class wave for kayakers. It's essential to book ahead.

★ Wildwaters Lodge LODGE $$$
(☎0772237400; www.wild-uganda.com; s/d incl full board US$615/780; @📶🏊) One of Uganda's best luxury hotels, Wildwaters lives up to its name by overlooking a raging stretch of the Nile from its stunning island location. Accessed via a boardwalk, the private thatched-roof suites have canvas walls and palatial interiors with gleaming polished floorboards, poster beds and sofas. All open up to balconies with outdoor claw-foot baths overlooking unhindered Nile views.

Eating

Due to its sizeable expat and NGO community, Jinja has some good eating options. The steady stream of travellers in town has contributed to the eating scene too, and has led to a string of rather hip cafes and coffee shops lining Main St. Various international cuisines dominate the selection, but Ugandan food is also available.

★ Deli CAFE $
(☎0794589400; 2 Main St; mains USh10,000-14,000; 📶) This industrial-chic deli and cafe is just the trick for homesick travellers. Tasty espresso drinks, brownies, lovely oversized salads, nachos and sandwiches on crusty fresh bread have patrons lining up. Seating is mostly at picnic tables on the shady front lawn. The deli stocks import items and wine as well as local meats and produce. Also delivers.

Source Café CAFE $
(☎0434-120911; www.source.co.ug; 20 Main St; mains from USh6000; ⏰7.30am-6pm Mon-Sat; 📶) A magnet for expats seeking reliable wi-fi (not free but cheap and fast), this attractive cafe does excellent French-press coffee, baked goods and sandwiches. The porch with mosaic tiles is a good place to watch the street action. There's also a nice gift shop and local coffee for sale, with proceeds going to development programs.

Leoz INDIAN $
(☎0434-120298; 11 Main St; mains USh11,000-18,000; ⏰9am-11pm) Locals like this friendly laid-back Nepali-owned restaurant, the last word in authentic South Asian food, from Indian *thalis* to *dhaal bhaat*, with some Ugandan dishes also available.

Moti Mahal INDIAN $$
(☎0757879048; Iganga Rd; mains USh17,000-22,000; ⏰9am-9.30pm) Jinja's best Indian food comes from this cavernous restaurant with a large downstairs dining room. The ambience is dull but the food isn't. Enjoy spicy curries, tandoor dishes and more. It also delivers.

Gately on the Nile INTERNATIONAL $$$
(☎0772469638; www.gately-on-nile.com; 47 Nile Cres; mains USh26,000-30,000; ⏰6am-9.30pm; 📶👶) The restaurant on the back porch of the popular boutique hotel of the same (p411) name exudes the atmosphere of a Balinese garden. The fusion menu serving butter chicken, burgers and Thai specialities shows plenty of international flair. Has a kids' menu too.

Black Lantern INTERNATIONAL $$$
(www.nileporch.com; mains USh17,000-45,000; ⏰7am-9.30pm; 📶) Bujagali's premier dining destination is set under an elegant traditional thatched-roof overlooking the water. The extensive menu showcases dishes from around the world. Barbecued spare ribs are the house speciality, but there are other original options, including Afro-Mexican nachos and tilapia (Nile perch) grilled in banana leaves. Check the Facebook page for jazz and party nights.

Jinja Sailing Club INTERNATIONAL $$$
(☎0700876082; www.jinjasailingclub.com; Pier Rd; mains USh15,000-35,000; ⏰9am-11pm; 📶🖋) Completely rebuilt in a sleek and modern resort style, this waterfront restaurant serves a long list of Indian, African and Western classics, with vegetarian options. It's also a good destination to enjoy cocktails on the lawn overlooking Lake Victoria.

Drinking & Nightlife

★ Bourbon BAR
(Bridge Cl; ⏰10am-2am) Right on the fast-flowing water, this open-air thatched bar with lounge divans and tables on a floating pontoon boat is the most ambient drinking establishment in Jinja. It's also lively, with DJs and late nights on weekends. Check the Facebook page for upcoming events.

Spot 6 BAR
(☎0776333331; 10 Main St; ⏰24hr) One of the livelier nightlife options.

Babez BAR
(☎0775568650; Nadiope Rd East; ⏰2pm-1am) Features DJ jams and dancing.

Shopping

A Bernadette ARTS & CRAFTS
(www.abernadette.com; ⏰10am-5pm) Young NYC fashionistas have partnered with local women to create well-made recycled bags and accessories in fun, bold designs. Items are fair-trade certified and available for online purchase. The shop is in Source of the Smile Guesthouse (p411).

Kilombera Workshop ARTS & CRAFTS
(☎0793439619; www.facebook.com/kilombera weaving; ⏰8.30am-5pm Mon-Fri, 9am-1pm Sat) Many of the colourful cotton textiles (place mats, table runners, bedspreads) for sale around Jinja are made on hand-operated looms at this Nile-side workshop. Visitors are welcome to stop by and watch the process. The showroom has gorgeous items for sale. It's signposted 200m off the road, halfway between Jinja and Bujagali.

Information

INTERNET ACCESS

You can get online at tons of places along Main St and wi-fi is available at nearly all hotels and restaurants.

MONEY

There are plenty of banks in the centre, but **Stanbic** (Busoga Rd; ⏰9am-4.30pm Mon-Fri, to 1pm Sat) offers parking and is not as busy.

POST

The **Main Post Office** (cnr Main St & Bell Ave) is right on Main St.

TOURIST INFORMATION

Tourist Centre (☎0434-122758; www.jinjatouristcentre.co.ug; Bell Ave) This new information centre in the Town Hall can also book day tours, car rental and safaris.

Visit Jinja (www.visitjinja.com) Has travel information and offers some tour bookings.

VISA EXTENSIONS

The **Immigration Office** (☎0782335700; Busoga Rd; ⏰9am-5pm Mon-Fri) can arrange visa extensions, and makes for a less hectic alternative to Kampala.

Getting There & Away

Coming from Kampala, be prepared for a slow and frustrating ride on the two-lane road to Jinja. The Nalubaale Power Station (formerly known as the Owen Falls Dam) provides a spectacular gateway into town, but don't take pictures – people have been arrested for doing so, even though there are no signs informing people of this law.

BUS

The **bus station** houses numerous bus services connecting Jinja to Kampala and beyond. Most rafting companies offer complimentary transport to/from Kampala; for those not rafting it's worth checking to see if there's a spare seat available (USh10,000).

The Pineapple Express (p400) shuttle makes a daily trip at 7.30am and 1.30pm for Kampala (US$14) and Entebbe (US$24).

Post Bus (p400) is the best option for public transport.

There are also frequent minibus taxis to Kampala (USh7000, two hours) and coasters to Kampala (USh7000) and Mbale (USh7000, two hours), from where you can link to Soroti or Busia on the Kenyan border. There's no need to travel to Nairobi in stages as you can book tickets on the big buses (USh42,000, 14 hours) coming from Kampala.

CAR

If you're driving yourself, the best route from Kampala is the longer but faster and almost completely truck-free road north through Kayunga. You can hire rentals through Wemtec (p493) or the **Tourist Centre**.

MINIVAN TAXI

The trip between Jinja and Kampala (USh15,000) takes around two hours by minibus taxi – or much longer, depending on the traffic. The gathering point is the **Taxi Park**. At about 7pm these minivan taxis to Kampala move out to the **Night-time Taxi Stage** (Clive Rd).

Getting Around

The centre of Jinja is compact enough to wander about on foot. Elsewhere you'll want a *boda-boda*.

Rafting companies transport clients to Bujagali (30 minutes) for free. Otherwise, **Pineapple Express** (p400) efficiently makes the trip or you can take a taxi (USh26,000).

Mbale

☎0454 / POP 96,200

A bustling provincial city, you'll pass through Mbale if you're planning an assault on Mt Elgon or are en route to Sipi Falls. The downtown hums with low-key chaos. Away from the dusty centre there are pockets of charm and it does have a scenic mountain backdrop, but there's no real reason to hang around here.

Sights

Nabugoye Synagogue SYNAGOGUE
(Nabugoye Hill) An unexpected find in this neck of the woods, the synagogue is a simple, yet appealing, rustic red-brick building (with plans to revamp). The Jewish Abayudaya community in the outskirts of Mbale on Nabugoye Hill dates from the early 20th century. Services in English and Hebrew are held on Fridays from 6pm to 8pm and Saturdays at 9am. There's also a guesthouse.

Former military leader Semei Kakungulu founded the sect in 1913, fusing elements of Judaism and Christianity with a disbelief in Western medicine, leading to a fallout with British rulers. During the 20th century the group withstood widespread persecution, particularly under Idi Amin, who outlawed Judaism and destroyed synagogues.

A special-hire taxi from Mbale costs USh30,000; a *boda-boda* is USh4000.

Activities

Foundation for Development of Needy Communities VOLUNTEERING
(FDNC; 0772494285; www.fdncuganda.or.ug) Runs a host of community development programs in the area. Volunteers can work with projects relating to community health projects, environmental issues and women in management.

Sleeping

Visitors Inn HOTEL
(0700470344; Nkokonjeru Rd; s/d USh30,000/50,000;) This newish multistorey hotel is set at the edge of downtown where it's less noisy at night. It's a great deal: immaculate bedrooms have tiny balconies and TVs, fan and canopy beds. The wi-fi can be weak.

Casa Del Turista HOSTEL $
(0772328085; https://casadelturistablog.wordpress.com; 18 Nkokonjeru Tce; dm/s/d US$12/18/26;) This friendly guesthouse is a relaxed place to hang out, with a great on-site cafe, spotless dorms and private rooms with a dash of style and en suite bathrooms. As the only hotel in town geared to international travellers, it's quite popular, so reserve ahead. The only downside is that common areas can feel overcrowded.

Mt Elgon Hotel HOTEL $$
(0773008903; www.mountelgonhotel.com; 30 Masaba Rd; s/d incl breakfast from US$90/110; restaurant 6am-11pm;) A colonial-era stalwart with modern flair, rooms here are spacious and quite plush. Amenities include a sauna, Jacuzzi, swimming pool and minigolf. It's in a quiet area outside the city, surrounded by verdant grounds. The high-end restaurant is popular with the general public, with a huge menu including local, Indian and continental fare.

Eating

★**Nurali's Café** INDIAN $
(0772445562; 5 Cathedral Ave; mains USh14,000-18,000; 8.30am-10.30pm;) This popular Indian restaurant delivers delicious flavours from the tandoor. The chicken tikka masala is melt-in-your-mouth good, plus there's excellent palak paneer and naan with big chunks of garlic. Add to that fast service and spice that hums on the tongue – if you wish. A friendly and fun place.

Eco Sham CAFE $
(0772328085; 18 Nkokonjeru Tce; mains USh10,000-20,000; 8am-10pm;) Inside the Casa del Turista, this cafe has quality food and top organic Mt Elgon coffee, with proceeds going to a local school. The rooftop tables with umbrellas are great for a sunset beer, though you won't get wait service up there. Popular with locals and tourists alike.

Information

MONEY

All the big banks are concentrated on the southwest end of Republic St, a few hundred metres from the clock tower.

TOURIST INFORMATION

Mt Elgon National Park Headquarters
(0454-433170; www.ugandawildlife.org; 19 Masaba Rd; 8am-5pm Mon-Fri, to 3pm Sat & Sun) Organise your Mt Elgon visit here, about 1km from the city centre.

Getting There & Away

BUS & MINIBUS

Post Bus (p400) heads to/from Kampala daily via Jinja. There are frequent buses or minibuses to Kampala (USh15,000, four hours), Jinja (USh10,000, three hours), Kumi (USh7000, one hour), Soroti (USh15,000, three hours), Moroto (USh30,000, nine to 12 hours) and Kotido (USh40,000, 10 to 12 hours) from the main taxi park off Manafa Rd. Behind it is the bus stand, with less-frequent transport to Jinja, Kampala and Soroti. Prices are similar to minibus prices.

Gateway (☎0414-234090; Lira-Mbale Rd) has a daily bus to Nairobi (USh42,000, 12 hours) departing at 3am.

TAXI

For Sipi Falls (USh7000, one hour), Kapchorwa (USh10,000, 1¼ hours) and Budadari (USh5000, 45 minutes), head to the **Kumi Rd taxi park** northeast of town. Services are infrequent to these smaller places so it's best to travel in the morning.

Mt Elgon National Park

Spread out over the slopes of a massive extinct volcano, **Mt Elgon National Park** (www.ugandawildlife.org; adult/child US$35/5, trekking per day incl fees & guide US$75) is a good place to spot various primates and lots of birds, including the rare Jackson's francolin, alpine chat and white-starred forest robin. Larger fauna, including leopards, hyenas, buffaloes and elephants, are far harder to spot, but most visitors come for the hiking and impressive landscapes that are peppered with cliffs, caves, gorges and waterfalls.

Trekking in Mt Elgon National Park offers some of East Africa's most memorable climbing experiences, and boasts a milder climate, lower elevation and much more reasonable prices than climbs in neighbouring Kenya or Tanzania. Mt Elgon has five major peaks and the highest, Wagagai (4321m), is on the Ugandan side. It's the second-tallest mountain in Uganda and the eighth tallest in Africa.

The lower slopes are covered in tropical montane forest with extensive stands of bamboo. Above 3000m the forest fades into heath and then afro-alpine moorland, which blankets the caldera, a collapsed crater covering some 40 sq km. The moorland is studded with rare plant species and you'll often see duiker bounding through the long grass and endangered lammergeier vultures overhead. In September it's decorated with wildflowers.

MT ELGON NATIONAL PARK

Why Go Uganda's second-highest peak, Wagagai (4321m); trekking routes into Kenya or Sipi Falls.

When to Go Year-round, but generally there's less rain from June to August and December to March. From September to October there are wildflowers.

Practicalities Decent trekking equipment can be rented at **Rose's Last Chance** (p416) in Budadari. The park is best accessed via Mbale, a three-hour drive from Kampala.

Budget Tips Rose's Last Chance can arrange a number of walks in the area that don't require paying for a park permit.

Trekking Mt Elgon

Preparation

Mt Elgon may be a relatively easy climb, but this is still a big, wild mountain. Rain, hail and thick mists aren't uncommon, even in dry season, and night-time temperatures frequently drop below freezing. Pack adequate clothing and at least one day's extra food, just in case. Altitude sickness is rarely a problem, but heed the warning signs. It's also wise to check the latest security situation, as there are occasional incidents along the Kenyan border; an armed escort is provided and included in your permit fee.

While you can climb Mt Elgon year-round, the best time is from June to August or December to March. The busiest times are June and July, though this coincides with rainy season. However, seasons are unpredictable and it can rain at any time. You can get information and organise your trek at the Mt Elgon National Park Headquarters (p414) in Mbale or at the visitor centres at each of the trailheads, which are all open in theory 8am to 5pm weekdays and to 3pm weekends, though these times can be flexible to say the least!

Even as the number of visitors on Mt Elgon increases, tourism remains relatively underdeveloped and no more than 250 people reach the caldera in the busiest months. It's possible to hike for days without seeing another climber. The climb is nontechnical and relatively easy, as far as 4000m-plus ascents go.

If you're not up for the full climb there are numerous options for day hikes.

Costs

Trekking on Mt Elgon costs US$75 per person per day, which covers park entry fees and a ranger-guide. Permits are issued at UWA offices at each trailhead. Guides are mandatory whether heading to the summit or just doing a day trip. Camping fees are USh15,000 extra per night and porters, who are highly recommended, charge USh17,500 per day for carrying 18kg. Cooks charge USh20,000 per day. Also factor in tips, which are highly appreciated.

Trails

There are three routes up the mountain. Many people combine different routes going up and down for maximum variety. We've given the standard travel times for the various routes, but if you're up to the challenge these can all be shortened by a day or two. On the other hand, you may want to add an extra day to further explore the caldera or visit the Suam Gorge, or let the guides take you to waterfalls and caves. If summiting at Wagagai, it only takes an extra hour to hit Jackson's Summit (4165m) via Jackson's Pool, a little crater lake. You must use designated campsites, all of which have tent pads, latrines, rubbish pits and nearby water sources.

Climbers have the option of continuing their trek into Kenya. Park staff at the headquarters will take you to the immigration office in Mbale for the requisite paperwork and then hand you off to the Kenya Wildlife Service at the hot springs in the caldera. It's a two-day hike down the Kenyan side.

There are also many options for **day hikes**, with the most popular being a trio of short loops around the Forest Exploration Centre at the start of the Sipi Trail. Rose's Last Chance offers day walks for USh50,000 (including lunch) or a two-day **Budadari to Sipi Falls** walk along the slopes of Mt Elgon, visiting villages and coffee plantations en route (USh350,000 per person including food, tents, guide and porter); no park permit required.

SASA TRAIL

The Sasa Trail is the original route to Wagagai, and still the busiest as it can easily be reached by public transport from Mbale. It's a three- to four-day round-trip to the summit with a 1650m ascent on day one. From Budadari, which is considered the trailhead, a road leads 5km to Bumasola (you can take a car up this leg if you want) then it's a short walk to the forest. Almost as soon as you enter the forest, you reach Mudangi Cliffs, which are scaled via ladders, then it's 2½ hours of pure bamboo forest. The second day is an easier walk. On summit day, it's four hours from your campsite to Wagagai.

SIPI TRAIL

The Sipi Trail, which begins at the Forest Exploration Centre in Kapkwai, has become a popular return route as it allows you to chill out at Sipi Falls following your trip to the top. It's a four- to seven-day round-trip, though you can opt to descend via the Sasa Trail, an easier route. On the first day you can camp inside the huge Tutum Cave, which has a small waterfall over its entrance and once attracted elephants who dug salt out of the rock, much like some caves on the Kenyan side still do.

PISWA TRAIL

Starting high, the Piswa Trail has a gentler ascent than the Sipi Trail. It's the best wildlife-watching route as it doesn't pass through bamboo stands, and it also offers the longest pass through the other-worldly moorland in the caldera. It's a six-day journey when returning by the Sasa Trail and seven days when coming back via the Sipi Trail. Piswa Trail is less used because it begins in the difficult-to-reach village of Kapkwata, above Sipi.

Sleeping

★Rose's Last Chance GUESTHOUSE $
(☎0752203292, 0772623206; www.roseslastchance.yolasite.com; Budadiri; camping/dm/s/d incl half board USh25,000/40,000/50,000/70,000) Located near the trailhead in Budadari, Rose's is a laid-back, comfortable, fun and friendly place that brings guests closer to the local scene. Testing local brews is a favourite activity and Rose sometimes brings in musicians and dancers at night. The dining room has good vibes and bedrooms are cosy and clean. It's close to the UWA office.

You can also study local cooking, dances and the Luguisu language here.

UWA Forest Exploration Centre GUESTHOUSE $
(☎0773427679, 0772674063; Kapkwai; camping/dm/s/d USh15,000/10,000/40,000/55,000) This lovely spot run by Uganda Wildlife Authority (UWA) is right at the Sipi trailhead and has a little restaurant. Book via the National Park Headquarters (p414) office in Mbale.

Suam Guesthouse GUESTHOUSE $
(☎0772674063; menpuwa@yahoo.ie; Suam; camping/r USh15,000/35,000) A budget UWA lodge (cold water only) at Suam trail where you'll need to bring your own food. Book in advance via the National Park Headquarters (p414) in Mbale.

UWA Kapkwata Guesthouse GUESTHOUSE $
(☎07734278679; Kapkwata; camping/dm with shared bath USh15,000/25,000, s/d USh30,000/55,000) This simple place serves the Piswa trailhead, just east of the park entrance gate. Dorms and cabins have shared bathrooms and there are basic meals available.

Getting There & Away

The park is best accessed via Mbale, a three-hour drive from Kampala.

SASA TRAIL

There are regular minibuses from Mbale to Budadari (USh5000, one hour).

SIPI TRAIL

There's no regular transport to the Forest Exploration Centre (p416), but minibuses between Mbale and Kapchorwa (USh11,000, 1½ hours) pass the signposted turn-off to Kapkwai, from where it's a 6km walk to the Forest Exploration Centre. A *boda-boda* from Sipi should cost USh10,000 to USh15,000 depending on how dry the road is; a fair special-hire price from Mbale to Kapkwai is around USh80,000. A more interesting way to get to the centre is to hire a guide at Sipi to walk you through the villages – about a 90-minute trip.

PISWA TRAIL

Getting to the Piswa trailhead in Kapkwata takes some effort. The excellent paved road ends at Kapchorwa. From here you'll have to take a minivan taxi to Kapkwata (USh15,000) for the often-rough 33km trip that can take up to four hours. They run until around 3pm, so it's possible to make it from Mbale in a day.

Sipi Falls

Sipi Falls, in the foothills of Mt Elgon, is a stunner – arguably the most beautiful waterfall in all Uganda. There are three falls separated by steep hillsides. Though the upper two are beautiful, it's the 95m main drop that attracts the crowds, and most lodgings look out on to it. The view of the wide plains disappearing into the distance below is also spectacular. It's well worth spending a night or two in this peacefully magnificent place, which also allows you time to enjoy some of the excellent walks in the area, including the show-stopping descent to the bottom of the falls.

Activities

Rock Climbing

The mainstay of **Rob's Rolling Rock** (☎0776963078, 07751963078; www.rollingrocksipifalls.wordpress.com; abseiling US$50, rock climbing US$40) is a 100m rappel alongside the main falls – providing the undisputed best views in Sipi. It has also bolted in 14 rock-climbing routes (easy to intermediate). There are long-term plans to open accommodation and a bar on the property.

Walks to Sipi Falls

There are some excellent walks on a network of well-maintained local trails with beautiful scenery in every direction. The most popular walk is to the bottom of the falls – during rainy season it's an awe-inspiring sight. It's a steep climb down through villages and crops, and a sweaty, exhausting climb back up. A cave behind the easy-to-reach second falls is really worth the climb. On a clear day you can see much of Uganda from the ridge at the top.

Locals don't allow tourists to ramble the trails on their own. Much of the route is private property, with landowners charging for passage. Per person, the going rate for guides is about USh15,000 to get to the bottom of the main drop and USh25,000 for the four-hour, 8km walk to all three.

There are also village walks and the forest walking trails at Mt Elgon National Park's Forest Exploration Centre (p416) nearby, though you have to pay the national park fees to hike there.

Coffee Tours

A highlight of visiting Sipi is a coffee tour that walks you through the whole process: from picking the coffee berries, to shelling them, grinding them with a traditional mortar and pestle, roasting them on an open fire and – of course – finishing with a fine cup of strong Arabic coffee (including a bag for you to take home). Tours cost USh25,000 per person and involve a village visit to one of the mudbrick houses that have a small coffee plantation plot. For a visit, ask the **Sipi Falls Tourism Guide Association** (☎0772646364, 0773068977; 🐾) 🍃.

Mountain Biking

Sipi River Lodge has developed a selection of mountain-biking routes ranging from hard-core technical rocky climbs to downhill sections; bike hire can also be arranged.

Sleeping

Moses' Campsite GUESTHOUSE $

(0752208302; camping USh10,000, bandas per person USh20,000) Sipi's original backpacker option, this small, laid-back operation has a good view of the falls from its wonderful rickety terrace and unhindered views of the plains below from a rocky cliff. The *bandas* are decent, the staff friendly and colobus monkeys often hang around the shady campground. For better or worse, the addition of a bar means music-filled evenings.

Crow's Nest GUESTHOUSE $

(0752515389; thecrowsnets@yahoo.com; camping/dm USh15,000/30,000, cabins per person from USh50,000) Set up by Peace Corps volunteers, these Scandinavian-style log cabins feature some private baths and views of all three waterfalls from their terraces (go for cabin 2 or 3). They can arrange cultural walks (USh30,000) that cover hunting traditions and spiritualism. And yes, someone really did make a mess of the email address: crowsnets, not nest!

★ **Sipi River Lodge** LODGE $$

(0751796109; www.sipiriverlodge.com; incl half board dm US$56, banda with shared bathroom s/d US$102/118, cottage s/d US$126/200) A real retreat set in lush gardens with porch rockers and a creek-side trail to the second waterfall. Dorms and *bandas* use separate bathrooms with individual room locks and plenty of space. Splurge on a cottage with gorgeous batiks, private deck and shower views of the falls. A great on-site restaurant attracts nonguests for espresso drinks and homemade meals.

Many of the ingredients on the menu come from the on-site vegetable garden. A nightly set menu (US$20, reserve ahead), with a vegan option, is served in an atmospheric dining room with a log fire and well-stocked bar. Activities range from Mt Elgon treks to mountain biking, fly fishing and coffee tours on the lodge plantation.

Lacam Lodge LODGE $$

(0752292554; www.lacamlodge.co.uk; incl breakfast camping USh43,000, per person with shared bathroom USh52,000, bandas s/d from USh133,000/220,000) This very attractive lodge sits astride the top of the big waterfall, with sideways, close-up views and breezes. Accommodation, from the three-bed dorms to the large *bandas*, is comfortable, and the service is good. Nonguests sometimes come to enjoy a meal with a view.

Sipi Falls Resort LODGE $$$

(0753153000; sipiresort@gmail.com; camping/s/d/tr USh30,000/160,000/190,000/230,000) Sublime waterfall views and affordable *bandas* with open-air private showers (cold) ensure a memorable stay. Hosts are friendly but beds can be lumpy and meal service, like in most places, is deplorably slow. Quantities of local French-press coffee is a big plus. The old house was used as a residence by the last British governor of Uganda.

Shopping

Sipi Women's Craft Shop ARTS & CRAFTS

(077768221381; 7am-7pm) These quality crafts, clothes and accessories are made by local women. They also sell Sipi coffee and honey. Proceeds from sales go to the community. It's on the outskirts of town as you approach from Mbale.

Getting There & Away

Minibus taxis run between Mbale and Sipi Falls (USh10,000, one hour), but can take a long time to fill up.

For the return trip, most minibuses start at Kapchorwa and are often full when they pass through Sipi, so you may end up waiting a while. Ask at your lodge if they know when any minibuses will start the trip in Sipi.

To Mbale expect to pay around USh50,000 for a special hire or USh20,000 for a *boda-boda*.

Nyero Rock Paintings

Of the many ancient rock-art sites scattered around eastern Uganda, this is one of the easiest to reach, and one of the few that's worth the effort to do so. The **main site** (off Ngora Rd; USh10,000), known as **Nyero 2**, is a big white wall covered in groups of red circles, boats and some vaguely human and animal forms. Archaeologists have yet to unravel the significance of the designs, who painted them and even when they did so. If the caretaker is around, he'll charge for an informative tour; otherwise local kids will show you around. **Nyero 1**, with a few more circles, lies just below the main site, while **Nyero 3**, where you probably won't notice the modest painting unless someone shows you, is a few hundred metres north. The surrounding countryside is littered with boulder-covered peaks and cacti, giving it a Wild West feel.

Getting There & Away

The rock paintings are 10km west of Kumi, just past Nyero village. Look for the small, white signpost. It's an easy day trip from Mbale, Sipi or even Jinja. Minibuses running between Mbale (USh7000, one hour) and Soroti (USh7000, one hour) are frequent and stop along the highway. Departing from the taxi park just north of the Kumi city centre to Ngora, shared car-taxis can drop you at the site (USh5000, 20 minutes), but departures are infrequent in the morning and rare in the afternoon. From Kumi the round-trip (including waiting time) by special hire costs USh35,000 and by *boda-boda* around USh6000.

NORTHEASTERN UGANDA

The ultraremote northeast represents a Uganda largely unknown to both visitors and the bulk of its population living down south. And for good reason – it's a long and rugged road to its principal draw, Kidepo Valley National Park, where lion prides, herds of zebra and waterbuck share the savannah with species found in no other Ugandan park such as cheetah and wild dogs. Bordering South Sudan and Kenya, it's a world apart in terms of culture and landscape – with knobby mountains and steep escarpments straight out of fiction. Acholi, Karamajong, Ik and Dodoth people call the region home. Gulu and Kitgum suffered for decades under LRA guerilla raids. Tribal conflict, acted out mostly in deadly cattle raids, made pastoral Karamojaland off limits for some time, though a decade-long disarmament has brought greater stability, with visitors following suit. Moroto is emerging as a fascinating destination to get close to Karamojan culture with sustainable tourism.

Kidepo Valley National Park

Considered one of the most remote safari parks in Africa, **Kidepo Valley National Park** (www.ugandawildlife.org; adult/child US$40/20) is most notable for harbouring a number of animals found nowhere else in Uganda, including cheetahs, bat-eared foxes, aardwolves, caracal and greater and lesser kudus. There are also large concentrations of elephants, zebras, buffaloes, bushbuck, giraffes, lions, jackals, leopards, hyenas and Nile crocodiles. The park also offers some of the most stunning scenery of any protected area in Uganda; the rolling, short-grass savannah of the 1442-sq-km park is ringed by mountains and cut by rocky ridges. Amazingly, most of the animals, including even the occasional lion, are content to graze and lounge right near the park accommodation, so you can see a whole lot without going very far – a kind of armchair safari.

KIDEPO VALLEY NATIONAL PARK

Why Go Stunning scenery; best variety of wildlife in Uganda including zebra, cheetah and ostrich to go with lion, giraffe and elephant; the chance to visit a Karamojong village.

When to Go November to January, when you might see some of the biggest buffalo herds in Africa. During rainy season (August to September) long grass can impede viewing, and safari track access can be problematic. But you're sure to see lots of animals any time.

Practicalities Can be reached in a day from Kampala if you have your own vehicle. Public transport takes a few days, with a night in Kitgum or Gulu; if approaching from the east you'll need to overnight in Moroto, Soroti or Kotdio.

Budget Tips Apoka Hostel has well-priced *bandas* at the park headquarters, as does Buffalo Base outside the park; consider getting a group to chip in to hire 4WD from Kampala.

Activities

Wildlife Drives

Kidepo is the only park in Uganda where Uganda Wildlife Authority (UWA) has a vehicle for hire to visitors (day/night US$90/120), but it's not always available. For those with their own vehicles, there's an extensive network of tracks in the park, with the Narus Valley being a top target for wildlife. Lions are often spotted lazing in rocky outcrops and climbing the branches of fig trees. Also popular are the borassus palm forest and Kanangorok hot springs by the Kidepo River near the South Sudan border; which is also the habitat of ostriches. With your own vehicle, night drives cost US$40 for guide and spotlight.

Note that only the Apoka gate (at Apoka Rest Camp) staffs ranger guides for morning safaris. It's a good idea to book yours a day in advance, as the staff is small.

Nature Walks

A great option for wildlife viewing is to venture out on foot, accompanied by armed rangers.

Cultural Tours

UWA can organise visits (US$30) to Karamojong and Ik villages with hiking at Mt Morungole, both memorable experiences allowing you to interact with these northeast tribal groups.

Sleeping

There are only a few lodgings, but there's something for every price range, from budget to luxury. If you want to be in the thick of the action, the park maintains several isolated campsites (USh15,000) with latrines, firewood and water, but you provide the tent. You'll be accompanied by an armed guard who can arrange firewood for cooking.

Buffalo Base GUESTHOUSE **$**
(0775193270; www.buffalobase.com; Karenga; s/d US$25/40;) Well outside the park in the small township of Karenga (8km from Kidepo's gate), this simple roadside guesthouse is a good option for those wanting to experience Karamoja culture by staying in a *manyata* (traditional Karamoja round hut). There are also basic rooms, and food is served in its pleasant restaurant. It can arrange cultural performances and park transport.

Wi-fi use (via memory stick) can be purchased.

Apoka Rest Camp BANDA **$**
(0392-899500, 0782637293; info@ugandawildlife.org; camping/s/d USh15,000/61,000/72,000, s/d with shared bathroom USh41,000/52,000) Run by Uganda Wildlife Authority (UWA), this campus of basic *bandas* is spread over a grassy site. There's plenty of wildlife about, so be sure to keep your distance and always carry a torch. A small restaurant (reserve ahead if possible) offers a limited menu (meals USh10,000) and cold beers to enjoy around the nightly campfire.

★ **Kidepo Savannah Lodge** LODGE **$$**
(in Kampala 0312-294894; www.naturelodges.biz/kidepo-savannah-lodge; Kalokudo Gate; s/d lazy camping incl full board US$60/110, s/d safari tent incl full board US$115/165) Just outside the park boundary, this stylish addition delivers excellent value. It sits on a low ridge with expansive park views and visiting zebra and waterbuck. Simpatico staff serve meals or chilled beers in the main lodge with ample lounging space. Deluxe safari tents feature decks, beds clad in Masai blankets and hot showers in attached open-air bathrooms.

Apoka Safari Lodge LODGE **$$$**
(0414-251182; www.wildplacesafrica.com; s/d incl full board & 2 activities US$725/1170;) A unique luxury property, Apoka Safari Lodge spoils you with 10 lovely rooms, fine dining and a swimming pool chiselled into rock. Large, thatched cottages with canvas walls and solar power look out on wildlife attracted to the on-site watering hole. Each cottage features an outdoor tub, stone showers and a writing desk that would suit Hemingway to a tee.

The swimming pool (US$25) is available to day visitors when no guests are booked. Meals are another possibility for nonguests (lunch/dinner US$30/45), depending on other bookings. Reception displays the skull of Kidepo's last rhino – shot by poachers in the early 1980s.

Nga'Moru Wilderness Camp LODGE **$$$**
(0785551911; http://ngamoru.blogspot.cl; per person incl full board US$120) This wild and peaceful spot just outside the park border has safari tents with hot solar-powered showers and huge cottages with prime views. Installations have seen some wear and a small dining area with little windows takes little advantage of the cool setting. Lions occasionally hang out here. Owner Patrick is an excellent source of info for northern Uganda.

WORTH A TRIP

JOURNEY THROUGH KARAMOJA

The far-less-travelled route up to Kidepo National Park heads through the wilds of Karamojaland in the eastern reaches of Uganda, a two- or three-day journey that takes you though some of the most stunning scenery in the country. You'll pass timeless plains peppered with tall jagged peaks and fields ablaze with sunflowers. You'll also encounter the Karamojong people – the highlight of the journey for most – pastoral herders recognisable by their traditional dress (similar to the Maasai). Males often sport dapper Dr Seuss–style top hats with a feather stuck in it, and brandish a cattle stick and a mini wooden stool (used as a seat, headrest and, in recent times, to steady their rifle for target practice).

Until very recently Karamoja has had a deserved reputation as a dangerous destination. In the past the Karamojong had been known to ambush highway travellers, sometimes to steal food or money. Safety has improved markedly since disarmament of the Karamong people by the Ugandan military in 2011–12 when 40,000 AK-47s were confiscated. The main concern these days comes not from the Karamoja but from occasional skirmishes between them and armed Turkana people from Kenya who cross the border looking to steal cattle.

An increasing number of tourists travel through these days without incident. However, it's still paramount to check security warnings and road conditions before setting out (national park staff will have the latest details) and again at every step of the way. Heavy rains can make sections of road impassable.

Coming from Kampala or Kidepo, the best spot to overnight is **Moroto**, the biggest and most prosperous of Karamoja towns, with leafy streets and many NGOs. Sustainable tour operator **Kara-Tunga Tours** (☎0784414528; www.kara-tunga.com; Independence Ave; day trip/overnight per person from US$35/75) offers stays in pastoral villages or traditional herders camps, outdoor adventures and fascinating cultural immersion with Karamajong through fantastic programs designed by a Dutch-Karamojan. Stay at their relaxed base **Kara-Tunga Guesthouse & Cafe** (☎0784414528; www.kara-tunga.com/guesthouse; Independence Ave; camping USh15,000, s/d incl breakfast USh57,000/77,000) or in the classic **Mt Moroto Hotel** (☎0392-897300; http://morotohotel.com; Moroto; r incl breakfast from USh75,000-140,000, cottage USh250,000;), banked up against the gorgeous mountain of the same name. Guided hiking is also a good option here. Moroto is 440km from Kampala; by car it's eight hours, but by bus (USh35,000) it's often around 12 hours, as many take the less-direct route through **Soroti**, another major town where you can overnight. The former government-run **Soroti Hotel** (☎0414-561269, 0705408000; hotelsoroti01@gmail.com; Serere Rd; s/d incl breakfast from US$35/40;) is a very good choice with large clean rooms, a bar and restaurant. Breaking up the journey from Kampala in Mbale (USh20,000, six hours) is another good option. From Moroto, you can also bus to Kidepo (USh30,000, four hours).

Further on is **Kotido**, a gritty, downtrodden town with a large NGO presence. You can stay at the **Kotido Resort** (☎0783933700; https://kotidoresorthotel.com; Lomukura St, Kotido; s/d incl breakfast US$14/28;), with clean rooms in a secure compound, but it's best to time it so you can push on. Just outside Kidepo, the village of **Kaabong** can be an interesting stop to take in the bustling roadside market and perhaps to purchase a plaid blanket to steel you against the chilly evenings of the north.

Getting There & Away

There are two routes to reach Kidepo. The vast majority of visitors take the route through to Kitgum via Gulu, which is the shorter route. Otherwise there's the more adventurous eastern route through spectacular scenery of Karamoja. Though Karamoja was once notorious for banditry, the area has gained increasing stability (in large part thanks to disarmament) and travellers in private vehicles are using this route with good results.

Undoubtedly your best bet is to rent a car, in which case you can make it in one day from Kampala to Kidepo if you get a very early start. Alternatively you could take a bus to Kitgum and negotiate a special-hire from there.

Kitgum

POP 57,000

Bustling Kitgum sees few travellers. The district suffered badly under the Lord's Resistance Army's (LRA's) reign of terror and today has a sizeable NGO population. If you are headed to Kidepo Valley National Park you could overnight here.

Sleeping & Eating

While the town's most popular option undergoes renovations, pickings are slim. However, there are basic sleeping options that will get you through the night.

There are inexpensive cafes on Ogwok Rd.

Acholi Pride GUESTHOUSE $
(0772687793; Ogwok Rd; r USh28,000, with shared bathroom USh13,000) Next door to UWA, this is by far the best cheapie in town, with simple, clean and functional rooms set around a courtyard. It's on a busy corner in town. Rooms have TV, mosquito net and fan.

Fugly's GUESTHOUSE $$
(0785551911; fuglys.limited@gmail.com; Church Cres; s/d incl breakfast USh80,000/160,000, with shared bathroom from USh50,000/100,000;) South African–owned Fugly's is popular with NGOs and diplomats for its good range of rooms, plenty of lawn, small pool and barbecue in the evening. When we visited it was closed for renovations; look for it to open in 2018.

Information

INTERNET ACCESS

There's an internet cafe across from **Acholi Pride**.

MONEY

There are several banks with ATMs.

TOURIST INFORMATION

UWA (0777478856; 4 Ogwok Rd; 8am-5.30pm Mon-Sat) A good source of information.

Getting There & Away

The Post Bus (p400) heads to Kampala daily, as does Homeland bus (USh35,000, eight hours) at 6.30am and 5pm. You can also head to Gulu (USh15,000, two hours).

Until around midday, trucks head east from Kitgum to Karenga (USh20,000, 3½ hours), 24km from the park's headquarters and lodging area. They depart from the little village in front of Stanbic bank. In Karenga you might get lucky and be able to hitch a ride, but you'll probably need a special-hire (USh40,000).

Gulu

0471 / POP 154,000

Unless you're here volunteering or en route to Kidepo Valley National Park, there's no real reason to visit Gulu. However, it's quite a pleasant stop, with friendly locals, a relaxed feel and nice spots to hang out. The largest town in northern Uganda, it was one of the hardest hit during the Lord's Resistance Army (LRA) conflict. It's a town in transition and, in a sure sign of optimism, restaurants are busy and people are arriving from elsewhere in the country hoping to cash in on the coming boom. And there's no shortage of *wazungus* (foreigners) about, with so many NGOs in town.

Sights

Taks Centre CULTURAL CENTRE
(0471-433906; www.takscentre.blogspot.co.uk; 3-5 Upper Churchill Dr; 8am-10pm Mon-Sat) It's worth popping into this happening community arts centre to see what's on, whether it be an art exhibition, fireside chat or cultural performance. They sell beautiful Ugandan crafts and there's also a restaurant serving local food and *banda* accommodation for USh50,000, including breakfast. Proceeds go to job training for local youth.

Activities

St Jude Children's Home VOLUNTEERING
(0782896897; www.stjudechildrenshome.com) A Catholic orphanage welcoming volunteers to work with children from teaching, games or sports, from one-week minimum stints to long-term. Accommodation inclusive.

Thrive-Gulu VOLUNTEERING
(0714366824; www.thrivegulu.org) Does a range of work involving rehabilitating those who suffered during the LRA, including child soldiers. Occasionally looking for skilled volunteers.

Sleeping

Gulu has a reasonable number of good hotels, but because of all the aid workers passing through, prices are usually higher than they should be.

Iron Donkey GUESTHOUSE $

(☎0793719563; www.facebook.com/irondonkeygulu; Olya Rd; s/d incl breakfast USh60,000/90,000;) With just nine rooms, this simple lodging above a popular cafe of the same name offers a mix of decent doubles, twins and bunk beds. It's popular with volunteer workers. All have shared bathrooms with hot showers.

Hotel Pearl Afrique HOTEL $

(☎0774072277; www.hotelpearlafrique.co; Paul Odong Rd; s/d incl breakfast from USh75,000/90,000;) A comfortable, good-value choice with spotless rooms, some with bathtubs. Pricier rooms are worth it, with tons more space. There's a restaurant and bar with live music on weekends.

Bomah Hotel HOTEL $$

(☎0779945063; http://bomahhotels.com; 8 Eden Rd; s/d/ste US$47/70/195; @) In a leafy part of town, the colonial-style Bomah is a smart option with 90 sparkling rooms in a hotel block set over many levels and more under construction. There's also an excellent gym overlooking the pool and a popular thatched-roof restaurant (mains USh18,000 to USh26,000).

Eating

Gulu is blessed with good restaurants serving meals at very reasonable prices. There's a Uchumi supermarket for those heading to Kidepo.

★**Elephante** CAFE $

(☎0783115811; Samuel Doe Rd; mains USh8000-18,000; 9am-10pm;) Gulu's hipsters flood this cute garden cafe serving wood-fired pizzas, burgers and Mexican fare. It's owned by a Portland native, which ensures quality espresso drinks and a good tea selection (in addition to beer and wine). If you had pizza in mind, be patient. It takes a long while to fire up the oven.

Iron Donkey Restaurant CAFE $

(☎0793719563; Olya Rd; mains USh12,000-20,000; 9am-7pm Tue-Sun) Start your day feasting on homemade pastries, crêpes or an American breakfast. Salads, sandwiches and tacos are served the rest of the day. It's no wonder that this bakery-cafe with international flair is a magnet for young NGO workers. The restaurant stays open for hotel guests after 7pm.

New Abyssinia ETHIOPIAN $

(☎0774423132; Labwar Rd; mains USh7000-11,000; 7.30am-midnight;) Serving delicious Ethiopian and Eritrean food, this friendly restaurant offers a welcome change of pace. To sample some of everything, try the Abyssinian special with *injera* (a spongy flatbread) and a variety of dishes. Vegan friendly.

Drinking & Nightlife

BJz PUB

(☎0771008142; Eden Rd; 8.30am-midnight, later Sat & Sun) Gulu's most popular drinking spot for locals and expats alike, with plenty of seating areas and live music on weekends.

Coffee Hut CAFE

(Awich Rd; coffee USh4000, wraps USh8000; 7am-8pm;) Across from the bus park, this modern cafe is the place to go for excellent coffee, juice, breakfast and tasty wraps.

Information

All major banks have branches here with ATMs.

Getting There & Away

To get here your best option is the Kampala–Gulu Post Bus (p400), which continues through to Kitgum. Otherwise buses and minivans run between Kampala and Gulu (USh30,000, five to six hours) all day long, departing from and arriving at Gulu's bus park. Much of this road is new and in excellent shape.

Those heading to Kidepo can get a bus to Kitgum (USh15,000, two hours). Minibus taxis to Masindi (USh15,000, four hours) are infrequent, so it may be quicker to take a minibus to Kigumba (USh15,000, 2½ hours) or Kitgum and transfer to Masindi (USh5000, 1½ hours). There are also taxis to Arua (USh30,000, four hours).

SOUTHWESTERN UGANDA

A lush region of clear lakes, thickly forested islands and misted mountains, the southwest offers a taste of the best of Uganda. Whether you're on world-class treks along the western Rift Valley or preferring the placid escapism of Lake Bunyonyi's numerous islands, this gorgeous and diverse area should not be missed. Terraced hills and farmland cover much of the region. But it's also Uganda's top wildlife-watching destination and one of the best places in the world to spot primates. A visit with the mountain gorillas on the steep slopes of Bwindi Impenetrable National Park ranks as one of Africa's top experiences. You can also go chimp trekking in Kibale Forest National Park, home to the greatest variety of primates on the planet. There are safari opportunities too, from famous tree-climbing lions that steal the show at Queen Elizabeth National Park, to its herds of giraffes, hippos and buffaloes.

Fort Portal

☎0483 / POP 54,300

The fort may be gone, but this dynamic and friendly town is definitely still a great portal to numerous places offering sublime scenery, amazing nature and genuine adventure. Here you can explore the beautiful Crater Lakes, track the chimps in Kibale Forest National Park or drop into Semuliki National Park with its hot springs and central African wildlife, while all the time having the pleasant hotels of Fort Portal to return to afterwards.

As the heartland of a verdant tea-growing area, Fort Portal enjoys a pleasantly mild year-round climate, while its central location makes it a very convenient base from which to explore the area, meaning that many travellers intend just to stay overnight but end up staying here for several days.

Sights

Mugusu Market MARKET

(Kasese Rd; daytime Wed) The Wednesday market, 11km south of Fort Portal, is the largest market in the west and attracts traders from all over, including many from the DRC selling fresh produce, clothing and bric-a-brac.

Tooro Botanical Garden GARDENS

(☎0752500630; incl tour USh10,000; 9am-5pm) These homegrown botanical gardens

Southwestern Uganda

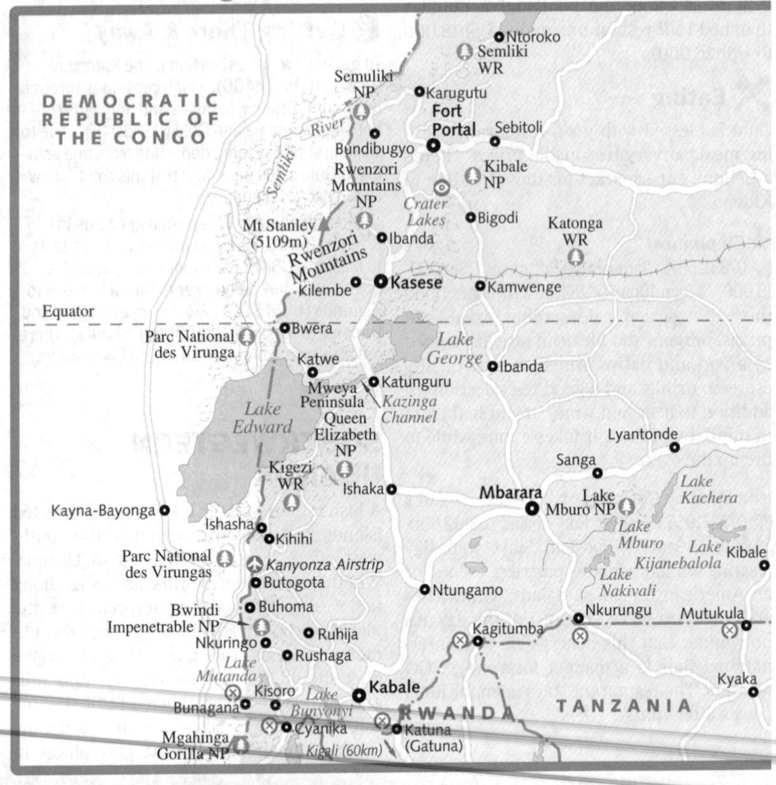

have a lot of well-signed indigenous plants and trees, as well as an organic farming project growing herbs, flowers, natural dyes and medicinal plants. Admission includes a tour through the extensive grounds that lasts just over an hour. Morning and late-afternoon birdwatching is a highlight (USh30,000 per person for a three-hour guided walk).

Tooro Palace PALACE
(guide USh5000) Looking down at town from its highest hill, the palace is worth a visit purely for its 360-degree panoramic views. It's the residence of King Oyo, who ascended the throne in 1995 at the age of three. A guide relates the history of the kingdom and explains the ceremonies that take place here, but you can't go inside.

The circular structure was built in 1963, but fell into ruin after the abolition of the royal kingdoms by Idi Amin. It was restored in 2001 after Colonel Gadaffi met the king and donated the money for repairs.

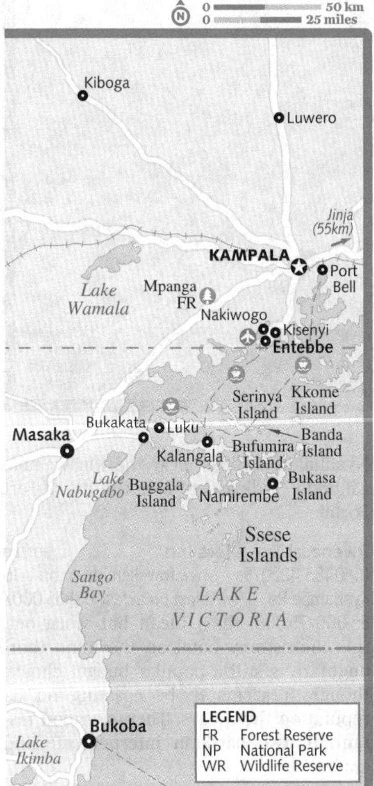

Karambi Royal Tombs TOMB
(Kasese Rd; USh10,000; 8am-6pm) These royal tombs, 4km south of town, make for a peaceful excursion. While from outside it's not much to look at, if you can find the caretaker he'll let you in for a look at the tombs, which house drums, spears and other personal effects of several of the Toro kings who are buried here. The cemetery outside is the resting place for various other royal family members.

Tours

Kabarole Tours & Safari TOURS
(0774057390, 0483-422183; https://kabarole-tours.com; 1 Moledina St; 8am-6pm Mon-Sat, 10am-4pm Sun) A local leader in community tourism and an impressive advocate for sustainable travel, Kabarole Tours can take you anywhere in Uganda, but focuses on this little corner of the country. Popular day trips include Crater Lakes, mountain-bike tours, birdwatching, village walks and treks in the foothills of the Rwenzoris. It can arrange gorilla permits for both Uganda and Rwanda.

Sleeping

Downtown Fort Portal is one of Uganda's noisiest places, and for that reason the best accommodation is concentrated in the scenic outskirts of town at Boma or the nearby Crater Lakes. That said, there are a few decent options in the town itself, and being central is far better if you don't have your own transport.

★YES Hostel HOSTEL $
(Youth Encouragement Services; 0787291183, 0772780350; www.yesugandahostel.weebly.com; Lower Kakiiza Rd; camping/dm USh12,000/25,000, d with shared bathroom USh40,000;) This wonderful project is the work of Carol Adans, a Hawaiian who moved to Uganda to make a difference over two decades ago, and boy, has she! YES supports the Mama Rescue Home, where 30 HIV+ children live, through its exceptional-value hostel with a peaceful pastoral setting. Rooms are configured as dorms, but usually you'll get one to yourself.

Breakfast is extra (USh12,000). There's a large kitchen (use per day USh5000), solar hot-water showers and *muzungu* (foreigner) meals are also offered. It's 3km from the centre; a *boda-boda* costs USh2000.

Fort Portal

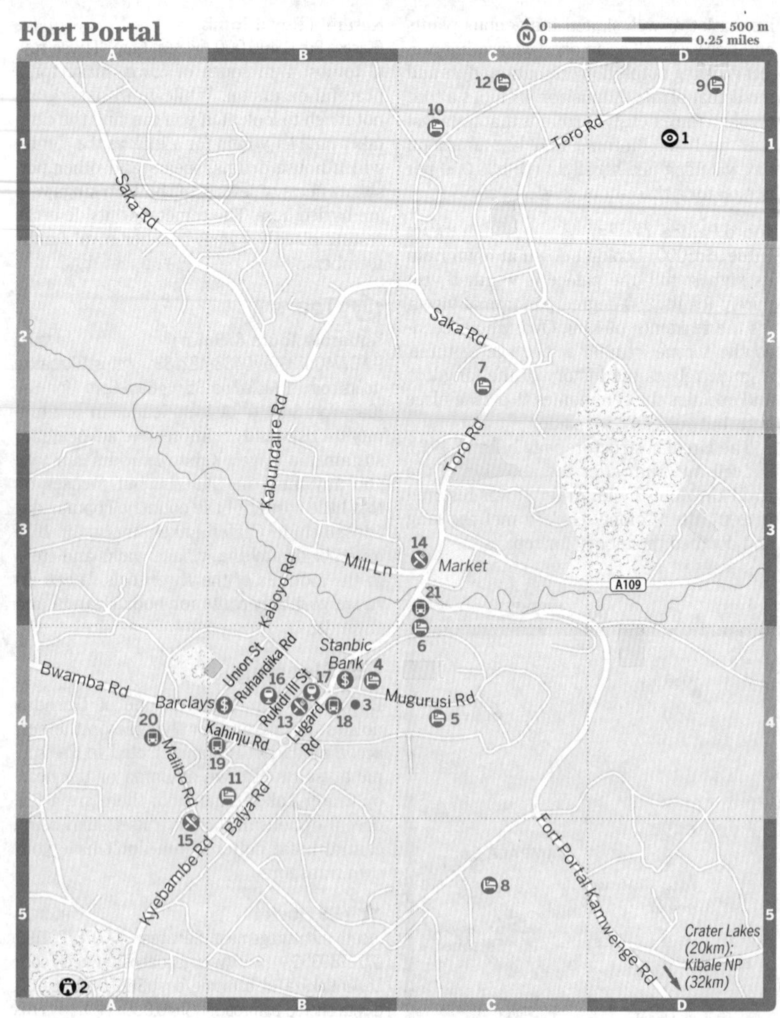

Daj Guesthouse HOTEL $
(☎0392-176279; Mugurusi Rd; s/d incl breakfast USh76,000/80,000; 📶) A good budget choice, this central hotel has some large, clean rooms with pastel walls. Some rooms feature flat-screen TV.

Mpora Rural Family HOMESTAY $
(☎0752555732; www.ugandahomestay.com; banda with shared bathroom per person incl full board US$24) This orphanage offers accommodation to help finance it (as well as the two schools) in a rural setting 15km from Fort Portal. It also hires mountain bikes and offers multiday cycling tours. It's located in Nyankuku, a village near the Kichwamba-Kihondo Trading Centre, northwest of Fort Portal.

Rwenzori Travellers Inn HOTEL $
(☎0483-422075; www.travellersinn.com; 16 Kyebambe Rd; s/tw/d incl breakfast USh55,000/65,000/75,000; @📶) Clean but worn out, this multistorey hotel on the main thoroughfare is still a popular budget choice, though it seems to be coasting on its reputation these days. There's a good restaurant, two bars, an internet cafe and craft shop.

Fort Portal

Sights
1 Tooro Botanical Garden D1
2 Tooro Palace A5

Activities, Courses & Tours
3 Kabarole Tours & Safari B4

Sleeping
4 Daj Guesthouse B4
5 Dutchess Guesthouse C4
6 Fort Motel C4
7 Golf Course View Guesthouse C2
8 Kalya Courts Hotel C5
9 Mountains of the Moon Hotel D1
10 Ruwenzori View Guesthouse C1
11 Rwenzori Travellers Inn B4
12 YES Hostel C1

Eating
13 Andrew & Brothers B4
Dutchess .... (see 5)
14 Gardens C3
15 Sweet Aromas Bakery A5

Drinking & Nightlife
16 Forest B4
17 Gluepot Bar B4

Transport
18 Kalita Transport Office B4
19 Link Coaches B4
20 Nyakaseke Taxi Park A4
21 Shared Taxis to Kamwenge & Rwaihamba C3

Golf Course View Guesthouse GUESTHOUSE $
(☎0772485602; golfcourse71@gmail.com; Rwenzori Rd; camping incl breakfast USh10,000, s/d incl breakfast USh50,000/60,000, with shared bathroom USh30,000/40,000) Just outside town, this relaxed guesthouse draws in shoestring lodgers. It has some faded colonial charm, with spacious, dark rooms that feature saggy beds and huge bathrooms. There's a restaurant, bar and kitchen for guest use. On a clear day there are lovely views of the Rwenzoris.

Fort Motel HOTEL $$
(☎0772501731; www.fortmotel.com; 2 Lugard Rd; s/d incl breakfast from US$80/110;) A great addition to Fort Portal's improving hotel scene, this stylish hotel has smart and ample rooms with balcony views, in-room safes and minifridges. There's also a sauna and gym.

Dutchess Guesthouse GUESTHOUSE $$
(☎0704879474, 0718746211; www.dutchessuganda.com; 11 Mugusrusi Rd; s/d/tr incl breakfast US$65/80/105, with shared bathroom US$50/65/90; P@) Dutchess offers excellent-value boutique rooms with plenty of flair, big beds, couches, power adaptors and safes for laptops. Sadly there are just a few rooms, so it's a good idea to book ahead. The excellent downstairs restaurant (p428) is another reason to stay here, as is its central location.

Mountains of the Moon Hotel HOTEL $$
(☎0775557840; www.mountainsofthemoonhotel.com; Nyaika Ave; s/d/tw from US$125/145/165; P@) With its classic country-club feel, this stately resort has 33 comfortable and well-equipped rooms set among peaceful, well-maintained grounds. It's the fanciest address in town, though the staff don't appear to have got that memo yet. Grounds are extensive and lush. There's a pool, gym, sauna and steamroom in addition to a decent (if rather slow) restaurant and lively bar.

Ruwenzori View Guesthouse GUESTHOUSE $$
(☎0483-422102, 0772722102; www.ruwenzoriview.com; Lower Kakiiza Rd, Boma; s/d USh135,000/195,000, with shared bathroom USh70,000/115,000; P) This blissful little guesthouse run by a Dutch-Anglo couple has a refreshingly rural and homely atmosphere. Rooms with attached bathrooms have private patios overlooking the superb garden and Rwenzori-mountain backdrop. Rates include a hearty breakfast, while its social dinners (USh35,000) served around the family table are an institution (nonguests welcome). Also sells exceptional local crafts.

Kalya Courts Hotel HOTEL $$
(www.kalyacourtshotel.com; Maguru Itaara Rd; s/d/tr USh100,000/180,000/200,000; P) This relative newcomer to Fort Portal has spacious gardens, clean rooms and bathrooms with hot water and some of the best water pressure in Uganda – exactly what you need after remote safari lodges. It's motel-like in style and a short walk from the town centre.

★ **Kyaninga Lodge** LODGE $$$
(☎0772999750; www.kyaningalodge.com; Lake Kyaninga; s/d incl full board US$265/395; P) The stunning Kyaninga Lodge, 10km northeast of Fort Portal, features eight epic thatched-roofed log cabins that soar high upon stilts. Joined by a wooden walking

platform, they are a spectacular sight – as are the views over Kyaninga Lake. The log cabins are spacious and private, with gleaming wooden floors and bathrooms with claw-foot baths, glass showers and marble countertops.

The restaurant also has amazing views, both from the outdoor deck and in the cosy Nepali teahouse-like restaurant. It's popular with nonguests for lunch (two courses USh50,000; reservations required). There's a swimming pool and sundeck too (nonguests USh10,000). It also hosts a marathon and triathlon yearly – see the website for details.

Eating

★Gardens AFRICAN $

(0772694482; Lugard Rd; mains USh10,000-30,000; 7am-11.30pm) Quite friendly and popular, this busy corner restaurant has a quality menu of foreign and local dishes including burgers, curries, pizza and African fare such as *firinda* (mashed skinless beans) and lots of *mochomo* (barbecued meat). There's a good liquor list, a large African lunch buffet and excellent local coffee too.

Sweet Aromas Bakery BAKERY $

(0790916151; Malibo Rd; mains USh4000; 8am-8pm;) Offering tasty baked goods, teas and fresh coffee, this tiny bakery and cafe can satisfy your sweet tooth. It's popular with expats.

Dutchess INTERNATIONAL $

(www.dutchessuganda.com; 11 Mugusrusi Rd; mains USh10,000-30,000; 7am-11pm;) Coveted by travellers, this elegant cafe has a creative menu featuring crocodile burgers, Flemish beef stew with Guinness and mash, and a selection of 46 excellent wood-fired pizzas, including a superb calzone. The only lacklustre offering on our last visit was the dessert menu. People linger here with their laptops. It's a nice, relaxing setting, but service can be surly.

Andrew & Brothers SUPERMARKET $

(Lugard Rd; 9am-7pm) For provisions, including wine, this is the best of several supermarkets in town.

Drinking & Nightlife

Forest BAR

(0772912349; Rukidi III St; 1pm-late) The most popular spot for a drink in Fort Portal, this Belgian-owned bar/club has outdoor seating and plenty of large screens showing sports.

Gluepot Bar BAR

(0702634499; Kaboyo Rd; 1pm-7am) In the town centre, Gluepot is a lively upstairs drinking spot.

Information

Barclays (Bwamba Rd) With ATM and currency exchange.

Stanbic Bank (Lugard Rd) Has an ATM.

Getting There & Away

BUS

Kalita (0756897920; www.kalita.co.ug; Lugard Rd) and **Link** (0312-108830; www.link.co.ug) have regular buses to Kampala (USh20,000, five hours). Both also head to Kasese (USh5000, two hours), but only Kalita makes the journey to Kabale (USh35,000, eight hours), via Katunguru (USh9000, 1½ hours) in Queen Elizabeth National Park.

TAXI

There are frequent departures from the **Nyakaseke Taxi Park** (Malibo Rd) to Kampala (USh18,000, four hours), Mbarara (USh20,000, 3½ hours), Ntoroko (USh15,000, 2½ hours), Bundibugyo (USh11,000, 1½ hours) and Hoima (36,000, five hours).

Minibuses (near Manga Bridge) and shared taxis to Kamwenge (for Kibale Forest National Park, USh15,000, 1½ hours) and Rwaihamba (for Lake Nkuruba, USh5000, 45 minutes) leave from the intersection near where the main road crosses the river.

SPECIAL HIRE

Drivers hang around the vacant lot by the Continental Hotel and charge from USh100,000 per day if you aren't travelling too far. Kabarole Tours (p425) has cars with driver for US$80 per day.

Crater Lakes

A dramatic landscape of crater lakes cupped under steep hillsides, the area south of Fort Portal offers travellers a scenic retreat ideal for long walks and road cycling. Much of the land is cultivated, but primates and plenty of birds occupy the lake shores. Emblazoned on Uganda's USh20,000 note, picturesque Lake Nyinambuga makes a worthwhile photo op. Of all the crater lakes, Lake Nkuruba is considered the most beautiful, surrounded by forest with black-and-white and red colobus.

Most lodges and guesthouses organise walks through local villages and places beyond (with entrance fees), such as Top of the World viewpoint on the highest hill behind Lake Nyamirima. The common wisdom is that the lakes are bilharzia-free, but we wouldn't risk it. Also be aware that a lone hippo inhabits Lake Nyabikere, so check with locals before plunging into the waters.

Sights

Top of the World VIEWPOINT
(USh5000) On the highest hill behind Lake Nyamirima, from this viewpoint you can see up to five lakes (depending on the air clarity).

Sleeping

Lodgings are scattered throughout the rural region on the shores of the crater lakes. Options are diverse, with plenty of good ones ranging from camping and *bandas* at community-run projects to luxury high-end lodges.

Lake Kifuruka Eco-Camp CABIN $
(☎0772562513; www.ecolodge-uganda.com; Lake Kifuruka; camping USh10,000, bandas s/d USh40,000/70,000, with shared bathroom USh20,000/40,000) Located 2km southwest of Rwaihamba this camp's log-cabin *bandas* are basic but clean, and proceeds go to funding local schools. It's a good spot for those seeking a more authentic local experience. It can also arrange village homestays.

Perhaps slightly less dazzling than the other crater lakes, brown Lake Kifuruka is attractive nevertheless. Other activities include canoe hire (USh15,000 per three hours), walks to all eight lakes or birdwatching (USh40,000 per person) or visits to Mahoma Falls (guided walk USh54,000). Staff are friendly and meals are available from USh7000.

Afritastic Planet Ruigo GUESTHOUSE $
(☎0782548326; planetruigo@afritastic.com; Lake Kasenda; camping incl breakfast US$10, banda incl breakfast US$13-25) This tiny refuge from the world sits right on the shore of Lake Kasenda looking up at the steep hills on the other side. Considering how few people come here, the three self-contained *bandas* are well maintained. The 'tree house' is secluded – it's on the other side of the lake and is great for those who want solitude.

Meals and activities can be arranged. There's plenty of thick forest for walking and you can easily wander over to nearby lakes Mulusi and Murigamire. Birdwatching and forest walks are rewarding. Little Lake Kasenda isn't at the end of the road, but it sure feels like it. There's no public transport here; your best bet is a *boda-boda* from Fort Portal (USh25,000).

Lake Nkuruba Nature Reserve Community Campsite BANDA $
(☎0773266067, 0782141880; www.nkuruba.com; Lake Nkuruba; camping USh10,000, s/d with shared bathroom USh36,000/52,000, cottage USh75,000) One of the best-value places around, and set on a forested lake that's exceptionally pristine for these parts. The hilltop camp sports excellent views and easy lake access. The *bandas* are basic, but clean and comfortable. The cottage is down on the lake shore for more privacy. Funds go towards community projects.

Meals are available (USh9000 to USh13,000), as are walks around the area (USh15,000 per person). There are plenty of birds here; keep your eye out for the great blue turaco. There are also black-and-white colobus monkeys, and it is possible to take night tours to spot bushbabies. You can hire bicycles (USh15,000 per day) and motorcycles for exploring on your own.

Chimpanzee Forest Guesthouse GUESTHOUSE $$
(☎0772486415; www.chimpanzeeforestguesthouse.com; Lake Nyabikere; camping US$10, s/d guesthouse incl full board US$80/120, cottage incl full board US$95/145; 📶) Not actually on Lake Nyabikere, but near enough to snag some views, is the wonderful Chimpanzee Forest Guesthouse. Set on manicured gardens overlooking tea plantations, there's a choice of renovated *bandas* or rooms in the atmospheric 1950s colonial building with a fireplace and a superb collection of antique books on Africa.

Some of the quality food here is grown on-site. Birdwatching and guided walks are also on the cards. The entrance is 300m south of the Kibale Forest National Park office on Fort Portal Rd.

Rweteera Safari Park & Tourist Camping LODGE $$
(☎0776862153; www.rweteerasafaripark.com; Lake Nyabikere; camping per person US$10, tented camping s/d incl breakfast US$35/50; 📶) Nothing fancy, this place on Lake Nyabikere still

WORTH A TRIP

AMABEERE CAVE

The reputed birthplace of King Ndahura, this small **cave** (incl guide US$10; ⏲8am-6pm) offers more cultural significance than natural wonder. The water dripping from the roof is milky white, hence the name Amabeere ('Breasts'). Most of the rock formations are broken, but it's fun to walk behind the waterfall covering it and past the wall of vines along the adjacent ridge.

It's 8km northwest of Fort Portal, signposted 1.5km off the Bundibugyo road; minibus taxis are USh3000 and take 30 minutes.

gets good feedback, with simple, comfortable tent camping by the lake. Any minibus (USh5000) heading south from Fort Portal can drop you right at the entrance.

Nyinabulitwa Country Resort & Safari Camp LODGE $$
(☎0712984929; www.nyinabulitwaresort.com; Lake Nyinabulitwa; camping incl breakfast US$15, s/d/tr full board US$60/100/150) An intimate little family-run place on the lake's south shore with five *bandas* and an excellent campground. With a beautiful garden setting, it's the perfect place to catch up on your journal. It runs boat trips (US$10 per person) around the lake and can deliver you to a tree house for bird- and primate-watching. Or paddle yourself for free.

A tranquil spot, the midsized Lake Nyinabulitwa, or 'Mother of Lakes', is set back a bit off the road to Kibale Forest National Park. It's 20km from Fort Portal, 1.5km off the main road just before Rweetera Trading Centre.

★**Papaya Lake Lodge** LODGE $$$
(☎0793388277; www.papayalakelodge.com; Lake Lyantonde; s/d incl full board US$390/550; 📶🏊) A stylish retreat with a rock 'n' roll heart, stunning Papaya Lake Lodge goes that extra mile. A gin cart for cocktail hour, antique masks and a bathroom sink fashioned on a fixed-gear bicycle are some of the original details. Spacious cottages with balconies face pretty Lake Lyantonde. The pièce de résistance: a ridgetop swimming pool overlooking two crater lakes.

There's also a lakeside bar and floating jetty where canoe trips start. Or if you prefer to laze, order an in-room massage.

★**Kluge's Guest Farm** GUESTHOUSE $$$
(☎0772440099; http://klugesguestfarm.com; lazy camping per person incl breakfast US$35, s/d incl half board US$145/205; 📶🏊) Whether you're drinking a beer with Stefan Kluge himself or watching monkeys skate across the treetops, this well-run retreat is unique. The cooking alone is some of the best in Uganda, served buffet style with homemade sausage, fresh breads and house hot sauce. Rooms are immaculate and beds divine. There's a sparkling little pool and roaring evening campfire.

Kids will enjoy the forest trail, playground and farm animals on-site. The hosts can arrange village walks and offer good travel advice. It's 15km from Fort Portal and well signposted.

Ndali Lodge LODGE $$$
(☎0772221309; www.ndalilodge.com; Lake Nyinambuga; d incl full board US$770; @📶🏊) With exquisite taste, this luxurious, colonial-style lodge on iconic Lake Nyinambuga has a stunning ridgetop location and is run by third-generation owners. Its elegant (but overpriced) cottages face west towards Mwamba and Rukwanzi lakes with the Rwenzori Mountains looming on the horizon. Day trippers can reserve ahead for a three-course lunch (US$25) served on a tranquil porch overlooking the lake.

ℹ Getting There & Away

Minibuses and shared taxis from Fort Portal to Rwaihamba pass Lake Nkuruba (USh5000, 45 minutes). A special-hire will set you back about USh30,000, and a *boda-boda* around USh10,000. For destinations around Lakes Nyabikere and Nyinabulitwa, take a minibus from Fort Portal's Mpanga Bridge towards Bigodi (USh9000, one hour).

For Lake Kifurka, take the same Bigodi-bound transport (USh5000) and ask to be dropped off at Rwaihamba market, from where you can get a *boda-boda* (USh2000) to your lodging.

Lake Kasenda is 35km south of Fort Portal and 11km south of Rwaihamba. You can drive here in 1½ hours: call your lodging to ask if the road is still in good enough shape for a car to make it. A special-hire taxi from Fort Portal should cost around USh80,000, but drivers are unlikely to know where it is.

Kibale Forest National Park

☎0483

This 795-sq-km **national park** (☎0483-425335; www.ugandawildlife.org; adult/child US$40/20) just outside Fort Portal is made up of dense tropical rainforest, within which dwell enormous numbers of primates. If you can't afford the lavish cost of mountain-gorilla tracking, then visiting one of the five habituated groups of chimpanzees here is a very worthy substitute, not to mention a far less financially draining one. Also regularly seen here are the rare red colobus and L'Hoest's monkeys.

Larger but rarely seen residents include bushbucks, sitatungas, buffaloes, leopards and quite a few forest elephants. There are also an incredible 250 species of butterfly and 372 species of bird here. The park visitor centre is at Kanyanchu, 35km southeast of Fort Portal.

Sights

Kihingami Wetlands Sanctuary NATURE RESERVE
(☎0774057390; ktours@infocom.co.ug; ⏲8am-5pm) This eco-tourism site, set up with the help of Fort Portal's Kabarole Tours (p425), preserves an attractive 13-sq-km valley that otherwise would have been gobbled up by the surrounding tea plantations. Despite its small size, a remarkable 230 bird species have been spotted here, including Jameson's wattle-eye and white-spotted flufftail. There's also a good chance of seeing red colobus monkeys and spotted-necked otters.

Local guides lead forest walks (USh25,000 per person) and birdwatching walks (USh25,000 per person), both at 7.30am and 3pm daily. You can also tour a fair-trade tea factory (USh25,000 per person) at 9am and 2pm.

Kihingami is 15km east of Fort Portal, just before the Sebitoli section of Kibale National Park. Book through Kabarole Tours or take any minibus (USh5000, 30 minutes) heading east from Fort Portal towards Sebitoli village.

Activities

Bigodi Wetland Sanctuary BIRDWATCHING, WALKING
(☎0772886865; www.bigoditourism.com; incl guide US$17; ⏲7.30am-5pm) Located 6km south of the Kibale National Park visitor centre at Kanyanchu (no park permit is required), Bigodi was established by a local development organisation to protect the 4-sq-km **Magombe Swamp** that's home to around 200 species of birds (highlights include papyrus gonolek, white-winged warbler and great blue turaco). It's also good for spotting butterflies and primates, with eight different species here, including grey-cheeked mangabey. Three-hour guided walks (USh40,000 per person, including binoculars and gumboots) depart on demand.

Other activities available include village walks (USh30,000 per person), Saturday-afternoon basket-weaving demonstrations, dance and drama performances, and fun interpretive meals (USh15,000 per person; book in advance) where your hosts share the stories behind the local food they serve you. Volunteer opportunities are also available. Any shared taxis (USh8000, 45 minutes) between Fort Portal and Kamwenge can drop you there.

Chimpanzee Tracking

With around a 90% chance of finding chimpanzees on any particular day, Kibale National Park is undoubtedly the most popular place to track them in Uganda. There's a morning (8am) and afternoon (2pm) departure, and while there are plenty of hills along the trails, the walking isn't difficult if you're in shape. Children aged 12 and under aren't permitted.

KIBALE FOREST NATIONAL PARK

Why Go The best place to track chimpanzees in the wild in Uganda; excellent birdwatching in nearby Bigodi Wetland Sanctuary.

When to Go Year-round; for chimpanzee habituation experience visit in low-season months of March, April, May and November.

Practicalities Regular minibuses to Kamwenge from Fort Portal. Prebooking chimpanzee permits is recommended.

Budget Tips While US$150 for chimpanzee tracking may seem expensive, bear in mind these fees include your park permit (US$40), and offer a more affordable alternative than visiting the gorillas. Public transport and inexpensive accommodation are available.

While you've a good chance of being issued a chimp permit (US$150) at the park, it occasionally gets booked out during holiday season, so reservations at the UWA office (p485) in Kampala are a good idea. Regular trackers get just one hour with the playful primates, but those on the **Chimpanzee Habituation Experience** (1/2/3 days US$220/440/660; ⏲Mar, Apr, May & Nov) can spend the whole day with them.

Note that chimpanzees have been in the process of being habituated in the Sebitoli sector, 12km east of Fort Portal, for some years now, but permits for this group were still not being issued to travellers.

Nature Walks

You'll be very lucky to see chimps on a nature walk (US$30 per person) but as nearly 1500 dwell here, you never know your luck, and there's a good chance you'll hear some scamper off through the treetops. With frequent sightings of owls, civets and the 12cm-long Demidoff's dwarf galago, night walks (US$40) can be very rewarding. A birdwatching tour with a guide costs US$30. Do be aware that you'll also need to pay the park entrance fee (US$40) to do one or more of these walks.

Sleeping

You can easily visit Kibale for the day while based in Fort Portal or the Crater Lakes, but the national park also has accommodation ranging from camping and budget guesthouses to luxury lodges within its boundaries.

Jacaranda Hilltop Guesthouse GUESTHOUSE $
(☎0774057390; Kasunga, Northern Sector; incl breakfast d USh90,000, s/d with shared bath USh52,000/75,000) Immersed within the tea plantations, this atmospheric colonial guesthouse is located inside the former residence of the tea-estate manager. Its simple rooms have a relaxed rural feel. Bikes are available for hire (per day US$10), perfect for exploring the surrounding countryside. It's well placed on the fringes of Kibale for walks into the park; and chimpanzee tracking once they're habituated.

It's 5km off Kampala Rd; any bus plying the Fort Portal route can drop you at the sign.

UWA Campsite CAMPGROUND $
(☎0486-424121; camping per person US$12) This pleasant campsite is enclosed by rainforest, but offers some attractive grass on which to pitch your tent. There are showers and toilets on-site and you can take meals at nearby Primate Lodge (p433) if you don't want to cook for yourself.

Tinka's Homestay GUESTHOUSE $
(☎0772468113; per person incl full board USh70,000) Tinka's rambling house is a relaxed, family atmosphere with just two guest rooms. It's 6km from Kibale HQ, right near the visitor centre of Bigodi Wetland Sanctuary, which is convenient if you're here to see birds as well as chimps. It also offers excellent traditional lunches (USh15,000 per person) that are absolute feasts – reserve in advance.

Kibale Forest Camp LODGE $$
(☎0779820695; www.naturelodges.biz/kibale-forest-camp; Bigodi; s/d incl half board lazy camping US$50/90, safari tent US$105/145) This welcoming and atmospheric camp sits deep in the forest with monkeys and birdlife. There are deluxe safari tents with stone floors and porches, solar power, fire-heated hot water and even ready-made 'lazy camping' for the budget minded. A safari-style restaurant and lounge occupies an attractive two-storey hut.

It's on the outskirts of Bigodi, 1km down a side road off Kamwenge Rd.

Chimps' Nest LODGE $$
(☎0774669107; www.chimpsnest.com; incl breakfast s/d with shared bathroom US$21/26, s/d cottage US$60/80, tree house US$140; @ 📶) Popular for its night-time wildlife walks, this lodge has very affordable basic rooms (don't mind the toilet three inches off the floor) and charming rustic cottages with outdoor showers. However, staff can be rather indifferent and meals are just so-so. Showers are heated by firewood. It's 4km down a rough road from Nkingo, straddling Kibale Forest and Magombe Swamp.

SLEEPING IN THE NORTHERN SECTOR

In the northern end of the park along Kampala Rd, this seldom-visited part of the forest will have more accommodation options when the chimpanzees who live here are fully habituated – this is expected to occur in the next few years. For the time being it sees little traffic, as park entrance fees are the same as for the chimp-tracking area but with less on offer.

★**Primate Lodge** LODGE $$$

(☎0414-267153; www.ugandalodges.com/primate; Kanyanchu; camping without breakfast US$14, s/d incl full board safari tent US$62/79, cottage US$204/286; 📶) Right in the park and next to the UWA headquarters, this deluxe forest lodge is perfectly located for chimp tracking. Luxury stone cottages have timber floors, windows on all sides, huge terraces and coffee delivered to the room in the morning. There's even a secluded tree house with occasional elephant views. Rooms have solar hot water and evening power.

Discounts available in low season.

Sebitoli Forest Camp LODGE $$$

(☎0392-175976, 0782761512; Sebitoli, Northern Sector; camping/d USh18,000/50,000) This UWA-run camp has a relaxing location surrounded by trees with black-and-white colobus monkeys. Rooms here are great value, with a canteen and friendly staff.

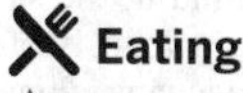

Eating

★**EcoBurrito** TEX-MEX $

(☎0780142926; www.ecoburrito.com; Bigodi; burritos USh9000-10,000; ⏰8am-5pm Mon-Fri) This brilliant and highly unexpected roadside find is likely to elicit squeals of glee from even the most seasoned Africa hands. An American doctoral student studying the chimps in the park trained locals in the ways of Tex-Mex, and EcoBurrito is the result. Enjoy succulent and delicious chapattis and tortillas stuffed full of tasty fillings and washed down with beer.

All proceeds to the project go to the local primary school, so you can finally rationalise your burrito consumption as charity work.

Getting There & Away

Minibuses to Kamwenge from Fort Portal pass the park visitor centre (USh15,000, one hour). For Sebitoli, take any minibus (USh4000, 30 minutes) heading east from Fort Portal.

Semuliki National Park

Semuliki National Park (☎0382-276424; www.ugandawildlife.org; adult/child US$35/5) covers 220 sq km of the valley floor connecting Uganda to the steamy jungles of central Africa and harbours some intriguing wildlife, although sightings are not always easy due to the thick vegetation. It's most famous for its primordial hot springs, sites for traditional rituals for the local Bamaga people.

SEMULIKI NATIONAL PARK

Why Go Sulphur hot springs; a feel for Congo tropical lowland rainforest; primate walks; birdwatching.

When to Go Year-round.

Practicalities Day trips are a popular option. Minibuses run from Fort Portal to Bundibugyo near park headquarters.

Budget Tips Public transport, UWA campsites and canteen meals make Semuliki an affordable park to visit, but bear in mind visits to the hot springs cost US$30 per person on top of park entry.

Birdwatchers come to see more than 440 bird species, particularly the central African species, such as the Congo serpent eagle, residing at their eastern limits. At least 133 of the 144 Guinea–Congo forest species have been recorded here and nearly 50 species are found nowhere else in East Africa. There are nine primate species, including De Brazza's monkey, and many mammals not found elsewhere in Uganda, such as Zenker's flying mice. Both the resident elephant and buffalo are the forest variety, smaller than their savannah brethren.

Sights

Most people come here to see Semuliki's two boiling sulphur hot springs. Entry costs US$30 per person (excluding park entry), which includes a guided walk.

The **female hot spring** is where women from the Bamaga clan would make sacrifices to the gods before bathing naked in the natural springs. Its soupy atmosphere has a distinct prehistoric feel, and features a small burbling geyser. Your guide can demonstrate the water's temperatures by boiling an egg – available from the information centre for USh500 each; though with the stench of sulphur it's probably the last thing you feel like eating.

A half-hour walk from the 'female' spring, the **male hot spring** is where the men carried out their sacrificial rituals. It is accessed via a muddy forest trail with plenty of primates and birdlife along the way. It leads to a verdant clearing of swamp where a boardwalk passes through sweeping grass and squawking frogs to the hot spring located in a 12m pool.

Activities

Birding or hiking require a UWA ranger guide (US$30). The guide will come with an armed guard from the Counter-Terrorism Unit, as this is a border area.

Walking Trails

Walking options include the 11km **Kirimia Trail**, which is a full-day romp through the heart of the forest and the favoured destination of birdwatchers, and the somewhat shorter but hillier **Red Monkey Trail**. Both end at the Semliki River, which forms the border between Uganda and the DRC.

Sleeping

Bumaga Campsite CAMPGROUND $
(☎0772367215; camping USh20,000, banda USh40,000-120,000) Bumaga is a pleasant, grassy campsite on the edge of the forest with several *bandas* and a campsite with showers and latrines. There's a lovely elevated dining area providing meals. You'll need to arrange accommodation at the UWA office at the Sempaya gate. The campsite is 2km past the gate.

Ntoroko Game Lodge LODGE $$$
(☎0756000598; www.ntorokogamelodge.com; camping per person US$50, s/d incl breakfast US$204/312; @wifi) Sitting directly on the shores of Lake Albert these ample thatched-roof tented camps have wooden floors, some claw-foot tubs and patios overlooking the water. Full board is available. There's a good selection of activities including walks, community visits and biking, as well as trips into the park.

Getting There & Away

Semuliki National Park is just 52km from Fort Portal, but plan on taking two hours to reach it in dry season. In wet season, check the state of the roads before heading out.

Semliki Wildlife Reserve

Once one of the best-stocked and most popular wildlife parks in East Africa, the **Semliki Wildlife Reserve** (☎0772649880; adult/child US$35/5) suffered significant poaching during the civil-war years and after the war with Tanzania. However, wildlife is recovering well and you may encounter waterbucks, reedbucks, bushbucks, chimpanzees, pygmy hippos, buffaloes, leopards, elephants and hyenas. A number of lions have also recently returned to the reserve, which is the oldest protected natural area in Uganda, having first been set aside in 1926.

Activities

Chimpanzee Tracking

Likely the best wildlife experience in the park is the morning chimp tracking (which UWA prefers to call a primate walk; per person US$30). The hiking is more difficult than in Kibale and you're less likely to encounter chimps (around a 30% chance), but if you do, the thinner forest means your views are superior. These are rare 'dry-habitat chimps' that spend considerable time in the savannah and so walk upright more often than others.

Wildlife Drives

With a line of mountains behind it, the savannah scenery from the main road is often superb, but the wildlife viewing along it isn't: Ugandan kob and baboons are the only sure things. It's best to get a ranger (US$20) from the park headquarters to lead you down other tracks.

Nature Walks

Rangers lead nature walks (per person US$30) in various places around the park, including Nyaburogo Gorge behind the headquarters (which has lots of primates and butterflies), along the shore of Lake Albert and – via a steep climb to great views atop the mountains – on the southeastern edge of the park.

Boat Trips

A Lake Albert boat trip will likely reveal hippos and crocodiles, but it's mostly undertaken by birdwatchers for the near-guaranteed shoebill stork sightings. Semliki Safari Lodge (p435) charges US$70 for a half-day on the water. You could also arrange the trip with fishers in Ntoroko village for about half the price, in a boat about half the size.

Sleeping

UWA Campsite CAMPGROUND $
(☎0772911499; www.ugandawildlife.org; camping USh15,000, banda with shared bathroom USh50,000) The small Uganda Wildlife Authority (UWA) campsite at Ntoroko is on

the shores of Lake Albert, meaning you often have hippos joining you in the evening. There are three *bandas* with shared bathrooms and a small canteen where staff prepare your meals.

Semliki Safari Lodge LODGE **$$$**
(☎0414-251182; www.wildplacesafrica.com; s/d incl full board & activities US$180/300;) One of the first luxury lodges in Uganda, with eight luxury tents set under *bandas,* all with sumptuous Persian carpets and four-poster beds. It's extremely good value for what you get, as prices include all food, one game drive or boat trip per day, transfers from the airport and local taxes.

Getting There & Away

Semliki can be reached very easily by public transport or your own wheels from Fort Portal, and even from Kampala if you fly.

AIR

Semliki Safari Lodge can arrange flights (one way US$236) from Entebbe airport.

CAR & MOTORCYCLE

From Fort Portal, head west towards Bundibugyo and then fork right at Karugutu, 27km from Fort Portal; the headquarters is 3km further. A car can handle travel inside the reserve, but ask about conditions between Fort Portal and Karugutu as the road can be quite poor.

MINIBUS & TRUCK

Connecting Fort Portal to Ntoroko (USh12,000, three hours), minibuses and trucks can drop you at the park headquarters. You could also get one of the more frequent Bundibugyo-bound vehicles and get off at Karugutu (USh6000, 1½ hours), to continue from there.

Kasese

☎0483 / POP 101,900

The long-closed Kilembe Copper Mines once brought great prosperity to this drab town, and the now-defunct train line from Kampala used to deposit a steady stream of visitors here. While a Chinese company plans to reopen mining, the only reason travellers come here is to stock up on provisions for a trip to the Rwenzori Mountains.

Nearby Kilembe, 12km away in the foothills of the Rwenzoris, is an interesting town to walk through with old mining equipment and company housing.

Activities

Rwenzori Mountaineering Services TREKKING
(RMS; ☎Kampala 0784308425, Kasese 0785257635, Nyakalengija 0755723581; www.rwenzorimountaineeringservices.com; 30 Rwenzori Rd) This community-run business is the best established in the area and has excellent guides who know the area like the backs of their hands. The standard seven-day, six-night Central Circuit trek costs US$700 per person. It's US$800 if you want to summit Margherita Peak.

Extra days cost US$125 and extra peaks are US$150. Gas cookers can be hired for US$60, or you can hire a cook for US$20 per day. Prices do not include equipment, but they do have the following for hire at US$25 a pop: climbing boots, crampons, harnesses, ice-axes, ropes, rubber boots and sleeping bags.

Sleeping

Sandton Hotel HOTEL **$**
(☎0701489055; www.sandtonhotelkasese.net; Rwenzori Rd; s/d incl breakfast US$48/62;) Kasese's answer to the Sheraton is this immaculate hotel built around two courtyards. There are small, pleasant rooms and car rental. But best of all, the on-site Indian restaurant serves wonderful curries, tikka masala and fish in chilli sauce (mains USh14,000 to USh17,000). Access the restaurant via Rwenzori Rd, the parking area is on Kilembe Rd.

White House Hotel GUESTHOUSE **$**
(☎0782536263; whitehse_hotel@yahoo.co.uk; 46 Henry Bwambale Rd; r USh40,000, s/d with shared bathroom USh23,000/37,000;) A mix of cleanliness and good prices makes White House one of Kasese's most popular budget options.

Hotel Margherita HOTEL **$$**
(☎0483-444015; www.hotel-margherita.com; Kasese-Kilembe Rd; s/d/ste/apt incl breakfast from US$70/95/140/190;) Though it once had a pedigree, Hotel Margherita's long-silent corridors and faded '70s decor make you feel like you're stepping on to the set of *The Shining*. The stunning grounds look out towards the Rwenzoris, and some rooms feature amazing views. It's 3km out of town on the road up to Kilembe. It has a good restaurant too.

Eating

Cafe Olimaco CAFE $
(0772480580; Stanley St; mains USh6000-14,000; 8am-11pm;) Sometimes with wi-fi, this cute cafe with patio seating offers satisfactory light meals, snacks and espresso drinks.

Titi's Market SUPERMARKET $
(Rwenzori Rd; 9am-7pm) A small supermarket.

City Top SUPERMARKET $
(Rwenzori Rd; 9am-6pm) Well-stocked supermarket.

Information

Barclays (cnr Margherita St & Rwenzori Rd; 9am-5pm Mon-Fri) Has an ATM and exchanges currency.

Stanbic Bank (Stanley St; 9am-5pm Mon-Fri, 10am-1pm Sat) Has an ATM and offers currency-exchange services.

Getting There & Away

Buses stop at the roundabout at the entrance to town. The quickest connection to Kampala (USh30,000, five hours) is the Link or Kalita bus via Fort Portal (USh6000, one hour).

Getting to Queen Elizabeth National Park is straightforward. Catch any Mbarara-bound vehicle to Katunguru (USh5000, 30 minutes).

Rwenzori Mountains National Park

The Unesco World Heritage–listed **Rwenzori Mountains National Park** (www.ugandawildlife.org; adult/child US$35/5) contains the tallest mountain range in Africa, including several peaks that are permanently covered by ice. The three highest peaks in the range are Margherita (5109m), Alexandria (5083m) and Albert (5087m), all on Mt Stanley, the third highest mountain in Africa. The mountain range, which isn't volcanic, stretches about 110km by 50km wide and is home to an extraordinary number of rare plants and animals, and new examples of both are still being discovered. Two mammals are endemic to the range, the Rwenzori climbing mouse and the Rwenzori red duiker, as are 19 of the 241 known bird species. Despite this, this is one of Uganda's less-visited national parks, and so nature lovers wanting to escape the safari crowds should definitely put it on their list.

Activities

Back in Uganda's heyday, the Rwenzoris were as popular with travellers as Mt Kilimanjaro and Mt Kenya, but this is definitely a more demanding expedition. The Rwenzoris (known locally as the 'Rain Maker') have a well-deserved reputation for being very wet and muddy, with trails that are often slippery and steep. There are treks available to suit all levels and needs, from one-day jaunts in the forest to 10-day treks with technical climbs. The six-day treks are the most popular.

Two companies offer trekking in the Rwenzoris: the popular Rwenzori Trekking Services (p437), which looks after the Kilembe Trail, and the community-owned Rwenzori Mountaineering Services (p435) based in Kasese, which arranges treks from Nyakalengija. The Muhoma Nature Trail is open to all, but Ruboni Community Campsite (p438) can assist with arranging guides, as can Uganda Wildlife Authority (UWA).

The best times to trek are from late December to mid-March and from mid-June to mid-August, when there's less rain. Even at these times, the higher reaches are often enveloped in mist, though this generally clears for a short time each day. April and October are the wettest months.

Guides, who are compulsory even if you've conquered the seven summits, are on perpetual standby so you can book in the morning and leave the same day.

Walking trails and huts are in pretty good shape, particularly on the Kilembe trail, where huts use polynum insulation to make life more comfortable. There are wooden pathways over the bogs and bridges over the larger rivers, lessening the impact of walkers on the fragile environment.

There have been reports of tour operators working with child porters, not engaging in environmentally sound practices or not offering the amount of food or quality of shelter promised. You also need to ensure your guides always boil your drinking water, or bring materials to purify it yourself. Seek detailed information about your trip before signing up and provide feedback to Lonely Planet if you have observations to share.

Note: trekkers should confirm that their travel insurance policy covers adventure/mountaineering activities above 4000m and rescue. Otherwise, rescue costs start at US$150 to US$10,000 per hour for a helicopter.

Rwenzori Mountains National Park

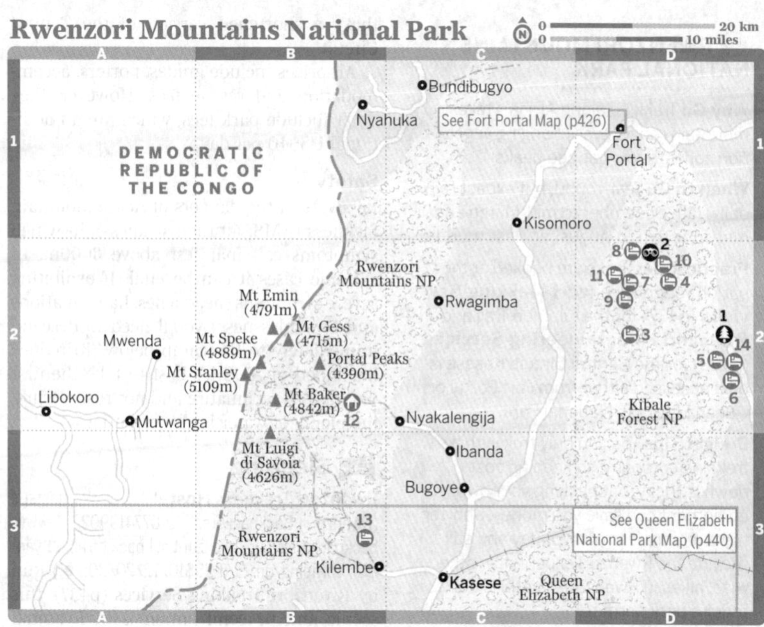

Rwenzori Mountains National Park

Sights
1 Kibale Forest National Park D2
2 Top of the World D2

Activities, Courses & Tours
Bigodi Wetland Sanctuary .... (see 14)
Chimpanzee Habituation Experience .... (see 1)
Rwenzori Trekking Services .... (see 13)

Sleeping
3 Afritastic Planet Ruigo D2
4 Chimpanzee Forest Guesthouse D2
5 Chimps' Nest D2
6 Kibale Forest Camp D2
7 Lake Kifuruka Eco-Camp D2
8 Lake Nkuruba Nature Reserve Community Campsite D2
9 Ndali Lodge D2
10 Nyinabulitwa Country Resort & Safari Camp D2
11 Papaya Lake Lodge D2
Primate Lodge .... (see 1)
12 Ruboni Community Campsite B2
13 Rwenzori Trekkers Hostel B3
Rweteera Safari Park & Tourist Camping .... (see 10)
14 Tinka's Homestay D2
UWA Campsite .... (see 1)

Eating
EcoBurrito .... (see 14)

Rwenzori Trekking Services TREKKING
(RTS; ☎Kampala 0774114499, Kilembe 0774199022; www.rwenzoritrekking.com; Kilembe) This company has breathed new energy into trekking in the Rwenzoris, with excellent reviews for its professional guides, quality equipment and safety measures, as well as comfortable mountain huts. A range of tailor-made treks are offered, from technical climbs to leisurely strolls in the forested foothills. With an office in the Rwenzori Trekkers Hostel.

Equipment

The routes to the peaks on Mt Stanley require the use of ice-axes, ropes and crampons (depending on conditions, you may have to rope in for Mts Baker and Speke), but you don't need mountaineering experience to reach the summits if your guide is experienced – the catch is that not all of them are. From all reports, the guides from Rwenzori Trekking Services are the most reliable.

RWENZORI MOUNTAINS NATIONAL PARK

Why Go Trekking along Africa's tallest mountain range; ever-changing vegetation zones; snow-capped peaks.

When to Go Year-round, but expect rain daily; late December to mid-March and mid-June to mid-August are less muddy.

Practicalities Treks are booked at the park through **Rwenzori Trekking Services** (p437) for the Kilembe Trail and **Rwenzori Mountaineering Services** (p435) for the Central Circuit. Kasese is best accessed either from Fort Portal or Queen Elizabeth National Park.

Budget Tips You can only trek with a trekking company, so keeping costs down is tricky, but packing your own equipment can save you money. Shorter treks require less of an outlay and still provide the Rwenzori experience; otherwise, hikes in Rwenzori's foothills don't require park permits.

No special equipment is required for a trek if you don't go on to the ice or snow (and if you do, this gear can be hired at the trailhead), but bring plenty of warm, waterproof clothing (temperatures often drop below 0°C). You'll also want a good sleeping bag. The most important item is a good, broken-in pair of trekking boots to get you over the slippery rock slabs, which can be quite treacherous at times. Rubber boots are also essential for the bogs – so ensure these are available. A small day pack is useful as your porters will travel at their own pace.

Before attempting a trek in the Rwenzoris get a copy of *Guide to the Rwenzori* (2006) by Henry Osmaston, which covers routes, natural history and all other aspects of the mountains. A good companion to Osmaston's opus is *Rwenzori Map & Guide*, an excellent large-scale contour map by Andrew Wielochowski.

Trekking Routes in the Rwenzoris

The peaks are accessed via two routes: the **Kilembe Trail** and the long-standing **Central Circuit** that starts from Nyakalengija village. For those short on time there's also the two- to three-day **Muhoma Nature Trail**, a 28km circuit set up by UWA in 2012 that's a shortened version of the Central Circuit.

All prices include guides, porters, accommodation and rescue fees. However, they don't include park fees, which are an additional US$40 per day.

Safety

Be aware of the dangers of Acute Mountain Sickness (AMS; altitude sickness), in which symptoms can manifest above 3000m. In extreme cases it can be fatal. If exhibiting severe symptoms (headaches, hallucinations and breathlessness) you'll need to descend immediately to the camp below. To reduce likelihood of AMS it's best to take the first day easy to acclimatise and not rush. Drinking plenty of water is also essential.

Sleeping

Rwenzori Trekkers Hostel HOSTEL $
(Rwenzori Backpackers; ☎0774199022; www.backpackers.co.ug/rwenzoribackpack.html; Kyanjuki; camping/dm/s/d US$10/12/20/30; P) Run by Rwenzori Trekking Services (p437), this scenic and peaceful option is in Kyanjuki just above Kilembe, 12km outside Kasese, and is a perfect starting point if you plan on tackling this side of the Rwenzori. Rooms, all with shared bathrooms, are in restored miners' housing and are slightly run-down with peeling linoleum floors, but they're fine for the price.

The restaurant has a great trekking menu comprising T-bone steaks, pasta and vegetarian options. The hostel does some excellent work in the community, and also offers village walks and cultural performances.

Ruboni Community Campsite HUT $
(☎0752503445; www.rubonicamp.com; near Nyakalengija; camping with/without tent US$5/15, banda per person incl breakfast US$25, r with shared bathroom per person incl breakfast US$20) This community-run place down the road from Nyakalengija is at the base of the hill just outside the park boundary, with an attractive setting and comfortable lodging. All profits go towards a health centre, tree-planting projects and more. It also offers guided walks into the hills outside the park, drumming lessons and traditional dance performances.

It's near the Nyakalengija entrance gate.

★ **Equator Snow Lodge** LODGE $$
(☎0414-258273; http://geolodgesafrica.com/index.php/equator-snow-lodges; Nyakalengija; s/d/

tr incl full board US$132/242/342;) Conveniently located for the Central (and Mahoma) Trail, this luxury mountain lodge at the foot of the Rwenzoris has large cottages with fireplaces, sunroofs and hardwood details with riverfront balconies surrounded by old-growth forest. There are superb trekking opportunities in the immediate area, even if you're not keen on a hard-core mountaineering expedition. Massages too. All up, excellent value.

It's near the Nyakalengija park entrance.

Getting There & Away

Nyakalengija is 25km from Kasese, though minibuses only run as far as Ibanda (USh5000, one hour). From here you can take a *boda-boda* to Nyakalengija (USh4000) or Ruboni Community Camp (USh3500). Chartering a special-hire taxi from Kasese will set you back USh80,000.

For Kilembe (USh3000, 30 minutes), take one of the frequent shared-car taxis from near the Shell petrol station on Kilembe Rd. A special-hire taxi will cost around USh40,000 and *boda-boda* around USh10,000.

Queen Elizabeth National Park

Few reserves in the world can boast such a high biodiversity rating and with landscapes including savannah, bushland, wetlands and lush forests. Covering 1978 sq km, scenic **Queen Elizabeth National Park** (0782387805; www.ugandawildlife.org; adult/child US$40/20; 6.30am-7pm, park gates 7am-7pm) is one of the most popular parks in Uganda. The park is inhabited by 96 species of mammals, including healthy numbers of hippos, elephants, lions and leopards as well as chimps and hyenas. The remote Ishasha sector, in the far south of the park, is famous for its tree-climbing lions; these females, who enjoy spending the long, hot afternoons snoozing photogenically in fig trees, are the most memorable sight in the entire park, but don't miss the superb birdlife (611 species), the wonderful boat trip on the Kazinga Channel or a walk through beautiful Kyambura (Chambura) Gorge, a little Eden brimming with chimpanzees and other primates.

Back in the 1970s, with its great herds of elephants, buffaloes, kobs, waterbucks, hippos and topis, Queen Elizabeth was one of the premier safari parks in Africa. But during the troubled 1980s, Ugandan and Tanzanian troops (which occupied the country after Amin's demise) did their ivory-grabbing, trophy-hunting best. Thankfully, animal populations have recovered since then with thanks to improved park security and an emphasis on antipoaching patrols.

Sights

Leopard Village VILLAGE
(0791492245; www.uganda-carnivores.org/leopard-village; Muhokya) Leopard Village is one of the communities within Queen Elizabeth National Park. It's possible to visit it on a tour run by Uganda Carnivore Program, which gives an insight in to how locals coexist with wildlife, and introduces you to other cultural activities. Tours usually meet at a park gate.

Salt Mine MINE
(0753393450; Katwe; US$10) The interesting village of **Katwe** on the north shore of Lake Edward, 4km west of Main gate (Kabatoro gate), is famous for its salt industry. Salt mining on the crater lake behind the village dates back to at least the 15th century, and today some 3000 people still use the same traditional methods. Women pull salt from evaporation ponds when it's dry enough (generally December to March and July to September) while men dig rock salt year-round.

Tours are booked at the Katwe Tourism Information Centre on the west side of the village, across from a defunct salt factory.

QUEEN ELIZABETH NATIONAL PARK

Why Go Tree-climbing lions; elephants; leopards; scenic savannah landscapes; boat rides along Kazinga Channel.

When to Go Year-round; the dry seasons (December to March and May to August) are most popular but most roads can be accessed in rainy season.

Practicalities Park gates open 7am to 7pm. Katunguru is the main village in the park's centre, linked by buses from Kampala and Kasese. Vehicles for wildlife drives can be hired from here too.

Budget Tips One of the most accessible parks by public transport; with some negotiation, safari vehicles can be arranged in Katunguru. Budget accommodation is available in most sectors of the park.

Queen Elizabeth National Park

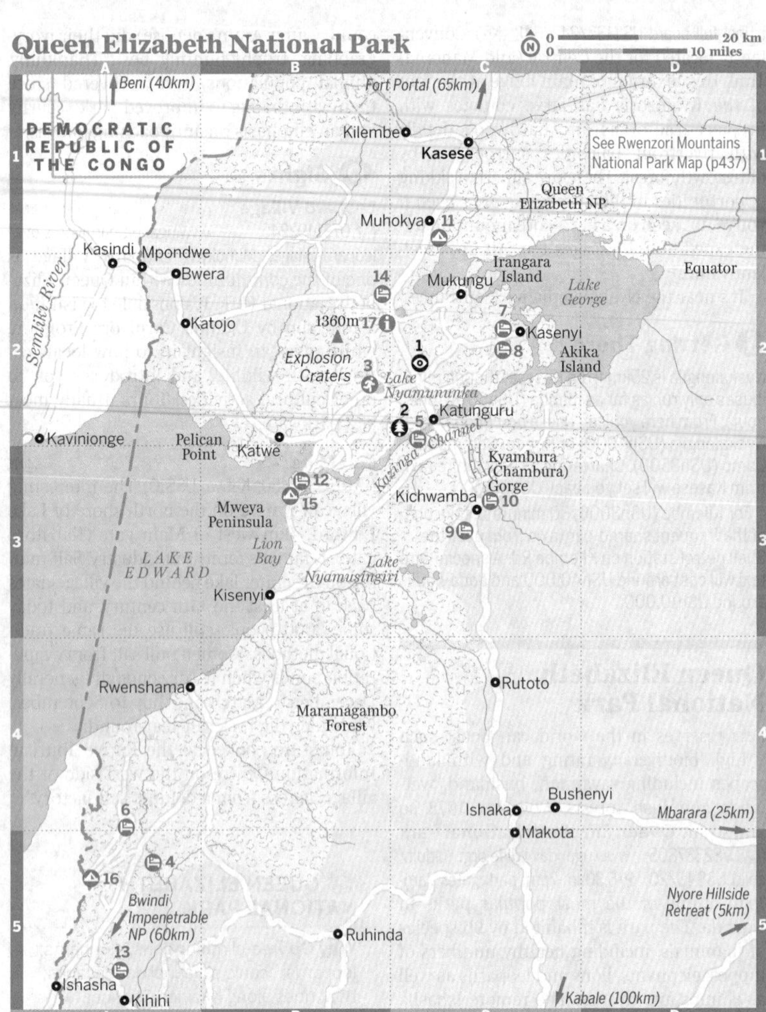

Equator LANDMARK

The equator crosses the northern sector of the park near Kasenyi and is marked with a circular monument on either side of the road, predictably popular with passers-by stopping for that quintessential holiday snap.

Activities

Uganda Carnivore Program WILDLIFE WATCHING

(www.uganda-carnivores.org; lion tracking per person US$150) This nonprofit is dedicated to the monitoring, research and conservation of predators in Uganda. Many of these animals are declining in number due to nearby population pressures and loss of habitat. Visitors can join their lion-tracking program by booking through UWA's Mweya Visitor Information Centre (p445). The Carnivore Program website has good information on the cause.

Uganda Balloon Safari BALLOONING

(☎0759002552; www.ugandaballoonsafari.com; Kasenyi gate; per person US$380; ⏰6am) If you've ever wondered what it would be like to safari from the air, here's your chance.

Queen Elizabeth National Park

Sights
1 Equator...C2
2 Queen Elizabeth National Park...C2

Activities, Courses & Tours
3 Explosion Crater Drive...B2

Sleeping
4 @The River...A5
5 Bush Lodge...C2
Enjojo Lodge...(see 4)
6 Ishasha Wilderness Camp...A4
7 Kasenyi Safari Camp...C2
8 Kasenyi Wild Game Lodge...C2
9 Katara Lodge...C3
Kingfisher Lodge...(see 9)
10 Kyambura Gorge Lodge...C3
11 Little Elephant Camp...C1
12 Mweya Safari Lodge...B3
13 Savannah Resort Hotel...A5
14 Simba Safari Camp...B2
15 UWA Campgrounds...B3
16 UWA Campsite & Bandas...A5
UWA Guesthouses & Cottages...(see 15)

Eating
Omwani Training Cafe...(see 10)
Tembo Canteen...(see 12)

Entertainment
Kikorongo Women Community...(see 14)

Information
Mweya Visitor Information Centre...(see 12)
17 Queens Pavilion...B2

These daily one-hour sunrise balloon rides (two-person minimum) float over the Kasenyi sector of the park, a good site for game drives. Upon landing you're treated to a bush breakfast replete with white linens. Run by a licensed operator. Booking ahead is essential.

Explosion Crater Drive SCENIC DRIVE
(near Mweya Peninsula) This 27km round-trip takes you through a sector not known for wildlife. What it does have are awesome craters, with some cupping pools that reflect the sky on clear days. At times you might even see elephants in them. Massive Kyemengo Crater is the largest. Go as an extension of your safari drive. Some hotels offer cycling excursions here.

Boat Trips

Almost every visitor takes the two-hour launch trip (US$30) up the Kazinga Channel to see the thousands of hippos and pink-backed pelicans, plus plenty of crocodiles, buffaloes and fish eagles. With a little luck, it's also possible to catch sight of one of the elephant herds and – very occasionally – see a lion or a leopard. The boat docks below Mweya Safari Lodge (p444), but you buy tickets at the Mweya Visitor Information Centre (p445) on top of the hill. Trips departs at 9am, 11am, 3pm and 5pm.

Wildlife Drives

Most wildlife-viewing traffic is in the northeast of the park in Kasenyi, which offers the best chance to see lions, elephants, waterbucks and kobs. It's also one of the most scenic sections of any park in Uganda, particularly in the morning when the savannah landscape shines golden and is dotted with cactus-like candelabra trees. Night game drives (US$30 per person, including guide) are also available, though you may have to hire a spotlight (US$20) to see anything. Pay for drives or book guides at any of the park gates or at the Mweya Visitor Information Centre (p445).

There's also a small network of trails between Mweya Peninsula and Katunguru gate that usually reveal waterbucks and kobs, elephants and, occasionally, leopards.

As well as being famous for its tree-climbing lions, Ishasha, in the south of the Queen Elizabeth National Park, is the only place to see topis and sitatungas.

You can get just about everywhere by car if it isn't raining, though having a 4WD is a good idea in Ishasha year-round. Taking a UWA ranger-guide (US$20) along for your drive is always a good idea, but more so in Ishasha than anywhere else because they know every fig tree in the area – the lions' preferred perches.

Wildlife Research Tours

An initiative introduced by UWA is a range of 'experiential tourism' activities to assure closer wildlife encounters. Most popular is **lion tracking** (using a combination of locator devices and radio collars) run by the Uganda Carnivore Program (p440) in vehicles provided by UWA that head off track; it also yields good leopard sightings. Other activities include mongoose tracking

ISHASHA TREE-CLIMBING LIONS

Somewhat off the beaten track in the far southern sector of the park, Ishasha is famous for its population of tree-climbing lions. It's one of the few places in Africa where lions are known to hang out in trees (you'll find them in Kidepo National Park too) and are often found lazing on the sprawling limbs of fig trees during the heat of the day. Generally the best time to spot them is outside the usual safari drive times (11am to 5pm, basically when they're not hunting). If it's wet, the lions generally won't climb.

(US$30), and assisting with the hippo census (US$100) and bird-species counts.

Chimpanzee Tracking

In the eastern region of the park, in the 100m-deep **Kyambura (Chambura) Gorge**, you can go chimpanzee tracking (per person US$50), with walks lasting from two to four hours and departing at 8am and 2pm. You have a semi-reasonable chance of finding the habituated troop, but visits are often unfruitful; mornings are probably the best bet. The gorge is a beautiful scar of green cutting through the savannah, and from the viewing platform you can sometimes see primates, including chimps, frolicking in the treetops below.

Bookings can be made at the Mweya Visitor Information Centre (p445), or you can just show up and hope there are spots available. Children under 15 years aren't permitted.

Nature Walks

Guided nature walks through the forest in Maramagambo are available (US$30 per person). Trips on the forest trails here are taken mostly by birdwatchers, though there are nine species of primate around and it's quite common to see pythons hunting and eating bats. Down at Ishasha, hippo encounters are pretty likely on short walks along the river and, if you're there early in the morning, there's a chance of spotting a giant forest hog. You won't see much on a walk at Mweya that you can't see just hanging around on your own. Book guided walks at any of the park gates or at the Mweya Visitor Information Centre (p445).

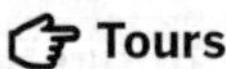

Tours

All tour operators can put together a short safari to Queen Elizabeth National Park. Kampala-based **Great Lakes Safaris** (Map p386; ☎0414-267153; http://safari-uganda.com; Biina Rd 1001, Kampala) has three-day trips departing every Wednesday and Friday and half-day hot-air-balloon safaris (US$380 per person), while Red Chilli Hideaway (p487) has four-day safaris from US$350 per person in groups of eight. For a more personal experience, ask at Little Elephant Camp (p443) (day trip US$130).

Sleeping

★Bush Lodge LODGE $
(☎0312-294894; www.naturelodges.biz/the-bush-lodge; Kazinga Channel; s/d incl full board lazy camping US$60/110, safari tent US$80/130, banda US$135/190) An excellent budget choice, this exceptionally run bush camp sits on the banks of Kazinga Channel frequented by elephants, forest pigs, warthogs and hippos. There are basic tents with beds (and power outlets), and private *bandas* and safari-tents with outdoor showers clad in bamboo and composting toilets. Meals are wonderful, with tables arranged atmospherically around the campfire.

At night guards walk you back to your tent, lest hippos be on the loose.

Simba Safari Camp LODGE $
(☎0704942646; www.ugandalodges.com/simba; Bwera Rd, Kikorongo; camping US$9, dm/s/d incl breakfast US$26/72/96;) Just outside the northern sector of the park, Simba is a good budget camp popular with many tour groups. Rooms are spotless with canopy beds and stone-floor showers. It has a social restaurant/bar and is in a convenient location for Kasenyi game drives. At the time of writing they were renovating and adding a new sector of upmarket lodgings.

To get here by public transport, take any bus from Kampala heading to Bwera and ask to be dropped off at Simba.

UWA Guesthouses & Cottages LODGE, COTTAGE $
(Mweya; s/tw/d USh52,000/82,000/102,000, tw with shared bathroom USh41,000, cottage USh250,000-300,000) In an effort to provide more affordable accommodation in Queen Elizabeth National Park, UWA has acquired a range of properties along Mweya. The pick are the cottages, which are basic but com-

fortable rooms in close proximity to the popular Tembo Canteen (p445). Take care walking in the evening as plenty of wild animals graze here.

Self-caterers, families and groups can opt for one of the bigger cottages equipped with fridge and cooking facilities, which can sleep six to eight people.

Suba Motel GUESTHOUSE **$**
(☎0392-905978; www.subamotel.com; Kihihi; s/d incl breakfast USh60,000/90,000; 📶) A clean, cheap and straightforward hotel with rooms arranged around a courtyard, and a good little restaurant that makes a useful pit stop for those passing through. It also has vehicles for rent and does airport pick-ups.

UWA Campgrounds CAMPGROUND **$**
(Mweya; camping USh15,000) Although the facilities are rustic, the setting is superb, making Mweya a great place to pitch a tent. Campsite 3, the main one, has little shade but is set away from the development on the peninsula and looks out over the channel. More isolated are campsites 1 and 2, which are 3.5km and 4.5km east of the visitor centre respectively.

They have nothing but pit toilets and good channel views, especially campsite 2.

Expect a lot of animal sightings and sounds; exercise extreme caution after dark. Book all camping at the visitor centre (p445) in Mweya before setting up your tent.

UWA Campsite & Bandas CAMPGROUND **$**
(☎0773595353; Ishasha; camping USh15,000, banda with shared bathroom USh41,000) A blissfully remote set-up with two basic *bandas* and a canteen serving local dishes (USh25,000). There are two lovely campsites on the Ishasha River, which forms the border with the DRC, where hippos can be spotted. Be vigilant moving at night as there's abundant wildlife. The border site hosts an army camp, so most uniformed officers aren't UWA.

Rwenzori Salaama Hotel LODGE **$**
(☎0782927350; Katunguru; s/d Ush36,000/47,000) If you get stuck in Katunguru, this basic lodge has the cheapest and cleanest rooms and a decent attached restaurant.

★**Little Elephant Camp** TENTED CAMP **$$**
(☎0780763884, 0776143353; http://littleelephantcamp.com; outside Kikorongo; d lazy camping US$50, d safari tent US$125) 🍃 This dream safari camp features a few impeccable tents outfitted with grills and your own personal kitchen and living-room tent. Comfortable and ultraprivate, it's ideal for groups or families. Your hosts are a lovely Canadian couple who have thought out every old-school adventure detail from custom-made director's chairs to wooden trunks and open-air solar-heated showers fenced behind each tent.

Guests cook for themselves, but can get a little help with cold drinks, salads, marinated steaks and chicken supplied by hosts for extra. Don't be surprised if you hear elephants trumpeting at night – the land abuts the northern end of Queen Elizabeth National Park. Hosts also can provide personalised safaris (half-day US$65) in their Land Cruiser.

@The River LODGE **$$**
(☎0772722688; www.attheriverishasha.com; Ishasha; camping/bush-camping per person US$12/180, tented camp with shared bathroom per person US$60, s/d incl full board US$95, s/d with shared bathroom incl full board US$70; 🏊) This quintessential Queen Elizabeth experience has a great riverside location, stilted *bandas* and good guiding. While its vibe and standards are similar to that of the luxury camps, @The River boasts far more affordable rates. It has a laid-back camp atmosphere, with a plunge pool and riverside beach. If you're up for adventure, try the bush camping option.

Kasenyi Wild Game Lodge LODGE **$$**
(☎0752652861; www.kasenyigamelodges.com; Kasenyi; per person incl breakfast US$50) Given its location close to the prime wildlife-viewing area, these well-spaced thatched *bandas* are good value. It can feel a little desolate, though. All have porches looking out to the salt lake, a popular stop on safari drives.

Savannah Resort Hotel HOTEL **$$**
(☎0777076086; www.savannahresorthotel.com; Kihihi; s/d/tr incl breakfast US$120/165/240; 📶🏊) Located 4km outside Kihihi near the airstrip, this pleasant hotel has a mix of comfortable rooms and *bandas* in a peaceful location surrounded by a golf course. Prices are steep considering the level of comfort here. A good on-site restaurant serves international and African dishes. It's a 30-minute drive to Ishasha.

Kingfisher Lodge LODGE **$$**
(☎0774159579; www.kingfisher-uganda.net; Kichwamba; s/d incl half board US$125/230; P@📶🏊) This little compound of whitewashed and thatched-roof towers is a tad

dated but it's well priced and has memorable Queen Elizabeth vistas. Rooms are smallish but nice and most have their own porch. Nonguests can use the pool (US$10).

★**Kyambura Gorge Lodge** LODGE **$$$**
(☎0414-322789; https://volcanoessafaris.com/kyambura-gorge-lodge-uganda; Kyambura; s/d US$336/560;) This former coffee factory is a top choice for those looking to slow things right down. Style looms large here, with abstract art and mismatched craft pieces that exude personality. Modern *bandas* feature outdoor showers, scavenged wood balconies, floor to ceiling windows and sofas where you can take in the savannah. The swimming pool is perfect for a sundowner and massage is free.

It supports a local women's coffee co-op. Low-season rates offer healthy discounts. If your rate does not include tours, note that they can only be paid for in cash.

★**Enjojo Lodge** LODGE **$$$**
(☎0772067070; www.enjojolodge.com; Ishasha; camping without/with tent incl breakfast US$15/20, lazy camping incl full board US$70, s/d cottage incl full board US$145/250) Providing a wonderful experience for guests, this ultrapopular Belgian resort suits all budgets. Beyond the warm welcome and helpful service, there's great Rwandan-French cuisine. Lodgings are well spaced, with cottages on a terraced boardwalk. It's run on solar, with hot showers even for campers, amid an acacia forest that's returning thanks to reforestation efforts. A pool is in the works.

Ishasha Wilderness Camp LODGE **$$$**
(☎0414-321479; www.ugandaexclusivecamps.com/ishasha-wilderness-camp; Ishasha; s/d incl full board US$475/720; @) The location right on the Ntungwe River is prime. At these prices this tented camp is less luxurious than you might expect, though its 10 tents are spacious, with elegant furnishings and wi-fi in a lovely thatched living room. One of the few lodges inside the park's boundaries, there's great wildlife guiding and an option for bush breakfasts or sundowners.

Remember that you will be paying park fees to get here, since it's inside the gate. Rates drop during low season (April, May and November).

Katara Lodge LODGE **$$$**
(☎0773011648; www.kataralodge.com; Kichwamba; s/d incl full board US$250/400; @) It's hard not to be seduced by this gorgeous place. Eight wood, thatch and canvas cottages are made for taking in the stunning savannah views and there's a saltwater pool for cooling off. The best bit: beds roll out on to a deck for sleeping under the stars. Includes vegetables from the on-site garden, rainwater harvesting and solar power.

Kasenyi Safari Camp LODGE **$$$**
(☎0791992038; www.kasenyisafaricamp.com; Kasenyi; cottages incl full board US$425;) This friendly American-Ugandan-owned luxury lodge features beautiful thatched tented-cottages with king-size canopy beds, decks and loungers with views to the salt lake. There's solar power providing hot water with great pressure and laundry service. The site is spread out in a location good for wildlife encounters. A swimming pool is on the cards.

Mweya Safari Lodge LODGE **$$$**
(☎0312-260260; www.mweyalodge.com; Mweya; s/d incl full board from US$227/402; @) Queen Elizabeth's iconic, classic safari lodge has a commanding location with excellent views over Lake Edward and Kazinga Channel, with herds of hippos and buffaloes. Set in a resort-like complex, it offers everything from hotel-style rooms (some cramped) to luxury tents and plush cottages, most with water views. Come sunset, the terrace overlooking the water is the place to be.

There's also a spa and health club (handy when you don't want to jog among lions). Even if you're not staying here it's worth popping in for a meal (mains from USh20,000) or a G&T at the atmospheric bar with Chesterfield couches, a fireplace and hunting relics from yesteryear (including a giant set of tusks). History buffs can stay where Queen Elizabeth was when she woke up to news that she was queen (cottage US$1190).

Eating

Omwani Training Cafe CAFE **$**
(☎0773985958; Kyambura; mains USh6000-10,000; ⌚9am-5pm) When you tire of all-inclusive lodge meals, come to this adorable cafe with tables in the backyard and chickens running loose. Service is slow but the end product is good – enormous *rolex* (eggs wrapped in chapatti), espresso drinks and addictive sweet-potato hash browns. If you order ahead, you can get delicious wood-fired pizza in the afternoon.

It's run by an NGO training local disadvantaged youth.

Tembo Canteen INTERNATIONAL $
(Mweya Peninsula; meals USh10,000-20,000; ⏲6.30am-11pm) A wonderful safari-style canteen, Tembo buzzes with campers, UWA staff, guides and drivers, all here for cheap, tasty food and cold beer. Head outdoors to its tables with epic lake views.

☆ Entertainment

Kikorongo Women Community LIVE PERFORMANCE
(☎0757548713; kikorongowomen@gmail.com; Kikorongo) Visit Kikorongo Women Community for performances and craft demonstrations.

ℹ Information

Mweya Visitor Information Centre (☎0392-700694; Mweya Peninsula; ⏲6.30am-6.30pm) Helpful and busy visitor centre on the Mweya Peninsula with good displays on the park (don't miss the extraordinary attempts at taxidermy), as well as maps and books for sale, and info on activities and UWA's accommodation and campgrounds.

Queens Pavilion (Kikorongo; ⏲8am-6pm; 📶) Near the equator monument, this stopover point has tourist info, a cafe with wi-fi and views over Lake George. It also sell maps and souvenirs.

ℹ Getting There & Away

AIR

Aerolink (p491) flies from Entebbe to the airstrip in Kihihi (US$283), which is convenient for visiting both the northern sector of Bwindi Impenetrable Forest and the southern sector of Queen Elizabeth National Park.

BUS

There are several direct buses to Katunguru (USh25,000, eight hours) from Kampala's main bus park including with Kalita, Link and Poko, which all go via Mbarara en route to Kasese (USh5000, one hour). Once in the park, arrange game drives through your hotel or a special-hire taxi in Katunguru.

Buses to Kasindi (USh4000, 45 minutes), where you can cross to Buera in the Democratic Republic of Congo, pass the Kikorongo junction north of the park.

CAR & MOTORCYCLE

Most people visit the park either as part of an organised tour or by renting a car. If you're driving, beware of animals crossing the road along the high-speed tarmac section, particularly at night. Petrol is available at Mweya, but it's pricier than in towns, so fill up before you head towards the park.

The road from Katunguru to the village of Ishasha cuts through the park and passes Ishasha gate. Although no park entry fees are needed to travel this road, you'll be fined US$150 if you're caught venturing off it and into the park. The Ishasha sector is 100km from Mweya down a pretty good road (due to oil exploration in the area) in the far south of the park.

From Ishasha, you can head south for Butogota and Bwindi Impenetrable National Park, reaching them in about two hours during dry season.

Bwindi Impenetrable National Park

As names go, there's hardly a more evocative African destination than the Impenetrable Forest of Bwindi. This swath of steep mountains covered in thick, steamy jungle is just as magnificent as it sounds. The 331-sq-km World Heritage-listed Bwindi Impenetrable National Park (☎0486-424121, 0414-355409; www.ugandawildlife.org; adult/child US$40/20; ⏲park office 7.45am-5pm) is one of Africa's most ancient habitats, even surviving the last Ice Age as most of the continent's other forests disappeared.

The combination of its broad altitude span (1160m to 2607m) and its antiquity has produced an incredible diversity of flora and fauna, resulting in some 120 mammal species and over 350 bird species calling Bwindi home. The stars of the show, however, are

> **ℹ BWINDI IMPENETRABLE NATIONAL PARK**
>
> **Why Go** Tracking mountain gorillas; forest walks with Twa people; birdwatching.
>
> **When to Go** December to March and June to September have the least rain, but permits are easier to obtain at other times.
>
> **Practicalities** The rainy season often brings delays due to landslides, so be sure to leave enough time to get here; ideally it's best to stay close to the region you'll be tracking gorillas in.
>
> **Budget Tips** During April, May and November gorilla permits are US$450. Budget accommodation is available; public transport is possible, but inconvenient and time-consuming.

Bwindi Impenetrable National Park

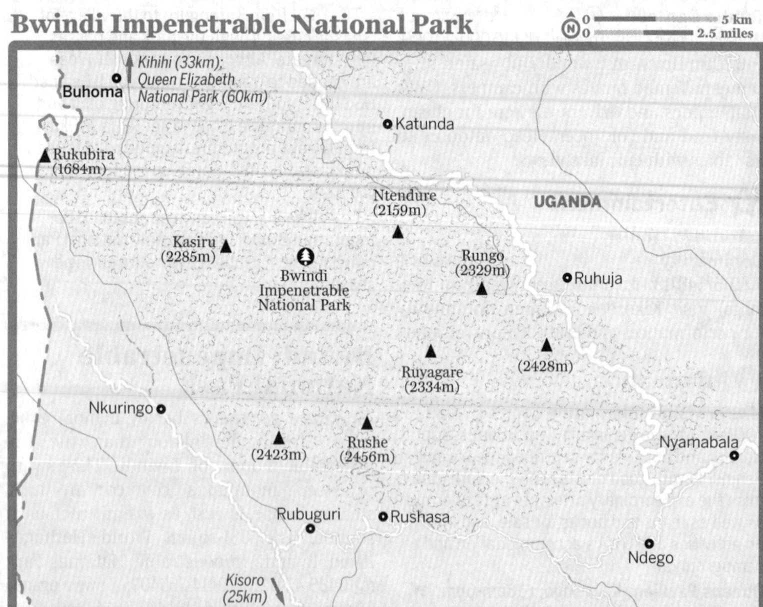

the approximately 400 mountain gorillas living here. This is one of the best places in the world to see mountain gorillas up close. Having a look at these critically endangered creatures up close is an unforgettable experience – don't miss it.

As well as its famous gorillas, lucky visitors might see forest elephants, 11 species of primate (including chimpanzees and L'Hoest's monkeys), duikers, bushbucks, African golden cats and the rare giant forest hog, as well as a host of bird and insect species. For birdwatchers it's one of the most exciting destinations in the country, with over 350 species, including 23 of the 24 endemic to the Albertine Rift and several endangered species, such as the African green broadbill. With a good guide, sighting daily totals of more than 150 species is possible. On the greener side of the aisle, Bwindi harbours eight endemic plants.

Activities

Batwa Cultural Experience CULTURAL
(☎0774977349; batwaempowerment@gmail.com; per person US$50) The Twa (Batwa) people were displaced from their forest habitat when Bwindi became a national park, but this community-owned initiative allows you to meet them and see how they lived in the forest. Activities include beekeeping, mushroom gathering, hunting demonstrations and crafts. Stories from Twa legend are told alongside traditional song and dance. Price depends on number of participants.

Nkuringo Walking Safaris SAFARI
(☎0774805580, Entebbe 0392-176327; info@nkuringosafaris.com; day tour for 2 people from US$70) Nkuringo Walking Safaris is a trekking specialist that offers popular treks through Bwindi Impenetrable Forest. It also offers a full raft of other Bwindi activities, as well as walking tours to other national parks in Uganda.

Gorilla Trekking

A genuine once-in-a-lifetime experience, hanging out with mountain gorillas is one of the most thrilling wildlife encounters in the world, and Bwindi Impenetrable National Park is a prime place to see them. There are theoretically 96 daily permits available to track gorillas in Bwindi. Permits cost US$600 (including park entry) and are booked through the UWA office (p485) in Kampala. Note you must be over 15 years of age to track the gorillas.

Trips leave from the park office nearest the group you'll be tracking at 8.30am daily, but you should report to park headquarters by 7.45am. If you are based in Kisoro or Kabale and plan on leaving early in the morning, be mindful that rainy season presents potential delays, such as landslides or getting trapped in thick mud.

With the help of trackers, chances of finding the gorillas are almost guaranteed. But mountainous and heavily forested terrain can present hikers with quite a challenge if the gorillas are a fair distance away. The path is often steep and slippery, and it can take anywhere from 30 minutes to five hours to reach them, so you'll need to be in reasonable shape. If you think you're going to struggle it's strongly advised you hire a porter (US$15) who can carry your day pack and lend a hand getting up and down the hill. Walking sticks are also a very good idea, and are sometimes provided by UWA.

Forest Walks

Even if you can't afford gorilla tracking, Bwindi is a rewarding park to visit just for a chance to explore the lush virgin rainforest. Several three- to four-hour nature walks run by the Uganda Wildlife Authority (UWA) penetrate the Impenetrable Forest around Buhoma. The walks begin at 9am and 2.15pm and cost US$30 per person (not including your park entry fee).

The **Waterfall Trail** leads to a magnificent 33m waterfall on the Munyaga River, but just as impressive is the rich forest ecosystems it passes through. This is the best trail for spotting both orchids and primates. Weather permitting, the **Muzabijiro Loop Trail** and **Rushura Hill Trail** offer excellent views south to the Virunga volcanoes and the Western Rift Valley in the DRC. The latter, which is a more difficult climb, also serves up views of Lake Edward and, on an exceptionally clear day, the Rwenzoris.

A longer but much easier trek is along the **River Ivi Trail**, which follows the path of a planned-but-never-built road between Buhoma and Nkuringo. It's 14km through the forest and then another 6km uphill along a road to Nkuringo village; you might be able to hitch this last part.

Tours

Ride 4 A Woman CYCLING
(0785999112; www.ride4awoman.org; Buhoma; bike rental from US$25) This NGO runs guided mountain-bike tours through the forest or village and rents out bikes if you want to go exploring yourself. It also has a clothing and craft store near Buhoma Hospital, where it offers sewing classes from USh30,000. All proceeds go to helping women in the community.

Buhoma Village Tourist Walk WALKING
(0772384965; www.buhomacommunity.com; US$15) Offered by the Buhoma Community Rest Camp (p448), these popular three- to four-hour walks head to the surrounding countryside to visit local healers, watch a Twa song-and-dance show and witness the none-too-appetising production of banana wine and gin (the bananas are mashed by foot).

Sleeping

Bwindi is surrounded by lodges, and these span nearly all price ranges, though with gorilla permits normally costing US$600, there's unsurprisingly a focus on upmarket accommodation. There are four main concentrations of lodges around the park, at Buhoma, Nkuringo, Rushaga and Ruhija. The distance between them is significant so it's essential to book gorilla permits before lodging so both coincide.

Rushaga Gorilla Camp CABIN $
(0774633331; http://rushaga.com; Rushaga; camping US$25, s/d safari tent incl breakfast US$90/140, s/d cabin incl breakfast US$60/80) This budget and midrange option hits a rare price point for Bwindi and proves both comfortable and economical. Safari tents with decks are lovely, but the budget row cabins aren't bad, with balconies looking out on the forest. There's also a nice campfire area with panoramic views. It's run by the group from Bunyonyi Overland Resort.

Gorilla Conservation Camp BANDA $
(0782509151; www.ctph.org/gorilla-conservation-camp; Buhoma; camping US$15, per person incl full board US$55;) A fantastic newer budget camp set up by the community, here you get sweeping views of Bwindi from its bucolic hilltop location above Buhoma. Accommodation is in raised self-contained safari tents with porches and ample rooms with hardwood floors and mosquito nets. It's popular with researchers and all proceeds go to gorilla conservation and community projects.

Ruhija Gorilla Friends Resort GUESTHOUSE $
(0754323546; bitarihorobert@gmail.com; Ruhija; camping with/without tent US$10/15, incl breakfast per person US$30, with shared bathroom US$25, cottage per person US$50) One of Bwindi's best-value options for budget travellers, here you can pitch a tent, use one of theirs, go for a room or – best of

all – the tented rooms with great views. Rooms are clean, water's hot and service is friendly. It's partnered with a Canadian development fund with proceeds going to the community.

Buhoma Community Rest Camp LODGE $

(☎0772384965; www.buhomacommunity.com; Buhoma; camping US$12, dm/r per person with shared bathroom incl full board US$60/96, r per person incl full board US$115;) Next door to the park headquarters, this rustic but pleasant camp is Bwindi's most popular budget option, looking directly out to lush forest. *Bandas* and safari tents are spaced out on a hill heading down the valley, and the best are at the bottom, which puts you right at the jungle; gorillas sometimes even pass by here.

Some of the profits go towards funding community-development projects.

Mist Lodge HOTEL $

(☎0784182010; mistlodgebuhoma@gmail.com; per person US$25) Lodge is a misnomer for this small concrete hotel, but it's still decent value for shoestring travellers. It's clean and simple, but breakfast costs extra.

BWINDI GORILLAS & PERMITS

Demand for gorilla permits exceeds supply for most of the year in Bwindi. During the 'low seasons' of April to May and October to November (the rainiest months), you may be able to confirm a space a week or two in advance of your trip. During the rest of the year it's not unheard of for permits to be booked up months in advance. If nothing is available that fits your schedule, check at the backpacker places in Kampala and Jinja, where the safari companies advertise excess permits they want to sell. It's no problem to buy these, even when someone else's name is on them. Cancellations and no-shows are rare, but you can get on the list at the park office: it's first-come, first-served. If you haven't prearranged a gorilla permit, this should be your number-one priority upon arrival in Kampala.

UWA offers discount permits during the low season months of April, May and November for US$450 instead of the usual US$600, making it the lowest possible price for gorilla tracking anywhere.

Buhoma

Nestled in the northwest corner of the park, Buhoma has three groups of gorillas: Rushegura (13 members), Mubare (11) and Habinyanza (17). As the first section of the park to open for gorilla tracking, Buhoma is by far the most developed in terms of tourist infrastructure, and with the most permits available it's also the most popular. Gorillas are probably the most accessible here too, sometimes as little as a 30-minute trek away.

Ruhija

In the northeast of the park, Ruhija has three groups: Bitukura (14 members), Oruzogo (17) and Kyaguriri (19). There's a good range of accommodation sprouting up here, but otherwise it's also accessible from Kabale or Buhoma, a two-hour drive either direction.

Nkuringo

While there's only one group in Nkuringo, a family of 11 that includes two silverbacks, it's regarded as one of the most entertaining and relaxed of the gorilla groups. Nkuringo is spectacularly set in the southwest of the park on a ridge opposite the wall of green that is Bwindi. From various spots you can spy Lake Edward, the Rwenzoris, all of the Virungas and even Nyiragongo Volcano by Goma in the DRC.

Rushaga

Located in the southeast of the park, Rushaga has 40 permits available for its five groups including Nshongi (family of eight gorillas, the most popular), Mishaya (eight), Kahungye (Bwindi's largest habituated group with 26 members), Busingye (nine) and Bweza (seven). This lovely thick tract of forest is also home to elephants. Another possibility in this sector is the gorilla habituation experience (per person US$1500). The permit process is the same and the difference is that visitors stay four hours with one group that is in the process of habituation.

Bwindi Backpackers LODGE $

(☎0772661854; www.bwindibackpackerslodge.com; Nkuringo; camping US$15, dm US$20-25, s/d US$45/90, s/d with shared bathroom US$30/60; 📶) Colourful and dilapidated, Bwindi Backpackers offers rare budget digs on the south side of the park. Basic, dark rooms have thick blankets and mosquito nets. Our gripe is with the shared bathrooms with puddles of standing water. The restaurant boasts the best views of all over the jungle canopy. Management is slow to help if there's a snag.

Nshongi Camp BANDA $

(☎0774231913; www.nshongicamp.altervista.org; Rushaga; camping US$5, banda s/d incl full board US$48/76) Right on the forest's edge, this simple but delightful camp has flat tent sites and dark mud-brick *bandas* with paraffin lamps and mosquito nets dispersed throughout the garden. Friendly owner Silver is a local, and is very knowledgeable about the area. It's only a short walk to the trailhead. There's no generator, so bring fully charged camera batteries.

Ruhija Community Rest Camp GUESTHOUSE $

(☎0771846635; camping US$10, room/cabin per person incl breakfast US$25-35) 🍃 With the entire forest at its feet, this community-run camp would be a good budget choice but for the water problems and poor management that can present frustrations for guests. The common area has a hostel vibe with fireplace, bar and board games. Proceeds go to water projects and a local orphanage. It also offers community walks.

Ichumbi Gorilla Lodge LODGE $$

(☎0772349040; http://ichumbigorillalodge.com; Rushaga; camping US$40, s/d incl full board US$130/150, s/d cottages incl full board US$150/240; 📶) Opened in 2016, this gorgeous lodge features stilted cottages sloped above the valley floor. Rooms feature African design accents, woven ceilings and terraces with views. There are canopy beds, huge shower heads and hot water, and very welcoming service.

Bakiga Lodge LODGE $$

(☎0774518421; www.bakigalodge.com; Ruhija; s/d tent incl full board from US$100/180, s/d cabin incl full board US$120/200; 📶) 🍃 Run by an NGO that protects local springs and constructs water projects, Bakiga Lodge offers terrific value with its mix of stilted log cabins and safari tents looking out to the forested hills. There's a pleasant common area with a fireplace and solar-powered showers and electricity. It has self-contained safari tents and two cabins. It's very popular.

Gorilla Valley Lodge LODGE $$

(☎0778531524; www.naturelodges.biz/gorilla-valley-lodge; Rushaga; s/d incl breakfast US$95/106) Gorilla Valley delivers the complete Bwindi experience: spectacular forest views, atmospheric bar and well-priced rooms with a rustic simplicity that one imagines would be to Dian Fossey's liking.

Gorilla Mist Camp LODGE $$

(☎0756563577; www.gorillamistcamp.com; s/d incl full board US$130/250; 📶) A solid midrange lodge with views of hilly surrounds from its stilted thatched-roof cottages and decked-out tents with hardwood furniture and carpets. Rooms and baths are spacious and run on solar power. Bathtubs and balconies add to its appeal.

★ **Bwindi Lodge** LODGE $$$

(☎0414-346464; www.volcanoessafaris.com/lodges/bwindi-lodge; Buhoma; s/d incl full board & activities US$300/500; 📶) 🍃 Eight stylish *bandas* with solar power, gorgeous textiles and warming fireplaces make up this ultraluxurious offering. Take a walk and go birding on the extensive grounds or enjoy a free massage. Gorillas have been spotted using the riverside path – it's just that chilled. Activities include game drives, tea-plantation visits, forest walks and visits to Batwa villages. Also supports community-based projects.

★ **Nkuringo Bwindi Gorilla Lodge** LODGE $$$

(☎0754805580; www.mountaingorillalodge.com; Nkuringo; s/d incl full board US$200/250, s/d cottages incl full board US$300/418; 📶) 🍃 A wonderful set-up with views looking out to the misty Virungas, the Nkuringo Gorilla Camp is an excellent pick for Nkuringo. Comfortable rooms and cottages mix safari-chic with boutique details. Little touches such as turn-over service, fabulous bathrobes and hot-water bottles go a long way.

The food is also good, served in the restaurant lit by paraffin lanterns with a bucket of glowing coals provided for warmth. It's a short walk from the Nkuringo trailhead.

Sanctuary Gorilla Forest Camp LODGE $$$

(www.sanctuaryretreats.com/uganda-camps-gorilla-forest; Buhoma; s/d incl full board US$600/1200; 📶) Of the most atmospheric of Bwindi's luxury lodges, this one is tucked within the park's boundaries. Its eight sumptuous safari tents have mahogany floorboards with private porches and are set on the forest's misty slopes. The campfire on the lawn is tailor-made for gorilla debriefing.

Buhoma Lodge LODGE $$$
(☎0414-321479, 0772721155; www.ugandaexclusivecamps.com/buhoma-lodge; Buhoma; s/d incl full board US$445/660; 📶) One of the few lodges inside the park, the refined Buhoma Lodge is perfect for those wanting to make their 'gorilla experience' that bit more memorable. Spacious stilted cottages feature polished-wood floors, claw-foot tubs and plenty of natural light. Each has a private porch with fantastic views of the dense forest and a stone bathtub with seats. Massage included.

There's also professional service and a useful information binder listing walks in the park.

Silverback Lodge LODGE $$$
(☎0789463757; http://silverbacklodge.com; s/d incl full board US$350/450; 📶) With lovely mountain views and enjoyable al fresco dining, Silverback proves to be a relaxing destination. Service is attentive but, for the price, rooms can be pretty small. It's partnered with some of Uganda's most well-known lodges.

Clouds Lodge LODGE $$$
(☎0414-251182; www.wildplacesafrica.com; Nkuringo; s/d incl full board US$834/1280; @) A joint project with the Uganda Safari Company, African Wildlife Foundation, International Gorilla Conservation Programme and the local community, this lodge offers a subtle sort of luxury, but if you can afford it, you'll enjoy it. Large stone cottages have big windows, original art and double-sided fireplaces, plus the services of a butler. Rates include drinks and laundry.

Gorilla Safari Lodge LODGE $$$
(☎0414-345742; www.crystallodgesuganda.com; Rushaga; s/d incl full board from US$271/424; 📶) This high-end lodge features solar-powered lodge cottages with claw-foot bath, petal-strewn bed and fireplace. However, it does seem somewhat less organised than the competition and it's close enough to the village for ambient noise to be present. It's a five-minute walk from the trailhead. Discounts available.

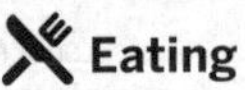

Eating

Bwindi Bar CAFE $
(Buhoma; mains USh8000; ⌚8am-8pm) A colourful haven on the main drag, this cute cafe serves organic espresso drinks with brownies and banana cake. For something more substantial, try a rolex (eggs wrapped in a chapatti), they're served gourmet style with goat's cheese and red-onion chutney. It's a nonprofit sponsored by Bwindi Lodge.

ℹ Getting There & Away

BUHOMA

Whether you have your own vehicle or not, getting to Buhoma can be complicated.

A special-hire vehicle is a good option, particularly if you can muster up a group to share the costs. The four-hour trip from Kabale to Buhoma costs around USh200,000/300,000 one-way/return.

By public transport there are several options involving uncomfortable and often hair-raising truck journeys. If you're lucky you'll get a pick-up truck direct to Buhoma from Kabale on Tuesday or Friday at around 10am (USh20,000, four to six hours). Otherwise you can try your luck with a truck from Kabale to Kihihi and disembark at Kanyantorogo (USh15,000, three hours). From here you'll need to get either another pick-up to Butogota (USh4000, 30 minutes) or wait for the bus from Kampala to pass (as early as 3pm, but usually later). Butogota is 17km northeast of Buhoma; for the last leg of the trip you have the option of catching the daily Green Bus at 8am, an infrequent pick-up to Buhoma (USh2000, one hour), or (most realistically) a special-hire taxi for USh72,000 or *boda-boda* for about USh20,000.

If you're heading to Buhoma from Kampala, there's a daily Bismarken bus to Butogota (USh44,000, 10 to 12 hours) departing Kampala's Buganda Bus Park (p400) around 6am; it departs in the other direction from Butogota at 3am.

If you're driving from Kabale to Buhoma, the best route is the long way through Kanungu (which can be done in a car if you're an experienced driver) rather than the rough road through Ruhija.

It's also possible to access Buhoma via walking through Bwindi Impenetrable National Park to Nkuringo, a lovely 12km stretch that takes five to seven hours. Contact Nkuringo Walking Safaris (p446) if this appeals, and they will arrange for you to be guided through the 'impenetrable' jungle.

Both Fly Uganda (p491) and Aerolink (p491) fly daily to Kihihi from Kampala (90 minutes), one hour away by car.

If you're coming from Queen Elizabeth National Park, Buhoma is best accessed from Kihihi, which is around 30 minutes outside Ishasha; a special-hire taxi is the most realistic option, costing around USh100,000 for the 40km journey.

NKURINGO

There are occasional trucks from Kabale to Nkuringo (USh20,000, four hours) but realistically you'll have to take a special-hire taxi (one-way USh100,000, 2½ hours) or *boda-boda* (USh35,000).

From Kisoro a truck travels to Nkuringo (USh10,000, three hours) on Monday and Thursday. It leaves Nkuringo around 8am and returns about 3pm. A special-hire taxi from Kisoro (1½ hours) costs around USh100,000 one-way or USh150,000 return. A *boda-boda* driver will charge you USh30,000, but it's a long, bottom-shaking ride. Be aware of the risks during rainy season when there can be lengthy delays due to the poor condition of the road.

The best way to travel from Nkuringo (you can also do it uphill from Kisoro) is to leave the road behind. Nkuringo Walking Safaris (p446) will lead you on a 22km trek to Kisoro via Lake Mutanda (this can be shortened with some driving) and then a 2½-hour paddle in a dugout canoe.

RUSHAGA

Located 54km from Kabale, Rushaga can be reached via a special-hire taxi (USh150,000, three hours), while a *boda-boda* is around USh35,000 one-way.

Otherwise it's 32km from Kisoro, which costs USh60,000 one-way and USh100,000 return by special-hire taxi (one hour) or USh15,000 by *boda-boda* one-way. Trucks (USh5000, two hours) depart in the afternoon on Monday and Thursday, and at 10am on Friday.

RUHIJA

Ruhija is about 50km (up to two hours) from Buhoma gate, and 52km from Kasese (a special-hire will cost about USh140,000 return). If you're chancing your luck with public transport, there are pick-up trucks (USh11,000, 2½ to three hours) that leave Kabale on Tuesday, Wednesday and Thursday, but there's no set departure time.

Kabale

0486 / POP 49,700

A dusty provincial town, Kabale is the kind of place most people get through as fast as possible. It is mostly of interest to travellers as a transport hub and gateway to both Lake Bunyonyi and Bwindi Impenetrable National Park, though given its proximity to both, most travellers try to avoid overnighting here and carry straight on to Bunyoni and Bwindi's far more obvious charms.

Sights

Great Lakes Museum MUSEUM

(www.greatlakesmuseum.co.ug; adult/child USh5000/4000; 7.30am-8pm) Along the highway on approach to Kabale, keep an eye out for this museum. It has a varied collection of artefacts and masks, information on clans, and quirky items such as displays on the evolution of phones and cameras. The cafe selling Ugandan coffee offers accommodation and mountain-bike hire.

It's 100km from Mbarara on the Kabale–Mbarara Road.

Kabale Arts Center MUSEUM

(0752558222; www.edirisa.org; Muhumuza Rd; incl guide USh20,000; 9am-9pm) Inside Kwanzi, this simple but worthwhile cultural museum houses a replica traditional homestead, built of sticks and papyrus, showing how the local Bakiga people lived a century ago. At the time of writing it was undergoing renovation but should be open by the time you read this.

Sleeping

Kwanzi HOSTEL $

(Edirisa; 0752558222; www.edirisa.org; Muhumuza Rd; dm USh16,000, tw/d with shared bathroom USh35,000/45,000; @) In a cool fuchsia corner building, this chilled-out guesthouse has very friendly staff and simple concrete rooms priced for the budget traveller. Beds sport thick blankets – it can get cold at 1863m! The rooftop restaurant is *the* spot to hang out in Kabale. It also offers canoe-trekking trips on Lake Bunyonyi and sustainable tours to Batwa villages.

Kabale Backpackers HOSTEL $

(0782421519; Muhumuza Rd; dm USh15,000, r per person excl breakfast USh20,000-35,000;) After an ownership change this hostel holds less appeal. It isn't particularly attuned to the needs of backpackers (paid wi-fi, very basic toilets), but it suits a basic budget. There's a pool table and cafe downstairs. Rooms are very simple, but beds have mosquito nets.

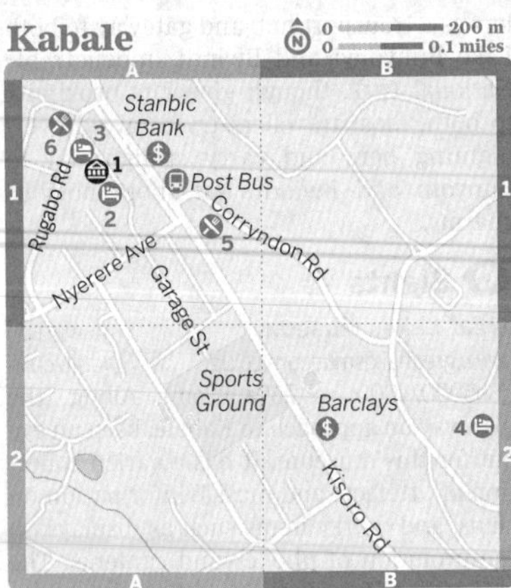

Kabale

Sights
1 Kabale Arts Center ... A1

Sleeping
2 Kabale Backpackers ... A1
3 Kwanzi ... A1
4 White Horse Inn ... B2

Eating
5 Cafe Barista ... A1
Kwanzi Cafe ... (see 3)
6 Little Ritz ... A1

White Horse Inn HOTEL $$
(☎0772459859, 0486-423336; www.whitehorseinnkabale.com; Rwamafa Rd; s/d incl breakfast USh105,000/150,000; wi-fi) Set on five grassy acres on the outskirts of town, this faded colonial hotel (built 1937) has hosted many a visiting dignitary, including Jimmy Carter and Bill Gates. With dated buildings flanked by brick columns, it now survives in the shadow of its glory days – but is a good midrange option for those who like their accommodation to have some character.

Eating

Kwanzi Cafe CAFE $
(☎0752558222; Muhumuza Rd; USh12,000-16,000; ⏰7am-10pm) This 2nd-storey open-air cafe with comfortable divans provides respite from dusty Kabale. A curbside blackboard announces the daily specials, though your meal still might take over an hour to assemble. Mains such as coconut curry and whole fried fish are served with rice or chapatis. There's also all-day breakfast: a faster option.

Cafe Barista CAFE $
(Kabale-Kisoro Rd; mains USh8000-20,000; ⏰8am-11pm) This friendly cafe on Kabale's main drag serves up pizzas, burgers and curries to hungry travellers. It also has decent coffee and pastries.

Little Ritz INTERNATIONAL $
(☎0703849039; Rugabo Rd; mains USh7000-25,000; ⏰7am-midnight) Located above the popular Hot Loaf Bakery, this rather dark and characterless place nevertheless offers an eclectic menu of Western, Indian, Chinese and African dishes that can be enjoyed outside on the balcony or inside by the fireplace.

Information

INTERNET ACCESS

Kabale Backpackers (p451) Internet access for USh40 per minute and paid wi-fi when it's functioning. There are several more internet cafes in town.

MONEY

If you are headed towards Lake Bunyonyi, stock up on cash at **Stanbic** (☎0486-22107; Kabale-Kisoro Rd; ⏰9am-4pm Mon-Fri) or **Barclays** (☎0486-422009; 190 Kabale-Kisoro Rd; ⏰8.30am-4pm Mon-Fri, 9am-1pm Sat).

TOURIST INFORMATION

Pick up a copy of the free *Gorilla Highlands* (www.gorillahighlands.com) pocket guide, which has information and history about the area including Bunyoni, Mgahinga and Bwindi. It's also available online.

Getting There & Away

BUS

The **Post Bus** (Kabale-Kisoro Rd) heads to Kabale to/from Kampala (USh25,000, eight hours) en route from/to Kisoro (USh14,000, two hours) at around 3pm from the post office. Other regular daily buses to Kampala (USh30,000) – including Horizon, Bismarken and Jaguar – also continue to/from Kisoro. You can catch these either at the main junction or in front of the Highland Hotel on the northwest side of town.

There are buses to Fort Portal (Ush35,000, eight hours) via Queen Elizabeth National Park and Kasese (Ush35,000, seven hours).

Jaguar goes to Kigali (USh15,000, four hours).

MINIBUS

Minibus taxis to the Rwandan border at Katuna (USh4000, 30 minutes) and on to Kigali are frequent.

TAXI

Shared taxis park near the Highland Hotel on the northwest side of town.

Lake Bunyonyi

Lake Bunyonyi ('place of many little birds') is undoubtedly the loveliest lake in Uganda. Its contorted shore encircles 29 islands, surrounded by steep terraced hillsides reminiscent of parts of Nepal. A magical place, especially with a morning mist rising off the placid waters, it has supplanted the Ssese Islands as *the* place for travellers to chill out on their way through Uganda, and has a selection of gorgeously remote and bucolic places to stay on distant islands, where you've only the birds for company. Best of all – unlike many lakes in East Africa – Bunyoni is bilharzia, croc and hippo free, and so its crystal-clear waters are all yours to swim in. Bliss.

Sights

Kyahugye Island WILDLIFE RESERVE

(www.bunyonyiecoresort.com; adult/child US$10/5) Run by Lake Bunyonyi Eco Resort (p455), this 35-acre island is worth a visit if you want to see to wildlife such as zebra, waterbuck, ipala and kob up close. All were brought here from Lake Mburo National Park (p461).

Bwama & Njuyeera (Sharp's) Islands HISTORIC SITE

Many boat drivers will take you to these islands, where British missionary Dr Leonard Sharp founded a leper colony and settled in 1921, but the story is more interesting than the sights. The colony on Bwama was shut down in the 1980s (there are two schools on the island now) and nearly all Njuyeera's history was stripped when it was converted into a (not recommended) hotel.

Akampeine Island HISTORIC SITE

Translating as Punishment Island, this tiny island was so named because it was once the place where unmarried pregnant women were dumped to die. Their only rescue from drowning or starvation was if a man who was too poor to pay a bride-price came over to claim the banished woman as his wife. There's nothing to see here, with just one spindly tree in its centre.

Activities

All guesthouses on the lake can arrange boat trips, either in motorboats or dugout canoes, which is still how most locals get about. This is one of the few places in Uganda where you can swim, with no crocodiles, hippos or bilharzia, so go ahead and jump in.

Canoeing

The best way to get intimate with Bunyonyi is by jumping in a canoe to paddle its peaceful waters. Excellent tours, which include some trekking, are offered by Kwanzi (p451) in Kabale, which range from five hours to its flagship three-day tours (www.canoetrekking.com; full day per person USh300,000). The longer tours offer a very up-close look at local life with village homestays and visits to the Batwa. Note prices are discounted for larger groups.

Otherwise it's easy enough to grab a dugout canoe on your own for a leisurely paddle; but practise before paddling off on an ambitious trip, as many travellers end up going round in circles, known locally as the *muzungu* corkscrew. Keep an eye out for otters, particularly along the shore during early morning and late afternoon.

Tours

All the guesthouses at Lake Bunyonyi can set you up with village walks to see, among other things, local blacksmiths *(abahesi)* who have replaced locally mined iron ore with scrap metal, but otherwise use traditional methods. But if you just want an easygoing amble along the lake shore, it's straightforward enough to find your own way around.

Batwa Today CULTURAL

(www.edirisa.org; from US$35) There are several Twa village tours in the area, but Batwa Today is the most recommended, aiming to deliver a more authentic exchange. Trips head to Echuya Forest, the former home of local Twa. While there are cultural performances, the experience is less contrived than those offered in Bwindi and Mghahinga. Rather than dwelling on the past, insights are offered from a more current context.

Arranged by the team from Kwanzi (p451) in Kabale, tours are led by Twa guides and sensitively balance preserving Twa culture and identity with improving living conditions, while minimising the human zoo element. Prices exclude transport.

Amagara Tours SAFARI
(☎0752296197; www.lakebunyonyi.net; Byoona Amagara, Itambira Island) Based at the Byoona Amagara resort on Lake Bunyonyi, this budget-focused company has great packages for all the national parks in the southwest, and is a great option for gorilla tracking, as well as Rwanda and DRC tours.

Sleeping

Lake Bunyoni has a good choice of accommodation, both on the mainland and on several of its many islands, where you'll find the most charming and remote options. Note that you may need to make a reservation in advance to enable the island hotels to pick you up at the Rutinda landing in town, where it's possible to leave your car in guarded car parks.

Seeds of Hope CABIN $
(☎0773092904; www.bunyonyilake.com; Itambira Island; cabins per person incl breakfast from US$25;) An excellent option, this small resort features round concrete cottages and wooden stilt cabins with balconies surrounded by a eucalyptus forest with water views. It's run by a British NGO with programs to help the local community. Cabins are immaculate, staff are very welcoming and there's a nice thatched restaurant and swimming dock in a lovely, peaceful spot.

Boat transport (USh25,000) is available from the mainland.

Bushara Island Camp LODGE $
(☎0772464585; www.busharaislandcamp.com; Bushara Island; camping without/with tent US$6/10, s/d safari tents US$35/40, d/tr cottages US$40/60, tree house US$58) One of Bunyonyi's best choices, this ultrarelaxed camp offers a wonderful selection of cottages and safari tents, all widely spaced through the eucalyptus forest. The 'tree-house' cottage set on stilts is wonderfully rustic and features a great balcony. All have memorable outdoor showers. With top service (breakfast delivered to your door), it's no surprise there are many return visitors.

The thatched-roof restaurant serves excellent food and has a roaring fireplace. A motorboat transfer from Rutinda is free unless you're camping (per trip USh15,000). Other perks are free birdwatching tours and a fun rope swing into the lake. It's run by the Church of Uganda to raise funds for community development projects.

Byoona Amagara LODGE $
(☎0752652788; www.lakebunyonyi.net; Itambira Island; camping/dm USh12,000/24,000, s/d/tr from USh40,000/60,000/75,000, geodome/cabin from USh50,000/60,000; @) Marooned perfectly on an idyllic island, Byoona Amagara bills itself as a backpacker's paradise bursting with personality. The rooms are built with all-natural materials and are very reasonably priced, though open-faced geodome huts are the pick of the litter, with extraordinary views. There's solar and some composting toilets.

The originality continues in the kitchen, which turns out tasty, creative dishes. Private rooms have a two-person minimum during peak holiday periods, and a 25% single supplement at other times. Boat transport (USh25,000) is available from Rutinda.

Gorilla View Backpackers HOSTEL $
(☎0772666331; Lake Bunyonyi; dm US$15, s/d incl breakfast US$35/40;) This perfectly serviceable backpacker haven has mixed dorms and a thatched restaurant. It's not waterfront, but there's a swimming dock across the road that you can access.

Crater Bay GUESTHOUSE $
(☎0486-426255; www.craterbaycottageslakebunyonyi.com; camping per person US$5, s/d with shared bathroom US$20/30, s/d tented camping incl breakfast US$20/25, s/d cottages incl breakfast US$50/70) A laid-back and inexpensive family-run resort, Crater Bay offers a cramped maze of *bandas* or tented camping overlooking the lake. It's good value on a shoestring, but there are more spacious resorts around. The garden has private areas to relax and there's a dock for water activities with canoes available.

Bunyonyi Overland Resort HOSTEL $
(☎0772409510; www.bunyonyioverland.com; camping with/without tent US$8/12, dm US$15, s/d from US$35/45, s/d cottage US$45/60;) Overland's sprawling lakeside camp caters to all kinds with four-bed dorms, overlander campsites and comfortable, self-contained cottages, of which the newer ones are much better, with lots of space, better light and rain showers. It's extremely popular, and its social bar is Bunyonyi's liveliest. Mountain bikes (US$10) and canoes (US$10) can be hired too.

★Birdnest@Bunyoni Resort RESORT $$
(☎0754252560; www.birdnestatbunyonyi.com; s/d/cottage US$160/190/210;) The Belgian-owned Birdnest is an impressive sight. It's the most upmarket choice in Bunyonyi, but remains excellent value. Open-plan rooms have vibrant decor, with lovely, private balconies looking out to the lake, while the outside terrace decking has a swimming pool with huge hammocks and free canoe hire. The secluded cottages (which sleep four) can only be reached by canoe.

The restaurant has a quality European menu and a good wine list. Nonguests can access wi-fi (USh10,000 per hour).

Lake Bunyonyi Eco Resort LODGE $$
(☎0392-080344; www.lakebunyonyiecoresort.com; Kyahugye Island; camping USh15,000, s/d incl full board US$90/100;) It's nice to find somewhere that does things a bit differently, and this Kyahugye Island resort fits the bill, with its small population of zebra, kob, impala and bushbuck (and one monkey) imported from Lake Mburo to Lake Bunyonyi. Rooms are in private, wooden thatched cottages with lake views. Call ahead to arrange pick-up from the pier to avoid the long climb.

Arcadia Cottages LODGE $$
(☎0793617741; www.arcadialodges.com/lake-bunyonyi.html; s/d incl breakfast US$100/140;) Built upon a hill, Arcadia has intoxicating views over the lake dotted with dozens of islands and a backdrop of the Virunga volcanoes in the distance. While they are adding more cottages, at present, the lower row are the best pick, boasting unhindered views, private porches and comfortable rooms. It also offers tours, birdwatching and boat rides.

Even if you won't be sleeping here, stop by for a meal for the sweeping panoramic views. On chilly nights a brazier of hot coals is provided, which makes things nice and cosy. It sits 2km uphill off the main road to the lake.

Nature's Prime Island BUNGALOW $$
(☎0772423215; www.naturesprimeisland.com; Akarwa Island; s/d safari tents incl breakfast from US$35/70, cabins incl breakfast US$40/80) Occupying a lovely little wooded island right near Rutinda, Nature Prime mixes it up with Scandinavian-style rustic log cabins and safari tents set on raised platforms. Use of canoes is complimentary, as is boat transfer. It offers a slew of extra activities that makes it popular with active guests.

Drinking & Nightlife

Lake View Coffee House CAFE
(Kachwekano; 7.30am-7.30pm) Grab a cup of local coffee or cold beer at this open-air cafe. There's little competition for ambience – it has a fantastic wooden deck with sweeping views over the lake. There's also a crafts shop.

Getting There & Away

Rutinda, where most of Bunyonyi's lodgings and the main jetty are found, is 9km from Kabale. To get here take a special-hire taxi (USh25,000) or *boda-boda* (motorcycle taxi; USh6000). Secure parking is available by the Rutinda landing for those driving here.

Kisoro

☎0486 / POP 17,560

While Kisoro – a gritty town with a frontier atmosphere – may not be much to look at, its verdant surrounds are undeniably beautiful. On a clear day the backdrop of the Virunga chain of volcanoes is stunning. Kisoro serves as a popular base for tourists, here primarily to see mountain gorillas in nearby Mgahinga Gorilla National Park (if they're this side of the border, that is), track golden monkeys or climb volcanoes. It's also a convenient base for those with gorilla permits in the southern sector of Bwindi Impenetrable National Park or even Parc National des Virunga at Djomba, just over the border in the DRC. If you're en route to/from Rwanda it makes a pleasant place to spend the night.

Cold winds blow through town, so pack that jacket.

Sights

Mgahinga Gorilla National Park and Lake Mutanda are the real attractions, just outside town. Kisoro's Monday and Thursday markets are large, colourful affairs that are well worth some of your time.

Tours

Mountain Gorilla Coffee Tours TOURS
(☎0777412288; wetalaj@gmail.com; Main St; 1/2 people US$30/45) These excellent coffee tours, run by knowledgeable guides, show guests the process from bean to cup, with a cupping session to compare notes on aromas

Kisoro

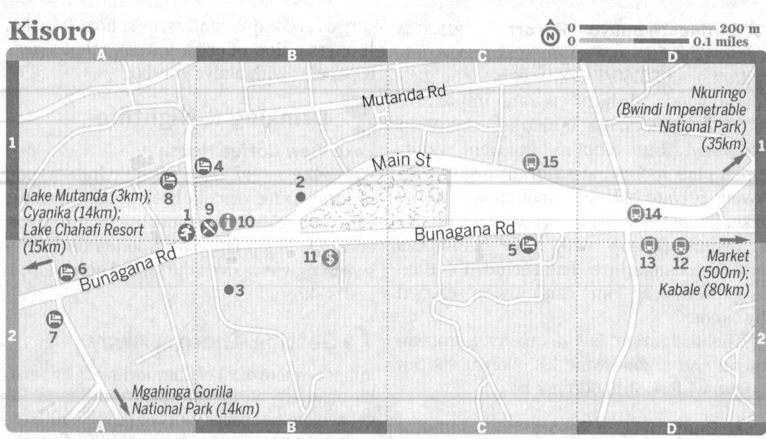

Kisoro

Activities, Courses & Tours
1 Mgahinga Community Development Organisation A1
2 Mountain Gorilla Coffee Tours B1
3 United Organisation for Batwa Development in Uganda B2

Sleeping
4 Golden Monkey Guesthouse B1
5 Mucha Bistro & Guesthouse C2
6 Sawasawa Guest House A2
7 Travellers Rest Hotel A2
8 Virunga Hotel A1

Eating
9 Coffee Pot Café B1

Information
10 Mgahinga Gorilla National Park Office B1
11 Stanbic Bank B2

Transport
Bismarken Bus .... (see 12)
12 Horizon Coaches D2
13 Jaguar Coaches D2
14 Post Bus D1
15 Taxi Park C1

and tastes. A bag of coffee is included in the price. It also rents out mountain bikes, and runs other tours, including canoeing Lake Mutanda, village homestays and Batwa cultural visits.

United Organisation for Batwa Development in Uganda CULTURAL
(UOBDU; ☎0486-430140; https://uobdu.wordpress.com; 3 Bazanyamaso Rd; 5hr tour US$80; ⊙8am-5.30pm) If you're interested in visiting a Twa (Batwa) village, this organisation will ensure that your trip is culturally sensitive. If you have the chance, do the Batwa Trail (p459) tour in Mgahinga Gorilla National Park.

Sleeping

Kisoro is backpacker-friendly, with decent midrange options as well. There are quality sleeping options at nearby Mgahinga Gorilla National Park and at Lake Mutanda.

Lake Chahafi Resort LODGE $
(☎0782754496; www.lakechahafiresort.com; Lake Chahafi; camping with/without tent incl breakfast US$8/12, dm/s/d/tr incl breakfast US$20/70/90/120) Located 15km outside Kisoro off the road to the Rwanda border, these cottages offer a great hideaway by the lake. There are plenty of activities including biking, birding and canoeing. The site has a remarkable history as the place of a WWI battle that saw British and Belgian troops up against the Germans in 1915; trenches can still be seen.

All meals are available and there's a bar.

Sawasawa Guest House GUESTHOUSE $
(☎0774472926; www.facebook.com/sawasawaguesthouse; Bunagana Rd; s/d incl breakfast US$25/35, with shared bathroom US$15/20) Run by a friendly team, low-key Sawasawa is popular with volunteers and NGOs. It makes an excellent budget choice with sparkling

rooms decked in matching bedspreads and feminine decor. It's run by some wonderful women and the food and Italian press coffee is also good.

Mucha Bistro & Guesthouse GUESTHOUSE $
(☎0784478605; www.hotel-mucha.com/bistroandguesthouse; Kabale-Kisoro Rd; s/d USh55,000/71,000; 📶) This German-Bulgarian–owned hotel has small but stylish rooms around a concrete courtyard. Its smart bistro is also a winner. Its flagship lodge is based in Lake Mutanda.

Golden Monkey Guesthouse HOSTEL $
(☎0772435148; www.goldenmonkeyguesthouse.com; dm/s/d US$10/30/40, r with shared bathroom US$15; 📶) Friendly and welcoming, Golden Monkey is a decent budget choice with restaurant. It also runs **Virunga Adventure Tours**, and can arrange trips across Uganda as well as decent-value transfers to the nearby parks.

Virunga Hotel HOSTEL $
(☎0782360820; camping/dm/r US$7/18/40, r with shared bathroom US$30) One of Kisoro's original backpackers, Virunga Hotel is where overland trucks end up. Its rear block has new, modern rooms. The cheapest rooms are rather cramped.

★ **Travellers Rest Hotel** HOTEL $$
(☎0772533029; www.gorillatours.com/accommodations/travellers-rest; Mahuabura Rd; s/d/tr incl breakfast US$85/100/130; @📶) A hotel with a history, it was once run by the so-called father of gorilla tourism, Walter Baumgärtel, and Dian Fossey regularly stayed here. Through various thoughtful touches such as Congolese crafts, this otherwise simple place has become a lovely little oasis. The garden has lots of shade and the restaurant features an atmospheric bar with fireplace.

The restaurant is one of the more reliable places to dine, with options ranging from pasta to omelettes and curries. It's also known for its buffet dinners (US$15), which are worth the splurge; visitors need to reserve by 3pm.

Eating

Coffee Pot Café CAFE $
(www.coffee-pot-cafe.com; Bunagana Rd; mains USh5000-15,000; ⏲8.30am-9.30pm; 📶) A smart German-owned cafe with decent coffee, burgers, BLTs and meatball dishes. It sells secondhand books and quality crafts next door.

Information

MONEY

There are several banks with ATMs, including **Stanbic** (☎0392-222206; Kabale-Kisoro Rd; ⏲9am-4pm).

TOURIST INFORMATION

Mgahinga Gorilla National Park Office (☎0414-680793; www.ugandawildlife.org; Kabale-Kisoro Rd; ⏲8am-5pm) The place to book your gorilla permits, they have information about everything in and around Kisoro.

Getting There & Away

Post Bus (Main St) heads to Kampala (USh25,000, eight hours) via Kabale (USh10,000, 1½ hours) daily at 6am. Several bus companies also have departures during the morning, as do minibus taxis. **Jaguar Coaches** (☎0777763491), **Horizon Coaches** and **Bismarken Bus** also go to Kampala and intermediate destinations.

The Rwandan border south of Kisoro at Cyanika is open 24 hours and it's a pretty simple, quick trip to Musanze (Ruhengeri). To the border a *boda-boda* is around USh5000; special-hire taxi is USh20,000.

To the southern section of Bwindi Impenetrable National Park, you can take a *boda-boda* (USh30,000) or taxi (USh80,000) from the **taxi park**.

Mgahinga Gorilla National Park

The tiny 34-sq-km **Mgahinga Gorilla National Park** (Map p522; ☎0486-430098; www.ugandawildlife.org; adult/child US$40/20) in the far southwest corner of the country is Uganda's sliver of the volcanic Virunga range, which extends in greater part to the dense tropical rainforests of eastern DRC and northern Rwanda. The 434-sq-km Virunga Conservation Area that is shared between the three countries is home to half the world's mountain-gorilla population.

Gorilla tracking is the main attraction, but it's less popular than Bwindi Impenetrable National Park, due to the one habituated family having a tendency to duck across the mountains into Rwanda or the DRC. But there's more on offer here than just gorillas. Elephants, buffaloes and serval are rarely seen, but they're also out there, and 115 species of bird flutter through the forests, including Rwenzori turaco and mountain black boo boo.

MGAHINGA GORILLA NATIONAL PARK

Why Go Mountain gorillas; golden monkeys; volcano trekking in the stunning Virungas; Batwa Trail.

When to Go Year-round, but be sure to check the gorillas are here, as they sometimes hang out on the Rwandan side. The dry seasons (mid-December to February and June to October) are best for tracking primates.

Practicalities Kisoro is a convenient base, though it's possible to stay in the park.

Budget Tips Golden-monkey tracking offers a more affordable alternative to tracking the gorillas. Nearby Kisoro is a very backpacker-friendly town, but there's also affordable lodging at Mgahinga Gorilla National Park and Lake Mutanda.

All activities are booked through UWA in Kisoro, or otherwise its office in Mgahinga.

Activities

Volunteering

A community initiative based around Mgahinga National Park and Kisoro, **Mgahinga Community Development Organisation** (☎Kisoro 0382-278763; www.mcdou.org; Kabale-Kisoro Rd, Kisoro) provides a range of opportunities including teaching, farming, animal conservation and beekeeping.

Gorilla Tracking

If you plan to come here specifically for gorillas, the first step is to check they're on this side of the border. When the gorillas are living on Ugandan soil, eight people can visit per day. The cost is US$600, including the entrance fee, a ranger-guide and armed guards. Due to the higher altitude, gorillas here have a fuzzier, more luxuriant coat compared to their cousins in Bwindi.

Some permits may be available last minute, so check with the UWA office (p456) in Kisoro, though it's ideal to buy them at least a month in advance.

Trips depart from park headquarters at 8.30am, but check in at the office (p457) in Kisoro the day before your trip to confirm your arrival.

Unlike permits for Bwindi, bookings for Mgahinga Gorilla National Park aren't taken at the UWA head office in Kampala. You must make your reservation by calling the park office (p457) in Kisoro no more than two weeks in advance. You pay at the park on the day of your tracking. Because of this system, tour operators rarely come here, making it a good place to get permits at the last minute. It is also possible to book permits in Kisoro for Rushaga at Bwindi Impenetrable National Park.

Golden Monkey Tracking

While inevitably overshadowed by the gorillas, golden monkeys (a very rare subspecies of the rare blue monkey found only in this part of the world) are another lure to Mgahinga. For US$90 (including park entry) you spend an hour with these beautiful creatures who live in large groups and are quite playful. Tracking starts at 8.30am, and the guides can find the habituated troop 85% of the time, though they are less easily spotted if it's raining.

If you're really into the idea, there are longer four-hour trips (US$100 excluding entry fees), which allow you to be involved with the habituation process.

Volcano Trekking

Mgahinga has three dormant volcanoes that can be climbed, which, though strenuous, require no mountaineering experience. Each volcano costs US$80 to climb, which includes park entry and a guide. The most popular climb is **Mt Sabyinyo** (3669m), which involves breathtaking walks along gorges and a few challenging ladder ascents, with the reward of getting to the third and final peak where you'll be standing in Uganda, Rwanda and the DRC all at once. It's a 14km, eight-hour trek.

There's also the 12km, seven-hour trek to the crater lake at the summit of **Mt Muhavura** (4127m). It's the tallest of the volcanoes and almost too perfect to be true, with views reaching all the way to the Rwenzori Mountains. **Mt Gahinga** (3474m) is the least taxing of the climbs, an 8km, six-hour trek up to its swampy summit through bamboo zone. All treks lead you into the otherworldly afro-alpine moorland, home of bizarre plants such as giant groundsel and lobelias.

Two less demanding treks (US$30 including guide), both about 10km long and great for birdwatchers, are the **Border**

Trail, which starts at Sabyinyo but then cuts back south along the Congolese border, and the **Gorge Trail**, which heads to a small waterfall in a gorge halfway up Sabyinyo. You could combine these into one longer trek.

Tours

Batwa Trail CULTURAL
(UWA Kisoro 0414-680793; incl guide US$80) Organised by UWA, forest tours led by local Twa (Batwa), explain how they used to live in the forest before being forcibly removed when it became a national park. The 3½-hour tours include Twa legends, demonstrations of hunting and fire lighting, and a visit to the 342m-long Garama Cave, a historic residing spot of the Twa, with a song-and-dance performance.

While at times it feels a bit contrived, the tour provides a much better insight to the Twa people than the often-depressing village visits. Ask your hotel or travel agency to arrange these tours, but do check that all your money goes to the Twa themselves, rather than to people in the middle.

Sleeping

Amajambere Iwacu Community Campground CAMPGROUND $
(Map p522; 0774954956, 0782306973; www.amajamberecamp.com; camping with/without tent US$10/15, dm US$15, s/d/tw banda incl breakfast US$30/50/40) Right at the park's gate, this friendly and extremely peaceful camp – set up and run by the local community – has a variety of rooms with nice verandas for relaxing. It's a good choice for those seeking a local experience, and has volunteer opportunities and hot meals available. Proceeds fund school projects in the area.

★ **Mt Gahinga Lodge** LODGE $$$
(Map p522; 0414-346464; www.volcanoessafaris.com; s/d incl full board US$330/550) Set within a rocky garden that blends in beautifully with the natural surrounds, this luxury lodge oozes charm. The homestead-style cottages have volcano views, playful, bold African decor and ample space, with sofas and fireplaces that take the damp edge off the forest. Rates include drinks and a massage – both perfect after a day's trekking.

To get here from Kisoro, go 14km in on the Mgahinga–Kisoro road and turn at the signpost for the park. It's on your right.

Getting There & Away

There's no scheduled transport along the rough 14km track between Kisoro and the park headquarters. A special-hire taxi (around USh60,000) or *boda-boda* (motorcycle taxi; USh10,000) are the most straightforward ways of getting to the park, but be prepared for a long, rough, slippery ride if it's wet.

Lake Mutanda

This scenic lake lies just north of Kisoro and stretches not far south of Bwindi, making it a relaxing base for your gorilla trip. It's a pretty spot, with a misty Virunga backdrop comprising a string of volcanoes and a lake ringed by papyrus swamp, and is a good alternative for those who find Lake Bunyonyi overdeveloped. There are also dugout canoes for hire if you fancy a paddle; you don't need to worry about hippos, crocodiles or bilharzia here. Lake Mutanda is also the starting point for eight-hour treks into Bwindi Impenetrable National Park with Nkuringo Walking Safaris (p446).

Sleeping

Mutanda Eco-Community Centre CABIN $
(0773107795; www.lakemutandacamp.com; camping per tent US$6, dm US$10, s/d cottage US$40/50) Run by the local community, these rickety stilted cabins (number 4 and 5 have excellent lake views) and grassy campground sit on the fringes of farmland. It's a welcoming place with a strong community presence – if there's a bush party, attend, though sleeping might not be an option. Hosts cook local food and rent out dugout canoes.

Keep an eye out for otters.

Mucha HOTEL $$
(0755700362; www.hotel-mucha.com; Bwindi Rd; s/d incl breakfast US$50/90;) While the idea of slick modern hotel rooms in such a pastoral setting is confounding, Mucha pulls it off. Choose between volcano views or creek-side rooms with modern amenities and big windows. The European restaurant with abstract art is a classy affair.

Chameleon Hill Lodge LODGE $$$
(in Kampala 0772721818; www.chameleonhill.com; s/d incl breakfast US$330/460;) Finally a lodge in Uganda that's trying something original, hilltop Chameleon provides a memorable first impression with a series of multicoloured surrealist chimney-stack

buildings. The flair doesn't stop there, with plenty of arty touches and colour in its 10 comfortable chalets, all with porches and soaring lake panoramas. There's a lauded restaurant and bar, and massages are available.

Mutanda Lake Resort LODGE $$$
(☎0789951943; www.mutandalakeresort.com; Mutanda Lake; s/d/tr incl breakfast US$130/170/250, lunch/dinner US$10/18;) In a superb location directly on the lake, this relaxed Dutch-owned resort has luxury safari tents raised on wooden platforms with self-contained bathrooms, lovely porches and polished wooden floorboards. It's within striking distance of gorillas at Nkuringo, Ruhija and Mgahinga. There are also boating options.

Access is via a very rough road that takes 40 minutes to go 16km.

Getting There & Away

Lake Mutanda is easily accessible from Kisoro. For the community centre, a *boda-boda* or special-hire taxi should cost USh5000 and USh20,000 respectively. The lodges are considerably further along, accessed via a hair-raising clifftop dirt road.

Mbarara

☎0485 / POP 195,000

Fast-growing Mbarara is Uganda's second-largest urban centre. There's one of the country's best museums nearby, though travellers might be turned off negotiating the chaotic, gritty downtown. Unless you're with an NGO or wanting to break up your trip, there's little reason to overnight.

Sights

★**Igongo Cultural Centre** MUSEUM
(www.igongo.co.ug; 12km Mbarara-Masaka Rd; adult/child USh20,000/3000; 7.30am-10pm) Located 12km from Mbarara on the road to Kampala, this cultural village features the best museum displays in Uganda. Set on the grounds of a former palace of the Ankole king, this quality museum explores the peoples of southwestern Uganda, particularly the Ankole, through artefacts, a cultural village replica and a heap of info. There's a restaurant serving traditional Ankole dishes, such as smoked Ankole cow's milk and boiled meats. There's also a new on-site hotel.

There's a great bookshop with an interesting selection of Ugandan reading material. Directly across from the centre is **Biharwe Eclipse Monument** atop Biharwe Hill. It was built to commemorate a victory for Ankole kingdom 500 years ago, following an eclipse that saw the invading king retreat in fear (and never return), spooked as day plunged into sudden darkness.

Sleeping

The best lodging options are on the outskirts of the city.

★**Nyore Hillside Retreat** CABIN $$
(☎0783356142; https://nyoreretreat.com; camping USh25,000, lazy camping from USh45,000, s/d cottages incl breakfast from USh150,000/200,000;) In the owner's family for generations, this hillside set of *bandas* provides a peaceful and welcoming retreat surrounded by coffee and banana plantations. Campers get tents with air mattresses and linens set in a garden. The on-site restaurant serves up wonderful curries. To get here, zigzag on the dirt roads 27km west of Mbarara.

Igongo Country Hotel HOTEL $$
(☎0704629921; Masaka Rd; s/d from US$100/120;) Away from the bustle of the centre, this comfortable hotel behind the cultural centre is a good choice if you want to overnight around Mbarara. The 52 smart, modern rooms have glass-walled bathrooms, robes and safes. There's an on-site restaurant and the excellent cultural centre itself, plus a swimming pool is in the works.

Lake View Resort Hotel HOTEL $$
(☎0772367972; www.lakeviewresorthotel.co.ug; off Fort Portal-Kasese Rd; s/d incl breakfast from US$65/80;) On the outskirts of town off the road to Kasese, this modern hotel sits in front of a tiny lake, and is a popular option for business travellers too. Nonguests can also use the pool (adult/child USh15,000/10,000).

Getting There & Away

Departing from side-by-side parks, there are frequent buses and minibuses to Kampala (USh15,000, 4½ hours), Masaka (USh10,000, 2½ hours) and Kabale (USh15,000, 3½ hours). For Kasese (USh15,000, three hours) and Queen Elizabeth National Park (Katunguru), jump on the daily Kalita bus at 11am. You can also catch the Kigali-bound buses that begin in Kampala.

Lake Mburo National Park

With exciting African wildlife watching in arm's reach of the capital, the 370-sq-km **Lake Mburo National Park** (☎0751046904; adult/child US$40/20; ⏰7am-6.30pm) is an increasingly common stop on the safari circuit. It's the only place in southern Uganda to see zebras and the only park in the country with impalas, slender mongoose and giant bush rats. You can also look for hyenas, leopards, topis, elands and recently reintroduced Rothschild's giraffes. Lions are rarely sighted – it's thought there's only one left here. Few big predators means there are horse-riding and mountain-biking opportunities. Some of the 325 bird species include martial eagles and red-faced barbets in the acacia-wooded savannah, and papyrus yellow warblers and African finfoots in the wetlands.

Adjacent to the park are the ranches of the Bahima people, who herd the famed long-horned Ankole cattle, a common sight here, unfortunately both inside and outside the park.

Activities

Launch Trips

The 1½-hour boat trips run by UWA are popular on Lake Mburo to get up close and personal with hippos, crocodiles and waterbirds. Trips cost US$15 per person and depart at 8am, 10am, noon, 2pm, 4pm and 5.30pm. For fewer than four guests it's US$40. Fishing permits (US$15) are also available, but you'll need to bring your own equipment.

Wildlife Drives

Animals are most abundant in the south during dry season (as this is where the permanent water is) and in the northeast in wet season. Guides cost US$20; night drives (US$30 per person) are also possible.

Wildlife Walks

Lake Mburo has some good nature walks (US$30 per person), particularly the guided early-morning **hyena walk** at 6.30am. The other popular pedestrian destination is an observation blind overlooking a salt lick. Both walks take two hours. Birdwatchers should ask about the Rubanga forest, which has a closed canopy in some places and you may find birds not yet recorded on the park's official list.

> **LAKE MBURO NATIONAL PARK**
>
> **Why Go** Most accessible park to Kampala; zebras, elands and impalas; healthy population of hippos and crocodiles; hyena nature walk; horse-riding safari.
>
> **When to Go** Year-round.
>
> **Practicalities** It's a 3½-hour drive from Kampala. Reservations for boat trips are recommended from June to August and in December.
>
> **Budget Tips** If you don't have your own vehicle, a combination of bus and *boda-boda* can get you to park headquarters, from where activities can be arranged. There's also camping and affordable *bandas*.

Horse-Riding Safaris

A novel way to explore the park is a horse-riding safari. Without the engine noise of a 4WD it's a peaceful way to get around to see wildlife and the park's lakes. Rides are booked through Mihingo Lodge (p462) and cost US$40 for one hour, US$130 for a half-day and US$300 for a full day with possible discounts for lodge guests. They can also arrange overnight and multiday trips.

Sleeping

UWA Campsites CAMPGROUND $
(camping per person USh15,000) There are three campsites, but most opt for the attractive Lakeside Camp 2, 1.25km from park headquarters. It also has the scenic Lakeside Restaurant (p462). If you have your own vehicle, consider Kingfisher Campsite 3, which is more rustic. Be mindful of encounters with wildlife, particularly hippos.

Rwonyo Rest Camp BANDA, CAMPGROUND $
(☎0392-711346; www.ugandawildlife.org; camping/dm USh15,000/20,000, s/d banda with shared bathroom USh35,000/40,000, s/d safari tents USh30,000/60,000) UWA's accommodation at the park headquarters has camping, simple *bandas* and safari tents on wooden platforms, all with shared bathroom facilities. Overall, it's a very nice set-up with a classic park feel. It sells beers and drinks, but the closest food is 1.25km away at the

Lakeside Restaurant or at upmarket Arcadia Cottages; UWA can arrange a *boda-boda* for USh12,000.

Eagles Nest Lake Mburo LODGE $$
(☎0777820071, 0312-294894; www.naturelodges.biz; s/d incl breakfast US$60/70) Up the top of an impossibly steep hill outside the park, this Dutch-owned lodge has memorable views out to Mburo's distant plains and lakes. Tented safari-style accommodation is simple, but fantastic value. Guests can get half or full board.

★**Mihingo Lodge** LODGE $$$
(☎0752410509; www.mihingolodge.com; s/d incl full board from US$370/520;) One of Uganda's best park lodges lies just outside Mburo's eastern border, with rustic tent-cottages spread along the ridge. All have amazing views, including a watering hole busy with zebras, impalas and waterhogs. Its luxurious pool also has views out to a salt lick. Another highlight is seeing its family of habituated bushbabies at night. It also runs horse-riding safaris.

Rwakobo Rock LODGE $$$
(☎0755211771; www.rwakoborock.com; safari tent per person US$50, r US$80, cottage per person incl full board US$125;) It may officially be outside the park, but you'll feel well and truly immersed within this eco lodging with soaring Mburo views from its namesake rock. *Bandas* are nestled away in the bush, while the thatched-roof restaurant has more views and excellent meals. Check the website for activities on offer including bike safaris, cultural walks, and game drive and walk combos.

Kimbla-Mantana Lake Mburo Camp LODGE $$$
(☎0414-320152, 0772401391; www.lakemburocamp.com; s/d incl full board US$220/330;) A classy camp offering luxury tents with commanding views of Lake Mburo (and sunsets behind the hills) available right from the hammocks on the big porches.

Arcadia Cottages LODGE $$$
(☎0486-26231; www.arcadialodges.com/lake-mburo.html; s/d incl full board US$170/210) Near but not right on the lake, this camp features bright, attractive cottages that are a melange of concrete, canvas, wood and thatch. Half and full board are available. The small daily menu always has something Italian on it; nonguests are welcome to dine here.

Eating

Lakeside Restaurant INTERNATIONAL $
(mains USh15,000-26,000; 7am-10pm) Serving typical Ugandan fare and more, scenic Lakeside Restaurant is good if you can spare a long time to wait for your food.

Getting There & Away

CAR

There are two possible ways into the park from the main Masaka–Mbarara road: Nshara and Sanga gates. If you're driving your own vehicle, it's better to use the Nshara, 13km after Lyantonde, because you'll see much more wildlife on the drive in.

SPECIAL-HIRE, BODA-BODA & MINIBUS

If you're hoping to hitch or arrange a special-hire taxi (USh60,000) or *boda-boda* (motorcycle taxi; USh15,000), it's best to use the route from the Sanga gate, 27km after Lyantonde and 40km from Mbarara. Minibus taxis to Sanga cost USh6000 from Mbarara (45 minutes) and USh10,000 from Masaka (two hours). It's about a 25km drive to Rwonyo from either gate.

If you're really rushed, Lake Mburo can be done as a day trip from Kampala. It's about a 3½-hour drive each way. A bus to Kampala is USh17,000.

Masaka

☎0481 / POP 104,000

A surprisingly happening little town, Masaka is a good place to break up a journey to the southwest, especially if you want to stake out the elusive shoebill at the nearby Ramsar site. In 1979 Masaka was trashed by the Tanzanian army during the war that ousted Idi Amin. While the scars remain very visible, these days Masaka has turned the corner. For most travellers, it's a stop en route to the Ssese Islands or Tanzania, and an otherwise good place to break your journey for a decent meal or coffee.

Sights

Nabajjuzi Wetlands NATURE RESERVE
(☎0414-540719; www.natureuganda.org) Just out of Masaka on the way to Mbarara, these Ramsar site–listed wetlands offer excellent opportunities to spy two of Uganda's most elusive animals: the shoebill stork and the sitatunga. The observatory, a basic ecotourism facility, organises birdwatching and nature walks with a community ecotourism initiative through Nature Uganda.

Camp Ndegeya Sculpture Park ARTS CENTRE
(0777006726; www.weaverbirdartcommunity.org) This community arts centre in Ndegeya village, 7km from Masaka, has a cool outdoor sculpture park and holds art events throughout the year, including Fiestart in August. A *boda-boda* here costs USh5000.

Sleeping

Banda Lodge BANDA $
(0792011010; www.banda.dk; 7 Kigamba Rd; dm US$10, s/d/q banda incl breakfast US$30/50/100;) The Danish owners of Cafe Frikadellen run this peaceful hillside guesthouse. It has a resort feel with smart, very affordable *bandas* arranged around an extremely inviting pool, and a restaurant with great views. It's within a large, unsigned compound. Day visitors (USh10,000) can use the pool from Monday to Saturday.

Villa Katwe GUESTHOUSE $
(0791000637; www.villakatwe.com; Somero Rd; s/d camping USh30,000/35,000, s/d/tr incl breakfast USh55,000/100,000/135,000;) Run by Robin and Wycliffe, a fun young Dutch-Ugandan couple (who are a good source of travel info), this chilled-out guesthouse has a homely atmosphere with social kitchen table and lounge with card games. There's also a backyard full of bunnies, and the **Your Way Tours** tour company.

Masaka Backpackers HOSTEL $
(0752619389; www.masakabackpackers.webklik.nl/page/home; camping from USh10,000, dm/s/d USh16,000/30,000/45,000;) This fun, friendly place 4.5km south of town has a rural feel and a helpful owner. It can arrange visits to the Nabajjuzi Wetlands and organise village tours. A *boda-boda* from Masaka costs around USh3000.

Eating

Grass Roots Cafe CAFE $
(0791869841; www.grassrootscafe.org; mains USh7000; 9.30am-8.30pm;) This cute little deli offers all-day breakfast, Turkish coffee and healthy wraps featuring hummus, spinach and avocado or falafel. Don't skip the fresh juice, with refreshing combos such as pineapple, cucumber and mint.

Valley Cave UGANDAN $
(47 Hobat St; mains USh3000-10,000; 7am-11pm) This popular eatery is a good spot to grab some local food.

Café Frikadellen DANISH, GREEK $$
(0775018586; www.facebook.com/cafefrikadellen; Plot 6, Circle Rd; mains USh13,000-27,000; 8am-10pm Mon-Fri, 10am-10pm Sat, noon-10pm Sun;) An expat fave, this Danish-owned eatery is best known for its Friday night all-you-can-eat barbecue (USh40,000) with many side salads, but also serves quality à la carte dishes from Greek to Danish, including a *frikadeller* (meatball) burger. Be prepared for painfully slow service. Proceeds from its craft shop go to an orphanage.

Plot 99 CAFE $$
(0700151649; www.plot99.ugogreen.eu; 99 Hill Rd, Kizungu; mains USh13,000-24,000; noon-10pm Mon, Wed & Thu, 10am-10pm Fri-Sun;) This chilled out Belgian-Dutch–owned coffeehouse serves everything from Belgian fries with mayo to thin-crust pizzas and Greek salads. It has great coffee too, and proceeds go to a locally based charity, U Go Green (www.ugogreen.eu). Offers free delivery.

Getting There & Away

Most minibuses pick up and drop off passengers at the Shell petrol station on Kampala Rd. Many buses, on the other hand, use the bypass rather than coming into town, so it's usually quickest to take a *boda-boda* (motorcycle taxi; USh3000) to nearby Nyendo for east-bound services and Kyabakuza for westbound services.

Bus service is frequent to Kampala (USh18,000, two hours) and Mbarara (USh10,000, 2½ hours), but less so to Kabale (USh20,000, five hours).

If you're crossing into Tanzania it's best to hop on the direct Friend Safaris bus from Kampala out at the junction.

Ssese Islands

If you're looking for a place to slow right down, Ssese's lush archipelago of 84 islands along Lake Victoria's northwestern shore boasts some stunning white-sand beaches. There's not much to do other than grab a good book and relax. There are canoes for hire, but swimming is not advised due to the risks of bilharzia, and some outlying islands have the occasional hippo and crocodile. Most guesthouses on the beach have nightly bonfires, which is a great way to relax with a few drinks after enjoying one of Ssese's famous sunsets.

The early 1990s saw the Ssese's popularity peak, but the suspension of the ferry service largely removed them from the *muzungu* (foreigner) map until a ferry began running from Entebbe in 2006.

History

Early in the 20th century, sleeping sickness hit the islands (Ssese equals Tsetse), which saw most of the original Bassese inhabitants flee. People slowly began to drift back about a decade and a half later, but it wasn't until the 1980s that serious settlement took place again. There are very few Bassese anymore and their Lussese language has all but died. The lack of settlement left the islands largely unspoiled, though things have changed dramatically in the recent past. Massive scars of deforestation are visible on many of the islands, and overfishing is an issue.

Sleeping

Almost all visitors limit themselves to Buggala or Banda islands. The electricity supply on the islands is erratic, though most lodges have generators.

Bugala Island

Few people venture far beyond Buggala Island (the most accessible of the islands), though it can be noisy. Most of the Buggala Island lodging is on attractive Lutoboka Bay, right where the ferry drops you off, and most hotels will pick you up for free.

Ssese Islands Beach Hotel HOTEL $
(0754444684; www.sseseislandsbeachhotel.com; Bugala Island; camping with/without tent USh35,000/30,000, s/d incl full breakfast from USh110,000/185,000;) While motel-style rooms may not suit an island getaway, at least they're set right on the beach with great views from their private porches. It backs on to a basic golf course; a hit is included in the rates.

Islands Club GUESTHOUSE $
(0787998034; www.sseseislandsclub.com; Kalangala, Bugala Island; s/d incl breakfast USh70,000/140,000) One of the first lodgings on the island, the wooden bungalows here have a real beachy feel to them, which may have something to do with their location on a blinding stretch of white sand. The spiced, fried tilapia (Nile perch) it serves is absolutely delicious and staff are friendly and helpful.

Brovad Sands Lodge RESORT $$
(0758660020; www.sseseislandsresorthotel.com; Bugala Island; s/d incl full board USh250,000/350,000;) A stunning property comprising large, plush thatched cottages in a tropical garden with a soaring *banda* restaurant and direct beach access. Though it has its imperfections (eg some shoddy materials), all is forgiven when lazing in its pool or hanging out on the beach by the bonfire. Bring your own mosquito net. Discounts available.

Banda Island

Banda Island is an old-school backpacker destination with a picturesque beach that's enjoying a resurgence.

★ **Banda Island Resort** GUESTHOUSE $
(0772222777, 0774728747; www.bandaisland.biz; Banda Island; incl full board camping USh110,000, dm & tented camping USh150,000, cottage USh195,000) Banda is exactly what an island escape should be: it has a picturesque beach and laid-back vibe, and days here feel like weeks. This decidedly rustic place nonetheless has running water, cold beer and hot showers. Accommodation is in comfortable cottages, decent dorms or tented camps. Food is a highlight. Hippos are common visitors come full moon.

The local catch contributes to anything from fish samosas to sensational fish burritos. Guests can paddle around in canoes, learn to sail, pass the days with lazy games of outdoor backgammon, or perform some quality control on the hammocks.

Information

MONEY

There are no banks on the Ssese Islands.

POST

There's a post office in Kalangala, the only full-on town – it's on Buggala Island.

Getting There & Away

BOAT & FERRY

Departure times from Buggala are at 1.30pm, arriving at Port Bell by 6pm. Fares are USh30,000/70,000 for economy/1st class; you'll need to arrive 30 minutes before departure.

TAXI

On Buggala Island, shared taxis run from Kalangala to Luku (USh7000, one hour), while coming from the mainland, shared taxis run from Nyendo (3km east of Masaka) to Bukakata

(USh5000, one hour). Taxis in both directions run to coincide with the car-ferry schedule, and neither is a fun trip as they're usually insanely overpacked with 15 passengers somehow squeezing into a five-seat car.

Getting Around

On Buggala Island, Kalangala trading centre is 2km uphill from the pier; a *boda-boda* costs USh3000.

Island hopping is not a popular activity. Thanks to high fuel costs, it's expensive to travel between islands. A special-hire boat from Buggala Island to Banda Island is upwards of US$75.

NORTHWESTERN UGANDA

Northwestern Uganda feels wilder and more remote than the country's principal destinations, but that's part of the attraction. Its primary calling card is the magnificent Murchison Falls National Park, the best all-round protected area for wildlife, balanced with the experience of evening bonfires at the bush camp or luxury lodge. If your timing is right on a game drive, it's Eden before the fall: roaming herds of elephants, leopards resting in trees and giraffes traipsing the savannah. Its raging namesake waterfall is where the Victoria Nile crashes through a narrow channel on its final descent into Lake Albert. Another highlight is the Budongo Forest Reserve, with a huge chimp population. For decades, the Lord's Resistance Army (LRA) and its war on civilians put most of northwestern Uganda effectively off limits. But now that the LRA has fled Uganda, this vast region is once again a prominent star on the traveller's map.

Getting There & Away

Most visitors to the region arrive overland with a tour operator or rental car. There's flight service from Entebbe to Murchison Falls National Park

Northwestern Uganda

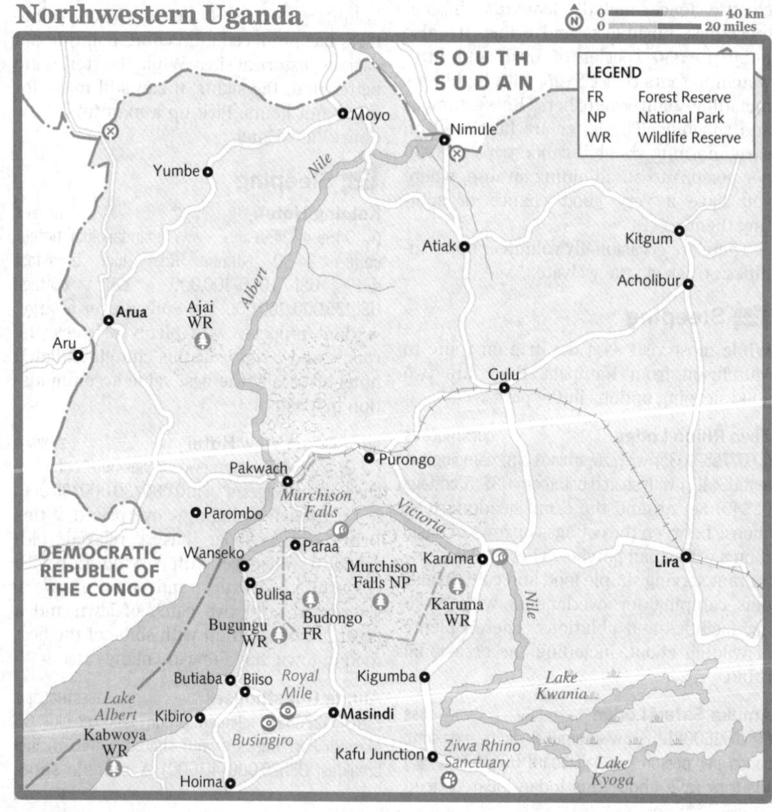

and major towns. Buses, *boda bodas* and shared taxis are used throughout the region, but in the national park and reserves you will need a 4WD vehicle to watch wildlife.

Ziwa Rhino Sanctuary

The Big Five are back. Twenty years after poachers shot the nation's last wild rhino in Uganda, Rhino Fund Uganda opened this private 70-sq-km reserve, 170km northwest of Kampala. There are now 19 southern white rhinos roaming the savannah and wetland, many of which were born in the wild in Uganda. The long-term goal for these magnificent beasts is to reintroduce them in Murchison Falls and Kidepo Valley National Parks.

While tracking rhinos on foot sounds a bit foolhardy, the fact that they're in the company of armed antipoacher rangers 24 hours a day, means they're well and truly used to human presence.

Other animals living inside the 6ft-tall electric fence include leopards, hippos, crocodiles, bushbucks and oribis. It's also home to 350 species of bird, and birdwatching tours cost US$25, with highlights including giant kingfishers, Ross's turacos and shoebills. The latter are best seen on early-morning shoebill canoe trips (US$30 per person) to an adjoining swamp, where you have a very good chance of spotting them.

There are occasionally volunteer opportunities, so ask via the website.

Sleeping

While most visit as a day trip en route to Murchison from Kampala, there are two good sleeping options in the park.

Ziwa Rhino Lodge GUESTHOUSE **$**
(0775521035; www.ziwarhino.com; camping per tent US$10, r with shared bathroom US$15, cottage US$40) Set around the camp headquarters, choose between the cottages or rows of basic rooms with small porches. There's also a restaurant serving simple food and cold drinks, plus camping for overlanders with cooking facilities and ablutions. There's plenty of wildlife about, including the occasional rhino.

Amuka Safari Lodge LODGE **$$$**
(0771600812; www.amukalodgeuganda.com; banda per person incl half board US$153;) Visitors rave about this lodge located deep in the sanctuary (a 20-minute drive from park headquarters). There are tasteful, secluded cottages and a common area with lovely decking, a swimming pool, a bar and an open-air restaurant.

Getting There & Away

All buses from Kampala heading to Gulu or Masindi pass nearby. Get off at little Nakitoma (USh15,000, three hours) and take a *boda-boda* 7km to the sanctuary gate for USh8000.

Masindi

0465 / POP 94,600

Fast-growing Masindi is a pleasant rural city with dusty streets and a faded colonial charm. It's the last place of any substance on the road to Murchison Falls National Park, and a good place to base yourself for the night and stock up on provisions.

Sights

For a **Walking Tour of Masindi**, a group of Voluntary Service Overseas (VSO) volunteers has produced a brochure pointing out various historical sites. While the stories are better than the sights, it can still make for a few fun hours. Pick up a map from New Court View Hotel.

Sleeping

Kolping Hotel HOTEL **$**
(0465-420458; www.ugandakolpinghotels.com; 24-30 Nthuha Rd; incl breakfast s/d USh70,000/100,000, s/d cottage USh125,000/150,000;) Spread over a large, verdant property with plenty of trees, the rooms and *bandas* at this church-affiliated hotel are easily the best-value accommodation in Masindi.

New Court View Hotel BANDA **$**
(0752446463; www.newcourtviewhotel.com; Hoima Rd; camping/s/d USh10,000/80,000/95,000;) Though slightly overpriced, this British-owned lodge has a relaxed, old-school traveller feel with cosy *bandas* with colourful bedcovers and tiny showers. There's an attractive patch of lawn and a great little restaurant with some of the best food in town, but a few too many cats.

Alinda Guesthouse GUESTHOUSE **$**
(0771226331; alindamasindi@yahoo.co.uk; 86 Masindi Port Rd; s/d with shared bathroom incl breakfast USh20,000/40,000) A reliable shoe-

stringer, friendly Alinda has big clean rooms right on the main road and a shared shower block with buckets.

Masindi Hotel HOTEL $$
(☎0465-420023; www.masindihotel.com; Hoima Rd; s/d incl full breakfast US$95/115; ⌚restaurant 5am-10pm; @📶) Built in 1923 by East Africa Railways and Harbours Company, Uganda's reportedly oldest hotel has hosted the likes of Ernest Hemingway, Katharine Hepburn and Humphrey Bogart. While its rooms are nothing flash, it exudes a certain romance perfect for a pre-safari jaunt. The 'Hemingway' bar remains the best place for a drink and the dining, with Indian fare, is outstanding.

Eating

Travellers' Corner AFRICAN, INTERNATIONAL $
(☎0776251510; Masindi Port Rd; mains USh15000-20,000; ⌚6.30am-11pm) This corner pub serves anything from tasty stews to Indian fare and fajitas. Choose between a tranquil courtyard sitting area and patio seating out front with people-watching aplenty.

Wat General Agencies SUPERMARKET $
(Commercial St; ⌚9am-7pm) If you forget to pack anything in Kampala, this small supermarket on Commercial St will come in handy.

Information

MONEY

Stanbic Bank (☎0465-20530; Kijunjubwa Rd; ⌚9am-4pm Mon-Fri) and **Barclays** (☎0465-4206739; Masindi Port Rd; ⌚8.30am-4pm Mon-Fri, 9am-1pm Sat) have ATMs.

POST

Post Office (☎0414-255511; Masindi Port Rd; ⌚8.30am-5pm Mon-Fri)

TOURIST INFORMATION

UWA Information Office (☎0465-420428; Masindi; ⌚7am-12.30pm & 2-6.30pm Mon-Fri, to noon Sat) Down a dirt road north of the post office; has national park information.

Getting There & Away

The Post Bus stops in Masindi on its way to and from Kampala (USh10,000, five hours) en route to Hoima. Otherwise **Link** (☎0465-421073; Masindi Port Rd) has regular buses to Kampala (USh12,000, 3½ hours) which leave from the **bus park** (off Masindi Port Rd) on Masindi Port Rd between 7.30am and 4.30pm.

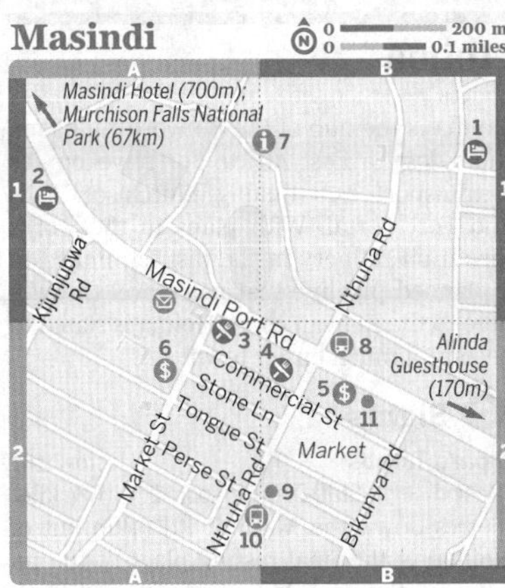

Masindi

Sleeping
1 Kolping Hotel B1
2 New Court View Hotel A1

Eating
3 Travellers' Corner A2
4 Wat General Agencies B2

Information
5 Barclays B2
6 Stanbic Bank A2
7 UWA Information Office B1

Transport
8 Buses to Kampala B2
9 Enyange B2
Link .... (see 8)
10 Taxi Park A2
11 Yebo Tours B2

For Gulu you'll need to jump on a bus or taxi to Kafu Junction (USh5000) on the main highway and catch a northbound bus there. Taxis line up at the **Taxi Park** (Perse St). There are also departures to Butiaba (USh13,000, three hours), Bulisa (USh20,000, 2½ hours) and Wanseko (USh20,000, 2½ hours).

As a gateway town to Murchison Falls National Park, Masindi is a good place to arrange transport hire into the park. Two recommended companies for hiring a 4WD are **Yebo Tours** (☎0772637493; yebotours2002@yahoo.com; Masindi Port Rd; 4WD tour per person US$145) and **Enyange** (☎0772657403; Perse St, Erika Kaheeru bldg; 4WD per day excl fuel US$90; ⌚7.30am-7pm Mon-Sat), opposite the taxi park.

Hoima

0465 / POP 100,600

Hoima is the hub of the Bunyoro Kingdom, the oldest in East Africa. For travellers it's a transport hub linking Murchison Falls and Fort Portal. With plans in the works for an oil refinery in the district, linked to a planned pipeline that will travel through here to the Kenyan coast, Hoima is slated to become a much busier town.

Sights

Mparo Tombs HISTORIC SITE

(Masindi Rd; USh10,000; sporadic) Two kilometres down the Masindi Rd (4km out of Hoima) is the final resting place of the renowned Bunyoro king Omukama ('King') Chwa II Kabalega and his son. Kabalega was a thorn in the side of the British for much of his reign until he was exiled to the Seychelles in 1899. Inside are his spears, bowls, throne and other personal effects on display above the actual resting place.

Karuziika Palace PALACE

(0782128229; arkbk.president@bunyoro-kitara.org; Main St) Due to tight security (the king has received death threats), this modern palace is almost never open. If you contact the palace a month in advance you may be able to visit the part-time home of the Bunyoro king and admire the throne room, which is draped with leopard and lion skins.

Sleeping

African Village Guest Farm BANDA $

(0772474972; camping US$8, bandas US$17-50) Located on a small dairy farm, there are nine *bandas* with balconies, and Betty and her daughters are great hosts. There's a restaurant on-site. It's a 10-minute drive outside Hoima; a *boda-boda* costs USh3000.

Kolping Hotel HOTEL $

(0465-420458; www.ugandakolpinghotels.com; 30 Butiaba Rd; s/d incl breakfast USh75,000/85,000;) Run by Catholic nuns, this sprawling hotel is a solid budget choice. It's dated but comfortable, with ample doubles set around different courtyards. Meals are available.

Miika Eco Resort COTTAGE $$$

(0392-002486; www.mereho.com; Butiaba Rd Km3; s/d incl breakfast US$180/240;) An ambitious project years in the making, this sprawling campus has gorgeous landscaped grounds. Business travellers and NGO employees take up some of the 64 rooms spread out in prim cottages with flat-screen TV and minifridge. There's a restaurant and a pool is in the works. Rooms are vastly overpriced, but internet deals make it significantly cheaper than listed prices.

Getting There & Away

The Post Bus goes to Kampala (USh13,000, four hours) via Masindi. Otherwise there are minibuses (USh14,000, three hours) and less-frequent buses to Kampala.

At the **bus park** (off Fort Portal Rd), there are also minibuses to Masindi (USh10,000, 1½ hours). For Fort Portal there's a coaster bus (USh25,000, five hours) that makes the run directly, but not every day. Otherwise it takes two minibuses to get to Fort Portal with a change in Kagadi (USh15,000, three hours).

Minibuses also run to Butiaba (USh10,000, two hours) in the morning plus Bulisa (USh15,000, three hours) and Wanseko (USh15,000, 3¼ hours) all day long.

Murchison Falls National Park

Uganda's largest national park, **Murchison Falls National Park** (0392-881348; www.ugandawildlife.org; adult/child US$40/20; 7am-7pm) is one of its very best; animals are in plentiful supply and the raging Murchison Falls, where the Victoria Nile crashes through the rock and descends dramatically towards Lake Albert, is an unforgettable sight. This is an exceptional place to see wildlife and a trip along the Nile should not be missed, not least in order to see the powerful Murchison Falls up close, a simply unforgettable experience.

Once one of Africa's most famous parks, Murchison had legendary numbers of animals, including as many as 15,000 elephants. Unfortunately during the war years poachers and troops wiped out practically all wildlife. However, while the park's rhino population was wiped out entirely, all other wildlife has recovered fast since peace returned: elephants, Rothschild giraffes, lions, antelope, waterbucks, buffaloes, hippos and crocodiles can all be seen with ease today.

For more information on the park, pick up a copy of *Murchison Falls Conservation Area Guidebook* (2004) by Shaun Mann at the park office.

History

During the 1960s, Murchison (3893 sq km; 5081 sq km with the adjoining Bugungu and Karuma Wildlife Reserves) was one of Africa's most famous parks; as many as 12 launches filled with eager tourists would buzz up the river to the falls each day. The park also had some of the largest concentrations of wildlife in Africa, including as many as 15,000 elephants. Though wildlife has recovered fast since peace came to Uganda, don't come to Murchison expecting a scene from the Serengeti. That said, even if there were no animals, the awesome power of Murchison Falls would make this park worth visiting.

In recent years, oil exploration within the park has caused concern in some quarters. With over 40% of Uganda's oil reserves under it, Murchison Falls has a struggle ahead of it, and a consortium of British, French and Chinese oil companies are now engaged in drilling, though at present the sites are in isolated sections of the park away from game drives.

Sights

★Top of the Falls WATERFALL

(trail US$15) Once described as the most spectacular thing to happen to the Nile along its 6700km length, the 50m wide Victoria Nile is squeezed here through a 6m gap in the rock and crashes through this narrow gorge with unbelievable power. The 45m waterfall was featured in the Katharine Hepburn and Humphrey Bogart film *The African Queen*. Murchison was even stronger back then, but in 1962 massive floods cut a second channel creating the smaller Uhuru Falls 200m to the north.

There's a beautiful walking trail from the top down to the river, and the upper stretch of this path offers views of Uhuru Falls, which a boat trip will not bring you close enough to to appreciate. Though it's straightforward, a ranger guide is required. If you take the launch trip, the captain will let you off at the trailhead and a ranger will meet you there. The boat can then pick you up later if there's an afternoon launch, or you can prearrange a car to take you out. This is also a good way for campers to get to the campsite at the top of the falls before returning to Paraa the next morning. The hike takes about 45 minutes from the bottom.

Activities

There are a number of activities to choose from here, the most popular of which are Nile boat trips, wildlife drives and nature walks. Chimpanzee tracking in Budongo Forest Reserve (p474) is a highlight.

Nile Boat Trips

The three-hour launch trip (US$30 per person) run by UWA from Paraa that heads up to the base of the falls is a highlight of the park for many visitors. There are abundant hippos, crocodiles and buffaloes; thousands of birds, including many fish eagles; and usually elephants along this 17km stretch of the Nile. In rainy season even shoebills might make an appearance. The trip climaxes with fantastic frontal views of Murchison Falls, around 500m from its base. Trips depart at 8am and 2pm. Cold drinks (including beers) are available, but no food. Bring sunscreen. A more cushy option is to take the same trip with Wild Frontiers (p471).

Another option, run by both Wild Frontiers and the UWA (US$150 per boat; departs at 7am), is a five-hour Nile Delta boat trip that heads downstream to the papyrus-filled delta where the Nile empties into Lake Albert. While it's less popular than the trip upstream to the falls, wildlife watching

> **MURCHISON FALLS NATIONAL PARK**
>
> **Why Go** Excellent wildlife watching from boat or car; Rothschild giraffe and lion; sheer power and fury of Murchison Falls; chimpanzee tracking in Budongo Forest Reserve.
>
> **When to Go** Year-round, but February to April is best as grass is lower.
>
> **Practicalities** Public transport can be used to get to the fringes of the park, but you'll need a vehicle to get within; numerous hostels offer budget tours, which are the best option for backpackers without wheels.
>
> **Budget** Lodges outside the northern sections of the park are accessible via buses from Kampala, from where you can organise safari drives into the park. Otherwise sign up for an organised tour run by Red Chilli or Backpackers, who both run well-priced three-day tours from Kampala.

Murchison Falls National Park

Murchison Falls National Park

Top Sights

1 Murchison Falls National Park B2
2 Top of the Falls B2

Sights

3 Budongo Forest Reserve B3

Activities, Courses & Tours

Kaniyo Pabidi Tourist Site .... (see 6)
Wild Frontiers .... (see 15)

Sleeping

4 Bakers Lodge A2
5 Boomu Women's Group B3
6 Budongo Eco Lodge B3
7 Bwana Tembo Safari Camp A1
8 Chobe Safari Lodge D2
Fort Murchison .... (see 7)
Heritage Safari Lodge .... (see 7)
Murchison River Lodge .... (see 4)
9 Murchison Safari Lodge A1
10 Murchison Tree House A2
11 Nile Safari Lodge A2
12 Pakuba Safari Lodge A2
13 Paraa Safari Lodge B2
Red Chilli Rest Camp .... (see 15)
Top of the Falls Campsite .... (see 2)
14 Yebo Tours Safari Camp A2

Information

15 Park Headquarters B2

is still very good, though perhaps not as reliable. You may see leopards lounging in trees and shoebill sightings are very common. Tour companies often book the UWA boat so you should be able to join for a fraction of the cost – ask at any park office.

Wildlife Drives

Pretty much all wildlife watching on land happens in the Buligi area, on the point between the Albert and Victoria Niles. Just about all the park's resident species might be seen in the savannah on the Albert, Queen and Victoria tracks, and the chances of spotting lions and leopard are quite good. There's very little wildlife south of the river, and driving in from Masindi or Pakwach you'll probably only see baboons and warthogs.

You'll want a minimum of four hours to get out there and back. Those with their own vehicle should definitely take a UWA ranger-guide (US$20) to boost their chances of sightings. Night drives (from 6pm to 10pm) enable travellers to see nocturnal animals and cost US$100 per vehicle. For self-drivers staying across the river, take note of the Paraa ferry schedule to avoid missing the last boat back in the evening at 7pm (get there 10 minutes earlier). On the off-chance you haven't organised a vehicle, budget travellers sometimes have luck hanging out at the ferry dock and finding space in someone's vehicle.

Nature Walks

The 1.5km guided nature walk along the north bank of the Nile run by Paraa Safari Lodge (p473) – US$30 per person – is popular with birdwatchers, but you're not likely to see many other animals.

Sport Fishing

Murchison is one of the world's best places to fish for the gargantuan Nile perch. The normal catch ranges from 20kg to 60kg, but the record haul is 108kg. You can fish from the shore or get a boat, but be mindful of crocodiles and hippos. Catfish and tiger fish are other popular catches. Being a national park, fishing here is strictly catch and release. Permits cost US$50 for one day or US$150 for four days. The best months are December to March and June to October. For more information, check out www.fishingmurchison.com.

Tours

Wild Frontiers BOAT, FISHING

(0773897275; www.wildfrontiers.co.ug) Offers the most comfortable boat trips up the Nile to the falls (US$32 per person; 2.30pm daily, 8.30am Monday, Wednesday, Friday). You can also book game drives (US$65 per person), cheese-and-wine sunset cruises (US$75 per person) and longer boat trips downstream to the papyrus-filled delta (US$55 per person) where the Nile empties into Lake Albert.

Full-day fishing trips start at US$115 per person (excluding permits).

Sleeping

Most of Murchison's lodges are located within the vicinity of the Paraa park headquarters, a convenient choice for wildlife drives and the falls. There are also more remote options in the far west, north and south sectors, providing a more peaceful experience.

Red Chilli Rest Camp HOSTEL $

(0772509150; www.redchillihideaway.com; Paraa; camping US$8, d safari tents US$35, tw/f banda US$55/90, d banda with shared bathroom US$40;) With good tours and buoyant staff, this is the most popular budget option in Murchison. Basic *bandas* are good value though not exactly grime-free, while safari tents get the job done. The restaurant-bar is set under a thatched roof with good river views and a roaring evening fire. Meals, all extra, are good value. Book well in advance.

Hippos regularly graze here at night, so bring a torch and give them a very wide berth.

Boomu Women's Group GUESTHOUSE $

(0772448950; www.boomuwomensgroup.org; Kichumbanyobo gate; camping per person USh12,000, bandas per person incl breakfast with shared bathroom USh50,000) Just outside the Kichumbanyobo gate, the simple *bandas* here are run by local women and offer an insight in to how rural Ugandans live. The money helps raise funds for a local preschool. There's a fascinating cooking tour (USh20,000 per person) among other activities. A *boda-boda* from Masindi costs USh12,000.

Yebo Tours Safari Camp BANDA $

(0772637493; Bugungu gate; camping US$10, bandas incl full board per person US$40) Yebo is a good budget option and one of the few camps in the park that actively celebrates its authentic local qualities. The basic mud-wall *bandas* have thatched roofs and little else, but are a real local experience, as is the tasty Ugandan cooking served in the canteen. Under construction is a new thatched lounge. It's 8km from Paraa.

It also offers safari tours out of Masindi.

Top of the Falls Campsite CAMPGROUND $

(camping USh15,000) On the river near the falls, this scenic and secluded camp has pit toilets and nothing else save the sounds of distant raging water and thousands of birds.

Murchison Safari Lodge HOSTEL $

(0776799899; Wankwar gate; incl full breakfast camping/dm USh20,000/40,000, banda with shared bathroom USh80,000) This bush camp in the northern sector, 7km from Wankwar gate (and 10km from Purongo town), has basic *bandas* and dorms in a peaceful spot, but lacks atmosphere. Still, the nearby watering hole attracts giraffes and the host is warm and welcoming. Most people who stay here are on a safari with Backpackers Hostel (p392) in Kampala.

★**Fort Murchison** LODGE $$

(☎0312-294894; www.naturelodges.biz/fort-murchison; Pakwach; incl half board s/d safari tent US$50/90, s/d US$125/200) Dutch-owned Nature Lodges' most ambitious venture takes the form of an ambient Islamic fort in a commanding location overlooking the Albert Nile. It has fine dining, good service and rooms oozing with safari style (go upstairs for the best views). The gorgeous rooftop deck has loungers shared with darting multicoloured agama lizards. There's a swimming pool and wi-fi in the works.

If you're looking for a more classic safari-style accommodation, there's tented camping set up on an expansive campsite. The rooftop bar is another perk.

★**Murchison River Lodge** LODGE $$

(☎0714000085; www.murchisonriverlodge.com; Bugungu gate; incl full board camping US$45, s/d safari tents US$130/220, with shared bathroom US$85/140, cottage US$175/280; 📶🏊) While firmly in the luxury category, Murchison River opens its doors to all budgets, whether you're here to pitch a tent, do some lazy camping or live it up in its lavish two-storey thatched cottages. Grounds are quite spread out. The safari-style open-air restaurant has good food and superb views of the Victoria Nile with elephants in the distance.

The top-notch shower block for campers is modern, clean and roomy for changing. Except for basic camping, prices include full board. However, campers can use the pool, making it a popular choice.

Murchison Tree House CABIN $$

(☎0773559335; www.murchisontreehouse.com; Wanseko Rd, Bugungu gate; camping US$8, banda/safari-tent/cottage/tree house per person incl full board US$50/50/120/170) This new locally owned lodge on 18 hectacres occupies some cool real estate at the end of the road on a breezy riverside spot. The tree house is actually a stilted waterfront cabin near the hippos. Tucked into the forest are pleasant cottages and safari tents with chemical toilets. Beware the marauding baboons – you'll be given an escort to avoid them.

It's 6.6km from Mubako gate.

Bwana Tembo Safari Camp LODGE $$

(☎0791217028; www.bwanatembosafaricamp.com; Bwana Tembo Rd, Pakwach; safari tent s/d incl full-board US$130/205, cottage US$130/230; 📶) Set on a grassy plot of land, this relaxed, Italian-owned camp has a mix of tented camping and cottages. Its homemade pastas and Italian meat dishes get rave reviews. It offers safari vehicles with driver for US$100 for a half day and US$180 for full-day trips.

Heritage Safari Lodge LODGE $$

(☎0792212618; www.heritagesafarilodge.com; Tangi gate, Pakwach; camping US$10, s/d incl breakfast lazy camping US$30/50, cottage US$60/80; 📶) This Ugandan-owned lodge has wonderful Acholi *bandas* built using traditional methods and decked out with comfortable interiors. All look over the Albert Nile, and elephants are regular visitors.

Bakers Lodge LODGE $$$

(☎0414-321479; www.wildfrontiers.com; Bugungu gate; per person incl full board US$280; 🏊) The luxury pick in Murchison, this classic safari pick occupies a prime location on the Victoria Nile with elegant riverfront digs. The style is nostalgic, with wooden trunks with leather straps, tea and cookies. Extras such as massages, a swimming pool and a minibar offer a welcome diversion. With its own dock and boats, it's ideal for fishing enthusiasts and boating.

There's also an option for private cruises, camping or wildlife drives on the northern bank and bush breakfasts.

Chobe Safari Lodge LODGE $$$

(☎0312-259390; www.chobelodgeuganda.com; Chobe gate; s/d/ste incl full board from US$217/397/457; @📶🏊) Isolated on the far-eastern reaches of the park, renovations have returned Chobe – one of Murchison's original 1950s lodges – to its former splendour. Its gorgeous river location is teeming with honking hippos, enjoyed from its classy outdoor restaurant. The upstairs standard rooms are the best pick with great views, lovely decor and balconies. Its three-tiered swimming pool is another highlight.

The place has the feel of a celebrity hideaway, and even has its own airstrip – though it's more popular with grazing buffaloes.

Nile Safari Lodge LODGE $$$

(☎0414-258273; www.geolodgesafrica.com; Bugungu gate; camping US$10, s/d incl full board US$171/272; 🏊) For a room with a view, Nile Safari is the pick of the lot, with each of its stilted cottages featuring superb Victoria Nile outlooks from private balconies. However, at these prices it's all a bit dated, though the outdoor showers are an experience. The place runs on solar and generator electricity.

For campers, the grassy Shoebill site (US$30 for tent hire) is a good spot by the river, though you'll need to pay extra to use the pool.

Pakuba Safari Lodge LODGE $$$
(☎0786657070, 0414-253597; www.pakubasafarilodge.com; Tangi gate; s/d US$163/189;) Overlooking the Albert Nile, this lodge deep inside the park was built on a site just up from the ruins of an old safari lodge formerly used by Idi Amin, now a picturesque ruin favoured as a hang-out by giraffes. Rooms are huge, stylish and rather minimalist, even if they're rather tightly packed together in terraced rows.

A pool was being added during our last visit.

Paraa Safari Lodge LODGE $$$
(☎0772788880; www.paraalodge.com; Paraa; s/d/ste incl full board US$220/349/436;) On the northern bank of the Nile, this classic African park lodge has a great location and stellar views, even if it has definitely aged in many respects since it opened in 1954. The rooms are well furnished and have marble bathrooms and terraces, though only the deluxe rooms have air-con. Go for an upstairs room for the best views.

Information

Park Headquarters (www.ugandawildlife.org; Paraa; 6.30am-6.30pm) Get info, buy permits, book tours and pay for ferry crossings across the Nile here.

Getting There & Away

AIR

There are regular flights from Entebbe (US$263, one hour) to Murchison's Pakuba airstrip via Aerolink (p491). Fly Uganda (p491) goes to Pakuba, Bugungu and Chobe airstrips for a similar rate from Kajjansi airfield between Entebbe and Kampala.

BUDGET TOURS

The three-day budget trips offered by Red Chilli Hideaway (p487) in Kampala leave at least thrice-weekly in high season (June to August and December to February), and include transport, park entrance fees, a launch trip, a wildlife drive and accommodation for US$320 per person, making it a great deal. Nearly all hostels in Kampala offer similar deals, but Red Chilli consistently gets the best feedback and keeps their prices impressively low.

BUGUNGU & KICHUMBANYOBO GATES

The **park headquarters** at Paraa is on the southern bank of the Victoria Nile. From Masindi you can take the direct route through the Kichumbanyobo gate or the longer, but more scenic, route west to Lake Albert and then enter the park via the western Bugungu gate. For those with their own vehicle, consider entering via one route and leaving by the other. Both routes go through Budongo Forest Reserve (p474), a recommended stopover.

There's no direct public transport into the park. The cheapest way into Murchison Falls National Park is to get to Bulisa or Wanseko, an interesting fishing village where the Nile empties into Lake Albert. Minibuses run to these neighbouring towns daily from Hoima and Masindi for USh15,000. You can go as far as Bulisa, from where you can get a *boda-boda* to take you to Paraa for around USh40,000. *Boda-boda* drivers are required to pay park admission but often don't, so negotiate a fee without the admission costs and you might get lucky.

NORTHERN GATES

With security now restored to northern Uganda, the northern gates – Chobe (near Karuma Falls on the Gulu Rd), Tangi (reached from Pakwach) and Wankwar (from Purongo) – are now viable options again.

The northern section of the park is surprisingly accessible from Kampala by public transport, with various bus companies making the trip to Pakwach (USh30,000, six hours) via Purongo (for Wankwar gate, USh25,000) and Karuma (for Chobe gate). Buses depart from Kampala's Arua Park at 1pm.

Getting Around

BOAT

A vehicle ferry crosses the river at Paraa. The crossings take five minutes and are scheduled approximately every hour between 7am and 7pm. The ferry holds just eight vehicles, but will make as many crossings as necessary to get everyone over. The one-day fare is USh5000 for passengers and USh25,000 and up for cars (depending on size). Unscheduled crossings cost USh120,000. Ferry fees are payable at a small booth near the landing.

CAR

Tracks within the park are generally well maintained and, although a 4WD is highly recommended, cars should have little trouble getting around. However, some tracks, especially in the Buligi area (where most wildlife drives are done), can be treacherous during wet season.

Fuel is available on the northern side of the Victoria Nile River at Paraa, but it costs about 10% more than in Masindi.

Budongo Forest Reserve

You will find Uganda's largest population of chimpanzees in the **Budongo Forest Reserve** (www.budongo.org; daylight) FREE, a large (825-sq-km) tract of virgin tropical forest on the southern fringes of Murchison Falls National Park. There are 800 chimps in the reserve and adjacent Kaniyo Pabidi. You can also see 366 bird species, but the huge mahogany trees are also worth a look. It's a great add-on to your Murchison Falls National Park visit. As it's actually part of the park, you'll need to pay those entry fees here if engaging in activities.

Activities

Activities in the reserve are organised through Budongo Eco Lodge and while they can be booked at the lodge itself, it's safer to prebook permits through Great Lakes Safaris (p442), the current concession holders. Low season runs from March until mid-June.

Chimpanzee Tracking

Chimpanzee-tracking trips take place daily and you have a good chance of finding the chimps, though it's not guaranteed. The walking is easy as the terrain is level, and walks last from two to four hours.

Treks cost US$75 during low season (March to mid-June), and US$85 during high season (mid-June to February), excluding national-park entry fees. Once you find the chimps, you get to spend an hour with them; two lucky visitors (October through June only) are allowed to spend a whole day for US$150 per person. Trekkers must be over 15 years old.

Kaniyo Pabidi Tourist Site WILDLIFE WATCHING

(MFCA) This site is regarded as one of the more reliable places to track chimpanzees in Uganda with an estimated 70% chance of finding them. You have to pay the park entry fee on top of the activity fee (US$85). It's on the main park road, 29km north of Masindi and inside the southern boundary of Murchison Falls National Park.

Kaniyo Pabidi isn't served by public transport, but it's possible to arrange a charter from Masindi for about USh60,000 or take a *boda-boda* or about USh15,000 (more if the guards make the driver pay admission fees).

Forest Walks

These worthwhile forest walks pass through East Africa's last remaining mahogany forest. The largest specimens are 60m tall and 300 years old. Black-and-white colobus monkeys and duiker are commonly seen. Guided walks cost US$15 for 2½ hours and US$20 for four hours.

Birdwatching

Those here for birdwatching usually seek Puvel's illadopsis, which isn't known anywhere else in East Africa. Other highly sought species are the rufous-sided broadbill and white-naped pigeon. Guided walks cost US$20 for a half day and US$35 for a full day.

Busingiro Tourist Site BIRDWATCHING

(3hr forest walk US$50) Busingiro Tourist Site, also within Budongo and 40km west of Masindi on the Bulisa Rd, is for the birdwatchers. It's a great place to add yellow-footed flycatcher and African pitta to your spotting list. There used to be chimp tracking here too, but when the chimps lost their fear of humans they started raiding local farms, forcing an end to the program. The chimps are still here though, so you may get lucky and meet them.

Visitors can only go unguided along the main road. Guided walks are charged per person. Busingiro is on the route used by minibuses heading for Bulisa from Masindi.

Royal Mile BIRDWATCHING

(half-day birding US$30) Royal Mile has some of the country's best birdwatching. There are some rare species, but more importantly, sightings are easy. The bird list exceeds 350 species, including several types of flycatcher, sunbird, kingfisher, hornbill and eagle. At dusk it's possible to view bat hawks. Since it's outside the national park, the only fees are for guided walks (guides required).

You'll need your own vehicle to get to the Royal Mile. The first turn-off is 25km from Masindi, marked by the Nyabyeya Forestry College signpost, and there's another, also with a college sign, closer to Busingiro.

Sleeping

There's one ecolodge with economical dorms in the reserve; otherwise accommodation options are plentiful at nearby Murchison Falls National Park or in Masindi.

Budongo Eco Lodge LODGE $$

(0414-696191; www.ugandalodges.com/budongo; Kaniyo Pabidi; dm/s/d/tr incl breakfast US$26/81/134/156;) Great value, this wooded camp has six handsome cabins and nice dorms with screen windows. There's solar power, hot water, rainwater catchment and eco-toilets. If you're interested in seeing chimps, this is one of Uganda's best-kept secrets, with excellent, personalised guiding that's respectful of the animals. The restaurant serves good food too.

Getting There & Away

The reserve is 30km north of Masindi. Most travellers come via private transport. From Masindi, there are minibuses (USh15,000) that pass the reserve on their way to Bulisa or Wanseko.

UNDERSTAND UGANDA

History

Independence

Unlike Kenya and, to a lesser extent, Tanzania, Uganda never experienced a large influx of European colonisers and the associated expropriation of land. Instead, farmers were encouraged to grow cash crops for export through their own cooperative groups. Consequently, Ugandan nationalist organisations sprouted much later than those in neighbouring countries, and, when they did, it happened along tribal lines. So exclusive were some of these that when Ugandan independence was discussed, the Baganda people considered secession.

By the mid-1950s, however, Lango school teacher Dr Milton Obote managed to put together a loose coalition headed by the Uganda People's Congress (UPC), which led Uganda to independence in 1962 with the promise that the Buganda kingdom would have autonomy. The *kabaka* (king), Edward Mutesa II, became the president of the new nation, and Milton Obote became Uganda's first prime minister.

It wasn't a particularly favourable time for Uganda to come to grips with independence. Civil wars were raging in neighbouring Sudan, the DRC and Rwanda, and refugees streamed into Uganda, adding to its problems. Also, it soon became obvious that Obote had no intention of sharing power with the *kabaka*. A confrontation loomed.

Obote moved in 1966, arresting several cabinet ministers and ordering his army chief of staff, Idi Amin, to storm the *kabaka's* palace in Kampala. The raid resulted in the flight of the *kabaka* and his exile in London, where he died in 1969. Following this coup, Obote proclaimed himself president, and the Buganda monarchy was abolished, along with those of the Bunyoro, Ankole, Toro and Busoga kingdoms. Meanwhile, Idi Amin's star was on the rise.

OPERATION ENTEBBE 1976 HOSTAGE RESCUE

The site of one of the most well-known hostage-rescue missions, Uganda's international airport in Entebbe received a hijacked Air France flight on 27 June 1976. Carrying 248 passengers, a Tel Aviv flight en route to Paris was hijacked by Palestinian and German terrorists and diverted to Libya, before eventually being given permission to land in Entebbe by Idi Amin, a pro-Palestine supporter. Demanding the release of 53 Palestine Liberation Organization (PLO) prisoners in return for the release of the hostages, terrorists held passengers in the main hall of the airport building (now the old terminal building, and a popular site for Israeli tourists) for over a week. Eventually all non-Jewish passengers were released, leaving around 105 hostages still detained.

In what's considered one of the most daring and dramatic hostage operations to ever take place, a covert operation comprised of an Israeli taskforce of around 100 commandos touched down in Entebbe at 11pm in a C-130 Hercules cargo plane. Several Mercedes rolled off the plane to give the appearance that it was part of Idi Amin's entourage, from which Israeli commandos emerged to storm the terminal. Within 30 minutes, seven terrorists and around 40 Ugandan soldiers were killed. Three Israeli hostages also died in the crossfire. The freed hostages were loaded on to the plane while Ugandan soldiers fired away, resulting in the death of one Israeli soldier: the brother of Israeli prime minister Benjamin Netanyahu. In the meantime, more than half of Uganda's airforce planes were destroyed by the Israelis to prevent retaliatory air strikes upon Israel. In response, Amin ordered the killing of 75-year-old Dora Bloch, a British-Jewish hostage who had remained in Kampala recovering in the hospital following the ordeal.

The Amin Years

Under Milton Obote's watch, events began to spiral out of control. Obote ordered his attorney general, Godfrey Binaisa, to rewrite the constitution consolidating virtually all powers in the presidency and then moved to nationalise foreign assets.

In 1969 a scandal broke out over US$5 million in funds and weapons allocated to the Ministry of Defence that couldn't be accounted for. An explanation was demanded of Idi Amin, who by then was commander of the Ugandan army, and when it wasn't forthcoming, Amin's deputy, Colonel Okoya, and some junior officers demanded his resignation. Shortly afterwards Okoya and his wife were shot dead in their Gulu home, and rumours began to circulate about Amin's imminent arrest. It never came. Instead, when Obote left for Singapore in January 1971 to attend the Commonwealth Heads of Government Meeting (CHOGM), Amin staged a coup. Uganda's former colonial masters, the British, who had probably suffered most under Obote's nationalisation program, were among the first to recognise the new regime. Obote went into exile in Tanzania.

So began Uganda's first reign of terror. All political activities were quickly suspended and the army was empowered to shoot on sight anyone suspected of opposition to the regime. Over the next eight years an estimated 300,000 Ugandans lost their lives, often in such brutal ways as being bludgeoned to death with sledgehammers and iron bars. Among those who suffered most were the Acholi and Lango people, who were decimated in waves of massacres; whole villages were wiped out. Next Amin turned on the professional classes. University professors, doctors, cabinet ministers, lawyers, businesspeople and even military officers who might have posed a threat to Amin were dragged from their offices and shot or simply never seen again.

Also targeted was the 70,000-strong Asian community. In 1972 they were given 90 days to leave the country. Amin and his cronies grabbed the billion-dollar booty the evictees were forced to leave behind squandering it on 'new toys for the boys' and personal excess. Amin then turned on the British, nationalising US$500 million worth of investments in tea plantations and other industries without compensation.

Meanwhile the economy collapsed; industrial activity ground to a halt; hospitals and rural health clinics closed; roads cracked and became riddled with potholes; cities became garbage dumps; and utilities fell apart. The prolific wildlife was machine-gunned by soldiers for meat, ivory and skins, and the tourism industry evaporated. The stream of refugees across the border became a flood.

Faced with chaos and an inflation rate that hit 1000%, Amin was forced to delegate more and more powers to the provincial

AMIN 'THE BUTCHER OF UGANDA'

Regarded as one of Africa's most notorious and ruthless dictators, the name Idi Amin continues to be synonymous with Uganda despite the passage of nearly four decades since he was ousted as president. Following his defeat in the Uganda–Tanzania war in 1979, Amin fled the country never to return, heading to Libya and Iraq before taking exile in Saudi Arabia, where he died from kidney failure in 2003, aged 78. He never faced justice for the atrocities committed, with an estimated 300,000 losing their lives under his rule. President in 1971–79, Amin will be remembered not only for executions, human-rights violations and ethnic persecution, but also for corruption and the transformation of the once prosperous Ugandan economy into financial ruin.

Amin was a highly charismatic leader who had the ability to charm most who he met. Physically imposing at 1.91m, with a broad build, Amin was a champion boxer who held Uganda's light heavyweight boxing championship in 1951–60. To many Africans, Amin was (and, for many, remains) highly respected for his fierce nationalism and the courage to stand up to colonial powers.

On the flip side, he was also known for his wild mood swings and paranoia. Henry Kyemba, one of Amin's most trusted ministers at the time, states in his autobiography *State of Blood* that Amin dabbled with cannibalism and blood rituals. Persistent rumours from exiled Ugandans also suggest that he kept the heads of his most prized enemies in a freezer, which he would take out on occasion to lecture them on their evil ways.

governors, who became virtual warlords in their areas. Towards the end of the Amin era, the treasury was so bereft of funds it was unable to pay the soldiers. One of the few supporters of Amin at the end of the 1970s was Colonel Gadaffi, who bailed out the Ugandan economy in the name of Islamic brotherhood (Amin had conveniently become a Muslim by this stage) and began an intensive drive to equip the Ugandan forces with sophisticated weapons.

The rot had spread too far, however, and was beyond the point where a few million dollars in Libyan largesse could help. Faced with a restless army beset with intertribal fighting, Amin looked for a diversion. He chose a war with Tanzania, ostensibly to teach that country a lesson for supporting anti-Amin dissidents. It was his last major act of recklessness, and in it lay his downfall.

War with Tanzania

On 30 October 1978 the Ugandan army rolled across northwestern Tanzania virtually unopposed and annexed more than 1200 sq km of territory. Meanwhile the air force bombed the Lake Victoria ports of Bukoba and Musoma.

Tanzanian President Julius Nyerere ordered a full-scale counterattack, but it took months to mobilise his ill-equipped and poorly trained forces. By early 1979 he had managed to scrape together a 50,000-strong people's militia, composed mainly of illiterate youngsters from the bush. This militia joined with the many exiled Ugandan liberation groups – united only in their determination to rid Uganda of Amin. The two armies met. East Africa's supposedly best-equipped and best-trained army threw down its weapons and fled, and the Tanzanians pushed on into the heart of Uganda. Kampala fell without a fight, and by April 1979 organised resistance had effectively ceased.

Amin fled the country and eventually ended up in Saudi Arabia where he died in 2003, never having faced justice.

Post-Amin Chaos

The Tanzanian action was criticised, somewhat half-heartedly, by the Organisation for African Unity (OAU; now called the African Union), but most African countries breathed a sigh of relief to see Amin finally brought to heel. All the same, Tanzania was forced to foot the entire bill for the war, estimated at US$500 million, a crushing blow for an already desperately poor country.

The rejoicing in Uganda was short-lived. The Tanzanian soldiers, who remained in the country, supposedly to assist with reconstruction and to maintain law and order, turned on the Ugandans when their pay did not arrive. They took what they wanted from shops at gunpoint, hijacked trucks arriving from Kenya with international relief aid and slaughtered yet more wildlife.

Once again, the country slid into chaos and gangs of armed bandits roamed the cities, killing and looting. Food supplies ran out and hospitals could no longer function. Nevertheless, thousands of exiled Ugandans began to answer the call to return home and help with reconstruction.

Yusuf Lule, a modest and unambitious man, was installed as president with Tanzanian President Julius Nyerere's blessing. But when he began speaking out against Nyerere, he was replaced by Godfrey Binaisa, sparking riots supporting Lule in Kampala. Meanwhile Obote bided his time in Dar es Salaam.

Binaisa quickly came under pressure to set a date for a general election and a return to civilian rule. Obote eventually returned from exile to an enthusiastic welcome in many parts of the country and swept to power in what is widely regarded as a rigged vote.

It was 1981 and the honeymoon with Obote proved short. Like Amin, Obote favoured certain tribes. Large numbers of civil servants and army and police commanders belonging to the tribes of the south were replaced with Obote supporters belonging to the tribes of the north. The State Research Bureau, a euphemism for the secret police, was re-established and the prisons began to fill up again; Obote was on course to complete the destruction that Amin had begun. More and more reports of atrocities and killings leaked out of the country. Mass graves unrelated to the Amin era were unearthed. The press was muzzled and Western journalists were expelled. It appeared that Obote was once again attempting to achieve absolute power. Intertribal tension was on the rise, and in mid-1985 Obote was overthrown in a coup staged by the army under the command of Tito Okello.

THE MISADVENTURES OF HEMINGWAY IN UGANDA

Despite Ernest Hemingway's well-known love of Africa, having based several novels and short stories here, he certainly could be forgiven for not looking back fondly upon his time spent in Uganda. Tallying the misfortune of two plane crashes within a week, his time here was a total disaster.

As a Christmas present to his fourth wife, Mary Welsh, in 1954, Hemingway arranged a scenic flight from Nairobi to the Congo, which en route took in spectacular aerial views of the Nile around Lake Albert. While circling Murchison Falls at a low altitude, the small plane clipped a telegraph wire, causing the plane to crash into dense forest. With relatively minor yet painful injuries including broken ribs and a dislocated shoulder, they emerged from the wreck to face a night stranded near the falls.

Anyone who's done the Murchison Falls launch trip can attest to its abundance of wildlife, and a night spent out in the open with crocodiles, hippos, elephants and leopards is far from ideal. Yet somehow they managed to survive the night, spent shooing off animals, and were fortuitously picked up by a passing boat en route to Butiaba the next day.

Undeterred by the shock of surviving a plane crash and in need of medical attention, Hemingway and Welsh decided to charter another flight to take them to Entebbe. Yet upon take off, the plane crashed in a ball of flames. The injuries they sustained were indeed far more serious this time, particularly for Hemingway who sustained a fractured skull while forcing his way out, as well as a ruptured liver, a collapsed intestine, several broken vertebrae and a burnt scalp (among other injuries). It was widely reported in the international media that he'd died in the crash. During time spent recovering in Nairobi, Hemingway was able to read over his obituaries.

The severity of his injuries prevented Hemingway from accepting his Nobel Prize for Literature 10 months later, and many believed he never physically or mentally recovered from the accidents. Hemingway wrote about the incident for *Look* magazine in 1954 in an article with the innocuous sounding title: 'The Christmas Gift'.

The NRA Takeover

Okello was not the only opponent of Obote. Shortly after Obote became president for the second time, a guerrilla army opposed to his tribally biased government was formed in western Uganda under the leadership of Yoweri Museveni.

A group of 27 soon swelled to a guerrilla force of about 20,000, many of them orphaned teenagers. In the early days few gave the guerrillas, known as the National Resistance Army (NRA), much of a chance, but the NRA had a very different ethos from the armies of Amin and Obote. New recruits were indoctrinated in the bush by political commissars and taught they had to be servants of the people, not oppressors. Discipline was tough. Anyone who got badly out of line was executed. Museveni was determined that the army would never again disgrace Uganda. A central thrust of the NRA was to win the hearts and minds of the people, who learned to identify with the persecuted Baganda in the infamous Luwero Triangle, where people suffered more than most under Obote's iron fist.

By the time Obote was ousted and Okello had taken over, the NRA controlled a large slice of western Uganda and was a power to be reckoned with. Museveni wanted a clean sweep of the administration, the army and the police. He wanted corruption stamped out and those who had been involved in atrocities during the Amin and Obote regimes brought to trial.

The fighting continued in earnest, and by January 1986 it was obvious that Okello's days were numbered. The surrender of 1600 government soldiers holed up in their barracks in the southern town of Mbarara brought the NRA to the outskirts of Kampala itself. With the morale of government troops low, the NRA launched an all-out offensive to take the capital. Okello's troops fled, almost without a fight, though not before looting whatever remained and carting it away in commandeered buses. It was a typical parting gesture, as was the gratuitous shooting-up of many Kampala high-rise offices.

During the following weeks, Okello's rabble were pursued and pushed north over the border into Sudan. The long nightmare was finally over.

Rebuilding

Despite Museveni's Marxist leanings, he proved to be a pragmatist after taking control. He appointed several arch-conservatives to his cabinet and made an effort to reassure the country's large Catholic community.

In the late 1980s, peace agreements were negotiated with most of the guerrilla factions who had fought for Okello or Obote and were still active in the north and northeast. Under an amnesty offered to the rebels, as many as 40,000 had surrendered by 1988, and many were given jobs in the NRA. In the northwest of the country, almost 300,000 Ugandans returned home from Sudan.

With peace came optimism: services were restored, factories and farmland that had lain idle for years were again put to use, the main roads were resurfaced, and the national parks' infrastructure was restored and revitalised in an attempt to undo the devastation wrought by years of war.

The 1990s

The stability and rebuilding that came with President Museveni's coming to power in 1986 was followed in the 1990s with economic prosperity and unprecedented growth. For much of the decade Uganda was the fastest-growing economy in Africa, becoming a favourite among investors. One of the keys to its success was the bold decision to invite back the Asians who, as in Kenya, had held a virtual monopoly on business and commerce. Not surprisingly, they were very hesitant about returning, but assurances were given and kept, and property was returned.

The darkness didn't end for northern Uganda, however, due to the Lord's Resistance Army (LRA), the last remaining rebel group founded during the time of the NRA rebellion. Its leader, Joseph Kony, grew increasingly delusional and paranoid and shifted his focus from attacking soldiers to attacking civilians in an attempt to found a government based on the biblical Ten Commandments.

His vicious tactics included torture, mutilation (slicing off lips, noses and ears), rape and abducting children to use as soldiers and sex slaves. Eventually over one million northerners fled their homes to Internally Displaced Persons (IDP) camps and tens of thousands of children became 'night commuters', walking from their villages each evening to sleep in schools and churches or on the streets of large and (sometimes) safer towns. In their half-hearted fight against the LRA, government forces reportedly committed their own atrocities too.

In 1993 a new draft constitution was adopted by the National Resistance Council (NRC). One surprising recommendation in the draft was that the country should adopt a system of 'no-party' politics. Given the potential for intertribal rivalry within a pluralist system, it was a sensible policy. Under the draft constitution, a Constituent Assembly was formed, and in 1994 elections for the assembly showed overwhelming support for the government. Also in 1993 the monarchies were restored, but with no actual political power.

Democratic 'no-party' elections were called for May 1996. The main candidates were President Museveni and Paul Ssemogerere, who had resigned as foreign minister in order to campaign. Museveni won a resounding victory, capturing almost 75% of the vote. The only area where Ssemogerere had any real support was in the anti-National Resistance Movement (NRM) north.

A New Millenium

Eventually Museveni shifted his position on political parties, and in July 2005 a referendum was held that overwhelmingly endorsed the change. This political shift was of much less concern to the average Ugandan than the other that occurred the same month; parliament approving a constitutional amendment scrapping presidential term limits. Museveni himself had put the two-term limit in place, but had regrets as the end of his tenure drew closer. It was alleged that MPs were bullied and bribed into voting for the change. International criticism was strong and even many Ugandans who backed Museveni were angry at his move. Nevertheless, Museveni convincingly won his fourth election in 2011 with 68.4% of the vote.

By the 2000s the LRA's campaign of terror had ebbed, though certainly not ceased. In 2002 the LRA lost its Sudanese support and the Ugandan military launched Operation Iron Fist, attacking the LRA's bases across the northern border. The mission failed and an angered Kony not only increased attacks in Uganda but also expanded his targets to areas such as Soroti that had not previously been affected. In the years that followed there were various ceasefires and nominal peace talks, but little progress was made until 2005, when the LRA fled to Garamba National Park in the DRC. After on-again, off-again talks a peace deal was reached in February 2008, though Kony then broke his promise to sign it and the LRA began abducting more child soldiers and even attacked a Sudanese army base.

While Kony and the LRA have dwindled to a tiny force since then and not been a threat to Ugandans for almost a decade now, efforts continue to find and bring Kony to justice. In 2013 US President Obama announced a US$5 million reward for Kony's capture. In March 2014 the USA deployed special operation troops and military aircraft to tackle the LRA in Central Africa Republic (where Kony is believed to be hiding), the DRC and Sudan, to go with the 5000 African Union troops already on the ground.

In May 2017 the six-year hunt for Kony, which included 100 US special forces working alongside the Ugandan military in Central African Republic, ended. The LRA, down to an estimated 120 soldiers, had become a downgraded threat dispersed into difficult jungle terrain. Kony, with a US$5 million bounty on his head, continues to remain missing though some believe that he has taken refuge in a disputed border area between Sudan and South Sudan.

Presidential elections were held on 18 February 2016 and Yoweri Museveni won once again, this time with 61% of the vote, extending his 30-year rule.

Uganda Today

When newcomers ask Africaphiles where to travel on the continent, Uganda is a ready response. With its relative stability, accessibility and the goodwill ease of its residents, the country is an increasingly attractive destination for visitors. That's not to say that locals don't have their own concerns. Keeping it safe and running smoothly for all is an everyday endeavour.

Keep Calm & Carry On

Surprising almost nobody, President Museveni won a thumping victory in the 2016 presidential elections, earning an impressive 61% of the vote. As he began his fifth term as president, Museveni looked more and more like one of the African big men he himself used to rage against, and though his popularity wanes, no credible opposition has arisen that can make an impact at the polls.

With violence and instability rocking both neighbouring South Sudan and DRC, Uganda's relative normalcy keeps domestic criticism at bay. Over 1.2 million refugees have poured over the border from South Sudan, fleeing war and famine. While Uganda is doing its best to absorb the newcomers, there is no resolution to the crisis in sight.

Though there's been no further incident since the horrific bombings in Kampala in 2010 that left 74 dead, threats of terrorism remain a concern. The ongoing involvement of Ugandan troops in peacekeeping missions in Somalia have put the nation firmly in the targets of the Al-Shadab militia group. In light of the Nairobi attacks in 2013, Kampala remains on high alert with thorough security checks at malls, bars and restaurants now an everyday part of life.

Tensions have also bubbled to the surface with ethnic clashes involving kingdom disputes. In 2016 a crackdown by government forces on King Mumbere's royal guards – accused of militia involvement – ended with 46 guards killed and the royal palace in flames. It's sadly not an isolated incident, and tribal disputes have become commonplace in Western Uganda in recent years.

Uganda's controversial anti-gay legislators – egged on by US evangelical churches with a presence in Uganda – also keep the country in the international media spotlight for all the wrong reasons. The 'miniskirt law' is another worrying sign of Draconian measures, in which under the vague 'anti-pornography' bill, women would effectively be banned from wearing skirts above the knees. The bill was misinterpreted by many, which led to ugly scenes with vigilantes taking to the streets to harass and abuse women wearing short skirts. Fortunately it's an aspect of the bill that since seems to have been relaxed, with no further incident.

The Anti-Gay Bill

Since the controversial anti-gay bill that proposed the death penalty for homosexual behaviour was first drafted in 2009, Uganda has predictably come under fire from the international community. Barack Obama described it as 'odious', as the USA and several European governments cut foreign aid in protest, while the World Bank postponed its US$90 million loan. Though all references to the death penalty have since been removed, it's a piece of legislation that continues to rear its ugly head.

In February 2014 the Uganda Anti-Homosexuality Act was officially passed by parliament and signed off by President Museveni. The law made provisions for a life prison sentence to be applied to those convicted of 'aggravated homosexuality', a term that incorporated homosexuals convicted of rape, sex with a minor or knowingly spreading HIV, as well as 'serial offenders' – a clause that remains vague. Furthermore, under the legislation, anyone who failed to report homosexual behaviour could be imprisoned for up to three years.

In August 2014 Uganda's constitutional court found the Anti-Homosexuality Act to be illegal and it was overturned. Not to be deterred, the government is planning to introduce new, further-reaching legislation, incorporating prison sentences for those seen to be 'promoting' homosexuality.

Though homosexuality has officially been illegal in Uganda since the British introduced these laws in the 19th century, it is rarely, if ever, policed. The influence of visiting US evangelists has been widely reported, with many suggesting their preaching played a hand in whipping up anti-gay sentiment and influencing the anti-homosexuality bill. The documentary *God Loves Uganda* (2013) provides an interesting analysis on the subject.

So what does all this mean for LGBTQI travellers to Uganda, and is it safe to travel there? There's no doubt Ugandan culture is generally homophobic, so (as in other East African nations) discretion is vital. If travellers follow the lead of the local and expat gay community, who remain very much underground, there shouldn't be any threat. Keep in mind that displays of public affection – whether couples are heterosexual, gay or lesbian – are largely considered socially taboo.

Culture

The National Psyche

Despite the years of terror and bloodshed, Ugandans are a remarkably positive and spirited people, and no one comes away from the country without a measure of admiration and affection for them. While locals can initially be very reserved and shy, once you break the ice you'll find them to be opinionated and eloquent conversationalists, and almost always unfailingly polite and engagingly warm.

Ugandans will often greet strangers on public transport or while walking in rural areas. The greeting comes not just with a simple 'hello' but also with asking how you and your family are doing – and the interest is genuine. In fact, you risk offending someone (though Ugandans would likely never show it) if you don't at least ask 'How are you?' before asking for information or beginning a conversation.

Many Ugandans fear a fractured future. The country has had a remarkable run since 1986 when Museveni saved the nation, but nationalism has never taken hold. Tribe comes first. In fact, many Baganda still desire independence. This tribal divide has always manifested itself in politics, but the re-emergence of political parties is exacerbating the problem.

There is also a serious north–south divide, and it doesn't appear to be closing with the advent of peace. Without Joseph Kony around to blame any more, northerners seem to be turning their resentment for the lack of prosperity and education opportunities towards the south; and not without some justification. During the war, many military officers used their power to swipe land, and today many of the new businesses in the north are owned, and new jobs taken, by carpetbaggers.

Daily Life

Life in Uganda has been one long series of upheavals for the older generations, while the younger generations, who now comprise the bulk of the population, have benefited from the newfound stability. Society has changed completely in urban areas in the past couple of decades, but in the countryside it's often business as usual.

Uganda has been heavily affected by HIV/AIDS. One of the first countries to be struck by an outbreak of epidemic proportions, Uganda acted swiftly in promoting AIDS awareness and safe sex. This was very effective in radically reducing infection rates throughout the country, and Uganda went from experiencing an infection rate of around 25% in the late 1980s to one that dropped as low as 4% in 2003.

But things have changed. Due in large part to pressure from the country's growing evangelical Christian population, led on this issue by President Museveni's outspoken wife (though the president himself has taken her lead), Uganda has reversed its policy on promoting condoms and made abstinence the focus of fighting the disease. The result is no surprise: the infection rate has since risen to 7.1%.

Education has been a real priority in Uganda and President Museveni has been keen to promote free primary education for all. It's a noble goal, but Uganda lacks the resources to realise it, and one-third of the population is illiterate. While more pupils are attending class, often the classes are hopelessly overcrowded and many teachers lack experience.

Agriculture remains the single most important component of the Ugandan economy, and employs 75% of the workforce. The main export crops include coffee, sugar, cotton, tea and fish. Crops grown for local consumption include maize, millet, rice, cassava, potatoes and beans.

Population

Uganda's population is estimated at 41.5 million, and its annual growth rate of 3.2% is one of the world's highest. The environmental impacts resulting from this population boom, such as deforestation and erosion, will only get worse with time. The median age is 15, with a life expectancy of 55 years.

Uganda is made up of a complex and diverse range of tribes. Lake Kyoga forms the northern boundary for the Bantu-speaking peoples, who dominate much of east, central and southern Africa and, in Uganda, include the Baganda (16.5%), Banyankole (9.6%), Basoga (8.8%) and Bagisu (4.9%). In the north are the Langi (6.3%) near Lake Kyoga and the Acholi (4.4%) towards the Sudanese border, who speak Nilotic languages. To the east are the Iteso (7%) and Karamojong (2%), who are related to the Maasai, and also speak Nilotic languages. Small numbers of Twa (Batwa) people live in the forests of the southwest. Non-Africans, including a sizeable community of Asians, comprise about 1% of the population.

Sport

The most popular sport in Uganda, as throughout most of Africa, is football (soccer) and it's possible to watch occasional international games at the Nelson Mandela Stadium on the outskirts of Kampala. There's also a domestic league (October to July), but few people follow it.

Cricket is also growing in popularity (matches are held at Lugogo Cricket Ground), while boxing has lost much of its popularity in recent years, though past world champions include John 'the Beast' Mugabi and Kassim 'the Dream' Ouma, a former child soldier.

The national basketball team, called the Silverbacks, made its debut at the 2015 FIBA Africa Championship.

Religion

Eighty-five percent of the population is Christian, split between Catholics (39.3%) and Protestants (45.1%), including a growing number of born-agains. Muslims, mostly northerners, compose 13.7% of the population. The Abayudaya are a small but devout group of native Jewish Ugandans living around Mbale.

Arts

Cinema

Hollywood put Uganda on the movie map with a big-screen version of *The Last King of Scotland* (2006) starring Forest Whitaker as the 'Big Daddy'. While not set in Uganda, much of the Hollywood classic *The African Queen* starring Humphrey Bogart and Katharine Hepburn was shot near Murchison Falls.

The conflict in the north has spawned many harrowing documentaries including *Invisible Children* (2006), *The Other Side of the Country* (2007) and *Uganda Rising* (2006). In a different vein is the Oscar-nominated *War/Dance* (2006), an inspiring tale of northern refugee schoolchildren competing in Uganda's National Primary and Secondary School Music and Dance Competition. *God Loves Uganda* (2013) is documentary that delves into the controversial anti-gay bill and the involvement of US evangelists.

Based on a true story, *The Queen of Katwe* (2016), directed by Mira Nair, recounts the struggles of a young chess player who came out of the slums to become a Woman Candidate Master after her performances at the World Chess Olympiads. The Disney movie stars David Oyelowo and Academy Award winner Lupita Nyong'o.

Books

Most of the interesting reading coming out of Uganda revolves around the country's darkest hours. Aristoc (p398) in Kampala stocks a good selection of local writers.

LITERATURE

Giles Foden's *The Last King of Scotland* (1998) chronicles the fictional account of Idi Amin's personal doctor as he slowly finds himself becoming confidant to the dictator. This best-selling novel weaves gruesome historical fact into its *Heart of Darkness*-esque tale.

The highly regarded and somewhat autobiographical *Abyssinian Chronicles* (2001) is the best-known work by Moses Isegawa. It tells the story of a young Ugandan coming of age during the turbulent years of Idi Amin and offers some fascinating insights into life in Uganda. A novel about a cursed clan, *Kintu* (2014) by Jennifer Nansubuga Makumbi, explores Buganda history and myth.

Waiting (2007), the fourth novel by Goretti Kyomuhendo, one of Uganda's pioneering female writers (and founder of Femrite: the Ugandan Women Writers' Association and publishing house), was published in the USA. It looks in on a rural family's daily life (and daily fear) as they await the expected arrival of marauding soldiers during the fall of Idi Amin. Femwrite titles include *A Woman's Voice* (1998) and *Words From a Granary* (2001), two collections of short stories.

Song of Lawino (1989) is a highly regarded poem (originally written in Acholi) by Okot p'Bitek about how colonialism led to a loss of culture.

Fong and the Indians (1968) by Paul Theroux is set in a fictional East African country that bears a remarkable likeness to Uganda, where he taught English for four years in the 1960s. It's set in pre-civil war days, and is at times both funny and bizarre as it details the life of a Chinese immigrant and his dealings with the Asians who control commerce in the country.

NONFICTION

Keen birdwatchers will be best served by *The Birds of East Africa* (2006) by Terry Stevenson and John Fanshawe, with *The Bird Atlas of Uganda* (2005) making a good secondary resource. Also available is *Butterflies of Uganda* (2004) by Nancy Carder et al.

The Uganda Wildlife Authority has published informative books on the natural history of some of the most popular national parks. They can be bought at the UWA office (p485) in Kampala, and occasionally at the parks themselves, although you may have to request them. Andrew Roberts' *Uganda's Great Rift Valley* (2006) is an entertaining study of the natural and human history of western Uganda.

Uganda: From the Pages of Drum (1994) is a lively compilation of articles that originally appeared in the now-defunct *Drum* magazine. These chronicle the rise of Idi Amin and the atrocities he committed, as well as President Museveni's bush war and his coming to power. It forms a powerful record of what the country experienced.

Ugandan Society Observed (2008) is another recommended collection of essays, these by expat Kevin O'Connor, that originally appeared in the *Daily Monitor* newspaper.

The Man with the Key has Gone! (1993) by Dr Ian Clarke is an autobiographical account of the time spent in Uganda's Luwero Triangle district by a British doctor and his family. It's a lively read and the title refers to a problem travellers may encounter in provincial Uganda.

Widely available in Uganda, Henry Kyemba's *State of Blood* (1977) is an inside story of the horrors committed by Idi Amin, with insight only one of his former ministers could provide.

Aboke Girls (2001) by Els de Temmerman is a heart-wrenching account of female child soldiers and an Italian nun's attempt to rescue them during LRA's decade-long reign of terror in northern Uganda. *The Wizard of the Nile* (2008), by reporter Matthew Green, chronicles the hunt for Joseph Kony.

Music & Dance

Kampala is the best place to experience live music and several local bands play at nightclubs each weekend. Try to catch the Afrigo Band and Maurice Kirya, Bobi Wine, plus the weeknightly events at the National Theatre.

Ugandan hip-hop is popular and original, particularly Luga-flow, or rapping in native tongues (Luga standing for Luganda, the Bantu language of the Bagandas). Babaluku was considered a pioneer of the form. Many feel that Uganda's modern rap has become more about entertainment than musicianship.

To listen to Ugandan music, from hip-hop to northern-style thumb piano playing, visit www.musicuganda.com.

Dance-troupe Triplets Ghetto Kids puts out great viral videos; go to https://tripletsghettokids.com. The most famous dancers in the country are the Ndere Troupe (p398). Made up of a kaleidoscope of Ugandan tribes, they perform traditional dances from all regions of the country.

Handicrafts

Uganda's most distinctive craft is bark-cloth, made by pounding the bark of a fig tree. Originally used for clothing and in burial and other ceremonies, these days it's turned into a multitude of items for sale to tourists including hats, bags, wall hangings, pillows and picture frames.

Ugandans also produce some really good raffia and banana-stem basketry, particularly the Toro of the west, who have the most intricate designs and still use natural dyes. Traditional products are easy to find, but the old methods have also been adopted to make new items such as table mats and handbags for sale to tourists.

Baganda drum-makers are well known: the best place to buy is at Mpambire, along the Masaka Rd. Uganda also has interesting pottery, though all the soapstone carving comes from Kenya and almost all the interesting woodwork is Congolese.

Environment

Uganda suffers the same environmental problems that plague the rest of the region: poaching, deforestation and overpopulation.

PRIMATE HABITUATION

When it comes to tracking mountain gorillas in the wild, one common question is how it's possible to safely get mere metres from these beautiful, yet intimidating beasts that can weigh in excess of 200kg and have the strength to rip your arms out of their sockets. The simple answer lies in whether the gorilla group is habituated or not. Habituation is the process by which a group of primates (or other animals) are slowly exposed to human presence to the point where they regard us neutrally. While habituated and nonhabituated gorillas are both considered wild, the latter are *truly* wild in the sense that they're unaccustomed to human presence, so they're either likely to flee into the forest or be downright dangerous and aggressive. Thankfully neither of these are the case when tracking gorillas in Bwindi – even though you might get the odd mock charge from a grumpy silverback.

The process of habituating gorillas is a long and patient affair that takes around two to three years. It's even longer for chimpanzees – normally around seven years before they're fully habituated. It involves spending time with a group every day and eventually winning over their trust, which is done by mimicking their behaviour: pretending to eat the same food as they do at the same time, grunting and even beating one's chest when they do. With gorillas, the first few weeks are fraught with danger for the human habitué, with repeated charges commonplace.

Habituation took place well before someone had the bright idea of charging tourists US$600 a pop to see the gorillas. It's a vital process for research that allows primatologists to observe the behavioural patterns of gorillas, chimps, golden monkeys, baboons etc. Some hold the view that the process of habituation is unethical: subjecting the creatures to our presence each day interferes with nature by changing their behavioural patterns. One example of things going wrong occurred in Busingiro on the edge of Murchison Falls National Park, where chimp tracking had to be abandoned when chimps lost their fear of humans and started raiding local farms. It also puts primates at risk of contagious ailments and disease, while making them more susceptible to attacks from poachers or nonhabituated 'wild' groups. But had there not been habituation of gorillas (and the tourist trade to go with it), there's every chance the species would've been wiped out by poachers decades ago.

Currently the biggest threat to Uganda's national parks and other protected areas comes from the oil industry. Significant oil finds in the Kabwoya Wildlife Reserve on Lake Albert have spurred invasive searches for more black gold in the Ishasha sector of Queen Elizabeth National Park and the delta area at Murchison Falls National Park. Providing the drilling companies explore and extract responsibly, there is hope for a sustainable marriage of interests; but conservationists are sceptical. Meanwhile, the World Health Organization released a pilot study in 2014 that found Kampala had particulate levels in the 'critical range', putting it on par with New Delhi for air pollution.

The Land

Uganda has an area of 241,038 sq km, which is small by African standards, but similar in size to Britain. Lake Victoria and the Victoria Nile river, which cuts through the heart of the country, combine to create one of the most fecund areas in Africa. Most of Uganda is a blizzard of greens, a lush landscape of rolling hills blanketed with fertile fields, where almost anything will grow if you stick it in the soil. The climate is drier in the north and some of the lands of the far northeast are semi-desert.

The tropical heat is tempered by the altitude, which averages more than 1000m in much of the country and is even higher in the cooler southwest. The highest peak is Mt Stanley (5109m) in the Rwenzori Mountains on the border with the DRC. A Chinese-funded US$6 billion copper-mining project in the region was shut down in June 2017 when a bribery scandal involving a former minister broke out.

Wildlife

Uganda can't compete with Kenya or Tanzania for sheer density of wildlife, but with 500 species of mammals, there is amazing diversity. You have a good chance of spotting all the classic African animals including lions, elephants, giraffes, leopard, hippos, zebras, hyenas and, up north, cheetahs and ostriches. Furthermore, with the opening of the Ziwa Rhino Sanctuary, the Big Five are all here again.

It's main attraction, however, is mountain gorillas. Uganda is home to more than half the world's mountain gorillas and viewing them in their natural environment is one of Uganda's highlights. On top of this, Uganda has a good number of chimpanzees and there are several places where you can track them. And with well over 1000 species recorded inside its small borders, Uganda is one of the best birdwatching destinations in the world.

GORILLA TRACKING

Gorilla tracking is one of the major draws for travellers in Uganda. These gentle giants live in two national parks: Bwindi Impenetrable and Mgahinga Gorilla.

CHIMPANZEE TRACKING

Chimpanzee tracking is a very popular activity in Uganda. The main areas are Kibale National Park, Budongo Forest Reserve in Murchison Falls National Park, Kyambura Gorge in Queen Elizabeth National Park and Toro-Semliki.

BIRDWATCHING

Uganda is one of the world's best birdwatching destinations, a twitcher's fantasy offering 1041 species; that's almost half the total found in all of Africa. Even nonbirdwatchers will be enthralled by the diversity of beauty among Uganda's birdlife.

A good starting point is Uganda Birding (www.birding-uganda.com), an excellent online resource with all there is to know – from birding hotspots and recommended tour operators to info on the birds themselves. Bird Uganda (www.birduganda.com) also has plenty of good info. The country's top guides are members of the Uganda Bird Guides Club (www.ugandabirdguides.org).

National Parks & Reserves

Uganda has an excellent collection of national parks and reserves. Twenty percent of your admission fees benefit local communities for things like construction of schools and health clinics, so you earn a warm fuzzy for every park you visit.

The **Uganda Wildlife Authority** (UWA; Map p388; ☎0414-355000; www.ugandawildlife.org; 7 Kira Rd; ⏰8am-5pm Mon-Fri, 9am-1pm Sat) administers all Uganda's protected areas. It's the place to make bookings to see the gorillas in Bwindi Impenetrable National Park, and should be the first port of call for those needing to book permits. It's also the place to reserve accommodation in the parks. Some other activities, such chimpanzee tracking, and launch trips in Murchison Falls and Queen Elizabeth National Parks in Kibale, can also be reserved here, though activities such as nature walks are arranged at the parks. Payments are accepted in shillings, dollars, euros and pounds in cash or Amex travellers cheques (1% commission). While credit cards aren't accepted, a new cashless 'smartcard' system was introduced to allow you to load up entry fees in Kampala before heading to the main national parks.

Most national parks charge US$35 to US$40 (US$5 to US$20 for children aged five to 15) and admission is valid for 24 hours. Other charges, which can add up quite fast, include vehicle entry (USh10,000/20,000/30,000 per motorcycle/car/4WD) for locally registered vehicles. If you're coming in with a foreign registered vehicle, the prices are very expensive (US$30/50/150 per motorcycle/car/4WD). Nature walks cost US$30 per person and rangers for wildlife-watching drives are US$20. Most prices are lower for Ugandan residents and much lower again for Ugandan citizens. For the most up-to-date prices, check the UWA website.

If you're pressed for time or money is no issue, you can charter flights to most of the parks.

LONG-HORNED ANKOLE

Sure there are the gorillas, the Big Five, and even shoebills, but one striking animal that also manages to turn heads, yet without getting its due credit, is the remarkable long-horned Ankole cow. Common in southwest Uganda, the domestic Ankole cattle is pretty much your ordinary cow except for one notable feature – its extreme horns that reach out as long as 2m, with some extending up to 3.7m! Revered among many pastoralist indigenous groups as a status symbol, animal numbers are unfortunately on the decline, as farmers continue to abandon them in favour of more-commercial breeds that yield more milk and meat.

The *Names of Ankole Cows* (2003) is a quirky book about these striking animals, available from the Igongo Cultural Centre (p460) bookshop.

Food & Drink

Local food is similar to elsewhere in the region, though ugali (a food staple usually made from maize flour or cassava) is called *posho,* and is far less popular than *matoke* (cooked plantains). Rice, cassava and potatoes are also common starches and vegetarians travelling beyond the main tourist destinations will end up eating these with beans quite often, although non-Ugandan meals are available at most hotels frequented by tourists.

Ugandan Cuisine

Ugandans eat a starch-heavy diet of *matoko, posho,* rice and potatoes with meat and vegetables. Stews and pleasant sauces, sometimes spicy, flavour dishes. Decent Indian food is available in most towns and can be a welcome alternative.

One uniquely Ugandan food is the *rolex,* a chapati rolled around an omelette. Grasshoppers are very popular during April and November and are sold by many street vendors.

Like all East Africans, Ugandans love their beer. Uganda Breweries and Nile Breweries are the two main local brewers, and they produce some drinkable lagers such as Nile, Club and Bell.

Waragi is the local millet-based alcohol and is relatively safe, although it can knock you around and give you a horrible hangover. It's similar to gin and goes down well with a splash of tonic. In its undistilled form it's known as *kasezi bong* and would probably send you blind if you drank enough of it.

Imported wines are quite expensive and not common beyond the tourist trail. Imported spirits are relatively cheaper, although, like wine, availability is somewhat restricted.

SURVIVAL GUIDE

Directory A–Z

BARGAINING

You'll usually need to bargain with *boda-boda* and special-hire drivers, though bear in mind that there are many honest drivers out there, and in many cases the price they propose is the standard fare for a journey.

SAFARI OPERATORS

By far the most convenient way to visit the parks is on an organised safari, with a good range of options that cover most budgets.

Gorilla Tours (☎0414-200221; www.gorillatours.com; 625 Lubowa Rise Rd) Gorillas are the speciality, but this company has itineraries covering all the major parks of southwest Uganda. The trips offer very good value, and it manages some of the country's best mid-range hotels.

Bird Uganda Safaris (☎0393-289048; www.birduganda.com) Herbert Byaruhanga, one of Uganda's pioneering birdwatchers, leads most of the trips himself but also enlists local guides at all the sites to ensure top spotting. Gorilla tracking and other wildlife encounters can be added to the mix.

Matoke Tours (Map p386; ☎0312-202907; www.matoketours.com; 1 Senfuka Rd) The Dutch-run Matoke team stands out for excellent and enthusiastic service for a midrange clientele, with trips ranging from classic safaris to more intrepid overland journeys to Kidepo Valley National Park and Karamojaland.

Red Chilli Hideaway (Map p386; ☎0772509150; www.redchillihideaway.com; 3-day safaris from US$320) An excellent choice for budget safaris to Murchison Falls and Queen Elizabeth National Parks. Also very affordable car-hire rates.

Kombi Tours (Map p388; ☎0792933773; www.kombitours.com; 13 Butoko St) Though style may outweigh practicality, the opportunity to get around Uganda in a vintage '70s VW Kombi (complete with original parts) makes this one of the coolest tour companies in the country. It offers both tailor-made trips and scheduled tours, and also has Land Cruisers for 4WD-accessible places.

CUSTOMS REGULATIONS

Uganda allows the importation of 200 cigarettes, 1L of spirits (over 25% volume of alcohol) or 2L of lighter alcoholic beverages (up to 25% volume of alcohol) as well as gifts and other items for personal use. Pornography is prohibited. Cultural artefacts and endangered species or related products are prohibited to export.

DANGERS & ANNOYANCES

Uganda is generally a very safe destination today. As a traveller your main dangers are those of mosquito-borne disease and dangerous driving. Gay travellers should be aware that recent evangelical-led campaigns against homosexuality have resulted in a high level of homophobia. Discretion is vital, as is taking serious safety precautions online: only meet contacts in a public place, and inform others where you are going and whom you are meeting.

Border Areas

After a disarmament program and resulting stabilisation, more people are travelling in the Karamojong area of the far northeast (though not within Kidepo Valley National Park); however, foreign governments still warn of banditry. Due to the instability of South Sudan and occasional conflict between Kenyan and Ugandan cattle-herding groups, the border areas in the far northwest have ongoing problems that may deter travellers. Various rebel groups hang out in the far eastern DRC and occasionally slip across the porous border to wreak havoc. Even with additional Ugandan troops in the area, the chances of this happening again cannot be completely discounted. Finally, there are smugglers and Kenyan rebels on and around Mt Elgon, though the risk to visitors is small.

ELECTRICITY

240V, 50 cycles; British three-pin plugs are used.

EMBASSIES & CONSULATES

Embassies and consulates are located in Kampala.

Australian Consulate (Map p388; ☎0312-515865; 40 Kyadondo Rd, Nakasero; ⌚9am-12.30pm & 2-5pm Mon-Fri)

Belgium Embassy (Map p388; ☎0414-349559; www.diplomatie.be/kampala; Lumumba Ave, Rwenzori House; ⌚8.30am-1pm & 2-4pm Mon-Thu, 8.30am-1pm Fri)

British High Commission (Map p388; ☎0312-312000; http://ukinuganda.fco.gov.uk; Windsor Loop, Kamwokya; ⌚8.30am-1pm & 2-5pm Mon-Thu, 8.30am-1pm Fri)

Burundi Embassy (Map p388; ☎0414-235850; 12a York Tce; ⌚visas 10am-1pm Mon-Thu)

Canadian Embassy (Map p388; ☎0414-258141; canada.consulate@utlonline.co.ug; 14 Parliament Ave; ⏲9.30am-noon &1-4.30pm Mon-Thu)

Danish Embassy (Map p388; ☎0312-363000; www.uganda.um.dk; 3 Lumumba Ave; ⏲8am-4pm Mon-Thu, to 2pm Fri)

DRC Embassy (Map p388; ☎0414-250099; 20 Philip Rd, Kololo; ⏲9am-4pm Mon-Fri)

Dutch Embassy (Map p388; ☎0414-346000; http://uganda.nlembassy.org; Nakasero Rd, Rwenzori Courts; ⏲10am-noon Mon-Thu by appointment)

Ethiopian Embassy (Map p388; ☎0414-348340; ethiokam@utlonline.co.org; 3 Kira Rd, Kitante Cl; ⏲8.30am-12.30pm & 2-5.30pm Mon-Fri)

French Embassy (Map p388; ☎0414-304500; www.ambafrance-ug.org; 16 Lumumba Ave; ⏲9am-5pm Mon-Thu, to 1pm Fri)

German Embassy (Map p388; ☎0414-501111; www.kampala.diplo.de; 15 Philip Rd, Kololo; ⏲8-11am Mon-Fri by appointment only)

Indian Embassy (Map p388; ☎0414-259398; 11 Kyadondo Rd; ⏲9.30am-12.30pm Mon-Fri)

Irish Embassy (Map p388; ☎0417-713000; www.embassyofireland.ug; 25 Yusuf Lule Rd, Nakasero; ⏲10am-noon & 2-4pm Mon-Fri)

Italian Embassy (Map p388; ☎0312-188000; www.ambkampala.esteri.it; 11 Lourdel Rd, Nakasero; ⏲10am-noon Tue-Thu)

Japanese Embassy (Map p388; ☎0414-349542; www.ug.emb-japan.go.jp; 8 Kyadondo Rd; ⏲8.30-12.30pm & 1.30-5.15pm Mon-Fri)

Kenyan High Commission (Map p388; ☎0414-258235; kampala@mfa.go.ke; 41 Nakasero Rd; ⏲9am-12.30pm & 2-4pm Mon-Fri)

Nigerian High Commission (Map p388; ☎0414-233691; www.nigeriahighcommissionkampala.org; 33 Nakasero Rd; ⏲10am-1pm Mon-Fri)

Rwandan Embassy (Map p388; ☎0414-344045; www.uganda.embassy.gov.rw; 2 Nakayima Rd, Kitante; ⏲9am-12.30pm Mon-Fri)

South African High Commission (Map p388; ☎0417-702100; www.dirco.gov.za/uganda; 15a Nakasero Rd; ⏲8.30am-noon Mon-Fri)

South Sudan Embassy (Map p388; ☎0414-271625; 2 Ssezibwa Rd; ⏲9am-noon Thu)

Sudan Embassy (Map p388; ☎0414-230001; www.mofa.go.ug/data/smenu/85/sudan.html; 21 Nakasero Rd; ⏲8.30am-3pm Mon-Thu, to 1pm Fri)

Tanzanian High Commission (Map p388; ☎0414-256272; Clement Hill Rd; ⏲9am-12.30pm & 2-5pm Mon-Thu, to 1pm Fri)

US Embassy (Map p386; ☎0414-259791; https://ug.usembassy.gov; Ggaba Rd, Nsambya; ⏲8-11.45am Mon-Wed, 8-10.45am Fri)

ETIQUETTE

Greetings Ugandans formally greet just about everyone, even if they are stopping someone for driving directions. Skipping this step gets you off to a poor start.

Bargaining Ugandans dislike arguments. If you have a conflict about charges at a hotel or the like, it's best to dig in your heels for a long but firm and polite discussion with a gentle joking welcome.

GAY & LESBIAN TRAVELLERS

Homosexuality has been illegal in Uganda since the time of British colonial rule, and in theory can result in a sentence of up to 14 years in prison. Not satisfied with this relative lenience, in 2014 the Ugandan government passed legislation that punished homosexuality with life imprisonment (watered down from the death sentence proposed by the original law), but this draconian measure was thrown out by the Constitutional Court. As you might expect, the gay community here remains very much underground. LGBTQI tourists are advised to likewise keep things discreet, although there's no need to be overly worried as foreigners are rarely the subject of investigation. Some lodgings will refuse to put two people of the same sex in a one-bed room.

HEALTH

Travel with your own comprehensive medical insurance, although you will find that medical help is inexpensive compared to costs in most Western countries. Bring a well-stocked first-aid kit. If you have a specific condition, it's wise to bring the medication you will need for the duration of your trip. The International Hospital (p399) in Kampala is the country's main private facility. Provincial cities have smaller, more limited facilities or clinics.

INTERNET ACCESS

Free wi-fi is available at all but the simplest hotels, as well as some better restaurants and cafes. However, it's much less likely (or very slow) in national parks and remote regions.

Smartphone users can easily purchase a local SIM card with data, and this remains the most reliable way to connect. Laptop users can get a wireless USB internet/dongle for around US$30. The best networks are MTN and Orange, which have reliable access for most parts of the country (but not in the remote parks).

Internet cafes can be found in cities and most medium-sized towns.

MAPS

Being both beautiful and useful, Uganda Maps national park maps, available at UWA offices, safari lodges and tour companies, are a great buy if you're headed to any of the national parks.

MONEY

ATMs

The biggest banks (Barclays, Stanbic, Centenary, Crane, Orient and Standard Chartered) have ATMs that accept international cards. Even many remote small towns will have at least one of these banks, though try not to let your cash run out as the system sometimes goes down and machines sometimes run out of cash.

Cash

The Ugandan shilling (USh) is a relatively stable currency that floats freely on international markets. Most tour operators and upmarket hotels quote in US dollars (a few in euros), but you can pay with shillings everywhere.

Notes in circulation are USh1000, USh5000, USh10,000, USh20,000 and USh50,000, and commonly used coins are USh50, USh100, USh200 and USh500.

US dollars are the most useful hard currency, especially in small towns, though euros and pounds sterling are also widely accepted.

If you're using dollars, try to avoid bills printed before 2006, as often they're not accepted (due to a higher risk of them being counterfeit notes). If exchanging dollars, small denominations *always* get a much lower rate than US$50 and US$100 notes – so ask for larger notes when you collect your money.

The best exchange rates by far are offered in Kampala. Forex bureaus offer slightly better rates than banks plus much faster service and longer hours; but they're rare outside Kampala.

Note that Uganda Wildlife Authority (UWA) offers fair exchange rates for park fees and accepts dollars, pounds and euros and either cash or travellers cheques.

Credit Cards

Credit cards are accepted at better hotels in larger cities, as well as smarter restaurants and safari lodges, but it's always a good idea to bring plenty of cash as a backup. There can often be a surcharge of 5% to 8% when making payments by cards, but these are slowly becoming rarer as companies become more accustomed to people paying this way. Visa is the most widely accepted card, but MasterCard is increasingly accepted.

Tipping

Tipping isn't expected in Uganda but, as wages are very low by Western standards, it will always be appreciated. The size of a given tip is up to the individual.

Restaurants USh1000 to USh1500 is enough in ordinary restaurants.

Rangers USh5000 to USh10,000 is reasonable for ranger-guides in national parks.

OPENING HOURS

Banks 9am–3pm Monday to Friday

Government offices 8.30am–5pm Monday to Friday

Restaurants 8am–10pm

Shops 8am–5pm Monday to Saturday

POST

Kampala's post office is slow but reliable; there's a chance things will go missing at provincial branches.

PUBLIC HOLIDAYS

New Year's Day 1 January

Liberation Day 26 January

International Women's Day 8 March

Easter (Good Friday, Holy Saturday and Easter Monday) March/April

Labour Day 1 May

Martyrs' Day 3 June

Heroes' Day 9 June

Independence Day 9 October

Christmas Day 25 December

Boxing Day 26 December

Banks and government offices also close on the major Muslim holidays.

TELEPHONE

The country code for Uganda is 256. To make an international call from Uganda, dial 000 or, on a mobile, the + button. If you're calling Uganda from outside the country, drop the 0 at the start of the phone number.

In case of emergency, dial 999 from a landline or 112 from a mobile phone.

Landline telephone connections, both domestic and international, are pretty good, but almost everyone (including businesses) operates on mobiles these days.

Mobile Phones

Mobile (cell) phones are very popular as the service is better than landlines, although there are still large areas of rural Uganda with little or no coverage. MTN and Orange currently have the best coverage across the country. All mobile numbers start with 07. Mobile phone companies sell SIM cards for USh2000 and then you buy airtime vouchers for topping up calling credit or data packs from street vendors.

TIME

East African Time (GMT/UTC plus three hours).

VISAS

Most passport holders visiting Uganda require visas, including citizens of the USA, Canada, EU, Australia and New Zealand. The process for obtaining visas was moved almost entirely online in July 2016. It's important to note that visas on arrival are no longer available without online approval first, and this can take up to five days.

To apply for your visa, go to the immigration website (www.visas.immigration.go.ug) and follow the instructions. You will have to upload a scan of both your passport photograph page and your yellow-fever certificate, and fill in an application form. Once submitted, you should have your approval notification within three working days. You should print this out and present it at immigration when you arrive in Uganda to get your visa on arrival.

When you get your visa on arrival, you'll need to pay in cash at the immigration desk. Single-entry tourist visas valid for up to 90 days cost US$50; however, do be sure to ask for a 90-day visa, or you'll probably be given 30 or 60 days. Your yellow-fever certificate may be required again, so bring it with you, though you don't need to bring a photo. Multiple-entry visas aren't available on arrival, but it is possible for embassies abroad to issue them (US$100 for six months).

Uganda is one of the countries covered by the East Africa Tourist (EAT) visa, and for those also visiting Kenya and Rwanda on the same trip it is a cheaper alternative. The visa costs US$100, is valid for 90 days and is multiple entry – it is available upon arrival or from embassies abroad. If acquiring the visa before travel, your first port of call must be the country through which you applied for the visa. If Uganda is your first destination, then you have to apply for the EAT visa in a Ugandan embassy abroad – you cannot get it by applying online and then obtaining it on arrival.

Visa Extensions

In Kampala, the **Immigration Office** (Map p388; 0414-595945; Jinja Rd; 9am-1pm & 2-5pm) is just east of the centre. Regardless of how many days you were given on your original tourist visa, you can apply for a free two-month extension. Submit a letter explaining the reason for your request, stating where you're staying and detailing when and how you'll be leaving the country. Attach a copy of your passport and plane ticket, if you have one. It takes seven days to process, but extensions are much quicker at immigration offices outside the capital, and these exist in most large towns, including Jinja and Fort Portal.

DEPARTURE TAX

The departure tax is included in the cost of airline tickets.

Getting There & Away

AIR

Entebbe International Airport (EBB; 0414-353000; http://entebbe-airport.com; Entebbe), about 40km south of the capital, is the only international airport in Uganda.

The following airlines service Entebbe.

British Airways (Map p388; 0414-257414; www.britishairways.com; Centre Court, Plot 4 Ternan Ave, Nakasero, Kampala; 8.30am-5pm Mon-Fri)

Brussels Airlines (Map p388; 0414-234201; www.brusselsairlines.com; 1 Lumumba Ave, Rwenzori House, Kampala; 9am-5pm Mon-Fri)

Emirates (Map p388; 0417-710444; www.emirates.com; Kimathi Ave, 1st fl Acacia Pl, Kololo; 9am-5pm Mon-Fri)

Ethiopian Airlines (Map p388; 0414-345577; www.ethiopianairlines.com; 1 Kimathi Ave, Kampala; 9am-5pm Mon-Fri)

Kenya Airways (Map p388; 0312-360000; www.kenya-airways.com; 14 Parliament Ave, Jubilee Insurance Bldg, Kampala; 9am-5pm Mon-Fri)

KLM (Map p388; 0414-338000; www.klm.com; 4 Parliament Ave, 3rd fl, Jubilee Insurance Bldg, Kampala; 8.30am-5pm Mon-Fri)

Qatar Airways (Map p388; 0417-800900; www.qatarairways.com; Nakasero Rd, Rwenzori Towers, 1st fl, Kampala; 9am-5pm Mon-Fri)

RwandAir (Map p388; 0414-344851; www.rwandair.com; Lumumba Ave, Garden City; 9am-5pm Mon-Fri)

South African Airways (Map p388; 0414-345772; www.flysaa.com; 42 Lugogo Bypass, ground fl, Kampala; 8am-5pm Mon-Fri, 9am-1pm Sat)

Turkish Airlines (Map p388; 0414-253433; www.turkishairlines.com; 15a Clement Hill Rd, 3rd fl, Ruth Towers, Kampala; 9am-5pm Mon-Fri)

LAND

Uganda shares land border crossings with Kenya, Rwanda, Tanzania, South Sudan and the DRC. Direct bus services connect the major cities in each country (with the exception of DRC), and local transport from towns nearer the border is available for those wanting to break their journey along the way.

Kenya

The busiest border crossing is at Busia on the direct route to Nairobi through Kisumu. Frequent minibuses link Jinja to Busia (USh10,000, two hours), and then again between Busia and Kisumu or Nairobi. The border crossing is straightforward, though there are a number of shady moneychangers – check everything twice.

The other busy border crossing to Kenya is through Malaba, a bit north of Busia and just east of Tororo. Finding onward transport from here to Nairobi is less frequent than at Busia.

To visit Mt Elgon National Park or Sipi Falls, the Suam border crossing, beyond which lies the Kenyan city of Kitale, may be convenient, but this is a pretty rough route. Trekkers in either the Ugandan or Kenyan national parks on Mt Elgon also have the option of walking over the border.

Most travellers avoid local transport altogether and opt for the direct buses running between Kampala and Nairobi, which range from luxurious to basic. You can also pick up these buses (or get dropped off on your way into Uganda) in Jinja. The journey takes about 12 to 13 hours.

Easy Coach (Map p388; ☎0757727273, 0776727270; www.easycoach.co.ke; Dewinton Rd, Kampala) Reputable company with modern buses. Daily departures to Nairobi (USh80,000) at 6.30am, 2pm and 7pm.

Queens Coach (Map p388; ☎0773002010; Yusuf Lule Rd, Kampala, Oasis Mall) Comfortable bus servicing Nairobi (USh75,000), departing 8pm.

Mash (Map p388; ☎0793234312; www.masheastafrica.com; 7 Dewinton Rd, Kampala) Twice-daily departures to Nairobi (USh70,000) at 5pm and 10pm.

Rwanda

There are two main border crossing points between Uganda and Rwanda: between Kabale and Kigali via Katuna (Gatuna on the Rwandan side), and between Kisoro and Musanze (Ruhengeri) via Cyanika. The Kagitumba border isn't very practical for most people, but there is public transport on both sides.

The busier crossing by far is at Katuna/Gatuna, and it can take over an hour to get through immigration stations on both sides. From Kabale there are lots of shared-car taxis to the border, and a few minibuses each morning (except Sunday) direct to Kigali. You can also wait at the main junction in the morning for the Kigali-bound buses from Kampala to pass through and hope they have free seats. On the Rwandan side there are minibuses travelling to Kigali (two hours) throughout the day. The border is open 24 hours.

From Kisoro to Cyanika there's no public transport, so you'll need to get a special-hire (USh35,000) or a *boda-boda* (motorcycle taxi; USh8000). Transport on the Rwandan side to Musanze (Ruhengeri) is frequent and the road in good condition; altogether it only takes about 1½ hours to travel between Kisoro and Musanze (Ruhengeri). The border is open 24 hours.

There's also the option of taking a direct bus between Kampala and Kigali (USh40,000), a seven- to nine-hour journey including a slow border crossing.

Jaguar Executive Coaches (Map p388; ☎0782811128; 30 Namirembe Rd, Kampala) Reliable company with daily services to Kigali at 7am, 9am, 8pm and 9pm. Also has a 'VIP' option with more comfortable seats.

Simba (Namayiba Terminal) (Map p388; Rashid Khamis Rd, Kampala) Daily buses to Kigali (USh40,000, 11 hours) at 2am.

Tanzania

The most commonly used direct route between Uganda and Tanzania is on the west side of Lake Victoria between Bukoba and Kampala, via Masaka; the border crossing is at Mutukula. Road conditions are good and the journey takes about six hours by bus from Kampala (you can also catch these buses in Masaka).

There's another border crossing located at Nkurungu, west of Mutukula, but the road is bad and little transport passes this way.

The journey to Dar es Salaam takes a day and a half via Nairobi.

Friends Safari (Map p388; ☎0788425952; Rashid Khamis Rd, Kampala) Recommended bus departs at 2pm for Bukoba (USh35,000, seven hours) and Mwanza (USh65,000, 12 hours) at 5am.

Falcon (Map p388; ☎0781338066; 4 Lumumba Ave, Kampala) Departs for Dar es Salaam (USh140,000, 28 hours) on Wednesday, Friday and Sunday at 5.30am.

Getting Around

AIR

Several airlines operate charter flights, which get you to the national parks in comfort (flights US$300 to US$500 one way).

Fly Uganda (☎0772706107; www.flyuganda.com; Kajjansi Airfield)

Aerolink (☎0317-333000; www.aerolinkuganda.com; Entebbe International Airport)

BICYCLE

Cycling opportunities are growing in Uganda for good reason. Once you get on country roads, the possibilities are nearly endless, with a pleasant climate and good scenery to fuel the trip. Consult with **Red Dirt Mountain Biking** (p387) in Kampala for tours, rentals or repairs.

BOAT

Boat travel in Uganda is limited to reaching the Ssese Islands, either by ferry from Nakiwogo (in Entebbe), Bukakata (east of Masaka) or small fishing boats operating from Kasenyi (also near Entebbe).

BUS

Standard buses and sometimes half-sized 'coasters' connect major towns on a daily basis. The longer your journey is, the more likely it will be on a bus rather than a minibus. Bus fares are usually a little less than minibus fares and buses stop far less frequently, which saves time. Buses generally leave Kampala at fixed departure times; however, when returning from provincial destinations, they usually leave when full. There are many reckless drivers, but buses are safer than minibuses. Night travel is best avoided.

The safest option is the post buses run by the Ugandan Postal Service (UPS). Post buses run daily (except Sunday) from Kampala to Kasese (via Mbarara), Kabale (via Masaka and Mbarara), Soroti (via Mbale) and Hoima (via Masindi).

Minibus

Uganda is the land of shared minibuses (called taxis, or occasionally matatus), and there's never any shortage of these blue-and-white minivans. Except for long distances, these are the most common vehicles between towns. There are official fares (you can check at the taxi-park offices if you want), but in reality the conductor charges whatever they think they can get, and not just for a *muzungu* (foreigner) but for locals as well. Ask fellow passengers the right price.

Minibuses leave when full and 'full' means exactly that. As soon as you're a fair distance away from towns, where police spot-checks are less likely, more passengers will be crammed in. As is clearly painted on their doors, minibuses are licensed to carry 14 passengers, but travelling with fewer than 18 is rare, and the number often well exceeds 20. For all but the shortest journeys, you're better off taking a bus as they stop less frequently and are safer due to their size. Many minibus and bus drivers drive too fast to leave any leeway for emergencies. Crash stories are regular features in the newspapers. Most crashes are head-on, so sit at the back for maximum safety.

Way-out-of-the-way places use shared-car taxis rather than minibuses, and these are similarly overloaded with passengers. If the roads are exceptionally bad, then the only choice is to sit with bags of maize and charcoal, empty jerrycans and other cargo in the backs of trucks.

CAR & MOTORCYCLE

There's a pretty good system of sealed roads between most towns in Uganda. Keep your wits about you when driving; cyclists, cows and large potholes often appear from nowhere.

The quality of *murram* (dirt) roads varies depending on whether it's the wet or dry season. In the dry, *murram* roads are very dusty and you'll end up choking behind trucks and minibuses while everything along the road gets covered in a fine layer of orange-brown dust. In wet season, a number of the *murram* roads become muddy mires, almost carrot soup, and may be passable only in a 4WD vehicle. If you're travelling around Uganda in wet season, always ask at the car-hire agency about the latest road conditions before setting off on a journey.

As with other transport, avoid travelling at night due to higher risks of accidents and banditry. Take care in the national parks where there's a US$500 fine for hitting animals and US$150 for off-track driving.

Driving Licences

If you have an International Driving Permit, you should bring it, although you really only need your local driving licence from home.

Fuel & Spare Parts

Petrol prices rise as you move out into provincial areas. Like everywhere in the world, petrol prices are highly volatile.

Filling and repair stations are found even in some small towns, but don't let the tank run too low or you may end up paying an extortionate amount to fuel up from a jerrycan in some really remote place.

Hire

Due to high taxes and bad roads, car-hire prices tend to be expensive compared to other parts of the world. Add fuel costs and there will be some real shock at the total price if you're considering driving around the country.

While all the major international franchises have offices in Kampala and at Entebbe International Airport, in virtually all instances it's better to deal with one of the local companies. Quoted prices for a small car with driver can range from US$50 to US$150. The highest prices are just rip-offs by companies who hope *wazungu* (foreigners) don't know any better, but with the others, the difference is in the details. Always ask about the number of free kilometres (and the price for exceeding them) and driver costs for food and lodging. Try negotiating with special-hire drivers, but generally speaking they aren't as reliable. Red Chilli backpackers (p392) offers very good rates for car hire.

Road Trip Uganda (p387) Popular company hiring self-drive fully equipped RAV4s from US$59 per day. Also offers a car with driver, travel itineraries and emergency car services.

Alpha Car Rentals (Map p388; ☎0772411232; www.alpharentals.co.ug; 3/5 Bombo Rd, Kampala, EMKA House; ⏲9am-6pm Mon-Fri) A car with driver costs USh80,000 for the day around Kampala, while a 4WD with driver is US$100 (the driver's food and lodging is included) if you head up-country, or US$70 for self-drive. It also has RAV4s from US$50 per day. All prices exclude fuel, but have unlimited mileage.

Wemtec (☎0772221113; wemtec@source.co.ug; 14 Spire Rd) Well-known company based in Jinja but delivers countrywide. Hires a variety of Land Rovers with driver from around USh200,000. Prices all-inclusive (minus fuel), with no limits on mileage.

Ashiraf Mwanje (☎0777129345; ashmwanje31@gmail.com) This helpful professional driver knows all of Uganda, speaks several local languages as well as English and offers private tours with his own 4WD vehicle.

HITCHING

Without your own transport, hitching is virtually obligatory in some situations, such as getting into national parks. Most of the lifts will be on delivery trucks, usually on top of the load at the back, which can be a very pleasant way to travel, though sun protection is a must. There's virtually always a charge for these rides.

TAP WATER

Avoid drinking tap water in Uganda. Water that is bottled, boiled or filtered should be fine.

Hitching is never entirely safe, and we don't recommend it. Travellers who hitch should understand that they are taking a small but potentially serious risk.

LOCAL TRANSPORT

Kampala has a local minibus network, as well as special-hire taxis for private trips. Elsewhere you'll have to rely solely on two-wheel taxis, known as *boda-bodas* as they originally shuttled people between border posts: from '*boda* to *boda*'. Never hesitate to tell a driver to slow down if you feel uncomfortable with his driving skills, or lack thereof. Outside Kampala, there are few trips within any town that should cost more than USh3000.

Boda-Bodas

While *boda-bodas* are perfect for getting through heavy traffic, they're also notorious for their high rate of accidents. Most incidents occur as a result of reckless young drivers: the *New Vision* newspaper has reported that on average there are five deaths daily as a result of *boda-boda* accidents. If you decide to use their services, get a recommendation from your hotel for a reliable, safe driver. It's also *very* wise to find a driver with a helmet you can borrow, and to insist they drive slowly.

Detour: Democratic Republic of the Congo

☎243 / POP 81.7 MILLION

Includes ➡

Goma 495
Parc National Des Virunga 498
Bukavu 501

Best Places to Eat

➡ Au Bon Pain (p497)
➡ Le Chalet (p497)
➡ Nyumbani Lounge (p497)
➡ Village Fatimata (p497)

Best Places to Stay

➡ Mikeno Lodge (p500)
➡ Tchegera Island Tented Camp (p500)
➡ Bukima Camp (p500)
➡ Caritas Guesthouse (p495)
➡ Lake Kivu Lodge (p496)

Why Go?

Carpeted by huge swaths of rainforest and punctuated by gushing rivers and smoking volcanoes, the Democratic Republic of Congo (DRC, formerly Zaire) is the ultimate African adventure. As much a geographical concept as a fully fledged nation, DRC has experienced one of the saddest chapters in modern history, suffering a brutal 20th century of colonial exploitation, authoritarian madness and what has been dubbed Africa's first 'world war', which finally ended in 2003 with the rise of the Kabila political dynasty.

While real stability remains many years away, the cautious development of DRC's enormous untapped mineral wealth and the presence of the world's largest UN peacekeeping force have bred optimism among its tormented but resilient population. At the same time, a small but fast-growing tourism industry, centred on the incredible Parc National des Virunga, has seen travellers return to what is easily one of Africa's most thrilling – and challenging – destinations.

When to Go

Goma

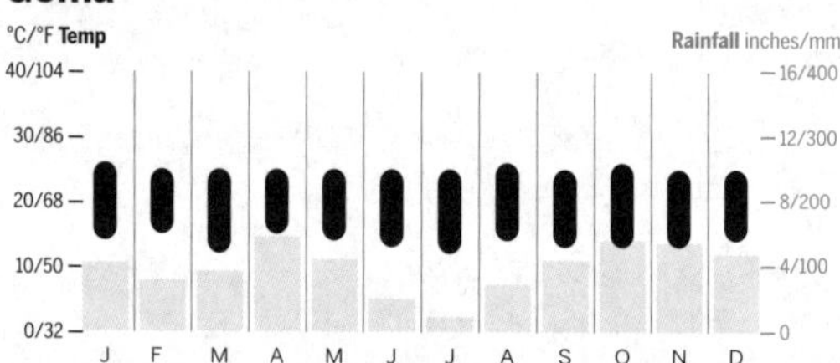

Dec–Mar Dry season for the north means slightly easier travel conditions.

Jan A good month to have the mountain gorillas totally to yourself.

Apr–Oct Dry season for the south and the best time to attempt overland routes across the country.

Goma

POP 1 MILLION

This likeable border town on Lake Kivu is unlike anywhere else in DRC, being home to an enormous UN and NGO presence that gives it an unusually cosmopolitan feel. Having been almost wiped off the map by the eruption of the nearby Nyiragongo volcano in 2002, Goma has done much rebuilding in the past decade and a half, and as a result the city has a surprisingly attractive centre. Indeed, it's fascinating to visit the parts of town that are covered in the lava field, and see how the resilient locals have gone back to their lives and rebuilt their houses in these new and challenging conditions.

People generally visit Goma en route to tracking mountain gorillas, climbing Nyiragongo or trekking in the Rwenzori Mountains. The city itself has no proper attractions, but it's a great pre- and post-Virunga hang-out, with some excellent sleeping and eating options.

Tours

Kivu Travel TOURS

(☎0992899667, in Belgium +32 495 58 68 07; www.kivutravel.com) A Belgian-Congolese company with an excellent reputation and great connections throughout the east, Kivu Travel has friendly and responsive staff who can help you plan most itineraries.

Okapi Tours & Travel TOUR COMPANY

(☎0994328077; www.okapitoursandtravel.org) Based in Goma, Okapi is run by Emmanuel and Bosco, who between them have a lot of experience and a vast network of contacts throughout eastern DRC. You can expect a high degree of friendly, personal advice.

Virunga Booking Office ADVENTURE, TOURS

(☎0991715401; www.visitvirunga.com; Blvd Kanyamulanga; ⌚8.30am-7pm Mon-Fri, 8.30am-12.30pm Sat) While most travellers book their Virunga adventures in advance, this helpful office in the centre of town is the place to come and book tours (including day trips) at the last minute.

Sleeping

Goma has a great range of sleeping options, from a few extremely basic guesthouses to luxurious lakeside properties with swimming pools and luscious gardens. Many visitors to Parc National des Virunga (p498) also base themselves in Goma and simply do day trips to the park, due to the high cost of accommodation there.

Caritas Guesthouse GUESTHOUSE $

(☎081679199; guesthousecaritas@yahoo.fr; off Ave de la Révolution; s/d from US$50/75; wi-fi) You've got a prime lakeside location here, including some lovely gardens, rooms with balconies and great views and a secure setting. The downside is the rather basic bathrooms and very unmemorable restaurant.

Hotel des Grands Lacs HOTEL $

(☎0997603103; hotelgrandslacs@gmail.com; Blvd Kanyamuhanga; r/apt US$30/60; P, air-con, wi-fi) Once Goma's grandest hotel, this colonial relic's grandeur has certainly failed, but its rooms are a great deal given their central location. The apartments have air-con, while wi-fi is only in the restaurant.

DRC FAST FACTS

Capital Kinshasa

Currency Congolese Franc (CDF), US dollar (US$)

Population 81.7 million

Languages French (official), Lingala, Swahili, Tshiluba

Money US dollars are accepted everywhere and moneychangers are omnipresent in DRC's cities. Somewhat reliable, internationally linked ATMs are common in the large cities.

Visas All visitors to DRC need visas, and they're not available on arrival. You must apply at the DRC embassy in your home country or country of residence.

Exchange Rates

Country	Currency	CDF
Australia	A$1	CDF1222
Canada	C$1	CDF1202
Eurozone	€1	CDF1932
Japan	¥100	CDF1479
NZ	NZ$1	CDF1140
UK	UK£1	CDF2188
US	US$1	CDF1571

For current exchange rates, see www.xe.com.

La Brise Guesthouse GUESTHOUSE $
(☎0998611089; labriseguesthouse@yahoo.fr; Ave la Corniche; r US$40-50;) This friendly budget hotel is right on the lake shore and offers clean, good-value rooms with mosquito nets. Room prices are determined by size and view calibre.

Detour: Democratic Republic of the Congo Highlights

❶ **Nyiragongo** (p498) Staring down in wonder at the lava lake of this magnificent active volcano is quite simply a once-in-a-lifetime experience.

❷ **Parc National des Virunga** (p498) Visiting the habituated mountain gorillas that thrive in the thick forests of Africa's oldest national park.

❸ **Parc National de Kahuzi-Biéga** (p501) Crossing gorgeous Lake Kivu to the friendly town of Bukavu, from where you can explore DRC's most overlooked national park.

❹ **Goma** (p495) Seeing Eastern DRC's capital is a fascinating experience – neither volcanic eruptions nor warlords can keep this survivor down!

Linda Hotel HOTEL $$
(☎0995487783; www.lindahotelgoma.com; Ave la Corniche; r US$60-80;) It's hard to miss this pink-painted lakeside compound, where a selection of seemingly randomly priced rooms is available. Despite a few eyebrow-raising art choices, rooms are exactly what you need in this price range and include mosquito nets, fridges, balconies and electric fans.

Lake Kivu Lodge HOTEL $$$
(☎0971868749; www.lackivulodge.com; Ave de la Paix; r US$130-180;) Goma's best hotel is some way out of the city centre, but makes the most of its gorgeous views over the lake. The cheapest rooms are on the small side and the bathrooms are in need of some work, but the standard-plus rooms come with some great extras including espresso machines, private gated terraces and four poster beds.

Ihusi Hotel HOTEL $$$
(☎0813129560; www.hotels.ihusigroup.com; 140 Blvd Kanyamuhanga; r incl full breakfast US$81-139;) Offering smart rooms across eight price categories and an open-air restaurant with sweeping views of Lake Kivu, the Ihusi is set in beautifully kept premises and is generally considered to be *the* place to stay in Goma. There's a large pool, tennis courts and gym.

Eating

You will eat well in Goma, where a large number of expats has ensured there are plenty of customers for a variety of eateries, ranging from formal dining in lakeside properties to more down-to-earth Congolese places in and around the city centre.

Mwajuma Shop SUPERMARKET $
(Blvd Kanyamuhanga; 8am-8pm Mon-Fri, 10am-8pm Sat) The best-stocked supermarket in Goma.

Le Petit Bruxelles INTERNATIONAL $
(Ave du Rond Point; mains US$7-13; noon-10pm Mon-Sat) Anything less like Brussels is a challenge to imagine, but this courtyard restaurant on a muddy street off Goma's central traffic roundabout does have a weird kind of charm all of its own. In the evenings, the barbecue is fired up and tasty seared steaks and cold beer are served up.

★Au Bon Pain BAKERY $$

(Ave Kanyamuhanga; mains US$9-15, sandwiches US$5; ⏰7am-7pm Mon-Sat, 10am-3pm Sun; 📶) The opening of this lifeline marked the beginning of a new era in Goma – and if that sounds like an exaggeration just look at the lovely pastries, the great coffee, the delicious sandwiches or the salads on offer. It's furiously popular at lunchtime, when you may have to wait for a seat.

To find it, look up – there's no sign at street level. It's on the 2nd floor, opposite the green Société Nationale d'Assurances building.

★Le Chalet INTERNATIONAL $$

(Ave de la Paix; mains US$12-18; ⏰11am-midnight; 📶) Ten minutes north of Goma's centre by *moto-taxi,* Le Chalet is a tranquil oasis of tropical gardens and calm, lakeside dining. The interesting menu runs beyond the standard meat dishes, and there's also excellent pizza from a wood-fired oven and good set-meal offers. Stick around after lunch for a spot of sunbathing and swimming.

The restaurant rents out kayaks and even a motorised pontoon (US$60 per hour), on which you can peek at the vast lakefront houses of DRC's political classes.

Nyumbani Lounge LEBANESE $$

(☎0829007748; Blvd Kanyamuhanga; ⏰6pm-midnight Mon-Thu, until 2am Fri-Sun; 📶🖉) With a menu that's more inventive than most you'll find in Goma, plus Levantine decor, comfortable banquettes and a large terrace that's perfect for al fresco dining or cocktail sipping, it's easy to see why this restaurant is so popular with expats. It's not easily spotted from the street, as it's on the 3rd floor of a commercial building.

Petit Paris FRENCH $$

(Chez Joseph; Ave des Mésanges; mains US$8-15; ⏰24hr) A charming and rightly popular place right in the middle of Goma's Quartier du Volcan, Petit Paris has busy main dining room, several smaller private rooms named after different French cities, a pool table and a bar where a good mix of locals and UN staff mix and enjoy the excellent Congolese-French cooking.

Village Fatimata BARBECUE $$

(☎0995636262; Ave Bougenvillier; mains US$12-17; ⏰9am-10pm) This is a good place to go for a taste of Congolese food and to escape the expat bubbles. Locals who come here for the grilled chicken, fish and goat ribs assure us it tastes better when washed down with a big, cold bottle of locally brewed Primus beer. The goat feast for six people costs US$28.

Drinking & Nightlife

There's much more going on in Goma after dark than in most cities in DRC – its large and wealthy expat community, vast UN workforce and people on NGO postings have to let off steam somewhere, although this tends to be in a private setting more than in a public one. Make friends with one expat in Goma and you'll quickly be able to find out what's going on; otherwise head to one of the nightclubs on Blvd Kanyamuhanga.

Chez Ntemba CLUB

(Blvd Kanyamuhanga; ⏰6pm-2am) This tiny place on Goma's main avenue is massively popular with a Congolese crowd who pack its mirrored-interior full come the weekends and spill out into the large 'garden' outside. It's sweaty, rough and ready – if possible go with locals or at least not alone.

Kivu Club CLUB

(Ave Bougenvillier; ⏰6pm-late, closed Tue) This large club is the main hang-out for Goma's expat partygoers. The empty swimming pool, red lighting and flat-screen TVs help make the whole place feel like a cross between a dilapidated hotel and a bar from a *Mad Max* film.

Shopping

Village des Artistes ARTS & CRAFTS

(Ave du Rond Point; ⏰7am-7pm) The Village des Artistes has a large and dusty selection of carved sculptures, wooden masks, ancestor figures, pots, drums, musical instruments and storage boxes. Don't be afraid to haggle.

Information

BIAC Bank (off Rond Point des Banques) Reliable ATM accepting international cards.

Raw Bank (Blvd Kanyamuhanga) Reliable ATM that accepts Visa and MasterCard.

Getting There & Away

Goma can be reached on daily flights from Kinshasa on **CAA Congo** (☎0820002776; www.caacongo.com; Goma International Airport) and

Congo Airways (☎0829781922; www.congoairways.com; Blvd 30 de Juin; ⏰8am–6pm Mon–Sat). There's also a connection four times a week to Addis Ababa on **Ethiopian Airlines** (☎0817006585; www.ethiopianairlines.com; Blvd du 30 Juin; ⏰8am–6pm Mon–Sat).

As the Rwandan border is just a couple of kilometres from the city centre, many people cross over from Gisenyi. The border crossing is very straightforward, with waiting buses and taxis leaving for Kigali as soon as you cross to the Rwandan side. Taxis wait on the DRC side of the border and will take you to anywhere in Goma for a few dollars.

Getting Around

Goma runs on SUVs, and it's a rarity to even see a normal-sized car on the street. For those without a driver, *moto-taxis* can be hailed anywhere in town and cost a flat fare of 500CDF.

Parc National Des Virunga

DRC's biggest single draw is this superb **national park** (☎0991715401; www.visitvirunga.org; Blvd Kanya Mulanga) – the first in Africa – which has been rejuvenated in recent years to offer a superb range of attractions. Trips here are normally focused on visits to the multiple groups of habituated mountain gorillas within the park, as well as to do the magnificent hike to the top of the active Nyiragongo volcano, where you can stare down into a bubbling lava lake in the massive crater below. However, there are many other activities on offer, including chimp treks, mountain climbing and birdwatching. This is Africa's hauntingly beautiful, beating heart and rarely is it possible to recommend somewhere so full-heartedly.

Having been the subject of the Oscar-nominated documentary *Virunga* in 2014, the park has been growing fast in popularity and its management team has risen to the challenge by impressively improving its accommodation and facilities. Do not miss this incredible place.

You'll either need to make arrangements directly with the park or book a tour with a travel agency to come to Virunga. Most tours begin and end in Goma, and due to the high cost of staying overnight in the park, many visitors base themselves in Goma and do day trips into the park. There is no public transport to the park and you'll need your own 4WD vehicle and driver to visit.

★Nyiragongo VOLCANO

(per person US$300) Perhaps DRC's most magnificent single sight, active volcano Nyiragongo soars above the city of Goma and the surrounding Virunga National Park and sends plumes of smoke into the sky, before becoming a flaming beacon visible for miles around after sundown. The trek to the top is an absolutely unmissable experience, with those who undertake the five-hour climb being rewarded with views into the volcano's explosive lava lake below.

Access to the volcano is only via travel agencies in Goma who arrange the trip through the Virunga National Park.

Senkwekwe Gorilla Orphanage WILDLIFE RESERVE

(⏰8am-4pm) Provided you make it back from your gorilla track in a timely fashion, it should be possible to visit the world's only mountain gorilla orphanage, which is integrated into the grounds of the Mikeno Lodge (p500). Named after the silverback who died defending the Rugendo group against gunmen in the infamous 2007 massacre, the orphanage is home to four gorillas, including Ndakasi and Ndeze, both massacre survivors.

Access to the orphanage is normally reserved for guests at the expensive hotel here – for whom it is free – but it may be possible to request a visit even if you're not a guest here; simply ask your travel agency to contact the Virunga National Park, which is also headquartered here.

Activities

All activities inside Virunga are run and strictly controlled by the **Institut Congolais pour la Conservation de la Nature** (ICCN; ☎0991715401; https://virunga.org/), which has overall control of Virunga and runs the park from its headquarters at Rumangabo.

Chimpanzee Tracking

Virunga park authorities offer chimp tracking near the headquarters at Rumangabo (US$100 per person). The habituated group consists of 12 individuals and chances of seeing them are generally excellent. Groups of four people leave Mikeno Lodge (p500) at 6am for the tracking and time with the group is limited to one hour. Unlike gorillas, chimps are fast moving, love to climb high into the canopy and are more wary of humans. This means you won't get as close

GORILLA TRACKING AT PARC NATIONAL DES VIRUNGA

There are few experiences in the world more memorable than coming face to face with a wild eastern mountain gorilla, and this is one the best places in the world for it. There are fewer than 900 mountain gorillas left in the world, and they are under constant threat from poachers who have massacred their numbers over the years.

There are six habituated families in Parc National des Virunga, and you will be assigned a group to visit by the rangers based on how many people are tracking and the current location of each group. The largest family, the Kabirizi, has 32 individuals and offers excellent opportunities to see infants and rambunctious youngsters. The Humba and Mapuwa groups are also sizeable families, each with 16 individuals. Humba is a ranger favourite because of the easy-going nature of the dominant silverback. The smaller groups, Rugendo, Munyaga and Lulengo, have about eight members each and are only visited when there are four or fewer trackers.

No matter which family you are assigned, you can expect a magical encounter, although this will differ from day to day, group to group and depending on the mood of the silverback. The ideal time to meet a gorilla family is from 10am to 11am (which means a 5.30am departure from Goma) when they will have finished foraging and are settling for a mid-morning rest. Youngsters are typically lively at this time, bounding over older siblings, climbing trees and generally annoying their parents as they relax. Older gorillas can often be seen grooming one another, sucking ants off twigs and climbing trees. The silverback will be doing whatever he damn well pleases.

The Trek

An entourage of armed rangers, trackers and a guide accompanies each group. The trackers leave at daybreak, locating the gorillas and radioing in their position so you won't have to climb every volcano in the Virunga massif in search of them. The machine gun–toting rangers are there for your protection and are standard practice in the park today.

All treks leave from one of three patrol posts, the most popular and the only one with accommodation is Bukima, the closest to Goma. If you arrive from the Ugandan border, you will most likely trek from either Jomba or Bikenge.

The treks can range from a 30-minute, sunny stroll to a five-hour ordeal up steep hills covered in dense forest in freezing cold rain. You need to be prepared for both.

The Encounter

Because gorillas are so genetically akin to humans, ICCN has imposed a number of strict rules to help minimise the chance of a disease jumping the species barrier and infecting the apes. Just like in Rwanda and Uganda, you will not be able to visit the gorillas if you are sick, nor will you be able to go to the toilet, eat, cough or blow your nose in their presence. But unlike in Rwanda and Uganda, you will also be required to wear a face mask to further reduce the potential for unwittingly transmitting a disease.

Visits are restricted to one hour and flash photography is banned. Your guide will tell you how to act while around the gorillas. Do exactly what they say, including the part about squatting low, eyes downcast in the face of a charge. Once you see the size of an adult silverback you will realise how difficult this will be.

Practicalities & Costs

You can arrange gorilla tracking with any travel agency or directly with the **Parc National des Virunga** (p498). The permit alone costs US$400 per person, and on top of that you'll need to pay for transport to and from Bukima. Visitor numbers are strictly limited, so it's a good idea to book your tracking well in advance, although obtaining permits is not generally as competitive as in Rwanda or Uganda is. Packages average around US$600 per person.

to a wild chimp as you will to a mountain gorilla, but don't let this deter you. This is a rare chance to meet our closest evolutionary cousins.

Climbing Nyiragongo Volcano

Beautiful and brooding, Nyiragongo Volcano (p498) is feared and respected by the people of Goma, over which is towers.

Having destroyed half the city in 2002, the volcano certainly deserves its reputation, but it's actually perfectly safe to climb as its serious eruptions can be reliably predicted. Those who do undertake the five-hour climb (US$300 per person) are rewarded with views from the crater's rim, down into the earth's smouldering heart and the world's largest lava lake. Wrapped up warm while watching the fiery glow of the lava light up the night sky is an incredibly surreal and utterly unforgettable display of the awesome power and scale of nature.

PREPARATION

As Nyiragongo's summit stands at 3468m, with a short but impressively steep section near the top, you will need to be moderately fit to tackle this beast. Guides and armed security are included with your permit, but consider hiring your own porter (US$12 per day; maximum weight carried 15kg) and cook (US$15 per day) at the small ranger post at the start of the climb.

Warm clothing is essential; nights are extremely cold on the summit and gloves, hats, fleeces and thick socks will go a long way towards making your experience more enjoyable. Do also ensure you have dry clothes to change into once you reach the summit, as you'll be sweating from the climb but soon freezing, which means you have a chance of catching hypothermia if you remain in wet clothes.

THE CLIMB

The hike to the rim is just 8km, but takes between four and six hours and is done in five stages. A walking stick is very useful (particularly on the steep descent) and you can buy one whittled by park employees for US$5 at the ranger post where you sign in. Climbers need to leave by 10am to ensure they reach the top by nightfall – do not be late as you will not be able to climb.

Accommodation on top, which is included in the permit cost, is in one of the super-simple A-frame shelters built on the crater's rim. Each one has two mattresses and two pillows, so you will need to bring your own sleeping bag (these can be rented from ICCN (p498) for US$5). Most commonly people come on a package that includes a chef, who will cook you dinner and breakfast the next day. This is a much better prospect than having to carry supplies up the volcano yourself.

Sleeping

All accommodation inside the national park is run by ICCN (p498), and while there are some superb accommodation options, sadly Virunga is not budget friendly at present. Most budget travellers base themselves in Goma and travel up to the park on day trips rather than spending the big bucks on the park lodge at Mikeno. There is talk of the park building more budget-friendly accommodation at Jomba near the Ugandan border and at Kibati, the starting point for Nyiragongo treks.

★Mikeno Lodge LODGE $$$
(☎0991715401; www.mikenolodge.com; s/d & tw incl meals US$316/450; P ☎) Easily the most luxurious and beautifully designed hotel in DRC, Mikeno Lodge is a pampering slice of bliss in the wilds of the Congo jungle. Each of the 12 vast bungalows is made of dark volcanic stone, rich mahogany and beautifully crafted thatched roofs. Inside they boast a cosy lounge, open fire and a bathroom with a stone-lined shower.

Meals are taken at the equally impressive main lodge, where an enormous terrace allows you to look directly into a forest canopy alive with colobus and blue monkeys. Food is excellent, service is attentive and there's even a gorilla orphanage (p498) on-site. In short, treat yourself.

Tchegera Island Tented Camp CAMPGROUND $$$
(☎0991715401; www.visitvirunga.org; per person incl full board US$216) Miles from the volcanic landscapes of Virunga proper, horseshoe-shaped Tchegera Island is in Lake Kivu, but officially also part of the national park (p498). It's an absolutely gorgeous place for kayaking, birdwatching and relaxing after climbing Nyiragongo, and the comfortable tents have their own hot-water bathrooms. A park permit and return boat transfer from Goma costs an additional US$100.

Bukima Camp TENTED CAMP $$$
(☎0991715401; www.visitvirunga.org; Bukima; s/d incl meals US$316/450) This magical spot is also the departure point for many of Virunga's gorilla-tracking excursions, which means you'll be able to sleep later by staying here. The campsite consists of eight luxurious tents with their own bathrooms, a large communal dining shelter

and some stunning views towards the mountains.

Getting There & Away

All transfers within the park are done with a military escort, and convoys to and from Goma (two hours' travel) are common in order to reduce the number of soldiers needed. Transfers are usually included with packages, but can also be ordered directly with ICCN (p498), the national park authorities. Bad roads make journeys long and not particularly comfortable.

Bukavu

POP 807,000

Bukavu is nestled along the gorgeously contorted shoreline at the southern tip of Lake Kivu, and is a pleasant and friendly town that boasts some of DRC's most attractive architecture, although this is best seen from the water. Bukavu is also the base for visiting the Parc National de Kahuzi-Biéga, Virunga's little-known neighbour, where you can track habituated eastern lowland gorillas (Grauer's gorillas) at relatively low prices.

Sights

★Parc National de Kahuzi-Biéga NATIONAL PARK
(☎English enquiries 0971300881, French enquiries 0822881012; http://kahuzibiega.wordpress.com) South Kivu's star attraction is this national park, where you can track habituated eastern lowland gorillas (Grauer's gorillas) for just US$400 per person, a relative bargain! The park also contains a chimp orphanage at Lwiro (US$30 per person), where between 40 and 50 chimps are kept in excellent conditions.

It's often possible to get gorilla permits for same-day hiking, and never a problem to get them with a few days' notice. Lodge Co-Co is the best place to arrange a trip. The starting point is at Tshivanga, 30km northwest of town. *Moto-taxis* there and back cost about US$20 to US$30, while hiring a taxi costs US$80.

It's also possible to arrange guides at the park to take you on some excellent hikes up the mountains (US$100 per day).

Idjwi Island ISLAND
Floating out in the middle of Lake Kivu, Idjwi Island is, at 340 sq km, the second-largest lake island in Africa. Isolated from Congo's decades of war, as well as missing out on what little development the mainland has seen, Idjwi is a wonderful place to escape the modern world, enjoy nature and the rich island culture. Lodging is available in small guesthouses and the speedboat between Bukavu and Goma stops here on request.

Sleeping

While tourists are a rarity these days, Bukavu once saw lots of visitors and has a number of well-established hotels. These are concentrated in the wealthier upper town near the Rwandan border, rather than downtown around the dock.

Esperance Guest House B&B $
(☎0999941197; lhenkinbrant@hotmail.com; 8 Ave Pangi, Ibanda; d incl breakfast US$40; wifi) There are only two rooms at the friendly little Esperance Guest House – and they both share a bathroom – but everything is kept polished and clean, and a good dinner is available for US$10 extra. Call ahead. Taxi drivers will know the nearby Hotel Horizon.

★Orchids Safari Club RESORT $$$
(☎0813126467; www.orchids-hotel.com; Ave Lt Dubois; s US$145-190, d US$180-225; P air-con @ wifi) This impressive hotel has gorgeous gardens overlooking the lake and the feel of a colonial-era country club. The rooms are spacious and very well appointed, with private terraces, smart furnishings, comfortable beds and large bathrooms.

Lodge Co-Co GUESTHOUSE $$$
(☎0993855752; www.lodgecoco.com; Ave Muhumba; s/d US$120/150; wifi) This Swiss-run guesthouse is the baby of Carlos, who has been tracking gorillas in the national park for decades. His love for the creatures shines through: each room features his gorilla photographs and the corridors are stuffed with local arts and crafts. It's an excellent base for anyone wanting to visit the gorillas with a true expert.

Eating

Karibu CONGOLESE $
(☎0993097044; off Ave Muhumba; mains US$5-13; ⏲9am-11pm) This fun and friendly bar and restaurant has a decidedly hip feel, with a crowd of locals around the pool table, a garden decorated with empty beer bottles and fairy lights, and a shop selling upcycled clothes with a Congolese touch. The menu

is of Congolese standards, as well as good pizza. It's in a side street behind the Horizon Hotel.

★ Orchids Safari Club Restaurant FRENCH $$$

(www.orchids-hotel.com; Ave Lt Dubois; mains US$20-30; ⏲7am-10pm; ❄📶) This smart restaurant inside the Orchids Safari Club (p501) hotel sees a scramble at lunchtime to bag one of its few lake-facing tables, and the views are well worth coming early for. The food is classical French cuisine with a few regional influences and local dishes.

ℹ Getting There & Away

Several boats a day connect Bukavu with Goma. Spend either US$15 for a spot on the shadeless, grossly overcrowded deck of a ferry (eight to 10 hours) or splurge US$50 for a *canot rapide* (speedboat; three hours). The latter is highly recommended, and runs in both directions twice a day. The scenery on the journey is gorgeous.

The road from Bukavu to Kisangani is terrible and not particularly safe, and so it's only advisable to arrive by air, boat or overland from Rwanda. **Kamembe Airport** (Aéroport de Kavumu), in the small town of Kavumu, 33km northwest of Bukavu, offers fights twice a week to Kinshasa via Goma.

Crossing into Rwanda from Bukavu is a cinch – take a taxi to the border (US$5) and then pick up onward transport to Kigali on the other side.

UNDERSTAND THE DEMOCRATIC REPUBLIC OF THE CONGO

DRC Today

Despite several years of progress and a relatively high degree of stability following the collapse of the M23 rebellion in 2013, DRC currently finds itself in the grip of a constitutional crisis that threatens to upset the all-too-fragile status quo. Under the DRC constitution, which sets a two-term limit to the presidency, incumbent president Joseph Kabila was due to step down in December 2016 having completed his second term as president. Rather than amending the constitution to do away with term limits, as has been done in several neighbouring countries, Kabila managed to persuade the country's electoral commission to postpone the elections due in late 2016 until early 2018, claiming that it was not possible to hold them sooner due to an inaccurate voter register. The DRC's highest court meanwhile ruled that Kabila could remain in office until the elections can be held, provoking popular fury that erupted into violence and demonstrations in Kinshasa and other large cities following the announcement in September 2016.

DRC's neighbours are now nervously watching events unfold, as it's clear that Kabila has no intention of relinquishing

OKAPI WILDLIFE RESERVE

Created to protect prime habitat of its bizarre namesake mammal, the okapi, this is one of the biggest parks in DRC. In addition to the okapis (*Okapia johnstoni*, also known as the forest giraffe), there are 17 resident primate species here and a fairly healthy elephant population. Combine this with excellent guided forest hikes (ranging from a few hours to several days) led by the Mbuti (pygmies) and the result is one of the best places in Central Africa to get the real genuine jungle experience – at least that was the case until the middle of 2012.

In June of that year a major attack on the park headquarters at Epulu and nearby villages by *mai-mai* (community) militia left six people dead, including park rangers. Thirteen okapi were killed and hundreds of people were forced to flee the area. A further attack by the same militia in 2015 saw the Zunguluka guard post burned down, and sadly at the moment it's not possible to visit this incredible place. For the latest news and for information about a possible reopening, check out www.okapiconservation.org.

If the security situation improves significantly enough to allow visitors again, then the road between Kisangani and Beni, which passes by the reserve, has been upgraded but there are still some horrendous sections. Allow at least a full day to travel from either Beni or Kisangani to Epulu – longer in the wet season.

power. Many fear another war is likely, if not inevitable. Indeed, DRC has never had a peaceful transfer of power in its history and so the end of the Kabila dynasty was seen by many as key to bolstering the country's titular democracy. Even though the divided opposition is ineffective, the tide of popular anti-government feeling is enormous, making it look rather unlikely that a peaceful solution will be found. In the meantime DRC needs effective government more than ever, with massive problems at almost all levels of society – from illiteracy and malnutrition to soaring HIV infection rates, endemic corruption, militia activity and crushing poverty.

Culture

Though DRC plays host to more than 250 ethnic groups (and over 700 different languages and dialects), four tribes dominate. The Kongo, Luba, Mongo and Mangbetu-Azande groupings collectively make up 45% of the population.

Half the population practises Roman Catholicism, while 20% are Protestant and 10% Muslim. The remaining 20% follow traditional beliefs or a religion that merges Christianity with indigenous ideas, such as Kimbanguism. Founded by faith-healer Simon Kimbangu in 1921 – that same year Belgian authorities, fearing his popularity, sentenced him to life in prison – it now has three million adherents.

Environment

Encompassing 18 different ecoregions and blanketing the greater part of the Congo River basin, DRC is Africa's most biologically rich country. Savannah covers much of the south and there's 37km of coast on the Atlantic, but tropical rainforests – home to all manner of creatures found nowhere else in the world, including bonobo and okapi – dominate the ecological scene.

The eastern border runs through a cornucopia of geological wonders, including Lake Tanganyika, the second-deepest lake in the world, and several other Great Rift Valley waters; the Rwenzori Mountains, which exceed 5000m; and several active volcanoes.

WARNING

Although rebel armies continue marauding around parts of DRC's east, these days most places are safe most of time. But this is a country where anything can happen, from rebellion to riots to volcanic eruptions. It's imperative to get up-to-the-minute information before travelling here.

SURVIVAL GUIDE

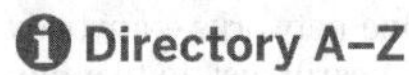

Directory A–Z

DANGERS & ANNOYANCES

DRC is fraught with potential danger, and almost any government website will warn you against travel here. This is alarmist, however: be sensible, ask for and follow local advice, keep your wits about you and you should be absolutely fine. There are, however, a large number of things to consider and be aware of.

There are still rebel armies and bandits (plus government soldiers, who are often just as dangerous) terrorising people in large swaths of northern and eastern DRC. North Kivu province around the city of Beni was particularly unstable at the time of writing. Political unrest is another danger: late 2016 saw violence that left many people dead in several cities in DRC, including Kinshasa.

Though the situation is improving, police and other officials, particularly those working in customs and immigration, frequently request money, though they rarely demand it. In all cases, being calm, friendly and confident is your best play. Do all you can to avoid handing over your passport (present copies instead) since it might cost you to get it back.

Photography in towns and cities across DRC attracts attention and should only be done if you're sure it's safe. The best plan is to ask a local, and if in doubt, don't take the photo. Travellers have been arrested for taking photos in Kinshasa and other towns. In the countryside things are generally easier, but avoid taking photos within sight of police.

ELECTRICITY

220V/50Hz; the European two-pin plug is the most common

EMERGENCY & IMPORTANT NUMBERS

There is no nationwide number for medical emergencies, so dial the nearest hospital in case of emergency.

DRC country code	243
Police	112
Fire	118

INTERNET ACCESS

Internet access in DRC is frustratingly slow. Very few hotel wi-fi networks actually work, and when they do they're incredibly slow. The most reliable internet access can be had via local mobile phone networks – anybody can register for a SIM card; just go to a mobile provider's office with your passport.

MONEY

US dollars are accepted everywhere and moneychangers are omnipresent in DRC's cities. Somewhat reliable, internationally linked ATMs are common in the large cities.

ATMs

Internationally linked ATMs are now common in Goma and Kisangani, though it's not unknown for them to run out of money or be out of order, so always carry back-up cash.

Cash

The local currency, the Congolese franc (CDF), is worthless outside of DRC. CDF1000 – just under one US dollar – is currently the biggest bill commonly available (though CDF5000 notes do exist), resulting in a big bundles of banknotes when you change money. For that reason most people pay for bigger items in US dollars.

Five-dollar US bills and upwards are fine; they just need to be clean and unmarked (not necessarily pristine). One-dollar notes are not usually accepted, so just use CDF1000 notes instead (it's widely accepted that US$1 is equal to CDF1000, despite it actually being slightly more).

Credit Cards

Credit cards are accepted in many DRC hotels, restaurants and upper-end shops, but fraud is a problem so cash is still best.

Changing Money

Moneychangers work on nearly every block of every city in DRC. They all change US dollars, plus sometimes euros and currencies from nearby countries. Rates are invariably better than the banks, but check your notes carefully.

Exchange Rates

Country	Currency	CDF
Australia	A$1	CDF775
Canada	C$1	CDF776
Eurozone	€1	CDF1116
Japan	¥100	CDF964
NZ	NZ$1	CDF731
UK	UK£1	CDF1295
US	US$1	CDF1028

For current exchange rates, see www.xe.com.

Tipping

Tipping is expected in smarter restaurants – around 5% to 7% is normal. Taxi drivers do not expect tips, though some will ask for one. It's a good idea to keep a stash of small bills (CDF500 is good) to tip with.

OPENING HOURS

Banks and offices 8.30am–3pm Monday to Friday, 8.30am–noon Saturday

Shops 8am–6pm Monday to Saturday

Restaurants noon–10pm

Bars 6pm–midnight

POST

The postal system in DRC remains unreliable and is not worth your time – if you need to send anything use a courier service such as FedEx or DHL.

PUBLIC HOLIDAYS

New Year's Day 1 January

Martyrs of Independence Day 4 January

Heroes' Day 16–17 January

Easter March/April

Labour Day 1 May

Liberation Day 17 May

Independence Day 30 June

Parents' Day 1 August

Christmas Day 25 December

TELEPHONE

Landlines are virtually extinct in DRC, with mobile phones having totally superseded them. There are no area codes.

Country code	+243
International access code	00

SIM cards cost very little in DRC and can be purchased from one of the major mobile-phone providers, including Airtel, Tigo and Vodacom. When going to buy one, be sure to bring your passport and go to an official office of the operator, rather than buying a SIM card from a street hawker. Only official vendors can register your SIM, which is necessary before it can be used.

TIME

Western DRC (including Kinshasa) is on GMT/UTC plus one hour, while eastern DRC (including Goma) is GMT/UTC plus two hours.

VISAS

The exact requirements for visas vary from embassy to embassy, but in general you will need proof of hotel booking, yellow fever vaccination and a legalised letter from a sponsor in DRC. Visa fees tend be between US$100 and US$200, and normally require several weeks to be processed.

The only current alternative to getting a visa at home is the two-week, single-entry tourist visa issued for people visiting Parc National des Virunga. The cost of this visa is US$105, and on top of that you'll need to purchase a mountain-gorilla trek permit, a Nyiragongo trek permit or accommodation at the Mikeno Lodge in order to get the paperwork issued. The visa limits you to visiting North Kivu province, and is issued on arrival, though all the bookings need to have been made several weeks in advance. See http://visitvirunga.org for more information.

Getting There & Away

Rwanda Whether you're heading to Goma or Bukavu, normally crossing from Rwanda couldn't be any easier. Transport from Kigali to the border towns of Gisenyi and Cyangugu is frequent, and from there you just walk into DRC and hire a *moto-taxi* to take you to your destination in town. In the case of Gisenyi, you cross directly into the city of Goma, and can even walk to your hotel.

Uganda The principal route to Uganda is from Beni to Kasindi, where you walk over the border and get another taxi to Kasese. Tour guides in Kisoro sometimes take clients across at Bunagana to see Parc National des Virunga's gorillas at Djomba.

Getting Around

Getting around the DRC can be a slog. The transport network is virtually nonexistent, there are danger areas to be avoided and even getting a visa can give you a migraine. So it's no surprise, then, that some travellers find it easier to just let someone else organise everything for them. The following tour companies are highly recommended and can help with everything from obtaining a visa to organising a full expedition down the Congo River.

Go Congo (☎0811837010; www.gocongo.com)

Kivu Travel (p495)

Okapi Tours & Travel (p495)

Rwanda

☎250 / POP 13 MILLION

Includes ➡

Kigali............... 507
Musanze (Ruhengeri).........517
Volcanoes National Park 520
Gisenyi (Rubavu) 527
Huye (Butare)....... 530
Nyungwe Forest National Park 534
Cyangugu (Rusizi)... 538
Kibuye (Karongi) ... 539
Akagera National Park 541

Best Places to Eat

- Heaven Restaurant (p515)
- Brachetto (p515)
- Sol et Luna (p514)
- Calafia (p529)
- Nehemiah's Best Coffee (p533)

Best Places to Stay

- Rwiza Village (p540)
- Five Volcanoes Boutique Hotel (p540)
- Bisate Lodge (p526)
- Virunga Lodge (p519)
- Cormoran Lodge (p540)

Why Go?

Rwanda is known as Le Pays des Mille Collines (Land of a Thousand Hills) thanks to the endless mountains in this scenically stunning little country. Nowhere are the mountains more majestic than the Virunga volcanoes in the northwest, and hidden among the bamboo forests are some of the world's last remaining mountain gorillas. For a change of scene, the shores of Lake Kivu conceal some of the best inland beaches on the continent, while Nyungwe Forest National Park protects extensive tracts of montane rainforest, and is home to many primates. But it's not all monkey business – Kigali, the capital, is safe and sophisticated.

Sure, Rwanda's name may evoke memories of the horrific genocide that brutalised this country in 1994, but it's all over and the country has embraced a promising and dynamic future. Rwanda remains stable, tourism is once again a key contributor to the economy, and you'll feel absolutely welcome.

When to Go

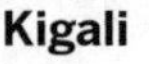

Kigali

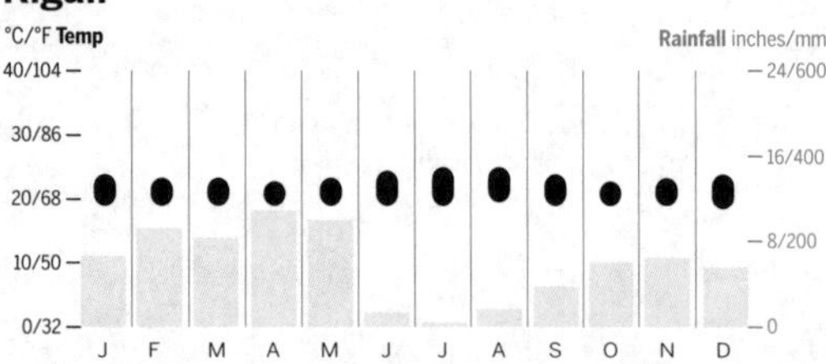

Jun–Aug & mid-Dec–mid-Mar Perfect climate for national parks and gorilla/chimp tracking.

Sep Baby gorillas are named during the Kwita Izina ceremony; ideal for hiking.

Apr–May Can by rainy, but fewer travellers means gorilla permits are easier to obtain.

Rwanda Highlights

1 Volcanoes National Park (p520) Hiking the forested slopes of the Virungas for a close encounter with mountain gorillas and golden monkeys.

2 Nyungwe Forest National Park (p534) Hacking through steamy rainforests in search of colobus monkeys and chimpanzees.

3 Kigali Genocide Memorial (p509) Confronting the horrors of the genocide at this haunting museum and memorial.

4 Ethnographic Museum (p532) Watching an Intore dance performance at the finest museum in the country, in Huye (Butare).

5 Kibuye (p539) Kicking back on the sandy shores of Lake Kivu with views of the islands out in the bay at this much-overlooked resort town.

6 Akagera National Park (p541) Going on safari in this quickly replenishing national park, where you can spot the Big Five.

7 Gisenyi (p527) Relaxing at one of the beach resorts, kayaking on Lake Kivu or cycling the Congo Nile trail.

KIGALI

POP 1.2 MILLION

Spanning several ridges and valleys, Kigali, with its lush hillsides, flowering trees, winding boulevards and bustling streets, is arguably one of the most attractive capital cities in Africa, as well as easily one of the cleanest and safest.

Despite bearing the brunt of the genocide's unspeakable horrors in 1994, Kigali has been the centre of Rwanda's nation-building efforts since that time and has seen massive amounts of state and foreign investment pouring in over the past two decades. Indeed, the rebirth of the capital has seen a cosmopolitanism arrive in the city and Kigali now boasts a slew of new skyscrapers, several international hotels and a host of excellent eating options. Few people leave Kigali without being impressed by this plucky and charismatic survivor. And being right in the centre of the country, it's a great base from where to organise your trip around Rwanda.

History

Kigali was founded in 1907 by German colonists, but did not become the capital until Rwandan independence in 1962. Although Rwandan power was traditionally centred on Huye (Butare), Kigali was chosen because of its central location. Walking Kigali's streets today, it is hard to imagine the horrors that unfolded here during those 100 days of madness in 1994, when an estimated one million Tutsis and moderate Hutus were systematically killed by the extremist Hutu militia, the Interahamwe.

RWANDA FACT FACTS

Area 26,338 sq km

Capital Kigali

Currency Rwandan franc (RFr)

Population 13 million

Languages Kinyarwanda, English, French

Money Most banks in larger towns have international ATMs. Credit cards are accepted at most tourist hotels. Bring US dollars or euros.

Visas Nearly all visitors require a visa for Rwanda, and as of January 2018 all nationalities can get one on arrival.

Exchange Rates

Australia	A$1	RFr663
Canada	C$1	RFr652
Europe	€1	RFr1048
Japan	¥100	RFr802
New Zealand	NZ$1	RFr618
UK	UK£1	RFr1187
USA	US$1	RFr851

For current exchange rates, see www.xe.com

Roadblocks, manned by the militia, were set up at strategic points throughout the city and tens of thousands of Rwandans were bludgeoned or hacked to death. People swarmed to the churches in search of sanctuary, but the killers followed them there and showed a complete lack of mercy or compassion.

While all of this horror took place for days and nights on end, the UN Assistance Mission for Rwanda (UNAMIR) stood by and watched, held back by the bureaucrats and politicians who failed to grasp the magnitude of what was unfolding and dithered over whether to get involved or not. In its defence, UNAMIR was bound by a restrictive mandate that prevented it from taking preliminary action, though it has been argued that more deliberate action could have saved untold lives.

After 10 Belgian peacekeepers were murdered at the start of the genocide, the Belgian government withdrew its contingent, leaving UNAMIR to fend for itself with a minimal mandate and no muscle. There was little the 250 troops that remained could do but watch, and rescue or protect the few that they could.

Even more unbelievable is the fact that a contingent of the Rwandan Patriotic Front (RPF) was holed up in the parliamentary compound throughout this period, a legacy of the Arusha 'peace' process. Like the UNAMIR troops, there was little they could do to stop such widespread killing, though they did mount some spectacular rescue missions from churches and civic buildings around the city.

When the RPF finally swept the *génocidaires* from power in early July 1994, Kigali was wrecked, much of the city's buildings were destroyed, and what little of the population remained alive were traumatised. As the Kigali Genocide Memorial so aptly puts it, Rwanda was dead.

Remarkably there are few visible signs of this carnage today. Kigali is now a dynamic and forward-looking city, the local economy is booming, investment is a buzzword, and buildings are springing up like mushrooms. In fact, so complete is the rebirth of the city that it's hard to imagine the events of the early 1990s happening here at all, which makes the various monuments and memorials to the genocide even more important.

Sights

★**Kigali Genocide Memorial** MEMORIAL
(☎0788309898; www.kgm.rw; KG 14 Ave; ⊙8am-4pm) FREE In the span of 100 days, an estimated one million Tutsis and moderate Hutus were systematically butchered by the Interahamwe army. This memorial honours the estimated 250,000 people buried here in mass graves and also has an excellent exhibition that tries to explain how it was that the world watched as the 1994 genocide unfolded. This is an intensely powerful and moving memorial for which you should dedicate at least half a day.

The informative audio tour (US$15) includes background on the divisive colonial experience in Rwanda. As the visit progresses, the exhibits become steadily more powerful, as you are confronted with the crimes that took place here and moving video testimony from survivors. If you have remained dispassionate until this point, you'll find that it will all catch up with you at the section that remembers the children who fell victim to the killers' machetes. Life-sized photos are accompanied by intimate details about their favourite toys, their last words and the manner in which they were killed.

The memorial concludes with sections on the search for justice through the international tribunal in Arusha as well as the local *gacaca* courts (traditional tribunals headed by village elders).

Upstairs is a moving section dedicated to informing visitors about other genocides that have taken place around the world and helping to set Rwanda's nightmare in a historical context.

After you've absorbed the museum displays, take a rose (by donation) to leave on one of the vast concrete slabs outside that cover the mass graves. There's also a wall of names, a rose garden, a gift shop and a pleasant cafe serving good coffee, lunch buffets (RFr2500), snacks and juices that is an ideal place to reflect and gather yourself before facing the outside world again.

Remembrance and Learning Tours across Rwanda can also be arranged through the Kigali Genocide Memorial.

It is located in the northern Kisozi district of the capital, which is a short *moto-taxi* ride from the centre (about RFr500).

Inema Arts Center GALLERY
(☎0783187646; www.inemaartcenter.com; KG 563 St; ⊙8am-6pm) FREE Opened in 2012, the privately run Inema Arts Center is a collective of 10 resident artists and guests. It's quickly established itself as the foremost modern art gallery in Kigali. As well as paintings, sculptures and contemporary takes on traditional crafts, there are dance and music performances several days a week and courses. Much of the art is for sale (and can be shipped internationally), but if you're not buying, you're welcome just to admire. There's a small on-site cafe.

Museum of Natural History MUSEUM
(☎0788573310; www.museum.gov.rw; KN 90 St; adult/child incl guide RFr6000/3000; ⊙8am-6pm) Kigali's best museum has exhibits on Rwanda's natural wonders and is housed in the 1907 residence of explorer Richard Kandt, reputed to be the first building in Kigali. The view from the garden is sensational and, looking over the urban sprawl, it's hard to imagine that it all started with this rather modest home. Few *moto-taxi* drivers have heard of the museum. Ask for Richard Kandt's house instead.

Nyanza Genocide Memorial MEMORIAL
(KK 15 Rd, Kicukiro; ⊙8am-5pm Mon-Fri) FREE Located in Kicukiro, a suburb southeast of the city centre towards the airport, there is little to see at this memorial other than the tiled tops of four mass graves believed to contain the remains of the 4000 Tutsis who took refuge in the Ecole Technique Officielle (ETO) grounds, and numerous unmarked wooden crosses.

Presidential Palace Museum MUSEUM
(☎0738742026; www.museum.gov.rw; KK 38 Ave, Kanombe; adult/child incl guide RFr6000/3000; ⊙8am-6pm) This former presidential palace on the eastern outskirts of the city has few exhibits, but it's interesting to explore, with 'secret' rooms and an odd presidential nightclub. Wreckage from Juvenal Habyarimana's presidential plane can still be seen where it was shot down – just over his garden wall. The perpetrators were never caught, but this act proved to be a rallying call for Hutu extremists and helped trigger the genocide.

Hotel des Mille Collines HISTORIC SITE
(Hotel Rwanda; ☎0788192530; www.millecollines.rw; KN 6 Ave) The inspiration for the film *Hotel Rwanda*, this still-functioning luxury

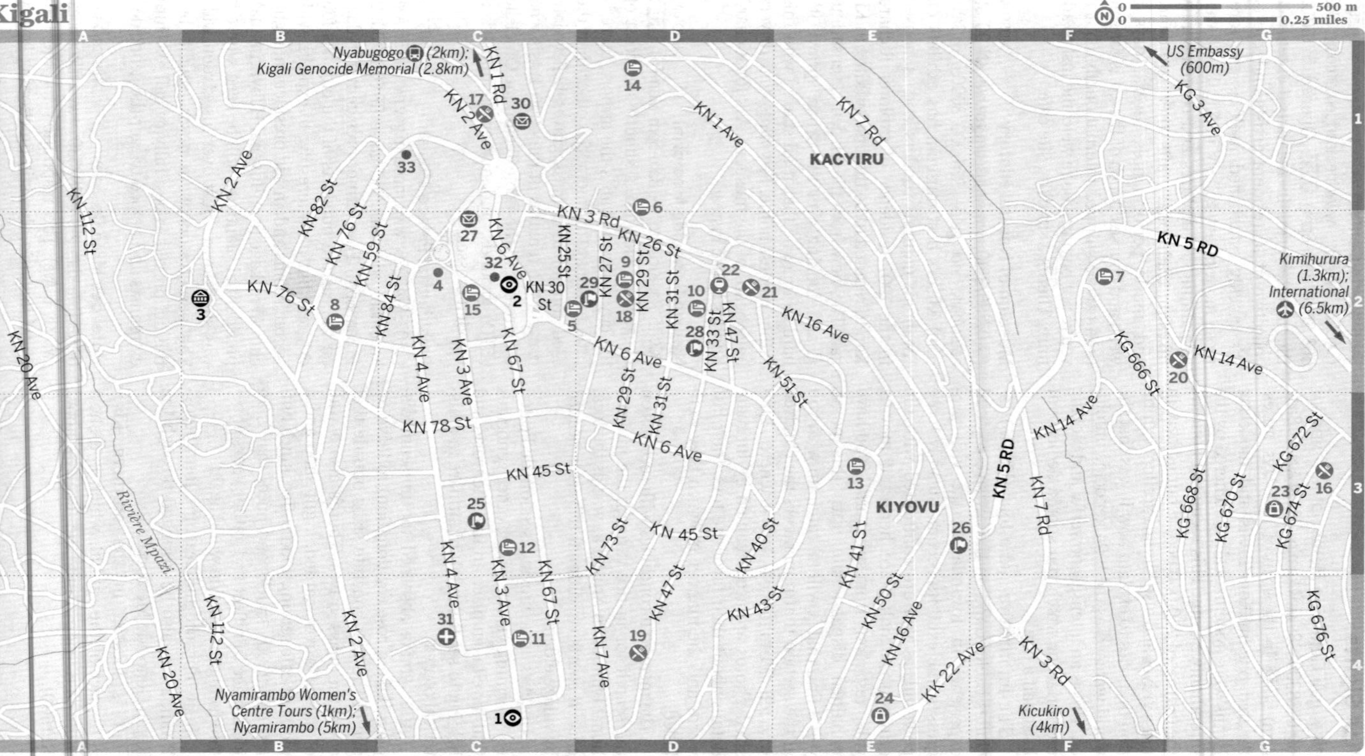
Kigali
0 500 m
0 0.25 miles
Nyabugogo (2km); Kigali Genocide Memorial (2.8km)
US Embassy (600m)
KG 3 Ave
KN 1 Rd
KN 2 Ave
KN 1 Ave
KN 7 Rd
KACYIRU
KN 112 St
KN 2 Ave
KN 82 St
KN 76 St
KN 59 St
KN 84 St
KN 76 St
KN 3 Rd
KN 26 St
KN 6 Ave
KN 25 St
KN 27 St
KN 29 St
KN 31 St
KN 30 St
KN 33 St
KN 47 St
KN 16 Ave
KN 5 RD
Kimihurura (1.3km); International (6.5km)
KG 666 St
KN 14 Ave
KN 20 Ave
KN 4 Ave
KN 3 Ave
KN 67 St
KN 6 Ave
KN 51 St
KN 78 St
KN 29 St
KN 31 St
KN 6 Ave
KN 14 Ave
KN 45 St
KIYOVU
KN 5 RD
KN 7 Rd
KG 668 St
KG 670 St
KG 672 St
KG 674 St
Rivière Mpazi
KN 45 St
KN 73 St
KN 40 St
KN 41 St
KN 47 St
KN 43 St
KN 50 St
KN 112 St
KN 2 Ave
KN 4 Ave
KN 3 Ave
KN 67 St
KN 7 Ave
KN 16 Ave
KK 22 Ave
KN 3 Rd
KG 676 St
KN 20 Ave
Nyamirambo Women's Centre Tours (1km); Nyamirambo (5km)
Kicukiro (4km)
A
B
C
D
E
F
G
1
2
3
4

Kigali

Sights
1 Camp Kigali Memorial C4
2 Hotel des Mille Collines C2
3 Museum of Natural History B2

Activities, Courses & Tours
4 RDB City Tour C2

Sleeping
5 5 Swiss Hotel C2
6 Centre Saint Paul D1
7 Discover Rwanda Youth Hostel F2
8 Gloria Hotel B2
9 Heaven Boutique Hotel & the Retreat D2
Hotel des Mille Collines .... (see 2)
10 Iris Guest House D2
11 Kigali Serena Hotel C4
12 Marriott C3
13 Park Inn by Radisson E3
14 Step Town Motel D1
15 Ubumwe Grande C2

Eating
16 Afrika Bite G3
17 Fantastic Restaurant C1
18 Heaven Restaurant D2
19 New Cactus D4
20 Shokola Cafe G2
21 Zaaffran D2

Drinking & Nightlife
22 Dolce D2

Shopping
23 Abraham Konga Collections G3
24 Caplaki E4

Information
25 Belgian Embassy C3
26 Canadian High Commission E3
27 DHL C2
28 French Embassy D2
29 German Embassy D2
30 Main Post Office C1
31 University Teaching Hospital of Kigali C4

Transport
32 Brussels Airlines C2
Ethiopian Airlines .... (see 27)
Kenya Airways .... (see 27)
KLM .... (see 27)
33 Qatar Airways C1
RwandAir .... (see 27)
Turkish Airlines .... (see 4)

hotel was owned by the Belgian airline Sabena in 1994. At the time of the genocide, the hotel's European managers were evacuated and control was given to local employee Paul Rusesabagina, who used his position to hide fleeing Tutsis and moderate Hutus, thus saving hundreds of lives.

Camp Kigali Memorial MEMORIAL
(KN 3 Ave; 8am-5pm) FREE The 10 stone columns you find here mark the spot where 10 Belgian UN peacekeepers were murdered on the first day of the genocide. Originally deployed to protect the home of moderate Prime Minister Agathe Uwilingiyimana, the soldiers were captured, disarmed and brought here by the Presidential Guard before being killed. Each stone column represents one of the soldiers and the horizontal cuts in it represent the soldier's age.

Tours

★ **Shadows of Africa** SAFARI
(0787067939, 0788356266; www.shadowsofafrica.com) Friendly and competent, this operator is easily one of the most professional tour companies in the country. The owner, Paul Ruganintwari, is a mine of local knowledge and can arrange all kinds of customised tours throughout Rwanda at competitive prices. He can also help book hotels. It also has branches in Tanzania, Kenya and Uganda – perfect if you want to combine several countries.

★ **New Dawn** CULTURAL
(0788558880; www.newdawnassociates.com; 1-4 people US$120) This well-run venture is a pioneer in community-based tourism in Rwanda and organises a life-enriching Millennium Village Tour for those who want to understand the post-genocide reconciliation process. During the one-day excursion, you'll visit a crafts centre, a farm, a school and a village where you'll meet survivors and perpetrators of the genocide, who will share their testimonies.

Terra Incognita Ecotours SAFARI
(0788385111; www.ecotours.com) A reputable outfit aiming at the midrange and upper end of the market. They do all the classic Rwandan trips.

Nyamirambo Women's Centre Tours TOURS
(0782111860; www.nwc-umutima.org; KN 7 Ave; per person RFr15,000, lunch RFr3000) The Nyamirambo Women's Centre (a local

NYAMATA & NTARAMA GENOCIDE MEMORIALS

During the genocide, victims fled to churches seeking refuge, only to find that some of the clergy was providing information to the Interahamwe. As a result of this lack of compassion, some of the most horrific massacres took place inside the sanctums of churches throughout Rwanda.

In **Ntarama church** (7am-5pm) FREE, about 25km south of Kigali, more than 5000 perished. The church has not been touched since the genocide ended and the bodies were removed. Today there are many bits of clothing scraps as well as skulls placed on shelves, and three mass graves next to the church.

Nyamata church (7am-5pm) FREE, about 30km south of Kigali, is a deeply disturbing genocide memorial where some 50,000 people died. Today the skulls and bones along with clothing scraps of the many victims are on display. While the visual remains of the deceased are a visceral sight, their inclusion here is to provide firm evidence to would-be genocide deniers.

Both of these memorials can be visited on a day trip from Kigali. From Nyabugogo bus terminal, take a bus or a *moto-taxi* to Nyanza bus terminal in Kicukiro, from where you can take a City Express bus to Ntarama or Nyamata (both RFr400).

self-help group) runs fun and interesting 2½-hour tours of the lively Nyamirambo area of the city. Tours take in the local market, a hair salon, the local mosque, tailors and music shop, among others. The tour finishes with a local lunch. It's a good way to get an insider's view of a non-touristy side of the city.

RDB City Tour HISTORY
(Rwanda Development Board; 0788313800; www.rwandatourism.com; KG 9 Ave; per person with own transport US$20, with RDB transport US$40; departs 8am or 2pm) Requiring a minimum of two people, this three-hour tour includes the Kigali Memorial Centre (p509), as well as a few other prominent buildings around town. It's not amazing value given the memorial currently has no entry charge, but the guides are very knowledgeable and can give a local's perspective on the capital. Tours leave from the RDB office.

Festivals & Events

Kigali Up MUSIC
(www.kigaliup.rw; RFr5000; Jul or Aug) Kigali's annual music festival features world music, blues, funk and roots artists from around the globe.

Rwanda Film Festival FILM
(www.rwandafilmfestival.net; Sep) The Rwanda Film Festival, otherwise known as Hillywood to locals, runs in cinemas around the city in September, showcasing new Rwandan film.

Sleeping

★ **Discover Rwanda Youth Hostel** HOSTEL $
(0782265679; www.discoverrwanda.hostel.com; KN 14 Ave; camping US$10, 4-/6-bed dm US$20/18, s with shared bathroom US$24-30, d/tw with shared bathroom US$45/42, d US$60; P@) This well-maintained backpackers' hostel set in verdant grounds offers a very sociable atmosphere, plenty of tours and excursions, and good-value meals. Accommodation-wise, there's something for everybody, from four- to six-bed dorms with shared bathrooms to private en suite rooms. And yes, there's even a small grassy area set aside for campers. There's a branch in Gisenyi.

Centre Saint Paul GUESTHOUSE $
(0252576371; cnpsaintpaul@yahoo.fr; off KN 3 Rd; s RFr17,000-24,000, d RFr24,000-40,000; P) This central Catholic Church–run complex has four blocks of spartan and simply furnished but serviceable rooms set around a well-manicured garden. Each room has its own bathroom, mosquito net and a small desk (presumably for reading your Bible at). Only breakfast and lunch meals are available.

★ **Gloria Hotel** HOTEL $$
(0785363180, 0788930233; www.gloriahotelrwanda.com; KN 59 St; s/d from US$70/90; P) This excellent, central midrange place appears sometimes to spill over into top end with its lavish buffet breakfast served in the gorgeous open-sided restau-

rant and charming staff that seem genuinely happy to see you. The rooms are fresh and modern with comfortable mattresses and neat carpets, and some come with balconies. One grumble: no lift. Brilliant value (by Kigali standards).

5 Swiss Hotel HOTEL $$
(☎0785511155; www.5swisshotel.com; KN 25 St; s US$100-130, d US$120-150; P❄📶) An attractive, secure compound in a residential area, this efficiently run haven of peace occupying a low-slung building is one of Kigali's most solid options, with 14 rooms that are well appointed and clean as a whistle. All have a private terrace or a balcony that opens onto a flourishing garden. There's an on-site restaurant with a limited menu.

Garr Hotel HOTEL $$
(☎0783831292; www.garrhotel.com; KG 9 Ave; s/d/tw US$95/110/130; P❄📶🏊) Head and shoulders above much of the competition in this price range, this homely hotel has large and rather classically styled rooms with wood furnishings and quality beds. It's in a smart part of town (but it's a long way from the city centre) and there's an on-site restaurant. The small swimming pool at the back of the garden is another nice touch.

Iris Guest House GUESTHOUSE $$
(☎0788465282, 0785806300; www.irisguesthouserw.com; KN 33 St; s/d/tw US$75/93/100; P📶) The Iris is a popular midrange guesthouse in Kigali. Although the furnishings in the 17 smallish rooms have seen better days, this place has that certain something that travellers can't get enough of. In short, it's a combination of friendly staff, good food (the attached restaurant specialises in French-influenced cuisine) and quiet, well-tended rooms. The pleasingly leafy little garden is another plus.

Step Town Motel HOTEL $$
(☎0785005662; www.step-town.com; KN 1 Ave; s/d US$55/65; P📶) Not far from the city centre, and down a quiet dusty lane (and a very steep hill!), this place, with its decent rooms and prim bathrooms, offers reasonable value by Kigali standards, especially if you can score a room with city views. There's also a garden terrace and a small bar-restaurant.

Hôtel Chez Lando HOTEL $$
(☎0788385300; www.chezlando.com; KG 201 St; s/d/tw US$71/94/118, bungalows & pavilions s/d US$118/153; P📶) A Kigali institution out in the suburb of Remera, the spotless rooms here are in well-proportioned single-storey units dotted around a lush garden. It's not worth paying extra for one of the pavilions or bungalows as the standard rooms are similar in style and comfort. Overall it's a pretty good deal, although it's slightly out of the way.

★Heaven Boutique Hotel & the Retreat BOUTIQUE HOTEL $$$
(☎0737886307; www.heavenrwanda.com; KN 29 St; s US$115-165, d US$145-195, Retreat s US$575-775, d US$675-875; P❄📶🏊) This American-run boutique hotel is a breath of fresh air in Kigali. The rooms are divided between three in the same building as the attached restaurant and 11 more recent rooms in a purpose-built villa just a little down the road, plus 11 opulent suites in the Retreat. Rooms are stylish and colourfully decorated and the welcome is warm. A gem.

Kigali Serena Hotel LUXURY HOTEL $$$
(☎0788184500; www.serenahotels.com; KN 3 Ave; d from US$240; P❄📶🏊) One of the top hotels in town, the Serena is still one place we never hear a bad word about. As inviting as the rooms and restaurants are, we think the real selling points are the hotel's impressive pool complex surrounded by greenery, and the congenial, relaxed atmosphere. Of all Kigali's top-end options, the Serena has the strongest African feel.

Marriott BUSINESS HOTEL $$$
(☎0222111111; www.marriott.com; KN 3 Ave; d from US$160; P❄📶🏊) You know exactly what you'll be getting at the sprawling Marriott: impersonal yet shiny-clean rooms and a host of top-notch facilities, including four restaurants, a fairly small swimming pool, a business centre, gift shops, a spa and a gym. Most rooms enjoy superb city views and there's a lovely garden in which to relax.

Park Inn by Radisson HOTEL $$$
(☎0788132500; www.parkinn.fr/hotel-kigali; KN 41 St; s/d from US$140/160; P📶🏊) You certainly won't fall in love with this mammoth, Y-shaped establishment with a colourful facade, but it's stocked with loads of amenities, including a (small) swimming pool, a gym, a restaurant, two bars and a disco. Service is prompt yet discreet, while the rooms (four categories) are good value for

the quality of bedding, the warmth of design and the overall size.

Ubumwe Grande BUSINESS HOTEL $$$
(☎0788165700; www.ubumwegrandehotel.com; KN 67 St; s US$190-240, d US$230-280; P❄📶🏊) Perched on a hill, this modern high-rise has the most dramatic city views you could ever hope for. The 153 rooms are spacious, elegantly restrained and come with a contemporary colour scheme (think grey, chocolate and beige), but the real steal is the uber-cool rooftop terrace, bar and pool. Extra inhouse perks include a good restaurant and a gym.

Hotel des Mille Collines HISTORIC HOTEL $$$
(☎0788192530; www.millecollines.rw; KN 6 Ave; s/d US$260/280; P❄📶🏊) Welcome to the real Hotel Rwanda. While a colonial South African hotel was used in the movie, the real deal is more of a motel-like construction that shelters neat but unexciting and petite rooms. Apart from its historical aura, the hotel's greatest attributes are the well-maintained pool in a beautifully landscaped garden and the excellent poolside restaurant and bar.

Eating

The dining scene in Kigali is increasingly sophisticated. There's some great local food available and, despite Rwanda's current dislike of all things French, locals still love French food and wine. All this means that eating in Kigali is generally far more rewarding than in many of the Anglophone East African countries.

Fantastic Restaurant RWANDAN $
(☎0788500278; KN 2 Ave; buffet RFr2300; ⊙11am-midnight) This colourful eatery overlooking a busy thoroughfare has excellent, speedy service and has become deservedly popular for its monster-sized, brilliant-value, all-day buffet specialising in Rwandan staples. There's live music on weekends from 7.30pm.

Afrika Bite RWANDAN $
(☎0788503888; KG 674 St; buffet RFr3500; ⊙noon-3pm & 6.30-10.30pm) This homely restaurant set in a villa surrounded by an enticing garden offers a great opportunity to sample Rwandan food at its finest. Lunch and dinner buffets are popular (come early).

★ **Pili-Pili** INTERNATIONAL $$
(☎0788585800; www.facebook.com/pilipilirwanda; KG 303 St; mains RFr5000-9000; ⊙5-11pm Mon, noon-1am Tue-Sun; 📶) Sassy Pili-Pili ticks all the right boxes: a vast open-air terrace with superb views, a nifty pool, an enticing ethnic chic two-storey interior and a congenial atmosphere. It's a popular bar and restaurant, known for its knockout burgers, grills, pizzas, salads and vast choice of drinks; it heats up to club temperature on weekend nights when DJs spin electronica and other beats.

★ **Sol et Luna** ITALIAN $$
(☎0788859593; www.soleluna-rwanda.com; KN 5 Rd; mains RFr4000-8000; ⊙6.30-10pm Mon, noon-3pm & 6.30-10pm Tue-Fri, noon-10pm Sat & Sun) Many locals and expats rave about this Italian kitchen, and we share their unbridled enthusiasm. The food here (and the trattoria-inspired decor, with a lovely open-air terrace) is clearly above average for Rwanda, with an assortment of flavoursome Italian dishes, including over 100 different pizzas! Something sweet to finish? Try the tiramisu.

★ **Zen** ASIAN $$
(☎0733503503; www.zenkigali.com; KG 9 Ave; mains RFr5500-9000; ⊙noon-3pm & 6-11pm Mon-Fri, noon-11pm Sat & Sun; 📶) With tinkling fountains and covered courtyard dining, this sublime restaurant offers Kigali's best Asian meals as well as Rwanda's first sushi dishes. This is where the well to do of Kigali come when they want to impress. It's a long way out of the city centre in a swanky neighbourhood.

★ **New Cactus** FRENCH $$
(☎0788678798; KN 47 St; mains RFr5000-9000; ⊙noon-2pm & 6-10.30pm; 📶) This attractive hacienda is set on a ridge where you can soak up the sparkling lights of Kigali by night or get a bird's-eye appreciation of the city during the day. It boasts a broad menu of French favourites as well as bounteous wood-fired pizzas and succulent pastas. For something different, try one of the delicious, spice-rich Congolese dishes.

Zaaffran INDIAN $$
(☎0783042504; KN 16 Ave; mains RFr5000-9000; ⊙11am-3pm & 5.30-11pm) There are a few excellent Indian restaurants in Kigali and Zaaffran, we reckon, is the pick of the lot. The menu is classic North Indian – tan-

dooris, tikkas, biryanis and masalas are all there, plus a few surprises – while the service is refreshingly earnest.

★ Brachetto ITALIAN $$$
(☎0787178133; KG 5 Ave; lunch buffet RFr7500-9500, mains RFr12,500-15,500; ⏲11.30am-2.30pm & 6-9.30pm Mon-Fri, 6-9.30pm Sat; 📶) Run by an Italian chef, this upmarket venue wouldn't be out of place in Milano, and gets top marks for its flawlessly prepared Italian specialties, including toothsome pasta dishes, risotto, grills, gourmet sandwiches and divine desserts (hmm, the dark chocolate mousse). It's also known for its great lunch buffet, which features a tempting selection of salads and desserts.

★ Heaven Restaurant INTERNATIONAL $$$
(☎0788486581; www.heavenrwanda.com; KN 29 St; mains RFr8000-16,000; ⏲7am-10.30pm Mon-Fri, 10am-10.30pm Sat & Sun; 📶) A highlight of the Kigali restaurant scene, Heaven has a relaxed, open-air deck bistro with a wide-ranging menu drawing from a variety of international influences. It's hugely popular with expats and travellers, so look elsewhere for local atmosphere, but do come here for an excellent and innovative menu that combines local flavours with international dishes. The weekend brunch (RFr12,600) is very popular.

Sakae ASIAN $$$
(☎0786597824; www.facebook.com/SakaeJapaneseRestaurant; off KG 270 St; mains RFr6000-12,000; ⏲10am-3pm & 6.30-11pm Mon-Sat) Set in an all-wood dining room, this widely acclaimed restaurant serves an exquisite selection of authentic Japanese, Korean and Chinese dishes – those in the know claim that the Beijing duck is among the very best this side of the Himalaya. Service is prompt and efficient.

Drinking & Nightlife

The good folk of Kigali take their drinking and partying pretty seriously and there are a number of decent bars around town, some of which turn into clubs as the night wears on. Most restaurants also double as bars. Kigali is generally an exceptionally safe place, which makes going out at night a relaxed affair, though take care after dark, as you would anywhere in Africa.

Dolce BAR
(KN 35 St; ⏲noon-midnight) Dolce ticks all the cool boxes: a great terrace with good city views, a congenial atmosphere, an enticing interior, plenty of cold beer, tasty brochettes (from RFr1000) and acceptable pizzas.

K-Club CLUB
(KG 9 Ave; Sat & Sun RFr5000; ⏲10pm-3am Mon-Thu, to 5am Fri-Sun) The general consensus is that K-Club is currently the best spot in town for a night out and come the weekends (the only time admission is charged), it's packed with a young and well-off crowd enjoying the cheap drinks, flashy atmosphere and air-conditioned dance floor. Dress up if you plan to join them.

Shopping

Local arts and crafts make for popular souvenirs and can be bought at many hotels and markets. You may also find yourself being offered items for sale by individuals on the street. Do be sure to check out the Inema Arts Center (p509) in Kigali for some impressive local art pieces.

Abraham Konga Collections ARTS & CRAFTS
(☎0785561626; www.abrahamkonga.com; KG 672 St; ⏲9am-9pm Tue-Sun) Abraham Konga is a jewellery designer who upcycles discarded materials to create necklaces and earrings of high quality. You'll also find basketware, woodcarvings, curios, clothing and *imigongo* paintings.

Caplaki ARTS & CRAFTS
(Coopérative des Artisans Plasticiens de Kigali; KK 2 Ave; ⏲8am-6pm) This association of more than 40 stalls has banded together to market itself as Caplaki, although each stall is an independent business. As you would expect, there is a great selection of Rwandan handicrafts on sale, but you'll also find lots of carvings and masks from the DRC, banana-fibre products from Uganda and items from Kenya.

Information

DANGERS & ANNOYANCES

By African standards Kigali is an exceptionally safe place. You have nothing to worry about walking around the city during the daytime. Even at night you'll normally be absolutely fine walking the streets, although do exercise basic precautions such as avoiding dark streets on your own or walking through shanty towns unaccompanied.

INTERNET ACCESS

Internet access is widespread and very cheap in Kigali. All but the cheapest hotels offer free wi-fi, as do many of the more upmarket cafes and restaurants. The Rwandan government is halfway through implementing a plan to provide free wi-fi in all public spaces across the city (and eventually across the country), but for most travellers the easiest option will be to purchase a SIM card with a data package from a local mobile phone provider such as MTN or Airtel.

MEDICAL SERVICES

Adventist Dental Clinic (0788777720; KG 567 St; 8am-6pm) About 3.5km from the centre of town in Kacyiru district, this place is run by an international dentist based in Kigali. If you can't find it, ask for the nearby Umubano Hotel.

King Faisal Hospital (0252588888; www.kfh.rw; KG 544 St) One of the best-equipped hospitals in Kigali. It underwent a major renovation in 2017.

University Teaching Hospital of Kigali (0252575462; KN 4 Ave, Kivoyu) The main state-run hospital in Kigali.

MONEY

Money is easy to get and easy to change throughout Rwanda and particularly in Kigali. There are ATMs at virtually every bank, most of which accept foreign credit cards, as well as foreign-exchange bureaus.

POST

DHL (Union Trade Centre, KN 4 Ave; 8am-5pm) Expensive but necessary if you need to send anything internationally.

Main Post Office (KN 1 Rd; 7am-5pm Mon-Fri, to 1pm Sat) In the centre.

TOURIST INFORMATION

Rwanda Tourism Information Centre – RDB (Rwanda Development Board; 0788313800; www.rwandatourism.com; KG 9 Ave, Kigali; 7am-5pm Mon-Fri, 8am-noon Sat & Sun) Rwanda's tourist authority has friendly staff who can help travellers make reservations to track the gorillas and golden monkeys at Volcanoes National Park as well as chimps at Nyungwe Forest National Park and various other activities around the country. Also runs Kigali city tours (from US$20 per person).

Getting There & Away

AIR

International airlines fly in and out of Kigali International Airport (p552), which is at Kanombe, 10km east of the city centre.

BUS

Several bus companies operate services to major towns and these are safer and less crowded than local minibuses. The **Nyabugogo bus terminal** (KN1 Rd), about 2km north of the city centre, is a bustling place where each bus company has a separate office and, in general, destinations and fares are listed on the wall of each office. The station is easily reached by *moto-taxi*. Buses usually depart from outside the office you bought your ticket at, but double-check. Most bus services dry up around mid-afternoon.

Capital Express Half-hourly departures for Kibuye (Karongi; RFr2500, 3½ hours) via Gitarama (RFr930, one hour).

Different Express Heads to the town of Gatuna, on the border with Uganda, every half hour (RFr1400, three hours).

Horizon Express To Nyanza (Nyabisindu; RFr1670, two hours) and Huye (Butare; RFr2510, three hours) every half hour.

Jaguar Executive Coaches Operates four daily buses to Kampala (Uganda; RFr8000 to RFr10,000, nine hours).

Kigali Safaris To Musanze (Ruhengeri; RFr1750, three hours) every half hour until 6.30pm.

Omega Express Hourly to Kibuye (Karongi; RFr2500, three hours) and Cyangugu (Kamembe; RFr5200, six hours).

Select Express Buses to the Rwanda–Tanzania border crossing of Rusumo (RFr3200, 3½ hours) every half hour.

Simba Coach Has a 5pm bus to Nairobi (Kenya; RFr27,000, 22 hours).

Stella To Kayonza (RFr1430, two hours) every half hour.

Trinity Express Operates seven daily buses to Kampala (Uganda; RFr10,000, nine hours) and a 4am bus to Dar es Salaam (Tanzania; RFr30,000, about 40 hours).

Virunga Express Good buses to Musanze (Ruhengeri; RFr1750, two hours) and Gisenyi (Rubavu; RFr3000, three hours) every half hour.

Volcano Express Reliable operator for Huye (Butare; RFr2510, 2½ hours) and Nyanza (Nyabisindu; RFr1670, 1¾ hours) every half hour.

CAR

Beyond Transport (0788356266; beyondtransport79@gmail.com; per day incl driver & fuel US$60-150; by reservation) This very reputable operator has excellent cars at competitive prices. A 4WD with driver and fuel well set you back US$150. For a RAV4, you'll pay between US$60 and US$80, including driver and fuel. Prices are negotiable.

Jean-Paul Birasa (☎0788517440; birasa jeanpaul@yahoo.fr; per day US$50-85, driver RFr20,000-25,000) If you just need a car and driver, Jean-Paul Birasa can organise no-frills car and jeep rental (the jeeps are small 4WDs such as a RAV4, which is fine for anywhere in Rwanda). For a driver, add RFr20,000 to RFr25,000 per day.

Getting Around

MINIBUS

Minibuses cruise the streets looking for passengers. All advertise their destination in the front window and run to districts throughout the city. They charge a flat price of RFr200.

MOTO-TAXI

These small Japanese trail bikes can be a swift way to get around Kigali and, unlike in many other parts of Africa, helmets are provided. Short hops are just RFr300 to RFr500, while trips out to the suburbs cost RFr700 to RFr1000.

TAXI

Taxis are not metered but a fare within the city centre costs, on average, RFr3000 to RFr4000, and double that out to the suburbs or later at night. A trip to the airport costs a standard RFr10,000.

NORTHWESTERN RWANDA

A formidable natural border between Rwanda, Uganda and the DRC, the Virunga volcanoes are where Rwanda really earns its nickname as the Land of a Thousand Hills. Home to the mighty mountain gorillas, the Rwandan Virungas are protected by Volcanoes National Park, the undisputed highlight of the country. The region is also home to the tranquil town of Gisenyi (Rubavu) on the sandy shores of Lake Kivu, Rwanda's top spot for a beach holiday. This may be the most developed part of the country for travellers, but you'll rarely feel overwhelmed by groups and will definitely remain a novelty for the friendly locals.

Musanze (Ruhengeri)

POP 86,700

For most travellers, Musanze (Ruhengeri) is the preferred staging post for the magnificent Volcanoes National Park, one of the best places in East Africa to track mountain gorillas. Since permit holders are required to check in at the park headquarters in nearby Kinigi at 7am on the day of tracking, staying in Musanze is a much safer and easier option than leaving from Kigali at the crack of dawn.

Musanze is a pleasant enough town to explore on foot, and it's situated near a number of interesting natural sights, with the massive Virunga volcanoes looming to the north and west.

Sights

Dian Fossey Gorilla Fund International – Karisoke Research Centre MUSEUM

(www.gorillafund.org; NR 4 Rd; 9am-4pm) FREE Right in the centre of Musanze, this high-quality research centre features an exhibit that comprises interpretive panels about mountain gorillas and the conservation efforts that Dian Fossey pioneered. It also shelters Dian Fossey artefacts, a 3D interactive model of the Virunga mountains and casts of real gorilla noseprints. Overall it makes a perfect introduction to a visit to the gorillas.

Nkotsi Village VILLAGE

(Nkotsi/Muko Village) Nkotsi village (also known as Muko) is a small village 7km southwest of Musanze. It's home to the **Red Rocks** (☎0789254315; www.redrocksrwanda.com; camping US$6-10, s/d US$20/30, safari tents s/d US$30/45, all with shared bathroom; P) camping and hostel, which, through the Hands of Hope organisation and Amahoro Tours (p518), organises a lively and interesting package of cultural activities open to all. These range from basket-weaving demonstrations (free) to learning how to brew (and yeah okay, drink) banana beer (US$25). Other activities include village walks (US$10), bee keeping (US$30), drumming lessons (US$25) and learning about traditional medicine (US$30).

It's best to arrange all activities in advance through either Red Rocks or Amahoro Tours.

Musanze Caves CAVE

(off NR 4 Rd; US$50) These four caves, 2km from the town centre along the road to Gisenyi, were created when different lava flows joined to create the Albertine Rift Valley. Bat roosts are a significant feature of the caves, as are huge roof collapses that create vast arrays of coloured light shafts.

Musanze (Ruhengeri)

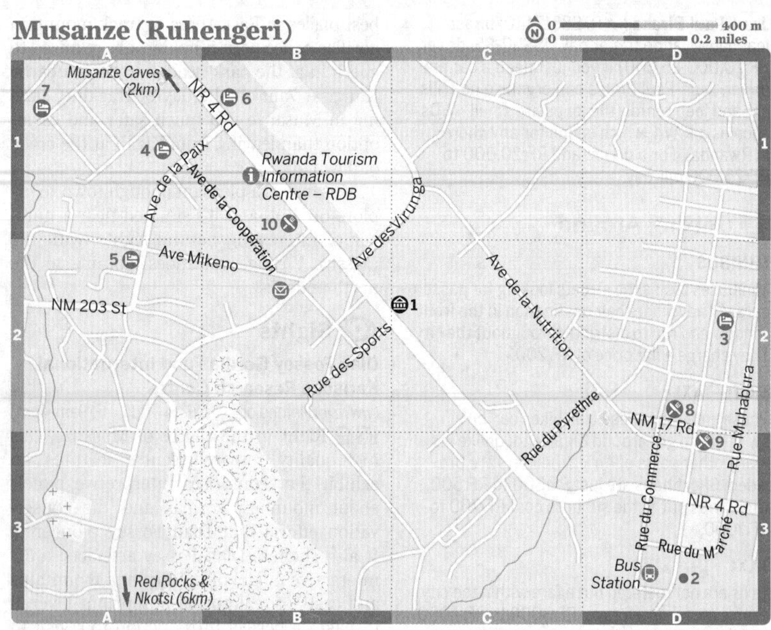

Tours

Kingfisher Journeys CANOEING
(☎0783811918; www.kingfisherjourneys.com; US$40; ⊙by reservation) This very well-run venture organises excellent canoeing trips down the Mukungwa River near Musanze. It's a great opportunity to soak up the rural atmosphere around Musanze and spot plenty of birds, including ibis, egrets, cranes, hammercocks, paradise flycatchers and weavers. Trips last about four hours and are guided. Prices include transfers.

Amahoro Tours CULTURE
(☎0788655223; www.amahoro-tours.com; ⊙by reservation) A small, locally run operator that can help arrange gorilla-tracking permits, cultural activities and homestays in the surrounding area at reasonable prices. The office is unsigned and down a small dirt alleyway behind the brick 'COODAF' building, near the bus station.

Sleeping

Volcano View Bed & Breakfast B&B $
(☎0784876354, 0788821820; www.volcanoviewrw.com; NM 222 St; d RFr30,000-34,000; P📶) Set in peaceful gardens two blocks off the main road in a residential neighbourhood, this appealing hideaway is run by Jane, who goes out of her way to make you feel at home. There are three comfy, airy and bright rooms and a relaxing lounge area. Meals can be arranged on request (RFr5000). It's a 20-minute walk northeast of the centre.

Amahoro Guesthouse – Red Rocks GUESTHOUSE $
(☎0788594521, 0784424866; www.amahoro-guesthouse.com; NM 20 St; camping US$10, dm/s/d US$15/35/50; P📶) Run by the excellent Amahoro Tours, Amahoro Guesthouse is the best budget place in town. The rooms are painted in bright, primary colours and there's a fresh, young feel to the place. There are three doubles with private facilities, two three-bed rooms that share a common bathroom, one four-bed dorm and two tents in the diminutive garden.

★ **La Locanda** B&B $$
(☎0782637996; www.lalocandarwanda.com; NM 215 St; s US$40, d US$60-80; P📶) This adorable guesthouse run by a helpful Italian resident is one of those whispered secrets that are passed around by word of mouth. The nine rooms in three brick villas are simple yet impeccably clean and colourful, and the welcoming lounge area is a good place to relax. Excellent meals (US$12) are also available. Brilliant value.

Musanze (Ruhengeri)

Sights

1 Dian Fossey Gorilla Fund International – Karisoke Research Centre C2

Activities, Courses & Tours

2 Amahoro Tours D3

Sleeping

3 Amahoro Guesthouse – Red Rocks D2
4 Garden House A1
5 Home Inn A2
6 Hotel Muhabura B1
7 La Locanda A1

Eating

8 Isange BF Restaurant D2
9 La Paillotte D3
10 Volcana Lounge B1

Garden House GUESTHOUSE **$$**
(☎0788405760, 0788427200; emgardner1@yahoo.co.uk; NM 202 St; s/d US$60/80; P Wi-Fi) This English-Rwandan-run guesthouse in a beautifully converted villa has five cute rooms with double glass doors giving views of the large, leafy gardens. The hosts are extremely kind, the dogs friendly and the breakfast, which consists of homemade breads, jams, fresh fruits and local honey, is as good as you'll get anywhere in Rwanda.

Home Inn HOTEL **$$**
(☎0788343127; www.homeinnhotel.com; NM 203 St; d/tw US$70/90; P Wi-Fi) Painted an alarming shade of apricot, the Home Inn has 17 fresh and bright rooms with 'gorgeously' garish bedspreads. The tiled bathrooms are spotless and many rooms have their own balcony that catches a refreshing breeze. Peaceful location. There's an on-site restaurant.

★ **Five Volcanoes Boutique Hotel** BOUTIQUE HOTEL **$$$**
(☎0789924969; www.fivevolcanoesrwanda.com; RN 8; d US$400-530; P Wi-Fi Pool) This is the best top-end option in Musanze and the best value in this price range. While it's certainly very pricey, you do get attentive and efficient staff, a great location between the town and the national park, very attractive accommodation and an excellent restaurant. Extras such as a good pool and even a complimentary shoe-cleaning service make all the difference.

★ **Virunga Lodge** LODGE **$$$**
(☎0252502452, 0788302069; www.volcanoessafaris.com; s/d incl full board US$991/1642; P Wi-Fi) One of the most stunningly situated places in the region, the Virunga Lodge, nestled on a ridge above Burera and Ruhondo lakes, offers incredible views across to the Virunga volcanoes, and is one of the finest lodges in Rwanda. Accommodation is in stone chalets decorated with local crafts and hardwood furnishings, though this place is definitely more 'bush chic' than opulent.

Rooms 5 to 8 are in high demand for they have fantastic views over both the towering volcanoes and Lake Ruhondo. Activities include nature walks and village visits. The lodge is a 30-minute drive from Musanze.

Eating

Isange BF Restaurant INTERNATIONAL **$**
(☎0783116655; www.facebook.com/IsangeBFRestaurant; NM 17 St; RFr1500-3500; ⌚7am-10pm Sun-Thu; Wi-Fi) Whether you're sitting al fresco on a snug terrace overlooking a garden or inside the pretty dining room decorated with African touches, dining at this cosy eatery is a treat. The menu roves from faultlessly cooked brochettes to burgers and from zesty salads to meat dishes.

La Paillotte ITALIAN **$**
(☎0785523561; off NR 4 Rd; mains RFr2500-5000; ⌚7am-11pm; Wi-Fi) This popular local haunt is streets ahead of the hotel restaurants in town, at least in terms of atmosphere. There's a funky interior and seating on a breezy roadside terrace. Woodfired pizzas are the most popular item on the menu, but there's also a selection of other dishes, including top-notch brochettes and homemade fries, as well as an in-house bakery.

STORYTELLER DINNERS

An interesting alternative and a memorable night out are the 'storytelling' meals organised by Amahoro Tours (p518). The idea is to bring together inquisitive tourists and community members who can exchange ideas and questions over the course of a local meal. The cost is US$30 per person, excluding the actual cost of the meal.

Volcana Lounge ITALIAN **$$**
(☎0728300753; NR 4 Rd; mains RFr4500-6500; ⏰11am-10pm) With a roaring wood fire in the corner, a sort of rainforest lodge atmosphere (despite being on Musanze's main street) and a laid-back feel, this is one of the most atmospheric places to eat and hang out in town. The menu consists primarily of Rwandan versions of pizza and pasta, as well as brochettes and a finger-licking chocolate mousse.

Information

MONEY

Banks with ATMs and currency-exchange services can be found in the centre. You'll also find foreign-exchange bureaus dotted around the market area, one block northeast of the bus station.

POST

Post Office (off Ave Mikeno; ⏰8am-noon & 2-4pm Mon-Fri) Basic telephone and postal services.

TOURIST INFORMATION

Rwanda Tourism Information Centre – RDB (Rwanda Development Board; ☎0252576514; www.rwandatourism.com; NR 4 Rd; ⏰7am-5pm) Located in the prefecture headquarters, this RDB office can offer advice about any RDB-organised activity, issue permits and book national-park activities. It also sells tickets for the Musanze caves.

Getting There & Away

From the town's **bus station** (Rue du Commerce), numerous bus companies offer scheduled half-hourly services between Musanze and Kigali (RFr1800, two hours) and between Musanze and Gisenyi (RFr1180, two hours). Some buses (and an armada of minibuses) travel to Cyanika (RFr480, 45 minutes) on the Rwanda–Uganda border. Several companies go direct to Kampala, Uganda (RFr8000 to RFr12,000, 12 hours).

Getting Around

There are few taxis in Musanze, but plenty of bicycle taxis and *moto-taxis* for those needing a rest. A typical fare from the town centre to the Hotel Muhabura is around RFr400 on a *moto-taxi*.

Volcanoes National Park

Volcanoes National Park (www.rwandatourism.com/destinations/volcanoes-national-park; gorilla permit US$1500, volcano trekking US$75-400), which runs along the border with the DRC and Uganda, is home to the Rwandan section of the Virungas. Comprising five volcanoes, the Virungas are utterly spellbinding and few would argue that this is not one of the most exciting national parks in Africa. Of all the extraordinary sights and attractions around the Virungas, the one that really draws people here are the mountain gorillas.

While most travellers are understandably driven by the desire to have a face-to-face encounter with real gorillas in the mist, rare golden monkeys, a troop of which have been habituated to human contact, can also be visited. There is a variety of rewarding climbing and trekking options in the park too. To get the most from the Virungas, give yourself as much time as you possibly can, as this is a park that absolutely rewards those who linger.

History

Belgian colonists, who intended to protect the mountain gorillas on Karisimbi, Bisoke and Mikeno in Rwanda and the Belgian Congo from poachers, first gazetted the Virungas as a national park in 1925. This small conservation triangle was the first protected area to be created on the continent of Africa. Four years later, the borders were extended further to form Parc National Albert (Albert National Park), a massive area that encompassed more than 8000 sq km.

Following the independence of the Congo in 1960 and Rwanda in 1962, Albert National Park was split into two entities, the Rwanda portion being assigned the name Parc National des Volcans. During the early years of Rwanda's fragile independence, it wasn't poaching or fighting that harmed the gorillas most, but rather a small daisy-like flower known as pyrethrum. Due to a large grant by the European Community (EC), the 1960s saw the conversion of half of Parc National des Volcans into commercial farms for pyrethrum, which can be processed into a natural insecticide.

By the early 1970s, poachers were making inroads on both sides of the Rwanda–Congo border as the demand for stuffed gorilla heads and hands (which were, depressingly, used as ashtrays) began to burgeon. Thankfully the plight of the mountain gorilla became an international issue following the work of the late Dian Fossey.

Gorilla tracking in Rwanda was first launched in 1979 by Amy Vedder and Bill

VOLCANOES NATIONAL PARK

Why Go Five bamboo- and rainforest-covered volcanoes that are sanctuaries to rare mountain gorillas and endangered golden monkeys.

When to Go The long dry season from June to September is the ideal time to track mountain gorillas as it is, well...drier.

Practicalities Reservations for gorilla tracking are sold out months in advance in high season, so make your booking as early as possible. Access to the park is via Musanze (Ruhengeri), although all trekkers need to report to the park headquarters in Kinigi (12km north of Musanze) at 7am on the day of their trek. The park does not provide transport to the trailheads.

Budget Tips Put simply, there's no cheap way to go and see the mountain gorillas. You can, however, have other equally memorable and much more adventurous experiences in the park for a more reasonable budget. Try trekking up some of the volcanoes and, to keep costs lower, stay in a guesthouse near Kinigi village.

Weber, who marketed the charismatic creatures to tourists on overland trips. By the late 1980s, the sale of gorilla permits was the country's third-largest revenue earner, which was enough to convince ordinary Rwandans that these great apes were indeed a valuable natural resource worth protecting.

In 1991 Rwanda was plunged into civil war, and Parc National des Volcans became a battlefield. By the time the perpetrators of the genocide swept across Rwanda in 1994, the park had been heavily land-mined and then abandoned as refugees fled into the neighbouring DRC. When the dust from the conflict settled, many observers were surprised to discover that the gorillas had weathered the violence remarkably well. However, it wasn't until 1999 that Parc National des Volcans was once again reopened to tourism. Since then tourism has boomed and gorilla tracking has once again become one of Rwanda's biggest earners. When the country changed one of its official languages from French to English in 2008, the park's name changed to Volcanoes National Park.

Sights

Gorilla Guardians Village CULTURAL CENTRE
(☎0788352009; www.cbtrwanda.org; US$20)

While most of the focus of Volcanoes National Park falls squarely onto the animals, this 'cultural village' puts the spotlight back onto the people. Visitors get to experience Rwandan village life by grinding seeds, firing bows and arrows, taking part in a traditional *intore* dance and even partaking in the marriage of a king to his queen.

Activities

Gorilla Tracking

An up-close encounter with the mountain gorillas while gorilla tracking (US$1500 per person) is the highlight of a trip to Africa for many visitors. A close-quarters encounter with a silverback male gorilla can be a hair-raising experience, especially if you've only ever seen large wild animals behind the bars of a cage or from the safety of a car. Yet despite their intimidating size, gorillas are remarkably nonaggressive animals, entirely vegetarian and quite safe to be around. You'll be given a safety briefing by park rangers before leaving to track the habituated gorilla groups.

GORILLA FAMILIES

There are 10 habituated gorilla groups (excluding those groups set aside solely for research purposes, which tourists are not allowed to visit) in Volcanoes National Park, including the **Susa group**, which has around 18 members. Although nearly everyone who shows up at the park headquarters is probably hoping to track the Susa group, the rangers usually select only the most able-bodied and all-round fit visitors. The Susa group is the hardest to reach – you need to trek for three to four hours up the slopes of Karisimbi at an altitude of more than 3000m.

The **Sabinyo group** (17 members) is a good choice for anyone who doesn't want a strenuous tracking experience, as it's usually easily found. The **Kwitonda group** is the largest, with 29 members. The **Agashya** (22 members) and **Amahura** (19 members) groups are also popular with visitors,

Volcanoes National Park

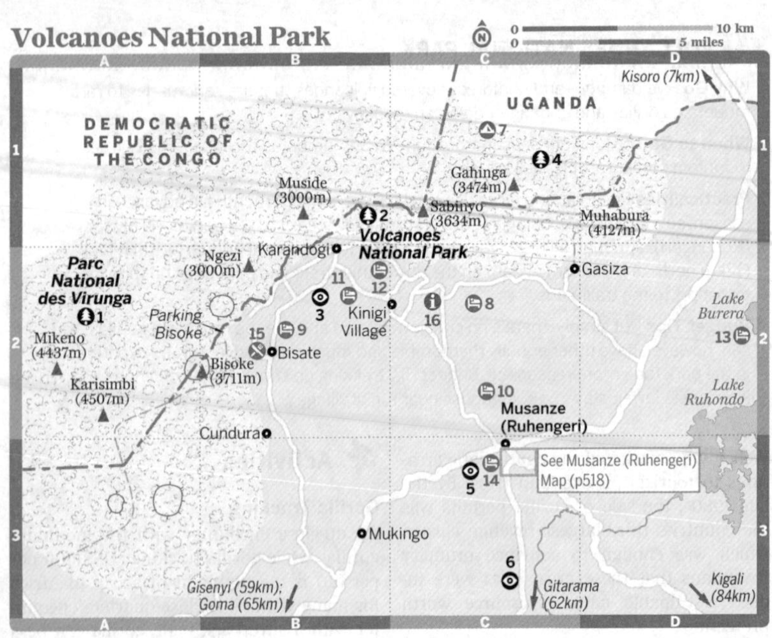

Volcanoes National Park

Top Sights

1 Parc National des Virunga A2
2 Volcanoes National Park B1

Sights

3 Gorilla Guardians Village B2
4 Mgahinga Gorilla National Park C1
5 Musanze Caves C3
6 Nkotsi Village C3

Sleeping

7 Amajambere Iwacu Community Campground C1
8 Amakoro Songa Kinigi Lodge C2
9 Bisate Lodge B2
10 Five Volcanoes Boutique Hotel C2
Gorilla Guardians Village .... (see 3)
Kinigi Guesthouse .... (see 16)
11 Mountain Gorilla View Lodge B2
Mt Gahinga Lodge .... (see 7)
Red Rocks .... (see 6)
12 Sabyinyo Silverback Lodge B2
13 Virunga Lodge D2
14 Volcano View Bed & Breakfast C3

Eating

15 Volcanoes Resto-Bar B2

Information

16 Volcanoes National Park Headquarters C2

although no matter which group you end up tracking, you're certain to have a memorable experience.

THE TREK

How hard is the trek to reach the gorillas? This is a question every other visitor seems to ask. It's a difficult question to answer, as it depends on which group of gorillas you go and see – some journeys are just a short stroll but others a half-day slog. You will most likely spend several hours scrambling through dense vegetation up steep, muddy hillsides, sometimes to altitudes of more than 3000m. At this altitude you will certainly be a little breathless, but someone of good fitness who does a reasonable amount of walking is unlikely to find the walk all that tough. If you're not used to walking though, it might be a very different story and you should request a group closer to the trailheads. At higher altitudes, you'll also have to contend with the thick overgrowth of stinging nettles, which can easily penetrate light clothing. As if fiery skin rashes weren't enough of a deterrent, it also rains a lot in this area and can get very cold. Oh, and when people say it gets muddy what they mean is it can get MUDDY.

THE ENCOUNTER

Visits to the gorillas are restricted to one hour, and flash photography is banned. While you are visiting the gorillas, do not eat, drink, smoke or go to the bathroom in their presence. If you have any potential airborne illness, do not go tracking as gorillas are extremely susceptible to human diseases.

In theory, visitors are requested to remain more than 5m from the gorillas at all times, though in practice the guides (and the gorillas) tend to flout this rule. Although no tourists have ever been harmed by the gorillas, you should give them the respect and wide berth you would any wild animal.

RESERVATIONS

The hefty US$1500 fee includes park entry, compulsory guides and guards. The number of people allowed to visit each of the groups is limited to a maximum of eight people per day, limiting the total number of daily permits to an absolute maximum of 80. Children under 15 are not allowed to visit the gorillas.

Gorilla permit bookings can be made through the RDB tourist office (p516) in Kigali or a Rwandan tour company. Those visiting on a tour package will have everything arranged for them, while independent travellers can secure permits if they make reservations early on. Frustratingly, it's not always easy to deal with the RDB by phone or email from overseas, so it's usually easier to book a permit through a Rwandan tour operator (although you will, of course, have to pay a small surcharge if doing it this way).

With demand often exceeding supply, you'll need to book well in advance if you want to be assured of a spot, especially during the peak seasons of December to January and July to August. Bookings made direct through RDB are secured with a full payment (via bank transfer); if you book through a Rwandan tour operator, you'll need to make a US$600 deposit, and full payment must be made one month before the day of your visit.

Independent travellers who have only decided to visit the gorillas in Rwanda once in the East Africa region can turn up at the RDB office in Kigali and try to secure a booking at the earliest available date. During the high season, waits of several days to more than a week are not uncommon.

You'll need to present yourself at 7am on the day that your permit is valid at the park headquarters (p526), 3km from Kinigi. It's worth emphasising that if you are late, your designated slot will be forfeited and your money will not be refunded.

WHAT TO BRING

You need to be prepared for a potentially long, wet and cold trek through rainforest. A pair of hiking shoes is a must, as is warm and waterproof clothing. The stinging nettles at higher elevations can really put a damper on the experience, so consider wearing trousers and long-sleeved shirts with a bit of thickness.

Despite the high altitudes and potentially cold temperatures, you also need to be prepared for the strong sun. Floppy hats, bandanas, sunglasses and lots of sunscreen are a good idea, as are plenty of cold water and hydrating fluids. Sugary snacks are also good for a quick energy boost.

When you check in at the park headquarters, you may be asked for identification by the park rangers. To avoid any potential hassles, carry your passport with you at all times in addition to your gorilla-tracking permit.

Porters (US$10) are available for the trek, though they're not absolutely necessary unless you're carrying a lot of gear. The guides, guards, drivers and any porters will expect a tip – the amount is up to you, and ultimately depends on the quality of the service. However, keep in mind that the locals know you're paying US$1500 for the privilege of gorilla tracking, so try not to be too stingy.

Golden Monkey Tracking

Golden monkey tracking (US$100 per person) is a relative newcomer on the wildlife scene of East Africa, but is rapidly rising in popularity. More like chimp-viewing than a gorilla encounter, these beautiful and active monkeys bound about the branches of bigger trees. If you're looking for a reason to spend an extra day in the park, don't miss the chance to track these rare animals.

Golden monkeys, which are a subspecies of the wider-spread blue monkey, are endemic to the Albertine Rift Valley and are distinguished by their gold body colouration, which contrasts sharply with black patches on their extremities. Classified as an endangered species, golden monkeys can only be seen in the Virungas, as deforestation and population growth in the Great Lakes region has greatly affected their home range.

Permits to track the golden monkeys are easy to get hold of – simply enquire at the RDB office in Kigali (p516) or Musanze (p520), or at the park headquarters (p526) in Kinigi. As with the gorillas, your time with the monkeys is limited to one hour. But unlike the gorillas, children are allowed to take part (permit price is the same as for adults).

Climbing & Trekking the Volcanoes

Dian Fossey was fascinated by the Virungas, and justifiably so. These stunning volcanoes serve as an evocative backdrop for a guided climb or trek. As you make your way along the ascents, you'll pass through some remarkable changes of vegetation, ranging from thick forests of bamboo and giant lobelia or hagenia on to alpine meadows. And there's further rewards in store: if the weather is favourable, you can enjoy spectacular views over the mountain chain.

There are several possibilities for climbing up to the summits of one or more of the volcanoes in the park, with treks ranging in length from several hours to two days. A guide is compulsory and is included in your trekking fee; additional porters are optional (US$20 per day). Note that it is forbidden to cut down trees or otherwise damage vegetation in the park, and you are only allowed to make fires in the designated camping areas.

One of the best parts of climbing and trekking the volcanoes is that you will be awarded ample opportunities to view wildlife (sans gorillas and golden monkeys, of course). The most common herbivores in the park are bushbucks and black-fronted duikers; buffaloes, bush pigs and giant forest hogs are infrequently spotted. Also, be sure to inspect the hollows of trees for hyraxes, genets, dormice, squirrels and forest pouched rats. The richest birdwatching zone is in the hagenia forests, where you can expect to see turaco, francolins, sunbirds, waxbills, crimson-wings and various hawks and buzzards.

KARISIMBI

Climbing Karisimbi (4507m), the highest summit in the Virungas, takes two long and taxing days. The track follows the saddle between Bisoke and Karisimbi, and then ascends the northwestern flank of the latter. Some five hours after beginning the trek, there is a metal shelter under which you can pitch your tent. The rocky and sometimes snow-covered summit is a further two to four hours walk through alpine vegetation.

To do this trek, take plenty of warm clothing, your own food, a sturdy tent (these can be rented from the park office for US$20) and a very good sleeping bag. It gets very cold, especially at the metal shelter, which is on a bleak shoulder of the mountain at 3660m. The wind whips through here, frequently with fog, so there is little warmth from the sun.

The two-day climb up Karisimbi costs US$400 for a solo climber or US$300 per person for groups of two or more, including park fees and a guide.

BISOKE CRATER LAKE

The most popular hike is the return trip up Bisoke crater lake, which takes six to seven hours from the car park at Bisoke. The well-defined track takes you up the steep southwestern flanks of the volcano to the rim (3630m), where you can see the crater lake. This climb costs US$75 per person, including park fees and a guide. From the park headquarters it's about a 30-minute drive to the trailhead.

DIAN FOSSEY'S GRAVE

Another popular trek is to the site of the former Karisoke Research Center, where Dian Fossey is buried alongside many of her primate subjects, including the famous Digit. From the park headquarters it's about a 30-minute drive to the trailhead, followed by a two- to three-hour hike to the ruins of the camp. This excursion costs US$75 per person, including park fees and a guide (though you are responsible

THE LIFE OF DIAN FOSSEY

When you realise the value of all life, you dwell less on what is past and concentrate more on the preservation of the future.

Dr Dian Fossey, zoologist (1932–85)

Dian Fossey was an American zoologist who spent the better part of her life at a remote camp high up on the slopes of the Virungas studying the mountain gorillas. Without her tenacious efforts to have poaching stamped out, and the work of committed locals since her violent murder, there possibly wouldn't be any of the great apes remaining in Rwanda.

Although trained in occupational therapy, in 1963 Fossey took out a loan and travelled to Tanzania where she met Dr Louis and Mary Leakey. At the time, she learned about the pioneering work of Jane Goodall with chimpanzees and George Schaller's groundbreaking studies on gorillas.

By 1966 Fossey had secured the funding and support of the Leakey family, and began conducting field research of her own. However, political unrest caused her to abandon her efforts the following year at Kabara (in the Democratic Republic of the Congo), and establish the Karisoke Research Center, a remote camp on Bisoke in the more politically stable Rwandan Virungas.

Fossey was catapulted to international stardom when her photograph was snapped by Bob Campbell in 1970 and splashed across the cover of *National Geographic*. Seizing her newfound celebrity status, Fossey embarked on a massive publicity campaign aimed at saving the mountain gorillas from impending extinction.

Tragically, Fossey was murdered on 26 December 1985. Her skull was split open by a *panga*, a type of machete used by local poachers to cut the heads and hands off gorillas. This bloody crime scene caused the media to speculate that poachers, who were angered by her conservationist stance, murdered her.

While this may have been the case, a good measure of mystery still surrounds Fossey's murder and despite the 1986 conviction of a former student, many people believe the murderer's true identity was never credibly established and her former student was merely a convenient scapegoat.

Following her death, Fossey was buried in the Virungas next to her favourite gorilla, Digit, who had previously been killed by poachers. Throughout her life Dian Fossey was a proponent of 'active conservation': the belief that endangered species are best protected through rigorous anti-poaching measures and habitat protection. As a result, she strongly opposed the promotion of tourism in the Virunga range, though the Dian Fossey Gorilla Fund International has changed its position on the issue since her untimely death.

Today Fossey is best known for her book *Gorillas in the Mist*, which is both a description of her scientific research and an insightful memoir detailing her time in Rwanda.

Parts of her life story were later adapted in the film *Gorillas in the Mist: The Story of Dian Fossey*, starring Sigourney Weaver. The movie was criticised for several fictitious scenes in which Fossey aggressively harasses local poachers, as well as its stylised portrayal of her affair with photographer Bob Campbell.

Dian Fossey's legacy is kept alive through the ongoing work of the Dian Fossey Gorilla Fund International (www.gorillafund.org), which has a research centre in Musanze.

for your own transportation to/from the trailhead).

NGEZI NATURE WALK

The return walk to Ngezi (about 3000m) takes two to three hours from the car park at Bisoke. This is one of the easiest of the treks, and at the right time of the day it is possible to see a variety of animals coming down from the hills to drink at streams and springs. This trek is slightly cheaper than the others at US$55 per person including a guide.

GAHINGA & MUHABURA

Climbing Gahinga (3474m; in Uganda) and Muhabura (4127m) is a two-day trip from Gasiza (US$200 per person including guide). The summit of the first volcano is reached after a climb of about four hours along a track that passes through a swampy saddle between the two mountains. The trip to the summit of Muhabura takes about four hours from the saddle. It is also possible to climb these volcanoes separately. For Gahinga, allow seven to eight hours for the return hike, and a minimum of nine hours for Muhabura. You'll need to be very fit to climb Muhabura as there's an altitude gain of more than 2000m. The trekking fee is US$100 for Muhabura and US$75 for Gahinga, including a guide.

Sleeping

Kinigi Guesthouse GUESTHOUSE $

(☎0786892045; kinigi2020@yahoo.fr; Kinigi; dm RFr10,000, s/d from RFr25,000/30,000; P 📶) We've heard mixed reports about these modest red-painted brick cottages that are within walking distance of the park headquarters. Some of the 11 rooms are rather dark and uninspiring, but the four-bed dorm is a good bet for shoestringers. It's set in a lovely garden with views of the towering Virungas.

★Bisate Lodge BOUTIQUE HOTEL $$$

(☎in South Africa +27 11 257 5000; www.wilderness-safaris.com/camps/bisate-lodge; Volcanoes National Park; d full board US$2800; P ❄ 📶) Now here's something really special – one of the most atmospheric places to stay in Rwanda. The location is among the best in the country, with incredible volcano views from the terrace; the architect-designed look, best described as 'ethnic chic', is stunning. Rooms are supremely comfortable with massive windows and lovely furnishings made of local materials.

★Sabyinyo Silverback Lodge LODGE $$$

(☎in Kenya +254 (20) 2734000; www.governorscamp.com; Volcanoes National Park; s/d incl full board US$1160/1850; P 📶) 🍃 If you want to splurge on your visit to the gorillas, then this is without a doubt the place to do it. Intimate and immaculate accommodation is in Venetian plaster cottages with Rwandese-style terracotta-tile roofs, spacious sitting areas, stylish en suite bathrooms and phenomenal volcano views. One quibble, though: access to the 10 units is a bit tricky (read: steep stairs).

Amakoro Songa Kinigi Lodge BOUTIQUE HOTEL $$$

(☎0727770101; www.songaafrica.com/amakoro-songa-lodge; Kinigi; s US$450-650, d US$800-900; P 📶) Between Kinigi and the Volcanoes National Park headquarters, this lovely, intimate venture has four spacious cottages dotted around a meticulously maintained garden. All have clean lines, contemporary decor and fabulous views of the surrounding volcanoes.

Gorilla Guardians Village HUT $$$

(☎0788352009; www.cbtrwanda.org; Gorilla Guardians Village; s/d incl full board US$100/170; P) 🍃 This recreation of a traditional village is one of the most original places to stay in the area. Although it is mainly used to provide day trippers with a 'cultural experience', you can also stay the night, and that's when things get interesting. Guests sleep in one of the cosy mud houses and are entertained long into the evening by local villagers.

Mountain Gorilla View Lodge LODGE $$$

(☎0788305708; www.3bhotels.com; Volcanoes National Park; s/d incl full board US$230/300; P 📶) These 38 rock cottages set in lush, grassy grounds and with impressive views down the volcano range are very large, functional and comfortable, and very well spaced. The attached bar and restaurant occupies an atmospheric thatched building with stone floors. Wi-fi is available at the restaurant only.

Eating

Volcanoes Resto-Bar CAFETERIA $

(☎0788495604; Volcanoes National Park; mains RFr2000-4000; ⏲7am-6pm) Conveniently located opposite the Bisoke car park, this small cafeteria arranged around attractive gardens dishes up simple meals and sells soft drinks and fruits. It also rents out raincoats, boots, gloves and gaiters. A great place to recharge the batteries after a visit to the gorillas or the climb up Bisoke or Karisimbi.

Information

Volcanoes National Park Headquarters (RDB; ☎0788771633; www.rwandatourism.com/destinations/volcanoes-national-park; Kinigi; ⏲6.30am-4pm Mon-Fri, to 12.30pm Sat & Sun) You are required to register at this office, 3km north of the village of Kinigi, at 7am on the day of your scheduled gorilla tracking. If you are late, your designated slot will be forfeited. This is also the place to arrange permits for golden monkey tracking, as well as climbs and treks in the Virunga volcanoes.

Getting There & Away

The main access point for Volcanoes National Park is the nearby town of Musanze (Ruhengeri).

The park headquarters is located about 3km north of the village of Kinigi. Kinigi is approximately 9km north of Musanze. Although it's possible to reach Kinigi by bus from Musanze, almost all visitors come to the park headquarters with their own wheels (usually via a tour operator).

From the park headquarters, a 4WD with high clearance is also necessary to reach the point where you start climbing up to where the gorillas are situated – most parking areas are located within a 30-minute drive. For solo travellers, the best option is to join a group in Musanze. Ask around at **Amahoro Tours** (p518) or **Hotel Muhabura** (0788364774; www.muhabura-hotel.com; NR 4 Rd; camping per tent US$20, s/d/tw US$45/55/70; P). The cost of hiring a vehicle and driver costs between US$80 and US$100 at either of these places.

Gisenyi (Rubavu)

POP 140,000

Gisenyi (Rubavu), right on the border with the DRC, is one of Rwanda's loveliest spots and the closest this landlocked country has to a beach resort. With some attractive stretches of sand fringed with all manner of tropical vegetation along Lake Kivu's long shore, Gisenyi is unsurprisingly a popular destination for wealthy Rwandans, expats and independent travellers alike. The town itself projects a languid air of some forgotten upcountry backwater, and that's part of its appeal. If you need some action, go on a boat tour, take a kayak excursion on majestic Lake Kivu or hit the Congo Nile Trail on foot or bicycle. One of the Great Lakes in the Albertine Rift Valley, it has a maximum depth of nearly 500m and is one of the 20 deepest and most voluminous lakes in the world.

Sights

Rubona Peninsula LANDMARK

Roughly 6km south of town (about RFr1000 by *moto-taxi*), along a lovely lakeshore road, the Rubona Peninsula is Lake Kivu at its finest. Hills rise steeply from the lake foreshore and are a patchwork of garden plots and small homesteads. The shore itself is often rocky, although there are enough sandy spots and places suitable for swimming. It's a very popular weekend destination, with a smattering of beach resorts.

Gisenyi Public Beach BEACH

The strip of sand beneath the main town is a justifiably popular place to take a dip. That said, some travellers imagining Caribbean sands are disappointed to discover the waters are grey-green and the sand coarse and yellowish. There is, however, plenty of it and, after days on the road, Lake Kivu represents a welcome opportunity to throw down a beach towel or do as the locals do and spread a picnic blanket under one of the many shade trees.

Pfunda Tea Estate FACTORY

(0786098239; www.birchalltea.co.uk; US$10; 7am-4pm Mon-Fri, to noon Sat) During the rainy season, at the height of production, the Pfunda Tea Factory processes up to 90 tonnes of tea from the surrounding plantations daily. Guided tours follow the tea production from arrival of the green leaf through to the withering, cutting, drying and sorting stages, before it is packaged for shipment to Mombasa (Kenya). The factory is about 9km from town on the road to Kigali and most easily reached by *moto-taxi* (about RFr1000).

Tours

★**Kingfisher Journeys** KAYAKING

(0783811918; www.kingfisherjourneys.com; US$60-90; by reservation) For something unique, sign on with this reputable outfit that runs half- and full-day guided kayak trips on Lake Kivu. Trips bring you to islets, fishing villages and various scenic spots, and there are astounding views of the hills and coastline. It can also arrange four-day trips down to Kibuye (US$420, including accommodation).

★**Rwandan Adventures** CYCLING, WALKING

(0786571414; www.rwandan-adventures.com; Rubona Peninsula; 8am-6pm) This Gisenyi-based tour company specialises in walking and cycling tours along the Congo Nile Trail and can organise fully guided tours. They also organise much shorter walking and cycling tours (US$45/70 for half-/full-day).

Gisenyi (Rubavu)

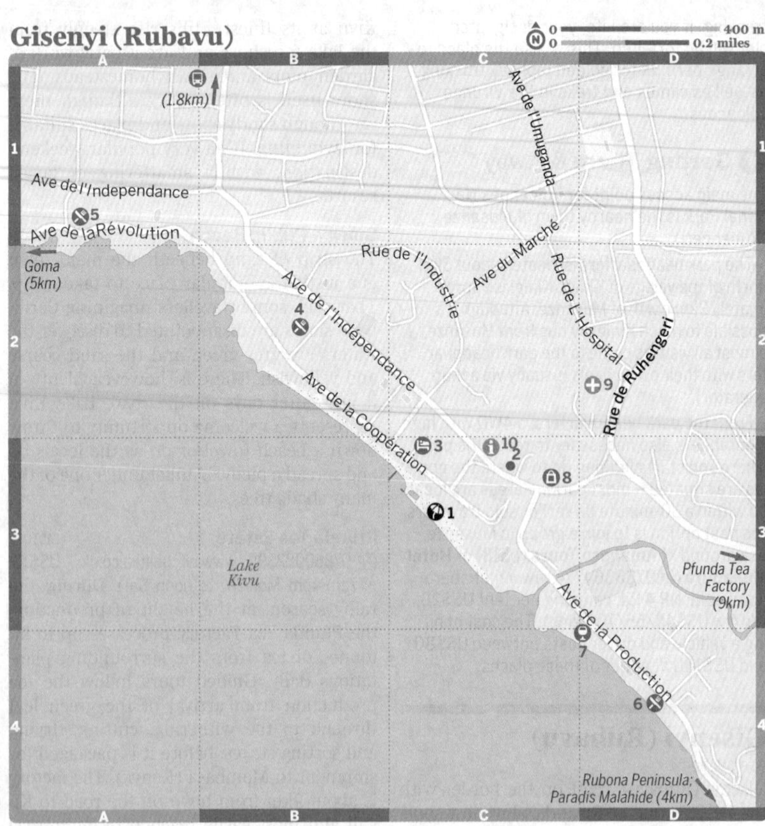

Their bikes are in tip-top condition and the guides are well qualified.

Green Hills Ecotours CULTURAL

(☎0722220000, 0788219495; www.greenhillsecotours.com; Ave de l'Indépendance; ⏲9am-5pm) Can arrange various cultural excursions around Gisenyi, including visits to Batwa communities who operate as potters. It can also organise cross-border visits to Virunga National Park in the DRC. There's a small crafts shop on the premises.

Sleeping

★ **Inzu Lodge** TENTED CAMP $

(☎0784179203; www.inzulodge.com; Rubona Peninsula; camping per tent US$25, d with shared bathroom US$40-47; P📶) By far the most unusual sleeping option in Gisenyi, this delightful oasis on a sloping hill that lords over majestic Lake Kivu offers comfortably equipped safari tents set on stone platforms with sweeping views. A grassy, partially shady plot is set aside for campers. The wonderfully cosy open-air restaurant serves an eclectic offering of Rwandan and Continental classics. A bonanza for budget-conscious visitors.

★ **Discover Rwanda Gisenyi Beach** HOSTEL $

(☎0781586272; www.discoverrwanda.net; Ave de la Coopération; camping per person US$10, dm US$17, s US$40-50, d US$50-60; P📶) A mere stone's throw away from the beach, Gisenyi's backpacker mecca is a relaxed and relatively orderly budget choice, with a full complement of facilities and hang-out areas in grassy grounds. The more expensive rooms and the eight-bed dorm occupy a former colonial building that brims with charm. The place has a very pleasant, convivial feel with an excellent bar and restaurant.

Gisenyi (Rubavu)

Sights
1 Gisenyi Public Beach C3

Activities, Courses & Tours
2 Green Hills Ecotours C3

Sleeping
3 Discover Rwanda Gisenyi Beach C3

Eating
4 Bistro Restaurant & Wine Garage B2
5 Calafia A1
6 Lakeside Restaurant & Beach Bar D4

Drinking & Nightlife
7 New Tam-Tam Bikini D4

Shopping
8 African Art Gallery C3

Information
9 Hôpital Gisenyi D2
10 Rwanda Tourism Information Centre – RDB C3

★**Palm Garden Lodge** BOUTIQUE HOTEL $$
(☎0788306830; www.palmgardenlodge.com; Rubona Peninsula; d US$65) A gem! Preferring intimacy to opulence, the Palm Garden is home to nine boutique-quality rooms decorated with well-chosen furnishings and antiques. Most rooms come with partial lake views (ask for the 'Remera', which has a balcony). The whole place oozes style and carefree charm. You can sit back on a sun lounger on the garden lawn and gaze down at the lake.

★**Paradis Malahide** HOTEL $$
(☎0788648650, 0788756204; www.paradisemalahide.com; Rubona Peninsula; s/d US$80/90; P 📶) Located along the shores of the Rubona Peninsula, this lodge continues to get wonderful reviews from loyal guests. Accommodation is in four apartments in a two-storey wooden house or in six circular stone bungalows scattered around an attractive tropical garden, but the highlight here is clearly the fab lakeside location. The atmospheric restaurant, which serves delicious Rwandan and international dishes, is another draw.

Palm Beach RESORT $$
(☎0785695577; www.palmbeachrubavu.com; Rubona Peninsula; d US$80-100; P 📶) The location (on a well-trimmed property fronting Lake Kivu) alone would make this one of Gisenyi's best options, but the six brick bungalows and four rooms in a circular building make this one of the best deals in the area. This mini resort is a particularly great find for sunbathers – the stretch of 'beach' here is the most alluring on the peninsula.

Eating

★**Calafia** CAFE $
(☎0787938145; www.calafiacafe.com; off Ave de la Révolution; mains RFr3000-5000; ⏲8am-8pm Mon-Thu, to 9pm Fri & Sat, 10am-6pm Sun; 📶) Four words: not to be missed. On the lakefront road near the DRC border, this wonderful conversion of an impressive mansion now hosts a superb cafe that is passionately run by a group of expat friends. Delicious sandwiches, yummy pastries (hmm, the banana cake) and frondy salads are supplemented by fish tacos, frittatas and excellent, ethically produced local coffee.

Bistro Restaurant & Wine Garage INTERNATIONAL $$
(☎0785368825; btwn Ave de l'Indépendance & Ave de la Coopération; mains RFr4000-6500; ⏲noon-9pm; 📶) This sassy eatery not far from the beach has an outdoor patio and becomes atmospheric at night. There's a small selection of well-executed dishes, including beef or tilapia (Nile perch) fillet, burgers with chips, brochettes and pizzas. Since wine also features strongly here, take the opportunity to get stuck into the list of well-chosen French tipples, available by the glass.

Lakeside Restaurant & Beach Bar INTERNATIONAL $$
(☎0787775405; www.facebook.com/LakesideGisenyi.Rwanda; Ave de la Production; mains RFr3500-7000; ⏲10am-10pm) This hip and classy lakefront resto-bar is as adept at serving up light bites as it is heartier meals. The menu is eclectic and inventive, and the breezy, sunset-friendly deck overlooking the beach is very atmospheric. A chill-out place by day, it gets really lively at night on weekends when DJs take over with African beats.

Drinking & Nightlife

New Tam-Tam Bikini BEER GARDEN
(Ave de la Production; ⏲10am-11pm) While we don't know who came up with the name, we can vouch for the great beachfront location.

This beach shack is a *very* popular spot for a beer and gets pleasingly raucous on the weekends when the drinking crowd rolls in from Kigali and the nearby DRC. Accompany your beachside beer with a plate of brochettes and chips.

Shopping

African Art Gallery ARTS & CRAFTS
(☎0782419298; Rue de Ruhengeri; ⊙9am-6pm) This small curio store has a varied and colourful collection of handicrafts from the DRC, Uganda and Rwanda, including lots of Congolese masks and other wooden items as well as necklaces, paintings and basketware.

Information

MEDICAL SERVICES

Hôpital Gisenyi (Rue de Ruhengeri; ⊙24hr) Gisenyi's best medical facility.

MONEY

Banks with ATMs and currency-changing services can be found along Rue de Ruhengeri in the centre. You'll also find foreign-exchange bureaus dotted around the market area and the bus station.

TOURIST INFORMATION

Rwanda Tourism Information Centre – RDB (Rwanda Development Board; www.rwandatourism.com; Ave de l'Indépendance; ⊙7am-5pm Mon-Fri, 8am-noon Sat & Sun) This office can book national park activities around the country and can also help with finding guides for the Congo Nile Trail.

Getting There & Away

BUS & MINIBUS

Gisenyi's **bus station** is 2km northwest of the town centre towards the DRC border. Various companies go between Gisenyi and Kigali (RFr3000, four hours) via Musanze (Ruhengeri; RFr1200, two hours). Departures are half hourly from 7am until 5pm. There are also several daily services between Gisenyi and Kibuye (Karongi; RFr3000, 3½ hours) between 5.30am and 4pm. Ask at the bus station as operators on these routes vary (but prices are the same).

There are a few daily buses to Kampala, Uganda (US$15 to US$20, 14 hours) that leave from a separate car park that lies 200m further west along the road. Prices are normally quoted in dollars for this route, but tickets are payable in francs (or dollars).

BOAT

There's a twice-weekly passenger **ferry service** (☎0781087996; Rubona Peninsula) between Gisenyi, Kibuye (Karongi) and Cyangugu (Rusizi). The boat makes the southbound trip from Gisenyi on Wednesdays and Saturdays, leaving from Rubona Peninsula at 7am. It arrives at Kibuye (RFr2500) around 10.30am and at Cyangugu (RFr5000) around 3.45pm. Boats head north from Cyangugu on Tuesdays and Fridays.

Getting Around

If you need wheels, *moto-taxis* swarm everywhere. From town to the bus station should cost around RFr400. It's a RFr1000 blast out to the Rubona Peninsula.

SOUTHWESTERN RWANDA

Rwanda's endless mountains and valleys keep rolling right down to the southwestern corner of the country near the border with Burundi. While the gorillas in Volcanoes National Park tend to garner almost everybody's attention, southwestern Rwanda is home to East Africa's largest montane forest, Nyungwe Forest National Park, one of the most primate-rich areas in the world. For outdoors enthusiasts, it also offers plenty of hiking opportunities. For some cultural sustenance, make a beeline for the historic colonial and intellectual centre of Huye (Butare), which plays host to one of East Africa's best ethnographic museums.

Huye (Butare)

POP 89,600

Huye is one of the most distinguished towns in Rwanda, having served as the country's most prominent intellectual centre since the colonial era, when it was known as Butare, a name most Rwandans still use for it. Home to the National University of Rwanda, the National Institute of Scientific Research and the excellent Ethnographic Museum, Huye may be a step down in size after the capital, but it's certainly no lightweight on the Rwandan stage. While Huye may have lost a bit of ground to Kigali after independence, today it still manages to maintain its political relevance, especially

WORTH A TRIP

MURAMBI GENOCIDE MEMORIAL

Nyamagabe (formerly called Gikongoro) and the satellite town of Murambi was the site of one of the most unforgettable horrors of the 1994 genocide. Refugees flocked to Murambi, the location of a half-built technical college, after being told that they would be safe there. It was merely a ploy though and on 21 April the army and Interahamwe militia moved in and, depending on whose doing the counting, between 27,000 and 40,000 people were murdered here.

Murambi Genocide Memorial (Nyamagabe; ⌚8am-4pm) is by far the most graphic of the many genocide memorials in Rwanda, as hundreds of bodies have been exhumed and preserved with powdered lime, and appear as they did when the killers struck.

A visit starts with well-presented museum-style information panels (many of which seem to lay the blame for it all on the French) and short films. You then walk through rooms with larger than life photographs of some of the victims and accounts from some of the few who survived.

Heading outside, you pass by some mass graves and then over to what were once planned to be classrooms. Many of these contain wooden racks filled with hundreds of preserved bodies. Wandering through these rooms the scene becomes more and more macabre, with many of the displayed corpses – men, women and children – still contorted in the manner in which they died. The last rooms are perhaps the most moving of all. These contain the toddlers and babies and, just as with the adults, you can sometimes get a good guess as to their final moments: some, presumably calling for their mothers, are still holding their arms out; another covers his or her eyes in what might be a vain attempt to hide from the killers. Many others have fractures in their skulls from the machetes.

As you can imagine from this description, Murambi can be overwhelming, and not everyone can stomach it. It is, however, another poignant reminder to us all of what came to pass here, and why it must never be allowed to happen again.

Nyamagabe is 28km west of Huye, and there are regular buses running between the two (RFr510, 50 minutes). The memorial is 2km beyond the town at Murambi. *Moto-taxis* can run you there for RFr500 if you don't fancy the walk.

since it's ruled by legions of Rwanda's academic elite.

While Huye isn't a tourist destination in the traditional sense, it's nevertheless an interesting stopover and the heavy concentration of liberal college students roaming the streets makes for an interesting contrast to the chaotic whirl of mercantile Kigali.

History

The tradition of Butare as an academic centre dates back to 1900 when it hosted the first Catholic mission in present-day Rwanda. As prominent intellectuals and religious figures were drawn to the area, Butare grew in favour among the Belgian occupiers. Following the death of Queen Astrid, the Swedish wife of King Leopold III, the town was renamed Astrida in 1935.

After independence in 1962, the town's name was changed back to Butare as it launched a strong bid to serve as the capital of Rwanda. Although Kigali was eventually chosen, due to its central location, Butare was selected to host the country's first university, which opened its doors to students in 1963.

In the early days of the 1994 genocide, Tutsis and moderate Hutus fled to Butare in the hope that its intellectual tradition would reign over the ensuing madness. For a short while, the Tutsi prefect of Butare, Jean-Baptiste Habyarimana, managed to maintain peace and order in the town.

Sadly, however, Habyarimana was quickly murdered by the Interahamwe and replaced by Colonel Tharcisse Muvunyi. Under his tenure, Butare was the site of horrific massacres that claimed the lives of nearly a quarter of a million people. Although Muvunyi fled to Britain after the genocide, he was eventually arrested and convicted.

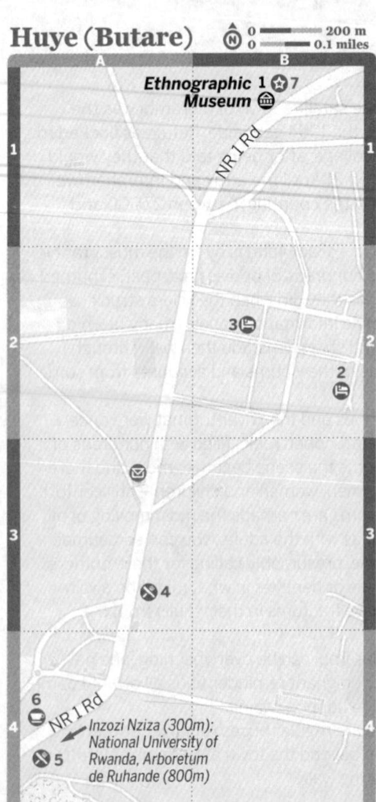

Huye (Butare)

Top Sights
1 Ethnographic Museum B1

Sleeping
2 Centre d'Accueil Mater Boni Consilii B2
3 Emmaus Hostel B2

Eating
4 Hotel Ibis Restaurant A3
5 Nehemiah's Best Coffee A4

Drinking & Nightlife
6 C&C Café Connexion A4

Entertainment
7 Traditional Rwandan Dance Troupe B1

In 2006 the name of the town was changed from Butare to Huye following an administrative reorganisation of Rwanda's 12 former provinces.

Sights

★Ethnographic Museum MUSEUM
(☎0730741093; www.museum.gov.rw; NR 1 Rd; adult/child RFr6000/3000; ⊙8am-6pm) This outstanding museum was given to the city as a gift from Belgium in 1989 to commemorate 25 years of independence. While the building itself is certainly one of the most beautiful structures in the city, the museum wins top marks for having one of the best ethnological and archaeological collections in the entire region. The seven exhibition halls contain some very interesting items and everything is unusually well lit and presented.

National University of Rwanda GARDENS
(off NR 1 Rd) Rwanda's finest institution of learning suffered terribly during the 1994 genocide, though today it has turned towards the future with hope and optimism. Strolling through its campus is a pleasant diversion, especially if you find yourself at the Arboretum de Ruhande. Started by the Belgians in 1934, this attractive and peaceful arboretum is a great place to learn about African flora while indulging in a bit of leafy shade.

Sleeping

Emmaus Hostel GUESTHOUSE $
(☎0788865736; s RFr13,000-20,000, d RFr18,000-25,000; P📶) Arguably the best budget option in town, this church-run abode arranged around a neat garden courtyard has a variety of clean rooms, including large and light-filled doubles. Breakfast is copious. It's about 200m east of the main street.

Hotel Barthos HOTEL $
(☎0783079269; NR 1 Rd; s RFr15,000, d RFr20,000-25,000; P📶) At the southern end of town close to the university campus, this four-storey building with a quirkily decorated facade – the owner is a well-known Rwandan sculptor – is a safe bet, with functional rooms that are inundated with natural light. It's on a rather noisy thoroughfare; if you're a light sleeper, ask for a room at the back.

★Centre d'Accueil Mater Boni Consilii HOTEL $$
(☎0788283903; www.mbcrwanda.com; s/d RFr30,000/70,000; P 📶) It's definitely unusual to find a church-run place offering such a comfortable hotel experience, but that's just what you get here. In a tranquil residential area 500m from the main road, the hotel provides plenty of peace and quiet, while its spotless rooms are an excellent deal, although the singles in the older wing are a bit pokey and feel old-fashioned.

Eating

★Nehemiah's Best Coffee CAFETERIA $
(☎0783880153; NR 1 Rd; snacks RFr1300-3000; ⏲6.30am-10pm Mon-Sat, 10am-10pm Sun; 📶) On the main drag running from the upper town to the university, this wonderful surprise serves up pastries, omelettes, burgers, freshly made smoothies and – most importantly of all – great coffee, making it by far the best spot in town for a light meal in cool surrounds. And yes, there's (fast) wi-fi. It's right next to Ecobank.

Inzozi Nziza CAFETERIA $
(NR 1 Rd; ice cream from RFr800; ⏲8am-8pm) Mmm, the homemade ice creams! Oh, the damn addictive banana cake! Also serves up omelettes (RFr2000), palate-pleasing salads (RFr1500), cookies and excellent coffee.

Hotel Ibis Restaurant FRENCH $$
(☎0788323000; NR 1 Rd; meals RFr3500-8000; ⏲11.30am-10pm; 📶) This hotel restaurant, with its open-air terrace and pleasantly faded dining room (there's a brighter room upstairs), is the most popular place in town for locals and tourists alike. It is justly revered for its tasty French-inspired cuisine with a bow to local ingredients. It also dishes up pizzas, pastas and a wholesome range of salads.

Drinking & Nightlife

C&C Café Connexion CAFE
(☎0786120712; NR 1 Rd; coffee RFr300-700; ⏲8am-7pm Mon-Sat, 10am-6pm Sun) An industrial space turned coffee shop, this very atmospheric place, which uses only the finest of beans, is dominated by a massive coffee-bean roaster and grinder and is the place in town for a caffeine boost. You can also buy fresh, export-quality Rwandan coffee here.

Entertainment

★Traditional Rwandan Dance Troupe DANCE
(☎0730741093; www.museum.gov.rw; Ethnographic Museum, NR 1 Rd; 1-5 people RFr50,000, 6-10 people RFr60,000) There is a traditional Rwandan dance troupe based in Huye, and its show is spectacular. The Intore dance originated in Burundi and involves elaborate costumes and superb drumming routines. Performances can be organised through the Ethnographic Museum (p532), and the larger the group size, the cheaper it will be per person. Note that prices substantially increase on weekends and during the evening.

Information

MONEY

Banks with exchange facilities and ATMs accepting international cards can be found along the main drag.

POST

Post Office (NR 1 Rd; ⏲8am-3pm) The main city post office.

Getting There & Away

The bus station is about 1km north of the town centre, near the Ethnographic Museum. There are regular services between Huye and Kigali (RFr2510, three hours), Nyamagabe (Gikongoro; RFr510, 50 minutes), Nyanza (Nyabisindu; RFr670, 45 minutes) and Cyangugu (Rusizi; RFr3000, four hours).

The road from Huye to Cyangugu passes through the Nyungwe Forest National Park and some spectacular virgin rainforest.

Nyanza (Nyabisindu)

POP 58,000

Culture buffs, Nyanza will appeal to you. The capital of the South Province boasts several worthwhile historical attractions. In 1899 Mwami Musinga Yuhi V established Rwanda's first permanent royal capital here. Until then, the royals had divided their time between 50 or so homes scattered throughout their kingdom. Today his traditional palace (well, actually a very good replica of it) and the first home built by his son and successor Mutara III Rudahigwa have been restored and form the King's Palace Museum – Nyanza's main draw.

After visiting Belgium and seeing the stately homes there, Mutara concluded his own home wasn't up to scratch and had a second, and altogether grander, palace built on nearby Rwesero Hill, which today is the National Arts Gallery.

Sights

King's Palace Museum – Rukari MUSEUM
(☎0788479170; www.museum.gov.rw; adult/child RFr6000/3000; ⏲8am-6pm) Situated on a hill 2km southwest of town, this fascinating museum is less about ancient history and more about royal residences. The displays centre on a replica king's 'palace'. Inclusive in the ticket price is a guided tour that helps explain some of the architectural idiosyncrasies inside the royal compound, including why the royal beer brewer's hut had an entrance without a lip, and other curiosities such as why the woman who looked after the king's milk was never able to marry.

National Arts Gallery – Rwesero MUSEUM
(www.museum.gov.rw; adult/child RFr6000/3000; ⏲8am-6pm) Rwanda's most prestigious art museum is housed inside what was meant to be King Mutara III Rudahigwa's new palace (he died before the building was completed in somewhat mysterious circumstances after a routine vaccination went wrong). Today it houses mostly contemporary paintings and stylistic sculptures on themes dealing with the genocide, unity and brotherhood. Keep hold of your ticket, as admission to this museum entitles you to a 30% discount at King's Palace Museum – Rukari.

Sleeping

Dayenu Hotel HOTEL $
(☎0788559220; s/d RFr25,000/35,000; P) This multistorey hotel in the centre of town has rooms with frilly bedspreads, not to mention rather flamboyant pink bedsheets. As well as the florid bedding, it also has a bar, a restaurant (serving Rwanda staples and pasta) and even a swimming pool in attractive gardens, which probably isn't what you'd have expected to find in dusty Nyanza.

Boomerang Hotel HOTEL $
(☎0788526617; s/d RFr10,000/12,000; P) On the slopes of Rwesero Hill, this no-frills local hotel and restaurant has presentable rooms (but saggy mattresses) and friendly staff. The hot water for the showers comes by the bucket.

Getting There & Away

Any of the minibuses or buses that ply the main road between Kigali and Huye (Butare) can drop you at the turn-off for Nyanza. From here you can catch a *moto-taxi* to town (5km, RFr400 to RFr600). Better still, catch a Volcano Express or Horizon bus directly to Nyanza from either Kigali (RFr1700, 1¾ hours) or Huye (RFr750, 45 minutes).

The King's Palace Museum – Rukari and the National Art Gallery – Rwesero are a further 2km from town and can be reached on foot or by *moto-taxi* (RFr500).

Nyungwe Forest National Park

Quite simply, **Nyungwe Forest National Park** (☎0788558880, 0788317027; www.nyungweforest.com; US$40-90; ⏲6am-6pm) is Rwanda's most important area of biodiversity, with no fewer than 1000 plant species, 13 species of primates, 75 species of other mammals, at least 275 species of birds and an astounding 120 species of butterflies. It has been rated the highest priority for forest conservation in Africa and its protected area covers one of the oldest rainforests in Africa. Despite its huge biodiversity, Nyungwe is little known outside of East Africa.

Nyungwe's strongest drawcard is the chance to track chimpanzees, which have been habituated over the years to human visits. While chimps tend to garner most of the spotlight here, sightings of troops of other monkeys, including Angolan colobi, Dent's monkeys, grey-cheeked mangabeys, olive baboons, vervet monkeys and diademed monkeys, are virtually guaranteed.

Another highlight is the simple pleasure of hiking along well-maintained trails over the lush, green valleys of the equatorial rainforest.

Activities

Chimpanzee Tracking

They may pale in size when compared to the hulking masses that are the mountain gorillas, but there is no denying the affinity that we humans have for chimpanzees. Sharing an estimated 94% of our genetic material, chimps display an incredible range of human-like behaviours ranging from tool use to waging war.

NYUNGWE FOREST NATIONAL PARK

Why Go Nyungwe Forest National Park enjoys some of the richest forest biodiversity in all of Africa. The park's star activities are tracking chimpanzees and the world's largest troop of colobus monkey (around 500). Both species have been habituated to humans.

When to Go Nyungwe can be visited year-round and the chimps often descend from the higher elevations (and are therefore easier to find) during the wet season.

Practicalities Most activities begin at the Uwinka Reception Centre or at the Gisakura Booking Office (but some then require a vehicle to reach the trailheads).

Budget Tips By showing a little resourcefulness, it's possible for budget travellers to visit Nyungwe and enjoy most of the activities. There's cheap accommodation available near both park offices and some walking trails begin close by.

Chimps are highly sociable creatures, and one of the few primates to form complex communities ranging upwards of 100 individuals. During the day these communities break down into smaller units that forage for food, a behaviour that has been dubbed 'fission-fusion' by anthropologists. Since they cover a greater daily distance than the relatively docile gorilla, chimpanzee tracking (US$90 per person) is a much more uncertain enterprise.

Chimpanzee habituation in Nyungwe is still very much a work in progress, and although you will almost certainly encounter them, it might not be all that close up. This is especially so because Nyungwe's chimps seem to spend longer periods of time high in the tree tops than many other East African chimps.

Much like gorilla tracking, you need to be prepared for lengthy hikes that can take up to several hours. However, the vegetation on the forest floor is much less dense than in the Virunga mountains where the gorillas live, so the walk is generally a little less tiring. In the rainy season you have a good chance of successfully tracking the chimps on the coloured trails (a network of trails of varying levels of difficulty), though in the dry season they have a tendency to head for higher elevations.

Although there are groups of chimps throughout Nyungwe, the habituated group that most people are taken to is actually located in the **Cyamudongo Forest**, a very small, isolated 'island' of forest surrounded by tea estates a little over an hour's drive from the park office at Gisakura. This group consists of about 40 individuals. At certain times, though, visitors might be taken to see a second habituated group, the Uwinka group, which is the largest with around 65 individuals. That said, this group, which is usually found within 12km of the Uwinka Reception Centre, is harder to access. Whichever group you end up visiting, having a car is something of a necessity for chimp tracking, as you'll need to arrange transportation for you and your guide to the trailhead. Be prepared for an early start – usually 5.30am from Gisakura. Porters are available at Cyamundongo (US$10).

Visits are limited to one hour.

Colobus Monkey Tracking

A subspecies of the widespread black-and-white colobus, the Angolan colobus is an arboreal Old World monkey that is distinguished by its black fur and long, silky white locks of hair. Weighing 10kg to 20kg, and possessing a dexterous tail that can reach lengths of 75cm, Angolan colobus are perfectly suited to a life up in the canopy.

Colobi are distributed throughout the rainforests of equatorial Africa, though they reach epic numbers in Nyungwe Forest National Park. While they may not be as a charismatic as chimps, colobi are extremely social primates that form enormous group sizes – one of the two semi-habituated troops in Nyungwe numbers no fewer than 500 individuals.

As you might imagine, finding yourself in the presence of literally hundreds of primates bounding through the treetops can be a mesmerising experience. Curious animals by nature, colobi in Nyungwe seem to almost revel in their playful interactions with human visitors.

Troops of Angolan colobus maintain fairly regimented territories, which is good news for those planning a colobus track (US$60 per person), as the semi-habituated group in Nyungwe tends to stick to the coloured trails. While watching wildlife is never a certainty, generally the trackers can find the colobus monkey troop in an hour or so.

There is a smaller, and often more accessible troop, of around 50 individuals near the **Gisakura Tea Plantation**. Be sure to ask which troop you'll be tracking when you make your reservation. This second troop is less worthwhile to visit as the walk is only about two to five minutes from the Gisakura park office and it feels like a lot of money to pay to stand in a tea field looking at monkeys you could almost see without leaving the park office!

Trekking Nyungwe Forest

In addition to tracking primates, Nyungwe Forest National Park has a number of superb walking trails that mostly begin at the Uwinka Reception Centre (p538).

It's not possible to walk in the park without a guide, and one is included when you pay your trek fees. Walks begin at set times; the first departures are around 9am, with further departures around 11am and 2pm.

NATURE WALKS

This network of trails was constructed in the late 1980s in an attempt to open up Nyungwe to tourists. While tourism in the national park remains relatively low-key, these six trails are nevertheless reasonably well maintained. Each trail is marked with a different colour. Hikers can choose trails ranging from the 2km-long **Buhoro Trail**, a proverbial walk in the woods, right up to the 10km-long **Imbaraga Trail**, which winds steeply up forested slopes and requires about six hours. Some of the most popular trails include the **Igishigishigi Trail** (2.1km, about 1½ hours), which has spectacular tree ferns and great views, and the **Umuyove Trail** (5.5km, 3½ hours), which has birds, colourful flowers, a waterfall and large mahogany trees. The **Irebero Trail** (3.6km, three hours) is noted for its stunning viewpoints.

Although you need to specifically request to engage in either chimpanzee or colobus tracking, in theory you could run across either primate while hiking the coloured trails. Even if you don't come across these two star billings, you're likely to spot some of Nyungwe's other 11 primates, as well as a whole slew of birdlife, and possibly even the odd mammal or two.

These trails originate from the Uwinka Reception Centre (p538) and cost US$40 per person.

A number of walking trails are also available in the Kitabi area and begin at the Kitabi Booking Office (p538). They're much less known than the ones around Uwinka. A guide is also compulsory and is included in your trekking fee (US$40 per person).

WATERFALL (ISUMO) TRAIL

While not as popular as the nature walks, the Waterfall Trail (per person US$50) is a stunner of a hike and one of the highlights of Nyungwe. It's one of the few treks that start from the Gisakura side of the park and takes three to five hours to complete depending on your fitness level. The trail winds up and down steep hillsides through primeval-looking rainforest where the trees are festooned in vines and mosses and the air is heavy and damp. The highlight (quite obviously) is a remote waterfall, where you can take a shallow dip and refresh your body after the hot and humid hike.

KAMIRANZOVU TRAIL

If you have your own wheels, the Kamiranzovu Trail (per person US$40) starts somewhere between Uwinka and Gisakura, and runs for about 4km to Kamiranzovu Swamp. Sadly, the last elephant was shot here in 1999, though the swamplands are still your best bet for spotting other large mammals. Even if you don't come across any other fauna, this trail is particularly famous for its rare species of orchids and birds, including the greater swamp warbler.

Birdwatching

Nyungwe has something of a legendary status among birdwatchers in East Africa, and is by far the country's top spot for birdwatching with some 300-plus species, which include no fewer than 27 Albertine Rift Valley endemics. However, the dense forest cover means actually getting a good view of a bird (or any other animal for that matter) can often be frustratingly hard, which means that only serious birders are likely to get feathered into excitement by many of the park's birds.

For those people, the dirt Rangiro Rd, which starts 1.5km east of Uwinka, and the Imbaraga, Umuyove and Kamiranzovu Trails are all highly recommended for birdwatching. The paved road through the park permits viewing at all levels of the forest: expect mountain buzzards and cinnamon-chested bee-eaters perched along here, plus numerous sunbirds, wagtails and flocks of waxbills. Other commonly sighted birds include francolins, turacos, African crowned eagles, hornbills and even Congo bay owls.

There are six specialist birding guides based in Nyungwe who need to be booked in advance for specalist birdwatching trips (per person US$50) – email or call one of the park's two reception centres. There are more than 27 endemics in the park, including Rwenzori turacos as well as other large forest species such as African crowned eagles and various hornbills. Depending on what you hope to see, the guide will choose a trail that maximises your chances of spotting your quarry.

If you're unsure of what to ask for, opt for the dirt Rangiro Rd. Thanks to the frequent changes in elevation along this route you have increased chances of spotting a good number of Nyungwe's fine feathered friends.

Canopy Walkway

Now's your chance to relive your *Indiana Jones* fantasies. The construction of a 160m-long and at times 70m-high canopy walkway is a big draw for visitors after something unusual. You won't encounter much wildlife while on the metallic suspension bridge, but you'll certainly appreciate the jungle anew from this unique monkey's-eye perspective. Access to the canopy walkway, which is on the Igishigishigi Trail, involves a preliminary 20- to 30-minute hike from Uwinka. Canopy tours begin at set times (8am, 10am, 1pm and 3pm), last about two hours and are guided (per person US$60).

Sleeping

Kitabi Cultural Village CAMPGROUND $
(☎0787260016; www.kitabiecocenter.com; Kitabi; camping US$15; P) For that 'end-of-the-earth' feeling, you could head to this lovely venture perched on a ridge about 300m from the main road. You'd be hard pressed to find a more peaceful setting to pitch your tent, within a grassy, manicured property blessed with sensational forest views. The ablution block is in top nick. Note that tents are available for hire (US$5).

EAR Gisakura Visitor Centre BUNGALOW $
(☎0788278766, 0784417866; gisakuravisitors16@yahoo.com; Gisakura; camping per tent excl breakfast RFr10,000, s/d RFr25,000/30,000; P) The superb bucolic location is the big selling point here. The four bungalows are scattered in a large patch of forest and represent good value if you're after creature comforts. Thanks to a canopy of trees the camping area gets plenty of shade and the on-site restaurant gets good reviews. It's signposted 200m from the main road.

Uwinka Campsite CAMPGROUND $
(☎0787109335; Uwinka; camping US$30; P) The campsite at the park's reception centre is currently the only option at Uwinka. There are several choice spots, many with impressive views overlooking the forest and one on a wooden platform under a shelter that's a godsend in the likely event of rain. The ablution block is cleaner than average, though showers (and toilets) come in buckets.

Gisakura Guest House GUESTHOUSE $
(☎0788675051; www.gisakuraguesthouserw.com; Gisakura; s/d with shared bathroom US$35/55; P 📶) This guesthouse offers accommodation in cramped and simple but functional rooms that share communal showers and toilets and are set in a beautiful garden. It's well managed and the staff are very friendly and helpful, but it's hard not to think that it's overpriced. There's an on-site restaurant. Lunch or dinner buffets cost US$8.

KCCEM Guesthouse GUESTHOUSE $
(☎0783506432; marozaba@yahoo.com; Kitabi; s/d/tw excl breakfast RFr12,000/18,000/20,000; P 📶) On the eastern park boundary, not far from the Kitabi Booking Office, this no-nonsense guesthouse is great value. The 20 en suite rooms occupy five brick blocks that are perfectly serviceable and clean. Decoratively it's a bit bland, but the quiet location, mountains views and great attached canteen (meals from RFr2500) ensure it's worth a second look.

★**Gisakura Family Hostel** GUESTHOUSE $$
(☎0781282368; gisakurahostel@gmail.com; Gisakura; s/d with shared bathroom RFr30,000/45,000; P 📶) On the main road

in Gisakura, this zesty number is a solid option with efficient staff and good facilities. Rooms are practical with no flouncy embellishments – just good lighting, back-friendly mattresses and salubrious (shared) bathrooms with hot water. There's an on-site restaurant that serves excellent meals at petite prices. Choice.

Nyungwe Top View Hill Hotel LODGE $$$
(☎0788306663; www.nyungwehotel.com; Gisakura; s/d US$135/200; P 📶) High on a hill above Gisakura, this efficiently run place has large and finely decorated cottages with panoramic views, excellent bathrooms and a tiny lounge area with fireplace (staff will light the fire for you on cold nights – which means most nights). The dining and reception area occupy an impressive circular building with a tall thatched roof and traditional paintings on the walls.

One & Only Nyungwe House LODGE $$$
(☎0787352279; www.oneandonlyresorts.com; Gisakura; d from US$800; P 📶 🏊) Located in the heart of a tea plantation with a stunning jungle backdrop, the former Nyungwe Forest Lodge, now part of the famous One & Only chain, is one of the most exclusive lodges in all Rwanda, with 22 fancy rooms and suites in six opulent wooden villas.

ℹ Information

Nyungwe Forest National Park is sliced in two parts by the Huye–Cyangugu road. Visitors can access the park through the Kitabi Booking Office, the Gisakura Booking Office or the Uwinka Reception Centre, which all lie along this road. For information online, see www.rwandatourism.com.

Uwinka Reception Centre (☎0788317027, 0788317028; nyungwe.reservation@gmail.com; Uwinka; ⏱7am-5pm) This reception centre is a little over halfway to Cyangugu from Huye (Butare). Most nature walks (as well as the Canopy Walkway) begin here. Note that this reception centre does not take bookings nor accept payments; guides and activities must be booked online or paid at either Kitabi Booking Office (at the eastern end of the park) or at Gisakura Booking Office (at the western end of the park).

It has a small but informative display on the ecology of the park, a cafeteria and an outdoor terrace area.

Gisakura Booking Office (☎0788317027, 0788317028; nyungwe.reservation@gmail.com; Gisakura; ⏱7am-5pm) This booking office can be found in Gisakura (near the tea plantation) and is the one most frequently used by park visitors. You can pay fees here and organise nature walks, birdwatching trips and chimpanzee tracking.

Kitabi Booking Office (☎0788317028, 0788317027; nyungwe.reservation@gmail.com; Kitabi) This booking office lies at the eastern end of the park. You can pay fees here and book nature walks, birdwatching trips and chimpanzee tracking. A number of nature walks also start here.

ℹ Getting There & Away

Regular buses travel between Huye (Butare; RFr4000, two hours, 90km) and Kamembe (for Cyangugu; one hour, 55km) throughout the day. Any one of these buses can drop you at Kitabi, Uwinka Reception Centre or Gisakura, but they charge the full RFr4000 fare.

The trouble is that having arrived, your ability to move around the park is severely limited if you don't have a car. If you're sticking to the nature walks and don't have your own transport, consider camping at Uwinka where most of the walks begin (although there are some that start close to Gisakura, plus there's a small group of habituated colobus within easy walking distance of Gisakura, and there are also nature trails around Kitabi).

Leaving is more problematic as many of the passing buses are full and you may have to wait some time before one will stop. The rangers on duty at either of the booking centres will normally phone one of the bus companies on your behalf and secure a seat. Once the ranger has made the booking he'll hold your fare as in the past some travellers go on to find lifts with other tourists and then refuse to pay for the empty seat that is being held for them.

Cyangugu (Rusizi)

POP 64,000

Clinging to the southern tip of Lake Kivu, and looking across to Bukavu in the DRC, Cyangugu (Rusizi) is an attractively situated town on the lake's shore. There's not much action, but it's a great place to relax for a day or two before (or after) exploring Nyungwe Forest National Park.

The town has two distinct settlements: Kamembe, the commercial heart (an important location for the processing of tea and cotton) found a few kilometres above the lake; and Cyangugu proper, which is much lower, far prettier, far quieter and right next to the DRC border.

Sleeping

Hotel du Lac – Kivu View Hotel HOTEL $

(☎0788307576; kivuview@yahoo.fr; d RFr15,000-60,000; P 📶) So close to the border it's almost in the DRC, this local landmark has a good mix of rooms, even though some of them have aged less than gracefully over the years. Cheaper rooms have cold showers only. It has a restaurant overlooking the river and serves a mix of local and international dishes.

★ **Emeraude Kivu Resort** HOTEL $$

(☎0787010900; www.emeraudekivuresort.rw; s/d US$100/120; P 📶) This well-regarded venture provides an excellent level of comfort and service. The sun-filled, spick-and-span rooms boast pristine bathrooms, well-sprung mattresses and cardiac-arresting lake views. Boat trips can easily be arranged. The fancy restaurant overlooking the lake is a joy.

Information

You'll find all the banks in Kamembe. Moneychangers near the border in Cyangugu will change Rwandan francs to DRC francs, although US dollars are the currency of choice for all but the smallest of purchases in the DRC.

Getting There & Away

Cyangugu is literally a stone's throw away from the DRC, and providing you have all your paperwork in place, you can walk across the bridge and into the Congo.

Moto-taxis for the short hop between Cyangugu and Kamembe cost RFr500.

Kibuye (Karongi)

POP 48,000

Be prepared to fall on your knees in awe: spread across a series of tongues jutting into Lake Kivu, Kibuye (Karongi) is one of the most scenic cities in Rwanda. The steep hills that fall into the deep green waters and the indented shoreline with a smattering of islands nearby make it extremely picturesque. It's also, even by Rwandan standards, a very clean and green little town where nothing much seems to happen in a hurry. In short, if you're after a mellow place to decompress, Kibuye is your answer.

History

During the 100 days of madness in 1994, Kibuye was the site of some of the most horrific and despicable mass killings in all of Rwanda. Prior to the outbreak of the genocide, more than 20% of the local population was Tutsi; in 1994 the Interahamwe killed an estimated nine out of every 10 Tutsi. While these scars still run deep, today the residents of Kibuye are working together as a community to embrace the prospect of future tourism. A couple of memorials to the slain victims ensure that the past is not forgotten, while the frames of new buildings are signs of a brighter future.

Sights

Museum of the Environment MUSEUM

(☎0730741093; www.museum.gov.rw; adult/student RFr6000/3000; ⏰8am-6pm) This smart museum on Kibuye's lake shore has educational displays about energy sources and the environmental impact of different types of fuel sources. It won't appeal to anyone who knows anything about sustainability, but there is an excellent rooftop garden with a collection of native plants, each with explanations of their use in traditional medicine.

Église St Pierre CHURCH

FREE While a good number of memorials in Rwanda are stark reminders of the past atrocities, the genocide memorial church of St Pierre is a beautiful, calm and evocative testament to the strength of the human spirit. The interior is adorned with colourful mosaics and vivid stained-glass windows, while outside a small brick annex displays skulls and bones from some of the 11,000 people who were killed by a drunken mob here.

Bisesero Genocide Memorial MEMORIAL

(Bisesero) FREE About 30km southeast from Kibuye, the small village of Bisesero is home to stunning scenery and a stirring genocide memorial.

During the early days of the genocide, more than 50,000 Tutsis fled here in the hope of evading the Interahamwe. For more than a month, these brave individuals were able to fend off their aggressors with little more than basic farming implements. On 13 May, a reinforced regiment of soldiers and militia descended on Bisesero, slaughtering more than half of the refugees. By the time the French arrived on the scene in June, there were fewer than 1300 Tutsis remaining.

Activities

Following the ring road around Lake Kivu's shores offers some amazing views and you're likely to find a few sandy patches where you can pause to laze or to take a cooling dip – do be aware that some locals claim Lake Kivu now has bilharzia (p647) in it.

Boat Trips

Every visitor to Kibuye seems to head out onto the wide blue yonder for a boat trip around the lake. The most popular excursion is a half-day tour (boat holding 12 people around RFr50,000) taking in six of the gorgeous forested islands and islets sitting offshore of Kibuye, including the Chapeau de Napoleon, which is home to thousands of birds.

Boats for charter can be found at the water's edge beneath the Museum of the Environment (p539). Rates aren't fixed and will depend on how far you wish to venture and for how long you wish to go.

Sleeping

Home St Jean GUESTHOUSE $
(☎0784725107; www.homesaintjean.com; dm US$12, s US$23-38, with shared bathroom US$15-20, d US$30-47, with shared bathroom US$23-27; P Wi-Fi) Sitting on its own hillside with stunning 270-degree views across Lake Kivu, this church-run pad has rooms of varying standards (and different prices) that are nothing too out of the ordinary but are well scrubbed and set in a manicured garden. There's even access to the lake via a steep footpath. Rooms 14 to 17 are the most comfortable.

★**Rwiza Village** BOUTIQUE HOTEL $$
(☎0788307356, 0789714551; www.rwizavillage.org; camping per tent US$40, s/d US$80/115; P Wi-Fi) In search of an escape? This lovely venture perched on a hillside sloping down to the lake (there's a pontoon for swimming) offers guests the chance to unplug in 10 cocoon-like, A-framed chalets built from local materials. They are set amid beautifully landscaped gardens, with the added bonus of breathtaking views. The attached restaurant concocts delicious vegetarian specialties. A winner.

★**Cormoran Lodge** LODGE $$$
(☎0728601515; www.cormoranlodge.com; s/d US$135/180; P Wi-Fi) Outside of town along a very rough road, this stunner of a lodge melds rock, lake and wood into a truly memorable place to stay. The rooms, which are all free-standing and spaced throughout landscaped grounds tumbling to the lake shore, are like luxurious tree houses on stilts and are built entirely out of logs and beach pebbles.

Information

Banks with ATMs are easy to find in the centre. They also change currencies.

Getting There & Away

BOAT

There's a twice-weekly passenger **ferry service** (☎0781087996) between Gisenyi (Rubavu), Kibuye (Karongi) and Cyangugu (Rusizi). The boat makes the southbound trip from Gisenyi on Wednesdays and Saturdays, leaving from Rubona Peninsula at 7am. It arrives at Kibuye (RFr2500) around 10.30am and at Cyangugu (RFr5000) around 3.45pm. Boats head north from Cyangugu on Tuesdays and Fridays.

Tickets are purchased on the boat.

BUS

The road linking Kibuye with Kigali is endlessly winding but in excellent shape, making Kibuye very accessible from the capital. Bus services to Kigali (RFr2500, 3½ hours) via Gitarama (RFr1700, two hours) start around 6am and continue hourly until 5.30pm.

There are also several daily services for Gisenyi (Rubavu; RFr3000, three hours) and Cyangugu (Rusizi; RFr2200, 3½ hours).

The **bus station** is right in the centre of town.

Getting Around

Moto-taxis wait for arriving buses in the centre of town. It's a RFr500 hop from here to Hotel Centre Bethany or Home St Jean.

EASTERN RWANDA

While much of Rwanda is characterised by equatorial rainforest, rolling hills, mountains and richly cultivated farmland, eastern Rwanda is something else entirely. Contiguous with the dry and flat savannah lands of Tanzania, this region is more reminiscent of the classic images of East African landscapes. While sights are scarce in this part of the country, Akagera National Park is one of Rwanda's highlights and another postgenocide success story. The park has done an impressive job of rehabilitating its decimated animal population since refugees flooded into the park during the genocide, and it's one of the most progressively run national parks in East Africa. And, since 2017, you can even spot all of Africa's iconic safari species – elephant, lion, leopard, rhino, buffalo, giraffe and zebra.

Akagera National Park

Call it a miracle. Created in 1934 to protect the lands surrounding the Kagera River, **Akagera National Park** (☎0786182871; www.african-parks.org/the-parks/akagera; per person US$40/25, vehicle US$20-40; ⏲6am-6pm) is back with a vengeance. It once protected nearly 10% of Rwanda and was considered to be one of the finest wildlife reserves in the whole of Africa. Sadly, due to the massive numbers of refugees who returned to Rwanda in the late 1990s, over half of the park was de-gazetted and resettled with new villages. Human encroachment facilitated poaching and environmental degradation and Akagera's wildlife was very nearly decimated. However, strict conservation laws, better management, the reintroduction of lions in 2015 and black rhinos in 2017, the revamping of old camps and the building of new ones has meant that Akagera is getting increasingly popular. Sure, it can't compete with its counterparts in Kenya or Tanzania, but its scenic landscapes, diverse habitats and rich wildlife are well worth the trip.

Sights

There are three distinct environments in the park: standard savannah as seen in much of the region; an immense swampy area along the border with Tanzania that contains six lakes and numerous islands, some of which are covered with forest; and a chain of low mountains on the flanks of the park with variable vegetation, ranging from short grasses on the summits to wooded savannah and dense thickets of forest.

Truth be told, you will be disappointed if you come here expecting concentrations of wildlife on a par with Kenya and Tanzania. Carnivores in Akagera are limited to rarely seen leopards (about 150 individuals) and hyenas as well as genets, servals and jackals. And lions? In 2015 seven individuals were flown from South Africa to Rwanda in a chartered plane and transported to Akagera.

AKAGERA NATIONAL PARK

Why Go While wildlife populations are still recovering, Akagera's strongest drawcard is its unique ecology: a mix of woodland habitats, swampy wetlands and jagged mountains.

When to Go The best time to visit is during the dry season (mid-May to September). November and April are the wettest months.

Practicalities Tsetse flies and mosquitoes can be bad enough to seriously detract from your safari enjoyment, so bring a good insect repellent. Akagera is really only accessible for those with their own transport.

Budget Tips Due to the necessity of hiring your own vehicle, Akagera is a tough park to explore on a budget. Costs can be reduced by camping and just going on a boat safari. However, you still need some kind of transport to both the campsite and the lake shore.

There are now 19 lions in the park, which bodes well. Eighteen black rhinos were also introduced to Akagera in 2017. Of the other large 'trophy' animals there are an estimated 90 elephants in the park, which are quite commonly seen. Buffalo are also present in reasonably healthy numbers (about 3000), and there are masses of hippos and crocs in the lakes. Antelope and other plains game are well represented, though herds tend to be small and the animals rather skittish. Common safari staples include impala, topi, zebra and waterbuck, as well as the majestic but rare roan antelope and the diminutive Oribi. Maasai giraffes, never native to the park, have been introduced and are faring well.

Of the primates, olive baboons and vervet monkeys are very common.

Even if you don't come across too many animals, you probably won't come across too many other wildlife-viewing drivers either, which means you can soak up the park's splendid nature in relative peace and isolation.

Activities

For all activities bar the wildlife drives in your own vehicle, you should book in advance through the park office (p543).

Wildlife Drives

For a classic wildlife drive, most people hire a 4WD safari jeep in Kigali, but this is very expensive (around US$300 per day including fuel from most reputable agencies). Park ranger guides or community freelance guides are both optionally available (US$25/40 per half-/full-day).

One long but worthwhile safari option is to enter the park at the main gate, pick up your guide and spend the day making your way to the park's northern Nyungwe gate (wildlife populations are much higher in the north). Once there, you could drop off your guide (with a *moto-taxi* fare to get him back to park headquarters) before returning to Kigali.

The other option is to rent one of the park's safari jeeps for US$180 for a half day and US$280 for a full day. Rates include a driver and a guide. You should arrange this in advance through the park office (p543).

Lake Ihema Boat Trips

Park authorities can arrange boat trips on Lake Ihema to see the hippo pods and some of the huge Nile crocodiles that are otherwise difficult to observe. This is also the best way to view the park's abundant water-birds, including swamp flycatchers, African fishing eagles, African darters and breeding colonies of noisy and smelly cormorants and open-bill storks. For our money this is the single nicest way of exploring the park. It's important to make a reservation through the park office (p543) at least an hour or so in advance. One-hour tours cost US$30 per person, while the sunset trip is US$40. Trips depart at 7.30am, 9am, 3pm and 4.30pm.

IMIGONGO SHOPPING IN EASTERN RWANDA

Eastern Rwanda is famous for its superb *imigongo* paintings. They consist of a series of geometric patterns made with cow dung, which are painted (usually in red, white and black colours made from local plants mixed with ash). In certain villages, including Kirehe (Nyararambi), some houses have their outer walls decorated with cow-dung paintings.

You can buy *imigongo* paintings in various shops and hotels around Rwanda, but if you're heading to Akagera National Park, it's well worth making a detour to Kirehe, where you can purchase such paintings and see how they are created at a few cooperatives, including **Chez Gasana** (☎0788436682; NR 4 Rd, Kirehe/Nyakarambi; ⏰7am-6pm) and **Coopérative Kakira Art Imigongo** (☎0788844779; NR 4 Rd, Kirehe/Nyakarambi; ⏰7am-noon & 2-6pm).

Birdwatching

Akagera lies on the great Nile Valley bird migration route, which means that you could potentially spot nearly 500 species of birds, including several endemics, more than 40 different kinds of raptors and, in wetland areas, the much sought after shoebill. It's Rwanda's best birdwatching destination outside of Nyungwe Forest National Park. The many kilometres of waterside habitat support African eagles, kingfishers, herons, ibises, storks, egrets, crakes, rails, cormorants, darts and pelicans. Seasonal visitors include large flocks of ducks, bee-eaters and terns, and the woodlands areas are particularly good places for barbets, shrikes, orioles and weavers. Birding guides can be arranged at the park's office (p543).

Behind-the-Scenes Tour

One of the most innovative and interesting activities offered is a behind-the-scenes tour (per person US$25), which requires a minimum of four people. You will get to meet and talk to rangers, antipoaching patrols and community-projects managers. It's a fascinating insight into the often very political world of modern wildlife conservation in East Africa and the day-to-day running of a protected zone. It's organised through the park office (p543) and you need to give at least a day or so notice. The tour lasts about 90 minutes.

Night Drive

As dusk comes and all the daylight wildlife heads off to bed somewhere, a whole new cast of rarely seen characters emerges from the gloom. A night drive gives you the opportunity to see some of these creatures – if you're lucky, leopards and hyenas. The safari (per person US$40), which starts at 5.30pm, lasts around two hours and requires a minimum of two participants.

Sleeping

Mutumba Campsite CAMPGROUND $
(Akagera National Park; camping US$25) Akagera's most spectacular campsite, Mutumba is perched on the Mutumba Hills, which form the highest point of the park. Needless to stay, the views are mesmerising. Firewood is provided and there's an ablution block with clean toilets (but no shower). It's protected by an electric fence.

Muyumbu Campsite CAMPGROUND $
(Akagera National Park; camping US$25) This attractive campsite perched on a ridge is blessed with stunning views of the lakes. Firewood is provided and there's an ablution block with clean toilets (but no shower). It's protected by an electric fence.

Lake Shakani Campsite CAMPGROUND $
(Akagera National Park; camping US$25) This basic yet ideally located campsite is right on the shores of Lake Shakani, a few kilometres northeast of the park headquarters. It offers firewood and a basic toilet (but no shower). Book through the park office. Note that this campsite is not fenced.

Akagera Game Lodge HOTEL $$
(0786182871, 0785201206; www.akageralodge.com; Akagera National Park; s US$100-140; P wi-fi pool) Built on a ridge near the park office, this motel-like place has large and well-appointed rooms with views over the hills to the hippo-filled lake below for a very good price. The restaurant (mains from RFr4000) is kind of soulless, but the food is tasty. Positives include a well-maintained pool and a play area for kids.

★ **Ruzizi Tented Lodge** TENTED CAMP $$$
(0787113300; www.ruzizilodge.com; Akagera National Park; s/d incl full board US$265/400; P wi-fi) Hidden under a tangle of dense riverine trees on the shore of Lake Ihema, this refined tented camp with an intimate feel – there are only nine units, all with lake views – is a delightfully relaxing place. While it's not as ornate as some top-end camps elsewhere in East Africa, it's a steal at this price.

Karenge Bush Camp TENTED CAMP $$$
(0787113300; www.african-parks.org/the-parks/akagera/visit-the-park/karenge-bush-camp; Akagera Nationa Park; s/d incl full board US$245/350; Jun-Aug & mid-Dec–Feb; P) What a fabulous setting! This temporary tented camp perched on the edge of an escarpment overlooking an incredible sweep of savannah offers six comfortable (but not luxurious) safari tents with private outside bathroom. Its location is ideal for morning wildlife drives around Kilala Plain, which maximises your chance of spotting lions and hyenas.

> WORTH A TRIP
>
> **RUSUMO FALLS**
>
> At Rusumo, right between the Rwandan and Tanzanian border posts, the gorgeous **Rusumo Falls** (Rusumo) are the largest waterfalls in Rwanda and a good side trip from Akagera National Park. As you would expect, the falls are at their best during the wet season. They're not tall, but you can expect an impressive rush of muddy water. You're allowed to drive (or walk) until the bridge between the two border posts – the best vantage point.

Eating

Park Office Cafeteria CAFETERIA $
(0782166015; Akagera National Park; sandwiches RFr2500; 6am-6pm) The cafeteria housed in the park visitor centre is a dream come true for coffee-lovers, with a choice of excellent Rwandan brews. It also serves cakes and generous sandwiches – a great option if you haven't brought your own lunch.

CTN – Akagera National Park Community Centre FAST FOOD $
(0781051999; Akagera National Park; mains RFr500-1500; 11am-10pm) Very few visitors have heard about this easy-to-miss canteen at the staff quarters (look for the small building behind the basketball court), which is open to all. The food – mostly brochettes, rice and French fries – is fresh, tasty and cheap. You can also hunker down in one of the five rooms in the adjoining building (from RFr7000). Bathrooms are shared.

Information

Note that park fees are valid for one night – in other words, if you arrive when the park opens at 6am and leave the next day at 6pm, you'll still pay US$40 (and not US$80).

Park Office (0786182871, 0782166015; www.african-parks.org/the-parks/akagera; Kiyonza; 6am-6pm) Just past the park's main gate at Kiyonza, the very helpful park office is where you need to book most activities. It also houses an interesting display on the park, and there's a cafeteria selling excellent coffee, cakes and sandwiches.

Getting There & Away

While in theory it's possible to get close to the park by public transport, Akagera is really only accessible for those with their own transport. Safari and tour companies in Kigali can arrange a vehicle with a driver or you can simply hire your own and self drive – a far cheaper option.

Although Akagera can be reached in about two hours from Kigali and is a feasible day trip from the capital, it does make sense to spend at least a night in the park to make the most of your trip.

Getting Around

A 4WD with high clearance is essential for driving inside the park. A vast network of dirt roads are there to explore on your own or with a guide.

UNDERSTAND RWANDA

History

Decolonisation & Independence

Rwanda and neighbouring Burundi were colonised by Germany and later Belgium, both of which played on ethnic differences to divide and conquer the population. Power was concentrated in the hands of the minority Tutsi, with the Tutsi *mwami* (king) playing the central role in political and legislative decision-making.

In 1956 Mwami Rudahigwa called for independence from Belgium, which influenced Rwanda's colonial occupiers to switch allegiance to the Hutu majority. The Tutsis favoured fast-track independence, while the Hutus wanted the introduction of democracy followed later by independence.

After the death of Rudahigwa in 1959, tribal tensions flared as the 'Hutu Revolution' resulted in the deaths of an estimated 20,000 to 100,000 Tutsis. Another 150,000 Tutsis were driven from the country, and forced to resettle as refugees in Uganda, Kenya and Tanzania.

Following independence in 1962, the Hutu majority came to power under Prime Minister Gregoire Kayibanda, who introduced quotas for Tutsis that limited their opportunities for education and work. In the fresh round of bloodshed that followed, thousands more Tutsis were killed, and tens of thousands fled across the borders.

Intertribal tensions erupted once again in 1972 when tens of thousands of Hutu were massacred in Burundi by the Tutsi-dominated government in reprisal for a coup attempt. The slaughter reignited old hatreds in Rwanda, which prompted Major General Juvenal Habyarimana to oust Kayibanda in 1973.

During the early years of his regime, Habyarimana made progress towards healing tribal divisions, and the country enjoyed relative economic prosperity. However, events unfolding in Uganda in the 1980s were to have a profound impact on the future of Rwanda.

In 1986 Yoweri Museveni became president of Uganda after his National Resistance Army (NRA) fought a brutal bush war to remove General Tito Okello from power. One of Museveni's key lieutenants was the current Rwandan president Paul Kagame, who capitalised on the victory by joining together with other exiled Tutsis to form the Rwandan Patriotic Front (RPF).

The Civil War Erupts

On 1 October 1990, 5000 well-armed soldiers of the RPF invaded Rwanda. All hell broke loose. Two days later at Habyarimana's request, France, Belgium and the DRC flew in troops to help the Rwandan army repel the invasion.

With foreign support assured, the Rwandan army went on a rampage against the Tutsis, as well as any Hutu suspected of having collaborated with the RPF. Thousands of people were shot or hacked to death, and countless others indiscriminately arrested, herded into football stadiums or police stations and left there without food or water for days.

Many died. Congolese Hutu troops joined in the carnage. Once again thousands of Tutsi refugees fled to Uganda. However, the initial setback for the RPF was only temporary as President Museveni was keen to see the repatriation of the now

250,000 Tutsi refugees living in western Uganda.

While he fervently denied such allegations, Museveni allegedly helped to reorganise and re-equip the RPF. In 1991, Kagame's forces invaded Rwanda for a second time, and by 1993 were garrisoned only 25km outside of Kigali.

With Habyarimana backed into a corner, the warring parties were brought to the negotiating table in Arusha, Tanzania. Negotiations stalled, hostilities were renewed, and French troops were flown in to protect foreign nationals in Kigali, though they were accused by the RPF of assisting the Rwandan army. A report released in 2008 by the Rwandan government accused the French government of committing war crimes, though all allegations were fervently denied by the French.

Meanwhile, with morale in the Rwandan army fading fast, the RPF launched an all-out offensive on the capital. Once again backed into a corner, Habyarimana invited the RPF to attend a conference of regional presidents. Power-sharing was on the agenda.

Tragically, on 6 April 1994, the aeroplane carrying Habyarimana and Cyprien Ntaryamira, the president of Burundi, was shot down by a surface-to-air missile while on approach to Kigali airport. It will probably never be known who fired the missile, though most observers believe it was Hutu extremists who had been espousing ethnic cleansing over the airwaves of Radio Télévision Libre des Mille Collines.

Regardless of who was responsible, the event unleashed one of the 20th century's worst explosions of bloodletting.

The Genocide

In the 100 days that followed, extremists among Habyarimana's Hutu political and military supporters embarked on a well-planned 'final solution' to the Tutsi 'problem'. One of the principal architects of the genocide was the cabinet chief of the Ministry of Defence, Colonel Theoneste Bagosora, who had been in charge of training the Interahamwe ('those who stand together') militia for more than a year.

One of Bagosora's first acts was to direct the army to kill the 'moderate' Hutu prime minister, Agathe Uwilingiyimana, as well as 10 Belgian UN peacekeepers. The killing of the UN peacekeepers prompted Belgium to withdraw all of its troops – precisely what Bagosora had calculated – which paved the way for the genocide to begin in earnest.

Rwandan army and Interahamwe death squads ranged at will over the countryside, killing, looting and burning, and roadblocks were set up in every town and city to prevent Tutsis from escaping. Every day, thousands of Tutsi and any Hutu suspected of sympathising with them or their plight were butchered on the spot. The streets of Kigali were littered with dismembered corpses, and the stench of rotting flesh was everywhere.

Those who attempted to take refuge in religious missions or churches often did so in vain. In some cases, it was the nuns and priests themselves who betrayed the fugitives to the death squads. Any mission that refused the death squads access was simply blown apart.

Perhaps the most shocking part of the tragedy was the willingness with which ordinary Hutu – men, women and even children as young as 10 years old – joined in the carnage. The perpetrators of the massacre were caught up in a tide of blind hatred, fear and mob mentality, which was inspired, controlled and promoted under the direction of their political and military leaders.

The UN Assistance Mission for Rwanda (UNAMIR) was in Rwanda throughout the genocide, but was powerless to prevent the killing due to an ineffective mandate. Although UN Force Commander Lieutenant General Romeo Dallaire had been warning senior UN staff and diplomats about the coming bloodshed, his warnings went unheeded.

The international community left Rwanda to face its fate. While the RPF eventually succeeded in pushing the Rwandan army and the Interahamwe into the DRC and Burundi, around a million people were killed, while another two million were huddled in refugee camps across the borders.

UNAMIR was finally reinforced and given a more open mandate in July, but it was in the words of Dallaire, 'too much, too late'. The genocide was already over – the RPF had taken control of Kigali.

The Aftermath

Of course, that is far from the end of the story. Within a year of the RPF victory, a legal commission was set up in Arusha, Tanzania, to try those accused of involvement in the genocide. However, many of the main perpetrators – the Interahamwe and former senior army officers – fled into exile beyond the reach of the RPF.

Some went to Kenya, where they enjoyed the protection of President Moi, who long refused to hand them over. Others – including Colonel Theoneste Bagosora, the principal architect of the genocide, and Ferdinand Nahimana, the director of the notorious Radio Télévision Libre des Mille Collines, which actively encouraged Hutus to butcher Tutsis – fled to Cameroon where they enjoyed the protection of that country's security boss, Jean Fochive. However, when Fochive was sacked by the newly elected president of Cameroon, Paul Biya, the Rwandan exiles were arrested.

Of greater importance were the activities of the Interahamwe and former army personnel in the refugee camps of the DRC and Tanzania. Determined to continue their fight against the RPF, they spread fear among the refugees that if they returned to Rwanda, they would be killed. When Rwanda began to demand the repatriation of the refugees, the grip of the Interahamwe on the camps was so complete that few dared move.

What was of most concern to the RPF was that the Interahamwe was using the refugee camps as staging posts for raids into Rwanda, with the complicity of the Congolese army. By 1996 Rwanda was openly warning the DRC that if these raids did not stop, the consequences would be dire.

The raids continued, and the RPF held true to its threat by mounting a lightning strike two-day campaign into the DRC, targeting one of the main refugee camps north of Goma. The Interahamwe fled deep into the jungles of the Congo, which allowed

THE SLOW HAND OF JUSTICE

Following a slow and shaky start, the **International Criminal Tribunal for Rwanda** (ICTR; http://unictr.unmict.org) managed to net most of the major suspects wanted for involvement in the 1994 genocide. After more than 20 years pursuing justice for the genocide's victims by ending impunity for its gravest perpetrators, the tribunal finished its operations in December 2015.

The tribunal was established in Arusha, Tanzania, in 1995, but was initially impeded in its quest for justice by the willingness of several African countries to protect suspects. Countries such as Cameroon, the DRC and Kenya long harboured Kigali's most wanted, frustrating the Rwandan authorities in their attempts to seek justice. However, due to changes in their attitude or government, many of the former ministers (including the former prime minister, Jean Kambanda) of the interim cabinet that presided over the country during the genocide were arrested.

While the architects of the tragedy were tried at the ICTR, Rwanda's judicial system found itself facing a backlog that would take a century to clear. With too many cases (in excess of 120,000) and too few jails to humanely detain such a large percentage of the population, an age-old solution was revived.

Across the country thousands of *gacaca* courts were set up and hundreds of thousands of judges appointed. Modelled on traditional hearings that were headed by village elders, these tribunals were empowered to identify and categorise suspects. Category 1 suspects who were thought to have organised, encouraged or instigated the genocide were remanded for processing in the formal judicial system. The *gacaca* court tried category 2 and 3 suspects, those accused of murder, bodily injury or causing property damage. Each court contained a minimum of 15 community-elected judges and was witnessed by 100 citizens. These small courts, the work of which has also come to a close, not only found many of the guilty but also provided closure for the families of their victims and helped relieve the burden the larger courts face. That said, the lack of due legal process raised some concerns among some international human rights groups.

hundreds of thousands of refugees to return home to Rwanda.

Events changed in October 1996 when a guerrilla movement known as the Alliance of Democratic Forces for the Liberation of Congo-Zaïre, led by Laurent Kabila, emerged with the secret support of Rwanda and Uganda. The rebels, ably supported by Rwandan and Ugandan regulars, swept through the eastern DRC, and by December were in control of every town and city in the region.

The Congolese army, alongside the Interahamwe and former Rwandan army personnel, retreated west in disarray towards Kisangani, looting and pillaging as they went. However, the grip the Interahamwe had on the refugee camps was finally broken, which allowed the remaining refugees to stream back into Rwanda, not only from the DRC but also from Tanzania.

Faced with a huge refugee resettlement task, the government began to build new villages throughout the country. Huge tracts of Parc National de l'Akagera were de-gazetted as a national park and given over to this 'villagisation' program, along with much of the northwest region, which had previously hosted some of the most intense battles of the civil war.

The Healing Begins

Rwanda has done a remarkable job healing its wounds and has achieved an astonishing level of safety and security in a remarkably short space of time – albeit with considerable help from a guilty international community that ignored the country in its darkest hour. Visiting Kigali today, it is hard to believe the horror that swept across this land in 1994.

On the international front, however, things have been rather less remarkable. In 1998 Rwanda and Uganda joined forces to oust their former ally Laurent Kabila who was then president of the DRC. What ensued was Africa's first great war, sucking in as many as nine neighbours at its height and costing an estimated three to five million deaths, mostly from disease and starvation.

Rwanda and Uganda soon fell out, squabbling over the rich resources that were there for the plunder in the DRC. Rwanda backed the Rally for Congolese Democracy, Uganda the Movement for the Liberation of the Congo and the two countries fought out a brutal and prolonged proxy war.

Peace treaties were signed in 2002 and foreign forces were withdrawn from the DRC, though, if and when an international inquiry is launched, Rwanda may find itself facing accusations of war crimes. Rwanda's motives for entering the fray were to wipe out remnants of the Interahamwe militia and former soldiers responsible for the genocide, but somewhere along the line, elements in the army may have lost sight of the mission. A leaked 2010 report by the UN High Commissioner for Human Rights has even accused the current Rwandan administration of committing genocide against Hutus in the DRC. And in 2012 a rebel militia in the DRC, the M23, took over large tracts of eastern DRC, including the Congolese side of the Virungas and even, briefly, Goma. Both Rwanda and Uganda have been accused of supporting and equipping the M23 rebels.

Back on the domestic front, Paul Kagame assumed the presidency in 2000 and was overwhelmingly endorsed at the ballot box in presidential elections in 2003 and 2010 that saw him take 95% and 93% of the vote respectively. However, his rule has become increasingly autocratic, with opposition groups silenced, civil society being stifled and many journalists being harassed and even imprisoned. A 2015 referendum gave Kagame a mandate to run again for election until 2034, with an incredible 98% of voters supporting a side-stepping of the constitution. While it's undeniable that Kagame is hugely popular in Rwanda, many commentators have suggested that the move is incompatible with the country's otherwise impressively progressive politics.

Rwanda Today

Rwanda is easily one of Africa's most progressive and better-run nations, and has done an impressive job of coming to terms with and moving on from its dark past. That said, the news is not all positive, with the increasingly autocratic rule of President Paul Kagame worrying many observers who see definite signs of the now veteran leader making moves to ensure he can remain in power long term.

Building National Unity

Despite all the efforts at nation building since the genocide, Rwanda remains the home of two tribes, the Hutu and the Tutsi. The Hutu presently outnumber the Tutsi by more than four to one and, while the RPF government is one of national unity with a number of Hutu representatives, it's viewed in some quarters as a Tutsi government ruling over a predominantly Hutu population.

However, the RPF government has done an impressive job of promoting reconciliation and restoring trust between the two communities. This is no small achievement after the horrors that were inflicted on the Tutsi community during the genocide of 1994, especially since it would have been all too easy for the RPF to embark on a campaign of revenge and reprisal.

On the contrary, Kagame and his government are attempting to build a society with a place for everyone, regardless of tribe. Officially there are no more Tutsis, no more Hutus, only Rwandans – idealistic perhaps, but it is realistically the best hope for the future. Rightly or wrongly, Paul Kagame has plenty of detractors, but on the surface, at least, it's hard not to see Rwanda today as anything other than buzzing with potential for the future.

Kagame is trying to leave the past behind and create a new Rwanda for Rwandans. Forget the past? No. But do learn from it and move on to create a new spirit of national unity.

Signs of Authoritarianism

Despite being a genuinely popular leader who many credit with single-handedly leading Rwanda's impressive transformation since 2000, Paul Kagame has in recent years displayed a worrying strain of authoritarianism and undertaken various measures that suggest he plans to remain in power indefinitely.

In 2015 an incredible 3.7 million Rwandans – over half the total number of people in the country registered to vote – signed a petition seeking a constitutional amendment to allow Kagame to stand again for re-election in 2017, and effectively clearing the way for him to run for office until 2034. When the matter was put to a referendum later the same year, an amazing 98% of the electorate supported the move, though there were reports of voter intimidation and coercion. While publicly stating that he has no plans to remain in power for decades, it certainly looks like Kagame wants to keep his options open and has little tolerance for people who oppose his policies.

Unsurprisingly, Kagame easily won the 2017 presidential election. His plans are to boost the modernisation of the country, continue the reconciliation process and reinforce the diplomatic influence of Rwanda within Central and East Africa.

Amnesty International has repeatedly reported declining press freedom, human rights abuses and repression of opposition parties, although much of the silencing of dissenting voices in Rwanda can be said to be the result of self-censorship on the part of a populace unwilling to provoke a government that has brought about peace and progress.

Culture

The National Psyche

Tribal conflict has torn Rwanda apart during much of the independence period, culminating in the horrific genocide that unfolded in 1994. With that said, there are basically two schools of thought when it comes to looking at Rwandan identity.

The colonial approach of the Belgians was to divide and rule, issuing ID cards that divvied up the population along strict tribal lines. They tapped the Tutsis as leaders to help control the Hutu majority, building on the foundations of precolonial society in which the Tutsi were considered more dominant. Later, as independence approached, they switched sides, pitting Hutu against Tutsi in a new conflict that simmered on and off until the 1990s when it exploded onto the world stage.

In the new Rwanda, the opposite is true. Tribal identities have been systematically eliminated and everyone is now treated as a Rwandan. The new government is at pains to present a singular identity and blames the Belgians for categorising the country along tribal lines and setting the stage for the savagery that followed. Rwanda was a peaceful place beforehand: Hutu and Tutsi lived side by side for generations and intermarriage was common – or so the story goes.

The truth, as is often the case, is probably somewhere in between. Rwanda was no oasis before the colonial powers arrived. However, Tutsis probably had a better time of it than Hutus, something that the Belgians were able to exploit as they sought control.

But it is true to say that there was no history of major bloodshed between the two peoples before 1959, and the foundations of the violence were laid by the Belgian insistence on ethnic identity and their cynical political manipulation of it. The leaders of the genocide merely took this policy to its extreme, first promoting tribal differences and then playing on them to manipulate a malleable population.

Daily Life

Urban Rwanda is a very sophisticated place. People start the day early before breaking off for a long lunch. Late dinners inevitably lead to drinking and socialising, which sometimes doesn't wind down until the early morning.

In rural areas people work long hours from dawn until dusk, but they also take a break during the hottest part of the day. However, it is a hard life for women in the countryside who seem burdened with the lion's share of the work, while many menfolk often sit around drinking and talking.

Faith is an important rock in the lives of many Rwandan people, with Christianity firmly rooted as the dominant religion. Churches from different denominations in Rwanda were tainted by their association with the genocide in 1994, though that doesn't seem to have dampened people's devotion to the faith.

Like many countries in Africa, Rwanda actively promotes universal primary education. Despite suffering terribly during the genocide, the education system continues to improve and the literacy rate, according to Unicef, stands at around 68%, up from 58% in 1991.

Economy

Rwanda's economy was decimated during the genocide – production ground to a halt, and foreign investors pulled out altogether. However, the current government has done a commendable job of stimulating the economy, which is now fairly stable and boasts steady growth and low inflation. Foreign investors are once again doing business in Kigali, and there are building projects springing up all over the capital. Tourism too has rebounded and is again the country's leading foreign-exchange earner.

The agricultural sector is the principal employer and a major export earner, contributing around 33% of Rwanda's GDP. Coffee is by far the largest export, accounting for about 60% of export income, while tea and pyrethrum (a natural insecticide) are also important crops. However, the vast majority of farmers live subsistence lives, growing plantain, sweet potato, beans, cassava, sorghum and maize.

LEAVE YOUR PLASTIC BAGS AT HOME

In an effort to preserve the natural beauty of Rwanda, the government enforces a strict ban on plastic bags throughout the country. Police at borders may even confiscate any plastic bags they find, although we have never heard about a visitor having their suitcases searched.

Population

The population exceeded 13 million in 2017, which gives Rwanda one of the highest population densities of any country in Africa. While tribal identities are very much a taboo subject in Rwanda, the population is believed to be about 84% Hutu, 15% Tutsi and 1% Twa. The Twa is a Central African indigenous group that has suffered from discrimination over the generations, though it is slowly gaining a political and cultural foothold.

Religion

About 65% of the population are Christians of various sects (Catholicism is predominant), a further 25% follow tribal religions, often with a dash of Christianity, and the remaining 10% are Muslim.

Arts

Rwanda's most famous dancers are the Intore troupe – their warrior-like displays are accompanied by a trance-like drumbeat similar to that of the famous Tambourinaires in Burundi.

Environment

The Land

In the 'Land of a Thousand Hills', it is hardly surprising to find that endless mountains stretch into the infinite horizon. Rwanda's 26,338 sq km of land is one of the most densely populated places on earth, and almost every available piece of land is under cultivation (except the national parks). Since most of the country is mountainous, this involves a good deal of terracing. Coffee and tea plantations take up considerable areas of land.

National Parks & Reserves

Due to its small size and high demand for cultivatable land, Rwanda only has a small network of national parks. The most popular protected area (and the focus of most visits to Rwanda) is Volcanoes National Park, a string of brooding volcanoes that provides a home for the rare mountain gorilla. Nyungwe Forest National Park, Rwanda's newest national park, is a tropical montane forest that is one of the richest primate destinations in the region. Akagera National Park, the third of Rwanda's parks, is on the up after habitat destruction during the civil war as well as postwar 'villagisation' – its impressive comeback includes growing wildlife populations and the reintroduction of both lions and rhinos.

Environmental Issues

Soil erosion, resulting from the overuse of land, is the most serious problem confronting Rwanda today. The terracing system in the country is fairly anarchic and, unlike much of Southeast Asia, the lack of coordinated water management has wiped out much of the topsoil on the slopes. This is potentially catastrophic for a country with too many people in too small a space, as it points to a food-scarcity problem in the future.

> **EATING PRICE RANGES**
>
> The following price ranges refer to a main course.
>
> $ less than RFr4000 (US$5)
>
> $$ RFr4000–RFr8000 (US$5–US$10)
>
> $$$ more than RFr8000 (US$10)

Food & Drink

In the rural areas of Rwanda, food is very similar to that in other East African countries. Popular meats include tilapia (Nile perch), goat, chicken and beef brochettes, though the bulk of most meals are centred on *ugali* (maize meal) and *matoke* (cooked plantains). In the cities, however, Rwanda's French roots are evident in the *plat du jour* (plate of the day), which is usually excellently prepared Continental-inspired cuisine.

SURVIVAL GUIDE

Directory A–Z

DANGERS & ANNOYANCES

Mention Rwanda to most people and they think of it as a highly dangerous place. However, it's actually one of the safest countries in East Africa to travel in today.

- Serious crime or hostility aimed specifically at travellers is very rare, and there's no more to worry about here than in most other countries.
- Kigali is a genuine contender for the safest capital in Africa, though, as in any big city, take care at night and don't take unnecessary risks.
- Never take photographs of anything connected with the government or military (post offices, banks, bridges, border crossings, barracks, prisons and dams) – cameras can and will be confiscated by the rather overzealous police or security services.

ELECTRICITY

Electricity in Rwanda is 240V, 50 cycles, and plugs are mainly two-pin.

EMBASSIES & CONSULATES

Australia's embassy in Nairobi (Kenya) handles Rwanda, while New Zealand's embassy in Addis Ababa (Ethiopia) is responsible for Rwanda. Ireland handles its affairs from its embassy in Kampala, Uganda.

Belgian Embassy (☎0252575553; http://rwanda.diplomatie.belgium.be; KN 3 Ave, Kigali)

British High Commission (☎0252556000; http://ukinrwanda.fco.gov.uk; KG 7 Ave, Kigali)

Burundi Embassy (☎0252587940; KG 7 Ave, Kigali)

Canadian High Commission (☎0252573210; KN 16 Ave, Kigali)

French Embassy (☎0252551800; http://ambafrance-rw.org; KN 33 St, Kigali)

German Embassy (☎0280575141; www.kigali.diplo.de; KN 27 St, Kigali)

Kenyan High Commission (☎0252583334; www.kenyahighcomkigali.org; KG 7 Ave, Kigali)

Netherlands Embassy (☎0280280281; www.netherlandsandyou.nl/your-country-and-the-netherlands/rwanda; KG 7 Ave, Kigali)

Tanzanian High Commission (☎0252505400; KG 9 Ave, Kigali)

Ugandan High Commission (☎0252503537; http://kigali.mofa.go.ug; KG 569 St, Kigali)

US Embassy (☎0252596400; https://rw.usembassy.gov; KG 3 Ave, Kigali)

GAY & LESBIAN TRAVELLERS

Rwanda is not nearly as homophobic as its East African neighbours, but that's not to say that gay people here don't face significant prejudice. Same-sex relations are not illegal in Rwanda, but that's about it. Gay people are not afforded any rights or protections such as partnership, but despite several attempts by religious groups, legislation to proscribe gay sex has not been successful. Just as it was in Uganda and Kenya a decade ago, homosexuality remains a taboo subject that most people simply never discuss or think about. Kigali has several gay-friendly locales, but otherwise, if you want to make contacts, online is the best bet. Always be cautious, however, and meet people in public places.

HEALTH

Good, Western-style medical care is available in Kigali, and to a lesser extent in Huye (Butare). Elsewhere, reasonable to good care is available in larger towns. If you fall ill in an unfamiliar area, ask staff at top-end hotels or resident expatriates where the best nearby medical facilities are; in an emergency, contact your embassy.

Well-stocked pharmacies are found in major towns. It's best to bring whatever you think you may need from home, including malaria pills and a malaria test kit. Always check the expiry date before buying medications, especially in smaller towns.

There's a high risk of contracting HIV from infected blood if you receive a blood transfusion in the region. The **BloodCare Foundation** (www.bloodcare.org.uk) is a useful source of safe, screened blood, which can be transported to any part of the world within 24 hours.

For Western standards, expect to pay Western prices.

INTERNET ACCESS

Internet access is widely available in all towns and cities. All midrange and top-end hotels, bar a few remote ecolodges, have wi-fi available (often in room but sometimes just around the reception area) and an increasing number of budget hotels, restaurants and cafes offer wi-fi. However, speeds are slow and service is often cut off for no reason.

A good alternative (or supplement) to hotel-provided wi-fi is to buy a local SIM card with data or an internet dongle from any of the main mobile-phone providers (MTN offers the best network coverage). This means you'll be able to get online in all but the most remote corners of Rwanda.

MONEY

Currency

The unit of currency is the Rwandan franc (RFr). It is divided into 100 centimes. Notes come in RFr100, RFr500, RFr1000, RFr5000 and RFr10,000 denominations. Coins come in RFr10, RFr20 and RFr50.

ATMs

Banks in all towns and cities have ATMs, but not all work with foreign credit cards. The notable exceptions are the Bank of Kigali, GT Bank and Ecobank, which work with both Visa and MasterCard.

Cash

Banks throughout the country can exchange US dollars or euros, although they can be very slow to do so. Most people use the foreign-exchange bureaus in Kigali and other larger towns instead, and this is quite safe. Foreign-exchange bureaus also offer slightly better rates.

Rwanda, like other African countries, is very particular on which notes it will or will not accept. Anything older than 2006 or deemed too dirty, crinkled or tatty will not be accepted. Denominations of US$50 or US$100 are preferred.

If you bring US dollars, note that you won't really need to change them, as most activities can be paid in US dollars and almost all hotels accept US dollars.

Credit Cards

Credit cards are increasingly accepted at midrange and top-end tourist hotels and restaurants. The Rwanda Tourism Information Centre (RDB) office (p516) in Kigali also accepts them, as do most national park offices (though lines are sometimes down at these).

OPENING HOURS

The following are common business hours in Rwanda. Sunday is the weekly holiday for offices and most shops.

Banks 8am–5pm Monday to Friday

Government offices 8am–5pm Monday to Friday

Restaurants Breakfast 7–10am, lunch 11am–3pm, dinner 6.30–10pm

Shopping centres 8am-10pm

PUBLIC HOLIDAYS

New Year's Day 1 & 2 January

National Heroes Day 1 February

Easter (Good Friday, Holy Saturday and Easter Monday) March/April

Genocide against the Tutsi Memorial Day 7 April

Labour Day 1 May

Independence Day 1 July

Liberation Day 4 July

Umuganura Day First Friday in August

Assumption 15 August

Christmas Day 25 December

Boxing Day 26 December

TELEPHONE

➡ Mobile-phone reception is excellent throughout the country.

➡ Most businesses use mobile phones rather than landlines.

➡ Mobile numbers begin with 078, 072 or 073.

➡ The main operators in Rwanda are MTN, Tigo and Airtel.

➡ It's cheap, fast and painless to get a Rwandan SIM card for your phone; just go to any operator with your passport.

➡ Top-up cards start from as little as RFr100. Mobile phone calls cost about RFr1 per second, although rates vary depending on when you call.

TIME

Rwanda is on GMT/UTC plus two hours. If you're coming from Uganda or Tanzania, be advised that Rwanda is one hour behind the rest of East Africa.

TOURIST INFORMATION

The Rwanda Development Board (RDB; www.rwandatourism.com) runs the state tourist board. Currently it has several tourist offices: one in Kigali, one in Musanze (Ruhengeri) and another one in Gisenyi (Rubavu). While they have only limited amounts of promotional information, the staff are – for East Africa – unusually well trained, knowledgeable and helpful.

VISAS

Almost everyone requires a visa to enter Rwanda.

➡ From January 2018 citizens from all nations (no longer just those from Australia, Germany, Israel, New Zealand, South Africa, Sweden, the UK and the USA) can automatically receive visas on arrival at Kigali International airport and all land borders.

➡ The cost of the 30-day tourist visa depends on your nationality. Citizens of Australia, Germany, Israel, New Zealand, South Africa, Sweden, the UK and the USA will pay US$30, while many others may need to hand over US$50.

➡ Another option is to apply for your visa online before you travel by registering at Rwanda Immigration (www.migration.gov.rw). Single-entry (V1) and conference visas (T6) take three days to process (both are valid for 30 days). You have the option to pay online or upon arrival.

➡ To extend your stay or apply for any other type of visa, you must do so at **Rwanda Directorate General of Immigration and Emigration** (☎0788152222; www.migration.gov.rw; KG 7 Ave, Kigali; ⏰application submission 7-11.30am Mon-Wed & Fri, visa collection 1-4.30pm Mon-Wed & Fri, 1-3.30pm Thu) in Kigali's Kacyiru district, about 7km northeast of the city centre near the US Embassy. For extensions you'll need to bring the appropriate form (available online), a passport-sized photo, your passport, a letter of introduction or a letter addressed to the Director of Immigration explaining why you require a visa, and RFr30,000. Extensions take five days to issue.

➡ Rwanda is one of the countries covered by the East Africa Tourist Visa, and for those also visiting Kenya and Uganda on the same trip it is a cheaper alternative. The visa costs US$100, is valid for 90 days and is multiple entry (if staying within the three countries) – it is available online (www.migration.gov.rw), upon arrival or from embassies abroad. If acquiring the visa before travel, your first port-of-call must be the country through which you applied for the visa. These visas can not be extended.

ℹ Getting There & Away

AIR

Rwanda has one international gateway for arrival by air, **Kigali International Airport** (KN 5 Rd, Kanombe), which is located at Kanombe, 10km east of Kigali's city centre.

Brussels Airlines (☎0788158000; www.brusselsairlines.com; Hotel des Mille Collines, KN 6 Ave, Kigali; ⏰8.30am-5pm Mon-Fri, to 12.30pm Sat) Operates six flights a week

DEPARTURE TAX

Taxes are included in the price of your ticket.

to/from Brussels (with onward connections to many European cities). Baggage can be checked in here on the day of departure between 10am and 1pm – very convenient as flights to Brussels leave at night.

Ethiopian Airlines (☎0788751585; www.ethiopianairlines.com; Union Trade Centre, KN 4 Ave, Kigali; ⊙8am-7.30pm Mon-Sat) Has two daily flights to/from Addis Ababa (Ethiopia) and good connections to elsewhere in Africa.

Kenya Airways (☎0782062524; www.kenya-airways.com; Union Trade Centre, KN 4 Ave, Kigali; ⊙8am-6pm Mon-Fri, 9am-6pm Sat) Has three daily flights to/from Nairobi.

KLM (☎0782062524; www.klm.com; Union Trade Centre, KN 4 Ave, Kigali; ⊙8am-6pm Mon-Fri, 9am-6pm Sat) Has two daily flights to/from Amsterdam (one via Nairobi). KLM bookings are handled by Kenya Airways.

Qatar Airways (☎0252553500; www.qatarairways.com; 11th fl, Kigali City Tower, KN 2 St, Kigali; ⊙8am-6pm Mon-Fri, 10am-2pm Sat) Daily flights to/from Doha.

RwandAir (☎0788177000; www.rwandair.com; Union Trade Centre, KN 4 Ave, Kigali; ⊙8am-9pm Mon-Fri, 9am-9pm Sat & Sun) Rwanda's national carrier flies to/from Accra (Ghana), Brussels (Belgium), Bujumbura (Burundi), Brazzaville (Congo), Cotonou (Benin), Dar es Salaam (Tanzania), Douala (Cameroon), Dubai (UAE), Entebbe (Uganda), Harare (Zimbabwe), Johannesburg (South Africa), Juba (South Sudan), Kilimanjaro (Tanzania), Lagos (Nigeria), Libreville (Gabon), London (UK), Lusaka (Zambia), Mombasa (Kenya), Mumbai (India) and Nairobi (Kenya). It has a good safety record.

Turkish Airlines (☎0786730231; www.turkishairlines.com; 4th fl, Pension Plaza, KN 4 Ave, Kigali; ⊙8.30am-5pm Mon-Fri) Daily flights to/from Istanbul.

LAND

International Buses

Different Express (p516) Heads to the Uganda border town of Gatuna every half hour (RFr1400, three hours).

Jaguar Executive Coaches (p516) Operates four daily buses from Kigali to Kampala (Uganda; RFr8000 to RFr10,000, nine hours).

Select Express (p516) Runs buses from Kigali to the Rwanda–Tanzania border crossing of Rusumo (RFr3200, 3½ hours) every half hour.

Simba Coach (p516) Has a 5pm bus to Nairobi (Kenya; RFr27,000, 22 hours).

Trinity Express (p516) For the ultimate in long bus rides, this company sends buses to Dar es Salaam (Tanzania; RFr30,000; about 36 hours) at 4am. The bus stops for four hours in the middle of the night near Dodoma. It also operates seven daily buses to Kampala (Uganda; RFr10,000, nine hours).

Border Crossings

Burundi The main border crossing between Rwanda and Burundi is via Huye (Butare) and Kayanza, on the Kigali–Bujumbura road. Although the border is open, this crossing is considered risky due to the unstable political situation in Burundi.

Tanzania Only one bus company, **Trinity Express** (p516), operates cross-border buses to Tanzania and this goes all the way to Dar es Salaam. But doing it, as most people do, in stages is no great hassle, with a number of companies sending frequent buses to the border, after which you can get another bus to the tiny Tanzanian town of Benako (marked as Kasulo on some maps), about 20km southeast of the frontier. From here get a bus to the town of Biharamulo, where you'll probably have to overnight. The following day catch a bus to Mwanza or Bukoba. From Mwanza you can connect to Arusha.

The DRC There are two crossings between Rwanda and the DRC; both are on the shores of Lake Kivu. To the north is the crossing between Gisenyi (Rubavu) and Goma. The southern border is between Cyangugu (Rusizi) and Bukavu. Providing the DRC remains politically stable and you have prearranged visas, the crossings are surprisingly straightforward, and you can walk across the borders directly from town to town.

Uganda There are two main crossing points for foreigners: between Kigali and Kabale via Gatuna/Katuna (called Gatuna on the Rwandan side and Katuna on the Ugandan side); and between Musanze (Ruhengeri) and Kisoro via Cyanika.

There are direct buses between Kigali/Musanze and Gisenyi and Kampala. Buses also run between Kigali and the border at Gatuna (RFr1400, three hours) throughout the day. Plenty of shared taxis (USh4000) and special-hire taxis (USh20,000 for the whole car) travel back and forth between Katuna and Kabale.

From Musanze (Ruhengeri) to Kisoro via Cyanika, the road is in excellent shape on the Rwandan side and in rather poor condition on the Ugandan side. Minibuses link either side of the border with Musanze (from RFr480, 25km).

Getting Around

AIR

RwandAir (p553) operates domestic flights between Kigali and Cyangugu (Rusizi; US$175). There are no other services within the country.

BICYCLE

Rwanda is an exceptionally hilly country, but it's also unusually scenic and has a very good road network by African standards. Cycling is certainly possible here, and for many locals it's their main way of getting around. Do expect lots of challenging hills, however (locals often hang on to the back of trucks to make it up to the top – not a very safe practice!), and also many freewheeling descents.

BOAT

Ferries on Lake Kivu connect the Rwandan ports of Cyangugu (Rusizi), Kibuye (Karongi) and Gisenyi (Rubavu) on a twice-weekly basis. Each leg costs RFr2500. Speedboat charters are another option between these ports, but they are prohibitively expensive.

BUS & MINIBUS

Rwanda has efficient and reliable public transport. Privately run buses cover the entire country and, with scheduled departure times, you won't find yourself waiting for hours while the driver scouts for more passengers. Tickets are bought in advance from a ticket office, which is usually the point of departure.

You will also find plenty of well-maintained, modern minibuses serving all the main routes. Head to the bus stand in any town between dawn and about 3pm and it is quite easy to find one heading to Kigali and nearby towns. Destinations are displayed in the front window and the fares are fixed. Neither buses nor minibuses are supposed to charge extra for baggage.

CAR & MOTORCYCLE

Cars are suitable for most of the country's main roads, but those planning to explore Akagera National Park will need a 4WD.

Car hire isn't well established in Rwanda, but there are plenty of small local agencies in Kigali that can organise something. Prices start at around US$50 per day if you're driving around the capital. If you prefer to have a car and driver, **Beyond Transport** (p516) is a very reputable operator that has excellent cars at competitive prices. A 4WD with driver and fuel will set you back US$150. For a small 4WD, such as a RAV4 (which is fine for anywhere in Rwanda), you'll pay between US$60 and US$80, including driver and fuel. Prices are negotiable. You can also contact Jean-Paul Birasa (p517), who can organise no-frills car and jeep rental with drivers.

Burundi

257 / POP 10.52 MILLION

Includes ➡

Burundi Today...... 556
History 557
Culture............ 558
Environment 558

Fast Facts

➡ **Area** 27,830 sq km

➡ **Capital** Bujumbura

➡ **Currency** Burundian franc (BIF)

➡ **Languages** Kirundi, French

➡ **Time** Central Africa Time (GMT/UTC plus two hours)

Introduction

Tiny Burundi is an incongruous mix of soaring mountains, languid lakeside communities and a tragic past blighted by ethnic conflict. Despite their troubles, Burundians have an irrepressible joie de vivre, and their smiles are as infectious as a rhythm laid down by a drummer from Les Tambourinaires (a Burundian dance group).

When civil war broke out in 1993, the economy was destroyed and the tourist industry succumbed to a quick death. When the war finally ended in 2005, a trickle of travellers returned to rediscover the steamy capital, Bujumbura, with its lovely Lake Tanganyika setting and some of the finest inland beaches on the continent.

The new peace, however, came to a shattering end in 2015 when President Nkurunziza decided to run for what many Burundians believed to be a constitution-breaking third term in office. Violence broke out before the election, and has escalated since. The entire country is now considered unsafe to visit.

Burundi at a Glance

➡ **Bujumbura** The sultry capital has great nightlife and delicious food.

➡ **Saga Beach** Soft white sands, warm waters and a stash of cool beach bars make this one of the most enticing inland beaches in Africa.

➡ **Chutes de la Karera** Four different waterfalls make up this gorgeous cascade.

➡ **Source du Nil** Burundi's very own pyramid, a memorial marking a small stream in Kasumo, at the southernmost source of the Nile.

➡ **Parc National de la Rusizi** Antelopes and hippos splash and stomp through this national park just outside Bujumbura.

UNDERSTAND BURUNDI

Burundi Today

The political situation in Burundi is highly unstable, with frequent acts of violence throughout the country. This instability is having a very negative impact on a country that has long been one of the poorest and least developed in East Africa.

According to both the International Monetary Fund (IMF) and World Bank, Burundi is one of the five poorest countries in the world. Civil wars, corruption, landlocked geography, poor education, HIV/AIDS and a lack of economic freedom have all but economically crippled the country, and today it is largely dependent on foreign aid.

The country sits at just 180 out of 186 countries on the Human Development Index and 64.9% of the population are thought to live below the poverty line. Although Burundi's largest industry is agriculture (employing around 90% of the workforce), the sheer number of people living in such a small country (Burundi is the second most densely populated country in Africa) means that not enough food is produced to keep everyone fed. According to the Global Hunger Index almost half of all households are food insecure and slightly over half of the children of Burundi have stunted growth due to a lack of food.

Economically things are grim as well, with the country recording a negative economic growth rate in 2016, which can primarily be put down to the unstable political situation and a recent contraction in food production.

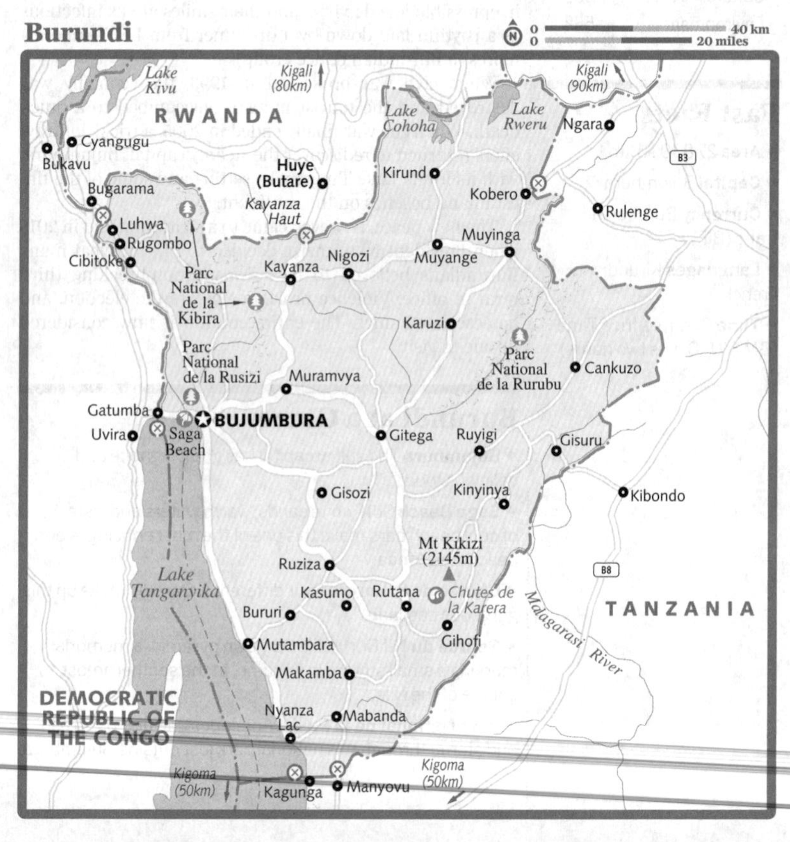

History

Independence & Coups

Burundi, like Rwanda, was colonised first by Germany and then later by Belgium, and like its northern neighbour, the Europeans played on ethnic differences to divide and conquer the population. Power was traditionally concentrated in the hands of the minority Tutsi, though Hutus began to challenge the concentration of power following independence in 1962.

In the 1964 elections, Tutsi leader Mwami Mwambutsa refused to appoint a Hutu prime minister, even though Hutu candidates attracted the majority of votes. Hutu frustration soon boiled over, and Hutu military officers and political figures staged an attempted coup. Although it failed, Mwambutsa was exiled to Switzerland, and replaced by a Tutsi military junta.

A wholesale purge of Hutu from the army and bureaucracy followed, and in 1972 another large-scale Hutu revolt resulted in more than 1000 Tutsi being killed. The Tutsi military junta responded with the selective genocide of elite Hutu; after just three months, an estimated 200,000 Hutu had been killed and another 100,000 had fled into neighbouring countries.

In 1976 Jean-Baptiste Bagaza came to power in a bloodless coup, and three years later he formed the Union pour le Progrès National (Uprona). His so-called democratisation program was largely considered to be a failure, and in 1987 his cousin Major Pierre Buyoya toppled him in another coup.

The new regime attempted to address the causes of intertribal tensions by gradually bringing Hutu representatives back into positions of power. However, there was a renewed outbreak of intertribal violence in northern Burundi during the summer of 1988; thousands were massacred and many more fled into neighbouring Rwanda.

A Bloody Civil War

Buyoya finally bowed to international pressure, and multiparty elections were held in June 1993. These brought a Hutu-dominated government to power, led by Melchior Ndadaye, himself a Hutu. However, Ndadaye's rule was to be short-lived, as by October of that year he had been assassinated by unknown military assailants in an attempted coup (a 1996 UN investigation accused the army command of being responsible for Ndadaye's death, but the report did not name names). The coup eventually failed, though thousands were massacred in intertribal fighting, and almost half a million refugees fled across the border into Rwanda.

In April 1994 Cyprien Ntaryamira, the new Hutu president, was killed in the same plane crash that killed Rwanda's President Juvénal Habyarimana – an event that ignited the subsequent genocide in Rwanda. In Burundi, Sylvestre Ntibantunganya was immediately appointed interim president, though both Hutu militias and the Tutsi-dominated army went on the offensive. No war was actually declared, but at least 100,000 people were killed in clashes between mid-1994 and mid-1996.

In July 1996 former president Major Pierre Buyoya again carried out a successful coup, and took over as the country's president with the support of the army. However, intertribal fighting continued between Hutu rebels and the Tutsi-dominated government and Tutsi militia. Hundreds of thousands of political opponents, mostly Hutus, were herded into 'regroupment camps', and bombings, murders and other horrific activities continued throughout the country.

WARNING

The security situation in Burundi is very unstable and low-level violence continues throughout much of the country. Most Western governments advise against all but essential travel to most of the country, including Bujumbura, and all travel to certain parts of the northwest and northeast.

If you do visit the country, the following precautions should apply:

- Do not walk around Bujumbura at night.
- The road north of Bujumbura towards Cibitoke should be avoided.
- Do not attempt to visit the Parc National de la Kibira or Parc National de la Ruvubu.
- Do not travel anywhere by road at night.
- Avoid the Democratic Republic of the Congo (DRC) border areas.
- Carry your passport at all times.

A Fragile Peace

At the end of 2002 the Forces for the Defence of Democracy (FDD), the largest rebel group, signed a peace deal. In April 2003 prominent Hutu Domitien Ndayizeye succeeded Buyoya as president, and a road map to elections was hammered out.

In 2004 the UN began operations in Burundi, sending more than 5000 troops to enforce the peace. Parliamentary elections were successfully held in 2005, and the former rebels, the FDD, emerged victorious. Pierre Nkurunziza, leader of the FDD, was sworn in as president in August. The 2010 elections were marred by violence and allegations of fraud and corruption. Despite international observers recognising the local elections as mainly free and fair, a growing mistrust of the incumbent's commitments to democracy saw all opposition withdraw their candidacy and Nkurunziza was re-elected unopposed.

Between 2010 and early 2015 the peace largely held and Burundi continued on its (very shaky) road to recovery: foreign investment started to arrive; the infrastructure of the country started to be overhauled; the economy climbed slowly upward, with tourism increasing; and for a few short years things looked more positive than they had in many a year.

But then in April 2015 Domitien Ndayizeye announced that he intended to run for a third term as president. Opposition parties said that this would be against the constitution, which limits a president to two terms. Ndayizeye, though, claimed that his first term didn't count as he was appointed by parliament and not voted for by the people. But the people weren't happy and by the end of April angry protests had broken out on the streets of Bujumbura. On 26 April six demonstrators were killed in clashes with police during a protest. This led to more protests, much more violence, a government shutdown of independent radio stations and media outlets, an attempted coup, and tens of thousands of people fleeing the worsening situation for Rwanda and Tanzania.

Despite the rapid breakdown in law and order, elections were held in late July 2015. These were boycotted by the opposition and Ndayizeye was duly re-elected. Since then low-level violence has continued throughout Burundi and an estimated 380,000 people had fled its borders by February 2017.

SATURDAY COMMUNITY WORK

Traditionally, from 8am to 11am every Saturday the country comes to a grinding halt. The reason? *Ibikorwa rusangi* – a time for obligatory community work. During these hours the populace is required to lend a hand on community projects for the greater good of their country. Shops, taxis, buses and restaurants are closed and instead rubbish is gathered, grass cut and drains dug. One of the few exceptions is international buses, which have special dispensation to operate.

Culture

Burundi's population comprises 84% Hutu,15% Tutsi and 1% Twa. Like Rwanda in 1994, Burundi has been torn apart by tribal animosities, and the conflict between Hutus and Tutsis has claimed hundreds of thousands of lives since independence. The Belgians masterminded the art of divide and rule, using the minority Tutsis to control the majority Hutus. Generations of intermarriage and cooperation went out the window, as the population was forced into choosing sides, Hutu or Tutsi. The pattern continued into independence as the minority Tutsis clung to power to protect their privileges, and marginalised the Hutu majority.

Although the recent violence hasn't been as much along ethnic lines as in the past, in mid-2017 a human rights groups reported a purge of Tutsis serving in the army, which could be setting a worrying trend for the future.

Environment

Taking up a mere 27,830 sq km, most of the country is made up of mountains that vanish into the horizon. Like its neighbour Rwanda, this is a very densely populated country and most areas that can be farmed are being utilised as such. There are three national parks worthy of the name and, at least prior to the latest round of violence, there were surprisingly healthy animal populations within them.

Understand East Africa

EAST AFRICA TODAY 560

More than 50 years after the countries of this region gained independence, many challenges remain, but there are bright spots too.

HISTORY 562

From humankind's earliest days, through migrations, colonialism and independence, East Africa's history reflects myriad influences.

LIFE IN EAST AFRICA 568

Daily life moves at its own pace, with hospitality, community solidarity and spirituality major themes.

ENVIRONMENT 573

Diverse landscapes and fragile ecosystems host a wealth of plants, birds and wildlife, some thriving, some endangered.

WILDLIFE & HABITAT 581

NATIONAL PARKS & RESERVES 605

East Africa's parks, reserves and conservancies range from open savannahs to dense mountain forests.

TRIBAL CULTURES 611

More than 300 different groups call East Africa home, each with fascinating and colourful traditions.

THE ARTS 619

Discover East Africa's lively arts scene, from Swahili-style architecture to Congo-inspired dance bands.

A TASTE OF EAST AFRICA 623

Learn about everything from ugali to decoding a menu in this guide to East African–style dining.

East Africa Today

More than five decades since most East African countries became independent, the region is at once a (somewhat fragile) beacon of stability for the rest of the continent and a canvas for some of the most pressing issues of our time. Despite major challenges, democracy remains the norm here. But questions of authoritarianism, ethnicity and terrorism never seem far away.

Best on Film

Out of Africa (1985) Caused a generation to dream of East Africa.

People of the Forest – The Chimps of Gombe (1988) Documentary following a chimpanzee family.

Echo of the Elephants (1993) Elephants of Amboseli National Park.

Hotel Rwanda (2004), **Shooting Dogs in Rwanda** (2005) Powerful stories from the Rwandan genocide.

The Last King of Scotland (2006) Idi Amin's Uganda.

Best in Print

Out of Africa (Karen Blixen, aka Isak Dinesen; 1937) Definitive account of colonial Kenya.

The Tree Where Man Was Born (Peter Matthiessen; 1972) Lyrical account of East Africa's people, wildlife and landscapes.

We Wish to Inform You That Tomorrow We Will Be Killed with Our Families (Philip Gourevitch; 1998) Searing study of Rwanda's 1994 genocide.

One Day I Will Write About This Place: A Memoir (Binyavanga Wainaina; 2011) Modern Kenyan childhood.

Lions in the Balance: Man-Eaters, Manes, and Men with Guns (Craig Packer; 2015) Behind-the-scenes look into the politics of lion conservation in Tanzania.

Ethnic Flashpoints

The spectre of ethnic identity stalks East Africa like few other places on the planet. The question lay at the heart of what happened in Burundi in 1993, in Rwanda in 1994 and in Kenya in 2007. More than a million East Africans lost their lives in these three conflicts in which a person's ethnic story took centre stage – in much of the region, the first question on locals' minds upon meeting a fellow countryman or countrywoman is still this: from which tribe do you come? As long as that question remains at the forefront of public debate and private loyalties, the potential for conflict continues.

There is, however, much to celebrate. Tanzania and, to a lesser extent, Uganda rarely make headlines, if at all, for issues of ethnic unrest – despite having more than 120 tribal groups, Tanzania is a model of nation-building and a place where ethnic conflict is extremely rare. More than that, four out of the five East African countries (Burundi is the exception) are at peace.

The Challenge of Democracy

Democracy's roots sink deeper into the East African soil with each passing election. While concerns remain as to whether opposition parties stand a real chance of victory in Uganda, Burundi and Rwanda, Kenya's experience suggests that the region's democratic institutions are stronger than many analysts dared hope. Ever since the widespread political and ethnic violence that followed the 2007 elections, Kenya and its friends hold their collective breath whenever the country votes.

Kenya's hotly contested 2017 elections ended peacefully. And then, in an event unprecedented in African politics, Kenya's highest court ruled in favour of an opposition challenge, the elections were annulled and new elections were scheduled. It was a landmark moment in East Africa's road to democracy. Sadly, however, the rerun was boycotted by the opposition, one of the country's electoral commissioners fled to the USA, and barely one-third of Kenyans cast their ballots (compared with 80% in the first round). Although Uhuru Kenyatta was declared the winner, the future appeared more uncertain than ever at the time of writing.

Presidents for Life?

For all the plaudits East Africa receives for its stability and regular roster of elections, three countries are, as of late 2017, run by men who can't seem to let go of power. Yoweri Museveni of Uganda (in power since 1986), Paul Kagame of Rwanda (2000) and Pierre Nkurunziza of Burundi (2005) have all amended their country's constitutions to allow themselves to seek additional presidential terms. The crackdown on opposition politicians and political protests that have accompanied the extensions is a worrying development.

Some would say that these three presidents are showing symptoms of a familiar African malady. The course of the 'illness' is simple. First, such presidents come to power as reformers and unifiers of troubled lands. Over time they become more authoritarian by degrees. Finally they convince themselves that their countries simply can't do without them. Uganda and Rwanda in particular appear to be on a consistently upward trajectory, lending power to their presidents' arguments that they remain indispensable. But the longer it continues, the greater the disquiet about what comes next.

The Coming Environmental Crisis

Drought has always stalked East Africa, with some parts of the region just one failed rainy season away from a major crisis. For all the growth in East Africa's urban middle class, much of the region's population continues to live at subsistence levels, wholly dependent upon the rains that sustain their crops or provide grazing for their livestock. Often these people live alongside national parks or private ranches and conservancies that are closed to them despite having what could be prime grazing or agricultural lands.

Failed rains in 2016 and again in 2017, especially in Kenya's north and west, prompted the large-scale movement of armed herders and gangs onto the Laikipia Plateau where many of the ranches are owned by white Kenyans. One prominent conservationist was killed, another was critically injured, and a number of lodges were burned to the ground. Things have quietened down since then, but there are fears that these may be the first shots in a climate-change war in a region with a rapidly growing population, increasingly unpredictable rains and contested yet scarce resources.

POPULATION: **164.5 MILLION**

AREA: **1,816,753 SQ KM**

HIGHEST POINT: **MT KILIMANJARO (5896M)**

HIGHEST GDP PER CAPITA: **KENYA (US$3400)**

LOWEST GDP PER CAPITA: **BURUNDI (US$800)**

belief systems

(% of population)

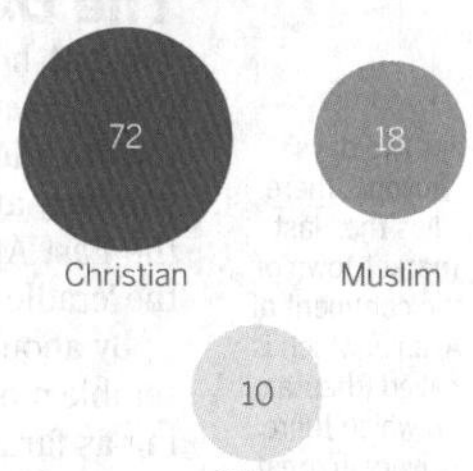

if East Africa were 100 people

33 would be Tanzanian
29 would be Kenyan
24 would be Ugandan
7 would be Burundian
7 would be Rwandan

population per sq km

EAST AFRICA | UK | USA

≈ 33 people

History

East Africa has one of the longest documented human histories of any region in the world. Home to some of humankind's earliest ancestors, it later became one of the great crossroads of the world, a constant ebb and flow of peoples drawn by trade and migration, exploration and exploitation. In more recent times, the region was profoundly marked by the struggles against colonialism and for independence, struggles that continue to shape the region's story to this day.

The Dawn of Humankind

Ancient hominid (human-like) skulls and footprints, some over three million years old, have been found at various sites in East Africa, including at Oldupai Gorge in Tanzania and Lake Turkana in Kenya. Although similarly ancient traces have also been found elsewhere on the continent, the East African section of the Great Rift Valley is popularly considered the 'cradle of humanity'.

'Two days' beyond, there lies the...last market-town of the continent of Azania, which is called Rhapta... in which there is ivory in great quantity, and tortoise-shell...' *(Periplus of the Erythraean Sea; 1st century AD)*

By about one million years ago, these early ancestors had come to resemble modern humans, and had spread well beyond East Africa, including as far as Europe and Asia. Roughly 100,000 years ago, and possibly earlier, *Homo sapiens* had arrived on the scene.

The earliest evidence of modern-day East Africans dates from around 10,000 years ago, when much of the region was home to Khoisan-speaking hunter-gatherer communities. On the western fringes of East Africa, including parts of the area that is now Rwanda and Burundi, there were also small populations of various so-called Pygmy groups.

The Great Migrations

Beginning between 3000 and 5000 years ago, a series of migrations began that were to indelibly shape the face of East Africa. Cushitic- and Nilotic-speaking peoples from the north and Bantu speakers from the west converged on the Khoisan and other peoples already in the area, creating over the centuries the rich tribal mosaic that is East Africa today.

The first to arrive were Cushitic-speaking farmers and cattle herders who made their way to the region from present-day Ethiopia, and set-

TIMELINE

c 25 million BC

Tectonic plates collide and East African plains buckle. Formation of the Great Rift Valley begins, as do changes that result ultimately in the formation of Kilimanjaro and other volcanoes.

c 3.7 million BC

Fossils found at Lake Turkana (Kenya) and at Laetoli (Tanzania) show that hominid (human-like) creatures wandered the East African plains over three million years ago.

c 100 BC

The first Bantu speakers arrive in the region, part of a series of great population migrations that continue to shape the face of modern-day East Africa.

tled both inland and along the coast. They moved mostly in small family groups, and brought with them traditions that are still practised by their descendents, including the Iraqw around Tanzania's Lake Manyara and the Gabbra and Rendille in northern Kenya.

The next major influx began around 1000 BC when Bantu-speaking peoples from West Africa's Niger Delta area began moving eastwards, arriving in East Africa around the 1st century BC. Thanks to their advanced agricultural skills and knowledge of ironworking and steel production – which gave them a great advantage in cultivating land and establishing settlements – these Bantu speakers were able to absorb many of the Cushitic and Khoisan speakers who were already in the region, as well as the Pygmy populations around the Great Lakes. Soon they became East Africa's most populous ethnolinguistic family – a status that they continue to hold today.

A final wave of migration began somewhat later when smaller groups of Nilotic peoples began to arrive in East Africa from what is now southern Sudan. This influx continued through to the 18th century, with the main movements taking place in the 15th and 16th centuries. Most of these Nilotic peoples – whose descendants include the present-day Maasai and Turkana – were pastoralists, and many settled in the less fertile areas of southern Kenya and northern Tanzania where their large herds would have sufficient grazing space.

Today the population diversity resulting from these migrations is one of the most fascinating aspects of travel in East Africa.

Monsoon Winds

As these migrations were taking place in the interior, coastal areas were being shaped by far different influences. Azania, as the East African coast was known to the ancient Greeks, was an important trading post as early as 400 BC, and had likely been inhabited even before then by small groups of Cushitic peoples, and by Bantu speakers. The *Periplus of the Erythraean Sea,* a navigator's guide written in the 1st century AD, mentions Raphta as the southernmost trading port. Although its location remains a mystery, it is believed to have been somewhere along the Kenyan or Tanzanian coast, possibly on the mainland opposite Manda or Paté Islands (north of Lamu), or further south near the Pangani or Rufiji estuaries.

Trade seems to have grown steadily throughout the early part of the first millennium. Permanent settlements were established as traders, first from the Mediterranean and later from Arabia and Persia, came ashore on the winds of the monsoon and began to intermix with the indigenous peoples, gradually giving rise to Swahili language and culture. The traders from Arabia also brought Islam, which by the 11th century had become entrenched.

Swahili Ruins

Kilwa Kisiwani (Tanzania)

Kaole Ruins (Tanzania)

Gede Ruins (Kenya)

Jumba la Mtwana (Kenya)

Takwa Ruins (Kenya)

Mnarani (Kenya)

Unesco World Heritage Sites

Kasubi Tombs (Uganda)

Lamu Old Town (Kenya)

Fort Jesus (Kenya)

Kondoa Rock-Art Sites (Tanzania)

Stone Town (Zanzibar Town, Tanzania)

Tombs of Buganda Kings, Kasubi (Uganda)

c AD 750–1200

Monsoon winds push Arab trading ships to the East African coast and Swahili civilisation is born. Settlements are established at Lamu, Gede, Kilwa and elsewhere along the coast.

1331

Moroccan traveller Ibn Battuta visits Kilwa (Tanzania) and finds a flourishing town of 10,000 to 20,000 residents, with a grand palace, mosque, inn and slave market.

15th century

The king of Malindi sends the Chinese emperor a giraffe. Vasco da Gama reaches East Africa en route to the Orient, stopping at Mombasa and Malindi before continuing to India.

c 1400–1700

In several waves, small bands of nomadic cattle herders migrate south from the Sudan into the Rift Valley – ancestors of the Maasai who today live in Kenya and Tanzania.

Between the 13th and 15th centuries these coastal settlements – including those at Shanga (on Paté Island), Gede, Lamu and Mombasa (all in present-day Kenya) and on the Zanzibar Archipelago and at Kilwa Kisiwani (both in Tanzania) – flourished, with trade in ivory, gold and other goods extending as far away as India and China.

Portuguese influence is still seen in East Africa's architecture, customs and language. The origin of the Swahili word *gereza* (jail), from Portuguese *igreja* (church), dates from the days when Portuguese forts contained both in the same compound.

Europeans & Arabs

The first European to reach East Africa was the intrepid Portuguese explorer Vasco da Gama, who arrived in 1498, en route to the Orient. Within three decades, the Portuguese had disrupted the old trading networks and subdued the entire coast, building forts at various places, including Kilwa and Mombasa. Portuguese control lasted until the early 18th century, when they were displaced by Arabs from Oman.

As the Omani Arabs solidified their foothold, they began to turn their sights westwards, developing powerful trade routes that stretched inland as far as Lake Tanganyika and central Africa. Commerce grew at such a pace that in the 1840s, the Sultan of Oman moved his capital from Muscat to Zanzibar Island.

The slave trade also grew rapidly during this period, driven in part by demand from European plantation holders on the Indian Ocean islands of Réunion and Mauritius. Soon slave traders, including the notorious Tippu Tip, had established stations at Tabora (Tanzania) and other inland towns. By the mid-19th century, the Zanzibar Archipelago had become the largest slave entrepôt along the East African coast, with nearly 50,000 slaves, abducted from as far away as Lake Tanganyika, passing through Zanzibar's market each year.

Modern Historical Sites

- *Kigali Genocide Memorial (Kigali, Rwanda)*
- *National Museum (Dar es Salaam, Tanzania)*
- *National Museum (Nairobi, Kenya)*
- *Uganda Museum (Kampala)*
- *Mwalimu Julius K Nyerere Museum (Butiama, Tanzania)*

Colonial Control

In addition to reports of the horrors of the still-ongoing regional slave trade, tales of the attractions of East Africa also made their way back to Europe, and Western interests were piqued. In 1890 Germany and Great Britain signed an agreement defining 'spheres of influence' for themselves, which formally established a British protectorate over the Zanzibar Archipelago. Most of what is now mainland Tanzania, as well as Rwanda and Burundi, came under German control as German East Africa (later Tanganyika), while the British took Kenya and Uganda.

The 19th century was also the era of various European explorers, including Gustav Fischer (a German whose party was virtually annihilated by the Maasai at Hell's Gate on Lake Naivasha in 1882), Joseph Thomson (a Scot who reached Lake Victoria via the Rift Valley lakes and the Aberdare Highlands in 1883) and Count Teleki von Szek (an Austrian who explored the Lake Turkana region and Mt Kenya in 1887). Anglican bishop James Hannington set out in 1885 to establish a diocese in Ugan-

1850–70

Zanzibar's slave market becomes the largest in East Africa. According to some estimates, up to 50,000 slaves pass through its gates each year.

1890

Britain and Germany create 'spheres of influence'. Zanzibar becomes a British 'protectorate'. After WWI the German area of Rwanda-Urundi (later to be Rwanda and Burundi) comes under Belgian control.

1899

Nairobi is founded in an area of rivers, plains and swamps traditionally known by the Maasai as *uaso nairobi* (cold water). Residents carry guns to defend against wild animals.

1905–07

In the Matumbi Hills near Kilwa (Tanzania), the mystic Kinjikitile stirs African labourers to rise up against their German overlords in what became known as the Maji Maji rebellion.

SWAHILI

The word Swahili ('of the coast', from the Arabic word *sāhil*) refers both to the Swahili language and the Islamic culture of the peoples inhabiting the East African coast from Mogadishu (Somalia) in the north down to Mozambique in the south. Both language and culture are a rich mixture of Bantu, Arabic, Persian and Asian influences.

Although Swahili culture began to develop in the early part of the first millennium AD, it was not until the 18th century, with the ascendancy of the Omani Arabs on Zanzibar, that it came into its own. Swahili's role as a lingua franca was solidified as it spread throughout East and Central Africa along the great trade caravan routes. European missionaries and explorers soon adopted the language as their main means of communicating with locals. In the second half of the 19th century, missionaries, notably the German Johann Ludwig Krapf, also began applying the Roman alphabet. Prior to this, Swahili had been written exclusively in Arabic script.

da, but was killed when he reached the Nile. Other explorers included Burton and Speke, who were sent to Lake Tanganyika in 1858 by the Royal Geographical Society, and the famous Henry Morton Stanley and David Livingstone.

By the turn of the 20th century, Europeans had firmly established a presence in East Africa. Both the British and German colonial administrations were busy building railways and roads to open their colonies to commerce, establishing hospitals and schools, and encouraging the influx of Christian missionaries. Kenya's fertile and climatically favourable highlands proved eminently suitable for European farmers to colonise. In Tanganyika, by contrast, large areas were unable to support agriculture and were plagued by the tsetse fly, which made cattle grazing and dairy farming impossible.

Africans and Africa played a key role in WWII. The East African Carrier Corps consisted of over 400,000 men, and the development of the atom bomb was entirely dependent on uranium from the Congo.

Independence

As the European presence in Africa solidified, discontent with colonial rule grew and demands for independence became more insistent. In the 1950s and early 1960s, the various nationalist movements coalesced and gained force across East Africa, culminating in the granting of independence to Tanzania (1961), Uganda, Rwanda and Burundi (all in 1962), and Kenya (1963). In Kenya, the path to independence was violent and protracted, with some of the underlying issues reflected in the country's current political difficulties; in Tanzania and Uganda the immediate pre-independence years were relatively peaceful, while in Rwanda and Burundi, long-existing tribal rivalries were a major issue – the effects of which are still being felt today.

1952

The Mau Mau rebellion begins as a protest against colonial land-grabbing in Kikuyu lands. By the time it is suppressed, thousands of Kikuyu have been killed or put into detention camps.

1961–63

Following a period of increasing discontent with colonial rule, the countries of East Africa gain independence, with Tanganyika (now Tanzania) leading the way in December 1961.

1978–79

Ugandan dictator Idi Amin invades Tanzania, burning villages along the Kagera River believed to harbour Ugandan rebels. Tanzania's army marches to Kampala to topple Amin and restore Milton Obote to power.

1994

The presidents of Rwanda and Burundi are killed when their plane is shot down during landing, unleashing the Rwandan genocide, leaving more than one million dead in its wake.

THE SLAVE TRADE

Slavery has been practised in Africa throughout recorded history. Initially, slaves were taken from coastal regions and shipped to Arabia, Persia and the Indian Ocean islands. Kilwa Kisiwani, off Tanzania's southern coast, was a major export gateway. As demand increased, traders made their way inland, and during the 18th and 19th centuries, slaves were being brought from as far away as Malawi and the Congo. By the 19th century, with the rise of the Omani Arabs, Zanzibar Island had eclipsed Kilwa Kisiwani as East Africa's major slave-trading depot. According to some estimates, by the 1860s from 10,000 to as many as 50,000 slaves were passing through Zanzibar's market each year. Overall, close to 600,000 slaves were sold through Zanzibar between 1830 and 1873, when a treaty with Britain paved the way for the trade's ultimate halt in the region in the early 20th century.

As well as the human horrors, the slave trade caused major social upheavals. In the south of present-day Tanzania, it fanned inter-clan warfare as ruthless entrepreneurs raided neighbouring tribes for slaves. In other areas, it promoted increased social stratification and altered settlement patterns. Some tribes began to build fortified settlements encircled by trenches, while others concentrated their populations in towns as self-defence. Another major societal change was the gradual shift in the nature of chieftaincy from religiously based to a position resting on military power or wealth.

The slave trade also served as an impetus for European missionary activity in East Africa, prompting the establishment of the first mission stations and missionary penetration of the interior. A tireless campaigner against the horrors of slavery was Scottish missionary-explorer David Livingstone (1813–74), whose efforts, combined with the attention attracted by his funeral, were an important influence mobilising British initiatives to halt human trafficking in the region. For more on the British campaign to end slavery, read Adam Hochschild's *Bury the Chains* (2005).

By the time slavery was abolished, between eight and 20 million Africans had been sold into slavery.

Kenya

In Kenya, the European influx increased rapidly during the first half of the 20th century, so that by the 1950s there were about 80,000 settlers in the country. Much of the land that was expropriated for their farms came from the homelands of the Kikuyu people. The Kikuyu responded by forming an opposition political association in 1920, and by instigating the Mau Mau rebellion in the 1950s, which marked a major turning point in Kenyan politics and ultimately led the way to independence.

7 August 1998

Within minutes of each another, Al-Qaeda truck bombs explode at the US embassies in Nairobi and Dar es Salaam, killing and injuring dozens.

Dec 2007–Jan 2008

Kenya is racked by post-election violence as hundreds are killed and thousands displaced from their homes in the Rift Valley and central areas.

2011

After attacks blamed on Somalia's al-Shabab militia, Kenya invades Somalia to try to drive the Islamists from power. The African Union, including soldiers from Uganda and Burundi, later take over the mission.

21 September 2013

Somalia's militant al-Shabab group attacks Nairobi's upmarket West Gate Shopping Mall. The siege lasts for days and ends with 67 people dead, including the attackers.

Tanganyika (Tanzania)

In Tanganyika (most of what is now mainland Tanzania, as well as Rwanda and Burundi), the unpopular German administration continued until the end of WWI, when the League of Nations mandated Tanzania to the British, and Rwanda and Burundi to the Belgians. British rule was equally unpopular, with the Brits neglecting development of Tanzania in favour of the more lucrative and fertile options available in Kenya and Uganda. Political consciousness soon began to coalesce in the form of farmers' unions and cooperatives through which popular demands were expressed. By the mid-20th century, there were over 400 such cooperatives, which soon joined to form the Tanganyika Africa Association (TAA), a lobbying group for the nationalist cause based in Dar es Salaam.

In 2013 the British government agreed to pay £19.9 million in costs and compensation to more than 5000 elderly Kenyans who suffered torture and abuse during the Mau Mau uprising in the 1950s.

Uganda

In Uganda, the British tended to favour the recruitment of the powerful Buganda people for the civil service. Members of other tribes, unable to acquire responsible jobs in the colonial administration or to make inroads into the Buganda-dominated commercial sector, were forced to seek other ways of joining the mainstream. The Acholi and Lango, for example, chose the army and became the tribal majority in the military. As resentment grew, the seeds were planted for the intertribal conflicts that were to tear Uganda apart following independence.

Zamani: A Survey of East African History (1968), edited by renowned Kenyan historian BA Ogot with JA Kieran, is a classic introduction to the region's precolonial and colonial history from an African perspective.

Rwanda & Burundi

In Rwanda and Burundi, the period of colonial rule was characterised by increasing power and privilege of the Tutsi. The Belgian administrators found it convenient to rule indirectly through Tutsi chiefs and their princes, and the Tutsi had a monopoly on the missionary-run educational system. As a result, long-existing tensions between the Tutsi and Hutu were exacerbated, igniting the spark that was later to explode in the 1993 Burundi and 1994 Rwanda genocides.

2015

Burundi's Constitutional Court clears the way for President Nkurunziza to stand for a third term. Despite widespread protests, Nkurunziza wins a third term as president with 70% of the vote.

2016

Already in power since 1986, Uganda's President Yoweri Museveni wins presidential election. Eighteen months later, government MPs introduce a bill removing presidential age limits.

2017

Rwandan President Paul Kagame easily wins re-election, after the results of a 2016 referendum allow him to stand for a third term.

2017

A largely peaceful Kenyan presidential election results in a victory for incumbent Jomo Kenyatta, but after an opposition legal challenge, the Supreme Court annuls the results and orders fresh election due to irregularities.

Life in East Africa

Traditional cultures hold East Africa together (and sometimes tear it apart). Feeding into these traditions are all manner of affiliations, and respect for one's elders, firmly held religious beliefs, traditional gender roles, *ujamaa* (familyhood) and even national identity all play their part in helping East Africans make sense of their worlds. Watching how these traditions equip East Africans to deal with the assault of modernity is one of the more interesting elements of travelling in the region.

Daily Life & Customs

Hospitality

It's a wild place, the East African bush, and hospitality counts because it has to. You never know if you'll soon be the one on the asking end – whether for a cup of water, a meal or a roof over your head for the night – and strangers are traditionally welcomed as family. In a region where it is commonplace for a 10km walk to get you to the nearest water source, the nearest medical clinic or the nearest primary school, time takes on an altogether different dimension. Daily rhythms are determined by the sun and the seasons, and arriving is the most important thing, not when or how. *Nitafika* (I will arrive). *Safiri salama* (Travel in peace). *Umefika* (You have arrived). *Karibu* (Welcome). Additional words are not necessary.

Support Networks

No monthly social security cheques arrive in the mail in East Africa, so community life is essential – for support in times of sickness and for the ageing, as well as for ensuring a proper upbringing for the young people. Mourning is a community affair, as is celebrating. It would be unheard of not to attend the funeral of your mother's second cousin once removed, just as it would be equally unheard of to miss celebrating the wedding of your father's stepbrother's neighbour. Salaried jobs are scarce, and if you're one of the lucky few to have found one, it's expected that you'll share your good fortune with the extended family. Throughout East African society, 'I' and 'me' are very much out, while 'our' and 'we' are in and always have been.

Life Expectancy

Burundi: 60.5 years

Kenya: 64 years

Rwanda: 60.1 years

Tanzania: 62.2 years

Uganda: 55.4 years

Extended family has traditionally provided a critical layer of support for East Africans. In recent decades, extended family has become increasingly important as parents migrate to cities for lucrative work, leaving their children to be cared for by grandparents, aunts and uncles. This fluid system has also enabled many to deal with the devastation wrought by the HIV/AIDS epidemic.

In all aspects of daily life, emphasis is on the necessary. If you do attend that funeral, forget bringing flowers; a bag of rice, or money, would be a more appropriate way of showing your solidarity with the bereaved.

Social Hierarchies

At all levels of society, invisible social hierarchies lend life a sense of order. Age-based groups play a central role among many tribes, and the elderly and those in positions of authority are respected. Men rule the roost in the working world and, at least symbolically, in the family as well. Although women arguably form the backbone of the economy throughout the region – with most juggling child-rearing plus work on the family farm or in an office – they are frequently marginalised when it comes to education and politics. Some positive contrasts to this situation are found in Kenya, which is notable for its abundance of nongovernment organisations, many headed by women, and in Uganda, where women play prominent roles in educational and literary circles.

In Swahili-speaking areas of East Africa, it's common for a woman to drop her own name, and become known as *Mama* followed by the name of her oldest son (or daughter, if she has no sons).

Ways of Belonging

With the exception of Tanzania, where local chieftaincies were abolished following independence, tribal identity and structures are strong. In fact, stay long enough and you'll quickly see the differences from country to country. Tanzanians, for example, almost always identify themselves as Tanzanian first, with other layers of identity (tribe, region etc) a distant second. The result is, on the surface at least, a remarkably harmonious society.

In Kenya, on the other hand, the situation is reversed and while most are proud to be Kenyan, national identity is only one (perhaps even a subordinate) way among many in which Kenyans understand their world. Family ties, the pull of religion and gender roles are all prominent issues in the public domain and in the daily lives of ordinary people. Perhaps even above all of these, the tribe remains an important aspect of a Kenyan's identity: upon meeting a fellow Kenyan, the first question on anyone's mind is, 'What tribe do you come from?'

The importance of tribe (or the political manipulation of tribal affiliations) has had disastrous consequences, as seen in the Burundian genocide in 1993, the Rwandan genocide in 1994 and in the 2007 post-election violence in Kenya. All three countries have since sought to overcome these divisions. Both Burundi and Rwanda have undergone significant programs of nation-building in which, for the most part, national identity is promoted as more important than tribal identity. In Kenya the 2010 constitution recognises the rights of ethnic minorities and even calls for the make-up of the cabinet to reflect the country's regional and ethnic diversity.

The Tanzanian town of Mto wa Mbu, close to Lake Manyara National Park, is famous for being the only place in the country (perhaps aside from major cities) where all of Tanzania's 120 tribal groups are present.

Multicultural Melting Pot

Almost since the dawn of humankind, outsiders have been arriving in East Africa and have been assimilated into its seething, simmering and endlessly fascinating cultural melting pot. From the Bantu-, Nilotic- and Cushitic-speaking groups that made their way to the region during the early migrations, to Arab and Asian traders, and colonial-era Europeans, a long stream of migrants have left their footprints. Today the region's modern face reflects this rich fusion of influences, with 300-plus tribal

HIV/AIDS IN EAST AFRICA

Together with malaria, AIDS is the leading cause of death in sub-Saharan Africa, and East Africa is no exception. According to the US government, in a 2016 ranking of countries with the most inhabitants living with HIV/AIDS, Kenya (1.6 million people), Uganda (almost 1.4 million) and Tanzania (1.4 million) all came within the 10 worst-affected countries. By another measure, 7.2% of Ugandans, 6.1% of Kenyans and 5.1% of Tanzanians have HIV/AIDS. In Uganda alone, there are nearly one million AIDS orphans under 17 years of age.

Encouragingly, AIDS awareness has improved in the region; East African governments now discuss the situation openly, and you'll notice AIDS-related billboards in Dar es Salaam, Nairobi, Kampala and elsewhere. Yet at the grassroots level in many areas, the stigma remains and, especially away from urban centres, real discussion remains limited. AIDS-related deaths are often kept quiet, with tuberculosis used euphemistically as a socially acceptable catch-all diagnosis. In one study in Kenya, over half of the women surveyed who had acquired HIV hadn't told their partners because they feared being beaten or abandoned.

groups, as well as small but economically significant pockets of Asians, Arabs and Europeans all rubbing shoulders.

Kenya's first permanent settlers from the Indian subcontinent were indentured workers, brought here from Gujarat and the Punjab by the British to build the Uganda Railway. After the railway was finished, the British allowed many workers to stay and start up businesses, and hundreds of *dukas* (small shops) were set up across the country. After WWII, the Indian community came to control large sectors of the East African economy. However, few gave their active support to the black nationalist movements in the run-up to independence, despite being urged to do so by India's prime minister, and many were hesitant to accept local citizenship after independence. This earned the widespread distrust of the African community and the African response reached a low point with the anti-Asian pogroms that swept Uganda during the reign of Idi Amin.

Kenyan athletes did well at the Rio Olympics, winning six gold, six silver and one bronze medal, ranking 15th, the highest of any African country. However, they nearly didn't make it to Rio after a series of failed drug tests and difficulties surrounding the compliance of the country's anti-doping agency.

Sports

Despite football-crazy fans, East African countries remain the great underachievers of African football. No East African team has ever won the African Cup of Nations and nor have any of the five countries ever qualified for the World Cup Finals.

On the international sports stage, Kenya's athletes have won gold medals in long-distance running events at every Olympics since 1968, save for 1976 and 1980 when Kenya did not participate.

The East African Safari Rally (www.eastafricansafarirally.com), which has been held annually since 1953, passes through Kenya, Uganda and Tanzania along public roadways, and attracts an international collection of drivers with their vintage (pre-1971) automobiles.

The epic Tour d'Afrique (www.tdaglobalcycling.com/tour-dafrique) bicycle race passes through East Africa (Kenya and Tanzania) en route between Cairo (Egypt) and Cape Town (South Africa).

Bao

It's not exactly sport, but *bao* (also known as *kombe, mweso* and by various other names) is one of East Africa's favourite pastimes. It's especially popular on the Zanzibar Archipelago and elsewhere along the coast, where you'll see men in their *kanzu* (white robe-like outer garment) and *kofia* (hat) huddled around a board watching two opponents play. The rules vary somewhat from place to place, but the game always involves trying to capture the pebbles or seeds of your opponent, which are set out on a board with rows of small hollows. Anything can substitute for a board, from finely carved wood to a flattened area of sand on the beach.

As of late 2017, Uganda was the highest-ranked East African team in the FIFA World Rankings (71st out of 206), followed by Kenya (88th), Rwanda (118th), Tanzania (125th) and Burundi (129th).

Religion

Christianity and Islam dominate spiritual life in East Africa, but there are also a sizeable number of adherents of traditional religions, as well as small communities of Hindus, Sikhs and Jains.

Christians are in the majority in all East African countries: Rwanda (88.9% of the population), Burundi (86%), Uganda (84.4%), Kenya (83%) and Tanzania (officially 61.4% but many of these people still practise traditional religions). Ninety-nine percent of Zanzibar's population is Muslim.

Christianity

The first Christian missionaries reached East Africa in the mid-19th century. Since then the region has been the site of extensive missionary activity, and today most of the major denominations are represented, including both Catholics and Protestants. In many areas, mission stations have been the major, and in some cases the only, channels for health care and education, with missions still sometimes providing the only schools and medical facilities in remote areas.

In addition to the main denominations, there is also an increasing number of home-grown African sects, especially in Kenya. Factors that are often cited for their growth include cultural resurgence, an ongoing struggle against neocolonialism and the alienation felt by many jobseekers who migrate to urban centres far from their homes.

Church services throughout East Africa are invariably very colourful and packed to overflowing. Even if you can't understand the language, it's worth going to listen to the unaccompanied choral singing, which East Africans do with such beauty and harmony.

Former Kenyan president Jomo Kenyatta once argued that female genital mutilation (FGM) was such an integral part of initiation rites and Kikuyu identity that its abolition would destroy the tribal system.

Islam

In 1984 archaeologists discovered a mosque's foundations in Lamu, Kenya, along with coins dating from AD 830, suggesting that Islam had a foothold on the East African coast as early as the 9th century, barely 100 years after the death of the Prophet Mohammed. It should be hardly surprising that Islam took hold so quickly in East Africa, given the region's trading connections with southern Arabia.

Further evidence suggests an Islamic presence in Zanzibar from at least the 11th century, while the famous traveller Ibn Battuta found that by the early 14th century, Islam was the dominant religion all along the East African coast as far as South Africa. These days, Islam here – in typical East African fashion – has developed in a considerably less dogmatic form than in other parts of the world.

Most East African Muslims are Sunnis, with a small minority of Shiites, primarily among the Asian community. The most influential of the various Shiite sects represented are the Ismailis, followers of the Aga Khan.

FEMALE GENITAL MUTILATION

Female genital mutilation (FGM), often euphemistically referred to as female circumcision, is the partial or total removal of the female external genitalia. FGM is usually carried out for reasons of cultural or gender identity, and it is entrenched in tribal life in some areas. Yet among the very real risks of the procedure are infection, shock and haemorrhage, as well as lifelong complications and pain with menstruation, urination, intercourse and childbirth. For women who have had infibulation – in which all or part of the external genitalia are removed, and the vaginal opening then narrowed and stitched together – unassisted childbirth is impossible, and many women and children die as a consequence.

Since the mid-1990s there have been major efforts to reduce the incidence of the practice, with slow but real progress. In both Kenya and Tanzania, FGM has been declared illegal with prison sentences for violators, although the number of prosecutions is miniscule and the practice continues in many areas. According to Unicef, an estimated 27% of Kenyan women (including 98% in Northeastern Province, near Somalia, but just 1% in Western Province) have undergone FGM: it is particularly prevalent among the Kisii and Maasai. In Tanzania the figures are estimated at around 15% and the practice is particularly common in the north.

In Uganda FGM was finally banned by the government in 2009, with penalties of 10 years' imprisonment for violators (or life, if the girl dies), although enforcement remains a concern. The main area where FGM is still practised is in northeastern Uganda, near the border with Kenya, with the national prevalence rate at around 1%.

Several nongovernmental women's organisations, in Kenya in particular, have taken a leading role in bringing FGM to the forefront of media discussion. There is also a growing movement towards alternative rites that offer the chance to maintain traditions while minimising the health complications, such as the practice of *ntanira na mugambo* (circumcision through words).

CONDUCT IN EAST AFRICA

East Africa comfortably mixes a generally conservative outlook on life with a great deal of tolerance and openness towards foreigners. Following are a few tips to smooth the way.

➡ While most East Africans are likely to be too polite to tell you so directly, they'll be privately shaking their head about travellers not wearing enough clothing or sporting tatty clothes. Especially along the Muslim coast, cover up your shoulders and legs, and avoid plunging necklines and skin-tight fits.

➡ Pleasantries count. Even if you're just asking for directions, take time to greet the other person. Handshake etiquette is also worth learning, and best picked up by observation. In many areas, East Africans often continue holding hands for several minutes after meeting, or even throughout an entire conversation.

➡ Don't eat or pass things with the left hand.

➡ Respect authority; losing your patience or undermining an official's authority will get you nowhere, while deference and a good-natured demeanour will see you through most situations.

➡ Avoid criticising the government of your host country, or offending locals with public nudity, open anger and public displays of affection (between people of the same or opposite sex).

➡ When visiting a rural area, seek out the chief or local elders to announce your presence, and ask permission before setting up a tent or wandering through a village – it will rarely be refused.

➡ Receive gifts with both hands, or with the right hand while touching the left hand to your right elbow. Giving a gift? Don't be surprised if the appreciation isn't expressed verbally.

Five pillars of Islam guide Muslims in their daily lives:

Haj (pilgrimage) It is the duty of every Muslim, who is fit and can afford it, to make the pilgrimage to Mecca at least once.

Sala (prayer; sometimes written *salat*) This is the obligation of prayer, done five times daily when muezzins call the faithful to pray, facing Mecca and ideally in a mosque.

Sawm (fasting) Ramadan commemorates the revelation of the Quran to Mohammed and is the month when Muslims fast from dawn to dusk.

Shahada (the profession of faith) 'There is no God but Allah, and Mohammed is his Prophet' is the fundamental tenet of Islam.

Zakat (alms) Giving to the poor is an essential part of Islamic social teaching.

Negotiations of bride price still play a major role in marriages in the region. Although cash is becoming an increasingly common replacement, cattle are still coveted in many areas.

Traditional Religions

The natural and spiritual worlds are part of the same continuum in East Africa, and mountain peaks, lakes, forests, certain trees and other natural features are viewed by many as dwellings of the supreme being or of the ancestors.

Most local traditional beliefs acknowledge the existence of a supreme deity. Many also hold that communication with this deity is possible through the intercession of the ancestors. The ancestors are thus accordingly honoured, and viewed as playing a strong role in protecting the tribe and family. Maintaining proper relations is essential for general well-being. However, among the Maasai, the Kikuyu and several other tribes, there is no tradition of ancestor worship, with the supreme deity (known as Ngai or Enkai) the sole focus of devotion.

Traditional medicine in East Africa is closely intertwined with traditional religion, with practitioners using divining implements, prayers, chanting and dance to facilitate communication with the spirit world.

Environment

The story of East Africa's natural environment is one of fragile abundance. It is the tale of a continent's extraordinary natural beauty and diversity, of all that we imagine Africa to be – from the Great Rift Valley to horizonless savannah, spectacular lakes and deep forests. Inhabiting these epic landforms are some of the last great herds of wildlife left on the planet. But these landforms and wild herds are under threat, making the urgency to see them that much greater.

The Land

Straddling the equator, edged to the east by the Indian Ocean and to the west by a chain of Rift Valley lakes, East Africa is as diverse geographically and environmentally as it is culturally.

Great Rift Valley

Africa's Great Rift Valley is one of the continent's defining landforms and this great gouge in the planet cuts a swath through the heart of East Africa. It was formed between 30 and eight million years ago, when the tectonic plates that comprise the African and Eurasian landmasses collided and then diverged again. As the plates moved apart, massive tablets of the earth's crust collapsed between them, resulting over the millennia in the escarpments, ravines, flatlands and lakes that mark much of East Africa today.

The Rift Valley is part of the Afro-Arabian rift system that stretches 5500km from the salty shores of the Dead Sea to the palm trees of Mozambique. The East African section of the Rift Valley consists of two branches formed where the main rift system divides north of Kenya's Lake Turkana. The western branch, or Western Rift Valley, makes its way past Lake Albert in Uganda through Rwanda and Burundi down to Lake Tanganyika, after which it meanders southeast to Lake Nyasa. Seismic and volcanic disturbances still occur throughout the western branch. The eastern branch, known as the Eastern or Gregory Rift, runs south from Lake Turkana past Lake Natron and Lake Manyara in Tanzania before joining again with the Western Rift in northern Malawi.

Peter Matthiessen's classic *The Tree Where Man Was Born* is an evocative and beautifully written 1960s picture of East Africa's physical, environmental and cultural make-up. His *Sand Rivers* (1981), a timeless account of a foot safari through the Selous Game Reserve, is lesser known but just as brilliant.

The forces that created the Rift Valley also gave rise to Africa's highest mountains, among them Mt Kilimanjaro, Mt Kenya, Uganda's Rwenzori Mountains and the DRC's Virunga Range. Most began as volcanoes and most are now extinct, but no fewer than 30 remain active, among them the DRC's Nyiragongo volcano. Other places where the escarpments of the Rift Valley are particularly impressive include Kenya's Rift Valley Province, the Nkuruman Escarpment east of Kenya's Masai Mara National Reserve, and the terrain around Ngorongoro Conservation Area (p120) and Lake Manyara National Park (p115) in Tanzania.

The Savannah

The African savannah – broad rolling grasslands dotted with lone acacia trees – is a quintessentially African landscape, so much so that it covers an estimated two-thirds of the African land mass.

Savannah is often located in a broad swath surrounding tropical rainforest. The term itself refers to a grasslands ecosystem. While trees may be (and usually are) present, such trees do not, under the strict definition of the term, form a closed canopy.

The East African savannah was formed during the Rift's great upheavals, when volcanic lava and ash rained down upon the lands surrounding the Rift's volcanoes, covering the landscape in fertile but shallow soils. Grasses, that most successful of plant forms, flourished as they needed little depth for their roots to grow. However, no other plants were able to colonise the savannah (the perfectly adapted acacia aside), as their roots were starved of space and nourishment.

Thus created, savannah flourishes in areas where there are long wet seasons alternating with long dry seasons, creating ideal conditions for the growth of dense, nutritious grasses. Shaped by fire – which both regenerate and devastate – and by grazing animals, savannah is a dynamic habitat in constant flux with its adjacent woodlands.

In East Africa, the most famous sweeps of savannah are found in Tanzania's Serengeti National Park (p123) and Kenya's Masai Mara National Reserve (p252).

Forests

East Africa's forests border the great rainforest systems of central Africa, which once formed part of the mighty Guineo–Congolian forest ecosystem. The most intact stands of rainforest are found in places such as the Rwenzori Mountains National Park (p436) in southwestern Uganda and the DRC's Virunga range, although important blocks of rainforest still exist in Rwanda and Burundi; in the latter two countries, the pressure on forests from soaring populations is particularly acute.

Kenya has few forests, although the Kakamega Forest Reserve (p268) shows what most of western Kenya must have once looked like, while the Arabuko Sokoke Forest Reserve (p331) is the largest surviving tract of coastal forest in East Africa. There are also small patches of tropical rainforest in Tanzania's Eastern Arc mountains, such as the Usambara Mountains.

Forest Cover

Tanzania: 36.8%

Kenya: 6.1%

Uganda: 14.1%

Rwanda: 18.4%

Burundi: 6.6%

DRC: 67.7%

Lakes

Lake Victoria, which is shared between Uganda, Tanzania and Kenya, is Africa's largest freshwater lake (and the second-largest by area in the world after the US's Lake Superior). Its surface covers an area of over 68,000 sq km. Water levels fluctuate widely, depending largely on the rains, with depths never more than 80m and more often lower than 10m. More than 90% of the lake falls within Tanzanian or Ugandan territory. Lake Victoria is also considered one of the sources of the Nile.

Lake Tanganyika is the world's longest freshwater lake and is estimated to have the second-largest volume of freshwater in the world (after Lake Baikal in Siberia), with 45% belonging to the DRC and 41% to Tanzania.

Lake Nyasa (also known as Lake Malawi), Africa's third-largest and second-deepest freshwater lake, is the Rift Valley's southernmost lake. Its waters reportedly contain more fish species than any other freshwater lake on earth.

About 6% (59,000 sq km) of mainland Tanzania is covered by inland lakes. The deepest is Lake Tanganyika, while the largest (and one of the shallowest) is Lake Victoria.

Besides providing fertile soil, the volcanic deposits of the Rift Valley have created alkaline waters in most Rift Valley lakes. Its largest is a sea of jade, otherwise known by the more boring name of Lake Turkana, which straddles the Ethiopian border in the north; Lake Turkana is the world's third-largest salt lake. Other important alkaline lakes include Bogoria, Nakuru, Elmenteita and Natron. These shallow soda lakes, formed by the valley's lack of decent drainage, experience high evaporation rates, which further concentrates the alkalinity. The strangely soapy and smelly waters are the perfect environment for the growth of microscopic blue-green algae, which in turn feed lesser flamingos, tiny crustaceans (food for greater flamingos) and insect larvae (food for soda-resistant fish). In 2011 Kenya's Rift Valley lake system (primarily lakes Nakuru, Elmenteita and Bogoria) was inscribed on Unesco's list of World Heritage Sites.

Wildlife

East Africa is arguably the premier wildlife-watching destination on earth. The wildlife that most visitors come to see ranges from the 'Big Five' (lion, buffalo, elephant, leopard and rhino) to some of the last great herds of zebras, hippos, giraffes, wildebeest and antelope left on earth, plus major populations of primates. These animals are not only impressive to watch but are also essential linchpins in a beautifully complex natural web where each species has its own niche in any given ecosystem.

In addition to the large animals, other players include over 60,000 insect species, several dozen types of reptiles and amphibians (including many snake species), and abundant marine life, both in the Indian Ocean and inland water systems. Completing the picture are close to 1500 different types of birds, including many rare ones – Tanzania, Kenya and Uganda are each home to more than 1000 species.

Seeing the 'Big Five' has become a mantra for African wildlife watchers, but few know it was coined by white hunters for the five species deemed most dangerous to hunt: elephant, lion, leopard, rhino and buffalo.

Endangered Species

Many of East Africa's most important species have become endangered over the past few decades as a result of poisoning, the ongoing destruction of their natural habitat, and merciless poaching for ivory, skins, horn and bush meat.

Elephants

In the 1970s and 1980s, the numbers of African elephants plummeted from an estimated 1.3 million to around 500,000 thanks to widespread poaching. In Kenya, elephant numbers fell from 45,000 in 1976 to just 5400 in 1988. The slaughter ended only in 1989 when the trade in ivory was banned under the Convention for International Trade in Endangered Species (Cites). When the ban was established, world raw ivory prices plummeted by 90%, and the market for poaching and smuggling was radically reduced. The same year, Kenyan President Daniel arap Moi dramatically burned 12 tons of ivory in Nairobi National Park as a symbol of Kenya's resolve in the battle against poachers.

But poaching is once again on the rise. Africa has lost more than 30,000 elephants a year since 2010 and in 2014, for the first time in decades, a critical threshold was crossed when more elephants were being

GOOD WILDLIFE READS

- *The Tree Where Man Was Born* (Peter Matthiessen; 1972) Classic, lyrical account of wildlife and traditional peoples in East Africa.
- *A Primate's Memoir: Love, Death and Baboons in East Africa* (Robert M Sapolsky; 2002) Wonderfully told memoir of working among the baboons of East Africa.
- *Ivory, Apes & Peacocks: Animals, Adventure and Discovery in the Wild Places of Africa* (Alan Root; 2012) Picaresque tale of the life of the late Alan Root, one of the pioneers in wildlife documentary film-making.
- *The Big Cat Man: An Autobiography* (Jonathan Scott; 2016) Jonathan Scott has been the companion to a generation of safari goers and armchair travellers. His autobiography is typically warm-hearted.
- *Don't Run, Whatever You Do: My Adventures as a Safari Guide* (Peter Allison; 2007) Light-hearted romp through adventures and misadventures of a safari guide. Set in Botswana but could easily be East Africa.

killed on the continent than were being born. Adding to the problem is the fact that elephant numbers had yet to recover from previous decades when poaching was rampant – in Tanzania's Selous Game Reserve, for example, there were more than 110,000 elephants in the late 1970s, but the latest survey found just 13,500.

The 2016 Great Elephant Census counted 352,271 African savanna elephants spread across 18 countries, a 30% decrease in seven years. In East Africa there was both good news and bad news. Kenya's elephant population, for example, was considered to be 'relatively stable' at 25,959, while Uganda's 4864 elephants were cause for optimism after the country's elephant population fell to just 800 during the 1980s. Tanzania, on the other hand, saw a catastrophic 60% decline in elephant numbers in the five years to 2016, with just 42,871 elephants and 2.6 carcasses spotted for every live elephant.

Amboseli Trust for Elephants (www.elephanttrust.org) and **Save the Elephants** (www.savetheelephants.org) are invaluable sources of information about East Africa's elephants.

East African governments remain on the frontline in the war against poaching, but other organisations are also active, such as the **Big Life Foundation** (www.biglife.org).

Black Rhinoceros

Black Rhino Hotspots

- *Ol Pejeta Conservancy (Kenya)*
- *Lake Nakuru National Park (Kenya)*
- *Ngorongoro Conservation Area (Tanzania)*
- *Selous Game Reserve (Tanzania)*
- *Tsavo West National Park (Kenya)*
- *Nairobi National Park (Kenya)*

These inoffensive vegetarians are armed with impressive horns that have made them the target of both white hunters and poachers; rhino numbers plummeted to the brink of extinction during the 20th century and the illegal trade in rhino horns is still driven by their use in traditional medicines in Asian countries and the demand for dagger handles in Yemen.

Despite having turned the situation around from the desperate lows of the 1980s, wildlife authorities in East Africa are again battling a recent upsurge in rhino poaching. It was in 2009 that the crisis again began to take hold. In the following year Kenya's Lewa Wildlife Conservancy lost its first rhinos to poaching in almost three decades. In the years since, all of the major rhino sanctuaries – Nairobi National Park, Solio Game Reserve, Lewa Wildlife Conservancy, Ol Pejeta Conservancy and Ngulia Rhino Sanctuary in Tsavo West National Park – have lost rhinos. Most worrying of all is that each of these have extremely high security and sophisticated anti-poaching programs. Then again, by 2017 the number of rhinos being poached from East Africa's parks and reserves had fallen, suggesting that the enhanced security measures were paying off.

There are two species of rhino – black and white – both of which are predominantly found in savannah regions. The black rhino is probably East Africa's most endangered large mammal – the black rhino population plum-

THE TSETSE FLY

The tsetse fly is one of the most persistent and annoying of all East African insects – we found them to be particularly troublesome, and their bite particularly painful, in Tanzania's Tarangire National Park and some areas of Serengeti National Park. Their bite can also be more than painful, causing sleeping sickness in both humans and domestic livestock (in whom the disease is called animal trypanosomiasis). But for all its nastiness, East Africa might not have the wildlife and wilderness areas that remain to this day were it not for the tsetse.

After the rinderpest outbreak devastated East Africa's livestock herds in the final years of the 19th century, the tsetse fly and wild animals (which appear immune to tsetse-borne diseases) moved in, rendering large swaths of the region unsuitable for human populations and their domestic livestock. In many cases, these areas would become the national parks that today protect the region's epic wildlife populations.

meted by over 97% between 1960 and 1992, with the low point reached in 1995 with just 2410 thought to remain in the wild. By 2014, numbers were thought to have rebounded to around 5000. Kenya has East Africa's largest share, with an estimated 650 to 700 black rhinos surviving in the wild.

Lions

Because lions are the easiest of the big cats to observe, few people realise that lions face an extremely uncertain future. No one quite knows how many lions there once were, but there were probably more than a million when colonial explorers arrived in East Africa in the 19th century. Now, as few as 20,000 are thought to remain and lions have disappeared from 80% of their historical range, according to Panthera, the leading cat conservation NGO, based in New York.

Across their range, numbers are falling alarmingly, thanks primarily to human encroachment and habitat loss. The poisoning of lions, either in retaliation for them killing livestock or encroaching onto farming lands, has also reached dangerous levels, to the extent that some lion conservationists predict that the lion could become regionally extinct in Kenya within 20 years.

More than half of the continent's total population resides in Tanzania, while in Kenya lion numbers have reached critical levels: fewer than 2000 lions are thought to remain in the country. Uganda is home to an estimated 400 lions, with the only viable populations in Queen Elizabeth National Park (p439), Murchison Falls National Park (p468) and Kidepo Valley National Park (p419). Lions are believed to be regionally extinct in Burundi, and had disappeared from Rwanda until the species was reintroduced into Akagera National Park (p541) in 2015 by African Parks (www.africanparks.org).

Lion Guardians (www.lionguardians.org) and **Living with Lions** (www.livingwithlions.org) are Kenyan organisations fighting to protect lions and are important sources of information. **Wildlife Direct** (www.wildlifedirect.org) is another useful source of information, particularly on the threats posed by poisoning. Check out also **Panthera** (www.panthera.org), **Big Life Foundation** (www.biglife.org) and **Ewaso Lions** (www.ewasolions.org).

There is no finer resource on Africa's wild cats than *Cats of Africa* (2005) by L Hunter. It is an authoritative but highly readable book covering their behaviour, conservation and ecology, with superb photos by G Hinde. The author is the president of Panthera (www.panthera.org), the leading cat conservation NGO.

Mountain Gorillas

Gorillas are the largest of the great apes and share 97% of their biological make-up with humans. They used to inhabit a swath of land that cut right across central Africa, but the last remaining eastern mountain gorillas number around 880 individuals, divided between two 300-plus populations in the forests of Uganda's Bwindi Impenetrable National Park (p445) and on the slopes of the Virunga volcanoes, encompassing Uganda's Mgahinga Gorilla National Park (p457), Rwanda's Volcanoes National Park (p520) and the DRC's Parc National des Virunga (p498).

Mountain gorilla numbers have held firm and even slightly increased over the past 15 years or so, despite the widely publicised execution-style killings of seven gorillas in Parc National des Virunga in 2007, ongoing threats from instability in the DRC, poaching, mining exploration, the Ebola and Marburg viruses and the trade in bush meat. The International Union for Conservation of Nature (IUCN) Red List of Threatened Species (www.iucnredlist.org) lists the eastern mountain gorilla as critically endangered.

Grevy's Zebras

Kenya (along with neighbouring Ethiopia) is home to the last surviving wild populations of Grevy's zebra. In the 1970s, approximately 15,000 Grevy's zebras were thought to survive in the wild. Just 2600 are estimated to remain and less than 1% of the Grevy zebra's historical range lies within protected areas. Distinguished from other zebra species by having narrow stripes and bellies free from stripes, the Grevy's zebra is found in the Lewa Wildlife Conservancy (p286), Ol Pejeta Conservancy (p284), Segera Retreat (p286) and the Samburu National Reserve (p347).

Giraffes

One of the most worrying developments in recent years has been the downgrading of the giraffe by the International Union for Conservation of Nature (IUCN) from Least Concern in 2010 to Vulnerable in 2016. The world's tallest land mammal remains widespread across East and southern Africa, but a precipitous 40% decline (from an estimated 151,702 to 163,452 individuals in 1985 to 97,562 in 2015) has brought the species' fate into sharp focus.

The main threats to the giraffe are illegal hunting, habitat loss, increasing human-wildlife conflict, civil conflict and encroaching human settlements.

Rothschild's Giraffes

The most endangered of the nine giraffe subspecies, the Rothschild's giraffe has recently been hauled back from the brink of extinction. At the forefront of the fight to save the Rothschild's giraffe (which, unlike other subspecies, has distinctive white 'stockings' with no orange-and-black markings below the knee) is the Giraffe Centre (p226) in Nairobi. Rothschild's giraffes are making a comeback, with populations having been reintroduced into the wild at Lake Nakuru National Park (p249) and Ruma National Park (p265) (both in Kenya). There's also a small population in Uganda's Murchison Falls National Park (p468).

African Wild Dogs

The International Union for Conservation of Nature (IUCN) Red List of Threatened Species (www.iucnredlist.org) lists the African wild dog as endangered, with no more than 6600 left on the continent (of which just 1400 are mature individuals). Most range across southern Africa, but southern Tanzania does have East Africa's most important regional populations. Your best chance of seeing the species is in Selous Game Reserve (p190), while they're also found in Ruaha National Park (p174). Kenya's only significant population is found on the Laikipia Plateau, but they are occasionally seen in the Masai Mara ecosystem. The species is thought to be extinct in Rwanda, Burundi and Uganda.

Cheetahs

The fastest land animal on earth (it can reach speeds of 75km/h in the first two seconds of its pursuit and at full speed may reach 115km/h), the cheetah in full flight is one of the most thrilling sights in the African wild. Cheetahs inhabit mostly open country, from the savannah to the desert, and they're most easily spotted in the major national parks of Kenya, Tanzania, Namibia, Botswana, South Africa and Zambia. A small number of cheetahs are also believed to survive in the Sahara of Algeria and Niger.

At the end of 2016, a scientific study by the Zoological Society of London, Panthera and the Wildlife Conservation Society confirmed what many conservationists in the field had long feared – the cheetah is in trouble. The latest estimates suggest that just 7100 cheetahs remain in the wild, all of which live in Africa save for an isolated population of around 50 in the deserts and mountains of central Iran.

Of the estimated 6600 adult cheetahs that remain, the International Union for Conservation of Nature (IUCN; www.iucnredlist.org) argued that there were just under 2000 cheetahs left in East Africa; between one-half and two-thirds are in southern Africa. More specifically, the IUCN estimated a population of 710 for the Serengeti–Mara–Amboseli–Tsavo regions, plus a further 450 spread across Samburu and the Laikipia Plateau.

WILDLIFE WATCHING: THE BASICS

- Most animals are naturally wary of people, so to minimise their distress (or aggression) keep as quiet as possible, avoid sudden movements and wear subdued colours when in the field.
- Avoid direct eye contact, particularly with primates, as this is seen as a challenge and may provoke aggressive behaviour.
- Good binoculars are an invaluable aid to observing wildlife at a distance and are essential for birdwatching.
- When on foot, stay downwind of animals wherever possible – they'll smell you long before they see or hear you.
- Never get out of your vehicle unless it's safe to do so.
- Always obey park regulations, including traffic speed limits; thousands of animals are needlessly killed on African roads every year.
- Follow your guide's instructions at all times – it may mean the difference between life and death on a walking safari.
- Never get between a mother and her young.
- Exercise care when boating or swimming, and be particularly aware of the dangers posed by crocodiles and hippos.
- Never feed wild animals – it encourages scavenging, may adversely affect their health and can cause animals to become aggressive towards each other and humans.

The major causes of the cheetah's decline are shrinking habitats and human encroachment, which results in increasing conflict between cheetahs and farmers; more than three-quarters of Africa's wild cheetahs live outside protected areas. Other problems include the smuggling of cheetah cubs out of the continent for sale as pets – baby cheetahs sell for as much as US$10,000 on the black market – with more than 1200 trafficked off the continent over the past decade, 85% of whom died in transit.

Organisations such as the **Mara Cheetah Project** (www.maracheetahs.org) and the Namibia-based **Cheetah Conservation Fund** (CCF; www.cheetah.org) are at the forefront of efforts to mitigate this conflict and are worth contacting to find out more.

Environmental Issues

East Africa is confronting some pressing environmental issues including deforestation, desertification, poaching, threats to endangered species and the impacts of tourism.

Deforestation

More than half of Africa's forests have been destroyed over the last century, and forest destruction continues on a large scale in parts of East Africa where forest areas today represent only a fraction of the region's original forest cover. On the Zanzibar Archipelago, for example, only about 5% of the dense tropical forest that once blanketed the islands still remains. In sections of the long Eastern Arc chain, which sweeps from southern Kenya down towards central Tanzania, forest depletion has caused such serious erosion that entire villages have had to be shifted to lower areas. In densely populated Rwanda and Burundi, many previously forested areas have been completely cleared to make way for agriculture.

Eastern Arc Mountains Information Source (www.easternarc.org) is an information clearing house for the many environmental and community-based projects being undertaken in the Eastern Arc range in Kenya and Tanzania.

Native hardwood such as ebony and mahogany is often used to make the popular carved wooden statue souvenirs sold in East Africa. Though this industry supports thousands of local families who may otherwise be without an income, it also consumes an estimated 80,000 trees annually. The World

CATTLE-FREE NATIONAL PARKS?

Nothing seems to disappoint visitors to Kenya's national parks more than the sight of herders shepherding their livestock to water sources within park boundaries. In the words of former Kenya Wildlife Service head Dr Richard Leakey: 'People don't pay a lot of money to see cattle'. The issue is, however, a complicated one.

On the one hand, what you are seeing is far from a natural African environment. For thousands of years people, and their herds of cattle, lived happily (and sustainably) alongside the wildlife, and their actions helped to shape the landscapes of East Africa. But with the advent of conservation and national parks, many of Kenya's tribal peoples, particularly pastoralists such as the Maasai and Samburu, found themselves and their cattle excluded from their ancestral lands or waterholes of last resort, often with little or no compensation or alternative incomes provided (although, of course, some do now make a living through tourism and conservation).

Having been pushed onto marginal lands, with rapidly growing populations and with limited access to alternative water sources in times of drought, many have been forced to forgo their traditional livelihoods and have taken to leading sedentary lifestyles. Those that continue as herders have little choice but to overgraze their lands. Such policies of exclusion tend to reinforce the perception among local peoples that wildlife belongs to the government and brings few benefits to local communities. This position is passionately argued in the excellent (if dated) book *No Man's Land* (2003) by George Monbiot.

At the same time, tourism is a major (and much-needed) source of revenue for East Africa and most visitors to the region want to experience a natural wilderness – on the surface at least, the national parks and reserves appear to provide this Eden-esque slice of Africa. It also remains questionable whether allowing herders and their livestock to graze within park boundaries would alleviate the pressures on over-exploited land and traditional cultures, or would instead simply lead to the degradation of Kenya's last remaining areas of relatively pristine wilderness.

Things get even more complicated when talking about private and community conservancies. Many Laikipia and Mara conservancies – **Ol Pejeta Conservancy** (p284) and **Segera Ranch** (p286) are two prominent examples – consider livestock to be an important part of habitat management, arguing that well-maintained livestock herds can help reduce tick infestations for wildlife. Carefully controlled grazing can also, they argue, actually assist in the regeneration of grassland ecosystems.

Wide Fund for Nature (WWF) and Unesco campaigned to promote the use of common, faster-growing trees, and many handicraft cooperatives now use wood taken from forests managed by the Forest Stewardship Council. If you buy a carving, ask if the wood is sourced from managed forests.

Tourism

Unregulated tourism and development pose serious threats to East Africa's ecosystems. In northern and eastern Zanzibar, for example, new hotels are being built at a rapid rate, without sufficient provision for waste disposal and maintenance of environmental equilibrium. Inappropriate visitor use is another aspect of the issue; prime examples are the tyre tracks criss-crossing off-road areas of Kenya's Masai Mara National Reserve, the litter found along some popular trekking routes on Mt Kilimanjaro, and the often rampant use of firewood by visitors and tour operators alike.

One positive development has been the rise of community-based conservation as tour operators, funding organisations and others recognise that East Africa's protected areas are unlikely to succeed in the long term unless local people obtain real benefits.

Among the most impressive projects are the private conservancies that have become a feature of conservation tourism in the Laikipia and Masai Mara regions of Kenya.

K_BOONNITROD / SHUTTERSTOCK ©

Mt Kilimanjaro National Park (p134)

Wildlife & Habitat

Think of East Africa and the word 'safari' comes to mind, but travel west from the big wildlife parks of Tanzania and Kenya and you cross through a world of gorgeous lakes and rivers, before ascending into a mystical realm of snowy, cloud-draped peaks that straddle Africa's continental divide. Many parts of the verdant western region remain relatively unknown and are seldom visited, providing welcome respite from overbooked safaris and lodges to the east. But no matter where you travel, East Africa – home to a dazzling number and variety of animals – is sure to amaze.

– David Lukas

Big Cats

The three big cats – leopards, lions and cheetahs – provide the high point for so many memorable Kenyan safaris. The presence of these apex predators, even the mere suggestion that they may be nearby, is enough to draw the savannah taut with attention. It's the lion's gravitas, roaring at night, stalking at sunset. It's the elusive leopard that remains hidden while in plain view. And it's the cheetah in a fluid blur of hunting perfection.

Leopard

Weight 30-60kg (female), 40-90kg (male); length 170-300cm More common than you realise, the leopard relies on expert camouflage techniques to stay hidden. During the day you might only spot one reclining in a tree after it twitches its tail, but at night there is no mistaking their bone-chilling groans. Best seen in Masai Mara NR, Serengeti NP.

Cheetah

Weight 40-60kg; length 200-220cm
The cheetah is a world-class sprinter. Although it reaches speeds of 112km/h, the cheetah runs out of steam after 300m and must cool down for 30 minutes before hunting again. This speed comes at another cost – the cheetah is so well adapted for running that it lacks the strength and teeth to defend its food or cubs from attack by other large predators. Best seen in Masai Mara NR, Serengeti NP, Tsavo East NP, Amboseli NP.

Lion

Weight 120-150kg (female), 150-225kg (male); length 210-275cm (female), 240-350cm (male) Those lions sprawled out lazily in the shade are actually Africa's most feared predators. Equipped with teeth that tear effortlessly through bone and tendon, they can take down an animal as large as a bull giraffe. Each group of adults (a pride) is based around generations of females that do the majority of the hunting; swaggering males typically fight among themselves and eat what the females catch. Best seen in Masai Mara NR, Serengeti NP, Selous GR, Ruaha NP.

1. Cheetahs **2.** Male and female lion **3.** Leopard

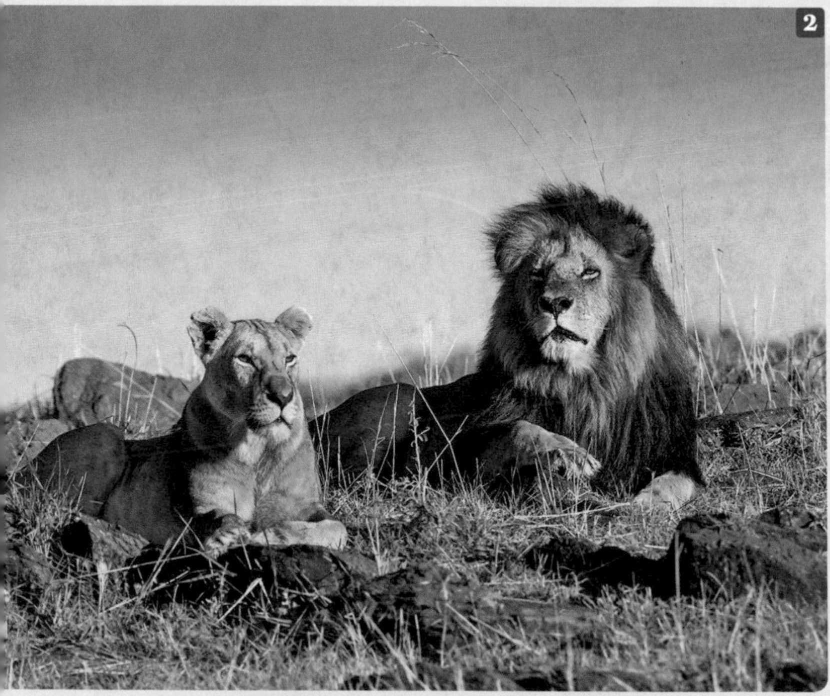

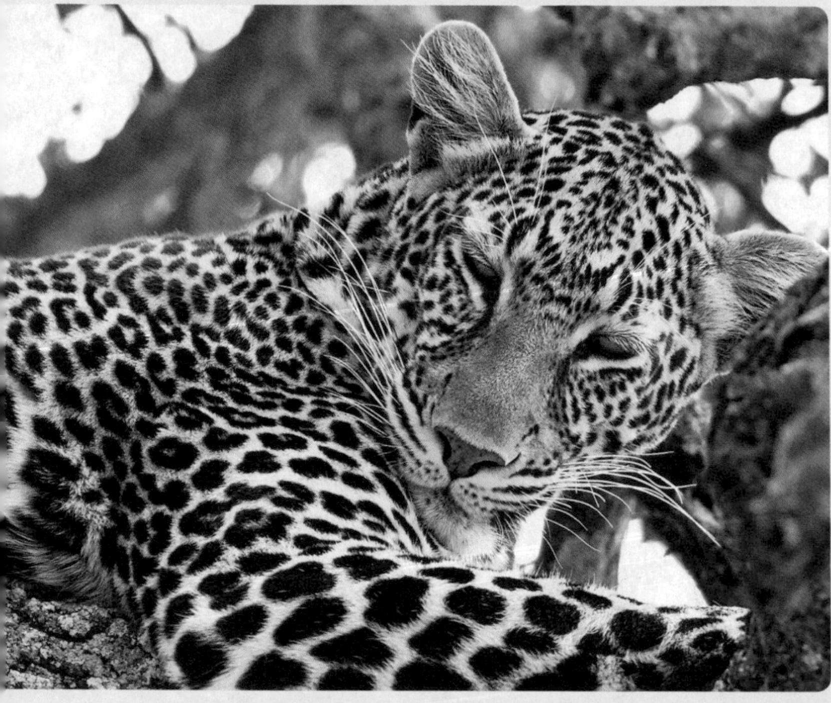

TRAVEL STOCK / SHUTTERSTOCK ©

1

2

. Serval **2.** Wildcats **3.** Caracal

Small Cats

While big cats get the lion's share of attention from tourists, East Africa's small cats are equally interesting though much harder to spot. You won't find these cats chasing down gazelles or wildebeest, instead look for them slinking around in search of rodents or making incredible leaps to snatch birds out of the air.

Wildcat

Weight 3-6.5kg; length 65-100cm Readily found on the outskirts of villages, or wherever there are abundant mice and rats, the wildcat looks like a common tabby and is in fact the direct ancestor of the domesticated housecat. The wildcat is best identified by its unmarked rufous ears and longish legs. Widely distributed but rarely seen.

Serval

Weight 6-18kg; length 90-130cm Twice as large as a housecat, with towering legs and large ears, the beautifully spotted serval is highly adapted for walking in tall grass and making prodigious leaps to catch rodents and birds. This elegant cat is often observed hunting in the daytime. Best seen in Masai Mara NR, Serengeti NP, Aberdare NP (black servals).

Caracal

Weight 8-19kg; length 80-120cm The caracal is a gorgeous tawny cat with long, pointy ears. This African version of the northern lynx has jacked-up hind legs like a feline dragster. These beanpole kickers enable this slender cat to make vertical leaps of 3m and swat birds out of the air. Widespread in East Africa's parks, although difficult to spot.

Ground Primates

East Africa is the evolutionary cradle of primate diversity, giving rise to more than 30 species of monkeys, apes and prosimians (the 'primitive' ancestors of modern primates), all of which have dextrous hands and feet.

Vervet Monkey

Weight 4-8kg; length 90-140cm Each troop of vervets is composed of females who defend home ranges passed down from generation to generation, and males who fight each other for bragging rights and access to females. Check out the extraordinary blue and scarlet colours of their sexual organs when they're aroused. Widespread throughout East Africa.

Chimpanzee

Weight 25-40kg; length 60-90cm Travelling to the forests of western East Africa to see chimpanzees may take you off the beaten path, but it's hard to deny the allure of these human-like primates, with deep intelligence and emotion lurking behind their familiar deep-set eyes. Researchers at Gombe and Mahale Mountains NPs are making startling discoveries about chimp behaviour. Best seen in Kabale Forest NP, Mahale Mountains NP, Gombe Stream NP, Nyungwe Forest NP.

Mountain Gorilla

Weight 70-115kg (female), 160-210kg (male); length 140-185cm Gorilla-viewing is a big draw in Uganda and Rwanda, so expect some effort or expense getting a coveted slot on a tour into gorilla habitat. Seems like a hassle? Just wait until you're face-to-face with a massive silverback male on his home turf and nothing else will matter! Best seen in Volcanoes NP, Bwindi Impenetrable NP, Mgahinga NP.

Olive Baboon

Weight 11-30kg (female), 22-50kg (male); length 95-180cm Although the formidable olive baboon has 5cm-long fangs and can kill a leopard, its best defence may be its ability to run up trees and shower intruders with liquid excrement. Widespread throughout East Africa.

1. Patas monkey **2.** Mother baboon with baby **3.** Chimpanzees

2

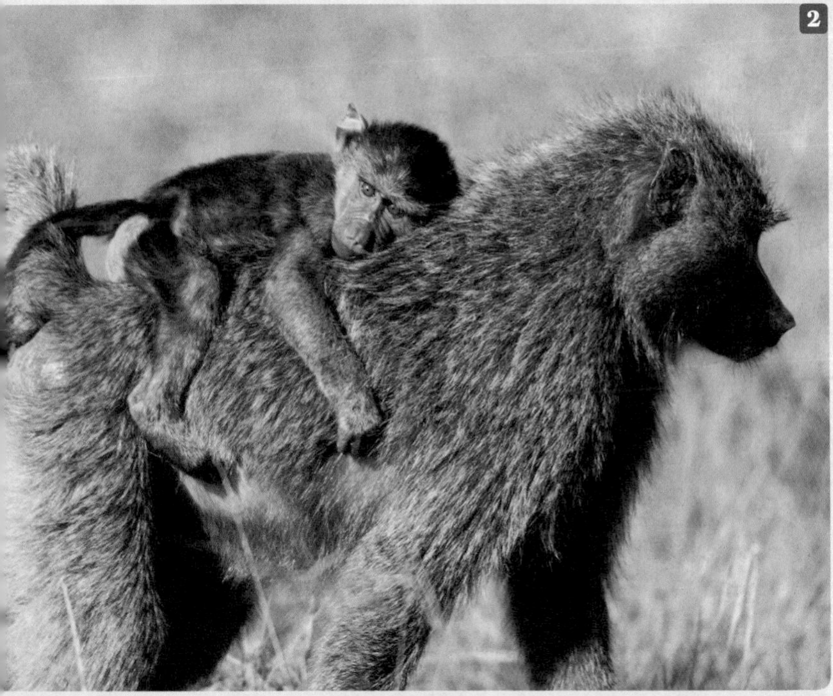

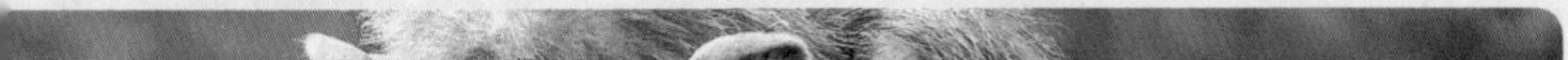

HENNER DAMKE / SHUTTERSTOCK ©

1

2

1. Black-and-white colobus **2.** Blue monkey **3.** Greater galago

Arboreal Primates

Forest primates are a diverse group that live entirely in trees. These agile, long-limbed primates generally stay in the upper canopy where they search for leaves and arboreal fruits. It might take the expert eyes of a professional guide to help you find some of these species.

Greater Galago

Weight 550-2000g; length 55-100cm A cat-sized nocturnal creature with a dog-like face, the greater galago belongs to a group of prosimians that have changed very little in 60 million years. Best known for its frequent bawling cries (hence the common name 'bushbaby'), the galago would be rarely seen except that it readily visits feeding stations at many popular safari lodges. Living in a world of darkness, galagos communicate with each other through scent and sound. Widespread throughout East Africa, including Nyungwe Forest NP, Rwanda Jozani Forest, Zanzibar.

Black-and-White Colobus

Weight 10-23kg; length 115-165cm The black-and-white colobus is one of East Africa's most popular primates due to the flowing white bonnets of hair across its black body. Like all colobus, this agile primate has a hook-shaped hand so it can swing through the trees with the greatest of ease. When two troops run into each other expect to see a real show. Best seen in Kakamega Forest, Lake Nakuru NP, Arusha NP, Nyungwe Forest NP.

Blue Monkey

Weight 4-12kg; length 100-170cm These long-tailed monkeys are widespread primates that have adapted to many forested habitats throughout sub-Saharan Africa, including some of the forested parks in Tanzania where they are among the easiest monkeys to spot. The versatile primates live in large social groups that spend their entire lives among trees. Best seen in Rwenzori Mountains National Park, Volcanoes NP, Lake Manyara NP.

Cud-Chewing Mammals

Africa is arguably most famous for its astounding variety of ungulates – hoofed mammals that include everything from buffaloes to giraffes. In this large family, the cud-chewing antelope are particularly numerous, with 40 different species in East Africa alone.

Wildebeest

Weight 140-290kg; length 230-340cm Few animals evoke the spirit of the African plain like the wildebeest. Over one million gather in vast, constantly moving herds on the Serengeti. Best seen in Masai Mara NR, Serengeti NP.

Thomson's Gazelle

Weight 15-35kg; length 95-150cm Lanky and exceptionally alert, the long-legged Thomson's gazelle is built for speed. The 400,000 living on the Serengeti Plains migrate with wildebeest and zebras. Widespread throughout southern Kenya and northern Tanzania.

African Buffalo

Weight 250-850kg; length 220-420cm Imagine a big cow with curling horns, and you have the African buffalo. Fortunately, they're usually docile – an angry or injured buffalo is an extremely dangerous animal. Widespread from central Kenya to southern Tanzania.

Gerenuk

Weight 30-50kg; length 160-200cm The gerenuk is one of the strangest creatures you'll ever see – a tall slender gazelle with a giraffe-like neck that stands on its hind legs to reach 2m-high branches. Best seen in Samburu NR, Amboseli NP.

Uganda Kob

Weight 60-120kg; length 170-200cm Kob gather in great numbers on the flood plains of Uganda, where males fight and show off their curved horns in front of gathered females.

1. Gerenuks 2. African buffalo 3. Kob 4. Thomson's gazelle

KRASNOVA EKATERINA / SHUTTERSTOCK ©

LARSEK / SHUTTERSTOCK ©

Hoofed Mammals

The continent has a surprising diversity of hoofed animals that have been at home here for millions of years. Those that don't chew cuds can be seen over a much broader range of habitats than the cud-chewing antelope. Without human intervention, Africa would be ruled by elephants, zebras, hippos and warthogs.

Black Rhinoceros

Weight 700-1400kg; length 350-450cm Pity the black rhinoceros for having a horn that is worth more than gold. Once widespread and abundant on open plains south of the Sahara, the slow-moving rhino has been poached to the brink of extinction. Best seen in Ol Pejeta Conservancy, Lake Nakuru NP, Nairobi NP, Meru NP, Ngorongoro Crater.

Plains Zebra

Weight 175-320kg; length 260-300cm Scientists first thought the stripes, each distinct as a human fingerprint, were to confuse predators by making it difficult to distinguish the outline of individual zebras in a herd. However, new studies suggest stripes help combat disease-carrying horseflies. Widespread throughout southern and central Kenya.

African Elephant

Weight 2200-3500kg (female), 4000-6300kg (male); height 2.4-3.4m (female), 3-4m (male) Bull elephants are commonly referred to as 'the king of beasts,' but elephant society is actually ruled by a lineage of elder females who lead each group along traditional migration routes between watering holes. Best seen in Amboseli NP, Tarangire NP, Serengeti NP, Tsavo East NP, Samburu NR.

Giraffe

Weight 450-1200kg (female), 1800-2000kg (male); height 3.5-5.2m The 5m-tall giraffe does such a good job reaching up to grab mouthfuls of leaves on high branches that stretching down to get a drink of water is difficult. Masai giraffes are widespread in Tanzania and southern Kenya, while Rothschild's giraffes and reticulated giraffes best seen in Lake Nakuru NP and Samburu NR respectively.

1. Giraffes **2.** African elephants **3.** Plains zebras

CINOBY / GETTY IMAGES ©

More Hoofed Mammals

This sampling of miscellaneous hoofed animals highlights the astonishing diversity in this major group of African wildlife. Every visitor wants to see elephants and giraffes, but don't pass up a chance to watch hyraxes or warthogs.

Rock Hyrax

Weight 1.8-5.5kg; length 40-60cm It doesn't seem like it, but those funny tailless squirrels you see lounging around on rocks are an ancient cousin to the elephant. You won't see some of the features that rock hyraxes share with their larger kin, but look for tusks when one yawns. Easily spotted in many Kenyan and Tanzanian parks.

Warthog

Weight 45-75kg (female), 60-150kg (male); length 140-200cm Despite their fearsome appearance and sinister tusks, only the largest male warthogs are safe from lions, cheetahs and hyenas. To protect themselves when attacked, most warthogs run for burrows, then back in while slashing wildly with their tusks. Widespread throughout East Africa.

Hippopotamus

Weight 510-3200kg; length 320-400cm The hippopotamus is one strange creature. Designed like a big grey floating beanbag with tiny legs, the 3000kg hippo spends all its time in or very near water, chowing down on aquatic plants. Placid? No way! Hippos display a tremendous ferocity and strength when provoked. Best seen in Masai Mara NR, Serengeti NP, Tsavo West NP.

1. Warthog **2.** Rock hyraxes **3.** Hippopotamuses

2

USO / GETTY IMAGES ©

LAYUE / SHUTTERSTOCK ©

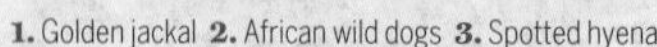

1. Golden jackal **2.** African wild dogs **3.** Spotted hyena
4. Banded mongoose

2

BCOSTELLOE / SHUTTERSTOCK ©

4

Carnivores

It is a sign of Africa's ecological richness that the continent supports a remarkable variety of predators. When it comes to predators, expect the unexpected and you'll return home with a lifetime of memories!

Banded Mongoose

Weight 1.5-2kg; length 45-75cm Bounding across the savannah on their morning foraging excursions, family groups search for delicious snacks like toads, scorpions and slugs. Easily spotted in many East African parks.

Spotted Hyena

Weight 40-90kg; length 125-215cm Living in groups that are ruled by females (who grow penis-like sexual organs), hyenas use bone-crushing jaws to disembowel terrified prey on the run. Widespread and easily seen throughout many East African parks.

Golden Jackal

Weight 6-15kg; length 85-130cm Through a combination of sheer fierceness and bluff, the trim little jackal manages to fill its belly while holding hungry vultures and hyenas at bay. Best seen in Masai Mara NR, Ngorongoro Crater.

Hunting Dog

Weight 20-35kg; length 100-150cm Organised in complex hierarchies maintained by rules of conduct, these social canids are incredibly efficient hunters, running in packs of 20 to 60 to chase down antelope and other animals. Sadly, these beautiful dogs are now highly endangered. Best seen in Laikipia, Selous GR, Ruaha NP.

Honey Badger (Ratel)

Weight 7-16kg; length 75-100cm Some Africans say they would rather face a lion than a honey badger, and even lions relinquish their kill when a badger shows up. It finds its favourite food by following honey guide birds to bee hives. It's also known as a 'ratel'. Best seen in Mikumi NP.

DMUSSMAN / SHUTTERSTOCK ©

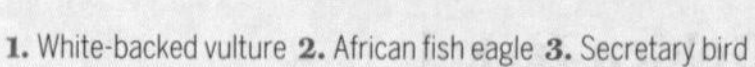

1. White-backed vulture **2.** African fish eagle **3.** Secretary bird
4. Bateleur

3

2

MINT IMAGES / ART WOLFE / GETTY IMAGES ©

4

Birds of Prey

East Africa has nearly 100 species of hawks, eagles, vultures and owls. More than 40 species have been spotted within a single park, making these some of the best places in the world to see an incredible variety of birds of prey.

White-Backed Vulture

Length 80cm Mingling around carcasses with lions, hyenas and jackals, vultures use their sheer numbers to compete for scraps of flesh and bone. Best seen in Masai Mara NR, Serengeti NP.

African Fish Eagle

Length 75cm This replica of the American bald eagle presents an imposing appearance but is most familiar for its loud, ringing vocalisations that have become known as 'the voice of Africa.' Best seen in Amboseli NP, Lake Baringo, Saadani NP.

Bateleur

Length 60cm French for 'tightrope-walker,' bateleur refers to this bird's distinctive low-flying aerial acrobatics. At close hand, look for its bold colour pattern and scarlet face. Widespread throughout East Africa.

Secretary Bird

Length 100cm With the body of an eagle and the legs of a crane, the secretary bird stands at 1.3m tall and walks up to 20km a day in search of vipers, cobras and other snakes, which it kills with lightning speed and agility. This idiosyncratic, grey-bodied raptor is commonly seen striding across the savannah. Best seen in Amboseli NP, Kidepo Valley NP, Mkomazi NP.

Augur Buzzard

Length 55cm Perhaps the most common raptor in the region, the augur buzzard occupies a wide range of wild and cultivated habitats. They hunt by floating motionlessly in the air then swooping down quickly to catch unwary critters. Widespread in western regions of East Africa.

18042011 / SHUTTERSTOCK ©

1. Shoebill **2.** Lesser flamingos **3.** Lilac-breasted roller **4.** Ostrich

2

ANTONIO JORGE NUNES / SHUTTERSTOCK ©

4

Other Birds

Birdwatchers from all over the world visit East Africa in search of the region's 1400 species of birds.

Lilac-Breasted Roller

Length 40cm Nearly everyone on safari gets to know the gorgeously coloured lilac-breasted roller. The roller gets its name from its tendency to 'roll' from side to side in flight as a way of showing off its iridescent blues, purples and greens. Commonly seen throughout East Africa.

Lesser Flamingo

Length 100cm Coloured deep rose-pink and gathering by the hundreds of thousands on shimmering salt lakes, the lesser flamingo creates one of Africa's most dramatic wildlife spectacles when they fly in formation or perform synchronised courtship. Best seen in Lake Natron, Lake Magadi and (depending on the year) Lake Nakuru NP and Lake Bogoria NR.

Ostrich

Length 200-270cm Standing at 270cm and weighing upwards of 130kg, these ancient flightless birds escape predators by running away at 70km/h or lying flat on the ground to resemble a pile of dirt. Widespread throughout Kenya, Uganda and northern Tanzania. Blue-legged Somali Ostrich commonly seen in Laikipia and Samburu NR.

Shoebill

Length 124cm The reclusive shoebill is one of the most highly sought-after birds in East Africa. Looking somewhat like a stout-bodied stork with an ugly old clog stuck on its face, the shoebill baffles scientists because it has no clear relative in the bird world. Best seen in Akagera NP, Mabamba Swamp.

Grey-Crowned Crane

Length 100cm Uganda's national bird is extremely elegant. Topped with a frilly yellow bonnet, this blue-grey crane dances wildly and shows off its red throat pouch during the breeding season. Best seen from central Kenya down into Tanzania, especially Amboseli NP.

Habitats

Nearly all the wildlife in East Africa occupies a specific type of habitat, and you will hear rangers and fellow travellers refer to these habitats repeatedly as they describe where to search for animals. If this is your first time in East Africa some of these habitats and their seasonal rhythms take some getting used to, but your wildlife-viewing experiences will be greatly enhanced if you learn how to recognise them and the animals you might expect to find in each one.

Savannah

Savannah is *the* classic East African landscape – broad rolling grasslands dotted with lone acacia trees. The openness and vastness of this landscape makes it a perfect home for large herds of grazing animals, and fast-sprinting predators like cheetahs. Shaped by fire and grazing animals, savannah is a dynamic habitat in constant flux with its adjacent woodlands. One of the best places in the world for exploring African savannah is found at Serengeti National Park.

High Mountains

High mountains are such a rare habitat in East Africa that the massive extinct volcanoes of Mts Kilimanjaro, Kenya and Elgon, and the remarkable highlands of the Rwenzori Mountains, stand out dramatically in the landscape. These isolated peaks are islands of montane forest, ethereal bogs, giant heathers, and moorlands perched high above the surrounding lowlands. The few animals that survive here are uniquely adapted to these bizarre landscapes.

Woodland

Tanzania is the only place in East Africa where you'll find dry woodlands, locally known as *miombo*. This important habitat provides homes for many birds, small mammals and insects. Here the trees form a continuous canopy that offers shelter from predators and harsh sunlight, and is a fantastic place to search for wildlife. In places where fingers of woodland mingle with savannah, animals such as leopards and antelope often gather to find shade and places to rest during the day. During the dry season, fires and elephants can wreak havoc on these woodlands, fragmenting large tracts of forest habitat into patches. Ruaha National Park in Tanzania is a great place to explore a wide diversity of mixed savannah and *miombo* habitats.

Semiarid Desert

Much of eastern and northern Kenya and parts of northeastern Tanzania see so little rainfall that shrubs and hardy grasses, rather than trees, are the dominant vegetation. This is not the classic landscape that many visitors come to see, and it doesn't seem like a great place for wildlife, but the patient observer will be richly rewarded. While it's true that the lack of water restricts larger animals such as zebras, gazelles and antelope to waterholes, this habitat explodes with plant and animal life whenever it rains. Tsavo East National Park in Kenya is a massive and gorgeous region of semiarid wilderness.

1. Mt Kenya (p289), Kenya's highest peak
2. Baobabs, Ruaha National Park (p174), Tanzania

1

ROGER DE LA HARPE / UIG / GETTY IMAGES ©

Lioness and cubs

National Parks & Reserves

East Africa's national parks and reserves rank among the best in Africa and some of the parks – Serengeti, Masai Mara and Mt Kilimanjaro to name just three – are the stuff of travellers' lore. Although some of the parks are under siege, and as much as 75% of the region's wildlife lives outside the protected areas, the region's national parks have ensured that East Africa remains one of the last repositories of charismatic megafauna left on the planet.

History

The idea of setting aside land to protect nature began during colonial times, and in many cases this meant forcibly evicting the local peoples from their traditional lands. Enforcement of any vague notions of conservation that lay behind the reserves was often lax, and local anger was fuelled by the fact that many parks were set aside as hunting reserves for white hunters with anything but conservation on their minds. Many of these hunters, having pushed some species to the brink of extinction, later became conservationists and by the middle of the 20th century, the push was on to establish the national parks and reserves that we see today.

Africa's oldest national park is Parc National des Virunga in the Democratic Republic of the Congo – it was set aside by the Belgian colonial authorities in 1925. It was more than 20 years later, in 1946, that Nairobi National Park became East Africa's first such officially protected area.

Protected Areas by Country

Tanzania: 38.4%

Kenya: 12.7%

Uganda: 26.3%

Rwanda: 7.6%

Burundi: 5.6%

Visiting National Parks & Reserves

Tanzania

With more than one-third of Tanzanian territory locked away as a national park, wildlife reserve or marine park, Tanzania has the widest selection of protected areas to choose from.

Park entry fees range from US$30 to US$100 per adult per day (US$10 to US$20 per child per day), depending on the park, with Serengeti (p123), Kilimanjaro (p134), Mahale Mountains (p160) and Gombe (p159) parks the most expensive.

Except at some of the less-visited parks, where credit-card machines are planned, all park fees must be paid electronically with a Visa card or MasterCard. It's also possible to pay using a 'smart card' available for purchase from CRDB and Exim banks.

Kenya

Kenya has 22 national parks, plus numerous marine parks and national reserves. Entry to some marine parks starts at US$20 per adult (US$15 per child) per 24 hours, while mainland parks start at US$25 (US$15 per child) and reach as much as US$80 (US$45 per child) for the Masai Mara National Reserve (p252). Vehicles cost extra, with US$10 per day the norm.

You must pay all park entry fees with a credit card (or M-Pesa, the phone app popular with locals).

Major National Parks & Reserves of East Africa

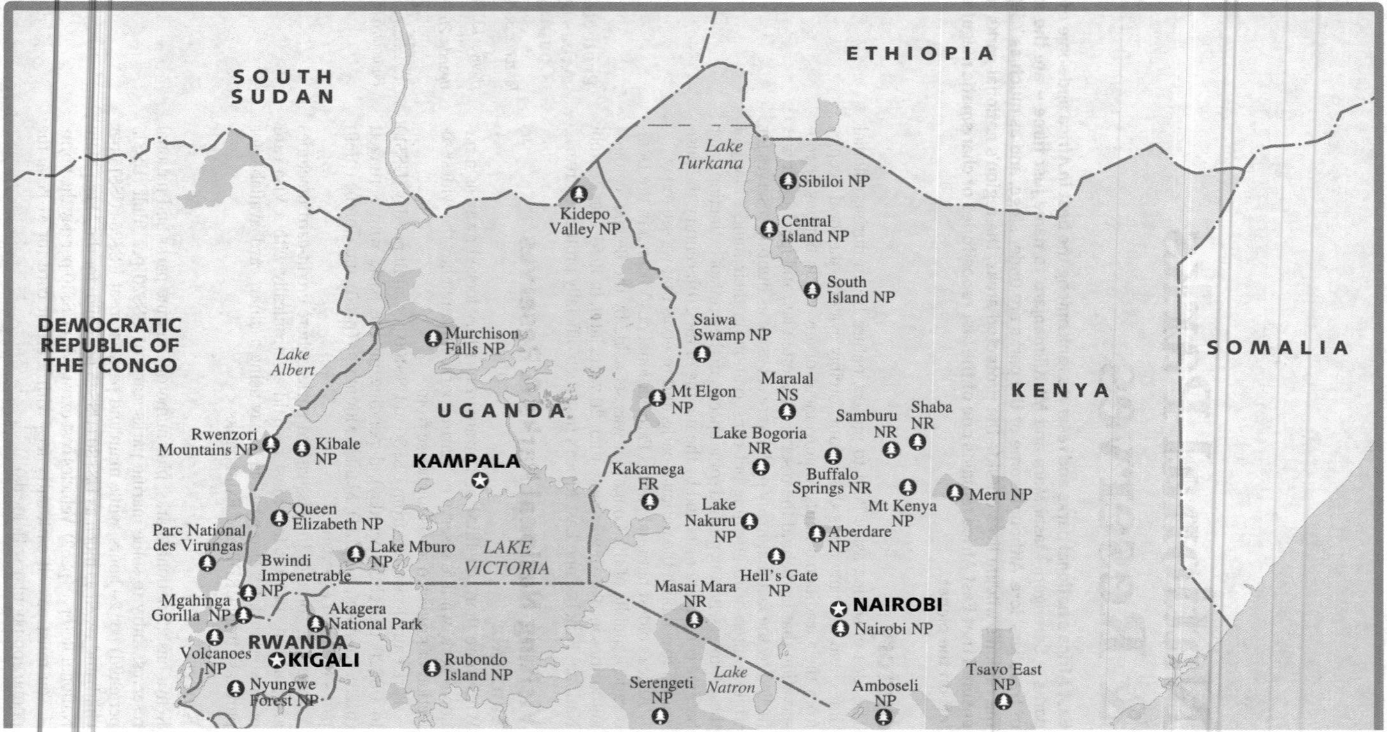

0 100 km
0 50 miles

ETHIOPIA
SOUTH SUDAN
SOMALIA
KENYA
UGANDA
DEMOCRATIC REPUBLIC OF THE CONGO
RWANDA
KAMPALA
NAIROBI
KIGALI
Lake Turkana
Lake Albert
LAKE VICTORIA
Lake Natron
Sibiloi NP
Central Island NP
South Island NP
Kidepo Valley NP
Saiwa Swamp NP
Murchison Falls NP
Mt Elgon NP
Maralal NS
Samburu NR
Shaba NR
Lake Bogoria NR
Buffalo Springs NR
Kakamega FR
Meru NP
Mt Kenya NP
Lake Nakuru NP
Aberdare NP
Hell's Gate NP
Masai Mara NR
Nairobi NP
Rwenzori Mountains NP
Kibale NP
Queen Elizabeth NP
Parc National des Virungas
Lake Mburo NP
Bwindi Impenetrable NP
Mgahinga Gorilla NP
Akagera National Park
Volcanoes NP
Nyungwe Forest NP
Rubondo Island NP
Serengeti NP
Amboseli NP
Tsavo East NP

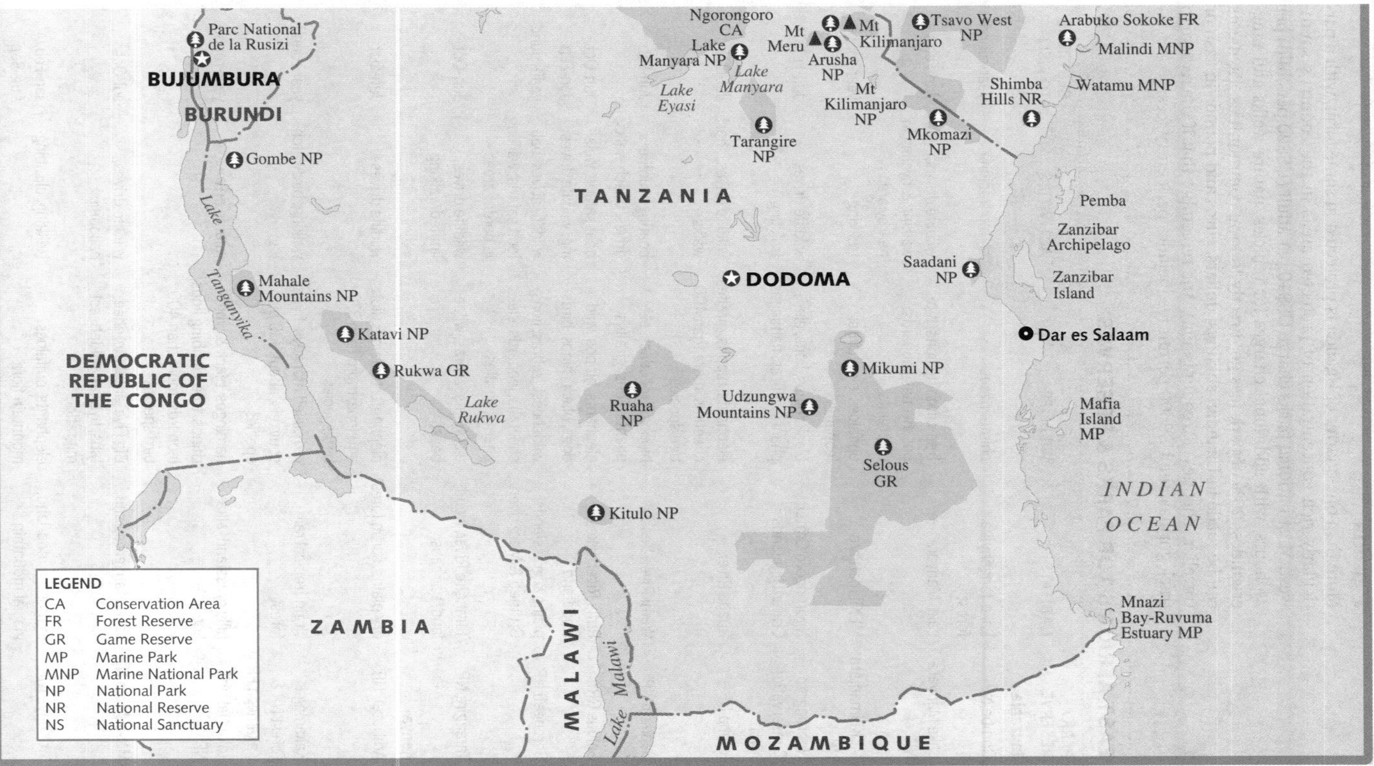

Parc National de la Rusizi
BUJUMBURA
BURUNDI
Gombe NP
Lake Tanganyika
Mahale Mountains NP
Katavi NP
Rukwa GR
Lake Rukwa
DEMOCRATIC REPUBLIC OF THE CONGO
ZAMBIA
MALAWI
Lake Malawi
MOZAMBIQUE
TANZANIA
Ngorongoro CA
Lake Manyara NP
Lake Manyara
Lake Eyasi
Mt Meru
Arusha NP
Mt Kilimanjaro
Mt Kilimanjaro NP
Tarangire NP
Tsavo West NP
Mkomazi NP
Shimba Hills NR
Arabuko Sokoke FR
Malindi MNP
Watamu MNP
Pemba
Zanzibar Archipelago
Zanzibar Island
Saadani NP
DODOMA
Dar es Salaam
Mikumi NP
Udzungwa Mountains NP
Ruaha NP
Selous GR
Kitulo NP
Mafia Island MP
INDIAN OCEAN
Mnazi Bay-Ruvuma Estuary MP
LEGEND
CA Conservation Area
FR Forest Reserve
GR Game Reserve
MP Marine Park
MNP Marine National Park
NP National Park
NR National Reserve
NS National Sanctuary

Uganda

More than one-quarter of Uganda is protected in some form, with a particularly rich concentration of protected areas in the country's southwest. Most national parks charge US$40 per adult (US$20 per child) per 24 hours, with additional charges for vehicles, nature walks and ranger-guides; 20% of park fees go directly to local communities. Payments can be made in Ugandan shillings, dollars, euros and pounds in cash or travellers cheques (1% commission). And remember that if you're here to track gorillas, the US$600 permit fee includes park entry fees.

EAST AFRICA'S TOP PARKS & RESERVES

PARK/ RESERVE	HABITATS	WILDLIFE	ACTIVITIES	BEST TIME TO VISIT
Tanzania				
Gombe NP	Lake Tanganyika, forest	chimpanzees	chimp tracking	year-round
Lake Manyara NP	Lake Manyara	tree-climbing lions, hippos, hyenas, leopards, elephants	wildlife drives, walking & cycling in nearby areas	Jun-Feb
Mt Kilimanjaro NP	Mt Kilimanjaro	buffaloes, elephants, leopards	trekking	year-round
Ngorongoro Conservation Area	Ngorongoro Crater, Crater Highlands	black rhinos, lions, elephants, zebras, flamingos	wildlife drives, trekking	Jun-Feb
Ruaha NP	Ruaha River	elephants, hippos, giraffes, cheetahs, more than 400 bird species	wildlife drives, short walks	Jul-Oct
Saadani NP	Wami River, beach	hippos, crocodiles, elephants, lions, giraffes	boating, wildlife drives, beach walks	Jun-Feb
Selous GR	Rufiji River, lakes, woodland	elephants, hippos, wild dogs, black rhinos, birds	boat safaris, walking, wildlife drives	Jun-Oct, Jan-Feb
Serengeti NP	plains & grasslands, Grumeti & Mara rivers	wildebeest, zebras, lions, cheetahs, leopards, elephants, giraffes	wildlife drives, balloon safaris, walking in border areas	year-round
Tarangire NP	Tarangire River, woodland, baobabs	elephants, zebras, wildebeest	wildlife drives, limited walking	Jun-Oct
Kenya				
Amboseli NP	dry plains, scrub forest	elephants, buffaloes, lions, antelope, more than 370 bird species	wildlife drives	Jun-Oct
Kakamega Forest NR & Kakamega FR	virgin tropical rainforest	red-tailed monkeys, flying squirrels, about 330 bird species	walking, birdwatching	year-round
Lake Nakuru NP	hilly grassland, alkaline lake	flamingos, black & white rhinos, tree-climbing lions, leopards, more than 400 bird species	wildlife drives	year-round
Masai Mara NR	savannah, grassland	Big Five, antelope, cheetahs, hyenas, wildebeest migration	wildlife drives, ballooning	Jul-Oct
Mt Kenya NP	rainforest, moorland, glacial mountain	elephants, buffaloes, mountain flora	trekking, climbing	Jan-Feb, Aug-Sep

Rwanda

Rwanda has three national parks worthy of the name and entry fees depend on the reason for your visit. A permit to track the gorillas in Volcanoes National Park (p520) costs US$1500, which includes park entry fees. Tracking chimpanzees (US$90) or golden monkeys (US$100) is considerably cheaper. Payments are usually made in cash, and preferably in US dollars.

PARK/ RESERVE	HABITATS	WILDLIFE	ACTIVITIES	BEST TIME TO VISIT
Nairobi NP	open plains with urban backdrop	black rhinos, lions, leopards, cheetahs, giraffes, more than 400 bird species	wildlife drives	year-round
Tsavo West & East NPs	plains, ancient volcanic cones	Big Five, cheetahs, giraffes, hippos, crocodiles, around 500 bird species	rock climbing, wildlife drives	year-round
Uganda				
Bwindi Impenetrable NP	primeval tropical forest	eastern mountain gorillas	gorilla tracking, birdwatching	May-Sep
Kibale Forest NP	lush forest	highest density of primates in Africa, including chimpanzees, red colobus & L'Hoest's monkeys	chimp tracking, forest elephant viewing	May-Aug
Mgahinga Gorilla NP	volcanoes	eastern mountain gorillas, golden monkeys, elephants	gorilla tracking, visiting Twa (Batwa) villages, birdwatching	Jun-Sep
Murchison Falls NP	thundering falls, the Victoria Nile	elephants, hippos, crocodiles, lions, leopards, hyenas, Rothschild's giraffes, Ugandan kob, more than 460 bird species	launch trip, wildlife drives, birdwatching	year-round
Queen Elizabeth NP	lakes, gorges, savannah	hippos, elephants, lions, leopards, chimpanzees, 611 recorded bird species	launch trip, chimp tracking, birdwatching	year-round
Rwenzori Mountains NP	Africa's highest mountain range	blue monkeys, chimpanzees, Rwenzori red duiker, 241 recorded bird species	trekking	Jun-Aug
Rwanda				
Volcanoes NP	towering volcanoes	eastern mountain gorillas, golden monkeys	gorilla & golden monkey tracking, volcano climbing	May-Sep
Nyungwe Forest NP	one of Africa's oldest rainforests, waterfalls	chimpanzees, Angolan colobus monkeys, about 275 bird species	chimp & colobus monkey tracking	May-Sep
Democratic Republic of the Congo				
Parc National des Virunga	volcanoes, dense rainforest	eastern mountain gorillas, chimpanzees, forest elephants, okapis	gorilla & chimp tracking, volcano climbing	May-Sep

The Conservancy Model

In Kenya, and to a much lesser extent in Tanzania, some of the most important conservation work is being done (and some of the most rewarding conservation tourism experiences are to be found) on private or community land.

Private Conservancies

The conservancy idea took hold on the large cattle ranches on Kenya's Laikipia Plateau and surrounding areas. One of the first to turn its attention to conservation was Lewa Downs, now the Lewa Wildlife Conservancy (p286), which in 1983 set aside part of its land as a rhino sanctuary. There are now more than 40 such conservancies scattered across Laikipia and northern regions, with more around the Masai Mara.

Top East African Conservancies

- *Lewa Wildlife Conservancy (Kenya)*
- *Ol Pejeta Conservancy (Kenya)*
- *Il Ngwesi (Kenya)*
- *Borana Conservancy (Kenya)*
- *Mara North Conservancy (Kenya)*
- *Olare-Orok Conservancy (Kenya)*
- *Olderikesi Conservancy (Kenya)*

The conservancy model differs from government-run national parks and reserves in a number of important ways:

- Nearly all conservancies focus on both wildlife conservation *and* community engagement and development; the conservancy entrance fees directly fund local community projects and wildlife programs. By giving local communities a stake in the protection of wildlife, so the argument goes, they are more likely to protect the wildlife in their midst.
- Access to conservancy land is, in most cases, restricted to those staying at the exclusive lodges and tented camps; Kenya's Ol Pejeta Conservancy (p284) is a notable exception. The result is a far more intimate wildlife-watching experience.
- Most private conservancies offer far more activities (including walking, horseback safaris and off-road driving) than national parks.

In Tanzania

Tanzania has only one private conservancy and it's officially a ranch: **Manyara Ranch Conservancy** (☎027-254 5284, 0683 918888; www.manyararanch.com), between Lake Manyara and Tarangire National Parks. There's also the **Enduimet Wildlife Management Area** (Map p136; ☎0787 903715; www.enduimet.org), which broadly functions in a similar way in the West Kilimanjaro region.

Community-Run Conservancies

Community conservancies are an extension of the private conservancy model. Rather than being owned by wealthy landowners or families, community conservancies are owned by entire communities and administered by community representatives. With financial and logistical support from outside sources, these communities have in many cases built ecolodges whose income now provides much-needed funds for their education, health and humanitarian projects.

Northern Kenya appears to provide particularly fertile ground for the community conservancy model, but there are also some excellent examples around Amboseli National Park and in the Masai Mara region.

Tribal Cultures

East Africa has a rich mosaic of tribal cultures, with over 300 different groups in an area roughly one-fourth of the size of Australia. Although many have very much entered the modern world, traditions remain strong, expressed through splendid ceremonial attire, pulsating dance rhythms, refined artistry and highly organised community structures. Experiencing these traditions will likely be a highlight of your travels.

Akamba

The Akamba, who live east of Nairobi towards Tsavo National Park, first migrated here from the south about 200 years ago in search of food. Because their own low-altitude land was poor, they were forced to barter for food stocks from the neighbouring Maasai (p616) and Kikuyu (p615) peoples. Soon they acquired a reputation as savvy traders, with business dealings (including in ivory, beer, honey, iron weapons and ornaments) extending from the coast inland to Lake Victoria and north to Lake Turkana. Renowned also for their martial prowess, many Akamba were drafted into Britain's WWI army, and today they are still well represented among Kenyan defence and law enforcement brigades.

In the 1930s, the British colonial administration settled large numbers of white farmers in traditional Akamba lands and tried to limit the number of cattle the Akamba could own by confiscating them. In protest, the Akamba formed the Ukamba Members Association, which marched en masse to Nairobi and squatted peacefully at Kariokor Market until their cattle were returned. Large numbers of Akamba were subsequently dispossessed to make way for Tsavo National Park.

All Akamba go through initiation rites at about the age of 12, and have the same age-based groups common to many of the region's peoples. Young parents are known as 'junior elders' (*mwanake* for men; *mwiitu* for women) and are responsible for the maintenance and upkeep of the village. They later become 'medium elders' *(nthele),* and then 'full elders' *(atumia ma kivalo),* with responsibility for death ceremonies and administering the law. The last stage of a person's life is that of 'senior elder' *(atumia ma kisuka),* with responsibility for holy places.

The Rosen Publishing Group (www.rosenpublishing.com) publishes the *Heritage Library of African Peoples*, aimed at late-primary and early-secondary school students. Although the entire East Africa set is available, individual titles (such as Luo, Kikuyu, Maasai and Samburu) are also easy to track down.

Baganda

Uganda's largest tribal group, the Baganda, comprises almost 20% of Uganda's population and is the source of the country's name ('Land of the Baganda'; their kingdom is known as Buganda). Although today the Baganda are spread throughout the country, their traditional lands are in the areas north and northwest of Lake Victoria, including Kampala. Due to significant missionary activity most Baganda are Christian, although animist traditions persist.

The Baganda, together with the neighbouring Haya (p613), have a historical reputation as one of East Africa's most highly organised tribes. Their traditional political system was based around the absolute power of the *kabaka* (king), who ruled through district chiefs. This system reached its zenith during the 19th century, when the Baganda came to

THE SWAHILI

The East African coast is home to the Swahili ('People of the Coast'), descendants of Bantu-Arab traders who share a common language and traditions. Although generally not regarded as a single tribal group, the Swahili have for centuries had their own distinct societal structures, and consider themselves to be a single civilisation.

Swahili culture first began to take on a defined form around the 11th century, with the rise of Islam. Today most Swahili are adherents of Islam, although it's generally a more liberal version than that practised in the Middle East. Thanks to this Islamic identity, the Swahili have traditionally considered themselves to be historically and morally distinct from peoples in the interior, with links eastwards towards the rest of the Islamic world.

Swahili festivals follow the Islamic calendar. The year begins with Eid al-Fitr, a celebration of feasting and almsgiving to mark the end of Ramadan fasting. The old Persian new year's purification ritual of Nauroz or Mwaka was also traditionally celebrated, with the parading of a bull anticlockwise through town followed by its slaughter and several days of dancing and feasting. In many areas, Nauroz has now become merged with Eid al-Fitr and is no longer celebrated. The festival of *maulidi* (marking the birth of the Prophet) is another Swahili festival, marked by decorated mosques and colourful street processions.

The World of the Swahili by John Middleton is a good place to start for anyone wanting to learn more about Swahili life and culture.

dominate various neighbouring groups, including the Nilotic Iteso (who now comprise about 8% of Uganda's population). Baganda influence was solidified during the colonial era, with the British favouring their recruitment to the civil service. During the chaotic Obote/Amin years of the late 1960s and early 1970s, the Bagandan monarchy was abolished; it was restored in 1993, although it has no political power.

Swahili's role as a lingua franca was solidified as it spread throughout East and Central Africa along the great trade caravan routes. Today it is spoken in more countries and by more people than any other language in sub-Saharan Africa.

El-Molo

The Cushitic-speaking El-Molo are a small tribe, numbering fewer than 4000 people. Historically the El-Molo were one of the region's more distinct groups, but in recent times they have been forced to adapt or relinquish many of their old customs in order to survive, and intermarriage with other tribes is common.

The El-Molo, whose ancestral home is on two small islands in the middle of Kenya's Lake Turkana, traditionally subsisted on fish, supplemented by the occasional crocodile, turtle, hippopotamus or bird. Over the years an ill-balanced diet and the effects of too much fluoride in the local water began to take their toll. The El-Molo became increasingly susceptible to disease and, thus weakened, to attacks from stronger tribes. Their numbers plummeted.

Today the El-Molo face an uncertain future. While some continue to eke out a living from the lake, others have turned to cattle herding or work in the tourism industry. Commercial fishing supplements their traditional subsistence existence and larger, more permanent settlements in Loyangalani, on Lake Turkana's southeastern shores, have replaced the El-Molo's traditional dome-shaped island homes.

Gusii (Kisii)

The Gusii (6% of Kenya's population) occupy the country's Western Highlands, east of Lake Victoria, forming a small Bantu-speaking island in a mainly Nilotic-speaking area. Primarily cattle herders and crop cultivators, they farm Kenya's cash crops – tea, coffee and pyrethrum – as well as market vegetables. They are also well known for their basketry and distinctive, rounded soapstone carvings.

Like many other tribal groups, Gusii society is clan based, with everyone organised into age sets. Medicine men *(abanyamorigo)*, in particular, hold a highly respected and privileged position, performing the role of doctor and social worker. One of their more peculiar practices is trepanning: the removal of sections of the skull or spine to aid maladies such as backache or concussion.

Hadzabe

The area close to Lake Eyasi in Tanzania is home to the Hadzabe (also known as Hadzapi, Hadza or Tindiga) people, who are believed to have lived here for nearly 10,000 years. The Hadzabe are often said to be the last true hunter-gatherers in East Africa and of the around 1000 who remain, between one-quarter and one-third still live according to traditional ways.

Traditional Hadzabe live a subsistence existence, usually in bands or camps of 20 to 30 people with no tribal or hierarchical structures. Families engage in communal child-rearing, and food and all other resources are shared throughout the camp. Camps are often moved, sometimes due to illness, death or the need to resolve conflicts, and they may even relocate to the site of a large kill, such as a giraffe. One enduring characteristic of Hadzabe society is that their possessions are so few that each person may carry everything they own on their backs when they travel.

The Hadzabe language is characterised by clicks and may be distantly related to that of southern Africa's San, although it shows only a few connections to Sandawe, the other click language spoken in Tanzania, and genetic studies have shown no close link between the Hadzabe and any other East African peoples.

Academic studies of the Hadzabe abound, but there is no finer treatment of the group than in the final chapter of Peter Matthiessen's *The Tree Where Man Was Born* (1972).

Haya

The Haya, who live west of Lake Victoria around Bukoba, have both Bantu and Nilotic roots, and are one of the largest tribes in Tanzania. They have a rich history, and in the precolonial era boasted one of the most highly developed early societies on the continent.

At the heart of traditional Haya society were eight different states or kingdoms, each headed by a powerful and often despotic *mukama* (ruler), who ruled in part by divine right. Order was maintained through a system of chiefs and officials, assisted by an age-group-based army. With the rise of European influence in the region, this era of Haya history came to an end. The various groups began to splinter, and many chiefs were replaced by persons considered more malleable and sympathetic to colonial interests.

Resentment of these propped-up leaders was strong, spurring the Haya to regroup and form the Bukoba Bahaya Union in 1924, which soon developed into the more influential and broad-based African Association. Together with similar groups established elsewhere in Tanzania, it constituted one of the country's earliest political movements and was an important force in the drive towards independence.

Hutu & Tutsi

The Hutu and the Tutsi are related peoples of Bantu origin who live in Burundi, Rwanda, eastern regions of the Democratic Republic of the Congo and Uganda. The Hutus are the majority ethnic group in both Burundi (where 85% of the population is Hutu and 14% Tutsi) and Rwanda (84% and 15% respectively).

Almost every aspect of shared Hutu-Tutsi history is disputed and ethnic conflicts between the two groups were a recurring theme throughout much of the 20th century. The Belgian colonial authorities favoured the Tutsi as the ruling elite. After independence, the battle for political power between the Hutu and Tutsi caused great instability in both Burundi and Rwanda. In 1993, an estimated 500,000 Burundians died in a little-reported genocide, followed a year later by the Rwandan genocide in which more than 800,000 people were killed.

Both Hutu and Tutsi speak the same Bantu language (Kinyarwanda in Rwanda, Kirundi in Burundi) and some scholars argue that the difference between the two groups is one of caste rather than any ethnic distinction. Intermarriage between the two groups was traditionally common. Both Hutu and Tutsi are predominantly Christian, although many maintain traditional beliefs in which the spirits of ancestors play an important role.

Kalenjin

The Kalenjin are one of Kenya's largest groups, with 12% of the country's population. Together with the Kikuyu (p615), Luo (p615), Luyha and Kamba, they account for about 70% of Kenya's population. Although often viewed as a single ethnic entity, the term 'Kalenjin' was actually coined in the 1950s to refer to a loose collection of several different Nilotic groups, including the Kipsigi, Nandi, Marakwet, Pokot and Tugen (former Kenyan president Daniel arap Moi's people). These groups speak different dialects of the same language (Nandi), but otherwise have distinct traditions and lifestyles. Due to the influence of arap Moi, the Kalenjin have amassed considerable political power in Kenya. They are also known for their female herbalist doctors, and for their many world-class runners.

The Kalenjin have age-set groups into which a man is initiated after circumcision. Administration of the law is carried out at the *kok* (an informal court led by the clan's elders).

The traditional homeland of the various Kalenjin peoples is along the western edge of the central Rift Valley area, including Kericho, Eldoret, Kitale, Baringo and the land surrounding Mt Elgon. Originally pastoralists, Kalenjin today are known primarily as farmers. An exception to this are the cattle-loving Kipsigi, whose cattle rustling continues to cause friction between them and neighbouring tribes.

The Nandi, who are the second largest of the Kalenjin communities, and comprise about one-third of all Kalenjin, settled in the Nandi Hills between the 16th and 17th centuries, where they prospered after learning agricultural techniques from the Luo and Luyha. They had a formidable military reputation and, in the late 19th century, managed to delay construction of the Uganda Railway for more than a decade until Koitalel, their chief, was killed.

Karamajong

The marginalised Karamojong, at home in Karamoja, in northeastern Uganda, are one of East Africa's most insulated, beleaguered and colourful tribes. As with the Samburu, Maasai (p616) and other Nilotic pastoralist peoples, life for the Karamojong centres on cattle, which are kept at night

FOREST DWELLERS

The clash between traditional and Western ways of life in East Africa is particularly apparent among the region's hunter-gatherer and forest-dwelling peoples. These include the Twa, who live in the western forests of Rwanda and Burundi, where they comprise less than 1% of the overall population, and the Hadzabe (or Hadza), in north-central Tanzania around Lake Eyasi. Typically these communities are among the most marginalised peoples in East African society.

For the Twa and the Hadzabe, the loss of land and forest is the loss of their only resource base. With the rise of commercial logging, the ongoing clearing of forests in favour of agricultural land, and the establishment of parks and conservation areas, the forest resources and wildlife on which they depend have dramatically decreased. Additional pressures come from hunting and poaching, and from nomadic pastoralists (many of whom have also been evicted from their own traditional areas) seeking grazing lands for their cattle.

Although some Hadzabe have turned to tourism and craft-making for subsistence, the benefits of these are sporadic. Some now only hunt for the benefit of tourists, and others have given up their traditional lifestyle completely. In Rwanda, the Twa have begun mobilising to gain increased political influence and greater access to health care and education.

in the centre of the family living compound and graze by day on the surrounding plains. Cattle are the main measure of wealth, ownership is a mark of adulthood, and cattle raiding and warfare are central parts of the culture. When cattle are grazed in dry-season camps away from the family homestead, the Karamojong warriors tending them live on blood from live cattle, milk and sometimes meat. In times of scarcity, protection of the herd is considered so important that milk is reserved for calves and children.

The Karamojong have long been subjected to often heavy-handed government pressure to abandon their pastoralist lifestyle; their plight has been exacerbated by periodic famines, as well as the loss of their traditional dry-season grazing areas with the formation of Kidepo Valley National Park in the 1960s. While current Ugandan president Yoweri Museveni has permitted the Karamojong to keep arms to protect themselves against raids from other groups, including the Turkana in neighbouring Kenya, government expeditions targeted at halting cattle raiding continue. These raids and expeditions, combined with easy access to weapons from neighbouring Sudan and a breakdown of law and order, have made the Karamoja area off-limits to outsiders in recent years.

The Kikuyu god, Ngai, is believed to reside on Mt Kenya, and many Kikuyu homes are still oriented to face the sacred peak. Some Kikuyu still come to its lower slopes to offer prayers and the foreskins of their young men – this was the traditional place for holding circumcision ceremonies.

Kikuyu

The Kikuyu, who comprise about 22% of Kenya's population and are the country's largest tribal group, have their heartland surrounding Mt Kenya. They are Bantu peoples who are believed to have migrated into the area from the east and northeast from around the 16th century onwards, and have undergone several periods of intermarriage and splintering. According to Kikuyu oral traditions, there are nine original *mwaki* (clans), each tracing its origins back to male and female progenitors known as Kikuyu and Mumbi. The administration of these clans, each of which is made up of many family groups *(nyumba),* was originally overseen by a council of elders, with great significance placed on the roles of the witch doctor, medicine man and blacksmith.

Initiation rites consist of ritual circumcision for boys and female genital mutilation for girls, though the latter is becoming less common. The practice was a source of particular conflict between the Kikuyu and Western missionaries during the late 19th and early 20th centuries. The issue eventually became linked with the independence struggle, and the establishment of independent Kikuyu schools.

The Kikuyu are also known for the opposition association they formed in the 1920s to protest European seizure of large areas of their lands, and for their subsequent instigation of the Mau Mau rebellion in the 1950s. Due to the influence of Jomo Kenyatta, Kenya's first president, the Kikuyu today are disproportionately represented in business and government (former president Mwai Kibaki was a Kikuyu, as is the current president, Uhuru Kenyatta). This has proved to be a source of ongoing friction with other groups.

Luo

The Luo live on the northeastern shores of Lake Victoria. They began their migration to the area from Sudan around the 15th century. Although their numbers are relatively small in Tanzania, in Kenya they comprise about 13% of the population and are the country's third-largest tribal group.

During the independence struggle, many of Kenya's leading politicians and trade unionists were Luo and they continue to form the backbone of the Kenyan political opposition.

The Luo have had an important influence on the East African musical scene. They are notable especially for their contribution to the highly popular *benga* style, which has since been adopted by musicians from many other tribes.

Instead of circumcision, the Luo traditionally extracted four to six teeth at initiation. It's still common to see Luo elders with several pegs missing.

The Luo were originally cattle herders, but the devastating effects of rinderpest in the 1890s forced them to adopt fishing and subsistence agriculture, which are the main sources of livelihood for most Luo today. Luo family groups consist of the man, his wife or wives, and their sons and daughters-in-law. The family unit is part of a larger grouping of families or *dhoot* (clans), several of which make up *ogandi* (a group of geographically related people), each led by a *ruoth* (chief). Traditional Luo living compounds are enclosed by fences, and include separate huts for the man and for each wife and son. The Luo consider age, wealth and respect as converging, with the result that elders control family resources and represent the family to the outside world.

Maasai

The Maasai are pastoral nomads who have actively resisted change, and many still follow the same lifestyle they have for centuries. Their traditional culture centres on their cattle, which, along with their land, are considered sacred. Cows provide many of their needs: milk, blood and meat for their diet, and hides and skins for clothing, although sheep and goats also play an important dietary role, especially during the dry season.

The Maasai's artistic traditions are most vividly seen in their striking body decoration and beaded ornaments. Women are famous for their magnificent beaded plate-like necklaces, while men typically wear the red-checked *shuka* (blanket) and carry a distinctive balled club.

Maasai society is patriarchal and highly decentralised. Maasai boys pass through a number of transitions during their life, the first of which is marked by the circumcision rite. Successive stages include junior warriors, senior warriors, junior elders and senior elders; each level is distinguished by its own unique rights, responsibilities and dress. Junior elders, for example, are expected to marry and settle down sometime between ages 30 and 40. Senior elders assume the responsibility of making wise and moderate decisions for the community. The most important group is that of the newly initiated warriors, *moran*, who are charged with defending the cattle herds.

Maasai women play a markedly subservient role and have no inheritance rights. Polygamy is widespread and marriages are arranged by the elders, without consulting the bride or her mother. Since most women are significantly younger than men at the time of marriage, they often become widows; remarriage is rare.

The Samburu, who live directly north of Mt Kenya, are closely related to the Maasai linguistically and culturally.

Makonde

The Makonde are famed throughout East Africa and beyond for their highly refined ebony woodcarvings. The tribe has its origins in northern Mozambique, where many Makonde still live, although in recent years a subtle split has begun to develop between the group's Tanzanian and Mozambican branches. Today most Tanzanian Makonde live in southeastern Tanzania on the Makonde plateau, although many members of the carving community have since migrated to Dar es Salaam.

Tanzania is the only African country boasting indigenous inhabitants from all of the continent's main ethnolinguistic families (Bantu, Nilo-Hamitic, Cushitic and Khoisan). They live in closest proximity around lakes Eyasi and Babati.

The Makonde are matrilineal. Although customs are gradually changing, children and inheritances normally belong to the woman, and it's still common for husbands to move to the villages of their wives after marriage. Makonde settlements are widely scattered (possibly a remnant of the days when the Makonde sought to evade slave raids), and there is no tradition of a unified political system. Despite this, a healthy sense of tribal identity has managed to survive. Makonde villages are typically governed by a hereditary chief and a council of elders. The Makonde traditionally practised body scarring, and many elders still sport facial markings and (for women) wooden lip plugs.

Because of their remote location, the Makonde have succeeded in remaining largely insulated from colonial and postcolonial influences. They are known in particular for their steady resistance to Islam. Today most Makonde follow traditional religions, with the complex spirit world given its fullest expression in their carvings.

LAND PRESSURES

During the colonial era in Kenya, it was largely Maasai land that was taken for European colonisation through two controversial treaties. The creation of Serengeti National Park in Tanzania and the continuing colonial annexation of Maasai territory put many of the traditional grazing lands and waterholes of the Maasai off-limits. During subsequent years, as populations of both the Maasai and their cattle increased, pressure for land became intense and conflict with the authorities was constant. Government-sponsored resettlement programs have met with only limited success, as Maasai traditions scorn agriculture and land ownership.

One consequence of this competition for land is that many Maasai ceremonial traditions can no longer be fulfilled. Part of the ceremony where a man becomes a *moran* (warrior) involves a group of young men around the age of 14 going out and building a small livestock camp after their circumcision ceremony. They then live alone there for up to eight years before returning to the village to marry. Today, while the tradition and desire to preserve the tradition survive, land is often unavailable.

Meru

Originally from the coast, the Meru now occupy the northeastern slopes of Mt Kenya and represent 6% of Kenya's population. Up until 1974 the Meru were led by a chief (the *mogwe*), but upon his death the last incumbent converted to Christianity. Strangely, many of their tribal stories mirror the traditional tales of the Old Testament. The practice of ancestor worship, however, is still widespread. They have long been governed by an elected council of elders *(njuuri)*, making them the only tribe practising a structured form of democratic governance prior to colonialism. The Meru now live on some of the most fertile farmland in Kenya and grow numerous cash crops. Subgroups of the Meru include the Chuka, Igembe, Igoji, Tharaka, Muthambi, Tigania and Imenti.

Pare

The Bantu-speaking Pare inhabit the Pare mountains in northeastern Tanzania, where they migrated several centuries ago from the Taita Hills area of southern Kenya.

The Pare are one of Tanzania's most educated groups. Despite their small numbers, they have been highly influential in shaping Tanzania's recent history. In the 1940s they formed the Wapare Union, which played an important role in the independence drive.

The Pare are also known for their rich oral traditions, and for their elaborate rituals centring on the dead. Near most villages are sacred areas in which the skulls of tribal chiefs are kept. When people die, they are believed to inhabit a netherworld between the land of the living and the spirit world. If they are allowed to remain in this state, ill fate will befall their descendants. As a result, rituals allowing the deceased to pass peacefully into the world of the ancestors hold great significance. Traditional Pare beliefs hold that when an adult male dies, others in his lineage will die as well until the cause of his death has been found and 'appeased'. Many of the possible reasons for death have to do with disturbances in moral relations within the lineage or in the village, or with sorcery.

Among the Pare, a deceased male's ghost influences male descendants for as long as the ghost's name is remembered. Daughters, too, are dependent on their father's goodwill. However, since property and status are transmitted through the male line, a ghost only has influence over his daughter's descendants until her death.

Sukuma & Nyamwezi

The Sukuma, Bantu speakers from southern Lake Victoria, comprise almost 15% of Tanzania's total population, although it is only relatively recently that they have come to view themselves as a single entity. They are closely related to the Nyamwezi, Tanzania's second-largest tribal group around Tabora.

AGE-BASED GROUPS

Age-based groups (in which all youths of the same age belong to a group, and pass through the various stages of life and their associated rituals together) continue to play an important role in tribal life throughout much of East Africa. Each group has its own leader and community responsibilities, and definition of the age-based groups is often highly refined. Among the Sukuma, for example, who live in the area south of Lake Victoria, each age-based group traditionally had its own system for counting from one to 10, with the system understood by others within the group, but not by members of other groups. Among the Maasai, who have one of the most highly stratified age-group systems in the region, males are organised into age groups and further into sub-groups, with inter-group rivalries and relationships one of the defining features of daily life.

Among the most famous Sukuma dances are the *banungule* (hyena dance) and the *bazwilili bayeye* (snake and porcupine dance). Before beginning, dancers are treated with traditional medicaments as protection from injury. It's not unheard of for the animals, too, to be given a spot of something to calm their tempers.

The Sukuma are renowned for their drumming and for their dancing. Lively meetings between their two competing dance societies, the Bagika and the Bagulu, are a focal point of tribal life.

The Sukuma are also known for their highly structured form of village organisation in which each settlement is subdivided into chiefdoms ruled by a *ntemi* (chief) in collaboration with a council of elders. Divisions of land and labour are made by village committees consisting of similarly aged members from each family in the village. These age-based groups perform numerous roles, ranging from assisting with the building of new houses to farming and other community-oriented work. As a result of this system, which gives most families at least a representational role in many village activities, Sukuma often view houses and land as communal property.

Turkana

The colourful Turkana are a Nilotic people who live in the harsh desert country of northwestern Kenya where they migrated from southern Sudan and northeastern Uganda. Although the Turkana only emerged as a distinct tribal group during the early to mid-19th century, they are notable today for their strong sense of tribal identification. The Turkana are closely related linguistically and culturally to Uganda's Karamojong (p614).

Like the Samburu and the Maasai (p616) (with whom they are also linguistically linked), the Turkana are primarily cattle herders, although in recent years increasing numbers have turned to fishing and subsistence farming. Personal relationships based on the exchange of cattle, and built up by each herd owner during the course of a lifetime, are of critical importance in Turkana society and function as a social security net during times of need.

The Turkana are famous for their striking appearance and traditional garb. Turkana men cover part of their hair with mud, which is then painted blue and decorated with ostrich and other feathers. Despite the intense heat of the Turkana lands, the main garment is a woollen blanket, often with garish checks. Turkana accessories include a stool carved out of a single piece of wood, a wooden fighting staff and a wrist knife. Tattooing is another hallmark of Turkana life. Witch doctors and prophets are held in high regard, and scars on the lower stomach are usually a sign of a witch doctor's attempt to cast out an undesirable spirit. Traditionally, Turkana men were tattooed on the shoulder and upper arm for killing an enemy – the right shoulder for killing a man, the left for a woman.

A surprising number of Turkana men still wear markings on their shoulders to indicate that they have killed another person.

In addition to personal adornment, other important forms of artistic expression include finely crafted carvings and refined a cappella singing. Ceremonies play a less significant role among the Turkana than among many of their neighbours, and they do not practise circumcision or female genital mutilation.

The Arts

East Africa's artistic traditions are lesser known than those from elsewhere on the continent, but that means there are some discoveries to be made. Outstanding literary and Swahili architectural traditions, in particular, give expression and voice to the region's fascinating local cultures, while Makonde woodcarving is one of the more refined in Africa. East Africans are also gaining plaudits in the cinema world, while local musicians have perfected the art of adapting better-known musical traditions into something irresistibly East African.

Swahili-Style Architecture

East Africa is one of the continent's architectural treasures, particularly for its colonial-era buildings and religious architecture, including both churches and mosques. The real highlights, however, are the old town areas of Zanzibar and Lamu (both Unesco World Heritage Sites) and of Mombasa, all of which display mesmerising combinations of Indian, Arabic, European and African characteristics in their buildings and street layouts.

In Lamu, Pate and elsewhere along the coast, Swahili architecture predominates. At the simplest level, Swahili dwellings are plain rectangular mud-and-thatch constructions, set in clusters and divided by small, sandy paths. More elaborate stone houses are traditionally constructed of coral and wood along a north–south axis, with flat roofs and a small open courtyard in the centre, which serves as the main source of light.

The various quarters or neighbourhoods in Swahili towns are symbolically anchored by a central mosque, usually referred to as the *msikiti wa Ijumaa* (Friday mosque). In a sharp break with Islamic architectural customs elsewhere, traditional Swahili mosques don't have minarets; the muezzin gives the call to prayer from inside the mosque, generally with the help of a loudspeaker.

Movies About East Africa

Born Free (1966)

Out of Africa (1985)

Hotel Rwanda (2004)

Shooting Dogs in Rwanda (2005)

The Constant Gardener (2005)

The Last King of Scotland (2006)

Cinema

East Africa's long languishing and traditionally underfunded film industry received a major boost with the opening of the Zanzibar International Film Festival (p71), also known as the Festival of the Dhow Countries. The festival, which has been held annually on Zanzibar Island since 1998, continues to be one of the region's premier cultural events. It serves as a venue for artists from the Indian Ocean basin and beyond, and has had several local prize winners, including two winners of the prestigious Golden Dhow Award. The first came in 1998 with *Maangamizi: The Ancient One,* shot in Tanzania and co-directed by Tanzanian Martin M'hando. M'hando is also known for his film, *Mama Tumaini (Women of Hope).* More recently, Kenya's Bob Nyanja won the coveted prize in 2011 for *The Rugged Priest,* in which an American Catholic priest battles the powers-that-be among the Maasai amid ethnic conflict in Kenya's Rift Valley.

Maasai women in traditional dress

Other regional winners of prizes at the Zanzibar festival have included *Makaburi Yatasema* (*Only the Stones are Talking;* 2003), a film about AIDS directed by Chande Omar Omar, and *Fimbo ya Baba* (*Father's Rod;* 2006), a Chande Omar Omar production also focusing on AIDS. In 2005 Tanzania's Beatrix Mugishawe won acclaim (and two prizes) for *Tumaini,* which focuses on AIDS orphans.

Rwandan Eric Kabera is known worldwide for *Keepers of Memory* (2004), as well as *100 Days* (produced with Nick Hughes; 2001) and *Through My Eyes* (2004), all sobering documentaries of the Rwandan genocide and its aftermath, and also ZIFF award winners.

In 2013 Kenyan actor Lupita Nyong'o became the first East African to win an Oscar. She was awarded Best Supporting Actress for her role in *12 Years a Slave.*

Rwanda has a small but notable film festival (www.rwandafilmfestival.net), spearheaded by Rwandan filmmaker Eric Kabera. It takes place in September or October (although dates vary) and is centred on Kigali, with screenings also in villages outside the capital.

East African Literature

East Africa's first-known Swahili manuscript is an epic poem dating from 1728 and written in Arabic script. However, it wasn't until the second half of the 20th century – once Swahili had become established as a regional language – that Swahili prose began to develop. One of the best known authors from this period was Tanzanian poet and writer Shaaban Robert (1909–62), who spearheaded development of a modern Swahili prose style. Among his works are the autobiographical *Maisha yangu* (*My Life*), and several collections of folk tales.

Arguably the region's most celebrated writer is Ngũgĩ wa Thiong'o (1938–). His harrowing criticism of the Kenyan establishment's neocolonialist politics landed him in jail for a year (described in *Detained: A Prison Writer's Diary;* 1982), lost him his job at Nairobi University and forced him into exile. His works include *Petals of Blood* (1977), *Matigari* (1987), *The River Between* (1965), *A Grain of Wheat* (1967), *Devil on the Cross* (1980) and *Wizard of the Crow* (2006). As a statement about the importance of reviving African languages as cultural media, Ngũgĩ wa Thiong'o wrote *Wizard of the Crow* in Gikuyu and then translated it himself into English. His latest works are memoirs: *Dreams in a Time of War* (2010), *In the House of the Interpreter* (2012) and *Birth of a Dream Weaver: A Writer's Awakening* (2016).

Other important regional writers include Binyavanga Wainaina (1971–; Kenya), Okot p'Bitek (1931–82; Uganda), Moses Isegawa (1963–; Uganda) and Abdulrazak Gurnah (1948–; Tanzania).

There is also a rich but often overlooked body of English-language literature written by East African women, particularly in Uganda. Watch out for Mary Karooro Okurut (1954–; Kenya), whose *A Woman's Voice: An Anthology of Short Stories by Ugandan Women* (2002) provides a good overview of the work of some of Uganda's female writers.

Another name to look for is that of the internationally recognised Kenyan writer Grace Ogot (1930–2015), whose work includes *Land Without Thunder* (1968), *The Strange Bride* (1989), *The Graduate* (1980) and *The Island of Tears* (1980). Born in Nyanza Province, she set many of her stories against the scenic background of Lake Victoria, and offers an insight into Luo culture in pre-colonial Kenya. Also from Kenya, Margaret Atieno Ogola (1958–2011) was the author of the celebrated novel *The River and the Source* (1994) and its sequel, *I Swear by Apollo* (2002), which follow the lives of four generations of Kenyan women in a rapidly evolving country.

East African Novels

Abyssinian Chronicles (Moses Isegawa; 1998)

Desertion (Abdulrazak Gurnah; 2005)

Wizard of the Crow: A Novel (Ngũgĩ wa Thiong'o; 2006)

Waiting (Goretti Kyomuhendo; 2007)

Ngoma: Music & Dance

Congolese Roots

The single greatest influence on the modern East African music scene has been the Congolese bands that began playing in Dar es Salaam and Nairobi in the early 1960s, and brought the styles of rumba and soukous into the East African context. Among the best known is Orchestre Super Matimila, which was propelled to fame by the late Congolese-born Remmy Ongala ('Dr Remmy'). Many of Ongala's songs (most are in Swahili) are commentaries on contemporary themes such as AIDS, poverty and hunger. Another of the Congolese bands is Samba Mapangala's Orchestra Virunga. Mapangala, a Congolese vocalist, first gained a footing in Uganda in the mid-1970s with a group known as Les Kinois before moving to Nairobi and forming Orchestra Virunga.

As Swahili lyrics replaced the original vocals, a distinct East African rumba style was born. Its proponents include Simba Wanyika (together with offshoot Les Wanyika), which had its roots in Tanzania but gained fame in the nightclubs of Nairobi.

British writer Giles Foden spent part of his childhood in East Africa and has written a number of books on the region, including novels *The Last King of Scotland* (1998) and *Zanzibar* (2002), and a 2004 nonfiction work, *Mimi and Toutou Go Forth: The Bizarre Battle for Lake Tanganyika.*

Benga

In the 1970s Kenyan benga music rose to prominence on the regional music scene. It originated among the Luo of western Kenya and is characterised by its clear electric guitar licks and pounding bass rhythms. Its ethnic roots were maintained, however, with the guitar taking the place of the traditional *nyatiti* (folk lyre), and the bass guitar replacing the drum, which originally was played by the *nyatiti* player with a toe ring. One of the best-known proponents of benga has been DO Misiani, whose group Shirati Jazz has been popular since the 1960s.

Dance

Throughout East Africa, dance plays a vital role in community life, although masked dance is not as common as it is in West Africa. A wide variety of drums and rhythms are used depending on the occasion, with

MAKONDE WOODCARVINGS

Tanzania's Makonde people are renowned for their woodcarvings. Among their most common carving styles are those with *ujamaa* motifs, and those known as *shetani,* which embody images from the spirit world.

Ujamaa carvings are designed as a totem pole or 'tree of life' containing interlaced human and animal figures around a common ancestor. Each generation is connected to those that preceded it, and gives support to those that follow. Tree of life carvings often reach several metres in height, and are almost always made from a single piece of wood.

Shetani carvings are much more abstract, and even grotesque, with the emphasis on challenging viewers to new interpretations while giving the carver's imagination free rein. Although Makonde carvings have inspired other East African woodcarvers, particularly among the Akamba people of southern Kenya, true Makonde carvings remain the finest examples of the genre.

many dances serving as expressions of thanks and praise, or as a means of communicating with the ancestors or telling a story. East Africa's most famous dance group is the globally acclaimed Les Tambourinaires du Burundi.

Kanga, Kikoi & Handicrafts

Women throughout East Africa wear brightly coloured lengths of printed cotton cloth, typically with Swahili sayings printed along the edge, known as kanga in Kenya, Tanzania and parts of Uganda. Many of the sayings are social commentary or messages – often indirectly worded, or containing puns and double meanings – that are communicated by the woman wearing the kanga. Others are simply a local form of advertising, such as those bearing the logo of political parties.

In coastal areas, you'll also see the *kikoi,* which is made of a thicker textured cotton, usually featuring striped or plaid patterns, and traditionally worn by men. Also common are batik-print cottons depicting everyday scenes, animal motifs or geometrical patterns.

Jewellery, especially beaded jewellery, is particularly beautiful among the Maasai and the Turkana. It is worn in ceremonies as well as in everyday life, and often indicates the wearer's wealth and marital status.

Basketry and woven items – all of which have highly functional roles in local society – also make lovely souvenirs.

For information about East African music, see www.eastafricanmusic.com, which provides a broad overview of the region's music. For kanga sayings, see www.glcom.com/hassan/kanga.html and www.mwambao.com/methali.htm, both of which provide a sampling of what is being said around you.

Visual Arts

East Africa is renowned for its exceptional figurative art, especially that crafted by Tanzania's Makonde, who are acclaimed throughout the region for their skill at bringing blocks of hard African blackwood (*Dalbergia melanoxylon* or, in Swahili, *mpingo*) to life in often highly fanciful depictions.

In comparison with woodcarving, painting has a much lower profile in East Africa. One of the more popular styles is Tanzania's Tingatinga painting, which takes its name from the self-taught artist Edward Saidi Tingatinga, who began the style in the 1960s. Tingatinga paintings are traditionally composed in a square format, and feature brightly coloured animal motifs set against a monochrome background.

A Taste of East Africa

East Africa's culinary tradition has generally emphasised feeding the masses as efficiently as possible, with little room for flair or innovation. Most meals centre on ugali, a thick, dough-like mass made from maize and/or cassava flour. While traditional fare may be bland but filling, there are some treats to be found. Many memorable eating experiences in the region are likely to revolve around dining al fresco in a safari camp, surrounded by the sights and sounds of the African bush.

The Street-Food Scene

Whether for the taste or simply the ambience, the street-food scene is one of the region's highlights. Throughout East Africa vendors hawk grilled maize, or deep-fried yams seasoned with a squeeze of lemon juice and a dash of chilli powder. Along the coast *pweza* (octopus) kebabs sizzle over the coals, and women squat near large, piping-hot pots of sweet *uji* (millet porridge). Other East African streetside favourites include *sambusas* (deep-fried pastry triangles stuffed with spiced mince meat) – but be sure they haven't been sitting around too long – *maandazi* (semi-sweet doughnut-like products) and *chipsi mayai* (a puffy omelette with chips mixed in). *Nyama choma* (seasoned barbecued meat) is found throughout the region and is especially popular in Kenya. Food trucks are starting to make an appearance in Nairobi, providing a more Western take on the street food experience.

Urojo is a filling, delicious soup with *kachori* (spicy potatoes), mango, limes, coconut, cassava chips, salad and sometimes *pili-pili* (hot pepper). Originally from Zanzibar, it's widely available along the coast.

Ugali & Other Staples

One of the most common staples in East Africa is ugali; it's known as *posho* in Uganda. Around Lake Victoria, the staple is just as likely to be *matoke* (cooked plantains), while along the coast rice with coconut milk is the norm. Whatever the staple, it's always accompanied by a sauce, usually with a piece of meat – often a rather tough piece of meat – floating around in it.

Vegetarian Cuisine

While there isn't much in East Africa that is specifically billed as 'vegetarian', you can find cooked rice and beans almost everywhere. The main challenges are keeping dietary variety and getting enough protein. In larger towns, Indian restaurants are wonderful for vegetarian meals. Elsewhere, Indian shop owners may have suggestions, while fresh yoghurt, peanuts and cashews, and fresh fruits and vegetables are all widely available. Most tour operators are willing to cater to special dietary requests, such as vegetarian, kosher or halal, with advance notice.

Pilau flavoured with spices and stock is the signature dish at traditional Swahili weddings. The expression 'going to eat pilau' means to go to a wedding.

Drinks

Water & Juice

Tap water is best avoided; also be wary of ice and fruit juices that may have been diluted with unpurified water. Bottled water is widely available, except in remote areas, where it's worth carrying a filter or purification tablets.

Soft drinks (sodas) are found almost everywhere. Freshly squeezed juices, especially pineapple, sugar cane and orange, are a treat, although check whether they have been mixed with safe water. Also refreshing, and never a worry hygienically, is the juice of the *dafu* (green) coconut. Western-style supermarkets sell imported fruit juices.

Especially along the coast, coffee vendors carry around a stack of coffee cups and a piping-hot kettle on a long handle with coals fastened underneath. They let you know they're coming by clacking together their metal coffee cups.

Coffee & Tea

Although East Africa exports high-quality coffee and tea, what's usually available locally is far inferior, and instant coffee is the norm. The situation is changing in major cities and tourist areas, albeit slowly. Both tea and coffee are generally drunk with lots of milk and sugar. On the coast, sip a smooth spiced tea *(chai masala)* or sample a coffee sold by vendors strolling the streets carrying a freshly brewed pot in one hand, cups and spoons in the other.

Beer & Wine

Among the most common beers are the locally brewed Tusker, Primus and Kilimanjaro, and South Africa's Castle Lager, which is also produced locally. Many locals prefer their beer warm, especially in Kenya, so getting a cold beer can be a task.

Nairobi is starting to see a proliferation of craft or boutique breweries – a most welcome addition to the region's drinking scene. Good-quality South African wines are readily available in major cities.

Locally produced home brews (fermented mixtures made with bananas or millet and sugar) are widely available. However, avoid anything distilled; in addition to being illegal, it's also often lethal.

Portuguese explorers in the colonial era introduced maize, cassava, potatoes and chillies from South America, all of which are now staples of the East African diet.

Dining Out

Three meals a day is the norm, with the main meal eaten at midday and breakfast frequently nothing more than tea or instant coffee and packaged white bread. In remote areas, many places are closed in the evening and street food is often the only option.

Hotelis & Night Markets

For dining local-style, find a local eatery, known as a *hoteli* in Swahili-speaking areas. The day's menu, rarely costing more than US$1, is usually written on a chalkboard. Rivalling *hotelis* for local atmosphere are the bustling night markets, where vendors set up grills along the roadside and sell *nyama choma* (seasoned barbecue meat) and other street food.

Restaurants

For Western-style meals, cities and main towns will have an array of restaurants, most moderately priced compared with their European counterparts. Every capital city has at least one Chinese restaurant. In many parts of East Africa, especially along the coast, around Lake Victoria and in Uganda, there's also usually a selection of Indian cuisine, found both at inexpensive eateries serving Indian snacks, as well as in pricier restaurants.

For a refreshingly African take on Kenyan cooking, with an emphasis on home cooking rather than restaurants, check out Talking to Nelly (www.talkingtonelly.com), a food blog from a Mombasa-based foodie.

Self-Catering

Supermarkets in main towns sell imported products, such as canned meat, fish and cheese.

Local Customs & Traditions

Typical East African style is to eat with the right hand from communal dishes in the centre of the table. It is not customary to share drinks. Children generally eat separately.

DINING EAST AFRICAN STYLE

If you're invited to join in a meal, the first step is hand washing. Your host will bring around a bowl and water jug; hold your hands over the bowl while the host pours water over them. Sometimes soap is provided, and a towel for drying off.

At the centre of the meal will be ugali or some other similar staple. Take some with the right hand from the communal pot (your left hand is used for wiping – and we don't mean your mouth!), roll it into a small ball with the fingers, making an indentation with your thumb, and dip it into the accompanying sauce. Don't soak the ugali too long (to avoid it breaking up in the sauce), and keep your hand lower than your elbow (except when actually eating) so the sauce doesn't drip down your forearm. Eating with your hand is a bit of an art and may seem awkward at first, but after a few tries it will start to feel more natural.

The underlying element in all meal invitations is solidarity between the hosts and the guests. If you receive an invitation to eat but aren't hungry, it's OK to explain that you have just eaten. However, still share a few bites of the meal in order to demonstrate your solidarity with the hosts, and to express your appreciation.

Don't be worried if you can't finish what's on your plate; this shows that you have been satisfied. But try to avoid being the one who takes the last handful from the communal bowl, as your hosts may think that they haven't provided enough.

Except for fruit, desserts are rarely served; meals conclude with another round of hand washing.

European-style restaurant dining, while readily available in major cities, is not an entrenched part of local culture. More common are meal-centred gatherings at home to celebrate special occasions.

Lunch is served between noon and 2.30pm, and dinner from about 6.30pm or 7pm to 10pm. The smaller the town, the earlier its dining establishments are likely to close; after about 7pm in rural areas it can be hard to find alternatives to street food. During Ramadan, many restaurants in coastal areas close completely during daylight fasting hours.

Cooking the East African Way (Constance Nabwire & Bertha Vining Montgomery, 2001) combines easy-to-follow recipes from across the region with interesting text on culinary traditions in Kenya and elsewhere.

Menu Decoder

bia – beer
biryani – rice dish, sometimes in a casserole form, often served with chicken or meat
chai – tea
chai ya asubuhi – breakfast
chakula cha jioni – dinner
chakula cha mchana – lunch
chakula kutoka bahari – seafood
chapati – Indian-style bread
chenye viungo – spicy
chipsi mayai – puffy omelette with chips mixed in
chumvi – salt
githeri – a mix of beans and corn
irio – mashed greens, potato and boiled corn or beans (see also *kienyeji*)
jusi – juice
kaa – crab
kahawa – coffee
karanga – peanut
kiazi – potato
kienyeji – mashed greens, potato and boiled corn or beans (see also *irio*)
kiti moto – fried or roasted pork bits, sold by the kilo, served with salad and fried plantain
kuku – chicken

WE DARE YOU

If you're lucky(!) and game (more to the point), you may be able to try various cattle-derived products beloved of the pastoral tribes of Kenya, Tanzania and elsewhere. Samburu, Pokot, Maasai and Karamojong warriors all have a taste for cattle blood. The blood is taken straight from the jugular, which does no permanent damage to the cattle. *Mursik* is made from milk fermented with grass ash, and is served in smoked gourds. It tastes and smells pungent, but it contains compounds that reduce cholesterol, enabling the warriors to live quite healthily on a diet of red meat, milk and blood.

kumbwe – snack
maji – water
maji ya machungwa – orange juice
maji ya madini – mineral water
mandazi – a semisweet doughnut served warm, with lashings of milk and brown sugar
masala chai – tea with cardamom and cinnamon
matoke – mashed green plantains
maziwa – milk
mboga – vegetable
mchuzi – sauce, sometimes with bits of beef and vegetables
mgahawa – restaurant
mishikaki – marinated grilled meat kebabs, usually beef
mkate mayai – literally 'bread eggs'; a wheat dough pancake, filled with minced meat and egg and fried on a hotplate
mkate wa kumimina – sesame-seed bread, found along the coast
mtindi – cultured milk, usually sold in small bags and delicious on a hot day
mukimo – sweet potatoes, corn, beans and plantains
mwanakondoo – lamb
nyama – meat
nyama choma – seasoned barbecued meat
nyama mbuzi – mutton
nyama ng'ombe – beef
nyama nguruwe – pork
nyama ya ndama – veal
pilau – rice dish, often served with chicken, meat or seafood, sometimes cooked in broth (a coastal speciality)
pilipili – pepper
posho – Ugandan version of *ugali*
samaki – fish
sambusas – deep-fried pastry triangles stuffed with spiced mincemeat; similar to Indian samosas
sukari – sugar
sukuma wiki – braised or stewed spinach
tambi – pasta
ugali – thick, dough-like mass made from maize and/or cassava flour
uji – thin, sweet porridge made from bean, millet or other flour
vitambua – small rice cakes resembling tiny, thick pancakes
wali – cooked rice
wali na kuku/samaki/nyama/maharagwe – cooked white rice with chicken/fish/meat/beans

Avoid handling or eating food with the left hand; in many areas, it's even considered impolite to give someone something with the left hand.

Survival Guide

SAFE TRAVEL 628
Common Dangers 628
By Country 629

DIRECTORY A-Z 630
Accommodation 630
Activities 631
Bargaining 632
Electricity 632
Emergency & Important Numbers 632
Etiquette 632
Gay & Lesbian Travellers 632
Insurance 633
Internet Access 633
Legal Matters 634
Maps 634
Money 635
Opening Hours 635
Photography 636
Post 636
Public Holidays 636
Telephone 636
Time 636
Toilets 636
Tourist Information 636
Travellers with Disabilities 637
Visas 637
Volunteering 637
Women Travellers 638
Work 639

TRANSPORT 640
GETTING THERE & AWAY 640
Entering the Country/Region 640
Air 640
Land 641
Sea 641
Tours 642
GETTING AROUND 642
Air 642
Bicycle 643
Boat 643
Bus 644
Car & Motorcycle 644
Hitching 645
Local Transport 645
Train 646

HEALTH 647
BEFORE YOU GO 647
Health Insurance 647
IN EAST AFRICA 647
Availability & Cost of Health Care 647
Infectious Diseases 647
Traveller's Diarrhoea 650
Environmental Hazards 650

LANGUAGE 652

Safe Travel

While there are significant risks in some areas of East Africa, most places are extremely safe.

➡ Street crime can be an issue in urban areas: carry only what you need with you.

➡ Lock your valuables away if leaving them in your hotel.

➡ Never travel East Africa's roads by night when the region's poor road-safety record gets worse.

➡ Banditry can be a concern in northeastern Kenya, northeastern Uganda and rural Burundi.

➡ Safari touts can be a nuisance in Nairobi and Arusha.

➡ Be wary of scams: the less you look like a gullible, newly arrived tourist, the less likely you'll be targeted.

COMMON DANGERS

Banditry

Banditry tends to occur in quite localised areas – northeastern Kenya, northeastern Uganda and rural Burundi are the most common trouble-spots, but these areas are well known and easily avoided, and even these are safer than they used to be. Always check the international travel advisories and make detailed enquiries locally – expats, police and local guides are usually reliable sources – before setting out.

Crime

Petty theft is a risk throughout East Africa, primarily in capital cities and tourist areas. The risks are especially high in crowded settings (markets, public transport, and bus and train stations) or in isolated areas (dark streets or deserted beaches). Muggings and violent crime are less frequent but nonetheless do occur. By following a few simple precautions, you'll minimise the risks.

➡ Avoid isolated areas, including beaches, at any time of day, but especially at night.

➡ In cities, especially Nairobi (Kenya), be alert for hustlers who will try any ploy to get you into a back alley and away from the watching eyes of onlookers.

➡ Don't tempt people by flaunting your wealth. Avoid external money pouches, dangling backpacks and camera bags, and leave jewellery, fancy watches, electronics and the like at home or in the hotel safe.

➡ When out walking, keep a small amount of cash separate from your other money and handy, so that you don't pull out large wads of bills for making purchases.

➡ Try not to look lost, even if you are. Walk purposefully and confidently, and don't refer to a guidebook or a map while on the street.

➡ Take particular care when arriving for the first time at a bus station, particularly in places such as Nairobi and Arusha (Tanzania). Try to spot the taxi area before disembarking, and make a beeline for it.

➡ Store valuables in a hotel safe, if there's a reliable one, ideally inside a lockable pouch.

➡ Keep the windows up in vehicles when stopped in traffic, and keep your bags out of sight.

➡ On buses and trains, never accept food or drink from fellow passengers. Also avoid travelling at night.

Road Accidents

Perhaps the most widespread threat to your safety comes from travelling on the region's roads. Road conditions vary, but driving standards are almost universally poor and high speeds are common.

To minimise the risk, consider the following:

➡ Never travel at night.

➡ Choose a full-sized bus over a minibus.

➡ If travelling in a matatu (usually a minivan), never take the seat next to the driver.

Scams

The region's thieves have invented numerous ways to separate you from your money. Most are deceptively simple, and equally simple to avoid.

- Be sceptical of anyone who approaches you on the street saying 'Remember me?' or claiming to be collecting donations for school fees. Your money has a better chance of reaching those most in need when channelled through registered charities or churches.
- You're walking along a busy city street, and suddenly find your way blocked by someone. Before you know it, his buddy has come up behind you and relieved you of your wallet, and they both disappear into the crowds.
- Someone strikes up a conversation and tries to sell you marijuana (*bangi* or *ganja*). Before you can shake them loose, police officers (sometimes legitimate, sometimes not) appear and insist that you pay a huge fine for being involved in the purchase of illegal drugs. Insist on going to the nearest police station before paying anything.
- A smooth-talker befriends you and his friend just happens to have a taxi. When you get in, you're joined by his buddies, who then force you to turn over your ATM card and PIN, and ride with them to various ATMs around the city until your account is emptied. Only take taxis from established ranks, and avoid getting into taxis with a 'friend' of the driver or someone else already in it.

GOVERNMENT TRAVEL ADVICE

The following government websites offer travel advisories and information for travellers:

- **Australian Department of Foreign Affairs & Trade** (www.smartraveller.gov.au)
- **Canadian Department of Foreign Affairs & International Trade** (www.voyage.gc.ca)
- **French Ministere des Affaires Etrangeres Europeennes** (www.diplomatie.gouv.fr/fr/conseils-aux-voyageurs)
- **Italian Ministero degli Affari Esteri** (www.viaggiaresicuri.mae.aci.it)
- **New Zealand Ministry of Foreign Affairs & Trade** (www.safetravel.govt.nz)
- **UK Foreign & Commonwealth Office** (www.gov.uk/foreign-travel-advice)
- **US Department of State** (www.travel.state.gov)

BY COUNTRY

Tanzania

Although you should take all the usual precautions, Tanzania is one of the safest countries in the region. Muggings and petty thefts do occur, especially in Dar es Salaam and Zanzibar, while touts can be a particular annoyance in Arusha, Mbeya and Zanzibar.

Kenya

As of late 2017, most Western governments were advising against all but essential travel within 60km of the Kenya–Somali border as well as the entire coast from Malindi to the Somali border (except Lamu and the Manda islands). The rest of the country was largely considered to be safe for travellers, but check the most recent reports to be sure.

It is also worth checking the prevailing situation in Laikipia, after violence affected a handful of ranches and lodges in 2017.

Nairobi is notorious for muggings and more serious crime, but the situation has improved and the greatest dangers are relatively easy to avoid. Crime can be a problem in Mombasa and other coastal areas, especially beach resorts.

Uganda

Uganda is generally safe for foreign travellers and Kampala is one of the region's safer large cities. The main issues used to come from bandits in the Karamojong area of far northeastern Uganda, but that threat has subsided and is no longer the subject of any travel advisories.

Democratic Republic of Congo

The DRC's reputation for violence is well known. Always check the security situation carefully and be aware that things can change rapidly in this troubled corner of Africa. At the time of research, small pockets of eastern DRC bordering Rwanda were considered relatively safe, at least by Congolese standards.

Rwanda

Few visitors to Rwanda experience any problems, although you should take the usual safety precautions. You should also always check the prevailing security situation close to Rwanda's borders with Burundi and the DRC.

Burundi

The security situation in Burundi has improved, but as of late 2017 the entire country still remains subject to political instability and violence, with travel advisories warning against all-but-essential travel to some areas and against all travel to the remainder.

Directory A-Z

Accommodation

East Africa has something for everyone, with accommodation ranging from no-frills rooms with communal bucket bath or simple campsites to some of Africa's most luxurious safari lodges.

Camping

- There are campsites in most national parks, and in or near many major towns. In some rural tourist areas, local villagers maintain campgrounds. Facilities range from none at all to full service, with hot showers and cooking areas.
- In Kenyan and Tanzanian parks there are both public campsites (usually very basic, with a toilet block with a couple of pit toilets, a water tap and perhaps public showers) and special campsites (which have even fewer facilities than the standard camps, but cost more because of their wilder locations and set-up costs). Public campsites can cost up to US$30/20 per adult/child and special campsites start at US$50/25 per person.
- Except for the national parks, prices average US$5 to US$10 per person per night.
- Camping away from established sites is not advisable; in rural areas, ask the village head or elders before pitching your tent. Camping is not recommended in Rwanda and Burundi, where camping options in any case range from limited to nonexistent.
- In coastal areas, bungalows or *bandas* (simple wooden or thatched huts, often with only a mattress and mosquito net) offer an alternative to camping.

Hostels, Guesthouses & Budget Hotels

- True hostels are rare, but mission hostels and guesthouses are scattered throughout the region. While intended primarily for missionaries and aid-organisation staff, they're generally happy to accommodate travellers if space is available. Most are clean, safe and good value.
- In budget guesthouses and hotels, you generally get what you pay for, though there's the occasional good deal. The cheapest ones (every town will have one) are poorly ventilated concrete-block rooms with sometimes clean sheets, shared toilets, cold showers or a bucket bath, mosquito net, sometimes a fan and often only a token lock on the door. Rates for this type of place average from US$5 per room per night. A few dollars more will get you a somewhat more comfortable room, often with a bathroom (although not always with running or hot water).
- Many budget places double as brothels, and at many of the cheapest ones solo women travellers are likely to feel uncomfortable. For peace and quiet, guesthouses without bars are the best choice.
- Backpackers and dormitory-style places aren't as common as in southern Africa, but there are a few, with prices slightly higher than you'd pay for a room in a basic local guesthouse.

Hotels, Lodges & Luxury Safari Camps

- Larger towns will have one or several midrange hotels, most with private bathrooms, hot water and a fan or an air-conditioner. Facilities range from faded to good value, and prices range from US$50 to US$200 per person.
- Major tourist areas also have a good selection of top-end accommodation, with prices ranging from about

BOOK YOUR STAY ONLINE

For more accommodation reviews by Lonely Planet authors, check out http://lonelyplanet.com/hotels/. You'll find independent reviews, as well as recommendations on the best places to stay. Best of all, you can book online.

US$200 upwards per person per night. On the safari circuits, top-end prices are generally all-inclusive or sold on a full-board basis.

➡ National parks often have 'permanent tented camps' or 'luxury tented camps'. These offer comfortable beds in canvas tents, usually with a private toilet, screened windows and most of the comforts of a hotel room, but with a wilderness feel.

➡ 'Mobile' or 'fly' camps are temporary camps set up for several nights, or for one season, and used for walking safaris or a more intimate bush experience away from the main tented camp.

ACCOMMODATION PRICE RANGES

The following price ranges refer to a standard double room in high season. Prices vary significantly across the region.

$ less than US$50

$$ US$50–US$200

$$$ more than US$200

Activities

Watching wildlife might get all of the attention when it comes to getting active in East Africa, and understandably so, but this is also a much-underrated destination for hiking, diving and snorkelling. Possibilities are numerous and can add depth or a whole new dimension to your visit.

Diving & Snorkelling

East Africa's Indian Ocean coast has some fabulous diving and/or snorkelling opportunities and caters to everyone from beginners to experienced divers. Take a diving beginner or refresher course, or simply snorkel off the back of a dhow – now there's a day you'll never forget.

WHEN TO GO

There are distinct seasons for diving in East Africa. October (or September) to March is the best time. From June to August it's often impossible to dive, especially in Kenya, due to the poor visibility caused by the heavy silt flow from some rivers. That said, some divers have taken the plunge in July and found visibility to be a very respectable 7m to 10m, although 4m is more common.

DIVE OPERATORS & SAFETY

When choosing a dive operator, quality rather than cost should be the priority. Consider the operator's experience and qualifications; the knowledge and competence of staff; and the condition of equipment and frequency of maintenance. Assess whether the overall attitude is serious and professional, and ask about safety precautions: radios, oxygen, boat reliability and back-up engines, emergency evacuation procedures, first-aid kits, safety flares and life jackets. On longer dives, do you get an energising meal, or just tea and biscuits?

There are decompression chambers in Matemwe on Zanzibar's east coast, in Mombasa in Kenya (although this latter one is an army facility, and not always available to the general public) and in Johannesburg (South Africa). Also check the **Divers Alert Network Southern Africa** (DAN; www.dansa.org) website; it's highly recommended to take out insurance coverage with DAN, whose coverage includes Kenya and Tanzania. All insurance should be arranged before coming to East Africa. Many general insurance policies exclude diving, so you'll likely need to pay a bit extra, but it's well worth it in comparison with the bills you will need to foot should something go wrong.

Be sure to allow a sufficient surface interval between the conclusion of your final dive and any onward flights. The Professional Association of Dive Instructors (PADI) recommends at least 12 hours, or more if you have

PRACTICALITIES

➡ **Discount Cards** An International Student Identity Card (ISIC) or the graduate equivalent is occasionally useful for discounts on some train fares, airline tickets and entry charges to museums and archaeological sites.

➡ **Newspapers** *The East African* (www.theeastafrican.co.ke). For a pan-African focus, see the BBC's *Focus on Africa, Business Africa* and *Africa Today*. For East African travel, check out *Travel Africa* (www.travelafricamag.com).

➡ **Radio** Kenya, Uganda and Tanzania: government-run national broadcasters have radio and TV transmissions in English. BBC's World Service and Deutsche Welle transmit in English and Swahili.

➡ **Smoking** Throughout East Africa (except in Burundi and eastern DRC), smoking is banned in all enclosed public areas, including restaurants, bars, hotels and public transport. There are expensive fines (even possible jail time) for breaches. In Uganda, the sale of e-cigarettes, flavoured tobacco and single cigarettes is banned.

➡ **Weights & Measures** The metric system is used.

been doing daily multiple dives for several days.

Hiking & Trekking

East Africa has some outstanding trekking possibilites, including many that include a climb to an epic summit. Almost all hikes and climbs in the region require local guides, and some require a full range of clothing, from lightweight for the semitropical conditions at lower altitudes to full winter gear for the high summits. Waterproof clothing and equipment is important at any altitude and in any season.

The best time to trek is from June to February – avoid the March to May rainy season.

Bargaining

Bargaining is expected by vendors in tourist areas, markets and many street stalls. Away from tourist areas and for non-tourist items, the price quoted will often be the 'real' price, so don't automatically assume that the quote you've been given is too high. It is *sometimes* possible to negotiate a discount for taxis (especially if chartered for a set period) and accommodation (depending on the season).

Emergency & Important Numbers

Country	Country Code	Emergency Number
Burundi	✆257	✆117 (police)
DRC	✆243	✆112 (police), ✆118 (fire)
Kenya	✆254	999
Rwanda	✆250	113
Tanzania	✆255	n/a
Uganda	✆256	✆999 (landline), ✆112 (mobile)

Electricity

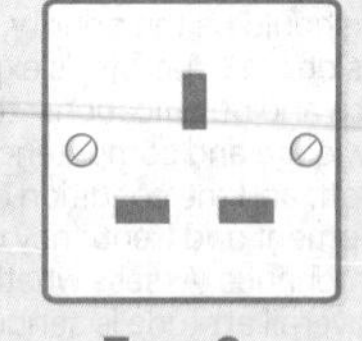

Type G
230-240V/50Hz

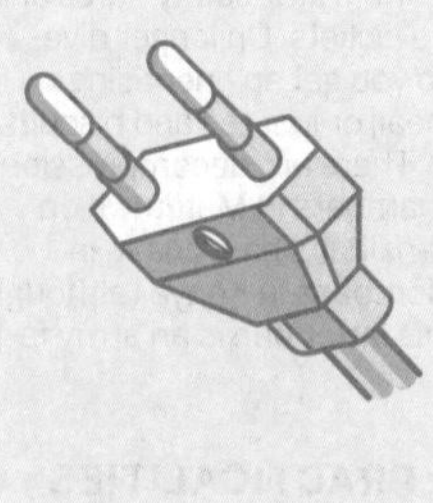

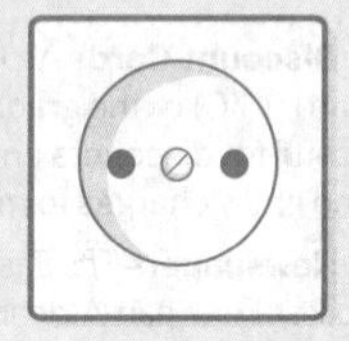

Type C
220-240V/50Hz

Etiquette

➡ **Greetings** Greetings are important. Never launch into a conversation, even when just asking for directions, without first greeting the person with whom you're speaking. Learning a few words in Swahili helps.

➡ **Eating** Never, ever handle food with the left hand! If others are eating with their hands, do the same, even if cutlery is provided. If eating in someone's home, leave a small amount on your plate to show your hosts that you've been satisfied.

➡ **Children** Don't hand out sweets/pens to children on the streets, since it encourages begging.

➡ **Patience** Impatience will get you nowhere in East Africa, where nothing is hurried. If in a frustrating situation, be patient, friendly and considerate. Never lose your temper as a confrontational attitude won't go down well.

➡ **Photography** Always ask before photographing people. Never photograph someone if they don't want you to. If you agree to send someone a photo, do so.

Gay & Lesbian Travellers

While there are very few prosecutions under the law, it is certainly better to be discreet as a gay foreigner in East Africa.

Officially, male homosexuality is illegal in Uganda, Tanzania and Kenya. While prosecutions rarely occur, discretion is advised as gay sexual relationships are culturally taboo, and public displays of affection, whether between people of the same or opposite sex, are frowned upon. In Uganda and Kenya in particular, anti-gay public discourse has become increasingly common.

Female homosexuality inhabits a grey area of legality and tends not to excite the same public outrage, but it still exists very much in the shadows.

Recent developments give little cause for optimism. In 2014 the Ugandan government tried to increase the punishment for homosexual acts to life imprisonment,

RESPONSIBLE DIVING

Wherever you dive, consider the following tips, and help preserve the ecology and beauty of the reefs:

- Never use anchors on a reef, and take care not to ground boats on coral.
- Avoid touching or standing on living marine organisms or dragging equipment across a reef. Polyps can be damaged by even the gentlest contact. If you must hold on to a reef, only touch exposed rock or dead coral.
- Be conscious of your fins. Even without contact, the surge from fin strokes near a reef can damage delicate organisms. Take care not to kick up clouds of sand, which can smother organisms.
- Practise and maintain proper buoyancy control. Major damage can be done by divers descending too fast and colliding with a reef.
- Take great care in underwater caves. Spend as little time within them as possible, as your air bubbles may be caught within the roof and thereby leave organisms high and dry. Take turns inspecting the interior of a small cave.
- Resist the temptation to collect or buy corals or shells – which you'll frequently be offered by vendors on the beaches – or to loot marine archaeological sites (mainly shipwrecks).
- Ensure that you take home all your rubbish and any litter you may find as well. Plastics in particular are a serious threat to marine life.
- Do not feed fish.
- Minimise your disturbance of marine animals, and never ride on the backs of turtles or attempt to touch dolphins.

but the law was thrown out by the Constitutional Court, while in July 2014, 40 people were arrested for 'suspected homosexuality' in a Nairobi nightclub. And in Zanzibar in 2017, 20 people were arrested while attending a HIV/AIDS education session. In October of the same year, three South African lawyers were accused of promoting homosexuality and deported from Tanzania after attending a meeting called to challenge a law preventing private health clinics from providing HIV/AIDS services.

Useful Resources

David Tours (www.davidtravel.com) Can arrange anything from balloon safaris to luxurious coastal hideaways, all with a gay focus.

Gay & Lesbian Coalition of Kenya (GALCK; www.galck.org) Local advocacy group that keeps a low profile, but that it exists at all in the public domain represents a scrap of progress.

Global Gayz (www.globalgayz.com/africa/kenya) Covers gay issues with country-by-country links.

Insurance

Before heading to East Africa, consider taking out a membership with the **African Medical & Research Foundation** (AMREF; ☎254-20-6002299, Nairobi emergency lines 254-20-315454/5; www.amref.org). A one-month Gold membership costs US$24 and covers two air ambulance evacuations and 24-hour medical treatment in all five East African countries.

- Shop around before choosing a policy, as those designed for short package tours in Europe may not be suitable for East Africa.
- Read the fine print: some policies specifically exclude 'dangerous activities', which can mean scuba diving, motorcycling and even trekking. A locally acquired motorcycle licence isn't valid under some policies.
- Most policies valid in East Africa require you to pay on the spot and claim later, so keep all documentation.
- Most importantly, check that the policy covers an emergency flight home or at least medical evacuation to Western-standard health facilities, and understand in advance the procedures you need to follow in an emergency.

Worldwide travel insurance is available at www.lonelyplanet.com/travel-insurance. You can buy, extend and claim online anytime – even if you're already on the road.

Internet Access

- Throughout East Africa, you'll find wi-fi in all but the very cheapest or most remote hotels, although speeds vary enormously.

- There are internet cafes in all capitals and major towns, although few last long. In rural areas, connections remain spotty.
- Prices average US$1 per hour; truly fast connections are rare.

Legal Matters

Apart from traffic offences such as speeding and driving without a seatbelt (which are mandatory in many areas for driver and front-seat passengers), the main area to watch out for is drug use and possession. Marijuana (*bangi* or *ganja*) is widely available in places such as Nairobi, Dar es Salaam and Zanzibar, and is frequently offered to tourists, invariably as part of a set-up involving the police or fake police. If you're caught, expect to pay a large bribe to avoid arrest or imprisonment.

If you're arrested for whatever reason, you can request to call your embassy, but the help they can give you will be limited.

If you get robbed, most insurance companies require a police report before they'll reimburse you. You can get these at the nearest police station, though it's usually a time-consuming process.

Maps

Recommended maps include the following:

- Nelles *Tanzania, Rwanda, Burundi* (1:1,500,000)
- Nelles *Kenya & Serengeti* (1:1,000,000)
- Nelles *Uganda* (1:700,000)
- Michelin *Africa: Central & South* (1:4,000,000)

RESPONSIBLE TREKKING

The huge number of visitors in some of East Africa's wilderness and trekking areas are beginning to take their toll. Mt Kilimanjaro is a prime example, although there are many others. Following are some tips for helping to preserve the region's delicate ecosystems and beauty:

- Carry out all your rubbish, and make an effort to carry out rubbish left by others. Sanitary napkins, tampons, condoms and toilet paper should be carried out despite the inconvenience. They burn and decompose poorly.
- Minimise waste by taking minimal packaging and no more food than you will need. Take reusable containers or stuff sacks.
- Contamination of water sources by human faeces can lead to the transmission of all sorts of nasties. Where there is a toilet, use it. Where there is none (as is the case in many of the region's trekking areas), bury your waste. Dig a small hole 15cm (6in) deep and at least 100m (320ft) from any watercourse. Cover the waste with soil and a rock. In snow, dig down to the soil. Also ensure that these guidelines are applied to a portable toilet tent if one is being used by a large trekking party.
- Don't use detergents or toothpaste in or near watercourses, even if they are biodegradable. For personal washing, use biodegradable soap (best purchased at home) and a water container at least 50m (160ft) away from the watercourse. Disperse the waste water widely to allow the soil to filter it fully. Wash cooking utensils 50m (160ft) from watercourses using a scourer, sand or snow instead of detergent.
- Hillsides and mountain slopes, especially at high altitudes, are prone to erosion. Stick to existing trails, and avoid short cuts. If a well-used trail passes through a mud patch, walk through the mud so as not to increase the size of the patch. Avoid removing the plant life that keeps topsoils in place.
- Don't depend on open fires for cooking. The cutting of wood for fires in popular trekking areas such as Kilimanjaro can cause rapid deforestation. Cook on a lightweight kerosene, alcohol or Shellite (white gas) stove and avoid those powered by disposable butane gas canisters.
- If you are trekking with a guide and porters, supply stoves for the whole team. In cold conditions, ensure that all members are outfitted with enough clothing so that fires are not a necessity for warmth. If you patronise local accommodation, try to select places that don't use wood fires to heat water or cook food.
- Ensure that you fully extinguish a fire after use. Spread the embers and flood them with water.

Money

Bring a mix of US dollars or euros in cash (post-2006 notes in large and small denominations); a credit card (Visa and MasterCard are most widely accepted) for withdrawing money from ATMs; and some travellers cheques as an emergency standby (although note that these are generally changeable in major cities only, and with very high commissions).

ATMs

There are ATMs in all capital cities and most major towns (except for Burundi, where they are found almost exclusively in Bujumbura, and to a lesser extent Rwanda). They take Visa, MasterCard or both (Visa only in Rwanda). Some banks in Kenya, Tanzania and Uganda also have machines linked to the Plus and Cirrus networks. However, despite their growing use, ATMs are out of order or out of cash with enough frequency that you should always have some sort of back-up funds. There are few ATMs away from major routes.

Black Market

Except possibly in Burundi, there is essentially no black market for foreign currency. Nevertheless, you'll still get shady characters sidling up beside you in Nairobi, Dar es Salaam and major tourist areas, trying to get you to change money and promising enticing rates. It's invariably a set-up; changing on the street should be avoided.

Cash

US dollars, followed by euros, are the most convenient foreign currencies and get the best rates. Other major currencies are readily accepted in major cities, but often not elsewhere, or at less favourable rates. You'll get higher rates for larger denomination bills (US$50 and US$100 notes), but carry a supply of smaller denomination notes as well, as change can be difficult to find.

Throughout the region, the only US dollar notes that are accepted for exchange are those from 2006 onward.

EATING PRICE RANGES

The following price ranges refer to a main course. What you get for these prices varies greatly across the region.

$ less than US$6

$$ US$6–US$12

$$$ more than US$12

Credit Cards

Visa and MasterCard can be used for some top-end hotels and a few tour operators, especially in major towns and in Kenya. However, they're best viewed as a standby unless you've confirmed things in advance with the establishment. In Burundi you'll need to rely almost exclusively on cash, although a few banks in major cities give cash advances against a credit card with a high commission. Some places, especially in Tanzania, attach a commission of about 5% to 10% to credit card payments.

Exchanging Money

You can change cash with a minimum of hassle at banks or foreign exchange (forex) bureaus in major towns and cities; rates and commissions vary, so it pays to shop around. In addition to regular banking hours, most forex bureaus are also open on Saturday mornings. Outside banking hours and away from an ATM, ask shop owners if they can help you out, rather than changing with someone on the street (which should always be avoided). It's better to say something like 'The banks are closed; do you know someone who could help me out?' rather than directly asking if they will change money.

Tipping

Small local businesses Tipping not expected.

Anywhere frequented by tourists Tips are expected.

Service charge If a service charge hasn't been included, round out the bill or calculate about 10%.

Guides and drivers Tips expected by those with whom you've spent a number of days; count on US$10 to US$15 per day per group.

Safari camps Most keep a box for tips that are shared among all staff.

Travellers Cheques

Throughout the region, travellers cheques either can't be changed at all (as in Rwanda, Burundi and Tanzania) or can only be changed in major cities, with high commissions and with great difficulty. They should not be relied upon. Where they can be changed, rates are lower than for cash. American Express and Thomas Cook are the most widely recognised; get your cheques in US dollars or euros. Bring a range of denominations because some banks charge a per-cheque levy. Carry the *original* purchase receipt with you (and separately from the cheques), as many banks and forex bureaus will ask to see it.

If your cheques are stolen, getting replacements while still in the region is generally not possible.

Opening Hours

The following apply, with some variations, in most countries of the region. Many shops and offices close for one to two hours between noon and 2pm, and on Friday afternoons for mosque services (especially coastal areas).

Banks 9am–3pm Monday to Friday, 9am–11am Saturday

Post offices 8.30am–5pm Monday to Friday, 9am–noon Saturday

Restaurants 11am–2pm and 5pm–9pm; some remain open between lunch and dinner

Shops 8.30am or 9am–3pm or 5pm Monday to Friday, 9am–11am Saturday

Supermarkets 8.30am–8.30pm Monday to Saturday, 10am–8pm Sunday

Photography

Nairobi has the best selection of camera equipment, followed by Dar es Salaam and Kampala, though it's best to bring what you'll need, including extra memory cards, with you.

Many internet cafes and speciality shops can help with transferring digital images to storage devices. It's a good idea to carry a USB converter for memory cards.

Whatever equipment you carry, be sure to keep it well protected against dust. *Lonely Planet's Guide to Travel Photography* (Richard I'Anson; 5th ed, 2016) is full of helpful tips for taking photographs while on the road.

Post

Postal services in East Africa are fairly reliable and you can find a post office in most large or medium-sized towns. Sending packages is at your own risk; for more assurance, use a courier service.

Letters sent from Kenya rarely go astray but can take two weeks to one month to reach Australia, Europe or the USA. As a general rule, it's best to send letters and parcels from capital city post offices.

Public Holidays

In Tanzania, parts of Kenya and Uganda, major Islamic holidays are also celebrated as public holidays. The dates depend on the moon and fall about 11 days earlier each year. The most important ones include the following:

Eid al-Fitr The end of Ramadan, and East Africa's most important Islamic celebration; celebrated as a two-day holiday in many areas.

Eid al-Kebir (Eid al-Haji) Commemorates the moment when Abraham was about to sacrifice his son in obedience to God's command, only to have God intercede at the last moment and substitute a ram. It coincides with the end of the pilgrimage (haj) to Mecca.

Eid al-Moulid (Maulidi) The birthday of the Prophet Mohammed.

Ramadan The annual 30-day fast when adherents do not eat or drink from sunrise to sunset. Although Ramadan is not a public holiday, restaurants are often closed during this time in coastal areas.

Telephone

Phone Codes

Throughout the region, except in Rwanda and Burundi, area codes must be used whenever you dial long-distance.

Mobile Phones

The mobile network reaches most areas of the region. Most companies sell prepaid starter packages for about US$2, and top-up cards are on sale at shops everywhere. Although several mobile companies have a presence throughout the region (meaning you can keep the same SIM card in different countries), it's cheaper to buy a local SIM card when you cross the border – roaming costs remain high across the region although agreements between governments are increasingly lowering costs.

Local SIM cards can be used in European and Australian phones. Other phones must be set to roaming.

Time

Time in Kenya, Uganda and Tanzania is GMT/UTC plus three hours year-round; in Rwanda and Burundi it's GMT/UTC plus two hours.

Toilets

Toilets vary from standard long drops to full-flush luxury conveniences. Most midrange and top-end hotels sport flushable sit-down types, although at the lower end of the price range, toilet seats are a rare commodity. Budget guesthouses often have squat toilets, sometimes equipped with a flush mechanism, but otherwise with a bucket and scoop.

Toilets with running water are a rarity outside major hotels. If you see a bucket with water nearby, use it for flushing. Paper (you'll invariably need to supply your own) should be deposited in the can that's usually in the corner.

Many of the upmarket bush camps have 'dry' toilets – just a fancy version of the long drop with a Western-style seat perched on the top.

Tourist Information

Rwanda is the only country in the region with functioning tourist offices of any use. Elsewhere, the private sector is a much better source of information. National tourist bodies include the following:

➡ **Kenya's Ministry of Tourism** (www.tourism.go.ke)

➡ **Rwanda Tourism** (Rwanda Development Board; ☎0788313800; www.rwandatourism.com; KG 9 Ave, Kigali; ⌚7am-5pm Mon-Fri, 8am-noon Sat & Sun)

➡ **Tanzania Tourist Board** (www.tanzaniatourist board.com)

➡ **Uganda Tourism Board** (www.visituganda.com)

Travellers with Disabilities

While there are few facilities specifically for people with disabilities, East Africans are generally quite accommodating, and willing to offer whatever assistance they can as long as they understand what you need. In general, Kenya and northern Tanzania are probably the easiest destinations, and safari companies in these areas often have experience taking people with disabilities on safari. Some considerations:

➡ While some newer lodges have wheelchair-accessible rooms, few hotels have lifts, many have narrow stairwells and there are generally no grips or rails in bathrooms.

➡ Many park lodges and camps are built on ground level. However, access paths, in an attempt to maintain a natural environment, are sometimes rough or rocky, and rooms or tents raised. It's best to enquire about access before booking.

➡ As far as we know, there are no Braille signboards at any parks or museums, nor any facilities for travellers who are deaf.

➡ In most places, taxis are small sedans. Minibuses are widely available in Kenya, Tanzania and Uganda, and can be chartered for transport and customised safaris. Large or wide-door vehicles can also be arranged through car-hire agencies in major cities, and often with safari operators as well.

Accessible Journeys (www.disabilitytravel.com) Offers a handful of Kenyan and Tanzanian safari tours.

Society for Accessible Travel & Hospitality (SATH; ☎USA 212-447 7284; www.sath.org) A good resource that gives advice on how to travel with a wheelchair, kidney disease, sight impairment or deafness.

Accessible Travel Online Resources

Download Lonely Planet's free Accessible Travel guides from http://lptravel.to/AccessibleTravel.

Lonely Planet's Travel for All community on Google Plus is a helpful initial contact.

Other contacts:

Access-Able Travel (www.access-abletravel.com.au)

Accessible Journeys (www.disabilitytravel.com)

Disability Horizons (www.disabilityhorizons.com)

Mobility International (www.miusa.org)

National Information Communication Awareness Network (www.nican.com.au)

Safari Guide Africa (www.safariguideafrica.com/safaris-for-the-disabled)

Tourism for All (www.tourismforall.org.uk)

Visas

➡ It's best to arrange visas in advance.

➡ Uganda no longer issues visas on arrival without pre-approval – apply online for a visa.

➡ Kenya was still issuing visas on arrival at the time of writing but e-visas available online are expected to replace those obtained on arrival.

➡ Tanzania still issues visas on arrival, but in theory that is only for travellers with no Tanzanian embassy or consulate in their home country.

➡ As of January 2018 Rwanda issues visas on arrival for all nationalities.

➡ For all countries, regulations are subject to change, so call the relevant embassy for an update.

➡ Once in East Africa, a single-entry visa for Kenya, Tanzania or Uganda allows you to visit either of the other two countries (assuming you've met their visa requirements and have been issued a visa) and then return to the original country without having to apply for a second visa for the original country. Thus, if you're in Tanzania on a single-entry visa, you can go to Kenya (assuming you also have a Kenyan visa), and then return to Tanzania without needing a new Tanzanian visa. This doesn't apply to Rwanda and other African countries, so if these are on your regional itinerary, it saves money to get a multiple-entry visa at the outset. Note that visas issued at airports and land borders are usually for single entry only.

➡ At most borders and at airport immigration where visas are available, visa fees must be paid in US dollars cash, although other major currencies are sometimes accepted (including at Nairobi's Jomo Kenyatta International Airport).

➡ Ensure that your passport has plenty of blank pages for entry and exit stamps, and is valid for at least six months after the conclusion of your planned travels.

➡ Carry extra passport-sized photos for visa applications.

➡ Proof of an onward ticket or sufficient funds is rarely required if you apply for a visa at land borders. It's occasionally requested at airports in the region, but generally only if you give immigration officials reason to doubt that you'll leave.

Volunteering

Volunteering can be a great way to reduce the ecological footprint of your trip. As a general rule, volunteering works best for both the traveller and the organisation

EAST AFRICAN TOURIST VISA

In 2014 the governments of Kenya, Uganda and Rwanda created a new East Africa Tourist Visa (EATV). Under the scheme, tourists are entitled to a 90-day, multiple-entry visa that covers travel in and out of these three countries for a single fee of US$100. Neither Burundi nor Tanzania are part of the EATV. The visas are available upon arrival at airports and most land crossings. Applications can also be made prior to travelling to the region, either at an embassy or consulate for one of the three countries in your home country or online. Although requirements vary from embassy to embassy, most applications require a single passport photo and a letter to the embassy outlining your travel plans.

With the visa duly in your passport, your first port-of-call must be the country through which you applied for the visa, whereafter there are no restrictions on travelling in or out of the three countries. No visa extensions are possible.

Apart from convenience, the EATV could save you money, with individual visas for most (but not all) nationalities costing US$50 for Kenya, US$50 for Uganda and US$30 for Rwanda.

For more information and links to online application forms, visit www.visiteastafrica.org/travel-guide/visa-information.

in question if you treat it as a genuine commitment rather than simply a fun extension of your trip. It's also preferable if you have a particular skill to bring to the experience, especially one that cannot be satisfied by local people.

Keep in mind that there is no such thing as a perfect volunteer placement. Generally speaking, you'll get as much out of a program as you're willing to put into it; the vast majority of volunteers in East Africa walk away all the better for the experience.

There are various opportunities for volunteering, generally teaching, or in environmental or health work; these are almost always best arranged prior to arriving in East Africa.

Camps International (www.campsinternational.com) organises community-focused budget and/or gap-year itineraries in Tanzania and Kenya.

Note that for any volunteering work involving children, you will require a criminal background check from your home country and/or previous countries of residence.

International Organisations

The following international organisations are good places to start gathering information on volunteering, although they won't necessarily always have projects on the go in East Africa.

Australian Volunteers International (www.australianvolunteers.com)

Coordinating Committee for International Voluntary Service (www.ccivs.org)

Earthwatch (www.earthwatch.org)

Idealist (www.idealist.org)

International Volunteer Programs Association (www.volunteerinternational.org)

Peace Corps (www.peacecorps.gov)

Step Together Volunteering (www.step-together.org.uk)

UN Volunteers (www.unv.org)

Volunteer Service Abroad (www.vsa.org.nz)

Voluntary Service Overseas (www.vso.org.uk)

Volunteer Abroad (www.goabroad.com/volunteer-abroad)

Worldwide Experience (www.worldwideexperience.com)

Women Travellers

East Africa (especially Kenya, Tanzania and Uganda) is a relatively easy region to travel in, either solo or with other women, especially when compared with parts of North Africa, South America and certain Western countries. In Rwanda and Burundi, verbal hassles, hisses and the like tend to be more common than elsewhere in the region, although things rarely go further than this. Otherwise you're unlikely to encounter any more specifically gender-related problems than you would elsewhere in the world and, more often than not, you'll meet only warmth, hospitality and sisterly regard.

To avoid unwanted attention, consider the following:

- Dressing modestly is the single most successful strategy for minimising unwanted attention. Wear trousers or a long skirt, and a conservative top with sleeves. Tucking your hair under a cap or scarf, or tying it back, also helps.
- Use common sense, trust your instincts and take the usual precautions when out and about. Try to avoid walking alone at night. Avoid isolated areas at all times, and be particularly cautious on beaches, many of which can become isolated very quickly. Hassling tends to be worse in tourist areas along the Kenyan coast than elsewhere in the region.

➡ If you find yourself with an unwanted suitor, explain that your husband (whether real or fictitious) or a large group of friends will be arriving imminently at that very place. The easiest response to the question of why you aren't married is to explain that you are still young (*bado kijana* in Swahili), which, whether you are or not, will at least have some humour value. As for why your family isn't with you, you can always explain that you will be meeting them later.

➡ Seek out local women, as this can enrich your trip tremendously. Good places to try include tourist offices, government departments or even your hotel, where at least some of the staff are likely to be formally educated young to middle-aged women. In rural areas, starting points include women teachers at a local school, or staff at a health centre.

➡ In mixed-race situations in some areas of the region – specifically if you're a black woman with a white male – some East Africans may assume that you're a prostitute. Taking taxis if you go out at night and ignoring any comments may help minimise problems here.

➡ Arrange tour and trekking guides through a reputable hotel or travel agency. Avoid freelance guides who approach you on the street.

➡ Ignore hissing and catcalls; don't worry about being rude, and don't feel the need to explain yourself.

➡ A limited selection of tampons is available at pharmacies or large supermarkets in major towns throughout the region. Elsewhere, the choice is usually limited to pads. Women will likely come to appreciate the benefits of Western-style consumer testing when using local sanitary products.

Work

➡ The most likely areas for employment are the safari industry, tourism, scuba diving and teaching. For safari-, diving- and tourism-related positions, competition is stiff and the best way to land something is to get to know someone already working in the business. Also check safari operator and lodge websites, some of which advertise vacant positions.

➡ Work and residency permits generally must be arranged through the employer or sponsoring organisation; residency permits normally should be applied for before arriving in the region. Be prepared for lots of bureaucracy.

➡ Most teaching positions are voluntary, and best arranged through voluntary agencies or mission organisations at home.

➡ Also start your search from home for international staff positions with aid agencies. There are numerous opportunities, especially in Kenya and Uganda. However, most organisations require applicants to go through their head office.

Transport

GETTING THERE & AWAY

East Africa is well connected by air to the rest of Africa, the Middle East and Europe, while land connections are very often overland epics. Flights and tours can be booked online at lonelyplanet.com/bookings.

Entering the Country/Region

Entering most countries of the region is usually hassle free, although there can be long queues at airport immigration and crossing land borders in your own vehicle always takes longer. A couple of countries in the region (Kenya and Uganda) are moving towards pre-arranged online visas, so don't always assume you can obtain a visa on arrival – plan ahead.

Air

It's quite easy to fly to East Africa, with flights arriving from Europe, the Middle East and elsewhere in Africa. From Australia and the USA, you'll most often have to transit through the Middle East or Johannesburg (from Australia) or Europe (from North America).

Airports & Airlines

Nairobi (Kenya) is East Africa's major air hub, and the best destination for finding special airfares. Other major gateways include Dar es Salaam and Arusha in Tanzania, and Entebbe in Uganda. There are also international airports in Kigali (Rwanda), Bujumbura (Burundi) and Zanzibar (Tanzania), and it's worth checking out cheap charter flights to Mombasa (Kenya) from Europe.

The main international airports are as follows:

Jomo Kenyatta International Airport (NBO; Map p232; ☎020-6822111, 0722205061; www.kaa.go.ke), Nairobi (Kenya)

Kilimanjaro International Airport (JRO; Map p136; ☎027-255 4252; www.kilimanjaroairport.co.tz), Arusha (Tanzania)

Julius Nyerere International Airport (DAR; ☎022-284 2402; www.taa.go.tz), Dar es Salaam (Tanzania)

Entebbe International Airport (EBB; ☎0414-353000; http://entebbe-airport.com; Entebbe) (Uganda)

Kigali International Airport (KN 5 Rd, Kanombe) (Rwanda)

Bujumbura International Airport (Burundi)

The following airlines fly to/from East Africa:

African Express Airways (www.africanexpress.co.ke) Connects Nairobi with East African and Middle Eastern destinations.

Air Mauritius (www.airmauritius.com) Mauritius to Nairobi.

CLIMATE CHANGE & TRAVEL

Every form of transport that relies on carbon-based fuel generates CO_2, the main cause of human-induced climate change. Modern travel is dependent on aeroplanes, which might use less fuel per kilometre per person than most cars but travel much greater distances. The altitude at which aircraft emit gases (including CO_2) and particles also contributes to their climate change impact. Many websites offer 'carbon calculators' that allow people to estimate the carbon emissions generated by their journey and, for those who wish to do so, to offset the impact of the greenhouse gases emitted with contributions to portfolios of climate-friendly initiatives throughout the world. Lonely Planet offsets the carbon footprint of all staff and author travel.

DEPARTURE TAX

Departure tax is included in the price of a ticket.

British Airways (www.britishairways.com) London to Nairobi, Dar es Salaam and Entebbe.

Brussels Airlines (www.brusselsairlines.com) Brussels to Bujumbura, Entebbe, Kigali and Nairobi.

Daallo Airlines (www.daallo.com) Dubai to Nairobi.

Egypt Air (www.egyptair.com.eg) Cairo to Nairobi, Dar es Salaam and Entebbe.

Emirates (www.emirates.com) Dubai to Nairobi, Dar es Salaam and Entebbe.

Ethiopian Airlines (www.ethiopianairlines.com) Vast international network to Addis Ababa, and then onward connections to Bujumbura, Dar es Salaam, Entebbe, Kigali, Kilimanjaro, Mombasa, Nairobi and Zanzibar.

Fly 540 (www.fly540.com) Juba (South Sudan) to Nairobi with connections around the region.

Kenya Airways (www.kenya-airways.com) Extensive African and wider international network to Nairobi, with onward connections to all East African capitals and Zanzibar.

KLM (www.klm.com) Amsterdam to Nairobi, Dar es Salaam, Kilimanjaro and Entebbe.

Linhas Aéreas de Moçambique (www.lam.co.mz) Maputo to Nairobi, Dar es Salaam, Kilimanjaro and Zanzibar.

Qatar Airways (www.qatarairways.com) Doha to Dar es Salaam, Entebbe and Kigali.

RwandAir (www.rwandair.com) Istanbul, Dubai, Brussels and a host of African cities to Kigali.

South African Airways (www.flysaa.com) Johannesburg to Dar es Salaam, Nairobi, Entebbe and Kigali.

Swiss International Airlines (www.swiss.com) Zurich to Dar es Salaam and Nairobi.

Tickets

- Airfares from Europe and North America to East Africa are highest in December and January, and again from June through August. They're lowest from March through May, except around the Easter holidays.
- London is the main discount airfare hub, and a good place to look for special deals, especially to Nairobi.
- When planning your trip, consider buying an open-jaw ticket, which enables you to fly into one country and out of another. This often works out more cheaply and more environmentally friendly than booking a standard return flight in and out of one city, plus a connecting regional flight.
- Charter flights are generally cheaper than scheduled flights, and are also worth considering. Some come as part of a package that includes accommodation, but most charter companies sell 'flight only' tickets.

Land

There are several possibilities for combining East Africa travels with overland travel elsewhere in Africa. For more on driving your own vehicle to the region, check out the somewhat dated *Adventure Motorcycling Handbook* (2001) by Chris Scott et al (useful especially if you're combining the Sahara and West Africa with East Africa) and *Africa by Road* (1995) by Bob Swain and Paula Snyder.

North & West Africa

For information on trans-Saharan routes, see Lonely Planet's *West Africa*, and check the website of **Chris Scott** (www.sahara-overland.com). Once through West Africa, most travellers fly from Douala (Cameroon) over the Central African Republic and Democratic Republic of the Congo (the DRC) via Addis Ababa to any of the East African capitals, from where you can continue overland.

Northeast Africa

The Nile route through northeast Africa goes from Egypt into Sudan (via Lake Nasser, and then on to Khartoum). From Khartoum, it's straightforward to make your way to Ethiopia, and then into Kenya. Note, however, that going in the other direction, obtaining Ethiopian visas in Kenya can be problematic.

There are regular flights between Juba (South Sudan) and Entebbe and even a bus service between the two countries. For all travel involving routings in Sudan and South Sudan, get an update on the security situation before setting your plans.

Southern Africa

The main gateways between southern and East Africa are Zambia and Malawi, both of which are readily reached from elsewhere in southern Africa. Once in Zambia, head to Kapiri Mposhi where you can get the Tanzania–Zambia Railway (Tazara) northeast to Mbeya (Tanzania). From Mbeya, continue by road or rail towards Dar es Salaam, and then by road towards Mombasa and Nairobi. Another route from Zambia goes to Mpulungu on the Zambian shore of Lake Tanganyika, from where you can travel by steamer to Kigoma. From Kigoma, head by rail east to Dar es Salaam or northeast by road towards Lake Victoria, Uganda and western Kenya.

From Malawi, after entering East Africa at Songwe River Bridge (at the Tanzanian border), head by bus to Mbeya and continue as outlined above.

Sea

There are no commercial ferries linking East Africa with other parts of the continent. On Lake Victoria, the main lake ferry connections to/from East Africa are between Malawi and Tanzania on Lake Nyasa, and between Zambia and Tanzania on Lake Tanganyika.

Tours

Organised tours can be low-budget affairs, where you travel in an 'overland truck' with 15 to 30 other people and some drivers/leaders, carrying tents and other equipment, buying food along the way, and cooking and eating as a group. At the other end of the spectrum are individually tailored tours, ranging in price from reasonable to very expensive.

Australia & New Zealand

African Wildlife Safaris (www.africanwildlifesafaris.com.au) Customised itineraries in Kenya, Uganda, Rwanda and Tanzania.

Classic Safari Company (www.classicsafaricompany.com.au) Upmarket customised itineraries in Kenya, Rwanda, Tanzania and Uganda, including gorilla tracking.

Peregrine Travel (www.peregrineadventures.com) Everything from overland truck tours to upmarket wildlife safaris and family safaris.

South Africa

Africa Travel Co (www.africatravelco.com) Overland tours combining eastern and southern Africa.

Wild Frontiers (www.wildfrontiers.com) A range of itineraries in Tanzania and Uganda.

UK

Abercrombie & Kent (www.abercrombiekent.co.uk) Customised luxury tours and safaris.

Africa-in-Focus (www.africa-in-focus.com) East and southern Africa overland tours and safaris.

African Initiatives (www.african-initiatives.org.uk) Fair-traded safaris in northern Tanzania.

Baobab Travel (www.baobabtravel.com) A culturally responsible operator with itineraries in Kenya and Tanzania.

Dragoman (www.dragoman.com) East Africa overland tours.

Expert Africa (www.expertafrica.com) A long-standing, experienced operator with a wide selection of itineraries in Tanzania, Kenya and Rwanda.

Nature Trek (www.naturetrek.co.uk) Respected company with a long-standing focus on wildlife and tours in Kenya, Rwanda, Tanzania and Uganda.

Responsible Travel (www.responsibletravel.com) Matches you up with ecologically and culturally responsible tour operators to plan an itinerary.

Safari Drive (www.safaridrive.com) Self-drive safaris, primarily in northern Tanzania and Kenya.

Tribes Tailormade Travel (www.tribes.co.uk) Fair-traded safaris and treks in Tanzania, Kenya, Uganda and Rwanda, including gorilla tracking.

Wildfoot Travel (www.wildfoottravel.com) Wildlife is the major focus of this UK-based operator.

USA & Canada

Abercrombie & Kent (www.abercrombiekent.com) Customised luxury tours and safaris.

Africa Adventure Company (www.africa-adventure.com) Upmarket specialist safaris in Kenya, Tanzania, Uganda and Rwanda.

African Horizons (www.africanhorizons.com) A small operator offering various packages throughout East Africa.

Deeper Africa (www.deeperafrica.com) Socially responsible, upmarket safaris in Kenya and Tanzania, and gorilla tracking in Uganda and Rwanda.

Eco-Resorts (www.eco-resorts.com) Socially responsible itineraries in Kenya, Tanzania and Rwanda.

Explorateur Voyages (www.explorateur.qc.ca) Itineraries in Kenya, Tanzania, Uganda and Rwanda.

Good Earth Tours (www.goodearthtours.com) Itineraries in Tanzania, Kenya and Uganda, with detours also to Rwanda.

International Expeditions (www.ietravel.com) Naturalist-oriented safaris in Kenya, Tanzania and Uganda.

Mountain Madness (www.mountainmadness.com) Upmarket treks on Mt Kilimanjaro, Mt Kenya, Mt Meru and the Rwenzoris.

Thomson Family Adventures (www.familyadventures.com) Family-friendly northern Tanzania safaris and Kilimanjaro treks.

Other

Access2Tanzania (www.access2tanzania.com) Customised, community-focused itineraries.

Basecamp Explorer (www.basecampkenya.com) Scandinavian-owned ecotourism operator offering comprehensive and often luxurious camping itineraries with an environmentally sustainable focus.

Hoopoe Safaris (www.hoopoe.com) Community-integrated luxury camping and lodge safaris in Tanzania.

Into Africa (www.intoafrica.co.uk) Specialises in 'fair-trade' trips providing insights into African life and directly supporting local communities.

GETTING AROUND

Air

Flying within East Africa is quite easy – Kenya Airways (www.kenya-airways.com) has the most flights connecting the region's capitals.

While air service within East Africa is relatively reliable, cancellations and delays should still be expected at any time. Always reconfirm your ticket, and allow cushion time between regional and intercontinental flights.

Airlines in East Africa

The main regional airlines that fly within East Africa include the following. In addition to these, both Kenya and Tanzania have numerous smaller companies that fly domestically within their own borders.

Air Kenya (Map p136; ☎in Kenya 020-391 6000; www.airkenya.com)

Kenya Airways (KQ; ☎22223542; www.kenya-airways.com; Blvd Lumumba)

Precision Air (☎022-219 1000, 0787 888417; www.precisionairtz.com)

RwandAir (Map p510; ☎0788177000; www.rwandair.com; Union Trade Centre, KN 4 Ave, Kigali; ⌚8am-9pm Mon-Fri, 9am-9pm Sat & Sun)

Air Passes

None of East Africa's airlines offers air passes that offer cheaper fares for regional flights.

Bicycle

Cycling can be an enjoyable, adventurous way to explore East Africa. When planning your trip, consider the following:

- Main sealed roads aren't good for cycling, as there's usually no shoulder and traffic moves dangerously fast.
- Distances are very long, often with nothing in between. Consider picking a base, and doing exploratory trips from there.
- Cycling is best well away from urban areas, in the early morning and late afternoon hours, and in the cooler, dry season between June and August.
- When calculating daily distances, plan on taking a break from the midday heat, and don't count on covering as much territory each day as you might in a northern European climate.
- Mountain bikes are best for flexibility and local terrain, and should be brought from home. While single-speed bicycles (and occasionally mountain bikes) can be rented in many towns (ask hotel staff or enquire at the local bicycle repair stand), they're only suitable for short rides.
- Other planning considerations include water (carry at least 4L), rampaging motorists (a small rear-view mirror is a worthwhile investment), sleeping (bring a tent) and punctures (thorn trees are a problem in some areas).
- Bring sufficient spares (including several spare inner tubes, a spare tyre and plenty of tube patches), and be proficient at repairs.
- Bicycles can be transported on minibuses and buses (though for express or luxury buses, you may need to make advance arrangements with the driver to stow your bike in the hold). There's also no problem or additional cost to bring your bicycle on any of the region's lake or coastal ferries. Cycling isn't permitted in national parks or wildlife reserves.
- As elsewhere in the world, don't leave your bike unattended unless it's locked, and secure all removable pieces. Taking your bike into a hotel room is generally no problem (and is a good idea).
- A recommended contact is the US-based International Bicycle Fund (www.ibike.org), a socially conscious, low-budget organisation that arranges tours in East Africa and provides information.

Boat

- On the Tanzanian section of Lake Victoria, there are passenger boats connecting Mwanza (Tanzania) with Bukoba, Ukerewe Island and various lakeside villages.
- In the Kenyan section of the lake, the only ferry transport is across the Winam Gulf between Mbita Point (near Homa Bay) and Luanda Kotieno, where matatus go to Kisumu. Small boats connect the mainland around Mbita Point with the Mfangano, Rusinga and Takawiri Islands.
- You might also find motorised canoes to Mfangano Island from Mbita Point.
- In Uganda, on Lake Victoria, small boats connect mainland villages with the Ssese Islands; there are also regular cargo boats from Kampala to Mwanza that accept passengers.
- On Lake Tanganyika, a passenger ferry connects Kigoma (Tanzania) with Mpulungu (Zambia).
- On Lake Nyasa, the main route is between Mbamba Bay and Itungi (both in Tanzania), via numerous lakeside villages. There's also a boat between Mbamba Bay and Nkhata Bay (Malawi).
- The main coastal routes are between Dar es Salaam, Zanzibar and Pemba, and the short run between the coast and the Lamu archipelago (Kenya).

Dhow Travel

With their billowing sails and graceful forms, dhows (ancient Arabic sailing vessels) have become a symbol of East Africa for adventure travellers. Yet despite their romantic reputation, the realities can be quite different. Before undertaking a longer journey, test things out with a short sunset or afternoon sail. Coastal hotels are good contacts for arranging reliable dhow travel. If you decide to give a local dhow a try, keep the following tips in mind:

- Be prepared for rough conditions. There are no facilities on board, except possibly a toilet hanging off the stern. Sailings are wind and tide dependent, and departures are often predawn.
- Journeys often take much longer than anticipated; bring extra water and sufficient food.
- Sun block, a hat and a covering are essential, as is waterproofing for your luggage and a rain jacket.

➡ Boats capsize and people are killed each year. Avoid overloaded boats and don't set sail in bad weather.

➡ Travel with the winds, which blow from south to north from approximately July to September and north to south from approximately November to late February. Note that what Westerners refer to as dhows are called either *jahazi* or *mashua* by most Swahili speakers. *Jahazi* are large, lateen-sailed boats. *Mashua* are smaller, and often with proportionately wider hulls and a motor. The *dau* has a sloped stem and stern. On lakes and inland waterways, the *mtumbwi* (dugout canoe) is in common use. Coastal areas, especially Zanzibar's east-coast beaches, are good places to see *ngalawa* (outrigger canoes).

Bus

Buses cover most routes and are generally safer and more reliable than minibuses, but where there's a train (eg between Nairobi and Mombasa), take it.

➡ **Kenya & Tanzania** You sometimes have the choice of going by 'luxury' or 'ordinary' bus. Luxury buses are more comfortable and more expensive, although not always quicker than ordinary buses. Some also have the dubious advantage of a video system, usually playing bad movies at full volume for the entire trip.

➡ **Uganda** Has mostly ordinary buses, although there are luxury buses on some cross-border routes.

➡ **Rwanda & Burundi** There are few full-size buses; especially in Burundi, minibuses are the rule.

BUS SAFETY

Public transport is a fine (and often the only) choice for getting around East Africa, but be savvy when using local buses and minibuses.

➡ Never accept food and drink from fellow passengers, even if it appears to be sealed.

➡ Avoid night travel, especially on long-distance routes such as Nairobi–Kampala.

➡ Be especially wary of pickpockets on minibuses, and when boarding.

➡ At bus stations, keep your luggage compact and your valuables well concealed.

➡ Road safety is a major issue. Get advice locally about the best (safest) bus lines, and stick to established lines.

➡ In minibuses in particular, under no circumstances should you sit in the 'death seat' next to the driver. Play it safe and sit in the middle seats away from the window.

Car & Motorcycle

Touring East Africa by car or motorcycle is quite feasible, although vehicle rental rates can be expensive.

Throughout East Africa, main roads are sealed and in reasonable states of repair. In rural areas, they range from decent to terrible, especially in the wet season when many secondary routes become impassable. Trips in remote areas require 4WD; motorcycles generally aren't permitted in national parks.

Whether you drive your own or a rental vehicle, expect stops at checkpoints where police and border officials will ask to see your driving licence, insurance paperwork and vehicle papers.

Bring Your Own Vehicle

➡ To bring your own vehicle into East Africa, you'll need to arrange a *carnet de passage*. This document allows you to take a vehicle duty-free into a country where duties would normally be payable. It guarantees that if a vehicle is taken into a country but not exported, the organisation that issued the *carnet* will accept responsibility for payment of import duties (generally between 100% and 150% of the new value of the vehicle). The *carnet* should also specify any expensive spare parts that you'll be carrying.

➡ To get a *carnet*, contact your national motoring organisation at home, which will give you an indemnity form for completion by either a bank or an insurance company. Once you have deposited a bond with a bank or paid an insurance premium, the motoring organisation will issue the *carnet*. The cost of the *carnet* itself is minimal; allow at least a week to complete the process.

➡ For longer trips, in addition to a *carnet* and mechanical knowledge, bring along a good collection of spares.

Driving Licences

If you're taking your own vehicle or considering hiring one in East Africa, arrange an International Driving Permit (IDP) before leaving home. They're available at minimal cost through your national motoring organisation.

Fuel & Spare Parts

➡ Fuel costs in the region average US$1.50 to US$1.75 per litre of petrol or diesel. Filling and repair stations are readily available in major towns but scarce elsewhere. In many areas, diesel is easier to find than petrol.

- Top your tank up at every opportunity and carry basic spares. For travel in remote areas and in national parks, also carry jerry cans with extra fuel.
- Petrol sold on the roadside is unreliable, as it's often diluted with water or kerosene. Diluting is also a common problem at established petrol stations in much of the region, so ask around locally before filling up.

Hire

Car, 4WD and motorcycle hire is expensive throughout East Africa, averaging US$100 to US$200 per day for a 4WD. Few agencies offer unlimited kilometres, and many require that you take a chauffeur (which is a good idea anyway). For self-drive rentals, you'll need a driving licence and often also an International Driving Permit. If you'll be crossing any borders, you'll need to arrange the necessary paperwork with the hire agency in advance.

Insurance

Throughout the region, liability insurance must generally be bought at the border upon entry. While cost and quality vary, in many cases you may find that you are effectively travelling uninsured, as there's often no way to collect on the insurance. With vehicle rentals, even if you're covered from other sources, it's recommended to take the full coverage offered by hire companies.

Road Rules

- Drive on the left: Tanzania, Kenya and Uganda.
- Drive on the right: Rwanda and Burundi.
- Roundabouts: traffic already in the roundabout has the right of way.

Road Conditions & Hazards

- Night-time road travel isn't recommended anywhere; if you must drive at night, be alert for stopped vehicles in the roadway without lights or hazard warnings.
- If you're not used to driving in Africa, watch for pedestrians, children and animals, as well as for oncoming vehicles on the wrong side of the road. Especially in rural areas, remember that many people have never driven themselves and are not aware of necessary braking distances and similar concepts; moderate your speed accordingly.
- Tree branches on the road are the local version of flares or hazard lights and mean there's a stopped vehicle, crater-sized pothole or similar calamity ahead.
- Passing (including on curves or other areas with poor visibility) is common practice and a frequent cause of accidents.

Hitching

Hitching is never entirely safe, and we don't recommend it. Travellers who hitch should understand that they are taking a small but potentially serious risk. If you do hitch, you'll be safer doing so in pairs and letting someone know of your plans.

Hitching may be your only option in remote areas, although it's rare that you'll get a free ride unless you're lucky enough to be offered a lift by resident expats, well-off locals or aid workers; even then, at least offer to make a contribution for petrol on longer journeys, or to pick up a meal tab. To flag down a vehicle, hold out your hand at about waist level and wave it up and down, with the palm to the ground; the common Western gesture of holding out your thumb isn't used.

A word of warning about taking lifts in private cars: smuggling across borders is common practice, and if whatever is being smuggled is found, you may be arrested even though you knew nothing about it. Most travellers manage to convince police that they were merely hitching a ride (passport stamps are a good indication of this), but the convincing can take a long time.

Local Transport

Minibus

- Most East Africans rely heavily on minibuses for transport. They're called matatus in Kenya, dalla-dallas in Tanzania, and taxis or matatus in Uganda.
- Except in Rwanda and Burundi, minibuses are invariably packed to bursting point, and this – combined with excessive speed, poor maintenance and driver recklessness – means that they're not the safest way of getting around. In fact, they can be downright dangerous, and newspaper reports of matatu and dalla-dalla crashes are a regular feature of life here. In Rwanda and Burundi, travelling in minibuses is generally safer.
- If you have a large backpack, think twice about boarding, especially at rush hour, when it will make the already crowded conditions even more uncomfortable for others.

Taxi

In Kenya, northern Tanzania and Uganda, shared taxis operate on some routes. These officially take between five and nine passengers, depending on size, leave when full and are usually faster, though more expensive, than bus travel. They're marginally more comfortable than minibuses but have their share of accidents too.

Private taxis for hire are found in all major towns. Use only reliable hotel taxis or those from established ranks, and avoid freelancers (known in Swahili-speaking areas as 'taxi bubu').

Motorcycle taxis (*boda-boda* in Kenya, Tanzania and Uganda; *moto-taxi* in Rwanda, Burundi and the DRC) are also widely available, at a fraction of the cost of standard vehicle taxis.

Truck

➡ In remote areas, trucks may be the only form of transport, and they're invariably the cheapest. For most regular runs there will be a 'fare', which is more or less fixed and is what the locals pay. It's usually equivalent to, or a bit less than, the bus fare for the same route. For a place in the cab, expect to pay about twice what it costs to travel on top of the load.

➡ Many truck lifts are arranged the night before departure at the 'truck park' – a compound or dust patch that you'll find in most towns. Ask around for a truck that's going your way, and be prepared to wait, especially on remote routes where there may be trucks leaving only once or twice a week. For longer trips, ask what to do about food and drink, and bring plenty of snacks and extra drinking water – enough for yourself and to share.

Train

➡ The main passenger lines are the recently upgraded Nairobi–Mombasa Madaraka Express route (Kenya), the Tazara 'express' line from Dar es Salaam to Mbeya (Tanzania), and the meandering Central line connecting Dar es Salaam with Kigoma (Tanzania).

➡ First class costs about double what the bus would cost, but is well worth it for the additional comfort. Second class is reasonably comfortable, but the savings over 1st class are marginal. Economy-class travel is cheap, crowded and uncomfortable. There are no assigned seats, and for long trips you'll probably wind up sitting and sleeping on the floor. Reservations for 1st class are best made as early as possible, although sometimes you'll get lucky and be able to book a cabin on the day of travel.

➡ In all classes, keep an eye on your luggage, especially at stops. In 1st and 2nd class, make sure the window is jammed shut at night to avoid the possibility of someone entering when the train stops (there's usually a piece of wood provided for this), and keep your cabin door shut.

➡ Food and drink (mainly soft drinks) are available on trains and from station vendors, but bring extra food and water. Have plenty of small change handy.

Health

If you stay up to date with your vaccinations and take basic preventive measures, you'd be unlucky to succumb to most of the health hazards covered here. The exception is malaria, which is a real risk throughout much of East Africa.

BEFORE YOU GO

Predeparture planning will save you trouble later.

- Get a check-up from your dentist and doctor if you have any regular medication or chronic illness (eg high blood pressure or asthma).
- Organise spare contact lenses and glasses (and take your optical prescription with you).
- Get a first-aid and medical kit together and arrange necessary vaccinations.
- Get an International Certificate of Vaccination ('yellow booklet') listing vaccinations you have received.
- Carry medications in their original (labelled) containers. If carrying syringes or needles, have a physician's letter documenting their medical necessity.

Health Insurance

Check whether your insurance plan will make payments directly to providers or reimburse you later for overseas health expenditures. Most doctors in East Africa expect cash payment.

Ensure that your travel insurance will cover any emergency transport required to get you at least as far as Nairobi (Kenya), or, preferably, home, by air and with a medical attendant if necessary. Consider temporary membership with the **African Medical & Research Foundation** (AMREF; ☎254-20-6002299, Nairobi emergency lines 254-20-315454/5; www.amref.org), which offers air evacuation in medical emergencies for most of East Africa.

IN EAST AFRICA

Availability & Cost of Health Care

Health care services can be excellent, especially in major cities, but as a general rule privately run hospitals and clinics offer better care than state-run hospitals. However, private hospitals can be expensive – a major reason why we recommend taking out travel insurance before travelling.

Infectious Diseases

With basic preventive measures, it's unlikely that you'll succumb to any of the infectious diseases present in East Africa.

Bilharzia (Schistosomiasis)

This disease is spread by flukes (minute worms) that are carried by a species of freshwater snail. Don't paddle or swim in any freshwater lakes or slow-running rivers anywhere in East Africa unless you have reliable confirmation that they are bilharzia-free. A blood test can detect antibodies if you might have been exposed, and treatment is possible in specialist travel clinics. If not treated the infection can cause kidney failure or permanent bowel damage.

Cholera

Cholera is spread via contaminated drinking water. The main symptom is profuse watery diarrhoea, which causes debilitation if fluids are not replaced quickly. An oral cholera vaccine is available but is not particularly effective. Pay close attention to good drinking water and avoid potentially contaminated food. Treatment is by fluid replacement (orally or via a drip), but sometimes antibiotics are needed. Self-treatment is not advised.

Dengue Fever

Mini-epidemics of this mosquito-borne disease crop up with some regularity in Tanzania, notably in Dar es Salaam. Symptoms include high fever, severe headache and body ache (dengue used

RECOMMENDED VACCINATIONS

The World Health Organization (www.who.int/en) recommends that all travellers be covered for diphtheria, tetanus, measles, mumps, rubella and polio, as well as for hepatitis B, regardless of their destination.

According to the Centers for Disease Control & Prevention (www.cdc.gov), the following vaccinations are recommended for East Africa: hepatitis A, hepatitis B, meningococcal meningitis, rabies and typhoid, and boosters for tetanus, diphtheria, polio and measles.

It is also advisable to be vaccinated against yellow fever (required for all visitors to Rwanda and the DRC). If travelling overland between Kenya and Tanzania, for example, you will be asked for proof of yellow fever vaccination.

to be known as breakbone fever). Some people develop a rash and experience diarrhoea. There is no vaccine, only prevention. The dengue-carrying *Aedes aegypti* mosquito is active day and night, so use DEET-mosquito repellent periodically throughout the day. See a doctor to be diagnosed and monitored (dengue testing is available in Dar es Salaam). There is no specific treatment, just rest and paracetamol – do not take aspirin as it increases the likelihood of haemorrhaging. Severe dengue is a potentially fatal complication.

Diptheria

Found throughout East Africa, diphtheria is spread through close respiratory contact. Vaccination is recommended for those likely to be in close contact with the local population in infected areas and is more important for long stays than for short-term trips.

Filariasis

Tiny worms migrating in the lymphatic system cause filariasis. The bite from an infected mosquito spreads the infection. Symptoms include localised itching and swelling of the legs and/or genitalia. Treatment is available.

Hepatitis A

Hepatitis A is spread through contaminated food (particularly shellfish) and water. It causes jaundice, and although rarely fatal, it can cause prolonged lethargy and delayed recovery. If you've had hepatitis A, don't drink alcohol for up to six months afterwards; once you've recovered, there won't be long-term problems. Early symptoms include dark urine and a yellow colour to the whites of the eyes, sometimes with fever and abdominal pain. Hepatitis A vaccine (Avaxim, VAQTA, Havrix) gives protection for up to a year; a booster after a year gives 10-year protection. Hepatitis A and typhoid vaccines can also be given as a single-dose vaccine (hepatyrix or viatim).

Hepatitis B

Hepatitis B is spread through infected blood, contaminated needles and sexual intercourse. It can also be spread from an infected mother to the baby during childbirth. It affects the liver, causing jaundice and occasionally liver failure. Most people recover completely, but some might be chronic carriers of the virus, which could lead eventually to cirrhosis or liver cancer. Those visiting high-risk areas for long periods or those with increased social or occupational risk should be immunised.

HIV

Human immunodeficiency virus (HIV), the virus that causes acquired immune deficiency syndrome (AIDS), is an enormous problem throughout East Africa. It's spread through infected blood and blood products, by sexual intercourse with an infected partner and from an infected mother to her baby during childbirth and breastfeeding. It can be spread through 'blood to blood' contact, such as with contaminated instruments during medical, dental, acupuncture and other body-piercing procedures, and through sharing used intravenous needles. If you think you might have been infected with HIV, a blood test is necessary.

Malaria

Malaria is endemic throughout East Africa (except at altitudes higher than 2000m, where risk of transmission is low). The disease is caused by a parasite in the bloodstream spread via the bite of the female *Anopheles* mosquito. There are several types of malaria, with falciparum malaria the most dangerous type and the predominant form in the region. Infection rates vary with climate and season. Rates are higher during the rainy season, but the risk exists year-round. It is extremely important to take preventive measures, even just for short visits.

There is no vaccination against malaria (yet). However, several different drugs are used for prevention with new ones in the pipeline. Up-to-date advice from a travel-health clinic is essential. The pattern of drug-resistant malaria changes rapidly, so what was advised several years ago might no longer be current.

ANTIMALARIAL A TO D

A – Awareness of the risk. No medication is totally effective, but protection of up to 95% is achievable with most drugs, as long as other measures have been taken.

B – Bites: avoid at all costs. Sleep in a screened room, use mosquito spray or coils and sleep under a permethrin-impregnated net at night. Cover up at night with long trousers and long sleeves, preferably with permethrin-treated clothing. Apply repellent to all areas of exposed skin in the evenings.

C – Chemical prevention (ie antimalarial drugs) is usually needed in malarial areas. Expert advice is needed as resistance patterns change and new drugs are in development. Most antimalarial drugs need to be started at least a week in advance and continued for four weeks after the last exposure to malaria.

D – Diagnosis. If you have a fever or flu-like illness within a year of travel to a malarial area, malaria is a possibility; immediate medical attention is necessary.

SYMPTOMS

Malaria's early stages include headaches, fevers, generalised aches and pains, and malaise, which could be mistaken for flu. Other symptoms can include abdominal pain, diarrhoea and a cough. Anyone who develops a fever while in East Africa or within two weeks after departure should assume malarial infection until blood tests prove negative, even if you have been taking antimalarial medication. If not treated, the next stage could develop within 24 hours, particularly if falciparum malaria is the parasite: jaundice, then reduced consciousness and coma (also known as cerebral malaria) followed by death. Treatment in hospital is essential; the death rate might still be as high as 10% even in the best intensive-care facilities.

SIDE EFFECTS & RISKS

Many travellers are under the impression that malaria is a mild illness, that treatment is always easy and successful and that taking antimalarial drugs causes more illness through side effects than actually getting malaria. Unfortunately, this is not true. Side effects of the medication depend on the drug taken. Doxycycline can cause heartburn and indigestion; mefloquine (Lariam) can cause anxiety attacks, insomnia and nightmares and (rarely) severe psychiatric disorders; chloroquine can cause nausea and hair loss; and proguanil can cause mouth ulcers. These side effects are not universal and can be minimised by taking medication correctly, eg with food. Also, some people should not take a particular antimalarial drug – for example, people with epilepsy should avoid mefloquine, and doxycycline should not be taken by pregnant women or children younger than 12.

If you decide against taking antimalarial drugs, you must understand the risks and be obsessive about avoiding mosquito bites. Use nets and insect repellent, and report any fever or flu-like symptoms to a doctor as soon as possible. Malaria in pregnancy frequently results in miscarriage or premature labour and the risks to both mother and foetus during pregnancy are considerable. Travel in East Africa when pregnant should be carefully considered.

STAND-BY TREATMENT

Carrying emergency stand-by treatment is essential for travel in remote areas. Seek your doctor's advice as to recommended medicines and dosages. However, this should be viewed as emergency treatment only and not as routine self-medication, and should only be used if you will be far from medical facilities and have been advised about the symptoms of malaria and how to use the medication. If you resort to emergency self-treatment, seek medical advice as soon as possible to confirm whether the treatment has been successful. In particular, you want to avoid contracting cerebral malaria, which can be fatal within 24 hours. Self-diagnostic kits, which can identify malaria in the blood from a finger prick, are available in the West and are worth buying.

Meningococcal Meningitis

Meningococcal infection is spread through close respiratory contact and is most likely contracted in crowded situations. Infection is uncommon in travellers. Vaccination is particularly recommended for long stays and is especially important towards the end of the dry season. Symptoms include fever, severe headache, neck stiffness and a red rash. Immediate medical treatment is necessary.

The ACWY vaccine is recommended for all travellers in sub-Saharan Africa. This vaccine is different from the meningococcal meningitis C vaccine given to children and adolescents in some countries; it is safe to be given both types of vaccine.

Rabies

Rabies is spread by receiving the bites or licks of an infected animal on broken skin. It is always fatal once the clinical symptoms start (which might be months after an infected bite), so postbite vaccination should be given as soon as possible. Postbite vaccination (whether or not you've been vaccinated before the bite) prevents the virus from spreading to the central nervous system. Animal handlers should be vaccinated, as should those travelling to remote areas where a reliable source of postbite vaccine is not available. Three preventive injections are needed over a month. If you haven't been vaccinated you will need a course of five injections starting 24 hours or as soon as possible after being exposed. If you have been vaccinated, you will need fewer postbite injections, and have more time to seek medical help.

Rift Valley Fever

This fever is spread occasionally via mosquito bites. The symptoms are of a fever and flu-like illness; and the good news is it's rarely fatal.

Trypanosomiasis (Sleeping Sickness)

Spread via the bite of the tsetse fly, it causes headache, fever and eventually coma. If you have headache and fever symptoms and have negative malaria tests, have yourself evaluated by a reputable clinic, where you should also be able to obtain treatment.

Tuberculosis (TB)

TB is spread through close respiratory contact and occasionally through infected milk or milk products. The BCG vaccine is recommended for those likely to be mixing closely with the local population, although it only provides moderate protection. It's more important for long stays than for short-term visits. Inoculation with the BCG vaccine is not available in all countries, but it is given routinely to many children in developing nations. It is a live vaccine and should not be given to pregnant women or immunocompromised individuals.

TB can be asymptomatic, only being picked up on a routine chest X-ray. Alternatively, it can cause a cough, weight loss or fever, months or even years after exposure.

Typhoid

This is spread through food or water contaminated by infected human faeces. The first symptom is usually a fever or a pink rash on the abdomen. Sometimes septicaemia (blood poisoning) can occur. A typhoid vaccine (typhim Vi, typherix) will give protection for three years. In some countries, the oral vaccine Vivotif is also available. Antibiotics are usually given as treatment, and death is rare unless septicaemia occurs.

Yellow Fever

Tanzania, Kenya, Uganda and Burundi no longer officially require you to carry a certificate of yellow fever vaccination unless you're arriving from an infected area (which includes from anywhere in East Africa). However, it's still sometimes asked for at some borders, and is a requirement in some neighbouring countries, including Rwanda. The vaccine is recommended for most visitors to Africa by the Centers for Disease Control & Prevention (www.cdc.gov). Also, there is always the possibility that a traveller without a legally required, up-to-date certificate will be vaccinated and detained in isolation at the port of arrival for up to 10 days, or possibly even repatriated.

Yellow fever is spread by infected mosquitoes. Symptoms range from a flu-like illness to severe hepatitis (liver inflammation), jaundice and death. The yellow fever vaccination must be given at a designated clinic and is valid for 10 years. It is a live vaccine and must not be given to immunocompromised or pregnant travellers.

Traveller's Diarrhoea

Diarrhoea is the most common travel-related illness. Sometimes dietary changes, such as increased spices or oils, are the cause. To help prevent diarrhoea: avoid tap water unless you're sure it's safe to drink; only eat fresh fruits or vegetables if cooked or peeled; and be wary of dairy products that might contain unpasteurised milk. Although freshly cooked food can often be a safe option, plates or serving utensils might be dirty, so be selective when eating food from street vendors (make sure that cooked food is piping hot all the way through).

If you develop diarrhoea, be sure to drink plenty of fluids, preferably lots of an oral rehydration solution containing water, and some salt and sugar. A few loose stools don't require treatment, but if you start having more than four or five stools a day, you should start taking an antibiotic (usually a quinoline drug, such as ciprofloxacin or norfloxacin) and an antidiarrhoeal agent (such as loperamide) if you are not within easy reach of a toilet. If diarrhoea is bloody, persists for more than 72 hours or is accompanied by fever, shaking chills or severe abdominal pain, you should seek medical attention.

Amoebic Dysentry

Contracted by consuming contaminated food and water, amoebic dysentery causes blood and mucus in the faeces. It can be relatively mild and tends to come on gradually, but seek medical advice if you think you have the illness, as it won't clear up without treatment (which is with specific antibiotics).

Giardiasis

This, like amoebic dysentery, is also caused by ingesting contaminated food or water. The illness usually appears a week or more after you have been exposed to the offending parasite. Giardiasis might cause only a short-lived bout of typical traveller's diarrhoea, but it can also cause persistent diarrhoea. Ideally, seek medical advice if you suspect you have giardiasis, but if you're in a remote area you could start a course of antibiotics, with medical follow-up when feasible.

Environmental Hazards

Altitude Sickness

The lack of oxygen at high altitudes (over 2500m) affects most people to some extent. Symptoms of Acute Mountain Sickness (AMS) usually develop in the first 24 hours at altitude, but may be delayed up to three weeks. Mild symptoms are headache, lethargy, dizziness, difficulty sleeping and loss of appetite. Severe symptoms are breathlessness, a dry, irritated cough (followed by the production of pink, frothy sputum), severe headache, lack of coordination, confusion, vomiting, irrational behaviour, drowsiness and unconsciousness. There's no rule as to what is too high: AMS can be fatal at 3000m, but 3500m to 4500m is the usual range when it can cause problems. *Symptoms should never be ignored;* trekkers die every year on East Africa's mountains, notably Mt Kilimanjaro.

Treat mild symptoms by resting at the same altitude until you have recovered, usually a day or two. Paracetamol or aspirin can be taken for headaches. If symptoms persist or grow worse, however, immediate descent is necessary; even 500m can help. Drug treatments should never be used to avoid descent or to enable further ascent. Diamox (acetazolamide) reduces the headache of AMS and helps the body acclimatise to the lack of oxygen. It is only available on prescription.

Suggestions for preventing AMS:

➡ Ascend slowly. On Mt Kilimanjaro, this means choosing one of the longer routes (eg Machame) that allow for a more gradual ascent. On Mt Kenya, it means spending at least three nights on the ascent.

➡ Sleep at a lower altitude than the greatest height reached during the day if possible ('climb high, sleep low').

➡ Drink extra fluids. Monitor hydration by ensuring that urine is clear and plentiful.

➡ Eat light, high-carbohydrate meals for more energy.

➡ Avoid alcohol, sedatives and tobacco.

Heat Exhaustion

This condition occurs following heavy sweating and excessive fluid loss with inadequate replacement of fluids and salt, and is particularly common in hot climates when taking unaccustomed exercise before full acclimatisation. Symptoms include headache, dizziness and tiredness. Dehydration is already happening by the time you feel thirsty – aim to drink sufficient water to produce pale, diluted urine. Self-treatment requires fluid replacement with water and/or fruit juice, and cooling by cold water and fans. Treatment of the salt-loss component consists of consuming salty fluids, as in soup, and adding a little more table salt to foods than usual.

TAP WATER

Don't drink tap water in East Africa unless it has been boiled, filtered or chemically disinfected (such as with iodine tablets). Never drink from streams, rivers and lakes. Also avoid drinking from pumps and wells; some do bring pure water to the surface, but the presence of animals can contaminate supplies. With bottled water, check that the bottles are properly sealed, and haven't just been refilled with ordinary tap water.

Insect Bites & Stings

Mosquitoes might not always carry malaria or dengue fever, but they (and other insects) can cause irritation and infected bites. To avoid these, take the same precautions as you would for avoiding malaria. Use DEET-based insect repellents. Excellent clothing treatments are also available, and mosquitoes that land on the treated clothing will die.

Bee and wasp stings cause real problems only to those who have a severe allergy to the stings (anaphylaxis). If you are one of these people, carry an 'epipen' – an adrenaline (epinephrine) injection, which you can give yourself. This could save your life.

Scorpions are frequently found in arid or dry climates. They can cause a painful sting that is sometimes life threatening. If stung by a scorpion, seek immediate medical assistance.

Bed bugs are often found in hostels and cheap hotels. They lead to very itchy, lumpy bites. Spraying the mattress with crawling insect killer after changing bedding will get rid of them.

Scabies is also frequently found in cheap accommodation. These tiny mites live in the skin, particularly between the fingers. They cause an intensely itchy rash. The itch is easily treated with malathion and permethrin lotion from a pharmacy; other members of the household also need treatment to avoid spreading scabies, even if they do not show any symptoms.

TSETSE FLIES

Tsetse flies can be unwelcome safari companions in some areas, delivering painful, swelling bites. To minimise the nuisance, wear thick, long-sleeved shirts and trousers in khaki or other drab shades, and avoid bright, contrasting and very dark clothing. The flies are also attracted by heat (eg the heat of a running car motor), so if you're idling, keep the windows rolled up.

Snake Bites

Avoid getting bitten! Do not walk barefoot, or stick your hand into holes or cracks. However, 50% of those bitten by venomous snakes are not actually injected with poison (envenomed). If you are bitten by a snake, do not panic. Immobilise the bitten limb with a splint (such as a stick) and apply a bandage over the site, with firm pressure, similar to bandaging a sprain. Do not apply a tourniquet, or cut or suck the bite. Get medical help as soon as possible so antivenom can be given if needed. Try to note the snake's appearance to help in treatment.

Language

SWAHILI

Swahili, the national language of Tanzania and Kenya, is also one of the most widely spoken African languages and the key language of communication in the East African region. Although the number of speakers of Swahili throughout East Africa is estimated to be well over 50 million, it's the mother tongue of only about 5 million people, and is predominantly used as a second language or a lingua franca by speakers of other African languages. Swahili belongs to the Bantu group of languages from the Niger-Congo family and can be traced back to the first millenium AD. It's hardly surprising that in an area as vast as East Africa many different dialects of Swahili can be found, but you'll be understood if you stick to the standard coastal form, as used in this book.

Most sounds in Swahili have equivalents in English. In our coloured pronunciation guides, ay should be read as in 'say', oh as the 'o' in 'role', dh as the 'th' in 'this' and th as in 'thing'. Note also that the sound ng can be found at the start of words in Swahili, and that Swahili speakers make only a slight distinction between r and l – instead of the hard 'r', try pronouncing a light 'd'. The stressed syllables are indicated with italics.

Basics

Jambo is a pidgin Swahili word, used to greet tourists who are presumed not to understand the language. If people assume you can speak a little Swahili, they might use the following greetings:

WANT MORE?

For in-depth language information and handy phrases, check out Lonely Planet's *Swahili Phrasebook* or *Africa Phrasebook*. You'll find them at **shop.lonelyplanet.com**.

Hello. (general)	*Habari?*	ha·*ba*·ree
Hello. (respectful)	*Shikamoo.*	shee·ka·*moh*
Goodbye.	*Tutaonana.*	too·ta·oh·*na*·na
Good ...	*Habari za ...?*	ha·*ba*·ree za ...
morning	*asubuhi*	a·soo·*boo*·hee
afternoon	*mchana*	m·*cha*·na
evening	*jioni*	jee·*oh*·nee
Yes.	*Ndiyo.*	n·*dee*·yoh
No.	*Hapana.*	ha·*pa*·na
Please.	*Tafadhali.*	ta·fa·*dha*·lee
Thank you (very much).	*Asante (sana).*	a·*san*·tay (*sa*·na)
You're welcome.	*Karibu.*	ka·*ree*·boo
Excuse me.	*Samahani.*	sa·ma·*ha*·nee
Sorry.	*Pole.*	*poh*·lay

How are you?
Habari? ha·*ba*·ree

I'm fine.
Nzuri./Salama./Safi. n·*zoo*·ree/sa·*la*·ma/*sa*·fee

If things are just OK, add *tu* too (only) after any of the above replies. If things are really good, add *sana sa*·na (very) or *kabisa* ka·*bee*·sa (totally) instead of *tu*.

What's your name?
Jina lako nani? jee·na *la*·koh *na*·nee

My name is ...
Jina langu ni ... jee·na *lan*·goo nee ...

Do you speak English?
Unasema Kiingereza? oo·na·*say*·ma kee·een·gay·*ray*·za

I don't understand.
Sielewi. see·ay·*lay*·wee

Accommodation

Where's a ...?	*... iko wapi?*	... ee·koh *wa*·pee
campsite	*Uwanja wa kambi*	oo·*wan*·ja wa *kam*·bee
guesthouse	*Gesti*	*gay*·stee
hotel	*Hoteli*	hoh·*tay*·lee
youth hostel	*Hosteli ya vijana*	hoh·*stay*·lee ya vee·*ja*·na

Do you have a ... room?	*Kuna chumba kwa ...?*	koo·na *choom*·ba kwa ...
double (one bed)	*watu wawili, kitanda kimoja*	*wa*·too wa·*wee*·lee kee·*tan*·da kee·*moh*·ja
single	*mtu mmoja*	*m*·too m·*moh*·ja
twin (two beds)	*watu wawili, vitanda viwili*	*wa*·too wa·*wee*·lee vee·*tan*·da vee·*wee*·lee

How much is it per ...?	*Ni bei gani kwa ...?*	nee bay *ga*·ne kwa ...
day	*siku*	*see*·koo
person	*mtu*	*m*·too
bathroom	*bafuni*	ba·*foo*·nee
key	*ufunguo*	oo·foon·*goo*·oh
toilet	*choo*	choh
window	*dirisha*	dee·*ree*·sha

Directions

Where's the ...?
... iko wapi? ... ee·koh *wa*·pee

What's the address?
Anwani ni nini? an·*wa*·nee nee *nee*·nee

How do I get there?
Nifikaje? nee·fee·*ka*·jay

How far is it?
Ni umbali gani? nee oom·*ba*·lee *ga*·nee

Can you show me (on the map)?
Unaweza kunionyesha (katika ramani)? oo·na·*way*·za koo·nee·oh·*nyay*·sha (ka·*tee*·ka ra·*ma*·nee)

It's ...	*Iko ...*	ee·koh ...
behind ...	*nyuma ya ...*	*nyoo*·ma ya ...
in front of ...	*mbele ya ...*	m·*bay*·lay ya ...
near ...	*karibu na ...*	ka·*ree*·boo na ...
next to ...	*jirani ya ...*	jee·*ra*·nee ya ...
on the corner	*pembeni*	paym·*bay*·nee
opposite ...	*ng'ambo ya ...*	ng·*am*·boh ya ...
straight ahead	*moja kwa moja*	*moh*·ja kwa *moh*·ja

KEY PATTERNS

To get by in Swahili, mix and match these simple patterns with words of your choice:

When's (the next bus)?
(Basi ijayo) itaondoka lini? (*ba*·see ee·*ja*·yoh) ee·ta·ohn·*doh*·ka *lee*·nee

Where's (the station)?
(Stesheni) iko wapi? (stay·*shay*·nee) ee·koh *wa*·pee

How much is (a room)?
(Chumba) ni bei gani? (choom·ba) nee bay ga·nee

I'm looking for (a hotel).
Natafuta (hoteli). na·ta·foo·ta (hoh·tay·lee)

Do you have (a map)?
Una (ramani)? oo·na (ra·ma·nee)

Please bring (the bill).
Lete (bili). *lay*·tay (bee·lee)

I'd like (the menu).
Nataka (menyu). na·*ta*·ka (*may*·nyoo)

I have (a reservation).
Nina (buking). *nee*·na (*boo*·keeng)

Turn ...	*Geuza ...*	gay·*oo*·za ...
at the corner	*kwenye kona*	*kway*·nyay *koh*·na
at the traffic lights	*kwenye taa za barabarani*	*kway*·nyay ta za ba·ra·ba·*ra*·nee
left	*kushoto*	koo·*shoh*·toh
right	*kulia*	koo·*lee*·a

Eating & Drinking

I'd like to reserve a table for ...	*Nataka kuhifadhi meza kwa ...*	na·*ta*·ka koo·hee·*fa*·dhee *may*·za kwa ...
(two) people	*watu (wawili)*	*wa*·too (wa·*wee*·lee)
(eight) o'clock	*saa (mbili)*	sa (m·*bee*·lee)

I'd like the menu.
Naomba menyu. na·*ohm*·ba *may*·nyoo

What would you recommend?
Chakula gani ni kizuri? cha·*koo*·la *ga*·nee nee kee·*zoo*·ree

Do you have vegetarian food?
Mna chakula bila nyama? m·na cha·*koo*·la *bee*·la *nya*·ma

I'll have that.
Nataka hicho. na·*ta*·ka *hee*·choh

Cheers!
Heri! hay·ree

That was delicious!
Chakula kitamu sana! cha·koo·la kee·ta·moo sa·na

Please bring the bill.
Lete bili. lay·tay bee·lee

I don't eat ...	*Sili ...*	see·lee ...
butter	*siagi*	see·a·gee
eggs	*mayai*	ma·ya·ee
red meat	*nyama*	nya·ma

beer	*bia*	bee·a
bottle	*chupa*	choo·pa
breakfast	*chai ya asubuhi*	cha·ee ya a·soo·boo·hee
coffee	*kahawa*	ka·ha·wa
cold	*baridi*	ba·ree·dee
dinner	*chakula cha jioni*	cha·koo·la cha jee·oh·nee
fish	*samaki*	sa·ma·kee
fork	*uma*	oo·ma
fruit	*tunda*	toon·da
glass	*glesi*	glay·see
hot	*joto*	joh·toh
juice	*jusi*	joo·see
knife	*kisu*	kee·soo
lunch	*chakula cha mchana*	cha·koo·la cha m·cha·na
market	*soko*	soh·koh
meat	*nyama*	nya·ma
plate	*sahani*	sa·ha·nee
restaurant	*mgahawa*	m·ga·ha·wa
spoon	*kijiko*	kee·jee·koh
tea	*chai*	cha·ee
vegetable	*mboga*	m·boh·ga
water	*maji*	ma·jee
wine	*mvinyo*	m·vee·nyoh

SIGNS

Mahali Pa Kuingia	Entrance
Mahali Pa Kutoka	Exit
Imefunguliwa	Open
Imefungwa	Closed
Maelezo	Information
Ni Marufuku	Prohibited
Choo/Msalani	Toilets
Wanaume	Men
Wanawake	Women

Emergencies

Help!	*Saidia!*	sa·ee·dee·a
Go away!	*Toka!*	toh·ka

I'm lost.
Nimejipotea. nee·may·jee·poh·tay·a

Call the police.
Waite polisi. wa·ee·tay poh·lee·see

Call a doctor.
Mwite daktari. m·wee·tay dak·ta·ree

I'm sick.
Mimi ni mgonjwa. mee·mee nee m·gohn·jwa

It hurts here.
Inauma hapa. ee·na·oo·ma ha·pa

I'm allergic to (antibiotics).
Nina mzio wa (viuavijasumu). nee·na m·zee·oh wa (vee·oo·a·vee·ja·soo·moo)

Where's the toilet?
Choo kiko wapi? choh kee·koh wa·pee

Shopping & Services

I'd like to buy ...
Nataka kununua ... na·ta·ka koo·noo·noo·a ...

I'm just looking.
Naangalia tu. na·an·ga·lee·a too

Can I look at it?
Naomba nione. na·ohm·ba nee·oh·nay

I don't like it.
Sipendi. see·payn·dee

How much is it?
Ni bei gani? ni bay ga·nee

That's too expensive.
Ni ghali mno. nee ga·lee m·noh

Please lower the price.
Punguza bei. poon·goo·za bay

ATM	*mashine ya kutolea pesa*	ma·shee·nay ya koo·toh·lay·a pay·sa
post office	*posta*	poh·sta
public phone	*simu ya mtaani*	see·moo ya m·ta·nee
tourist office	*ofisi ya watalii*	o·fee·see ya wa·ta·lee

Time, Dates & Numbers

The Swahili time system starts six hours later than the international one – it begins at sunrise (about 6am year-round). So, *saa mbili* sa m·bee·lee (lit: clocks two) means '2 o'clock Swahili time' and '8 o'clock European time'.

QUESTION WORDS

What?	*Nini?*	*nee*·nee
When?	*Wakati?*	wa·*ka*·tee
Where?	*Wapi?*	*wa*·pee
Who?	*Nani?*	*na*·nee

What time is it?
Ni saa ngapi? — nee sa n·*ga*·pee

It's (10) o'clock.
Ni saa (nne). — nee sa (*n*·nay)

Half past (10).
Ni saa (nne) na nusu. — nee sa (*n*·nay) na *noo*·soo

morning	*asubuhi*	a·soo·*boo*·hee
afternoon	*mchana*	m·*cha*·na
evening	*jioni*	jee·*oh*·nee
yesterday	*jana*	*ja*·na
today	*leo*	*lay*·oh
tomorrow	*kesho*	*kay*·shoh

Monday	*Jumatatu*	joo·ma·*ta*·too
Tuesday	*Jumanne*	joo·ma·*n*·nay
Wednesday	*Jumatano*	joo·ma·*ta*·noh
Thursday	*Alhamisi*	al·ha·*mee*·see
Friday	*Ijumaa*	ee·joo·*ma*
Saturday	*Jumamosi*	joo·ma·*moh*·see
Sunday	*Jumapili*	joo·ma·*pee*·lee

1	*moja*	*moh*·ja
2	*mbili*	m·*bee*·lee
3	*tatu*	*ta*·too
4	*nne*	*n*·nay
5	*tano*	*ta*·noh
6	*sita*	*see*·ta
7	*saba*	*sa*·ba
8	*nane*	*na*·nay
9	*tisa*	*tee*·sa
10	*kumi*	*koo*·mee
20	*ishirini*	ee·shee·*ree*·nee
30	*thelathini*	thay·la·*thee*·nee
40	*arobaini*	a·roh·ba·*ee*·nee
50	*hamsini*	ham·*see*·nee
60	*sitini*	see·*tee*·nee
70	*sabini*	sa·*bee*·nee
80	*themanini*	thay·ma·*nee*·nee
90	*tisini*	tee·*see*·nee
100	*mia moja*	*mee*·a *moh*·ja
1000	*elfu*	*ayl*·foo

Transport

Which ... goes to (Mbeya)?	*... ipi huenda (Mbeya)?*	... *ee*·pee hoo·*ayn*·da (m·*bay*·a)
bus	*Basi*	*ba*·see
ferry	*Kivuko*	kee·*voo*·koh
minibus	*Daladala* (Tan)/ *Matatu* (Ken)	da·la·*da*·la/ ma·*ta*·too
train	*Treni*	*tray*·nee

When's the ... bus?	*Basi ... itaondoka lini?*	*ba*·see ... ee·ta·ohn·*doh*·ka *lee*·nee
first	*ya kwanza*	ya *kwan*·za
last	*ya mwisho*	ya *mwee*·shoh
next	*ijayo*	ee·*ja*·yoh

A ... ticket to (Iringa).	*Tiketi moja ya ... kwenda (Iringa).*	tee·*kay*·tee *moh*·ja ya ... *kwayn*·da (ee·*reen*·ga)
1st-class	*daraja la kwanza*	da·*ra*·ja la *kwan*·za
2nd-class	*daraja la pili*	da·*ra*·ja la *pee*·lee
one-way	*kwenda tu*	*kwayn*·da too
return	*kwenda na kurudi*	*kwayn*·da na koo·*roo*·dee

What time does it get to (Kisuma)?
Itafika (Kisumu) saa ngapi? — ee·ta·*fee*·ka (kee·*soo*·moo) sa n·*ga*·pee

Does it stop at (Tanga)?
Linasimama (Tanga)? — lee·na·see·*ma*·ma (*tan*·ga)

I'd like to get off at (Bagamoyo).
Nataka kushusha (Bagamoyo). — na·*ta*·ka koo·*shoo*·sha (ba·ga·*moh*·yoh)

I'd like to hire a ...	*Nataka kukodi ...*	na·*ta*·ka koo·*koh*·dee ...
4WD	*forbaifor*	*fohr*·ba·ee·fohr
bicycle	*baisikeli*	ba·ee·see·*kay*·lee
car	*gari*	*ga*·ree
motorbike	*pikipiki*	pee·kee·*pee*·kee

regular	*kawaida*	ka·wa·*ee*·da
unleaded	*isiyo na risasi*	ee·see·yoh na ree·*sa*·see

Is this the road to (Embu)?
Hii ni barabara kwenda (Embu)? — hee nee ba·ra·*ba*·ra *kwayn*·da (*aym*·boo)

Where's a petrol station?
Kituo cha mafuta kiko wapi? — kee·*too*·oh cha ma·*foo*·ta *kee*·ko *wa*·pee

(How long) Can I park here?
Naweza kuegesha hapa (kwa muda gani)? na·*way*·za koo·ay·*gay*·sha *ha*·pa (kwa *moo*·da *ga*·ni)?

I need a mechanic.
Nahitaji fundi. na·hee·*ta*·jee *foon*·dee

I have a flat tyre.
Nina pancha. *nee*·na *pan*·cha

I've run out of petrol.
Mafuta yamekwisha. ma·*foo*·ta ya·may·*kwee*·sha

FRENCH

French is the official language in Burundi (along with Kirundi) and Rwanda (along with the English and the national language, Kinyarwanda).

French has nasal vowels (represented in our pronunciation guides by o or u followed by an almost inaudible nasal consonant sound m, n or ng). Note also the 'funny' *u* (ew in our guides) and the deep-in-the-throat *r*. The last syllable in a word is lightly stressed.

Hello.	*Bonjour.*	bon·zhoor
Goodbye.	*Au revoir.*	o·rer·vwa
Excuse me.	*Excusez-moi.*	ek·skew·zay·mwa
Sorry.	*Pardon.*	par·don
Yes./No.	*Oui./Non.*	wee/non
Please.	*S'il vous plaît.*	seel voo play
Thank you.	*Merci.*	mair·see
You're welcome.	*De rien.*	der ree·en

How are you?
Comment allez-vous? ko·mon ta·lay·voo

Fine, and you?
Bien, merci. Et vous? byun mair·see ay voo

What's your name?
Comment vous appelez-vous? ko·mon voo·za·play voo

My name is ...
Je m'appelle ... zher ma·pel ...

Do you speak English?
Parlez-vous anglais? par·lay·voo ong·glay

I don't understand.
Je ne comprends pas. zher ner kom·pron pa

What time is it?
Quelle heure est-il? kel er ay til

How much is it?
C'est combien? say kom·byun

Where are the toilets?
Où sont les toilettes? oo son lay twa·let

Can you show me (on the map)?
Pouvez-vous m'indiquer (sur la carte)? poo·vay·voo mun·dee·kay (sewr la kart)

I'm lost.
Je suis perdu/perdue. zhe swee·pair·dew (m/f)

Help!
Au secours! o skoor

Leave me alone!
Fichez-moi la paix! fee·shay·mwa la pay

Call a doctor.
Appelez un médecin. a·play un mayd·sun

Call the police.
Appelez la police. a·play la po·lees

I'm ill.
Je suis malade. zher swee ma·lad

What's the local speciality?
Quelle est la spécialité locale? kel ay la spay·sya·lee·tay lo·kal

Cheers!
Santé! son·tay

a ... room	*une chambre ...*	ewn shom·brer ...
single	*à un lit*	a un lee
double	*avec un grand lit*	a·vek un gron lee

a ... ticket	*un billet ...*	un bee·yay ...
one-way	*simple*	sum·pler
return	*aller et retour*	a·lay ay rer·toor

1	*un*	un
2	*deux*	der
3	*trois*	trwa
4	*quatre*	ka·trer
5	*cinq*	sungk
6	*six*	sees
7	*sept*	set
8	*huit*	weet
9	*neuf*	nerf
10	*dix*	dees
20	*vingt*	vung
30	*trente*	tront
40	*quarante*	ka·ront
50	*cinquante*	sung·kont
60	*soixante*	swa·sont
70	*soixante-dix*	swa·son·dees
80	*quatre-vingts*	ka·trer·vung
90	*quatre-vingt-dix*	ka·trer·vung·dees
100	*cent*	son
1000	*mille*	meel

GLOSSARY

The following is a list of words and acronyms from Burundi (B), Kenya (K), Rwanda (R), Tanzania (T) and Uganda (U) that appear in this book. For a glossary of food and drink terms, see p625.

askari – security guard, watchman

ASP (T) – Afro-Shirazi Party on Zanzibar Archipelago

banda – thatched-roof hut with wooden or earthen walls; simple wooden and stone-built accommodation

bangi – marijuana; also ganja

bao – a board game widely played in East Africa

baraza – the stone seats seen along the outside walls of houses in the Stone Towns of Zanzibar and Lamu, used for chatting and relaxing

Big Five, the – the five archetypal large African mammals: lion, buffalo, elephant, leopard and rhino

boda-boda (U) – bicycle taxi

boma – a living compound; in colonial times, a government administrative office

bui-bui – black cover-all garment worn by some Islamic women outside the home

CCM (T) – Chama Cha Mapinduzi (Party of the Revolution); Tanzania's governing political party

chai – tea

Cites – Convention on International Trade in Endangered Species

dalla-dalla (T) – minibus

dhow – traditional Arabic sailing vessel, common along the coast

duka – small shop or kiosk

fly camp – a camp away from the main tented camps or lodges, for the purpose of enjoying a more authentic bush experience

forex – foreign exchange bureau

gacaca (R) – traditional tribunal headed by village elders

gof – volcanic crater

injera – unleavened bread

Interahamwe (R) – Hutu militia

kabaka (U) – king

kanga – printed cotton wraparound, incorporating a Swahili proverb, worn by Tanzanian women

karibu – Swahili for welcome

kikoi – printed cotton wraparound traditionally worn by men in coastal areas

KWS (K) – Kenya Wildlife Service

makuti – palm thatching

manyatta (K) – Maasai or Samburu livestock camp often surrounded by a circle of thorn bushes

matatu (K) – minibus

Maulid – birth of the prophet Mohammed and Muslim feast day, celebrated in many areas of East Africa

mihrab – prayer niche in a mosque showing the direction of Mecca

moran (K) – Maasai or Samburu warrior

mpingo – African blackwood

muzungu – white person, foreigner (plural wazungu)

mwami (B; R) – king

NCA (T) – Ngorongoro Conservation Area

Ngai – Kikuyu god

ngoma – dance and drumming

NRA (U) – National Resistance Army

NRM (U) – National Resistance Movement

nyatiti – traditional folk lyre

panga – machete, carried by many people in the east African countryside

RMS (U) – Rwenzori Mountaineering Services

RPF (R) – Rwandan Patriotic Front

shetani – literally, demon or something supernatural; in art, a style of carving embodying images from the spirit world

shuka – tie-dyed sarong

soukous – dance style

taarab (T) – Zanzibari music combining African, Arabic and Indian influences

Tanapa (T) – Tanzania National Parks Authority

TANU (T) – Tanganyika African National Union

tilapia – Nile perch

TTB (T) – Tanzania Tourist Board

Ucota – Uganda Community Tourism Association

uhuru – freedom or independence

ujamaa (T) – familyhood, togetherness

Unguja (T) – Swahili name for Zanzibar Island

UWA (U) – Uganda Wildlife Authority

ZNP – Zanzibar Nationalist Party

ZPPP – Zanzibar & Pemba People's Party

Behind the Scenes

SEND US YOUR FEEDBACK

We love to hear from travellers – your comments keep us on our toes and help make our books better. Our well-travelled team reads every word on what you loved or loathed about this book. Although we cannot reply individually to your submissions, we always guarantee that your feedback goes straight to the appropriate authors, in time for the next edition. Each person who sends us information is thanked in the next edition – the most useful submissions are rewarded with a selection of digital PDF chapters.

Visit **lonelyplanet.com/contact** to submit your updates and suggestions or to ask for help. Our award-winning website also features inspirational travel stories, news and discussions.

Note: We may edit, reproduce and incorporate your comments in Lonely Planet products such as guidebooks, websites and digital products, so let us know if you don't want your comments reproduced or your name acknowledged. For a copy of our privacy policy visit lonelyplanet.com/privacy.

OUR READERS

Many thanks to the travellers who used the last edition and wrote to us with helpful hints, useful advice and interesting anecdotes: Bastien Poirier, Bennett Garner, David Bomford, Dian & Jeff Schubel, Gertrud Dietze, Hektor Krome, Jon Didrichsen, Julie Woods, Kathryn Savage, Mirjam Fritz

AUTHOR THANKS

Anthony Ham

Heartfelt thanks to Matt Phillips, my Africa friend and editor of long standing for continuing to entrust me with a corner of the earth I adore. Warmest thanks also to Peter Ndirangu Wamae, another companion of the African road over many years. Carole and Donald Boag were wonderful hosts in the Serengeti, and thanks to Mary Fitzpatrick for her enduring wisdom. To my family, Marina, Carlota and Valentina: thank you for sharing my love of Africa and for giving me so many special memories there.

Ray Bartlett

My family. Matt P, editor extraordinaire. Sachi, Maha, Bintee, Dorocella, Zhen, Dawson, Ruge, Sauda, Paschal, Mr Gara, Happiness, Mr Bita, Mariam, Hezron, Placilia, Will I Am, Jullyan, Novart, George, Rachel, Elizabeth, Megan and Evan, Eustocia, Ratna, Dharmesh, Loyce, Jacky, Clara, William, Peter, Paul, Gabriel, Enock, Chesco, Yusuph, Abdullah, Siwema, Khatib, Antonny, Jabiri, Charles, Juma, Francisco, Neema, Nixon, Novart, Nuru, Kalfan, Hussein, Chris and Louise, Miho-san, and the incredible people of Tanzania. Thank you for such a lovely time in your sweet, special country.

Jean-Bernard Carillet

A huge thanks to everyone who made this trip a pure joy, including Paul, Natasha, Bruce and Alphonse, and all the travellers I met while on the road. At Lonely Planet, a big thanks to Matt for his trust.

Shawn Duthie

Thank you to my wife, Lucy, for looking after Kai while I had fun in Kenya. Many thanks also to the staff at Lonely Planet, particularly Matt Phillips, Neill Coen and Paul Clammer for all of the advice and support. In Kenya, my utmost thanks to everyone who helped with information and advice, especially Rob Andrew, Sophie Grant and my drinking buddies in North Horr.

David Else

Many thanks go first to the travellers and Zanzibaris that I met along the way; their insights and stories were invaluable. Big thanks also to my old pal Peter Bennett for local knowledge. And the biggest thanks to Corinne, my wife, for keeping the home fires burning while I'm on the road.

Mary Fitzpatrick

So many people helped during the research and writing for this project. I'd especially like to thank Nassor in Newala, Sultan in Dar es Salaam, Abdullah in Somanga and Eustacia in Selous Game Reserve.

A special thank you also to Destination Editor Matt Phillips and to my Tanzania coauthors. My biggest thanks goes to Rick, Christopher, Dominic and Gabriel for their entertaining company during research and patience and good humour during write-up.

Anna Kaminski

I'd like to thank Matt for entrusting me with the Kenyan coast, Stuart for the advice, and everyone who helped me along the way. In particular: Carol in Shela, Rachel on Manda, Arnold and Kesh in Lamu Town, Paul in Watamu, Suleiman in Mombasa, my driver Fauz, my wonderful hosts in Malindi and Diani, my Kaya Kinondo guide, and the boat captains who got me to Pate and Kiwayu islands safely.

Carolyn McCarthy

It was a joy to travel throughout Uganda on this research trip. I am indebted to Aimee Dowl and Derek Kverno for their hospitality, and numerous tips and insights. Ashiraf Mwanje was the best driver a *muzungu* could find. Thanks for keeping us safe. And a Nile Special to Wendy for the good company.

Gratitude also goes out to all those we met along the way for being so gracious, good humoured and helpful: *Neyanziza Neyanzege*!

Helena Smith

Asante Elidady for a warm welcome and Art for arranging it, Mwisho Msumai for the lowdown on Morogoro, and Joas Kahembe in Babati. In Iringa thanks to Bill Allen, Owen Flagel and Joan Mayer for a great night out, and Rajipa David for a great day out. Jessica Klink, Cori Van Dyke and especially Amy Glasser shared knowledge of Mbeya and Matema. Thanks too to Amelia in Mbeya, Erica Zelfand for help with Tukuyu, and Moyo Jacob Mwagobele in Matema.

ACKNOWLEDGEMENTS

Climate map data adapted from Peel MC, Finlayson BL & McMahon TA (2007) 'Updated World Map of the Köppen-Geiger Climate Classification', Hydrology and Earth System Sciences, 11, 163–344.

Cover photograph: Cheetah cub with its mother, Masai Mara, Kenya; Jonathan and Angela Scott/AWL ©

THIS BOOK

This 11th edition of Lonely Planet's *East Africa* guidebook was researched and written by Anthony Ham, Ray Bartlett, Stuart Butler, Jean-Bernard Carillet, Shawn Duthie, David Else, Mary Fitzpatrick, Anna Kaminski, Tom Masters, Carolyn McCarthy and Helena Smith. The previous edition was written by Anthony Ham, Stuart Butler, Mary Fitzpatrick and Trent Holden. This guidebook was produced by the following:

Destination Editor Matt Phillips

Product Editors Will Allen, Elizabeth Jones, Saralinda Turner

Regional Senior Cartographer Diana Von Holdt

Cartographer Mick Garrett

Book Designer Jessica Rose

Assisting Editors Janet Austin, Sarah Bailey, Judith Bamber, Michelle Bennett, Nigel Chin, Peter Cruttenden, Melanie Dankel, Andrea Dobbin, Kellie Langdon, Rosie Nicholson, Lauren O'Connell, Kristin Odijk, Simon Williamson

Cover Researcher Naomi Parker

Thanks to Hannah Cartmel, Grace Dobell, Susan Paterson

Index

A

Aberdare National Park 279-81, **280**
accommodation 630-1, *see also individual locations*
  language 653, 656
activities 23-6, 631-2, *see also individual activities*
Adamson, George 243, 298, 299
Adamson, Joy 243, 299, 348
adventure sports 82, 330, 409, *see also individual sports*
African buffaloes *see* buffaloes
African elephants *see* elephants
African fish eagles 599, **598-9**
African wild dogs *see* wild dogs
air travel 640-1, 642-3
  Kenya 373-4, 375
  Rwanda 552-3, 554
  Tanzania 211-12, 215-16
  Uganda 490, 491
airlines 640-1, 642-3
airports 640-1
Akagera National Park 541-4
Akamba people 611
altitude sickness 650-1
Amani Nature Reserve 99
Amboseli National Park 16, 300-3, **303**, **16**
Amin, Idi 476-7, 477
amoebic dysentery 650
animals, *see* wildlife
ankole cows 486
Arabuko Sokoke Forest Reserve 331-2
archaeological sites, *see also* rock-art sites, ruins
  Hyrax Hill Prehistoric Site, Kenya 246
  Isimila Stone Age Site, Tanzania 172-3
  Katuruka Heritage Site, Tanzania 151
  Oldupai Gorge, Tanzania 123
  Thimlich Ohinga Archaeological Site, Kenya 265
architecture 73, 619
area codes 19, 632
arts 619-22, *see also individual arts*
arts centres *see also* museums & galleries
  32° East Ugandan Arts Trust, Uganda 384
  Camp Ndegeya Sculpture Park, Uganda 463
  College of Arts, Tanzania 93
  Inema Arts Center, Rwanda 509
  Kabale Arts Center, Uganda 451
  Kazuri Beads & Pottery Centre, Kenya 230
  Neema Crafts, Tanzania 171
Arusha 103-9, **104-5**
Arusha National Park 109-12, **108**
ATMs 635
augur buzzards 599

B

Babati 142
baboons 586, **587**
  Kenya 249, 274, 282, 321, 331
  Rwanda 534, 541
  Tanzania 115, 159, 170
  Uganda 434, 470
Bagamoyo 93-4
Baganda people 611-12
balloon safaris 40, 126, 255, 367, 440-1
banded mongooses 597, **597**
banditry 368, 628
bao 570
Baragoi 352-3
bargaining 486, 488, 632
bateleurs 599, **599**
bathrooms 636
beaches 22
  Bofa Beach, Kenya 328
  Diani Beach, Kenya 323-6, **324**
  Gisenyi Public Beach, Rwanda 527
  Jakobsen's Beach, Tanzania 157
  Jangwani Beach, Tanzania 63
  Jimbizi Beach, Tanzania 194
  Kanga Beach, Tanzania 187
  Kunduchi Beach, Tanzania 63
  Mange Beach, Tanzania 187
  Marimbani Beach, Tanzania 187
  Masoko Pwani, Tanzania 194
  Matvilla Beach, Tanzania 143
  Mwamahunga Beach, Tanzania 157
  Shangani Beach, Tanzania 197
  Shela Beach, Kenya 337
  Tiwi Beach, Kenya 322, **324**
  Vumawinbi Beach, Tanzania 91
bicycle travel, *see* cycling
big cats 20, 582-3 *see also individual species*
bilharzia 647
birds 598-601 *see also individual species*
birdwatching 608-9
  Akagera National Park, Rwanda 542
  Amboseli National Park, Kenya 300-2
  Budongo Forest Reserve, Uganda 474
  Bwindi Impenetrable National Park, Uganda 445-6
  Crater Lakes, Uganda 429
  Entebbe, Uganda 402
  Fort Portal, Uganda 424-5
  Jinja, Uganda 409
  Kakamega Forest, Kenya 268
  Kibale Forest National Park, Uganda 431
  Lake Baringo, Kenya 250
  Lake Manyara National Park, Tanzania 115
  Lake Rukwa, Tanzania 165
  Mabamba Swamp Wetlands, Uganda 406
  Mikumi National Park, Tanzania 170
  Murchison Falls National Park, Uganda 469, 471
  Nyungwe Forest National Park, Rwanda 536-7
  Parc National des Virunga, DRC 498
  Ruaha National Park, Tanzania 174
  Rubondo Island National Park, Tanzania
  Saadani National Park, Tanzania 94
  Selous Game Reserve, Tanzania 190
  Semuliki National Park, Tanzania 433-4
  Tanzania 207
  Uganda 485
  Volcanoes National Park, Rwanda 524
  Ziwa Rhino Sanctuary, Uganda 466
black market 635
black rhinoceroses *see* rhinoceroses
black-and-white colobus 589, **17**, **588-9**
  Kenya 274, 276, 324

Map Pages **000**
Photo Pages **000**

Rwanda 535-6
Tanzania 149
Uganda 402, 428, 474
blue monkeys 589, **588**
boat travel 641-2, 643-4
Kenya 375
Rwanda 554
Tanzania 215, 216-17
Uganda 492
boda-bodas 379, 493
books 560, 575, 620-1
food 625
peoples 611
wildlife 36, 127, 575, 577
Borana Conservancy 288
border crossings
Kenya 374-5
Rwanda 553
Tanzania 212-15
Uganda 490-1
bribes 377
budgeting 19
Budongo Forest Reserve 474-5
Buffalo Springs National Reserve 347-8, **346**
buffaloes 590, **591**
Kenya 226, 245, 249, 252, 261, 274, 279, 286, 288, 321, 349, 350
Rwanda 524, 541
Tanzania 115, 124, 135, 160, 164, 170, 174, 190, 193
Uganda 419, 434, 441, 468, 469
Bukavu 501-2
Bukoba 150-2, **151**
Burundi 50, 555-8, **556**
culture 558
currency 555
economy 556
environment 558
history 557-8
language 555
politics 556
safety 557, 629
time 555
bus travel 644, 645-6
Kenya 375-6, 379, 380
Rwanda 554
Tanzania 217, 218
Uganda 492
bushwalking *see* hiking
business hours 19, 635-6, *see also individual countries*
Butare 530-3, **532**
buzzards 599
Bwindi Impenetrable National Park 45, 445-51, **446**

C

camping 630
canoeing, *see* kayaking & canoeing
car travel 644-5
driving licences 217, 377, 492, 644
hire 217, 377-8, 492-3, 554, 645
insurance 645
Kenya 376-9
road accidents 217-18, 378, 628, 645
road rules 218, 378-9, 645
Rwanda 554
Tanzania 217-18
Uganda 492-3
caracals 585, **585**
cathedrals, *see* churches & cathedrals
cats 584-5
cattle 580
caves
Amabeere Cave, Uganda 430
Elkony Caves, Kenya 276
Musanze Caves, Rwanda 517
Shetani Caves, Kenya 305
cell phones 18
Central Island National Park 357
Chake Chake 87-9, **88**
chameleons **15**
Changuu 77-8
cheetahs 578-9, 582, **13**, **582**
Kenya 226, 252, 258, 259, 260, 300-1, 305, 3008, 309-10
Tanzania 123, 125, 174
Uganda 419
Cherangani Hills 355-6
children, travel with 47-8
chimpanzee tracking 39
Budongo Forest Reserve, Uganda 474
Gombe National Park, Tanzania 159
Kibale Forest National Park, Uganda 13, 431-2, **13**
Mahale Mountains National Park, Tanzania 160-1
Nyungwe Forest National Park, Rwanda 534-5
Parc National des Virunga, DRC 498-9
Queen Elizabeth National Park, Uganda 442
Semliki Wildlife Reserve, Uganda 434
Tanzania 207
Uganda 485
chimpanzees 13, 484, 586, **13**, **586-7**
sanctuaries 284-5, 401-2
Tanzania 149, 160
Uganda 431, 434, 439
cholera 647
Christianity 570-1
Chumbe Island Coral Park 78
churches & cathedrals
Anglican Cathedral 67
Catholic Cathedral (Songea) 184
Catholic Cathedral (Tabora) 155
Catholic Cathedral (Zanzibar Town) 65
Église St Pierre 539
Holy Ghost Cathedral 315
Namirembe Cathedral 385
Ntarama Church 512
Nyamata Church 512
Rubaga Cathedral 387
cinema, *see* films
climate 23-6, *see also individual countries*
climbing 245, 417, *see also* hiking
coffee 417
colobus monkeys *see* black-and-white colobus, red colobus
community projects, *see* volunteering
conservancies 610
Borana Conservancy, Kenya 288
Lewa Wildlife Conservancy, Kenya 286-8
Manyara Ranch Conservancy, Tanzania 610
Mara North Conservancy, Kenya 259-60
Naboisho Conservancy, Kenya 260
Ol Pejeta Conservancy, Kenya 284-5
Olare-Orok Conservancy, Kenya260-1
Olderikesi Conservancy, Kenya 261-2
consulates, *see* embassies
costs 19, 631, 635
courses
cooking 81
language 209, 370
cows 486
cranes 601
Crater Lakes 428-30
credit cards 635
crime 368-9, 628, *see also* safety
cuisine, *see* food
cultural tourism
Bwindi Impenetrable National Park, Uganda 446
Gisenyi (Rubavu), Rwanda 528
Kidepo Valley National Park, Uganda 420
Kigali, Rwanda 511
Kisoro, Uganda 456
Kondoa Rock-Art Sites, Tanzania 141
Lake Bunyonyi, Uganda 453-4
Lake Eyasi, Tanzania 119
Mgahinga Gorilla National Park, Uganda 459
Mto wa Mbu, Tanzania 114
Musanze (Ruhengeri), Rwanda 518
Ruaha National Park, Tanzania 175
Tanzania 101
culture 560-1, 568-72, 611-18
currency 18
customs regulations
Kenya 368
Tanzania 207
Uganda 487
Cyangugu 538-9
cycling 643
Bwindi Impenetrable National Park, Uganda 447
Congo Nile Trail, Rwanda 527-8
Crater Lakes, Uganda 428
Diani Beach, Kenya 324
Hell's Gate National Park, Kenya 245
Jinja, Uganda 410
Kampala, Uganda 387
Kenya 367, 375
Mto wa Mbu, Tanzania 114
Njombe, Tanzania 177
Nungwi, Tanzania 79

cycling *continued*
  Rwanda 554
  safaris 39-40
  Sipi Falls, Uganda 418
  Uganda 491
  Ukerewe Island, Tanzania 149

D

dalla-dallas 218-19
dance 621-2
  Rwanda 533, 550
  Uganda 483-4
dangers, *see* safety
Dar es Salaam 53-63, **56**, **58**
  accommodation 53-9
  food 59-60
  internet access 61
  medical services 61
  money 61
  nightlife 60
  safety 60-1
  shopping 60
  sights 53
  tourist information 61
  travel to/from 61-2
  travel within 62-3
deforestation 579-80
Democratic Republic of the Congo (DRC) 50, 494-505, **496**
  accommodation 494
  area codes 504-5
  business hours 504-5
  climate 494
  culture 503
  electricity 503
  emergencies 504
  exchange rates 495
  food 494
  highlights 496
  internet access 504
  language 495
  money 495, 504
  opening hours 504
  politics 502-3
  postal services 504
  safety 503, 629
  telephone services 504-5
  time 505
  travel seasons 494
  travel to/from 505
  travel within 505
  visas 495, 505
dengue fever 647-8
desert 602
dhow travel 216-17, 643-4
Diani Beach 323-6, **324**
diarrhoea 650
diptheria 648
disabilities, travellers with 372, 637
diving & snorkelling 22, 631-2, 633
  Chumbe Island Coral Park, Tanzania 78
  Dar es Salaam's southern beaches, Tanzania 63-4
  Diani Beach, Kenya 325
  Kenya 367
  Kigomasha Peninsula, Tanzania 91
  Kilifi, Kenya 328-9
  Kisite Marine National Park, Kenya 327
  Lake Nyasa, Tanzania 183
  Lake Tanganyika, Tanzania 158
  Mafia, Tanzania 188
  Mahale Mountains National Park, Tanzania 161
  Malindi, Kenya 333-5
  Mikindani, Tanzania 200
  Mnemba Island, Tanzania 81
  Pemba, Tanzania 87
  Tiwi Beach, Kenya 322
  Wasini Island, Kenya 327
  Watamu, Kenya 330
  Zanzibar Island, Tanzania 70, 79-81
Dodoma 139-41, **140**
dolphins 85, **21**
drinks 623-4
  coffee 417
  tea 268
driving, *see* car travel
driving licences 217, 377, 492, 644
dysentery 650

E

eagles 599, **598-9**
Eldoret 270-2, **271**
electricity 632
elephants 20-1, 575-6, 592, **16**, **593**
  Kenya 226-30, 252, 260, 279, 286, 287, 288, 300-2, 305, 309-10, 321, 322, 331, 347, 349, 350
  Rwanda 541
  Tanzania 112, 115, 121, 123-6, 135, 149, 160, 164, 170, 174-5, 190, 193
  Uganda 419, 434, 439, 441, 446, 468-9
Eliye Springs 357-8
El-Molo people 612
embassies
  Kenya 369-70
  Rwanda 550-1
  Tanzania 208
  Uganda 487-8
emergencies
  language 654
emergency services 19, 632, *see also individual countries*
endangered species 575-9
Entebbe 401-5, **402**
environment 602-3
  Burundi 558
  Democratic Republic of the Congo 503
  Kenya 360-1, 362-5
  Rwanda 550
  Tanzania 205-6
  Uganda 484-6
environmental issues 550, 561, 579-80
equator 406
etiquette 572, 632
events 23-6
exchange rates
  Democratic Republic of the Congo 495
  Kenya 221
  Rwanda 508
  Tanzania 53
  Uganda 384

F

female genital mutilation 571
ferry travel, *see* boat travel
Festival of the Dhow Countries 24
festivals 23-6
field guides 36
filariasis 648
films 560, 619-20
fishing 188, 409, 471
flamingos 115-6, 117, 119, 249, 250, 357, 601, **600-1**
food 623-6, 635, *see also individual locations*
  customs 624-5
  language 625-6, 653-4
forests
  Arabuko Sokoke Forest Reserve, Kenya 331-2
  Budongo Forest Reserve, Uganda 474-5
  Jozani Forest, Tanzania 82
  Kakamega Forest, Kenya 268-70, 270, **269**
  Kaya Kinondo, Kenya 323
  Kibale Forest National Park, Uganda 431-3
  Kiwengwa-Pongwe Forest Reserve, Tanzania 82
  Mazumbai Forest Reserve, Tanzania 101
  Mbizi Forest Reserve, Tanzania 165
  Mpanga Forest Reserve, Uganda 406
  Ndelemai Forest, Tanzania 101
  Ngezi Forest Reserve, Tanzania 90
  Nyungwe Forest National Park, Rwanda 534-8
Fort Portal 424-8, **426**
Fossey, Dian 524-5
French language 656

G

galagos 589
Gandhi, Mahatma 410
gardens, *see* parks & gardens
gay travellers 632-3
  Kenya 370
  Rwanda 551
  Tanzania 209
  Uganda 480-1, 488
gazelles 590, **591**
Gede Ruins 332
genocide (Rwanda) 508, 509, 511, 512, 531, 539, 545, 546-7
geography 573-5
gerenuks 590, **590**
giardiasis 650
giraffes 578, 592, 593, **16**
  Kenya 226, 242, 245, 249, 252, 265, 286, 288, 301, 305, 321, 347
  Rwanda 541
  Tanzania 94, 149, 160, 164, 170
  Uganda 419, 461, 468
Gisenyi 527-30, **528**

golden jackals 597, **596**
golden monkey tracking 458, 523-4
Goma 495-8
Gombe National Park 159-60
Goodall, Dr Jane 159
gorilla tracking 41-6, 485, **46**
Parc National des Virunga, DRC 46, 499
Volcanoes National Park, Rwanda 11, 46, 521-3, **11**
Bwindi Impenetrable National Park, Uganda 45, 446-7, 448
Mgahinga Gorilla National Park, Uganda 45, 458
gorillas 11, 484, 577, 586, **11**, **43**
Great Rift Valley 573
greater galagos 589
Grevy's zebras *see* zebras
grey-crowned cranes 601
Gulu 422-3
Gusii people 612-13

H

habitats 602-3
Hadzabe people 613
handicrafts 484, 622
Haya people 613
health 647-51
insurance 647
tsetse flies 576, 651
vaccinations 648
water 493, 651
heat exhaustion 651
Hell's Gate National Park 245-6, **245**
Hemingway, Ernest 478
hepatitis 648
hiking 21, 632, 634, *see also* national parks & reserves
Babati, Tanzania 142
Kenya 367, 368
Mt Meru, Tanzania 110
Ol Doinyo Lengai, Tanzania 117
Rwenzori Mountains National Park, Uganda 435-6
Sipi Falls, Uganda 417
Tanzania 207
Tukuyu, Tanzania 181-2
Uluguru Mountains, Tanzania 168
hippopotamuses 594, **594-5**
Kenya 242, 249, 252, 285, 299, 301, 308, 310
Rwanda 541
Tanzania 94, 115, 126, 142, 149, 160, 164, 170, 174-5, 190, 194
Uganda 439, 441-2, 461, 466, 468-9
historic sites, *see also* archaeological sites, ruins
Akampeine Island, Uganda 453
Bagamoyo Town, Tanzania 93
Boma, Tanzania 200
Bwama Island, Uganda 453
Chole, Tanzania 187
Fort Jesus, Kenya 312-14
Hamamni Persian Baths, Tanzania 67
Hotel des Mille Collines, Rwanda 509-11
House of Wonders, Tanzania 65
Juani, Tanzania 187
Karambi Royal Tombs, Uganda 425
Kasubi Tombs, Uganda 385
Kidichi Persian Baths, Tanzania 67
Lamu Fort, Kenya 337-9
Livingstone's Tembe, Tanzania 155
Mengo Palace, Uganda 384
Mparo Tombs, Uganda 468
Njuyeera (Sharp's) Island, Uganda 453
Old Dispensary, Tanzania 67
Old Fort, Tanzania 65
Slave Market, Tanzania 200
Tooro Palace, Uganda 425
Toten Island, Tanzania 98
Uganda Martyrs' Shrine, Uganda 385
Wamala Tombs, Uganda 385
history 562-7, *see also individual countries*
hitching 645
Kenya 379
Tanzania 218
Uganda 493
HIV/AIDS 569, 648
Hoima 468
holidays 636
Homa Bay 264-5
honey badgers 597
horse riding 207, 287, 408-9, 461
hot springs 433
hunting dogs 597
Huye 530-3, **532**
hyenas 597, **596**
hyraxes 594, **595**

I

Il Ngwesi Group Ranch 288
imigongo 542
immigration 640
insect bites 651
insurance
car 645
health 647
travel 633
International Camel Derby 25, 351
internet access 633-4, *see also individual locations*
internet resources 19
accessible travel 637
air tickets 641
food 624
safaris 33
travel advice 629
volunteering 638
Iringa 171-4, **172**
Isiolo 345-7, **343**
Islam 571-2
islands 21-2
Akampeine Island, Uganda 453
Bwama Island, Uganda 453
Central Island National Park, Kenya 357
Chole, Tanzania 187
Chumbe Island, Tanzania 78
Idjwi Island, DRC 501
Jibondo, Tanzania 187
Juani, Tanzania 187
Kyahugye Island, Uganda 453
Mafia, Tanzania 185-90, **185**
Misali Island, Tanzania 87
Mnemba Island, Tanzania 81
Ndere Island National Park, Kenya 263
Ngamba Island Chimpanzee Sanctuary, Uganda 401
Njuyeera (Sharp's) Island, Uganda 453
Pemba, Tanzania 85-91, **86**
Rubondo Island National Park, Tanzania 149-50
South Island National Park, Kenya 353
Ssese Islands, Uganda 463-5
Toten Island, Tanzania 98
Ukerewe Island, Tanzania 149
Wasini Island, Kenya 327-8
Zanzibar Island, Tanzania 65-85, **66**
Iten 272
itineraries 27-31, **27**, **28**, **29**, **30**, **31**
safaris 37-8

J

jackals 597, **596**
Jambiani 84-5
Jangwani Beach 63
Jinja 406-13, **408**
Jozani-Chwaka National Park 82

K

Kabale 451-3, **452**
Kakamega Forest 268-70, 270, **269**
Kalenjin people 614
Kampala 384-401, **386**, **388-9**
accommodation 391-5
activities 387
drinking 397-8
emergencies 399
entertainment 398
festivals & events 391
food 395-7
important numbers 399
internet access 399
medical services 399
money 399
nightlife 397-8
postal services 399
safety 398-9
shopping 398
sights 384-7
tourist information 399
tours 387, 390-1
travel to/from 399-400
travel within 400-1

kanga 622
Karamajong people 614-15
Karamoja 421
Karatu 118-19
Karongi 539-40
Kasese 435-6
Katavi National Park 163-5
Kaya Kinondo 323
kayaking & canoeing
  Dar es Salaam's southern beaches, Tanzania 63-64
  Gisenyi (Rubavu), Rwanda 527
  Jinja, Uganda 410
  Lake Bunyonyi, Uganda 453
  Lake Nyasa, Tanzania 182
  Mabamba Swamp Wetlands, Uganda 406
  Mida Creek, Kenya 333
  Musanze (Ruhengeri), Rwanda 518
  safaris 40
  Ssese Islands, Uganda 463
  Zanzibar Island, Tanzania 70
Kendwa 80-1
Kenya 49, 220-380, **222-3**, **241**, **253**, **277**, **301**, **313**, **344-5**
  accommodation 220, 365-7
  activities 367-8
  books 361-2
  business hours 371
  climate 220
  consulates 369-70
  culture 361
  customs regulations 368
  embassies 369-70
  exchange rates 221
  food 220
  highlights 222-3
  history 358-60
  internet access 370
  language 221
  legal matters 370
  money 221, 371
  music 361, 362-3
  opening hours 371
  politics 360
  postal services 371-2
  public holidays 372
  religion 361
  safety 342, 368-9, 629
  telephone services 372
  time 372
  tourist information 372
  travel seasons 220
  travel to/from 373-5
  travel within 375-80
  visas 221, 372-3
  volunteering 373
Kericho 266-8, **267**
Kibale Forest National Park 431-3
Kibera 231
Kibuye 539-40
Kidepo Valley National Park 419-21
Kigali 507-17, **510**
  accommodation 512-14
  drinking 515
  festivals & events 512
  food 514-15
  history 508
  internet access 516
  medical services 516
  money 516
  nightlife 515
  postal services 516
  safety 515
  shopping 515
  sights 509-11
  tourist information 516
  tours 511-12
  travel to/from 516-17
  travel within 517
Kigoma 156-9, **156**
Kigomasha Peninsula 90-1
kikoi 622
Kikuyu people 615
Kilifi 328-9
Kilwa Kisiwani 196-7
Kilwa Masoko 194-6, **194**
Kisii 266
Kisii people 612-13
Kisii soapstone 266
Kisoro 455-7, **456**
Kisumu 262-4, **262**
Kitale 272-4, **273**
kitesurfing
  Diani Beach, Kenya 324
  Malindi, Kenya 333
  Watamu, Kenya 330
  Zanzibar Island, Tanzania 79, 84
Kitgum 422
Kiwengwa 82
Kiweni 89
Kizimkazi 85
kob 590, **590-1**
Kondoa Rock-Art Sites 141-2
Kunduchi Beach 63

L

Laikipia Plateau 14, 281-9, **277**
Lake Baringo 250, **251**
Lake Bogoria 250, **251**
Lake Bunyonyi 453-5
Lake Eyasi 119
Lake Manyara National Park 115-17
Lake Mburo National Park 461-2
Lake Mutanda 459-60
Lake Naivasha 242-5, **243**
Lake Nakuru National Park 247, 249-51, **248**, **35**
Lake Natron 117-18
Lake Nyasa 182-4
Lake Tanganyika 158
Lake Victoria 143-52, 262-5, **144**
lakes 574-5
Lamu 337-43, **338**
landscapes 602-3
language 652-7
  courses 209, 370
  food glossary 625-6
  French 656
  Swahili 652-6
legal matters 634
Lekurruki Community Ranch 288-9
leopards 582, **582-3**
  Kenya 226, 249, 252, 259, 279, 304-5, 308, 310, 350
  Rwanda 541
  Tanzania 123-6, 135, 160, 170
  Uganda 419, 434, 439, 441, 461, 466, 470
lesbian travellers 632-3
  Kenya 370
  Rwanda 551
  Tanzania 209
  Uganda 480-1, 488
lesser flamingos *see* flamingos
Lewa Wildlife Conservancy 286-8
LGBT travellers 632-3
  Kenya 370
  Rwanda 551
  Tanzania 209
  Uganda 480-1, 488
lilac-breasted rollers 601, **600**
lions 577, 582, **35**, **583**, **604**
  Kenya 221, 249, 252, 256, 259, 260, 261, 285, 288, 300-1, 304-5, 309, 310, 349
  Rwanda 541
  Tanzania 112, 115, 122, 123-7, 160, 164, 170, 175, 193
  Uganda 419, 434, 439, 441, 442, 468, 470
literature, see books
Lodwar 356-7
Loita Hills 261
Longonot National Park 242
Loyangalani 353-5
Luo people 615-16
Lushoto 99-100, **99**

M

Maasai people 255-6, 258, 616
Mabamba Swamp Wetlands 406
Machame 137-8
Mafia 185-90, **185**
Mahale Mountains National Park 160-2
Maji Maji rebellion 202
Makambako 177
Makonde people 616
Makonde Plateau 201
Makonde woodcarving 622
malaria 648-9
Malindi 332-7, **334**
mammals 590-1, 592-3, 594-5
maps 634
  Kenya 370-1
  Tanzania 209
  Uganda 488
Mara North Conservancy 259-60
Marafa Depression 336
Maralal 351-2, **352**
Marangu 133-4
Marich Pass 355-6
marine parks & reserves
  Dar es Salaam Marine Reserves, Tanzania 206
  Kisite Marine National Park, Kenya 327
  Mafia Island Marine Park, Tanzania 187
  Malindi Marine National Park, Kenya 332

Maziwe Marine Reserve, Tanzania 206
Mnazi Bay-Ruvuma Estuary Marine Park, Tanzania 206
Tanga Coelacanth Marine Park, Tanzania 206
Tanzania 206
Watamu Marine National Park, Kenya 330
markets
Central Market, Uganda 408
Darajani Market, Tanzania 67
Fish Market (Bagamoyo), Tanzania 93
Fish Market (Mtwara), Tanzania 197, 199
Kisumu Main Market, Kenya 263
Lamu Market, Kenya 337
Mtwara, Tanzania 197
Mugusu Market, Uganda 424
Mwaloni Market, Tanzania 145
Mwigobero Market, Tanzania 143
Night Market, Tanzania 195
Pottery Market, Tanzania 182
Songea, Tanzania 184
Spice Market, Kenya 315
Usambara Mountains, Tanzania 100
Marsabit 349-50
Marsabit National Park 350-1, **350**
Masai Mara National Reserve 13, 252-8, **254-5**
Masaka 462-3
Masasi 201
Masindi 466-7, **467**
matatus, *see* bus travel
Matema 182-3
Matemwe 81-2
Matthews Range 349
Mbale 413-15
Mbamba Bay 183-4
Mbarara 460
Mbeya 178-81, **179**, **180**
measures 631
medical services 647
memorials
Bisesero Genocide Memorial, Rwanda 539
Camp Kigali Memorial, Rwanda 511
Kigali Genocide Memorial, Rwanda 509
Murambi Genocide Memorial, Rwanda 531
Ntarama Church, Rwanda 512
Nyamata Church, Rwanda 512
Nyanza Genocide Memorial, Rwanda 509
meningococcal meningitis 649
Meru 298, **297**
Meru National Park 298-300, **299**
Meru people 617
Mgahinga Gorilla National Park 45, 457-9
Michamvi Peninsula 83
Mida Creek 333
Mikindani 200-1
Mikumi National Park 170-1
minibuses, *see* bus travel
Mkoani 89
mobile phones 18, 636-7
Mombasa 312-21, **314**, **318**
accommodation 315-16
activities 315
drinking 317
festivals & events 315
food 316-17
medical services 319
money 319
nightlife 317
postal services 319
safaris 316
safety 319
shopping 317-19
sights 312-15
tourist information 319
tours 316
travel to/from 319-20
travel within 320-1
Mombasa Carnival 26, 315
money 18, 631, 635, *see also individual countries*
mongooses 597, **597**
monkeys 17, 586, 588-9, 589, **17**, **586**, **588**
Morogoro 168-70, **169**
Moshi 129-33, **130**
mosques
Mandhry Mosque, Kenya 315
National Mosque, Uganda 385
motorcycle travel, *see* car travel
mountain gorillas, *see* gorillas
movies, *see* films
Mpanda 162-3
Mpanga Forest Reserve 406
Mt Elgon National Park 274-7, 415-17, **275**
Mt Kenya National Park 289-97, **289**, **292**, **294**, **603**
Mt Kilimanjaro National Park 12, 134-7, **136**, **12**, **581**
Mt Meru 110-11
Mtae 100-1
Mto wa Mbu 114
Mtwara 197-200, **198**
Murchison Falls National Park 468-73, **470**
Musanze 517-20, **518**
museums & galleries
Afri Mak Arts & Crafts Group, Tanzania 197
Afriart Gallery, Uganda 393
AKA Gallery at Tulifanya, Uganda 393
Baden-Powell Museum, Kenya 278
Catholic Museum, Tanzania 93-4
Dian Fossey Gorilla Fund International – Karisoke Research Centre, Rwanda 517
Elsamere, Kenya 242
Ethnographic Museum, Rwanda 532
Fort Jesus, Kenya 312-14
Great Lakes Museum, Uganda 451
Igongo Cultural Centre, Uganda 460
Inema Arts Center, Rwanda 509
Iringa Boma, Tanzania 171-2
Karen Blixen's House & Museum, Kenya 230
Karibu Art Gallery, Uganda 393
King's Palace Museum – Rukari, Rwanda 534
Kitale Museum, Kenya 273
Lamu Museum, Kenya 337
Maji Maji Museum, Tanzania 184
Makerere Art Gallery, Uganda 393
Museum of Natural History, Rwanda 509
Museum of the Environment, Rwanda 539
Mwalimu Julius K Nyerere Museum, Tanzania 143
Nafasi Art Space, Tanzania 53
National Arts Gallery – Rwesero, Rwanda 534
National Museum, Kenya 221
National Museum & House of Culture, Tanzania 53
Nommo Gallery, Uganda 393
Old Law Courts, Kenya 315
Oldupai Museum, Tanzania 123
Presidential Palace Museum, Rwanda 509
Princess Salme Museum, Tanzania 67-70
Sukuma Museum, Tanzania 148
Swahili House, Kenya 337
Treasures of Africa Museum, Kenya 272-3
Uganda Art Gallery, Uganda 393
Uganda Museum, Uganda 385
Umoja Art Gallery, Uganda 393
Village Museum, Tanzania 53
music 204, 621
Musoma 143-4
Mwaluganje Elephant Sanctuary 322
Mwanza 145-8, **146-7**

N

Naboisho Conservancy 260
Nairobi 221-40, **224-5**, **228-9**, **236**
accommodation 231-4
drinking 235-6
emergencies 238
entertainment 236-8
festivals & events 230-1
food 234-5
medical services 238-9
money 239
nightlife 235-6
postal services 239
safety 237
shopping 238
sights 221-30
travel to/from 238, 239-40
travel within 239, 240

Nakuru 246-9, **246**
Nanyuki 282-4, **283**
Naro Moru 297-8
Narok 251-2
national parks & reserves 605-10, **606-7**, *see also* marine parks & reserves
- Aberdare National Park, Kenya 279-81, **280**
- Akagera National Park 541-4, Rwanda
- Amboseli National Park, Kenya 16, 300-3, **303**, 16
- Arusha National Park, Tanzania 109-12, **108**
- Buffalo Springs National Reserve, Kenya 347-8, **346**
- Bwindi Impenetrable National Park, Uganda 45, 445-51, **446**
- Central Island National Park, Kenya 357
- Gombe National Park, Tanzania 159-60
- Hell's Gate National Park, Kenya 245-6, **245**
- Jozani-Chwaka National Park, Tanzania 82
- Katavi National Park, Tanzania 163-5
- Kenya 363-4
- Kibale Forest National Park, Uganda 431-3
- Kidepo Valley National Park, Uganda 419-21
- Lake Manyara National Park, Tanzania 115-17
- Lake Mburo National Park, Uganda 461-2
- Lake Nakuru National Park, Kenya 247, 249-51, **248**, 35
- Longonot National Park, Kenya 242
- Mahale Mountains National Park, Tanzania 160-2
- Marsabit National Park, Kenya 350-1, **350**
- Masai Mara National Reserve, Kenya 13, 252-8, **254-5**
- Meru National Park, Kenya 298-300, **299**
- Mgahinga Gorilla National Park, Uganda 45, 457-9
- Mikumi National Park, Tanzania 170-1
- Mt Elgon National Park, Kenya 274-7, **275**
- Mt Elgon National Park, Uganda 415-17,
- Mt Kenya National Park, Kenya 289-97, **289**, **292**, **294**, 603
- Mt Kilimanjaro National Park, Tanzania 12, 134-7, 12, 581
- Murchison Falls National Park, Uganda 468-73, **470**
- Nairobi National Park, Kenya 221-6, **232-3**
- Ndere Island National Park, Kenya 263
- Nyungwe Forest National Park, Rwanda 17, 534-8
- Parc National de Kahuzi-Biéga, DRC 501
- Parc National des Virunga, DRC 46, 498-501
- Queen Elizabeth National Park, Uganda 439-45, **440**
- Ruaha National Park, Tanzania 174-7, 602-3
- Rubondo Island National Park, Tanzania 149-50
- Ruma National Park, Kenya 265-6
- Rwanda 550
- Rwenzori Mountains National Park, Uganda 15, 436-9, **437**
- Saadani National Park, Tanzania 94-5
- Saiwa Swamp National Park, Kenya 274
- Samburu National Reserve, Kenya 347-8, **346**
- Semuliki National Park, Uganda 433-4
- Serengeti National Park, Tanzania 13, 123-9, **124-5**
- Shaba National Reserve, Kenya 347-8, **346**
- Shimba Hills National Reserve, Kenya 321-2
- Sibiloi National Park, Kenya 354
- South Island National Park, Kenya 353
- Tanzania 205-19
- Tarangire National Park, Tanzania 112-14
- Tsavo East National Park, Kenya 309-11, **306-7**
- Tsavo West National Park, Kenya 303-9, **306-7**
- Uganda 485-6
- Volcanoes National Park, Rwanda 46, 520-7, **522**, 46

National Resistance Army (NRA) 478
Ndoto Mountains 349
newspapers 631
Ngezi Forest Reserve 90
ngoma 621
Ngorongoro Conservation Area 14, 119-23, 206, **120-1**, 14
Ngorongoro Crater 122-3
night drives
- Akagera National Park, Rwanda 542
- Amboseli National Park, Kenya 302
- Kidepo Valley National Park, Uganda 420
- Lake Manyara National Park, Tanzania 115
- Lake Mburo National Park, Uganda 461
- Murchison Falls National Park, Uganda 470-1
- Ruaha National Park, Tanzania 176
- Serengeti National Park, Tanzania 126
- Tarangire National Park, Tanzania 113

Nile River 17, 407-8, 469-70, **17**
Njombe 177-8
Nungwi 78-80
Nyabisindu 533-4
Nyahururu 282
Nyamwezi people 617-18
Nyanza 533-4
Nyeri 277-9, **278**
Nyero Rock Paintings 418-19
Nyungwe Forest National Park 17, 534-8

O

Ol Doinyo Lengai 117
Ol Pejeta Conservancy 284-5
Olare-Orok Conservancy 260-1
Olderikesi Conservancy 261-2
Oldupai Gorge 123
olive baboons *see* baboons
opening hours 19, 635-6, *see also individual countries*
Operation Entebbe 475
ostriches 174, 226, 309, 310, 347, 420, 601, 601

P

painting 622
Paje 83-4
Pangani 95-7
Parc National des Virunga 46, 498-501
Pare people 617
parks & gardens
- Entebbe Botanical Gardens, Uganda 402
- Forodhani Gardens, Tanzania 65
- Kakamega Forest Reserve, Kenya 268-9
- National University of Rwanda, Rwanda 532
- Source of the Nile Gardens, Uganda 408
- Tooro Botanical Garden, Uganda 424-5

passports 640
patas monkeys 586
Pemba 85-91, **86**
photography 636
plains zebras *see* zebras
planning, *see also individual countries*
- budgeting 19
- calendar of events 23-6
- children, travel with 47-8
- East Africa basics 18-19
- East Africa country overviews 49
- gorilla tracking 41-6
- internet resources 19
- itineraries 27-31, **27**, **28**, **29**, **30**, **31**
- safaris 32-40
- travel seasons 18, 23-6

plastic bags 365, 549
politics 560-1, *see also individual countries*
Pongwe 82-3
population 561
postal services 636, *see also individual countries*
primates 20, 586-7, 588-9, *see also individual species*
public holidays 636, *see also individual countries*

Map Pages **000**
Photo Pages 000

Q

Queen Elizabeth National Park 439-45, **440**

R

rabies 649
radio 631
rafting, *see* white-water rafting
ratels 597
red colobus 82, 160, 428, 431
religion 561, 570-2
  Kenya 361
  Rwanda 549
  Tanzania 204
  Uganda 482
rhinoceroses 363, 576-7, 592, **21**
  Kenya 221, 226-7, 230, 249, 252, 279, 284, 286, 287, 288, 299, 305, 363
  Rwanda 541
  Tanzania 123-4, 190
  Uganda 466
Rift Valley fever 649
road accidents 217-18, 378, 628, 645
road rules 218, 378-9
rock climbing, *see* climbing
rock hyraxes 594, **595**
rock-art sites 141-2, 172, 418-19
Rothschild's giraffes *see* giraffes
Ruaha National Park 174-7, **602-3**
Rubavu 527-30, **528**
Rubondo Island National Park 149-50
Ruhengeri 517-20, **518**
ruins 22, *see also* archaeological sites, historic sites
  Gede Ruins, Kenya 332
  Jumba la Mtwana, Kenya 330
  Kaole Ruins, Tanzania 93
  Kilwa Kisiwani, Tanzania 196, 196-7
  Maruhubi Palace, Tanzania 67
  Mkame Ndume Ruins, Tanzania 87
  Mnarani, Kenya 328
  Mtoni Palace, Tanzania 67
  Ras Mkumbuu Ruins, Tanzania 87
  Songo Mnara, Tanzania 197
Ruma National Park 265-6
Rusizi 538-9
Rwanda 50, 506-54, **507**
  accommodation 506
  business hours 552
  climate 506
  consulates 550-1
  culture 548-9
  dance 533, 550
  economy 549
  electricity 550
  embassies 550-1
  environment 550
  exchange rates 508
  food 506, 550
  genocide 508, 509, 511, 512, 531, 539, 545, 546-7
  health 551
  highlights 507
  history 544-7
  internet access 551
  language 508
  money 508, 551-2
  politics 547-8
  public holidays 552
  religion 549
  safety 550, 629
  telephone services 552
  time 552
  tourist information 552
  travel seasons 506
  travel to/from 552-3
  travel within 554
  visas 508, 552
Rwenzori Mountains National Park 15, 436-9, **437**

S

Saadani National Park 94-5
safaris 32-40
  balloon safaris 40
  camel safaris 40
  canoe safaris 40
  cycling safaris 39-40
  DIY safaris 40
  hiking safaris 39-40
  Kenya 38, 227
  Rwanda 38
  Tanzania 37-8
  Uganda 38
  vehicle safaris 38-9
  walking safaris 39-40
safety 628-9, 647-51 *see also* road accidents
  banditry 368, 628
  Burundi 629
  DRC 629
  Kenya 319, 342, 343, 368-9, 629
  road, *See* road accidents
  Rwanda 629
  Tanzania 207-8, 218, 629
  Uganda 629
Saiwa Swamp National Park 274
Samburu National Reserve 347-8, **346**
Sauti za Busara 23, 71
savannah 573-4, 602
scams 137, 369, 628-9
schistosomiasis 647
secretary birds 599, **598**
Segera Ranch 286
Selous Game Reserve 16, 190-4, **190**, **16**
Selous-Niassa Wildlife Corridor 193
Semliki Wildlife Reserve 434-5
Semuliki National Park 433-4
Serengeti National Park 13, 123-9, **124-5**
servals 585, **584-5**
Shaba National Reserve 347-8, **346**
Shela Beach 337
Shimba Hills National Reserve 321-2
Shimoni 326-7
shoebills 406, 601, **600**
shopping, *see also individual locations*
  language 654
Sibiloi National Park 354
Sipi Falls 417-18
skydiving 325
slave trade 566
sleeping sickness 650
small cats 584-5
smoking 631
snake bites 651
snorkelling, *see* diving & snorkelling
soapstone 266
Songea 184-5
Soni 101-3
spas 70
sports 482, 570
spotted hyenas 597, **596**
Ssese Islands 463-5
Stone Town 12, **68-9**, **12**, *see also* Zanzibar Town
Sumbawanga 165-7
Swahili 565
Swahili language 612, 652-6
Swahili people 612
synagogues 414

T

taarab 204
Tabora 154-6, **154**
Tanga 97-9, **96-7**
Tanzania 49, 52-219, **54-5**, **92**, **102**, **139**, **153**, **166-7**, **186**
  accommodation 52, 206-7
  activities 207
  business hours 210
  climate 52
  consulates 208
  customs regulations 207
  embassies 208
  etiquette 208-9
  exchange rates 53
  food 52
  highlights 54-5
  history 201-3
  internet access 209
  language 53
  money 53, 209-10
  opening hours 210
  public holidays 210
  safety 207-8, 218, 629
  telephone services 210
  time 211
  tourist information 211
  travel seasons 52
  travel to/from 211-15
  travel within 215-19
  visas 53, 211
  volunteering 211
Tarangire National Park 112-14
taxis 645-6
  Kenya 379
  Tanzania 219
tea 268
telephone services 18
temples
  Kampala Hindu Temple, Uganda 385
  Lord Shiva Temple, Kenya 315
Thomson's gazelles 590, **591**
time 18, 636, *see also individual countries*
tipping 40, 635
Tiwi Beach 322, **324**

toilets 636
tourist information 636-7
tours 642, *see also individual locations*, safaris
train travel 646
  Kenya 380
  Tanzania 219
travel to/from East Africa 640-2
travel within East Africa 642-6
traveller's diarrhoea 650
travellers cheques 635
trekking, *see* hiking
tribal groups 611-18
trypanosomiasis 650
Tsavo East National Park 309-11, **306-7**
Tsavo West National Park 303-9, **306-7**
tsetse flies 576, 651
tuberculosis 650
tuk-tuks 379
Tukuyu 181-2
Tumbe 90
Tunduru 185
Turkana people 618
turtles 187
Tutsi people 613-14
typhoid 650

U

ugali 623
Uganda 50, 381-493, **382-3**, **407**, **424-5**, **465**
  accommodation 381
  books 483
  business hours 489
  climate 381
  consulates 487-8
  culture 481-2
  customs regulations 487
  dance 483-4
  electricity 487
  environment 484-6
  etiquette 488
  exchange rates 384
  films 482-3
  food 381, 486
  health 488-93
  highlights 382-3
  history 475-80
  internet access 488
  language 384
  money 384, 489
  music 483-4
  politics 480-1
  postal services 489
  public holidays 489
  religion 482
  safety 487, 629
  telephone services 489
  time 489
  travel seasons 381
  travel within 491-3
  visas 384, 489-90
  volunteering 387, 402-3, 414, 422, 458
  wildlife 485
Uganda kob 590, **590-1**
Ukerewe Island 149
Usambara Mountains 99-103

V

vacations 636
vaccinations 648
vegetarian travellers 623
vervet monkeys 586
viewpoints
  Crater Lakes, Uganda 429
  Kakamega Forest, Kenya 269
  Lake Manyara National Park, Tanzania 115
  Lake Nakuru National Park, Kenya 249
  Nakuru, Kenya 246-7
  Tsavo West National Park, Kenya 308
visas 18, 637, 638, *see also individual countries*
visual arts 204, 393, 622
Voi 311-12
volcanoes
  Central Island volcano, Kenya 357
  Mgahinga Gorilla National Park, Uganda 458-9
  Mt Elgon, Uganda 415-6
  Mt Kenya, Kenya 293
  Mt Kilimanjaro, Tanzania 134-5
  Mt Longonot, Kenya 242
  Mt Rungwe, Tanzania 182
  Ngorongoro Crater, Tanzania 122
  Nyiragongo, DRC 498, 499-500
  Shetani Lava Flows, Kenya 304-5
  Teleki, Kenya 357, **15**
  Volcanoes National Park, Rwanda 46, 520-7, **522**, **46**
Volcanoes National Park 11, 46, 520-7, **522**, **11**, **46**
volunteering 637-8
  Kenya 373
  Tanzania 211
  Uganda 387, 402-3, 414, 422, 458
vultures 599, **598**

W

walking tours 341
warthogs 594, **594**
Wasini Island 327-8
Watamu 329-31
water 493, 651
water sports 79, 80, *see also individual water sports*
waterfalls
  Adamson's Falls, Kenya 299
  Chania Falls, Kenya 281
  Gura Falls, Kenya 281
  Karura Falls, Kenya 281
  Luhuji Falls, Tanzania 177
  Makalia Falls, Kenya 249
  Murchison Falls, Uganda 469
  Rusumo Falls, Rwanda 543
  Sipi Falls, Uganda 417-18
  Thomson's Falls, Kenya 282
weather 23-6
weights 631
West Kilimanjaro 138
Western Highlands 265-77
Wete 89-90
whale sharks 187
white-backed vultures 599, **598**
white-water rafting
  Jinja, Uganda 17, 409-10, **17**
  Kenya 368
wild dogs 170, 174, 190, 193, 288, 349, 578, **14**, **596-7**
wildcats 585, **584**
wildebeest 112, 115, 123, 125, 170, 252, 259, 300-1, 590
  migration 11, 24, 37, 128, 257, 259, **10-11**
wildlife 581-604, *see also individual species*
  Kenya 249, 363
  Tanzania 205
  Uganda 485
wildlife drives
  Akagera National Park, Rwanda 542
  Amboseli National Park, Kenya 300, 304
  Kidepo Valley National Park, Uganda 420
  Lake Mburo National Park, Uganda 461
  Masai Mara National Reserve, Kenya 253-4
  Murchison Falls National Park, Uganda 470-1
  Naboisho Conservancy, Kenya 260
  Queen Elizabeth National Park, Uganda 441
  Ruaha National Park, Tanzania 175
  Saadani National Park, Tanzania 95
  Selous Game Reserve, Tanzania 191
  Semliki Wildlife Reserve, Uganda 434
  Serengeti National Park, Tanzania 126
wildlife reserves & sanctuaries *see also* national parks & reserves
  Bigodi Wetland Sanctuary, Uganda 431
  Colobus Conservation Centre, Kenya 324
  Crescent Island, Kenya 242
  David Sheldrick Wildlife Trust, Kenya 226-30
  Donkey Sanctuary, Kenya 337
  Enduimet Wildlife Management Area, Tanzania 610
  Fruit Bat Sanctuary, Tanzania 187
  Giraffe Centre, Kenya 226
  Gogo River Bird Sanctuary, Kenya 226
  Kihingami Wetlands Sanctuary, Uganda 431
  Kyahugye Island, Uganda 453
  Mnarani Marine Turtle Conservation Pond, Tanzania 78
  Mwaluganje Elephant Sanctuary, Kenya 322
  Nabajjuzi Wetlands, Uganda 462

Map Pages **000**
Photo Pages **000**

Ngamba Island Chimpanzee Sanctuary, Uganda 401
Ngulia Rhino Sanctuary, Kenya 305
Okapi Wildlife Reserve, DRC 502
Rhino Sanctuary, Kenya 299
Selous Game Reserve, Tanzania 16, 190-4, **190**, **16**
Selous-Niassa Wildlife Corridor, Tanzania 193
Semliki Wildlife Reserve, Uganda 434-5
Senkwekwe Gorilla Orphanage, DRC 498
Tanzania 205-6
Watamu Turtle Watch, Kenya 330
Ziwa Rhino Sanctuary, Uganda 466
women travellers 638-9
woodcarving 622
woodland 602
work 639

Y

yellow fever 650
yoga 78-9

Z

Zanzibar Archipelago 64-91, **64**
Zanzibar Island 65-85, **66**
Zanzibar Song & Dance 23
Zanzibar Town 12, 65-77, **68-9**, **12**
accommodation 72-4
activities 70
entertainment 75-6
festivals & events 71-2
food 74-5
internet access 76
medical services 76
money 76
nightlife 75
safety 76
shopping 75, 76-8
sights 65-70
tourist information 76
tours 71
travel to/from 77
travel within 77
zebras 577-8, 592, **13**, **592-3**
Kenya 226, 242, 245, 249, 252, 259, 265, 286, 300-1, 304, 347
Rwanda 541
Tanzania 112, 115, 123, 164, 170
Uganda 419, 453, 461
Ziwa Rhino Sanctuary 466
zoos
Bio-Ken Snake Farm & Laboratory, Kenya 330
Chimpanzee Sanctuary, Kenya 284-5
Endangered Species Enclosure, Kenya 284
Mt Kenya Wildlife Conservancy Animal Orphanage, Kenya 283
Uganda Reptiles Village, Uganda 402
Uganda Wildlife Education Centre, Uganda 401-2

Map Legend

Sights

- Beach
- Bird Sanctuary
- Buddhist
- Castle/Palace
- Christian
- Confucian
- Hindu
- Islamic
- Jain
- Jewish
- Monument
- Museum/Gallery/Historic Building
- Ruin
- Shinto
- Sikh
- Taoist
- Winery/Vineyard
- Zoo/Wildlife Sanctuary
- Other Sight

Activities, Courses & Tours

- Bodysurfing
- Diving
- Canoeing/Kayaking
- Course/Tour
- Sento Hot Baths/Onsen
- Skiing
- Snorkelling
- Surfing
- Swimming/Pool
- Walking
- Windsurfing
- Other Activity

Sleeping

- Sleeping
- Camping
- Hut/Shelter

Eating

- Eating

Drinking & Nightlife

- Drinking & Nightlife
- Cafe

Entertainment

- Entertainment

Shopping

- Shopping

Information

- Bank
- Embassy/Consulate
- Hospital/Medical
- Internet
- Police
- Post Office
- Telephone
- Toilet
- Tourist Information
- Other Information

Geographic

- Beach
- Gate
- Hut/Shelter
- Lighthouse
- Lookout
- Mountain/Volcano
- Oasis
- Park
- Pass
- Picnic Area
- Waterfall

Population

- Capital (National)
- Capital (State/Province)
- City/Large Town
- Town/Village

Transport

- Airport
- Border crossing
- Bus
- Cable car/Funicular
- Cycling
- Ferry
- Metro station
- Monorail
- Parking
- Petrol station
- Subway station
- Taxi
- Train station/Railway
- Tram
- Underground station
- Other Transport

Routes

- Tollway
- Freeway
- Primary
- Secondary
- Tertiary
- Lane
- Unsealed road
- Road under construction
- Plaza/Mall
- Steps
- Tunnel
- Pedestrian overpass
- Walking Tour
- Walking Tour detour
- Path/Walking Trail

Boundaries

- International
- State/Province
- Disputed
- Regional/Suburb
- Marine Park
- Cliff
- Wall

Hydrography

- River, Creek
- Intermittent River
- Canal
- Water
- Dry/Salt/Intermittent Lake
- Reef

Areas

- Airport/Runway
- Beach/Desert
- Cemetery (Christian)
- Cemetery (Other)
- Glacier
- Mudflat
- Park/Forest
- Sight (Building)
- Sportsground
- Swamp/Mangrove

Note: Not all symbols displayed above appear on the maps in this book

Shawn Duthie

Central Highlands & Laikipia, Northern Kenya Originally from Canada, Shawn has been travelling, studying and working around the world for the past 13 years. A love of travel merged with an interest in international politics, which led to several years of lecturing at the University of Cape Town and, now, a stint as a freelance political risk consultant specialising in African countries. Shawn lives in South Africa and takes any excuse to travel around this amazing continent.

David Else

Zanzibar Archipelago (Tanzania) David Else is a professional freelance writer specialising in travel, trekking, cycling, walking and outdoor adventure activities. Since the 1980s he's been writing guidebooks for Lonely Planet and other publishers, and on a wide range of travel topics for magazines, newspapers and websites. In three decades of covering Africa, David has written for many Lonely Planet guidebooks, including *West Africa, Southern Africa, Malawi, Zambia, Gambia & Senegal* and *Trekking in East Africa*. He now lives in the UK, where he's worked on several editions of guides to Great Britain and England.

Read more about David at:
lonelyplanet.com/members/davidelse

Mary Fitzpatrick

Dar es Salaam, Northeastern Tanzania, Southeastern Tanzania Originally from the USA, Mary spent her early years dreaming of how to get across an ocean or two to more exotic locales. Following graduate studies, she set off for Europe. Her fascination with languages and cultures soon led her further south to Africa, where she has spent the past two decades living and working as a professional travel writer all around the continent. She focuses particularly on East and Southern Africa, including Mozambique and Tanzania.

Read more about Mary at:
lonelyplanet.com/members/maryf

Anna Kaminski

South Coast, North Coast (Kenya) Originally from the Soviet Union, Anna grew up in Cambridge, UK. She graduated from the University of Warwick with a degree in Comparative American Studies, a background in the history, culture and literature of the Americas and the Caribbean, and an enduring love of Latin America. Her restless wanderings led her to settle briefly in Oaxaca and Bangkok, and her flirtation with criminal law saw her volunteering as a lawyer's assistant in the courts, ghettos and prisons of Kingston, Jamaica. Anna has contributed to almost 30 Lonely Planet titles. She calls London home.

Read more about Anna at:
lonelyplanet.com/members/AnnaCohenKaminski

Tom Masters

Democratic Republic of the Congo Dreaming since he could walk of going to the most obscure places on earth, Tom has always had a taste for the unknown. This has led to a writing career that has taken him all over the world, including North Korea, the Arctic, Congo and Siberia. Despite a childhood spent in the English countryside, as an adult Tom has always called London, Paris and Berlin home. He currently lives in Berlin and can be found online at www.tommasters.net.

Read more about Tom at:
lonelyplanet.com/members/tommasters

Carolyn McCarthy

Uganda Carolyn McCarthy specialises in travel, culture and adventure in the Americas. She has written for *National Geographic, Outside, BBC Magazine, Sierra Magazine, Boston Globe* and other publications. A former Fulbright fellow and Banff Mountain Grant recipient, she has documented life in the most remote corners of Latin America. Carolyn has contributed to 40 guidebooks and anthologies for Lonely Planet, including Colorado, USA, Argentina, Chile, Trekking in the Patagonian Andes, Panama, Peru and USA National Parks guides. For more information, visit www.carolynmccarthy.org or follow her Instagram travels @mccarthyoffmap.

Helena Smith

Central Tanzania, Southern Highlands Helena is an award-winning writer and photographer covering travel, outdoors and food. She has written guidebooks on destinations from Fiji to northern Norway. Helena is from Scotland but was partly brought up in Malawi, so Africa always feels like home. She also enjoys global travel in her multicultural home area of Hackney and wrote, photographed and published Inside Hackney, the first guide to the borough (https://insidehackney.com). Her 1000-word autobiography won *Vogue*'s annual writing contest, and she's a winner of the *Independent on Sunday*'s travel writing competition.

Read more about Helena at:
lonelyplanet.com/members/helena_smith

OUR STORY

A beat-up old car, a few dollars in the pocket and a sense of adventure. In 1972 that's all Tony and Maureen Wheeler needed for the trip of a lifetime – across Europe and Asia overland to Australia. It took several months, and at the end – broke but inspired – they sat at their kitchen table writing and stapling together their first travel guide, *Across Asia on the Cheap*. Within a week they'd sold 1500 copies. Lonely Planet was born.

Today, Lonely Planet has offices in Franklin, London, Melbourne, Oakland, Dublin, Beijing and Delhi, with more than 600 staff and writers. We share Tony's belief that 'a great guidebook should do three things: inform, educate and amuse'.

OUR WRITERS

Anthony Ham

Nairobi, Southeastern Kenya, Southern Rift Valley, Western Kenya, Northern Tanzania Anthony is a freelance writer and photographer who specialises in Spain, East and Southern Africa, the Arctic and the Middle East. When he's not writing for Lonely Planet, Anthony writes about and photographs Spain, Africa and the Middle East for newspapers and magazines in Australia, the UK and US. Anthony also wrote the Plan Your Trip, Understand and Survival Guide sections.

Read more about Anthony at:
lonelyplanet.com/members/anthony_ham

Ray Bartlett

Lake Victoria, Western Tanzania Ray Bartlett has been travel writing for nearly two decades, bringing Japan, Korea, Mexico, and many parts of the United States to life in rich detail for top-industry publishers, newspapers and magazines. His acclaimed debut novel *Sunsets of Tulum*, set in Yucatán, was a Midwest Book Review 2016 Fiction pick. Among other pursuits, he surfs regularly and is an accomplished Argentine tango dancer. Follow him on Facebook, Twitter or Instagram, or contact him for questions or motivational speaking opportunities via www.kaisora.com, his website.

Jean-Bernard Carillet

Rwanda Jean-Bernard is a Paris-based freelance writer and photographer who specialises in Africa, France, Turkey, the Indian Ocean, the Caribbean and the Pacific. He loves adventure, remote places, islands, outdoors, archaeological sites and food. His insatiable wanderlust has taken him to 114 countries across six continents, and it shows no sign of waning. It has inspired lots of articles and photos for travel magazines and some 70 Lonely Planet guidebooks, both in English and in French.

Read more about Jean-Bernard at:
lonelyplanet.com/members/jbcarillet

Stuart Butler

Burundi Stuart has been writing for Lonely Planet for a decade and during this time he's come eye to eye with gorillas in the Congolese jungles, met a man with horns on his head who could lie in fire, huffed and puffed over snow-bound Himalayan mountain passes, interviewed a king who could turn into a tree, and had his fortune told by a parrot. Oh, and he's met more than his fair share of self-proclaimed gods. When not on the road for Lonely Planet, he lives on the beautiful beaches of Southwest France with his wife and two young children. His website is www.stuartbutlerjournalist.com.

Read more about Stuart at:
lonelyplanet.com/members/stuartbutler

OVER PAGE MORE WRITERS

Published by Lonely Planet Global Limited
CRN 554153
11th edition – Jul 2018
ISBN 978 1 78657 574 6

10 9 8 7 6 5 4 3 2 1
Printed in Singapore